LONDON
Mini Street Atlas

CONTENTS

Key to Map Pages	2-3
Large Scale Map Pages	4-27
Map Pages	28-125
Congestion Charging Zone	126-127
Index to Streets, etc.	128-343
Index to Hospitals	344-348
Index to Stations	349-352
Underground Map	back cover

SCALE

Map Pages 28-125
1:21477 Approx. 3 inches to 1 mile

0   ⅛   ¼ Mile

0   100 200 300 Metres
4.66 cm to 1 km   7.49 cm to 1 mile

Map Pages 4-11
1:10560 6 inches to 1 mile

0   ¹⁄₁₆   ⅛ Mile

0   100   200 Metres
9.47 cm to 1km   15.24 cm to 1 mile

Geographers' A-Z Map Company Ltd.

Fairfield Road, Borough Green, Sevenoaks, Kent TN15 8PP
Enquiries & Trade Sales 01732 781000   Retail Sales 01732 783422
www.a-zmaps.co.uk

Edition 5 2005   Edition 5A 2006   Copyright © Geographers' A-Z Map Co. Ltd.

Ordnance Survey® This product includes mapping data licensed from Ordnance Survey® with the permission of the Controller of Her Majesty's Stationery Office.
© Crown Copyright 2005. All rights reserved. Licence number 100017302

2 | **KEY TO MAP PAGES**

Kingsbury | HENDON | HORNSEY

	Golders Green		Highgate		
28	29	30	31	32	33	34

Neasden | Cricklewood

HAMPSTEAD

42	43	44	45	46	47	48

WILLESDEN | | | | CAMDEN TOWN | ISLIN

Kensal Green | Kilburn | MARYLEBONE | | FINS

56	57	58	59	60	61	62

A40 | | | | *LARGE SC*

ACTON | | PADDINGTON | WEST END *SECTIO* | Holborn

Shepherd's Bush

70	71	72	73	74	75	76

KENSINGTON | | Westminster | LAM

CHISWICK | HAMMERSMITH | CHELSEA

84	85	86	87	88	89	90

BARNES | FULHAM | BATTERSEA

PUTNEY | CLAPHAM | BRIX

98	99	100	101	102	103	104

Roehampton | WANDSWORTH

Richmond Park | Balham

112	113	114	115	116	117	118

WIMBLEDON | Tooting | STREATHAM

SCALE

```
0        1        2 Miles
0    1    2    3 Kilometres
```

MITCHAM

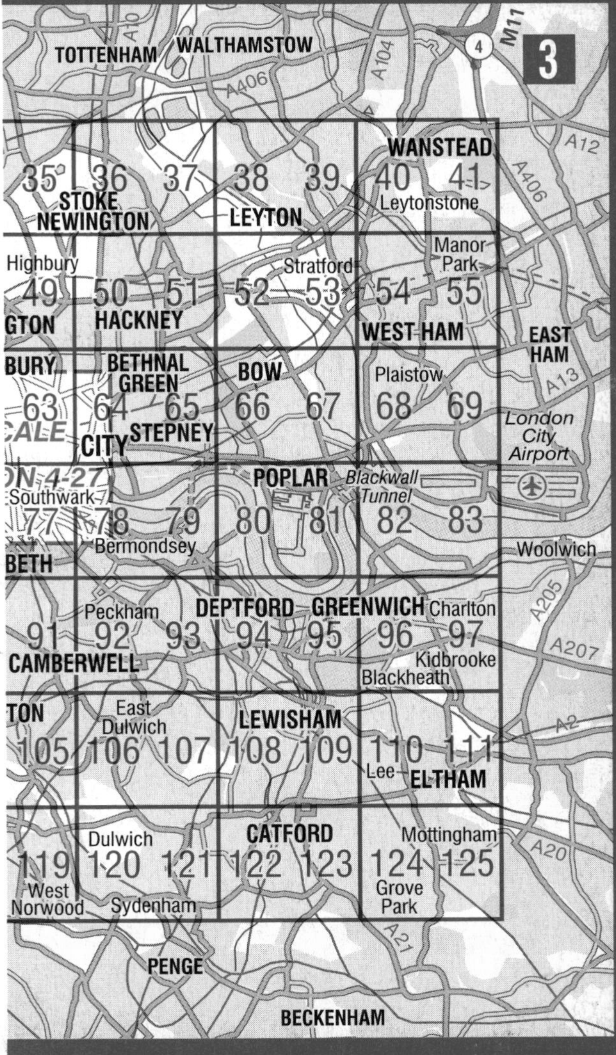

TOTTENHAM WALTHAMSTOW

4

3

M11

A104

A406

A10

A12

A406

WANSTEAD

35 36 37 38 39 40 41

STOKE NEWINGTON

Leytonstone

LEYTON

Manor Park

Highbury

Stratford

49 50 51 52 53 54 55

GTON HACKNEY

WEST HAM

EAST HAM

A13

BURY BETHNAL GREEN BOW Plaistow

63 64 65 66 67 68 69

CALE

CITY STEPNEY

London City Airport

ON-4-27

POPLAR Blackwall Tunnel

Southwark

77 78 79 80 81 82 83

Bermondsey

BETH

Woolwich

A205

Peckham DEPTFORD GREENWICH Charlton

91 92 93 94 95 96 97

CAMBERWELL

Kidbrooke

Blackheath

A207

TON East Dulwich LEWISHAM

105 106 107 108 109 110 111

Lee ELTHAM

A2

Dulwich CATFORD Mottingham

A20

119 120 121 122 123 124 125

West Norwood Sydenham

Grove Park

A21

PENGE

BECKENHAM

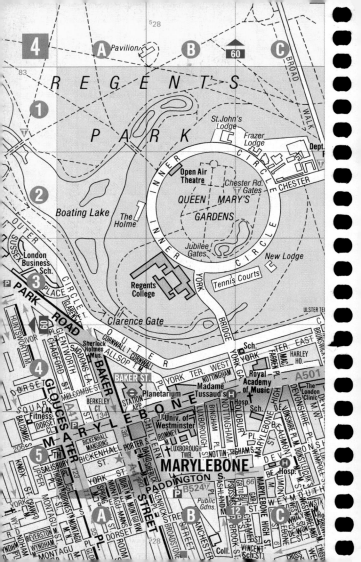

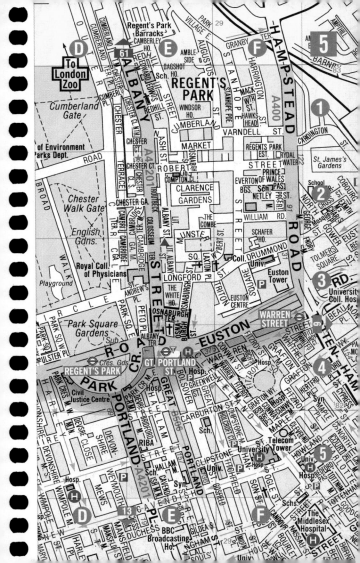

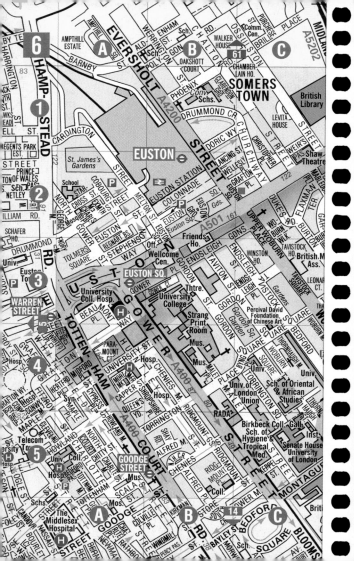

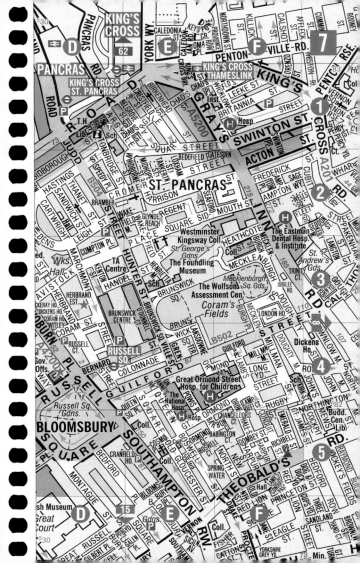

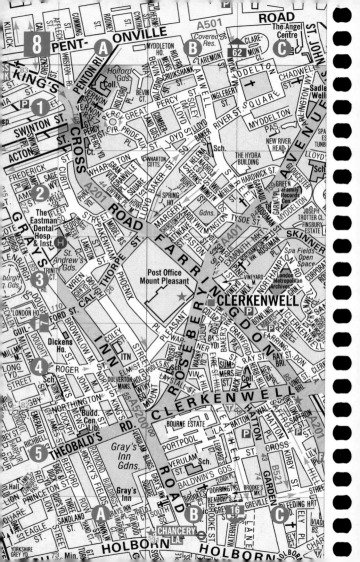

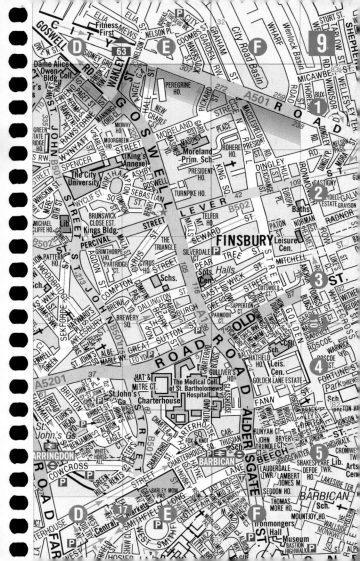

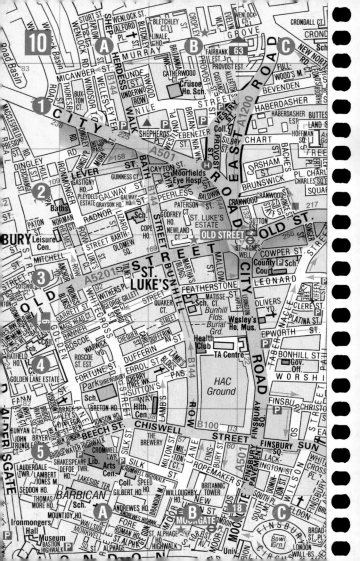

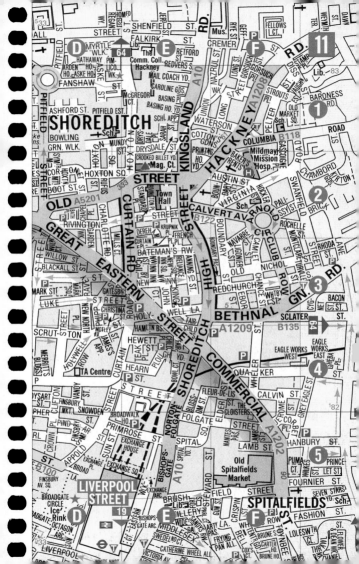

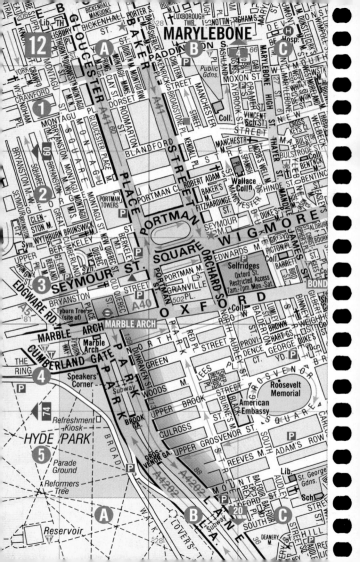

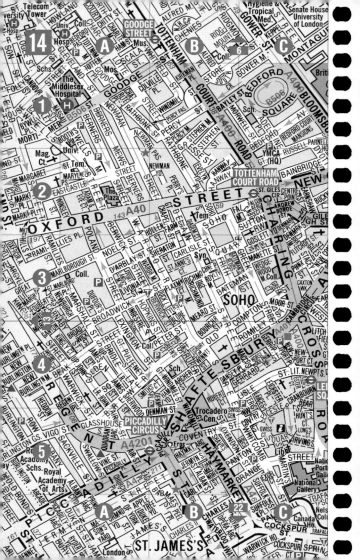

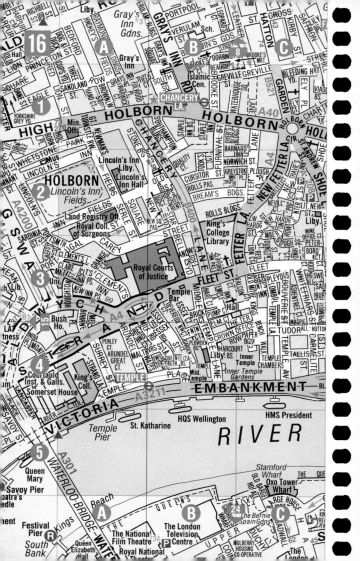

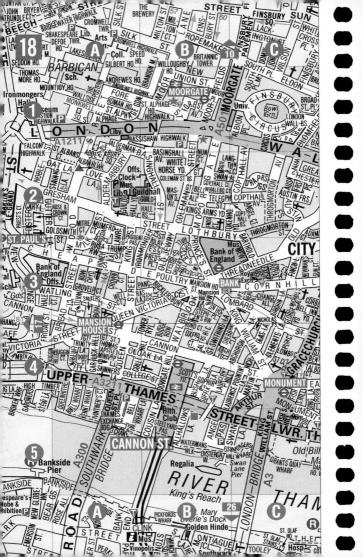

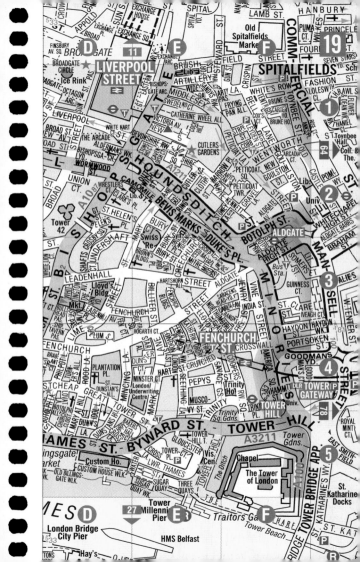

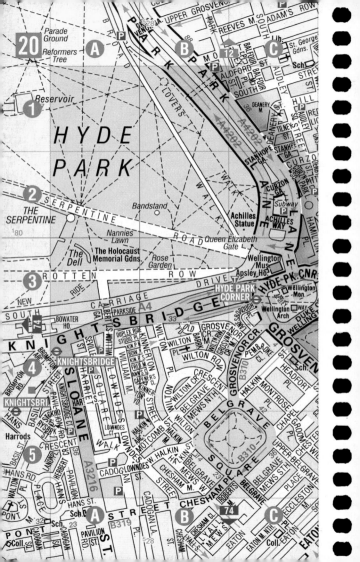

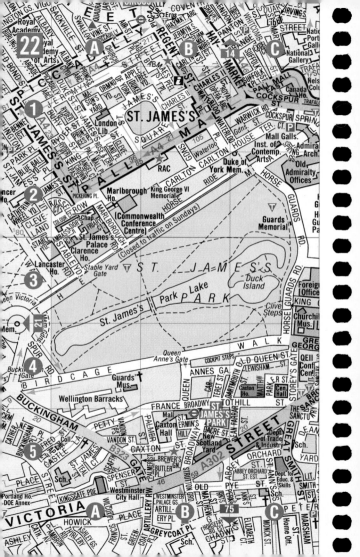

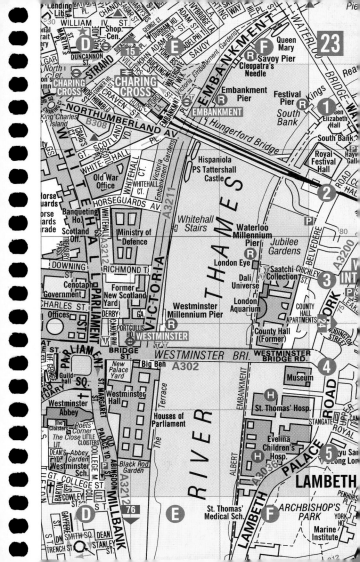

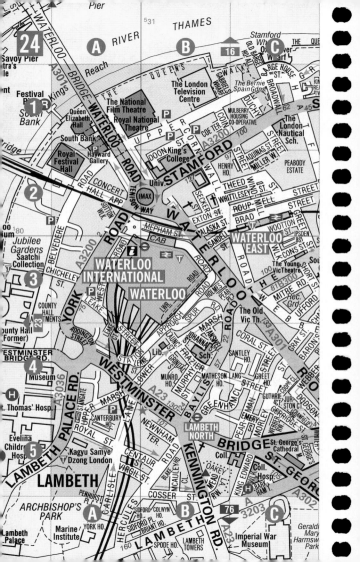

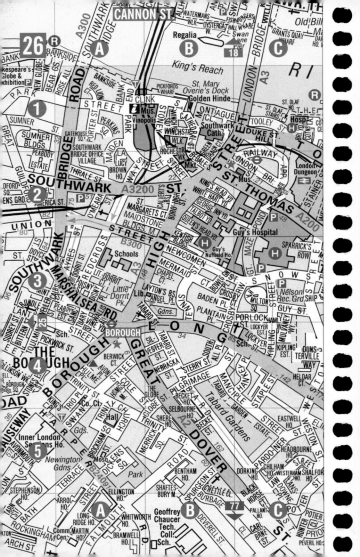

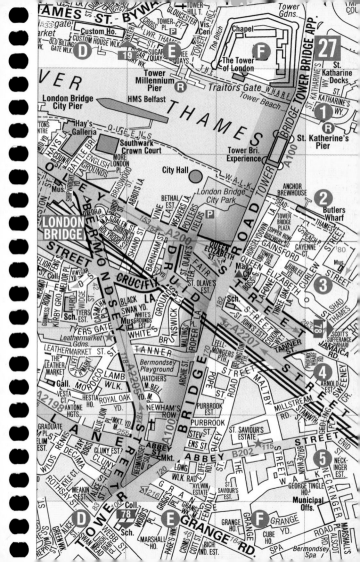

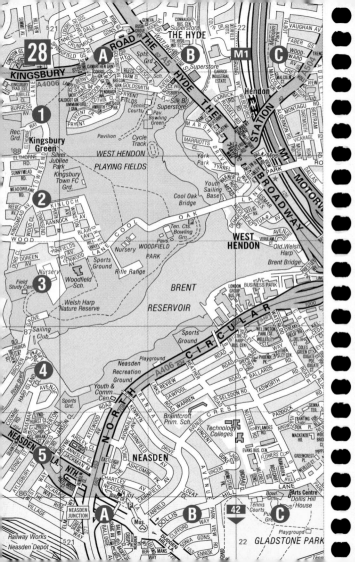

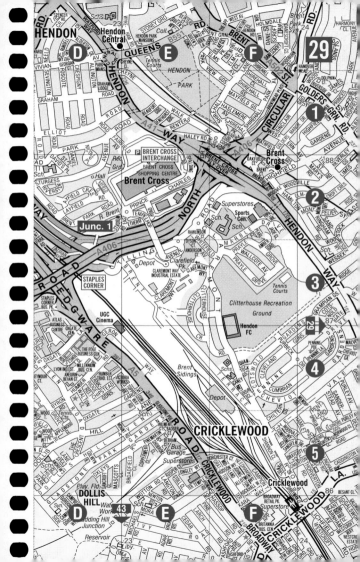

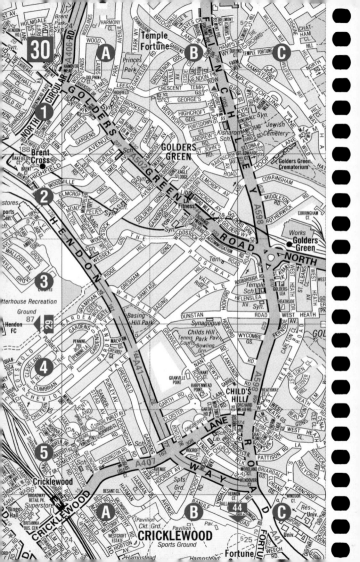

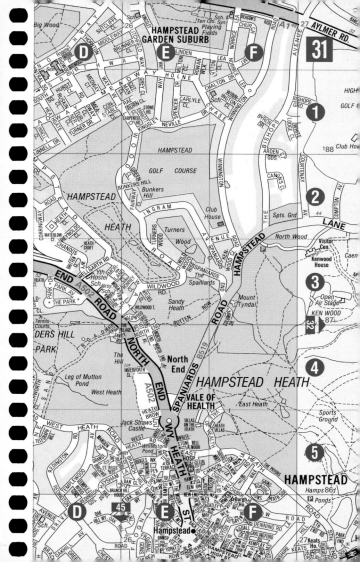

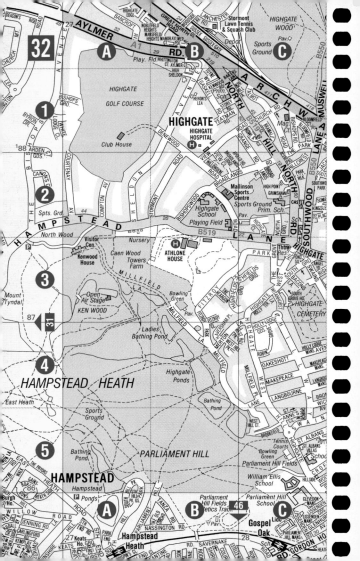

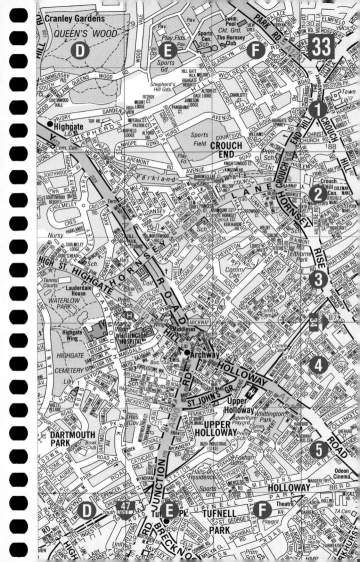

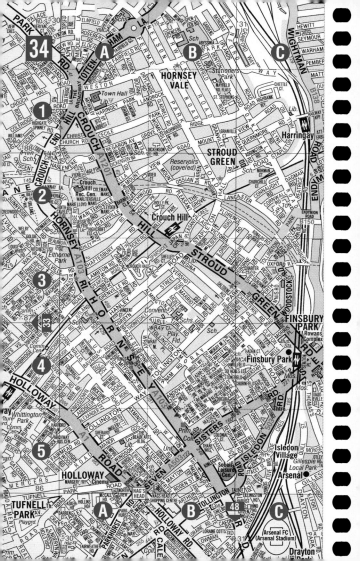

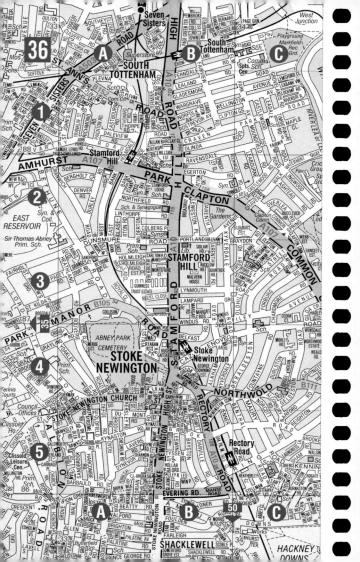

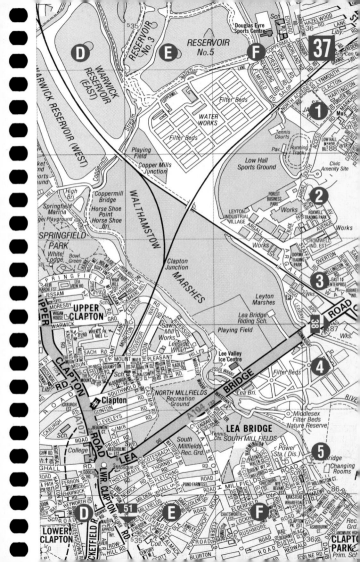

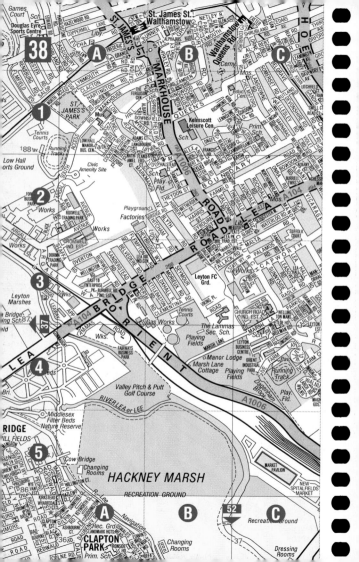

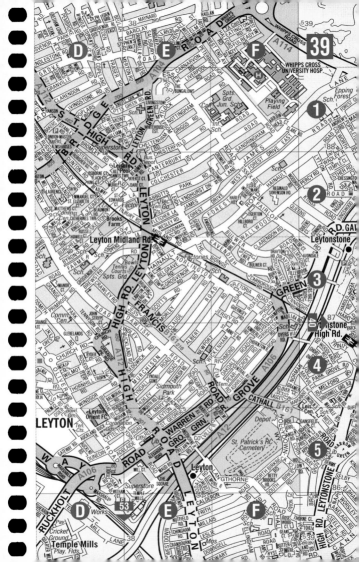

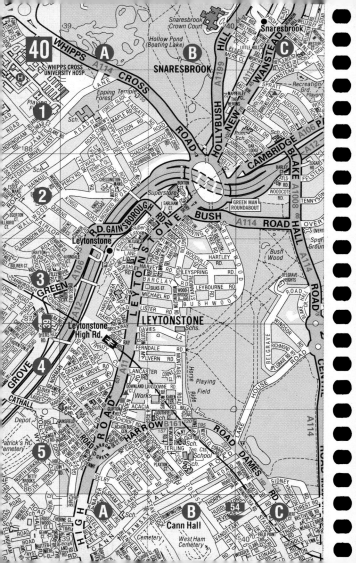

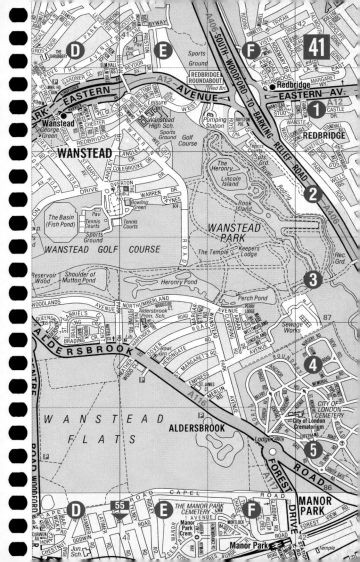

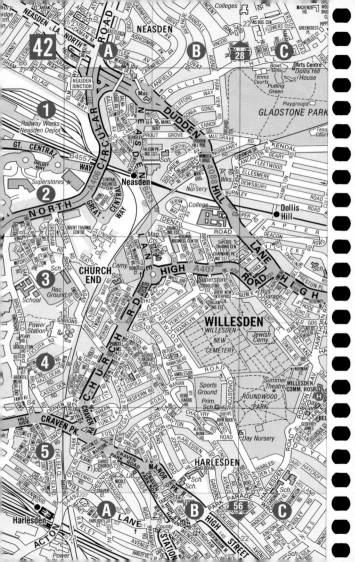

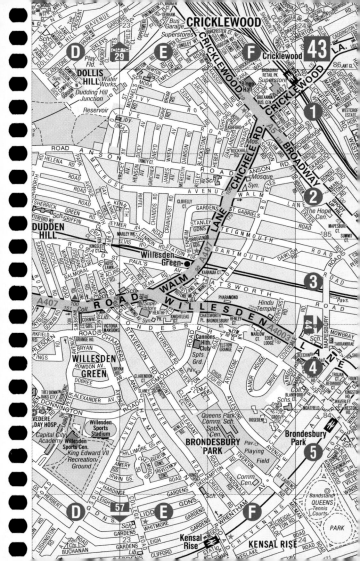

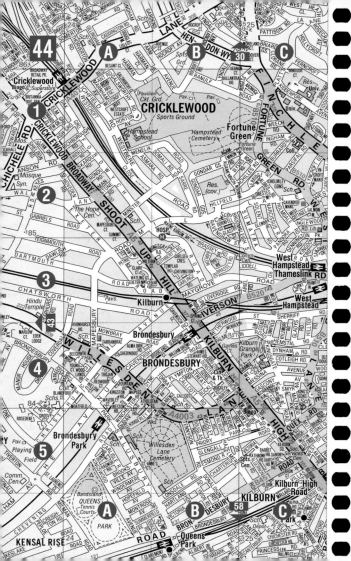

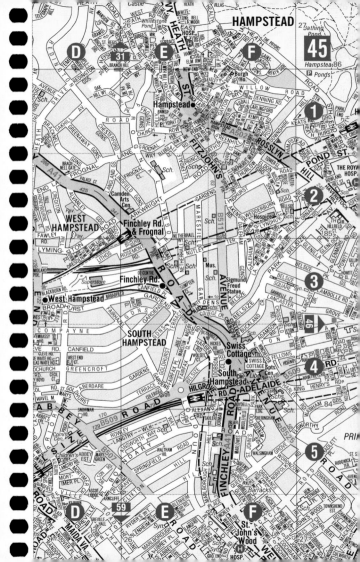

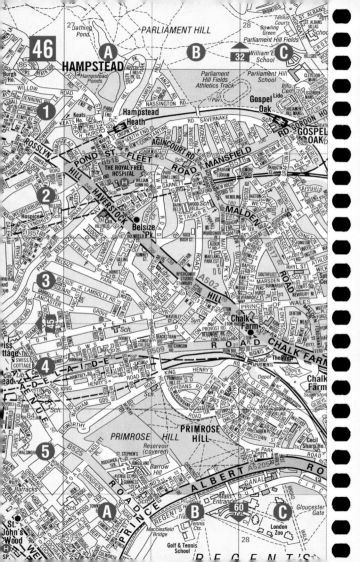

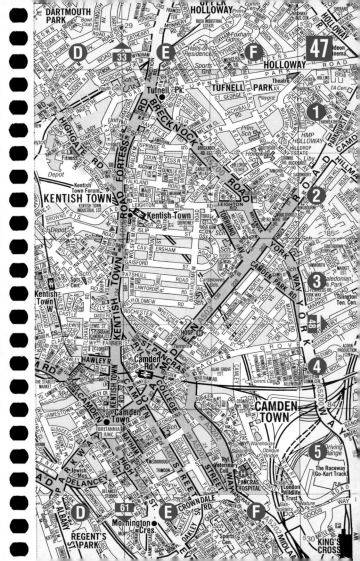

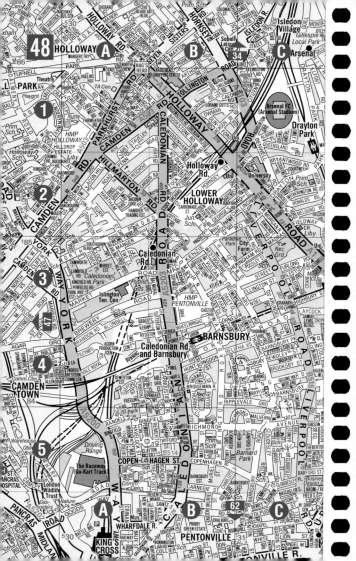

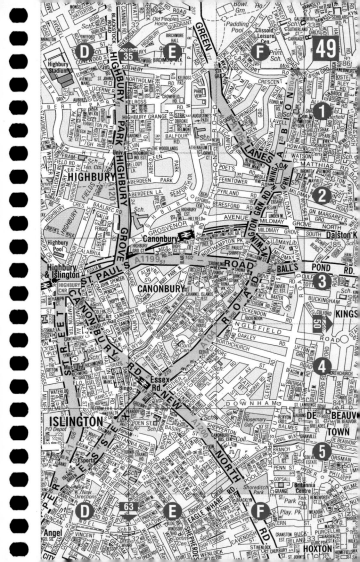

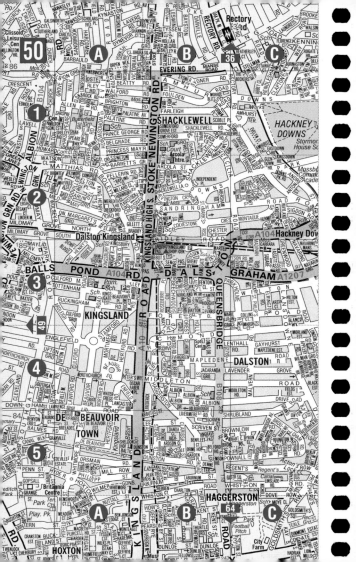

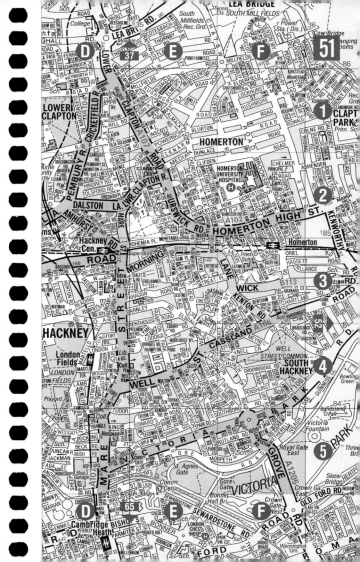

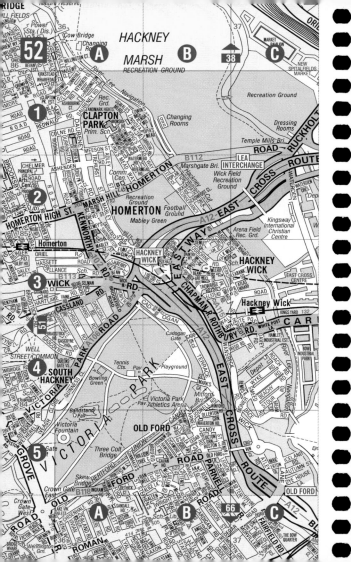

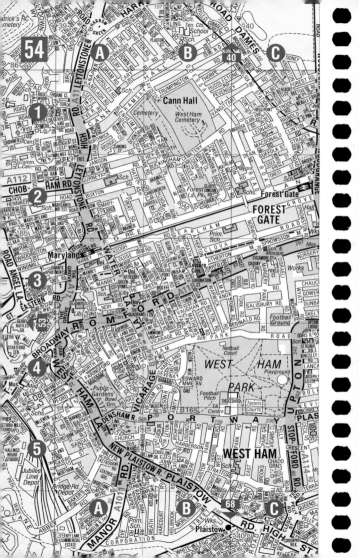

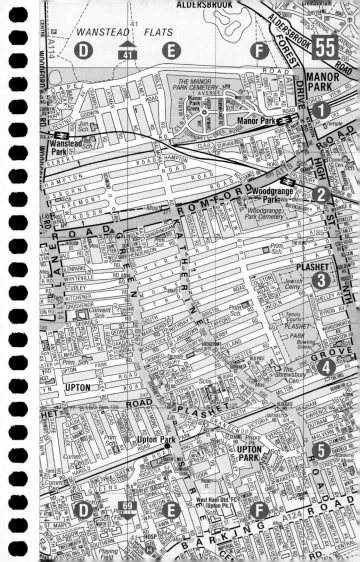

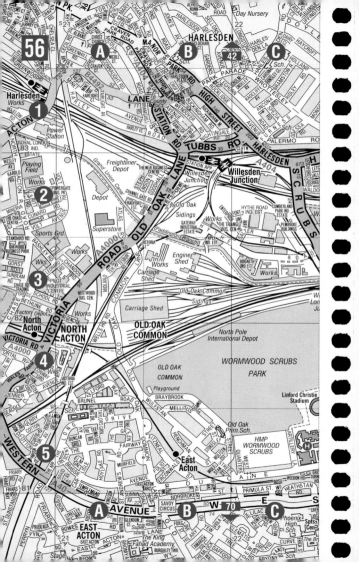

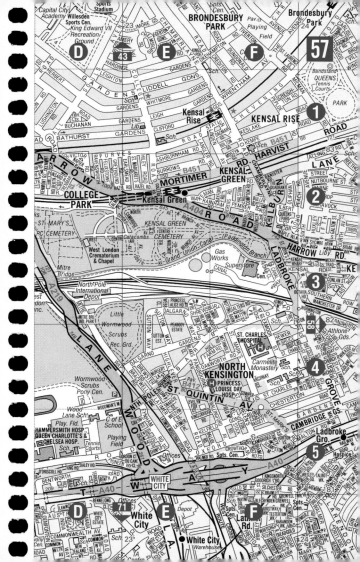

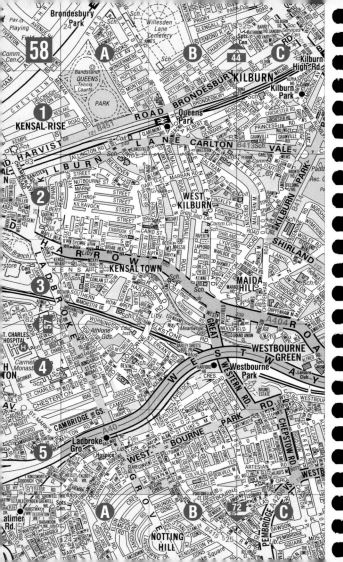

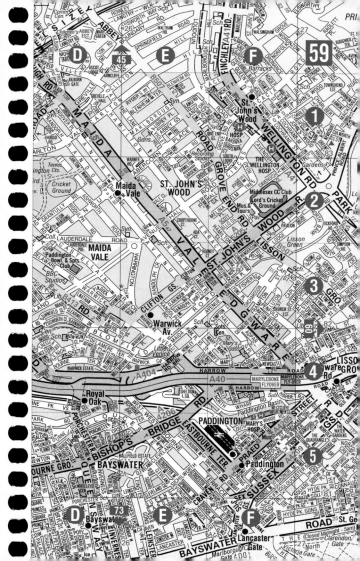

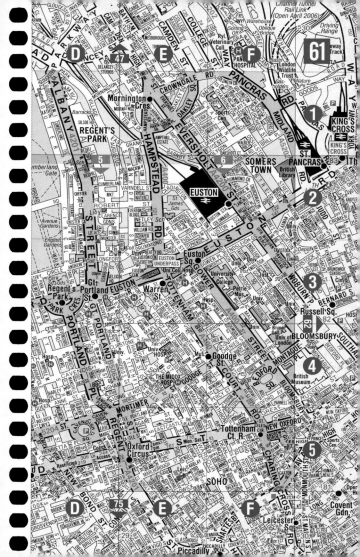

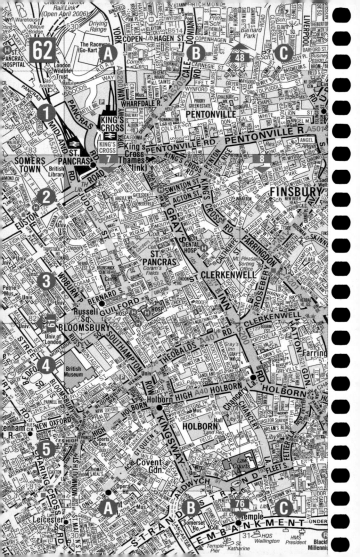

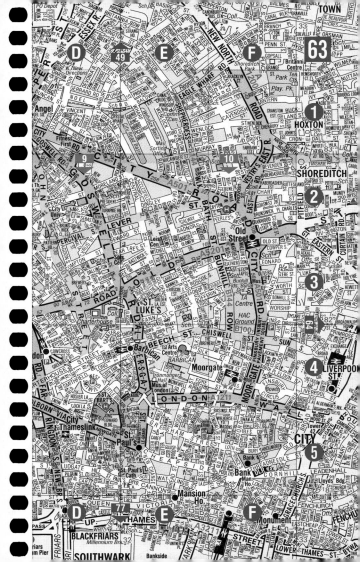

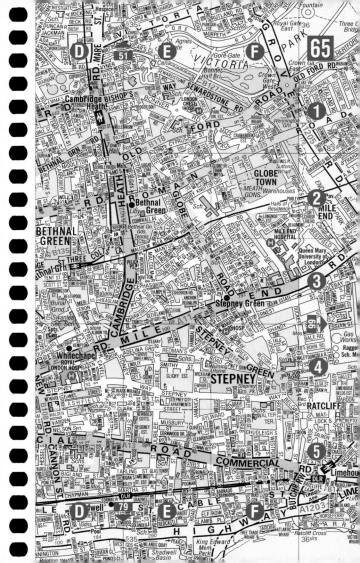

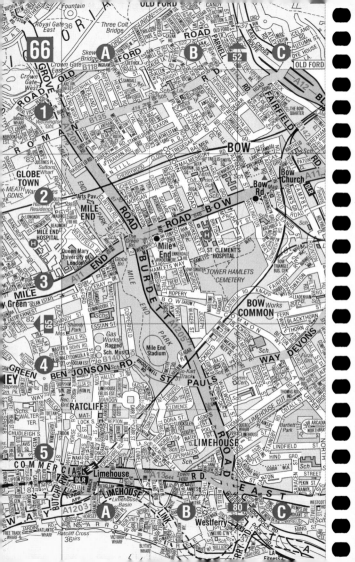

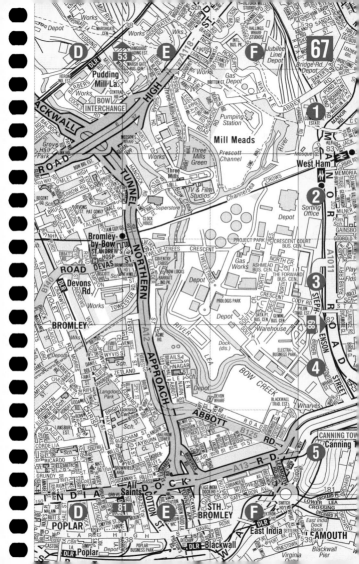

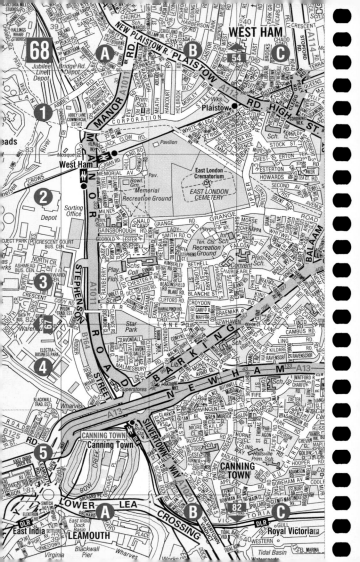

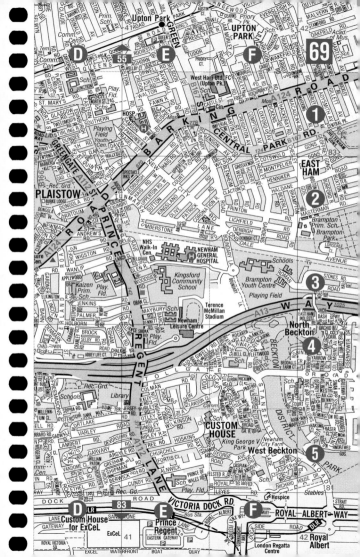

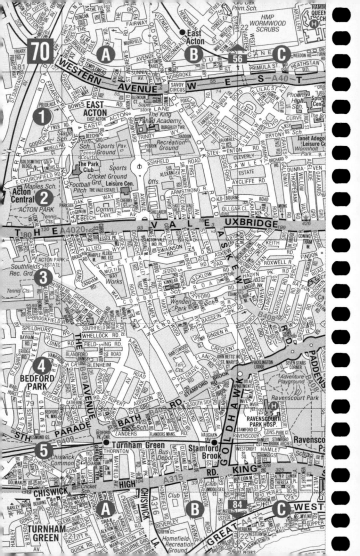

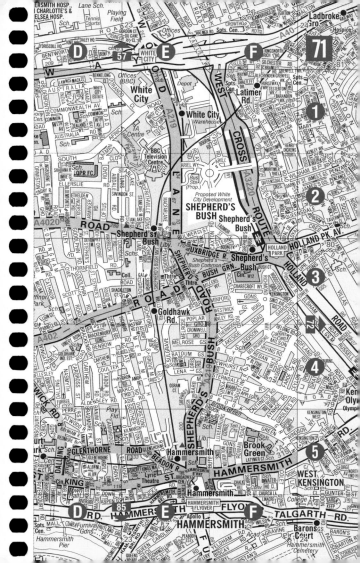

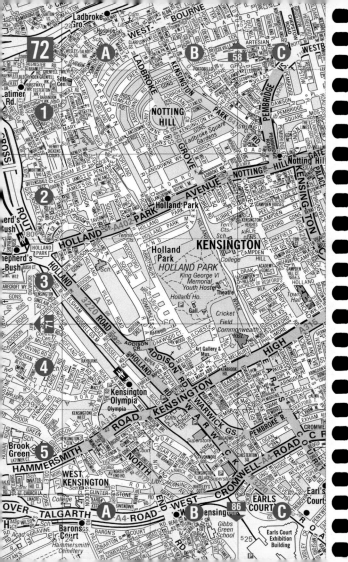

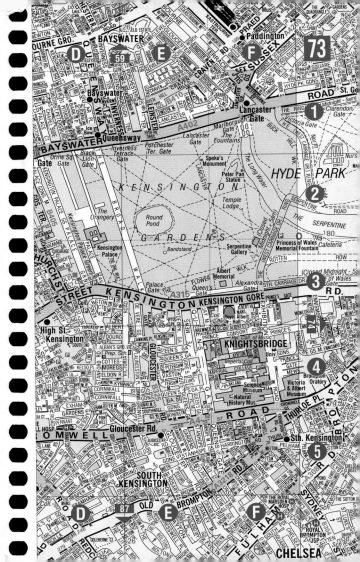

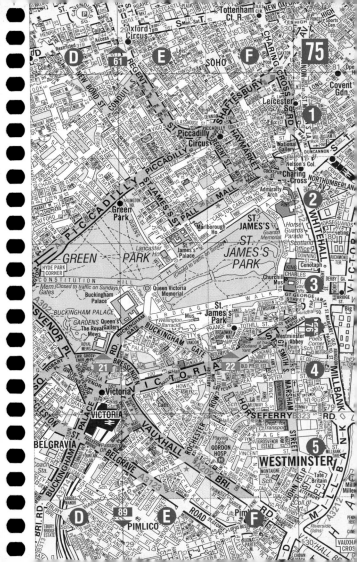

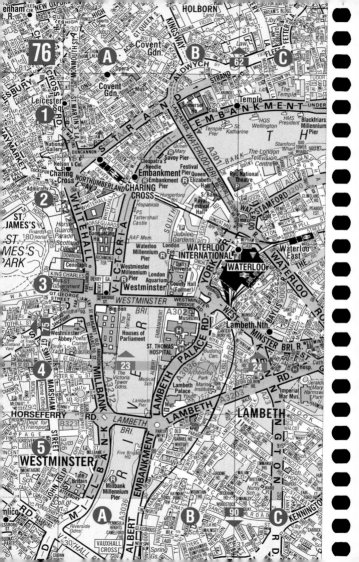

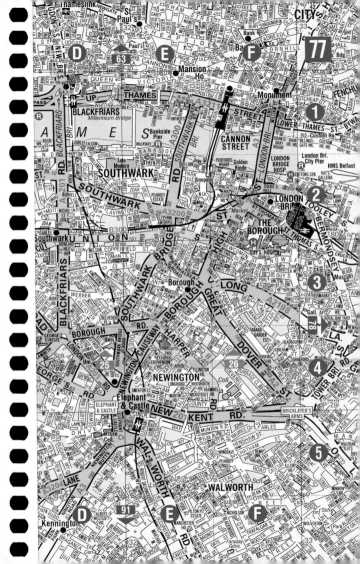

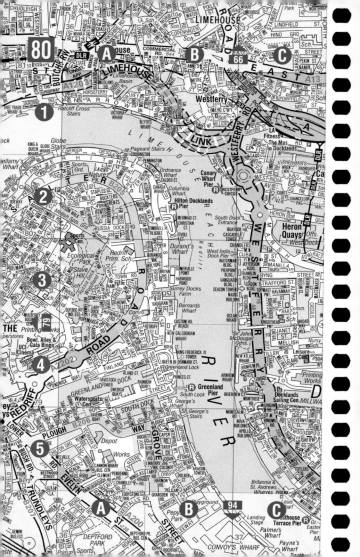

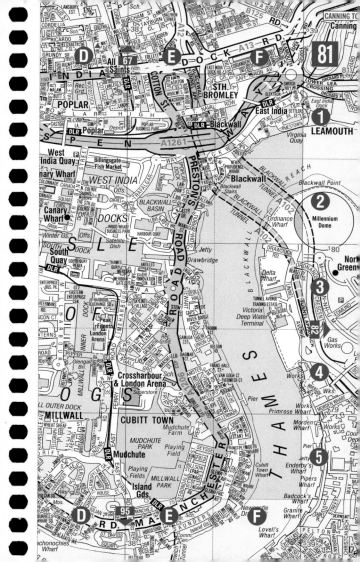

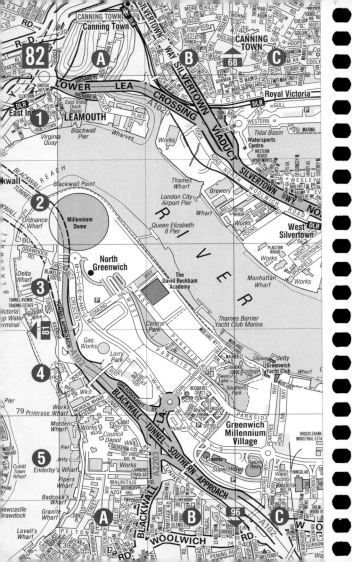

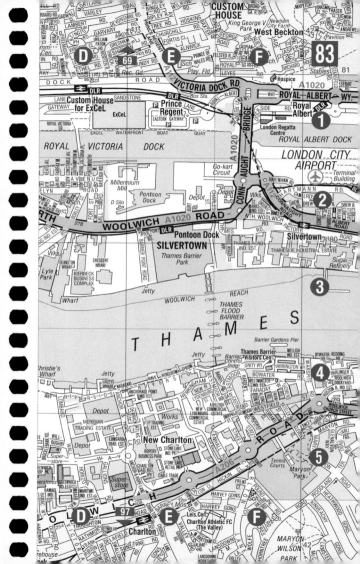

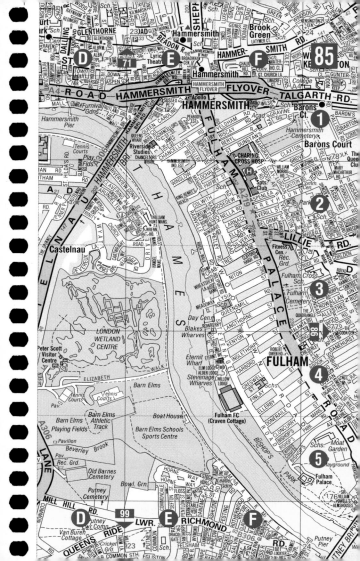

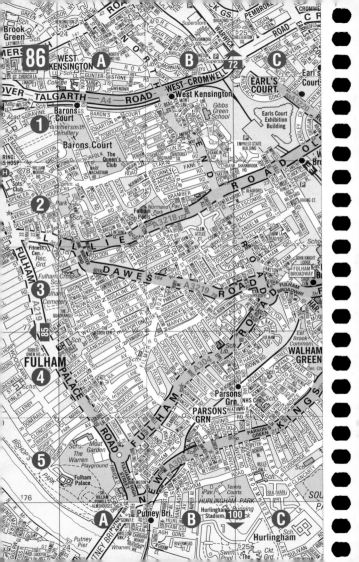

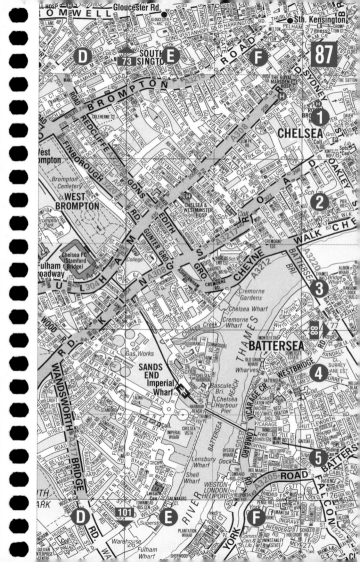

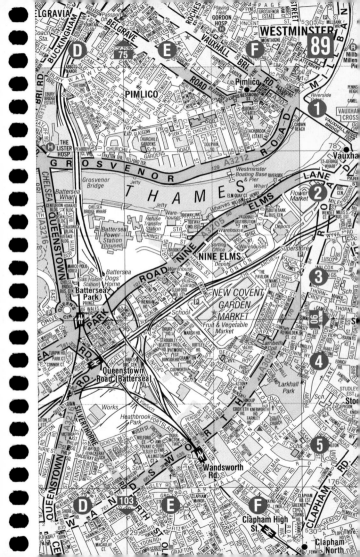

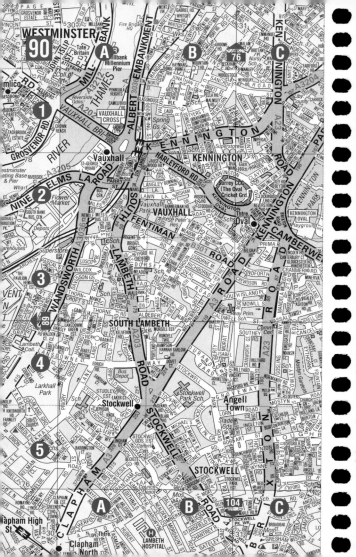

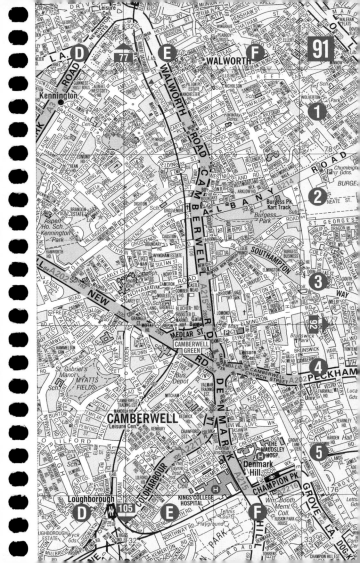

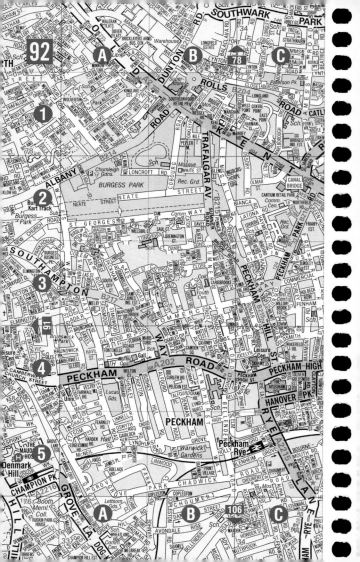

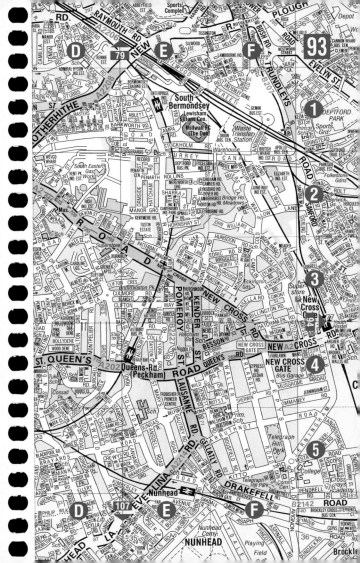

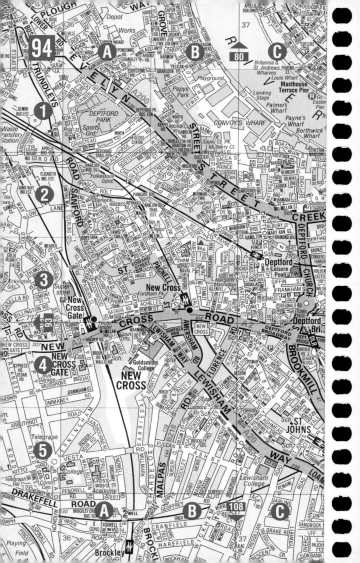

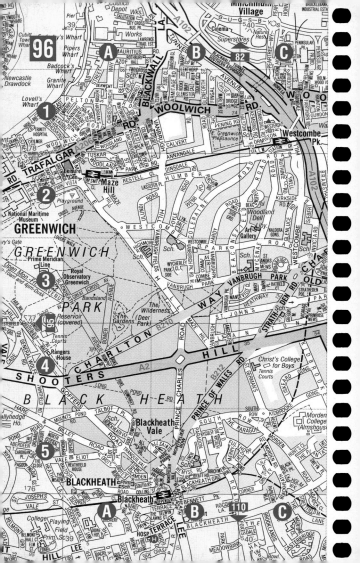

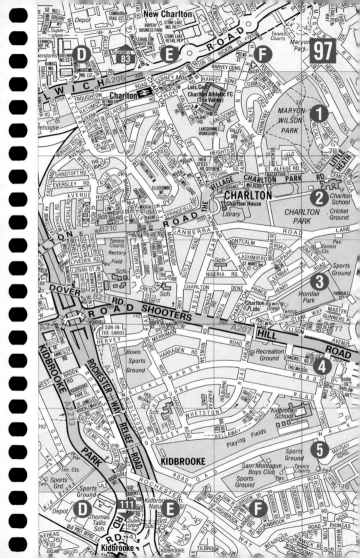

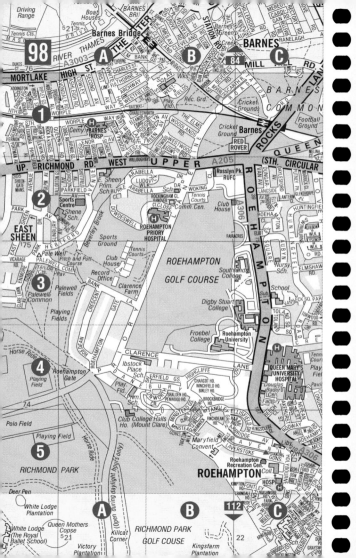

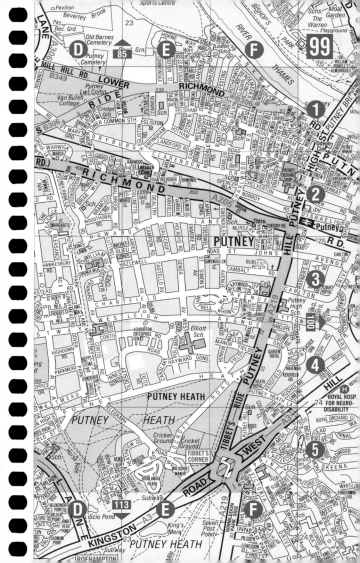

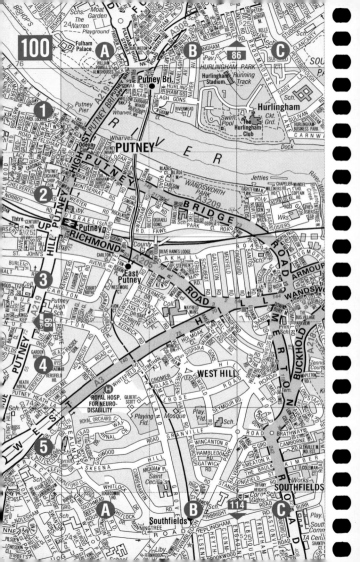

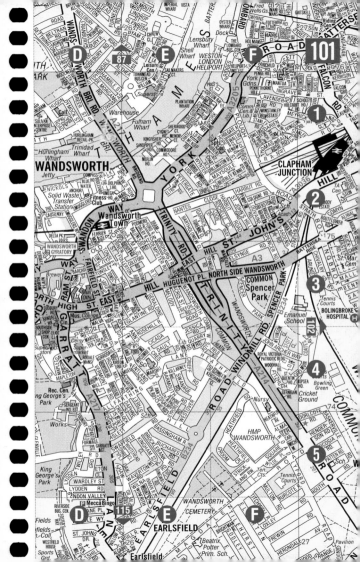

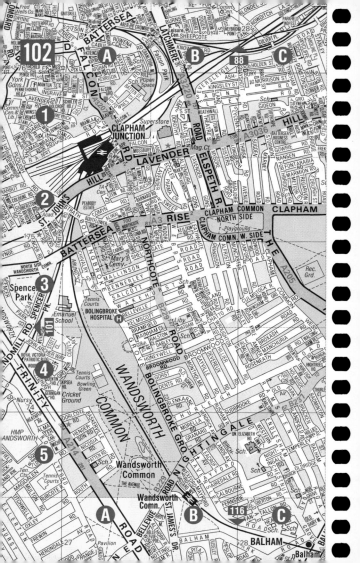

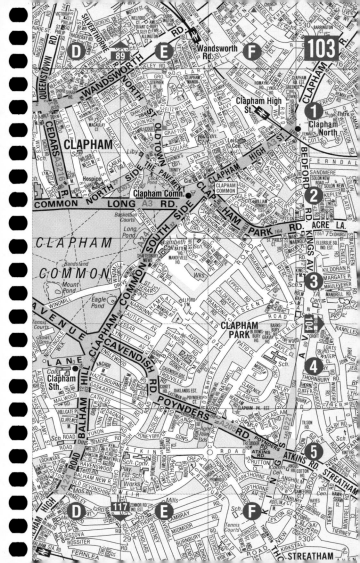

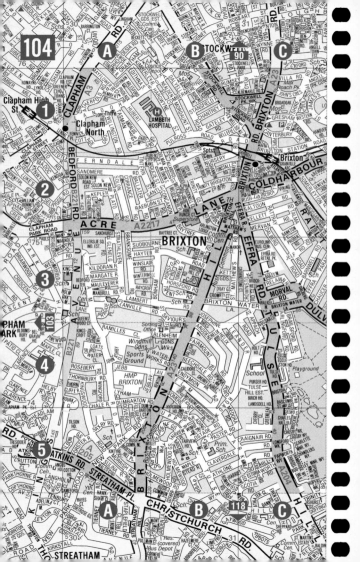

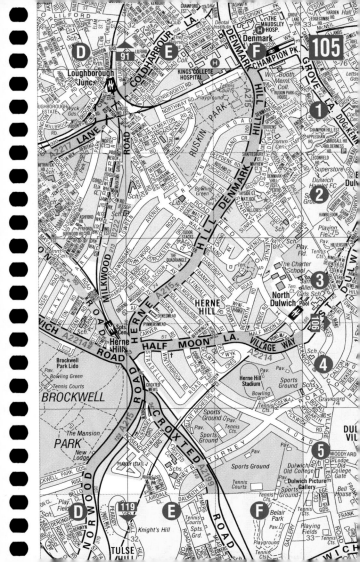

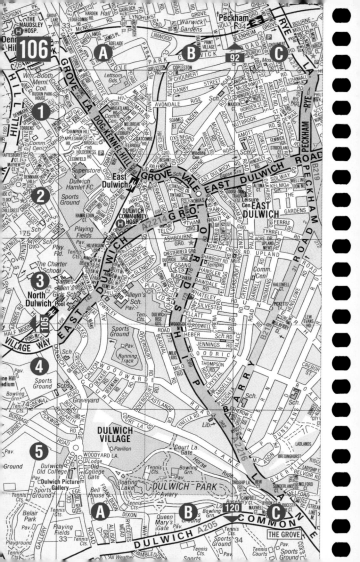

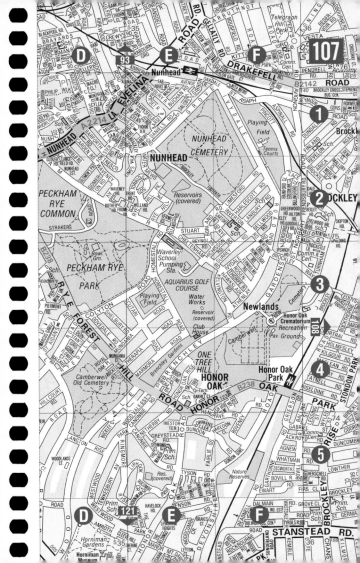

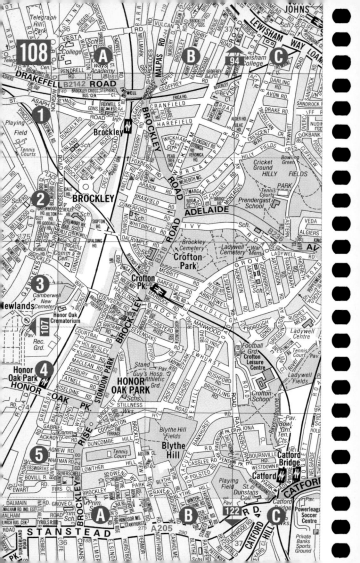

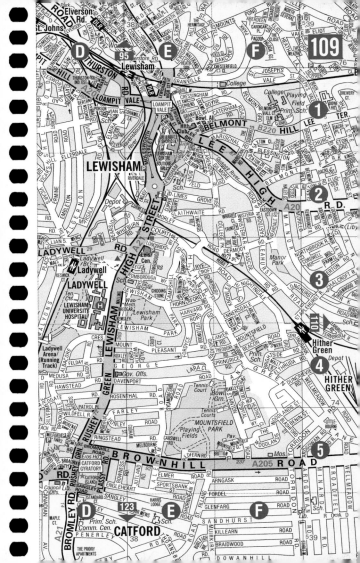

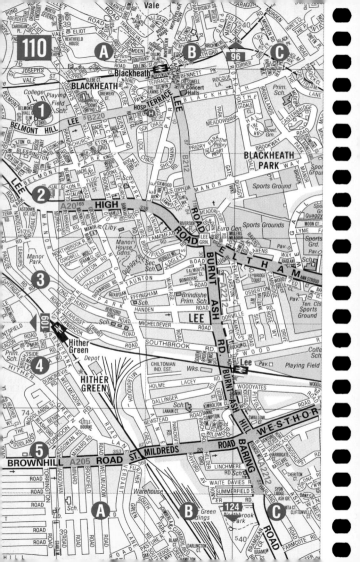

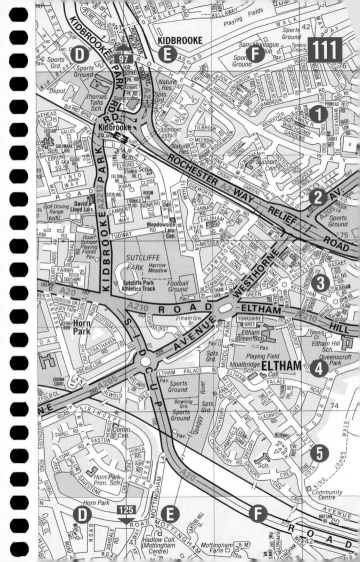

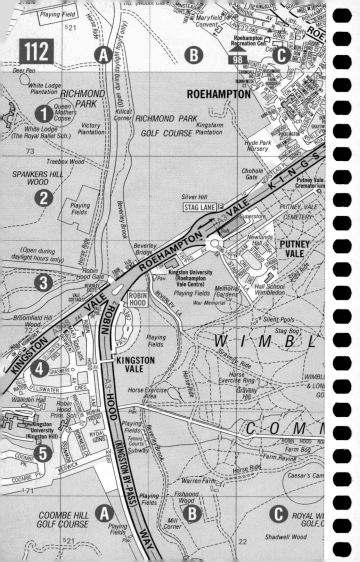

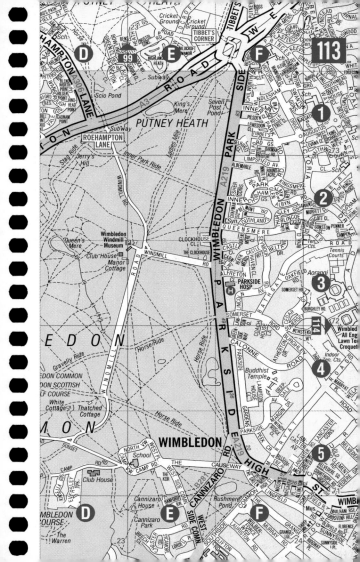

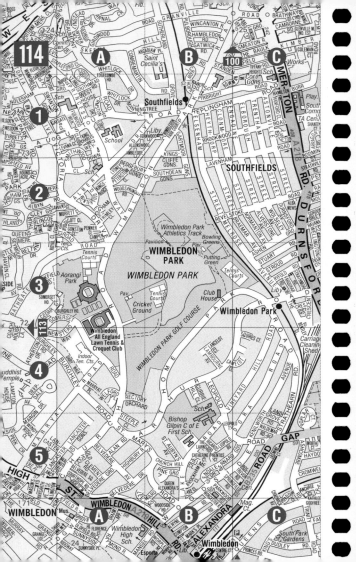

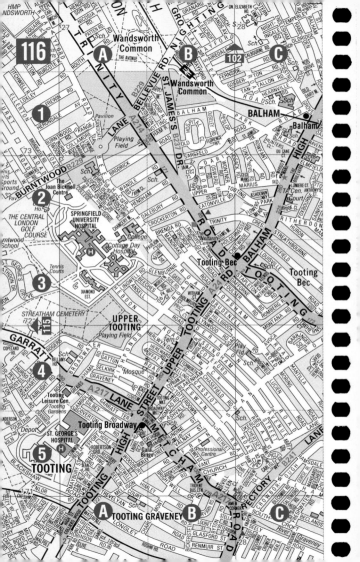

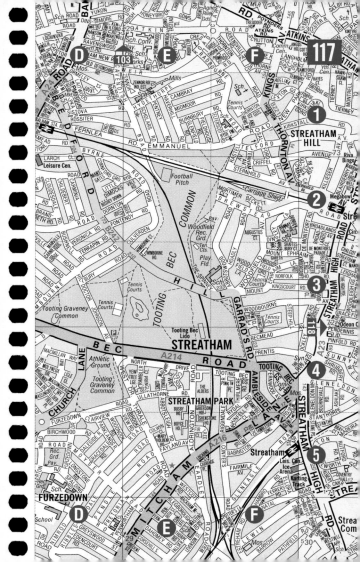

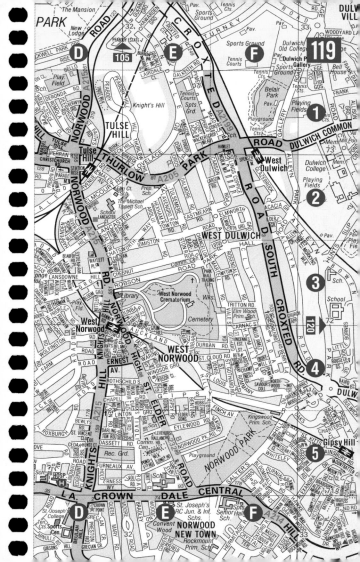

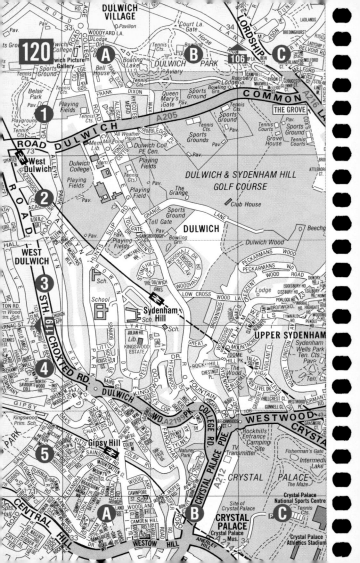

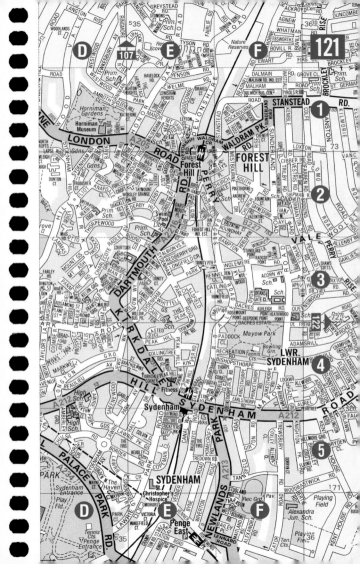

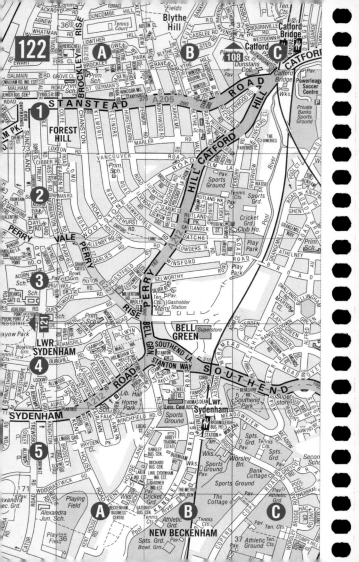

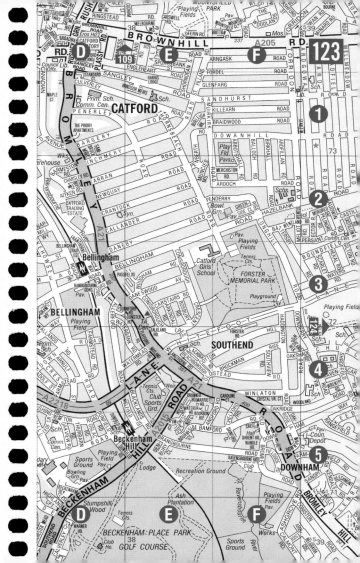

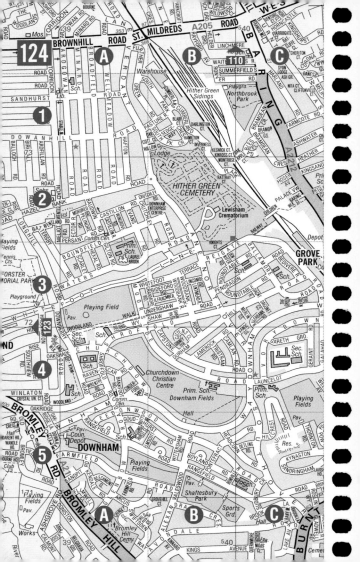

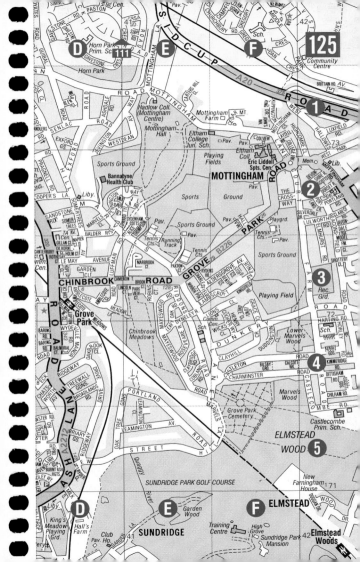

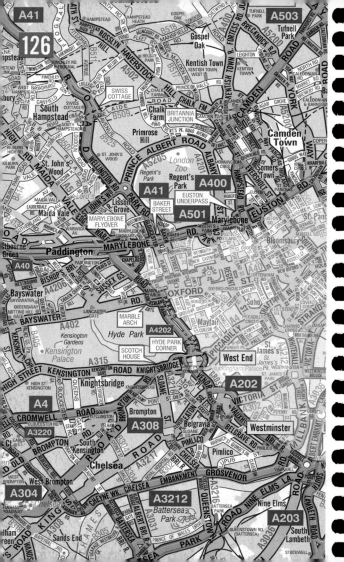

CONGESTION CHARGING ZONE

- Zone applies Mon-Fri 7.00am to 6-30pm excluding public holidays.
- Daily charge allows unlimited travel within and multiple access to the zone.
- Payment must be made on the day of travel or in advance.
- You can pay by telephone (0845 900 1234), via the website (www.cclondon.com), by post, by mobile phone SMS text message or at selected petrol stations and retail outlets.
- Exemptions include motorcycles, mopeds and bicycles. Registration for discount schemes, including disabled and residents, is available from Transport for London.
- There is a penalty charge for late or non-payment of the fee.
- For full details see the Transport for London website (www.cclondon.com).

INDEX

Including Streets, Places & Areas, Industrial Estates,
Selected Flats & Walkways, Junction Names and
Selected Places of Interest.

HOW TO USE THIS INDEX

1. Each street name is followed by its Postcode District (or, if outside the London Postcodes, by its Locality Abbreviation(s)) and then by its map reference;
   e.g. **Abbeville Rd.** SW4 . . . .4E **103** is in the SW4 Postcode District and is to be found in square 4E on page **103**. The page number is shown in bold type.

2. A strict alphabetical order is followed in which Av., Rd., St., etc. (though abbreviated) are read in full and as part of the street name; e.g. **Abbotsleigh Rd.** appears after **Abbots La.** but before **Abbots Mnr.**

3. Streets and a selection of flats and walkways too small to be shown on the maps, appear in the index with the thoroughfare to which it is connected shown in brackets;
   e.g. **Abady Ho.** SW1 . . . .5F **75** (off Page St.)

4. Addresses that are in more than one part are referred to as not continuous.

5. Places and areas are shown in the index in **BLUE TYPE** and the map reference is to the actual map square in which the town centre or area is located and not to the place name shown on the map; e.g. **ALDERSBROOK** 4D **41**

6. An example of a selected place of interest is Admiralty Arch 1C **22** (2F **75**)

7. Junction names are shown in the index in **BOLD TYPE**; e.g. **ANGEL** 1C **62**

8. Map references for entries that appear on large scale pages **4-27** are shown first, with small scale map references shown in brackets; e.g. **Abbey Orchard St.** SW1 . . . .5B **22** (4F **75**)

GENERAL ABBREVIATIONS

All. : Alley
App. : Approach
Arc. : Arcade
Av. : Avenue
Bk. : Back
Blvd. : Boulevard
Bri. : Bridge
B'way. : Broadway
Bldg. : Building
Bldgs. : Buildings
Bus. : Business
C'way. : Causeway
Cen. : Centre
Chu. : Church
Chyd. : Churchyard
Circ. : Circle
Cir. : Circus
Cl. : Close
Coll. : College
Comn. : Common
Cnr. : Corner
Cott. : Cottage
Cotts. : Cottages
Ct. : Court
Cres. : Crescent
Cft. : Croft
Dr. : Drive
E. : East
Emb. : Embankment

Ent. : Enterprise
Est. : Estate
Fld. : Field
Flds. : Fields
Gdn. : Garden
Gdns. : Gardens
Gth. : Garth
Ga. : Gate
Gt. : Great
Grn. : Green
Gro. : Grove
Hgts. : Heights
Ho. : House
Ho's. : Houses
Ind. : Industrial
Info. : Information
Junc. : Junction
La. : Lane
Lit. : Little
Lwr. : Lower
Mnr. : Manor
Mans. : Mansions
Mkt. : Market
Mdw. : Meadow
Mdws. : Meadows
M. : Mews
Mt. : Mount
Mus. : Museum
Nth. : North

Pal. : Palace
Pde. : Parade
Pk. : Park
Pas. : Passage
Pav. : Pavilion
Pl. : Place
Pct. : Precinct
Prom. : Promenade
Quad. : Quadrant
Ri. : Rise
Rd. : Road
Rdbt. : Roundabout
Shop. : Shopping
Sth. : South
Sq. : Square
Sta. : Station
St. : Street
Ter. : Terrace
Twr. : Tower
Trad. : Trading
Up. : Upper
Va. : Vale
Vw. : View
Vs. : Villas
Vis. : Visitors
Wlk. : Walk
W. : West
Yd. : Yard

Beck : **Beckenham**
Brom : **Bromley**
Chst : **Chislehurst**

Ilf : **Ilford**
King T :
    Kingston Upon Thames

Wfd G : **Woodford Green**

02 Cen. NW3 . . . . . 3E **45**
198 Gallery 4D **105**
   (off Railton Rd.)

A

Abady Ho. SW1 . . . . 5F **75**
   (off Page St.)
Abherley M. SW4 . . . . . 1D **103**
Abbess Cl. SW2 . . . . . 1D **119**
Abbeville M. SW4 . . . . . 2F **103**
Abbeville Rd.
   SW4 . . . . 4E **103**
Abbey Bus. Cen.
   SW8 . . . . 4E **89**
Abbey Cl. E5 . . . . 1C **50**
   SW8 . . . . 4F **89**
Abbey Ct. NW8 . . . . . 1E **59**
   (off Abbey Rd.)
   SE17 . . . . 1E **91**
   (off Macleod St.)
Abbey Dr. SW17 . . . . 5C **116**
Abbey Est. NW8 . . . . . 5D **45**
Abbeyfield Est. SE16 . . 5E **79**
Abbeyfield Rd. SE16 . . 5E **79**
   (not continuous)
Abbey Gdns. NW8 . . . 1E **59**
   SE16 . . . . 5C **78**
   W6 . . . . 2A **86**
Abbey Ho. E15 . . . . . . 1A **68**
   (off Baker's Row)
   NW8 . . . . 2E **59**
   (off Garden Rd.)
Abbey La. E15 . . . . . . 1E **67**
Abbey La. Commercial Est.
   E15 . . . . 1A **68**
Abbey Life Ct. E16 . . . . 4D **69**
Abbey Lodge NW8 . . . 2A **60**
   (off Park Rd.)
Abbey M. E17 . . . . 1C **38**
Abbey Orchard St.
   SW1 . . . . 5B **22** (4F **75**)
Abbey Orchard St. Est.
   SW1 . . . . 5C **22** (4F **75**)
   (not continuous)
Abbey Rd. E15 . . . . 1F **67**
   NW6 . . . . 4D **45**
   NW8 . . . . 5D **45**
Abbey St. E13 . . . . 3C **68**
   SE1 . . . . 5E **27** (4B **78**)
Abbey Trad. Est.
   SE26 . . . . 5B **122**
Abbot Ct. SW8 . . . . 3A **90**
   (off Hartington Rd.)
Abbot Ho. E14 . . . . 1D **81**
   (off Smythe St.)
Abbotsbury Cl. E15 . . . 1E **67**
   W14 . . . . 3A **72**
Abbotsbury M. SE15 . . 1E **107**
Abbotsbury Rd. W14 . . . 3A **72**

Abbotshade Rd. SE16 . . 2F **79**
Abbotshall Rd. SE6 . . 1F **123**
Abbot's Ho. W14 . . . . . 4B **72**
   (off St Mary Abbots Ter.)
Abbots La.
   SE1 . . . . . 2E **27** (2A **78**)
Abbotsleigh Rd.
   SW16 . . . . 4E **117**
Abbots Mnr. SW1 . . . . . 5D **75**
Abbots Pk. SW2 . . . . . 1C **118**
Abbot's Pl. NW6 . . . . . 5D **45**
Abbot's Rd. E6 . . . . 5F **55**
Abbots Ter. N8 . . . . 1A **34**
Abbotstone Rd.
   SW15 . . . . 1E **99**
Abbot St. E8 . . . . 3B **50**
Abbots Wlk. W8 . . . . . 4D **73**
Abbotswell Rd. SE4 . . 3B **108**
Abbotswood Rd.
   SE22 . . . . 2A **106**
   SW16 . . . . 3F **117**
Abbott Rd. E14 . . . . . . 4E **67**
   (not continuous)
Abbotts Cl. N1 . . . . 3E **49**
Abbotts Ho. SW1 . . . . . 1F **89**
   (off Aylesford St.)
Abbotts Pk. Rd. E10 . . . 2E **39**
Abbotts Wharf E14 . . . 5C **66**
   (off Stainsby Pl.)
Abchurch La.
   EC4 . . . . . . 4C **18** (1F **77**)
   (not continuous)
Abchurch Yd.
   EC4 . . . . . . 4B **18** (1F **77**)
Abdale Rd. W12 . . . . . . 2D **71**
Abel Ho. SE11 . . . . 2C **90**
   (off Kennington Rd.)
Aberavon Rd. E3 . . . . . 2A **66**
Abercorn Cl. NW8 . . . . 2E **59**
Abercorn Ho. SE10 . . . 3D **95**
   (off Tarves Way)
Abercorn Mans. NW8 . . 1E **59**
   (off Abercorn Pl.)
Abercorn Pl. NW8 . . . . 2E **59**
Abercorn Way SE1 . . . 1C **92**
Abercrombie St.
   SW11 . . . . 5A **88**
Aberdale Rd. SE16 . . . 3F **79**
   (off Garter Way)
Aberdare Gdns. NW6 . . 4D **45**
Aberdeen Ct. W9 . . . . . 3E **59**
   (off Maida Va.)
Aberdeen La. N5 . . . . . 2E **49**
Aberdeen Mans. WC1 . . 3D **7**
   (off Kenton St.)
Aberdeen Pk. N5 . . . . . 2E **49**
Aberdeen Pl. NW8 . . . . 3F **59**
Aberdeen Rd. N5 . . . . . 1E **49**
   NW10 . . . . 2B **42**
Aberdeen Sq. E14 . . . . 2B **80**
Aberdeen Ter. SE3 . . . . 5F **95**
Aberdeen Wharf E1 . . 2D **79**
   (off Wapping High St.)
Aberdour St. SE1 . . . . . 5A **78**

Aberfeldy Ho. SE5 . . . . . 3D **91**
   (not continuous)
Aberfeldy St. E14 . . . . . 4E **67**
   (not continuous)
Aberford Gdns. SE18 . . 4F **97**
Abergeldie Rd.
   SE12 . . . . 4D **111**
Abernethy Rd. SE13 . . 2A **110**
Abersham Rd. E8 . . . . . 2B **50**
Abingdon W14 . . . . 5B **72**
   (off Kensington Village)
Abingdon Cl. NW1 . . . . 3F **47**
   SE1 . . . . 5B **78**
   (off Bushwood Dr.)
Abingdon Ct. W8 . . . . . 4C **72**
   (off Abingdon Vs.)
Abingdon Gdns. W8 . . . 4C **72**
Abingdon Ho. E2 . . . . . . 3F **11**
   (off Boundary St.)
Abingdon Lodge W8 . . . 4C **72**
Abingdon Rd. W8 . . . . . 4C **72**
Abingdon St.
   SW1 . . . . 5D **23** (4A **76**)
Abingdon Vs. W8 . . . . . 4C **72**
Abinger Gro. SE8 . . . . . 2B **94**
Abinger Ho. SE1 . . . . . . 4B **26**
   (off Gt. Dover St.)
Abinger M. W9 . . . . 3C **58**
Abinger Rd. W4 . . . . . . 4A **70**
Ablett St. SE16 . . . . 1E **93**
Abney Gdns. N16 . . . . . 4B **36**
Abney Pk. Ter. N16 . . . 4B **36**
   (off Cazenov Rd.)
Aboyne Rd. NW10 . . . . 5A **28**
   SW17 . . . . 3F **115**
Abyssinia Cl. SW11 . . 2A **102**
Abyssinia Rd. N8 . . . . . 1B **34**
Abyssinia Rd.
   SW11 . . . . 2A **102**
Acacia Bus. Cen.
   E11 . . . . 5A **40**
Acacia Cl. SE8 . . . . 5A **80**
Acacia Gdns. NW8 . . . 1F **59**
Acacia Gro. SE21 . . . . 2F **119**
Acacia Pl. NW8 . . . . . . 1F **59**
Acacia Rd. E11 . . . . 4A **40**
   E17 . . . . 1A **38**
   NW8 . . . . 1F **59**
Academy Apartments
   E8 . . . . 2D **51**
   (off Dalston La.)
   E8 . . . . 2D **51**
   (off Institute Pl.)
Academy Bldgs. N1 . . . 1D **11**
   (off Fanshaw St.)
Academy Ct. E2 . . . . . . 2E **65**
   (off Kirkwall Pl.)
Academy Gdns. W8 . . . 3C **72**
Academy Ho. E3 . . . . . . 4D **67**
   (off Violet Rd.)
Acanthus Dr. SE1 . . . . . 1C **92**
Acanthus Rd. SW11 . . 1C **102**
Accommodation Rd.
   NW11 . . . . 3B **30**

Acfold Rd. SW6 . . . . 4D 87
Achilles Cl. SE1 . . . . 1C 92
Achilles Ho. E2 . . . . 1D 65
   (off Old Bethnal Grn. Rd.)
Achilles Rd. NW6 . . . . . . 2C 44
Achilles Statue
. . . . 2C 20 (2C 74)
Achilles St. SE14 . . . . . . 3A 94
Achilles Way
W1 . . . . 2C 20 (2C 74)
Acklam Rd. W10 . . . . 4A 58
   (not continuous)
Ackmar Rd. SW6 . . . . . . 4C 86
Ackroyd Dr. E3 . . . . 4A 66
Ackroyd Rd. SE23 . . . . . 5F 107
Acland Cres. SE5 . . . . . 1F 105
Acland Ho. SW9 . . . . 4B 90
Acland Rd. NW2 . . . . 3D 43
Acme Ho. E14 . . . . 4E 67
Acol Ct. NW6 . . . . 4C 44
Acol Rd. NW6 . . . . 4C 44
Acorn Ct. E6 . . . . 4F 55
Acorn Gdns. W3 . . . . 4A 56
Acorn Pde. SE15 . . . . 3D 93
Acorn Production Cen.
N7 . . . . 4A 48
Acorn Wlk. SE16 . . . . 2A 80
Acorn Way SE23 . . . . . . 3F 121
Acre Dr. SE22 . . . . 2C 106
Acre La. SW2 . . . . 2A 104
Acre Rd. SW19 . . . . 5F 115
Acris St. SW18 . . . . 3E 101
Acton Ho. E8 . . . . 5B 50
   (off Lee St.)
Acton La. NW10 . . . . 1A 56
Acton M. E8 . . . . 5B 50
Acton Pk. Est. W3 . . . . . 3A 70
Acton St. WC1 . . 2F 7 (2B 62)
Acton Va. Ind. Pk.
W3 . . . . 3A 70
Acuba Rd. SW18 . . . . . . 2D 115
Ada Ct. N1 . . . . 5E 49
   (off Packington St.)
W9 . . . . 2E 59
Ada Gdns. E14 . . . . 5F 67
E15 . . . . 5B 54
Ada Ho. E2 . . . . 5C 50
   (off Ada Pl.)
Adair Rd. W10 . . . . 3A 58
Adair Twr. W10 . . . . 3A 58
   (off Appleford Rd.)
Ada Kennedy Ct.
SE10 . . . . 3E 95
   (off Greenwich Sth. St.)
Adam & Eve Ct. W1 . . . . 2A 14
Adam & Eve M. W8 . . . . 4C 72
Adam Cl. SE6 . . . . 4B 122
Adam Ct. SE11 . . . . 5D 77
   (off Opal St.)
SW7 . . . . 5E 73
   (off Gloucester St.)
Adams Ct. E17 . . . . 1A 38
EC2 . . . . 2C 18 (5A 64)
Adams Gdns. Est.
SE16 . . . . 3E 79
Adams Ho. E14 . . . . 5F 67
   (off Aberfeldy St.)
Adams M. SW17 . . . . . . 2B 116
Adamson Rd. E16 . . . . . . 5C 68
NW3 . . . . 4F 45

Adams Pl. E14 . . . . 2D 81
   (off Nth. Colonnade, The)
N7 . . . . 2B 48
Adamsrill Rd. SE26 . . . . 4F 121
Adam's Row
W1 . . . . 5C 12 (1C 74)
Adam St.
WC2 . . . . 5E 15 (1A 76)
Adam Wlk. SW6 . . . . 3E 85
Ada Pl. E2 . . . . 5C 50
Adare Wlk. SW16 . . . . . . 3B 118
Ada Rd. SE5 . . . . 3A 92
Adastral Ho. WC1 . . . . . . 5F 7
   (off New North St.)
Ada St. E8 . . . . 5D 51
Ada Workshops E8 . . . . . 5D 51
Adderley Gro.
SW11 . . . . 3C 102
Adderley St. E14 . . . . . . 5E 67
Addey Ho. SE8 . . . . 3B 94
Addington Ct.
SW14 . . . . 1A 98
Addington Gro.
SE26 . . . . 4A 122
Addington Ho. SW9 . . . . . 5B 90
   (off Stockwell Rd.)
Addington Rd. E3 . . . . . . 2C 66
E16 . . . . 3A 68
N4 . . . . 1C 34
Addington Sq. SE5 . . . . . 2F 91
   (not continuous)
Addington St.
SE1 . . . . 4A 24 (3B 76)
Addis Ho. E1 . . . . 4E 65
   (off Lindley St.)
Addisland Ct. W14 . . . . . 3A 72
   (off Holland Vs. Rd.)
Addison Av. W11 . . . . . . 2A 72
Addison Bri. Pl. W14 . . . 5B 72
Addison Cres. W14 . . . . . 4A 72
   (not continuous)
Addison Dr. SE12 . . . . . . 3D 111
Addison Gdns. W14 . . . . 4F 71
Addison Gro. W4 . . . . . . 4A 70
Addison Ho. NW8 . . . . . . 2F 59
   (off Grove End Rd.)
Addison Pk. Mans.
W14 . . . . 4F 71
   (off Richmond Way)
Addison Pl. W11 . . . . 2A 72
Addison Rd. E11 . . . . 1C 40
W14 . . . . 3A 72
Addle Hill
EC4 . . . . 3E 17 (5D 63)
Addlestone Ho. W10 . . . . 4E 57
   (off Sutton Way)
Addle St.
EC2 . . . . 2A 18 (5E 63)
Addy Ho. SE16 . . . . 5E 79
Adela Ho. W6 . . . . 1E 85
   (off Queen Caroline St.)
Adelaide Av. SE4 . . . . . . 2B 108
Adelaide Cl. SW9 . . . . . . 2C 104
Adelaide Cl. NW8 . . . . . . 5F 45
   (off Abbey Rd.)
Adelaide Gro. W12 . . . . . 2C 70
Adelaide Ho. E15 . . . . . . 1B 68
SE5 . . . . 5A 92
W11 . . . . 5B 58
   (off Portobello Rd.)

Adelaide Rd. E10 . . . . . . 5D 39
NW3 . . . . 4F 45
SW18 . . . . 3C 100
Adelaide St.
WC2 . . . . 5D 15 (1A 76)
Adela St. W10 . . . . 3A 58
Adelina Gro. E1 . . . . 4E 65
Adelina M. SW12 . . . . . . 1F 117
Adelina Yd. E1 . . . . 4E 65
   (off Adelina Gro.)
Adeline Pl.
WC1 . . . . 1C 14 (4F 61)
Adelphi Ct. E8 . . . . 4B 50
   (off Celandine Dr.)
SE16 . . . . 3F 79
   (off Garter Way)
W4 . . . . 2A 84
Adelphi Ter.
WC2 . . . . 5E 15 (1A 76)
Adelphi Theatre 5E 15
   (off Strand)
Adeney Cl. W6 . . . . 2F 85
Aden Gro. N16 . . . . 1F 49
Aden Ho. E1 . . . . 4E 65
   (off Duckett St.)
Adenmore Rd. SE6 . . . . . 5C 108
Aden Ter. N16 . . . . 1F 49
Adeyfield Ho. EC1 . . . . . . 2C 10
   (off Cranwood St.)
Adie Rd. W6 . . . . 4E 71
Adine Rd. E13 . . . . 3D 69
Adler St. E1 . . . . 5C 64
Adley St. E5 . . . . 2A 52
Admiral Ct. SW10 . . . . . . 4E 87
   (off Admiral Sq.)
W1 . . . . 1B 12
   (off Blandford St.)
Admiral Ho. SW1 . . . . . . 5E 75
   (off Willow Pl.)
SE16 . . . . 1D 93
Admiral M. W10 . . . . 3F 57
Admiral Pl. SE16 . . . . . . 2A 80
Admirals Ct. SE1 . . . . . . 2F 27
   (off Horselydown La.)
Admiral's Ga. SE10 . . . . . 4D 95
Admiral Sq. SW10 . . . . . 4E 87
Admiral St. SE8 . . . . 5C 94
Admirals Wlk. NW3 . . . . . 5E 31
Admirals Way E14 . . . . . 3C 80
Admiralty Arch
. . . . 1C 22 (2F 75)
Admiralty Cl. SE8 . . . . . . 3C 94
Admiral Wlk. W9 . . . . 4C 58
Adolf St. SE6 . . . . 4D 123
Adolphus Rd. N4 . . . . . . 4D 35
Adolphus St. SE8 . . . . . . 3B 94
Adpar St. W2 . . . . 4F 59
Adrian Av. NW2 . . . . 3D 29
Adrian Boult Ho. E2 . . . . 2D 65
   (off Mansford St.)
Adrian Ho. N1 . . . . 5B 48
   (off Barnsbury Est.)
SW8 . . . . 3A 90
   (off Wyvil Rd.)
Adrian M. SW10 . . . . . . 2D 87
Adriatic Bldg. E14 . . . . . . 1A 80
   (off Horseferry Rd.)
Adriatic Ho. E1 . . . . 3F 65
   (off Ernest St.)

Adron Ho. *SE16* *5E 79*
  (off Millender Wlk.)
Adstock Ho. *N1* *4D 49*
  (off Sutton Est., The)
Advance Rd. SE27 . . . . 4E 119
Adventurers Ct. *E14* *1F 81*
  (off Newport Av.)
Adys Lawn *NW2* 3D 43
Ady's Rd. SE15 . . . . . . 1B 106
Aegean Apartments
  E16 . . . . *1C 82*
  (off Western Gateway)
Aegon Ho. *E14* *4D 81*
  (off Lanark Sq.)
Affleck St. *N1* 1F 7 (1B 62)
Afghan Rd. SW11 . . . . . . 5A 88
Afsil Ho. *EC1* *1C 16*
  (off Viaduct Bldgs.)
Aftab Ter. *E1* *3D 65*
  (off Tent St.)
Agamemnon Rd.
  NW6 . . . . 1B 44
Agar Gro. NW1 . . . . 4E 47
Agar Gro. Est. NW1 . . . . 4F 47
Agar Pl. NW1 . . . . 4E 47
Agar St.
  WC2 . . . . . . 5D 15 (1A 76)
Agate Cl. E16 . . . . 5F 69
Agate Rd. W6 . . . . 4E 71
Agatha Cl. E1 . . . . 2D 79
Agave Rd. NW2 . . . . 1E 43
Agdon St. EC1 . . 3D 9 (3D 63)
Agincourt Rd. NW3 . . . . 1B 46
Agnes Ho. *W11* *1F 71*
  (off St Ann's Rd.)
Agnes Rd. W3 . . . . 2B 70
Agnes St. E14 . . . . 5B 66
Agnew Rd. SE23 . . . . . 5F 107
Aigburth Mans. *SW9* . . *3C 90*
  (off Mowll St.)
Aileen Wlk. E15 . . . . . . 4B 54
Ailsa St. E14 . . . . 4E 67
Ainger M. *NW3* *4B 46*
  (off Ainger Rd., not continuous)
Ainger Rd. NW3 . . . . . . 4B 46
Ainsdale *NW1* *1F 5*
  (off Harrington St.)
Ainsdale Dr. SE1 . . . . . 1C 92
Ainsley St. E2 . . . . 2D 65
Ainslie Wlk. SW12 . . . . 5D 103
Ainsty Est. SE16 . . . . . . 3F 79
Ainsty St. SE16 . . . . 3E 79
Ainsworth Cl. NW2 . . . . 5C 28
  SE15 . . . . 5A 92
Ainsworth Ho. *NW8* . . . *5D 45*
  (off Ainsworth Way)
Ainsworth Rd. E9 . . . . . 4E 51
Ainsworth Way NW8 . . . 5E 45
Aintree Av. E6 . . . . 5F 55
Aintree Est. *SW6* *3A 86*
  (off Aintree St.)
Aintree St. SW6 . . . . . . 3A 86
Aird Ho. *SE1* *5F 25*
  (off Rockingham St.)
Airdrie Cl. N1 . . . . 4B 48
Airedale Av. W4 . . . . . . 5B 70
Airedale Av. Sth. W4 . . 1B 84
Airedale Rd. SW12 . . . 5B 102
Airlie Gdns. W8 . . . . . . 2C 72
Air St. W1 . . . . . . 5A 14 (1E 75)

Aisgill Av. W14 . . . . 1B 86
  (not continuous)
Aislibie Rd. SE12 . . . . . 2A 110
Aiten Pl. W6 . . . . 5C 70
Aithan Ho. *E14* *5B 66*
  (off Copenhagen Pl.)
Aitken Cl. E8 . . . . 5C 50
Aitken Rd. SE6 . . . . . . 2D 123
Ajax Ho. *E2* *1D 65*
  (off Old Bethnal Grn. Rd.)
Ajax Rd. NW6 . . . . 1B 44
Akbar Ho. *E14* *5D 81*
  (off Cahir St.)
Akehurst St. SW15 . . . . 4C 98
Akenside Rd. NW3 . . . . 2F 45
Akerman Rd. SW9 . . . . 5D 91
Akintaro Ho. *SE8* *2B 94*
  (off Alverton St.)
Alamaro Lodge
  SE10 . . . . 4B 82
Aland Ct. SE16 . . . . 4A 80
Alan Hocken Way
  E15 . . . . 1A 68
Alan Preece Ct. NW6 . . 4F 43
Alan Rd. SW19 . . . . . . 5A 114
Alanthus Cl. E12 . . . . . 4C 110
Alaska Bldgs. SE1 . . . . 5A 78
Alaska St.
  SE1 . . . . . . 2B 24 (2C 76)
Alastor Ho. *E14* *4E 81*
  (off Strattondale St.)
Albacore Cres.
  SE13 . . . . 4D 109
Alba Gdns. NW11 . . . . . 1A 30
Alba M. SW18 . . . . 2C 114
Alban Highwalk EC2 . . . 2A 18
  (not continuous)
Albany *W1* 5F 13 (1E 75)
Albany Ct. E10 . . . . 2C 38
  NW8 . . . . 1F 59
  (off Abbey Rd.)
  NW10 . . . . *2D 57*
  (off Trenmar Gdns.)
Albany Courtyard
  W1 . . . . . . 5A 14 (1E 75)
Albany Mans. SW11 . . . 3A 88
Albany M.
  BR1: Brom 5C 124
  N1 . . . . 4C 48
  SE5 . . . . 2E 91
Albany Pl. N7 . . . . 1C 48
Albany Rd. E10 . . . . . . 2C 38
  E12 . . . . 1F 55
  E17 . . . . 1A 38
  N4 . . . . 1C 34
  SE5 . . . . 2F 91
  SW19 . . . . 5D 115
Albany St.
  NW1 . . . . 1E 5 (1D 61)
Albany Ter. NW1 . . . . . . 4E 5
Alba Pl. W11 . . . . 5B 58
Albatross Way SE16 . . . 3F 79
Albemarle SW19 . . . . . 2F 113
Albemarle Ho. *SE8* . . . *5B 80*
  (off Foreshore)
  SW9 . . . . 1C 104
Albemarle St.
  W1 . . . . 5E 13 (1D 75)
Albemarle Way
  EC1 . . . . 4D 9 (3D 63)

Alberta Est. *SE17* *1D 91*
  (off Alberta St.)
Alberta Ho. *E14* *2E 81*
  (off Gaselee St.)
Alberta St. SE17 . . . . . . 1D 91
Albert Av. SW8 . . . . 3B 90
Albert Barnes Ho.
  SE1 . . . . *4E 77*
  (off New Kent Rd.)
Albert Bigg Point *E15* . . *1E 67*
  (off Godfrey St.)
Albert Bri. SW8 . . . . . . 3A 88
Albert Bri. Rd. SW11 . . 3A 88
Albert Carr Gdns.
  SW16 . . . . 5A 118
Albert Cl. E9 . . . . 5D 51
Albert Cotts. *E1* *4C 64*
  (off Deal St.)
Albert Ct. E7 . . . . 1C 54
  SW7 . . . . 4F 73
Albert Ct. Ga. *SW7* *3B 74*
  (off Knightsbridge)
Albert Dr. SW19 . . . . . 2A 114
Albert Emb.
  SE1 . . . . . . 5F 23 (4B 76)
  (Lambeth Pal. Rd.)
  SE1 . . . . 1A 90
  (Vauxhall Bri.)
Albert Gdns. E1 . . . . . . 5F 65
Albert Ga.
  SW1 . . . . . . 3A 20 (3B 74)
Albert Gray Ho.
  SW10 . . . . *3F 87*
  (off Worlds End Est.)
Albert Hall Mans.
  SW7 . . . . 3F 73
  (not continuous)
Albert Memorial 3F 73
Albert M. *E14* *1A 80*
  (off Northey St.)
  N4 . . . . 3B 34
  SE4 . . . . 2A 108
  W8 . . . . 4E 73
Albert Pal. Mans.
  SW11 . . . . *4D 89*
  (off Lurline Gdns.)
Albert Pl. W8 . . . . 4D 73
Albert Rd. E10 . . . . 4E 39
  E16 . . . . 2F 83
  E17 . . . . 1C 38
  N4 . . . . 3B 34
  N15 . . . . 1A 36
  NW6 . . . . 1B 58
Albert Sq. E15 . . . . 2A 54
  SW8 . . . . 3B 90
Albert Starr Ho. *SE8* . . *5F 79*
  (off Bush Rd.)
Albert St. NW1 . . . . 5D 47
Albert Studios SW11 . . 4B 88
Albert Ter. NW1 . . . . . . 5C 46
  W6 . . . . *1C 84*
  (off Beavor La.)
Albert Ter. M. NW1 . . . . 5C 46
Albert Way SE15 . . . . . 3D 93
Albert Westcott Ho.
  SE17 . . . . *1D 91*
  (off Middleton Rd.)
Albery Theatre 4D 15
  (off St Martin's La.)

Albion Av. SW8........5F 89
Albion Bldgs. N1.....1A 62
  (off Albion Yd.)
Albion Cl. W2........1A 74
Albion Ct. W6.........5D 71
  (off Albion Pl.)
Albion Dr. E8.........4B 50
Albion Est. SE16......3F 79
Albion Gdns. W6......5D 71
Albion Ga. W2........1A 74
  (off Albion St., not continuous)
Albion Gro. N16.......1A 50
Albion Ho. SE8........3C 94
  (off Watsons St.)
Albion M. N1..........5C 48
  W2................1A 74
  W6................5D 71
Albion Pde. N16.......1F 49
Albion Pl.
  EC1.........5D 9 (4D 63)
  EC2.........1C 18 (4F 63)
  W6................5D 71
Albion Rd. N16........1F 49
Albion Sq. E8.........4A 50
  (not continuous)
Albion St. SE16.......3F 79
  W2................5A 60
Albion Ter. E8........4A 50
Albion Vs. Rd.
  SE26.............3E 121
Albion Wlk. N1........1A 62
  (off York Way)
Albion Way
  EC1....1F 17 (4E 63)
  SE13.............2E 109
Albion Wharf SW11....3A 88
Albion Yd. E1.........4D 65
  N1................1A 62
Albon Ho. SW18.......4D 101
  (off Neville Gill Cl.)
Albrighton Rd. SE22...1A 106
Albury Ho. SW3.......4E 25
  (off Boyfield St.)
Albury M. E12.........4E 41
Albury St. SE8........2C 94
Albyn Rd. SE8........4C 94
Alcester Cres. E5.....4D 37
Alconbury Rd. E5......4C 36
Aldam Pl. N16.........5B 36
Aldbourne Rd. W12....2B 70
  (not continuous)
Aldbridge St. SE17....1A 92
Aldburgh M.
  W1........2C 12 (5C 60)
  (not continuous)
Aldbury Ho. SW3......5A 74
  (off Marlborough St.)
Aldebert Ter. SW8.....3A 90
Aldeburgh Cl. E5......4D 37
Aldeburgh Pl. SE10....5C 82
  (off Aldeburgh St.)
Aldeburgh St. SE10....1C 96
Alden Av. E15.........2B 68
Aldenham Ho. NW1....1A 6
  (off Aldenham St.)
Aldenham St.
  NW1.......1A 6 (1E 61)
Alden Ho. E8..........5D 51
  (off Duncan Rd.)
Aldensley Rd. W6......4D 71

Alderbrook Rd.
  SW12.............4D 103
Alderbury Rd. SW13...2C 84
Alder Cl. SE15........2B 92
Alder Gro. NW2.......4C 28
Alder Ho. NW3.........3B 46
  SE4...............1C 108
  SE15...............2B 92
  (off Cator St.)
Alder Lodge SW6......4E 85
Aldermanbury
  EC2........2A 18 (5E 63)
Aldermanbury Sq.
  EC2........1A 18 (4E 63)
Aldermans Wlk.
  EC2.....1D 19 (4A 64)
Alder M. N19..........4E 33
Aldermoor Rd. SE6....3B 122
Alderney Ho. N1.......3E 49
  (off Arran Wlk.)
Alderney Rd. E1.......3F 65
Alderney St. SW1.....5D 75
Alders, The SW16.....4E 117
ALDERSBROOK......4D 41
Aldersbrook Rd. E11...4D 41
  E12...............4D 41
Alders Cl. E11........4D 41
Aldersford Cl. SE4....3F 107
Aldersgate St.
  EC1........5F 9 (4E 63)
Aldersgrove Av.
  SE9..............3F 125
Aldershot Rd. NW6....5B 44
Alderson St. W10.....3A 58
Alderton Cl. NW10....5A 28
Alderton Cres. NW4...1D 29
Alderton Rd. SE24....1E 105
Alderton Way NW4....1D 29
Alderville Rd. SW6....5B 86
Alderwick Ct. N7......3B 48
  (off Cornelia St.)
Aldford Ho. W1........1B 20
  (off Park St.)
Aldford St.
  W1...........1C 20 (2C 74)
ALDGATE..........5B 64
Aldgate E1............2F 19
  (off Whitechapel High St.)
  EC3.......3E 19 (5A 64)
Aldgate Av.
  E1............2F 19 (5B 64)
Aldgate Barrs E1......2F 19
Aldgate High St.
  EC3.......3F 19 (5B 64)
Aldgate Triangle E1...5C 64
  (off Coke St.)
Aldham Ho. SE14.....5B 94
  (off Malpas Rd.)
Aldine Ct. W12........3E 71
  (off Aldine St.)
Aldine Pl. W12........3E 71
Aldine St. W12........3E 71
Aldington Ct. E8......4C 50
  (off London Flds. W. Side)
Aldington Rd. SE18...4F 83
Aldis M. SW17........5A 116
Aldis St. SW17........5A 116
Aldred Rd. NW6......2C 44
Aldren Rd. SW17......3E 115
Aldrich Ter. SW18.....2E 115

Aldrick Ho. N1........5B 48
  (off Barnsbury Est.)
Aldridge Rd. Vs.
  W11................4B 58
Aldrington Rd.
  SW16.............5E 117
Aldsworth Cl. W9.....3D 59
Aldwick Ho. SE13....4E 109
Aldworth Gro. SE13...4E 109
Aldworth Rd. E15.....4A 54
Aldwych WC2....4F 15 (5B 62)
Aldwych Ct. E8........4B 50
  (off Middleton Rd.)
Aldwych Theatre......3F 15
  (off Aldwych)
Aldwyn Ho. SW8......3A 90
  (off Davidson Gdns.)
Alestan Beck Rd. E16..5F 69
Alexa Cl. W8..........5C 72
Alexander Av. NW10...4D 43
Alexander Evans M.
  SE23.............2F 121
Alexander Fleming Mus.
  ....5F 59
  (off Praed St.)
Alexander Ho. E14....4C 80
  (off Tiller Rd.)
Alexander M. W2......5D 59
Alexander Pl. SW7....5A 74
Alexander Rd. N19....5A 34
Alexander Sq. SW3....5A 74
Alexander St. W2.....5C 58
Alexander Studios
  SW11.............2F 101
  (off Haydon Way)
Alexandra Av. SW11...4C 88
  W4................3A 84
Alexandra Cl. SE8.....2B 94
Alexandra Cotts.
  SE14..............4B 94
Alexandra Ct. SW7....5E 72
  (off Queen's Ga.)
  W2................1D 73
  (off Moscow Rd.)
  W9................3E 59
  (off Maida Va.)
Alexandra Cres.
  BR1: Brom.......5B 124
Alexandra Dr. SE19...5A 120
Alexandra Gdns. W4...3A 84
Alexandra Gro. N4....3D 35
Alexandra Ho. E16....2D 83
  (off Wesley Av.)
Alexandra Mans.
  SW3..............2F 87
  (off King's Rd.)
Alexandra M. SW19...5B 114
Alexandra National Ho.
  N4................3D 35
Alexandra Pl. NW8....5E 45
Alexandra Rd. E10....5E 39
  E17................1B 38
  NW8...............5E 45
  SE26.............5F 121
  SW14.............1A 98
  SW19.............5B 114
  W4................3A 70
Alexandra St. E16.....4C 68
  SE14..............3A 94

Alexandra Ter. *E14* 1D **95**
   (off Westferry Rd.)
Alexandra Wlk.
  SE19 . . . . 5A **120**
Alexandra Yd. E9 . . . . 5F **51**
Alexis St. SE16 . . . . 5C **78**
Alfearn Rd. E5 . . . . 1E **51**
Alford Ct. *N1* *1A **10***
   (off Shepherdess Wlk.,
   not continuous)
Alford Ho. N6 . . . . 1E **33**
Alford Pl. N1 . . 1A **10** (1E **63**)
Alfreda St. SW11 . . . . . . 4D **89**
Alfred Ho. *E9* *2A **52***
   (off Homerton Rd.)
E12 . . . . *4F **55***
   (off Tennyson Av.)
Alfred M. W1 . . . 5B **6** (4F **61**)
Alfred Nunn Ho.
  NW10 . . . . 5B **42**
Alfred Pl. WC1 . . 5B **6** (4F **61**)
Alfred Rd. E15 . . . . 2B **54**
  W2 . . . . 4C **58**
Alfred St. E3 . . . . 2B **66**
Alfreton Cl. SW19 . . . . . 3F **113**
Alfriston Rd. SW11 . . . . 3B **102**
Algar Ho. SE1 . . . . 4D **25**
Algarve Rd. SW18 . . . 1D **115**
Algernon Rd. NW4 . . . . . 1C **28**
  NW6 . . . . 5C **44**
  SE13 . . . . 2D **109**
Algiers Rd. SE13 . . . . . 2C **108**
Alice Gilliatt Ct. *W14* . . *2B **86***
   (off Star Rd.)
Alice La. E3 . . . . 5B **52**
Alice Owen Technology Cen.
  EC1 . . . . *1D **9***
   (off Goswell Rd.)
Alice Shepherd Ho.
  E14 . . . . *3E **81***
   (off Manchester Rd.)
Alice St. SE1 . . 5D **27** (4A **78**)
   (Decima St.)
  SE1 . . . . . 5D **27** (4A **78**)
   (Rothsay St.)
Alice Thompson Cl.
  SE12 . . . . 2E **125**
Alice Walker Cl.
  SE24 . . . . 2D **105**
Alie St. E1 . . . . 3F **19** (5B **64**)
Alison Ct. SE1 . . . . 1C **92**
Aliwal M. SW11 . . . . . . 2A **102**
Aliwal Rd. SW11 . . . . . . 2A **102**
Alkerden Rd. W4 . . . . . . 1A **84**
Alkham Rd. N16 . . . . 4B **36**
Allan Barclay Ct. N15 . . 1B **36**
Allanson Ct. *E10* *4C **38***
   (off Leyton Grange Est.)
Allard Gdns. SW4 . . . . . 3F **103**
Allardyce St. SW4 . . . . 2B **104**
Allcott Ho. *W12* *5D **57***
   (off Du Cane Rd.)
Allcroft Rd. NW5 . . . . . . 2C **46**
Allenby Rd. SE23 . . . . . 3A **122**
Allen Ct. *E17* *1C **38***
   (off Yunus Khan Cl.)
Allendale Cl. SE5 . . . . . . 5F **91**
  SE26 . . . . 5F **121**
Allen Edwards Dr.
  SW8 . . . . 4A **90**

Allenford Ho. *SW15* . . . *4B **98***
   (off Tunworth Cres.)
Allen Rd. E3 . . . . 1B **66**
  N16 . . . . 1A **50**
Allensbury Pl. NW1 . . . . 4F **47**
Allen St. W8 . . . . 4C **72**
Allenswood SW19 . . . 1A **114**
Allerford Rd. SE6 . . . . . 3D **123**
Allerton Ho. *N1* *1B **10***
   (off Fairbank Est.)
Allerton Rd. N16 . . . . . . 4E **35**
Allerton St.
  N1 . . . . 1B **10** (2F **63**)
Allerton Wlk. N7 . . . . . . 4B **34**
Allestree Rd. SW6 . . . . . 3A **86**
Alleyn Cres. SE21 . . . . 2F **119**
Alleyn Ho. *SE1* *5C **26***
   (off Burbage Cl.)
Alleyn Pk. SE21 . . . . . . 2F **119**
Alleyn Rd. SE21 . . . . . 3F **119**
Allfarthing La.
  SW18 . . . . 4D **101**
Allgood St. E2 . . . . 1B **64**
Allhallows La.
  EC4 . . . . 5B **18** (1F **77**)
Allhallows Rd. E6 . . . . . 4F **69**
Alliance Rd. E13 . . . . . . 4E **69**
Allied Ind. Est. W3 . . . . 3A **70**
Allied Way W3 . . . . 3A **70**
Allingham M. *N1* *1E **63***
   (off Allingham St.)
Allingham St. N1 . . . . . . 1E **63**
Allington Cl. SW19 . . . 5F **113**
Allington Ct. *SW1* *5E **21***
   (off Allington St.)
  SW8 . . . . 5E **89**
Allington Rd. NW4 . . . . 1D **29**
  W10 . . . . 2A **58**
Allington St.
  SW1 . . . . 5E **21** (4D **75**)
Allison Cl. SE10 . . . . . . 4E **95**
Allison Gro. SE21 . . . . 1A **120**
Alliston Ho. *E2* *2B **64***
   (off Gibraltar Wlk.)
Allitsen Rd. NW8 . . . . . 1A **60**
   (not continuous)
All Nations Ho. *E8* *4D **51***
   (off Martello St.)
Allnutt Way SW4 . . . . . 3F **103**
Alloa Rd. SE8 . . . . 1F **93**
Allom Ho. *W11* *1A **72***
   (off Clarendon Rd.)
Allonby Ho. *E14* *4A **66***
   (off Aston St.)
Alloway Rd. E3 . . . . 2A **66**
Allport Ho. *SE5* *1F **105***
   (off Denmark Hill)
Allport M. *E1* *3E **65***
   (off Hayfield Pas.)
All Saints Cl. SW8 . . . . 4A **90**
All Saints Ct. *E1* *1E **79***
   (off Johnson St.)
  SW11 . . . . *3D **89***
   (off Prince of Wales Dr.)
All Saints Dr. SE3 . . . . 5A **96**
   (not continuous)
All Saints Ho. W11 . . . . *4B **58***
   (off All Saints Rd.)
All Saints Pas.
  SW18 . . . . 3C **100**

All Saints Rd. W11 . . . . 4B **58**
All Saints St. N1 . . . . . . 1B **62**
All Saints Twr. E10 . . . . 2D **39**
Allsop Pl.
  NW1 . . . . 4A **4** (3B **60**)
All Souls Av. NW10 . . . 1D **57**
All Souls' Pl.
  W1 . . . . 1E **13** (4D **61**)
Allwood Cl. SE26 . . . . . 4F **121**
Alma Birk Ho. NW6 . . . . 4A **44**
Almack Rd. E5 . . . . 1E **51**
Alma Gro. SE1 . . . . 5B **78**
Alma Pl. NW10 . . . . 2D **57**
Alma Rd. SW18 . . . . . . 2E **101**
Alma Sq. NW8 . . . . 1E **59**
Alma St. E15 . . . . 3F **53**
  NW5 . . . . 3D **47**
Alma Ter. *E3* *5B **52***
   (off Beale Rd.)
  SW18 . . . . 5F **101**
  W8 . . . . 4C **72**
Almeida St. N1 . . . . 5D **49**
Almeida Theatre 5D **49**
   (off Almeida St.)
Almeric Rd. SW11 . . . . 2B **102**
Almington St. N4 . . . . . 3B **34**
Almond Cl. SE15 . . . . . 5C **92**
Almond Rd. SE16 . . . . . 5D **79**
Almorah Rd. N1 . . . . 4F **49**
Alnwick Rd. E16 . . . . . . 5E **69**
  SE12 . . . . 4D **111**
Alperton St. W10 . . . . . 3B **58**
Alphabet Sq. E3 . . . . . . 4C **66**
Alpha Bus. Cen. E17 . . 1B **38**
Alpha Cl. NW1 . . . . 3A **60**
Alpha Gro. E14 . . . . 3C **80**
Alpha Ho. NW6 . . . . 1C **58**
  NW8 . . . . *3A **60***
   (off Ashbridge St.)
  SW4 . . . . 2B **104**
Alpha Pl. NW6 . . . . 1C **58**
  SW3 . . . . 2A **88**
Alpha Rd. SE14 . . . . . . 4B **94**
Alpha St. SE15 . . . . . . 5C **92**
Alpine Gro. E9 . . . . 4E **51**
Alpine Rd. E10 . . . . 4D **39**
  SE16 . . . . 5E **79**
Alric Av. NW10 . . . . 4A **42**
Alroy Rd. N4 . . . . 2C **34**
Alsace Rd. SE17 . . . . . 1A **92**
Alscot Rd.
  SE1 . . . . 5F **27** (5B **78**)
   (not continuous)
Alscot Rd. Ind. Est.
  SE1 . . . . 4B **78**
Alscot Way SE1 . . . . . . 5B **78**
Alston Rd. SW17 . . . . 4F **115**
Altenburg Gdns.
  SW11 . . . . 2B **102**
Althea St. SW6 . . . . . . 5D **87**
Althorpe M. SW11 . . . . 4F **87**
Althorp Rd. SW17 . . . . 1B **116**
Altima Ct. SE22 . . . . . 2C **106**
Altior Ct. N6 . . . . 1E **33**
Alton Rd. SW15 . . . . . 1C **112**
Alton St. E14 . . . . 4D **67**
Aluna Ct. SE15 . . . . . . 1E **107**
Alvanley Gdns. NW6 . . . 2D **45**
Alverstone Av.
  SW19 . . . . 2C **114**

Alverstone Ho. SE11 . . . 2C 90
Alverstone Ho. NW2 . . . 4E 43
Alverton St. SE8 . . . 1B 94
  (not continuous)
Alvey St. SE17 . . . 1A 92
Alvington Cres. E8 . . . 2B 50
Alwold Cres. SE12 . . . 4D 111
Alwyne La. N1 . . . 4D 49
Alwyne Pl. N1 . . . 3E 49
Alwyne Rd. N1 . . . 4E 49
  SW19 . . . 5B 114
Alwyne Sq. N1 . . . 3E 49
Alwyne Vs. N1 . . . 4D 49
Alyth Gdns. NW11 . . . 1C 30
Alzette Ho. E2 . . . 1F 65
  (off Mace St.)
Amazon St. E1 . . . 5C 64
Ambassadors Ct. E8 . . . 4B 50
  (off Holly St.)
  SW1 . . . 2A 22
Ambassador Sq. E14 . . . 5D 81
Ambassadors Theatre
  . . . . 4C 14
  (off West St.)
Ambergate St. SE17 . . . 1D 91
Amber Gro. NW2 . . . 3F 29
Amberley Gro.
  SE26 . . . 5D 121
Amberley Rd. E10 . . . 2C 38
  W9 . . . 4C 58
Amber Wharf E2 . . . 5B 50
  (off Nursery La.)
Amblecote Cl. SE12 . . . 3D 125
Amblecote Mdws.
  SE12 . . . 3D 125
Amblecote Rd.
  SE12 . . . 3D 125
Ambler Rd. N4 . . . 5D 35
Ambleside
  BR1: Brom . . . 5F 123
  NW1 . . . 1E 5
  SW19 . . . 1A 114
Ambleside Av.
  SW16 . . . 4F 117
Ambleside Cl. E9 . . . 2E 51
  E10 . . . 2D 39
Ambleside Gdns.
  SW16 . . . 5F 117
Ambleside Point
  SE15 . . . 3E 93
  (off Tustin Est.)
Ambleside Rd. NW10 . . . 4B 42
Ambrosden Av.
  SW1 . . . 5A 22 (4E 75)
Ambrose Av. NW11 . . . 2A 30
Ambrose Ho. E14 . . . 4C 66
  (off Selsey St.)
Ambrose M. SW11 . . . 5B 86
Ambrose St. SE16 . . . 5D 79
Ambrose Wlk. E3 . . . 1C 66
Amelia Ho. W6 . . . 1E 85
  (off Queen Caroline St.)
Amelia St. SE17 . . . 1E 91
Amen Cnr.
  EC4 . . . 3E 17 (5D 63)
  SW17 . . . 5B 116
Amen Ct.
  EC4 . . . 3E 17 (5D 63)
America Sq.
  EC3 . . . 4F 19 (1B 78)

America St.
  SE1 . . . 2F 25 (2E 77)
Amerland Rd.
  SW18 . . . 3B 100
Amersham Gro.
  SE14 . . . 3B 94
Amersham Rd. SE14 . . . 4B 94
Amersham Va. SE14 . . . 3B 94
Amery Ho. SE17 . . . 1A 92
  (off Kinglake St.)
Amesbury Av. SW2 . . . 2A 118
Amesbury Twr. SW8 . . . 5E 89
Ames Cotts. E14 . . . 4A 66
  (off Maroon St.)
Ames Ho. E2 . . . 1F 65
  (off Mace St.)
Amethyst Rd. E15 . . . 1F 53
AMF Bowling . . . 1E 109
Amherst Ho. SE16 . . . 3F 79
  (off Wolfe Cres.)
Amhurst Pde. N16 . . . 2B 36
  (off Amhurst Pk.)
Amhurst Pk. N16 . . . 2F 35
Amhurst Pas. E8 . . . 1C 50
Amhurst Rd. E8 . . . 2D 51
  N16 . . . 1B 50
Amhurst Ter. E8 . . . 1C 50
Amias Ho. EC1 . . . 3F 9
  (off Central St.)
Amiel St. E1 . . . 3E 65
Amies St. SW11 . . . 1B 102
Amigo Ho. SE1 . . . 5C 24
  (off Morley St.)
Amina Way SE16 . . . 4C 78
Amity Rd. E15 . . . 4B 54
Ammanford Grn.
  NW9 . . . 1A 28
Ammonite Ho. E15 . . . 4B 54
Amner Rd. SW11 . . . 4C 102
Amor Rd. W6 . . . 4E 71
Amory Ho. N1 . . . 5B 48
  (off Barnsbury Est.)
Amott Rd. SE15 . . . 1C 106
Amoy Pl. E14 . . . 1C 80
  (not continuous)
Ampthill Est. NW1 . . . 1E 61
Ampthill Sq.
  NW1 . . . 1A 6 (1E 61)
Ampton Pl.
  WC1 . . . 2F 7 (2B 62)
Ampton St.
  WC1 . . . 2F 7 (2B 62)
Amroth Cl. SE23 . . . 1D 121
Amroth Grn. NW9 . . . 1A 28
Amstel Ct. SE15 . . . 3B 92
  (off Garnies Cl.)
Amsterdam Rd. E14 . . . 4E 81
Amundsen Ct. E14 . . . 1C 94
  (off Napier Av.)
Amwell Ct. Est. N4 . . . 4E 35
Amwell St.
  EC1 . . . 1B 8 (2C 62)
Amyruth Rd. SE4 . . . 3C 108
Anatola Rd. N19 . . . 4E 33
Anchor SW18 . . . 2D 101
Anchorage Ho. E14 . . . 1F 81
  (off Clove Cres.)

Anchorage Point E14 . . . 3B 80
  (off Cuba St.)
Anchorage Point Ind. Est.
  SE7 . . . 4E 83
Anchor & Hope La.
  SE7 . . . 4E 83
Anchor Brewhouse
  SE1 . . . 2F 27 (2B 78)
Anchor Ct. SW1 . . . 5F 75
  (off Vauxhall Bri. Rd.)
Anchor Ho. E16 . . . 4B 68
  (off Barking Rd.)
  E16 . . . 5E 69
  (off Prince Regent La.)
  EC1 . . . 3F 9
  (off Old St.)
Anchor M. SW12 . . . 4D 103
Anchor Retail Pk. E1 . . . 3E 65
Anchor Rd. E12 . . . 4F 41
Anchor St. SE16 . . . 5D 79
Anchor Ter. E1 . . . 3E 65
Anchor Wharf E3 . . . 4D 67
  (off Yeo St.)
Anchor Yd.
  EC1 . . . 3A 10 (3E 63)
Ancill Cl. W6 . . . 2A 86
Ancona Rd. NW10 . . . 1C 56
Andalus Rd. SW9 . . . 1A 104
Andaman Ho. E1 . . . 4A 66
  (off Duckett St.)
Anderson Cl. W3 . . . 5A 56
Anderson Cl. NW2 . . . 3E 29
Anderson Ho. E14 . . . 1E 81
  (off Woolmore St.)
  SW17 . . . 5F 115
  W12 . . . 5D 57
  (off Du Cane Rd.)
Anderson Rd. E9 . . . 3F 51
Anderson Sq. N1 . . . 5D 49
  (off Gaskin St.)
Anderson St. SW3 . . . 1B 88
Anderton Cl. SE5 . . . 1F 105
Andover Av. E16 . . . 5F 69
Andover Pl. NW6 . . . 1D 59
Andover Rd. N7 . . . 4B 34
Andoversford Ct.
  SE15 . . . 2A 92
  (off Bibury Cl.)
Andre St. E8 . . . 2C 50
Andrew Borde St.
  WC2 . . . 2C 14 (5F 61)
Andrew Ct. SE23 . . . 2F 121
Andrewes Gdns. E6 . . . 5F 69
Andrewes Highwalk
  EC2 . . . 1A 18
Andrewes Ho. EC2 . . . 1A 18
Andrew Pl. SW8 . . . 3F 89
Andrew Reed Ho.
  SW18 . . . 5A 100
  (off Linstead Way)
Andrews Crosse WC2 . . . 3B 16
Andrews Ho. NW3 . . . 4B 46
  (off Fellows Rd.)
Andrew's Rd. E8 . . . 5D 51
Andrew St. E14 . . . 5E 67
Andrews Wlk. SE17 . . . 2D 91
Anerley Hill SE19 . . . 5B 120
Aneurin Bevan Ct.
  NW2 . . . 4D 29
Anfield Cl. SW12 . . . 5E 103

ANGEL 1C 62
Angela Davies Ind. Est.
SE24 . . . . 2D 105
Angel All. E1 . . . . 5B 64
(off Whitechapel High St.)
Angel Cen., The N1 . . . 1C 8
Angel Cl.
EC2 . . . . . . 2C 18 (5F 63)
SW1 . . . . . . 2A 22 (2E 75)
Angel Ga. EC1 . . . . . . 1E 9
(not continuous)
Angelina Ho. SE15 . . . 4C 92
(off Goldsmith Rd.)
Angelis Apartments
N1 . . . . 1E 9
(off Graham St.)
Angel La. E15 . . . . 3F 53
Angell Pk. Gdns.
SW9 . . . . 1C 104
Angell Rd. SW9 . . . . . . 1C 104
ANGELL TOWN 4C 90
Angell Town Est.
SW9 . . . . 5C 90
Angel M. E1 . . . . 1D 79
N1 . . . . 1C 62
SW15 . . . . 5C 98
Angel Pas.
EC4 . . . . . . 5B 18 (1F 77)
Angel Pl. SE1 . . 3B 26 (3F 77)
Angel Sq. EC1 . . . . 1D 63
Angel St. EC1 . . 2F 17 (5E 63)
Angel Wlk. W6 . . . . . . 5E 71
Angel Yd. N6 . . . . 3C 32
Angerstein Bus. Pk.
SE10 . . . . 5C 82
Angerstein La. SE3 . . . 4B 96
Anglebury W2 . . . . 5C 58
(off Talbot Rd.)
Angler's La. NW5 . . . . 3D 47
Anglesea Ter. W6 . . . . 4D 71
Anglesey Ho. E14 . . . . 5C 66
(off Lindfield St.)
Angles Rd. SW16 . . . . 4A 118
Anglia Ho. E14 . . . . . . 5A 66
(off Salmon La.)
Anglian Rd. E11 . . . . . 5F 39
Anglo Rd. E3 . . . . 1B 66
Angrave Ct. E8 . . . . . . 5B 50
(off Scriven St.)
Angrave Pas. E8 . . . . . 5B 50
Angus Ho. SW2 . . . . . . 5F 103
Angus Rd. E13 . . . . . . 2E 69
Angus St. SE14 . . . . . . 3A 94
Anhalt Rd. SW11 . . . . . 3A 88
Anley Rd. W14 . . . . . . 3F 71
Annabel Cl. E14 . . . . . 5D 67
Annandale Rd. SE10 . . 2B 96
W4 . . . . 1A 84
Anna Neagle Cl. E7 . . . 1C 54
Anne Compton M.
SE12 . . . . 5B 110
Anne Goodman Ho.
E1 . . . . 5E 65
(off Jubilee St.)
Annesley Cl. NW10 . . . 5A 28
Annesley Ho. SW9 . . . 4C 90
Annesley Rd. SE3 . . . . 4D 97
Annesley Wlk. N19 . . . 4E 33
Anne St. E13 . . . . 3C 68

Annette Cres. N1 . . . . . 4E 49
Annette Rd. N7 . . . . . . 5B 34
(not continuous)
Annie Besant Cl. E3 . . 5B 52
Anning St.
EC2 . . . . 3E 11 (3A 64)
Annis Rd. E9 . . . . 3A 52
Ann La. SW10 . . . . 2F 87
Ann Moss Way SE16 . . 4E 79
Ann's Cl. SW1 . . . . 4A 20
Ann's Pl. E1 . . . . 1F 19
Ann Stroud Ct. SE12 . . 3C 110
Ansar Gdns. E17 . . . . . 1B 38
Ansdell Rd. SE15 . . . . . 5E 93
Ansdell St. W8 . . . . . . 4D 73
Ansdell Ter. W8 . . . . . . 4D 73
Ansell Ho. E1 . . . . 4E 65
(off Mile End Rd.)
Ansell Rd. SW17 . . . . . 3A 116
Anselm Rd. SW6 . . . . . 2C 86
Ansford Rd.
BR1: Brom 5E 123
Ansleigh Pl. W11 . . . . 1F 71
Anson Ho. E1 . . . . 3A 66
(off Shandy St.)
SW1 . . . . 2E 89
(off Churchill Gdns.)
Anson Rd. N7 . . . . 1E 47
NW2 . . . . 1D 43
Anstey Ho. E9 . . . . 5E 51
(off Templecombe Rd.)
Anstey Rd. SE15 . . . . . 1C 106
Anstice Cl. W4 . . . . . . 3A 84
Antenor Ho. E2 . . . . . . 1D 65
(off Old Bethnal Grn. Rd.)
Anthony Cope Ct. N1 . . 1C 10
(off Chart St.)
Anthony Ho. NW8 . . . . 3A 60
(off Ashbridge St.)
Anthony St. E1 . . . . . . 5D 65
Antigua Wlk. SE19 . . . 5F 119
Antilles Bay E14 . . . . . 3E 81
Antill Rd. E3 . . . . 2A 66
Antill Ter. E1 . . . . 5F 65
Antonine Hgts. SE1 . . . 4D 27
Anton St. E8 . . . . 2C 50
Antony Ho. SE14 . . . . . 3F 93
(off Barborough St.)
SE16 . . . . 5E 79
(off Raymouth Rd.)
Antrim Gro. NW3 . . . . 3B 46
Antrim Mans. NW3 . . . 3B 46
Antrim Rd. NW3 . . . . . 3B 46
Apex Ind. Est. NW10 . . 5C 80
Aphrodite Ct. E14 . . . . 5C 80
(off Homer Dr.)
Apollo Bldg. E14 . . . . . 5C 80
Apollo Bus. Cen. SE8 . 1F 93
Apollo Ct. E1 . . . . 1C 78
(off Thomas More St.)
SW9 . . . . 4C 90
(off Southey Rd.)
Apollo Ho. E2 . . . . 1D 65
(off St Jude's Rd.)
N6 . . . . 2B 32
SW10 . . . . 3F 87
(off Milman's St.)
Apollo Pl. E11 . . . . 5A 40
SW10 . . . . 3F 87

Apollo Theatre
Soho 4B 14
(off Shaftesbury Av.)
Victoria 4E 75
(off Wilton Rd.)
Apothecary St.
EC4 . . . . 3D 17 (5D 63)
Appach Rd. SW2 . . . . . 3C 104
Apple Blossom Ct.
SW8 . . . . 3F 89
(off Pascal St.)
Appleby Cl. N15 . . . . . 1F 35
Appleby Rd. E8 . . . . . . 4C 50
E16 . . . . 5B 68
Appleby St. E2 . . . . . . 1B 64
Appledore Cl.
SW17 . . . . 2B 116
Appleford Ho. W10 . . . 3A 58
(off Bosworth Rd.)
Appleford Rd. W10 . . . 3A 58
Applegarth Ho. SE1 . . 3E 25
SE15 . . . . 3C 92
(off Bird in Bush Rd.)
Applegarth Rd. W14 . . 4F 71
Apple Rd. E11 . . . . 5A 40
Appleshaw Ho. SE5 . . 1A 106
Appleton Rd. SE9 . . . . 1F 111
Apple Tree Yd.
SW1 . . . . 1A 22 (2E 75)
Applewood Cl. NW2 . . 5D 29
Applewood Dr. E13 . . . 3D 69
Appold St.
EC2 . . . . 5D 11 (4A 64)
Apprentice Way E5 . . . 1D 51
Approach, The NW4 . . 1F 29
W3 . . . . 5A 56
Approach Cl. N16 . . . . 1A 50
Approach Rd. E2 . . . . . 1E 65
April Ct. E2 . . . . 1C 64
(off Teale St.)
April Glen SE23 . . . . . 3F 121
April St. E8 . . . . 1B 50
Apsley Cen., The
NW2 . . . . 4C 28
Apsley House 3C 20
Apsley Ho. E1 . . . . 4E 65
(off Stepney Way)
NW8 . . . . 1F 59
(off Finchley Rd.)
Apsley Way NW2 . . . . 4C 28
W1 . . . . 3C 20 (3C 74)
(not continuous)
Aquarius Bus. Pk.
NW2 . . . . 3C 28
(off Priestley Way)
Aquila St. NW8 . . . . . . 1F 59
Aquinas St.
SE1 . . . . 2C 24 (2C 76)
Arabella Dr. SW15 . . . 2A 98
Arabian Ho. E1 . . . . . . 3A 66
(off Ernest St.)
Arabin Rd. SE4 . . . . . . 2A 108
Aragon Ho. E16 . . . . . . 2C 82
(off Capulet M.)
Aragon Twr. SE8 . . . . . 5B 80
Aral Ho. E1 . . . . 3F 65
(off Ernest St.)
Arapiles Ho. E14 . . . . . 5F 67
(off Blair St.)
Arbery Rd. E3 . . . . 2A 66

Arbon Ct. N1 . . . . 5E **49**
(off Linton St.)
Arbor Ct. N16 . . . . 4F **35**
Arboretum Ct. N1 . . . . . 3F **49**
(off Dove Rd.)
Arborfield Cl. SW2 . . 1B **118**
Arborfield Ho. E14 . . . . 1C **80**
(off E. India Dock Rd.)
Arbour Ho. E1 . . . . 5F **65**
(off Arbour Sq.)
Arbour Sq. E1 . . . . 5F **65**
Arbury Ter. SE26 . . . . . 3C **120**
Arbuthnot Ho. SE14 . . 5F **93**
Arbutus St. E8 . . . . 5B **50**
Arcade, The EC2 . . . . . 1D **19**
N7 . . . . 1A **48**
(off Macready Pl.)
Arcadia Ct. E1 . . . . 2F **19**
Arcadia St. E14 . . . . . . 5C **66**
Archangel St. SE16 . . 3F **79**
Archbishop's Pl.
SW2 . . . . 5B **104**
Archdale Ct. W12 . . . . . 2D **71**
Archdale Ho. SE1 . . . . . 5D **27**
(off Long La.)
Archdale Rd. SE22 . . 3B **106**
Archel Rd. W14 . . . . 2B **86**
Archer Ho. SE14 . . . . . . 4A **94**
SW11 . . . . 4F **87**
W11 . . . . 1B **72**
(off Westbourne Gro.)
Archers Lodge SE16 . . 1C **92**
(off Culloden Cl.)
Archer Sq. SE14 . . . . . 2A **94**
Archer St.
W1 . . . . 4B **14** (1F **75**)
Archery Cl. W2 . . . . 5A **60**
Archery Steps W2 . . . . 1A **74**
(off St George's Flds.)
Arches, The NW1 . . . . . 4D **47**
SW8 . . . . 3F **89**
WC2 . . . . 1E **23**
(off Villiers St.)
Arches Leisure Cen. . . 2A **96**
Archibald M.
W1 . . . . 5D **13** (1C **74**)
Archibald Rd. N7 . . . . . 1F **47**
Archibald St. E3 . . . . . 2C **66**
Archie St.
SE1 . . . . 4E **27** (3A **78**)
Arch St. SE1 . . . . 4E **77**
ARCHWAY 4E **33**
Archway Bus. Cen.
N19 . . . . 5F **33**
Archway Cl. N19 . . . . . 4E **33**
SW19 . . . . 3D **115**
W10 . . . . 4F **57**
Archway Leisure Cen.
. . . . 4E **33**
Archway Mall N19 . . . . 4E **33**
Archway M. SW15 . . . 2A **100**
(off Putney Bri. Rd.)
Archway Rd. N6 . . . . . . 1C **32**
N19 . . . . 1C **32**
Archway St. SW13 . . . 1A **98**
Arcola St. E8 . . . . 2B **50**
Arcola Theatre 1B **50**
Arctic St. NW5 . . . . 2D **47**
Arcus Rd.
BR1: Brom 5A **124**

Ardbeg Rd. SE24 . . . . 3F **105**
Arden Ct. Gdns. N2 . . . 1F **31**
Arden Cres. E14 . . . . . . 5C **80**
Arden Est. N1 . . . . 1A **64**
Arden Ho. N1 . . . . 1D **11**
SE11 . . . . 5B **76**
(off Black Prince Rd.)
SW9 . . . . 5A **90**
(off Grantham Rd.)
Ardent Ho. E3. . . . . 1A **66**
(off Roman Rd.)
Ardfillan Rd. SE6 . . . . 1F **123**
Ardgowan Rd. SE6 . . 5A **110**
Ardilaun Rd. N5 . . . . . . 1E **49**
Ardleigh Rd. N1 . . . . . . 3A **50**
Ardley Cl. NW10 . . . . . 5A **28**
SE6 . . . . 3A **122**
Ardlui Rd. SE27 . . . . . . 2E **119**
Ardmere Rd. SE13 . . . 4F **109**
Ardoch Rd. SE6 . . . . . 2F **123**
Ardshiel Cl. SW15 . . . . 1F **99**
Ardwell Rd. SW2 . . . . 2A **118**
Ardwick Rd. NW2 . . . . . 1C **44**
Arena Bus. Cen. N4 . . . 1E **35**
Arena Ind. Est. N4 . . . . 1D **35**
Ares Ct. E14 . . . . 5C **80**
(off Homer Dr.)
Arethusa Ho. E14 . . . . . 5C **80**
(off Cahir St.)
Argall Av. E10 . . . . 2F **37**
Argall Way E10 . . . . . . 3F **37**
Argon M. SW6 . . . . 3C **86**
Argos Ct. SW9 . . . . 4C **90**
(off Caldwell St.)
Argos Ho. E2 . . . . 1D **65**
(off Old Bethnal Grn. Rd.)
Argosy Ho. SE8 . . . . . . 5A **80**
Argyle Ho. E14 . . . . . . 4E **81**
Argyle Pl. W6. . . . . 5D **71**
Argyle Rd. E1 . . . . 3F **65**
E15 . . . . 1A **54**
E16 . . . . 5D **69**
Argyle Sq.
WC1 . . . . 1E **7** (2A **62**)
Argyle St.
WC1 . . . . 1D **7** (2A **62**)
Argyle Wlk. WC1 . . . . . 2A **62**
Argyle Way SE16 . . . . . 1C **92**
Argyll Cl. SW9 . . . . 1B **104**
Argyll Mans. SW3 . . . . 2F **87**
W14 . . . . 5A **72**
(off Hammersmith Rd.)
Argyll Rd. W8 . . . . 3C **72**
Argyll St. W1 . . . 3F **13** (5E **61**)
Arica Ho. SE16 . . . . 4D **79**
(off Slippers Pl.)
Arica Rd. SE4 . . . . 2A **108**
Ariel Ct. SE11 . . . . 5D **77**
Ariel Rd. NW6 . . . . 3C **44**
Ariel Way W12 . . . . 2E **71**
Aristotle Rd. SW4 . . . 1F **103**
Ark, The W6 . . . . 1F **85**
(off Talgarth Rd.)
Arkindale Rd. SE6 . . . 3E **123**
Arkley Cres. E17 . . . . . 1B **38**
Arkley Rd. E17 . . . . 1B **38**
Arklow Ho. SE17 . . . . . 2F **91**
Arklow Rd. SE14 . . . . . 2B **94**
Arklow Rd. Trad. Est.
SE8 . . . . 2A **94**

Arkwright Ho. SW2 . . 5A **104**
(off Streatham Pl.)
Arkwright Rd. NW3 . . . 2E **45**
Arlesey Cl. SW15 . . . 3A **100**
Arlesford Rd. SW9 . . . 1A **104**
Arlingford Rd. SW2 . . 3C **104**
Arlington Av. N1 . . . . . . 5E **49**
(not continuous)
Arlington Cl. SE13 . . . 3F **109**
Arlington Ho. EC1 . . . . . 1C **8**
(off Arlington Way)
SE8 . . . . 2B **94**
(off Evelyn St.)
SW1 . . . . 1F **21** (2E **75**)
W12 . . . . 2D **71**
(off Tunis Rd.)
Arlington Lodge
SW2 . . . . 2B **104**
Arlington Pl. SE10 . . . . 3E **95**
Arlington Rd. NW1. . . . 5D **47**
Arlington Sq. N1. . . . . . 5E **49**
Arlington St.
SW1 . . . . 1F **21** (2E **75**)
Arlington Way
EC1 . . . . 1C **8** (2C **62**)
Armada Ct. SE8 . . . . . . 2C **94**
Armadale Rd. SW6 . . . 3C **86**
Armada St. SE8 . . . . . . 2C **94**
(off McMillan St.)
Armagh Rd. E3. . . . . . . 5B **52**
Arminger Rd. W12 . . . . 2D **71**
Armitage Rd. NW11 . . 3A **30**
SE10 . . . . 1B **96**
Armour Cl. N7 . . . . 3B **48**
Armoury Rd. SE8 . . . . . 5D **95**
Armoury Way SW18. . 3C **100**
Armsby Ho. E1 . . . . 4E **65**
(off Stepney Way)
Armstrong Rd. SW7 . . 4F **73**
W3 . . . . 2B **70**
Arnal Cres. SW18 . . . 5A **100**
Arncliffe NW6. . . . . 1D **59**
Arndale Wlk. SW18 . . 3D **101**
Arne Ho. SE11 . . . . 1B **90**
(off Worgan St.)
Arne St. WC2. . . 3E **15** (5A **62**)
Arne Wlk. SE3 . . . . . . 2B **110**
Arneway St. SW1 . . . . . 4F **75**
Arnewood Cl. SW15 . . 1C **112**
Arngask Rd. SE6 . . . . . 5F **109**
Arnhem Pl. E14 . . . . . . 4C **80**
Arnhem Way SE22 . . . 3A **106**
Arnhem Wharf E14. . . 4B **80**
Arnold Cir.
E2. . . . . 2F **11** (2B **64**)
Arnold Est.
SE1 . . . . 4F **27** (3B **78**)
(not continuous)
Arnold Ho. SE3 . . . . . . 3E **97**
(off Shooters Hill Rd.)
SE17 . . . . 1D **91**
(off Doddington Gro.)
Arnold Mans. W14 . . . 2B **86**
(off Queen's Club Gdns.)
Arnold Rd. E3 . . . . 2C **66**
Arnot Ho. SE5. . . . . 3E **91**
(off Comber Gro.)
Arnott Cl. W4. . . . . 5A **70**
Arnould Av. SE5 . . . . . 2F **105**
Arnside St. SE17 . . . . . 2F **91**

Arnulf St. SE6........ 4D **123**
Arnulls Rd. SW16 .... 5D **119**
Arodene Rd. SW2..... 4B **104**
Arragon Rd. E6 ...... 5F **55**
  SW18 .... 1C **114**
Arran Ct. NW10 ...... 5A **28**
Arran Dr. E12 .... 3F **41**
Arran Ho. E14........ 2E **81**
        (off Raleana Rd.)
Arran Rd. SE6 .... 2D **123**
Arran Wlk. N1........ 4E **49**
Arrol Ho.
  SE1 .... 5A **26** (4E **77**)
Arrow Ct. SW5........ 5C **72**
     (off W. Cromwell Rd.)
Arrowhead Ct. E11 .... 1F **39**
Arrow Rd. E3 .... 2D **67**
Arrows Ho. SE15 ..... 3E **93**
       (off Clifton Way)
Arrowsmith Ho. SE11.. 1B **90**
       (off Wickham St.)
Arsenal FC. 1C **48**
Artemis Ct. E14 ...... 5C **80**
       (off Homer Dr.)
Artesian Cl. NW10 .... 4A **42**
Artesian Rd. W2...... 5C **58**
Artesian Wlk. E11 .... 5A **40**
Arthingworth St. E15 .. 5A **54**
Arthur Ct. SW11...... 4C **88**
  W2 .... 5D **59**
      (off Queensway)
  W10. .... 5F **57**
     (off Silchester Rd.)
Arthur Deakin Ho. E1.. 4C **64**
       (off Hunton St.)
Arthurdon Rd. SE4 .... 3C **108**
Arthur Henderson Ho.
  SW6 .... 5B **86**
       (off Fulham Rd.)
Arthur Horsley Wlk.
  E7 .... 2B **54**
    (off Twr. Hamlets Rd.)
Arthur Rd. N7........ 1B **48**
  SW19 .... 5B **114**
Arthur St.
  EC4........ 4C **18** (1F **77**)
Artichoke Hill E1 ..... 1D **79**
Artichoke M. SE5 ..... 4F **91**
      (off Artichoke Pl.)
Artichoke Pl. SE5 ..... 4F **91**
Artillery Ho. E15. ..... 3A **54**
Artillery La.
  E1. .... 1E **19** (4A **64**)
  W12 .... 5C **56**
Artillery Pas. E1 ...... 1F **19**
Artillery Pl.
  SW1 .... 5B **22** (4F **75**)
Artillery Row
  SW1 .... 5B **22** (4E **75**)
Artisan Ct. E8 .... 3C **50**
Artisan M. NW10 ..... 2F **57**
      (off Warfield Rd.)
Artisan Quarter
  NW10 .... 2F **57**
     (off Wellington Rd.)
Artizan St. E1 .... 2F **19**
Arts Theatre. 4D **15**
     (off St Martin's St.)
Arundel Bldgs. SE1 .... 4A **78**
      (off Swan Mead)

Arundel Cl. E15 ...... 1A **54**
  SW11 .... 3A **102**
Arundel Ct. SE16 ..... 1D **93**
      (off Varcoe Rd.)
  SW3 .... 1A **88**
      (off Jubilee Pl.)
  SW13 .... 2D **85**
     (off Arundel Ter.)
Arundel Gdns. W11 ... 1B **72**
Arundel Gt. Ct.
  WC2........ 4A **16** (1B **76**)
Arundel Gro. N16...... 2A **50**
Arundel Mans. SW6.... 4B **86**
     (off Kelvedon Rd.)
Arundel Pl. N1........ 3C **48**
Arundel Sq. N7....... 3C **48**
Arundel St.
  WC2........ 4A **16** (1B **76**)
Arundel Ter. SW13..... 2D **85**
Arvon Rd. N5 .... 2C **48**
     (not continuous)
Asbridge Ct. W6....... 4D **71**
     (off Dalling Rd.)
Ascalon Ho. SW8...... 3E **89**
     (off Thessaly Rd.)
Ascalon St. SW8 ...... 3E **89**
Ascham St. NW5 ...... 2E **47**
Ascot Ct. NW8 .... 2F **59**
     (off Grove End Rd.)
Ascot Ho. NW1........ 1E **5**
  W9 .... 3C **58**
     (off Harrow Rd.)
Ascot Lodge NW6 ..... 5D **45**
Ascot Rd. N15. .... 1F **35**
  SW17 .... 5C **116**
Ashanti M. E8 .... 2E **51**
Ashbee Ho. E2 .... 2E **65**
     (off Portman Pl.)
Ashbourne Ct. E5. ..... 1A **52**
Ashbourne Gro.
  SE22 .... 2B **106**
  W4 .... 1A **84**
Ashbridge Rd. E11..... 2A **40**
Ashbridge St. NW8 .... 3A **60**
Ashbrook Rd. N19 ..... 3F **33**
Ashburn Gdns. SW7.... 5E **73**
Ashburnham Gro.
  SE10. .... 3D **95**
Ashburnham Mans.
  SW10 .... 3E **87**
    (off Ashburnham Rd.)
Ashburnham Pl.
  SE10. .... 3D **95**
Ashburnham Retreat
  SE10. .... 3D **95**
Ashburnham Rd.
  NW10 .... 2E **57**
  SW10 .... 3E **87**
Ashburnham Twr.
  SW10 .... 3F **87**
     (off Worlds End Est.)
Ashburn Pl. SW7 ...... 5E **73**
Ashburton Ent. Cen.
  SW15 .... 4E **99**
Ashburton Gro. N7 .... 1C **48**
Ashburton Ho. W9..... 3B **58**
     (off Fernhead Rd.)
Ashburton Rd. E16..... 5C **68**
Ashburton Ter. E13..... 1C **68**
Ashbury Pl. SW19 .... 5E **115**

Ashbury Rd. SW11.... 1B **102**
Ashby Ct. NW8 .... 3F **59**
     (off Pollitt Dr.)
Ashby Gro. N1 .... 4E **49**
     (not continuous)
Ashby Ho. N1 .... 4E **49**
     (off Essex Rd.)
  SW9 .... 5D **91**
Ashby M. SE4........ 5B **94**
  SW2 .... 3A **104**
     (off Prague Pl.)
Ashby Rd. SE4 .... 5B **94**
Ashby St. EC1 ... 2E **9** (2D **63**)
Ashchurch Gro.
  W12 .... 4C **70**
Ashchurch Pk. Vs.
  W12 .... 4C **70**
Ashchurch Ter.
  W12 .... 4C **70**
Ashcombe Rd.
  SW19 .... 5C **114**
Ashcombe St. SW6 .... 5D **87**
Ashcroft Ho. SW8..... 4E **89**
     (off Wadhurst Rd.)
Ashcroft Sq. W6....... 5E **71**
Ashdale Ho. N4 ...... 2F **35**
Ashdale Rd. SE12 .... 1D **125**
Ashdene SE15 .... 3D **93**
Ashdon Rd. NW10 .... 5B **42**
Ashdown Cres.
  NW5 .... 2C **46**
Ashdown Ho. SW1 .... 5A **22**
Ashdown Wlk. E14 .... 5C **80**
     (off Copeland Dr.)
Ashdown Way
  SW17 .... 2C **116**
Ashenden SE17 ...... 5E **77**
     (off Deacon Way)
Ashenden Rd. E5 ..... 2A **52**
Ashen Gro. SW19. .... 3C **114**
Ashentree Ct.
  EC4................ 3C **16**
Asher Way E1........ 1C **78**
Ashfield Ct. SW9 ..... 5A **90**
     (off Clapham Rd.)
Ashfield Ho. W14..... 1B **86**
    (off W. Cromwell Rd.)
Ashfield Rd. N4 ...... 1E **35**
  W3 .... 2B **70**
Ashfield St. E1........ 4D **65**
Ashfield Yd. E1. ...... 4E **65**
Ashford Ct. NW2...... 1F **43**
Ashford Ho. SE8...... 2B **94**
  SW9 .... 2D **105**
Ashford Pas. NW2 .... 1F **43**
Ashford Rd. NW2 ..... 1F **43**
Ashford St.
  N1. .... 1D **11** (2A **64**)
Ash Gro. E8 .... 5D **51**
     (not continuous)
  NW2 .... 1F **43**
  SE12 .... 1C **124**
Ashgrove Ct. W9 ..... 4C **58**
     (off Elmfield Way)
Ashgrove Ho. SW1..... 1F **89**
     (off Lindsay Sq.)
Ashgrove Rd.
  BR1: Brom 5F **123**

Ash Ho. E14 . . . . 3E 81
  (off E. Ferry Rd.)
SE1 . . . . 5B 78
  (off Longfield Est.)
W10 . . . . 3A 58
  (off Heather Wlk.)
Ashington Ho. E1 . . . . 3D 65
  (off Barnsley St.)
Ashington Rd. SW6 . . . 5B 86
Ashlake Rd. SW16 . . . . 4A 118
Ashland Pl.
W1 . . . . 5B 4 (4C 60)
Ashleigh Commercial Est.
SE7 . . . . 4E 83
Ashleigh Point SE23 . . 3F 121
Ashleigh Rd. SW14 . . . 1A 98
Ashley Ct. SW1 . . . . 4E 75
  (off Morpeth Ter.)
Ashley Cres. SW11 . . . 1C 102
Ashley Gdns.
SW1 . . . . 5A 22 (4E 75)
  (not continuous)
Ashley Pl.
SW1 . . . . 5F 21 (4E 75)
Ashley Rd. E7 . . . . 4E 55
N19 . . . . 3A 34
SW19 . . . . 5D 115
Ashlin Rd. E15 . . . . 1F 53
Ashlone Rd. SW15 . . . . 1E 99
Ashmead Bus. Cen.
E16 . . . . 3F 67
Ashmead Ho. E9 . . . . 2A 52
  (off Homerton Rd.)
Ashmead M. SE8 . . . . . . 5C 94
Ashmead Rd. SE8 . . . . . 5C 94
Ashmere Gro. SW2 . . . 2A 104
Ash M. NW5 . . . . 2E 47
Ashmill St. NW1 . . . . . . 4A 60
Ashmole Pl. SW8 . . . . . 2B 90
  (not continuous)
Ashmole St. SW8 . . . . . 2B 90
Ashmore NW1 . . . . 4F 47
  (off Agar Gro.)
Ashmore Cl. SE15 . . . . 3B 92
Ashmore Ho. W14 . . . . 4A 72
  (off Russell Rd.)
Ashmore Rd. W9 . . . . . 1B 58
Ashmount Est. N19 . . . 2F 33
Ashmount Rd. N19 . . . . 2E 33
Ashness Rd. SW11 . . . . 3B 102
Ashpark Ho. E14 . . . . 5B 66
  (off Norbiton Rd.)
Ash Rd. E15 . . . . 2A 54
Ashtead Rd. E5 . . . . 2C 36
Ashton Hgts. SE23 . . . 1E 121
Ashton Ho. SW9 . . . . . . 3C 90
Ashton Rd. E15 . . . . . . 2F 53
Ashton St. E14 . . . . 1E 81
Ash Tree Ho. SE5 . . . . . . 3E 91
  (off Pitman St.)
Ashurst Gdns. SW2 . . . 1C 118
Ashvale Rd. SW17 . . . . 5B 116
Ashville Rd. E11 . . . . . . 4F 39
Ashwater Rd. SE12 . . . 1C 124
Ashwin St. E8 . . . . 3B 50
Ashworth Cl. SE5 . . . . . 5F 91
Ashworth Mans. W9 . . . . . 2D 59
  (off Elgin Av.)
Ashworth Rd. W9 . . . . . 2D 59

Aske Ho. N1 . . . . 1D 11
  (not continuous)
Asker Ho. N7 . . . . 1A 48
Aske St. N1 . . . . . 1D 11 (2A 64)
Askew Cres. W12 . . . . . 3B 70
Askew Est. W12 . . . . 2B 70
  (off Uxbridge Rd.)
Askew Rd. W12 . . . . . . 3B 70
Askham Ct. W12 . . . . . 2C 70
Askham Rd. W12 . . . . . 2C 70
Askill Dr. SW15 . . . . . . 3A 100
Asland Rd. E15 . . . . . . 5A 54
Aslett St. SW18 . . . . . . 5D 101
Asmara Rd. NW2 . . . . . 2A 44
Asmuns Hill NW11 . . . . 1C 30
Asmuns Pl. NW11 . . . . 1B 30
Asolando Dr.
SE17 . . . . 5E 77
Aspect Ct. E14 . . . . 3E 81
  (off Manchester Rd.)
Aspen Cl. N19 . . . . 4E 33
Aspen Gdns. W6 . . . . . 1D 85
Aspen Ho. SE15 . . . . . . 2E 93
  (off Sharratt St.)
Aspenlea Rd. W6 . . . . . 2F 85
Aspen Lodge W8 . . . . . . 4D 73
  (off Abbots Wlk.)
Aspen Way E14 . . . . . . 1D 81
Aspern Gro. NW3 . . . . . 2A 46
Aspinall Rd. SE4 . . . . . 1F 107
  (not continuous)
Aspinden Rd. SE16 . . . 5D 79
Aspley Rd. SW18 . . . . . 3D 101
Assam St. E1 . . . . 5C 64
  (off White Chu. La.)
Assata St. N1 . . . . 3D 49
Assembly Pas. E1 . . . . . 4E 65
Association Gallery, The
                3D 11
  (off Leonard St.)
Astbury Bus. Pk.
SE15 . . . . 4E 93
Astbury Ho. SE11 . . . . . 4C 76
  (off Lambeth Wlk.)
Astbury Rd. SE15 . . . . . 4E 93
Astell St. SW3 . . . . 1A 88
Aste St. E14 . . . . 3E 81
Astey's Row N1 . . . . . . 4E 49
Astle St. SW11 . . . . . . 5C 88
Astley Av. NW2 . . . . . . 2E 43
Astley Ho. SE1 . . . . 1B 92
  (off Rowcross St.)
SW13 . . . . 2D 85
  (off Wyatt Dr.)
W2 . . . . 4C 58
  (off Alfred Rd.)
Aston Ho. SW8 . . . . 4F 89
W11 . . . . 1B 72
  (off Westbourne Gro.)
Aston St. E14 . . . . 4A 66
Aston Ter. SW12 . . . . . 4D 103
Astonville St. SW18 . . . 1C 114
Astor Ct. E16 . . . . 5E 69
  (off Ripley Rd.)
SW6 . . . . 3E 87
  (off Maynard Cl.)
Astoria, The 2C 14
  (off Falconberg M.)
Astoria Ct. E8 . . . . 4B 50
  (off Queensbridge Rd.)

Astoria Mans.
SW16 . . . . 3A 118
Astoria Wlk. SW9 . . . . . 1C 104
Astra Ho. SE14 . . . . 2B 94
  (off Arklow Rd.)
Astrop M. W6 . . . . 4E 71
Astrop Ter. W6 . . . . 3E 71
Astwood M. SW7 . . . . . 5E 73
Atalanta St. SW6 . . . . . 3F 85
Atheldene Rd.
SW18 . . . . 1D 115
Athelney St. SE6 . . . . . 3C 122
Athelstane Gro. E3 . . . 1B 66
Athelstane M. N4 . . . . . 3C 34
Athelstan Gdns. NW6 . . 4A 44
Athenaeum Ct. N5 . . . . 1E 49
Athene Pl. EC4 . . . . 2C 16
  (off St Andrew St.)
Athenia Ho. E14 . . . . 5F 67
  (off Blair St.)
Athenlay Rd. SE15 . . . 3F 107
Athens Gdns. W9 . . . . . . 3C 58
  (off Harrow Rd.)
Atherden Rd. E5 . . . . . 1E 51
Atherfold Rd.
SW9 . . . . 1A 104
Atherstone Ct. W2 . . . . . 4D 59
  (off Delamere Ter.)
Atherstone M. SW7 . . . 5E 73
Atherton Dr. SW19 . . . 4F 113
Atherton Leisure Cen.
                3B 54
Atherton M. E7 . . . . 3B 54
Atherton Rd. E7 . . . . . . 3B 54
SW13 . . . . 3C 84
Atherton St. SW11 . . . . 5A 88
Athlone Cl. E5 . . . . 2D 51
Athlone Ho. E1 . . . . 5E 65
  (off Sidney St.)
Athlone Rd. SW2 . . . . . 5B 104
Athlone St. NW5 . . . . . 3C 46
Atholl Ho. W9 . . . . 2E 59
  (off Maida Va.)
Athol Sq. E14 . . . . 5E 67
Atkin Bldg. WC1 . . . . 5A 8
  (off Raymond Bldgs.)
Atkinson Ct. E10 . . . . . . 2D 39
  (off Kings Cl.)
Atkinson Ho. E2 . . . . 1C 64
  (off Pritchards Rd.)
E13 . . . . 3B 68
  (off Sutton Rd.)
SE17 . . . . 5F 77
  (off Catesby St.)
Atkinson Rd. E16 . . . . . 4E 69
Atkins Rd. E10 . . . . 1D 39
SW12 . . . . 5E 103
Atlanta Ho. SE16 . . . . . . 4A 80
  (off Brunswick Quay)
Atlantic Ct. E14 . . . . 1F 81
  (off Jamestown Way)
Atlantic Ho. E1 . . . . 4A 66
  (off Harford St.)
Atlantic Rd. SW9 . . . . . 2C 104
Atlantic Wharf E1 . . . . . 1F 79
Atlas Bus. Cen. NW2 . . 3D 29
Atlas Gdns. SE7 . . . . . . 5E 83
Atlas M. E8 . . . . 3B 50
N7 . . . . 3B 48

Atlas Rd. E13 . . . . 1C **68**
  NW10 . . . . 2A **56**
Atlas Wharf E9 . . . . 3C **52**
Atley Rd. E3 . . . . 5C **52**
Atney Rd. SW15 . . . . . 2A **100**
Atrium Apartments
  N1 . . . . 5F **49**
   (off Felton St.)
Atterbury Rd. N4 . . . . . . 1C **34**
Atterbury St. SW1 . . . . 5A **76**
Attewood Av. NW10 . . 5A **28**
Attilburgh Ho. SE1 . . . . 5F **27**
   (off Abbey St.)
Attleborough Ct.
  SE23 . . . . 2C **120**
Attneave St.
  WC1 . . . . 2B **8** (2C **62**)
Atwater Ct. SW2 . . . . 1C **118**
Atwell Cl. E10 . . . . 1D **39**
Atwell Rd. SE15 . . . . . . 5C **92**
Atwood Ho. W14 . . . . . . 5B **72**
   (off Beckford St.)
Atwood Rd. W6 . . . . 5D **71**
Aubert Ct. N5 . . . . 1D **49**
Aubert Pk. N5 . . . . 1D **49**
Aubert Rd. N5 . . . . 1D **49**
Aubrey Beardsley Ho.
  SW1 . . . . 5E **75**
   (off Vauxhall Bri. Rd.)
Aubrey Mans. NW1 . . . . 4A **60**
   (off Lisson St.)
Aubrey Moore Point
  E15 . . . . 1E **67**
   (off Abbey La.)
Aubrey Pl. NW8 . . . . . . 1E **59**
Aubrey Rd. N8 . . . . 1A **34**
  W8 . . . . 2B **72**
Aubrey Wlk. W8 . . . . . . 2B **72**
Auburn Cl. SE14 . . . . . . 3A **94**
Aubyn Hill SE27 . . . . . 4E **119**
Aubyn Sq. SW15 . . . . . 3C **98**
Auckland Hill SE27 . . . 4E **119**
Auckland Ho. W12 . . . . 1D **71**
   (off White City Est.)
Auckland Rd. E10 . . . . . 5D **39**
  SW11 . . . . 2A **102**
Auckland St. SE11 . . . . 1B **90**
Auden Pl. NW1 . . . . 5C **46**
   (not continuous)
Audley Cl. SW11 . . . . 1C **102**
Audley Dr. E16 . . . . 2D **83**
Audley Rd. NW4 . . . . . 1C **28**
Audley Sq.
  W1 . . . . 1C **20** (2C **74**)
Audrey St. E2 . . . . 1C **64**
Augurs La. E13 . . . . 2D **69**
Augusta St. E14 . . . . . . 5D **67**
Augustine Rd. W14 . . . . 4F **71**
Augustus Cl. W12 . . . . . 3D **71**
Augustus Ct. SW16 . . . 2F **117**
Augustus Ho. NW1 . . . . 1F **5**
   (off Augustus St.)
Augustus Rd. SW19 . . . 1F **113**
Augustus St.
  NW1 . . . . 1E **5** (1D **61**)
Aulton Pl. SE11 . . . . . . 1C **90**
Auriga M. N1 . . . . 2F **49**
Auriol Ho. W12 . . . . 2D **71**
   (off Ellerslie Rd.)
Auriol Rd. W14 . . . . 5A **72**

Aurora Bldg. E14 . . . . . . 2E **81**
   (off Blackwall Way)
Aurora Ho. E14 . . . . 5D **67**
   (off Kerbey St.)
Austen Ho. NW6 . . . . . . 2C **58**
   (off Cambridge Rd.)
Austin Cl. SE23 . . . . . . 5A **108**
Austin Ct. E6 . . . . 5E **55**
  SE15 . . . . 1C **106**
   (off Philip Wlk.)
Austin Friars
  EC2 . . . . 2C **18** (5F **63**)
   (not continuous)
Austin Friars Pas.
  EC2 . . . . 2C **18**
Austin Friars Sq.
  EC2 . . . . 2C **18**
Austin Ho. SE14 . . . . . . 3B **94**
   (off Achilles St.)
Austin Rd. SW11 . . . . . . 4C **88**
Austin St. E2 . . . 2F **11** (2B **64**)
Austin Ter. SE1 . . . . 5C **24**
   (off Morley St.)
Australian War Memorial
  . . . . 3C **20**
   (off Duke of Wellington Pl.)
Australia Rd. W12 . . . . . 1D **71**
Austral St. SE11 . . . . . . 5D **77**
Autumn Cl.
  SW19 . . . . 5E **115**
Autumn St. E3 . . . . 5C **52**
Avalon Rd. SW6 . . . . . . 4D **87**
Avarn Rd. SW17 . . . . . . 5B **116**
Avebury Ct. N1 . . . . 5F **49**
   (off Imber St.)
Avebury Rd. E11 . . . . . . 3F **39**
Avebury St. N1 . . . . 5F **49**
Aveline St. SE11 . . . . . . 1C **90**
Ave Maria La.
  EC4 . . . . 3E **17** (5D **63**)
Avenell Mans.
  N5 . . . . 1D **49**
Avenell Rd. N5 . . . . 5D **35**
Avenfield Ho. W1 . . . . . . 4A **12**
   (off Park La.)
Avening Rd. SW18 . . . 5C **100**
Avening Ter.
  SW18 . . . . 5C **100**
Avenons Rd. E13 . . . . . . 3C **68**
Avenue, The E11 . . . . . . 1D **41**
  NW6 . . . . 5F **43**
  SE10 . . . . 3F **95**
  SW4 . . . . 3C **102**
  SW18 . . . . 5A **102**
  W4 . . . . 4A **70**
Avenue Cl. NW8 . . . . . . 5A **46**
Avenue Ct. NW2 . . . . . . 5B **30**
  SW3 . . . . 5B **74**
   (off Draycott Av.)
Avenue Gdns. SW14 . . . 1A **98**
Avenue Ho. NW8 . . . . . . 1A **60**
  NW10 . . . . 1D **57**
   (off All Souls Av.)
Avenue Lodge NW8 . . . 4F **45**
   (off Avenue Rd.)
Avenue Mans. NW3 . . . 2D **45**
   (off Finchley Rd.)
Avenue Pk. Rd.
  SE27 . . . . 2D **119**

Avenue Rd. E7 . . . . 1D **55**
  N6 . . . . 2E **33**
  N15 . . . . 1F **35**
  NW3 . . . . 4F **45**
  NW8 . . . . 4F **45**
  NW10 . . . . 1B **56**
Averill St. W6 . . . . 2F **85**
Avery Farm Row
  SW1 . . . . 5C **74**
Avery Row
  W1 . . . . 4D **13** (1D **75**)
Aviary Ct. E16 . . . . 4B **68**
Avignon Rd. SE4 . . . . . 1F **107**
Avington Ct. SE1 . . . . . . 5A **78**
   (off Old Kent Rd.)
Avis Sq. E1 . . . . 5F **65**
Avoca Rd. SW17 . . . . . 4C **116**
Avocet Cl. SE1 . . . . 1C **92**
Avon Ct. SW15 . . . . . . 3A **100**
  W9 . . . . 4C **58**
   (off Elmfield Way)
Avondale Av. NW2 . . . . 5A **28**
Avondale Cl. E11 . . . . . . 3A **40**
  E16 . . . . 4A **68**
Avondale Cres.
  IG4: Ilf 1F **41**
Avondale Ho. SE1 . . . . . 1C **92**
   (off Avondale Sq.)
Avondale Pk. Gdns.
  W11 . . . . 1A **72**
Avondale Pk. Rd.
  W11 . . . . 1A **72**
Avondale Pavement
  SE1 . . . . 1C **92**
Avondale Ri. SE15 . . . . 1B **106**
Avondale Rd. E16 . . . . . 4A **68**
  E17 . . . . 2C **38**
  N15 . . . . 1D **35**
  SE9 . . . . 2F **125**
  SW14 . . . . 1A **98**
  SW19 . . . . 5D **115**
Avondale Sq. SE1 . . . . . 1C **92**
Avon Ho. W8 . . . . 4C **72**
   (off Allen St.)
  W14 . . . . 5B **72**
   (off Kensington Village)
Avonhurst Ho. NW2 . . . 4A **44**
Avonley Rd. SE14 . . . . . 3E **93**
Avonmore Gdns.
  W14 . . . . 5B **72**
Avonmore Pl. W14 . . . . 5A **72**
Avonmore Rd. W14 . . . . 5A **72**
Avonmouth St.
  SE1 . . . . 5F **25** (4E **77**)
Avon Pl. SE1 . . . 4A **26** (3E **77**)
Avon Rd. SE4 . . . . 1C **108**
Avro Ho. SW8 . . . . 3D **89**
   (off Havelock Ter.)
Axminster Rd. N7 . . . . . 5A **34**
Aybrook St.
  W1 . . . . 1B **12** (4C **60**)
Aycliffe Rd. W12 . . . . . . 2C **70**
Ayerst Ct. E10 . . . . 2E **39**
Aylesbury Cl. E7 . . . . . . 3B **54**
Aylesbury Ho. SE15 . . . 2C **92**
   (off Friary Est.)
Aylesbury Rd. SE17 . . . 1F **91**
Aylesbury St.
  EC1 . . . . 4D **9** (3D **63**)
  NW10 . . . . 5A **28**

Aylesford Ho. *SE1* *4C 26*
    (off Long La.)
Aylesford St. SW1. . . . . . .1F 89
Aylesham Cen., The
  SE15. . . . . .4C 92
Aylestone Av. NW6. . . . .4F 43
Aylmer Ct. N2. . . . . .1B 32
Aylmer Ho. SE10. . . . . .1F 95
Aylmer Pde. N2. . . . . . . .1B 32
Aylmer Rd. E11 . . . . . . .3B 40
  N2. . . . . .1A 32
  W12 . . . . .3B 70
Aylton Est. SE16. . . . . . .3E 79
Aylward Rd. SE23. . . . . .2F 121
Aylward St. E1 . . . . .5E 65
    (Jamaica St.)
  E1 . . . . .5E 65
    (Jubilee St.)
Aylwin Est.
  SE1. . . . . .5E 27 (4A 78)
Aynhoe Mans.
  W14. . . . . .5F 71
    (off Aynhoe Rd.)
Aynhoe Rd. W14. . . . . . .5F 71
Ayres Cl. E13 . . . . .2C 68
Ayres St.
  SE1 . . . . . .3A 26 (3E 77)
Ayrsome Ho. N16. . . . . .5A 36
Ayrton Gould Ho. E2. . .2F 65
    (off Roman Rd.)
Ayrton Rd. SW7. . . . . . .4F 73
Aysgarth Rd. SE21 . . . .5A 106
Ayshford Ho. E2. . . . . . .2D 65
    (off Viaduct St.)
Ayston Ho. SE16. . . . . .5F 79
    (off Plough Way)
Ayton Ho. SE5. . . . . . . .3F 91
    (off Edmund St.)
Aytoun Pl. SW9. . . . . . . .5B 90
Aytoun Rd. SW9. . . . . . .5B 90
Azalea Ho. SE14. . . . . . .3B 94
    (off Achilles St.)
Azania M. NW5 . . . . . . .3D 47
Azenby Rd.
  SE15. . . . . .5B 92
Azof St. SE10 . . . . .5A 82
Azov Ho. E1 . . . . .3A 66
    (off Commodore St.)
Azure Ho. E2. . . . . .2C 64
    (off Buckfast St.)

B

Baalbec Rd. N5 . . . . .2D 49
Babington Ct. WC1. . . . . .5F 7
Babington Ho. SE1 . . . . .3A 26
    (off Disney St.)
Babington Rd.
  SW16. . . . . .5F 117
Babmaes St.
  SW1. . . . . . .5B 14 (1F 75)
Bacchus Wlk. N1 . . . . . .1A 64
    (off Regan Way)
Bache's St.
  N1. . . . . . . .1C 10 (2F 63)
Back All. EC3 . . . . .3E 19
Bk. Church La. E1 . . . . .5C 64
Back Hill EC1. . . .4C 8 (3C 62)
Backhouse Pl. SE17. . . .5A 78

Back La. N8 . . . . .1A 34
  NW3. . . . . .1E 45
    (off Long La.)
Back Passage EC1 . . . . . .5E 9
    (off Long La.)
Bacon Gro. SE1 . . . . . . .4B 78
Bacon's College Sports Cen.
  . . . . .2A 80
Bacons La. N6 . . . . .3C 32
Bacon St.
  E1. . . . . . . .3F 11 (3B 64)
  E2 . . . . .3B 64
Bacton NW5 . . . . .2C 46
Bacton St. E2 . . . . .2E 65
Baddesley Ho. SE11 . . .1B 90
    (off Jonathan St.)
Baddow Wlk. N1. . . . . . .5E 49
    (off New Nth. Rd.)
Baden Pl.
  SE1. . . . . . .3B 26 (3F 77)
Baden Powell Ho.
  SW7. . . . . .5E 73
    (off Queen's Ga.)
Badger Ct. NW2 . . . . . . .5E 29
Badminton M. E16. . . . .2C 82
Badminton Rd.
  SW12. . . . . .4C 102
Badric Ct. SW11. . . . . . .5F 87
Badsworth Rd. SE5 . . . .4E 91
Baffin Way E14. . . . . . . .2E 81
Bagley's La. SW6 . . . . . .4D 87
Bagnigge Ho. WC1. . . . . .2B 8
    (off Margery St.)
Bagshot Ho. NW1. . . . . .1E 5
Bagshot St. SE17. . . . . .1A 92
Baildon E2 . . . . .1E 65
    (off Cyprus St.)
Baildon St. SE8 . . . . . . .3B 94
Bailey Cotts. E14 . . . . . .4A 66
    (off Maroon St.)
Bailey Ho. SW10. . . . . .3D 87
    (off Coleridge Gdns.)
Bailey M. SW2. . . . . . . .3C 104
Bailey Pl. SE26. . . . . . . .5F 121
Bainbridge St.
  WC1. . . . . . .2C 14 (5F 61)
Baird Cl. E10 . . . . .3C 38
Baird Gdns. SE19. . . . . .4A 120
Baird Ho. W12 . . . . .1D 71
    (off White City Est.)
Baird St. EC1. . . .3A 10 (3E 63)
Baizdon Rd. SE3 . . . . . .5A 96
Baker Ho. WC1 . . . . .4E 7
    (off Colonnade)
Baker Pas. NW10. . . . . .5A 42
Baker Rd. NW10 . . . . . . .5A 42
Bakers Av. E17. . . . . . . .1D 39
Baker's Fld. N7 . . . . .1A 48
Bakers Hall Ct.
  EC3. . . . . .5D 19
Bakers Hill E5. . . . . .3E 37
Bakers La. N6 . . . . .1B 32
Baker's M.
  W1. . . . . . . .2B 12 (5C 60)
Bakers Pas. NW3 . . . . . .1E 45
    (off Heath St.)
Baker's Rents
  E2. . . . . . . .2F 11 (2B 64)
Baker's Row E15 . . . . . .1A 68
  EC1 . . . . . . .4B 8 (3C 62)
BAKER STREET 4B 60

Baker St.
  NW1. . . . . . . .4A 4 (3B 60)
  W1. . . . . .4A 4 (3B 60)
Baker's Yd. EC1 . . . . .4B 8
Bakery Cl. SW9. . . . . . . .3B 90
Bakery Pl. SW11 . . . . . .2B 102
Balaam Leisure Cen.
  . . . . .3C 68
Balaam St. E13 . . . . .3C 68
Balaclava Rd. SE1 . . . . .5B 78
Bala Grn. NW9. . . . . .1A 28
    (off Ruthin Cl.)
Balchen Rd. SE3. . . . . . .5F 97
Balchier Rd. SE22 . . . . .4D 107
Balcombe Ho. NW1 . . . .3A 60
    (off Taunton Pl.)
Balcombe St.
  NW1. . . . . . . .5A 4 (3B 60)
Balcorne St. E9 . . . . .4E 51
Balder Ri. SE12. . . . . . . .2D 125
Balderton Flats W1 . . . .3C 12
    (off Balderton St.)
Balderton St.
  W1. . . . . . . .3C 12 (5C 60)
Baldock St. E3. . . . . .1D 67
Baldrey Ho. SE10. . . . . .1B 96
    (off Blackwall La.)
Baldry Gdns. SW16. . . .5B 118
Baldwin Cres. SE5 . . . . .4E 91
Baldwin Ho. SW2 . . . . . .1C 118
Baldwins Gdns.
  EC1 . . . . . . .5B 8 (4C 62)
Baldwin St.
  EC1. . . . . . . .2B 10 (2F 63)
Baldwin Ter. N1 . . . . . . .1E 63
Balearic Apartments
  E16. . . . . .1C 82
    (off Western Gateway)
Bale Rd. E1 . . . . .4A 66
Balfern Gro. W4 . . . . . . .1A 84
Balfern St. SW11 . . . . . .5A 88
Balfe St. N1 . . . . .1A 62
Balfour Ho. W10 . . . . . . .4F 57
    (off St Charles Sq.)
Balfour M.
  W1. . . . . . . .1C 20 (2C 74)
Balfour Pl. SW15. . . . . . .2D 99
  W1. . . . . . . .5C 12 (1C 74)
Balfour Rd. N5. . . . . .1E 49
Balfour St. SE17. . . . . . .5F 77
Balfron Twr. E14. . . . . . . .5E 67
BALHAM 1C 116
Balham Continental Mkt.
  SW12. . . . . .1D 117
    (off Shipka Rd.)
Balham Gro. SW12 . . . .5C 102
Balham High Rd.
  SW12. . . . . .3C 116
  SW17. . . . . .3C 116
Balham Hill SW12 . . . . .5D 103
Balham Leisure Cen.
  . . . . .2D 117
Balham New Rd.
  SW12. . . . . .5D 103
Balham Pk. Rd.
  SW12. . . . . .1B 116
Balham Sta. Rd.
  SW12. . . . . .1D 117
Balin Ho. SE1. . . . . .3B 26
    (off Long La.)

Balkan Wlk. E1. . . . . . . 1D 79
Balladier Wlk. E14. . . . . 4D 67
Ballamore Rd.
  BR1: Brom 3C 124
Ballance Rd. E9 . . . . 3F 51
Ballantine St. SW18 . . 2E 101
Ballantrae Ho. NW2 . . . 1B 44
Ballard Ho. SE10 . . . . . . 2D 95
  (off Thames St.)
Ballards Rd. NW2 . . . . . 4C 28
Ballast Quay SE10 . . . . 1F 95
Ballater Rd. SW2 . . . . . 2A 104
Ball Ct. EC3 . . . . 3C 18
  (off Cornhill)
Ballina St. SE23 . . . . . . 5F 107
Ballin Ct. E14 . . . . 3E 81
  (off Stewart St.)
Ballingdon Rd.
  SW11 . . . . 4C 102
Balliol Rd. W10 . . . . 5E 57
Balloch Rd. SE6 . . . . . . 1F 123
Ballogie Av. NW10 . . . . 1A 42
Ballow Cl. SE5 . . . . 3A 92
Balls Pond Pl. N1 . . . . . 3F 49
Balls Pond Rd. N1 . . . . . 3F 49
Balman Ho. SE16 . . . . . 5F 79
  (off Rotherhithe New Rd.)
Balmer Rd. E3 . . . . 1B 66
Balmes Rd. N1 . . . . 5F 49
Balmoral Apartments
  W2 . . . . 4A 60
  (off Praed St.)
Balmoral Cl. SW15 . . . . 4F 99
Balmoral Ct. SE12 . . . . 4D 125
  SE16 . . . . 2F 79
  (off King & Queen Wharf)
  SE17 . . . . 1F 91
  (off Lytham St.)
  SE27 . . . . 4E 119
Balmoral Gro. N7 . . . . . . 3B 48
Balmoral Ho. E14 . . . . . . 4D 81
  (off Lanark Sq.)
  E16 . . . . 2D 83
  (off Keats Av.)
  W14 . . . . 5A 72
  (off Windsor Way)
Balmoral M. W12. . . . . . 4B 70
Balmoral Rd. E7 . . . . . . 1E 55
  E10 . . . . 4D 39
  NW2 . . . . 3D 43
Balmore Cl. E14 . . . . 5E 67
Balmore St. N19 . . . . . . 4E 33
Balmuir Gdns. SW15 . . . 2E 99
Balnacraig Av. NW10 . . 1A 42
Balniel Ga. SW1 . . . . . . 1F 89
Balsam Ho. E14 . . . . 1D 81
  (off E. India Dock Rd.)
Baltic Apartments
  E16 . . . . 1C 82
  (off Western Gateway)
Baltic Cl. SE16 . . . . 3F 79
Baltic Ho. SE5 . . . . 5E 91
Baltic Pl. N1 . . . . 5A 50
Baltic St. E.
  EC1 . . . . 4F 9 (3E 63)
Baltic St. W.
  EC1 . . . . 4F 9 (3E 63)
Baltimore Ho. SE11 . . . . 5C 76
  (off Hotspur St.)
Balvaird Pl. SW1 . . . . . . 1F 89

Balvernie Gro.
  SW18 . . . . 5B 100
Balvernie M. SW18 . . . . 5C 100
Bamber Rd. SE15 . . . . . 4B 92
Bamborough Gdns.
  W12 . . . . 3E 71
Bamford Ct. E15 . . . . . . 2D 53
  (off Clays La.)
Bamford Rd.
  BR1: Brom 5E 123
Bampton Rd. SE23 . . . . 3F 121
Banbury Ct. WC2 . . . . . 4D 15
Banbury Ho. E9 . . . . 4F 51
Banbury Rd. E9 . . . . 4F 51
Banbury St. SW11 . . . . . 5A 88
Banchory Rd. SE3 . . . . . 3D 97
Bancroft Av. N2 . . . . 1A 32
Bancroft Ct. SW8 . . . . . . 3A 90
  (off Allen Edwards Dr.)
Bancroft Ho. E1 . . . . 3E 65
  (off Cephas St.)
Bancroft Rd. E1 . . . . 2E 65
Banfield Rd. SE15 . . . . . 1D 107
Bangalore St. SW15 . . . 1E 99
Banim St. W6. . . . . 5D 71
Banister Ho. E9 . . . . 2F 51
  SW8 . . . . 4E 89
  (off Wadhurst St.)
  W10 . . . . 2A 58
  (off Bruckner St.)
Banister M. NW6 . . . . . . 4D 45
Banister Rd. W10 . . . . . . 2F 57
Bank, The N6 . . . . 3D 33
Bank End
  SE1 . . . . 1A 26 (2E 77)
Bankfoot Rd.
  BR1: Brom 4A 124
Bankhurst Rd. SE6 . . . . 5B 108
Bank La. SW15 . . . . 3A 98
Bank of England
  . . . . 3B 18 (5F 63)
Bank of England Mus.
  . . . . 3C 18
Bank of England Offices
  EC4 . . . . 3F 17
Banks Ho. SE1 . . . . 5F 25
  (off Rockingham St.)
Bankside SE1 . . 5F 17 (1E 77)
  (not continuous)
Bankside Art Gallery
  . . . . 5E 17 (1D 77)
Bankside Way SE19 . . 5A 120
Bank St. E14 . . . . 2D 81
Bankton Rd. SW2 . . . . . 2C 104
Bankwell Rd. SE13 . . . . 2A 110
Bannatyne's Health Club
  Grove Park. 2D 125
Bannerman Ho. SW8 . . 2B 90
Banner St.
  EC1 . . . . 4A 10 (3E 63)
Banning St. SE10 . . . . . 1A 96
Bannister Cl. SW2 . . . . 1C 118
Bannister Ho. SE14 . . . 2F 93
  (off John Williams Cl.)
Banqueting House
  . . . . 2D 23 (2A 76)
Banstead St. SE15 . . . . 1E 107
Banting Ho. NW2 . . . . . 5C 28
Bantock Ho. W10 . . . . . 2A 58
  (off Third Av.)

Bantry Ho. E1 . . . . 3F 65
  (off Ernest St.)
Bantry St. SE5 . . . . 3F 91
Banyard Rd. SE16 . . . . . 4D 79
Baptist Gdns.
  NW5 . . . . 3C 46
Barandon Rd. W11 . . . . 1F 71
  (off Grenfell Rd.)
Barandon Wlk. W11 . . . 1F 71
Barbanel Ho. E1 . . . . . . 3E 65
  (off Cephas St.)
Barbara Brosnan Ct.
  NW8 . . . . 1F 59
Barbauld Rd. N16 . . . . . 5A 36
Barber Beaumont Ho.
  E1 . . . . 2F 65
  (off Bancroft Rd.)
Barbers All. E13 . . . . . . 2D 69
Barbers All. E15 . . . . . . 1D 67
Barbican Arts Cen.
  . . . . 5A 10 (4E 63)
Barbican Cinema 5A 10
  (in Arts Cen.)
Barbican Theatre 5A 10
  (off Silk St.)
Barbican Trade Cen.
  EC1 . . . . 5A 10
  (off Beech St.)
Barb M. W6 . . . . 4E 71
Barbon All. EC2 . . . . 2E 19
  (off Houndsditch)
Barbon Cl.
  WC1 . . . . 5E 7 (4B 62)
Barchard St. SW18 . . . 3D 101
Barchester St. E14 . . . . 4D 67
Barclay Cl. SW6 . . . . . . 3C 86
Barclay Ho. E9 . . . . 4E 51
  (off Well St.)
Barclay Path E17 . . . . . . 1E 39
Barclay Rd. E11 . . . . . . 3B 40
  (not continuous)
  E13 . . . . 3E 69
  E17 . . . . 1E 39
  SW6 . . . . 3C 86
Barcombe Av. SW2 . . . 2A 118
Bardell Ho. SE1 . . . . 3C 78
  (off Parkers Row)
Bardolph Rd. N7 . . . . . . 1A 48
Bard Rd. W10 . . . . 1F 71
Bardsey Pl. E1 . . . . 3E 65
  (off Mile End Rd.)
Bardsey Wlk. N1 . . . . . . 3E 49
  (off Douglas Rd. Nth.)
Bardsley Ho. SE10 . . . . 2E 95
  (off Bardsley La.)
Bardsley La. SE10 . . . . 2E 95
Barents Ho. E1 . . . . 3F 65
  (off White Horse La.)
Barfett St. W10 . . . . 3B 58
Barfield Rd. E11 . . . . . . 3B 40
Barfleur La. SE8. . . . . . . 5B 80
Barford St. N1 . . . . 5C 48
Barforth Rd. SE15 . . . . . 1D 107
Barge Ho. St.
  SE1 . . . . 1C 24 (2C 76)
Bargery Rd. SE6 . . . . . . 1D 123
Bargrove Cres. SE6 . . . 2B 122
Barham Ho. SE17 . . . . . 1A 92
  (off Kinglake St.)
Baring Cl. SE12 . . . . . . 2C 124

Baring Ho. *E14* *5C 66*
   (off Canton St.)
Baring Rd. SE12 . . . . . . *5C 110*
Baring St. N1 . . . . *5F 49*
Barker Dr. NW1 . . . . *4E 47*
Barker M. SW4 . . . . . . *2D 103*
Barkers Arc. W8 . . . . *3D 73*
Barker St. SW10 . . . . *2E 87*
Barker Wlk. SW9 . . . . . . *3F 117*
Barkham Ter. SE1 . . . . . . *5C 24*
Barking Rd. E6 . . . . *1E 69*
  E13 . . . . *1E 69*
  E16 . . . . *4B 68*
  (not continuous)
Bark Pl. W2 . . . . *1D 73*
Barkston Gdns. SW5 . . . . *5D 73*
Barkway Ct. *N4* *4E 35*
  (off Queen's Dr.)
Barkwith Ho. *SE14* *2F 93*
  (off Cold Blow La.)
Barkworth Rd. SE16 . . . . . *1D 93*
Barlborough St. SE14 . . . . *3F 93*
Barlby Gdns. W10 . . . . . . *3F 57*
Barlby Rd. W10 . . . . *4E 57*
Barleycorn Way E14 . . . . . *1B 80*
Barley Mow Pas. EC1 . . . . *5E 9*
  W4 . . . . *1A 84*
Barley Shotts Bus. Pk.
  W10 . . . . *4B 58*
Barling *NW1* *3D 47*
  (off Castlehaven Rd.)
Barlings Ho. *SE4* *2F 107*
  (off Frendsbury Rd.)
Barlow Dr. SE18 . . . . *4F 97*
Barlow Ho. *N1* *1B 10*
  (off Fairbank Est.)
  SE16 . . . . *5D 79*
  (off Rennie Est.)
  W11 . . . . *1A 72*
  (off Walmer Rd.)
Barlow Pl.
  W1 . . . . *5E 13 (1D 75)*
Barlow Rd. NW6 . . . . *3B 44*
Barlow St. SE17 . . . . *5F 77*
Barmeston Rd. SE6 . . . . *2D 123*
Barmouth Rd. SW18 . . . . *4E 101*
Barnabas Rd. E9 . . . . *2F 51*
Barnaby Ct. *SE16* *3C 78*
  (off Scott Lidgett Cres.)
Barnaby Pl. *SW7* *5F 73*
  (off Old Brompton Rd.)
Barnard Gro. E15 . . . . . . *4B 54*
Barnard Ho. *E2* *2D 65*
  (off Ellsworth St.)
Barnard Lodge *W9* *4C 58*
  (off Admiral Wlk.)
Barnard M. SW11 . . . . . *2A 102*
Barnardo Gdns. E1 . . . . . *1F 79*
Barnardo St. E1 . . . . *5F 65*
Barnard Rd. SW11 . . . . *2A 102*
Barnards Ho. *SE16* *3B 80*
  (off Wyatt Cl.)
Barnard's Inn EC1 . . . . . . *1B 16*
Barnbrough *NW1* *5E 47*
  (off Camden St.)
Barnby Sq. E15 . . . . *5A 54*
Barnby St. E15 . . . . *5A 54*
  NW1 . . . . *1A 6 (1E 61)*
Barn Cl. *NW5* *2F 47*
  (off Torriano Av.)

Barn Elms Athletic Track
  . . . . *5D 85*
Barn Elms Pk. SW15 . . . . *1E 99*
BARNES *5B 84*
Barnes Av. SW13 . . . . . . *3C 84*
Barnes Cl. E12 . . . . *1F 55*
Barnes Ct. E16 . . . . *4E 69*
  N1 . . . . *4C 48*
Barnes High St.
  SW13 . . . . *5B 84*
Barnes Ho. *E2* *1E 65*
  (off Wadeson St.)
  SE14 . . . . *2F 93*
  (off John Williams Cl.)
Barnes St. E14 . . . . *5A 66*
Barnes Ter. SE8 . . . . *1B 94*
Barnet Gro. E2 . . . . *2C 64*
Barnett St. E1 . . . . *5D 65*
Barney Cl. SE7 . . . . *1E 97*
Barn Fld. NW3 . . . . *2B 46*
Barnfield Cl. N4 . . . . *2A 34*
  SW17 . . . . *3F 115*
Barnfield Pl. E14 . . . . *5C 80*
Barnham St.
  SE1 . . . . *3E 27 (3A 78)*
BARNSBURY *4B 48*
Barnsbury Est. N1 . . . . . . *5B 48*
  (not continuous)
Barnsbury Gro. N7 . . . . . . *4B 48*
Barnsbury Ho. SW4 . . . . *4F 103*
Barnsbury Pk. N1 . . . . . . *4C 48*
Barnsbury Rd. N1 . . . . . . *1C 62*
Barnsbury Sq. N1 . . . . . . *4C 48*
Barnsbury St. N1 . . . . . . *4C 48*
Barnsbury Ter. N1 . . . . . . *4B 48*
Barnsdale Av. E14 . . . . . . *5D 81*
Barnsdale Rd. W9 . . . . . . *3B 58*
Barnsley St. E1 . . . . *3D 65*
Barnstable La.
  SE13 . . . . *2E 109*
Barnstaple Ho. *SE10* *3D 95*
  (off Devonshire Dr.)
  SE12 . . . . *3B 110*
  (off Taunton Rd.)
Barnston Wlk. *N1* *5E 49*
  (off Popham St.)
Barn St. N16 . . . . *4A 36*
Barnwell Ho. *SE5* *4A 92*
  (off St Giles Rd.)
Barnwell Rd. SW2 . . . . . *3C 104*
Barnwood Cl. W9 . . . . . . *3D 59*
Baroness Rd.
  E2 . . . . *1F 11 (2B 64)*
Baronsclere Ct. N6 . . . . . *2E 33*
BARONS COURT *1A 86*
Baron's Ct. Rd. W14 . . . . *1A 86*
Barons Court Theatre
  . . . . *1A 86*
  (off Comeragh Rd.)
Barons Keep W14 . . . . . . *1A 86*
Baronsmead Rd.
  SW13 . . . . *4C 84*
Baron's Pl.
  SE1 . . . . . . *4C 24 (3C 76)*
Baron St. N1 . . . . *1C 62*
Baron Wlk. E16 . . . . *4B 68*
Barque M. SE8 . . . . *2C 94*
Barratt Ho. *N1* *4D 49*
  (off Sable St.)
Barratt Ind. Pk. E3 . . . . . *3E 67*

Barret Ho. NW6 . . . . *5C 44*
  SW9 . . . . *1B 104*
  (off Benedict Rd.)
Barrett Ho. *SE17* *1E 91*
  (off Browning St.)
Barrett's Gro. N16 . . . . . . *2A 50*
Barrett St.
  W1 . . . . *3C 12 (5C 60)*
Barrhill Rd. SW2 . . . . . . *2A 118*
Barriedale SE14 . . . . *5A 94*
Barrie Est. W2 . . . . *1F 73*
Barrie Ho. *W2* *1E 73*
  (off Lancaster Ga.)
Barrier App. SE7 . . . . *4F 83*
Barrier Point Rd.
  E16 . . . . *2E 83*
Barrington Sq. SW17 . . . *4C 116*
Barrington Cl. NW5 . . . . . *2C 46*
Barrington Ct. SW4 . . . . . *5A 90*
Barrington Rd. SW9 . . . . *1D 105*
Barrow Ct. *SE6* *1B 124*
  (off Cumberland Pl.)
Barrowgate Rd. W4 . . . . . *1A 84*
Barrow Hill Est. NW8 . . . . *1A 60*
  (off Barrow Hill Rd.)
Barrow Hill Rd. NW8 . . . . *1A 60*
Barrow Rd. SW16 . . . . . . *5F 117*
Barry Av. N15 . . . . *1B 36*
Barry Ho. *SE16* *5D 79*
  (off Rennie Est.)
Barry Rd. SE22 . . . . *4C 106*
Barset Rd. SE15 . . . . . . *1E 107*
  (not continuous)
Barston Rd. SE27 . . . . . . *3E 119*
Barstow Cres. SW2 . . . . *1B 118*
Barter St.
  WC1 . . . . *1E 15 (4A 62)*
Bartholomew Cl.
  EC1 . . . . *1E 17 (4E 63)*
  (not continuous)
  SW18 . . . . *2E 101*
Bartholomew Ct. *E14* *1F 81*
  (off Newport Av.)
  EC1 . . . . *3A 10*
  (off Old St.)
Bartholomew La.
  EC2 . . . . *3C 18 (5F 63)*
Bartholomew Pl. EC1 . . . *1F 17*
Bartholomew Rd.
  NW5 . . . . *3E 47*
Bartholomew Sq. E1 . . . . *3D 65*
  EC1 . . . . *3A 10 (3E 63)*
Bartholomew St. SE1 . . . *4F 77*
Bartholomew Vs.
  NW5 . . . . *3E 47*
Bartle Rd. W11 . . . . *5A 58*
Bartlett Ct. E14 . . . . *5C 66*
Bartlett Ct.
  EC4 . . . . *2C 16 (5C 62)*
Bartletts Pas. *EC4* *2C 16*
  (off Fetter La.)
Barton Cl. E9 . . . . *2E 51*
  SE15 . . . . *1D 107*
Barton Ct. *W14* *1A 86*
  (off Baron's Ct. Rd.)
Barton Ho. *N1* *4D 49*
  (off Sable St.)
  SW6 . . . . *1D 101*
  (off Wandsworth Bri. Rd.)
Barton Rd. W14 . . . . *1A 86*

Barton St.
SW1 . . . . 5D **23** (4A **76**)
Bartonway *NW8* . . . *5F 45*
(off Queen's Ter.)
Bartram Rd. SE4 . . . . . 3A **108**
Bartrip St. E9 . . . . 3B **52**
Barville Cl. SE4 . . . . . 2A **108**
Barwell Ho. *E2* *3C 64*
(off Menotti St.)
Barwick Rd. E7. . . . . . 1D **55**
Bascombe St. SW2 . . 4C **104**
Baseline Bus. Studios
W11 . . . . *1F 71*
(off Barandon Wlk.)
Basevi Way SE8 . . . . . . 2C **94**
Bashley Rd. NW10 . . . 3A **56**
Basildon Ct. *W1* *5C 4*
(off Devonshire St.)
Basil Gdns. SE27 . . . . 5E **119**
Basil Ho. *SW8* *3A 90*
(off Wyvil Rd.)
Basil St.
SW3 . . . . 5A **20** (4B **74**)
Basin App. E14. . . . . . 5A **66**
Basing Ct. SE15 . . . . . 4B **92**
Basingdon Way SE5 . . 2F **105**
Basinghall Av.
EC2. . . . . . . 2B **18** (5F **63**)
Basinghall St.
EC2. . . . . . . 2B **18** (5F **63**)
Basing Hill NW11 . . . . 3B **30**
Basing Ho. Yd.
E2. . . . . 1E **11** (2A **64**)
Basing Pl. E2. . 1E **11** (2A **64**)
Basing Pl. SW11 . . . . . 5B **58**
Basire St. N1 . . . . 5E **49**
Baskerville Gdns.
NW10 . . . . 1A **42**
Baskerville Rd.
SW18 . . . . 5A **102**
Basket Gdns. SE9 . . . . 3F **111**
Baslow Wlk. E5. . . . . . 1F **51**
Basnett Rd. SW11 . . . 1C **102**
Basque *SE16* *3F 79*
(off Garter Way)
Bassano St. SE22 . . . . 3B **106**
Bassein Pk. Rd. W12. . 3B **70**
Bassett Rd. E7 . . . . . . 1F **55**
W10. . . . . 5F **57**
Bassett St. NW5 . . . . . 3C **46**
Bassingbourn Ho. *N1* . *4C 48*
(off Sutton Est., The)
Bassingham Rd.
SW18 . . . . 5E **101**
Bassishaw Highwalk
EC2 . . . . 1A **18**
Basswood Cl. SE15 . . 1D **107**
Basterfield Ho. *EC1* . . *4F 9*
(off Golden La. Est.)
Bastion Highwalk
EC2 . . . . 1F **17**
Bastion Ho. *EC2* . . . *1A 18*
(off London Wall)
Bastwick St.
EC1. . . . . 3F **9** (3E **63**)
Basuto Rd. SW6 . . . . . 4C **88**
Batavia Ho. *SE14* . . . *3A 94*
(off Batavia Rd.)
Batavia M. SE14. . . . . 3A **94**
Batavia Rd. SE14 . . . . 3A **94**

Batchelor St. N1. . . . . 5C **48**
Bateman Ho. *SE17*. . . *2D 91*
(off Otto St.)
Bateman's Bldgs.
W1 . . . . 3B **14**
Bateman's Row
EC2 . . . . 3E **11** (3A **64**)
Bateman St.
W1 . . . . 3B **14** (5F **61**)
Bates Point *E13* *5C 54*
(off Pelly Rd.)
Bate St. E14 . . . . 1B **80**
Bath Cl. SE15. . . . . . . 3D **93**
Bath Ct. EC1 . . . . 4B **8**
SE26. . . . . 3C **120**
(off Droitwich Cl.)
Bathgate Rd. SW19 . . 3F **113**
Bath Gro. *E2*. *1C 64*
(off Horatio St.)
Bath Ho. *E2* *3C 64*
(off Ramsey St.)
SE1 . . . . *5A 26*
(off Bath Ter.)
Bath Pl. EC2 . . 2D **11** (2A **64**)
W6 . . . . *1E 85*
(off Peabody Est.)
Bath Rd. E7. . . . . 3F **55**
W4 . . . . 5A **70**
Baths App. SW6. . . . . 3B **86**
Bath St.
EC1. . . . . . . 2A **10** (2E **63**)
Bath Ter. SE1 . . 5F **25** (4E **77**)
Bathurst Gdns.
NW10 . . . . 1D **57**
Bathurst Ho. *W12* . . . *1D 71*
(off White City Est.)
Bathurst M. W2 . . . . . 5F **59**
Bathurst St. W2 . . . . . 1F **73**
Batley Pl. N16 . . . . . . 5B **36**
Batley Rd. N16 . . . . . . 5B **36**
Batman Cl. W12. . . . . . 2D **71**
Batoum Gdns. W6 . . . . 4E **71**
Batson Ho. *E1* *5C 64*
(off Fairclough St.)
Batson St. W12 . . . . . . 3D **70**
Battenberg Wlk.
SE19 . . . . 5A **120**
Batten Cotts. *E14* . . . *4A 66*
(off Maroon St.)
Batten Ho. SW4 . . . . . 3E **103**
W10 . . . . *2A 58*
(off Third Av.)
Batten St. SW11. . . . . 1A **102**
Battersby Rd. SE6 . . . 2F **123**
BATTERSEA 4C **88**
Battersea Bri. SW11. . 3F **87**
Battersea Bri. Rd.
SW11 . . . . 3A **88**
Battersea Bus. Cen.
SW11 . . . . 1C **102**
Battersea Chu. Rd.
SW11 . . . . 4F **87**
Battersea High St.
SW11 . . . . 4F **87**
(not continuous)
Battersea Pk. 3B **88**
Battersea Pk. Children's Zoo
. . . . 3C **88**
Battersea Pk. Equestrian Cen.
. . . . 5A **88**

Battersea Pk. Rd.
SW8 . . . . 5A **88**
SW11 . . . . 5A **88**
Battersea Ri. SW11 . . 3A **102**
Battersea Sports Cen.
. . . . 1F **101**
Battersea Sq. SW11. . . 4F **87**
Battishill St. N1 . . . . . 4D **49**
Battlebridge Ct. *N1* . . *1A 62*
(off Wharfdale Rd.)
Battle Bri. La.
SE1 . . . . 2D **27** (2A **78**)
Battle Bri. Rd. NW1 . . 1A **62**
Battle Ct. SW19 . . . . . 5E **115**
Battledean Rd. N5 . . . . 2D **49**
Battle Ho. *SE15* *2C 92*
(off Haymerle Rd.)
Batty St. E1 . . . . 5C **64**
Baudwin Rd. SE6 . . . . 2A **124**
Baulk, The SW18 . . . . 5C **100**
Bavaria Rd. N19. . . . . . 4A **34**
. . . . *(not continuous)*
Bavent Rd. SE5 . . . . . . 5E **91**
Bawdale Rd. SE22 . . . 3B **106**
Bawtree Rd. SE14 . . . . 3A **94**
Baxendale St. E2 . . . . . 2C **64**
Baxter Rd. E16. . . . . . . 5E **69**
N1. . . . . 3F **49**
Bay Ct. *E1*. *3F 65*
(off Frimley Way)
Bayer Ho. *EC1* *4F 9*
(off Golden La. Est.)
Bayes Cl. SE26. . . . . . 5E **121**
Bayes Ct. *NW3*. *4B 46*
(off Primrose Hill Rd.)
Bayfield Ho. *SE4* . . . *2F 107*
(off Coston Wlk.)
Bayfield Rd. SE9 . . . . 2F **111**
Bayford Ho. *E8* *4D 51*
(off Bayford St.)
Bayford Rd. NW10 . . . 2F **57**
Bayford St. E8. . . . . . . 4D **51**
Bayford St. Bus. Cen.
E8 . . . . *4D 51*
(off Sidworth St.)
Bayham Pl. NW1 . . . . . 5E **47**
Bayham Rd. W4 . . . . . 4A **70**
Bayham St. NW1 . . . . . 5E **47**
Bayley St.
WC1 . . . . 1B **14** (4F **61**)
Baylis Rd.
SE1 . . . . 4B **24** (3C **76**)
Baynes M. NW3 . . . . . 3F **45**
Baynes St. NW1 . . . . . 4E **47**
Bayonne Rd. W6 . . . . . 2A **86**
Bayston Rd. N16 . . . . . 5B **36**
BAYSWATER 1E **73**
Bayswater Rd. W2 . . . 1D **73**
Baythorne St. E3 . . . . . 4B **66**
Bayton Ct. *E8* *4C 50*
(off Lansdowne Dr.)
Baytree Ct. SW2. . . . . 2B **104**
Baytree Rd. SW2 . . . . 2B **104**
Bazalgette Ho. *NW8* . . *3F 59*
(off Orchardson St.)
Bazeley Ho. *SE1* *4D 25*
(off Library St.)
Bazely St. E14 . . . . . . 1E **81**
BBC Broadcasting House
. . . . 1E **13** (4D **61**)

BBC Television Cen. 1E 71
BBC Worldwide 5E 57
   (off Wood La.)
Beacham Cl. SE7 . . . . 1F 97
Beachborough Rd.
  BR1: Brom 4E 123
Beachcroft Rd. E11 . . . 5A 40
Beachcroft Way
  N19 . . . . 3F 33
Beach Ho. SW5 . . . . 1C 86
   (off Philbeach Gdns.)
Beachy Rd. E3 . . . . 4C 52
Beacon Bingo Hall . . . 1F 43
Beacon Ga. SE14 . . . . . 1F 107
Beacon Hill N7 . . . . 2A 48
Beacon Ho. E14 . . . . 1D 95
   (off Burrells Wharf Sq.)
  SE5 . . . . 3A 92
   (off Southampton Way)
Beacon Rd. SE13 . . . . . 4F 109
Beaconsfield Cl.
  SE3 . . . . 2C 96
Beaconsfield Rd.
  E10 . . . . 4A 38
  E16 . . . . 3B 68
  E17 . . . . 1B 38
  NW10 . . . . 3B 42
  SE3 . . . . 3B 96
  SE9 . . . . 2F 125
  SE17 . . . . 1F 91
Beaconsfield Ter. Rd.
  W14 . . . . 4A 72
Beaconsfield Wlk.
  SW6 . . . . 4B 86
Beacontree Rd. E11 . . . 3B 40
Beadman Pl. SE27 . . . . 4D 119
Beadman St. SE27 . . . . 4D 119
Beadnell Rd. SE23 . . . . 1F 121
Beadon Rd. W6 . . . . 5E 71
Beak St. W1 . . . . 4A 14 (1E 75)
Beale Pl. E3 . . . . 1B 66
Beale Rd. E3 . . . . 5B 52
Beames Rd. NW10 . . . . . 5A 42
Beaminster Ho. SW8 . . 3B 90
   (off Dorset Rd.)
Beamish Ho. SE16 . . . . 5D 79
   (off Rennie Est.)
Beanacre Cl. E9 . . . . . . 3B 52
Beardall St.
  EC4 . . . . . . 2D 17 (5D 63)
Beardell St. SE19 . . . . . 5B 120
Beardsfield E13 . . . . . . 1C 68
Bear Gdns.
  SE1 . . . . 1F 25 (2E 77)
Bear La. SE1 . . 1E 25 (2D 77)
Bearstead Ri. SE4 . . . . 3B 108
Bear St. WC2 . . . 4C 14 (1F 75)
Beaton Cl. SE15 . . . . . . 4B 92
Beatrice Cl. E13 . . . . . . 3C 68
Beatrice Ho. W6 . . . . . . 1E 85
   (off Queen Caroline St.)
Beatrice Pl. W8 . . . . 4D 73
Beatrice Rd. E17 . . . . . . 1C 38
  N4 . . . . 2C 34
  SE1 . . . . 5C 78
Beatrix Ho. SW5 . . . . . . 1D 87
   (off Old Brompton Rd.)
Beatson Wlk. SE16 . . . . . 2A 80
   (not continuous)
Beattie Ho. SW8 . . . . . . 4E 89

Beatty Ho. E14 . . . . 3C 80
   (off Admirals Way)
  NW1 . . . . 3F 5
   (off Drummond St.)
  SW1 . . . . 1E 89
   (off Dolphin Sq.)
Beatty Rd. N16 . . . . 1A 50
Beatty St. NW1 . . . . 1E 61
Beauchamp Pl. SW3 . . . 4A 74
Beauchamp Rd. E7 . . . . 4D 55
  SW11 . . . . 2A 102
Beauchamp St.
  EC1 . . . . 1B 16 (4C 62)
Beauchamp Ter.
  SW15 . . . . 1D 99
Beauclerc Rd. W6 . . . . . 4D 71
Beauclerk Ho.
  SW16 . . . . 3A 118
Beaufort Cl. SW15 . . . . . 5D 99
Beaufort Ct. E14 . . . . . . 3C 80
   (off Admirals Way)
  SW6 . . . . 2C 86
Beaufort Gdns. NW4 . . . 1E 29
  SW3 . . . . 4A 74
Beaufort Ho. E16 . . . . . 2D 83
   (off Fairfax M.)
  SW1 . . . . 1F 89
   (off Aylesford St.)
Beaufort M. SW6 . . . . . . 2B 86
Beaufort St. SW3 . . . . . . 2F 87
Beaufort Ter. E14 . . . . . 1E 95
   (off Ferry St.)
Beaufoy Ho. SE27 . . . . 3D 119
  SW8 . . . . 3B 90
   (off Rita Rd.)
Beaufoy Wlk. SE11 . . . . 5B 76
Beaulieu Av. E16 . . . . . . 2D 83
  SE26 . . . . 4D 121
Beaulieu Cl. SE5 . . . . . 1F 105
Beaulieu Lodge E14 . . . 4F 81
   (off Schooner Cl.)
Beaumaris Grn. NW9 . . 1A 28
Beaumont W14 . . . . 5B 72
   (off Kensington Village)
Beaumont Av. W14 . . . . 1B 86
Beaumont Bldgs.
  WC2 . . . . 3E 15
   (off Martlett Ct.)
Beaumont Ct. E1 . . . . . . 2A 66
  E5 . . . . 5D 37
  W1 . . . . 5C 4
   (off Beaumont St.)
Beaumont Cres. W14 . . . 1B 86
Beaumont Gdns.
  NW3 . . . . 5C 30
Beaumont Gro. E1 . . . . . 3F 65
Beaumont Ho. E10 . . . . 2D 39
  E15 . . . . 5B 54
   (off John St.)
Beaumont Lodge E8 . . . 3C 50
   (off Greenwood Rd.)
Beaumont M.
  W1 . . . . 5C 4 (4C 60)
Beaumont Pl.
  W1 . . . . 3A 6 (3E 61)
Beaumont Ri. N19 . . . . . 3F 33
Beaumont Rd. E10 . . . . 2D 39
   (not continuous)
  E13 . . . . 2D 69
  SW19 . . . . 5A 100

Beaumont Sq. E1 . . . . . . 4F 65
Beaumont St.
  W1 . . . . 5C 4 (4C 60)
Beaumont Ter. SE13 . . . 5A 110
   (off Wellmeadow Rd.)
Beaumont Wlk. NW3 . . . 4B 46
Beauvale NW1 . . . . 4C 46
   (off Ferdinand St.)
Beauval Rd. SE22 . . . . . 4B 106
Beaux Arts Bldg., The
  N7 . . . . 5A 34
Beavor Gro. W6 . . . . 1C 84
   (off Beavor La.)
Beavor La. W6 . . . . 1C 84
Beccles St. E14 . . . . 5B 66
Bechervaise Ct. E10 . . . 3D 39
   (off Leyton Grange Est.)
Bechtel Ho. W6 . . . . 5F 71
   (off Hammersmith Rd.)
Beck Cl. SE13 . . . . 4D 95
Beckenham Bus. Cen.
  BR3: Beck 5A 122
Beckenham Hill Est.
  BR3: Beck 5D 123
Beckenham Hill Rd.
  BR3: Beck, Lon 5D 123
  SE6 . . . . 5D 123
Beckers, The N16 . . . . . 1C 50
Becket Ho. E16 . . . . 2D 83
   (off Constable Av.)
  SE1 . . . . 4B 26
Becket St.
  SE1 . . . . 5B 26 (4F 77)
Beckett Cl. NW10 . . . . . 3A 42
  SW16 . . . . 2F 117
Beckett Ho. E1 . . . . 4E 65
   (off Jubilee St.)
  SW9 . . . . 5A 90
Beckfoot NW1 . . . . 1A 6
   (off Ampthill Est.)
Beckford Cl. W14 . . . . . 5B 72
Beckford Ho. N16 . . . . . 2A 50
Beckford Pl. SE17 . . . . . 1E 91
Beckham Ho. SE11 . . . . 5B 76
Becklow Gdns. W12 . . . 3C 70
   (off Becklow Rd.)
Becklow M. W12 . . . . . . 3C 70
   (off Becklow Rd.)
Becklow Rd. W12 . . . . . 3B 70
   (not continuous)
Beck Rd. E8 . . . . 5D 51
Beckton Rd. E16 . . . . . . 4B 68
Beckway St. SE17 . . . . . 5A 78
   (not continuous)
Beckwith Ho. E2 . . . . . . 1D 65
   (off Wadeson St.)
Beckwith Rd. SE24 . . . . 3F 105
Beclands Rd. SW17 . . . 5C 116
Becmead Av. SW16 . . . . 4F 117
Becondale Rd.
  SE19 . . . . 5A 120
Becquerel Ct. SE10 . . . 4B 82
Bective Pl. SW15 . . . . . 2B 100
Bective Rd. E7 . . . . 1C 54
  SW15 . . . . 2B 100
Bedale St.
  SE1 . . . . 2B 26 (2F 77)
Beddalls Farm Ct. E6 . . 4F 69
Bedefield
  WC1 . . . . 2E 7 (2A 62)

Bede Ho. SE4 . . . . 4B 94
  (off Clare Rd.)
Bedford Av.
  WC1 . . . . 1C 14 (4F 61)
Bedfordbury
  WC2 . . . . . . 4D 15 (1A 76)
Bedford CI. W4 . . . . 2A 84
Bedford Cnr. W4 . . . . . . 5A 70
  (off South Pde.)
Bedford Ct.
  WC2 . . . . . . 5D 15 (1A 76)
  (not continuous)
Bedford Ct. Mans.
  WC1 . . . . 1C 14
Bedford Gdns. W8 . . . . 2C 72
Bedford Hill SW12 . . . 1D 117
  SW16 . . . . 1D 117
Bedford Ho. SW4 . . . . . 2A 104
  (off Solon New Rd. Est.)
Bedford M. SE6 . . . . . . 2D 123
BEDFORD PARK 4A 70
Bedford Pk. Cnr. W4 . . 5A 70
Bedford Pk. Mans.
  W4 . . . . 5A 70
Bedford Pas. SW6 . . . . . 3A 86
  (off Dawes Rd.)
  W1 . . . . 5A 6 (4E 61)
Bedford Pl.
  WC1 . . . . 5D 7 (4A 62)
Bedford Rd. N8 . . . . 1F 33
  SW4 . . . . 2A 104
  W4 . . . . 4A 70
Bedford Row
  WC1 . . . . . . 5A 8 (4B 62)
Bedford Sq.
  WC1 . . . . 1C 14 (4F 61)
Bedford St.
  WC2 . . . . . . 4D 15 (1A 76)
Bedford Ter. SW2 . . . . 3A 104
Bedford Way
  WC1 . . . . 4C 6 (3F 61)
Bedgebury Gdns.
  SW19 . . . . 2A 114
Bedgebury Rd. SE9 . . . 2F 111
Bedivere Rd.
  BR1: Brom 3C 124
Bedlam M. SE11 . . . . . . 5C 76
  (off Walnut Tree Wlk.)
Bedmond Ho. SW3 . . . . . 1A 88
  (off Ixworth Pl.)
Bedser CI. SE11 . . . . . . 2B 90
Bedwell Ho. SW9 . . . . . 5C 90
Beeby Rd. E16 . . . . 4D 69
Beech Av. W3 . . . . 2A 70
Beech CI. SE8 . . . . 2C 94
  SW15 . . . . 5C 98
  SW19 . . . . 5E 113
Beech Ct. W9 . . . . 4C 58
  (off Elmfield Way)
Beech Cres. Ct. N5 . . . 1D 49
Beechcroft Av. NW11 . . 2B 30
Beechcroft CI.
  SW16 . . . . 5B 118
Beechcroft Ct. NW11 . . 2B 30
  (off Beechcroft Av.)
Beechcroft Rd.
  SW17 . . . . 2A 116
Beechdale Rd. SW2 . . 4B 104
Beechdene SE15 . . . . . 4D 93
  (off Carlton Gro.)

Beechen Pl. SE23 . . . . 2F 121
Beeches Ho. SW17 . . . 3A 116
Beechey Ho. E1 . . . . 2D 79
  (off Watts St.)
Beechfield Rd. N4 . . . . 1E 35
  SE6 . . . . 1B 122
Beech Gdns. EC2 . . . . . 5F 9
  (off Beech St.)
Beech Ho. SE16 . . . . . . 3E 79
  (off Ainsty Est.)
Beechmont CI.
  BR1: Brom 5A 124
Beechmore Rd.
  SW11 . . . . 4B 88
Beecholme Est. E5 . . . 5D 37
Beech St. EC2 . . . 5F 9 (4E 63)
Beech Tree Cl. N1 . . . . 4C 48
Beechwood Ct. W4 . . . . 2A 84
Beechwood Gro. W3 . . 1A 70
Beechwood Ho. E2 . . . . 1C 64
  (off Teale St.)
Beechwood Rd. E8 . . . 3B 50
Beechwoods Ct.
  SE19 . . . . 5B 120
Beechworth NW6 . . . . . 4A 44
Beechworth Cl. NW3 . . 4C 30
Beecroft La. SE4 . . . . . 3A 108
Beecroft M. SE4 . . . . . 3A 108
Beecroft Rd. SE4 . . . . . 3A 108
Beehive Cl. E8 . . . . 4B 50
Beehive Pl. SW9 . . . . . 1C 104
Beemans Row
  SW18 . . . . 2E 115
Bee Pas. EC3 . . . . 3D 19
  (off Lime St.)
Beeston Cl. E8 . . . . 2C 50
Beeston Ho. SE1 . . . . . 5B 26
  (off Burbage Cl.)
Beeston Pl.
  SW1 . . . . . . 5E 21 (4D 75)
Beethoven St. W10 . . . 2A 58
Begbie Rd. SE3 . . . . . . 4E 97
Begonia Wlk. W12 . . . 5B 56
Beira St. SW12 . . . . . . 5D 103
Bekesbourne St. E14 . . 5A 66
Beldanes Lodge
  NW10 . . . . 4C 42
Belfast Rd. N16 . . . . . . 4B 36
Belfont Wlk. N7 . . . . . . 1A 48
  (not continuous)
Belford Ho. E8 . . . . 5B 50
Belfort Rd. SE15 . . . . . 5E 93
Belfry CI. SE16 . . . . . . 1D 93
Belfry Rd. E12 . . . . 4F 41
Belgrade Rd. N16 . . . . 1A 50
Belgrave Ct. E2 . . . . . . 1D 65
  (off Temple St.)
  E13 . . . . 3E 69
  E14 . . . . 1B 80
  (off Westferry Cir.)
  SW8 . . . . 3E 89
  (off Ascalon St.)
Belgrave Gdns. NW8 . . 5D 45
Belgrave Hgts. E11 . . . 3C 40
Belgrave Ho. SW9 . . . 3C 90
Belgrave M. Nth.
  SW1 . . . . . . 4B 20 (3C 74)
Belgrave M. Sth.
  SW1 . . . . . . 5C 20 (4C 74)
Belgrave M. W. SW1 . . 5B 20

Belgrave Pl.
  SW1 . . . . . . 5C 20 (4C 74)
Belgrave Rd. E10 . . . . 3E 39
  E11 . . . . 4C 40
  E13 . . . . 3E 69
  E17 . . . . 1C 38
  SW1 . . . . 5D 75
  SW13 . . . . 3B 84
Belgrave Sq.
  SW1 . . . . . . 5B 20 (4C 74)
Belgrave St. E1 . . . . . . 4F 65
Belgrave Yd.
  SW1 . . . . 5D 21
BELGRAVIA 4C 74
Belgravia Ct. SW1 . . . . 4D 75
  (off Ebury St.)
Belgravia Gdns.
  BR1: Brom 5A 124
Belgravia Ho. SW1 . . . . 5B 20
  (off Halkin Pl.)
  SW4 . . . . 4F 103
Belgravia Workshops
  N19 . . . . 4A 34
  (off Marlborough Rd.)
Belgrove St.
  WC1 . . . . 1E 7 (2A 62)
Belham Wlk. SE5 . . . . . 4F 91
Belinda Rd. SW9 . . . . 1D 105
Belitha Vs. N1 . . . . 4B 48
Bella Best Ho. W1 . . . . 1D 89
  (off Westmoreland Ter.)
Bellamy Cl. E14 . . . . . . 3C 80
  W14 . . . . 1B 86
Bellamy Ho. W17 . . . . 4F 115
Bellamy's Ct. SE16 . . . 2F 79
  (off Abbotshade Rd.)
Bellamy St. SW12 . . . 5D 103
Bellasis Av. SW2 . . . . 2A 118
Bell Dr. SW18 . . . . 5A 100
Bellefields Rd.
  SW9 . . . . 1B 104
Bellenden Rd. SE15 . . . 4B 92
Belleville Rd.
  SW11 . . . . 3A 102
Bellevue Pde.
  SW17 . . . . 1B 116
Bellevue Pl. E1 . . . . 3E 65
Bellevue Rd. SW13 . . . 5C 84
  SW17 . . . . 1A 116
Bellew St. SW17 . . . . 3E 115
Bellfield CI. SE3 . . . . . 3C 96
Bellflower Cl. E6 . . . . . 4F 69
Bell Gdns. E10 . . . . 3C 38
  (off Church Rd.)
Bellgate M. NW5 . . . . 1D 47
BELL GREEN 4A 122
Bell Grn. SE26 . . . . 4B 122
Bell Grn. La. SE26 . . . 5B 122
Bell Ho. SE10 . . . . 2E 95
  (off Haddo St.)
Bellina M. NW5 . . . . . . 1D 47
BELLINGHAM 3C 122
Bellingham Grn.
  SE6 . . . . 3C 122
Bellingham Rd.
  SE6 . . . . 3D 123
Bellingham Trad. Est.
  SE6 . . . . 3D 123
Bell Inn Yd.
  EC3 . . . . 3C 18 (5F 63)

Bell La. E1 . . . . . 1F **19** (4B **64**)
E16 . . . . 2B **82**
Bellmaker Ct. E3 . . . . 4C **66**
Bell Mdw. SE19 . . . . . 5A **120**
Bell Moor NW3 . . . . **5E 31**
(off E. Heath Rd.)
Bello Cl. SE24 . . . . 5D **105**
Bellot Gdns. SE10 . . . . . 1A **96**
(off Bellot St.)
Bellot St. SE10 . . . . . . 1A **96**
Bells All. SW6 . . . . 5C **86**
Bellsize Ct. NW3 . . . . . . 2F **45**
Bell St. NW1 . . . . 4A **60**
SE18 . . . . 4F **97**
Belltrees Gro.
SW16 . . . . 5B **118**
Bell Wharf La.
EC4 . . . . 5A **18** (1E **77**)
Bellwood Rd. SE15 . . . . 2F **107**
Bell Yd. WC2 . . 2B **16** (5C **62**)
Bell Yd. M.
SE1 . . . . 4E **27** (3A **78**)
Belmont Cl. SW4 . . . . . 1E **103**
Belmont Ct. N5 . . . . 1E **49**
NW11 . . . . 1B **30**
Belmont Gro. SE13 . . . . 1F **109**
W4 . . . . 5A **70**
Belmont Hall Ct.
SE13 . . . . 1F **109**
Belmont Hill SE13 . . . . . 1E **109**
Belmont M. SW19 . . . . . 2F **113**
Belmont Pde. NW11 . . . . 1B **30**
Belmont Pk. SE13 . . . . . 2F **109**
Belmont Pk. Cl.
SE13 . . . . 2A **110**
Belmont Pk. Rd. E10 . . . 1D **39**
Belmont Rd. SW4 . . . . . 1E **103**
Belmont St. NW1 . . . . . . 4C **46**
Belmore Ho. N7 . . . . 2F **47**
Belmore La. N7 . . . . 2F **47**
Belmore St. SW8 . . . . . . 4F **89**
Beloe Cl. SW15 . . . . 2C **98**
Belsham St. E9 . . . . 3E **51**
Belsize Av. NW3 . . . . 3F **45**
Belsize Ct. Garages
NW3 . . . . 2F **45**
(off Belsize La.)
Belsize Cres. NW3 . . . . . 2F **45**
Belsize Gro. NW3 . . . . . 3A **46**
Belsize La. NW3 . . . . 3F **45**
Belsize M. NW3 . . . . 3F **45**
Belsize Pk. NW3 . . . . . . 3F **45**
Belsize Pk. Gdns.
NW3 . . . . 3F **45**
Belsize Pk. M. NW3 . . . . 3F **45**
Belsize Pl. NW3 . . . . 2F **45**
Belsize Rd. NW6 . . . . . . 5D **45**
Belsize Sq. NW3 . . . . . . 3F **45**
Belsize Ter. NW3 . . . . . . 3F **45**
Beltane Dr. SW19 . . . . . 3F **113**
Belthorn Cres.
SW12 . . . . 5E **103**
Belton Rd. E7 . . . . 4D **55**
E11 . . . . 1A **54**
NW2 . . . . 3C **42**
Belton Way E3 . . . . 4C **66**
Beltran Rd. SW6 . . . . . . 5D **87**
Belvedere, The
SW10 . . . . **4E 87**
(off Chelsea Harbour)

Belvedere Av. SW19 . . . 5A **114**
Belvedere Bldgs.
SE1 . . . . 4E **25** (3D **77**)
Belvedere Ct. N1 . . . . . . 5A **50**
(off De Beauvoir Cres.)
NW2 . . . . 3F **43**
(off Willesden La.)
SW15 . . . . 2E **99**
Belvedere Dr.
SW19 . . . . 5A **114**
Belvedere Gro.
SW19 . . . . 5A **114**
Belvedere M. SE3 . . . . . 3D **97**
SE15 . . . . 1E **107**
Belvedere Pl.
SE1 . . . . 4E **25** (3D **77**)
SW2 . . . . 2B **104**
Belvedere Rd. E10 . . . . . 3A **38**
SE1 . . . . 3A **24** (2B **76**)
Belvedere Sq.
SW19 . . . . 5A **114**
Belvoir Rd. SE22 . . . . . 5C **106**
Bembridge Cl. NW6 . . . . 4A **44**
Bembridge Ho. SE8 . . . . **5B 80**
(off Longshore)
SW18 . . . . **4D 101**
(off Iron Mill Rd.)
Bemersyde Point E13 . . 2D **69**
(off Dongola Rd. W.)
Bemerton Est. N1 . . . . . 4A **48**
Bemerton St. N1 . . . . . . 5B **48**
Bemish Rd. SW15 . . . . . 1F **99**
Benbow Ct. W6 . . . . **4E 71**
(off Benbow Rd.)
Benbow Ho. SE8 . . . . . . 2C **94**
(off Benbow St.)
Benbow Rd. W6 . . . . 4D **71**
Benbow St. SE8 . . . . . . 2C **94**
Benbury Cl.
BR1: Brom 5E **123**
Bence Ho. SE8 . . . . 5A **80**
(off Rainsborough Av.)
Bendall M. NW1 . . . . . . **4A 60**
(off Bell St.)
Bendemeer Rd.
SW15 . . . . 1F **99**
Benden Ho. SE13 . . . . . **3E 109**
(off Monument Gdns.)
Bendish Rd. E6 . . . . 4F **55**
Bendon Valley
SW18 . . . . 5D **101**
Benedict Rd. SW9 . . . . . 1B **104**
Ben Ezra Ct. SE17 . . . . . **5E 77**
(off Asolando Dr.)
Benfleet Ct. E8 . . . . 5B **50**
Bengal Ct. EC3 . . . . 3C **18**
(off Birchin La.)
Bengal Ho. E1 . . . . 4F **65**
(off Duckett St.)
Bengeworth Rd.
SE5 . . . . 1E **105**
Benham Cl. SW11 . . . . . 1F **101**
Benham Ho. SW10 . . . . . 3D **87**
(off Coleridge Gdns.)
Benham's Pl. NW3 . . . . . 1E **45**
Benhill Rd. SE5 . . . . 3F **91**
Benhurst Ct. SW16 . . . . 5C **118**
Benhurst La. SW16 . . . . 5C **118**
Benin St. SE13 . . . . 5F **109**
Benjamin Cl. E8 . . . . . . 5C **50**

Benjamin Franklin House
. . . . 1D **23**
(off Craven St.)
Benjamin St.
EC1 . . . . 5D **9** (4D **63**)
Ben Jonson Cl. N1 . . . . . 1A **64**
Ben Jonson Ho. EC2 . . . 5A **10**
Ben Jonson Pl. EC2 . . . . 5A **10**
Ben Jonson Rd. E1 . . . . 4F **65**
Benledi St. E14 . . . . 5F **67**
Bennelong Cl. W12 . . . . 1D **71**
Bennerley Rd. SW11 . . . 3A **102**
Bennet's Hill
EC4 . . . . 4E **17** (1E **77**)
Bennet St.
SW1 . . . . 1F **21** (2E **75**)
Bennett Ct. N7 . . . . 5B **34**
Bennett Gro. SE13 . . . . . 4D **95**
Bennett Ho. SW1 . . . . . . **5F 75**
(off Page St.)
Bennett Pk. SE3 . . . . . . 1B **110**
Bennett Rd. E13 . . . . . . 3E **69**
N16 . . . . 1A **50**
SW9 . . . . 5C **90**
Bennett St. W4 . . . . 2A **84**
Bennett's Hill SW1 . . . . . 4F **75**
Benn St. E9 . . . . 3A **52**
Bensbury Cl. SW15 . . . . 5D **99**
Ben Smith Way SE16 . . . 4C **78**
Benson Av. E6 . . . . 1E **69**
Benson Ho. E2 . . . . **3F 11**
(off Ligonier St.)
SE1 . . . . 2C **24**
(off Hatfields)
Benson Quay E1 . . . . . . 1E **79**
Benson Rd. SE23 . . . . . 1E **121**
Bentfield Gdns. SE9 . . . 3F **125**
Bentham Ct. N1 . . . . **4E 49**
(off Ecclesbourne Rd.)
Bentham Ho. SE1 . . . . . 5B **26**
Bentham Rd. E9 . . . . . . 3F **51**
Bentinck Cl. NW8 . . . . . 1A **60**
Bentinck Ho. W12 . . . . . 1D **71**
(off White City Est.)
Bentinck M.
W1 . . . . 2C **12** (5C **60**)
Bentinck St.
W1 . . . . 2C **12** (5C **60**)
Bentley Cl. SW19 . . . . . 3C **114**
Bentley Ct. SE13 . . . . . . 2E **109**
(off Whitburn Rd.)
Bentley Dr. NW2 . . . . . . 5B **30**
Bentley Ho. SE5 . . . . . . 4A **92**
(off Peckham Rd.)
Bentley Rd. N1 . . . . 3A **50**
Bentons La. SE27 . . . . . 4E **119**
Benton's Ri. SE27 . . . . . 5F **119**
Bentworth Ct. E2 . . . . . . 3C **64**
(off Granby St.)
Bentworth Rd. W12 . . . . 5D **57**
Benville Ho. SW8 . . . . . . **3B 90**
(off Oval Pl.)
Benwell Rd. N7 . . . . 1C **48**
Benwick Cl. SE16 . . . . . 5D **79**
Benworth St. E3 . . . . . . 2B **66**
Benyon Cl. N1 . . . . 5A **50**
(off De Beauvoir Est.)
Benyon Ho. EC1 . . . . 1C **8**
(off Myddelton Pas.)

Benyon Rd. N1 . . . . 5F **49**
Berberis Ho. *E3* 4C *66*
    (off Gale St.)
Berber Pl. E14 . . . . 1C **80**
Berber Rd. SW11 . . . . . 3B **102**
Berenger Twr. *SW10*. . . .3F *87*
    (off Worlds End Est.)
Berenger Wlk.
   SW10 . . . . .3F *87*
    (off Worlds End Est.)
Berens Rd. NW10. . . . . . 2F **57**
Beresford Rd. N5 . . . . . . 2F **49**
Beresford Ter. N5 . . . . . . 2E **49**
Berestede Rd. W6 . . . . 1B **84**
Bere St. E1 . . . . 1F **79**
Bergen Ho. *SE5* 5E *91*
    (off Carew St.)
Bergen Sq. SE16 . . . . . . 4A **80**
Berger Rd. E9 . . . . 3F **51**
Berghem M. W14 . . . . . 4F **71**
Bergholt Cres. N16. . . . . 2A **36**
Bergholt M. NW1 . . . . . 4E **47**
Berglen Ct. E14 . . . . 5A **66**
Bering Sq. E14 . . . . 1C **94**
Bering Wlk. E16. . . . . . . 5F **69**
Berisford M. SW18. . . .4E **101**
Berkeley Ct. NW1. . . . . . 4A **4**
   NW10 . . . . 1A **42**
   NW11 . . . . 2B *30*
    (off Ravenscroft Av.)
Berkeley Gdns. W8 . . . . 2C *72*
Berkeley Ho. *SE8* 1B *94*
    (off Grove St.)
Berkeley M.
   W1. . . . . .3A **12** (5B **60**)
Berkeley Rd. E12 . . . . . 2F **55**
   N8 . . . . 1F **33**
   N15 . . . . 1F **35**
   SW13 . . . . 4C **84**
Berkeley Sq.
   W1 . . . . .5E **13** (1D **75**)
Berkeley St.
   W1 . . . . .5E **13** (1D **75**)
Berkeley Twr. *E14*. 2B *80*
    (off Westferry Cir.)
Berkeley Wlk. *N7*. 4B *34*
    (off Durham Rd.)
Berkley Gro. NW1 . . . . 4C **46**
Berkley Rd. NW1 . . . . . 4B **46**
Berkshire Ho. SE6 . . . . 4C **122**
Berkshire Rd. E9 . . . . . 3B **52**
Bermans Way NW10 . . . 1A **42**
BERMONDSEY 3C **78**
Bermondsey Sq.
   SE1 . . . . . . 5E **27** (4A **78**)
Bermondsey St.
   SE1 . . . . . . 2D **27** (2A **78**)
Bermondsey Trad. Est.
   SE16 . . . . 1E **93**
Bermondsey Wall E.
   SE16 . . . . 3C **78**
Bermondsey Wall W.
   SE16 . . . . 3C **78**
Bernard Angell Ho.
   SE10 . . . . .2F *95*
    (off Trafalgar Rd.)
Bernard Ashley Dr.
   SE7. . . . . 1D **97**
Bernard Cassidy St.
   E16 . . . . 4B **68**

Bernard Gdns.
   SW19 . . . . 5B **114**
Bernard Mans. *WC1* 4D *7*
    (off Bernard St.)
Bernard Rd. N15 . . . . . . 1B **36**
Bernard Shaw Ct.
   NW1 . . . . .4E *47*
    (off St Pancras Way)
Bernard St.
   WC1. . . . . . . .4D **7** (3A **62**)
Bernard Sunley Ho.
   SW9 . . . . .3C *90*
    (off Sth. Island Pl.)
Bernays Gro. SW9 . . . . 2B **104**
Berners Ho. *N1* 1C *62*
    (off Barnsbury Est.)
Berners M.
   W1 . . . . .1A **14** (4E **61**)
Berners Pl.
   W1 . . . . .2A **14** (5E **61**)
Berners Rd. N1 . . . . 5D **49**
Berners St.
   W1 . . . . .1A **14** (4E **61**)
Berner Ter. *E1* 5C *64*
    (off Fairclough St.)
Bernhardt Cres. NW8. . . 3A **60**
Berridge M. NW6. . . . . . 2C **44**
Berridge Rd. SE19 . . . . 5F **119**
Berriman Rd. N7 . . . . . . 5B **34**
Berry Cotts. *E14* 5A *66*
    (off Maroon St.)
Berryfield Rd. SE17. . . . 1D **91**
Berry Ho. *E1*. 3D *65*
    (off Headlam St.)
Berry La. SE21. . . . . . . 4F **119**
Berryman's La.
   SE26 . . . . 4F **121**
Berry Pl. EC1. . . . .2E **9** (2D **63**)
Berry St. EC1. . . . .3E **9** (3D **63**)
Bertal Rd. SW17. . . . . . 4F **115**
Berthon St. SE8 . . . . . . 3C **94**
Bertie Rd. NW10 . . . . . . 3C **42**
   SE26 . . . . 5F **121**
Bertram Rd. NW4. . . . . . 1C **28**
Bertram St. N19. . . . . . . 4D **33**
Bertrand Ho. SW16 . . . .3A *118*
    (off Leigham Av.)
Bertrand St. SE13 . . . . 1D **109**
Berwick Ct. SE1. . . . . . 4A **26**
Berwick Rd. N22 . . . . . . 5D **69**
Berwick St.
   W1 . . . . .2A **14** (5E **61**)
Berwyn Rd. SE24. . . . . 1D **119**
Beryl Rd. W6 . . . . 1F **85**
Besant Cl. NW2 . . . . . . 5A **30**
Besant Ct. N1. . . . . 2F **49**
Besant Ho. *NW8*. 5E *45*
    (off Boundary Rd.)
Besant Pl. SE22 . . . . . 2B **106**
Besant Rd. NW2. . . . . . 1A **44**
Besant Wlk. N7 . . . . . . 4B **34**
Besford Ho. *E2*. 1C *64*
    (off Pritchard's Rd.)
Besley St. SW16 . . . . . 5E **117**
Bessborough Gdns.
   SW1 . . . . 1F **89**
Bessborough Pl.
   SW1 . . . . 1F **89**
Bessborough Rd.
   SW15 . . . . 1C **112**

Bessborough St.
   SW1 . . . . 1F **89**
Bessemer Ct. NW1. . . . .4E *47*
    (off Rochester St.)
Bessemer Pk. Ind. Est.
   SE24. . . . . 2D **105**
Bessemer Rd. SE5. . . . . 5E **91**
Bessingham Wlk.
   SE4 . . . . .2F *107*
    (off Aldersford Cl.)
Besson St. SE14. . . . . . 4E **93**
Bessy St. E2 . . . . 2E **65**
Bestwood Dr. *SE8*. 5F *79*
    (off Rotherhithe New Rd.)
Beswick M. NW6 . . . . . . 3D **45**
Beta Pl. SW4 . . . . . . 2B **104**
Bethal Est. SE1 . . . . 2E **27**
Bethel Cl. NW4 . . . . 1F **29**
Bethell Av. E16. . . . . 3B **68**
Bethersden Ho. *SE17*. . .1A *92*
    (off Kinglake St.)
Bethlehem Ho. *E14*. . . .1B *80*
    (off Limehouse C'way.)
BETHNAL GREEN 2D **65**
Bethnal Green Cen. for
   Sports & Performing Arts
   . . . . 2B **64**
Bethnal Green Mus. of
   Childhood 2E **65**
Bethnal Grn. Rd.
   E1. . . . . .3F **11** (3B **64**)
   E2. . . . . .3F **11** (3B **64**)
Bethune Cl. N16. . . . . . . 3A **36**
Bethune Rd. N16 . . . . . . 2F **35**
   NW10 . . . . 3A **56**
Bethwin Rd. SE5 . . . . . . 3D **91**
Betsham Ho. *SE1* 3B *26*
    (off Newcomen St.)
Betterton Ho. *WC2* 3E *15*
    (off Betterton St.)
Betterton St.
   WC2. . . . . . . .3D **15** (5A **62**)
Bettons Pk. E15 . . . . . . 5A **54**
Bettridge Rd. SW6. . . . . 5B **86**
Betts Ho. *E1*. 1D *79*
    (off Betts St.)
Betts M. E17. . . . . 1B **38**
Betts Rd. E16. . . . . 1D **83**
Betts St. E1 . . . . 1D **79**
Betty Brooks Ho. E11 . . . 5F **39**
Betty May Gray Ho.
   E14 . . . . .5E *81*
    (off Pier St.)
Beulah Hill SE19. . . . . . 5D **119**
Beulah Rd. E17 . . . . 1C **38**
Bevan Ho. *WC1* 5E *7*
    (off Boswell St.)
Bevan St. N1 . . . . 5E **49**
Bev Callender Cl.
   SW8 . . . . 1D **103**
Bevenden St.
   N1 . . . . .1C **10** (2F **63**)
Beveridge Rd.
   NW10 . . . . 4A **42**
Beverley Cl. SW11 . . . 2F **101**
   SW13 . . . . 5C **84**
Beverley Cotts.
   SW15 . . . . 3A **112**
Beverley Ct. SE4 . . . . . 1B **108**
    (not continuous)

Beverley Gdns.
NW11 . . . . 2A **30**
SW13 . . . . 1B **98**
Beverley Ho.
BR1: Brom 5F **123**
(off Brangbourne Rd.)
Beverley La. SW15 . . 3B **112**
Beverley Path SW13 . . 5B **84**
Beverley Rd. E6 . . . . . 2F **69**
SW13 . . . . 1B **98**
W4 . . . . 1B **84**
Beversbrook Rd. N19 . . 5F **33**
Beverstone Rd.
SW2 . . . . 3B **104**
Beverston M. W1 . . . . 1A **12**
Bevill Allen Cl.
SW17 . . . . 5B **116**
Bevin Cl. SE16 . . . . 2A **80**
Bevin Ct. WC1 . . 1A **8** (2B **62**)
Bevington Path SE1 . . . 4F **27**
Bevington Rd. W10 . . . 4A **58**
Bevington St. SE16 . . . 3C **78**
Bevin Ho. *E2* 2E **65**
(off Butler St.)
Bevin Sq. SW17 . . . . . 3B **116**
Bevin Way
WC1 . . . . 1B **8** (1C **62**)
Bevis Marks
EC3 . . . . 2E **19** (5A **64**)
Bew Cl. SE22 . . . . 5C **106**
Bewdley St. N1 . . . . 4C **48**
Bewick M. SE15 . . . . . . 3D **93**
Bewick St. SW8 . . . . . . 5D **89**
Bewley Ho. *E1* 1D **79**
(off Bewley St.)
Bewley St. E1 . . . . 1E **79**
Bewlys Rd. SE27 . . . . . 5D **119**
Bexhill Rd. SE4 . . . . . . 4B **108**
Bexhill Wlk. E15 . . . . . . 5A **54**
Bexley Ho. SE4 . . . . . . 2A **108**
Bianca Rd. SE15 . . . . . . 2C **92**
Bibury Cl. SE15 . . . . . . 2A **92**
(not continuous)
Bickenhall Mans. W1 . . . . 5A **4**
(not continuous)
Bickenhall St.
W1 . . . . 5A **4** (4B **60**)
Bickersteth Rd.
SW17 . . . . 5B **116**
Bickerton Rd. N19 . . . . 4E **33**
Bickley Rd. E10 . . . . . . 2D **39**
Bickley St. SW17 . . . . 5A **116**
Bicknell Ho. *E1* 5C **64**
(off Ellen St.)
Bicknell Rd. SE5 . . . . . 1E **105**
Bidborough St.
WC1 . . . . 2D **7** (2A **62**)
Biddenham Ho. *SE16* . . 5F **79**
(off Plough Way)
Bidder St. E16 . . . . 3A **68**
(not continuous)
Biddesden Ho. *SW3* . . . 5B **74**
(off Cadogan St.)
Biddestone Rd. N7 . . . 1B **48**
Biddulph Mans. *W9* . . . 2D **59**
(off Elgin Av.)
Biddulph Rd. W9 . . . . . 2D **59**
Bideford Rd.
BR1: Brom 3B **124**
Bidwell St. SE15 . . . . . 4D **93**

Big Ben 4E **23** (3A **76**)
Biggerstaff Rd. E15 . . . 5E **53**
Biggerstaff St. N4 . . . . 4C **34**
Biggs Row SW15 . . . . . 1F **99**
Big Hill E5 . . . . 3D **37**
Bigland St. E1 . . . . 5D **65**
Bignold Rd. E7 . . . . 1C **54**
Bigwood Ct. NW11 . . . 1D **31**
Bigwood Rd.
NW11 . . . . 1D **31**
Bilberry Ho. *E3* 4C **66**
(off Watts Gro.)
Billingford Cl.
SE4 . . . . 2F **107**
Billing Cl. *E1* 5F **65**
(off Bower St.)
Billingley *NW1* 5E **47**
(off Pratt St.)
Billing Pl. SW10 . . . . . . 3D **87**
Billing Rd. SW10 . . . . . 3D **87**
Billingsgate Fish Market
. . . . 2D **81**
Billing St. SW10 . . . . . . 3D **87**
Billington Rd.
SE14 . . . . 3F **93**
Billiter Sq. EC3 . . . . 3E **19**
Billiter St.
EC3 . . . . 3E **19** (5A **64**)
Billson St. E14 . . . . 5E **81**
Bilsby Gro. SE9 . . . . . . 4F **125**
Bilton Towers *W1* 3A **12**
(off Gt. Cumberland Pl.)
Bina Gdns. SW5 . . . . . . 5E **73**
Binbrook Ho. W10 . . . . 4E **57**
(off Sutton Way)
Binden Rd. W12 . . . . . . 4B **70**
Binfield Rd.
SW4 . . . . 4A **90**
Bingfield St. N1 . . . . 5A **48**
(not continuous)
Bingham Ct. *N1* 4D **49**
(off Halton Rd.)
Bingham Pl.
W1 . . . . 5B **4** (4C **60**)
Bingham St. N1 . . . . 3F **49**
Bingley Rd. E16 . . . . . . 5E **69**
Binley Ho. SW15 . . . . . . 4B **98**
Binney St.
W1 . . . . 3C **12** (5C **60**)
Binnie Ct. *SE10* 3D **95**
(off Greenwich High Rd.)
Binnie Ho. *SE1* 5F **25**
(off Bath Ter.)
Binns Rd. W4 . . . . 1A **84**
Binns Ter. W4 . . . . 1A **84**
Bircham Path *SE4* 2F **107**
(off Aldersford Cl.)
Birch Cl. E16 . . . . 4A **68**
N19 . . . . 4E **33**
SE15 . . . . 5C **92**
Birchdale Rd. E7 . . . . . . 2E **55**
Birchen Cl. NW9 . . . . . 4A **28**
Birchen Gro. NW9 . . . . 4A **28**
Birches, The E12 . . . . . 1F **55**
SE7 . . . . 2D **97**
Birchfield Ho. *E14* 1C **80**
(off Birchfield St.)
Birchfield St. E14 . . . . . 1C **80**
Birch Gro. E11 . . . . 1A **54**
SE12 . . . . 5B **110**

Birch Ho. SE14 . . . . . . 4B **94**
SW2 . . . . 4C **104**
(off Tulse Hill)
W10 . . . . 3A **58**
(off Droop St.)
Birchington Ct. *NW6* . . 5D **45**
(off W. End La.)
Birchington Ho. E5 . . . . 2D **51**
Birchington Rd. N8 . . . . 1F **33**
NW6 . . . . 5C **44**
Birchin La.
EC3 . . . . 3C **18** (5F **63**)
Birchlands Av.
SW12 . . . . 5B **102**
Birchmere Lodge
SE16 . . . . 1D **93**
(off Sherwood Gdns.)
Birchmere Row SE3 . . . 5B **96**
Birchmore Hall N5 . . . . 5E **35**
Birchmore Wlk. N5 . . . . 5E **35**
Birch Va. Ct. *NW8* 3F **59**
(off Pollitt Dr.)
Birchwood Dr. NW3 . . . 5D **31**
Birchwood Rd.
SW17 . . . . 5D **117**
Birdbrook Ho. *N1* 4E **49**
(off Popham Rd.)
Birdbrook Rd. SE3 . . . . 2E **111**
Birdcage Wlk.
SW1 . . . . 4F **21** (3E **75**)
Birdhurst Rd. SW18 . . 3E **101**
Bird in Bush BMX Track
. . . . 3D **93**
(off Bird in Bush Rd.)
Bird in Bush Rd.
SE15 . . . . 3C **92**
Bird-in-Hand Pas.
SE23 . . . . 2E **121**
Bird in Hand Yd.
NW3 . . . . 1E **45**
(off Holly Bush Va.)
NW3 . . . . 1E **45**
(Perrin's Ct.)
Birdlip Cl. SE15 . . . . . . 2A **92**
Birdsall Ho. SE5 . . . . . 1A **106**
Birdsfield La. E3 . . . . . . 5B **52**
Birkbeck College 5C **6**
Birkbeck Hill SE21 . . . 1D **119**
Birkbeck M. E8 . . . . 2B **50**
Birkbeck Rd. SE21 . . . 2E **119**
Birkbeck Rd. E8 . . . . . . 2B **50**
SW19 . . . . 5D **115**
Birkbeck St. E2 . . . . . . 2D **65**
Birkdale Cl. SE16 . . . . . 1D **93**
Birkenhead St.
WC1 . . . . 1E **7** (2A **62**)
Birkhall Rd. SE6 . . . . . 1F **123**
Birkwood Cl. SW12 . . 5F **103**
Birley Lodge *NW8* 1F **59**
(off Acacia Rd.)
Birley St. SW11 . . . . . . 5C **88**
Birnam Rd. N4 . . . . 4C **34**
Birrell Ho. *SW9* 5B **90**
(off Stockwell Rd.)
Birse Cres. NW10 . . . . 5A **28**
Birstall Rd. N15 . . . . 1A **36**
Biscay Ho. *E1* 3F **65**
(off Mile End Rd.)
Biscayne Av. E14 . . . . . 2F **81**

Biscay Rd. W6 . . . . 1F 85
Biscoe Way SE13 . . . . . 1F 109
Biscott Ho. E3 . . . . 3D 67
Bisham Gdns. N6 . . . . . 3C 32
Bishopgate Chu. Yd.
   EC2 . . . . 4A 64
Bishop King's Rd.
   W14 . . . . 5A 72
Bishop's Av. E13 . . . . . . 5D 55
   SW6 . . . . 5F 85
Bishops Av., The N2 . . . 2F 31
Bishop's Bri. Rd. W2 . . . 5D 59
Bishop's Cl. N19 . . . . . . 5E 33
Bishops Ct. EC4 . . . . . . 2D 17
   W2 . . . . 5D 59
   (off Bishop's Bri. Rd.)
   WC2 . . . . 2B 16
Bishopsdale Ho.
   NW6 . . . . 5C 44
   (off Kilburn Va.)
Bishopsgate
   EC2 . . . . . . 3D 19 (5A 64)
Bishopsgate Arc. EC2 . . 1E 19
Bishopsgate Institute &
   Libraries 1E 19
   (off Bishopsgate)
Bishops Grn. N2 . . . . . . 1A 32
Bishops Ho. SW8 . . . . . . 3A 90
   (off Sth. Lambeth Rd.)
Bishop's Mans. SW6 . . . 5F 85
   (not continuous)
Bishops Mead SE5 . . . . . 3E 91
   (off Camberwell Rd.)
Bishop's Pk. Rd.
   SW6 . . . . 5F 85
Bishops Rd. N6 . . . . 1C 32
   SW6 . . . . 4A 86
   SW11 . . . . 3A 88
Bishop's Ter. SE11 . . . . . 5C 76
Bishopsthorpe Rd.
   SE26 . . . . 4F 121
Bishop St. N1 . . . . 5E 49
Bishop's Way E2 . . . . . . 1D 65
Bishops Wood Almshouses
   E5 . . . . 1D 51
   (off Lwr. Clapton Rd.)
Bishopswood Rd. N6 . . . 2B 32
Bishop Way NW10 . . . . . 4A 42
Bishop Wilfred Wood Cl.
   SE15 . . . . 5C 92
Bishop Wilfred Wood Ct.
   E13 . . . . 1E 69
   (off Pragel St.)
Bissextile Ho. SE13 . . . . 5D 95
Bisson Rd. E15 . . . . 1E 67
Bittern Ct. SE8 . . . . 2C 94
Bittern Ho. SE1 . . . . 4F 25
   (off Gt. Suffolk St.)
Bittern St.
   SE1 . . . . . . 4F 25 (3E 77)
Blackall St.
   EC2 . . . . . . 3D 11 (3A 64)
Blackbird Yd. E2 . . . . . . 2B 64
Black Boy La. N15 . . . . . 1E 35
Blackburne's M.
   W1 . . . . 4B 12 (1C 74)
Blackburn Rd. NW6 . . . . 3D 45
Blackett St. SW15 . . . . . 1F 99
Blackford's Path
   SW15 . . . . 5C 98

Blackfriars Bri.
   SE1 . . . . . . 5D 17 (1D 77)
Blackfriars Ct. EC4 . . . . 4D 17
Black Friars La.
   EC4 . . . . . . 4D 17 (5D 63)
   (not continuous)
Blackfriars Pas.
   EC4 . . . . . . 4D 17 (1D 77)
Blackfriars Rd.
   SE1 . . . . . . 1D 25 (3D 77)
Blackfriars Underpass
   EC4 . . . . . . 4D 17 (1C 76)
BLACKHEATH 5B 96
Blackheath Av. SE10 . . . 3F 95
Blackheath Bus. Est.
   SE10 . . . . 4E 95
   (off Blackheath Hill)
Blackheath Concert Halls
   . . . . 1B 110
Blackheath Gro. SE3 . . . 5B 96
Blackheath Hill SE10 . . . 4E 95
BLACKHEATH PARK . . . 2C 110
Blackheath Pk. SE3 . . . . 1B 110
Blackheath Ri. SE13 . . . . 5E 95
   (not continuous)
Blackheath Rd. SE10 . . . 4D 95
BLACKHEATH VALE 5B 96
Blackheath Va. SE3 . . . . 5A 96
Blackheath Village
   SE3 . . . . 5B 96
Black Horse Ct. SE1 . . . 5C 26
Blackhorse Rd. SE8 . . . . 2A 94
Blacklands Rd. SE6 . . . . 4E 123
Blacklands Ter. SW3 . . . 5B 74
Black Lion La. W6 . . . . . 5C 70
Black Lion M. W6 . . . . . . 5C 70
Blackmans Yd. E2 . . . . . 3C 64
   (off Grimsby St.)
Blackmore Ho. N1 . . . . . 5B 48
   (off Barnsbury Est.)
Black Path E10 . . . . 2A 38
Blackpool Rd. SE15 . . . . 5D 93
Black Prince Rd. SE1 . . . 5B 76
   SE11 . . . . 5B 76
Blackshaw Rd.
   SW17 . . . . 4E 115
Blacks Rd. W6 . . . . 1E 85
Blackstock M. N4 . . . . . . 4D 35
Blackstock Rd. N4 . . . . . 4D 35
   N5 . . . . 4D 35
Blackstone Est. E8 . . . . . 4C 50
Blackstone Rd. NW2 . . . 2E 43
   (off Churchill Gdns.)
Black Swan Yd.
   SE1 . . . . . . 3E 27 (3A 78)
Blackthorn Ct. E11 . . . . . 1F 53
   (off Hall Rd.)
Blackthorne Ct. SE15 . . . 3B 92
   (off Cator St.)
Blackthorn St. E3 . . . . . . 3C 66
Blacktree M. SW9 . . . . . 1C 104
BLACKWALL 2E 81
Blackwall La. SE10 . . . . 1A 96
Blackwall Trad. Est.
   E14 . . . . 4F 67
Blackwall Tunnel E14 . . 2F 81
   (not continuous)
Blackwall Tunnel App.
   E14 . . . . 5E 67

Blackwall Tunnel
   Northern App.
   E3 . . . . 1C 66
   E14 . . . . 1C 66
Blackwall Tunnel
   Southern App.
   SE10 . . . . 4A 82
Blackwall Way E14 . . . . 2E 81
Blackwater Cl. E7 . . . . . 1B 54
Blackwater Ho.
   NW8 . . . . 4F 59
   (off Church St.)
Blackwell Cl. E5 . . . . . . 1F 51
Blackwood Ho. SW4 . . . 4F 103
Blackwood Ho. E1 . . . . . 3D 65
   (off Collingwood St.)
Blackwood St. SE17 . . . 1F 91
Blade M. SW15 . . . . 2B 100
Bladen Ho. E1 . . . . 5F 65
   (off Dunelm St.)
Blades Ct. SW15 . . . . . . 2B 100
   W6 . . . . 1D 85
   (off Lower Mall)
Blades Ho. SE11 . . . . . . 2C 90
   (off Kennington Oval)
Bladon Cl. SW16 . . . . . . 5A 118
Blagdon Rd. SE13 . . . . . 4D 109
Blagrove Rd. W10 . . . . . 4A 58
Blair Av. NW9 . . . . 2A 28
Blair Cl. N1 . . . . 3E 49
Blair Ct. NW8 . . . . 5F 45
   SE6 . . . . 1B 124
Blairderry Rd. SW2 . . . . 2A 118
Blairgowrie Ct. E14 . . . . 5F 67
   (off Blair St.)
Blair Ho. SW9 . . . . 5B 90
Blair St. E14 . . . . 5E 67
Blake Ct. NW6 . . . . 2C 58
   (off Malvern Rd.)
   SE16 . . . . 1D 93
   (off Stubbs Dr.)
Blake Gdns. SW6 . . . . . 4D 87
Blake Hall Cres. E11 . . . 3C 40
Blake Hall Rd. E11 . . . . 2C 40
Blake Ho. E14 . . . . 3C 80
   (off Admirals Way)
   SE1 . . . . . . 5B 24 (4C 76)
   SE8 . . . . 2C 94
   (off New King St.)
Blakeley Cotts.
   SE10 . . . . 3F 81
Blakemore Rd.
   SW16 . . . . 3A 118
Blakeney Cl. E8 . . . . 2C 50
   NW1 . . . . 4F 47
Blakenham Rd.
   SW17 . . . . 4B 116
Blaker Ct. SE7 . . . . 3E 97
   (not continuous)
Blake Rd. E16 . . . . 3B 68
Blaker Rd. E15 . . . . 1E 67
Blakes Cl. W10 . . . . 4E 57
Blake's Rd. SE15 . . . . . . 3A 92
Blanchard Way E8 . . . . . 3C 50
Blanch Cl. SE15 . . . . 3E 93
Blanchedowne SE5 . . . . 2F 105
Blanche St. E16 . . . . 3B 68
Blandfield Rd.
   SW12 . . . . 5C 102

Blandford Ct. *N1* 4A **50**
  (off St Peter's Way)
NW6 . . . . 4F **43**
Blandford Ho. SW8 . . . 3B **90**
  (off Richborne Ter.)
Blandford Rd. W4 . . . . . 4A **70**
Blandford Sq. NW1 . . . 3A **60**
Blandford St.
  W1 . . . . 2A **12** (5B **60**)
Bland Ho. *SE11* 1B **90**
  (off Vauxhall St.)
Bland St. SE9 . . . . 2F **111**
Blann Cl. SE9 . . . . 4F **111**
Blantyre St. SW10 . . . . 3F **87**
Blantyre Twr. SW10 . . . 3F **87**
  (off Blantyre St.)
Blantyre Wlk. SW10 . . . 3F **87**
  (off Worlds End Est.)
Blashford *NW3* 4B **46**
  (off Adelaide Rd.)
Blashford St. SE13 . . . . 5F **109**
Blasker Wlk. E14 . . . . . 1D **95**
Blaxland Ho. *W12* 1D **71**
  (off White City Est.)
Blazer Cl. NW8 . . . . . . 2F **59**
  (off St John's Wood Rd.)
Blechynden Ho. W10 . . 5F **57**
  (off Kingsdown Cl.)
Blechynden St. W10 . . . 1F **71**
Bledlow Ho. *NW8* 3F **59**
  (off Capland St.)
Bleeding Heart Yd.
  EC1 . . . . 1C **16**
Blegborough Rd.
  SW16 . . . . 5E **117**
Blemundsbury *WC1* . . . 5F **7**
  (off Dombey St.)
Blendon Row *SE17* . . . 5F **77**
  (off Townley St.)
Blendworth Point
  SW15 . . . . 1D **113**
Blenheim Cl. SE12 . . . 1D **125**
Blenheim Cl. N19 . . . . . 4A **34**
  SE16 . . . . 2F **79**
  (off King & Queen Wharf)
Blenheim Cres. W11 . . 1A **72**
Blenheim Gdns. NW2 . . 3E **43**
  SW2 . . . . 4B **104**
Blenheim Gro. SE15 . . . 5C **92**
Blenheim Ho. *E16* 2D **83**
  (off Constable Av.)
Blenheim Pas. NW8 . . . 1E **59**
  (not continuous)
Blenheim Rd. E6 . . . . . . 2F **69**
  E15 . . . . 1A **54**
  NW8 . . . . 1E **59**
  W4 . . . . 4A **70**
Blenheim St.
  W1 . . . . 3D **13** (5D **61**)
Blenheim Ter. NW8 . . . 1E **59**
Blenkarne Rd.
  SW11 . . . . 4B **102**
Blessington Cl.
  SE13 . . . . 1F **109**
Blessington Rd.
  SE13 . . . . 1F **109**
Bletchley Ct. N1 . . . . . . 1B **10**
  (not continuous)
Bletchley St.
  N1 . . . . 1A **10** (1F **63**)

Bletsoe Wlk. N1 . . . . . . 1E **63**
Blick Ho. *SE16* 4E **79**
  (off Neptune St.)
Blincoe Cl. SW19 . . . . . 2F **113**
Bliss Cres. SE13 . . . . . 5D **95**
Blissett St. SE10 . . . . . 4E **95**
Bliss M. W10 . . . . 2A **58**
Blisworth Ho. *E2* 5C **50**
  (off Whiston Rd.)
Blithfield St. W8 . . . . . . 4D **73**
Bloemfontein Av.
  W12 . . . . 2D **71**
Bloemfontein Rd.
  W12 . . . . 1D **71**
Bloemfontein Way
  W12 . . . . 2D **71**
Blomfield Ct. *W9* 3E **59**
  (off Maida Va.)
Blomfield Mans.
  W12 . . . . 2E **71**
  (off Stanlake Rd.)
Blomfield Rd. W9 . . . . . 4D **59**
Blomfield St.
  EC2 . . . . 1C **18** (4F **63**)
Blomfield Vs. W2 . . . . . 4D **59**
Blondel St. SW11 . . . . . 5C **88**
Blondin St. E3 . . . . 1C **66**
Bloomburg St. SW1 . . . 5F **75**
Bloomfield Ct. N6 . . . . . 1C **32**
Bloomfield Ho. *E1* 4C **64**
  (off Old Montague St.)
Bloomfield Pl. W1 . . . . . 4E **13**
Bloomfield Rd. N6 . . . . . 1C **32**
Bloomfield Ter. SW1 . . . 1C **88**
Bloom Gro. SE27 . . . . . 3D **119**
Bloomhall Rd. SE19 . . . 5F **119**
Bloom Pk. Rd. SW6 . . . 3B **86**
BLOOMSBURY
  . . . . 5D **7** (4A **62**)
Bloomsbury Ct. WC1 . . 1E **15**
Bloomsbury Ho.
  SW4 . . . . 4F **103**
Bloomsbury Pl.
  SW18 . . . . 3E **101**
  WC1 . . . . 5E **7** (4A **62**)
Bloomsbury Sq.
  WC1 . . . . 1E **15** (4A **62**)
Bloomsbury St.
  WC1 . . . . 1C **14** (4F **61**)
Bloomsbury Theatre . . . 3B **6**
Bloomsbury Way
  WC1 . . . . 1D **15** (4A **62**)
Blore Cl. SW8 . . . . 4F **89**
Blore Ct. W1 . . . . 3B **14**
Blore Ho. *SW10* 3D **87**
  (off Coleridge Gdns.)
Blossom St.
  E1 . . . . 4E **11** (3A **64**)
Blount Ho. *E14* 4A **66**
  (off Maroon St.)
Blount St. E14 . . . . 5A **66**
Bloxam Gdns. SE9 . . . . 3F **111**
Bloxhall Rd. E10 . . . . . 3B **38**
Blucher Rd. SE5 . . . . . . 3E **91**
Blue Anchor La.
  SE16 . . . . 5C **78**
Blue Anchor Yd. E1 . . . 1C **78**
Blue Ball Yd.
  SW1 . . . . 2F **21** (2E **75**)
Bluebell Av. E12 . . . . . . 2F **55**

Bluebell Cl. E9 . . . . 5E **51**
  SE26 . . . . 4B **120**
Blue Elephant Theatre
  . . . . 3E **91**
  (off Bethwin Rd.)
Bluegate M. E1 . . . . . . 1D **79**
Blue Lion Pl.
  SE1 . . . . 5D **27** (4A **78**)
Blueprint Apartments
  SW12 . . . . 5D **103**
  (off Balham Gro.)
Blue Water SW18 . . . . 2D **101**
Blundell Cl. E8 . . . . 2C **50**
Blundell St. N7 . . . . 4A **48**
Blurton Rd. E5 . . . . 1E **51**
Blyth Cl. E14 . . . . 5F **81**
Blythe Cl. SE6 . . . . 5B **108**
BLYTHE HILL 5B **108**
Blythe Hill SE6 . . . . . . 5B **108**
Blythe Hill La. SE6 . . . . 5B **108**
Blythe Hill Pl. SE23 . . . 5A **108**
Blythe Ho. SE11 . . . . . . 2C **90**
Blythe M. W14 . . . . 4F **71**
Blythendale Ho. *E2* . . . 1C **64**
  (off Mansford St.)
Blythe W14 . . . . 4F **71**
  (not continuous)
Blythe St. E2 . . . . 2D **65**
Blythe Va. SE6 . . . . 1B **122**
Blyth Hill Pl. *SE23* 5A **108**
  (off Brockley Pk.)
Blyth Rd. E17 . . . . 2B **38**
Blyth's Wharf E14 . . . . . 1A **80**
Blythwood Rd. N4 . . . . . 2A **34**
Boades M. NW3 . . . . . . 1F **45**
Boadicea St. N1 . . . . . . 5B **48**
Boardwalk Pl. E14 . . . . 2E **81**
Boarley Ho. *SE17* 5A **78**
  (off Massinger St.)
Boathouse Cen., The
  W10 . . . . 3F **57**
  (off Canal Cl.)
Boathouse Wlk.
  SE15 . . . . 3B **92**
  (not continuous)
Boat Lifter Way SE16 . . 5A **80**
Boat Quay E16 . . . . 1E **83**
Bob Anker Cl. E13 . . . . 2C **68**
Bobbin Cl. SW4 . . . . . . 1E **103**
Bob Marley Way
  SE24 . . . . 2C **104**
Bocking St. E8 . . . . 5D **51**
Boddicott Cl. SW19 . . . 2A **114**
Boddington Ho. *SE14* . . 4E **93**
  (off Pomeroy St.)
  SW13 . . . . 2D **85**
  (off Wyatt Dr.)
Bodeney Ho. *SE5* 4A **92**
  (off Peckham Rd.)
Boden Ho. *E1* 4C **64**
  (off Woodseer St.)
Bodington Ho. W12 . . . 3F **71**
Bodley Mnr. Way
  SW2 . . . . 5C **104**
Bodmin St. SW18 . . . . 1C **114**
Bodney Rd. E8 . . . . 2D **51**
Bogart Ct. *E14* 1C **80**
  (off Premiere Pl.)
Bohemia Pl. E8 . . . . . . 3E **51**
Bohn Rd. E1 . . . . 4A **66**

Boileau Rd. SW13 . . . . . 3C 84
Boisseau Ho. E1 . . . . . . 4E 65
   (off Stepney Way)
Bolden St. SE8 . . . . 5D 95
Boldero Pl. NW8 . . . . . . 3A 60
   (off Gateforth St.)
Boleyn Ho. E16. . . . . . . 2C 82
   (off Southey M.)
Boleyn Rd. E6 . . . . 1F 69
E7 . . . . 4C 54
N16. . . . . 2A 50
Bolina Rd. SE16 . . . . . . 1E 93
Bolingbroke Gro.
  SW11 . . . . 2A 102
Bolingbroke Rd. W14 . . . 4F 71
Bolingbroke Wlk.
  SW11 . . . . 4F 87
Bolney Ga. SW7 . . . . . . 3A 74
Bolney St. SW8 . . . . . . 3B 90
Bolsover St.
  W1 . . . . 4E 5 (3D 61)
Bolt Ct. EC4 . . . . 3C 16
Bolton Cres. SE5 . . . . . . 3D 91
Bolton Gdns. NW10 . . . . 1F 57
  SW5 . . . . 1D 87
Bolton Gdns. M.
  SW10 . . . . 1E 87
Bolton Ho. SE10 . . . . . . 1A 96
   (off Trafalgar Rd.)
Bolton Pl. NW8 . . . . 5D 45
   (off Bolton Rd.)
Bolton Rd. E15 . . . . 3B 54
  NW8 . . . . 5D 45
  NW10 . . . . 5A 42
Boltons, The SW10 . . . . 1E 87
Boltons Ct. SW5 . . . . . . 1D 87
   (off Old Brompton Rd.)
Boltons Pl. SW5 . . . . . . 1E 87
Bolton St.
  W1 . . . . 1E 21 (2D 75)
Bolton Studios SW10 . . . 1E 87
Bolton Wlk. N7 . . . . 4B 34
   (off Durham Rd.)
Bombay Ct. SE16 . . . . . . 3E 79
   (off St Marychurch St.)
Bombay St. SE16 . . . . . . 5D 79
Bomore Rd. W11 . . . . . . 1A 72
Bonar Rd. SE15 . . . . 3C 92
Bonchurch Rd. W10 . . . . 4A 58
Bond Ct. EC4 . . . 4B 18 (1F 77)
Bond Ho. NW6 . . . . 1B 58
   (off Rupert Rd.)
  SE14 . . . . 3A 94
   (off Goodwood Rd.)
Bonding Yd. Wlk.
  SE16 . . . . 4A 80
Bond St. E15. . . . . 2A 54
  W4 . . . . 5A 70
Bondway SW8 . . . . 2A 90
Bonfield Rd. SE13 . . . . . 2E 109
Bonham Rd. SW2 . . . . . . 3B 104
Bonheur Rd. W4 . . . . . . 3A 70
Bonhill St.
  EC2. . . . . 4C 10 (3F 63)
Bonita M. SE4. . . . . 1F 107
Bon Marche Ter. M.
  SE27. . . . . 4A 120
   (off Gypsy Rd.)
Bonner Rd. E2 . . . . 1E 65
Bonner St. E2 . . . . 1E 65

Bonneville Gdns.
  SW4 . . . . 4E 103
Bonnington Ho. N1. . . . . 1B 62
Bonnington Sq.
  SW8 . . . . 2B 90
Bonny St. NW1. . . . . 4E 47
Bonsor Ho. SW8. . . . . . . 4E 89
Bonsor St. SE5. . . . . 3A 92
Bonville Rd.
  BR1: Brom 5B 124
Booker Cl. E14. . . . . 4B 66
Boones Rd. SE13 . . . . . . 2A 110
Boone St. SE13 . . . . 2A 110
Boord St. SE10. . . . . 4A 82
Boothby Rd. N19 . . . . . . 4F 33
Booth Cl. E9. . . . . 5D 51
Booth La. EC4. . . . . 4F 17
Booth's Pl.
  W1 . . . . 1A 14 (4E 61)
Boot St. N1 . . . . 2D 11 (2A 64)
Border Cres. SE26. . . . . . 5D 121
Border Rd. SE26 . . . . 5D 121
Bordon Wlk. SW15. . . . . . 5C 98
Boreas Wlk. N1 . . . . 1E 9
Boreham Av. E16. . . . . . . 5C 68
Boreham Cl. E11 . . . . 3E 39
Boreman Ho. SE10. . . . . . 2E 95
   (off Thames St.)
Borland Rd. SE15. . . . . . . 2E 107
Borneo St. SW15 . . . . . . 1E 99
BOROUGH, THE
  . . . . 4A 26 (3F 77)
Borough High St.
  SE1 . . . . 4A 26 (3E 77)
Borough Mkt. SE1 . . . . . 2B 26
Borough Rd.
  SE1 . . . . 5E 25 (4D 77)
Borough Sq. SE1 . . . . . . 4F 25
Borrett Cl. SE17 . . . . 1E 91
Borrodaile Rd.
  SW18 . . . . 4D 101
Borrowdale NW1 . . . . . . 2F 5
   (off Robert St.)
Borthwick M. E15. . . . . . 1A 54
Borthwick Rd. E15 . . . . . 1A 54
  NW9 . . . . 1B 28
Borthwick St. SE8 . . . . . 1C 94
Bosbury Rd. SE6 . . . . . . 3E 123
Boscastle Rd. NW5 . . . . 5D 33
Boscobel Ho. E8 . . . . . . 3D 51
Boscobel Pl. SW1 . . . . . 5C 74
Boscobel St. NW8 . . . . . 3F 59
Boscombe Av. E10 . . . . . 2F 39
Boscombe Cl. E5 . . . . . . 2A 52
Boscombe Rd.
  SW17 . . . . 5C 116
  W12 . . . . 2C 70
Boss Ho. SE1 . . . . 3F 27
   (off Boss St.)
Boss St. SE1 . . . 3F 27 (3B 78)
Boston Gdns. W4 . . . . . . 2A 84
Boston Pl. NW1 . . . . 3B 60
Boston Rd. E6. . . . . 2F 69
  E17 . . . . 1C 38
Bosun Cl. E14. . . . . 3C 80
Boswell Ho. W14 . . . . . . 4F 71
   (off Blythe Rd.)
  WC1 . . . . 5E 7 (4A 62)
Boswell Ho. WC1 . . . . . . 5E 7
   (off Boswell St.)

Boswell St.
  WC1 . . . . 5E 7 (4A 62)
Bosworth Ho. W10 . . . . . 3A 58
   (off Bosworth Rd.)
Bosworth Rd. W10 . . . . . 3A 58
Botha Rd. E13 . . . . 4D 69
Bothwell Cl. E16 . . . . . . 4B 68
Bothwell St. W6 . . . . . . 2F 85
Botolph All. EC3. . . . . . . 4D 19
Botolph La.
  EC3. . . . . 5D 19 (1A 78)
Botts M. W2 . . . . 5C 58
Boughton Ho. SE1 . . . . . 3B 26
   (off Tennis St.)
Boulcott St. E1 . . . . 5F 65
Boulevard, The SW6 . . . . 4E 87
  SW17 . . . . 2C 116
  SW18 . . . . 2D 101
Boulogne Ho. SE1 . . . . . 5F 27
   (off Abbey St.)
Boulter Ho. SE14 . . . . . . 4E 93
   (off Kender St.)
Boundaries Rd.
  SW12 . . . . 2B 116
Boundary Av. E17. . . . . . 2B 38
Boundary Ho. SE5 . . . . . 3E 91
Boundary La. E13. . . . . . 2F 69
  SE17 . . . . 2E 91
Boundary Pas.
  E1. . . . . 3F 11 (3B 64)
Boundary Rd. E13 . . . . . 1E 69
  E17 . . . . 2B 38
  NW8 . . . . 5D 45
  SW19 . . . . 5F 115
Boundary Row
  SE1 . . . . 3D 25 (3D 77)
Boundary St.
  E2. . . . . 2F 11 (2B 64)
Boundfield Rd. SE6 . . . . 3A 124
Bourbon Ho. SE6 . . . . . . 5E 123
Bourchier St.
  W1 . . . . 4B 14 (1F 75)
   (not continuous)
Bourdon Pl. W1 . . . . 4E 13
Bourdon St.
  W1 . . . . 5D 13 (1D 75)
  SW4 . . . . 4A 104
Bourke Cl. NW10 . . . . . . 3A 42
Bourlet Cl.
  W1 . . . . 1F 13 (4E 61)
Bournbrook Rd. SE3 . . . . 1F 111
Bourne Est.
  EC1 . . . . 5B 8 (4C 62)
Bourne M.
  W1 . . . . 3C 12 (5C 60)
Bournemouth Cl.
  SE15 . . . . 5C 92
Bournemouth Rd.
  SE15 . . . . 5C 92
Bourne Pl. W4 . . . . 1A 84
Bourne Rd. E7 . . . . 5B 40
  N8 . . . . 1A 34
Bournes Ho. N15 . . . . . . 1A 36
   (off Chisley Rd.)
Bourneside Gdns.
  SE6 . . . . 5E 123
Bourne St. SW1 . . . . 5C 74
Bourne Ter. W2 . . . . 4D 59
Bournevale Rd.
  SW16 . . . . 4A 118

Bournville Rd. SE6 . . . . . 5C **108**
Bousfield Rd. SE14 . . . . . 5F **93**
Boutflower Rd.
  SW11 . . . . 2E **102**
Boutique Hall SE13 . . . . 2E **109**
Bouverie M. N16 . . . . . . 4A **36**
Bouverie Pl. W2 . . . . 5F **59**
Bouverie Rd. N16 . . . . . 3A **36**
Bouverie St.
  EC4 . . . . . . 3C **16** (5C **62**)
Boveney Rd. SE23 . . . . . 5F **107**
Bovill Rd. SE23 . . . . 5F **107**
Bovingdon Cl. N19 . . . . . 4E **33**
Bovingdon Rd. SW6 . . . . 4D **87**
BOW 2B **66**
Bowater Cl. SW2 . . . . . 4A **104**
Bowater Ho. EC1 . . . . 4F **9**
  (off Golden La. Est.)
  SW1 . . . . 3A **20**
Bowater Pl. SE3 . . . . 3D **97**
Bowater Rd. SE18 . . . . . 4F **83**
Bow Bri. St. E3 . . . . 2D **67**
Bow Brook, The E2 . . . . . 1F **65**
  (off Mace St.)
Bow Chyd. EC4 . . . . 3E **17**
BOW COMMON 4C **66**
Bow Comn. La. E3 . . . . . 3B **66**
Bowden St. SE11 . . . . . . 1C **90**
Bowditch SE8 . . . . 5B **80**
  (not continuous)
Bowdon Rd. E17 . . . . 2C **38**
Bowen Dr. SE21 . . . . . . 3A **120**
Bowen St. E14 . . . . 5D **67**
Bower Av. SE10 . . . . 4A **96**
Bowerdean St. SW6 . . . . 4D **87**
Bower Ho. SE14 . . . . 4F **93**
  (off Besson St.)
Bowerman Av. SE14 . . . . 2A **94**
Bowerman Ct. N19 . . . . . 4F **33**
  (off St John's Way)
Bower St. E1 . . . . 5F **65**
Bowes-Lyon Hall E16 . . . 2C **82**
  (off Wesley Av.,
  not continuous)
Bowes Rd. W3 . . . . 1A **70**
Bowfell Rd. W6 . . . . 2E **85**
Bowhill Cl. SW9 . . . . 3C **90**
Bowie Cl. SW4 . . . . 5F **103**
Bow Ind. Pk. E15 . . . . . . 4C **52**
BOW INTERCHANGE 1D **67**
Bowland Rd. SW4 . . . . . 2F **103**
Bowland Yd. SW1 . . . . . 4A **20**
Bow La. EC4 . . . 3A **18** (5E **63**)
Bowl Ct. EC2 . . . . 4E **11** (3A **64**)
Bowles Rd. SE1 . . . . 2C **92**
Bowley Cl. SE19 . . . . . . 5B **120**
Bowley Ho. SE16 . . . . . . 4C **78**
Bowley La. SE19 . . . . . . 5B **120**
Bowling Grn. Cl.
  SW15 . . . . 5D **99**
Bowling Grn. La.
  EC1 . . . . . . 3C **8** (3C **62**)
Bowling Grn. Pl.
  SE1 . . . . 3B **26** (3F **77**)
Bowling Grn. St.
  SE11 . . . . 2C **90**
Bowling Grn. Wlk.
  N1 . . . . 1D **11** (2A **64**)
Bow Locks E3 . . . . 3E **67**
Bowman Av. E16 . . . . . . 1B **82**

Bowman M. SW18 . . . . . 1B **114**
Bowman's Bldgs.
  NW1 . . . . 4A **60**
  (off Penfold Pl.)
Bowmans Lea SE3 . . . . . 5E **107**
Bowman's M. E1 . . . . . . 1C **78**
  N7 . . . . 5A **34**
Bowman's Rd. N4 . . . . . . 5A **34**
Bowmore Wlk. NW1 . . . . 4F **47**
Bowness Cl. E8 . . . . 3B **50**
  (off Beechwood Rd.)
Bowness Cres.
  SW15 . . . . 5A **112**
Bowness Ho. SE15 . . . . . 3E **93**
  (off Hillbeck Cl.)
Bowness Rd. SE6 . . . . . . 5D **109**
Bowood Rd. SW11 . . . . . 3C **102**
Bow Quarter, The E3 . . . 1C **66**
Bow Rd. E3 . . . . 2B **66**
Bowry Ho. E14 . . . . 4B **66**
  (off Wallwood St.)
Bowsprit Point E14 . . . . . 4C **80**
  (off Westferry Rd.)
Bow St. E15 . . . . 2A **54**
  WC2 . . . . . . 3E **15** (5A **62**)
Bow Triangle Bus. Cen.
  E3 . . . . 3C **66**
Bowyer Ho. N1 . . . . 5A **50**
  (off Mill Row)
Bowyer Pl. SE5 . . . . 3E **91**
Bowyer St. SE5 . . . . 3E **91**
Boxall Rd. SE21 . . . . . . 4A **106**
Boxley St. E16 . . . . 2D **83**
Boxmoor Ho. W11 . . . . . 2F **71**
  (off Queensdale Cres.)
Box Tree Ho. SE8 . . . . . 2A **94**
Boxworth Gro. N1 . . . . . . 5B **48**
Boyce Ho. SW16 . . . . . . 5E **117**
  W10 . . . . 2B **58**
  (off Bruckner St.)
Boyce Way E13 . . . . 3C **68**
Boydell Ct. NW8 . . . . . . 4F **45**
  (not continuous)
Boyd Rd. SW19 . . . . 5F **115**
Boyd St. E1 . . . . 5C **64**
Boyfield St.
  SE1 . . . . 4E **25** (3D **77**)
Boyland Rd.
  BR1: Brom 5B **124**
Boyle St. W1 . . 4F **13** (1E **75**)
Boyne Rd. SE13 . . . . 1E **109**
Boyne Ter. M. W11 . . . . . 2B **72**
Boyson Rd. SE17 . . . . . . 2E **91**
  (not continuous)
Boyson Wlk. SE17 . . . . . 2F **91**
Boyton Cl. E1 . . . . 3E **65**
Boyton Ho. NW8 . . . . 1F **59**
  (off Wellington Rd.)
Brabant Ct. EC3 . . . . 4D **19**
Brabazon St. E14 . . . . . . 5D **67**
Brabner Ho. E2 . . . . 2C **64**
  (off Wellington Rd.)
Brabourne Cl. SE19 . . . . 5A **120**
Brabourn Gro. SE15 . . . . 5E **93**
Bracer Ho. N1 . . . . 1A **64**
  (off Whitmore Est.)
Bracewell Rd. W10 . . . . . 4E **57**
Bracey M. N4 . . . . 4A **34**
Bracey St. N4 . . . . 4A **34**
Bracken Av. SW12 . . . . . 4C **102**

Brackenbury N4 . . . . 3C **34**
  (off Osborne Rd.)
Brackenbury Gdns.
  W6 . . . . 4D **71**
Brackenbury Rd. W6 . . . . 4D **71**
Brackenfield Cl. E5 . . . . . 5D **37**
Bracken Gdns.
  SW13 . . . . 5C **84**
Bracken Ho. E3 . . . . 4C **66**
  (off Devons Rd.)
Brackley Av. SE15 . . . . . 1E **107**
Brackley Cl. NW8 . . . . . . 3F **59**
  (off Pollitt Dr.)
Brackley Rd. W4 . . . . . . 1A **84**
Brackley St.
  EC1 . . . . . . 5A **10** (3E **63**)
Brackley Ter. W4 . . . . . . 1A **84**
Bracklyn Ct. N1 . . . . 1F **63**
  (not continuous)
Bracklyn St. N1 . . . . 1F **63**
Bracknell Gdns.
  NW3 . . . . 1D **45**
Bracknell Ga. NW3 . . . . . 2D **45**
Bracknell Way NW3 . . . . 1D **45**
Bradbeer Ho. E2 . . . . . . 2E **65**
  (off Cornwall Av.)
Bradbourne St. SW6 . . . . 5C **86**
Bradbury M. N16 . . . . . . 2A **50**
  (off Bradbury St.)
Bradbury St. N16 . . . . . . 2A **50**
Braddyll St. SE10 . . . . . . 1A **96**
Bradenham SE17 . . . . . . 2F **91**
  (off Bradenham Cl.)
Bradenham Cl. SE17 . . . 2F **91**
Braden St. W9 . . . . 3D **59**
Bradfield Ct. NW1 . . . . . . 4D **47**
  (off Hawley Rd.)
Bradfield Rd. E16 . . . . . . 3C **82**
Bradford Cl. SE26 . . . . . 4D **121**
Bradford Ho. W14 . . . . . 4F **71**
  (off Spring Va. Ter.)
Bradford Rd. W3 . . . . . . 3A **70**
Bradgate Rd. SE6 . . . . . 4D **109**
Brading Cres. E11 . . . . . 4D **41**
Brading Rd. SW2 . . . . . . 5B **104**
Brading Ter. W12 . . . . . . 4C **70**
Bradiston Rd. W9 . . . . . . 2B **58**
Bradley Cl. N7 . . . . 3A **48**
Bradley Ho. SE16 . . . . . . 5E **79**
  (off Raymouth Rd.)
Bradley M. SW17 . . . . . . 1B **116**
Bradley Rd. SE19 . . . . . . 5E **119**
Bradley's Cl. N1 . . . . 1C **62**
Bradmead SW8 . . . . 3D **89**
Bradmore Pk. Rd.
  W6 . . . . 5D **71**
Bradshaw Cl. SW19 . . . . 5C **114**
Bradshaw Cotts. E14 . . . 5A **66**
  (off Repton St.)
Bradstock Ho. E9 . . . . . . 4F **51**
Bradstock Rd. E9 . . . . . . 3F **51**
Brad St. SE1 . . . 2C **24** (2C **76**)
Bradwell Ho. NW6 . . . . . 5D **45**
  (off Mortimer Cres.)
Brady Ho. SW8 . . . . 4E **89**
  (off Corunna Rd.)
Brady St. E1 . . . . 3D **65**
Braemar SW15 . . . . 4F **99**
Braemar Av. NW10 . . . . . 5A **28**
  SW19 . . . . 2C **114**

Braemar Cl. SE16 . . . . . 1D **93**
(off Masters Dr.)
Braemar Ct. SE6 . . . . 1B **124**
Braemar Ho. W9 . . . . 2E **59**
(off Maida Va.)
Braemar Rd. E13 . . . . . 3B **68**
Braeside
BR3: Beck 5C **122**
Braes St. N1 . . . . 4D **49**
Braganza St. SE17 . . . . 1D **91**
Braham Ho. SE11 . . . . . 1B **90**
Braham Mus. 3B **78**
(off Maguire St.)
Braham St. E1 . . . 3F **19** (5B **64**)
Braid Av. W3 . . . . 5A **56**
Braid Ho. SE10 . . . . . . 4E **95**
(off Blackheath Hill)
Braidwood Pas. EC1 . . . . 5F **9**
(off Aldersgate St.)
Braidwood Rd. SE6 . . . 1F **123**
Braidwood St.
SE1 . . . . . . 2D **27** (2A **78**)
Brailsford Rd. SW2 . . 3C **104**
Braintree Ho. E1 . . . . . . 3E **65**
(off Malcolm Rd.)
Braintree St. E2 . . . . . . 2E **65**
Braithwaite Ho. EC1 . . . 3B **10**
(off Bunhill Row)
Braithwaite Twr. W2 . . . 4F **59**
(off Hall Pl.)
Bramah Grn. SW9 . . . . . 4C **90**
Bramah Tea & Coffee Mus.
. . . . 3F **27** (2E **77**)
Bramalea Cl. N6 . . . . . . 1C **32**
Bramall Cl. E15 . . . . . . 2B **54**
Bramall Ct. N7 . . . . 2B **48**
(off George's Rd.)
Bramber WC1 . . . . 2D **7**
Bramber Rd. W14 . . . . . 2B **86**
Bramble Gdns. W12 . . . 1B **70**
Bramble Ho. E3 . . . . . . 4C **66**
(off Devons Rd.)
Brambles, The
SW19 . . . . 5B **114**
(off Woodside)
Brambling Ct. SE8 . . . . 2B **94**
(off Abinger Gro.)
Bramcote Gro. SE16 . . . 1E **93**
Bramcote Rd. SW15 . . . 2D **99**
Bramdean Cres.
SE12 . . . . 1C **124**
Bramdean Gdns.
SE12 . . . . 1C **124**
Bramerton NW6 . . . . . . 4F **43**
(off Willesden La.)
Bramerton St. SW3 . . . 2A **88**
Bramfield Ct. N4 . . . . . . 4E **35**
(off Queens Dr.)
Bramfield Rd.
SW11 . . . . 4A **102**
Bramford Rd. SW18 . . . 2E **101**
Bramham Gdns.
SW5 . . . . 1D **87**
Bramhope La. SE7 . . . . 2D **97**
Bramlands Cl.
SW11 . . . . 1A **102**
Bramley Cres. SW8 . . . 3F **89**
Bramley Ho. SW15 . . . . 4B **98**
(off Tunworth Cres.)
W10 . . . . 5F **57**

Bramley Rd. W10 . . . . . . 5F **57**
(not continuous)
Brampton WC1 . . . . 1F **15**
(off Red Lion Sq.)
Brampton Cl. E5 . . . . . . 4D **37**
Brampton Gdns. N15 . . 1E **35**
Brampton Rd. E6 . . . . . 2F **69**
N15 . . . . 1E **35**
Bramshaw Rd. E9 . . . . . 3F **51**
Bramshill Gdns.
NW5 . . . . 5D **33**
Bramshill Rd. NW10 . . 1B **56**
Bramshot Av. SE7 . . . . 2C **96**
Bramshurst NW8 . . . . . 5D **45**
(off Abbey Rd.)
Bramston Rd. NW10 . . 1C **56**
SW17 . . . . 3E **115**
Bramwell Ho.
SE1 . . . . . . 5A **26** (4E **77**)
SW1 . . . . 1E **89**
(off Churchill Gdns.)
Bramwell M. N1 . . . . . . 5B **48**
Brancaster Ho. E1 . . . . 2F **65**
(off Moody St.)
Brancaster Rd.
SW16 . . . . 3A **118**
Branch Hill NW3 . . . . . 5D **31**
Branch Hill Ho. NW3 . . 5D **31**
Branch Pl. N1 . . . . 5F **49**
Branch Rd. E14 . . . . . . 1A **80**
Branch St. SE15 . . . . . . 3A **92**
Brand Cl. N4 . . . . 3D **35**
Brandlehow Rd.
SW15 . . . . 2B **100**
Brandon Ho. SE17 . . . . 2D **91**
Brandon Ho.
BR3: Beck 5D **123**
(off Beckenham Hill Rd.)
Brandon Mans. W14 . . . 2A **86**
(off Queen's Club Gdns.)
Brandon M. EC2 . . . . . . 1B **18**
Brandon Rd. N7 . . . . . . 4A **48**
Brandon St. SE17 . . . . . 5E **77**
(not continuous)
Brandram M. SE13 . . . . 2A **110**
(off Brandram Rd.)
Brandram Rd. SE13 . . . 1A **110**
Brandreth Rd.
SW17 . . . . 2D **117**
Brand St. SE10 . . . . . . 3E **95**
Brangbourne Rd.
BR1: Brom 5E **123**
Brangton Rd. SE11 . . . 1B **90**
Brangwyn Ct. W14 . . . . 4A **72**
(off Blythe Rd.)
Branksea St. SW6 . . . . 3A **86**
Branksome Ho. SW8 . . . 3B **90**
(off Meadow Rd.)
Branksome Rd.
SW2 . . . . 3A **104**
Branscombe NW1 . . . . 5E **47**
(off Plender St.)
Branscombe St.
SE13 . . . . 1D **109**
Bransdale Cl. NW6 . . . . 5C **44**
Brantwood Ho. SE5 . . . 3E **91**
(off Wyndam Est.)
Brantwood Rd.
SE24 . . . . 3E **105**
Brasenose Dr. SW13 . . . 2E **85**

Brassett Point E15 . . . . . 5A **54**
(off Abbey Rd.)
Brassey Ho. E14 . . . . . . 5D **81**
(off Cahir St.)
Brassey Rd. NW6 . . . . . . 3B **44**
Brassey Sq. SW11 . . . 1C **102**
Brassie Av. W3 . . . . 5A **56**
Brass Talley All.
SE16 . . . . 3F **79**
Brasted Cl. SE26 . . . . . 4E **121**
Brathay NW1 . . . . 1A **6**
(off Ampthill Est.)
Brathway Rd. SW18 . . . 5C **100**
Bratley St. E1 . . . . 3C **64**
Bravington Pl. W9 . . . . . 3B **58**
Bravington Rd. W9 . . . . 1B **58**
Bravingtons Wlk. N1 . . . . 1E **7**
(off York Way)
Brawne Ho. SE17 . . . . . 2D **91**
(off Brandon Est.)
Braxfield Rd. SE4 . . . . . 2A **108**
Braxted Pk. SW16 . . . . 5B **118**
Bray NW3 . . . . 4A **46**
Brayards Rd. SE15 . . . . 5D **93**
Brayards Rd. Est.
SE15 . . . . 5E **93**
(off Brayards Rd.)
Braybrook St. W12 . . . . 4B **56**
Brayburne Av.
SW4 . . . . 5E **89**
Bray Ct. SW16 . . . . 5A **118**
Bray Cres. SE16 . . . . . . 3F **79**
Braydon Rd. N16 . . . . . . 3C **36**
Bray Dr. E16 . . . . 1B **82**
Brayfield Ter. N1 . . . . . . 4C **48**
Brayford Sq. E1 . . . . . . 5E **65**
Bray Pas. E16 . . . . 1C **82**
Bray Pl. SW3 . . . . 5B **74**
Bread St.
EC4 . . . . . . 3A **18** (5E **63**)
(not continuous)
Breakspears M. SE4 . . . 5B **94**
Breakspears Rd.
SE4 . . . . 2B **108**
Breamore Cl. SW15 . . . 1C **112**
Breamore Ho. SE15 . . . 3C **92**
(off Friary Est.)
Bream's Bldgs.
EC4 . . . . . . 2B **16** (5C **62**)
Bream St. E3 . . . . 4C **52**
Breasley Cl. SW15 . . . . 2D **99**
Brechin Pl. SW7 . . . . . . 5E **73**
Brecknock Rd. N7 . . . . . 2F **47**
N19 . . . . 1E **47**
Brecknock Rd. Est.
N19 . . . . 1E **47**
Brecon Grn. NW9 . . . . . 1A **28**
Brecon Ho. W2 . . . . 5E **59**
(off Hallfield Est.)
Brecon M. NW5 . . . . . . 2F **47**
Brecon Rd. W6 . . . . 2A **86**
Bredel Ho. E14 . . . . 4C **66**
(off St Paul's Way)
Bredgar SE13 . . . . 3D **109**
Bredgar Rd. N19 . . . . . . 4E **33**
Bredhurst Cl. SE20 . . . . 5E **121**
Bredinghurst SE22 . . . . 5C **106**
Bredin Ho. SW10 . . . . . 3D **87**
(off Coleridge Gdns.)
Breer St. SW6 . . . . 1D **101**

Breezers Ct. E1 . . . . 1C 78
(off Highway, The)
Breezer's Hill E1. . . . . . . 1C 78
Bremner Rd. SW7 . . . . . 4E 73
Brenchley Gdns.
SE23 . . . . 4E 107
Brenda Rd. SW17 . . . . . 2B 116
Brendon Av. NW10 . . . . 1A 42
Brendon St. W1 . . . . 5A 60
Brenley Gdns. SE9 . . 2F 111
Brenley Ho. SE1 . . . . . . 3B 26
(off Tennis St.)
Brennand Ct. N19 . . . . . 5E 33
Brent Ct. NW11 . . . . 2F 29
BRENT CROSS 2E 29
Brent Cross Fly-Over
NW2 . . . . 2F 29
NW4 . . . . 2F 29
Brent Cross Gdns.
NW4 . . . . 1F 29
BRENT CROSS INTERCHANGE
. . . . 1E 29
Brent Cross Shop. Cen.
NW4 . . . . 2E 29
Brentfield Gdns.
NW2 . . . . 2F 29
Brentfield Ho. NW10 . . 4A 42
Brentfield Rd. NW10 . . 3A 42
Brent Grn. NW4 . . . . . . 1E 29
Brent Ho. E9 . . . . 3E 51
(off Frampton Pk. Rd.)
Brenthouse Rd. E9 . . . . 4E 51
Brenthurst Rd. NW10 . . 3B 42
Brentmead Pl. NW11 . . 1F 29
Brent New Ent. Cen.
NW10 . . . . 3B 42
Brenton St. E14 . . . . 5A 66
Brent Pk. Rd. NW4 . . . . 2D 29
NW9 . . . . 2D 29
(not continuous)
Brent Rd. E16 . . . . 5C 68
Brent St. NW4 . . . . 1F 29
Brent Ter. NW2 . . . . 3E 29
(not continuous)
Brent Trad. Cen.
NW10 . . . . 2A 42
Brent Vw. Rd. NW9 . . . . 1C 28
Brentwood Ho. SE18. . . 3F 97
(off Portway Gdns.)
Brentwood Lodge
NW4 . . . . 1F 29
(off Holmdale Gdns.)
Bressenden Pl.
SW1 . . . . 5E 21 (4D 75)
Breton Highwalk EC1 . . 5A 10
(off Golden La.)
Breton Ho. EC2. . . . . . . 4A 10
SE1 . . . . 5F 27
(off Abbey St.)
Brett Cl. N16. . . . . 4A 36
Brettell St. SE17 . . . . . . 1F 91
Brett Ho. Cl. SW15 . . . . 5F 99
Brettinghurst SE1 . . . . 1C 92
(off Avondale Sq.)
Brett Pas. E8 . . . . 2D 51
Brett Rd. E8 . . . . 2D 51
Brewer's Grn. SW1 . . . . 5B 22
Brewer's Hall Gdn.
EC2. . . . . 1A 18
(off London Wall)

Brewer St.
W1 . . . . 4A 14 (1E 75)
Brewery, The
EC2 . . . . 5B 10 (4E 63)
Brewery Ind. Est., The
N1. . . . . 1A 10
(off Wenlock Rd.)
Brewery Rd. N7 . . . . 4A 48
Brewery Sq.
EC1 . . . . 3D 9 (3D 63)
SE1 . . . . 2F 27
Brewhouse La. E1 . . . . . 2D 79
SW15 . . . . 1A 100
Brewhouse Wlk.
SE16 . . . . 2A 80
Brewhouse Yd.
EC1 . . . . 3D 9 (3D 63)
Brewster Gdns. W10 . . 4E 57
Brewster Ho. E14 . . . . . 1B 80
(off Three Colt St.)
SE1 . . . . 5B 78
(off Dunton Rd.)
Brewster Rd. E10. . . . . . 3D 39
Briant Ho. SE1 . . . . 5B 24
Briant St. SE14. . . . . . . 4F 93
Briar Ct. SW15 . . . . 2D 99
(off Harbridge Av.)
Briardale Gdns.
NW3 . . . . 5C 30
Briar Rd. NW2 . . . . 1E 43
Briar Wlk. SW15 . . . . . . 2D 99
W10 . . . . 3A 58
Briarwood Rd. SW4 . . . 3F 103
Briary Cl. NW3. . . . . 4A 46
Briary Ct. E16. . . . . 5B 68
Briary Gdns.
BR1: Brom 5D 125
Brickbarn Cl. SW10 . . . 3E 87
(off King's Barn)
Brickfield Rd.
SW19 . . . . 4D 115
Brick La. E1 . . . . 4B 64
E2. . . . . 2F 11 (2B 64)
Brick Lane Music Hall
. . . . 2F 83

BRICKLAYER'S ARMS
. . . . 5F 77
Bricklayers Arms Bus. Cen.
SE1 . . . . 5A 78
Brick St. W1 . . 2D 21 (2D 75)
Brickwood Cl. SE26 . . . 3D 121
Brideale Cl. SE15. . . . . . 2B 92
Bride Ct. EC4 . . . . 3D 17
Bride La. EC4. . . . 3D 17 (5D 63)
Bridel M. N1 . . . . 5D 49
(off Colebrook Row)
Brides Pl. N1 . . . . 4A 50
(off De Beauvoir Rd.)
Bride St. N7 . . . . 3B 48
Bridewain St.
SE1 . . . . 5F 27 (4B 78)
(not continuous)
Bridewell Pl. E1. . . . . . . 2D 79
EC4 . . . . 3D 17 (5D 63)
Bridford M.
W1 . . . . 5E 5 (4D 61)
Bridge, The SW8 . . . . . . 3D 89
(off Queenstown Rd.)
Bridge App. NW1 . . . . . . 4C 46
Bridge Av. W6 . . . . 5E 71

Bridge Av. Mans. W6 . . . 1E 85
(off Bridge Av.)
Bridge Cl. W10 . . . . 5F 57
Bridge Ct. E10 . . . . 3B 38
E14 . . . . 1F 81
(off Newport Av.)
Bridgefoot SE1 . . . . 1A 90
Bridge Gdns. N16. . . . . . 1F 49
Bridge Ho. E9 . . . . 3F 51
(off Shepherds La.)
NW3 . . . . 4C 46
(off Adelaide Rd.)
NW10 . . . . 1F 57
(off Chamberlayne Rd.)
SE4 . . . . 2B 108
SW1 . . . . 1D 89
(off Ebury Bri.)
W2. . . . . 4F 59
(off Nth. Wharf Rd.)
Bridgehouse Ct. SE1 . . . 4D 25
(off Blackfriars Rd.)
Bridge Ho. Quay E14 . . . 2E 81
Bridgeland Rd. E16 . . . . 1C 82
Bridge La. NW11 . . . . . . 1B 30
SW11 . . . . 4A 88
Bridge Leisure Cen., The
. . . . 4B 122
Bridgeman Ho. E9 . . . . . 4E 51
(off Frampton Pk. Rd.)
Bridgeman Rd. N1. . . . . 4B 48
Bridgeman St. NW8 . . . . 1A 60
Bridge Mdws. SE14 . . . . 2F 93
Bridgend Rd. SW18 . . . . 2E 101
Bridgen Ho. E1. . . . . . . 5D 65
(off Nelson St.)
Bridgepark SW18 . . . . . 3C 100
Bridge Pl. SW1 . . . . 5D 75
Bridgepoint Lofts E7. . . 4E 55
Bridgeport Pl. E1 . . . . . 2C 78
Bridge Rd. E15 . . . . 4F 53
E17 . . . . 2B 38
NW10 . . . . 3A 42
Bridges Ct. SW11 . . . . . 1F 101
(not continuous)
Bridges Ho. SE5. . . . . . . 3F 91
(off Elmington St.)
Bridgeside Ho. N1 . . . . . 1E 63
(off Wharf Rd.)
Bridges Pl. SW6. . . . . . . 4B 86
Bridge St.
SW1. . . . . 4D 23 (3A 76)
Bridge Ter. E15. . . . . . . 4F 53
Bridgetown Cl.
SE19 . . . . 5A 120
Bridge Vw. W6 . . . . 1E 85
Bridgewalk Hgts. SE1 . . 3C 26
(off Weston St.)
Bridgewater Highwalk
EC2 . . . . 5F 9
Bridgewater Rd. E15 . . . 5E 53
Bridgewater Sq.
EC2. . . . . 5F 9 (4E 63)
Bridgewater St.
EC2. . . . . 5F 9 (4E 63)
Bridge Way NW11 . . . . . 1B 30
Bridgeway St. NW1 . . . . 1E 61
Bridge Wharf E2 . . . . . . 1F 65
Bridge Yd.
SE1. . . . . 1C 26 (2F 77)
Bridgford St. SW18 . . . 3E 115

Bridgnorth Ho. *SE15* . . . 2C **92**
   (off Friary Est.)
Bridgwater Ho. *W2*. *5E* **59**
   (off Hallfield Est.)
Bridle La.
  W1. . . . . 4A **14** (1E **75**)
Bridport *SE17*. *1F* **91**
   (off Date St.)
Bridport Ho. *N1*. *5F* **49**
   (off Bridport Pl.)
Bridport Pl. N1 . . . . *5F* **49**
   (not continuous)
Bridstow Pl. W2. . . . . 5C **58**
Brief St. SE5. . . . . 4D **91**
Brierfield *NW1* *5E* **47**
   (off Arlington Rd.)
Brierley Rd. E11. . . . . 1F **53**
  SW12 . . . . 2E **117**
Brierly Gdns. E2. . . . . 1E **65**
Brigade St. *SE3* *5B* **96**
   (off Tranquil Va.)
Briggeford Cl. E5 . . . . . . 4C **36**
Briggs Ho. *E2* *1F* **11**
   (off Chambord St.)
Brightfield Rd.
  SE12 . . . . 3A **110**
Brightling Rd. SE4. . . . . 4B **108**
Brightlingsea Pl. E14. . . 1B **80**
Brightman Rd.
  SW18 . . . . 1F **115**
Brighton Av. E17. . . . . . . 1B **38**
Brighton Bldgs. *SE1* . . . *5D* **27**
   (off Tower Bri. Rd.)
Brighton Gro. SE14 . . . . . 4A **94**
Brighton Rd. N16. . . . . . . 1A **50**
Brighton Ter. SW9 . . . . . 2B **104**
Brightside Rd. SE13 . . . 4F **109**
Bright St. E14. . . . . 5D **67**
Brightwell Cres.
  SW17 . . . . 5B **116**
Brig M. SE8 . . . . 2C **94**
Brigstock Ho. SE5. . . . . . 5E **91**
Brill Pl. NW1 . . . . 1C **6** (1F **61**)
Brimsdown Ho. E3 . . . . . 3D **67**
Brimstone Ho. *E15*. . . . *4A* **54**
   (off Victoria St.)
Brindley Ho. *W2*. *4C* **58**
   (off Alfred Rd.)
Brindley St. SE14. . . . . . 4B **94**
Brindley Way
  BR1: Brom 5C **124**
Brinklow Ho. *W2* *4D* **59**
   (off Torquay St.)
Brinkworth Way E9. . . . . 3B **52**
Brinsley Ho. *E1* *5E* **65**
   (off Tarling St.)
Brinsley St. E1. . . . . 5D **65**
Brinton Wlk. SE1 . . . . . . 2D **25**
Brion Pl. E14 . . . . 4E **67**
Brisbane Ho. *W12* *1D* **71**
   (off White City Est.)
Brisbane Rd. E10. . . . . . . 4D **39**
Brisbane Road Stadium
  . . . . 5D **39**
Brisbane St. SE5. . . . . . . 3F **91**
Briscoe Cl. E11. . . . . 4B **40**
Briscoe Rd. SW19 . . . . . 5F **115**
Briset Rd. SE9 . . . . 1F **111**
Briset St. EC1. . . 5D **9** (4D **63**)
Briset Way N7. . . . . 4B **34**

Bristol Gdns. SW15 . . . . . 5E **99**
  W9 . . . . 3D **59**
Bristol Ho. *SE11*. *4C* **76**
   (off Lambeth Wlk.)
Bristol M. W9. . . . . 3D **59**
Bristol Rd. E7 . . . . 3E **55**
Briston Gro. N8 . . . . 1A **34**
Bristowe Cl. SW2. . . . . . 4C **104**
Bristow Rd. SE19. . . . . . 5A **120**
Britain & London Vis. Cen.
  . . . . *1B* **22**
   (off Regent St.)
Britain at War Experience
  . . . . 2D **27**
Britannia Bri. *E14* *5B* **66**
   (off Commercial Rd.)
Britannia Bus. Cen.
  NW2 . . . . 1F **43**
Britannia Cl. SW4. . . . . . 2F **103**
Britannia Ga. E16. . . . . . 2C **82**
BRITANNIA JUNC. **5D 47**
Britannia Leisure Cen.
  . . . . 5F **49**
Britannia Rd. E14. . . . . . 5C **80**
  SW6 . . . . 3D **87**
   (not continuous)
Britannia Row N1. . . . . . . 5D **49**
Britannia St.
  WC1 . . . . 1F **7** (2B **62**)
Britannia Wlk.
  N1 . . . . 1B **10** (1F **63**)
   (Murray Gro.)
  N1 . . . . 1B **10** (2F **63**)
   (Nile St.)
Britannia Way *SW6* *3D* **87**
   (off Britannia Rd.)
Britannic Highwalk
  EC2. . . . . *1B* **18**
   (off Moor La.)
Britannic Twr. EC2 . . . . . 5B **10**
British Cartoon Cen., The
  . . . . *4E* **7**
   (off Bernard St.)
British Genius Site 3C **88**
British Gro. W4 . . . . 1B **84**
British Gro. Pas. W4 . . . 1B **84**
British Gro. Sth. *W4* . . . *1B* **84**
   (off British Gro. Pas.)
British Library
  . . . . 1C **6** (2F **61**)
British Mus. . . 1D **15** (4A **62**)
British St. E3 . . . . 2B **66**
British Telecom Cen.
  EC1 . . . . 2F **17**
British Wharf Ind. Est.
  SE14 . . . . 1F **93**
Britley Ho. *E14*. *5B* **66**
   (off Copenhagen Pl.)
Brittain Ho. SE9 . . . . . . 1F **125**
Brittany Point SE11 . . . . 5C **76**
Britten Cl. NW11 . . . . . . 3D **31**
Britten Cl. E15. . . . . 1F **67**
Britten St. SW3 . . . . 1A **88**
Britten Ct. SE6 . . . . 5F **109**
Britton St.
  EC1 . . . . 4D **9** (3D **63**)
BRIXTON 2B **104**
Brixton Academy *1C* **104**
   (off Stockwell Rd.)
Brixton Hill SW2 . . . . . . 5A **104**

Brixton Hill Ct. SW2. . . . 3B **104**
Brixton Hill Pl. SW2. . . . 5A **104**
Brixton Oval SW2. . . . . . 2C **104**
Brixton Recreation Cen.
  . . . . *1C* **104**
   (off Brixton Sta. Rd.)
Brixton Rd. SE11 . . . . . . 2C **90**
  SW9 . . . . 2C **104**
Brixton Sta. Rd.
  SW9 . . . . 1C **104**
Brixton Water La.
  SW2 . . . . 3B **104**
Broadbent Cl. N6 . . . . . . 3D **33**
Broadbent St.
  W1. . . . . 4D **13** (1D **75**)
Broadbridge Cl. SE3 . . . 3C **96**
Broad Comn. Est.
  N16. . . . . *3C* **36**
   (off Osbaldeston Rd.)
Broad Ct.
  WC2 . . . . 3E **15** (5A **62**)
Broadfield NW6 . . . . 3D **45**
Broadfield Cl. NW2 . . . . . 5E **29**
Broadfield La. NW1 . . . . . 4A **48**
Broadfield Rd. SE6 . . . . 5A **110**
Broadfields Way
  NW10 . . . . 2B **42**
Broadford Ho. *E1* *3A* **66**
   (off Commodore St.)
Broadgate EC2 . . . . 1D **19**
Broadgate Circ.
  EC2 . . . . 1D **19** (4A **64**)
Broadgate Ice Rink. 1D **19**
Broadlands Ho. E1 . . . . . 5E **69**
Broadgates Ct. *SE11* . . . *1C* **90**
   (off Cleaver St.)
Broadgates Rd.
  SW18 . . . . 1F **115**
Broadhinton Rd.
  SW4 . . . . 1D **103**
Broadhurst Cl. NW6 . . . . 3E **45**
Broadhurst Gdns.
  NW6 . . . . 3D **45**
Broadlands Av.
  SW16 . . . . 2A **118**
Broadlands Cl. N6 . . . . . 2C **32**
  SW16 . . . . 2A **118**
Broadlands Lodge
  N6. . . . . 2B **32**
Broadlands Rd.
  BR1: Brom 4D **125**
  N6. . . . . 2B **32**
Broad La.
  EC2 . . . . 5D **11** (4A **64**)
  N8. . . . . 1B **34**
Bradley St. NW8. . . . . . . 4F **59**
Bradley Ter. NW1. . . . . . 3A **60**
Broadmayne *SE17* *1F* **91**
   (off Portland St.)
Broadmead SE6 . . . . . . 3C **122**
Broadwall SE1 . . . . 5A **72**
Broadoak Ct. SW9 . . . . . 1C **104**
Broadoak Ho. *NW6* . . . *5D* **45**
   (off Mortimer Cres.)
Broad Sanctuary
  SW1 . . . . 4C **22** (3F **75**)
Broadstone Ho. *SW8* . . . *3B* **90**
   (off Dorset Rd.)
Broadstone Pl.
  W1 . . . . 1B **12** (4C **60**)

Broad St. Av.
EC2 . . . . 1D **19** (4A **64**)
Broad St. Pl. EC2 . . . . 1C **18**
Broad Wlk.
NW1 . . . . 1C **4** (5C **46**)
SE3 . . . . 3F **93**
W1 . . . . 5A **12** (1B **74**)
Broad Wlk., The W8 . . . 2D **73**
Broadwalk Ct. W8 . . . . 2C **72**
    (off Palace Gdns. Ter.)
Broadwalk Ho.
EC2 . . . . 5D **11** (3A **64**)
SW7 . . . . 3E **73**
    (off Hyde Pk. Ga.)
Broad Wlk. La.
NW1 . . . . 2B **30**
Broadwall
SE1 . . . . 1C **24** (2C **76**)
Broadwater Rd.
SW17 . . . . 4A **116**
Broadway E13 . . . . . . 1D **69**
E15 . . . . 4F **53**
SW1 . . . . 4B **22** (4F **75**)
Broadway, The N8 . . . 1A **34**
NW9 . . . . 1B **28**
SW13 . . . . 5A **84**
Broadway Arc. W6 . . . . 5E **71**
    (off Hammersmith B'way.)
Broadway Cen., The
W6 . . . . 5E **71**
Broadway Chambers
W6 . . . . 5E **71**
    (off Hammersmith B'way.)
Broadway Ho.
BR1: Brom 5F **123**
    (off Bromley Rd.)
E8 . . . . 5D **51**
    (off Ada St.)
Broadway Mkt. E8 . . . . 5D **51**
SW17 . . . . 4B **116**
Broadway Mkt. M.
E8 . . . . 5C **50**
Broadway M. E5 . . . . . 2B **36**
Broadway Pde. N8 . . . 1A **34**
Broadway Retail Pk.
NW2 . . . . 1F **43**
Broadway Shop. Mall
SW1 . . . . 5B **22** (4F **75**)
Broadway Squash &
Fitness Cen. 5F **71**
    (off Chalk Hill Rd.)
Broadway Theatre, The
Catford 5D **109**
Broadwick St.
W1 . . . . 4A **14** (1E **75**)
Broadwood Ter. W8 . . . 5B **72**
Broad Yd. EC1 . . 4D **9** (3D **63**)
Brocas Cl. NW3 . . . . . 4A **46**
Brockbridge Ho.
SW15 . . . . 4B **98**
Brockham Cl. SW19 . . 5B **114**
Brockham Dr. SW2 . . . 5B **104**
Brockham Ho. NW1 . . . 5E **47**
    (off Bayham Pl.)
SW2 . . . . 5B **104**
    (off Brockham Dr.)
Brockham St.
SE1 . . . . 5A **26** (4E **77**)
Brockill Cres. SE4 . . . 2A **108**

Brocklebank Ind. Est.
SE7 . . . . 5C **82**
Brocklebank Rd. SE7 . . 5D **83**
SW18 . . . . 5E **101**
Brockhurst St.
SE14 . . . . 3F **93**
BROCKLEY 2F **107**
Brockley Cross SE4 . . 1A **108**
Brockley Cross Bus. Cen.
SE4 . . . . 1A **108**
Brockley Footpath
SE4 . . . . 3A **108**
    (not continuous)
SE15 . . . . 2E **107**
Brockley Gdns. SE4 . . . 5B **94**
Brockley Gro. SE4 . . . . 3B **108**
Brockley Hall Rd.
SE4 . . . . 3A **108**
Brockley Jack Theatre
. . . . 3A **108**
Brockley M. SE4 . . . . 3A **108**
Brockley Pk. SE23 . . . 5A **108**
Brockley Ri. SE23 . . . 1A **122**
Brockley Rd. SE4 . . . . 1B **108**
Brockley Vw. SE23 . . . 5A **108**
Brockley Way SE4 . . . . 3F **107**
Brockman Ri.
BR1: Brom 4F **123**
Brockmer Ho. E1 . . . . . 1D **79**
    (off Crowder St.)
Brock Pl. E3 . . . . 3D **67**
Brock Rd. E13 . . . . . . 4D **69**
Brock St. SE15 . . . . . . 1E **107**
Brockway Cl. E11 . . . . 4A **40**
Brockweir E2 . . . . 1E **65**
    (off Cyprus St.)
Brockwell Ct. SW2 . . . 3C **104**
Brockwell Ho. SE11 . . . 2B **90**
    (off Vauxhall St.)
Brockwell Pk. 4D **105**
Brockwell Pk. Gdns.
SE24 . . . . 5C **104**
Brockwell Pk. Lido . . 4D **105**
Brockwell Pk. Row
SW2 . . . . 5C **104**
Brodia Rd. N16 . . . . . . 5A **36**
Brodie Ho. SE1 . . . . . . 1B **92**
    (off Cooper's Rd.)
Brodie St. SE1 . . . . . . 1B **92**
Brodlove La. E1 . . . . . . 1F **79**
Brodrick Rd. SW17 . . . 2A **116**
Broken Wharf
EC4 . . . . 4F **17** (1E **77**)
Brokesley St. E3 . . . . . 2B **66**
Broke Wlk. E8 . . . . 5B **50**
Bromar Rd. SE5 . . . . . 1A **106**
Bromell's Rd. SW4 . . . 2E **103**
Bromfelde Rd. SW4 . . 1F **103**
Bromfelde Wlk. SW4 . . 5F **89**
Bromfield St. N1 . . . . . 5C **48**
Bromhead St. E1 . . . . . 5E **65**
    (off Jubilee St.)
Bromhead St. E1 . . . . . 5E **65**
Bromleigh Ct. SE23 . . 2C **120**
Bromleigh Ho. SE1 . . . 5F **27**
    (off Abbey St.)
BROMLEY 2D **67**
Bromley Hall Rd.
E14 . . . . 4E **67**
Bromley High St. E3 . . 2D **67**

Bromley Hill
BR1: Brom 5A **124**
Bromley Pl.
W1 . . . . 5F **5** (4E **61**)
Bromley Rd.
BR1: Brom 1D **123**
E10 . . . . 1D **39**
SE6 . . . . 1D **123**
Bromley St. E1 . . . . . . 4F **65**
BROMPTON 4A **74**
Brompton Arc. SW3 . . . 4A **20**
Brompton Cotts.
SW10 . . . . 2E **87**
    (off Hollywood Rd.)
Brompton Oratory 4A **74**
Brompton Pk. Cres.
SW6 . . . . 2D **87**
Brompton Pl. SW3 . . . . 4A **74**
Brompton Rd.
SW1 . . . . 4A **20** (5A **74**)
SW3 . . . . 4A **20** (5A **74**)
Brompton Sq. SW3 . . . 4A **74**
Bromwich Av. N6 . . . . 4C **32**
Bromyard Av. W3 . . . . 1A **70**
Bromyard Ho. SE15 . . . 3D **93**
    (off Commercial Way)
Bromyard Leisure Cen.
. . . . 2A **70**
Bron Ct. NW6 . . . . 5C **44**
BRONDESBURY 4B **44**
Brondesbury Ct. NW2 . . 3F **43**
Brondesbury M. NW6 . . 4C **44**
BRONDESBURY PARK
. . . . 5A **44**
Brondesbury Pk.
NW2 . . . . 3D **43**
NW6 . . . . 4E **43**
Brondesbury Rd.
NW6 . . . . 1B **58**
Brondesbury Vs.
NW6 . . . . 1B **58**
Bronsart Rd. SW6 . . . . 3A **86**
Bronte Cl. E7 . . . . 1C **54**
Bronte Cl. W14 . . . . . . 4F **71**
    (off Girdler's Rd.)
Bronte Ho. N16 . . . . . . 2A **50**
NW6 . . . . 2C **58**
SW4 . . . . 5E **103**
Bronti Cl. SE17 . . . . . . 1E **91**
Bronwen Ct. NW8 . . . . 2F **59**
    (off Grove End Rd.)
Bronze St. SE8 . . . . . . 3C **94**
Brookbank Rd.
SE13 . . . . 1C **108**
Brook Cl. SW17 . . . . . 2C **116**
Brook Ct. E11 . . . . 5A **40**
E15 . . . . 2D **53**
    (off Clays La.)
SE12 . . . . 3E **125**
Brookdale Rd. SE6 . . . 5D **109**
    (not continuous)
Brook Dr. SE11 . . . . . . 4C **76**
Brooke Ho. SE14 . . . . 4A **94**
Brookehowse Rd.
SE6 . . . . 2C **122**
Brooke Rd. E5 . . . . 5C **36**
N16 . . . . 5B **36**
Brooke's Ct.
EC1 . . . . 5B **8** (4C **62**)
Brooke's Mkt. EC1 . . . . 5C **8**

Brooke St.
EC1 . . . . . 1B **16** (4C **62**)
Brookfield N6 . . . . 5C **32**
Brookfield Pk. NW5 . . . 5D **33**
Brookfield Rd. E9 . . . . 3A **52**
W4 . . . . 3A **70**
Brook Gdns. SW13 . . . 1B **98**
Brook Ga.
W1 . . . . . . 5A **12** (1B **74**)
BROOK GREEN 5F **71**
Brook Grn. W6 . . . . . 4F **71**
Brook Grn. Flats
W14. . . . . 4F 71
(off Dunsany Rd.)
Brook Ho. W6 . . . . *5E 71*
(off Shepherd's Bush Rd.)
Brook Ho's. NW1 . . . . . *1E 61*
(off Cranleigh St.)
Brooking Rd. E7 . . . . . 2C **54**
Brooklands Av.
SW19 . . . . 2D **115**
Brooklands Ct. NW6 . . 4B **44**
Brooklands Pk. SE3 . . 1C **110**
Brooklands Pas. SW8 . . 4F **89**
Brook La.
BR1: Brom 5C **124**
SE3 . . . . 5D **97**
Brook Lodge NW11 . . . *1F 29*
(off Nth. Circular Rd.)
Brookmarsh Ind. Est.
SE10 . . . . 3D **95**
Brook M. WC2 . . . . . . 3C **14**
Brook M. Nth. W2. . . . . 1E **73**
Brookmill Rd. SE8 . . . . 4C **94**
Brook Rd. NW2. . . . . . 4B **28**
Brooksbank St. E9 . . . . 3E **51**
Brooksby M. N1 . . . . . . 4C **48**
Brooksby St. N1 . . . . . . 4C **48**
Brooksby's Wlk. E9. . . . 2F **51**
Brooks Ct. SW8 . . . . . . 3E **89**
Brooks Farm 2D **39**
Brookside Rd. N19. . . . 4E **33**
NW11 . . . . 1A **30**
Brooks Lodge N1 . . . . . *1A 64*
(off Hoxton St.)
Brooks M.
W1. . . . . 4D **13** (1D **75**)
Brook Sq. SE18. . . . . . 4C **97**
Brooks Rd. E13. . . . . . 5C **54**
Brook St. W1. . . 4D **13** (1D **75**)
W2. . . . . 1F **73**
Brooksville Av. NW6. . . 5A **44**
Brookview Rd.
SW16 . . . . 5E **117**
Brookville Rd. SW6 . . . 3B **86**
Brookway SE3 . . . . . 1C **110**
Brookwood Av. SW13. . 5B **84**
Brookwood Ho. SE1 . . . *4E 25*
(off Webber St.)
Brookwood Rd.
SW18 . . . . 1B **114**
Broome Way SE5 . . . . 3F **91**
Broomfield E17. . . . . . 2B **38**
NW1 . . . . *4C 46*
(off Ferdinand St.)
Broomfield Ct. SE16. . . *4C 78*
(off Ben Smith Way)
Broomfield Ho. SE17. . *5A 78*
(off Massinger St.)
Broomfield St. E14. . . . 4C **66**

Broomgrove Rd.
SW9 . . . . 5B **90**
Broomhill Rd.
SW18 . . . . 3C **100**
Broomhouse La.
SW6 . . . . 5C **86**
(not continuous)
Broomhouse Rd.
SW6 . . . . 5C **86**
Broomsleigh Bus. Pk.
SE26. . . . . 5B **122**
Broomsleigh St.
NW6 . . . . 2B **44**
Broomwood Rd.
SW11 . . . . 4B **102**
Broseley Gro. SE26 . . 5A **122**
Brougham Rd. E8. . . . . 5C **50**
Brougham St. SW11 . . 5B **88**
Brough Cl. SW8 . . . . . . 3A **90**
Broughton Dr. SW9 . . 2C **104**
Broughton Gdns. N6. . . 1E **33**
Broughton Rd. SW6 . . . 5D **87**
Broughton Rd. SW8 . . . 5C **88**
Broughton St. Ind. Est.
SW11 . . . . 5C **88**
Browne Ho. SE8. . . . . . *3C 94*
(off Deptford Chu. St.)
Brownfield Area E14 . . 5D **67**
Brownfield St. E14. . . . 5D **67**
Brown Hart Gdns.
W1 . . . . . . 4C **12** (1C **74**)
Brownhill Rd. SE6 . . . 5D **109**
Browning Cl. W9 . . . . . 3E **59**
Browning Ho.
N16 . . . . *1A 50*
(off Shakspeare Wlk.)
SE14 . . . . *4A 94*
(off Loring Rd.)
W12 . . . . *5E 57*
(off Wood La.)
Browning M.
W1. . . . . . . 1C **12** (4D **61**)
Browning Rd. E11 . . . . 2B **40**
Browning St. SE17 . . . 1E **91**
Brownlow Ho. SE16 . . . *3C 78*
(off George Row)
Brownlow M.
WC1 . . . . . . 4A **8** (3B **62**)
Brownlow Rd. E7 . . . . . 1C **54**
E8 . . . . 5B **50**
NW10 . . . . 4A **42**
Brownlow St.
WC1 . . . . . 1A **16** (4B **62**)
Browns Arc. W1 . . . . . . *5A 14*
(off Regent St.)
Brown's Bldgs.
EC3 . . . . . . 3E **19** (5A **64**)
Browns La. NW5 . . . . . 2D **47**
Brown St. W1 . . . . 5B **60**
BROWNSWOOD PARK
. . . . 4D **35**
Brownswood Rd. N4 . . 5D **35**
Broxash Rd. SW11. . . 4C **102**
Broxbourne Rd. E7. . . . 5C **40**
Broxholme Ho. SW6 . . . *4D 87*
(off Harwood Rd.)
Broxholm Rd. SE27 . . 3C **118**
Broxted Rd. SE6. . . . . 2B **122**
Broxwood Way NW8 . . 5A **46**
Bruce Cl. W10 . . . . 4F **57**

Bruce Hall M.
SW17 . . . . 4C **116**
Bruce Ho. W10 . . . . . . 4F **57**
Bruce Rd. E3 . . . . 2D **67**
NW10 . . . . 4A **42**
Bruckner St. W10. . . . . 2A **58**
Brudenell Rd.
SW17 . . . . 3B **116**
Bruford Ct. SE8 . . . . . . 2C **94**
Bruges Pl. NW1 . . . . . . *4E 47*
(off Randolph St.)
Brune Ho. E1 . . . . 1F **19**
Brunei Gallery
. . . . 5C **6** (4F **61**)
Brunei Engine House Mus.
. . . . 3E **79**
Brunel Est. W2 . . . . 4C **58**
Brunel Ho. E14. . . . . . . *1D 95*
(off Ship Yd.)
Brunel Rd. E17. . . . . . . 1A **38**
SE16. . . . . 3E **79**
W3 . . . . 4A **56**
Brunel St. E16 . . . . 5B **68**
Brune St. E1 . . . 1F **19** (4B **64**)
Brunlees Ho. SE1 . . . . . *5F 25*
(off Bath Ter.)
Brunner Cl. NW11 . . . . 1D **31**
Brunner Ho. SE6. . . . . . 4E **123**
Brunner Rd. E17. . . . . . 1A **38**
Brunswick Cen.
WC1 . . . . . . 3D **7** (3A **62**)
Brunswick Cl. Est.
EC1 . . . . . . 2D **9** (2D **63**)
Brunswick Ct. EC1. . . . . *2D 9*
(off Tompion St.)
SE1 . . . . . . 4E **27** (3A **78**)
SW1 . . . . 5F **75**
(off Regency St.)
Brunswick Gdns.
W8 . . . . 2C **72**
Brunswick Ho. E2 . . . . . *1B 64*
(off Thurtle Rd.)
SE16. . . . . *4A 80*
(off Brunswick Quay)
Brunswick Mans. WC1. . *3E 7*
(off Handel St.)
Brunswick M. SW16. . . 5F **117**
W1 . . . . . . 2A **12** (5B **60**)
Brunswick Pk. SE5. . . . 4A **92**
Brunswick Pl.
N1 . . . . 2C **10** (2F **63**)
NW1 . . . . 4C **4** (3C **60**)
(not continuous)
Brunswick Quay SE16. . 4F **79**
Brunswick Rd. E10 . . . 3E **39**
E14 . . . . 5E **67**
Brunswick Sq.
WC1 . . . . . . 3E **7** (3A **62**)
Brunswick V. SE5. . . . . 4A **92**
Brunton Pl. E14 . . . . . . 5A **66**
Brushfield St.
E1 . . . . 5E **11** (4A **64**)
Brushwood Cl. E14 . . . 4D **67**
Brussels Rd. SW11 . . . 2F **101**
Bruton La.
W1 . . . . 5E **13** (1D **75**)
Bruton Pl.
W1 . . . . 5E **13** (1D **75**)
Bruton St.
W1 . . . . 5E **13** (1D **75**)

Brutus Ct. SE11 . . . . . 5D 77
(off Kennington La.)
Bryan Av. NW10 . . . . 4D 43
Bryan Ho. NW10 . . . . 4D 43
  SE16 . . . . 3B 80
Bryan Rd. SE16 . . . . . 3B 80
Bryan's All. SW6 . . . . 5D 87
Bryanston Ct. W1 . . . . 2A 12
(not continuous)
Bryanston Rd. N8 . . . 1F 33
Bryanston Mans.
  W1 . . . . 5A 4
(off York St.)
Bryanston M. E.
  W1 . . . . 1A 12 (4B 60)
Bryanston M. W.
  W1 . . . . . . 2A 12 (4B 60)
Bryanston Pl. W1 . . . 4B 60
Bryanston Sq.
  W1 . . . . . . 2A 12 (5B 60)
Bryanston St.
  W1 . . . . . . 3A 12 (5B 60)
Bryant Ct. E2 . . . . 1B 64
(off Whiston Rd.,
not continuous)
Bryant St. E15 . . . . . . 4F 53
Bryantwood Rd. N7 . . 2C 48
Bryce Ho. SE14 . . . . . 2F 93
(off John Williams Cl.)
Brydale Ho. SE16 . . . 5F 79
(off Rotherhithe New Rd.)
Bryden Cl. SE26 . . . . 5A 122
Brydges Pl.
  WC2 . . . . . . 5D 15 (1A 76)
Brydges Rd. E15 . . . . 2F 53
Brydon Wlk. N1 . . . . . 5A 48
Bryer Cl. EC2 . . . . 5F 9
Bryett Rd. N7 . . . . . . 5A 34
Bryher Ct. SE11 . . . . . 1C 90
(off Sancroft St.)
Brymay Cl. E3 . . . . . . 1C 66
Brynmaer Rd.
  SW11 . . . . 4B 88
Bryony Rd. W12 . . . . 1C 70
Buccleugh Ho. E5 . . . 2C 36
Buchanan Ct. SE16 . . . 5F 79
(off Worgan St.)
Buchanan Gdns.
  NW10 . . . . 1D 57
Buchan Rd. SE15 . . . 1E 107
Bucharest Rd.
  SW18 . . . . 5E 101
Buckden Cl. SE12 . . . 4C 110
Buckfast St. E2 . . . . . 2C 64
Buck Hill Wlk. W2 . . . 1F 73
Buckhold Rd. SW18 . . 4C 100
Buckhurst Ho. N7 . . . 2F 47
Buckhurst St. E1 . . . . 3D 65
Buer Rd. SW6 . . . . . . 5A 86
Buckingham Arc.
  WC2 . . . . 5D 15
Buckingham Chambers
  SW1 . . . . 5E 75
(off Greencoat Pl.)
Buckingham Ga.
  SW1 . . . . . 5F 21 (4E 75)
Buckingham La.
  SE23 . . . . 5A 108
Buckingham Mans.
  NW6 . . . . 2D 45
(off W. End La.)

Buckingham M. N1 . . . 3A 50
  NW10 . . . . 1B 56
  SW1 . . . . 5F 21
Buckingham Palace
  . . . . 4E 21 (3D 75)
Buckingham Pal. Rd.
  SW1 . . . . . . 5E 21 (5D 75)
Buckingham Pl.
  SW1 . . . . . 5F 21 (4E 75)
Buckingham Rd. E10 . . 5D 39
  E11 . . . . 1E 41
  E15 . . . . 2B 54
  N1 . . . . 3A 50
  NW10 . . . . 1B 56
Buckingham St.
  WC2 . . . . . . 1E 23 (1A 76)
Buckland Cl. N1 . . . . . 1A 64
(off St John's Est.)
Buckland Cres. NW3 . . 4F 45
Buckland Rd. E10 . . . . 4E 39
Buckland St. N1 . . . . . 1F 63
Bucklebury NW1 . . . . . 3F 5
(off Stanhope St.)
Bucklers All. SW6 . . . 2B 86
(not continuous)
Bucklersbury
  EC4 . . . . . . 3B 18 (5F 63)
Bucklersbury Pas.
  EC4 . . . . 5F 63
Buckle St. E1 . . . . 5B 64
Buckley Cl. SE23 . . . 5D 107
Buckley Ct. NW6 . . . . 4B 44
Buckley Rd. NW6 . . . . 4B 44
Buckmaster Cl.
  SW9 . . . . 1C 104
(off Stockwell Rd.)
Buckmaster Ho. N7 . . 1B 48
Buckmaster Rd.
  SW11 . . . . 2A 102
Bucknall St.
  WC2 . . . . . . 2C 14 (5A 62)
Bucknell Cl. SW2 . . . 2B 104
Buckner Rd. SW2 . . . 2B 104
Bucknill Ho. SW1 . . . . 1D 89
(off Ebury Bri. Rd.)
Buckridge Ho. EC1 . . . 5B 8
(off Portpool La.)
Buckstone Cl. SE23 . . 4E 107
Buck St. NW1 . . . . . . 4D 47
Buckters Rents SE16 . . 2A 80
Buckthorne Rd. SE4 . . 3A 108
Bude Cl. E17 . . . . 1B 38
Budge Row
  EC4 . . . . . . 4B 18 (1F 77)
Budge's Wlk. W2 . . . . 2E 73
(off Broad Wlk., The)
Budleigh Ho. SE15 . . . 3C 92
(off Bird in Bush Rd.)
Bugsby's Way SE7 . . . 5B 82
  SE10 . . . . 5B 82
Bulbarrow NW8 . . . . . 5D 45
(off Abbey Rd.)
Bulinga St. SW1 . . . . . 5A 76
(off John Islip St.)
Bullace Row SE5 . . . . 4F 91
Bullard's Pl. E2 . . . . . 2E 65
Bulleid Way SW1 . . . . 5D 75
Bullen Ho. E1 . . . . 3D 65
(off Collingwood St.)

Bullen St. SW11 . . . . . 5A 88
Buller Cl. SE15 . . . . . 3C 92
Buller Rd. NW10 . . . . 2F 57
Bullingham Mans.
  W8 . . . . 3C 72
(off Pitt St.)
Bull Inn Ct. WC2 . . . . 5E 15
Bullivant St. E14 . . . . 1E 81
Bull Rd. E15 . . . . 1B 68
Bulls Gdns. SW3 . . . . 5A 74
(not continuous)
Bulls Head Pas.
  EC4 . . . . . . 4A 18 (1E 77)
Bull Wharf La.
  EC4 . . . . 5A 18
(off Bull Wharf La.)
Bull Wharf Wlk. EC4 . . 5A 18
(off Bull Wharf La.)
Bull Yd. SE15 . . . . . . 4C 92
Bulmer M. W11 . . . . . 1C 72
Bulmer Pl. W11 . . . . . 2C 72
Bulow Est. SW6 . . . . . 4D 87
(off Pearscroft Rd.)
Bulstrode Pl.
  W1 . . . . 1C 12 (4C 60)
Bulstrode St.
  W1 . . . . 2C 12 (5C 60)
Bulwer Ct. E11 . . . . . 3F 39
Bulwer Ct. Rd. E11 . . . 3F 39
Bulwer Rd. E11 . . . . . 2F 39
Bulwer St. W12 . . . . . 2E 71
Bunbury Ho. SE15 . . . 3C 92
(off Fenham Rd.)
Bungalows, The E10 . . 1E 39
Bunhill Row
  EC1 . . . . 3B 10 (3F 63)
Bunhouse Pl. SW1 . . . 1C 88
Bunkers Hill NW11 . . . 2E 31
Bunning Way N7 . . . . 4A 48
Bunsen Ho. E3 . . . . . . 1A 66
(off Grove Rd.)
Bunsen St. E3 . . . . . . 1A 66
Bunyan Ct. EC2 . . . . . 5F 9
Buonaparte M. SW1 . . 1F 89
Burbage Cl.
  SE1 . . . . . . 5B 26 (4F 77)
Burbage Ho. N1 . . . . . 5F 49
(off Poole St.)
  SE14 . . . . 2F 93
(off Samuel Cl.)
Burbage Rd. SE21 . . . 4E 105
  SE24 . . . . 4E 105
Burcham St. E14 . . . . 5D 67
Burchell Ho. SE11 . . . 1B 90
(off Jonathan St.)
Burchell Rd. E10 . . . . 3D 39
  SE15 . . . . 4D 93
Burcote Rd. SW18 . . . 5F 101
Burden Ho. SW8 . . . . 3A 90
(off Thorncroft St.)
Burden Way E11 . . . . 4D 41
Burder Cl. N1 . . . . . . 3A 50
Burder Rd. N1 . . . . . . 3A 50
Burdett M. NW3 . . . . . 3F 45
  W2 . . . . 5D 59
Burdett Rd. E3 . . . . . . 3A 66
  E14 . . . . 3A 66
Burfield Cl. SW17 . . . 4F 115
Burford Rd. E6 . . . . . . 2F 69
  E15 . . . . 5F 53
  SE6 . . . . 2B 122
Burford Wlk. SW6 . . . 3E 87

Burge Rd. E7 . . . . 1F 55
Burges Gro. SW13 . . . . . 3D 85
Burgess Av. NW9 . . . . . . 1A 28
Burgess Bus. Pk. SE5 . . . 3F 91
Burgess Hill NW2 . . . . . . 1C 44
Burgess Pk. Kart Track
 . . . . 2F 91
Burgess Rd. E15 . . . . 1A 54
Burgess St. E14 . . . . 4C 66
Burge St.
 SE1 . . . . 5C 26 (4F 77)
Burgh House 1F 45
Burghill Rd. SE26 . . . . . . 4A 122
Burghley Hall Cl.
 SW19 . . . . 1A 114
Burghley Ho. SW19 . . . 3A 114
Burghley Rd. E11 . . . . . . 3A 40
 NW5 . . . . 1D 47
 SW19 . . . . 4F 113
Burghley Twr. W3 . . . . . . 1B 70
Burgh St. N1 . . . . 1D 63
Burgon St.
 EC4 . . . . 3E 17 (5D 63)
Burgos Gro. SE10 . . . . . . 4D 95
Burgoyne Rd. N4 . . . . . . 1D 35
 SW9 . . . . 1B 104
Burke Cl. SW15 . . . . 2A 98
Burke Lodge E13 . . . . . . 2D 69
Burke St. E16 . . . . 4B 68
 (not continuous)
Burland Rd. SW11 . . . . . . 3B 102
Burleigh Ho. SW3 . . . . . . 2F 87
 (off Beaufort St.)
 W10 . . . . 4A 58
 (off St Charles Sq.)
Burleigh Pl. SW15 . . . . . 3F 99
Burleigh St.
 WC2 . . . . . . 4F 15 (1B 76)
Burleigh Wlk. SE6 . . . . . 1E 123
Burley Ho. E1 . . . . 5F 65
 (off Chudleigh St.)
Burley Rd. E16 . . . . 5E 69
Burlington Arc.
 W1 . . . . 5F 13 (1E 75)
Burlington Cl. W9 . . . . . . 3C 58
Burlington Gdns.
 SW6 . . . . 5A 86
 W1 . . . . 5F 13 (1E 75)
Burlington La. W4 . . . . . . 3A 84
Burlington M. SW15 . . . . 3B 100
Burlington Pl. SW6 . . . . . 5A 86
Burlington Rd. SW6 . . . . 5A 86
Burma M. N16 . . . . 1F 49
Burma Rd. N16 . . . . 1F 49
Burmarsh NW5 . . . . 3C 46
Burma Ter. SE19 . . . . 5A 120
Burmester Rd.
 SW17 . . . . 3E 115
Burnaby St. SW10 . . . . . 3E 87
Burnand Ho. W14 . . . . . . 4F 71
 (off Redan St.)
Burnard Pl. N7 . . . . 2B 48
Burnaston Ho. E5 . . . . . . 5C 36
Burnbury Rd. SW12 . . . . 1E 117
Burne Jones Ho.
 W14 . . . . 5A 72
Burnell Wlk. SE1 . . . . . . 1B 92
 (off Abingdon Cl.)
Burness Cl. N7 . . . . 3B 48
Burne St. NW1 . . . . 4A 60

Burnett Cl. E9 . . . . 2E 51
Burnett Ho. SE13 . . . . . . 5E 95
 (off Lewisham Hill)
Burney St. SE10 . . . . 3E 95
Burnfoot Av. SW6 . . . . . . 4A 86
Burnham NW3 . . . . 4A 46
Burnham Cl. SE1 . . . . . . 5B 78
Burnham Ct. W2 . . . . 1D 73
 (off Moscow Rd.)
Burnham Est. E2 . . . . . . 2E 65
 (off Burnham St.)
Burnham St. E2 . . . . 2E 65
Burnham Way SE26 . . . . 5B 122
Burnhill Cl. SE15 . . . . . . 3D 93
Burnley Rd. NW10 . . . . . 2B 42
 SW9 . . . . 5B 90
Burnsall St. SW3 . . . . . . 1A 88
Burns Cl. SW19 . . . . 5F 115
Burns Ho. E2 . . . . 2E 65
 (off Cornwall Av.)
 SE17 . . . . 1D 91
 (off Doddington Gro.)
Burnside Cl. SE16 . . . . . 2F 79
Burns Rd. NW10 . . . . . . 5B 42
 SW11 . . . . 5B 88
Burnt Ash Hgts.
 BR1: Brom 5D 125
Burnt Ash Hill SE12 . . . 4B 110
 (not continuous)
Burnt Ash La.
 BR1: Brom 5C 124
Burnt Ash Rd. SE12 . . . 3B 110
Burnthwaite Rd. SW6 . . . 3B 86
Burntwood Cl.
 SW18 . . . . 1A 116
Burntwood Grange Rd.
 SW18 . . . . 1F 115
Burntwood La.
 SW17 . . . . 3E 115
Burntwood Vw.
 SE19 . . . . 5B 120
Buross St. E1 . . . . 5D 65
Burrage Ct. SE16 . . . . . . 5F 79
 (off Worgan St.)
Burrard Ho. E2 . . . . 1E 65
 (off Bishop's Way)
Burrard Rd. E16 . . . . 5D 69
 NW6 . . . . 2C 44
Burr Cl. E1 . . . . 2C 78
Burrell St.
 SE1 . . . . 1D 25 (2D 77)
Burrells Wharf Sq.
 E14 . . . . 1D 95
Burrell Towers E10 . . . . 2C 38
Burrhill Ct. SE16 . . . . 4F 79
 (off Worgan St.)
Burroughs Cotts. E14 . . 4A 66
 (off Halley St.)
Burrow Ho. SW9 . . . . . . 5C 90
 (off Stockwell Pk. Rd.)
Burrow Rd. SE22 . . . . . . 2A 106
Burrows M.
 SE1 . . . . 3D 25 (3D 77)
Burrows Rd. NW10 . . . . . 2E 57
Burrow Wlk. SE21 . . . . . 5E 105
Burr Rd. SW18 . . . . 1C 114
Bursar St.
 SE1 . . . . 2D 27 (2A 78)
Burslem St. E1 . . . . 5C 64
Burstock Rd. SW15 . . . . 2A 100

Burston Rd. SW15 . . . . . 3F 99
Burtley Cl. N4 . . . . 3E 35
Burton Bank N1 . . . . 4F 49
 (off Yeate St.)
Burton Ct. SW3 . . . . 1B 88
 (off Franklin's Row,
 not continuous)
Burton Gro. SE17 . . . . . . 1F 91
Burton Ho. SE16 . . . . 3D 79
 (off Cherry Gdn. St.)
Burton La. SW9 . . . . 5C 90
 (not continuous)
Burton Pl.
 WC1 . . . . 2C 6 (2F 61)
Burton Rd. NW6 . . . . 4B 44
 SW9 . . . . 5D 91
 (Akerman Rd.)
 SW9 . . . . 5C 90
 (Evesham Wlk.)
Burton St.
 WC1 . . . . 2C 6 (2F 61)
Burtonwood Ho. N4 . . . . 2F 35
Burtop Rd. Est.
 SW17 . . . . 3E 115
Burt Rd. E16 . . . . 2E 83
Burtt Ho. N1 . . . . 1D 11
 (off Aske St.)
Burtwell La. SE27 . . . . . 4F 119
Burwash Ho. SE1 . . . . . . 4C 26
 (off Kipling St.)
Burwell Cl. E1 . . . . 5D 65
Burwell Rd. E10 . . . . 3A 38
Burwell Rd. Ind. Est.
 E10 . . . . 3A 38
Burwell Wlk. E3 . . . . 3C 66
Burwood Ho. SW9 . . . . . 2D 105
Burwood Pl. W2 . . . . 5A 60
Bury Cl. SE16 . . . . 2F 79
Bury Ct. EC3 . . . 2E 19 (5A 64)
Bury Pl.
 WC1 . . . . 1D 15 (4A 62)
Bury St. EC3 . . . 3E 19 (5A 64)
 SW1 . . . . 1A 22 (2E 75)
Bury Wlk. SW3 . . . . 5A 74
Busbridge Ho. E14 . . . . . 4C 66
 (off Brabazon St.)
Busby Ho. SW16 . . . . . . 4E 117
Busby M. NW5 . . . . 3F 47
Busby Pl. NW5 . . . . 3F 47
Bushbaby Cl.
 SE1 . . . . 5D 27 (4A 78)
Bushberry Rd. E9 . . . . . . 3A 52
Bush Cotts. SW18 . . . . . 3C 100
Bush Ct. W12 . . . . 3F 71
Bushell Cl. SW2 . . . . 2B 118
Bushell St. E1 . . . . 2C 78
Bushey Down SW12 . . . 2D 117
Bushey Hill Rd. SE5 . . . . 4A 92
Bushey Rd. E13 . . . . 1E 69
 N15 . . . . 1A 36
Bush Ind. Est. N19 . . . . . 5E 33
Bushnell Rd. SW17 . . . . 2D 117
Bush Rd. E8 . . . . 5D 51
 E11 . . . . 2B 40
 SE8 . . . . 5F 79
 (off Rotherhithe New Rd.)
Bush Theatre 3E 71
Bushwood E11 . . . . 3B 40

Bushwood Dr. SE1 . . . . . 5B 78
Business Design Cen.
. . . . 5C 48
. . . . (off Upper St.)
Butcher Row E1 . . . . . . 1F 79
E14 . . . . 1F 79
Butchers Rd. E16 . . . . . 5C 68
Bute Gdns. W6 . . . . 5F 71
Bute St. SW7 . . . . 5F 73
Bute Wlk. N1 . . . . 3F 49
Butfield Ho. E9 . . . . 3E 51
. . . . (off Stevens Av.)
Butler Ho. E2 . . . . 2E 65
. . . . (off Bacton St.)
E14 . . . . 5B 66
. . . . (off Burdett St.)
SW9 . . . . 4D 91
. . . . (off Lothian Rd.)
Butler Pl.
SW1 . . . . . . 5B 22 (4F 75)
Butler Rd. NW10 . . . . . . 4B 42
Butlers & Colonial Wharf
SE1 . . . . 3F 27
. . . . (off Shad Thames)
Butler St. E2 . . . . 2E 65
Butlers Wharf SE1 . . . . . 3F 27
. . . . (off Gainsford St.)
Butley Ct. E3 . . . . 1A 66
. . . . (off Ford St.)
Butterfield Cl. SE16 . . . 3D 79
Butterfields E17 . . . . . . 1E 39
Butterfly Wlk. SE5 . . . . . 4F 91
. . . . (off Denmark Hill)
Buttermere NW1 . . . . . . 1E 5
. . . . (off Augustus St.)
Buttermere Cl. E15 . . . . 1F 53
SE1 . . . . 5B 78
Buttermere Ct. NW8 . . . . 5F 45
. . . . (off Boundary Rd.)
Buttermere Dr.
SW15 . . . . 3A 100
Buttermere Wlk. E8 . . . . 3B 50
Butterwick W6 . . . . 5F 71
Butterworth Ter.
SE17 . . . . 1E 91
. . . . (off Sutherland Wlk.)
Buttesland St.
N1 . . . . 1C 10 (2F 63)
Butts Rd.
BR1: Brom 5A 124
Buxhall Cres. E9 . . . . . . 3B 52
Buxted Rd. E8 . . . . 4B 50
SE22 . . . . 2A 106
Buxton Ct. E11 . . . . 2B 40
N1 . . . . 1A 10
Buxton M. SW4 . . . . 5F 89
Buxton Rd. E6 . . . . 2F 69
E15 . . . . 2A 54
N19 . . . . 3F 33
NW2 . . . . 3D 43
SW14 . . . . 1A 98
Buxton St. E1 . . . . 3B 64
Byam St. SW6 . . . . 5E 87
Byards Ct. SE16 . . . . . . 5F 79
. . . . (off Worgan St.)
Bye, The W3 . . . . 5A 56
Byelands Cl. SE16 . . . . . 2F 79
Byfeld Gdns. SW13 . . . . 4C 84
Byfield Cl. SE16 . . . . . . 3B 80
Byford Cl. E15 . . . . 4A 54

Bygrove St. E14 . . . . . . 5D 67
. . . . (not continuous)
Byne Rd. SE26 . . . . 5E 121
Byng Pl.
WC1 . . . . 4C 6 (3F 61)
Byng St. E14 . . . . 3C 80
Byrne Rd. SW12 . . . . . . 1D 117
Byron Av. E12 . . . . 3F 55
Byron Cl. E8 . . . . 5C 50
SE26 . . . . 4A 122
SW16 . . . . 5A 118
Byron Ct. NW6 . . . . 4E 45
. . . . (off Fairfax Rd.)
SE22 . . . . 1C 120
W9 . . . . 3C 58
. . . . (off Lanhill Rd.)
WC1 . . . . 3F 7
. . . . . (off Mecklenburgh Sq.)
Byron Dr. N2 . . . . 1F 31
Byron M. NW3 . . . . 1A 46
W9 . . . . 3C 58
Byron Rd. E10 . . . . 3D 39
NW2 . . . . 4D 29
Byron St. E14 . . . . 5D 67
Bythorn St. SW9 . . . . . . 1B 104
Byton Rd. SW17 . . . . . . 5B 116
Byward St.
EC3 . . . . 5E 19 (1A 78)
Bywater Ho. SE18 . . . . . 4F 83
Bywater Pl. SE16 . . . . . 2A 80
Bywater St. SW3 . . . . . . 1B 88
Byway E11 . . . . 1E 41
Bywell Pl. W1 . . . . 1F 13
Byworth Wlk. N19 . . . . . 3A 34

C

Cabbell St. NW1 . . . . . . 4A 60
Cable Ho. WC1 . . . . 1B 8
. . . . (off Gt. Percy St.)
Cable Pl. SE10 . . . . 4E 95
Cable St. E1 . . . . 1C 78
Cable Trade Pk. SE7. . . . 5E 83
Cabot Ct. SE16 . . . . 5F 79
. . . . (off Worgan St.)
Cabot Sq. E14 . . . . 2C 80
Cabot Way E6 . . . . 5F 55
Cabul Rd. SW11 . . . . . . 5A 88
Caci Ho. W14 . . . . 5B 72
. . . . . . (off Kensington Village)
Cactus Cl. SE15 . . . . . . 5A 92
Cactus Wlk. W12 . . . . . 5B 56
Cadbury Way SE16. . . . . 4B 78
Caddington Rd. NW2 . . . 5A 30
Cadell Cl. E2 . . . . 1B 64
Cade Rd. SE10 . . . . 4F 95
Cader Rd. SW18. . . . . . 4E 101
Cadet Dr. SE1 . . . . 5B 78
Cadet Pl. SE10 . . . . 1A 96
Cadiz St. SE17 . . . . 1E 91
Cadley Ter. SE23 . . . . . 2E 121
Cadman Cl. SW9 . . . . . . 3D 91
Cadmore Ho. N1 . . . . . . 4D 49
. . . . (off Sutton Est., The)
Cadmus Cl. SW4 . . . . . . 1F 103
Cadmus Ct. SW9 . . . . . . 4C 90
. . . . (off Southey Rd.)
Cadnam Lodge E14 . . . . 4E 81
. . . . (off Schooner Cl.)

Cadnam Point
SW15 . . . . 1D 113
Cadogan Cl. E9 . . . . 4B 52
Cadogan Ct. SW3 . . . . . 5B 74
. . . . (off Draycott Av.)
Cadogan Gdns. SW3 . . . 5B 74
Cadogan Ga. SW1 . . . . . 5B 74
Cadogan Ho. SW3 . . . . . 2F 87
. . . . (off Beaufort St.)
Cadogan La.
SW1 . . . . . . 5B 20 (4C 74)
Cadogan Mans. SW3 . . . 5B 74
. . . . (off Cadogan Gdns.)
Cadogan Pl.
SW1 . . . . . . 5A 20 (4B 74)
Cadogan Sq.
SW1 . . . . . . 5A 20 (4B 74)
Cadogan Gdns. SW3 . . . 5B 74
Cadogan Ter. E9 . . . . . . 3B 52
Cadoxton Av. N15 . . . . . 1B 36
Caedmon Rd. N7 . . . . . . 1B 48
Caernarvon Ho. E16 . . . 2D 83
. . . . (off Audley Dr.)
W2 . . . . 5E 59
. . . . (off Hallfield Est.)
Caesar Ct. E2 . . . . 1F 65
. . . . (off Palmer's Rd.)
Cafe Gallery 4E 79
Cahill St.
EC1 . . . . 4A 10 (3E 63)
Cahir St. E14 . . . . 5D 81
Caird St. W10 . . . . 2A 58
Cairncross M. N8 . . . . . 1A 34
. . . . (off Felix Av.)
Cairnfield Av. NW2 . . . . 5A 28
Cairns Rd. SW11 . . . . . 3A 102
Caister Ho. N7 . . . . 3B 48
Caister Ho. E15 . . . . . . 5B 54
. . . . (off Caistor Pk. Rd.)
Caistor M. SW12 . . . . . 5D 103
Caistor Pk. Rd. E15 . . . 5B 54
Caistor Rd. SW12 . . . . 5D 103
Caithness Ho. N1 . . . . . 5B 48
. . . . (off Twyford St.)
Caithness Rd. W14 . . . . 4F 71
Calabria Rd. N5 . . . . . . 3D 49
Calais Ga. SE5 . . . . 4D 91
Calais St. SE5 . . . . 4D 91
Calbourne Rd.
SW12 . . . . 5B 102
Calcott Ct. W14 . . . . . . 4A 72
. . . . (off Blythe Rd.)
Calcott Wlk. SE9. . . . . . 4F 125
Calcraft Ho. E2 . . . . 1E 65
. . . . (off Bonner Rd.)
Caldecot Rd. SE5 . . . . . 5E 91
Caldecott Way E5 . . . . . 5F 37
Calder Ct. SE16 . . . . . . 2B 80
Calderon Ho. NW8 . . . . . 1A 60
. . . . (off Townshend Est.)
Calderon Pl. W10 . . . . . 4E 57
Calderon Rd. E11 . . . . . 1E 53
Caldervale Rd. SW4 . . . 3F 103
Caldew St. SE5 . . . . 3F 91
Caldicot Grn. NW9 . . . . 1A 28
Caldwell Ho. SW13 . . . . 3E 85
. . . . (off Trinity Chu. Rd.)
Caldwell St. SW9 . . . . . 3B 90
Caldy Wlk. N1 . . . . 4E 49
Caleb St. SE1 . . . 3F 25 (3E 77)

Caledonia Ho. *E14* *5A 66*
   (off Salmon La.)
Caledonian Rd.
  N1 . . . . 1E 7 (1A 62)
  N7 . . . . 1B 48
Caledonian Sq.
  NW1 . . . . 3F 47
Caledonian Wharf
  E14 . . . . 5F 81
Caledonia St.
  N1 . . . . 1E 7 (1A 62)
Cale St. *SW3* 1A 88
Caletock Way *SE10* . . . 1B 96
Calgarth *NW1* *1A 6*
   (off Ampthill Est.)
Calgary Ct. *SE16* 3E 79
   (off Canada Est.)
Caliban Twr. *N1* *1A 64*
   (off Arden Est.)
Calico Ho. *EC4* *3A 18*
   (off Well Ct.)
Calico Row *SW11* 1E 101
Calidore Cl. *SW2* 4B 104
Callaby Ter. *N1* 3F 49
Callaghan Cl. *SE13* 2A 110
Callahan Cotts. *E1* *4E 65*
   (off Lindley St.)
Callander Rd. *SE6* 2D 123
Callcott Ct. *NW6* 4B 44
Callcott Rd. *NW6* 4B 44
Callcott St. *W8* 2C 72
Callendar Rd. *SW7* 4F 73
Callingham Cl. *E14* 4B 66
Callis Rd. *E17* 1B 38
Callow St. *SW3* 2F 87
Cally Swimming Pool
  . . . . 5B 48
Calmington Rd. *SE5* 2A 92
Calmont Rd.
  BR1: Brom 5F 123
Calonne Rd. *SW19* 4F 113
Calshot Ho. *N1* *1B 62*
   (off Calshot St.)
Calshot St. *N1* 1F 7 (1B 62)
Calstock *NW1* *5E 47*
   (off Royal College St.)
Calstock Ho. *SE11* *1C 90*
   (off Kennings Way)
Calthorpe St.
  WC1 . . . . 3A 8 (3B 62)
Calton Av. *SE21* 4A 106
Calverley Cl.
  BR3: Beck 5D 123
Calverley Gro. *N19* 3F 33
Calvert Av.
  E2 . . . . 2E 11 (2A 64)
Calvert Ho. *W12* *1D 71*
   (off White City Est.)
Calverton *SE5* *2A 92*
   (off Albany Rd.)
Calvert Rd. *SE10* 1B 96
Calvert's Bldgs.
  SE1 . . . . 2B 26 (2F 77)
Calvert St. *NW1* 5C 46
Calvin St. *E1* . . . 4F 11 (3B 64)
Calydon Rd. *SE7* 1D 97
Calypso Cres. *SE15* 3B 92
Calypso Way *SE16* 4B 80
Camarthen Grn. *NW9* . . . 1A 28
Cambalt Rd. *SW15* 3F 99

Cambay Ho. *E1* *3A 66*
   (off Harford St.)
Camber Ho. *SE15* 2E 93
Camberley Ho. *NW1* . . . 1E 5
Cambert Way *SE3* . . . 2D 111
CAMBERWELL 4F 91
Camberwell Chu. St.
  SE5 . . . . 4F 91
Camberwell Glebe
  SE5 . . . . 4A 92
CAMBERWELL GREEN
  . . . . 4F 91
Camberwell Grn.
  SE5 . . . . 4F 91
Camberwell Gro. *SE5* . . 4F 91
Camberwell Leisure Cen.
  . . . . 4F 91
Camberwell New Rd.
  SE5 . . . . 2C 90
Camberwell Pl. *SE5* 4E 91
Camberwell Rd. *SE5* . . . 2E 91
Camberwell Sta. Rd.
  SE5 . . . . 4E 91
Camberwell Trad. Est.
  SE5 . . . . 4D 91
Camborne Rd.
  SW18 . . . . 5C 100
Cambourne M. *W11* . . . 5A 58
Cambray Rd. *SW12* . . . 1E 117
Cambria Ho. *E14* *5A 66*
   (off Salmon La.)
  SE26 . . . . *4C 120*
   (off High Level Dr.)
Cambrian Cl. *SE27* . . . 3D 119
Cambrian Grn. *NW9* . . . *1A 28*
   (off Snowden Dr.)
Cambrian Rd. *E10* 2C 38
Cambria Rd. *SE5* 1E 105
Cambria St. *SW6* 3D 87
Cambridge Arc. *E9* *4E 51*
   (off Elsdale St.)
Cambridge Av. *NW6* . . . 1C 58
  W2 . . . . 2E 57
Cambridge Cir.
  WC2 . . . . 3C 14 (5F 61)
Cambridge Cl. *E17* 1B 38
Cambridge Ct. *E2*. *1D 65*
   (off Cambridge Heath Rd.)
  N16. . . . . *2A 36*
   (off Amhurst Pk.)
  NW6 . . . . 1C 58
  W2 . . . . *4A 60*
   (off Edgware Rd.)
  W6 . . . . *5E 71*
   (off Shepherd's Bush Rd.)
Cambridge Cres. *E2*. . . . 1D 65
Cambridge Dr. *SE12* . . 3C 110
Cambridge Gdns.
  NW6 . . . . 1C 58
  W10 . . . . 5F 57
Cambridge Ga.
  NW1 . . . . 3D 5 (3D 61)
Cambridge Ga. M.
  NW1 . . . . 3E 5 (3D 61)
Cambridge Gro. *W6*. . . . 5D 71
Cambridge Heath Rd.
  E1 . . . . 4D 65
Cambridge Ho. *W6* *5D 71*
   (off Cambridge Gro.)
Cambridge Pk. *E11* 2C 40

Cambridge Pk. Rd.
  E11 . . . . 2C 40
   (off Lonsdale Rd.)
Cambridge Pl. *W8* 3D 73
Cambridge Rd. *E11* 1B 40
  NW6 . . . . 1C 58
   (not continuous)
  SW11 . . . . 4B 88
  SW13 . . . . 5B 84
Cambridge Sq. *W2* 5A 60
Cambridge St. *SW1* . . . 5D 75
Cambridge Ter.
  NW1 . . . . 2D 5 (2D 61)
Cambridge Ter. M.
  NW1 . . . . 2E 5 (2D 61)
Cambridge Theatre *3D 15*
   (off Earlham St.)
Cambus Rd. *E16* 4C 68
Cam Ct. *SE15* 2B 92
Camden Arts Cen. 2D 45
Camden Ct. *NW1* *4E 47*
   (off Rousden St.)
Camden Gdns.
  NW1 . . . . 4D 47
Camden High St.
  NW1 . . . . 4D 47
Camden Hill Rd.
  SE19 . . . . 5A 120
Camden Ho. *SE8* 1B 94
Camdenhurst St. *E14*. . . 5A 66
Camden La. *N7*. 2F 47
Camden Lock Market
  . . . . *4D 47*
   (off Camden Lock Pl.)
Camden Lock Pl.
  NW1 . . . . 4D 47
Camden Market *5D 47*
   (off Dewsbury Ter.)
Camden M. *NW1* 4E 47
Camden Pk. Rd.
  NW1 . . . . 3F 47
Camden Pas. *N1* 5D 49
   (not continuous)
Camden Peoples Theatre
  . . . . *3F 5*
   (off Hampstead Rd.)
Camden Rd. *E11* 1D 41
  E17 . . . . 1B 38
  N7 . . . . 1A 48
  NW1 . . . . 4E 47
Camden Row *SE3* 5A 96
Camden Sq. *NW1* 4F 47
   (not continuous)
  SE15 . . . . 4B 92
Camden St. *NW1* 4E 47
Camden Studios
  NW1 . . . . *5E 47*
   (off Camden St.)
Camden Ter. *NW1*. 3F 47
CAMDEN TOWN 5D 47
Camden Wlk. *N1* 5D 49
   (not continuous)
Cameford Ct. *SW2* 5A 104
Camelford *NW1* *5E 47*
   (off Royal College St.)
Camelford Ct. *W11* 5A 58
Camelford Ho. *SE1* 1A 90
Camelford Wlk. *W11* . . . 5A 58
Camellia Ho. *SE8*. *3B 94*
   (off Idonia St.)

Camellia St. SW8. . . . . . 3A 90
(not continuous)
Camelot Cl. SW19 . . . . . 4B 114
Camelot Ho. NW1 . . . . . . 3F 47
Camel Rd. E16 . . . . 2F 83
Camera Pl. SW10 . . . . . . 2F 87
Cameret Ct. W11 . . . . . . 3F 71
(off Holland Rd.)
Cameron Ho. NW8 . . . . . . 1A 60
(off St John's Wood Ter.)
SE5 . . . . 3E 91
Cameron Pl. E1 . . . . 5D 65
SW16 . . . . 2C 118
Cameron Rd. SE6 . . . . . 2B 122
Cameron Ter. SE12 . . . . 3D 125
Camerton Cl. E8 . . . . 3B 50
Camilla Rd. SE16. . . . . . . 5D 79
Camlan Rd.
  BR1: Brom 4B 124
Camlet St.
  E2. . . . . 3F 11 (3B 64)
Camley St. NW1 . . . . 4F 47
Camomile St.
  EC3 . . . . 2E 19 (5A 64)
Campana Rd. SW6. . . . . . 4C 86
Campania Bldg. E1. . . . . . 1F 79
(off Jardine Rd.)
Campbell Cl. SW16 . . . . . 4F 117
Campbell Ct. SE21 . . . . . 1C 120
SW7 . . . . 4E 73
(off Gloucester Rd.)
Campbell Gordon Way
  NW2 . . . . 1D 43
Campbell Ho. SW1. . . . . . 1E 89
(off Churchill Gdns.)
W12 . . . . 1D 71
(off White City Est.)
Campbell Rd. E3 . . . . 2C 66
E15 . . . . 1B 54
Campbell Wlk. N1 . . . . . . 5A 48
(off Outram Pl.)
Campdale Rd. N7 . . . . . . 5F 33
Campden Gro. W8 . . . . . . 3C 72
Campden Hill W8 . . . . . . 3C 72
Campden Hill Ct. W8 . . . . 3C 72
Campden Hill Gdns.
  W8 . . . . 2C 72
Campden Hill Ga.
  W8 . . . . 3C 72
Campden Hill Mans.
  W8 . . . . 2C 72
(off Edge St.)
Campden Hill Pl.
  W11 . . . . 2B 72
Campden Hill Rd.
  W8 . . . . 2C 72
Campden Hill Sq.
  W8 . . . . 2B 72
Campden Ho. NW6 . . . . . 4F 45
(off Harben Rd.)
W8 . . . . 2C 72
(off Sheffield Ter.)
Campden Ho. Cl. W8 . . . . 3C 72
Campden Ho's. W8 . . . . . 2C 72
Campden Ho. Ter.
  W8 . . . . 2C 72
(off Kensington Ch. St.)
Campden St. W8 . . . . 2C 72
Campen Cl. SW19 . . . . . . 2A 114
Camperdown St. E1 . . . . . 5B 64

Campfield Rd. SE9. . . . . . 5F 111
Campion Rd. SW15 . . . . . 2E 99
Campion Ter. NW2 . . . . . . 5F 29
Camplin St. SE14 . . . . . . 3F 93
Camp Rd. SW19 . . . . 5D 113
(not continuous)
Campshill Pl. SE13 . . . . . 3E 109
Campshill Rd.
  SE13. . . . . 3E 109
Campus Rd. E17 . . . . 1B 38
Camp Vw. SW19 . . . . 5D 113
Cam Rd. E15. . . . . 5F 53
Canada Est. SE16. . . . . . . 4E 79
Canada Gdns. SE13 . . . . 3E 109
Canada Ho. SE16. . . . . . . 4A 80
(off Brunswick Quay)
Canada Memorial 3F 21
(off Green Pk.)
Canada Pl. E14 . . . . 2D 81
(off Up. Bank St.)
Canada Sq. E14 . . . . 2D 81
Canada St. SE16 . . . . 3F 79
Canada Way W12 . . . . . . 1D 71
Canada Wharf SE16 . . . . 2B 80
Canadian Av. SE6 . . . . . . 1D 123
Canal App. SE8 . . . . 1A 94
Canal Blvd. NW1 . . . . 3F 47
CANAL BRIDGE 2C 92
Canal Bldg. N1 . . . . 1E 63
(off Shepherdess Wlk.)
Canal Cl. E1 . . . . 3A 66
W10 . . . . 3F 57
Canal Gro. SE15 . . . . 2D 93
Canal Mkt. NW1 . . . . 4D 47
(off Castlehaven Rd.)
Canal Path E2. . . . . 5B 50
Canalside Activity Cen.
  . . . . 3F 57
Canal St. SE5 . . . . 2F 91
Canal Wlk. N1 . . . . 5F 49
SE26 . . . . 5E 121
Canal Way W10 . . . . 3F 57
Canberra Rd. SE7. . . . . . . 2E 97
Canbury M. SE26 . . . . . . 3C 120
Cancell Rd. SW9 . . . . 4C 90
Candahar Rd. SW11 . . . . 5A 88
Candida Ct. NW1 . . . . 4D 47
Candid Ho. NW10 . . . . . . 2D 57
(off Trenmar Gdns.)
Candle Gro. SE15 . . . . . . 1D 107
Candlelight Ct. E15 . . . . . 3B 54
(off Romford Rd.)
Candler St. N15 . . . . 1F 35
Candover St.
  W1 . . . . 1F 13 (4E 61)
Candy St. E3. . . . . 5B 52
Caney M. NW2 . . . . 4F 29
Canfield Gdns. NW6 . . . . 4D 45
Canfield Ho. N15. . . . . . . 1A 36
(off Albert Rd.)
Canfield Pl. NW6 . . . . 3E 45
Canford Rd. SW11 . . . . . 3C 102
Canham Rd. W3 . . . . 3A 70
CANN HALL 1A 54
Cann Hall Rd. E11 . . . . . . 1A 54
Cann Ho. W14 . . . . 4A 72
(off Russell Rd.)
Canning Cross SE5 . . . . . 5A 92
Canning Ho. W12. . . . . . . 1D 71
(off Australia Rd.)

Canning Pas. W8 . . . . 4E 73
(not continuous)
Canning Pl. W8 . . . . 4E 73
Canning Pl. M. W8. . . . . . 4E 73
(off Canning Pl.)
Canning Rd. E15 . . . . 1A 68
N5. . . . . 5D 35
CANNING TOWN 5B 68
CANNING TOWN 5A 68
Cannizaro Rd.
  SW19 . . . . 5E 113
Cannock Ho. N4 . . . . 2E 35
Cannon Ct. EC1 . . . . 3E 9
(off Brewhouse Yd.)
Cannon Dr. E14 . . . . 1C 80
Cannon Hill NW6 . . . . . . 2C 44
Cannon Ho. SE11 . . . . . . 5B 76
(off Beaufoy Wlk.)
Cannon La. NW3 . . . . 5F 31
Cannon Pl. NW3 . . . . 5F 31
Cannons Health Club
  Cannon St. 5B 18
  Fulham 4F 85
  Willesden Green 4E 43
Cannon St.
  EC4 . . . . 3F 17 (5E 63)
Cannon St. Rd. E1. . . . . . 5D 65
Cannon Wharf Bus. Cen.
  SE8. . . . . 5A 80
Cannon Workshops
  E14 . . . . 1C 80
(off Cannon Dr.)
Canon All. EC4 . . . . 3F 17
(off Queen's Head Pas.)
Canon Beck Rd.
  SE16 . . . . 3E 79
Canonbie Rd. SE23 . . . . . 5E 107
CANONBURY 3E 49
Canonbury Bus. Cen.
  N1. . . . . 5E 49
Canonbury Ct. N1 . . . . . . 4D 49
(off Hawes St.)
Canonbury Cres. N1. . . . . 4E 49
Canonbury Gro. N1 . . . . . 4E 49
Canonbury Hgts. N1. . . . . 3F 49
(off Dove Rd.)
Canonbury La. N1 . . . . . . 4D 49
Canonbury Pk. Nth.
  N1. . . . . 3E 49
Canonbury Pk. Sth.
  N1. . . . . 3E 49
Canonbury Pl. N1 . . . . . . 3D 49
(not continuous)
Canonbury Rd. N1 . . . . . . 3D 49
Canonbury Sq. N1 . . . . . . 4D 49
Canonbury St. N1 . . . . . . 4E 49
Canonbury Vs. N1 . . . . . . 4D 49
Canon Row
  SW1. . . . . . . 4D 23 (3A 76)
(not continuous)
Canon's Cl. N2 . . . . 2F 31
Canons Ct. E15. . . . . 1A 54
Canon St. N1 . . . . 5E 49
Canrobert St. E2 . . . . 1D 65
Cantelowes Rd. NW1 . . . . 3F 47
(not continuous)
Canterbury Av.
  IG1: Ilf 2F 41
Canterbury Cl. SE5. . . . . . 5E 91
(off Lilford Rd.)

Canterbury Ct. NW6 . . . . 1C 58
(off Canterbury Rd.)
SE12 . . . . 3D 125
SW9 . . . . 3C 90
Canterbury Cres.
SW9 . . . . 1C 104
Canterbury Gro.
SE27 . . . . 4C 118
Canterbury Ho.
SE1 . . . . . . 5A 24 (4B 76)
Canterbury Ind. Pk.
SE15 . . . . 2E 93
Canterbury Pl. SE17 . . . 1D 91
Canterbury Rd. E10 . . . . 2E 39
NW6 . . . . 1B 58
(not continuous)
Canterbury Ter. NW6 . . 1C 58
Cantium Retail Pk.
SE1 . . . . 2C 92
Canton St. E14 . . . . 5C 66
Cantrell Rd. E3 . . . . 3B 66
Canute Gdns. SE16 . . . 5F 79
Canvey St.
SE1 . . . . 1F 25 (2E 77)
Cape Henry Ct. E14 . . . . 1F 81
(off Jamestown Way)
Cape Ho. E8 . . . . 3B 50
(off Dalston La.)
Capel Ct. EC2 . . . . 3C 18
(off Bartholomew La.)
Capel Ho. E9 . . . . 4E 51
(off Loddiges Rd.)
Capel Rd. E7 . . . . 1D 55
E12 . . . . 1D 55
Capener's Cl. SW1 . . . . 4A 20
Capern Rd. SW18 . . . . 1E 115
Cape Yd. E1 . . . . 1C 78
Capital E. Apartments
E16 . . . . 1C 82
(off Western Gateway)
Capital Wharf E1 . . . . . 2C 78
Capland Ho. NW8 . . . . . 3F 59
(off Capland St.)
Capland St. NW8 . . . . . 3F 59
Caple Ho. SW10 . . . . . . 3E 87
(off King's Rd.)
Caple Rd. NW10 . . . . . . 1B 56
Capper St.
WC1 . . . . 4A 6 (3E 61)
Capstan Ct. E1 . . . . 1E 79
(off Wapping Wall)
Capstan Ho. E14 . . . . . . 1F 81
(off Clove Cres.)
E14 . . . . 5E 81
(off Stebondale St.)
Capstan Rd. SE8 . . . . . . 5B 80
Capstan Sq. E14 . . . . . . 3E 81
Capstan Way SE16 . . . . 2A 80
Capstone Rd.
BR1: Brom 4B 124
Capulet M. E16 . . . . 2C 82
Capworth St. E10 . . . . . 3C 38
Caradoc Cl. W2 . . . . 5C 58
Caradoc St. SE10 . . . . . 1A 96
Caradon Cl. E11 . . . . . . 3A 40
Caranday Vs. W11 . . . . . 2F 71
(off Norland Rd.)
Caravel Cl. E14 . . . . 4C 80
Caravel M. SE8 . . . . 2C 94
Caraway Cl. E13 . . . . . . 4D 69

Caraway Hgts. E14 . . . . . 1E 81
(off Poplar High St.)
Carbis Rd. E14 . . . . 5B 66
Carbrooke Ho. E9 . . . . . 5E 51
(off Templecombe Rd.)
Carburton St.
W1 . . . . 5E 5 (4D 61)
Cardale St. E14 . . . . 3E 81
Carden Rd. SE15 . . . . . 1D 107
Cardiff Ho. SE15 . . . . . . 2C 92
(off Friary Est.)
Cardigan Pl. SE3 . . . . . . 5F 95
Cardigan Rd. E3 . . . . . . 1B 66
SW13 . . . . 5C 84
Cardigan St. SE11 . . . . . 1C 90
Cardigan Wlk. N1 . . . . . . 4E 49
(off Ashby Gro.)
Cardinal Bourne St.
SE1 . . . . 5C 26 (4F 77)
Cardinal Cap All.
SE1 . . . . 2E 77
Cardinal Ct. E1 . . . . 1C 78
(off Thomas More St.)
Cardinal Hinsley Cl.
NW10 . . . . 1C 56
Cardinal Pl. SW15 . . . . . 2F 99
Cardinals Way N19 . . . . 3F 33
Cardine M. SE15 . . . . . . 3D 93
Cardington St.
NW1 . . . . 1A 6 (2E 61)
Cardozo Rd. N7 . . . . 2A 48
Cardross Ho. W6 . . . . . . 4D 71
(off Cardross St.)
Cardross St. W6 . . . . . . 4D 71
Cardwell Rd. N7 . . . . . . 1A 48
Career Ct. SE16 . . . . . . 3F 79
(off Christopher Cl.)
Carew Cl. N7 . . . . 4B 34
Carew Ct. SE14 . . . . 2F 93
(off Samuel Cl.)
Carew Rd. SE5 . . . . 5E 91
Carey Ct. SE5 . . . . 3E 91
Carey Gdns. SW8 . . . . . 4E 89
Carey La.
EC2 . . . . 2F 17 (5E 63)
Carey Mans. SW1 . . . . . 5F 75
(off Rutherford St.)
Carey Pl. SW1 . . . . 5F 75
Carey St.
WC2 . . . . 3A 16 (5B 62)
Carfax Pl. SW4 . . . . 2F 103
Carfree Cl. N1 . . . . 4C 48
Cargill Rd. SW18 . . . . . 1D 115
Carholme Rd. SE23 . . . . 1B 122
Carinthia Ct. SE16 . . . . . 5A 80
(off Plough Way)
Carisbrooke Gdns.
SE15 . . . . 3B 92
Carisbrooke Ho.
SW15 . . . . 2D 47
Carker's La. NW5 . . . . . . 2D 47
Carleton Gdns. N19 . . . . 2E 47
Carleton Rd. N7 . . . . 2E 47
Carleton Vs. NW5 . . . . . 2E 47
Carlile Cl. E3 . . . . 1B 66
Carlingford Rd. NW3 . . . 1F 45
Carlisle Av.
EC3 . . . . 3F 19 (5B 64)
W3 . . . . 5A 56
Carlisle Gdns. IG1: Ilf. . . 1F 41
Carlisle La.
SE1 . . . . 5A 24 (4B 76)

Carlisle Mans. SW1 . . . . 5E 75
(off Carlisle Pl.)
Carlisle Pl.
SW1 . . . . 5F 21 (4E 75)
Carlisle Rd. E10 . . . . . . 3C 38
N4 . . . . 2C 34
NW6 . . . . 5A 44
Carlisle St.
W1 . . . . 3B 14 (5F 61)
Carlisle Wlk. E8 . . . . 3B 50
Carlisle Way SW17 . . . . 5C 116
Carlos Pl.
W1 . . . . 5C 12 (1C 74)
Carlow St. NW1 . . . . 1E 61
Carlson Ct. SW15 . . . . . 2B 100
Carlton Cl. NW3 . . . . . . 4C 30
Carlton Ct. SW9 . . . . . . 4D 91
W9 . . . . 1D 59
(off Maida Va.)
Carlton Dr. SW15 . . . . . 3F 99
Carlton Gdns.
SW1 . . . . 2B 22 (2F 75)
Carlton Gro. SE15 . . . . . 4D 93
Carlton Hill NW8 . . . . . . 1D 59
Carlton Ho. NW6 . . . . . . 1C 58
(off Canterbury Ter.,
not continuous)
SE16 . . . . 3F 79
(off Wolfe Cres.)
Carlton Ho. Ter.
SW1 . . . . 2B 22 (2F 75)
Carlton Lodge N4 . . . . . . 2C 34
(off Carlton Rd.)
Carlton Mans. N16 . . . . . 3B 36
NW6 . . . . 4C 44
(off W. End La.)
W9 . . . . 2D 59
Carlton M. NW6 . . . . 2C 44
(off West Cotts.)
NW6 . . . . 2C 44
(West Kilburn)
Carlton Rd. E11 . . . . 3B 40
E12 . . . . 1F 55
N4 . . . . 2C 34
Carlton Sq. E1 . . . . 3F 65
(not continuous)
Carlton St.
SW1 . . . . 5B 14 (1F 75)
Carlton Ter. SE26 . . . . . 3F 121
Carlton Ter. St. E7 . . . . . 4E 55
Carlton Twr. Pl. SW1 . . . 4B 74
Carlton Va. NW6 . . . . . . 1B 58
Carlton Vs. SW15 . . . . . 3A 100
Carlwell St. SW17 . . . . . 5A 116
Carlyle Cl. N2 . . . . 1E 31
NW10 . . . . 5A 42
Carlyle Ct. SW6 . . . . 4D 87
(off Imperial Rd.)
SW10 . . . . 4E 87
(off Chelsea Harbour Dr.)
Carlyle Ho. N16 . . . . 5A 36
SW3 . . . . 3F 65
Carlyle Pl. SW15 . . . . . . 2F 99
Carlyle Rd. E12 . . . . 1F 55
Carlyle's House 2A 88
(off Cheyne Row)
Carlyle Sq. SW3 . . . . . . 1F 87
Carmalt Gdns. SW15 . . . 2E 99
Carmarthen Pl.
SE1 . . . . 3D 27 (3A 78)

Carmel Ct. W8 . . . . 3D 73
　(off Holland St.)
Carmelite St.
　EC4 . . . . . . 4C 16 (1C 76)
Carmel Lodge SW6 . . . 2C 86
　(off Lillie Rd.)
Carmen St. E14 . . . . . . 5D 67
Carmichael Cl.
　SW11 . . . . 1F 101
Carmichael Ct.
　SW13 . . . . 5B 84
　(off Grove Rd.)
Carmichael Ho. E14 . . . 1E 81
　(off Poplar High St.)
Carmichael M.
　SW18 . . . . 5F 101
Carminia Rd. SW17 . . . 2D 117
Carnaby St.
　W1 . . . . 3F 13 (5E 61)
Carnac St. SE27 . . . . . . 4F 119
Carnarvon Rd. E10 . . . . 1E 39
　E15 . . . . 3B 54
Carnbrook Rd. SE3 . . . 1F 111
Carnegie Pl. SW19 . . . . 3F 113
Carnegie St. N1 . . . . . . 5B 48
Carnie Lodge SW3 . . . 1D 117
Carnival Ho. SE1 . . . . . 3F 27
　(off Gainsford St.)
Carnoustie Dr. N1. . . . . 4B 48
　(not continuous)
Carnwath Rd. SW6 . . . . 1C 100
Carolina Cl. E15 . . . . . . 2A 54
Caroline Cl. SW16 . . . . 3B 118
　W2 . . . . 1D 73
　(off Bayswater Rd.)
Caroline Ct. SE6 . . . . . . 4F 123
Caroline Gdns.
　E2 . . . . 1E 11 (2A 64)
　SE15 . . . . 3D 93
Caroline Ho. W6 . . . . . . 1E 85
　(off Queen Caroline St.)
　W2 . . . . 1D 73
Caroline Pl. SW11 . . . . 5C 88
　W2 . . . . 1D 73
Caroline Pl. M. W2 . . . 1D 73
Caroline Ter. SW1 . . . . 5C 74
Caroline Wlk. W6 . . . . . 2A 86
　(off Lillie Rd.)
Carol St. NW1 . . . . 5E 47
Caronia Ct. SE16 . . . . . 5A 80
　(off Plough Way)
Carpenter Ho. E14 . . . . 4C 66
　(off Burgess St.)
　NW11 . . . . 1E 31
Carpenters Bus. Pk.
　E15 . . . . 4D 53
Carpenters Ct. NW1 . . . 5E 47
　(off Pratt St.)
Carpenters M. N7 . . . . . 2A 48
Carpenters Pl. SW4 . . . 2F 103
Carpenter's Rd. E15 . . . 3C 52
Carpenter St.
　W1 . . . . 5D 13 (1D 75)
Carradale Ho. E14 . . . . 5E 67
　(off St Leonard's Rd.)
Carrara Cl. SE24 . . . . . . 2C 104
　SW9 . . . . 2D 105
Carrara M. E8 . . . . 3C 50
Carrara Wharf SW6 . . . 1A 100
Carriage Dr. E. SW11 . . 3C 88

Carriage Dr. Nth.
　SW11 . . . . 2C 88
　(Carriage Dr. E.)
　SW11 . . . . 3B 88
　(Parade, The)
Carriage Dr. Sth.
　SW11 . . . . 4B 88
　(not continuous)
Carriage Dr. W.
　SW11 . . . . 3B 88
Carriage Pl. N16. . . . . . 5F 35
　SW16 . . . . 5E 117
Carrick Ho. N7 . . . . 3B 48
　(off Caledonian Rd.)
Carrick M. SE8 . . . . 2C 94
Carrington Ct.
　SW11 . . . . 2A 102
　(off Barnard Rd.)
Carrington Gdns. E7 . . . 1C 54
Carrington Ho. W1. . . . . 2D 21
　(off Carrington St.)
Carrington St.
　W1 . . . . 2D 21 (2D 75)
Carrol Cl. NW5 . . . . 1D 47
Carroll Cl. E15 . . . . 2B 54
Carroll Ho. W2 . . . . 1F 73
　(off Craven Ter.)
Carronade Ct. N7 . . . . . 2B 48
Carron Cl. E14 . . . . 5D 67
Carroun Rd. SW8 . . . . . 3B 90
Carr St. E14 . . . . 4A 66
Carslake Rd.
　SW15 . . . . 4E 99
Carson Rd. E16 . . . . 3C 68
　SE21 . . . . 2F 119
Carstairs Rd. SE6 . . . . . 3E 123
Carston Cl. SE12 . . . . . 3B 110
Carswell Rd. SE6 . . . . . 5E 109
Cartel Cl. EC4 . . . . 3D 17
Carteret Ho. W12. . . . . . 1D 71
　(off White City Est.)
Carteret St.
　SW1 . . . . . . 4B 22 (3F 75)
Carteret Way SE8 . . . . . 5A 80
Carter Ho. E1 . . . . 1F 54
Carter La.
　EC4 . . . . 3E 17 (5D 63)
Carter Pl. SE17. . . . . . . 1E 91
Carter Rd. E13 . . . . 5D 55
　SW19 . . . . 5F 115
Carters Cl. NW5 . . . . . . 2F 47
　(off Torriano Av.)
Carters La. SE23 . . . . . . 2A 122
Carter St. SE17 . . . . 2E 91
Carter's Yd. SW18 . . . . . 3C 100
Carthew Rd. W6 . . . . . . 4D 71
Carthew Vs. W6 . . . . . . 4D 71
Carthusian St.
　EC1 . . . . 5F 9 (4E 63)
Cartier Circ. E14 . . . . . . 2D 81
Carting La.
　WC2 . . . . 5E 15 (1A 76)
Cartmel NW1 . . . . 1F 5
　(off Hampstead Rd.)
Carton Ho. SE16 . . . . . . 4C 78
　(off Marine St.)
　W11 . . . . 1F 71
　(off St Ann's Rd.)

Cartwright Gdns.
　WC1 . . . . 2D 7 (2A 62)
Cartwright Ho. SE1 . . . . 4E 77
　(off County St.)
Cartwright St. E1 . . . . . 1B 78
Cartwright Way
　SW13 . . . . 3D 85
Carvel Ho. E14 . . . . 1E 95
　(off Manchester Rd.)
Carver Rd. SE24 . . . . . . 4E 105
Cary Rd. E11 . . . . 1A 54
Carysfort Rd. N16 . . . . . 5F 35
Casby Ho. SE16 . . . . . . 4C 78
　(off Marine St.)
Cascades Twr. E14 . . . . 2B 80
Casella Rd. SE14 . . . . . 3F 93
Casewick Rd. SE27 . . . 5C 118
Casey Cl. NW8 . . . . 2A 60
Casimir Rd. E5 . . . . 4E 37
Casino Av. SE24 . . . . . . 3E 105
Caspian Ho. E1 . . . . 4F 65
　(off Shandy St.)
Caspian St. SE5 . . . . . . 3F 91
Caspian Wlk. E16 . . . . . 5F 69
Casselden Rd. NW10 . . 4A 42
Cassell Ho. SW9 . . . . . 5A 90
　(off Stockwell Gdns. Est.)
Cassidy Rd. SW6 . . . . . 3C 86
　(not continuous)
Cassiobury Rd. E17 . . . 1A 38
Cassland Rd. E9 . . . . . . 4F 51
Casslee Rd. SE6 . . . . . . 5B 108
Casson Ho. E1 . . . . 4C 64
　(off Spelman St.)
Castalia Sq. E14. . . . . . 3E 81
Castellain Mans. W9. . . 3D 59
　(off Castellain Rd.,
　　not continuous)
Castellain Rd. W9 . . . . . 3D 59
Castell Ho. SE8 . . . . . . 3C 94
Castello Av. SW15 . . . . 3E 99
CASTELNAU 2D 85
Castelnau SW13 . . . . . . 4C 84
Castelnau Gdns.
　SW13 . . . . 2D 85
Castelnau Mans.
　SW13 . . . . 2D 85
　(off Castelnau, not continuous)
Castelnau Row
　SW13 . . . . 2D 85
Casterbridge NW6 . . . . 5D 45
　(off Abbey Rd.)
　W11 . . . . 5B 58
　(off Dartmouth Cl.)
Casterbridge Rd.
　SE3 . . . . 1C 110
Casterton St. E8. . . . . . 3D 51
Castillon Rd. SE6 . . . . . 2A 124
Castlands Rd. SE6 . . . . 2B 122
Castleacre W2 . . . . 5A 60
　(off Hyde Pk. Cres.)
Castle Baynard St.
　EC4 . . . . 4E 17 (1D 77)
Castlebrook Cl. SE11 . . 5D 77
Castle Climbing Cen., The
　. . . . . 4E 35
Castle Cl. E9 . . . . 2A 52
　SW19 . . . . 3F 113
Castlecombe Dr.
　SW19 . . . . 5F 99

Castlecombe Rd.
SE9 . . . . 4F 125
Castle Ct. EC3 . . . . 3C 18
(off Birchin La.)
SE26 . . . . 4A 122
Castle Dr. IG4: Ilf 1F 41
Castleford Ct. NW8 . . . . 3F 59
(off Henderson Dr.)
Castlehaven Rd.
NW1 . . . . 4D 47
Castle Ho. SE1 . . . . 5E 77
(off Walworth Rd.)
SW8 . . . . 3A 90
(off Sth. Lambeth Rd.)
Castle Ind. Est. SE17 . . . 5E 77
Castle La.
SW1 . . . . . . 5A 22 (4E 75)
Castlemaine SW11 . . . 5B 88
Castlemain St. E1 . . . . 4D 65
Castle Mead SE5 . . . . . 3E 91
Castle M. NW1 . . . . . . 3D 47
SW17 . . . . 4A 116
Castle Pl. NW1 . . . . . . 3D 47
W4 . . . . 5A 70
Castle Point E13 . . . . . 1E 69
(off Boundary Rd.)
Castlereagh St. W1 . . . . 5B 60
Castle Rd. NW1 . . . . . . 3D 47
Castle St. E6 . . . . 1E 69
Castleton Ho. E14 . . . . . 5E 81
(off Pier St.)
Castleton Rd. SE9 . . . . 4F 125
Castletown Rd. W14 . . . 1A 86
Castleview N4 . . . . 4E 35
Castle Way SW19 . . . . . 3F 113
Castle Wharf E14 . . . . . 1A 82
(off Orchard Pl.)
Castlewood Rd. N15 . . . 1C 36
N16 . . . . 1C 36
Castle Yd. N6 . . . . 2C 32
SE1 . . . . . . 1E 25 (2D 77)
Castor La. E14 . . . . 1D 81
Caterham Rd. SE13 . . . 1F 109
Catesby Ho. E9 . . . . 4E 51
(off Frampton Pk. Rd.)
Catesby St. SE17 . . . . . 5F 77
CATFORD. 5D 109
Catford Art Gallery . 5D 109
Catford B'way.
SE6 . . . . 5D 109
CATFORD GYRATORY
. . . . 5D 109
Catford Hill SE6 . . . . . 1B 122
Catford Island SE6 . . . 5D 109
Catford M. SE6 . . . . . . 5D 109
Catford Rd. SE6 . . . . . 5C 108
Catford Trad. Est.
SE6 . . . . 2D 123
Cathall Leisure Cen. . 4A 40
Cathall Rd. E11 . . . . . . 4F 39
Cathay Ho. SE16 . . . . . 3D 79
Cathay St. SE16 . . . . . . 3D 79
Cathcart Hill N19 . . . . . 5E 33
Cathcart Rd. SW10 . . . 2D 87
Cathcart St. NW5 . . . . . 3D 47
Cathedral Lodge EC1 . . 5F 9
(off Aldersgate St.)
Cathedral Mans.
SW1 . . . . 5E 75
(off Vauxhall Bri. Rd.)

Cathedral Piazza
SW1 . . . . . . 5F 21 (4E 75)
Cathedral St.
SE1 . . . . . . 1B 26 (2F 77)
Catherall Rd. N5 . . . . . 5E 35
Catherine Ct.
SW19 . . . . 5B 114
Catherine Griffiths Ct.
EC1 . . . . 3C 8
(off Northampton Rd.)
Catherine Gro. SE10 . . 4D 95
Catherine Ho. N1 . . . . . 5A 50
(off Whitmore Est.)
Catherine Pl.
SW1 . . . . . . 5F 21 (4E 75)
Catherine St.
WC2 . . . . . . 4F 15 (1B 76)
Catherine Wheel All.
E1 . . . . 1E 19 (4A 64)
(not continuous)
Catherine Wheel Yd.
SW1 . . . . 2F 21
Catherwood Ct.
N1 . . . . 1B 10
(off Murray Gro.,
not continuous)
Cathles Rd. SW12 . . . 4D 103
Cathnor Rd. W12 . . . . . 3D 71
Catling Cl. SE23 . . . . . 3E 121
Catlin St. SE16 . . . . . . 1C 92
Cato Rd. SW4 . . . . 1F 103
Cator Rd. SE26 . . . . . . 5F 121
Cator St. SE15 . . . . 3B 92
(E. Surrey Gro.)
SE15 . . . . 2B 92
(Ebley Cl.)
Cato St. W1 . . . . 4A 60
Catton St.
WC1 . . . . . . 1F 15 (4B 62)
Caudwell Ter.
SW18 . . . . 4F 101
Caughley Ho. SE11 . . . . 4C 76
(off Lambeth Wlk.)
Caulfield Rd.
SE15 . . . . 5D 93
Causeway, The
SW18 . . . . 3D 101
(not continuous)
SW19 . . . . 5E 113
Causton Cotts. E14 . . . 5A 66
Causton Ho. SE5 . . . . . 2E 91
Causton Rd. N6 . . . . . . 2D 33
Cautley Av. SW4 . . . . . 3E 103
Cavalry Gdns.
SW15 . . . . 3B 100
Cavan Ho. E3 . . . . 5B 52
Cavaye Pl. SW10 . . . . . 1E 87
Cavell Ho. N1 . . . . 5A 50
(off Colville Est.)
Cavell St. E1 . . . . 4D 65
Cavendish Av. NW8 . . . 1F 59
NW8 . . . . 2D 59
Cavendish Cl. NW6 . . . . 3B 44
NW8 . . . . 2D 59
Cavendish Ct. EC3 . . . . 2E 19
SE6 . . . . 1D 123
(off Bromley Rd.)
Cavendish Dr. E11 . . . . 3F 39
Cavendish Gdns.
SW4 . . . . 4E 103

Cavendish Ho.
NW8 . . . . 1F 59
(off Wellington Rd.)
Cavendish Mans. EC1 . . 4B 8
(off Rosebery Av.)
NW6 . . . . 2C 44
Cavendish M. Nth.
W1 . . . . 5E 5 (4D 61)
Cavendish M. Sth.
W1 . . . . 1E 13 (4D 61)
Cavendish Pde.
SW4 . . . . 4D 103
(off Clapham Comn. Sth. Side)
Cavendish Pl. SW4 . . . 3F 103
W1 . . . . 2E 13 (5D 61)
Cavendish Rd. N4 . . . . 1D 35
NW6 . . . . 4A 44
SW12 . . . . 4D 103
Cavendish Sq.
W1 . . . . 2E 13 (5D 61)
Cavendish St. N1 . . . . . 1F 63
Cavendish Ter. E3 . . . . . 2B 66
(Rusholme)
Cave Rd. E13 . . . . 2D 69
Caversham Ho.
SE15 . . . . 2C 92
(off Haymerle Rd.)
Caversham Rd. NW5 . . . 3E 47
Caversham St.
SW3 . . . . 2B 88
Caverswall St. W12 . . . 5E 57
Cavour Ho. SE17 . . . . . 1D 91
(off Alberta Est.)
Cawnpore St. SE19 . . . 5A 120
Caxton Ct. SW11 . . . . . 5A 88
Caxton Gro. E3 . . . . . . 2C 66
Caxton Rd. SW19 . . . . 5E 115
W12 . . . . 3F 71
Caxton St.
SW1 . . . . . . 5B 22 (4E 75)
Caxton St. Nth. E16 . . . 5B 68
Caxton Wlk.
WC2 . . . . . . 3C 14 (5F 61)
Cayenne Ct.
SE1 . . . . . . 3F 27 (3B 78)
Cayton Pl. EC1 . . . . . . 2B 10
Cayton St.
EC1 . . . . . . 2B 10 (2F 63)
Cazenove Rd. N16 . . . . 4B 36
Cearns Ho. E6 . . . . 5F 55
Cecil Ct. NW6 . . . . 4D 45
SW10 . . . . 2E 87
(off Fawcett St.)
WC2 . . . . . . 5D 15 (1A 76)
Cecile Pk. N8 . . . . 1A 34
Cecilia Rd. E8 . . . . 2B 50
Cecil Rhodes Ho.
NW1 . . . . 1F 61
(off Goldington St.)
Cecil Rd. E11 . . . . 5B 40
E13 . . . . 5C 54
NW10 . . . . 5A 42
Cecil Sharp House . . 5C 46
Cedar Cl. E3 . . . . 5B 52
SE21 . . . . 1E 119
Cedar Ct. N1 . . . . 4E 49
SE1 . . . . 5D 78
(off Royal Oak Td.)
SE7 . . . . 2E 97
SW19 . . . . 3F 113
Cedar Hgts. NW2 . . . . . 3B 44

Cedar Ho. E14 . . . . 3E 81
(off Manchester St.)
SE14 . . . . 4F 93
SE16 . . . . 3F 79
(off Woodland Cres.)
W8 . . . . 4D 73
(off Marloes Rd.)
Cedarhurst Dr. SE9 . . 3E 111
Cedar Mt. SE9. . . . . . 1F 125
Cedarne Rd. SW6 . . . . 3D 87
Cedar Pl. SE7 . . . . . . 1E 97
Cedar Rd. NW2. . . . . . 1E 43
Cedars, The E15. . . . . 4B 54
Cedars Av. E17 . . . . . . 1C 38
Cedars Cl. SE13 . . . . . 1F 109
Cedars M. SW4 . . . . 2D 103
(not continuous)
Cedars Rd. E15 . . . . . . 3A 54
SW4 . . . . 1D 103
SW13 . . . . 5C 84
Cedar Tree Gro.
SE27. . . . . 5D 119
Cedar Way NW1 . . . . . 4F 47
Cedar Way Ind. Est.
NW1 . . . . 4F 47
Cedra Ct. N16. . . . . . . 3C 36
Celandine Cl. E14 . . . . 4C 66
Celandine Dr. E8 . . . . 4B 50
Celandine Way E15 . . . 2A 68
Celbridge M. W2 . . . . 4D 59
Celestial Gdns.
SE13 . . . . 2F 109
Celia Ho. N1. . . . . 1A 64
(off Arden Est.)
Celia Rd. N19. . . . . . . 1E 47
Celtic St. E14 . . . . . . 4D 67
Cemetery La. SE7. . . . 2F 97
Cemetery Rd. E7 . . . . 2B 54
Cenacle Cl. NW3 . . . . 5C 30
Cenotaph 3D 23 (3A 76)
Centaur St.
SE1 . . . . . . 5A 24 (4B 76)
Central Av. E11. . . . . . 4F 39
E12. . . . . 5F 41
SW11 . . . . 3B 88
Central Bus. Cen.
NW10 . . . . 2A 42
Central Church Sports Club
. . . . 2F 121
Central Cir. NW4 . . . . 1D 29
Central Hill SE19 . . . . 5E 119
Central Ho. E15 . . . . . 1D 67
Central Mall SW18. . . 4D 101
(off South Mall)
Central Mans. NW4 . . . 1D 29
(off Watford Way)
Central Markets (Smithfield)
. . . . 1D 17
Central Pk. Rd. E6 . . . 1F 69
Central St Martins College of
Art & Design 1F 15
Central Sq. NW11 . . . . 1D 31
Central St.
EC1. . . . . . . 1F 9 (2E 63)
Central Wharf E14 . . . 5C 66
(off Thomas Rd.)
Centre Av. NW10 . . . . 2E 57
W3 . . . . 2A 70
Centre Ct. Shop. Cen.
SW19 . . . . 5B 114

Centre Dr. E7 . . . . 1E 55
Cen. for the Magic Arts, The
. . . . 3A 6
(off Stephenson Way)
Centre Hgts. NW3. . . . 4F 45
(off Finchley Rd.)
Centre Point SE1 . . . . 1C 92
Centrepoint WC2 . . . . 2C 14
Centre Point Ho.
WC2 . . . . 2C 14
(off St Giles High St.)
Centre Rd. E7. . . . . . . 4C 40
E11. . . . . 4C 40
Centre St. E2 . . . . 1D 65
Centric Cl. NW1 . . . . . 5C 46
Centurion Bldg.
SW8 . . . . 2D 89
Centurion Cl. N7 . . . . 4B 48
Centurion La. E3 . . . . 5B 52
Century Cl. NW4. . . . . 1F 29
Century Ho. SW15 . . . 2F 99
Century M. E5. . . . . . . 1E 51
Century Yd. SE23. . . . 2E 121
Cephas Av. E1 . . . . . . 3E 65
Cephas Ho. E1. . . . . . 3E 65
(off Doveton St.)
Cephas St. E1. . . . . . . 3E 65
Cerise Rd. SE15. . . . . 4C 92
Cerney M. W2. . . . . . . 1F 73
Cervantes Ct. W2. . . . 5D 59
Cester St. E2 . . . . 5C 50
Ceylon Rd. W14 . . . . . 4F 71
Chabot Dr. SE15. . . . . 1D 107
Chadacre Ct. E15. . . . 5C 54
(off Vicars Cl.)
Chadacre Ho. SW9 . . . 2D 105
(off Loughborough Pk.)
Chadbourn St. E14. . . 4D 67
Chadd Grn. E13 . . . . . 5C 54
(not continuous)
Chadston Ho. N1 . . . . 4D 49
(off Halton Rd.)
Chadswell WC1 . . . . . 2E 7
(off Cromer St.)
Chadwell St.
EC1 . . . . . . 1C 8 (2C 62)
Chadwick Av. SW19. . . 5C 114
Chadwick St. SW15 . . . 5B 98
Chadwick Rd. E11. . . . 1A 40
NW10 . . . . 5B 42
SE15. . . . . 5B 92
Chadwick St.
SW1 . . . . . . 5B 22 (4F 75)
Chadwin Rd. E13. . . . . 4D 69
Chadworth Ho. EC1 . . . 2F 9
(off Lever St.)
N4. . . . . 3E 35
Chagford St.
NW1 . . . . 4A 4 (3B 60)
Chailey St. E5 . . . . . . 5E 37
Chalbury Wlk. N1. . . . . 1B 62
Chalcot Cres. NW1. . . . 5B 46
Chalcot Gdns. NW3 . . . 3B 46
Chalcot M. SW16. . . . . 3A 118
Chalcot Rd. NW1. . . . . 4C 46
Chalcot Sq. NW1 . . . . 4C 46
(not continuous)
Chalcroft Rd. SE13. . . 3A 110
Chaldon Rd. SW6. . . . 3A 86
Chale Rd. SW2. . . . . . 4A 104

Chalfont Ct. NW1 . . . . . 4A 4
(off Baker St.)
Chalfont Ho. SE16. . . . 4D 79
(off Keetons Rd.)
Chalford NW3 . . . . 3E 45
(off Finchley Rd.)
Chalford Rd. SE21. . . . 4F 119
CHALK FARM. 4C 46
Chalk Farm Rd. NW1. . 4C 46
Chalk Hill Rd. W6. . . . . 5F 71
Chalk Rd. E13 . . . . . . 4D 69
Chalkwell Ho. E1 . . . . 5F 65
(off Pitsea St.)
Challenge Cl.
NW10 . . . . 5A 42
Challenger Ho. E14 . . . 1A 80
(off Victory Pl.)
Challice Way SW2 . . . . 1B 118
Challoner Cres. W14 . . 1B 86
Challoner St. W14 . . . . 1B 86
Chalmers Wlk. SE17 . . 2D 91
(off Hillingdon St.)
Chalsey Rd. SE4 . . . . . 2B 108
Chalton Dr. N2 . . . . . . 1F 31
Chalton Ho. NW1 . . . . . 1B 6
(off Chalton St.)
Chalton St.
NW1. . . . . . . 1B 6 (1E 61)
(not continuous)
Chamberlain Cotts.
SE5 . . . . 4F 91
Chamberlain Ho. E1. . . 1E 79
(off Cable St.)
NW1 . . . . 1C 6
SE1 . . . . 4B 24
(off Westminster Bri. Rd.)
Chamberlain St.
NW1 . . . . 4B 46
Chamberlayne Mans.
NW10 . . . . 2F 57
(off Chamberlayne Rd.)
Chamberlayne Rd.
NW10 . . . . 5E 43
Chamberlens Garages
W6 . . . . 5D 71
(off Dalling Rd.)
Chambers, The
SW10 . . . . 4E 87
(off Chelsea Harbour Dr.)
Chambers La. NW10 . . 4D 43
Chambers Pl. N7. . . . . 1A 48
Chambers St. SE16 . . . 3C 78
Chamber St. E1. . . . . . 1B 78
Chambers Wharf
SE16 . . . . 3C 78
Chambon Pl. W6 . . . . . 5C 71
Chambord St.
E2. . . . . 2F 11 (2B 64)
Chamomile Ct. E17 . . . 1C 38
(off Yunus Khan Cl.)
Champion Cres.
SE26 . . . . 4A 122
Champion Gro. SE5 . . . 1F 105
Champion Hill SE5 . . . 1F 105
Champion Hill Est.
SE5 . . . . 1A 106
Champion Hill Stadium
. . . . 2A 106
Champion Pk. SE5 . . . 5F 91
Champion Rd. SE26. . . 4A 122

Champlain Ho. *W12*. . . . 1D **71**
(off White City Est.)
Champness Cl.
SE27 . . . . 4F **119**
Chancel Ind. Est.
NW10 . . . . 2B **42**
Chancellor Gro.
SE21 . . . . 2E **119**
Chancellor Ho. *E1* 2D **79**
(off Green Bank)
Chancellor Pas. E14. . . 2C **80**
Chancellors Ct. WC1 . . 5F **7**
Chancellor's Rd. W6 . . 1E **85**
Chancellor's St. W6 . . . 1E **85**
Chancellors Wharf
W6 . . . . 1E **85**
Chancel St.
SE1 . . . . . . 2D **25** (2D **77**)
Chancery Bldgs. *E1* . . . 1D **79**
(off Lowood St.)
Chancery La.
WC2 . . . . 1A **16** (5C **62**)
Chancery M. SW17 . . . 2A **116**
Chance St.
E1 . . . . 3F **11** (3B **64**)
E2 . . . . 3F **11** (3B **64**)
Chandler Av. E16 . . . . . 4C **68**
Chandler Ho. *NW6* . . . 5B **44**
(off Willesden La.)
WC1 . . . . 4E **7**
(off Colonnade)
Chandlers Ct. SE12 . . 1D **125**
Chandlers M. E14. . . . . 3C **80**
Chandler St. E1 . . . . . . 2D **79**
Chandlers Way
SW2 . . . . 5C **104**
Chandler Way SE15 . . . 3A **92**
(Innis St.)
SE15 . . . . 2A **92**
(St George's Way)
Chandlery, The *SE1* . . . 5C **24**
(off Gerridge St.)
Chandlery Ho. *E1* 5C **64**
(off Bk. Church La.)
Chandos Pl.
WC2 . . . . 5D **15** (1A **76**)
Chandos Rd. E15 . . . . . 2F **53**
NW2 . . . . 2E **43**
NW10 . . . . 3A **56**
Chandos St.
W1 . . . . 1E **13** (4D **61**)
Chandos Way NW11. . . 3D **31**
Change All.
EC3. . . . . 3C **18** (5F **63**)
Channel Ga. Rd.
NW10 . . . . 2A **56**
Channel Ho. *E14* 4A **66**
(off Aston St.)
Channel Islands Est.
N1 . . . . 3E **49**
(off Guernsey Rd.)
Channelsea Path E15 . . 5F **53**
Channelsea Rd. E15. . . 5F **53**
Chantrey Ho. SW9 . . . 1B **104**
Chantry Cl. W9 . . . . . . 3C **58**
Chantry Cres. NW10. . . 3B **42**
Chantry Sq. W8 . . . . . . 4D **73**
Chantry St. N1 . . . . 5D **49**
Chant Sq. E15. . . . . . . 4F **53**
Chant St. E15 . . . . 4F **53**

Chapel Av. E12 . . . . . . 5F **41**
Chapel Cl. NW10 . . . . . 2B **42**
Chapel Ct.
SE1 . . . . 3B **26** (3F **77**)
Chapel Ho. St. E14 . . . 1D **95**
Chapelier Ho.
SW18 . . . . 2C **100**
Chapel Mkt. N1 . . . . . . 1C **62**
Chapel of St John the
Evangelist 5F **19**
(in Tower of London)
Chapel of St Peter & St Paul
. . . . 2F **95**
(in Old Royal Naval College)
Chapel Path *E11* 1D **41**
(off Woodbine Pl.)
Chapel Pl.
EC2 . . . . 2D **11** (2A **64**)
N1 . . . . 1C **62**
W1 . . . . 3D **13** (5D **61**)
Chapel Rd. SE27 . . . . . 4D **119**
Chapel Side W2 . . . . . . 1D **73**
Chapel St. NW1 . . . . . . 4A **60**
SW1 . . . . 5C **20** (4C **74**)
Chapel Way N7 . . . . . . 5B **34**
Chapel Yd. *SW18*. 3D **101**
(off Wandsworth High St.)
Chaplin Cl.
SE1 . . . . 3C **24** (3C **76**)
Chaplin Rd. E15. . . . . . 1B **68**
NW2 . . . . 3C **42**
Chapman Ho. *E1* 5D **65**
(off Bigland St.)
Chapman Pl. N4. . . . . . 4D **35**
Chapman Rd. E9 . . . . . 3B **52**
Chapmans Pk. Ind. Est.
NW10 . . . . 3B **42**
Chapman Sq.
SW19 . . . . 2F **113**
Chapman St. E1. . . . . . 1D **79**
Chapone Pl.
W1 . . . . 3B **14** (5F **61**)
Chapter Chambers
SW1 . . . . 5F **75**
(off Chapter St.)
Chapter House
. . . . 3F **17** (5D **63**)
Chapter Rd. NW2. . . . . 2C **42**
SE17. . . . . 1D **91**
Chapter St. SW1. . . . . . 5F **75**
Charcot Ho. SW15 . . . . 4B **98**
Charcroft Ct. *W14*. 3F **71**
(off Minford Gdns.)
Chardin Ho. SW9. . . . . 4C **90**
(off Gosling Way)
Chardin Rd. W4 . . . . . . 5A **70**
Chardmore Rd. N16. . . 3C **36**
Charecroft Way W12 . . 3F **71**
W14. . . . . 3F **71**
Charfield Ct. *W9* 3D **59**
(off Shirland Rd.)
Charford Rd. E16 . . . . . 4C **68**
Chargeable La. E13 . . . 3B **68**
Chargeable St. E16 . . . 3B **68**
Chargrove Cl. SE16 . . . 3F **79**
Charing Cross SW1 . . . 1D **23**
Charing Cross Rd.
WC2. . . . . 2C **14** (5F **61**)
Charing Cross Sports Club
. . . . 2F **85**

Charing Cross Underground
Shop. Cen. WC2 . . . 5D **15**
Charing Ho. *SE1*. 3C **24**
(off Windmill Wlk.)
Chariot Cl. E3. . . . . 5C **52**
Charlbert Ct. *NW8* 1A **60**
(off Charlbert St.)
Charlbert St. NW8 . . . . 1A **60**
Charlecote Gro.
SE26 . . . . 3D **121**
Charles II Pl. SW3 . . . . 1B **88**
Charles II St.
SW1 . . . . 1B **22** (2F **75**)
Charles Auffray Ho.
E1 . . . . 4E **65**
(off Smithy St.)
Charles Barry Cl.
SW4 . . . . 1E **103**
Charles Coveney Rd.
SE15 . . . . 4B **92**
Charles Darwin Ho.
E2 . . . . 2D **65**
(off Canrobert St.)
Charles Dickens Ho.
E2 . . . . 2C **64**
(off Mansford St.)
Charlesfield SE9. . . . . . 3E **125**
Charles Flemwell M.
E16. . . . . 2C **82**
Charles Gardner Ct.
N1 . . . . 1C **10**
(off Haberdasher St.)
Charles Haller St.
SW2 . . . . 5C **104**
Charles Harrod Ct.
SW13 . . . . 2E **85**
(off Somerville Av.)
Charles Ho. W14 . . . . . 5B **72**
(off Kensington High St.)
Charles La. NW8 . . . . . 1A **60**
Charles MacKenzie Ho.
SE16. . . . . 5C **78**
(off Linsey St.)
Charles Pl.
NW1 . . . . 2A **6** (2E **61**)
Charles Rd. E7 . . . . 4E **55**
Charles Rowan Ho.
WC1 . . . . 2B **8**
(off Margery St.)
Charles Simmons Ho.
WC1 . . . . 2B **8**
(off Margery St.)
Charles Sq.
N1 . . . . 2C **10** (2F **63**)
Charles Sq. Est. N1 . . . 2C **10**
Charles St. E16 . . . . . . 2E **83**
SW13 . . . . 5A **84**
W1 . . . . 1D **21** (2D **75**)
Charleston St. SE17. . . 5E **77**
Charles Townsend Ho.
EC1. . . . . 3D **9**
(off Skinner St.)
Charles Uton Ct. E8 . . . 1C **50**
Charles Whincup Rd.
E16. . . . . 2D **83**
Charlesworth Ho.
E14 . . . . 5B **66**
(off Dod St.)
Charlesworth Pl.
SW13 . . . . 1A **98**

Charleville Cir.
SE26 . . . . 5C **120**
Charleville Mans.
W14 . . . . *1A 86*
   (off Charleville Rd.)
Charleville Rd. W14. . . . 1A **86**
Charlie Chaplin Wlk.
SE1 . . . . *2A 24*
   (off Waterloo Rd.)
Charlmont Rd.
SW17 . . . . 5A **116**
Charlotte Ct. N8 . . . . . . 1F **33**
SE1 . . . . *5A 78*
   (off Old Kent Rd.)
W6 . . . . *5C 70*
   (off Invermead Cl.)
Charlotte Despard Av.
SW11 . . . . 4C **88**
Charlotte Ho. *E16.* *2D 83*
   (off Fairfax M.)
W6 . . . . *1E 85*
   (off Queen Caroline St.)
Charlotte M.
W1. . . . . 5A **6** (4E **61**)
W10. . . . . 5F **57**
W14 . . . . 5A **72**
Charlotte Pl. SW1. . . . . 5E **75**
W1. . . . . 1A **14** (4E **61**)
Charlotte Rd.
EC2 . . . . 2D **11** (2A **64**)
SW13 . . . . 4B **84**
Charlotte Row SW4 . . 1E **103**
Charlotte St.
W1. . . . . 5A **6** (4E **61**)
Charlotte Ter. N1 . . . . . 5B **48**
Charlow Cl. SW6 . . . . . 5E **87**
CHARLTON 3F **97**
Charlton Athletic FC . . *1E 97*
Charlton Chu. La.
SE7 . . . . 1E **97**
Charlton Ct. E2 . . . . 5B **50**
Charlton Dene SE7 . . . . 3E **97**
Charlton Ga. Bus. Pk.
SE7 . . . . 5E **83**
Charlton House *2F 97*
Charlton King's Rd.
NW5 . . . . 2F **47**
Charlton La. SE7. . . . . . 5B **83**
Charlton Lido *3F 97*
Charlton Pk. La. SE7 . . . 3F **97**
Charlton Pk. Rd. SE7 . . . 2F **97**
Charlton Pl. N1 . . . . . . 1D **63**
Charlton Rd. NW10 . . . . 5A **42**
SE3 . . . . 3C **96**
SE7 . . . . 3C **96**
Charlton Way SE3. . . . . 4A **96**
Charlwood Ho. *SW1* *5F 75*
   (off Vauxhall Bri. Rd.)
Charlwood Ho's. *WC1* . . . *2E 7*
   (off Midhope St.)
Charlwood Pl. SW1 . . . . 5E **75**
Charlwood Rd. SW15 . . . 2F **99**
Charlwood St. SW1 . . . . 1E **89**
   (not continuous)
Charlwood Ter. SW15 . . . 2F **99**
Charmans Ho. *SW3* *3A 90*
   (off Wandsworth Rd.)
Charminster Rd.
SE9 . . . . 4F **125**
Charmouth Ho. SW8 . . . 3B **90**

Charnock Ho. *W12.* *1D 71*
   (off White City Est.)
Charnock Rd. E5 . . . . . . 5D **37**
Charnwood Gdns.
E14 . . . . 5C **80**
Charnwood St. E5 . . . . . 4D **37**
Charrington St. NW1 . . . 1F **61**
Charsley Rd. SE6. . . . 2D **123**
Charter Ct. N4 . . . . 3C **34**
Charterhouse 4E **9**
Charter Ho. *WC2* *3E 15*
   (off Crown Ct.)
Charterhouse Bldgs.
EC1 . . . . 4E **9** (3E **63**)
Charterhouse M.
EC1 . . . . 5E **9** (4D **63**)
Charterhouse Rd. E8 . . . 1C **50**
Charterhouse Sq.
EC1 . . . . 5E **9** (4D **63**)
Charterhouse St.
EC1 . . . . 1C **16** (4C **62**)
Charteris Rd. N4 . . . . . . 3C **34**
NW6 . . . . 5B **44**
Charters St. SE19. . . . 5A **120**
Chartes Ho. *SE1* *5E 27*
   (off Stevens St.)
Chartfield Av. SW15 . . . 3D **99**
Chartfield Sq. SW15 . . . 3F **99**
Chartham Ct. *SW9* *1C 104*
   (off Canterbury Cres.)
Chartham Gro.
SE27 . . . . 3D **119**
Chartham Ho. *SE1* *5C 26*
   (off Weston St.)
Chart Ho. *E14.* *1D 95*
   (off Burrells Wharf Sq.)
Chartley Av. NW2. . . . . 5A **28**
Chartridge *SE17* *2F 91*
   (off Westmoreland Rd.)
Chart St. N1. . . . 1C **10** (2F **63**)
Charwood SW16. . . . . . 4C **118**
Chase, The E12 . . . . . . 1F **55**
SW4 . . . . 1D **103**
Chase Cen., The
NW10 . . . . 2A **56**
Chasefield Rd.
SW17 . . . . 4B **116**
Chaseley St. E14 . . . . . 5A **66**
Chasemore Ho. *SW6* . . . *3A 86*
   (off Williams Cl.)
Chase Rd. NW10 . . . . . 3A **56**
Chase Rd. Trad. Est.
NW10 . . . . 3A **56**
Chaston Pl. NW5 . . . . . . 2C **46**
   (off Grafton Ter.)
Chater Ho. *E2* *2F 65*
   (off Roman Rd.)
Chateris Community
Sports Cen. 5C **44**
Chatfield Rd. SW11 . . . 1E **101**
Chatham Cl. NW11 . . . . 1C **30**
Chatham Pl. E9 . . . . 3E **51**
Chatham Rd. SW11 . . . . 4B **102**
Chatham St. SE17 . . . . 5F **77**
Chats Palace Arts Cen.
. . . . 2F **51**
Chatsworth Av.
BR1: Brom 4D **125**
Chatsworth Ct. *W8.* *5C 72*
   (off Pembroke Rd.)

Chatsworth Est. E5. . . . . 1F **51**
Chatsworth Ho. *E16.* . . . *2D 83*
   (off Wesley Av.)
Chatsworth Lodge
W4 . . . . *1A 84*
   (off Bourne Pl.)
Chatsworth Pl. NW2. . . . 3E **43**
Chatsworth Rd. E5 . . . . . 5E **37**
E15 . . . . 2B **54**
NW2 . . . . 3E **43**
   (not continuous)
Chatsworth Way
SE27 . . . . 3D **119**
Chatterton M. *N4* *5D 35*
   (off Chatterton Rd.)
Chatterton Rd. N4 . . . . . 5D **35**
Chatto Rd. SW11 . . . . . 3B **102**
Chaucer Ct. N16. . . . . . . 1A **50**
Chaucer Dr. SE1. . . . . . . 5B **78**
Chaucer Ho. *SW1*. *1E 89*
   (off Churchill Gdns.)
Chaucer Mans. *W14* . . . *2A 86*
   (off Queen's Club Gdns.)
Chaucer Rd. E7 . . . . 3C **54**
E11 . . . . 1C **40**
SE24 . . . . 3C **104**
Chaucer Theatre *2F 19*
   (off Braham St.)
Chaucer Way SW19 . . . 5F **115**
Chaulden Ho. *EC1* *2C 10*
   (off Cranwood St.)
Chauntler Cl. E16. . . . . . 5D **69**
Cheadle Ct. NW8 . . . . . . 3F **59**
   (off Henderson Dr.)
Cheadle Ho. *E14* *5B 66*
   (off Copenhagen Pl.)
Cheam St. SE15. . . . . . 1E **107**
Cheapside
EC2 . . . . 3A **18** (5E **63**)
Chearsley *SE17* *5E 77*
   (off Deacon Way)
Cheddington Ho. *E2* . . . *5C 50*
   (off Whiston Rd.)
Chedworth Cl. E16. . . . . 5B **68**
Cheesemans Ter.
W14 . . . . 1B **86**
   (not continuous)
Cheethams Rd. E12 . . . 5F **41**
Chelford Rd.
BR1: Brom 5F **123**
Chelmer Rd. E9 . . . . 2F **51**
Chelmsford Cl. W6. . . . . 2F **85**
Chelmsford Ho. *N7* *1B 48*
   (off Holloway Rd.)
Chelmsford Rd. E11 . . . 3F **39**
E17 . . . . 1C **38**
Chelmsford Sq.
NW10 . . . . 5E **43**
CHELSEA 1A **88**
Chelsea Bri. SW1 . . . . . 2D **89**
SW8 . . . . 3D **89**
Chelsea Bri. Bus. Cen.
SW8 . . . . 3D **89**
Chelsea Bri. Rd.
SW1 . . . . 1C **88**
Chelsea Bri. Wharf
SW8 . . . . 2D **89**
Chelsea Cinema *1A 88*
Chelsea Cloisters
SW3 . . . . 5A **74**
Chelsea Cl. NW10 . . . . . 5A **42**

Chelsea College of
Art & Design 1A 88
Chelsea Cres. NW2 . . . 3B 44
SW10 . . . . 4E 87
Chelsea Emb. SW3 . . . 2A 88
Chelsea Farm Ho. Studios
SW10 . . . . 2F 87
(off Moravian Pl.)
Chelsea FC 3D 87
Chelsea Gdns. SW1 . . . 1C 88
Chelsea Ga. SW1 . . . . 1C 88
(off Ebury Bri. Rd.)
Chelsea Harbour
SW10 . . . . 4E 87
Chelsea Harbour Design Cen.
SW10 . . . . 4E 87
(off Chelsea Harbour Dr.)
Chelsea Harbour Dr.
SW10 . . . . 4E 87
Chelsea Lodge SW3 . . . 2B 88
(off Tite St.)
Chelsea Mnr. Ct.
SW3 . . . . 2A 88
Chelsea Mnr. Gdns.
SW3 . . . . 1A 88
Chelsea Mnr. St.
SW3 . . . . 1A 88
Chelsea Pk. Gdns.
SW3 . . . . 2F 87
Chelsea Physic Garden
. . . . 2B 88
Chelsea Reach Twr.
SW10 . . . . 3F 87
(off Worlds End Est.)
Chelsea Sports Cen. . . 1A 88
Chelsea Sq. SW3 . . . . 1F 87
Chelsea Studios
SW6 . . . . 3D 87
(off Fulham Rd.)
Chelsea Towers SW3 . . 2A 88
(off Chelsea Mnr. Gdns.)
Chelsea Village SW6 . . 3D 87
(off Fulham Rd.)
Chelsea Vista SW6 . . . 5E 87
Chelsea Wharf SW10 . . 3F 87
(off Lots Rd.)
Chelsfield Gdns.
SE26 . . . . 3E 121
Chelsfield Ho. SE17 . . 5A 78
(off Massinger St.)
Chelsham Rd. SW4 . . . 1F 103
Cheltenham Gdns. E6 . . 1F 69
Cheltenham Rd. E10 . . 1E 39
SE15 . . . . 2E 107
Cheltenham Ter.
SW3 . . . . 1B 88
Chelverton Rd. SW15 . . 2F 99
Chelwood Ho. W2 . . . . 5F 59
(off Gloucester Sq.)
Chelwood Wlk. SE4 . . 2A 108
Chenappa Cl. E13 . . . . 2C 68
Cheney Ct. SE23 . . . . 1F 121
Cheneys Rd. E11 . . . . 5A 40
Chenies, The NW1 . . . . 1F 61
(off Pancras Rd.)
Chenies Ho. W4 . . . . . 3B 84
(off Corney Reach Way)
Chenies M.
WC1 . . . . 4B 6 (3F 61)
Chenies Pl. NW1 . . . . . 1F 61

Chenies St.
WC1 . . . . 5B 6 (4F 61)
Cheniston Gdns. W8 . . 4D 73
Chepstow Cl. SW15 . . 3A 100
Chepstow Cnr. W2 . . . 5C 58
(off Chepstow Pl.)
Chepstow Ct. W11 . . . 1C 72
(off Chepstow Vs.)
Chepstow Cres. W11 . . 1C 72
Chepstow Pl. W2 . . . . 5C 58
Chepstow Rd. W2 . . . . 5C 58
Chepstow Vs. W11 . . . 1B 72
Chequers Ct. EC1 . . . . 4A 10
(off Chequer St.)
Chequers Ho. NW8 . . . 3A 60
(off Jerome Cres.)
Chequer St.
EC1 . . . . 4A 10 (3E 63)
(not continuous)
Cherbury Ct. N1 . . . . . 1F 63
(off St John's Est.)
Cherbury St. N1 . . . . . 1F 63
Cheriton Ct. SE12 . . . . 5C 110
Cheriton Sq. SW17 . . . 2C 116
Cherry Cl. SW2 . . . . . 5C 104
Cherry Ct. W3 . . . . . . 2A 70
Cherry Gdn. Ho.
SE16 . . . . 3D 79
(off Cherry Gdn. St.)
Cherry Gdn. St. SE16 . . 3D 79
Cherry Laurel Wlk.
SW2 . . . . 4B 104
Cherry Orchard SE7 . . 2E 97
Cherry Tree Cl. E9 . . . 5E 51
Cherry Tree Ct. NW1 . . 4E 47
(off Camden St.)
SE7 . . . . 2E 97
Cherry Tree Dr.
SW16 . . . . 3A 118
Cherry Tree Rd. E15 . . 2A 54
Cherry Tree Ter. SE1 . . 4E 27
(off Whites Grounds)
Cherry Tree Wlk.
EC1 . . . . 4A 10 (3E 63)
Cherrywood Cl. E3 . . . 2A 66
Cherrywood Dr.
SW15 . . . . 3F 99
Chertsey Rd. E11 . . . . 4F 39
Chertsey St. SW17 . . . 5C 116
Cherwell Ho. NW8 . . . 3F 59
(off Church St. Est.)
Cheryls Cl. SW6 . . . . . 4D 87
Cheseman St. SE26 . . 3D 121
Chesham Cl. SW1 . . . . 5B 20
Chesham Flats W1 . . . 4C 12
(off Brown Hart Gdns.)
Chesham M. SW1 . . . . 5B 20
Chesham Pl.
SW1 . . . . 5B 20 (4C 74)
(not continuous)
Chesham Rd. SW19 . . . 5F 115
Chesham St.
SW1 . . . . 5B 20 (4C 74)
Cheshire Cl. SE4 . . . . 5B 94
Cheshire St. EC4 . . . . 3C 16
(off Fleet St.)
Cheshire St. E2 . . . . . 3B 64
Chesholm Rd. N16 . . . . 5A 36
Cheshunt Ho. NW6 . . . 5D 45
(off Mortimer Cres.)

Cheshunt Rd. E7 . . . . 3D 55
Chesil Ct. E2 . . . . 1E 65
SW3 . . . . 2A 88
Chesilton Rd. SW6 . . . 4B 86
Chesley Gdns. E6 . . . . 1F 69
Chesney St. W9 . . . . . 3C 58
(off Shirland Rd.)
Chesney Ho. SE13 . . . 2F 109
(off Mercator Rd.)
Chesney St. SW11 . . . 4C 88
Chessington Ho.
SW8 . . . . 5F 89
Chessington Mans.
E10 . . . . 2C 38
E11 . . . . 2A 40
Chesson Rd. W14 . . . . 2B 86
Chester Cl.
SW1 . . . . 4D 21 (3D 75)
SW13 . . . . 1D 99
Chester Cl. Nth.
NW1 . . . . 1E 5 (2D 61)
Chester Cl. Sth.
NW1 . . . . 2E 5 (2D 61)
Chester Cotts. SW1 . . 5C 74
(off Bourne St.)
Chester Ct.
NW1 . . . . 1E 5 (2D 61)
SE5 . . . . 3F 91
(off Lomond Gro.)
SE8 . . . . 1F 93
Chester Cres. E8 . . . . 2B 50
Chesterfield Cl.
SE13 . . . . 5F 95
Chesterfield Gdns.
N4 . . . . 1D 35
SE10 . . . . 4F 95
W1 . . . . 1D 21 (2D 75)
Chesterfield Gro.
SE22 . . . . 3B 106
Chesterfield Hill
W1 . . . . 1D 21 (2D 75)
Chesterfield Ho. W1 . . 1C 20
(off Chesterfield Gdns.)
Chesterfield M. N4 . . . 1D 35
Chesterfield Rd. E10 . . 1E 39
Chesterfield St.
W1 . . . . 1D 21 (2D 75)
Chesterfield Wlk.
SE10 . . . . 4F 95
Chesterfield Way
SE15 . . . . 3E 93
Chesterford Gdns.
NW3 . . . . 1D 45
Chesterford Ho. SE18 . . 4F 97
(off Tellson Av.)
Chester Ga.
NW1 . . . . 2D 5 (2D 61)
Chester Ho.
SE8 . . . . 2B 94
SW1 . . . . 5D 75
(off Eccleston Pl.)
SW9 . . . . 3C 90
(off Brixton Rd.)
Chesterman Cl.
W4 . . . . 3A 84
(off Corney Reach Way)
Chester M.
SW1 . . . . 5D 21 (4D 75)
Chester Pl.
NW1 . . . . 1D 5 (2D 61)

Chester Rd. E7 . . . . 4F 55
  E11 . . . . 1D 41
  E16 . . . . 3A 68
  E17 . . . . 1F 37
  N19 . . . . 4D 33
  NW1 . . . . 2C 4 (2C 60)
  SW19 . . . . 5E 113
Chester Row SW1 . . . . . 5C 74
Chester Sq. SW1 . . . . . . 5C 74
Chester Sq. M.
  SW1 . . . . 5D 21
Chester St. E2 . . . . 3C 64
  SW1 . . . . . . 5C 20 (4C 74)
Chester Ter.
  NW1 . . . . 1D 5 (2D 61)
  (not continuous)
Chesterton Cl.
  SW18 . . . . 3C 100
Chesterton Rd. E13 . . . . 2C 68
  W10 . . . . 4F 57
Chesterton Sq. W8 . . . . . 5C 72
Chesterton Ter. E13 . . . . 2C 68
Chester Way SE11 . . . . . 5C 76
Chestnut All. SW6 . . . . . 2B 86
Chestnut Av. E7 . . . . 1D 55
  E12 . . . . 4F 41
Chestnut Cl. N16 . . . . . . 4F 35
  SE6 . . . . 5E 123
  SE14 . . . . 4B 94
  SW16 . . . . 4C 118
Chestnut Cl. SW6 . . . . . . 2B 86
  W8 . . . . 4D 73
  (off Abbots Wlk.)
Chestnut Dr. E11 . . . . . . 1C 40
Chestnut Gro.
  SW12 . . . . 5C 102
Chestnut Ho. W4 . . . . . . 5A 70
  (off Orchard, The)
Chestnut Pl. SE26 . . . . . 4B 120
Chestnut Rd. SE27 . . . . . 3D 119
Chestnuts, The N5 . . . . . 1E 49
  (off Highbury Grange)
Chettle Cl. SE1 . . . . 5B 26
Chettle Ct. N8 . . . . 1C 34
Chetwode Ho. NW8 . . . . . 3A 60
  (off Grendon St.)
Chetwode Rd.
  SW17 . . . . 3B 116
Chetwood Wlk. E6 . . . . . 4F 69
  (off Greenwich Cres.)
Chetwynd Rd. NW5 . . . . . 1D 47
Cheval Pl. SW7 . . . . 4A 74
Cheval St. E14 . . . . 4C 80
Chevening Rd. NW6 . . . . 1F 57
  SE10 . . . . 1B 96
Cheverell Ho. E2 . . . . . . 1C 64
  (off Pritchard's Rd.)
Cheverton Rd. N19 . . . . . 3F 33
Chevet St. E9 . . . . 2A 52
Chevington NW2 . . . . . . 3B 44
Cheviot Ct. SE14 . . . . . . 2E 93
  (off Avonley Rd.)
Cheviot Gdns.
  NW2 . . . . 4F 29
  SE27 . . . . 4D 119
Cheviot Ga. NW2 . . . . . . 4A 30
Cheviot Ho. E1 . . . . 5D 65
  (off Commercial Rd.)
Cheviot Rd. SE27 . . . . . . 5C 118
Chevron Cl. E16 . . . . 5C 68

Cheylesmore Ho.
  SW1 . . . . 1D 89
  (off Ebury Bri. Rd.)
Cheyne Cl. NW4 . . . . . . 1E 29
Cheyne Ct. SW3 . . . . . . 2B 88
Cheyne Gdns.
  SW3 . . . . 2A 88
Cheyne M. SW3 . . . . . . 2A 88
Cheyne Pl. SW3 . . . . . . 2B 88
Cheyne Row SW3 . . . . . 2A 88
Cheyne Wlk. NW4 . . . . . 1E 29
  SW3 . . . . 2A 88
  (not continuous)
  SW10 . . . . 3F 87
Chichele Rd. NW2 . . . . . 2F 43
Chicheley St.
  SE1 . . . . 3A 24 (3B 76)
Chichester Cl. SE3 . . . . . 3E 97
Chichester Ct. NW1 . . . . 4E 47
  (off Royal Coll. St.)
Chichester Ho. NW6 . . . . 1C 58
  SW9 . . . . 3C 90
  (off Brixton Rd.)
Chichester M. SE27 . . . . 4C 118
Chichester Rents
  WC2 . . . . 2B 16
Chichester Rd. E11 . . . . . 5A 40
  NW6 . . . . 1C 58
  W2 . . . . 4D 59
Chichester St. SW1 . . . . 1E 89
Chichester Way E14 . . . . 5F 81
Chicksand Ho. E1 . . . . . 4C 64
  (off Chicksand St.)
Chicksand St. E1 . . . . . . 4B 64
  (not continuous)
Chiddingstone SE13 . . . . 3E 109
Chiddingstone St.
  SW6 . . . . 5C 86
Chigwell Hill E1 . . . . 1D 79
Chilcombe Ho. SW15 . . . 5C 98
  (off Fontley Way)
Chilcot Cl. E14 . . . . 5D 67
Childebert Rd.
  SW17 . . . . 2D 117
Childeric Rd. SE14 . . . . . 3A 94
Childerley St. SW6 . . . . . 4A 86
Childers St. SE8 . . . . . . 2A 94
Child La. SE10 . . . . 4B 82
  (off School Bank Rd.)
Children's Discovery Cen.
  . . . . 4F 53
CHILD'S HILL 5C 30
Childs Hill Wlk. NW2 . . . . 5B 30
  (off Cricklewood La.)
Child's M. SW5 . . . . 5C 72
  (off Child's Pl.)
Child's Pl. SW5 . . . . 5C 72
Child's St. SW5 . . . . 5C 72
Child's Wlk. SW5 . . . . . . 5C 72
  (off Child's St.)
Chilham Ho.
  SE1 . . . . 5C 26 (4F 77)
  SE15 . . . . 2E 93
Chilham Rd. SE9 . . . . . . 4F 125
Chillianwallan Memorial
  . . . . 2C 88
Chillerton Rd.
  SW17 . . . . 5C 116
Chillingford Ho.
  SW17 . . . . 4E 115

Chillington Dr.
  SW11 . . . . 2F 101
Chillingworth Rd. N7 . . . . 2C 48
Chiltern Ct. NW1 . . . . . . 4A 4
  (off Baker St.)
  SE14 . . . . 3E 93
  (off Avonley Rd.)
Chiltern Gdns.
  NW2 . . . . 5F 29
Chiltern Rd. E3 . . . . 3C 66
Chiltern St.
  W1 . . . . 5B 4 (4C 60)
Chilthorne Cl. SE6 . . . . . 5B 108
Chilton Gro. SE8 . . . . . . 5F 79
Chiltonian Ind. Est.
  SE12 . . . . 4B 110
Chilton Rd. E2 . . . . 3B 64
Chilver St. SE10 . . . . . . 1B 96
Chilworth Ct. SW19 . . . . 1F 113
Chilworth M. W2 . . . . . . 5F 59
Chilworth St. W2 . . . . . . 5E 59
Chimney Ct. E1 . . . . 2D 79
  (off Brewhouse La.)
China Ct. E1 . . . . 2D 79
  (off Asher Way)
China Hall M. SE16 . . . . . 4E 79
China M. SW2 . . . . 5B 104
China Walk SE11 . . . . . . 5B 76
China Wharf SE1 . . . . . . 3C 78
Chinbrook Cres.
  SE12 . . . . 3D 125
Chinbrook Rd. SE12 . . . . 3D 125
Ching Ct. WC2 . . . . 3D 15
  (off Monmouth St.)
Chingley Cl.
  BR1: Brom 5A 124
Chinnock's Wharf
  E14 . . . . 1A 80
  (off Narrow St.)
Chipka St. E14 . . . . 3E 81
  (not continuous)
Chipley St. SE14 . . . . . . 2A 94
Chippendale Ho.
  SW1 . . . . 1D 89
  (off Churchill Gdns.)
Chippendale St. E5 . . . . . 5F 37
Chippenham Gdns.
  NW6 . . . . 2C 58
Chippenham M. W9 . . . . 3C 58
Chippenham Rd. W9 . . . . 3C 58
Chipperfield Ho.
  SW3 . . . . 1A 88
  (off Ixworth Pl.)
Chipstead Gdns.
  NW2 . . . . 4D 29
Chipstead St. SW6 . . . . . 4C 86
Chip St. SW4 . . . . 1F 103
Chisenhale Rd. E3 . . . . . 1A 66
Chisholm Ct. W6 . . . . . . 1C 84
Chisledon Wlk. E9 . . . . . 3B 52
  (off Osborne Rd.)
Chisley Rd. N15 . . . . 1A 36
Chiswell Sq. SE3 . . . . . . 5D 97
Chiswell St.
  EC1 . . . . 5B 10 (4E 63)
  SE5 . . . . 3F 91
  (off Edmund St.)
CHISWICK 1A 84
Chiswick Comn. Rd.
  W4 . . . . 5A 70

Chiswick Community
  Sports Hall 3A **84**
Chiswick High Rd.
  W4 . . . . 1A **84**
Chiswick House 2A **84**
Chiswick La. W4 . . . . 1A **84**
Chiswick La. Sth.
  W4 . . . . 2B **84**
Chiswick Mall W4 . . . 2B **84**
  W6 . . . . 2B **84**
Chiswick Sq. W4 . . . . 2A **84**
Chiswick Wharf W4 . . 2B **84**
Chitty St. W1 . . . . 5A **6** (4E **61**)
Chivalry Rd.
  SW11 . . . . 3A **102**
Chobham Gdns.
  SW19 . . . . 2F **113**
Chobham Rd. E15 . . . . 2F **53**
Chocolate Studios
  N1 . . . . 1B **10**
    (off Shepherdess Pl.)
Cholmeley Cres. N6 . . 2D **33**
Cholmeley Lodge N6 . 3D **33**
Cholmeley Pk. N6 . . . 3D **33**
Cholmley Gdns. NW6 . 2C **44**
Cholmondeley Av.
  NW10 . . . . 1C **56**
Choppin's Ct. E1 . . . . 2D **79**
Chopwell Cl. E15 . . . . 4F **53**
Choumert Gro. SE15 . . 5C **92**
Choumert M. SE15 . . . 5C **92**
Choumert Rd. SE15 . . 1B **106**
Choumert Sq. SE15 . . 5C **92**
Chow Sq. E8 . . . . 2B **50**
Chrisp Ho. SE10 . . . . . 2A **96**
    (off Maze Hill)
Chrisp St. E14 . . . . . . 4D **67**
    (not continuous)
Christchurch Av.
  NW6 . . . . 5F **43**
Christ Chu. Ct.
  NW10 . . . . 5A **42**
Christchurch Ct. EC4 . . 2E **17**
    (off Warwick La.)
Christchurch Hill
  NW3 . . . . 5F **31**
Christchurch Ho.
  SW2 . . . . 1B **118**
    (off Christchurch Rd.)
Christchurch Pas.
  NW3 . . . . 5E **31**
Christchurch Pl. SW8 . 5F **89**
Christchurch Rd. N8 . . 1A **34**
  SW2 . . . . 1B **118**
Christchurch Sq. E9 . . 5E **51**
Christchurch St. SW3 . 2B **88**
Christchurch Ter.
  SW3 . . . . 2B **88**
    (off Christchurch St.)
Christchurch Way
  SE10 . . . . 1A **96**
Christian Ct. SE16 . . . 2B **80**
Christian Pl. E1 . . . . . 5C **64**
    (off Burslem St.)
Christian St. E1 . . . . . 5C **64**
Christie Ct. N19 . . . . . 4A **34**
Christie Ho. SE10 . . . . 1B **96**
    (off Blackwall La.)
Christie Rd. E9 . . . . . . 3A **52**
Christina Sq. N4 . . . . . 3D **35**

Christina St.
  EC2 . . . . 3D **11** (3A **64**)
Christopher Cl. SE16 . . 3F **79**
Christopher Pl.
  NW1 . . . . 1C **6** (2F **61**)
Christophers M. W11 . . 2A **72**
Christopher St.
  EC2 . . . . 4C **10** (3F **63**)
Chryssell Rd. SW9 . . . 3C **90**
Chubworthy St. SE14 . 2A **94**
Chudleigh Rd. NW6 . . 4F **43**
  SE4 . . . . 3B **108**
Chudleigh St. E1 . . . . 5F **65**
Chulsa Rd. SE26 . . . . 5D **121**
Chumleigh Gdns.
  SE5 . . . . 2A **92**
    (off Chumleigh St.)
Chumleigh St. SE5 . . . 2A **92**
Church App. SE21 . . . 3F **119**
Church Av. E12 . . . . . . 5F **41**
  NW1 . . . . 3D **47**
Churchbury Rd. SE9 . . 5F **111**
Church Cloisters EC3 . 5D **19**
Church Cl. W8 . . . . . . 3D **73**
Church Ct. SE16 . . . . . 3B **80**
    (off Rotherhithe St.)
Church Cres. E9 . . . . . 4F **51**
Churchcroft Cl.
  SW12 . . . . 5C **102**
Churchdown
  BR1: Brom 4A **124**
CHURCH END 3A **42**
Church Entry EC4 . . . . 3E **17**
Churchfield Mans.
  SW6 . . . . 5B **86**
    (off New Kings Rd.)
Churchfields SE10 . . . 2E **95**
Church Gth. N19 . . . . . 4F **33**
    (off St John's Gro.)
Church Ga. SW6 . . . . . 1A **100**
Church Grn. SW9 . . . . 4C **90**
Church Gro. SE13 . . . . 3D **109**
Church Hill SW19 . . . . 5B **114**
Church Ho. EC1 . . . . . . 3E **9**
    (off Compton St.)
  SW1 . . . . 5C **22**
    (off Gt. Smith St.)
Churchill Ct. N4 . . . . . 2C **34**
Churchill Gdns. SW1 . 1E **89**
Churchill Gdns. Rd.
  SW1 . . . . 1D **89**
Churchill Mus.
  (Cabinet War Rooms)
  . . . . 3C **22** (3F **75**)
Churchill Pl. E14 . . . . 2D **81**
Churchill Rd. E16 . . . . 5E **69**
  NW2 . . . . 3D **43**
  NW5 . . . . 1D **47**
Churchill Wlk. E9 . . . . 2E **51**
Church La. E11 . . . . . . 3A **40**
  SW17 . . . . 5B **116**
Churchley Rd.
  SE26 . . . . 4D **121**
Church Mead SE5 . . . . 3E **91**
    (off Camberwell Rd.)
Churchmead Rd.
  NW10 . . . . 3C **42**
Church Mt. N2 . . . . . . 1F **31**
Church Pas. EC2 . . . . . 2A **18**
    (off Guildhall Yd.)

Church Path E11 . . . . . 1C **40**
  N5 . . . . 2D **49**
  NW10 . . . . 4A **42**
  SW14 . . . . 1A **98**
    (not continuous)
Church Pl.
  SW1 . . . . 5A **14** (1E **75**)
Church Ri. SE23 . . . . . 2F **121**
Church Rd. E10 . . . . . . 3C **38**
  E12 . . . . 2F **55**
  N1 . . . . 3E **49**
  N6 . . . . 1C **32**
  NW10 . . . . 4A **42**
  SW13 . . . . 5B **84**
  SW19 . . . . 5A **114**
Church Rd. Almshouses
  E10 . . . . 4D **39**
    (off Church Rd.)
Church Rd. Ind. Est.
  E10 . . . . 3C **38**
Church Row NW3 . . . . 1E **45**
  SW6 . . . . 3D **87**
    (off Park Rd.)
Church St. E15 . . . . . . 5A **54**
  NW8 . . . . 4F **59**
  W2 . . . . 4F **59**
  W4 . . . . 2B **84**
Church St. Est. NW8 . . 3F **59**
Church St. Nth. E15 . . 5A **54**
Church St. Pas. E15 . . 5A **54**
    (off Church St.)
Church Ter. SE13 . . . . 1A **110**
Church Va. SE23 . . . . . 2F **121**
Church Wlk. N6 . . . . . 5C **32**
  N16 . . . . 5F **35**
    (not continuous)
  NW2 . . . . 5B **30**
  SW13 . . . . 4C **84**
  SW15 . . . . 3D **99**
Churchward Ho. W14 . 1B **86**
    (off Ivatt Pl.)
Churchway
  NW1 . . . . 1C **6** (2F **61**)
    (not continuous)
Churchwell Path E9 . . 2E **51**
Churchyard Pas. SE5 . 5F **91**
Churchyard Row
  SE11 . . . . 5D **77**
Church Yd. Wlk. W2 . . 4F **59**
    (off St Mary's Sq.)
Churnfield N4 . . . . 4C **34**
Churston Av. E13 . . . . 5D **55**
Churston Cl. SW2 . . . 1C **118**
Churton Pl. SW1 . . . . 5E **75**
Churton St. SW1 . . . . 5E **75**
Chusan Pl. E14 . . . . . . 5B **66**
Chute Ho. SW9 . . . . . . 5C **90**
    (off Stockwell Pk. Rd.)
Cibber Rd. SE23 . . . . . 2F **121**
Cicada Rd. SW18 . . . . 4E **101**
Cicely Ho. NW8 . . . . . 1F **59**
    (off Cochrane St.)
Cicely Rd. SE15 . . . . . 4C **92**
Cinderella Path
  NW11 . . . . 3D **31**
Cinderford Way
  BR1: Brom 4A **124**
Cine Lumiere 5F **73**
    (off Queensberry Pl.)

Cineworld Cinema 3D 101
Cinnabar Wharf Central
E1 . . . . 2C 78
(off Wapping High St.)
Cinnabar Wharf E.
E1 . . . . 2C 78
(off Wapping High St.)
Cinnabar Wharf W.
E1 . . . . 2C 78
(off Wapping High St.)
Cinnamon Cl. SE15 . . . . . 3B 92
Cinnamon Row
SW11 . . . . 1E 101
Cinnamon St. E1 . . . . 2D 79
Cinnamon Wharf SE1 . . 3B 78
(off Shad Thames)
Circa Apartments
NW1 . . . . 4C 46
Circle, The NW2 . . . . . 5A 28
SE1 . . . . 3F 27
(off Queen Elizabeth St.)
Circus Lodge NW8 . . . . 2F 59
(off Circus Rd.)
Circus M. W1 . . . . 4B 60
(off Enford St.)
Circus Pl.
EC2. . . . . . . 1C 18 (4F 63)
Circus Rd. NW8 . . . . . . 2F 59
Circus St. SE10. . . . . . . 3E 95
Cirencester St. W2. . . . 4D 59
Cissbury Ho. SE26 . . . 3C 120
Cissbury Rd. N15 . . . . 1F 35
Citadel Pl. SE11. . . . . . 1B 90
Citizen Ho. N7 . . . . 1C 48
Citizen Rd. N7 . . . . 1C 48
Citrus Ho. SE8 . . . . 1B 94
(off Alverton St.)
City Bus. Cen. SE16 . . . 4E 79
City Central Est. EC1 . . . 2F 9
(off Seward St.)
City Cross Bus. Cen.
SE10. . . . . 5A 82
City Gdn. Row
N1 . . . . 1E 9 (1D 63)
City Harbour E14 . . . . 4D 81
(off Selsdon Way)
City Hgts. SE1. . . . . . . 2E 27
(off Weavers La.)
CITY OF LONDON
. . . . 3B 18 (5F 63)
City of London Almshouses
SW9 . . . . 2B 104
City of London Crematorium
E12 . . . . 5F 41
City of London Point
N7 . . . . 3F 47
(off York Way)
City of Westminster College
. . . . 4B 14 (1E 75)
City Pav. EC1 . . . . 5D 9
(off Britton St.)
City Rd. EC1 . . 1D 9 (1D 63)
City Twr. EC2 . . . . 1B 18
(off Basinghall St.)
City University
. . . . 2D 9 (2D 63)
City University Saddlers
Sports Cen.
. . . . 3E 9 (3D 63)

Cityview SE7. . . . . 2E 97
City Vw. Ct. SE22 . . . 5C 106
City Wlk. Apartments
EC1 . . . . 2F 9
(off Seward St.)
Clabon M. SW1 . . . . . . 4B 74
Clack St. SE16 . . . . 3E 79
Clacton Rd. E6 . . . . 2F 69
E17 . . . . 1A 38
Claire Cl. NW2 . . . . 3A 44
Claire Pl. E14. . . . . 4C 80
Clairville Rd.
SW16 . . . . 5D 117
Clairville Point
SE23 . . . . 3F 121
(off Dacres Rd.)
Clancarty Rd. SW6. . . . 5C 86
Clandeboye Ho. E15 . . 5B 54
(off John St.)
Clandon Ho. SE1 . . . . . 4E 25
(off Webber St.)
Clandon St. SE8 . . . . . 5C 94
Clanricarde Gdns.
W2 . . . . 1C 72
CLAPHAM 2E 103
CLAPHAM COMMON
. . . . 2F 103
Clapham Comn. Nth. Side
SW4 . . . . 2B 102
Clapham Comn. Sth. Side
SW4 . . . . 4D 103
Clapham Comn. W. Side
SW4 . . . . 2B 102
(not continuous)
Clapham Cres. SW4 . . . 2F 103
Clapham High St.
SW4 . . . . 2F 103
CLAPHAM JUNCTION
. . . . 1A 102
Clapham Junc. App.
SW11 . . . . 1A 102
Clapham Leisure Cen.
. . . . 1F 103
Clapham Mnr. Ct.
SW4 . . . . 1E 103
Clapham Mnr. St.
SW4 . . . . 1E 103
CLAPHAM PARK 5F 103
Clapham Pk. Est.
SW4 . . . . 4F 103
Clapham Pk. Rd.
SW4 . . . . 2E 103
Clapham Pk. Ter.
SW2 . . . . 3A 104
(off Kings Av.)
Clapham Picturehouse
. . . . 2E 103
Clapham Rd. SW9 . . . 1A 104
Clapham Rd. Est.
SW4 . . . . 1A 104
(not continuous)
Clapton Comn. E5 . . . . 2B 36
CLAPTON PARK 1F 51
Clapton Pk. Est. E5. . . . 1F 51
Clapton Pas. E5 . . . . . . 2E 51
Clapton Sq. E5 . . . . 2E 51
Clapton Ter. N16 . . . . . 3C 36
Clapton Way E5. . . . . . 1C 50
Clara Grant Ho. E14. . . 4C 80
(off Mellish St.)

Clara Nehab Ho.
NW11 . . . . 1B 30
(off Leeside Cres.)
Clare Ct. WC1. . . . . 2E 7
(off Judd St.)
Claredale Ho. E2 . . . . . 1D 65
(off Claredale St.)
Claredale St. E2. . . . . . 1C 64
Clare Gdns. E7. . . . . . . 1C 54
W11 . . . . 5A 58
Clare La. N1 . . . . 4E 49
Clare Lawn Av.
SW14 . . . . 3A 98
Clare Mkt.
WC2. . . . . . 3A 16 (5B 62)
Clare M. SW6 . . . . 3D 87
Claremont Cl.
N1 . . . . 1C 8 (1C 62)
SW2 . . . . 1A 118
Claremont Gro.
W4 . . . . 3A 84
Claremont Rd. E7 . . . . 2D 55
E11 . . . . 5F 39
N6 . . . . 2E 33
NW2 . . . . 2F 29
W9 . . . . 1A 58
Claremont Sq.
N1 . . . . 1B 8 (1C 62)
Claremont St. SE10. . . 2D 95
Claremont Vs. SE5 . . . 3F 91
(off Southampton Way)
Claremont Way NW2 . . 3E 29
(not continuous)
Claremont Way Ind. Est.
NW2 . . . . 3E 29
Clarence Av. SW4. . . . 5F 103
Clarence Ct. W6. . . . . . 5D 71
(off Cambridge Gro.)
Clarence Cres. SW4 . . . 4F 103
Clarence Gdns.
NW1. . . . . . . 2E 5 (2D 61)
Clarence Ga. Gdns.
NW1 . . . . 4A 4
(off Glentworth St.)
Clarence House 3A 22
Clarence La. SW15 . . . 4A 98
Clarence M. E5 . . . . . . 2D 51
SE16 . . . . 2E 79
SW12 . . . . 5D 103
Clarence Pl. E5 . . . . . . 2D 51
Clarence Rd. E5. . . . . . 1D 51
E12 . . . . 1E 55
E16 . . . . 3A 68
NW6 . . . . 4B 44
SE8 . . . . 2D 95
SE9 . . . . 2F 125
SW19 . . . . 5D 115
Clarence Ter.
NW1. . . . . . . 3A 4 (3B 60)
Clarence Wlk. SW4 . . . 5A 90
Clarence Way NW1 . . . 4D 47
W2 . . . . 1A 74
Clarendon Cl. E9 . . . . . 4E 51
W2 . . . . 1A 74
Clarendon Ct. NW2 . . . 4E 43
Clarendon Cross
W11 . . . . 1A 72
Clarendon Dr. SW15 . . 2E 99
Clarendon Flats W1 . . 3C 12
(off Balderton St.)
Clarendon Gdns. W9 . . . 3E 59

Clarendon Gro.
NW1 . . . . . . 1B 6 (2F 61)
Clarendon Ho. NW1 . . . . . 1A 6
(off Werrington St.)
Clarendon M. W2 . . . . . . 1A 74
Clarendon Pl. W2 . . . . . . 1A 74
Clarendon Ri. SE13 . . 2E 109
Clarendon Rd. E11 . . . . 3F 39
E17 . . . . 1D 39
W11 . . . . 1A 72
Clarendon St. SW1 . . . 1D 89
Clarendon Ter. W9 . . . 3E 59
Clarendon Wlk. W11 . . 5A 58
Clarens St. SE6 . . . . 2B 122
Clare Pl. SW15. . . . . . 5B 98
Clare Point NW2 . . . . . 3F 29
(off Whitefield Av.)
Clare Rd. E11 . . . . . . 1F 39
NW10 . . . . 4C 42
SE14 . . . . 4B 94
Clare St. E2 . . . . . . 1D 65
Clareville Gro. SW7 . . 5E 73
Clareville Gro. M.
SW7 . . . . 5E 73
Clareville St. SW7 . . . 5E 73
Clarewood Ct. W1 . . . . 4B 60
(off Seymour Pl.)
Clarewood Wlk.
SW9 . . . . 2C 104
Clarges M.
W1 . . . . . . 1D 21 (2D 75)
Clarges St.
W1 . . . . . . 1E 21 (2D 75)
Claribel Rd. SW9 . . . . 5D 91
Claridge Ct. SW6 . . . . 5B 86
Clarion Ho. E3 . . . . . . 1A 66
(off Roman Rd.)
SW1 . . . . 1E 89
(off Moreton Pl.)
W1 . . . . 3B 14
(off St Anne's Ct.)
Clarissa Ho. E14 . . . . 5D 67
(off Cordela St.)
Clarissa St. E8 . . . . . 5B 50
Clarke Path N16 . . . . 3C 36
Clarke's M.
W1 . . . . 5C 4 (4C 60)
Clark Ho. SW10 . . . . . 3E 87
(off Coleridge Gdns.)
Clarkson Rd. E16 . . . . 5B 68
Clarkson Row NW1 . . . 1E 61
(off Mornington Ter.)
Clarkson St. E2 . . . . . 2D 65
Clark's Pl.
EC2 . . . . 2D 19 (5A 64)
Clark St. E1 . . . . 4D 65
Classic Mans. E9 . . . . 4D 51
(off Wells St.)
Claude Rd. E10. . . . . . 4E 39
E13. . . . . 5D 55
SE15 . . . . 5D 93
Claude St. E14 . . . . . 5C 80
Claudia Jones Way
SW2 . . . . 4A 104
Claudia Pl. SW19. . . . 1A 114
Claughton Rd. E13 . . . 1E 69
Clavell St. SE10 . . . . 2E 95
Claverdale Rd.
SW2 . . . . 5B 104
Clavering Av. SW13. . . 2D 85

Clavering Ho. SE13 . . . 2F 109
(off Blessington Rd.)
Clavering Rd. E12 . . . . 3F 41
Claverton St. SW1 . . . 1E 89
Clave St. E1 . . . . 2E 79
Claxton Gro. W6 . . . . . 1F 85
Claxton Path SE4 . . . . 2F 107
(off Coston Wlk.)
Claybank Gro.
SE13 . . . . 1D 109
Claybridge Rd.
SE12 . . . . 4E 125
Claybrook Rd. W6 . . . . 2F 85
Claydon SE17 . . . . . . 5E 77
(off Deacon Way)
Clayhill Cres. SE9 . . . 4F 125
Claylands Pl. SW8 . . . 3C 90
Claylands Rd. SW8 . . . 2B 90
Claypole Ct. E17 . . . . . 1C 38
(off Yunus Khan Cl.)
Claypole Rd. E15. . . . . 1E 67
Clays La. E15. . . . . . . 2D 53
Clays La. Cl. E15. . . . . 2D 53
Clay St. W1 . . . 1A 12 (4B 60)
Clayton Cres. N1 . . . . 5A 48
Clayton Dr. SE8 . . . . . 1A 94
Clayton Ho. E9 . . . . . . 4E 51
(off Frampton Pk. Rd.)
SW13 . . . . 3E 85
(off Trinity Chu. Rd.)
Clayton M. SE10 . . . . . 4F 95
Clayton Rd. SE15 . . . . 4C 92
Clayton St. SE11 . . . . 2C 90
Clearbrook Way E1 . . . 5E 65
Clearwater Ter. W11 . . 3A 72
(off Lorne Gdns.)
Clearwell Dr. W9 . . . . 3D 59
Cleaver Ho. NW3 . . . . 4B 46
(off Adelaide Rd.)
Cleaver Sq. SE11 . . . . 1C 90
Cleaver St. SE11 . . . . 1C 90
Cleeve Hill SE23 . . . . 1D 121
Cleeve Way SW15 . . . 5B 98
Cleeve Workshops E2 . . 2E 11
(off Boundary Rd.)
Clegg Ho. SE3 . . . . . . 2D 111
SE16. . . . . 4E 79
(off Moodkee St.)
Clegg St. E1 . . . . 2D 79
E13. . . . . 1D 69
Cleland Ho. E2 . . . . . . 1E 65
(off Sewardstone Rd.)
Clematis St. W12. . . . . 1C 70
Clem Attlee Ct. SW6 . . 2B 86
Clem Attlee Pde.
SW6 . . . . 2B 86
(off Nth. End Rd.)
Clemence St. E14 . . . . 4B 66
Clement Av. SW4 . . . . 2F 103
Clement Cl. NW6 . . . . 4E 43
Clement Ho. SE8 . . . . 5A 80
W10 . . . . 4E 57
(off Dalgarno Gdns.)
Clementina Rd. E10. . . 3B 38
Clement Rd. SW19 . . . 5A 114
Clement's Av. E16 . . . . 1C 82
Clement's Inn
WC2 . . . . . . 3A 16 (5B 62)
Clement's Inn Pas.
WC2 . . . . 3A 16

Clements La.
EC4 . . . . 4C 18 (1F 77)
Clement's Rd. SE16. . . 4C 78
Clemson Ho. E8 . . . . . 5B 50
Clennam St.
SE1 . . . . 3A 26 (3E 77)
Clenston M.
W1 . . . . . . 2A 12 (5B 60)
Cleopatra's Needle
. . . . 5F 15 (2A 76)
Clephane Rd. N1 . . . . 3E 49
Clephane Rd. Nth.
N1 . . . . 3E 49
Clephane Rd. Sth.
N1 . . . . 3F 49
Clere Pl. EC2. . . 3C 10 (3F 63)
Clere St. EC2. . . 3C 10 (3F 63)
CLERKENWELL
. . . . 3B 8 (3C 62)
Clerkenwell Cl.
EC1 . . . . 3C 8 (3C 62)
(not continuous)
Clerkenwell Grn.
EC1 . . . . 4C 8 (3C 62)
Clerkenwell Rd.
EC1 . . . . 4B 8 (3C 62)
Clermont Rd. E9. . . . . 5E 51
Clevedon Cl. N16. . . . . 5B 36
Clevedon Mans.
NW5 . . . . 1C 46
Clevedon Pas. N16 . . . 4B 36
Cleve Ho. NW6 . . . . . 4D 45
Cleveland Av. W4. . . . . 5B 70
Cleveland Gdns. N4 . . . 1E 35
NW2 . . . . 4F 29
SW13 . . . . 5B 84
W2 . . . . 5E 59
Cleveland Gro. E1 . . . . 3E 65
Cleveland Mans.
SW9 . . . . 3C 90
(off Mowll St.)
W9 . . . . 3C 58
Cleveland M.
W1 . . . . 5F 5 (4E 61)
Cleveland Pl.
SW1 . . . . . . 1A 22 (2E 75)
Cleveland Rd. N1 . . . . 4F 49
SW13 . . . . 5B 84
Cleveland Row
SW1 . . . . . . 2F 21 (2E 75)
Cleveland Sq. W2 . . . . 5E 59
Cleveland St.
W1 . . . . 4E 5 (3D 61)
Cleveland Ter. W2 . . . . 5E 59
Cleveland Way E1 . . . . 3E 65
Cleveley Cl. SE7 . . . . . 5F 83
Cleveleys Rd. E5 . . . . 5D 37
Cleverly Est.
W12 . . . . 2C 70
Cleve Rd. NW6 . . . . . 4D 45
Cleves Ho. E16. . . . . . 2C 82
(off Southey M.)
Cleves Rd. E6. . . . . . . 5F 55
Clewer Ct. E10 . . . . . . 3C 38
(off Leyton Grange Est.)
Cley Ho. SE4 . . . . 2F 107
Clichy Est. E1 . . . . . . 4E 65
Clichy Ho. E1 . . . . 4E 65
(off Stepney Way)
Clifden Rd. E5 . . . . . . 2E 51

Cliffe Ho. *SE10* *1B* **96**
(off Blackwall La.)
Clifford Ct. *W2* *4D* **59**
(off Westbourne Pk. Vs.)
Clifford Dr. SW9 . . . . 2D **105**
Clifford Gdns. NW10 . . 1E **57**
Clifford Haigh Ho.
SW6 . . . . 3F **85**
Clifford Ho.
BR3: Beck. *5D* **123**
(off Calverley Cl.)
W14 . . . . *5B* **72**
(off Edith Vs.)
Clifford Rd. E16 . . . . 3B **68**
N1 . . . . 5A **50**
Clifford's Inn Pas.
EC4 . . . . 3B **16** (5C **62**)
Clifford St.
W1 . . . . 5F **13** (1E **75**)
Clifford Way NW10 . . . . 1B **42**
Cliff Rd. NW1 . . . . 3F **47**
Cliffsend Ho. *SW9* *4C* **90**
(off Cowley Rd.)
Cliff Ter. SE8 . . . . 5C **94**
Cliffview Rd. SE13 . . . . 1C **108**
Cliff Vs. NW1 . . . . 3F **47**
Cliff Wlk. E16 . . . . 4B **68**
Clifton Av. W12 . . . . 2B **70**
Clifton Ct. N4 . . . . 4C **34**
NW8 . . . . *3F* **59**
(off Maida Va.)
SE15 . . . . 3D **93**
Clifton Cres. SE15 . . . . 3D **93**
Clifton Est. SE15 . . . . . . 4D **93**
Clifton Gdns. N15 . . . . . 1B **36**
NW11 . . . . 1B **30**
W4 . . . . 5A **70**
(not continuous)
W9 . . . . 3E **59**
Clifton Ga. SW10 . . . . . . 2E **87**
Clifton Gro. E8 . . . . 3C **50**
Clifton Hill NW6 . . . . 1D **59**
NW8 . . . . 1D **59**
Clifton Ho. *E2* *3F* **11**
(off Club Row)
E11 . . . . 4A **40**
W2 . . . . 5F **59**
Clifton Ri. SE14 . . . . 3A **94**
(not continuous)
Clifton Rd. E7 . . . . 3F **55**
E16 . . . . 4A **68**
N8 . . . . 1F **33**
NW10 . . . . 1C **56**
SW19 . . . . 5F **113**
W9 . . . . 3E **59**
Clifton St.
EC2 . . . . 4D **11** (3A **64**)
Clifton Ter. N4 . . . . 4C **34**
Clifton Vs. W9 . . . . 4E **59**
Cliftonville Ct. SE12 . . 1C **124**
Clifton Wlk. *W6* *5D* **71**
(off King St.)
Clifton Way SE15 . . . . . 3D **93**
Climsland Ho.
SE1 . . . . 1C **24** (2C **76**)
Clinch Ct. *E16* *4C* **68**
(off Plymouth Rd.)
Clinger Ct. *N1* *5A* **50**
(off Hobbs Pl. Est.)

Clink Exhibition, The
. . . . 1B **26**
Clink St. SE1 . . 1B **26** (2F **77**)
Clink Wharf
SE1 . . . . *1B* **26**
(off Clink St.)
Clinton Rd. E3 . . . . 2A **66**
E7 . . . . 1C **54**
Clipper Cl. SE16 . . . . 3F **79**
Clipper Ho. *E14* *1E* **95**
(off Manchester Rd.)
Clipper Way SE13 . . . . . 2E **109**
Clipstone M.
W1 . . . . 5F **5** (4E **61**)
Clipstone St.
W1 . . . . 5E **5** (4D **61**)
Clissold Ct. N4 . . . . 4E **35**
Clissold Cres. N16 . . . . . 5F **35**
Clissold Leisure Cen.
. . . . 5F **35**
Clissold Rd. N16 . . . . 5F **35**
Clitheroe Rd. SW9 . . . . . 5A **90**
Clitherow Ho.
NW2 . . . . 3E **29**
Clitterhouse Cres.
NW2 . . . . 3E **29**
Clitterhouse Rd.
NW2 . . . . 3E **29**
Clive Ct. W9 . . . . 3E **59**
Cliveden Ho. *E16* *2C* **82**
(off Fitzwilliam M.)
Cliveden Pl. SW1 . . . . . . 5C **74**
Clive Ho. *SE10* *2E* **95**
(off Haddo St.)
Clive Lloyd Ho. *N15* 1E **35**
(off Woodlands Pk. Rd.)
Clive Pas. SE21 . . . . 3F **119**
Clive Rd. SE21 . . . . 3F **119**
SW19 . . . . 5A **116**
Cloak La.
EC4 . . . . 4A **18** (1E **77**)
Clochar Ct. NW10 . . . . . 5B **42**
Clock Ho. E3 . . . . 2E **67**
Clockhouse, The
SW19 . . . . 3E **113**
Clockhouse Cl.
SW19 . . . . 2E **113**
Clock Ho. Pde. E11 . . . . 1D **41**
Clockhouse Pl.
SW15 . . . . 4A **100**
Clock Mus., The 2A **18**
Clock Pl. *SE1* *5D* **77**
(off Newington Butts)
Clock Twr. M. N1 . . . . 5E **49**
Clock Twr. Pl. N7 . . . . . . 3A **48**
Cloister Ho. NW2 . . . . . . 5B **30**
Cloisters, The 5D **23**
Cloisters, The E1 . . . . . . 4F **11**
SW9 . . . . 4C **90**
Cloisters Bus. Cen.
SW8 . . . . *3D* **89**
(off Battersea Pk. Rd.)
Clonbrock Rd. N16 . . . . 1A **50**
Cloncurry St. SW6 . . . . . 5F **85**
Clonmel Rd. SW6 . . . . . . 3B **86**
Clonmore St. SW18 . . 1B **114**
Clorane Gdns. NW3 . . . 5C **30**
Close, The SE3 . . . . 5F **95**
Cloth Ct. EC1 . . . . 1E **17**
Cloth Fair
EC1 . . . . 1E **17** (4D **63**)

Clothier St.
E1 . . . . 2E **19** (5A **64**)
Cloth St. EC1 . . . . 5F **9** (4E **63**)
Cloudesdale Rd.
SW17 . . . . 2D **117**
Cloudesley Pl. N1 . . . . . 5C **48**
Cloudesley Rd. N1 . . . . 5C **48**
(not continuous)
Cloudesley Sq. N1 . . . . 5C **48**
Cloudesley St. N1 . . . . . 5C **48**
Clova Rd. E7 . . . . 3B **54**
Clove Cres. E14 . . . . 1E **81**
Clove Hitch Quay
SW11 . . . . 1E **101**
Clovelly Ct. NW2 . . . . . . 2E **43**
Clovelly Ho. *W2* *5E* **59**
(off Hallfield Est.)
Clovelly Way E1 . . . . 5E **65**
Clover Cl. E11 . . . . 4F **39**
Clover M. SW3 . . . . 2B **88**
Clove St. E13 . . . . 3C **68**
Clowders Rd. SE6 . . . . . 3B **122**
Cloysters Grn. E1 . . . . . . 2C **78**
Club Row E1 . . 3F **11** (3B **64**)
E2 . . . . 3F **11** (3B **64**)
Clunbury St. N1 . . . . 1F **63**
Cluny Est.
SE1 . . . . 5D **27** (4A **78**)
Cluny M. SW5 . . . . 5C **72**
Cluny Pl.
SE1 . . . . 5D **27** (4A **78**)
Cluse Ct. *N1* *1E* **63**
(off St Peters St.,
not continuous)
Clutton St. E14 . . . . 4D **67**
Clyde Ct. *NW1* *1F* **61**
(off Hampden Cl.)
Clyde Flats SW6 . . . . 3B **86**
(off Rhylston Rd.)
Clyde Pl. E10 . . . . 2D **39**
Clydesdale Ho. *W11* . . . *5B* **58**
(off Clydesdale Rd.)
Clydesdale Rd. W11 . . . 5B **58**
Clyde St. SE8 . . . . 2B **94**
Clyde Ter. SE23 . . . . 2E **121**
Clyde Va. SE23 . . . . 2E **121**
Clyde Wharf E16 . . . . 2C **82**
Clynes Ho. *E2* *2F* **65**
(off Knottisford St.)
Clyston St. SW8 . . . . 5E **89**
Coach & Horses Yd.
W1 . . . . 4E **13** (1E **75**)
Coach Ho. La. N5 . . . . . . 1D **49**
SW19 . . . . 4F **113**
Coach Ho. M. SE23 . . . 4F **107**
Coach Ho. Yd. *NW3* . . . *1E* **45**
(off Heath St.)
SW18 . . . . 2D **101**
Coachmaker M.
SW4 . . . . *1A* **104**
(off Fenwick Pl.)
Coach Yd. M. N19 . . . . . . 3A **34**
Coaldale Wlk. SE21 . . . 5E **105**
Coalecroft Rd. SW15 . . 2E **99**
Coalport Ho. *SE11* *5C* **76**
(off Walnut Tree Wlk.)
Coates Av. SW18 . . . . . 4A **102**
Coate St. E2 . . . . 1C **64**
Cobalt Sq. *SW8* *2B* **90**
(off Sth. Lambeth Rd.)

Cobbetts Av. IG4: Ilf 1F **41**
Cobbett St. SW8 . . . . . . 3B **90**
Cobble La. N1 . . . . 4D **49**
Cobble M. N5 . . . . 5E **35**
Cobbold Ct. *SW1* *5F 75*
(off Elverton St.)
Cobbold Ind. Est.
NW10 . . . . 3B **42**
Cobbold M. W12 . . . . . . 3B **70**
Cobbold Rd. E11 . . . . . . 5B **40**
NW10 . . . . 3B **42**
W12 . . . . 3A **70**
Cobb's Ct. EC4 . . . . 3E **17**
Cobb's Hall *W6* *2F 85*
(off Fulham Pal. Rd.)
Cobbsthorpe Vs.
SE26 . . . . 4F **121**
Cobb St. E1 . . . . 1F **19** (4B **64**)
Cobden Ho. *E2* *2C 64*
(off Nelson Gdns.)
NW1 . . . . *1E 61*
(off Arlington Rd.)
Cobden M. SE26 . . . . . . 5D **121**
Cobden Rd. E11 . . . . 5A **40**
Cobham Cl. SW11 . . . . . 4A **102**
Cobham M. NW1 . . . . . . 4F **47**
Cobland Rd.
SE12 . . . . 4E **125**
Coborn Rd. E3 . . . . 1B **66**
Coborn St. E3 . . . . 2B **66**
Cobourg Rd. SE5 . . . . . . 2B **92**
Cobourg St.
NW1 . . . . 2A **6** (2E **61**)
Coburg Cl. SW1 . . . . 5E **75**
Coburg Cres. SW2 . . . . 1B **118**
Coburg Dwellings *E1* . . . *5E 65*
(off Hardinge St.)
Cochrane Cl. *NW8* *1F 59*
(off Cochrane St.)
Cochrane Cl. EC10 . . . . . 3C **38**
(off Leyton Grange Est.)
Cochrane Ho. *E14* *3C 80*
(off Admirals Way)
Cochrane M. NW8 . . . . . 1F **59**
Cochrane St. NW8 . . . . . 1F **59**
Cochrane Theatre *1E 15*
(off Southampton Row)
Cockburn Ho. *SW1* *1F 89*
(off Aylesford St.)
Cockerell Rd. E17 . . . . . 2A **38**
Cock Hill E1 . . . . 1E **19** (4A **64**)
Cock La.
EC1 . . . . 1D **17** (4D **63**)
Cockpit Steps SW1 . . . . 4B **22**
Cockpit Theatre *3A 60*
(off Gateforth St.)
Cockpit Yd.
WC1 . . . . 5A **8** (4B **62**)
Cockspur Ct.
SW1 . . . . 1C **22** (2F **75**)
Cockspur St.
SW1 . . . . 1C **22** (2F **75**)
Coda Cen., The SW6 . . . 3A **86**
Code St. E1 . . . . 3B **64**
Codicote Ho. *SE8* *5F 79*
(off Chilton Gro.)
Codicote Ter. N4 . . . . . . 4E **35**
Codling Cl. E1 . . . . 2C **78**
Codrington Ct. E1 . . . . . 3D **65**
SE16 . . . . 1A **80**

Codrington Hill
SE23 . . . . 5A **108**
Codrington M. W11 . . . . 5A **58**
Cody Rd. E16 . . . . 3F **67**
Coffey St. SE8 . . . . 3C **94**
Coin St. SE1 . . . 1B **24** (2C **76**)
(not continuous)
Coity Rd. NW5 . . . . 3C **46**
Cokers La. SE21 . . . . . . 1F **119**
Coke St. E1 . . . . 5C **64**
Colas M. NW6 . . . . 5C **44**
Colbeck M. SW7 . . . . . . 5D **73**
Colberg Pl. N16 . . . . 2B **36**
Colborne Ho. *E14* *1C 80*
(off E. India Dock Rd.)
Colby M. SE19 . . . . 5A **120**
Colby Rd. SE19 . . . . 5A **120**
Colchester Rd. E10 . . . . 2E **39**
E17 . . . . 1C **38**
Colchester St. E1 . . . . . 5B **64**
Coldbath Sq.
EC1 . . . . 3B **8** (3C **62**)
Coldbath St. SE13 . . . . . 4D **95**
Cold Blow La. SE14 . . . . 3F **93**
(not continuous)
Coldharbour E14 . . . . . . 3E **81**
Coldharbour La.
SE5 . . . . 1E **105**
SW9 . . . . 2C **104**
Coldharbour Pl. SE5 . . . 5E **91**
Coldstream Gdns.
SW18 . . . . 4B **100**
Colebeck M. N1 . . . . 3D **49**
Colebert Av. E1 . . . . 3E **65**
Colebert Ho. *E1* *3E 65*
(off Colebert Av.)
Colebrook Cl. SW15 . . . 5F **99**
Colebrook Ct. *SW3* *5A 74*
(off Makins St.)
Colebrooke Dr. E11 . . . . 2E **41**
Colebrooke Pl. N1 . . . . . 5D **49**
Colebrooke Row N1 . . . . 1D **63**
Colebrook Ho. *E14* *5D 67*
(off Ellesmere St.)
Coleby Path SE5 . . . . . . 3F **91**
Colechurch Ho. *SE1* *1C 92*
(off Avondale Sq.)
Coleford Rd. SW18 . . . . 3E **101**
Colegrave Rd. E15 . . . . . 2F **53**
Colegrove Rd. SE15 . . . 2B **92**
Coleherne Ct. SW5 . . . . 1D **87**
Coleherne Mans.
SW5 . . . . *1D 87*
(off Old Brompton Rd.)
Coleherne M. SW10 . . . . 1D **87**
Coleherne Rd. SW10 . . . 1D **87**
Colehill Gdns. SW6 . . . . 5A **86**
Colehill La. SW6 . . . . . . 4A **86**
Cole Ho. *SE1* *4B 24*
(off Baylis Rd.)
Coleman Ct. SW18 . . . . 5C **100**
Coleman Flds. N1 . . . . . 5E **49**
Coleman M. N8 . . . . 2A **34**
Coleman Rd. SE5 . . . . . . 3A **92**
Coleman St.
EC2 . . . . 2B **18** (5F **63**)
Coleman St. Bldgs.
EC2 . . . . 2B **18**
Colenso Rd. E5 . . . . 1E **51**
Coleraine Rd. SE3 . . . . . 2B **96**

Coleridge Av. E12 . . . . . 3F **55**
Coleridge Cl. SW8 . . . . . 5D **89**
Coleridge Ct. *W14* *4F 71*
(off Blythe Rd.)
Coleridge Gdns. NW6 . . 4E **45**
SW10 . . . . 3D **87**
Coleridge Ho. *SE17* *1E 91*
(off Browning St.)
SW1 . . . . *1E 89*
(off Churchill Gdns.)
Coleridge La. N8 . . . . . . 1A **34**
Coleridge Rd. N4 . . . . . . 4C **34**
N8 . . . . 1F **33**
Coleridge Sq. SW10 . . . . 3E **87**
(off Coleridge Gdns.)
Coles Grn. Ct. NW2 . . . . 4C **28**
Coles Grn. Rd. NW2 . . . . 3C **28**
Coleshill Flats *SW1* *5C 74*
(off Pimlico Rd.)
Colestown St. SW11 . . . 5A **88**
Cole St. SE1 . . . 4A **26** (3E **77**)
Colet Ct. *W6* *5F 71*
(off Hammersmith Rd.)
Colet Flats *E1* *5A 66*
(off Troon St.)
Colet Gdns. W14 . . . . . . 5F **71**
Colet Ho. *SE17* *1D 91*
(off Doddington Gro.)
Coley St. WC1 . . . . 4A **8** (3B **62**)
Colfe & Hatcliffe Glebe
SE13 . . . . 3D **109**
(off Lewisham High St.)
Colfe Rd. SE23 . . . . 1A **122**
Colin Dr. NW9 . . . . 1B **28**
Colinette Rd. SW15 . . . . 2E **99**
Colin Rd. NW10 . . . . 3C **42**
Colin Winter Ho. *E1* *3E 65*
(off Nicholas Rd.)
Coliseum Theatre *5D 15*
(off St Martin's La.)
Coliston Pas. SW18 . . . . 5C **100**
Coliston Rd. SW18 . . . . . 5C **100**
Collamore Av. SW18 . . . 1A **116**
Collard Pl. NW1 . . . . 4D **47**
Collards Almshouses
E17 . . . . *1E 39*
(off Maynard Rd.)
College App. SE10 . . . . . 2E **95**
College Cl. E9 . . . . 2E **51**
College Cres. *NW3* *3F 45*
(off College Cres.)
SW3 . . . . *1B 88*
(off West Rd.)
W6 . . . . *1E 85*
(off Queen Caroline St.)
College Cres. NW3 . . . . . 3E **45**
College Cross N1 . . . . . . 4C **48**
College E. E1 . . . . 4B **64**
College Gdns. IG4: Ilf . . . 1F **41**
SE21 . . . . 1A **120**
SW17 . . . . 2A **116**
(not continuous)
College Gro. NW1 . . . . . 5E **47**
College Hill
EC4 . . . . 4A **18** (1E **77**)
College La. NW5 . . . . . . 1D **47**
College Mans. *NW6* *5A 44*
(off Winchester Av.)

College M. N1 . . . . 4C **48**
(off College Cross,
not continuous)
SW1 . . . . 5D **23**
SW18 . . . . 3D **101**
College of Arms 4F **17**
College Pde. NW6 . . . . . . 5A **44**
COLLEGE PARK 2D **57**
College Pk. Cl.
SE13 . . . . 2F **109**
College Pl. NW1 . . . . 5E **47**
SW10 . . . . 3E **87**
College Point E15. . . . . . . 3B **54**
College Rd. E17 . . . . 1E **39**
NW10 . . . . 1E **57**
SE19 . . . . 5A **106**
SE21 . . . . 5A **106**
College Row E9 . . . . 2F **51**
College St.
EC4 . . . . 4A **18** (1E **77**)
College Ter. E3 . . . . 2B **66**
College Vw. SE9 . . . . . . 1F **125**
College Yd. NW5 . . . . 1D **47**
Collent St. E9 . . . . 3E **51**
Collerston Ho. SE10 . . . . . 1B **96**
(off Armitage Rd.)
Colless Rd. N15 . . . . 1B **36**
Collett Rd. SE16 . . . . . . 4C **78**
Collier St. N1 . . . . 1B **62**
Collingbourne Rd.
W12 . . . . 2D **71**
Collingham Gdns.
SW5 . . . . 5D **73**
Collingham Pl. SW5 . . . . . 5D **73**
Collingham Rd. SW5 . . . . . 5D **73**
Collington St. SE10 . . . . 1F **95**
Collingtree Rd.
SE26 . . . . 4E **121**
Collingwood Ho. E1 . . . . . 3D **65**
(off Darling Row)
SE16 . . . . 3D **79**
(off Cherry Gdn. St.)
SW1 . . . . 1F **89**
(off Dolphin Sq.)
W1 . . . . 5F **5**
(off Clipstone St.)
Collingwood Rd. E17 . . . . 1C **38**
Collingwood St. E1 . . . . . 3D **65**
Collins Ct. E8 . . . . 3C **50**
Collins Ho. E14 . . . . 1E **81**
(off Newby St.)
E15 . . . . 5B **54**
(off John St.)
SE10 . . . . 1B **96**
(off Armitage Rd.)
Collinson Ct. SE1 . . . . . . 4F **25**
(off Gt. Suffolk St.)
Collinson Ho. SE15 . . . . 3C **92**
(off Peckham Pk. Rd.)
Collinson St.
SE1 . . . . 4F **25** (3E **77**)
Collinson Wlk.
SE1 . . . . 4F **25** (3E **77**)
Collins Rd. N5 . . . . 1E **49**
Collins Sq. SE3 . . . . 5B **96**
Collins St. SE3 . . . . 5A **96**
(not continuous)
Collin's Yd. N1 . . . . 5D **49**
Collison Pl. N16 . . . . 3A **36**
Coll's Rd. SE15 . . . . 4E **93**

Collyer Pl. SE15 . . . . 4C **92**
Colman Rd. E16 . . . . 4E **69**
Colmans Wharf E14 . . . . . 4D **67**
(off Morris Rd.)
Colmore M. SE15 . . . . . . 4D **93**
Colnbrook St.
SE1 . . . . 5D **25** (4D **77**)
Colne Rd. E5 . . . . 1A **52**
Colne St. E13 . . . . 2C **68**
Cologne Rd. SW11 . . . . . 2F **101**
Colombo St.
SE1 . . . . 2D **25** (2D **77**)
Colombo Street Sports Cen. &
Community Cen.
. . . . 2D **25**
(off Colombo St.)
Colomb St. SE10 . . . . . . 1A **96**
Colonial Ct. N7. . . . . 5B **34**
Colonnade
WC1 . . . . 4E **7** (3A **62**)
Colonnade, The SE8 . . . . 5B **80**
Colonnades, The W2 . . . . 5D **59**
Colosseum Ter. NW1 . . . . 2E **5**
Colour Ct. SW1 . . . . 2A **22**
Colson Way SW16 . . . . . 4E **117**
Colstead Ho. E1 . . . . 5D **65**
(off Watney Mkt.)
Colston Rd. E7 . . . . 3F **55**
Colthurst Cres. N4 . . . . . 4D **35**
Coltman St. E14 . . . . 5A **66**
(off Maroon St.)
SE10 . . . . 2E **95**
(off Welland St.)
Columbas Dr. NW3 . . . . . 3F **31**
Columbia Point SE16 . . . . 4E **79**
(off Surrey Quays Rd.)
Columbia Rd.
E2 . . . . 1F **11** (2B **64**)
E13 . . . . 3B **68**
Columbia Road Flower Market
. . . . 1F **11**
(off Columbia Rd.)
Columbine Av. E6 . . . . . . 4F **69**
Columbine Way SE13 . . . . 5E **95**
Columbus Ct. SE16 . . . . . 2E **79**
(off Rotherhithe St.)
Columbus Ct. Yd.
E14 . . . . 2C **80**
Colva Wlk. N19 . . . . 4D **33**
Colverson Ho. E1 . . . . . . 4E **65**
(off Lindley St.)
Colview Ct. SE9 . . . . . . 1F **125**
Colvestone Cres. E8. . . . . 2B **50**
Colville Ct. SE1 . . . . 5A **50**
Colville Est. W. E2 . . . . . 2B **64**
(off Turin St.)
Colville Gdns. W11 . . . . . 5B **58**
(not continuous)
Colville Ho. E2 . . . . 1E **65**
(off Waterloo Gdns.)
Colville Ho's. W11 . . . . . 5B **58**
Colville M. W11 . . . . 5B **58**
Colville Pl.
W1 . . . . 1A **14** (4E **61**)
Colville Rd. E11 . . . . 5E **39**
W11 . . . . 5B **58**
Colville Sq. W11 . . . . 5B **58**
Colville Ter. W11 . . . . . . 5B **58**

Colvin Cl. SE26 . . . . 5E **121**
Colvin Rd. E6 . . . . 4F **55**
Colwell Rd. SE22 . . . . . . 3B **106**
Colwick Cl. N6 . . . . 2F **33**
Colwith Rd. W6 . . . . 2E **85**
Colworth Gro.
SE17 . . . . 5E **77**
Colworth Rd. E11. . . . . . . 1A **40**
Colwyn Cl. SW16 . . . . . . 5E **117**
Colwyn Grn. NW9 . . . . . . 1A **28**
(off Snowdon Dr.)
Colwyn Ho.
SE1 . . . . 5B **24** (4C **76**)
Colwyn Rd. NW2 . . . . . . 5D **29**
Colyer Cl. N1 . . . . 1B **62**
Colyton La. SW16 . . . . . . 5C **118**
Colyton Rd. SE22 . . . . . 3D **107**
Combe, The
NW1 . . . . 2E **5** (2D **61**)
Combe Av. SE3 . . . . 3B **96**
Combedale Rd. SE10 . . . . 1C **96**
Combemartin Rd.
SW18 . . . . 5A **100**
Combe M. SE3 . . . . 3B **96**
Comber Cl. NW2 . . . . . . 5D **29**
Comber Gro. SE5 . . . . . . 3E **91**
Comber Ho. SE5 . . . . . . 3E **91**
Combermere Rd.
SW9 . . . . 1B **104**
Comberton Rd. E5 . . . . . 4D **37**
Comedy Store 5B **14**
(off Oxendon St.)
Comedy Theatre 5B **14**
(off Panton St.)
Comeragh M. W14 . . . . . 1A **86**
Comeragh Rd. W14 . . . . . 1A **86**
Comerell Pl. SE10 . . . . . 1B **96**
Comerford Rd. SE4 . . . . . 2A **108**
Comet Cl. E12 . . . . 1F **55**
Comet Pl. SE8 . . . . 3C **94**
(not continuous)
Comet St. SE8 . . . . 3C **94**
Comfort St. SE15 . . . . . . 2A **92**
Commercial Dock Path
SE16 . . . . 4B **80**
(off Gulliver St.)
Commercial Rd. E1 . . . . . 5C **64**
E14 . . . . 5A **66**
Commercial St.
E1 . . . . 4F **11** (3B **64**)
Commercial Way
SE15 . . . . 3B **92**
Commerell St. SE10 . . . . 1A **96**
Commodity Quay E1. . . . . 1B **78**
Commodore St. SE8 . . . . 4C **94**
(off Albyn Rd.)
Commodore Ho. E14 . . . . 1E **81**
(off Poplar High St.)
SW18 . . . . 1E **101**
Commodore Sq.
SW10 . . . . 4E **87**
Commodore St. E1 . . . . . 3A **66**
Common, The E15 . . . . . 3A **54**
Commondale SW15 . . . . . 1E **99**
Commonfield La.
SW17 . . . . 5A **116**
Common Mile Cl.
SW4 . . . . 3F **103**
Common Rd. SW13. . . . . 1D **99**
W4 . . . . 5A **70**

Commonwealth Av.
W12 . . . . 1D **71**
(not continuous)
Commonwealth
Conference Cen.
. . . . 2A **22** (2E **75**)
Commonwealth Institute
. . . . 4B **72**
Community La. N7 . . . . . 2F **47**
Community Rd. E15 . . . . 2F **53**
Como Rd. SE23 . . . . . . 2A **122**
Compass Ct. *SE1* 2F **27**
(off Shad Thames)
Compass Ho. SW18 . . 2D **101**
Compass Point *E14* . . . *1B **80***
(off Grenade St.)
Compayne Gdns.
NW6 . . . . 4D **45**
Compton Av. E6 . . . . . . 1F **69**
N1 . . . . 3D **49**
N6 . . . . 2A **32**
Compton Cl. E3 . . . . . 4C **66**
NW1 . . . . 2E **5**
NW11 . . . . 5F **29**
SE15 . . . . 3C **92**
Compton Ct. SE19 . . . 5A **120**
Compton Pas.
EC1 . . . . 3E **9** (3D **63**)
Compton Pl.
WC1 . . . . 3D **7** (3A **62**)
Compton Rd. N1. . . . . . 3D **49**
NW10 . . . . 2F **57**
SW19 . . . . 5B **114**
Compton St.
EC1 . . . . 3D **9** (3D **63**)
Compton Ter. N1 . . . . . 3D **49**
Comus Ho. *SE17* *5A **78***
(off Comus Pl.)
Comus Pl. SE17 . . . . . 5A **78**
Comyn Rd. SW11 . . . . 2A **102**
Comyns Cl. E16 . . . . . 4B **68**
Conant Ho. *SE11* 2D **91**
(off St Agnes Pl.)
Conant M. E1 . . . . 1C **78**
Concanon Rd. SW2 . . 2B **104**
Concert Hall App.
SE1 . . . . 2A **24** (2B **76**)
Concordia Wharf *E14* . . 2E **81**
(off Coldharbour)
Condell Rd. SW8 . . . . . 4E **89**
Conder St. E14 . . . . . . 5A **66**
Condray Pl. SW11 . . . . 3A **88**
Conduit Av. SE10 . . . . . 4F **95**
Conduit Ct. WC2. . . . . . 4D **15**
Conduit M. W2 . . . . 5F **59**
Conduit Pas. *W2* *5F **59***
(off Conduit Pl.)
Conduit Pl. W2 . . . . . . 5F **59**
Conduit St.
W1. . . . . 4E **13** (1D **75**)
Conewood St. N5 . . . . . 5D **35**
Coney Acre SE21 . . . . 1E **119**
Coney Way SW8 . . . . . 2B **90**
Congers Ho. SE8 . . . . . 3C **94**
Congreve Ho. N16 . . . . 2A **50**
Congreve St. SE17 . . . . 5A **78**
Congreve Wlk. *E16* *4F **69***
(off Fulmer Rd.)
Conifer Gdns.
SW16 . . . . 3A **118**

Conifer Ho. *SE4* 2B **108**
(off Brockley Rd.)
Coniger Rd. SW6 . . . . . 5C **86**
Coningham Ct. *SW10*. . . 3E **87**
(off King's Rd.)
Coningham M. W12. . . . 2C **70**
Coningham Rd.
W12 . . . . 3D **71**
Coningsby Rd. N4 . . . . 2D **35**
Conington Rd. SE13. . . 5D **95**
Conisborough Cres.
SE6 . . . . 3E **123**
Conisbrough *NW1* 5E **47**
(off Bayham St.)
Coniston *NW1* 1F **5**
(off Harrington St.)
Coniston Cl. SW13. . . . 3B **84**
Coniston Ct. *SE16*. 3F **79**
(off Eleanor Cl.)
W2 . . . . 5A **60**
(off Kendal St.)
Coniston Way N7 . . . . 4A **48**
Coniston Gdns. NW9 . . 1A **28**
Coniston Ho. *E3*. 3D **66**
(off Southern Gro.)
SE5 . . . . 3E **91**
(off Wyndham St.)
Coniston Rd.
BR1: Brom 5A **124**
Coniston Wlk. E9 . . . . . 2E **51**
Conlan St. W10 . . . . . . 3A **58**
Conley Rd. NW10. . . . . 3A **42**
Conley St. SE10 . . . . . . 1A **96**
Connaught Bri. E16 . . . 2F **83**
Connaught Bus. Cen.
NW9 . . . . 1B **28**
Connaught Cl. E10 . . . . 4F **37**
W2 . . . . 5A **60**
(off Connaught St.)
Connaught Ho.
NW10 . . . . 2D **57**
(off Trenmar Gdns.)
W1 . . . . 5D **13**
(off Davies St.)
Connaught Lodge *N4* . . 2C **34**
(off Connaught Rd.)
Connaught M. NW3 . . . 1A **46**
SE11 . . . . 5C **76**
(off Walcot Sq.)
SW6 . . . . 4A **86**
Connaught Pl. W2. . . . . 1B **74**
Connaught Rd. E11. . . . 3F **39**
E16 . . . . 2F **83**
E17 . . . . 1C **38**
N4 . . . . 2C **34**
NW10 . . . . 5A **42**
Connaught Rdbt.
E16 . . . . 1F **83**
(off Victoria Dock Rd.)
Connaught Sq. W2. . . . 5B **60**
Connaught St. W2 . . . . 5A **60**
Connell Ct. *SE14* 2F **93**
(off Myers La.)
Connor Cl. E11. . . . . . . 2A **40**
Connor Ct. SW11 . . . . 4D **89**
Connor St. E9 . . . . 5F **51**
Conrad Ho. *E14* 1A **80**
(off Victory Pl.)
E16 . . . . 2D **83**
(off Wesley Av.)

Conrad Ho. N16 . . . . . . 2A **50**
(off Matthias Rd.)
SW8 . . . . 3A **90**
(off Wyvil Rd.)
Consort Ho. *E14*. 1D **95**
(off St Davids Sq.)
W2 . . . . 1D **73**
(off Queensway)
Consort Lodge *NW8* . . . 5B **46**
(off Prince Albert Rd.)
Consort Rd. SE15. . . . . 4D **93**
Cons St. SE1 . . 3C **24** (3C **76**)
Constable Av. E16 . . . . 2D **83**
Constable Cl. NW11 . . . 1D **31**
Constable Ct. *SE16* . . . 1D **93**
(off Stubbs Dr.)
Constable Ho. NW3 . . . 4B **46**
SE21 . . . . 3A **120**
Constance Allen Ho.
W10. . . . . 5F **57**
(off Bridge Cl.)
Constance St. E16 . . . . 2F **83**
Constant Ho. *E14* *1D **81***
(off Harrow La.)
Constantine Ct. *E1*. . . . 5C **64**
(off Fairclough St.)
Constantine Rd.
NW3 . . . . 1A **46**
Constitution Hill
SW1 . . . . 3D **21** (3D **75**)
Content St. SE17 . . . . . 5F **77**
Convent Gdns. W11 . . . 5A **58**
Conway Gro. W3 . . . . . 4A **56**
Conway Ho. *E14*. 5C **80**
(off Cahir St.)
Conway M. W1 . . . . . . 4F **5**
Conway Rd. NW2 . . . . 4E **29**
Conway St.
W1 . . . . 4F **5** (3E **61**)
(not continuous)
Conybeare NW3 . . . . . 4A **46**
Conyer's Rd. SW16 . . . 5F **117**
Conyer St. E3. . . . . 1A **66**
Cook Ct. *SE16*. 2E **79**
(off Rotherhithe St.)
Cookes Cl. E11. . . . . . . 4B **40**
Cookham Cres. SE16 . . 3F **79**
Cookham Ho. *E2*. 3F **11**
(off Montclare St.)
Cook's Rd. E15. . . . . . . 1D **67**
SE17. . . . . 2D **91**
Coolfin Rd. E16 . . . . . . 5C **68**
Coolhurst Rd. N8 . . . . . 1F **33**
Cool Oak La. NW9 . . . . 2A **28**
Coomassie Rd. W9 . . . . 3B **58**
Coombe Ho. N7 . . . . . . 2F **47**
Coombe Lodge SE7 . . . 2E **97**
Coombe Pk.
KT2: King T. 5A **112**
Coomber Ho. *SW6*. . . . 1D **101**
(off Wandsworth Bri. Rd.)
Coombe Rd. NW10 . . . . 5A **28**
SE26 . . . . 4D **121**
W4 . . . . 1A **84**
Coombs St.
N1 . . . . 1E **9** (1D **63**)
Coomer M. SW6 . . . . . . 2B **86**
Coomer Pl. SW6 . . . . . 2B **86**
Coomer Rd. SW6 . . . . . 2B **86**

Cooper Cl.
SE1 . . . . 4C **24** (3C **76**)
Cooper Ct. E15 . . . . . . 2D **53**
Cooper Ho. NW8 . . . . . . 3F **59**
   (off Lyons Pl.)
Cooper Rd. NW4 . . . . . 1F **29**
NW10 . . . . 2B **42**
Coopersale Rd. E9 . . . . 2F **51**
Coopers Cl. E1 . . . . 3E **65**
Coopers Ct. *E3* *3B 66*
   (off Eric St.)
Coopers La. E10 . . . . . . 3D **39**
NW1 . . . . 1F **61**
   (not continuous)
SE12 . . . . 2D **125**
Coopers Lodge *SE1* . . . *3F 27*
   (off Tooley St.)
Cooper's Rd. SE1 . . . . . 1B **92**
Coopers Row
EC3 . . . . . . 4F **19** (1B **78**)
Cooper St. E16 . . . . 4B **68**
Coopers Wlk. E15 . . . . . 2A **54**
Cooper's Yd. SE19 . . . . 5A **120**
Cope Ho. EC1 . . . . 2A **10**
Copeland Dr. E14 . . . . . 5C **80**
Copeland Ho. *SE11* . . . *4C 76*
   (off Lambeth Wlk.)
SW17 . . . . 4F **115**
Copeland Rd. E17 . . . . . 1D **39**
SE15 . . . . 5C **92**
Copeman Cl. SE26 . . . . 5E **121**
Copenhagen Ho. *N1* . . . *5B 48*
   (off Barnsbury Est.)
Copenhagen Pl. E14 . . . 5B **66**
   (not continuous)
Copenhagen St. N1 . . . . 5A **48**
Cope Pl. W8 . . . . 4C **72**
Cope St. SE16 . . . . 5F **79**
Copford Wlk. *N1* *5E 49*
   (off Popham St.)
Copgate Path SW16 . . . 5B **118**
Copleston M. SE15 . . . . 5B **92**
Copleston Pas. SE5 . . . . 5B **92**
Copleston Rd. SE15 . . . 1B **106**
Copley Cl. SE17 . . . . . . 2E **91**
Copley Pk. SW16 . . . . . 5B **118**
Copley St. E1 . . . . 4F **65**
Coppelia Rd. SE3 . . . . . 2B **110**
Copperas St. SE8 . . . . . 2D **95**
Copperbeech Cl.
NW3 . . . . 2F **45**
Copperfield Ho. *SE1* . . . *3C 78*
   (off Wolseley St.)
W1 . . . . *5C 4*
   (off Marylebone High St.)
W11 . . . . *2F 71*
   (off St Ann's Rd.)
Copperfield Rd. E3 . . . . 3A **66**
Copperfield St.
SE1 . . . . . 3E **25** (3D **77**)
Coppermead Cl.
NW2 . . . . 5E **29**
Copper Mill La.
SW17 . . . . 4E **115**
Coppermill La. E17 . . . . 1E **37**
   (not continuous)
Copper Row SE1 . . . . . . 2F **27**
Copperworks, The
N1 . . . . *1A 62*
   (off Railway St.)

Coppice Dr. SW15 . . . . . 4D **99**
Coppock Cl. SW11 . . . . . 5A **88**
Copse Cl. SE7 . . . . 2D **97**
Captain Ho. SW18 . . . 2C **100**
Copthall Av.
EC2 . . . . 2C **18** (5F **63**)
   (not continuous)
Copthall Bldgs. EC2 . . . 2C **18**
Copthall Cl.
EC2 . . . . 2B **18** (5F **63**)
Copthorne Av.
SW12 . . . . 5F **103**
Coptic St.
WC1 . . . . 1D **15** (4A **62**)
Coral Apartments
E16 . . . . *1C 82*
   (off Western Gateway)
Coral Ho. E1 . . . . *3A 66*
   (off Harford St.)
Coral Row SW11 . . . . . 1E **101**
Coral St. SE1 . . . . 4C **24** (3C **76**)
Coram Ho. *W4* *1A 84*
   (off Wood St.)
WC1 . . . . 3D **7**
Coram St.
WC1 . . . . 4D **7** (3A **62**)
Corbden Cl. SE15 . . . . . 4B **92**
Corbet Ct.
EC3 . . . . 3C **18** (5F **63**)
Corbet Ho. *N1* *1C 62*
   (off Barnsbury Est.)
Corbet Pl. E1 . . . 5F **11** (4B **64**)
Corbett Ho. SE26 . . . . . 4B **122**
Corbett Ho. *SW10* *2E 87*
   (off Cathcart Rd.)
Corbett Rd. E11 . . . . . . 1E **41**
Corbetts La. SE16 . . . . . 5E **79**
   (not continuous)
Corbetts Pas. *SE16* . . . *5E 79*
   (off Corbetts La.)
Corbetts Wharf *SE16* . . *3D 79*
   (off Bermondsey Wall E.)
Corbicum E11 . . . . 2A **40**
Corbidge Ct. *SE8* *2D 95*
   (off Glaisher St.)
Corbiere Ho. *N1* *5F 49*
   (off De Beauvoir Est.)
Corbridge Cres. E2 . . . 1D **65**
Corbyn St. N4 . . . . 3A **34**
Corby Way E3 . . . . 3C **66**
Cordelia Cl. SE24 . . . . 2D **105**
Cordelia Ho. *N1* *1A 64*
   (off Arden Est.)
Cordelia St. E14 . . . . . . 5D **67**
Cording St. E14 . . . . . . 4D **67**
Cordwainers Ct. *E9* . . . *4E 51*
   (off St Thomas's Sq.)
Cordwainers Wlk.
E13 . . . . 1C **68**
Cord Way E14 . . . . 4C **80**
Cordwell Rd. SE13 . . . . 3A **110**
Corelli Ct. *SW5* *5C 72*
   (off W. Cromwell Rd.)
Corelli Rd. SE3 . . . . 5F **97**
Corfe Ho. *SW8* *3B 90*
   (off Dorset Rd.)
Corfield St. E2 . . . . 2D **65**
Coriander Av. E14 . . . . . 5F **67**
Corinne Rd. N19 . . . . . . 1E **47**
Corker Wlk. N7 . . . . 4B **34**

Cork Sq. E1 . . . . 2D **79**
Cork St. W1 . . . . 5F **13** (1E **75**)
Cork St. M. W1 . . . . 5F **13**
Cork Tree Ho. *SE27* . . *5D 119*
   (off Lakeview Rd.)
Corlett St. NW1 . . . . . . 4A **60**
Cormont Rd. SE5 . . . . . 4D **91**
Cormorant Ct. *SE8* . . . *2B 94*
   (off Pilot Cl.)
Cormorant Lodge *E1* . . *2C 78*
   (off Thomas More St.)
Cormorant Rd. E7 . . . . . 2B **54**
Cornbury Ho. *SE8* *2B 94*
   (off Evelyn St.)
Cornelia St. N7 . . . . 3B **48**
Cornell Bldg. *E1* *5C 64*
   (off Coke St.)
Corner Fielde SE3 . . . . 1B **118**
Corner Grn. SE3 . . . . . . 5C **96**
Corner Ho. St. WC2 . . . 1D **23**
Corney Reach Way
W4 . . . . 3A **84**
Corney Rd. W4 . . . . 2A **84**
Cornflower Ter.
SE22 . . . . 4D **107**
Cornford Gro.
SW12 . . . . 2D **117**
Cornhill EC3 . . . 3C **18** (5F **63**)
Cornick Ho. *SE16* *4D 79*
   (off Slippers Pl.)
Cornish Ho. *SE17* *2D 91*
   (off Brandon Est.)
Cornmill La. SE13 . . . . 1E **109**
Cornmow Dr. NW10 . . . . 2B **42**
Cornthwaite Rd. E5 . . . . 5E **37**
Cornwall Av. E2 . . . . . . 2E **65**
Cornwall Cres. W11 . . . 5A **58**
Cornwall Gdns.
NW10 . . . . 3D **43**
SW7 . . . . 4D **73**
Cornwall Gdns. Wlk.
SW7 . . . . 4D **73**
Cornwall Gro. W4 . . . . . 1A **84**
Cornwallis Ct. *SW8* . . . *4A 90*
   (off Lansdowne Grn.)
Cornwallis Ho. *SE16* . . *3D 79*
   (off Cherry Gdn. St.)
W12 . . . . 1D **71**
   (off India Way)
Cornwallis Rd. N19 . . . . 4A **34**
Cornwallis Sq. N19 . . . . 4A **34**
Cornwall Mans.
SW10 . . . . *3E 87*
   (off Cremorne Rd.)
W14 . . . . *4F 71*
   (off Blythe Rd.)
Cornwall M. Sth.
SW7 . . . . 4E **73**
Cornwall M. W. SW7 . . . 4D **73**
Cornwall Rd. N4 . . . . . . 2C **34**
N15 . . . . 1F **35**
SE1 . . . . 1B **24** (2C **76**)
   (off Seaton Cl.)
Cornwall Sq. *SE11* . . . *1D 91*
Cornwall St. E1 . . . . . . 1D **79**
Cornwall Ter.
NW1 . . . . 4A **4** (3B **60**)
Cornwall Ter. M. NW1 . . 4A **4**
Corn Way E11 . . . . 5F **39**
Cornwell Cres. E7 . . . . . 1E **55**

Cornwood Dr. E1. . . . . . .5E 65
Corona Bldg. E14 . . . . . .2E 81
   (off Blackwall Way)
Corona Rd. SE12 . . . . . .5C 110
Coronation Av.
  N16 . . . . .1B 50
Coronation Ct. E15 . . . . .3B 54
  W10 . . . . .4E 57
   (off Brewster Gdns.)
Coronation Rd. E13 . . . . .2E 69
Coroners Ct. NW1 . . . . . .5F 47
   (off Camley St.)
Coronet Cinema 2C 72
   (off Notting Hill Ga.)
Coronet St.
  N1 . . . . .2D 11 (2A 64)
Corporation Row
  EC1 . . . . .3C 8 (3C 62)
Corporation St. E15 . . . . .1A 68
  N7 . . . . .2A 48
Corrance Rd. SW2 . . . . .2A 104
Corringham Ct.
  NW11 . . . . .2C 30
Corringham Ho. E1 . . . . .5F 65
   (off Pitsea St.)
Corringham Rd.
  NW11 . . . . .2C 30
Corringway NW11 . . . . . .2D 31
Corris Grn. NW9 . . . . . .1A 28
Corry Dr. SW9 . . . . . . .2D 105
Corry Ho. E14 . . . . .1D 81
   (off Wade's Pl.)
Corsehill St. SW16 . . . . .5E 117
Corsham St.
  N1 . . . . .2C 10 (2F 63)
Corsica St. N5 . . . . . . .3D 49
Corsley Way E9 . . . . . . .3B 52
   (off Osborne Rd.)
Cortayne Rd. SW6 . . . . . .5B 86
Cortis Rd. SW15 . . . . . .4D 99
Cortis Ter. SW15 . . . . . .4D 99
Corunna Rd. SW8 . . . . . .4E 89
Corunna Ter. SW8 . . . . . .4E 89
Corvette Sq. SE10 . . . . .2F 95
Coryton Path W9 . . . . . .3B 58
   (off Ashmore Rd.)
Cosbycote Av. SE24 . . . . .3E 105
Cosgrove Ho. E2 . . . . . .5C 50
   (off Whiston Rd.)
Cosmo Pl.
  WC1 . . . . .5E 7 (4A 62)
Cosmur Cl. W12 . . . . . .4B 70
Cossall Wlk. SE15 . . . . .5D 93
Cossar M. SW2 . . . . . . .3C 104
Cosser St.
  SE1 . . . . . . .5B 24 (4C 76)
Costa St. SE15 . . . . . . .5C 92
Coston Wlk. SE4 . . . . . .2F 107
Cosway Mans. NW1 . . . . .4A 60
   (off Shroton St.)
Cosway St. NW1 . . . . . .4A 60
Cotall St. E14 . . . . .4C 66
Coteford St. SW17 . . . . .4B 116
Cotesbach Rd. E5 . . . . . .5E 37
Cotes Ho. NW8 . . . . . . .3A 60
   (off Broadley St.)
Cotham St. SE17 . . . . . .5E 77
Cotherstone Rd.
  SW2 . . . . .1B 118
Cotleigh Rd. NW6 . . . . . .4C 44

Cotman Cl. NW11 . . . . . .1E 31
  SW15 . . . . .4F 99
Cotman Ho. NW8 . . . . . .1A 60
   (off Townshend Est.)
Cotswold Ct. EC1 . . . . . .3F 9
Cotswold Gdns. E6 . . . . .2F 69
  NW2 . . . . .4F 29
Cotswold Ga. NW2 . . . . . .3A 30
Cotswold M. SW11 . . . . . .4F 87
Cotswold St. SE27 . . . . . .4D 119
Cottage Cl. E1 . . . . .3E 65
   (off Hayfield Pas.)
Cottage Grn. SE5 . . . . . .3F 91
Cottage Gro. SW9 . . . . . .1A 104
Cottage Pl. SW3 . . . . . . .4A 74
Cottage Rd. N7 . . . . .2B 48
Cottage St. E14 . . . . . . .1D 81
Cottage Wlk. N16 . . . . . .5B 36
Cottenham Rd. SE14 . . . . .3A 94
Cottesloe Ho. NW8 . . . . . .3F 59
   (off Jerome Cres.)
Cottesloe M. SE1 . . . . . .5C 24
   (off Emery St.)
Cottesloe Theatre 1B 24
  (in Royal National Theatre)
Cottesmore Ct. W8 . . . . .4D 73
   (off Stanford Rd.)
Cottesmore Gdns.
  W8 . . . . .4D 73
Cottingham Rd. SW8 . . . . .3B 90
Cottington St. SE11 . . . . .1C 90
Cottle Way SE16 . . . . . .3D 79
   (off Paradise St.)
Cotton Av. W3 . . . . .5A 56
Cotton Cl. E11 . . . . .4A 40
Cotton Hill
  BR1: Brom 4E 123
Cotton Ho. SW2 . . . . . . .5A 104
Cotton Row SW11 . . . . . .1E 101
Cottons Cen.
  SE1 . . . . . . .1D 27 (2A 78)
Cotton's Gdns.
  E2 . . . . .1E 11 (2A 64)
Cottons La.
  SE1 . . . . . . .1C 26 (2F 77)
Cotton St. E14 . . . . .1E 81
Cottrell Ct. SE10 . . . . . .5B 82
Cottrill Gdns. E8 . . . . . . .3D 51
Coulgate St. SE4 . . . . . .1A 108
Coulson St. SW3 . . . . . .1B 88
Coulter Rd. W6 . . . . . . .4D 71
Councillor St. SE5 . . . . . .3E 91
Counter Ct. SE1 . . . . . . .2B 26
   (off Borough High St.)
Counter St.
  SE1 . . . . . . .2D 27 (2A 78)
Countess Rd. NW5 . . . . . .2E 47
County Gro. SE5 . . . . . . .4E 91
County Hall Apartments
  SE1 . . . . .3F 23
County Hall (Former)
     . . . . .3F 23 (3B 76)
County St. SE1 . . . . .4E 77
Courland Gro. SW8 . . . . . .4F 89
Courland St. SW8 . . . . . .4F 89
Courtauld Ho. E2 . . . . . .5C 50
   (off Goldsmiths Row)
Courtauld Institute Galleries
     . . . . .4F 15
Courtauld Rd. N19 . . . . . .3A 34

Court Cl. NW8 . . . . .4F 45
   (off Boydell Ct.,
      not continuous)
Courtenay Av. N6 . . . . . .2A 32
Courtenay M. E17 . . . . . .1A 38
Courtenay Pl. E17 . . . . . .1A 38
Courtenay Rd. E11 . . . . . .5B 40
Courtenay Sq. SE11 . . . . .1C 90
Courtenay St. SE11 . . . . .1C 90
Court Farm Rd. SE9 . . . . .2F 125
Courtfield Gdns.
  SW5 . . . . .5D 73
Courtfield Ho. EC1 . . . . . .5B 8
   (off Baldwins Gdns.)
Courtfield M. SW5 . . . . . .5E 73
Courtfield Rd. SW7 . . . . . .5E 73
Court Gdns. N7 . . . . .3C 48
   (not continuous)
Courthill Rd. SE13 . . . . . .2E 109
Courthope Ho. SE16 . . . . .4E 79
   (off Lower Rd.)
  SW8 . . . . .3A 90
   (off Hartington Rd.)
Courthope Rd. NW3 . . . . . .1B 46
  SW19 . . . . .5A 114
Courtland Rd. E6 . . . . . . .5F 55
Courtlands Av.
  SE12 . . . . .3D 111
Court La. SE21 . . . . .4A 106
Court La. Gdns.
  SE21 . . . . .5A 106
Courleigh NW11 . . . . . . .1B 30
Courtmead Cl. SE24 . . . . .4E 105
Courtnell St. W2 . . . . . . .5C 58
Courtney Ct. N7 . . . . . . .2C 48
Courtney Ho. W14 . . . . . .4A 72
   (off Russell Rd.)
Courtney Rd. N7 . . . . . . .2C 48
Courtrai Rd. SE23 . . . . . .4A 108
Court Royal SW15 . . . . . .3A 100
Courtside N8 . . . . .1F 33
  SE26 . . . . .3D 121
Court St. E1 . . . . .4D 65
Courtville Ho. W10 . . . . . .2A 58
   (off Third Av.)
Courtyard, The E3 . . . . . .1C 66
  EC3 . . . . .3C 18
  (in Royal Exchange)
  N1 . . . . .4B 48
  NW1 . . . . .4C 46
Courtyard Theatre, The
  King's Cross 1A 62
   (off York Way)
Cousin La.
  EC4 . . . . .5B 18 (1F 77)
Couthurst Rd. SE3 . . . . . .2D 97
Coutt's Cres. NW5 . . . . . .5C 32
Couzens Ho. E3 . . . . . . .4B 66
   (off Weatherley Cl.)
Covell Ct. SE8 . . . . .3C 94
COVENT GARDEN
     . . . . .4E 15 (1A 76)
Covent Garden
     . . . . .4E 15 (1A 76)
Covent Gdn.
  WC2 . . . . .4E 15 (1A 76)
Coventry Cl. NW6 . . . . . .1C 58
Coventry Cross E3 . . . . . .3E 67
Coventry Hall SW16 . . . . .5A 118
Coventry Rd. E1 . . . . . . .3D 65

Coventry St.
W1 . . . . 5B **14** (1F **75**)
Coverdale Rd. NW2 . . . . 4F **43**
W12 . . . . 3D **71**
Coverley Cl. E1 . . . . . . 4C **64**
Coverley Point SE11 . . . 5B **76**
    (off Tyers St.)
Coverton Rd. SW17 . . . 5A **116**
Covington Way
SW16 . . . . 5B **118**
    (not continuous)
Cowcross St.
EC1 . . . . 5D **9** (4D **63**)
Cowdenbeath Path
N1 . . . . 5B **48**
Cowden St. SE6 . . . . . 4C **122**
Cowdrey Rd. SW19 . . . 5D **115**
Cowick Rd. SW17 . . . . 4B **116**
Cowley La. E11 . . . . . . 5A **40**
Cowley Rd. E11 . . . . . . 1D **41**
SW9 . . . . 4C **90**
    (not continuous)
SW14 . . . . 1A **98**
W3 . . . . 2B **70**
Cowley St.
SW1 . . . . 5D **23** (4A **76**)
Cowling Cl. W11 . . . . . . 2A **72**
Cowper Av. E6 . . . . 5F **55**
Cowper Ho. SE17 . . . . . 1E **91**
    (off Browning St.)
SW1 . . . . 1F **89**
    (off Aylesford St.)
Cowper Rd. N16 . . . . . . 2A **50**
SW19 . . . . 5E **115**
Cowper's Ct. EC3 . . . . . 3C **18**
    (off Birchin La.)
Cowper St.
EC2 . . . . 3C **10** (3F **63**)
Cowper Ter. W10 . . . . . . 4F **57**
Cowthorpe Rd. SW8 . . . 4F **89**
Cox Ho. W6 . . . . 2A **86**
    (off Field Rd.)
Coxmount Rd. SE7 . . . . 1F **97**
Cox's Ct. E1 . . . . 1F **19**
Coxson Way
SE1 . . . . 4F **27** (3B **78**)
Cox's Wlk. SE21 . . . . . . 1C **120**
Crabtree Cl. E2 . . . . 1B **64**
Crabtree Ct. E15 . . . . . . 2D **53**
Crabtree La. SW6 . . . . . 3E **85**
    (not continuous)
Crabtree Wlk. SE15 . . . 4B **92**
    (off Peckham Rd.)
Crace St. NW1 . . 1B **6** (2F **61**)
Craddock Rd. NW5 . . . . 3C **46**
Crafts Council & Gallery
. . . . 1C **62**
Cragie Ho. SE1 . . . . 5B **78**
    (off Balaclava Rd.)
Craigerne Rd. SE3 . . . . 3D **97**
Craignair Rd. SW2 . . . . 5C **104**
Craig's Ct.
SW1 . . . . 1D **23** (2A **76**)
Craik Ct. NW6 . . . . 1B **58**
    (off Carlton Va.)
Crail Row SE17 . . . . . . 5F **77**
Cramer St.
W1 . . . . 1C **12** (4C **60**)
Crammond Cl. W6 . . . . . 2A **86**
Crampton Ho. SW8 . . . . 4E **89**

Crampton Rd. SE20 . . . 5E **121**
Crampton St. SE17 . . . . 5E **77**
Cranberry La. E16 . . . . . 3A **68**
Cranbourn All.
WC2 . . . . 4C **14**
    (off Cranbourn St.)
Cranbourne Gdns.
NW11 . . . . 1A **30**
Cranbourne Pas.
SE16 . . . . 3D **79**
Cranbourne Rd. E12 . . . 2F **55**
E15 . . . . 1E **53**
Cranbourn Ho. SE16 . . . 3D **79**
    (off Marigold St.)
Cranbourn St.
WC2 . . . . 4C **14** (1F **75**)
Cranbrook NW1 . . . . 5E **47**
    (off Camden St.)
Cranbrook Est. E2 . . . . . 1F **65**
Cranbrook Rd. SE8 . . . . 4C **94**
W4 . . . . 1A **84**
Cranbrook St. E2 . . . . . . 1F **65**
Cranbury Rd. SW6 . . . . 5D **87**
Crandley Ct. SE8 . . . . . . 5A **80**
Crane Ct. EC4 . . . . 5C **62**
Crane Gro. N7 . . . . 3C **48**
Crane Ho. E3 . . . . 1A **66**
    (off Roman Rd.)
SE15 . . . . 4B **92**
Crane Mead SE16 . . . . . 5F **79**
    (not continuous)
Crane St. SE10 . . . . 1F **95**
SE15 . . . . 4B **92**
Cranfield Cl. SE27 . . . . . 3E **119**
Cranfield Ct. W1 . . . . . . 4A **60**
    (off Homer St.)
Cranfield Ho. WC1 . . . . . 5D **7**
Cranfield Rd. SE4 . . . . . 1B **108**
Cranfield Row SE1 . . . . 5C **24**
Cranford Cotts. E1 . . . . 1F **79**
    (off Cranford St.)
Cranford St. E1 . . . . 1F **79**
Cranford Way N8 . . . . . . 1B **34**
Cranhurst Rd. NW2 . . . . 2E **43**
Cranleigh Ho's. NW1 . . . 1E **61**
    (off Cranleigh St.)
Cranleigh M. SW11 . . . . 5A **88**
Cranleigh St. NW1 . . . . 1E **61**
CRANLEY GARDENS . . . 1D **33**
Cranley Gdns. SW7 . . . . 1E **87**
Cranley M. SW7 . . . . 1E **87**
Cranley Pl. SW7 . . . . 5F **73**
Cranley Rd. E13 . . . . . . 4D **69**
Cranmer Ct. SW3 . . . . . . 5A **74**
SW4 . . . . 1F **103**
Cranmere Ct. SE5 . . . . . 4E **91**
Cranmer Ho. SW9 . . . . . 3C **90**
    (off Brixton Rd.)
Cranmer Rd. E7 . . . . 1D **55**
SW9 . . . . 3C **90**
Cranmer Ter. SW17 . . . . 5F **115**
Cranmore Rd.
BR1: Brom 3B **124**
Cranston Est. N1 . . . . . . 1F **63**
Cranston Rd. SE23 . . . . 1A **122**
Cranswick Rd. SE16 . . . 1D **93**
Crantock Rd. SE6 . . . . . 2D **123**
Cranwell Cl. E3 . . . . 3D **67**
Cranwich Rd. N16 . . . . . 2F **35**
Cranwood Ct. EC1 . . . . . 2C **10**

Cranwood St.
EC1 . . . . 2C **10** (2F **63**)
Cranworth Gdns.
SW9 . . . . 4C **90**
Craster Rd. SW2 . . . . . . 5B **104**
Crathie Rd. SE12 . . . . . 4D **111**
Craven Cl. N16 . . . . 2C **36**
Craven Cottage 4F **85**
Craven Ct. NW10 . . . . . . 5A **42**
Craven Gdns.
SW19 . . . . 5C **114**
Craven Hill W2 . . . . 1E **73**
Craven Hill Gdns. W2 . . 1E **73**
    (not continuous)
Craven Hill M. W2 . . . . . 1E **73**
Craven Lodge W2 . . . . . 1E **73**
    (off Craven Hill)
Craven M. SW11 . . . . . . 1C **102**
Craven Pk. NW10 . . . . . 5A **42**
Craven Pk. M. NW10 . . . 4A **42**
Craven Pk. Rd. N15 . . . . 1B **36**
NW10 . . . . 5A **42**
Craven Pas. WC2 . . . . . 1D **23**
    (off Craven St.)
Craven Rd. NW10 . . . . . 5A **42**
W2 . . . . 1E **73**
Craven St.
WC2 . . . . 1D **23** (2A **76**)
Craven Ter. W2 . . . . 1E **73**
Craven Wlk. N16 . . . . . . 2C **36**
Crawford Bldgs. W1 . . . 4A **60**
    (off Homer St.)
Crawford Est. SE5 . . . . . 5E **91**
Crawford Mans. W1 . . . 4A **60**
    (off Crawford St.)
Crawford M.
W1 . . . . 1A **12** (4B **60**)
Crawford Pas.
EC1 . . . . 4C **8** (3C **62**)
Crawford Pl. W1 . . . . . . 5A **60**
Crawford Point E16 . . . . 5B **68**
    (off Wouldham Rd.)
Crawford Rd. SE5 . . . . . 4E **91**
Crawford St.
W1 . . . . 1A **12** (4A **60**)
Crawley Rd. E10 . . . . . . 3D **39**
Crawshay Ct. SW9 . . . . 4C **90**
Crawthew Gro.
SE22 . . . . 2B **106**
Crayford Cl. E6 . . . . 5F **69**
Crayford Ho. SE1 . . . . . 4C **26**
    (off Long La.)
Crayford Rd. N7 . . . . . . 1F **47**
Crayle Ho. EC1 . . . . 3E **9**
    (off Malta St.)
Crealock St. SW18 . . . . 4D **101**
Creasy Est. SE1 . . . . . . 4A **78**
Crebor St. SE22 . . . . . . 4C **106**
Credenhill Ho. SE15 . . . 3D **93**
Credenhill St.
SW16 . . . . 5E **117**
Crediton Hill NW6 . . . . . 2D **45**
Crediton Rd. E16 . . . . . . 5C **68**
NW10 . . . . 5F **43**
Credon Rd. E13 . . . . . . 1E **69**
SE16 . . . . 1D **93**
Creechurch La.
EC3 . . . . 3E **19** (5A **64**)
    (not continuous)
Creechurch Pl. EC3 . . . . 3E **19**

Creed Ct. E1 . . . . 2A 66
EC4 . . . . 3E 17
Creed La.
EC4 . . . . 3E 17 (5D 63)
Creek Ho. W14 . . . . 4A 72
(off Russell Rd.)
Creek Rd. SE8 . . . . 2C 94
SE10 . . . . 2C 94
Creekside SE8 . . . . 3D 95
Creeland Gro. SE6 . . . 1B 122
Crefeld Cl. W6 . . . . 2A 86
Creighton Av. E6 . . . . . 1F 69
Creighton Cl. W12 . . . . 1C 70
Creighton Rd. NW6 . . . 1F 57
Cremer Bus. Cen.
E2 . . . . 1F 11
(off Cremer St.)
Cremer Ho. SE8 . . . . . 3C 94
(off Deptford Chu. St.)
Cremer St.
E2 . . . . . . 1F 11 (1B 64)
Cremorne Est. SW10 . . 2F 87
Cremorne Rd. SW10 . . 3E 87
Creon Ct. SW9 . . . . . . 3C 90
(off Caldwell St.)
Crescent EC3 . . 4F 19 (1B 78)
Crescent, The E17 . . . . 1A 38
NW2 . . . . 5D 29
SW13 . . . . 5B 84
SW19 . . . . 3C 114
W3 . . . . 5A 56
Crescent Arc. SE10 . . . 2E 95
(off Creek Rd.)
Crescent Ct. SW4 . . . . 3F 103
(off Park Hill)
Crescent Ct. Bus. Cen.
E16 . . . . 3F 67
Crescent Gdns.
SW19 . . . . 3C 114
Crescent Gro. SW4 . . . 2E 103
Crescent Ho. EC1 . . . . . 4F 9
(off Golden La. Est.)
SE13 . . . . 5D 95
Crescent La. SW4 . . . . 2E 103
Crescent Pl. SW3 . . . . . 5A 74
Crescent Rd. E6 . . . . . . 5E 55
E10 . . . . 4D 39
E13 . . . . 5C 54
N8 . . . . 1F 33
Crescent Row
EC1 . . . . 4F 9 (3E 63)
Crescent Stables
SW15 . . . . 3A 100
Crescent St. N1 . . . . . . 4B 48
Crescent Way SE4 . . . . 1C 108
Crescent Wharf E16 . . . 3D 83
Crescent Wood Rd.
SE26 . . . . 3C 120
Cresford Rd. SW6 . . . . 4D 87
Crespigny Rd. NW4 . . . 1D 29
Cressal Ho. E14 . . . . . . 4C 80
(off Tiller Rd.)
Cresset Rd. E9 . . . . 3E 51
Cresset St. SW4 . . . . . . 1F 103
Cressida Rd. N19 . . . . . 3E 33
Cressingham Rd.
SE13 . . . . 1E 109
Cressington Cl. N16 . . . 2A 50
Cress M. BR1: Brom . . . 5F 123

Cresswell Gdns. SW5 . . 1E 87
Cresswell Ho. SE3 . . . . 1B 110
Cresswell Pl. SW10 . . . 1E 87
Cressy Ct. E1 . . . . 4E 65
W6 . . . . 4D 71
Cressy Ho's. E1 . . . . . . 4E 65
(off Hannibal Rd.)
Cressy Pl. E1 . . . . 4E 65
Cressy Rd. NW3 . . . . . . 2B 46
Cresta Ho. NW3 . . . . . . 4F 45
(off Finchley Rd.)
Crestfield St.
WC1 . . . . . . 1E 7 (2A 62)
Crest Rd. NW2 . . . . 4B 28
Crestway SW15 . . . . . . 4C 98
Creswick Wlk. E3 . . . . . 2C 66
Crewe Pl. NW10 . . . . . . 2B 56
Crewdson Rd. SW9 . . . 3C 90
Crewkerne Ct. SW11 . . 4F 87
(off Bolingbroke Wlk.)
Crews St. E14 . . . . 5C 80
Crewys Rd. NW2 . . . . . 4B 30
SE15 . . . . 5D 93
Crichton St. SW8 . . . . . 5E 89
Cricketers Ct. SE11 . . . 5D 77
(off Kennington La.)
Cricketers M. SW18 . . . 3D 101
Cricketers Wlk.
SE26 . . . . 5E 121
Cricketfield Rd. E5 . . . . 1D 51
Cricket La.
BR3: Beck 5A 122
Cricklade Av. SW2 . . . . 2A 118
CRICKLEWOOD 5A 30
Cricklewood B'way.
NW2 . . . . 5E 29
Cricklewood La. NW2 . . 1F 43
Cridland St. E15 . . . . . . 5B 54
Crieff Rd. SW18 . . . . . . 4E 101
Criffel Av. SW2 . . . . . . 2F 117
Crimscott St.
SE1 . . . . . . 5E 27 (4A 78)
Crimsworth Rd. SW8 . . 4F 89
Crinan St. N1 . . . . 1A 62
Cringle St. SW8 . . . . . . 3E 89
Cripplegate St.
EC2 . . . . . . 5A 10 (4E 63)
Crispe Ho. N1 . . . . 5B 48
(off Barnsbury Est.)
Crispian Cl. NW10 . . . . 1A 42
Crispin St. E1 . . 1F 19 (4B 64)
Crisp Rd. W6 . . . . 1E 85
Cristowe Rd. SW6 . . . . 5B 86
Criterion Ct. E8 . . . . . . 4B 50
(off Middleton Rd.)
Criterion M. N19 . . . . . 4F 33
Criterion Theatre 5B 14
(off Piccadilly)
Crockerton Rd.
SW17 . . . . 2B 116
Croft, The NW10 . . . . . 1B 56
Croft Cl. SE13 . . . . 4E 109
Croftdown Rd. NW5 . . . 5C 32
Crofters Ct. SE8 . . . . . . 5A 80
(off Croft St.)
Croft Ho. W10 . . . . 2A 58
(off Third Av.)
Croftongate Way
SE4 . . . . 3A 108

Crofton Leisure Cen.
. . . . 4C 108
CROFTON PARK 3B 108
Crofton Pk. Rd. SE4 . . 4B 108
Crofton Rd. E13 . . . . . . 3D 69
Crofton Ter. E5 . . . . . . 4A 92
Crofton Ter. E5 . . . . . . 2A 52
Crofts Ho. E2 . . . . 1C 64
(off Teale St.)
Crofts St. E1 . . . . 1C 78
Croftway NW3 . . . . 1C 44
Crogsland Rd. NW1 . . . 4C 46
Cromartie Rd. N19 . . . . 2F 33
Cromarty Ct. SW2 . . . . 3B 104
Cromarty Ho. E1 . . . . . 4A 66
(off Ben Jonson Rd.)
Crombie M. SW11 . . . . 5A 88
Crome Rd. NW10 . . . . . 3A 42
Cromer Ct. E10 . . . . . . 2F 39
SW17 . . . . 5C 116
Cromer St.
WC1 . . . . . . 2D 7 (2A 62)
Cromer Ter. E8 . . . . . . 2C 50
Cromer Vs. Rd.
SW18 . . . . 4B 100
Cromford Path E5 . . . . 1F 51
Cromford Rd. SW18 . . . 3C 100
Crompton Ct. SW3 . . . . 5A 74
Crompton Ho. SE1 . . . . 4E 77
(off County St.)
W2 . . . . 3F 59
(off Hall Pl.)
Crompton St. W2 . . . . . 3F 59
Cromwell Av. N6 . . . . . . 3D 33
W6 . . . . 1D 85
Cromwell Cl. E1 . . . . . . 2C 78
Cromwell Cres. SW5 . . 5C 72
Cromwell Gdns. SW7 . . 4F 73
Cromwell Gro. W6 . . . . 4E 71
Cromwell Highwalk
EC2 . . . . 5A 10
Cromwell Ind. Est.
E10 . . . . 3A 38
Cromwell Lodge E1 . . . 3E 65
(off Cleveland Gro.)
Cromwell M. SW7 . . . . 5F 73
Cromwell Pl. EC2 . . . . . 5A 10
(off Beech St.)
N6 . . . . 3D 33
SW7 . . . . 5F 73
Cromwell Rd. E7 . . . . . 4E 55
E17 . . . . 1E 39
SW5 . . . . 5C 72
SW7 . . . . 5C 72
SW9 . . . . 4D 91
SW19 . . . . 5C 114
Cromwell Twr. EC2 . . . 5A 10
Crondace Rd. SW6 . . . 4C 86
Crondall Ct. N1 . . . . . . 1C 10
Crondall Ho. SW15 . . . 5C 98
Crondall St.
N1 . . . . 1C 10 (1F 63)
Crone Ct. NW6 . . . . . . 1B 58
(off Denmark Rd.)
Cronin St. SE15 . . . . . . 3B 92
Crooked Billet Yd.
E2 . . . . . . 2E 11 (2A 64)
Crooke Rd. SE8 . . . . . . 1A 94
Crookham Rd. SW6 . . . 4B 86

Croombs Rd. E16 . . . . . 4E 69
Croom's Hill SE10 . . . . . 3E 95
Croom's Hill Gro.
  SE10 . . . . 3E 95
Cropley Ct. *N1* *1F 63*
  (off Cropley St.,
    not continuous)
Cropley St.
  N1 . . . . 1B 10 (1F 63)
Cropthorne Ct. W9 . . . . 2E 59
Crosby Ct.
  SE1 . . . . 3B 26 (3F 77)
Crosby Ho. E7 . . . . 3C 54
  E14 . . . . 4E 81
    (off Manchester Rd.)
Crosby Rd. E7 . . . . 3C 54
Crosby Row
  SE1 . . . . 4B 26 (3F 77)
Crosby Sq.
  EC3 . . . . . . 3D 19 (5A 64)
Crosby Wlk. E8 . . . . 3B 50
  SW2 . . . . 5C 104
Crosby Way SW2 . . . . . 5C 104
Crosier Cl. SE3 . . . . 4F 97
Crosland Pl.
  SW11 . . . . 1C 102
Cross Av. SE10 . . . . 2F 95
Crossbrook Rd. SE3 . . . 5F 97
Cross Cl. SE15 . . . . 5D 93
Crossfield Ho. *W11* . . . *1A 72*
  (off Mary Pl.)
Crossfield Rd. NW3 . . . . 3F 45
Crossfield St. SE8 . . . . . 3C 94
  (not continuous)
Crossford St. SW9 . . . . . 5B 90
Cross Keys Cl.
  W1 . . . . 1C 12 (4C 60)
Cross Keys Sq. *EC1* . . . *1F 17*
  (off Little Britain)
Cross La.
  EC3 . . . . . . 5D 19 (1A 78)
    (not continuous)
Crossleigh Ct. *SE14* . . *3B 94*
  (off New Cross Rd.)
Crosslet St. SE17 . . . . . 5F 77
Crosslet Va. SE10 . . . . . 4D 95
Crossley St. N7 . . . . 3C 48
Crossmount Ho. *SE5* . . *3E 91*
  (off Bowyer St.)
Cross Rd. SE5 . . . . 5A 92
Cross St. N1 . . . . 5D 49
  SE5 . . . . 1F 105
  SW13 . . . . 5A 84
Crossthwaite Av.
  SE5 . . . . 2F 105
Crosswall
  EC3 . . . . . . 4F 19 (1B 78)
Crossway N16 . . . . 2A 50
Crossway, The SE9 . . . . 2F 125
Crossway Ct. SE4 . . . . . 5A 94
Crossways Ter. E5 . . . . . 1E 51
Croston St. E8 . . . . 5C 50
CROUCH END 2F 33
Crouch End Hill N8 . . . . 2F 33
Crouch Hall Ct. N19 . . . 3A 34
Crouch Hall Rd. N8 . . . . 1F 33
Crouch Hill N4 . . . . 1A 34
  N8 . . . . 1A 34
Crouch Hill Recreation Cen.
  . . . . 2A 34

Crouchman's Cl.
  SE26 . . . . 3B 120
Crowborough Rd.
  SW17 . . . . 5C 116
Crowder St. E1 . . . . 1D 79
Crowfield Ho. N5 . . . . . . 1E 49
Crowfoot Cl. E9 . . . . 2B 52
Crowhurst Cl. SW9 . . . . 5C 90
Crowhurst Ho.
  SW9 . . . . 5B 90
    (off Aytoun Rd.)
Crowland Ho. *NW8* . . . *5E 45*
  (off Springfield Rd.)
Crowland Rd. N15 . . . . . 1B 36
Crowland Ter. N1 . . . . . . 4F 49
Crowline Wlk. N1 . . . . . . 3E 49
Crowmarsh Gdns.
  SE23 . . . . 5E 107
Crown Cl. E3 . . . . 5C 52
  NW6 . . . . 3D 45
Crown Cl. Bus. Cen.
  E3 . . . . 5C 52
    (off Crown Cl.)
Crown Ct. EC2 . . . . 3A 18
  SE12 . . . . 4D 111
  WC2 . . . . . . 3E 15 (5A 62)
Crown Dale SE19 . . . . . 5D 119
Crowndale Ct. *NW1* . . *1F 61*
  (off Crowndale Rd.)
Crowndale Rd. NW1 . . . 1E 61
Crownfield Rd. E15 . . . . 1F 53
Crown Hill Rd. NW10 . . 5B 42
Crown La. SW16 . . . . . . 5C 118
Crown La. Gdns.
  SW16 . . . . 5C 118
Crown Lodge *SW3* . . . *5A 74*
  (off Elystan St.)
Crown M. *E1* *4F 65*
  (off White Horse La.)
  E13 . . . . 5E 55
  W6 . . . . 5C 70
Crown Office Row
  EC4 . . . . . . 4B 16 (1C 76)
Crown Pas.
  SW1 . . . . . . 2A 22 (2E 75)
Crown Pl.
  EC2 . . . . . . 5D 11 (4A 64)
    (not continuous)
  NW5 . . . . 3D 47
  SE16 . . . . 1D 93
Crown Point SE19 . . . . . 5D 119
Crown Reach SW1 . . . . 1F 89
Crownstone Ct.
  SW2 . . . . 3C 104
Crownstone Rd.
  SW2 . . . . 3C 104
Crown St. SE5 . . . . 3E 91
Crown Wharf *E14* *2E 81*
  (off Coldharbour)
  SE8 . . . . 1B 94
    (off Grove St.)
Crows Rd. E15 . . . . 2F 67
Crowther Cl. *SW6* *2B 86*
  (off Bucklers All.)
Crowthorne Cl.
  SW18 . . . . 5B 100
Crowthorne Rd. W10 . . 5F 57
Croxley Rd. W9 . . . . 2B 58
Croxted Cl. SE21 . . . . . . 5E 105
Croxted M. SE24 . . . . . . 4E 105

Croxted Rd. SE21 . . . . . 5E 105
  SE24 . . . . 5E 105
Croxteth Ho. SW8 . . . . . 5F 89
Croydon Ho. *SE1* *3C 24*
  (off Wootton St.)
Croydon Rd. E13 . . . . . . 3B 68
Crozier Ho. SE3 . . . . . . 1D 111
  SW8 . . . . *3B 90*
    (off Wilkinson St.)
Crozier Ter. E9 . . . . 2F 51
Crucifix La.
  SE1 . . . . 3E 27 (3A 78)
Cruden Ho. *SE17* *2D 91*
  (off Brandon Est.)
Cruden St. N1 . . . . 5D 49
Cruikshank Ho. *NW8* . . *1A 60*
  (off Townshend Rd.)
Cruikshank Rd. E15 . . . . 1A 54
Cruikshank St.
  WC1 . . . . . . 1B 8 (2C 62)
Crummock Gdns.
  NW9 . . . . 1A 28
Crusader Ind. Est. N4 . . 1E 35
Crusoe M. N16 . . . . 4F 35
Crutched Friars
  EC3 . . . . . . 4E 19 (1A 78)
Crutchley Rd. SE6 . . . . . 2A 124
CRYSTAL PALACE 5B 120
Crystal Palace Athletics
  Stadium 5C 120
Crystal Palace Mus.
  . . . . 5B 120
Crystal Palace National
  Sports Cen. 5C 120
Crystal Palace Pde.
  SE19 . . . . 5B 120
Crystal Pal. Pk. Rd.
  SE26 . . . . 5C 120
Crystal Pal. Rd.
  SE22 . . . . 4B 106
Crystal Ter. SE19 . . . . . 5F 119
Crystal Vw. Ct.
  BR1: Brom 4F 123
Crystal Wharf N1 . . . . . 1D 63
Cuba St. E14 . . . . 3C 80
Cube Ho.
  SE16 . . . . . . 5F 27 (4B 78)
Cubitt Ho. SW4 . . . . 4E 103
Cubitt Steps E14 . . . . . . 2C 80
Cubitt St.
  WC1 . . . . . . 2A 8 (2B 62)
Cubitt's Yd. WC2 . . . . . . 4E 15
Cubitt Ter. SW4 . . . . 1E 103
CUBITT TOWN 5E 81
Cuddington *SE17* *5E 77*
  (off Deacon Way)
Cudham St. SE6 . . . . . . 5E 109
Cudworth Ho. SW8 . . . . 4E 89
Cudworth St. E1 . . . . . . 3D 65
Cuff Cres. SE9 . . . . 4F 111
Cuffley Ho. *W10* *4E 57*
  (off Sutton Way)
Cuff Point *E2* *1F 11*
  (off Columbia Rd.)
Culford Gdns. SW3 . . . . 5B 74
Culford Gro. N1 . . . . 3A 50
Culford Mans. *SW3* . . . *5B 74*
  (off Culford Gdns.)
Culford M. N1 . . . . 3A 50
Culford Rd. N1 . . . . 4A 50

Culham Ho. *E2* 2F **11**
(off Palissy St.)
Culling Rd. SE16 . . . . . . 4E **79**
Cullingworth Rd.
NW10 . . . . 2C **42**
Culloden Cl. SE16 . . . . 1C **92**
Cullum St.
EC3 . . . . . . 4D **19** (1A **78**)
Cullum Welch Ct.
N1 . . . . 1C **10**
(off Haberdasher St.)
Cullum Welch Ho. EC1 . . 4F **9**
(off Goswell Rd.)
Culmore Rd. SE15 . . . . 3D **93**
Culmstock Rd.
SW11 . . . . 3C **102**
Culpeper Ho. E14 . . . . . 5A **66**
Culpepper Ct. *SE11* . . 5C **76**
(off Kennington Rd.)
Culross Bldgs. *NW1* . . 1A **62**
(off Battle Bri. Rd.)
Culross Ho. W10 . . . . . . 5F **57**
(off Bridge Cl.)
Culross St.
W1 . . . . 5B **12** (1C **74**)
Culverden Rd.
SW12 . . . . 2E **117**
Culverhouse WC1 . . . . . 1F **15**
(off Red Lion Sq.)
Culverhouse Gdns.
SW16 . . . . 3B **118**
Culverley Rd. SE6 . . . . 1D **123**
Culvert Pl. SW11 . . . . . 5C **88**
Culvert Rd. N15 . . . . . . 1A **36**
SW11 . . . . 5B **88**
Culworth Ho. NW8 . . . . 1A **60**
(off Allitsen Rd.)
Culworth St. NW8 . . . . 1A **60**
Culzean Cl. SE27 . . . . 3D **119**
Cumberland Cl. E8 . . . 3B **50**
Cumberland Ga. *SW1* . . 1D **89**
(off Cumberland Ga.)
Cumberland Cres.
W14 . . . . 5A **72**
(not continuous)
Cumberland Gdns.
WC1 . . . . 1B **8** (2C **62**)
Cumberland Ga.
W1 . . . . 4A **12** (1B **74**)
Cumberland Ho.
E16 . . . . 2C **82**
(off Wesley Av.)
Cumberland Mans.
W1 . . . . 5B **60**
(off George St.)
Cumberland Mkt.
NW1 . . . . 1E **5** (2D **61**)
Cumberland Mills Sq.
E14 . . . . 1F **95**
Cumberland Pk. Ind. Est.
NW10 . . . . 2C **56**
Cumberland Pl.
NW1 . . . . 1D **5** (2D **61**)
SE6 . . . . 1B **124**
Cumberland Rd. E12 . . 1F **55**
E13 . . . . 4D **69**
SW13 . . . . 4B **84**
Cumberland St. SW1 . . 1D **89**
Cumberland Ter.
NW1 . . . . 1D **5** (1D **61**)

Cumberland Ter. M.
NW1 . . . . 1D **5**
(not continuous)
Cumbrian Gdns. NW2 . . 4F **29**
Cuming Mus. 5E **77**
(off Walworth Rd.)
Cumming St.
N1 . . . . 1A **8** (1B **62**)
Cumnor Cl. SW9 . . . . . 5B **90**
(off Robsart St.)
Cunard Pl.
EC3 . . . . . . 3E **19** (5A **64**)
Cunard Rd. NW10 . . . . 2A **56**
Cunard Wlk. SE16 . . . . 5F **79**
Cundy Rd. E16 . . . . 5E **69**
Cundy St. SW1 . . . . . . 5C **74**
Cunliffe St. SW16 . . . . 5E **117**
Cunningham Ho.
SE5 . . . . 3F **91**
(off Elmington Est.)
Cunningham Pl.
NW8 . . . . 3F **59**
Cupar Rd. SW11 . . . . . 4C **88**
Cupola Cl.
BR1: Brom 5D **125**
Cureton St. SW1 . . . . . 5F **75**
Curlew Ho. SE4 . . . . . 2A **108**
(off St Norbert Rd.)
SE15 . . . . 4B **92**
Curlew St.
SE1 . . . . 3F **27** (3B **78**)
Curness St. SE13 . . . . 2E **109**
Curnick's La. SE27 . . . 4E **119**
Curran Ho. SW3 . . . . . 5A **74**
(off Lucan Pl.)
Curricle St. W3 . . . . . . 2A **70**
Currie Hill Cl.
SW19 . . . . 4B **114**
Currie Ho. E14 . . . . . . 5F **67**
(off Abbott Rd.)
Cursitor St.
EC4 . . . . . . 2B **16** (5C **62**)
Curtain Pl.
EC2 . . . . . . 3E **11** (2A **64**)
Curtain Rd.
EC2 . . . . . . 2E **11** (3A **64**)
Curtis Dr. W3 . . . . 5A **56**
Curtis Fld. Rd.
SW16 . . . . 4B **118**
Curtis Ho. SE17 . . . . . 1F **91**
(off Morecambe St.)
Curtis St. SE1 . . . . 5B **78**
Curtis Way SE1 . . . . . . 5B **78**
Curve, The W12 . . . . . 1C **70**
Curwen Av. E7 . . . . 1D **55**
Curwen Rd. W12 . . . . . 3C **70**
Curzon Cinema
Mayfair 2D **21**
(off Curzon St.)
Soho 4C **14**
(off Shaftesbury Av.)
Curzon Ga. SW6 . . . . . 4E **87**
(off Imperial Rd.)
Curzon Cres. NW10 . . 4A **42**
Curzon Ga.
W1 . . . . 2C **20** (2C **74**)
Curzon Sq.
W1 . . . . 2C **20** (2C **74**)
Curzon St.
W1 . . . . 2C **20** (2C **74**)

Custance Ho. N1 . . . . . 1B **10**
(off Fairbank Est.)
Custance St.
N1 . . . . 1B **10** (2F **63**)
CUSTOM HOUSE 5E **69**
Custom House
. . . . 5D **19** (1A **78**)
Custom Ho. Reach
SE16 . . . . 3B **80**
Custom Ho. Wlk.
EC3 . . . . . . 5D **19** (1A **78**)
Cut, The SE1 . . 3C **24** (3C **76**)
Cutbush Ho. N7 . . . . . 2F **47**
Cutcombe Rd. SE5 . . . 5E **91**
Cuthbert Harrowing Ho.
EC1 . . . . 4F **9**
(off Golden La. Est.)
Cuthbert Ho. W2 . . . . . 4F **59**
(off Hall Pl.)
Cuthbert St. W2 . . . . . 4F **59**
Cuthill Wlk. SE5 . . . . . 4F **91**
Cutlers Gdns. EC2 . . . 1E **19**
Cutlers Sq. E14 . . . . . . 5C **80**
Cutler St. E1 . . 2E **19** (5A **64**)
Cutty Sark 2E **95**
Cutty Sark Gdns.
SE10 . . . . 2E **95**
(off King William Wlk.)
Cyclops M. E14 . . . . . . 5C **80**
Cygnet Cl. NW10 . . . . . 2A **42**
Cygnet Ho. SW18 . . . . 1E **101**
Cygnet Ho. Nth. E14 . . 5D **67**
(off Chrisp St.)
Cygnet Ho. Sth. E14 . . 5D **67**
(off Chrisp St.)
Cygnet St. E1 . . 3F **11** (3B **64**)
Cygnus Bus. Cen.
NW10 . . . . 2B **42**
Cynthia St. N1 . . 1A **8** (1B **62**)
Cyntra Pl. E8 . . . . 4D **51**
Cypress Gdns. SE4 . . . 3A **108**
Cypress Ho. SE14 . . . . 4F **93**
SE16 . . . . 3F **79**
(off Woodland Cres.)
Cypress Pl.
W1 . . . . 4A **6** (3E **61**)
Cyprus Cl. N4 . . . . 1D **35**
Cyprus Pl. E2 . . . . 1E **65**
Cyprus St. E2 . . . . 1E **65**
(not continuous)
Cyrena Rd. SE22 . . . . 4B **106**
Cyril Mans.
SW11 . . . . 4B **88**
Cyril St. EC1 . . . . 3E **9**
Cyrus St. EC1 . . . . 3E **9**
Czar St. SE8 . . . . 2C **94**

D

Dabbs La. EC1 . . . . 4C **8**
(off Farringdon Rd.)
Dabin Cres. SE10 . . . . 4E **95**
Dacca St. SE8 . . . . 2B **94**
Dace Rd. E3 . . . . 5C **52**
Dacre Gdns. SE13 . . . 2A **110**
Dacre Ho. SW3 . . . . . . 2F **87**
(off Beaufort St.)
Dacre Pk. SE13 . . . . . 1A **110**
Dacre Pl. SE13 . . . . . . 1A **110**

Dacre Rd. E11 . . . . 3B **40**
E13 . . . . 5D **55**
Dacres Est. SE23 . . . . 3F **121**
Dacres Ho. SW4 . . . . 1D **103**
Dacres Rd. SE23 . . . . 2F **121**
Dacre St.
SW1 . . . . 5B **22** (4F **75**)
Daffodil St. W12 . . . . . . 1B **70**
Dafforne Rd. SW17 . . . 3C **116**
Da Gama Pl. E14 . . . . 1C **94**
Dagenham Rd. E10 . . . . 3B **38**
Dagmar Ct. E14 . . . . . . 4E **81**
Dagmar Gdns. NW10 . . 1F **57**
Dagmar Pas. N1 . . . . . . 5D **49**
(off Cross St.)
Dagmar Rd. N4 . . . . . . 2C **34**
SE5 . . . . 4A **92**
Dagmar Ter. N1 . . . . . . 5D **49**
Dagnall St. SW11 . . . . . 5B **88**
Dagnan Rd. SW12 . . . 5D **103**
Dagobert Ho. E1 . . . . . . 4E **65**
(off Smithy St.)
Dagonet Gdns.
BR1: Brom 3C **124**
Dagonet Rd.
BR1: Brom 3C **124**
Dahomey Rd. SW16 . . 5E **117**
Dain Ct. W8 . . . . 5C **72**
(off Lexham Gdns.)
Dainford Cl.
BR1: Brom 5F **123**
Daintry Way E9 . . . . 3B **52**
Dairy Cl. NW10 . . . . . . 5C **42**
Dairyman Cl. NW2 . . . . 5F **29**
Dairy M. SW9 . . . . 1A **104**
Dairy Wlk. SW19 . . . . 4A **114**
Daisy Dobbings Wlk.
N19 . . . . 2A **34**
(off Jessie Blythe La.)
Daisy La. SW6 . . . . . . 1C **100**
Daisy Rd. E16 . . . . 3A **68**
Dakin Pl. E1 . . . . 4A **66**
Dakota Gdns. E6 . . . . . . 3F **69**
Dalberg Rd. SW2 . . . . 2C **104**
(not continuous)
Dalby Rd. SW18 . . . . . 2E **101**
Dalby St. NW5 . . . . 3D **47**
Dalebury Rd. SW17 . . 2B **116**
Dale Cl. SE3 . . . . 1C **110**
Daleham Gdns. NW3 . . 2F **45**
Daleham M. NW3 . . . . . 3F **45**
Dalehead NW1 . . . . 1F **5**
(off Hampstead Rd.)
Dale Ho. NW8 . . . . 5E **45**
(off Boundary Rd.)
SE4 . . . . 2A **108**
Dale Lodge N6 . . . . . . 1E **33**
Dalemain M. E16 . . . . . 2C **82**
Dale Rd. NW5 . . . . 2C **46**
SE17 . . . . 2D **91**
Dale Row W11 . . . . . . 5A **58**
Daleside Rd. SW16 . . 5D **117**
Dale St. W4 . . . . 1A **84**
Daleview Rd. N15 . . . . 1A **36**
Daley Ho. W12 . . . . . . 5D **57**
Daley St. E9 . . . . 3F **51**
Daley Thompson Way
SW8 . . . . 5D **89**
Dalgarno Gdns. W10 . . 4E **57**
Dalgarno Way W10 . . . 3E **57**

Dalgleish St. E14 . . . . . 5A **66**
Daling Way E3 . . . . 5A **52**
Dali Universe
. . . . 3F **23** (3B **76**)
Dalkeith Ct. SW1 . . . . . 5F **75**
(off Vincent St.)
Dalkeith Ho. SW9 . . . . 4D **91**
(off Lothian Rd.)
Dalkeith Rd. SE21 . . . 1E **119**
Dallas Rd. NW4 . . . . . . 2C **28**
SE26 . . . . 3D **121**
Dallinger Rd. SE12 . . 4B **110**
Dalling Rd. W6 . . . . . . 5D **71**
Dallington Sq. EC1 . . . . 3E **9**
(off Berry St.)
Dallington St.
EC1 . . . . 3E **9** (3D **63**)
Dalmain Rd. SE23 . . . 1F **121**
Dalmeny Av. N7 . . . . . 1F **47**
Dalmeny Rd. N7 . . . . . 5F **33**
(not continuous)
Dalmeyer Rd. NW10 . . 3B **42**
Dalmore Rd. SE21 . . . 2E **119**
Dalo Lodge E3 . . . . . . 4C **66**
(off Gale St.)
Dalrymple Rd. SE4 . . 2A **108**
DALSTON 3B **50**
Dalston La. E8 . . . . 3B **50**
Dalton Ho. SE14 . . . . . 2F **93**
(off John Williams Cl.)
SW1 . . . . 1D **89**
(off Ebury Bri. Rd.)
Dalton St. SE27 . . . . . 2D **119**
Dalwood St. SE5 . . . . . 4A **92**
Dalyell Rd. SW9 . . . . . 1B **104**
Damascene Wlk.
SE21 . . . . 1E **119**
Damask Cres. E16 . . . . 3A **68**
Damer Ter. SW10 . . . . . 3E **87**
Dames Rd. E7 . . . . 5C **40**
Dame St. N1 . . . . 1E **63**
Damien Ct. E1 . . . . 5D **65**
(off Damien St.)
Damien St. E1 . . . . 5D **65**
Damory Ho. SE16 . . . . . 5D **79**
(off Abbeyfield St.)
Danbury St. N1 . . . . . 1D **63**
Danby Ho. E9 . . . . 4E **51**
(off Frampton Pk. Rd.)
Danby St. SE15 . . . . . 1B **106**
Dancer Rd. SW6 . . . . . 4B **86**
Dando Cres. SE3 . . . . 1D **111**
Dandridge Cl. SE10 . . 1B **96**
Dandridge Ho. E1 . . . . . 5F **11**
(off Lamb St.)
Danebury Av. SW15 . . 4A **98**
(not continuous)
Daneby Rd. SE6 . . . . . 3D **123**
Danecroft Rd. SE24 . . 3E **105**
Danehurst St. SW6 . . . 4A **86**
Danemere St. SW15 . . 1E **99**
Dane Pl. E3 . . . . 1A **66**
Danescombe SE12 . . . 1C **124**
Danes Ct. NW8 . . . . . . 5B **46**
(off St Edmund's Ter.)
Danescroft NW4 . . . . . 1F **29**
Danescroft Av. NW4 . . 1F **29**
Danescroft Gdns.
NW4 . . . . 1F **29**

Danesdale Rd. E9 . . . . 3A **52**
Danesfield SE5 . . . . . . 2A **92**
(off Albany Rd.)
Danes Ho. W10 . . . . . . 4E **57**
(off Sutton Way)
Dane St.
WC1 . . . . 1F **15** (4B **62**)
Daneswood Av. SE6 . . 3E **123**
Daneville Rd. SE5 . . . . 4F **91**
Dangan Rd. E11 . . . . . 1C **40**
Daniel Bolt Cl. E14 . . . 4D **67**
Daniel Cl. SW17 . . . . 5A **116**
Daniel Gdns. SE15 . . . 3B **92**
Daniell Ho. N1 . . . . . . 1F **63**
(off Cranston St.)
Daniel Pl. NW4 . . . . . . 2D **29**
Dan Leno Wlk. SW6 . . 3D **87**
Dan Mason Dr. W4 . . . 5A **84**
Dansey Pl. W1 . . . . . . 4B **14**
Danson Rd. SE17 . . . . 1D **91**
Dante Pl. SE11 . . . . . . 5D **77**
Dante Rd. SE11 . . . . . 5D **77**
Danube Ct. SE15 . . . . . 3B **92**
(off Daniel Gdns.)
Danube St. SW3 . . . . . 1A **88**
Danvers Ho. E1 . . . . . . 5C **64**
(off Christian St.)
Danvers St. SW3 . . . . . 2F **87**
Da Palma Ct. SW6 . . . 2C **86**
(off Anselm Rd.)
Daphne St. SW18 . . . 4E **101**
Daplyn St. E1 . . . . 4C **64**
D'Arblay St.
W1 . . . . 3A **14** (5E **61**)
Darcy Ho. E8 . . . . 5D **51**
(off London Flds. E. Side)
Dare Ct. E10 . . . . 2E **39**
Darent Ho.
BR1: Brom 5F **123**
NW8 . . . . 4F **59**
(off Church St.)
Darenth Rd. N16 . . . . . 2B **36**
Darfield NW1 . . . . 5E **47**
(off Bayham St.)
Darfield Rd. SE4 . . . . 3B **108**
Darfield Way W10 . . . . 5F **57**
Darfur St. SW15 . . . . . 1F **99**
Darien Ho. E1 . . . . 4F **65**
(off Shandy St.)
Darien Rd. SW11 . . . . 1F **101**
Daring Ho. E3 . . . . 1A **66**
(off Roman Rd.)
Dark Ho. Wlk.
EC3 . . . . 5D **19** (1F **77**)
Darlan Rd. SW6 . . . . . 3B **86**
Darley Ho. SE11 . . . . . 1B **90**
(off Laud St.)
Darley Rd. SW11 . . . . 4B **102**
Darling Rd. SE4 . . . . . 1C **108**
Darling Row E1 . . . . . . 3D **65**
Darlington Ct. SE6 . . . 1B **124**
Darlington Ho. SW8 . . 3F **89**
(off Hemans St.)
Darlington Rd.
SE27 . . . . 5D **119**
Darnall Ho. SE10 . . . . . 4E **95**
(off Royal Hill)
Darnaway Pl. E14 . . . . 4E **67**
(off Aberfeldy St.)

Darnay Ho. SE16 . . . . . . 4C 78
Darnley Ho. E14 . . . . . . 5A 66
   (off Camdenhurst St.)
Darnley Rd. E9 . . . . 3E 51
Darnley Ter. W11 . . . . 2F 71
Darrell Rd. SE22 . . . . . . 3C 106
Darren Cl. N4 . . . . 2B 34
Darren Ct. N7 . . . . 1A 48
Darsley Dr. SW8 . . . . 4F 89
Dartford Ho. SE1 . . . . . . 5B 78
   (off Longfield Est.)
Dartford St. SE17 . . . . . . 2E 91
Dartington NW1 . . . . 5E 47
   (off Plender St.)
Dartington Ho. SW8 . . . . . 5F 89
   (off Union Gro.)
W2 . . . . 4D 59
   (off Senior St.)
Dartle Ct. SE16 . . . . 3C 78
   (off Scott Lidgett Cres.)
Dartmoor Wlk. E14 . . . . . 5C 80
   (off Charnwood Gdns.)
Dartmouth Cl. W11 . . . . . 5B 58
Dartmouth Ct. SE10 . . . . . 4E 95
Dartmouth Gro. SE10 . . . . 4E 95
Dartmouth Hill SE10 . . . . 4E 95
DARTMOUTH PARK 5D 33
Dartmouth Pk. Av.
   NW5 . . . . 5D 33
Dartmouth Pk. Hill
   N19 . . . . 3D 33
   NW5 . . . . 3D 33
Dartmouth Pk. Rd.
   NW5 . . . . 1D 47
   W4 . . . . 2A 84
Dartmouth Rd. NW2 . . . . 3F 43
   NW4 . . . . 1C 28
   SE23 . . . . 3D 121
   SE26 . . . . 3D 121
Dartmouth Row SE10 . . . 5E 95
Dartmouth St.
   SW1 . . . . 4C 22 (3F 75)
Dartmouth Ter. SE10 . . . . 4F 95
Dartrey Twr. SW10 . . . . . 3E 87
   (off Worlds End Est.)
Dartrey Wlk. SW10 . . . . . 3E 87
Dart St. W10 . . . . 2A 58
Darville Rd. N16 . . . . 5B 36
Darwen Pl. E2 . . . . 1D 65
Darwin Ct. NW1 . . . . 5D 47
   SE17 . . . . 5F 77
   (off Barlow St.)
Darwin Ho. SW1 . . . . 2E 89
   (off Grosvenor Rd.)
Darwin St. SE17 . . . . 5F 77
   (not continuous)
Daryngton Ho. SW8 . . . . 3A 90
   (off Hartington Rd.)
Dashwood Rd. N8 . . . . . . 1B 34
Dassett Rd. SE27 . . . . . . 5D 119
Data Point Bus. Cen.
   E16 . . . . 3F 67
Datchelor Pl. SE5 . . . . . . 4F 91
Datchet Ho. NW1 . . . . . . 1E 5
   (off Augustus St.)
Datchet Rd. SE6 . . . . 2B 122
Datchworth Ho. N1 . . . . 4D 49
   (off Sutton Est., The)
Date St. SE17 . . . . 1F 91

Daubeney Rd. E5 . . . . . . 1A 52
Daubeney Twr. SE8 . . . . 1B 94
   (off Bowditch)
Dault Rd. SW18 . . . . 4E 101
Dauncey Ho. SE1 . . . . . . 4D 25
Davenant Rd. N19 . . . . . 4F 33
Davenant St. E1 . . . . 4C 64
Davenport Ho. SE11 . . . . 5C 76
   (off Walnut Tree Wlk.)
Davenport Rd. SE6 . . . . 4D 109
Daventry Av. E17 . . . . . . 1C 38
Daventry St. NW1 . . . . . 4A 60
Daver Ct. SW3 . . . . 1A 88
Davern Cl. SE10 . . . . 5B 82
Davey Cl. N7 . . . . 3B 48
Davey Rd. E9 . . . . 4C 52
Davey's Ct. WC2 . . . . . . 4D 15
Davey St. SE15 . . . . 2B 92
David Beckham Academy, The
   . . . . 3B 82
Davidge Ho. SE1 . . . . . . 4C 24
   (off Coral St.)
Davidge St.
   SE1 . . . . 4D 25 (3D 77)
David Ho. SW8 . . . . 3A 90
   (off Wyvil Rd.)
David Lee Point E15 . . . . 5A 54
   (off Leather Gdns.)
David Lloyd Leisure
   Kidbrooke 2D 111
   South Kensington . . . 5D 73
   (in Point West)
David M. W1 . . . . 5A 4 (4B 60)
Davidson Gdns. SW8 . . . 3A 90
Davidson Terraces E7 . . 2D 55
   (off Claremont Rd.,
   not continuous)
David's Rd. SE23 . . . . . . 1E 121
David St. E15 . . . . 3F 53
Davies La. E11 . . . . 4A 40
Davies M.
   W1 . . . . 4D 13 (1D 75)
Davies St.
   W1 . . . . 3D 13 (5D 61)
Da Vinci Ct. SE16 . . . . . . 1D 93
   (off Rossetti Rd.)
Davis Ho. W12 . . . . 1D 71
   (off White City Est.)
Davis Rd. W3 . . . . 2B 70
Davis St. E13 . . . . 1D 69
Davisville Rd. W12 . . . . . 3C 70
Dawes Ho. SE17 . . . . 5F 77
   (off Orb St.)
Dawes Rd. SW6 . . . . 3A 86
Dawes St. SE17 . . . . 1F 91
Dawlish Av. SW18 . . . . . 2D 115
Dawlish Rd. E10 . . . . 3E 39
   NW2 . . . . 3F 43
Dawnay Gdns. SW18 . . . 2F 115
Dawnay Rd. SW18 . . . . . 2F 115
Dawn Cres. E15 . . . . 5F 53
Dawpool Rd. NW2 . . . . . 4B 28
Dawson Ho. E2 . . . . 2E 65
   (off Sceptre Rd.)
Dawson Pl. W2 . . . . 1C 72
Dawson Rd. NW2 . . . . . . 2E 43
Dawson St.
   E2 . . . . 1F 11 (1B 64)
Day Ho. SE5 . . . . 3E 91
   (off Bethwin Rd.)

Daylesford Av. SW15 . . . 2C 98
Daysbrook Rd. SW2 . . . . 1B 118
Dayton Ct. SE15 . . . . 4E 93
Deacon Ho. SE11 . . . . . . 5B 76
   (off Black Prince Rd.)
Deacon M. N1 . . . . 4F 49
Deacon Rd. NW2 . . . . . . 2C 42
Deacon's Ri. N2 . . . . 1F 31
Deacons Ter. N1 . . . . 3E 49
   (off Harecourt Rd.)
Deacon Way SE17 . . . . . 5E 77
Deal Ho. SE15 . . . . 2F 93
   (off Lovelinch La.)
Deal Porters Wlk.
   SE16 . . . . 3F 79
Deal Porters Way
   SE16 . . . . 4E 79
Deal Rd. SW17 . . . . 5C 116
Deal's Gateway SE10 . . . 4C 94
Deal St. E1 . . . . 4C 64
Dealtry Rd. SW15 . . . . . . 2E 99
Deal Wlk. SW9 . . . . 3C 90
Dean Abbott Ho. SW1 . . 5F 75
   (off Vincent St.)
Dean Bradley St. SW1 . . 4A 76
Dean Cl. E9 . . . . 2E 51
   SE16 . . . . 2F 79
Dean Ct. SW8 . . . . 3A 90
   (off Thorncroft St.)
Deancross St. E1 . . . . . . 5E 65
Deanery M. W1 . . . . 1C 20
Deanery Rd. E15 . . . . . . 3A 54
Deanery St.
   W1 . . . . 1C 20 (2C 74)
Dean Farrar St.
   SW1 . . . . 5C 22 (4F 75)
Dean Ho. E1 . . . . 5E 65
   (off Tarling St.)
   SE14 . . . . 3A 94
   (off New Cross Rd.)
Dean Rd. NW2 . . . . 3E 43
Dean Ryle St. SW1 . . . . . 5A 76
Dean's Bldgs. SE17 . . . . 5F 77
Dean's Ct.
   EC4 . . . . 3E 17 (5D 63)
Deans Ga. Cl. SE23 . . . . 3F 121
Deanshanger Ho.
   SE8 . . . . 5F 79
   (off Chilton Gro.)
Dean's M.
   W1 . . . . 2E 13 (5D 61)
Dean Stanley St.
   SW1 . . . . 5D 23 (4A 76)
Dean St. E7 . . . . 2C 54
   W1 . . . . 2B 14 (5F 61)
Dean's Yd. SW1 . . . . 5C 22
Dean Trench St.
   SW1 . . . . 5D 23 (4A 76)
Deason St. E15 . . . . 5E 53
Deauville Ct. SE16 . . . . . 3F 79
   (off Eleanor Cl.)
   SW4 . . . . 4E 103
De Barowe M. N5 . . . . . . 1D 49
Debdale Ho. E2 . . . . 5C 50
   (off Whiston Rd.)
De Beauvoir Ct. N1 . . . . 4F 49
   (off Northchurch Rd.)
De Beauvoir Cres.
   N1 . . . . 5A 50

De Beauvoir Est. N1 . . . . 5A **50**
De Beauvoir Pl. N1 . . . . 3A **50**
De Beauvoir Rd. N1 . . . . 5A **50**
De Beauvoir Sq. N1 . . . . 4A **50**
DE BEAUVOIR TOWN
 . . . . 5C **50**
Debenham Ct. E8 . . . . . . 5C **50**
 (off Pownall Rd.)
Debham Ct. NW2 . . . . . . 5E **29**
Debnams Rd. SE16 . . . . . 5E **79**
De Bruin Ct. E14 . . . . . . 1E **95**
 (off Ferry St.)
Decima St.
SE1 . . . . . . 5D **27** (4A **78**)
Deck Cl. SE16 . . . . 2F **79**
De Crespigny Pk.
SE5 . . . . 5F **91**
Deeley Rd. SW8 . . . . . . 4F **89**
Deepdale SW19 . . . . . . 4F **113**
Deepdene Gdns.
SW2 . . . . 5B **104**
Deepdene Point
SE23 . . . . 3F **121**
Deepdene Rd. SE5 . . . 2F **105**
Deerbrook Rd.
SE24 . . . . 1D **119**
Deerdale Rd. SE24 . . . . 2E **105**
Deerfield Cotts. NW9 . . 1B **28**
Deerhurst Ho. SE15 . . . . 2C **92**
 (off Haymerle Rd.)
Deerhurst Rd. NW2 . . . . 3F **43**
SW16 . . . . 5B **118**
Deeside Rd. SW17 . . . . 3F **115**
Dee St. E14 . . . . 5E **67**
Defoe Cl. SE16 . . . . 3B **80**
SW17 . . . . 5A **116**
Defoe Ho. EC2 . . . . 5A **10**
Defoe Pl. EC2 . . . . 5F **9**
 (off Beech St.)
SW17 . . . . 4B **116**
Defoe Rd. N16 . . . . 5A **36**
De Frene Rd. SE26 . . . 4F **121**
Dehar Cres. NW9 . . . . . 2B **28**
Dekker Ho. SE5 . . . . 3F **91**
 (off Elmington Est.)
Dekker Rd. SE21 . . . . . 4A **106**
Delacourt Rd. SE3 . . . . 3D **97**
Delafield Ho. E1 . . . . 5C **64**
 (off Christian St.)
Delafield Rd. SE7 . . . . . 1D **97**
Delaford Rd. SE16 . . . . 1D **93**
Delaford St. SW6 . . . . . 3A **86**
Delamere St. W2 . . . . . . 4D **59**
Delamere Ter. W2 . . . . . 4D **59**
Delancey Pas. NW1 . . . . 5D **47**
 (off Delancey St.)
Delancey St. NW1 . . . . 5D **47**
Delancey Studios
NW1 . . . . 5D **47**
Delany Ho. SE10 . . . . . . 2E **95**
 (off Thames Rd.)
Delarch Ho. SE1 . . . . . . 4D **25**
De Laune St. SE17 . . . . 1D **91**
Delaware Mans. W9 . . 3D **59**
 (off Delaware Rd.)
Delaware Rd. W9 . . . . . 3D **59**
Delawyk Cres. SE24 . . 4E **105**
Delfina Studio Trust . . . 3D **27**
 (off Bermondsey St.)
Delft Way SE22 . . . . . . 3A **106**

Delhi St. N1 . . . . 5A **48**
 (not continuous)
Delia St. SW18 . . . . 5D **101**
Delius Gro. E15 . . . . 1F **67**
Della Path E5 . . . . 5C **36**
Dell Cl. E15 . . . . 5F **53**
Dellow Ho. E1 . . . . 1D **79**
 (off Dellow St.)
Dellow St. E1 . . . . 1D **79**
Dell's M. SW1 . . . . 5E **75**
 (off Churton Pl.)
Delmaine Ho. E14 . . . . . 5A **66**
 (off Maroon St.)
Delmare Cl. SW9 . . . . . 2B **104**
Delme Cres. SE3 . . . . . 5D **97**
Delmerend Ho. SW3 . . . 1A **88**
 (off Ixworth Pl.)
Deloraine Ho. SE8 . . . . 4C **94**
Delorme St. W6 . . . . 2F **85**
Delta Bldg. E14 . . . . 5E **67**
 (off Ashton St.)
Delta Cl. NW2 . . . . 4C **28**
Delta Pk. SW18 . . . . . . 2D **101**
Delta Point E2 . . . . 2C **64**
Delta St. E2 . . . . 2C **64**
Delverton Ho. SE17 . . . . 1D **91**
 (off Delverton Rd.)
Delverton Rd. SE17 . . . 1D **91**
Delvino Rd. SW6 . . . . . . 4C **86**
De Montfort Pde.
SW16 . . . . 3A **118**
De Montfort Rd.
SW16 . . . . 3A **118**
De Morgan Rd.
SW6 . . . . 1D **101**
Dempster Rd. SW18 . . 3E **101**
Den, The 1E **93**
Denbigh Cl. NW10 . . . . 4A **42**
W11 . . . . 1B **72**
Denbigh Ct. E6 . . . . 2F **69**
Denbigh Ho. SW1 . . . . . 5A **20**
 (off Hans Pl.)
W11 . . . . 1B **72**
 (off Westbourne Gro.)
Denbigh M. SW1 . . . . . . 5E **75**
 (off Denbigh St.)
Denbigh Pl. SW1 . . . . . 1E **89**
Denbigh Rd. E6 . . . . 2F **69**
W11 . . . . 1B **72**
Denbigh St. SW1 . . . . . 5E **75**
 (not continuous)
Denbigh Ter. W11 . . . . 1B **72**
Denby Ct. SE11 . . . . . . 5B **76**
 (off Lambeth Wlk.)
Dence Ho. E2 . . . . 2C **64**
 (off Turin St.)
Denchworth Ho. SW9 . . 5C **90**
Dene Cl. SE4 . . . . 1A **108**
Denehurst Gdns.
NW4 . . . . 1E **29**
Denesmead SE24 . . . . 3E **105**
Denewood Rd. N6 . . . . 1B **32**
Denford St. SE10 . . . . . 1B **96**
 (off Glenforth St.)
Dengie Wlk. N1 . . . . 5E **49**
 (off Basire St.)
Denham Ct. SE26 . . . . 3D **121**
 (off Kirkdale)
Denham Ho. W12 . . . . . 1D **71**
 (off White City Est.)

Denham St. SE10 . . . . . 1C **96**
Denholme Rd. W9 . . . . . 2B **58**
Denison Ho. E14 . . . . . . 5C **66**
 (off Farrance St.)
Denison Rd. SW19 . . . 5F **115**
Denis Way SW4 . . . . . . 1F **103**
Denland Ho. SW8 . . . . . 3B **90**
 (off Dorset Rd.)
Denman Ho. N16 . . . . . 4A **36**
Denman Pl. W1 . . . . 4B **14**
Denman St. SE15 . . . . . 4B **92**
Denman St.
W1 . . . . 5B **14** (1F **75**)
Denmark Gro. N1 . . . . . 1C **62**
Denmark Hill SE5 . . . . . 4F **91**
Denmark Hill Est.
SE5 . . . . 2F **105**
Denmark Mans. SE5 . . 5E **91**
 (off Coldharbour La.)
Denmark Pl. E3 . . . . 2C **66**
WC2 . . . . 2C **14** (5F **61**)
Denmark Rd. NW6 . . . . 1B **58**
 (not continuous)
SE5 . . . . 4E **91**
Denmark St. E11 . . . . . 5A **40**
E13 . . . . 4D **69**
WC2 . . . . 2C **14** (5F **61**)
Denmead Ho. SW15 . . 4B **98**
 (off Highcliffe Dr.)
Denne Ter. E8 . . . . 5B **50**
Dennett's Rd. SE14 . . . 4E **93**
Denning Cl. NW8 . . . . . 2E **59**
Denning Point E1 . . . . . 2F **19**
 (off Commercial St.)
Denning Rd. NW3 . . . . . 1F **45**
Dennington Cl. E5 . . . . 4E **37**
Dennington Pk. Rd.
NW6 . . . . 3C **44**
Dennison Point E15 . . . 4E **53**
Denny Cl. E6 . . . . 4F **69**
Denny Cres. SE11 . . . . 1C **90**
Denny St. SE11 . . . . . . 1C **90**
Densham Ho. NW8 . . . . 1F **59**
 (off Cochrane St.)
Densham Rd. E15 . . . . . 5A **54**
Denstone Ho. SE15 . . . 2C **92**
 (off Haymerle Rd.)
Denton NW1 . . . . 3C **46**
Denton Ho. N1 . . . . 4D **49**
 (off Halton Rd.)
Denton Rd. N8 . . . . 1B **34**
Denton St. SW18 . . . . . 4D **101**
Denton Way E5 . . . . 5F **37**
Dents Rd. SW11 . . . . . 4B **102**
Denver Rd. N16 . . . . . . 2A **36**
Denwood SE23 . . . . . . 3F **121**
Denyer St. SW3 . . . . . . 5A **74**
Denys Ho. EC1 . . . . 5B **8**
 (off Bourne Est.)
Denzil Rd. NW10 . . . . . 2B **42**
Deodar Rd. SW15 . . . 2A **100**
Depot App. NW2 . . . . . 1F **43**
Depot Rd. W12 . . . . 1E **71**
Depot St. SE5 . . . . 2F **91**
DEPTFORD 3C **94**
Deptford Bri. SE8 . . . . 4C **94**
Deptford B'way. SE8 . . 4C **94**

Deptford Bus. Pk.
  SE15 . . . . 2E **93**
Deptford Chu. St.
  SE8 . . . . 2C **94**
Deptford Creek Bri.
  SE8 . . . . *2D* **95**
  (off Creek Rd.)
Deptford Ferry Rd.
  E14 . . . . 5C **80**
Deptford Grn. SE8 . . . . 2C **94**
Deptford High St.
  SE8 . . . . 2C **94**
Deptford Pk. Bus. Cen.
  SE8 . . . . 1A **94**
Deptford Strand SE8 . . 5B **80**
Deptford Trad. Est.
  SE8 . . . . 1A **94**
Deptford Wharf SE8 . . 5B **80**
De Quincey Ho. *SW1* . . . *1E* **89**
  (off Lupus St.)
De Quincey M. E16 . . . 2C **82**
Derby Ga.
  SW1 . . . . 3D **23** (3A **76**)
  (not continuous)
Derby Hill SE23 . . . . . . 2E **121**
Derby Hill Cres.
  SE23 . . . . 2E **121**
Derby Ho. *SE1* *5C* **76**
  (off Walnut Tree Wlk.)
Derby Lodge *WC1* *1F* **7**
  (off Britannia St.)
Derby Rd. E7 . . . . 4F **55**
  E9 . . . . 5F **51**
Derbyshire St. E2 . . . . . 2C **64**
  (not continuous)
Derby St. W1 . . . 2C **20** (2C **74**)
Dereham Ho. *SE4* *2F* **107**
  (off Frendsbury Rd.)
Dereham Pl.
  EC2 . . . . 2E **11** (2A **64**)
Derek Walcott Cl.
  SE24 . . . . 3D **105**
Dericote St. E8 . . . . . . 5D **51**
Dering St.
  W1 . . . . 3D **13** (5D **61**)
Dering Yd.
  W1 . . . . 3E **13** (5D **61**)
Derinton Rd. SW17 . . . 4B **116**
Dermody Gdns.
  SE13 . . . . 3F **109**
Dermody Rd. SE13 . . . 3F **109**
Deronda Est. SW2 . . . . 1D **119**
Deronda Rd. SE24 . . . . 1D **119**
Derrick Gdns. SE7 . . . . 4E **83**
Derry St. W8 . . . . 3D **73**
Dersingham Rd. NW2 . . 5A **30**
Derwent *NW1* *2F* **5**
  (off Robert St.)
Derwent Av. NW9 . . . . . 1A **28**
  SW15 . . . . 4A **112**
Derwent Ct. *SE16* *3F* **79**
  (off Eleanor Cl.)
Derwent Gro. SE22 . . . 2B **106**
Derwent Ho. *E3* *3B* **66**
  (off Southern Gro.)
  SW7 . . . . *5E* **73**
  (off Cromwell Rd.)
Derwent Ri. NW9 . . . . . 1A **28**
Derwent St. SE10 . . . . 1A **96**
Desborough Cl. W2 . . . 4D **59**

Desborough Ho.
  W14 . . . . *2B* **86**
  (off Nth. End Rd.)
Desborough St. *W2* . . . *4D* **59**
  (off Cirencester St.)
Desenfans Rd.
  SE21 . . . . 4A **106**
Desford Rd. E16 . . . . . . 3A **68**
Design Mus. 3B **78**
Desmond St. SE14 . . . . 2A **94**
Desmond Tutu Dr.
  SE23 . . . . 1B **122**
Despard Rd. N19 . . . . . 3E **33**
Dethick Ct. E3 . . . . . . 5A **52**
Detling Ho. *SE17* *5A* **78**
  (off Congreve St.)
Detling Rd.
  BR1: Brom 5C **124**
Detmold Rd. E5 . . . . . . 4E **37**
Devas St. E3 . . . . 3D **67**
Devenay Rd. E15 . . . . . 4B **54**
Deventer Cres.
  SE22 . . . . 3A **106**
De Vere Gdns. W8 . . . . 3E **73**
Deverell St.
  SE1 . . . . 5B **26** (4F **77**)
De Vere M. *W8* *4E* **73**
  (off De Vere Gdns.)
Devereux Ct. WC2 . . . . 3B **16**
Devereux La. SW13 . . . 3D **85**
Devereux Rd. SW11 . . . 4B **102**
Devitt Ho. *E14* *1D* **81**
  (off Wade's Pl.)
Devizes St. N1 . . . . . . 5F **49**
Devon Gdns. N4 . . . . . . 1D **35**
Devonia Rd. N1 . . . . . . 1D **63**
Devon Mans. *SE1* *3F* **27**
  (off Tooley St.)
Devonport W2 . . . . . . 5A **60**
Devonport M. W12 . . . 3D **71**
Devonport Rd. W12 . . . 2D **71**
  (not continuous)
Devonport St. E1 . . . . . 5F **65**
Devons Est. E3 . . . . . . 2D **67**
Devonshire Cl. E15 . . . 1A **54**
  W1 . . . . 5D **5** (4D **61**)
Devonshire Ct. *E1* *2E* **65**
  (off Bancroft Rd.)
  WC1 . . . . 5E **7**
  (off Boswell St.)
Devonshire Dr. SE10 . . 3D **95**
Devonshire Gro.
  SE15 . . . . 2D **93**
Devonshire Hall *E9* . . . *3E* **51**
  (off Frampton Pk. Rd.)
Devonshire Ho. *E14* . . . *5C* **80**
  (off Westferry Rd.)
  NW6 . . . . *3B* **44**
  (off Kilburn High Rd.)
  SE1 . . . . *5B* **25**
  (off Bath Ter.)
  SW1 . . . . *1F* **89**
  (off Lindsay Sq.)
Devonshire M. *SW10* . . *2F* **87**
  (off Park Wlk.)
  W4 . . . . 1A **84**
Devonshire M. Nth.
  W1 . . . . 5D **5** (4D **61**)
Devonshire M. Sth.
  W1 . . . . 5D **5** (4D **61**)

Devonshire M. W.
  W1 . . . . 4C **4** (3C **60**)
Devonshire Pas. W4 . . 1A **84**
Devonshire Pl. NW2 . . 5C **30**
  W1 . . . . 4C **4** (3C **60**)
  W8 . . . . 4D **73**
Devonshire Pl. M.
  W1 . . . . 4C **4** (4C **60**)
Devonshire Rd. E16 . . . 5D **69**
  E17 . . . . 1C **38**
  SE9 . . . . 2F **125**
  SE23 . . . . 1E **121**
  W4 . . . . 1A **84**
Devonshire Road
  Nature Reserve 5F **107**
Devonshire Row
  EC2 . . . . 1E **19** (4A **64**)
Devonshire Row M.
  W1 . . . . 4E **5**
Devonshire Sq.
  EC2 . . . . 1E **19** (5A **64**)
Devonshire St.
  W1 . . . . 5C **4** (4C **60**)
  W4 . . . . 1A **84**
Devonshire Ter. W2 . . . 5E **59**
Devons Rd. E3 . . . . . . 2D **67**
Devon St. SE15 . . . . . . 2D **93**
Devon Wharf E14 . . . . 4E **67**
De Walden Ho. *NW8* . . . *1A* **60**
  (off Allitsen Rd.)
De Walden St.
  W1 . . . . 1C **12** (4C **60**)
Dewar St. SE15 . . . . . . 1C **106**
Dewberry Gdns. E6 . . . 4F **69**
Dewberry St. E14 . . . . 4E **67**
Dewey Rd. N1 . . . . . . 1C **62**
Dewey St. SW17 . . . . . 5B **116**
Dewhurst Rd. W14 . . . 4F **71**
Dewsbury Ho. NW10 . . 2C **42**
Dewsbury Ter. NW1 . . 5D **47**
D'Eynsford Rd. SE5 . . . 4F **91**
Dhonau Ho. *SE1* *5B* **78**
  (off Longfield Est.)
Diadem Ct. W1 . . . . . . 2B **14**
Dial Wlk., The *W8* *3D* **73**
  (off Broad Wlk., The)
Diamond Est. SW17 . . . 3A **116**
Diamond Ho. *E3* *1A* **66**
  (off Roman Rd.)
Diamond St. SE15 . . . . 3A **92**
Diamond Ter. SE10 . . . 4E **95**
Diamond Way SE8 . . . 2C **94**
Diana Ho. SW13 . . . . . 4B **84**
Diana Cl. SE8 . . . . 2B **94**
Diana, Princess of Wales
  Memorial Fountain . . . 3F **73**
Diana, Princess of Wales
  Memorial Walk 2D **73**
  (in Kensington Gardens)
Dibden Ho. SE5 . . . . . . 3A **92**
Dibden St. N1 . . . . . . 5E **49**
Dibdin Ho. W9 . . . . . . 1D **59**
Dicey Av. NW2 . . . . . . 1E **43**
Dickens Est. SE1 . . . . . 3C **78**
  SE16 . . . . 4C **78**
Dickens House 4A **8**
Dickens Ho. NW6 . . . . . *2C* **58**
  (off Malvern Rd.)
  NW8 . . . . *3F* **59**
  (off Fisherton St.)

Dickens Ho. *SE17* 1D **91**
(off Doddington Gro.)
WC1 . . . . 3D **7**
Dickens M. *EC1* 5D **9**
(off Turnmill St.)
Dickenson Ho. N8 . . . . . 1B **34**
Dickenson Rd. N8 . . . . . 2A **34**
Dickens Rd. E6 . . . . 1F **69**
Dickens Sq.
SE1 . . . . 5A **26** (4E **77**)
Dickens St. SW8 . . . . . . 5D **89**
Dickinson Ct. *EC1* *3E **9***
(off Brewhouse Yd.)
Dicksee Ho. *NW8* *3F **59***
(off Lyons Pl.)
Dickson Ho. *E1* 5D **65**
(off Philpot St.)
Dickson Rd. SE9 . . . . . . 1F **111**
Dieppe Cl. W14 . . . . 1B **86**
Digby Bus. Cen. *E9* *3F **51***
(off Digby Rd.)
Digby Cres. N4 . . . . 4E **35**
Digby Mans. *W6* *1D **85***
(off Hammersmith Bri. Rd.)
Digby Rd. E9 . . . . 3F **51**
Digby St. E2 . . . . 2E **65**
Diggon St. E1 . . . . 4F **65**
Dighton Ct. SE5 . . . . . . 2E **91**
Dighton Rd. SW18 . . . . 3E **101**
Dignum St. N1 . . . . 1C **62**
Digswell St. N7 . . . . . . 3C **48**
Dilhorne Cl. SE12 . . . . . 3D **125**
Dilke St. SW3 . . . . 2B **88**
Dillwyn Cl. SE26 . . . . . 4A **122**
Dilston Gro. SE16 . . . . . 5E **79**
Dilton Gdns. SW15 . . . . 1C **112**
Dimes Pl. W6 . . . . 5D **71**
Dimond Cl. E7 . . . . 1C **54**
Dimsdale Wlk. E13 . . . . 1C **68**
Dimson Cres. E3 . . . . . . 2C **66**
Dingle Gdns. E14 . . . . . 1C **80**
Dingley La. SW16 . . . . . 2F **117**
Dingley Pl.
EC1 . . . . 1A **10** (2E **63**)
Dingley Rd.
EC1 . . . . 2F **9** (2E **63**)
Dingwall Gdns.
NW11 . . . . 1C **30**
Dingwall Rd. SW18 . . . . 5E **101**
Dinmont Est. E2 . . . . . . 1C **64**
Dinmont Ho. *E2* 1C **64**
(off Pritchard's St.)
Dinmont St. E2 . . . . 1D **65**
Dinmore Ho. *E9* 5E **51**
(off Templecombe Rd.)
Dinnington Ho. *E1* 3D **65**
(off Coventry Rd.)
Dinsdale Rd. SE3 . . . . . 2B **96**
Dinsmore Rd. SW12 . . . 5D **103**
Dinton Ho. *NW8* *3A **60***
(off Lilestone St.)
Dinton Rd. SW19 . . . . . 5F **115**
Diprose Lodge
SW17 . . . . 4F **115**
Dirleton Rd. E15 . . . . . . 5B **54**
Disbrowe Rd.
W6 . . . . 2A **86**
Discovery Bus. Pk.
SE16 . . . . *4C **78***
(off St James's Rd.)

Discovery Ho. *E14* 1E **81**
(off Newby Pl.)
Discovery Wlk. E1 . . . . . 2D **79**
Disney Pl.
SE1 . . . . 3A **26** (3E **77**)
Disney St.
SE1 . . . . 3A **26** (3E **77**)
Disraeli Gdns.
SW15 . . . . 2B **100**
Disraeli Rd. E7 . . . . 3C **54**
SW15 . . . . 2A **100**
Diss St. E2 . . . . . 1F **11** (1B **64**)
Distaff La.
EC4 . . . . 4F **17** (1E **77**)
Distillery La. W6 . . . . . . 1E **85**
Distillery Rd. W6 . . . . . . 1E **85**
Distin St. SE11 . . . . 5C **76**
Ditch All. SE13 . . . . 4D **95**
Ditchburn St. E14 . . . . . 1E **81**
Dittisham Rd. SE9 . . . . 4F **125**
Divisional Rd. E12 . . . . . 4F **41**
Divis Way *SW15* *4D **99***
(off Dover Pk. Dr.)
Dixon Clark Ct. N1 . . . . 3D **49**
Dixon Ho. *W10* 5F **57**
(off Darfield Way)
Dixon Rd. SE14 . . . . 4A **94**
Dixon's All. SE16 . . . . . . 3D **79**
Dobree Av. NW10 . . . . . 4D **43**
Dobson Cl. NW6 . . . . . . 4F **45**
Dobson Ho. *SE5* *3F **91***
(off Edmund St.)
SE14 . . . . *2F **93***
(off John Williams Cl.)
Doby Ct. EC4 . . . . 4A **18**
Dock Cotts. *E1* 1E **79**
(off Highway, The)
Dockers Tanner Rd.
E14 . . . . 4C **80**
Dockhead SE1 . . . . 3B **78**
Dockhead Wharf *SE1* . . 4F **27**
(off Shad Thames)
Dock Hill Av. SE16 . . . . . 2F **79**
Dockley Rd. SE16 . . . . . 4C **78**
Dockley Rd. Ind. Est.
SE16 . . . . *4C **78***
(off Dockley Rd.)
Dock Offices *SE16* *4E **79***
(off Surrey Quays Rd.)
Dock Rd. E16 . . . . 1B **82**
Dockside Rd. E16 . . . . . 1F **83**
Dock St. E1 . . . . 1C **78**
Doctor Johnson Av.
SW17 . . . . 3D **117**
Doctors Cl. SE26 . . . . . 5E **121**
Docwra's Bldgs. N1 . . . 3A **50**
Dodbrooke Rd.
SE27 . . . . 3C **118**
Dodd Ho. *SE16* *5D **79***
(off Rennie Est.)
Doddington Gro.
SE17 . . . . 2D **91**
Doddington Pl. SE17 . . . 2D **91**
Dodson St.
SE1 . . . . 4C **24** (3C **76**)
Dod St. E14 . . . . 5B **66**
Dog & Duck Yd. WC1 . . . 5F **7**
Doggett Rd. SE6 . . . . . . 5C **108**

Dog Kennel Hill
SE22 . . . . 1A **106**
Dog Kennel Hill Est.
SE22 . . . . 1A **106**
(off Albrighton Rd.)
Dog La. NW10 . . . . 1A **42**
Doherty Rd. E13 . . . . . . 3C **68**
Dolben Ct. SE8 . . . . 5B **80**
Dolben St.
SE1 . . . . . . 2D **25** (2D **77**)
(not continuous)
Dolby Rd. SW6 . . . . 5B **86**
Dolland Ho. *SE11* *1B **90***
(off Newburn St.)
Dolland St. SE11 . . . . . . 1B **90**
Dollar Bay Ct. *E14* *3E **81***
(off Lawn Ho. Cl.)
DOLLIS HILL 4D **29**
Dollis Hill Av. NW2 . . . . 5D **29**
Dollis Hill La. NW2 . . . . 1B **42**
Dolman Rd. W4 . . . . 5A **70**
Dolman St. SW4 . . . . . 2B **104**
Dolphin Ct. SE16 . . . . . 3F **79**
Dolphin Ct. NW11 . . . . . 1A **30**
SE8 . . . . 2B **94**
(off Wotton Rd.)
Dolphin Ho. SW18 . . . . 2D **101**
Dolphin La. E14 . . . . . . 1D **81**
Dolphin Sq. SW1 . . . . . 1E **89**
W4 . . . . 3A **84**
Dolphin Twr. *SE8* *2B **94***
(off Abinger Gro.)
Dombey Ho. *SE1* *3C **78***
(off Wolseley St.)
W11 . . . . *2F **71***
(off St Ann's Rd.)
Dombey St.
WC1 . . . . 5F **7** (4B **62**)
(not continuous)
Domecq Ho. *EC1* *3E **9***
(off Dallington St.)
Dome Hill Pk. SE26 . . . 4B **120**
Domelton Ho.
SW18 . . . . *4D **101***
(off Iron Mill Rd.)
Domett Cl. SE5 . . . . . . 2F **105**
Domfe Pl. E5 . . . . 1E **51**
Domingo St.
EC1 . . . . 3F **9** (3E **63**)
Dominica Cl. E13 . . . . . 1F **69**
Dominion Ct. *E8* *4B **50***
(off Middleton Rd.)
Dominion Ho. *E14* 1D **95**
(off St Davids Sq.)
Dominion St.
EC2 . . . . 5C **10** (4F **63**)
Dominion Theatre 2C **14**
(off Tottenham Ct. Rd.)
Donald Hunter Ho.
E7 . . . . 2D **55**
(off Woodgrange Rd.)
Donald Rd. E13 . . . . . . 5D **55**
Donaldson Rd. NW6 . . . 5B **44**
Donato Dr. SE15 . . . . . . 2A **92**
Doncaster Gdns. N4 . . . 1E **35**
Donegal Ho. *E1* *3D **65***
(off Cambridge Heath Rd.)
Donegal St. N1 . . . . 1B **62**
Doneraile Ho. *SW1* 1D **89**
(off Ebury Bri. Rd.)

Doneraile St. SW6 . . . . . 5F 85
Dongola Rd. E1 . . . . 4A 66
  E13 . . . . 2D 69
Dongola Rd. W. E13. . . 2D 69
Donkey All. SE22 . . . . . . 5C 106
Donkin Ho. SE16 . . . . . . 5D 79
  (off Rennie Est.)
Donmar Warehouse Theatre
  . . . . 3D 15
  (off Earlham St.)
Donnatt's Rd. SE14 . . . . 4B 94
Donne Cl. SE24 . . . . 4E 105
Donne Ho. E14 . . . . 5C 66
  (off Dod St.)
  SE14 . . . . 2F 93
  (off Samuel Cl.)
Donnelly Ct. SW6. . . . . . 3A 86
  (off Dawes Rd.)
Donne Pl. SW3 . . . . 5A 74
Donnington Ct. NW1 . . . 4D 47
  (off Castlehaven Rd.)
  NW10 . . . . 4D 43
Donnington Mans.
  NW10 . . . . 5E 43
  (off Donnington Rd.)
Donnington Rd.
  NW10 . . . . 4D 43
Donoghue Cotts. E14 . . . 4A 66
  (off Galsworthy Av.)
Donovan Ct. SW10 . . . . . 1F 87
  (off Drayton Gdns.)
Donovan Av. E1 . . . . 1E 79
  (off Cable St.)
Don Phelan Cl. SE5 . . . . 4F 91
Doon St. SE1 . . 2B 24 (2C 76)
Dora Ho. E14 . . . . 5B 66
  (off Rhodeswell Rd.)
  W11. . . . . 1F 71
  (off St Ann's Rd.)
Dorando Cl. W12 . . . . . . 1D 71
Doran Mnr. N2 . . . . 1B 32
  (off Gt. North Rd.)
Doran Wlk. E15 . . . . 4E 53
Dora Rd. SW19 . . . . 5C 114
Dora St. E14 . . . . 5B 66
Dora Way SW9 . . . . 5C 90
Dorchester Ct. N1. . . . . . 4A 50
  (off Englefield Rd.)
  NW2 . . . . 5F 29
  SE24 . . . . 3E 105
Dorchester Dr. SE24. . . . 3E 105
Dorchester Gro. W4 . . . . 1A 84
Dorchester Ter. NW2 . . . 5F 29
  (off Needham Ter.)
Dordrecht Rd. W3 . . . . . 2A 70
Doreen Av. NW9 . . . . . . 3A 28
Doreen Capstan Ho.
  E11 . . . . 5A 40
  (off Apollo Pl.)
Doria Rd. SW6 . . . . 5B 86
Doric Ho. E2 . . . . 1F 65
  (off Mace St.)
Doric Way
  NW1. . . . . . 1B 6 (2F 61)
Doris Emmerton Ct.
  SW11 . . . . 2E 101
Doris Rd. E7 . . . . 4C 54
Dorking Cl. SE8 . . . . 2B 94
Dorking Ho.
  SE1. . . . . 5C 26 (4F 77)

Dorlcote Rd. SW18 . . . . 5A 102
Dorman Way NW8 . . . . . 5F 45
  E10 . . . . 3F 37
Dorma Trad. Pk.
  E10 . . . . 3F 37
Dormay St. SW18 . . . . . 3D 101
Dormer Cl. E15 . . . . 3B 54
Dormstone Ho. SE17 . . . 5A 78
  (off Beckway St.)
Dornberg Cl. SE3 . . . . . . 3C 96
Dornberg Rd. SE3 . . . . . 3D 97
Dorncliffe Rd. SW6 . . . . 5A 86
Dorney NW3 . . . . 4A 46
Dornfell St. NW6 . . . . . . 2B 44
Dornton Rd. SW12. . . . . 2D 117
Dorothy Rd. SW11 . . . . . 1B 102
Dorrell Pl. SW9 . . . . 1C 104
Dorrien Wlk. SW16 . . . . 2F 117
Dorrington St.
  EC1 . . . . 5B 8 (4C 62)
Dorrit Ho. W11. . . . . 2F 71
  (off St Ann's Rd.)
Dorrit St.
  SE1 . . . . 3A 26 (3E 77)
Dorryn Ct. SE26 . . . . 5F 121
Dors Cl. NW9 . . . . 3A 28
Dorset Bldgs.
  EC4 . . . . 3D 17 (5D 63)
Dorset Cl.
  NW1. . . . . . . 5A 4 (4B 60)
Dorset Ct. N1 . . . . 4A 50
  (off Hertford Rd.)
Dorset Ho. NW1 . . . . 5A 4
  (off Gloucester Pl.)
Dorset M.
  SW1 . . . . 5D 21 (4D 75)
Dorset Pl. E15 . . . . 3F 53
Dorset Ri.
  EC4 . . . . 3D 17 (5D 63)
Dorset Rd. E7 . . . . 4E 55
  SE9 . . . . 2F 125
  SW8 . . . . 3A 90
Dorset Sq.
  NW1. . . . . . . 4A 4 (3B 60)
Dorset St.
  W1 . . . . 1A 12 (4B 60)
Dorton Cl. SE15 . . . . 3A 92
Dorville Cres. W6 . . . . . . 4D 71
Dorville Rd. SE12 . . . . . . 3B 110
Doughty Ct. E1 . . . . 2D 79
  (off Prusom St.)
Doughty Ho. SW10 . . . . . 2E 87
  (off Netherton Gro.)
Doughty M.
  WC1 . . . . 4F 7 (3B 62)
Doughty St.
  WC1 . . . . 3F 7 (3B 62)
Douglas Ct. NW6 . . . . . . 4C 44
  (off Quex Rd.)
Douglas Est. N1 . . . . 3E 49
  (off Oransay Rd.)
Douglas Eyre Sports Cen.
  . . . . 1F 37
Douglas Johnstone Ho.
  SW6 . . . . 2B 86
  (off Clem Attlee Ct.)
Douglas M. NW2 . . . . . . 5A 30
Douglas Path E14 . . . . . . 1E 95
  (off Manchester Rd.)
Douglas Pl. SW1 . . . . . . 5F 75
  (off Douglas St.)

Douglas Rd. E16 . . . . . . 4C 68
  N1 . . . . 4E 49
  NW6 . . . . 5B 44
Douglas Rd. Nth. N1 . . . 3E 49
Douglas Rd. Sth. N1 . . . 3E 49
Douglas St. SW1 . . . . . . 5F 75
Douglas Waite Ho.
  NW6 . . . . 4C 44
Douglas Way SE8. . . . . . 3C 94
  (Octavius St.)
  SE8 . . . . 3B 94
  (Stanley St.)
Doulton Ho. SE11. . . . . . 4B 76
  (off Lambeth Wlk.)
Doulton M. NW6 . . . . . . 3D 45
Dounesforth Gdns.
  SW18 . . . . 1D 115
Douro Pl. W8 . . . . 4D 73
Douro St. E3. . . . . 1C 66
Douthwaite Sq. E1 . . . . . 2C 78
Dove App. E6 . . . . 4F 69
Dove Commercial Cen.
  NW5 . . . . 2E 47
Dovecote Gdns.
  SW14 . . . . 1A 98
Dove Ct. EC2 . . . . 3B 18
Dovedale Bus. Est.
  SE15 . . . . 5C 92
  (off Blenheim Gro.)
Dovedale Rd. SE22 . . . . 3D 107
Dovehouse St. SW3 . . . . 1F 87
Dove M. SW5 . . . . 5E 73
Dover Cl. NW2 . . . . 4F 29
Dovercourt Est. N1 . . . . 3F 49
Dovercourt Rd.
  SE22 . . . . 4A 106
Doverfield Rd. SW2. . . . . 5A 104
Dover Flats SE1 . . . . 5A 78
Dover Ho. SE15 . . . . 2E 93
Dover Ho. Rd. SW15 . . . 2C 98
Dover Pk. Dr. SW15. . . . 4D 99
Dover Patrol SE3 . . . . . . 5D 97
Dover Rd. E12 . . . . 4E 41
  SE19 . . . . 5F 119
Dover St. W1. . 5E 13 (1D 75)
Dover Yd. W1 . . . . 1F 21
Dovet Ct. SW9 . . . . 4B 90
Doveton Ho. E1 . . . . 3E 65
  (off Doveton St.)
Doveton St. E1 . . . . 3E 65
Dove Wlk. SW1 . . . . 1C 88
Dovey Lodge N1 . . . . . . 4C 48
  (off Bewdley St.)
Dowanhill Rd. SE6 . . . . . 1F 123
Dowdeswell Cl.
  SW15 . . . . 2A 98
Dowding Ho. N6. . . . . . . 2C 32
  (off Hillcrest)
Dowdney Cl. NW5 . . . . . 2E 47
Dowe Ho. SE3 . . . . 1A 110
Dowes Ho. SW16 . . . . . . 3A 118
Dowgate Hill
  EC4 . . . . 4B 18 (1F 77)
Dowland St. W10 . . . . . . 2A 58
Dowlas St. SE5 . . . . 3A 92
Dowler Ho. E1 . . . . 5C 64
  (off Burslem St.)

Downbury M.
SW18 . . . . 3C **100**
Downderry Rd.
BR1: Brom 3F **123**
Downend Ct. SE15 . . . . . . 2A **92**
(off Longhope Cl.)
Downer's Cott.
SW4 . . . . 2E **103**
Downey Ho. E1 . . . . 3F **65**
(off Globe Rd.)
Downfield Cl. W9 . . . . . 3D **59**
DOWNHAM 5F **123**
Downham Ct. N1 . . . . . . 4F **49**
(off Downham Rd.)
Downham Ent. Cen.
SE6 . . . . 2B **124**
Downham La.
BR1: Brom 5F **123**
Downham Rd. N1 . . . . . 4F **49**
Downham Way
BR1: Brom 5F **123**
Downing St.
SW1 . . . . 3D **23** (3A **76**)
Dowland St. E11 . . . . . . 4A **40**
Down Pl. W6 . . . . 5D **71**
Downs Ct. Pde. E8 . . . 2D **51**
(off Amhurst Rd.)
Downsell Rd. E15 . . . . 1E **53**
Downsfield Rd. E17 . . 1A **38**
Downshire Hill NW3 . . 1F **45**
Downside Cres. NW3 . . 2A **46**
Downs La. E5 . . . . 1D **51**
Downs Pk. Rd. E5 . . . . 2B **50**
E8 . . . . 2B **50**
Downs Rd. E5 . . . . 1C **50**
Down St. W1 . . . 2D **21** (2D **75**)
Down St. M.
W1 . . . . 2D **21** (2D **75**)
Downton Av. SW2 . . . . 2A **118**
Downtown Rd. SE16 . . . 3A **80**
Dowrey St. N1 . . . . 5C **48**
Dowson Cl. SE5 . . . . . 2F **105**
Dowson Ho. E1 . . . . 5F **65**
(off Bower St.)
Doyce St.
SE1 . . . . 3F **25** (3E **77**)
Doyle Gdns. NW10 . . . . 5C **42**
Doyle Ho. SW13 . . . . . . 3E **85**
(off Trinity Chu. Rd.)
D'Oyley St. SW1 . . . . . 5C **74**
Doynton St. N19 . . . . . . 4D **33**
Draco Ga. SW15 . . . . . 1E **99**
Draco St. SE17 . . . . . . 2E **91**
Dragonfly Cl. E13 . . . . 2D **69**
Dragon Rd. SE15 . . . . . 2A **92**
Dragon Yd.
WC1 . . . . 2E **15** (5A **62**)
Dragoon St.
SE8 . . . . 1B **94**
Drake Cl. SE16 . . . . . . 3F **79**
Drake Ct. SE1 . . . . 4A **26**
(off Swan St.)
W12 . . . . 3E **71**
(off Scott's Rd.)
Drakefell Rd. SE4 . . . 1A **108**
SE14 . . . . 5F **93**
Drakefield Rd.
SW17 . . . . 3C **116**
Drake Hall E16 . . . . . . 2D **83**
(off Wesley Av.)

Drake Ho. E1 . . . . 4E **65**
(off Stepney Way)
E14 . . . . 1A **80**
(off Victory Pl.)
SW1 . . . . 2F **89**
(off Dolphin Sq.)
Drakeland Ho. W9 . . . . 3B **58**
(off Fernhead Rd.)
Drakeley Ct. N5 . . . . . . 1D **49**
Drake Rd. SE4 . . . . . . 1C **108**
Drakes Ct. SE23 . . . . . 1E **121**
Drakes Courtyard
NW6 . . . . 4B **44**
Drake St.
WC1 . . . . 1F **15** (4B **62**)
Draper Ho. SE1 . . . . . . 5D **77**
(off Elephant & Castle)
Draper Pl. N1 . . . . 5D **49**
(off Dagmar Ter.)
Drapers Gdns.
EC2 . . . . 2C **18** (5F **63**)
Drapers Rd. E15 . . . . . 1F **53**
Drappers Way SE16 . . 5C **78**
Drawdock Rd. SE10 . . . 3F **81**
Draxmont SW19 . . . . . 5A **114**
Draycot Rd. E11 . . . . . 1D **41**
Draycott Av. SW3 . . . . 5A **74**
Draycott Cl. NW2 . . . . . 5F **29**
SE5 . . . . 3F **91**
(not continuous)
Draycott M. SW6 . . . . 5B **86**
(off Laurel Bank Gdns.)
Draycott Pl. SW3 . . . . 5B **74**
Draycott Ter. SW3 . . . 5B **74**
Drayford Cl. W9 . . . . . . 3B **58**
Dray Gdns. SW2 . . . . 3B **104**
Draymans M. SE15 . . . 5B **92**
Drayson M. W8 . . . . . . 3C **72**
Drayton Gdns. SW10 . . 1E **87**
Drayton Ho. E11 . . . . . 3F **39**
SE5 . . . . 3F **91**
(off Elmington Rd.)
Drayton Pk. N5 . . . . . . 1C **48**
Drayton Pk. M. N5 . . . 2C **48**
Drayton Rd. E11 . . . . . 3F **39**
NW10 . . . . 5B **42**
Dreadnought St.
SE10 . . . . 4A **82**
Dreadnought Wharf
SE10 . . . . 2D **95**
(off Thames St.)
Dresden Cl. NW6 . . . . . 3D **45**
Dresden Ho. SE11 . . . . 5B **76**
(off Lambeth Wlk.)
Dresden Rd. N19 . . . . . 3E **33**
Dressington Av.
SE4 . . . . 4C **108**
Drewery Ct. SE3 . . . . . 1A **110**
Drewett Ho. E1 . . . . 5C **64**
(off Christian St.)
Drew Ho. SW16 . . . . . 3A **118**
Drew Rd. E16 . . . . 2F **83**
(not continuous)
Drewstead Rd.
SW16 . . . . 2F **117**
Driffield Rd. E3 . . . . . 1A **66**
Drill Hall Arts Cen. . . . 5B **6**
(off Chenies St.)
Drinkwater Ho. SE5 . . 3F **91**
(off Picton St.)

Drive, The N7 . . . . 3B **48**
(not continuous)
NW10 . . . . 5B **42**
NW11 . . . . 2A **30**
SW6 . . . . 5A **86**
Drive Mans. SW6 . . . . 5A **86**
(off Fulham Rd.)
Driveway, The E17 . . . 1D **39**
(off Hoe St.)
Dr Johnson's House . . 3C **16**
(off Pemberton Row)
Droitwich Cl. SE26 . . 3C **120**
Dromore Rd.
SW15 . . . . 4A **100**
Dron Ho. E1 . . . . 4E **65**
(off Adelina Gro.)
Droop St. W10 . . . . 2F **57**
Drovers Pl. SE15 . . . . . 3E **93**
Druce Rd. SE21 . . . . . 4A **106**
Druid St. SE1 . . 3E **27** (3A **78**)
Drummond Cres.
NW1 . . . . 1B **6** (2F **61**)
Drummond Ga. SW1 . . 1F **89**
Drummond Ho. E2 . . . . 1C **64**
(off Goldsmiths Row)
Drummond Rd. E11 . . . 1E **41**
SE16 . . . . 4D **79**
Drummond St.
NW1 . . . . 3F **5** (3E **61**)
Drum St. E1 . . . . 5B **64**
Drury Ho. SW8 . . . . . . 4E **89**
Drury La.
WC2 . . . . 2E **15** (5A **62**)
Drury Lane Theatre . . . 3F **15**
(off Catherine St.)
Drury Way NW10 . . . . . 2A **42**
Dryad St. SW15 . . . . . . 1F **99**
Dryburgh Ho. SW1 . . . 1D **89**
(off Abbots Mnr.)
Dryburgh Rd. SW15 . . 1D **99**
Dryden Ct. SE11 . . . . . 5D **77**
Dryden Mans. W14 . . . 2A **86**
(off Queen's Club Gdns.)
Dryden Rd. SW19 . . . . 5E **115**
Dryden St.
WC2 . . . . 3E **15** (5A **62**)
Dryfield Wlk. SE8 . . . . 2C **94**
Drylands Rd. N8 . . . . . 1A **34**
Drysdale Dwellings
E8 . . . . 2B **50**
(off Dunn St.)
Drysdale Ho. N1 . . . . . . 1E **11**
(off Drysdale St.)
Drysdale Pl.
N1 . . . . 1E **11** (2A **64**)
Drysdale St.
N1 . . . . 1E **11** (2A **64**)
Dublin Av. E8 . . . . 5C **50**
Ducal St. E2 . . . . 2B **64**
Du Cane Cl. W12 . . . . . 5E **57**
Du Cane Ct. SW17 . . . 1C **116**
Du Cane Rd. W12 . . . . 5B **56**
Ducavel Ho. SW2 . . . . 1B **118**
Duchess M.
W1 . . . . 1E **13** (4D **61**)
Duchess of Bedford Ho.
W8 . . . . 3C **72**
(off Duchess of Bedford's Wlk.)
Duchess of Bedford's Wlk.
W8 . . . . 3C **72**

Duchess St.
W1 . . . . 1E **13** (4D **61**)
Duchess Theatre 4F **15**
(off Catherine St.)

Duchy St.
SE1 . . . . . . 1C **24** (2C **76**)
(not continuous)

Ducie St. SW4 . . . . . . 2B **104**
Duckett M. N4 . . . . 1D **35**
Duckett M. N4 . . . . 1C **34**
Duckett St. E1 . . . . 3F **65**
Duck La. W1 . . . . 3B **14**
Du Cros Rd. W3 . . . . . . 2A **70**
DUDDEN HILL 2D **43**
Dudden Hill La.
NW10 . . . . 1B **42**
Dudden Hill Pde.
NW10 . . . . 1B **42**
Duddington Cl.
SE9 . . . . 4F **125**
Dudley Ct. W1 . . . . 5B **60**
(off Up. Berkeley St.)
WC2 . . . . 2D **15** (5A **62**)
Dudley Ho. W2 . . . . 4F **59**
(off Nth. Wharf Rd.)
Dudley M. SW2 . . . . 4C **104**
Dudley Rd. NW6 . . . . . 1A **58**
SW19 . . . . 5C **114**
Dudley St. W2 . . . . 4F **59**
Dudlington Rd. E5 . . . . 4E **37**
Dudmaston M.
SW3 . . . . 1F **87**
(off Fulham Rd.)
Dudrich M. SE22 . . . 3B **106**
Duffell Ho. *SE11* 1B **90**
(off Loughborough St.)
Dufferin Av. EC1 . . . . . 4B **10**
Dufferin Ct. *EC1* 4B **10**
(off Dufferin St.)
Dufferin St.
EC1 . . . . 4A **10** (3E **63**)
Duff St. E14 . . . . 5D **67**
Dufour's Pl.
W1 . . . . 3A **14** (5E **61**)
Dugard Way SE11 . . . . 5D **77**
Duggan Dr.
BR7: Chst 5F **125**
Duke Humphrey Rd.
SE3 . . . . 4A **96**
Duke of Wellington Pl.
SW1 . . . . 3C **20** (3C **74**)
Duke of York Column
(Memorial) 2C **22**
Duke of York Sq.
SW3 . . . . 5B **74**
Duke of York's Theatre
. . . . 5D **15**
(off St Martin's La.)
Duke of York St.
SW1 . . . . . . 1A **22** (2E **75**)
Duke Rd. W4 . . . . 1A **84**
Duke's Av. W4 . . . . . . 1A **84**
Dukes Ct. SE13 . . . . . . 5E **95**
SW14 . . . . 5A **84**
Duke's Head Yd. N6 . . 3D **33**
Duke Shore Wharf
E14 . . . . 1B **80**
Duke's Ho. *SW1* 5F **75**
(off Vincent St.)
Dukes La. W8 . . . . . . 3D **73**

Duke's La. Chambers
W8 . . . . 3D **73**
(off Dukes La.)

Duke's La. Mans.
W8 . . . . 3D **73**
(off Dukes La.)

Duke's M. W1 . . . . 2C **12**
Duke's Pl.
EC3 . . . . 3E **19** (5A **64**)
Dukes Point *N6* 3D **33**
(off Dukes Head Yd.)
Duke's Rd.
WC1 . . . . 2C **6** (2F **61**)
Dukesthorpe Rd.
SE26 . . . . 4F **121**
Duke St.
SW1 . . . . . . 1A **22** (2E **75**)
W1 . . . . 2C **12** (5C **60**)
Duke St. Hill
SE1 . . . . 1C **26** (2F **77**)
Duke St. Mans. *W1* . . . *3C* **12**
(off Duke St.)
Duke's Yd.
W1 . . . . 4C **12** (1C **74**)
Dulas St. N4 . . . . 3B **34**
Dulford St. W11 . . . . . 1A **72**
Dulka Rd. SW11 . . . . 3B **102**
Dulverton *NW1* *5E* **47**
(off Royal College St.)
Dulverton Mans.
WC1 . . . . 4A **8**
DULWICH 2A **120**
Dulwich Bus. Cen.
SE23 . . . . 1F **121**
Dulwich Comn.
SE21 . . . . 1A **120**
SE22 . . . . 1A **120**
Dulwich Hamlet F.C. . 2A **106**
Dulwich Lawn Cl.
SE22 . . . . 3B **106**
Dulwich Leisure Cen.
. . . . 2C **106**
Dulwich Oaks, The
SE21 . . . . 3A **120**
Dulwich Picture Gallery
. . . . 5F **105**
Dulwich Ri. Gdns.
SE22 . . . . 3B **106**
Dulwich Rd. SE24 . . . 3C **104**
Dulwich Upper Wood
Nature Pk. 5B **120**
DULWICH VILLAGE . . 5A **106**
Dulwich Village
SE21 . . . . 4F **105**
Dulwich Wood Av.
SE19 . . . . 4A **120**
Dulwich Wood Pk.
SE19 . . . . 4A **120**
Dumain Ct. *SE11* 5D **77**
(off Opal St.)
Dumbarton Ct. SW2 . . 4A **104**
Dumbarton Rd.
SW2 . . . . 4A **104**
Dumont Rd. N16 . . . . 5A **36**
Dumpton Pl. NW1 . . . . 4C **46**
Dunbar Ct. E7 . . . . . . 3C **54**
Dunbar St. SE27 . . . . 3E **119**
Dunbar Wharf *E14* . . 1B **80**
(off Narrow St.)
Dunboyne Rd. NW3 . . . 2B **46**

Dunbridge Ho. SW15 . . 4B **98**
(off Highcliffe Dr.)
Dunbridge St. E2 . . . . . 3C **64**
Duncan Gro. W3 . . . . . 5A **56**
Duncan Ho. *NW3* 4B **46**
(off Fellows Rd.)
SW1 . . . . 1E **89**
(off Dolphin Sq.)
Duncannon Ho. *SW1* . . 1F **89**
(off Lindsay Sq.)
Duncannon St.
WC2 . . . . 5D **15** (1A **76**)
Duncan Rd. E8 . . . . . . 5D **51**
Duncan St. N1 . . . . . . 1D **63**
Duncan Ter. N1 . . . . . . 1D **63**
(not continuous)
Dunch St. E1 . . . . 5D **65**
Duncombe Hill
SE23 . . . . 5A **108**
Duncombe Rd. N19 . . . 3F **33**
Duncrievie Rd.
SE13 . . . . 4F **109**
Dundalk Ho. *E1* 5E **65**
(off Clark St.)
Dundalk Rd. SE4 . . . . 1A **108**
Dundas Ho. *E2* 1E **65**
(off Bishop's Way)
Dundas Rd. SE15 . . . . 5E **93**
Dundee Ct. *E1* 2D **79**
(off Wapping High St.)
Dundee Ho. *W9* 2E **59**
(off Maida Va.)
Dundee Rd. E13 . . . . . 1D **69**
Dundee St. E1 . . . . . . 2D **79**
Dundee Wharf E14 . . . 1B **80**
Dundonald Ho. *E14* . . . 3D **81**
(off Admirals Way)
Dundonald Rd. NW10 . . 5F **43**
Dunedin Ho. E10 . . . . 5D **39**
Dunelm Gro. SE27 . . . 3E **119**
Dunelm St. E1 . . . . . . 5F **65**
Dunfield Gdns. SE6 . . 5D **123**
Dunfield Rd. SE6 . . . . 5D **123**
(not continuous)
Dunford Rd. N7 . . . . . . 1B **48**
Dungarvan Av. SW15 . . 2C **98**
Dunhill Point SW15 . . 1C **112**
Dunkeld Ho. *E14* 5F **67**
(off Abbott Rd.)
Dunkery Rd. SE9 . . . . 4F **125**
Dunkirk St. SE27 . . . . 4E **119**
Dunlace Rd. E5 . . . . . . 1E **51**
Dunlin Ho. *SE16* 5F **79**
(off Tawny Way)
Dunloe Ct. E2 . . . . 1B **64**
Dunloe St. E2 . . . . 1B **64**
Dunlop Pl. SE16 . . . . . 4B **78**
Dunmore Point *E2* 2F **11**
(off Gascoigne Pl.)
Dunmore Rd. NW6 . . . 5A **44**
Dunmow Ho. *SE11* 1B **90**
(off Newburn St.)
Dunmow Rd. E15 . . . . 1F **53**
Dunmow Wlk. *N1* 5E **49**
(off Popham St.)
Dunnage Cres. SE16 . . 5A **80**
(not continuous)
Dunnico Ho. *SE17* 1A **92**
(off East St.)

Dunn's Pas. WC1 . . . . . . 2E 15
Dunn St. E8 . . . . 2B 50
Dunollie Pl. NW5 . . . . . . 2E 47
Dunollie Rd. NW5 . . . . . . 2E 47
Dunoon Gdns. SE23 . . . . 5F 107
Dunoon Ho. N1 . . . . 5B 48
(off Bemerton Est.)
Dunoon Rd. SE23 . . . . . . 5E 107
Dunraven Rd. W12 . . . . . . 2C 70
Dunraven St.
  W1 . . . . 4A 12 (1B 74)
Dunsany Rd. W14 . . . . . . 4F 71
Dunsford Way
  SW15 . . . . 4D 99
Dunsmure Rd. N16 . . . . . . 3A 36
Dunstable M.
  W1 . . . . 5C 4 (4C 60)
Dunstan Ho's. E1 . . . . 4E 65
(off Stepney Grn.)
Dunstan Rd. NW11 . . . . . . 3B 30
Dunstan's Gro.
  SE22 . . . . 4D 107
Dunstan's Rd. SE22 . . . . 5C 106
Dunster Ct.
  EC3 . . . . 4E 19 (1A 78)
Dunster Gdns. NW6 . . . . . . 4B 44
Dunster Ho. SE6 . . . . . . 3E 123
Dunsterville Way
  SE1 . . . . 4C 26 (3F 77)
Dunston Rd. E8 . . . . 5B 50
  SW11 . . . . 5C 88
Dunston St. E8 . . . . 5B 50
Dunton Ct. SE23 . . . . . . 2D 121
Dunton Rd. E10 . . . . 2D 39
  SE1 . . . . 1B 92
Duntshill Rd. SW18 . . . . 1D 115
Dunworth M. W11 . . . . . . 5B 58
Duplex Ride
  SW1 . . . . 4A 20 (3B 74)
Dupree Rd. SE7 . . . . 1D 97
Durand Gdns. SW9 . . . . . . 4B 90
Durands Wlk. SE16 . . . . . . 3B 80
Durant St. E2 . . . . 1C 64
Durban Ct. E7 . . . . 4F 55
Durban Ho. W12 . . . . 1D 71
(off White City Est.)
Durban Rd. E15 . . . . 2A 68
  SE27 . . . . 4E 119
Durdans Ho. NW1 . . . . . . 4D 47
(off Farrier St.)
Durell Ho. SE16 . . . . 3F 79
(off Wolfe Cres.)
Durford Cres. SW15 . . . . 1D 113
Durham Cl. NW6 . . . . 1C 58
(off Kilburn Pk. Rd.,
  not continuous)
Durham Hill
  BR1: Brom 4B 124
Durham Ho. St. WC2 . . . . 5E 15
Durham Pl. SW3 . . . . 1B 88
Durham Rd. E12 . . . . 1F 55
  E16 . . . . 3A 68
  N7 . . . . 4B 34
Durham Row E1 . . . . 4F 65
Durham St. SE11 . . . . 1B 90
Durham Ter. W2 . . . . 5D 59
Durham Yd. E2 . . . . 2D 65
Durley Rd. N16 . . . . 2A 36
Durlston Rd. E5 . . . . 4C 36
Durnford Ho. SE6 . . . . . . 3E 123

Durnford St. N15 . . . . . . 1A 36
  SE10 . . . . 2E 95
Durning Rd. SE19 . . . . . . 5F 119
Durnsford Av. SW19 . . . . 2C 114
Durnsford Rd.
  SW19 . . . . 2C 114
Durrell Rd. SW6 . . . . 4B 86
Durrels Ho. W14 . . . . 5B 72
(off Warwick Gdns.)
Durrington Rd. E5 . . . . . . 1A 52
Durrington Twr.
  SW8 . . . . 5E 89
Durrisdeer Ho. NW2 . . . . . 1B 44
(off Lyndale)
Dursley Cl. SE3 . . . . 5C 97
Dursley Gdns. SE3 . . . . . . 4F 97
Dursley Rd. SE3 . . . . 5C 97
Durward St. E1 . . . . 4D 65
Durweston M. W1 . . . . 5A 4
Durweston St.
  W1 . . . . 1A 12 (4B 60)
Dutch Yd. SW18 . . . . . . 3C 100
Dutton St. SE10 . . . . 4E 95
Dye Ho. La. E3 . . . . 5C 52
Dyer's Bldgs.
  EC1 . . . . 1B 16 (4C 62)
Dyers Hall Rd. E11 . . . . . . 3A 40
Dyers Hill Rd. E11 . . . . . . 4F 39
Dyers La. SW15 . . . . 2D 99
Dylan Rd. SE24 . . . . . . 2D 105
Dylways SE5 . . . . 2F 105
Dymes Path SW19 . . . . . 2F 113
Dymock St. SW6 . . . . . . 1D 101
Dyneley Rd. SE12 . . . . . 3E 125
Dynevor Rd. N16 . . . . 5A 36
Dynham Rd. NW6 . . . . . . 4C 44
Dyott St.
  WC1 . . . . 2C 14 (5F 61)
Dysart St.
  EC2 . . . . 4D 11 (3F 63)
Dyson Ct. NW2 . . . . 3E 29
Dyson Ho. SE10 . . . . 1B 96
(off Blackwall La.)
Dyson Rd. E11 . . . . 1A 40
  E15 . . . . 3B 54

E

Eade Rd. N4 . . . . 2E 35
Eagle Cl. SE16 . . . . 1E 93
Eagle Ct.
  EC1 . . . . 5D 9 (4D 63)
Eagle Hill SE19 . . . . 5F 119
Eagle Ho. E1 . . . . 3D 65
(off Headlam St.)
  N1 . . . . 1F 63
(off Eagle Wharf Rd.)
Eagle Lodge NW11 . . . . . . 2B 30
Eagle M. N1 . . . . 3A 50
Eagle Pl. SW1 . . . . 5A 14
  SW7 . . . . 1E 87
Eagle St.
  WC1 . . . . 1F 15 (4B 62)
Eagle Wharf Ct. SE1 . . . . 2F 27
(off Lafone St.)
Eagle Wharf E. E14 . . . . . 1A 80
(off Narrow St.)
Eagle Wharf Rd. N1 . . . . . 1E 63

Eagle Wharf W. E14 . . . . . 1A 80
(off Narrow St.)
Eagle Works E. E1 . . . . . . 4F 11
Eagle Works W.
  E1 . . . . 4F 11 (3B 64)
Ealdham Sq. SE9 . . . . . . 2E 111
Eamont Ct. NW8 . . . . 1A 60
(off Eamont St.)
Eamont St. NW8 . . . . 1A 60
Eardley Cres. SW5 . . . . . 1C 86
Eardley Rd. SW16 . . . . . 5E 117
Earldom Rd. SW15 . . . . . . 2E 99
Earlham Ct. E11 . . . . 2B 40
Earlham Gro. E7 . . . . 2B 54
Earlham St.
  WC2 . . . . 3C 14 (5A 62)
Earl Ho. NW1 . . . . 3A 60
(off Lisson Gro.)
Earlom Ho. WC1 . . . . 2B 8
(off Margery St.)
EARL'S COURT 1C 86
Earls Court
  Exhibition Building
  . . . . 1C 86
Earl's Ct. Gdns. SW5 . . . . 5D 73
Earls Ct. Rd. SW5 . . . . . . 4C 72
  W8 . . . . 4C 72
Earl's Ct. Sq. SW5 . . . . . 1D 87
Earlsferry Way N1 . . . . . . 4A 48
  . . . . (not continuous)
EARLSFIELD 1E 115
Earlsfield Rd. SW18 . . . . 1E 115
Earlsmead Rd. NW10 . . . . 2E 57
Earls Ter. W8 . . . . 4B 72
Earlsthorpe M.
  SW12 . . . . 4C 102
Earlsthorpe Rd.
  SE26 . . . . 4F 121
Earlstoke St.
  EC1 . . . . 1D 9 (2D 63)
Earlston Gro. E9 . . . . 5D 51
Earl St. EC2 . . . . 5D 11 (4F 63)
  . . . . (not continuous)
Earls Wlk. W8 . . . . 4C 72
Earlswood Cl. SE10 . . . . . 2A 96
Earlswood St. SE10 . . . . . 1A 96
Early M. NW1 . . . . 5D 47
Earnshaw St.
  WC2 . . . . 2C 14 (5F 61)
Earsby St. W14 . . . . 5A 72
  . . . . (not continuous)
Eashing Point
  SW15 . . . . 1D 113
(off Wanborough Dr.)
Easleys M.
  W1 . . . . 2C 12 (5C 60)
East 10 Ent. Pk. E10 . . . . 3A 38
EAST ACTON 1B 70
E. Acton Arc. W3 . . . . . . 5A 56
E. Acton Ct. W3 . . . . 1A 70
E. Acton La. W3 . . . . 2A 70
E. Arbour St. E1 . . . . 5F 65
East Bank N16 . . . . 2A 36
East Block SE1 . . . . 3A 24
(off York Rd.)
Eastbourne M. W2 . . . . . . 5E 59
Eastbourne Rd. E15 . . . . . 5A 54
  N15 . . . . 1A 36
  SW17 . . . . 5C 116
Eastbourne Ter. W2 . . . . . 5E 59

Eastbrook Rd. SE3 . . . . . .4D 97
Eastbury Gro. W4. . . . . . .1A 84
Eastbury Ter. E1 . . . . .3F 65
Eastcastle St.
  W1. . . . . .2F 13 (5E 61)
Eastcheap
  EC3 . . . . .4D 19 (1A 78)
E. Churchfield Rd.
  W3. . . . . .2A 70
Eastcombe Av. SE7 . . . . .2D 97
Eastcote St. SW9 . . . . . . .5B 90
E. Cross Cen. E15 . . . . . .3C 52
E. Cross Route E3 . . . . . .4B 52
  E9. . . . . .2B 52
                        (Homerton)
  E9. . . . . .4B 52
                        (Old Ford)
  E15 . . . . .2B 52
Eastdown Ct. SE13 . . . . .2F 109
Eastdown Ho. E8 . . . . . . .1C 50
Eastdown Pk. SE13. . . . .2F 109
EAST DULWICH 2B 106
E. Dulwich Gro.
  SE22 . . . . .3A 106
E. Dulwich Rd.
  SE22 . . . . .2B 106
          (not continuous)
Eastern Av. E11 . . . . .1D 41
  IG4: Ilf. 1F 41
Eastern Gateway E16 . . . .1E 83
Eastern Quay Apartments
  E16. . . . . .2D 83
          (off Portsmouth M.)
Eastern Rd. E13 . . . . .1D 69
  E17 . . . . .1E 39
  SE4 . . . . .2C 108
E. Ferry Rd. E14. . . . . . . .5D 81
Eastfields Av. SW18. . . . .2C 100
Eastfield St. E14. . . . . . . .4A 66
East Gdns. SW17 . . . . . . .5A 116
EAST HAM 2F 69
E. Ham Ind. Est. E6 . . . . . .3F 69
E. Harding St.
  EC4 . . . . .2C 16 (5C 62)
E. Heath Rd. NW3 . . . . . . .5E 31
East Hill SW18 . . . . .3D 101
E. India Bldgs. E14 . . . . . .1C 80
          (off Saltwell St.)
E. India Ct. SE16. . . . . . . .3E 79
          (off St Marychurch St.)
E. India Dock Ho.
  E14 . . . . .5E 67
E. India Dock Rd.
  E14 . . . . .5C 66
Eastlake Ho. NW8. . . . . . .3F 59
          (off Frampton St.)
Eastlake Rd. SE5 . . . . . . .5E 91
Eastlands Cres.
  SE21 . . . . .4B 106
East La. SE16. . . . . .3C 78
          (Chambers St.)
  SE16. . . . . .3C 78
          (Scott Lidgett Cres.)
Eastlea M. E16. . . . . .3A 68
Eastleigh Cl. NW2 . . . . . . .5A 28
Eastleigh Wlk. SW15 . . . . .5C 98
East Lodge E16. . . . . .2C 82
          (off Wesley Av.)
E. London Crematorium
  E13 . . . . .2B 68

Eastman Ho. SW4 . . . . . .4E 103
Eastman Rd. W3 . . . . .3A 70
East Mascalls SE7 . . . . . .2E 97
Eastmearn Rd.
  SE21 . . . . .2E 119
Eastmoor Pl. SE7 . . . . . . .4F 83
Eastmoor St. SE7 . . . . . . .4F 83
East Mt. St. E1 . . . . .4D 65
          (not continuous)
Eastney St. SE10 . . . . . . .1F 95
Easton St.
  WC1. . . . . .3B 8 (3C 62)
East Parkside
  SE10 . . . . .3A 82
East Pas. EC1 . . . . .5F 9
East Pl. SE27 . . . . .4E 119
East Point SE1 . . . . .1C 92
E. Poultry Av.
  EC1 . . . . .1D 17 (4D 63)
East Rd. E15. . . . . .5C 54
  N1 . . . . .2B 10 (2F 63)
  SW3 . . . . .1C 88
East Row E11. . . . . .1C 40
  W10 . . . . .3A 58
Eastry Ho. SW8 . . . . .3A 90
          (off Hartington Rd.)
EAST SHEEN 2A 98
E. Sheen Av. SW14 . . . . . .3A 98
East Smithfield
  E1. . . . . .5F 19 (1B 78)
East St. SE17 . . . . .1E 91
E. Surrey Gro. SE15. . . . . .3B 92
E. Tenter St. E1 . . . . .5B 64
East Va. SW3 . . . . .1B 70
Eastville Av. NW11 . . . . . .1B 30
Eastway E9. . . . . .3B 52
Eastwell Ho. SE1 . . . . . . .5C 26
Eastwood Cl. N7. . . . . . . .2C 48
Eatington Rd. E10. . . . . . .1F 39
Eaton Cl. SW1 . . . . .5C 74
Eaton Dr. SW9 . . . . .2D 105
Eaton Ga. SW1. . . . . .5C 74
Eaton Ho. E14 . . . . .1B 80
          (off Westferry Cir.)
  SW11 . . . . .4F 87
Eaton La.
  SW1. . . . . .5E 21 (4D 75)
Eaton Mans. SW1 . . . . . . .5C 74
          (off Bourne St.)
Eaton M. Nth.
  SW1. . . . . . . .5C 20 (5C 74)
Eaton M. Sth. SW1 . . . . . .5C 74
Eaton M. W. SW1. . . . . . . .5C 74
Eaton Pl.
  SW1. . . . . . . .5C 20 (5C 74)
Eaton Row SW1. . . . . . . .4D 75
Eaton Sq.
  SW1. . . . . . . .5C 20 (5C 74)
Eaton Ter. E3 . . . . .2A 66
  SW1. . . . . .5C 74
Eaton Ter. M. SW1. . . . . . .5C 74
          (off Eaton Ter.)
Eatonville Rd.
  SW17 . . . . .2B 116
Eatonville Vs.
  SW17 . . . . .2B 116
Ebbisham Dr. SW8. . . . . .2B 90
Ebbsfleet Rd. NW2. . . . . .2A 44
Ebdon Way SE3 . . . . . . .1D 111
Ebenezer Ho. SE11 . . . . .5D 77

Ebenezer Mussel Ho.
  E2. . . . . .1E 65
          (off Patriot Sq.)
Ebenezer St.
  N1 . . . . .1B 10 (2F 63)
Ebley Cl. SE15 . . . . .2B 92
Ebner St. SW18 . . . . .3D 101
Ebony Ho. E2 . . . . .2C 64
          (off Buckfast St.)
Ebor Cotts. SW15. . . . . . .3A 112
Ebor St. E1. . . . . . .3F 11 (3B 64)
Ebsworth St.
  SE23 . . . . .5F 107
Eburne Rd. N7 . . . . .5A 34
Ebury Bri. SW1 . . . . .1D 89
Ebury Bri. Est. SW1 . . . . . .1D 89
Ebury Bri. Rd. SW1 . . . . . .1C 88
Ebury M. SE27 . . . . .3D 119
  SW1. . . . . .5D 75
Ebury M. E. SW1 . . . . .4D 75
Ebury Sq. SW1 . . . . .5C 74
Ebury St. SW1 . . . . .5C 74
Ecclesbourne Rd. N1. . . . .4E 49
Eccles Rd. SW11 . . . . . . .2B 102
Eccleston Bri. SW1 . . . . . .5D 75
Eccleston Ho.
  SW2 . . . . .4C 104
Eccleston M.
  SW1. . . . . . . .5C 20 (4C 74)
Eccleston Pl. SW1. . . . . . .5D 75
Eccleston Sq. SW1 . . . . . .5D 75
Eccleston Sq. M.
  SW1. . . . . .5D 75
Eccleston St. SW1 . . . . . . .4D 75
Eckford St. N1 . . . . .1C 62
Eckington Ho. N15 . . . . . .1F 35
          (off Fladbury Rd.)
Eckstein Rd. SW11 . . . . . .2A 102
Eclipse Rd. E13 . . . . .4D 69
Ecology Cen. and
  Arts Pavilion 2A 66
Ector Rd. SE6. . . . . .2A 124
Edans Ct. W12 . . . . .3B 70
Edbrooke Rd. W9 . . . . . . .3C 58
Eddisbury Ho. SE26. . . . . .3D 120
Eddiscombe Rd.
  SW6 . . . . .5B 86
Eddystone Rd. SE4 . . . . . .3A 108
Eddystone Twr. SE8 . . . . .1A 94
Edenbridge Cl. SE16 . . . .1D 93
          (off Masters Dr.)
Edenbridge Rd. E9 . . . . . .4F 51
Eden Cl. NW3. . . . . .4C 30
Eden Ct. NW3 . . . . .4C 72
Edencourt Rd.
  SW16 . . . . .5D 117
Eden Gro. E17 . . . . .1D 39
  N7 . . . . .2B 48
Edenham Way W10 . . . . . .3B 58
Eden Ho. NW8 . . . . .3A 60
          (off Church St.)
Edenhurst Av. SW6 . . . . . .1B 100
Eden Lodge NW6 . . . . . . .4F 43
Eden M. SW17 . . . . .3E 115
Eden Rd. E17. . . . . .1D 39
  SE27 . . . . .4D 119
Edensor Gdns. W4 . . . . . .3A 84
Edensor Rd. W4 . . . . .3A 84
Edenvale St. SW6 . . . . . . .5E 87
Eden Way E3 . . . . .5B 52

Edgar Ho. *E9* 2A **52**
  (off Homerton Rd.)
E11 . . . . 2C **40**
SW8 . . . . 3A **90**
  (off Wyvil Rd.)
Edgar Kail Way
SE22 . . . . 2A **106**
Edgarley Ter. SW6 . . . . . 4A **86**
Edgar Rd. E3 . . . . 2D **67**
Edgcott Ho. *W10* 4E **57**
  (off Sutton Way)
Edge Bus. Cen., The
NW2 . . . . 4D **29**
Edgecombe Ho. SE5 . . . 5A **92**
SW19 . . . . 1A **114**
Edgecot Gro. N15 . . . . . 1A **36**
Edgehill Ho. SW9 . . . . . 5D **91**
Edgeley La. SW4 . . . . 1F **103**
Edgeley Rd. SW4 . . . . 1F **103**
Edgel St. SW18 . . . . . . 2D **101**
Edgepoint Cl. SE27 . . . 5D **119**
Edge St. W8 . . . . 2C **72**
Edgeworth Ho. *NW8* . . 5E **45**
  (off Boundary Rd.)
Edgeworth Rd. SE9 . . . 2E **111**
Edgson Ho. *SW1* 1D **89**
  (off Ebury Bri. Rd.)
Edgware Rd. NW2 . . . . 3D **29**
W2 . . . . 3A **12** (3F **59**)
Edinburgh Cl. E2 . . . . . . 1E **65**
Edinburgh Ct. *SE16* . . . 2F **79**
  (off Rotherhithe St.)
Edinburgh Ga. SW1 . . . . 3B **74**
Edinburgh Ho. *W9* 2D **59**
  (off Maida Va.)
Edinburgh Rd. E13 . . . . 1D **69**
E17 . . . . 1C **38**
  (not continuous)
Edington NW5 . . . . 3C **46**
Edison Bldg. E14 . . . . . 3C **80**
Edison Ct. SE10 . . . . . . 4B **82**
Edison Rd. N8 . . . . 1F **33**
Edis St. NW1 . . . . 5C **46**
Edith Brinson Ho.
  E14 . . . . 5F **67**
  (off Oban St.)
Edith Cavell Cl. N19 . . . 2A **34**
Edith Gro. SW10 . . . . . . 2E **87**
Edith Ho. *W6* 1E **85**
  (off Queen Caroline St.)
Editha St. SW9 . . . . . . 1A **104**
Edith Neville Cotts.
  NW1 . . . . 1B **6**
  (off Drummond Cres.)
Edith Ramsay Ho. *E1* . . 4A **66**
  (off Duckett St.)
Edith Rd. E6 . . . . 4F **55**
E15 . . . . 2F **53**
SW19 . . . . 5D **115**
W14 . . . . 5A **72**
Edith Row SW6 . . . . . . 4D **87**
Edith St. E2 . . . . 1C **64**
Edith Summerskill Ho.
  SW6 . . . . 3B **86**
  (off Clem Attlee Est.)
Edith Ter. SW10 . . . . . . 3E **87**
Edith Vs. W14 . . . . 5B **72**
Edith Yd. SW10 . . . . . . 3E **87**
Edmeston Cl. E9 . . . . . . 3A **52**
Edmond Ct. SE14 . . . . . 4E **93**

Edmonton Ct. *SE16* . . . 4E **79**
  (off Canada Est.)
Edmund Halley Way
SE10 . . . . 3A **82**
Edmundsbury Ct. Est.
  SW9 . . . . 2B **104**
Edmund St. SE5 . . . . . . 3F **91**
Ednam Ho. *SE15* 2C **92**
  (off Haymerle Rd.)
Edna St. SW11 . . . . 4A **88**
Edred Ho. *E9* 1A **52**
  (off Lindisfarne Way)
Edrich Ho. SW4 . . . . . . 4A **90**
Edric Ho. *SW1* 5F **75**
  (off Page St.)
Edric Rd. SE14 . . . . 3F **93**
Edward VII Mans.
  NW10 . . . . 2F **57**
  (off Chamberlayne Rd.)
Edward Bond Ho. *WC1* . . 2E **7**
  (off Cromer St.)
Edward Cl. NW2 . . . . . . 1F **43**
Edward Ct. E16 . . . . 4C **68**
Edward Dodd Ct. *N1* . . . 1C **10**
  (off Haberdasher St.)
Edward Edward's Ho.
  SE1 . . . . 2D **25**
Edwardes Pl. W8 . . . . . . 4B **72**
Edwardes Sq. W8 . . . . . 4B **72**
Edward Ho. SE11 . . . . . . 1B **90**
  (off Newburn St.)
Edward Mann Cl. *E1* . . . 5F **65**
  (off Caroline St.)
Edward M.
  NW1 . . . . 1E **5** (2D **61**)
Edward Pl. SE8 . . . . 2B **94**
Edward Rd. E17 . . . . . . 1F **37**
Edward Robinson Ho.
  SE14 . . . . 3F **93**
  (off Reaston St.)
Edward's Cotts. N1 . . . . 3D **49**
Edward's La. N16 . . . . . . 4A **36**
Edwards M. N1 . . . . 4C **48**
  W1 . . . . 3B **12** (5C **60**)
Edward Sq. N1 . . . . 5B **48**
  SE16 . . . . 2A **80**
Edward St. E16 . . . . 3C **68**
  (not continuous)
  SE8 . . . . 2B **94**
  SE14 . . . . 3A **94**
Edward Temme Av.
  E15 . . . . 4B **54**
Edward Tyler Rd.
  SE12 . . . . 2E **125**
Edwina Gdns.
  IG4: Ilf. 1F **41**
Edwin Ho. SE15 . . . . . . 3C **92**
Edwin's Mead E9 . . . . . 1A **52**
Edwin St. E1 . . . . 3E **65**
  E16 . . . . 4C **68**
Edwyn Ho. *SW18* 4D **101**
  (off Neville Gill Cl.)
Effie Pl. SW6 . . . . 3C **86**
Effie Rd. SW6 . . . . 3C **86**
Effingham Rd. SE12 . . . 3A **110**
Effort St. SW17 . . . . . . 5A **116**
Effra Ct. *SW2* 3B **104**
  (off Brixton Hill)
Effra Pde. SW2 . . . . . . 3C **104**

Effra Rd. SW2 . . . . 2C **104**
  SW19 . . . . 5D **115**
Effra Rd. Retail Pk.
  SW2 . . . . 3C **104**
Egbert St. NW1 . . . . 5C **46**
Egbury Ho. *SW15* 4B **98**
  (off Tangley Gro.)
Egeremont Rd. SE13 . . 5D **95**
Egerton Ct. E11 . . . . . . 2F **39**
Egerton Cres. SW3 . . . . 5A **74**
Egerton Dr. SE10 . . . . . 4D **95**
Egerton Gdns. NW10 . . 5E **43**
  SW3 . . . . 5A **74**
Egerton Gdns. M.
  SW3 . . . . 4A **74**
Egerton Pl. SW3 . . . . . . 4A **74**
Egerton Rd. N16 . . . . . . 2B **36**
Egerton Ter. SW3 . . . . . 4A **74**
Egham Cl. SW19 . . . . . 2A **114**
Egham Rd. E13 . . . . 4D **69**
Eglantine Rd. SW18 . . . 3E **101**
Eglington Ct. SE17 . . . . 2E **91**
Egliston M. SW15 . . . . . 1E **99**
Egliston Rd. SW15 . . . . 1E **99**
Eglon M. NW1 . . . . 4B **46**
Egmont St. SE14 . . . . . 3F **93**
Egremont Ho. *SE13* . . . 5D **95**
  (off Russett Way)
Egremont Rd. SE27 . . . 3C **118**
Egret Ho. *SE16* 5F **79**
  (off Tawny Way)
Eider Cl. E7 . . . . 2B **54**
Eider Ct. *SE8* 2B **94**
  (off Pilot Cl.)
Eisenhower Dr. E6 . . . . 4F **69**
Elaine Gro. NW5 . . . . . . 2C **46**
Elam Cl. SE5 . . . . 5D **91**
Elam St. SE5 . . . . 5D **91**
Elan Ct. E1 . . . . 4D **65**
Eland Ho. *SW1* 5F **21**
  (off Bressenden Pl.)
Eland Rd. SW11 . . . . . 1B **102**
Elba Pl. SE17 . . . . 5E **77**
Elbe St. SW6 . . . . 5E **87**
Elborough St. SW18 . . . 1C **114**
Elbourne Ct. *SE16* 4F **79**
  (off Worgan St.)
Elbourn Ho. *SW3* 1A **88**
  (off Cale St.)
Elbury Dr. E16 . . . . 5C **68**
Elcho St. SW11 . . . . . . 3A **88**
Elcot Av. SE15 . . . . 3D **93**
Elder Av. N8 . . . . 1A **34**
Elderberry Gro.
  SE27 . . . . 4E **119**
Elderfield Ho. E14 . . . . 1C **80**
Elderfield Pl. SW17 . . . 4D **117**
Elderfield Rd. E5 . . . . . 1F **51**
Elderflower Way E15 . . . 4A **54**
Elder Gdns. SE27 . . . . 5E **119**
Elder Rd. SE27 . . . . . . 5E **119**
Elder St. E1 . . . . 5F **11** (3B **64**)
  (not continuous)
Elderton Rd. SE26 . . . . 4A **122**
Elder Wlk. *N1* 5D **49**
  (off Popham St.)
Elderwood Pl. SE27 . . . 5E **119**
Eldon Ct. NW6 . . . . 5C **44**
Eldon Gro. NW3 . . . . . . 2F **45**
Eldon Rd. W8 . . . . 4D **73**

Eldon St. EC2.... 1C **18** (4F **63**)
Eldridge Ct. SE16..... 4C **78**
Eleanor Cl. SE16.... 3F **79**
Eleanor Gro. SW13.. 1A **98**
Eleanor Ho. *W6* 1E **85**
　　(off Queen Caroline St.)
Eleanor Rathbone Ho.
　N6 .... 2F **33**
　　(off Avenue Rd.)
Eleanor Rd. E8........ 3D **51**
　E15................. 3B **54**
Eleanor St. E3...... 2C **66**
Electra Bus. Pk. E16... 4F **67**
Electric Av. SW9.... 2C **104**
Electric La. SW9.... 2C **104**
　　(not continuous)
Elektron Ho. E14..... 1F **81**
ELEPHANT & CASTLE
　.................... 4D **77**
Elephant & Castle
　SE1................ 5D **77**
Elephant & Castle Superbowl
　.................... 5E **77**
　　(off Walworth Rd.)
Elephant La. SE16... 3E **79**
Elephant Rd. SE17... 5E **77**
Elfindale Rd. SE24.. 3E **105**
Elford Cl. SE3..... 2D **111**
Elford M. SW4..... 3E **103**
Elfort Rd. N5....... 1C **48**
Elfrida Cres. SE6... 4C **122**
Elf Row E1.......... 1E **79**
Elgar Av. NW10..... 3A **42**
　　(not continuous)
Elgar Cl. E13........ 1E **69**
　SE8................ 3C **94**
Elgar Ct. *W14* 4A **72**
　　(off Blythe Rd.)
Elgar Ho. *NW6* 4E **45**
　　(off Fairfax Rd.)
　SW1 .... 1D **89**
　　(off Churchill Gdns.)
Elgar St. SE16...... 4A **80**
Elgin Av. W9........ 3B **58**
　W12................ 4D **71**
Elgin Cl. W12....... 3D **71**
Elgin Ct. W9........ 3D **59**
Elgin Cres. W11..... 1A **72**
Elgin Est. *W9* 3C **58**
　　(off Elgin Av.)
Elgin Ho. *E14* 5D **67**
　　(off Ricardo St.)
Elgin Mans. W9..... 2D **59**
Elgin M. W11....... 5A **58**
Elgin M. Nth. W9... 2D **59**
Elgin M. Sth. W9... 2D **59**
Elgood Cl. W11..... 1A **72**
Elgood Ho. *NW8* 1F **59**
　　(off Wellington Rd.)
Elham Ho. E5....... 2D **51**
Elia M. N1...... 1D **9** (1D **63**)
Elias Pl. SW8...... 2C **90**
Elia St. N1...... 1E **9** (1D **63**)
Elim Est.
　SE1....... 5D **27** (4A **78**)
Elim St. SE1.... 5C **26** (4F **77**)
　　(not continuous)
Elim Way E13...... 2B **68**
Eliot Bank SE23.... 2D **121**
Eliot Cotts. SE3..... 5A **96**

Eliot Ct. SW18...... 4D **101**
Eliot Gdns. SW15.... 2C **98**
Eliot Hill SE13...... 5E **95**
Eliot M. NW8........ 1E **59**
Eliot Pk. SE13....... 5E **95**
Eliot Pl. SE3........ 5A **96**
Eliot Va. SE3........ 5F **95**
Elizabeth Av. N1..... 5E **49**
Elizabeth Barnes Ct.
　SW6 .... 5D **87**
　　(off Marinefield Rd.)
Elizabeth Bri. SW1... 5D **75**
Elizabeth Cl. E14.... 5D **67**
　W9................. 3E **59**
Elizabeth Ct. SW1... 5C **22**
　SW10............... 2F **87**
　　(off Milman's St.)
Elizabeth Fry M. E8... 4D **51**
Elizabeth Gdns. W3.. 2B **70**
Elizabeth Ho. *SE11* .. 5C **76**
　　(off Reedworth St.)
　W6 .... 1E **85**
　　(off Queen Caroline St.)
Elizabeth Ind. Est.
　SE14............... 2F **93**
Elizabeth M. NW3... 3A **46**
Elizabeth Rd. E6.... 5F **55**
　N15................ 1A **36**
Elizabeth Sq. *SE16* .. 1C **74**
　　(off Sovereign Cres.)
Elizabeth St. SW1... 5C **74**
Elkington Point *SE11*. 5C **76**
　　(off Lollard St.)
Elkington Rd. E13... 3D **69**
Elkstone Rd. W10.... 4B **58**
Ellaline Rd. W6...... 2F **85**
Ella M. NW3......... 1B **46**
Elland Ho. *E14*...... 5B **66**
　　(off Copenhagen Pl.)
Elland Rd. SE15.... 2E **107**
Ella Rd. N8......... 2A **34**
Ellenborough Ho.
　W12 .... 1D **71**
　　(off White City Est.)
Ellenborough Pl.
　SW15............... 2C **98**
Ellen St. E1......... 5C **64**
Ellen Terry Ct. *NW1*.. 4D **47**
　　(off Farrier St.)
Ellen Wilkinson Ho.
　E2 .... 2F **65**
　　(off Usk St.)
　SW6 .... 2B **86**
　　(off Clem Attlee Ct.)
Ellerby St. SW6..... 4F **85**
Ellerdale Cl. NW3... 1E **45**
Ellerdale Rd. NW3... 2E **45**
Ellerdale St. SE13.. 2D **109**
Ellerslie Gdns. NW10. 5C **42**
Ellerslie Rd. W12... 2D **71**
Ellerslie Sq. Ind. Est.
　SW2................ 3A **104**
Ellerton Rd. SW13... 4C **84**
　SW18............... 1F **115**
Ellery St. SE17..... 1F **91**
Ellery St. SE15..... 5D **93**
Ellesmere Cl. E11... 1B **40**

Ellesmere Ct. W4.... 1A **84**
Ellesmere Rd. E3.... 1A **66**
　NW10............... 2C **42**
Ellesmere St. E14... 5D **67**
Ellingfort Rd. E8.... 4D **51**
Ellingham Rd. E15... 1F **53**
　W12................ 3C **70**
Ellington Ho.
　SE1......... 5A **26** (4E **77**)
Ellington St. N7..... 3C **48**
Elliot Cl. E15....... 4A **54**
Elliot Ho. *W1* 4A **60**
　　(off Cato St.)
Elliot Rd. NW4...... 1D **29**
　SW9................ 4D **91**
　W4................. 5A **70**
Elliott's Pl. N1..... 5D **49**
Elliott Sq. NW3..... 4A **46**
Elliotts Row SE11... 5D **77**
Ellis Cl. NW10...... 3D **43**
Elliscombe Mt. SE7.. 2E **97**
Elliscombe Rd. SE7.. 2E **97**
Ellisfield Dr. SW15.. 5C **98**
Ellis Franklin Ct.
　NW8 .... 1E **59**
　　(off Abbey Rd.)
Ellis Ho. *SE17*...... 1F **91**
　　(off Brandon St.)
Ellison Ho. *SE13* 5D **95**
　　(off Lewisham Rd.)
Ellison Rd. SW13.... 5B **84**
Ellis St. SW1....... 5C **74**
Ellora Rd. SW16.... 5F **117**
Ellsworth St. E2.... 2D **65**
Ellwood Ct. *W9* 3D **59**
　　(off Clearwell Dr.)
Elm Bank Gdns.
　SW13............... 5A **84**
Elmbourne Rd.
　SW17............... 3D **117**
Elmbridge Wlk. E8... 4C **50**
Elm Cl. E11......... 1D **41**
　N19................ 4E **33**
　NW4............... 1F **29**
Elm Ct. EC4........ 3B **16**
　SE13............... 1F **109**
　W9................. 4C **58**
　　(off Admiral Wlk.)
Elmcourt Rd. SE27.. 2D **119**
Elmcroft N6......... 2E **33**
Elmcroft Av. NW11.. 2B **30**
Elmcroft Cres. NW11. 2A **30**
Elmcroft St. E5..... 1E **51**
Elmer Ho. *NW1* 4A **60**
　　(off Penfold St.)
Elmer Rd. SE6..... 5E **109**
Elmfield Av. N8..... 1A **34**
Elmfield Rd. E17.... 1F **37**
　SW17............... 2C **116**
Elmfield Way W9.... 4C **58**
Elm Friars Wlk.
　NW1................ 4F **47**
Elm Grn. W3........ 5A **56**
Elmgreen Cl. E15... 5A **54**
Elm Gro. N8........ 1A **34**
　NW2................ 1F **43**
　SE15............... 5B **92**
Elm Gro. Rd. SW13.. 4C **84**
Elm Hall Gdns. E11.. 1D **41**
　　(not continuous)

Elm Ho. *E14* 3E **81**
   (off E. Ferry Rd.)
W10 . . . . 3A **58**
   (off Briar Wlk.)
Elmhurst Mans.
SW4 . . . . 1F **103**
Elmhurst Rd. *E7* 4D **55**
SE9 . . . . 2F **125**
Elmhurst St. *SW4* 1F **103**
Elmington Est. *SE5* . . 3F **91**
Elmington Rd. *SE5* . . . 3F **91**
Elmira St. *SE13* 1D **109**
Elm La. *SE6* 2B **122**
Elm Lodge *SW6* 4E **85**
Elmore Ho. *SW9* 5D **91**
Elmore Rd. *E11* 5E **39**
Elmore St. *N1* 4E **49**
Elm Pk. *SW2* 4B **104**
Elm Pk. Av. *N15* 1B **36**
Elm Pk. Chambers
SW10 . . . . 1F **87**
   (off Fulham Rd.)
Elm Pk. Gdns. *SW10* . . 1F **87**
SW10 . . . . 1F **87**
Elm Pk. Ho. *SW10* . . . 1F **87**
Elm Pk. La. *SW3* 1F **87**
Elm Pk. Mans. *SW10* . . 2E **87**
   (off Park Wlk.)
Elm Pk. Rd. *E10* 3A **38**
SW3 . . . . 2F **87**
Elm Pl. *SW7* 1F **87**
Elm Quay Ct. *SW8* . . . 2F **89**
Elm Rd. *E7* 3B **54**
E11 . . . . 4F **39**
E17 . . . . 1E **39**
Elm Row *NW3* 5E **31**
Elms, The *E12* 3F **55**
SW13 . . . . 1B **98**
Elms Av. *NW4* 1F **29**
Elmscott Rd.
BR1: Brom 5A **124**
Elms Cres. *SW4* 4E **103**
Elmshaw Rd. *SW15* . . . 3C **98**
Elmslie Point *E3* *4B 66*
   (off Leopold St.)
Elms M. *W2* 1F **73**
Elms Rd. *SW4* 3E **103**
ELMSTEAD 5F **125**
Elmstone Rd. *SW6* . . . 4C **86**
Elm St. *WC1* 4A **8** (3B **62**)
Elm Ter. *NW2* 5C **30**
NW3 . . . . 1A **46**
Elmton Ct. *NW8* *3F 59*
   (off Cunningham Pl.)
Elmton Way *E5* 5C **36**
Elm Tree Cl. *NW8* 2F **59**
Elm Tree Ct. *NW8* . . . *2F 59*
   (off Elm Tree Rd.)
SE7 . . . . 2E **97**
Elm Tree Rd. *NW8* . . . 2F **59**
Elm Wlk. *NW3* 4C **30**
Elm Way *NW10* 1A **42**
Elmwood Ct. *E10* *3C 38*
   (off Goldsmith Rd.)
SW11 . . . . 4D **89**
Elmwood Ho. *NW10* . . *1D 57*
   (off All Souls Av.)
Elmwood Rd. *SE24* . . . 3F **105**
Elmworth Gro. *SE21* . . 2F **119**
Elnathan M. *W9* 3D **59**

Elphinstone Ct.
SW16 . . . . 5A **118**
Elphinstone St. *N5* . . . 1D **49**
Elrington Rd. *E8* 3C **50**
Elsa Cotts. *E14* *4A 66*
   (off Halley St.)
Elsa St. *E1* 4A **66**
Elsdale St. *E9* 3E **51**
Elsden M. *E2* 1E **65**
Elsenham St. *SW18* . . 1B **114**
W14 . . . . 3A **72**
Elsham Rd. *E11* 5A **40**
Elsham Ter. *W14* *4A 72*
   (off Elsham Rd.)
Elsie La. Ct. *W2* *4C 58*
   (off Westbourne Pk. Vs.)
Elsiemaud Rd. *SE4* . . 3B **108**
Elsie Rd. *SE22* 2B **106**
Elsinore Gdns. *NW2* . . 5A **30**
Elsinore Ho. *N1* *5C 48*
   (off Denmark Gro.)
SE5 . . . . 5E **91**
   (off Denmark Rd.)
W6 . . . . 1F **85**
   (off Fulham Pal. Rd.)
Elsinore Rd. *SE23* . . . 1A **122**
Elsley Rd. *SW11* 1B **102**
Elspeth Rd. *SW11* . . . 2B **102**
Elstead Ho. *SW2* *5B 104*
   (off Redlands Way)
Elsted St. *SE17* 5F **77**
Elstow Grange *NW6* . . 4F **43**
Elswick Rd. *SE13* 5D **95**
Elswick St. *SW6* 5E **87**
Elsworthy Ri. *NW3* . . . 4A **46**
Elsworthy Rd. *NW3* . . 5A **46**
Elsworthy Ter. *NW3* . . 4A **46**
Elsynge Rd. *SW18* . . . 3F **101**
ELTHAM 5F **111**
Eltham Grn. *SE9* 3F **111**
Eltham Grn. Rd.
SE9 . . . . 2E **111**
Eltham High St.
SE9 . . . . 5F **111**
Eltham Hill *SE9* 3F **111**
Eltham Pal. Rd.
SE9 . . . . 4E **111**
Eltham Rd. *SE9* 3B **110**
SE12 . . . . 3B **110**
Elthiron Rd. *SW6* 4C **86**
Elthorne Rd. *N19* 4F **33**
NW9 . . . . 2A **28**
Elthorne Way *NW9* . . . 1A **28**
Elthruda Rd. *SE13* . . . 4F **109**
Elton Ho. *E3* *5B 52*
   (off Candy St.)
Elton Pl. *N16* 2A **50**
Eltringham St.
SW18 . . . . 2E **101**
Elvaston M. *SW7* 4E **73**
Elvaston Pl. *SW7* 4E **73**
Elveden Ho. *SE24* . . . 3D **105**
Elver Gdns. *E2* 2C **64**
Elverson Rd. *SE8* 5D **95**
Elverton St. *SW1* 5F **75**
Elvino Rd. *SE26* 5A **122**
Elvis Rd. *NW2* 3E **43**
Elwin St. *E2* 2C **64**
Elwood St. *N5* 5D **35**
Elworth Ho. *SW8* *3B 90*
   (off Oval Pl.)
Elwyn Gdns. *SE12* . . . 5C **110**

Ely Cotts. *SW8* 3B **90**
Ely Ct. *EC1* 1C **16**
NW6 . . . . 1C **58**
   (off Chichester Rd.)
Ely Ho. *SE15* *3C 92*
   (off Friary Est.)
Elyne Rd. *N4* 1C **34**
Ely Pl. *EC1* 1C **16** (4C **62**)
Ely Rd. *E10* 1E **39**
Elysium Pl. *SW6* *5B 86*
   (off Elysium St.)
Elysium St. *SW6* 5B **86**
Elystan Pl. *SW3* 1A **88**
Elystan St. *SW3* 5A **74**
Elystan Wlk. *N1* 5C **48**
Embankment *SW15* . . . 5F **85**
   (not continuous)
Embankment Gdns.
SW3 . . . . 2B **88**
Embankment Pl.
WC2 . . . . 1E **23** (2A **76**)
Embassy Ct. *NW8* *1F 59*
   (off Wellington Rd.)
Embassy Ho. *NW6* . . . 4D **45**
Embassy Theatre *4F 45*
   (off College Cres.)
Emba St. *SE16* 3C **78**
Emberton *SE5* *2A 92*
   (off Albany Rd.)
Emberton Ct. *EC1* *2D 9*
   (off Tompion St.)
Embleton Rd. *SE13* . . 2D **109**
Emden St. *SW6* 4D **87**
Emerald Cl. *E16* 5F **69**
Emerald Rd. *NW10* . . . 5A **42**
   (not continuous)
Emerald St.
WC1 . . . . 5F **7** (4B **62**)
Emerson St.
SE1 . . . . 1F **25** (2E **77**)
Emery Hill St. *SW1* . . . 4E **75**
Emery St.
SE1 . . . . 5C **24** (4C **76**)
Emery Theatre *5D 67*
   (off Annabel Cl.)
Emily Pl. *N7* 1C **48**
Emily St. *E16* *5B 68*
   (off Jude St.)
Emlyn Gdns. *W12* 3A **70**
Emlyn Rd. *W12* 3A **70**
Emmanuel Ct. *E10* . . . 2D **39**
Emmanuel Ho. *SE11* . . 5C **76**
Emmanuel Rd.
SW12 . . . . 1E **117**
Emma Rd. *E13* 1B **68**
Emma St. *E2* 1D **65**
Emminster *NW6* *5D 45*
   (off Abbey Rd.)
Emmott Cl. *E1* 3A **66**
NW11 . . . . 1E **31**
Emperor's Ga. *SW7* . . 4E **73**
Empingham Ho. *SE8* . . *5F 79*
   (off Chilton Ho.)
Empire Cinema *4C 14*
   (off Leicester Sq.)
Empire Sq. *N7* 5A **34**
Empire Wharf *E3* *5A 52*
   (off Old Ford Rd.)
Empire Wharf Rd.
E14 . . . . 5F **81**

Empress App. SW6 . . . . 1C 86
Empress Av. E12. . . . . . 4E 41
Empress M. SW6 . . . . . 1C 86
Empress Pl. SW6 . . . . . 1C 86
Empress State Bldg.
SW6 . . . . 1C 86
Empress St. SE17. . . . . 2E 91
Empson St. E3 . . . . . . 3D 67
Emsworth Ct.
SW16 . . . . 3A 118
Emsworth St. SW2. . . . 2B 118
Emu Rd. SW8. . . . . . . 5D 89
Enbrook St. W10 . . . . . 2A 58
Enclave, The SW13 . . . 5B 84
Endeavour Way
SW19 . . . . 4D 115
Endell St.
WC2. . . . . . . 2D 15 (5A 62)
Enderby St. SE10 . . . . 1F 95
Endlesham Rd.
SW12 . . . . 5C 102
Endsleigh Gdns.
WC1 . . . . 3B 6 (3F 61)
Endsleigh Pl.
WC1 . . . . 3C 6 (3F 61)
Endsleigh St.
WC1 . . . . 3C 6 (3F 61)
Endwell Rd. SE4. . . . . 5A 94
Endymion Rd. N4 . . . . . 2C 34
SW2 . . . . 4B 104
Energen Cl. NW10 . . . . 3A 42
Energize Fitness Club
. . . . 1A 86
(in Hammersmith &
West London College)
Enfield Cloisters N1 . . . 1D 11
(off Fanshaw St.)
Enfield Ho. SW9 . . . . . 5A 90
(off Stockwell Rd.)
Enfield Rd. N1 . . . . . . 4A 50
Enford St. W1. . . . . . . 4B 60
Engadine St. SW18 . . . 1B 114
Engate St. SE13 . . . . . 2E 109
Engine Cl. SW1 . . . . . 2A 22
(off Ambassador's Ct.)
England's La. NW3. . . . 3B 46
Englefield NW1 . . . . . . 2F 5
(off Clarence Gdns.)
Englefield Rd. N1 . . . . 4F 49
Engleheart Rd. SE6 . . . 5D 109
Englewood Rd.
SW12 . . . . 4D 103
English Grounds
SE1 . . . . 2D 27 (2A 78)
English St. E3 . . . . . . 3B 66
Enid St. SE16. . . 5F 27 (4B 78)
Enmore Gdns. SW14 . . 3A 98
Enmore Rd. SW15 . . . . 2E 99
Ennerdale NW1 . . . . . . 1F 5
(off Varndell St.)
Ennerdale Ct. E11 . . . . 2C 40
(off Cambridge Rd.)
Ennerdale Dr. NW9. . . . 1A 28
Ennerdale Ho. E3 . . . . 3B 66
Ennersdale Rd. SE13 . . 3F 109
Ennis Ho. E14. . . . . . . 5D 67
(off Vesey Path)
Ennismore Av. W4 . . . . 5B 70
Ennismore Gdns.
SW7 . . . . 3A 74

Ennismore Gdns. M.
SW7 . . . . 4A 74
Ennismore M. SW7 . . . 4A 74
Ennismore St. SW7 . . . 4A 74
Ennis Rd. N4 . . . . 3C 34
Ensbury Ho. SW8. . . . . 3B 90
(off Carroun Rd.)
Ensign Ho. E14 . . . . . . 3C 80
(off Admirals Way)
Ensign Ind. Cen. E1 . . . 1C 78
(off Ensign St.)
Ensign St. E1 . . . . 1C 78
Ensor M. SW7. . . . . . . 1F 87
Enterprise Bus. Pk.
E14 . . . . 3D 81
Enterprise Cen., The
BR3: Beck. 5A 122
(off Cricket La.)
Enterprise Ho. E9 . . . . 4E 51
(off Tudor Gro.)
E14. . . . . 1D 95
(off St Davids Sq.)
Enterprise Ind. Est.
SE16 . . . . 1E 93
Enterprise Row N15. . . 1B 36
Enterprise Way
NW10 . . . . 2B 56
SW18 . . . . 2C 100
Enterprise Way SE8 . . . 5B 80
Epcot M. NW10. . . . . . 2F 57
Epirus M. SW6. . . . . . 3C 86
Epirus Rd. SW6 . . . . . 3B 86
Epping Cl. E14. . . . . . 5C 80
Epping Pl. N1. . . . . . . 3C 48
Epple Rd. SW6. . . . . . 4B 86
Epsom Rd. E10. . . . . . 1E 39
Epworth St.
EC2. . . . . . . 4C 10 (3F 63)
Equity Sq. E2 . . . . 2B 64
(off Shacklewell St.)
Erasmus St. SW1 . . . . 5F 75
Erconwald St. W12 . . . 5B 56
Eresby Ho. SW7. . . . . . 3A 74
(off Rutland Ga.)
Eresby Pl. NW6 . . . . . 4C 44
Erica Ho. SE4. . . . . . . 1B 108
Erica St. W12. . . . . . . 1C 70
Eric Cl. E7 . . . . 1C 54
Ericcson Cl. SW18. . . . 3C 100
Eric Fletcher Ct. N1 . . . 4E 49
(off Essex Rd.)
Eric Liddell Sports Cen.
. . . . 2F 125
Eric Rd. E7 . . . . 1C 54
NW10 . . . . 3B 42
Eric Shipman Ter. E13. . 3C 68
(off Balaam St.)
Ericson Ho. SE13 . . . . 2F 109
(off Blessington Rd.)
Eric St. E3 . . . . 3B 66
Eric Wilkins Ho. SE1 . . 1C 92
(off Old Kent Rd.)
Eridge Rd. W4 . . . . . . 4A 70
Erlanger Rd. SE14 . . . . 4F 93
Erlich Cotts. E1. . . . . . 4E 65
(off Sidney St.)
Ermine Rd. N15. . . . . . 1B 36
SE13 . . . . 2D 109
Ernest Av. SE27 . . . . . 4D 119

Ernest Harriss Ho.
W9 . . . . 3C 58
(off Elgin Av.)
Ernest St. E1. . . . . . . 3F 65
Ernshaw Pl. SW15 . . . . 3A 100
Eros 5B 14 (1F 75)
Eros Ho. Shops
SE6. . . . . 5D 109
(off Brownhill Rd.)
Erpingham Rd. SW15. . . 1E 99
Errington Rd. W9 . . . . . 3B 58
Errol St. EC1 . . . 4A 10 (3E 63)
Erskine Hill NW11 . . . . 1C 30
Erskine Ho. SW1 . . . . . 1E 89
(off Churchill Gdns.)
Erskine M. NW3. . . . . . 4B 46
(off Erskine Rd.)
Erskine Rd. NW3 . . . . . 4B 46
Esam Way SW16 . . . . . 5C 118
Escott Gdns. SE9 . . . . 4F 125
Esher Gdns. SW19 . . . . 2F 113
Eskdale NW1 . . . . 1F 5
(off Stanhope St.)
Esk Rd. E13 . . . . 3C 68
Esmar Cres. NW9. . . . . 2C 28
Esmeralda Rd. SE1 . . . 5C 78
Esmond Ct. W8 . . . . . . 4D 73
(off Thackeray St.)
Esmond Gdns. W4 . . . . 5A 70
Esmond Rd. NW6. . . . . 5B 44
W4 . . . . 5A 70
Esmond St. SW15 . . . . 2A 100
Esparto St. SW18. . . . . 5D 101
Esporta Health & Fitness
Finchley Rd. 3E 45
(in 02 Centre)
Grove Park. 4A 84
Islington 5D 49
Wandsworth 2D 101
Wimbledon 5B 114
Esprit Ct. E1 . . . . 1F 19
(off Brune St.)
Essendine Rd. W9 . . . . 2C 58
Essex Ct. EC4. . . . . . . 3B 16
SW13 . . . . 5B 84
Essex Gdns. N4 . . . . . 1D 35
Essex Gro. SE19 . . . . . 5F 119
Essex Ho. E14 . . . . . . 5D 67
(off Giraud St.)
Essex Mans. E11 . . . . . 2F 39
Essex Pk. M. SW3 . . . . 2A 70
Essex Rd. E10 . . . . . . 1E 39
E17 . . . . 1A 38
N1. . . . . 5D 49
NW10 . . . . 4A 42
Essex Rd. Sth. E11. . . . 2F 39
Essex St. E7 . . . . 2C 54
WC2. . . . . 3B 16 (5C 62)
Essex Vs. W8. . . . . . . 3C 72
Essex Wharf E5. . . . . . 4F 37
Essian St. E1 . . . . 4A 66
Estate Way E10 . . . . . 3B 38
Estcourt Rd. SW6. . . . . 3B 86
Estella Ho. W11 . . . . . 1F 71
(off St Ann's Rd.)
Estelle Rd. NW3. . . . . . 1B 46
Esterbrooke St. SW1 . . 5F 75
Este Rd. SW11. . . . . . 1A 102
Esther Rd. E11 . . . . . . 2A 40
Estoria Cl. SW2 . . . . . 5C 104

Estorick Collection of Modern
Italian Art 3D 49
Estreham Rd. SW16 . . . . 5F 117
Eswyn Rd. SW17 . . . . . 4A 116
Etal Ho. *N1* 4D 49
(off Sutton Est., The)
Etcetera Theatre 4D 47
(off Camden High St.)
Etchingham Rd. E15. . . . 1E 53
Eternit Wlk. SW6 . . . . . 4E 85
Ethelbert St. SW12 . . . . 1D 117
Ethelburga St. SW11 . . . 4A 88
Ethelburga Twr.
SW11 . . . . 4A 88
(off Maskelyne Cl.)
Ethelden Rd. W12 . . . . 2D 71
Ethel Rd. E16 . . . . 5D 69
Ethel St. SE17 . . . . 5E 77
Etheridge Rd. NW4 . . . 2E 29
(not continuous)
Etherow St. SE22 . . . . 5C 106
Etherstone Grn.
SW16 . . . . 4C 118
Etherstone Rd.
SW16 . . . . 4C 118
Ethnard Rd. SE15 . . . . 2D 93
Etloe Ho. E10 . . . . 3C 38
Etloe Rd. E10 . . . . 4C 38
Eton Av. NW3 . . . . 4F 45
Eton Cl. SW18 . . . . 5D 101
Eton Coll. Rd. NW3 . . . 3B 46
Eton Ct. NW3 . . . . 4F 45
Eton Garages NW3 . . . . 3A 46
Eton Gro. SE13 . . . . . . 1A 110
Eton Hall NW3 . . . . . . 3B 46
Eton Ho. *N5* 1D 49
(off Leigh Rd.)
Eton Mnr. Ct. *E10* 4C 38
(off Leyton Grange Est.)
Eton Pl. NW3 . . . . 4C 46
Eton Ri. NW3 . . . . 3B 46
Eton Rd. NW3 . . . . 4B 46
Eton Vs. NW3 . . . . 3B 46
Etta St. SE8 . . . . 2A 94
Ettrick St. E14 . . . . 5E 67
(not continuous)
Eugene Cotter Ho.
SE17 . . . . 5F 77
(off Tatum St.)
Eugenia Rd. SE16 . . . . 5E 79
Euro Cl. NW10 . . . . . . 3C 42
Eurolink Bus. Cen.
SW2 . . . . 3C 104
Europa Pl. EC1. . 2F 9 (2E 63)
Eustace Bldg. SW8 . . . 2D 89
Eustace Ho. *SE11* 5B 76
(off Old Paradise St.)
Eustace Rd. E6 . . . . . 2F 69
SW6 . . . . 3C 86
Euston Cen.
NW1 . . . . 3F 5 (3E 61)
(not continuous)
Euston Gro. *NW1* 2B 6
(off Euston Sq.)
Euston Rd.
NW1 . . . . 4F 5 (3D 61)
(not continuous)
Euston Sq. NW1 . . . . 2F 61
Euston Sta. Colonnade
NW1 . . . . 2B 6 (2F 61)

Euston St.
NW1 . . . . 2A 6 (2E 61)
Euston Twr.
NW1 . . . . 3F 5 (3E 61)
Evandale Rd. SW9 . . . . 5C 90
Evangelist Rd. *EC4* 3D 17
(off Black Friars La.)
Evangelist Ho.
NW5 . . . . 1D 47
Evans Bus. Cen.
NW2 . . . . 5C 28
Evans Cl. E8 . . . . 3B 50
Evans Ho. *SW8* 3F 89
(off Wandsworth Rd.)
W12 . . . . 1D 71
(off White City Est.)
Evans Rd. SE6 . . . . . . 2A 124
Evanston Gdns.
IG4: IIf 1F 41
Evelina Mans. SE5 . . . . 3F 91
Evelina Rd. SE15 . . . . 1E 107
Evelyn Ct. E8 . . . . 1C 50
N1 . . . . 1B 10
(off Evelyn Wlk.,
not continuous)
Evelyn Denington Ct.
N1 . . . . 4D 49
(off Sutton Est., The)
Evelyn Fox Ct. W10 . . . 4E 57
Evelyn Gdns. SW7 . . . 1E 87
Evelyn Ho. *SE14* 4A 94
(off Loring Rd.)
W12 . . . . 3B 70
(off Cobbold Rd.)
Evelyn Lowe Est.
SE16 . . . . 4C 78
Evelyn Mans. *SW1* 5F 21
(off Carlisle Pl.)
W14 . . . . 2A 86
(off Queen's Club Gdns.)
Evelyn Rd. E16 . . . . . . 2C 82
SW19 . . . . 5D 115
Evelyn St. SE8 . . . . . . 5A 80
Evelyn Wlk.
N1 . . . . 1B 10 (1F 63)
Evelyn Yd.
W1 . . . . 2B 14 (5F 61)
Evenwood Cl. SW15. . 3A 100
Everard Ho. *E1* 5C 64
(off Boyd St.)
Everatt Cl. SW18 . . . . 4B 100
Everdon Rd. SW13 . . . . 2C 84
Everest Pl. E14 . . . . . . 4E 67
Everett Ho. *SE17* 1F 91
(off East St.)
Evergreen Sq. E8 . . . . 4B 50
Everilda St. N1 . . . . . . 5B 48
Evering Rd. E5 . . . . . . 5B 36
N16 . . . . 5B 36
Everington St. W6 . . . . 2F 85
(not continuous)
Everitt Rd. NW10 . . . . 2A 56
Everleigh St. N4 . . . . . 3B 34
Eve Rd. E11 . . . . 1A 54
E15 . . . . 1A 68
Eversholt St.
NW1 . . . . 1A 6 (1E 61)
Evershot Rd. N4 . . . . 3B 34
Eversleigh Rd. E6. . . . 5F 55
SW11 . . . . 1B 102

Eversley Ho. *E2* 2C 64
(off Gossett St.)
Eversley Pk. SW19 . . . 5D 113
Eversley Rd. SE7 . . . . 2D 97
Everthorpe Rd.
SE15 . . . . 1B 106
Everton Bldgs.
NW1 . . . . 2F 5 (2E 61)
Evesham Ho. *E2* 1E 65
(off Old Ford Rd.)
NW8 . . . . 5E 45
(off Abbey Rd.)
Evesham Rd. E15. . . . 4B 54
Evesham St. W11 . . . . 1F 71
Evesham Wlk. SE5 . . . 5F 91
SW9 . . . . 5C 90
Evesham Way
SW11 . . . . 1C 102
Ewald Rd. SW6 . . . . . 5B 86
Ewart Pl. E3 . . . . 1B 66
Ewart Rd. SE23. . . . . 5F 107
Ewe Cl. N7 . . . . 3A 48
Ewelme Rd. SE23. . . . 1E 121
Ewen Cres. SW2 . . . . 5C 104
Ewen Henderson Ct.
SE14 . . . . 3A 94
(off Goodwood Rd.)
Ewen Ho. *N1* 5B 48
(off Barnsbury Est.)
Ewer St. SE1 . . 2F 25 (2E 77)
Ewhurst Cl. E1 . . . . . . 4E 65
Ewhurst Rd. SE4 . . . . 4B 108
Exbury Ho. E9. . . . . . . 4E 51
SW1 . . . . 1F 89
(off Rampayne St.)
Exbury Rd. SE6 . . . . . 2C 122
ExCeL. 1D 83
Excel Cl. WC2 . . . . . . 5C 14
Excel Marina E16. . . . . 1C 82
Excelsior Gdns. SE13. . 5E 95
Excelsior Ind. Est.
SE15 . . . . 2E 93
Excel Waterfront E16. . 1D 83
Exchange Arc.
EC2 . . . . 5E 11 (4A 64)
Exchange Bldg. *E1* . . . 4F 11
(off Commercial St.)
Exchange Ct.
WC2 . . . . 5E 15 (1A 76)
Exchange Ho. EC2 . . . 5E 11
SW1 . . . . 5F 75
(off Vauxhall Bri. Rd.)
Exchange Mans.
NW11 . . . . 2B 30
Exchange Pl.
EC2 . . . . 5D 11 (4A 64)
Exchange Sq.
EC2 . . . . 5D 11 (4A 64)
Exchange St.
EC1 . . . . 2F 9 (2E 63)
Exeter Ct. *NW6*. 1C 58
(off Cambridge Rd.)
Exeter Ho. *SE15*. 2C 92
(off Friary Est.)
SW15 . . . . 4E 99
W2 . . . . 5E 59
(off Hallfield Est.)
Exeter Mans. NW2 . . . 3A 44
Exeter M. NW6 . . . . . . 3D 45
SW6 . . . . 3C 86

Exeter Rd. E16 . . . . 4C 68
E17 . . . . 1C 38
NW2 . . . . 2A 44
Exeter St.
WC2 . . . . 4E 15 (1A 76)
Exeter Way SE14 . . . . . . 3B 94
Exford Gdns. SE12 . . . . . 1D 125
Exford Rd. SE12 . . . . . . 2D 125
Exhibition Cl. W12 . . . . . 1E 71
Exhibition Rd.
SW7 . . . . 3F 73
Exmoor Ho. E3 . . . . 1A 66
(off Gernon Rd.)
Exmoor St. W10 . . . . 3F 57
Exmouth Ho. E14 . . . . . . 5D 81
(off Cahir St.)
EC1 . . . . 3B 8
(off Pine St.)
Exmouth Mkt.
EC1 . . . . 3B 8 (3C 62)
Exmouth M.
NW1 . . . . 2A 6 (2E 61)
Exmouth Pl. E8 . . . . 4D 51
Exmouth Rd. E17 . . . . . . 1B 38
Exning Rd. E16 . . . . 3B 68
Exon St. E1 . . . . 5E 65
Exonbury NW8 . . . . 5D 45
(off Abbey Rd.)
Exon St. SE17 . . . . 1A 92
Export Ho. SE1 . . . . 4E 27
(off Tower Bri. Rd.)
Express Newspapers
SE1 . . . . 1D 25
(off Blackfriars Rd.)
Exton St.
SE1 . . . . 2B 24 (2C 76)
Eyhurst Cl. NW2 . . . . . . 4C 28
Eyelwood Rd. SE27 . . . . 5E 119
Eynella Rd. SE22 . . . . . 5B 106
Eynham Rd. W12 . . . . . . 5E 57
Eynsford Ho. SE1 . . . . . . 4B 26
(off Crosby Row)
SE15 . . . . 2E 93
SE17 . . . . 5A 78
(off Beckway St.)
Eyot Gdns. W6 . . . . 1B 84
Eyot Grn. W4 . . . . 1B 84
Eyre Ct. NW8 . . . . 1F 59
Eyre St. Hill
EC1 . . . . 4B 8 (3C 62)
Eythorne Rd. SW9 . . . . . 4C 90
Ezra St. E2 . . . . 2B 64

F

F1 City Go-Kart Circuit
. . . . 2E 83
(off Connaught Bri.)
Faber Gdns. NW4 . . . . . . 1C 28
Fabian Rd. SW6 . . . . 3B 86
Facade, The SE23 . . . . . 2E 121
Factory Rd. E16 . . . . 2F 83
Fairacres SW15 . . . . 2B 98
Fairbairn Grn.
SW9 . . . . 4D 91
Fairbank Est.
N1 . . . . 1B 10 (1F 63)
Fairbridge Rd. N19 . . . . . 4F 33
Fairburn Ct. SW15 . . . . . 3A 100

Fairburn Ho. W14 . . . . . . 1B 86
(off Ivatt Pl.)
Fairby Ho. SE1 . . . . 5B 78
(off Longfield Est.)
Fairby Rd. SE12 . . . . . . 3D 111
Faircharm Trad. Est.
SE8 . . . . 3D 95
Fairchild Cl. SW11 . . . . . 5F 87
Fairchild Ho. E9 . . . . 4E 51
(off Frampton Pk. Rd.)
N1 . . . . 1D 11
(off Fanshaw St.)
Fairchild Pl. EC2 . . . . . . 4E 11
Fairchild St.
EC2 . . . . 3E 11 (3A 64)
Fairclough St. E1 . . . . . . 5C 64
Fairdale Gdns.
SW15 . . . . 2D 99
Fairfax Gdns. SE3 . . . . . 4E 97
Fairfax Mans. NW3 . . . . . 3E 45
(off Finchley Rd.)
Fairfax M. E16 . . . . 2D 83
SW15 . . . . 2E 99
Fairfax Pl. NW6 . . . . 4E 45
W14 . . . . 4A 72
Fairfax Rd. NW6 . . . . . . 4E 45
W4 . . . . 4A 70
Fairfield E1 . . . . 4E 65
(off Redman's Rd.)
NW1 . . . . 5E 47
(off Arlington Rd.)
Fairfield Av. NW4 . . . . . . 1D 29
Fairfield Cl. NW10 . . . . . 5C 42
Fairfield Dr. SW18 . . . . . 3D 101
Fairfield Gdns. N8 . . . . . 1A 34
Fairfield Gro. SE7 . . . . . 2F 97
Fairfield Rd. E3 . . . . 1C 66
N8 . . . . 1A 34
Fairfield St. SW18 . . . . . 3D 101
Fairfoot Rd. E3 . . . . 3C 66
Fairford SE6 . . . . 1C 122
Fairford Ho. SE11 . . . . . 5C 76
Fairhazel Gdns. NW6 . . . 3D 45
Fairhazel Mans.
NW6 . . . . 4E 45
(off Fairhazel Gdns.)
Fairholme Rd. W14 . . . . . 1A 86
Fairholt Cl. N16 . . . . 3A 36
Fairholt Rd. N16 . . . . . . 3F 35
Fairholt St. SW7 . . . . . . 4A 74
Fairland Rd. E15 . . . . . . 3B 54
Fairlawn SE7 . . . . 3E 97
Fairlawn Ct. SE7 . . . . . . 3E 97
(not continuous)
Fairlawn Mans. SE14 . . . 4F 93
Fairlawn Pk. SE26 . . . . . 5A 122
Fairlie Gdns. SE23 . . . . . 5E 107
Fairlight Av. NW10 . . . . . 1A 56
(not continuous)
Fairlight Ct. NW10 . . . . . 1A 56
Fairlight Rd. SW17 . . . . . 4F 115
Fairlop Cl. E11 . . . . 3F 39
Fairlop Rd. E11 . . . . 2F 39
Fairmead Gdns.
IG4: Ilf 1F 41
Fairmead Ho. E9 . . . . . . 1A 52
Fairmead Rd. N19 . . . . . 5F 33
Fairmile Av. SW16 . . . . . 5F 117
Fairmont Av. E14 . . . . . . 2E 81
Fairmount Rd. SW2 . . . . 4B 104

Fairstead Wlk. N1 . . . . . 5E 49
(off Popham St.)
Fair St. SE1 . . . . . 3E 27 (3A 78)
Fairthorn Rd. SE7 . . . . . 1C 96
Fairview Cl. SE26 . . . . . 5A 122
Fairview Ho. SW2 . . . . . 5B 104
Fairview Ho. SW2 . . . . . 5B 104
Fairview Pl. SW2 . . . . . 5B 104
Fairview Rd. N15 . . . . . 1B 36
Fairwall Ho. SE5 . . . . . . 4A 92
Fairway, The W3 . . . . . . 5A 56
Fairway Cl. NW11 . . . . . 2E 31
Fairway Ct. SE16 . . . . . . 3F 79
(off Christopher Cl.)
Fairways Bus. Pk.
E10 . . . . 4A 38
Fairweather Rd.
N16 . . . . 1C 36
Fairwyn Rd. SE26 . . . . . 4A 122
Fakruddin St. E1 . . . . . . 3C 64
Falcon WC1 . . . . 5E 7
(off Old Gloucester St.)
Falconberg Ct.
W1 . . . . 2C 14 (5F 61)
Falconberg M.
W1 . . . . 2C 14 (5F 61)
Falcon Cl.
SE1 . . . . 1E 25 (2D 77)
Falcon Ct.
EC4 . . . . 3C 16 (5C 62)
N1 . . . . 5E 49
(off City Gdn. Row)
Falconer Wlk. N7 . . . . . . 4B 34
Falconet Ct. E1 . . . . 2D 79
(off Wapping High St.)
Falcon Gro. SW11 . . . . . 1A 102
Falcon Highwalk EC2 . . . 1F 17
Falcon Ho. E14 . . . . . . 1D 95
(off St Davids Sq.)
Falcon La. SW11 . . . . . 1A 102
Falcon Lodge W9 . . . . . 4C 58
(off Admiral Wlk.)
Falcon Pk. Ind. Est.
NW10 . . . . 1A 42
Falcon Point
SE1 . . . . 5E 17 (1D 77)
Falcon Rd. SW11 . . . . . 5A 88
Falcon St. E13 . . . . 3B 68
Falcon Ter. SW11 . . . . . 1A 102
Falcon Way E14 . . . . . . 5D 81
Falconwood Ct. SE3 . . . . 5B 96
(off Montpelier Row)
Falkirk Ct. SE16 . . . . . . 2F 79
(off Rotherhithe St.)
Falkirk Ho. W9 . . . . 1D 59
(off Maida Va.)
Falkirk St.
N1 . . . . 1E 11 (1A 64)
Falkland Ho. SE6 . . . . . 4E 123
W8 . . . . 4D 73
W14 . . . . 1B 86
(off Edith Vs.)
Falkland Pl. NW5 . . . . . . 2E 47
Falkland Rd. NW5 . . . . . 2E 47
Fallodon Ho. W11 . . . . . 4B 58
(off Tavistock Cres.)
Fallow Ct. SE16 . . . . . . 1C 92
(off Argyle Way)
Fallsbrook Rd.
SW16 . . . . 5E 117
Falmouth Cl. SE12 . . . . . 3B 110

Falmouth Gdns.
IG4: Ilf 1F **41**
Falmouth Ho. *SE11* . . . 1C **90**
(off Seaton Cl.)
W2 . . . . 1A **74**
(off Clarendon Pl.)
Falmouth Rd.
SE1 . . . . . 5A **26** (4E **77**)
Falmouth St. E15 . . . . 2F **53**
Falmouth Way E17 . . . 1B **38**
Falstaff Ho. *SE11* 5D **77**
(off Opal St.)
Falstaff Ho. *N1* 1D **11**
(off Crondall St.)
Fambridge Cl. SE26 . . 4B **122**
Fane Ho. E2 . . . . 5E **51**
Fane St. W14 . . . . 2B **86**
Fan Mus., The 3E **95**
Fann St. EC1 . . . . . 4F **9** (3E **63**)
EC2 . . . . 4F **9** (3E **63**)
(not continuous)
Fanshaw St.
N1 . . . . 1D **11** (2A **64**)
Fanthorpe St. SW15 . . . 1E **99**
Faraday Cl. N7 . . . . 3B **48**
Faraday Ho. *E14* 1B **80**
(off Brightlingsea Pl.)
SE1 . . . . 4A **26**
(off Cole St.)
Faraday Lodge SE10 . . 4B **82**
Faraday Mans. *W14* . . . 2A **86**
(off Queen's Club Gdns.)
Faraday Mus.
. . . . 5F **13** (1E **75**)
Faraday Rd. E15 . . . . . 3B **54**
SW19 . . . . 5C **114**
W10 . . . . 4A **58**
Faraday Way SE18 . . . . 4F **83**
Fareham St.
W1 . . . . 2B **14** (5F **61**)
Faringford Rd. E15 . . . . 4A **54**
Fariweather Ho. N7 . . . 1A **48**
Farjeon Ho. *NW6* 4F **45**
(off Hilgrove Rd.)
Farjeon Rd. SE3 . . . . . 4F **97**
Farleigh Pl. N16 . . . . . 1B **50**
Farleigh Rd. N16 . . . . . 1B **50**
Farley Ct. *NW1* 4B **4**
(off Allsop Pl.)
Farley Rd. SE26 . . . . . 3D **121**
Farley Rd. SE6 . . . . . 5D **109**
Farlington Pl. SW15 . . 5D **99**
Farlow Rd. SW15 . . . . . 1F **99**
Farlton Rd. SW18 . . . 1D **115**
Farm Av. NW2 . . . . 5A **30**
SW16 . . . . 4A **118**
Farm Cl. SW6 . . . . 3C **86**
Farmcote Rd. SE12 . . 1C **124**
Farmdale Rd. SE10 . . . 1C **96**
Farmer Rd. E10 . . . . . . 3D **39**
Farmer's Rd. SE5 . . . . 3D **91**
Farmer St. W8 . . . . 2C **72**
Farmfield Rd.
BR1: Brom 5A **124**
Farmilo Rd. E17 . . . . . 2B **38**
Farm La. SW6 . . . . 2C **86**
(not continuous)
Farm La. Trad. Est.
SW6 . . . . 2C **86**
Farmleigh Ho. SW9 . . 3D **105**

Farm Pl. W8 . . . . 2C **72**
Farm Rd. E12 . . . . 4F **41**
NW10 . . . . 5A **42**
Farmstead Rd. SE6 . . 4D **123**
Farm St. W1 . . . 5D **13** (1D **75**)
Farm Wlk. NW11 . . . . . 1B **30**
Farnaby Ho. *W10* 2B **58**
(off Bruckner St.)
Farnaby Rd. SE9 . . . . 2E **111**
Farnan Rd. SW16 . . . . 5A **118**
Farnborough Ho.
SW15 . . . . 1C **112**
Farncombe St. SE16 . . 3C **78**
Farndale Ct. SE18 . . . . 3F **97**
Farndale Ho. *NW6* 5D **45**
(off Kilburn Va.)
Farnell M. SW5 . . . . . . 1D **87**
Farnham Ho. *NW1* 3A **60**
(off Harewood Av.)
Farnham Pl.
SE1 . . . . . 2E **25** (2D **77**)
Farnham Royal SE11 . . 1B **90**
Farningham Ho. N4 . . . 2F **35**
Farnley Ho. SW8 . . . . . 5F **89**
Farnsworth Ct. *SE10* . . . 4B **82**
(off Greenroof Way)
Farnworth Ho. *E14* 5F **81**
(off Manchester Rd.)
Faroe Rd. W14 . . . . . . 4F **71**
Farquhar Rd. SE19 . . . 5B **120**
SW19 . . . . 3C **114**
Farrance St. E14 . . . . . 5C **66**
Farrell Ho. *E1* 5E **65**
(off Ronald St.)
Farren Rd. SE23 . . . . 2A **122**
Farrer Ho. SE8 . . . . 3C **94**
Farriers Ho. *EC1* 4A **10**
(off Errol St.)
Farriers M. SE15 . . . . 1E **107**
Farrier St. NW1 . . . . . . 4D **47**
Farrier Wlk. SW10 . . . 2E **87**
Farringdon La.
EC1 . . . . . 4C **8** (3C **62**)
Farringdon Rd.
EC1 . . . . . 3B **8** (3C **62**)
Farringdon St.
EC4 . . . . . 1D **17** (4D **63**)
Farrins Rents SE16 . . . 2A **80**
Farrow La. SE14 . . . . . 3E **93**
Farrow Pl. SE16 . . . . . 4A **80**
Farthingale Wlk. E15 . . 4F **53**
Farthing All. SE1 . . . . . 3C **78**
Farthing Flds. E1 . . . . 2D **79**
Fashion & Textile Mus.
. . . . 3E **27**
Fashion St.
E1 . . . . 1F **19** (4B **64**)
Fassett Rd. E8 . . . . . . 3C **50**
Fassett Sq. E8 . . . . . . 3C **50**
Faulkners All.
EC1 . . . . . 5D **9** (4D **63**)
Faulkner St. SE14 . . . . 4E **93**
Faunce Ho. *SE17* 2D **91**
(off Doddington Gro.)
Faunce St. SE17 . . . . . 1D **91**
Favart Rd. SW6 . . . . . . 4C **86**
Faversham Ho. *NW1* . . . 5E **47**
(off Bayham Pl.)
SE17 . . . . 1A **92**
(off Kinglake St.)

Faversham Rd. SE6 . . 5B **108**
Fawcett Cl. SW11 . . . . . 5F **87**
SW16 . . . . 5C **118**
Fawcett Est. E5 . . . . . . 3C **36**
Fawcett Rd. NW10 . . . . 4B **42**
Fawcett St. SW10 . . . . 2E **87**
Fawe Pk. M. SW15 . . . 2B **100**
Fawe Pk. Rd. SW15 . . 2B **100**
Fawe St. E14 . . . . 4D **67**
Fawkham Ho. *SE1* 5B **78**
(off Longfield Est.)
Fawley Lodge E14 . . . . . 5F **81**
(off Millennium Dr.)
Fawley Rd. NW6 . . . . . 2D **45**
Fawnbrake Av. SE24 . . 3D **105**
Fawn Rd. E13 . . . . 1E **69**
Fawood Av. NW10 . . . . 4A **42**
Faygate Rd. SW2 . . . . 2B **118**
Fayland Av. SW16 . . . . 5E **117**
Fazeley Ct. *W9* 4C **58**
(off Elmfield Way)
Fearnley Ho. SE5 . . . . . 5A **92**
Fearon St. SE10 . . . . . 1C **96**
Feathers Pl. SE10 . . . . 2F **95**
Featherstone Av.
SE23 . . . . 2D **121**
Featherstone St.
EC1 . . . . . 3B **10** (3F **63**)
Featley Ho. SW9 . . . . 1D **105**
Felbridge Cl. SW16 . . . 4C **118**
Felbridge Ho. SE22 . . 1A **106**
Felday Rd. SE13 . . . . . 4D **109**
Felden St. SW6 . . . . . . 4B **86**
Feldman Cl. N16 . . . . . 3C **36**
Felgate M. W6 . . . . 5D **71**
Felix Av. N8 . . . . 1A **34**
Felixstowe Rd.
NW10 . . . . 2D **57**
Felix St. E2 . . . . 1D **65**
Fellbrigg Rd. SE22 . . . 3B **106**
Fellbrigg St. E1 . . . . . . 3D **65**
Fellmongers Path
SE1 . . . . 4F **27**
Fellows Ct.
E2 . . . . 1F **11** (1B **64**)
(not continuous)
Fellows Rd. NW3 . . . . . 4F **45**
Felltram M. *SE7* 1C **96**
(off Felltram Way)
Felltram Way SE7 . . . . 1C **96**
Felmersham Cl.
SW4 . . . . 2A **104**
Felsberg Rd. SW2 . . . 4A **104**
Felsham M. *SW15* 1F **99**
(off Felsham Rd.)
Felsham Rd. SW15 . . . 1E **99**
Felstead Gdns. E14 . . 1E **95**
Felstead Rd. E9 . . . . . . 3B **52**
E11 . . . . 2C **40**
Felstead St. E9 . . . . . . 3B **52**
Felstead Wharf E14 . . . 1E **95**
Felsted Rd. E16 . . . . . . 5F **69**
Felton Ho. *N1* 5F **49**
(off Branch Pl.)
SE3 . . . . 2D **111**
Felton St. N1 . . . . 5F **49**
Fenchurch Av.
EC3 . . . . . 3D **19** (5A **64**)
Fenchurch Bldgs.
EC3 . . . . . 3E **19** (5A **64**)

Fenchurch Pl.
  EC3 . . . . . 4E **19** (5A **64**)
Fenchurch St.
  EC3 . . . . . 4D **19** (1A **78**)
Fen Ct. EC3 . . . 4D **19** (5A **64**)
Fendall St.
  SE1 . . . . . . 5E **27** (4A **78**)
      (not continuous)
Fendt Cl. E16 . . . . 5B **68**
Fenelon Pl. W14 . . . . . . 5B **72**
Fenham Rd. SE15 . . . . . . 3C **92**
Fen La. SW13 . . . . 4D **85**
Fennel Cl. E16 . . . . 3A **68**
Fenner Cl. SE16 . . . . . . 5D **79**
Fenner Ho. E1 . . . . 2D **79**
      (off Watts St.)
Fenner Sq. SW11 . . . . . . 1F **101**
Fenning St.
  SE1 . . . . . . 3D **27** (3A **78**)
Fenn St. E9 . . . . 2F **51**
Fenstanton N4 . . . . 3B **34**
      (off Marquis St.)
Fen St. E16 . . . . 1B **82**
Fentiman Rd. SW8 . . . . . 2A **90**
Fenton Cl. E8 . . . . 3B **50**
  SW9 . . . . 5B **90**
Fenton House 1E **45**
      (off Windmill Hill)
Fenton Ho. SE14 . . . . . . 3A **94**
Fentons Av. E13 . . . . . . 2D **69**
Fenton St. E1 . . . . 5D **65**
Fenwick Gro. SE15 . . . . . 1C **106**
Fenwick Pl. SW9 . . . . . . 1A **104**
Fenwick Rd. SE15 . . . . . 1C **106**
Ferdinand Ho. NW1 . . . . . 4C **46**
      (off Ferdinand Pl.)
Ferdinand Pl. NW1 . . . . . 4C **46**
Ferdinand St. NW1 . . . . . 4C **46**
Ferguson Cen., The
  E17 . . . . 1A **38**
Ferguson Cl. E14 . . . . . . 5C **80**
Ferguson Dr. W3 . . . . . . 5A **56**
Ferguson Ho. SE10 . . . . . 4E **95**
Fergus Rd. N5 . . . . 2D **49**
Fermain Ct. E. N1 . . . . . 5A **50**
      (off De Beauvoir Est.)
Fermain Ct. Nth. N1 . . . . 5A **50**
      (off De Beauvoir Est.)
Fermain Ct. W. N1 . . . . . 5A **50**
      (off De Beauvoir Est.)
Ferme Pk. Rd. N8 . . . . . . 1A **34**
Fermor Rd. SE23 . . . . . . 1A **122**
Fermoy Rd. W9 . . . . 3B **58**
Fernbank M. SW12 . . . . . 4E **103**
Fernbrook Cres.
  SE13 . . . . 4A **110**
      (off Leahurst Rd.)
Fernbrook Rd. SE13 . . . . 3A **110**
Ferncliff Rd. E8 . . . . 2C **50**
Fern Cl. N1 . . . . 1A **64**
Fern Ct. SE14 . . . . 5F **93**
Ferncroft Av. NW3 . . . . . 5C **30**
Ferndale Community
  Sports Cen. 1B **104**
Ferndale Rd. E7 . . . . . . 4D **55**
  E11 . . . . 4A **40**
  N15 . . . . 1B **36**
  SW4 . . . . 2A **104**
  SW9 . . . . 2A **104**
Ferndene Rd. SE24 . . . . . 2E **105**

Ferndown Lodge E14 . . . . 4E **81**
      (off Manchester Rd.)
Ferndown Rd. SE9 . . . . . 5F **111**
Fernhall Dr. IG4: Ilf. 1F **41**
Fernhead Rd. W9 . . . . . . 1B **58**
Fernholme Rd.
  SE15 . . . . 3F **107**
Fernhurst Rd. SW6 . . . . . 4A **86**
Fernlea Rd. SW12 . . . . . 1D **117**
Fernsbury St.
  WC1 . . . . 2B **8** (2C **62**)
Fernshaw Cl. SW10 . . . . . 2E **87**
Fernshaw Rd. SW10 . . . . 2E **87**
Fernside NW11 . . . . 4C **30**
Fernside Rd. SW12 . . . . . 1B **116**
Ferns Rd. E15 . . . . 3B **54**
Fern St. E3 . . . . 3C **66**
Fernthorpe Rd.
  SW16 . . . . 5E **117**
Ferntower Rd. N5 . . . . . . 2F **49**
Fern Wlk. SE16 . . . . 1C **92**
Fernwood SW19 . . . . . . 1B **114**
Fernwood Av. SW16 . . . . 4F **117**
Ferranti Cl. SE18 . . . . . . 4F **83**
Ferrers Rd. SW16 . . . . . 5F **117**
Ferrey M. SW9 . . . . 5C **90**
Ferriby Cl. N1 . . . . 4C **48**
Ferrier Ind. Est.
  SW18 . . . . 2D **101**
      (off Ferrier St.)
Ferrier Point E16 . . . . . . 4C **68**
      (off Forty Acre La.)
Ferrier St. SW18 . . . . . . 2D **101**
Ferrings SE21 . . . . 3A **120**
Ferris Rd. SE22 . . . . 2C **106**
Ferron Rd. E5 . . . . 5D **37**
Ferrybridge Ho.
  SE11 . . . . 4C **76**
      (off Lambeth Wlk.)
Ferry Ho. E5 . . . . 3D **37**
      (off Harrington Hill)
Ferry La. SW13 . . . . 2B **84**
Ferry Rd. SW13 . . . . 3C **84**
Ferry St. E14 . . . . 1E **95**
Festing Rd. SW15 . . . . . 1F **99**
Festival Ct. E8 . . . . 4B **50**
      (off Holly St.)
Festoon Way E16 . . . . . . 1F **83**
Fetter La.
  EC4 . . . . . . 3C **16** (5C **62**)
      (not continuous)
Fettes Ho. NW8 . . . . 1F **59**
      (off Wellington Rd.)
Ffinch St. SE8 . . . . 3C **94**
Field Cl. NW2 . . . . 4C **28**
Field Ct. SW19 . . . . 3D **114**
  WC1 . . . . 1A **16** (4B **62**)
Fieldgate Mans. E1 . . . . . 4C **64**
      (off Fieldgate St.)
      (not continuous)
Fieldgate St. E1 . . . . . . 4C **64**
Field Ho. NW6 . . . . 2F **57**
      (off Harvist Rd.)
Fieldhouse Rd.
  SW12 . . . . 1E **117**
Fielding Ho. NW6 . . . . . . 2C **58**
  W4 . . . . 2A **84**
      (off Devonshire Rd.)
Fielding M. SW13 . . . . . . 2D **85**
      (off Jenner Pl.)

Fielding Rd. W4 . . . . 4A **70**
  W14 . . . . 4F **71**
Fieldings, The SE23 . . . . 1E **121**
Fieldsway Ho. SE17 . . . . 2E **91**
Field Point E7 . . . . 1C **54**
Field Rd. E7 . . . . 1B **54**
  W6 . . . . 1A **86**
Fields Est. E8 . . . . 4C **50**
Fieldside Rd.
  BR1: Brom 5F **123**
Field St. WC1 . . . . . . 1F **7** (2B **62**)
Fieldsway Ho. N5 . . . . . . 2C **48**
Fieldview SW18 . . . . 1F **115**
Fieldway Cres. N5 . . . . . 2C **48**
Fife Rd. E16 . . . . 4C **68**
Fife Ter. N1 . . . . 1B **62**
Fifield Path SE23 . . . . . . 3F **121**
Fifth Av. W10 . . . . 2A **58**
Fig Tree Cl. NW10 . . . . . 5A **42**
Figure Ct. SW3 . . . . 1B **88**
      (off West Rd.)
Filey Av. N16 . . . . 3C **36**
Filigree Ct. SE16 . . . . . . 2B **80**
Fillebrook Rd. E11 . . . . . 3F **39**
Filmer Chambers
  SW6 . . . . 4A **86**
      (off Filmer Rd.)
Filmer Rd. SW6 . . . . 4A **86**
Filton Ct. SE14 . . . . 3E **93**
      (off Farrow La.)
Finborough Ho.
  SW10 . . . . 2E **87**
      (off Finborough Rd.)
Finborough Rd.
  SW10 . . . . 1D **87**
Finborough Theatre, The
  . . . . 2D **87**
      (off Finborough Rd.)
Finch Av. SE27 . . . . 4F **119**
Finchdean Ho. SW15 . . . . 5B **98**
Finch Ho. SE8 . . . . 3D **95**
      (off Bronze St.)
Finch La.
  EC3 . . . . . . 3C **18** (5F **63**)
Finchley Pl. NW8 . . . . . . 1F **59**
Finchley Rd. NW2 . . . . . . 1B **30**
  NW3 . . . . 1C **44**
  NW8 . . . . 5F **45**
  NW11 . . . . 1B **30**
Finch Lodge W9 . . . . 4C **58**
      (off Admiral Wlk.)
Finch M. SE15 . . . . 4B **92**
Finch's Ct. E14 . . . . 1D **81**
Finden Rd. E7 . . . . 2E **55**
Findhorn St. E14 . . . . . . 5E **67**
Findon Cl. SW18 . . . . . . 4C **100**
Findon Rd. W12 . . . . 3C **70**
Fingal St. SE10 . . . . 1B **96**
Fingest Ho. NW8 . . . . . . 3A **60**
      (off Lilestone St.)
Finland Rd. SE4 . . . . 1A **108**
Finland St. SE16 . . . . . . 4A **80**
Finlay St. SW6 . . . . 4B **85**
Finmere Ho. N4 . . . . 2E **35**
Finnemore Ho. N1 . . . . . 5E **49**
      (off Britannia Row)
Finn Ho. N1 . . . . 1C **10**
      (off Bevenden St.)
Finnis St. E2 . . . . 2D **65**
FINSBURY 3F **9** (2C **62**)

Finsbury Av.
EC2 . . . . 1C **18** (4F **63**)
(not continuous)
Finsbury Av. Sq. EC2 . . 5D **11**
Finsbury Cir.
EC2 . . . . 1C **18** (4F **63**)
Finsbury Est.
EC1 . . . . 2C **8** (2C **62**)
Finsbury Leisure Cen.
. . . . 3F **9** (2E **63**)
Finsbury Mkt.
EC2 . . . . 4D **11** (3A **64**)
(Clifton St.)
EC2 . . . . 5D **11** (4A **64**)
(Pindar St.)
FINSBURY PARK 3C **34**
Finsbury Pk. Av. N4 . . 1E **35**
Finsbury Pk. Rd. N4 . . . 4D **35**
(not continuous)
Finsbury Pavement
EC2 . . . . 5C **10** (4F **63**)
Finsbury Sq.
EC2 . . . . 4C **10** (3F **63**)
Finsbury St.
EC2 . . . . 5B **10** (4F **63**)
Finsen Rd. SE5 . . . . . 2E **105**
Finstock Rd. W10 . . . . 5F **57**
Finwhale Ho. *E14* 4D **81**
(off Glengall Gro.)
Fiona Ct. NW6 . . . . . . 1C **58**
Firbank Cl. E16 . . . . . . 4F **69**
Firbank Rd. SE15 . . . . 5D **93**
Fircroft Rd. SW17 . . . . 2B **116**
Firecrest Dr. NW3 . . . . 5D **31**
Firefly Gdns. E6 . . . . . 3F **69**
Fir Gro. Rd. SW9 . . . . 5C **90**
Firhill Rd. SE6 . . . . . 4C **122**
Fir Ho. *W10* 3A **58**
(off Droop St.)
Firle Ho. *W10* 4E **57**
(off Sutton Way)
Firs, The E6 . . . . 4F **55**
SE26 . . . . 5D **121**
(Border Rd.)
SE26 . . . . 5E **121**
(Waverley Ct.)
Firsby Rd. N16 . . . . . . 3C **36**
Firs Cl. SE23 . . . . . 5A **108**
First Av. E13 . . . . . . 2C **68**
SW14 . . . . 1A **98**
W3 . . . . 2B **70**
W10 . . . . 3B **58**
First St. SW3 . . . . . . 5A **74**
Firth Gdns. SW6 . . . . 4A **86**
Firth Ho. *E2* 2C **64**
(off Barnet Gro.)
Firtree Cl. SW16 . . . . 5E **117**
Fir Tree Ho. *SE14* 3E **93**
(off Avonley Rd.)
Fir Trees Cl. SE16 . . . . 2A **80**
Fisher Athletic FC 2F **79**
Fisher Ho. *E1* 1E **79**
(off Cable St.)
N1 . . . . 5C **48**
(off Barnsbury Est.)
Fishermans Dr. SE16 . . 3F **79**
Fisherman's Pl. W4 . . . 2B **84**
Fisherman's Wlk.
E14 . . . . 2C **80**
Fisher's Cl. SW16 . . . 3F **117**

Fishers Ct. SE14 . . . . . 4F **93**
Fisher's La. W4 . . . . . 5A **70**
Fisher St. E16 . . . . . . 4C **68**
WC1 . . . . 1F **15** (4B **62**)
Fisherton St. NW8 . . . . 3F **59**
Fishmongers Hall Wharf
EC4 . . . . 5B **18**
Fishponds Rd.
SW17 . . . . 4A **116**
Fish St. Hill
EC3 . . . . 5C **18** (1F **77**)
Fish Wharf
EC3 . . . . 5C **18** (1F **77**)
Fisons Rd. E16 . . . . . . 2C **82**
Fitness First Health Club
Islington 1D **9** (1D **63**)
Lewisham 1E **109**
Tooting Bec 3C **116**
(off Balham High Rd.)
Fitrooms 2B **86**
Fitzalan St. SE11 . . . . . 5C **76**
Fitzgeorge Av. W14 . . . 5A **72**
Fitzgerald Av. SW14 . . 1A **98**
Fitzgerald Ct. *E10* 3D **39**
(off Leyton Grange Est.)
Fitzgerald Ho. *E14* . . . 5D **67**
(off E. India Dock Rd.)
SW9 . . . . 5C **90**
Fitzgerald Rd. E11 . . . . 1C **40**
SW14 . . . . 1A **98**
Fitzhardinge Ho. *W1* . . 2B **12**
(off Portman Sq.)
Fitzhardinge St.
W1 . . . . 2B **12** (5C **60**)
Fitzhugh Gro. SW18 . . 4F **101**
Fitzjames Av. W14 . . . 5A **72**
Fitzjohn's Av. NW3 . . . 1E **45**
Fitzmaurice Ho.
SE16 . . . . 5D **79**
(off Rennie Est.)
Fitzmaurice Pl.
W1 . . . . 1E **21** (2D **75**)
Fitzneal St. W12 . . . . 5B **56**
FITZROVIA 5E **5**
Fitzroy Cl. N6 . . . . . . 3B **32**
Fitzroy Ct. N6 . . . . . . 1E **33**
W1 . . . . 4A **6**
Fitzroy Ho. *E14* 4B **66**
(off Wallwood St.)
SE1 . . . . 1B **92**
(off Coopers La.)
Fitzroy M. W1 . . . . . . 4F **5**
Fitzroy Pk. N6 . . . . . . 3B **32**
Fitzroy Rd. NW1 . . . . 5C **46**
Fitzroy Sq. W1 . . 4F **5** (3E **61**)
Fitzroy St. W1 . . 4F **5** (3E **61**)
(not continuous)
Fitzroy Yd. NW1 . . . . 5C **46**
Fitzsimmons Ct.
NW10 . . . . 5A **42**
Fitzwarren Gdns. N19 . . 3E **33**
Fitzwilliam Hgts.
SE23 . . . . 2E **121**
Fitzwilliam M. E16 . . . . 2C **82**
Fitzwilliam Rd.
SW4 . . . . 1E **103**
Five Bell All. *E14* 5B **66**
(off Three Colt St.)
Fives Ct. SE11 . . . . . 4D **77**
Fiveways Rd. SW9 . . . . 5C **90**

Flack Ct. E10 . . . . 2D **39**
Fladbury Rd. N15 . . . . 1F **35**
Fladgate Rd. E11 . . . . 1A **40**
Flamborough Ho.
SE15 . . . . 4C **92**
(off Clayton Rd.)
Flamborough St.
E14 . . . . 5A **66**
Flamborough Wlk.
E14 . . . . 5A **66**
(off Flamborough St.)
Flamingo Ct. *SE8* 3C **94**
(off Hamilton St.)
Flamstead Ho. *SW3* . . . 1A **88**
(off Cale St.)
Flamsteed Rd. SE7 . . . 1F **97**
Flanchford Rd. W12 . . . 4B **70**
Flanders Ct. E17 . . . . . 2A **38**
Flanders Mans. W4 . . . 5B **70**
Flanders Rd. W4 . . . . . 5A **70**
Flanders Way E9 . . . . 3F **51**
(not continuous)
Flank St. E1 . . . . 1C **78**
Flansham Ho. *E14* . . . 5B **66**
(off Clemence St.)
Flask Wlk. NW3 . . . . . 1E **45**
Flatford Ho. SE6 . . . . 4E **123**
Flatiron Yd. *SE1* 2A **26**
(off Union St.)
Flavell M. SE10 . . . . . 1A **96**
Flaxman Ct. W1 . . . . . 3B **14**
WC1 . . . . 2C **6**
(off Flaxman Ter.)
Flaxman Ho. W4 . . . . . 1A **84**
(off Devonshire St.)
Flaxman Leisure Cen.
. . . . 5E **91**
Flaxman Rd. SE5 . . . 1D **105**
Flaxman Ter.
WC1 . . . . . . 2C **6** (2F **61**)
Flecker Ho. *SE5* 3F **91**
(off Lomond Gro.)
Fleece Wlk. N7 . . . . . 3A **48**
Fleetbank Ho. *EC4* . . . 3C **16**
(off Salisbury Sq.)
Fleet Bldg. EC4 . . . . . 2D **17**
(off Birkenhead St.)
Fleetfield *WC1* 1E **7**
(off Birkenhead St.)
Fleet Ho. *E14* 1A **80**
(off Victory Pl.)
Fleet Pl. EC4. . . 2D **17** (5D **63**)
(not continuous)
Fleet Rd. NW3 . . . . . . 2A **46**
Fleet Sq. WC1 . . 2A **8** (2B **62**)
Fleet St. EC4 . . 3B **16** (5C **62**)
Fleet St. Hill E1 . . . . . 3C **64**
Fleetway *WC1* 1E **7**
(off Birkenhead St.)
Fleetwood Cl. E16 . . . . 4F **69**
Fleetwood Rd. NW10 . . 2C **42**
Fleetwood St. N16 . . . 4A **36**
Fleming Ct. W9 . . . . . 3C **58**
Fleming Ct. W2 . . . . . 4F **59**
(off St Mary's Sq.)
Fleming Ho. N4 . . . . . 3E **35**
SE16 . . . . 3C **78**
(off George Row)
Fleming Lodge W9 . . . 4C **58**
(off Admiral Wlk.)
Fleming Rd. SE17 . . . 2D **91**

Flemming Cl. *SW10* *2E 87*
   (off Park La.)
Flempton Rd. E10 . . . . . 3A 38
Fletcher Bldgs. *WC2* . . . *3E 15*
   (off Martlett Ct.)
Fletcher Ho. *SE15* *3E 93*
   (off Clifton Way)
Fletcher La. E11 . . . . . . 2E 39
Fletcher Path SE8 . . . . . 3C 94
Fletcher St. E1 . . . . 1C 78
Fletching Rd. E5 . . . . . . 5E 37
SE7 . . . . 2E 97
Fleur-de-Lis St.
   E1 . . . . 4E 11 (3B 64)
Fleur Gates SW19 . . . . . 5F 99
Flimwell Cl.
   BR1: Brom 5A 124
Flinders Ho. *E1* *2D 79*
   (off Green Bank)
Flint Cl. E15 . . . . 4B 54
Flintmill Cres. SE3 . . . . . 5F 97
   (not continuous)
Flinton St. SE17 . . . . . . 1A 92
Flint St. SE17 . . . . 5F 77
Flitcroft St.
   WC2 . . . . . . 3C 14 (5F 61)
Flitton Ho. *N1* *4D 49*
   (off Sutton Est., The)
Flock Mill Pl. SW18 . . . 1D 115
Flockton St. SE16 . . . . . 3C 78
Flodden Rd. SE5 . . . . . . 4E 91
Flood St. SW3 . . . . 1A 88
Flood Wlk. SW3 . . . . . . 2A 88
Flora Cl. E14 . . . . 5D 67
Flora Gdns. *W6* *5D 71*
   (off Albion Gdns.)
Floral Pl. N1 . . . . 2F 49
Floral St.
   WC2 . . . . . . 4D 15 (1A 76)
Florence Cantwell Wlk.
   N19 . . . . 2A 34
   (off Jessie Blythe La.)
Florence Cl. E5 . . . . 5C 36
   N1 . . . . 4D 49
   (off Florence St.)
   SW19 . . . . 5A 114
   W9 . . . . 2E 59
   (off Maida Va.)
Florence Ho. *SE16* *1D 93*
   (off Rotherhithe New Rd.)
   W11 . . . . 1F 71
   (off St Ann's Rd.)
Florence Mans. *NW4* . . *1D 29*
   (off Vivian Av.)
Florence Nightingale Mus.
   . . . . 4F 23 (3B 76)
Florence Rd. E6 . . . . 5E 55
   E13 . . . . 1C 68
   N4 . . . . 2B 34
   (not continuous)
   SE14 . . . . 4B 94
   SW19 . . . . 5D 115
Florence Ter. E16 . . . . . . 3B 68
   N1 . . . . 4D 49
Florence Ter. SE14 . . . . . 4B 94
   SW15 . . . . 3A 112
Florence Way
   SW12 . . . . 1B 116
Flores Ho. *E1* *4F 65*
   (off Shandy St.)

Florey Lodge *W9* *4C 58*
   (off Admiral Wlk.)
Florfield Pas. *E8* *3D 51*
   (off Florfield Rd.)
Florfield Rd. E8 . . . . 3D 51
Florian SE5 . . . . 4A 92
Florian Rd. SW15 . . . . . 2A 100
Florida St. E2 . . . . 2C 64
Florin Ct. *SE1* *4F 27*
   (off Tanner St.)
Floris Pl. SW4 . . . . 1E 103
Florys Ct. SW19 . . . . . . 1A 114
Floss St. SW15 . . . . 5E 85
Flower & Dean Wlk.
   E1 . . . . 1F 19 (4B 64)
Flower M. NW11 . . . . 1A 30
Flowerpot Cl. N15 . . . . . 1B 36
Flowers Cl. NW2 . . . . . . 5C 28
Flowersmead SW17 . . . . 2C 116
Flowers M. N19 . . . . 4E 33
Flower Wlk., The
   SW7 . . . . 3E 73
Floyd Rd. SE7 . . . . 1E 97
Fludyer St. SE13 . . . . . . 2A 110
Flynn Ct. *E14* *1C 80*
   (off Garford St.)
Foley Ho. *E1* *5E 65*
   (off Tarling St.)
Foley St. W1 . . . 1F 13 (4E 61)
Folgate St.
   E1 . . . . 5E 11 (4A 64)
   (not continuous)
Foliot Ho. *N1* *1B 62*
   (off Priory Grn. Est.)
Foliot St. W3 . . . . 5B 56
Follett Ho. *SW10* *3F 87*
   (off Worlds End Est.)
Follett St. E14 . . . . 5E 67
Follingham Ct. *N1* *1E 11*
   (off Drysdale Pl.)
Folly M. W11 . . . . 5B 58
Folly Wall E14 . . . . 3E 81
Fonda Ct. *E14* *1C 80*
   (off Premiere Pl.)
Fontarabia Rd.
   SW11 . . . . 2C 102
Fontenelle Gdns.
   SE5 . . . . 4A 92
Fontenoy Ho. *SE11* . . . *5D 77*
   (off Kennington La.)
Fontenoy Rd. SW12 . . . 2D 117
Fonthill M. N4 . . . . 4B 34
Fonthill Rd. N4 . . . . 3B 34
Fontley Way SW15 . . . . 5C 98
Footpath, The SW15 . . . 4C 98
Forber Ho. *E2* *2E 65*
   (off Cornwall Av.)
Forbes Cl. NW2 . . . . 5C 28
Forbes St. E1 . . . . 5C 64
Forburg Rd. N16 . . . . . . 3C 36
Ford Cl. E3 . . . . 1A 66
Fordel Rd. SE6 . . . . 1E 123
Fordham St. E1 . . . . 5C 64
Fordingley Rd. W9 . . . . . 2B 58
Fordington Ho.
   SE26 . . . . 3C 120
Fordmill Rd. SE6 . . . . . . 2C 122
Ford Rd. E3 . . . . 1B 66
Fords Pk. Rd. E16 . . . . . 4C 68
Ford Sq. E1 . . . . 4D 65

Ford St. E3 . . . . 5A 52
   E16 . . . . 5B 68
Fordwych Rd. NW2 . . . . . 1A 44
Fordyce Rd. SE13 . . . . . 4E 109
Foreign St. SE5 . . . . 5D 91
Foreland Ho. *W11* *1A 72*
   (off Walmer Rd.)
Foreshore SE8 . . . . 5B 80
Forest Bus. Pk. E10 . . . . 2F 37
Forest Cl. E11 . . . . 1C 40
Forest Cft. SE23 . . . . . . 2D 121
Forest Dr. E12 . . . . 5F 41
Forest Dr. E. E11 . . . . . . 2F 39
Forest Dr. W. E11 . . . . . 2E 39
Forester Ho. *E14* *1A 80*
   (off Victory Pl.)
Forester Rd. SE15 . . . . . 1D 107
FOREST GATE 2C 54
Forest Ga. Retreat
   E7 . . . . 2C 54
   (off Odessa Rd.)
Forest Glade E11 . . . . . . 1A 40
Forest Gro. E8 . . . . 3B 50
FOREST HILL 2F 121
Forest Hill Bus. Cen.
   SE23 . . . . 2E 121
   (off Clyde Va.)
Forest Hill Ind. Est.
   SE23 . . . . 2E 121
Forest Hill Pool 2E 121
Forest Hill Rd.
   SE22 . . . . 3D 107
Forestholme Cl.
   SE23 . . . . 2E 121
Forest La. E7 . . . . 2A 54
   E15 . . . . 2A 54
Forest Lodge *SE23* . . . *3E 121*
   (off Dartmouth Rd.)
Forest Point *E7* *2D 55*
   (off Windsor Rd.)
Fore St. EC2 . . . 1A 18 (4E 63)
Fore St. Av.
   EC2 . . . . . . 1B 18 (4F 63)
Forest Rd. E7 . . . . 1C 54
   E8 . . . . 3B 50
   E11 . . . . 2F 39
Forest Side E7 . . . . 1D 55
Forest St. E7 . . . . 2C 54
Forest Vw. E11 . . . . 2B 40
Forest Vw. Av. E10 . . . . 1F 39
Forest Vw. Rd. E12 . . . . 1F 55
Forest Way N19 . . . . 4E 33
Forfar Rd. SW11 . . . . . . 4C 88
Forge Pl. NW1 . . . . 3C 46
Forges Rd. E12 . . . . 4F 41
Forman Pl. N16 . . . . 1B 50
Formby Ct. *N7* *2C 48*
   (off Morgan Rd.)
Formosa Ho. *E1* *3A 66*
   (off Ernest St.)
Formosa St. W9 . . . . . . 3D 59
Formunt Cl. E16 . . . . 4B 68
Forres Gdns. NW11 . . . . 1C 30
Forrester Path
   SE26 . . . . 4E 121
Forset Ct. *W2* *5A 60*
   (off Edgware Rd.)
Forset St. W1 . . . . 5A 60
Forster Ho.
   BR1: Brom 4F 123

Forster Rd. E17 . . . . . . 1A 38
SW2 . . . . 5A 104
Forston St. N1 . . . . 1E 63
Forsyth Gdns. SE17 . . . 2D 91
Forsyth Ho. E9 . . . . 4E 51
  (off Frampton Pk. Rd.)
SW1 . . . . 1E 89
  (off Tachbrook St.)
Fortescue Av. E8 . . . . . 4D 51
Fortess Gro. NW5 . . . . . 2E 47
Fortess Rd. NW5 . . . . . 2D 47
Fortess Wlk. NW5 . . . . . 2D 47
Fortess Yd. NW5 . . . . . 1D 47
Forthbridge Rd.
SW11 . . . . 2C 102
Fortis Cl. E16 . . . . 5E 69
Fortnam Rd. N19 . . . . . 4F 33
Fort Rd. SE1 . . . . 5B 78
Fortrose Cl. E14 . . . . . . 5F 67
Fortrose Gdns. SW2 . . 1A 118
Fort St. E1 . . . 1E 19 (4A 64)
E16 . . . . 2D 83
Fortuna Cl. N7 . . . . 3B 48
Fortune Ct. E8 . . . . 4B 50
  (off Queensbridge Rd.)
Fortunegate Rd.
NW10 . . . . 5A 42
FORTUNE GREEN 1C 44
Fortune Grn. Rd.
NW6 . . . . 1C 44
Fortune Ho. EC1 . . . . . . 4A 10
  (off Fortune St.)
SE11 . . . . 5C 76
  (off Marylee Way)
Fortune St.
EC1 . . . . 4A 10 (3E 63)
Fortune Theatre 3E 15
  (off Russell St.)
Fortune Way NW10 . . . 2C 56
Forty Acre La. E16 . . . . 4C 68
Forum Magnum Sq.
SE1 . . . . 3A 24
  (off York Rd.)
Forward Bus. Cen., The
E16 . . . . 3F 67
Fosbrooke Ho. SW8 . . . 3A 90
  (off Davidson Gdns.)
Fosbury M. W2 . . . . 1D 73
Foscote Ct. W9 . . . . 3C 58
  (off Foscote M.)
Foscote M. W9 . . . . 3C 58
Foscote Rd. NW4 . . . . . 1D 29
Foskett Rd. SW6 . . . . . 5B 86
Fossdene Rd. SE7 . . . . 1D 97
Fossil Rd. SE13 . . . . . 1C 108
Foss Rd. SW17 . . . . . 4F 115
Foster Ct. E16 . . . . 1B 82
  (off Tarling Rd.)
NW1 . . . . 4E 47
  (off Royal College St.)
Foster Ho. SE14 . . . . . 4B 94
Foster La.
EC2 . . . . . 2F 17 (5E 63)
Foster Rd. E13 . . . . 3C 68
W3 . . . . 1A 70
W4 . . . . 1A 84
Foster's Way SW18 . . . 1D 115
Fothergill Cl. E13 . . . . . 1C 68
Foubert's Pl.
W1 . . . . 3F 13 (5E 61)

Foulden Rd. N16 . . . . . 1B 50
Foulden Ter. N16 . . . . . 1B 50
Foulis Ter. SW7 . . . . . . 1F 87
Foulser Rd. SW17 . . . . 3B 116
Founders Ct. EC2 . . . . . 2B 18
Founders Ho. SW1 . . . . 1F 89
  (off Aylesford St.)
Foundling Ct. WC1 . . . . 3D 7
  (off Brunswick Cen.)
Foundling Mus., The
. . . . 3E 7 (3A 62)
Foundry Cl. SE16 . . . . . 2A 80
Foundry Ho. E14 . . . . . 4D 67
  (off Morris Rd.)
Foundry M. NW1 . . . . . . 3A 6
Foundry Pl. E1 . . . . 4E 65
  (off Redman's Rd.)
SW18 . . . . 5D 101
Fountain Ct.
EC4 . . . . . 4B 16 (1C 76)
SE23 . . . . 2F 121
SW1 . . . . 5D 75
  (off Buckingham Pal. Rd.)
Fountain Dr. SE19 . . . . 4B 120
Fountain Grn. Sq.
SE16 . . . . 3C 78
Fountain Ho. NW6 . . . . 4A 44
W1 . . . . 1B 20
  (off Park St.)
Fountain M. N5 . . . . . . 1E 49
  (off Highbury Grange)
NW3 . . . . 3B 46
Fountain Pl. SW9 . . . . . 4C 90
Fountain Rd. SW17 . . . 5F 115
Fountayne Rd. N16 . . . . 4C 36
Fountain Sq. SW1 . . . . 5D 75
Fount St. SW8 . . . . 3F 89
Fournier St.
E1 . . . . 5F 11 (4B 64)
Fourscore Mans. E8 . . . 4C 50
  (off Shrubland Rd.)
Four Seasons Cl. E3 . . 1C 66
Fourth Av. W10 . . . . . . 3A 58
Fovant Ct. SW8 . . . . . . 5E 89
Fowey Cl. E1 . . . . 2D 79
Fowey Ho. SE11 . . . . . . 1C 90
  (off Kennings Way)
Fowler Cl. SW11 . . . . . 1F 101
Fowler Ho. N15 . . . . . . 1F 35
  (off South Gro.)
Fowler Rd. E7 . . . . 1C 54
N1 . . . . 5D 49
Fowlers M. N19 . . . . . . 4E 33
  (off Holloway Rd.)
Fownes St. SW11 . . . . 1A 102
Fox & Knot St. EC1 . . . . 5E 9
Foxberry Rd. SE4 . . . . 1A 108
Foxborough Gdns.
SE4 . . . . 3C 108
Foxbourne Rd.
SW17 . . . . 2C 116
Fox Cl. E1 . . . . 3E 65
E16 . . . . 4C 68
Foxcombe Cl. E6 . . . . . 1F 69
Foxcombe Rd.
SW15 . . . . 1C 112
Foxcote SE5 . . . . 1A 92
Foxcroft WC1 . . . . 1A 8
  (off Penton Ri.)
Foxes Dale SE3 . . . . . 1C 110

Foxfield NW1 . . . . 5D 47
  (off Arlington Rd.)
Foxglove St. W12 . . . . . 1B 70
Foxham Rd. N19 . . . . . 5F 33
Foxhole Rd. SE9 . . . . . 3F 111
Foxley Cl. E8 . . . . 2C 50
Foxley Rd. SW9 . . . . . . 3C 90
Foxley Sq. SW9 . . . . . . 4D 91
Foxmore St. SW11 . . . . 4B 88
Fox Rd. E16 . . . . 4B 68
Foxwell M. SE4 . . . . . 1A 108
Foxwell St. SE4 . . . . . 1A 108
Foxwood Rd. SE3 . . . . 2B 110
Foyle Rd. SE3 . . . . 2B 96
Framfield Rd. N5 . . . . . 2D 49
Framlingham Cl.
E5 . . . . 4E 37
Frampton NW1 . . . . . . 4F 47
  (off Wrotham Rd.)
Frampton Ho. NW8 . . . . 3F 59
  (off Frampton St.)
Frampton Pk. Est. E9 . . 4E 51
Frampton Pk. Rd. E9 . . 3E 51
Frampton St. NW8 . . . . 3F 59
Francemary Rd.
SE4 . . . . 3C 108
Frances Ct. E17 . . . . . . 1C 38
Franche Ct. Rd.
SW17 . . . . 3E 115
Francis Barber Cl.
SW16 . . . . 5B 118
Franciscan Rd.
SW17 . . . . 5B 116
Francis Chichester Way
SW11 . . . . 4C 88
Francis Cl. E14 . . . . . . 5F 81
Francis Ct. EC1 . . . . . . 5D 9
SE14 . . . . 2F 93
  (off Myers La.)
Francis Ho. E17 . . . . . . 1B 38
N1 . . . . 5A 50
  (off Colville Est.)
SW10 . . . . 3D 87
  (off Coleridge Gdns.)
Francis M. SE12 . . . . . 5C 110
Francis Rd. E10 . . . . . . 3E 39
Francis St. E15 . . . . . . 2A 54
SW1 . . . . 5A 22 (5E 75)
Francis Wlk. N1 . . . . . . 5B 48
Franconia Rd. SW4 . . . 3F 103
Frank Beswick Ho.
SW6 . . . . 2B 86
  (off Clem Attlee Ct.)
Frank Burton Cl. SE7 . . 1D 97
Frank Dixon Cl.
SE21 . . . . 5A 106
Frank Dixon Way
SE21 . . . . 1A 120
Frankfurt Rd. SE24 . . . 3E 105
Frankham Ho. SE8 . . . . 3C 94
  (off Frankham St.)
Frankham St. SE8 . . . . 3C 94
Frank Ho. SW8 . . . . . . 3A 90
  (off Wyvil Rd.)
Frankland Cl. SE16 . . . 4D 79
Frankland Rd. SW7 . . . 4F 73
Franklin Bldg. E14 . . . . 3C 80
Franklin Cl. SE13 . . . . 4D 95
SE27 . . . . 3D 119

Franklin Ho. *E1* 2D *79*
              (off Watts St.)
Franklin Pl. SE13 . . . . . . 4D *95*
Franklin Sq. W14 . . . . . . 1B *86*
Franklin's Row SW3 . . . . 1B *88*
Franklin St. E3 . . . . 2D *67*
  N15 . . . . 1A *36*
Franklyn Rd. NW10 . . . 3B *42*
Frank Soskice Ho.
  SW6 . . . . *2B 86*
        (off Clem Attlee Ct.)
Frank St. E13 . . . . 3C *68*
Frank Whymark Ho.
  SE16 . . . . 3E *79*
         (off Rupack St.)
Fransfield Gro.
  SE26 . . . . 3D *121*
Frans Hals Ct. E14 . . . . 4F *81*
Franthorne Way
  SE6 . . . . 2D *123*
Fraser Cl. E6 . . . . 5F *69*
Fraser Ct. *E14* *1E 95*
          (off Ferry St.)
Fraser Rd. E17 . . . . 1D *39*
Fraser St. W4 . . . . 1A *84*
Frazier St.
  SE1 . . . . . . 4B *24* (3C *76*)
Frean St. SE16 . . . . 4C *78*
Frearson Ho. *WC1* *1A 8*
         (off Penton Ri.)
Freda Corbet Cl.
  SE15 . . . . 3C *92*
Frederica St. N7 . . . . . . 4B *48*
Frederick Charrington Ho.
  E1 . . . . *3E 65*
         (off Wickford St.)
Frederick Cl. W2 . . . . . . 1B *74*
Frederick Ct. *SW3* *5B 74*
     (off Duke of York Sq.)
Frederick Cres.
  SW9 . . . . 3D *91*
Frederick Rd. SE17 . . . . 2D *91*
Frederick's Pl.
  EC2 . . . . . . 3B *18* (5F *63*)
Frederick Sq. *SE16* *1A 80*
      (off Sovereign Cres.)
Frederick's Row
  EC1 . . . . . . 1D *9* (2D *63*)
Frederick St.
  WC1 . . . . . . 2F *7* (2B *62*)
Frederick Ter. E8 . . . . . . 4B *50*
Frederic M. SW1 . . . . . . 4A *20*
Frederic St. E17 . . . . . . 1A *38*
Fred Styles Ho. SE7 . . . . 2E *97*
Fred White Wlk. N7 . . . . 3A *48*
Freedom St. SW11 . . . . 5B *88*
Freegrove Rd. N7 . . . . . 2A *48*
       (not continuous)
Freeling Ho. *NW8* *5F 45*
       (off Dorman Way)
Freeling St. N1 . . . . 4B *48*
       (Carnoustie Dr.)
  N1 . . . . 4A *48*
       (Pembroke St.)
Freemantle St. SE17 . . . 1A *92*
Freemasons Rd. E16 . . . 4D *69*
Free Trade Wharf E1 . . . 1F *79*
Freke Rd. SW11 . . . . . 1C *102*
Fremantle Ho. *E1* *3D 65*
       (off Somerford St.)

Fremont St. E9 . . . . 5D *51*
       (not continuous)
French Ordinary Ct.
  EC3 . . . . 4E *19*
French Pl. E1 . . 2E *11* (2A *64*)
Frendsbury Rd. SE4 . . . 2A *108*
Frensham Dr. SW15 . . . 3B *112*
       (not continuous)
Frensham St. SE15 . . . . 2C *92*
Frere St. SW11 . . . . 5A *88*
Freshfield Av. E8 . . . . . . 4B *50*
Freshfield Cl. SE13 . . . 2F *109*
Freshford St. SW18 . . . 3E *115*
Freshwater Cl.
  SW17 . . . . 5C *116*
Freshwater Ct. *W1* *4A 60*
       (off Crawford St.)
Freshwater Rd.
  SW17 . . . . 5C *116*
Freston Rd. W10 . . . . . . 1F *71*
  W11 . . . . 1F *71*
Freswick Ho. *SE8* *5F 79*
       (off Chilton Gro.)
Freud Mus., The 3E *45*
Frewell Ho. *EC1* *5B 8*
       (off Bourne Est.)
Frewin Rd. SW18 . . . . . 1F *115*
Friar M. SE27 . . . . 3D *119*
Friars Av. SW15 . . . . . . 3B *112*
Friars Cl. SE1 . . . . 2E *25*
Friars Gdns. W3 . . . . . . 5A *56*
Friars Mead E14 . . . . . . 4E *81*
Friars Pl. La. W3 . . . . . . 1A *70*
Friars Rd. E6 . . . . 5F *55*
Friar St. EC4 . . 3E *17* (5D *63*)
Friars Way W3 . . . . 5A *56*
Friary Ct. SW1 . . . . 2A *22*
Friary Est. SE15 . . . . . . 2C *92*
       (not continuous)
Friary Rd. SE15 . . . . . . 3C *92*
  W3 . . . . 5A *56*
Friday St.
  EC4 . . . . 4F *17* (1E *77*)
Frideswide Pl. NW5 . . . . 2E *47*
Friern Rd. SE22 . . . . . . 5C *106*
Frigate Ho. *E14* *5E 81*
       (off Stebondale St.)
Frigate M. SE8 . . . . 2C *94*
Frimley Cl. SW19 . . . . . 2A *114*
Frimley St. *E1* *3F 65*
       (off Frimley Way)
Frimley Way E1 . . . . 3F *65*
Frinstead Ho. *W10* *1F 71*
       (off Freston Rd.)
Frinton Rd. E6 . . . . 2A *68*
  N15 . . . . 1A *36*
Friston St. SW6 . . . . . . 5D *87*
Frith Ho. *NW8* *3F 59*
     (off Frampton St.)

Frith Rd. E11 . . . . 1E *53*
Frith St. W1 . . . 3B *14* (5F *61*)
Frithville Ct. *W12* *2E 71*
      (off Frithville Gdns.)
Frithville Gdns.
  W12 . . . . 2E *71*
Frobisher Ct. *SE10* *2F 95*
     (off Old Woolwich Rd.)
  SE23 . . . . 2D *121*
  W12 . . . . *3E 71*
       (off Lime Gro.)
Frobisher Cres. *EC2* . . . *5A 10*
       (off Beech St.)
Frobisher Gdns. E10 . . . 2D *39*
Frobisher Ho. *E1* *2D 79*
       (off Watts St.)
  SW1 . . . . 2F *89*
       (off Dolphin Sq.)
Frobisher Pas. E14 . . . . 2C *80*
Frobisher Pl. Pioneer Cen.
  SE15 . . . . 4E *93*
Frobisher St. SE10 . . . . 2A *96*
Frogley Rd. SE22 . . . . . 2B *106*
Frogmore SW18 . . . . . 3C *100*
Frogmore Ind. Est.
  N5 . . . . 2E *49*
Frognal NW3 . . . . 1E *45*
Frognal Cl. NW3 . . . . . . 2E *45*
Frognal Ct. NW3 . . . . . . 3E *45*
Frognal Gdns. NW3 . . . 1E *45*
Frognal La. NW3 . . . . . . 2D *45*
Frognal Pde. NW3 . . . . . 3E *45*
Frognal Ri. NW3 . . . . . . 5E *31*
Frognal Way NW3 . . . . . 1E *45*
Froissart Rd. SE9 . . . . 3F *111*
Frome Ho. SE15 . . . . . 2D *107*
Frome St. N1 . . . . 1E *63*
Frontenac NW10 . . . . . 4D *43*
Frostic Wlk. E1 . . . . 4C *64*
Froude St. SW8 . . . . . . 5D *89*
Fruiterers Pas. *EC4* . . . *5A 18*
     (off Queen St. Pl.)
Fryday Gro. M.
  SW12 . . . . *5E 103*
       (off Weir Rd.)
Fryent Cres. NW9 . . . . . 1A *28*
Fryent Flds. NW9 . . . . . 1A *28*
Fryent Gro. NW9 . . . . . 1A *28*
Fry Ho. E6 . . . . 4E *55*
Frying Pan All. E1 . . . . . 1F *19*
Fry Rd. E6 . . . . 4F *55*
  NW10 . . . . 5B *42*
Fulbeck Ho. *N7* *3B 48*
       (off Sutterton St.)
Fulbeck Rd. N19 . . . . . . 1E *47*
Fulbourne St. E1 . . . . . 4D *65*
Fulbrook M. N19 . . . . . . 1E *47*
Fulcher Ho. *N1* *5A 50*
      (off Colville Est.)
  SE8 . . . . 1B *94*
Fulford St. SE16 . . . . . . 3D *79*
FULHAM 5A *86*
FULHAM BROADWAY
  . . . . 3C *86*
Fulham B'way. SW6 . . . 3C *86*
Fulham B'way. Shop. Cen.
  SW6 . . . . 3C *86*
      (off Fulham B'way.)
Fulham B'way. SW6 . . . 4C *86*
Fulham FC 4F *85*

Fulham High St.
SW6 . . . . 5A 86
Fulham Palace 5A 86
Fulham Pal. Rd.
SW6 . . . . 1E 85
W6 . . . . 1E 85
Fulham Pk. Gdns.
SW6 . . . . 5B 86
Fulham Pk. Rd. SW6 . . 5B 86
Fulham Pools 2A 86
Fulham Rd. SW3 . . . . 3D 87
SW6 . . . . 4A 86
(not continuous)
SW10 . . . . 3D 87
Fuller Cl. E2 . . . . . . 3C 64
(off Cheshire St.)
Fuller's Griffin Brewery &
Vis. Cen. 2B 84
Fullerton Rd. SW18 . . 3D 101
Fullwood's M.
N1 . . . . 1C 10 (2F 63)
Fulmar Ho. SE16 . . . . 5F 79
(off Tawny Way)
Fulmead St. SW6 . . . . 4D 87
Fulmer Ho. NW8 . . . . 3A 60
(off Mallory St.)
Fulmer Rd. E16 . . . . . 4F 69
Fulneck E1 . . . . 4E 65
(off Mile End Rd.)
Fulready Rd. E10 . . . . 1F 39
Fulthorp Rd. SE3 . . . . 5B 96
Fulton M. W2 . . . . . . 1E 73
Fulwood Pl.
WC1 . . . . . . 1A 16 (4B 62)
Fulwood Wlk.
SW19 . . . . 1A 114
Funland 5B 14
(in Trocadero Cen)
Furber St. W6 . . . . . . 4D 71
Furley Ho. SE15 . . . . 3C 92
(off Peckham Pk. Rd.)
Furley Rd. SE15 . . . . 3C 92
Furlong Rd. N7 . . . . . 3C 48
Furmage St. SW18 . . 5D 101
Furneaux Av. SE27 . . 5D 119
Furness Ho. SW1 . . . . 1D 89
(off Abbots Mnr.)
Furness Rd. NW10 . . . 1C 56
SW6 . . . . 5D 87
Furnival Mans. W1 . . . 1F 13
(off Wells St.)
Furnival St.
EC4 . . . . . . 2B 16 (5C 62)
Furrow La. E9 . . . . . . 2E 51
Fursecroft W1 . . . . . . 5B 60
(off George St.)
Further Grn. Rd.
SE6 . . . . 5A 110
FURZEDOWN 5D 117
Furzedown Dr.
SW17 . . . . 5D 117
Furzedown Rd.
SW17 . . . . 5D 117
Furzefield Rd. SE3 . . . 2D 97
Furze St. E3 . . . . . . 4C 66
Fusion Health & Leisure Cen.
. . . . 5D 77
Fye Foot La. EC4 . . . . 4F 17
(off Queen Victoria St.,
not continuous)

Fyfield N4 . . . . 4C 34
(off Six Acres Est.)
Fyfield Ct. E7 . . . . . . 3C 54
Fyfield Rd. SW9 . . . . 1C 104
Fynes St. SW1 . . . . . 5F 75

G

Gable Ct. SE26 . . . . . 4D 121
Gables Cl. SE5 . . . . . 4A 92
SE12 . . . . 1C 124
Gabriel Ho. SE11 . . . . 5B 76
Gabrielle Ct.
NW3 . . . . 3F 45
Gabriel M. NW2 . . . . . 4B 30
Gabriel St. SE23 . . . . 5F 107
Gabriels Wharf
SE1 . . . . . . 1B 24 (2C 76)
Gaddesden Ho. EC1 . . 2C 10
(off Cranwood St.)
Gadebridge Ho. SW3 . . 1A 88
(off Cale St.)
Gadsbury Cl. NW9 . . . 1B 28
Gadsden Ho. W10 . . . 3A 58
(off Hazlewood Cres.)
Gadwall Cl. E16 . . . . . 5D 69
Gage Brown Ho. W10 . . 5F 57
(off Bridge Cl.)
Gage Rd. E16 . . . . . . 4A 68
Gage St. WC1 . . 5E 7 (4A 62)
Gainford Ho. E2 . . . . . 2D 65
(off Ellsworth St.)
Gainford St. N1 . . . . . 5C 48
Gainsborough Ct.
SE16 . . . . 1D 93
(off Stubbs Dr.)
SE21 . . . . 2A 120
W12 . . . . 3E 71
Gainsborough Gdns.
NW3 . . . . 5F 31
NW11 . . . . 2B 30
Gainsborough Ho.
E14 . . . . 1A 80
(off Victory Pl.)
SW1 . . . . 5F 75
(off Erasmus St.)
Gainsborough Mans.
W14 . . . . 2A 86
(off Queen's Club Gdns.)
Gainsborough M.
SE26 . . . . 3D 121
Gainsborough Rd.
E11 . . . . 2A 40
E15 . . . . 2A 68
W4 . . . . 5B 70
Gainsborough St. E9 . . 3B 52
Gainsborough Studios E.
N1 . . . . 5F 49
(off Poole St.)
Gainsborough Studios Nth.
N1 . . . . 5F 49
(off Poole St.)
Gainsborough Studios Sth.
N1 . . . . 5F 49
(off Poole St.)
Gainsborough Studios W.
N1 . . . . 5F 49
(off Poole St.)

Gainsfield Ct. E11 . . . . 5A 40
Gainsford St.
SE1 . . . . . . 3F 27 (3B 78)
Gairloch Ho. NW1 . . . . 4F 47
(off Stratford Vs.)
Gairloch Rd. SE5 . . . . 5A 92
Gaisford St. NW5 . . . . 3E 47
Gaitskell Ct. SW11 . . . 5A 88
Gaitskell Ho. E6 . . . . . 5F 55
E17 . . . . 2A 92
(off Villa St.)
Galahad Rd.
BR1: Brom 4C 124
Galata Rd. SW13 . . . . 3C 84
Galatea Sq. SE15 . . . 1D 107
Galaxy Bldg. E14 . . . . 5C 80
(off Crews St.)
Galaxy Ho. EC2 . . . . . 3C 10
(off Leonard St.)
Galbraith St. E14 . . . . 4E 81
Galena Arches W6 . . . 5D 71
(off Galena Rd.)
Galena Ho. W6 . . . . . 5D 71
(off Galena Rd.)
Galena Rd. W6 . . . . . 5D 71
Galen Pl.
WC1 . . . . . . 1E 15 (4A 62)
Galesbury Rd.
SW18 . . . . 4E 101
Gales Gdns. E2 . . . . . 2D 65
Gale St. E3 . . . . 4C 66
Galgate Cl. SW19 . . . 1F 113
Galleon Cl. SE16 . . . . 3F 79
Galleon Ho. E14 . . . . 5E 81
(off Glengarnock Av.)
Gallery Ct. SE1 . . . . . 4B 26
(off Pilgrimage St.)
SW10 . . . . 2E 87
(off Gunter Gro.)
Gallery Rd. SE21 . . . . 1F 119
Galleywall Rd. SE16 . . 5D 79
Galleywall Rd. Trad. Est.
SE16 . . . . 5D 79
(off Galleywall Rd.)
Galleywood Ho. W10 . . 4E 57
(off Sutton Way)
Gallia Rd. N5 . . . . . . 2D 49
Gallions Rd. SE7 . . . . 5D 83
Galliver Pl. E5 . . . . . . 1D 51
Gallon Cl. SE7 . . . . . 5E 83
Gallus Sq. SE3 . . . . . 1D 111
Galloway Rd. W12 . . . 2C 70
Galsworthy Av. E14 . . . 4A 66
Galsworthy Cl. NW2 . . 1A 44
Galsworthy Cres. SE3 . 4E 97
Galsworthy Ho. W11 . . 5A 58
(off Elgin Cres.)
Galsworthy Rd. NW2 . . 1A 44
Galsworthy Ter. N16 . . 5A 36
Galton St. W10 . . . . . 2A 58
Galveston Ho. E1 . . . . 3A 66
(off Harford St.)
Galveston Rd.
SW15 . . . . 3B 100
Galway Cl. SE16 . . . . 1D 93
(off Masters Dr.)

Galway Ho. *E1* *4F 65*
  (off White Horse La.)
EC1 . . . . 2A 10
Galway St.
EC1 . . . . 2A 10 (2E 63)
Gambetta St. SW8 . . . . . 5D 89
Gambia St.
SE1 . . . . . . 2E 25 (2D 77)
Gambier Ho. *EC1* *2A 10*
  (off Mora St.)
Gambole Rd. SW17 . . . . 4A 116
Gamlen St. SW15 . . . . . 2F 99
Gamuel Cl. E17 . . . . 1C 38
Gandhi Cl. E17 . . . . 1C 38
Gandolfi St. SE15 . . . . . 2A 92
Ganton St.
W1 . . . . 4F 13 (1E 75)
Gap Rd. SW19 . . . . 5C 114
Garbett Ho. *SE17* *2D 91*
  (off Doddington Gro.)
Garbutt Pl.
W1 . . . . 5C 4 (4C 60)
Garden Cl. SE12 . . . . . . 3D 125
SW15 . . . . 5E 99
Garden Cl. EC4 . . . . 4B 16
Garden Ho., The *W6* . . . *2F 85*
  (off Bothwell St.)
Garden La.
BR1: Brom 5D 125
SW2 . . . . 1B 118
Garden M. W2 . . . . 1C 72
Garden Pl. E8 . . . . 5B 50
Garden Rd. NW8 . . . . . . 2E 59
Garden Row
SE1 . . . . . . 5D 25 (4D 77)
Garden Royal SW15 . . . . 4F 99
Gardens, The SE22 . . . . 2C 106
Garden St. E1 . . . . 4F 65
Garden Ter. SW1 . . . . . . 1F 89
SW7 . . . . 3A 74
  (off Trevor Pl.)
Garden Vw. E7 . . . . 1E 55
Garden Wlk.
EC2 . . . . . . 2D 11 (2A 64)
Gardiner Av. NW2 . . . . . 2E 43
Gardiner Cl. E11 . . . . . . 1D 41
Gardner Ct. *EC1* *3D 9*
  (off Brewery Sq.)
N5 . . . . 1E 49
Gardner Ind. Est.
SE26 . . . . 5B 122
Gardner Rd. E13 . . . . . . 3D 69
Gardners La.
EC4 . . . . . . 4F 17 (1E 77)
Gard St. EC1 . . . 1E 9 (2D 63)
Gareth Ct. SW16 . . . . . . 3F 117
Gareth Gro.
BR1: Brom 4C 124
Garfield Ct. *NW6* *4A 44*
  (off Willesden La.)
Garfield M. SW11 . . . . . 1C 102
Garfield Rd. E13 . . . . . . 3B 68
SW11 . . . . 1C 102
SW19 . . . . 5E 115
Garford St. E14 . . . . 1C 80
Garganey Ct. *NW10* *3A 42*
  (off Elgar Av.)
Garland Ct. *E14* *1C 80*
  (off Premiere Pl.)

Garlick Hill
EC4 . . . . . . 4A 18 (1E 77)
Garlies Rd. SE23 . . . . . 3A 122
Garlinge Rd. NW2 . . . . . 3B 44
Garnault M. EC1 . . . . 2C 8
Garnault Pl.
EC1 . . . . . . 2C 8 (2C 62)
Garner St. E2 . . . . 1C 64
Garnet Ho. *E1* *2E 79*
  (off Garnet St.)
Garnet Rd. NW10 . . . . . 3A 42
Garnet St. E1 . . . . 1E 79
Garnett Rd. NW3 . . . . . 2B 46
Garnham Cl. N16 . . . . . 4B 36
Garnham St. N16 . . . . . 4B 36
Garnies Cl. SE15 . . . . . 3B 92
Garrad's Rd. SW16 . . . . 3F 117
Garrard Wlk. NW10 . . . . 3A 42
Garratt Cl. SW18 . . . . . 5D 101
Garratt La. SW17 . . . . . 3E 115
SW18 . . . . 4D 101
Garratt Ter. SW17 . . . . 4A 116
Garraway Ct. *SW13* *3E 85*
  (off Wyatt Dr.)
Garrett Cl. W3 . . . . 4A 56
Garrett Ho. *SE1* *3D 25*
  (off Burrows M.)
W12 . . . . 5D 57
  (off Du Cane Rd.)
Garrett St.
EC1 . . . . . . 3A 10 (3E 63)
Garrick Av. NW11 . . . . . 1A 30
Garrick Cl. SW18 . . . . . 2E 101
Garrick Cl. *E8* *4B 50*
  (off Jacaranda Gro.)
Garrick Ho. W1 . . . . . . 2D 21
W4 . . . . 2A 84
Garrick Ind. Est.
NW9 . . . . 1B 28
Garrick Rd. NW9 . . . . . 1B 28
Garrick St.
WC2 . . . . . . 4D 15 (1A 76)
Garrick Theatre *5D 15*
  (off Charing Cross Rd.)
Garrick Yd. WC2 . . . . . 4D 15
Garsdale Ter. *W14* *1B 86*
  (off Aisgill Av.)
Garsington M. SE4 . . . . 1B 108
Garson Ho. *W2* *1F 73*
  (off Gloucester Ter.)
Garston Ho. *N1* *4D 49*
  (off Sutton Est., The)
Garter Way SE16 . . . . . 3F 79
Garth Ho. NW2 . . . . . . 4B 30
Garthorne Rd. SE23 . . . 5F 107
Garthorne Road
  Nature Reserve 5F 107
Garth Rd. NW2 . . . . . . 4B 30
Gartmoor Gdns.
SW19 . . . . 1B 114
Garton Pl. SW18 . . . . . 4E 101
Gartons Way SW11 . . . . 1E 101
Garvary Rd. E16 . . . . . . 5D 69
Garway Rd. W2 . . . . . . 5D 59
Gascoigne Pl.
E2 . . . . 1F 11 (2B 64)
  (not continuous)
Gascony Av. NW6 . . . . . 4C 44
Gascoyne Ho. E9 . . . . . 4A 52
Gascoyne Rd. E9 . . . . . 4F 51

Gaselee St. *E14* *2E 81*
  (off Baffin Way)
Gaskarth Rd. SW12 . . . . 4D 103
Gaskell Rd. N6 . . . . 1B 32
Gaskell St. SW4 . . . . . . 5A 90
Gaskin St. N1 . . . . 5D 49
Gaspar Cl. *SW5* *5D 73*
  (off Courtfield Gdns.)
Gaspar M. SW5 . . . . . . 5D 73
Gassiot Rd. SW17 . . . . 4B 116
Gasson Ho. *SE14* *2F 93*
  (off John Williams Cl.)
Gastein Rd. W6 . . . . . . 2F 85
Gastigny Ho. EC1 . . . . . 2A 10
Gataker Ho. *SE16* *4D 79*
  (off Slippers Pl.)
Gataker St. SE16 . . . . . 4D 79
Gatcombe Ho. SE22 . . . 1A 106
Gatcombe Rd. E16 . . . . 2C 82
N19 . . . . 5F 33
Gate Cinema *2C 72*
  (off Notting Hill Ga.)
Gateforth St. NW8 . . . . . 3A 60
Gate Hill Ct. *W11* *2B 72*
  (off Ladbroke Ter.)
Gatehouse Sq. SE1 . . . 1A 26
Gatehouse Theatre 3C 32
Gateley Ho. *SE4* *2F 107*
  (off Coston Wlk.)
Gateley Rd. SW9 . . . . . 1B 104
Gate Lodge *W9* *4C 58*
  (off Admiral Wlk.)
Gate M. SW7 . . . . 3A 74
  (off Rutland Ga.)
Gatesborough St.
EC2 . . . . . . 3D 11 (3A 64)
Gates Cl. SE17 . . . . . . 1E 91
Gatesden WC1 . . 2F 7 (2A 62)
Gateside Rd.
SW17 . . . . 3B 116
Gate St. WC2 . . 2F 15 (5B 62)
Gate Theatre, The *2C 72*
  (off Pembridge Rd.)
Gateway SE17 . . . . 2E 91
Gateway Arc. *N1* *1D 63*
  (off Upper St.)
Gateway Bus. Cen.
BR3: Beck 5A 122
Gateway Ind. Est.
NW10 . . . . 2B 56
Gateway M. E8 . . . . . . 2B 50
Gateway Rd. E10 . . . . . 5D 39
Gateways, The *SW3* . . . *5A 74*
  (off Sprimont Pl.)
Gathorne St. E2 . . . . . . 1F 65
Gatliff Cl. *SW1* *1D 89*
  (off Ebury Bri. Rd.)
Gatliff Rd. SW1 . . . . . . 1D 89
  (not continuous)
Gatonby St. SE15 . . . . . 4B 92
Gattis Wharf *N1* *1A 62*
  (off New Wharf Rd.)
Gatton Rd. SW17 . . . . . 4A 116
Gatwick Ho. *E14* *5B 66*
  (off Clemence St.)
Gatwick Rd. SW18 . . . . 5B 100
Gauden Cl. SW4 . . . . . . 1F 103
Gauden Rd. SW4 . . . . . 5F 89
Gaugin Ct. *SE16* *1D 93*
  (off Stubbs Dr.)

Gaumont Ter. *W12* *3E 71*
   (off Lime Gro.)
Gaunt St.
  SE1 . . . . 5F 25 (4E 77)
Gautrey Rd. SE15 . . . . . 5B 93
Gavel St. SE17 . . . . 5F 77
Gaverick M. E14 . . . . . 5C 80
Gavestone Cres.
  SE12 . . . . 5D 111
Gavestone Rd.
  SE12 . . . . 5D 111
Gaviller Pl. E5 . . . . 1D 51
Gawber St. E2 . . . . 2E 65
Gawsworth Cl. E15 . . . . 2B 54
Gay Cl. NW2 . . . . 2D 43
Gaydon Ho. *W2* *4D 59*
   (off Bourne Ter.)
Gayfere St.
  SW1 . . . . 5D 23 (4A 76)
Gayford Rd. W12 . . . . . . 3B 70
Gay Ho. N16 . . . . 2A 50
Gayhurst *SE17* *2F 91*
   (off Hopwood Rd.)
Gayhurst Ho. *NW8* *3A 60*
   (off Mallory St.)
Gayhurst Rd. E8 . . . . . . 4C 50
Gaymead *NW8* *5D 45*
   (off Abbey Rd.)
Gaynesford Rd.
  SE23 . . . . 2F 121
Gay Rd. E15 . . . . 1F 67
Gaysley Ho. SE11 . . . . 5C 76
   (off Hotspur St.)
Gay St. SW15 . . . . 1F 99
Gayton Cres. NW3 . . . . . 1F 45
Gayton Rd. NW3 . . . . . . 1F 45
Gayville Rd. SW11 . . . . 4B 102
Gaywood Cl. SW2 . . . . 1B 118
Gaywood St.
  SE1 . . . . . . 5E 25 (4D 77)
Gaza St. SE17 . . . . 1D 91
Gaze Ho. *E14* *5F 67*
   (off Blair St.)
Gean Ct. E11 . . . . 1F 53
Gearing Cl. SW17 . . . . 4C 116
Geary Rd. NW10 . . . . . . 2C 42
Geary St. N7 . . . . 2B 48
Gedling Pl.
  SE1 . . . . 5F 27 (4B 78)
Geere Rd. E15 . . . . 5B 54
Gees Ct. W1 . . . . 3C 12 (5C 60)
Gee St. EC1 . . . . . 3F 9 (3E 63)
Geffrye Est. N1 . . . . 1A 64
Geffrye Est. N1 . . . . 1A 64
Geffrye Mus. 1F 11
Geffrye St.
  E2 . . . . 1F 11 (1B 64)
Geldart Rd. SE15 . . . . . 3D 93
Geldeston Rd. E5 . . . . . 4C 36
Gellatly Rd. SE14 . . . . . 5E 93
Gemini Bus. Cen.
  E16 . . . . 3F 67
Gemini Bus. Est.
  SE14 . . . . 1F 93
Gemini Ct. *E1* *1C 78*
   (off Vaughan Way)
General Wolfe Rd.
  SE10 . . . . 4F 95
Geneva Ct. NW9 . . . . . . 1A 28
Geneva Dr. SW9 . . . . . 2C 104

Genoa Av. SW15 . . . . . 3E 99
Genoa Ho. *E1* *3F 65*
   (off Ernest St.)
Gentry Gdns. E13 . . . . . 3C 68
Geoffrey Cl. SE5 . . . . . 5E 91
Geoffrey Ct. SE4 . . . . . 5B 94
Geoffrey Gdns.
  E6 . . . . 1F 69
Geoffrey Ho. *SE1* 5C 26
   (off Pardoner St.)
Geoffrey Jones Ct.
  NW10 . . . . 5C 42
Geoffrey Rd. SE4 . . . . 1B 108
George Beard Rd.
  SE8 . . . . 5B 80
George Belt Ho. *E2* . . . *2F 65*
   (off Smart St.)
George Ct. WC2 . . . . . . 5E 15
George Downing Est.
  N16 . . . . 4B 36
George Eliot Ho.
  SW1 . . . . *5E 75*
   (off Vauxhall Bri. Rd.)
George Elliston Ho.
  SE1 . . . . *1C 92*
   (off Old Kent Rd.)
George Eyre Ho.
  NW8 . . . . *1F 59*
   (off Cochrane St.)
George Gillett Ct.
  EC1 . . . . 3A 10
George Inn Yd.
  SE1 . . . . 2B 26 (2F 77)
George La. SE13 . . . . 4D 109
George Lansbury Ho.
  NW10 . . . . 4A 42
George Lindgren Ho.
  SW6 . . . . *3B 86*
   (off Clem Attlee Ct.)
George Loveless Ho.
  E2 . . . . *1F 11*
   (off Diss St.)
George Lowe Ct. *W2* . . *4D 59*
   (off Bourne Ter.)
George Mathers Rd.
  SE11 . . . . 5D 77
George M. NW1 . . . . . . 2A 6
George Peabody Ct.
  NW1 . . . . *4A 60*
   (off Burne St.)
George Potter Ho.
  SW11 . . . . *5F 87*
   (off George Potter Way)
George Potter Way
  SW11 . . . . 5F 87
George Row SE16 . . . . 3C 78
George's Rd. N7 . . . . . 2B 48
George's Sq. *SW6* . . . *2B 86*
   (off Nth. End Rd.)
George St. E16 . . . . 5B 68
   (not continuous)
  W1 . . . . 2A 12 (5B 60)
George Tingle Ho.
  SE1 . . . . 5F 27
Georgetown Cl.
  SE19 . . . . 5A 120
Georgette Pl. SE10 . . . . 3E 95
George Walter Ct.
  SE16 . . . . *5E 79*
   (off Millender Wlk.)

George Wyver Cl.
  SW19 . . . . 5A 100
George Yd.
  EC3 . . . . 3C 18 (5F 63)
  W1 . . . . 4C 12 (1C 74)
Georgiana St. NW1 . . . . 5E 47
Georgian Ct. E9 . . . . . . 5E 51
  NW4 . . . . 1D 29
  SW16 . . . . 4A 118
Georgian Ho. *E16* *2C 82*
   (off Capulet M.)
Georgina Gdns. E2 . . . . 2B 64
Geraint Rd.
  BR1: Brom 4C 124
Geraldine Rd.
  SW18 . . . . 3E 101
Geraldine St.
  SE11 . . . . . . 5D 25 (4D 77)
Gerald M. *SW1* *5C 74*
   (off Gerald Rd.)
Gerald Rd. E16 . . . . 3B 68
  SW1 . . . . 5C 74
Gerard Rd. SW13 . . . . . 4B 84
Gerards Cl. SE16 . . . . . 1E 93
Germander Way E15 . . . 2A 68
Gernigan Ho. SW18 . . . 4F 101
Gernon Rd. E3 . . . . 1A 66
Geron Way NW2 . . . . . . 4D 29
Gerrard St. SE14 . . . . . *3E 93*
   (off Briant St.)
Gerrard Pl.
  W1 . . . . 4C 14 (1F 75)
Gerrard Rd. N1 . . . . 1D 63
Gerrard St.
  W1 . . . . 4C 14 (1F 75)
Gerridge Ct. *SE1* 5C 24
   (off Gerridge St.)
Gerridge St.
  SE1 . . . . 5C 24 (4C 76)
Gerry Raffles Sq. E15 . . 4F 53
Gertrude St. SW10 . . . . 2E 87
Gervase St. SE15 . . . . . 3D 93
Ghent Ct. SE6 . . . . . . 2C 122
Ghent Way E8 . . . . 3B 50
Giant Arches Rd.
  SE24 . . . . 5E 105
Gibbings Ho. *SE1* *4E 25*
   (off King James St.)
Gibbins Rd. E15 . . . . . . 4E 53
Gibbon Ho. *NW8* *3F 59*
   (off Fisherton St.)
Gibbon Rd. SE15 . . . . . 5E 93
  W3 . . . . 1A 70
Gibbon's Rents *SE1* . . . 2D 27
Gibbons Rd. NW10 . . . . 3A 42
Gibbon Wlk. SW15 . . . . 2C 98
Gibbs Av. SE19 . . . . . . 5F 119
Gibbs Cl. SE19 . . . . . . 5F 119
Gibbs Grn. W14 . . . . . . 1B 86
   (not continuous)
Gibbs Grn. Cl. W14 . . . 1B 86
Gibbs Sq. SE19 . . . . . . 5F 119
Gibney Ter.
  BR1: Brom 4B 124
Gibraltar Wlk. *E2* *2B 64*
   (off Padbury Ct.)
Gibson Cl. E1 . . . . 3E 65
Gibson Gdns. N16 . . . . 4B 36
Gibson Rd. SE11 . . . . . 5B 76
Gibsons Hill SW16 . . . . 5D 119

Gibson Sq. N1 . . . . 5C 48
Gibson St. SE10 . . . . . 1A 96
Gideon Rd. SW11 . . . . 1C 102
Gielgud Theatre 4B 14
   (off Shaftesbury Av.)
Giesbach Rd. N19 . . . . 4F 33
Giffen Sq. Mkt. SE8 . . . 3C 94
   (off Giffen St.)
Giffin St. SE8 . . . . 3C 94
Gifford Ho. SE10 . . . . . 1F 95
   (off Eastney St.)
SW1 . . . . 1E 89
   (off Churchill Gdns.)
Gifford St. N1 . . . . 4A 48
Gift La. E15 . . . . 5A 54
Gilbert Bri. EC2 . . . . . 5A 10
   (off Gilbert Ho.)
Gilbert Collection 4A 16
   (off Lancaster Pl.)
Gilbert Ho. E2 . . . . 2F 65
   (off Usk St.)
EC2 . . . . 5A 10
SE8 . . . . 2C 94
SW1 . . . . 1D 89
   (off Churchill Gdns.)
SW8 . . . . 3A 90
   (off Wyvil Rd.)
SW13 . . . . 3D 85
   (off Trinity Chu. Rd.)
Gilbert Pl.
WC1 . . . . 1D 15 (4A 62)
Gilbert Rd. SE11 . . . . . 5C 76
Gilbert Scott SW18 . . . 4A 100
Gilbert Sheldon Ho.
W2 . . . . 4F 59
   (off Edgware Rd.)
Gilbertson Ho. E14 . . . . 4C 80
   (off Mellish St.)
Gilbert St. E15 . . . . . . 1A 54
W1 . . . . 3C 12 (5C 60)
Gilbey Rd. SW17 . . . . . 4A 116
Gilbeys Yd. NW1 . . . . . 4C 46
Gilby Ho. E9 . . . . 3F 51
Gilda Cres. N16 . . . . . 3C 36
Gildea St.
W1 . . . . 1E 13 (4D 61)
Gilden Cres. NW5 . . . . 2C 46
Giles Coppice SE19 . . . 4B 120
Giles High St.
WC2 . . . . 2C 14 (5F 61)
Giles Ho. SE16 . . . . . . 4C 78
   (off Old Jamaica Rd.)
Gilesmead SE5 . . . . . . 4F 91
Gilkes Cres. SE21 . . . . 4A 106
Gilkes Pl. SE21 . . . . . . 4A 106
Gillam Ho. SE16 . . . . . 5E 79
   (off Silwood St.)
Gillan Ct. SE12 . . . . . . 3D 125
Gill Av. E16 . . . . 5C 68
Gillender St. E3 . . . . . . 3E 67
E14 . . . . 3E 67
Gillespie Rd. N5 . . . . . 5C 34
Gillett Av. E6 . . . . 1F 69
Gillett Pl. N16 . . . . . . 2A 50
Gillett St. N16 . . . . . . 2A 50
Gillfoot NW1 . . . . 1F 5
   (off Hampstead Rd.)
Gillian St. SE13 . . . . . 3D 109
Gillies St. NW5 . . . . . 2C 46
Gilling Ct. NW3 . . . . . 3A 46

Gillingham M. SW1 . . . . 5E 75
Gillingham Rd. NW2 . . . 5A 30
Gillingham Row
SW1 . . . . 5E 75
Gillingham St. SW1 . . . 5E 75
Gillison Wlk. SE16 . . . . 4D 79
Gilman Dr. E15 . . . . . . 5B 54
Gilman Ho. E2 . . . . 1C 64
   (off Pritchard's Rd.)
Gill St. E14 . . . . 5B 66
Gilmore Rd. SE13 . . . . . 2F 109
Gilpin Av. SW14 . . . . . 2A 98
Gilpin Cl. W2 . . . . 4E 59
   (off Porteus Rd.)
Gilpin Rd. E5 . . . . 1A 52
Gilray Ho. W2 . . . . 1F 73
   (off Gloucester Ter.)
Gilstead Rd. SW6 . . . . 5D 87
Gilston Rd. SW10 . . . . 1E 87
Gilton Rd. SE6 . . . . . . 3A 124
Giltspur St.
EC1 . . . . . . 2E 17 (5D 63)
Ginsburg Yd. NW3 . . . . 1E 45
Gipsy Hill SE19 . . . . . 4A 120
Gipsy La. SW15 . . . . . 1D 99
Gipsy Moth IV 2E 95
Gipsy Rd. SE27 . . . . . 4E 119
Gipsy Rd. Gdns.
SE27 . . . . 4E 119
Giralda Cl. E16 . . . . . . 4F 69
Giraud St. E14 . . . . . . 5D 67
Girdler's Rd. W14 . . . . 5F 71
Girdlestone Wlk. N19 . . . 4E 33
Girdwood Rd.
SW18 . . . . 5A 100
Girling Ho. N1 . . . . . . 5A 50
   (off Colville St.)
Gironde Rd. SW6 . . . . . 3B 86
Girton Rd. SE26 . . . . . 5F 121
Girton Vs. W10 . . . . . . 5F 57
Gisburn Ho. SE15 . . . . 2C 92
   (off Friary Est.)
Gissing Wlk. N1 . . . . . 4C 48
Gittens Cl.
BR1: Brom 4B 124
Given Wilson Wlk.
E13 . . . . 1B 68
Gladding Rd. E12 . . . . 1F 55
Glade, The SE7 . . . . . . 3E 97
Gladesmore Community
   School & Sports Cen.
   . . . . 1C 36
Gladesmore Rd. N15 . . . 1B 36
Gladiator St. SE23 . . . . 5A 108
Glading Ter. N16 . . . . . 5B 36
Gladsmuir Rd. N19 . . . 3E 33
Gladstone Ct. SW1 . . . . 5F 75
   (off Regency St.)
Gladstone Ct. Bus. Cen.
SW8 . . . . 4D 89
   (off Pagden St.)
Gladstone Ho. E14 . . . . 5C 66
   (off E. India Dock Rd.)
Gladstone M. NW6 . . . . 4B 44
Gladstone Pde. NW2 . . . 4E 29
Gladstone Pk. Gdns.
NW2 . . . . 5D 29
Gladstone Pl. E3 . . . . . 1B 66
Gladstone St.
SE1 . . . . 5D 25 (4D 77)

Gladstone Ter. SE27 . . . 5E 119
   (off Bentons La.)
SW8 . . . . 4D 89
Gladwell Rd.
BR1: Brom 5C 124
N8 . . . . 1B 34
Gladwin Ho. NW1 . . . . 1A 6
   (off Werrington St.)
Gladwyn Rd. SW15 . . . 1F 99
Gladys Dimson Ho.
E7 . . . . 2B 54
Gladys Rd. NW6 . . . . . 4C 44
Glaisher St. SE8 . . . . . 2C 94
Glamis Pl. E1 . . . . 1E 79
Glamis Rd. E1 . . . . . . 1E 79
Glanville Rd. SW2 . . . . 3A 104
Glasbrook Rd. SE9 . . . . 5F 111
Glaserton Rd. N16 . . . . 2A 36
Glasford St.
SW17 . . . . 5B 116
Glasgow Ho. W9 . . . . . 1D 59
   (off Maida Va.)
Glasgow Rd. E13 . . . . . 1D 69
Glasgow Ter. SW1 . . . . 1E 89
Glasier Ct. E15 . . . . . . 4A 54
Glass Art Gallery, The
   . . . . 3A 78
Glasshill St.
SE1 . . . . 3E 25 (3D 77)
Glass Ho. SE1 . . . . . . 4D 27
   (off Royal Oak Yd.)
Glasshouse Flds. E1 . . . 1F 79
Glasshouse St.
W1 . . . . 5A 14 (1E 75)
Glasshouse Wlk.
SE11 . . . . 1A 90
Glasshouse Yd.
EC1 . . . . 4F 9 (3E 63)
Glasslyn Rd. N8 . . . . . 1F 33
Glass St. E2 . . . . 3D 65
Glassworks Studios
E2 . . . . 1E 11
   (off Basing Pl.)
Glastonbury Ct. SE14 . . 3E 93
   (off Farrow La.)
Glastonbury Ho.
SE12 . . . . 3B 110
   (off Wantage Rd.)
SW1 . . . . 1D 89
   (off Abbots Mnr.)
Glastonbury Pl. E1 . . . . 5E 65
Glastonbury St. NW6 . . 2B 44
Glaucus St. E3 . . . . . . 4D 67
Glazbury Rd. W14 . . . . 5A 72
Glazebrook Cl. SE21 . . . 2F 119
Glebe, The SE3 . . . . . . 1A 110
SW16 . . . . 4F 117
Glebe Cl. W4 . . . . 1A 84
Glebe Cl. SE3 . . . . 1A 110
   (off Glebe, The)
Glebe Ho. SE16 . . . . . 4D 79
   (off Slippers Pl.)
Glebe Hyrst SE19 . . . . 4A 120
Glebelands E10 . . . . . . 4D 39
Glebelands Cl. SE5 . . . 1A 106
Glebe Pl. SW3 . . . . . . 2A 88
Glebe Rd. E8 . . . . 4B 50
NW10 . . . . 3C 42
SW13 . . . . 5C 84
Glebe St. W4 . . . . 1A 84

Glebe Ter. E3 . . . . 2D 67
  W4 . . . . 1A 84
Gledhow Gdns. SW5 . . . 5E 73
Gledstanes Rd. W14 . . 1A 86
Glegg Pl. SW15 . . . . 2F 99
Glenaffric Av. E14. . . . . 5E 81
Glen Albyn Rd.
  SW19 . . . . 2F 113
Glenallan Ho. W14. . . . 5B 72
   (off Nth. End Cres.)
Glenalvon Way SE18 . . 5F 83
Glenarm Rd. E5 . . . . 1E 51
Glenavon Rd. E15 . . . . . 4A 54
Glenbow Rd.
  BR1: Brom 5A 124
Glenbrook Rd. NW6 . . . 2C 44
Glenburnie Rd.
  SW17 . . . . 3B 116
Glencairne Cl. E16 . . . . 4F 69
Glencoe Mans. SW9 . . . 3C 90
   (off Mowll St.)
Glendale Dr. SW19. . . 5B 114
Glendall St. SW9 . . . . . 2B 104
Glendarvon St. SW15 . . 1F 99
Glendower Gdns.
  SW14 . . . . 1A 98
Glendower Pl. SW7 . . . 5F 73
Glendower Rd.
  SW14 . . . . 1A 98
Glendown Ho. E8 . . . . . 2C 50
Glendun Ct. W3 . . . . . . 1A 70
Glendun Rd. W3. . . . . . 1A 70
Gleneagle M. SW16 . . 5F 117
Gleneagle Rd.
  SW16 . . . . 5F 117
Gleneagles Cl. SE16 . . 1D 93
Gleneldon M. SW16. . . 4A 118
Gleneldon Rd.
  SW16 . . . . 4A 118
Glenelg Rd. SW2 . . . . . 3A 104
Glenfarg Rd. SE6 . . . . . 1E 123
Glenfield Rd. SW12 . . 1E 117
Glenfinlas Way SE5 . . . 3D 91
Glenforth St. SE10 . . . . 1B 96
Glengall Gro. E14 . . . . . 4D 81
Glengall Pas. SE15 . . . . 5C 44
   (off Priory Pk. Rd.,
   not continuous)
Glengall Rd. NW6 . . . . . 5B 44
  SE15. . . . . 1B 92
Glengall Ter. SE15 . . . . 2B 92
Glengarnock Av. E14 . . 5E 81
Glengarry Rd. SE22 . . 3A 106
Glenhurst Av. NW5. . . . 1C 46
Glenilla Rd. NW3. . . . . . 3A 46
Glenister Rd. SE10 . . . . 1B 96
Glenkerry Ho. E14 . . . . 5E 67
   (off Burcham St.)
Glenloch Rd. NW3 . . . . 3A 46
Glenluce Rd. SE3 . . . . . 2C 96
Glen M. E17 . . . . 1B 38
Glenmore Rd. NW3 . . . 3A 46
Glennie Ct. SE22 . . . . . 1C 120
Glennie Ho. SE10. . . . . 4E 95
   (off Blackheath Hill)
Glennie Rd. SE27. . . . . 3E 118
Glenparke Rd. E7 . . . . . 3D 55
   (not continuous)
Glenridding NW1 . . . . . 1A 6
   (off Ampthill Est.)

Glen Rd. E13 . . . . 3E 69
  E17 . . . . 1B 38
Glenrosa St. SW6. . . . . 5E 87
Glenroy St. W12. . . . . . 5E 57
Glensdale Rd. SE4. . . . 1B 108
Glenshaw Mans.
  SW9 . . . . 3C 90
   (off Brixton Rd.)
Glentanner Way
  SW17 . . . . 3F 115
Glen Ter. E14 . . . . 3E 81
   (off Manchester Rd.)
Glentham Gdns.
  SW13 . . . . 2D 85
Glentham Rd. SW13 . . 2C 84
Glenthorne M. W6. . . . . 5D 71
Glenthorne Rd. W6 . . . 5D 71
Glenthorpe Av.
  SW15 . . . . 2C 98
Glenton Rd. SE13. . . . . 2A 110
Glentworth St.
  NW1 . . . . 4A 4 (3B 60)
Glenville Gro. SE8 . . . . 3B 94
Glenville M. SW18 . . . 5D 101
Glenville M. Ind. Est.
  SW18 . . . . 5C 100
Glenwood Av. NW9 . . . 3A 28
Glenwood Rd. N15. . . . 1D 35
  SE6. . . . . 1B 122
Glenworth Av. E14 . . . . 5F 81
Gliddon Dr. E5 . . . . 1C 50
Gliddon Rd. W14 . . . . . 5A 72
Global App. E3. . . . . . . 1D 67
Globe, The
  SE1 . . . . 4B 26 (3E 77)
Globe Pond Rd.
  SE16 . . . . 2A 80
Globe Rd. E1 . . . . 2E 65
  E2 . . . . 2E 65
   (not continuous)
  E15 . . . . 2B 54
Globe Rope Wlk.
  E14 . . . . 5D 81
   (off E. Ferry Rd.)
Globe St.
  SE1 . . . . 5B 26 (4F 77)
Globe Ter. E2 . . . . 2E 65
GLOBE TOWN 2F 65
Globe Town Mkt. E2 . . . 2F 65
Globe Wharf SE16 . . . . 1F 79
Globe Yd. W1. . . . . 3D 13
Gloucester Arc. SW7 . . 5E 73
Gloucester Av. NW1. . . 4C 46
Gloucester Cir. SE10 . . 3E 95
Gloucester Cl. NW10 . . 4A 42
Gloucester Ct.
  EC3 . . . . 5E 19 (1A 78)
  NW11 . . . . 2B 30
   (off Golders Grn. Rd.)
  SE22 . . . . 1C 120
Gloucester Cres.
  NW1 . . . . 5D 47
Gloucester Dr. N4 . . . . 4D 35
Gloucester Gdns.
  NW11 . . . . 2B 30
  W2 . . . . 5E 59
Gloucester Ga. NW1 . . 1D 61
   (not continuous)
Gloucester Ga. M.
  NW1 . . . . 1D 61

Gloucester Ho. E16 . . . 2C 82
   (off Gatcombe Rd.)
  NW6 . . . . 1C 58
   (off Cambridge Rd.)
  SW9 . . . . 3C 90
Gloucester M. E10 . . . . 2C 38
  W2 . . . . 5E 59
Gloucester M. W. W2. . 5E 59
Gloucester Pl.
  NW1. . . . . 4A 4 (3B 60)
  W1. . . . . 5A 4 (3B 60)
Gloucester Pl. M.
  W1. . . . . 1A 12 (4B 60)
Gloucester Rd. E10 . . . 2C 38
  E11 . . . . 1D 41
  SW7 . . . . 4E 73
Gloucester Sq. E2 . . . . 5C 50
  W2. . . . . 5F 59
Gloucester St. SW1 . . . 1E 89
Gloucester Ter. W2 . . . 5D 59
Gloucester Wlk. W8. . . 3C 72
Gloucester Way
  EC1 . . . . 2C 8 (2C 62)
Glover Ho. NW6 . . . . . . 4E 45
   (off Harben Rd.)
  SE15. . . . . 2D 107
Glycena Rd. SW11. . . . 1B 102
Glyn Ct. SW16 . . . . 3C 118
Glynde M. SW3 . . . . . . 4A 74
   (off Walton St.)
Glynde Reach WC1 . . . 2E 7
Glynde Rd. SE4. . . . . . 4B 108
Glynfield Rd. NW10 . . . 4A 42
Glyn Rd. E5. . . . . 5F 37
Glyn St. SE11. . . . . 1B 90
Glynwood Ct. SE23. . . 2E 121
Goater's All. SW6 . . . . . 3B 86
   (off Dawes Rd.)
Godalming Rd. E14 . . . 4D 67
Godbold Rd. E15 . . . . . 3A 68
Goddard Pl. N19. . . . . . 5E 33
Godfree Ct. SE1 . . . . . . 3B 26
   (off Long La.)
Godfrey Ho. EC1. . . . . . 2B 10
Godfrey St. E15. . . . . . . 1E 67
  SW3 . . . . 1A 88
Goding St. SE11. . . . . . 1A 90
Godley Cl. SE14 . . . . . . 4E 93
Godley Rd. SW18. . . . . 1F 115
Godliman St.
  EC4 . . . . 3E 17 (5D 63)
Godman Rd. SE15 . . . . 5D 93
Godolphin Ho. NW3 . . . 4A 46
   (off Fellows Rd.)
Godolphin Pl. W3. . . . . 1A 70
Godolphin Rd. W12 . . . 2D 71
   (not continuous)
Godson Rd. SE1 . . . . . . 5C 26
   (off Pardoner St.)
Godwin Cl. N1 . . . . 1E 63
Godwin Ct. NW1. . . . . . 1E 61
   (off Chalton St.)
Godwin Ho. NW6 . . . . . 1D 59
   (off Tollgate Gdns.,
   not continuous)
Godwin Rd. E7 . . . . 1D 55
Goffers Rd. SE3 . . . . . . 4A 96
Golborne Gdns. W10 . . 3A 58
Golborne Ho. W10 . . . . 3A 58
   (off Adair Rd.)

Golborne M. W10 . . . . . 4A 58
Golborne Rd. W10 . . . . . 4A 58
Goldcrest Cl. E16 . . . . . 4F 69
Golden Cross M.
   W11 . . . . 5B 58
   (off Portobello Rd.)
Golden Hinde 1B 26 (2F 77)
Golden Hind Pl. SE8 . . . 5B 80
   (off Grove St.)
Golden La.
   EC1 . . . . 3F 9 (3E 63)
Golden La. Est.
   EC1 . . . . 4F 9 (3E 63)
Golden Lane Leisure Cen.
   . . . . 4F 9
   (off Golden La. Est.)
Golden Plover Cl.
   E16 . . . . 5C 68
Golden Sq.
   W1 . . . . 4A 14 (1E 75)
Golden Yd. NW3 . . . . . . 1E 45
   (off Holly Mt.)
Golders Ct. NW11 . . . . . 2B 30
Golders Gdns. NW11 . . . 2A 30
GOLDERS GREEN 1A 30
Golders Grn. Crematorium
   NW11 . . . . 2C 30
Golders Grn. Cres.
   NW11 . . . . 2B 30
Golders Grn. Rd.
   NW11 . . . . 1A 30
Golderslea NW11 . . . . . 3C 30
Golders Mnr. Dr.
   NW11 . . . . 1F 29
Golders Pk. Cl.
   NW11 . . . . 3C 30
Golders Way NW11 . . . . 2B 30
Goldhawk Ind. Est.
   W6 . . . . 4D 71
Goldhawk M. W12 . . . . . 3D 71
Goldhawk Rd. W6 . . . . . 5B 70
   W12 . . . . 5B 70
Goldhurst Ter. NW6 . . . . 4D 45
Goldie Ho. N19 . . . . 2F 33
Golding St. E1 . . . . 5C 64
Golding Ter. E1 . . . . . . 5C 64
   SW11 . . . . 5C 88
Goldington Bldgs.
   NW1 . . . . 5F 47
   (off Royal College St.)
Goldington Cres.
   NW1 . . . . 1F 61
Goldington St. NW1 . . . . 1F 61
Goldman Cl. E2 . . . . 3C 64
Goldmark Ho. SE3 . . . . 1D 111
Goldney Rd. W9 . . . . . . 3C 58
Goldsboro' Rd. SW8 . . . 4F 89
Goldsborough Ho.
   E14 . . . . 1D 95
   (off St Davids Sq.)
Goldsmith Av. E12 . . . . . 3F 55
   NW9 . . . . 1A 28
Goldsmith Ct. WC2 . . . . 2E 15
   (off Stukeley St.)
Goldsmith Rd. E10 . . . . 3C 38
   SE15 . . . . 4C 92
Goldsmith's Bldgs.
   W3 . . . . 2A 70
Goldsmiths Cl. W3 . . . . 2A 70
Goldsmiths College . . . 4A 94

Goldsmith's Pl. NW6 . . . 5D 45
   (off Springfield La.)
Goldsmith's Row E2 . . . 1C 64
Goldsmith's Sq. E2 . . . . 1C 64
Goldsmith St.
   EC2 . . . . 2A 18 (5E 63)
Goldsworthy Gdns.
   SE16 . . . . 1E 93
Goldthorpe NW1 . . . . . . 5E 47
   (off Camden St.)
Goldwell Ho. SE22 . . . . 1A 106
Goldwin Cl. SE14 . . . . . 4E 93
Goldwing Cl. E16 . . . . . 5C 68
Gollogly Ter. SE7 . . . . . 1E 97
Gomm Rd. SE16 . . . . . . 4E 79
Gondar Gdns. NW6 . . . . 2B 44
Gonson St. SE8 . . . . . . 2D 95
Gonston Cl. SW19 . . . . . 2A 114
Gonville St. SW6 . . . . . 1A 100
Gooch Ho. E5 . . . . 5D 37
   EC1 . . . . 5B 8
   (off Portpool La.)
Goodall Ho. SE4 . . . . . . 2F 107
Goodall Rd. E11 . . . . . . 5E 39
Goodfaith Ho. E14 . . . . . 1D 81
   (off Simpson's Rd.)
Goodge Pl.
   W1 . . . . 1A 14 (4E 61)
Goodge St.
   W1 . . . . 1A 14 (4E 61)
Goodhall St. NW10 . . . . 2B 56
   (not continuous)
Goodhart Pl. E14 . . . . . . 1A 80
Goodhope Ho. E14 . . . . 1D 81
   (off Poplar High St.)
Gooding Cl. N7 . . . . 3A 48
Gooding Ho. SE7 . . . . . 1E 97
Goodman Cres.
   SW2 . . . . 2A 118
Goodman Rd. E10 . . . . . 2E 39
Goodman's Ct. E1 . . . . . 1F 19
Goodman's Stile E1 . . . . 5C 64
Goodmans Yd.
   E1 . . . . 4F 19 (1B 78)
Goodrich Ct. W10 . . . . . 5F 57
Goodrich Ho. E2 . . . . . . 1E 65
   (off Sewardstone Rd.)
Goodrich Rd. SE22 . . . . 4B 106
Goodson Rd. NW10 . . . . 4A 42
Goodson St. N1 . . . . . . 1C 62
Goodspeed Ho. E14 . . . 1D 81
   (off Simpson's Rd.)
Goods Way NW1 . . . . . . 1A 62
Goodway Gdns. E14 . . . 5F 67
Goodwill Ho. E14 . . . . . 1D 81
   (off Simpson's Rd.)
Goodwin Cl. SE16 . . . . . 4B 78
Goodwin Rd. W12 . . . . . 3C 70
Goodwins Ct.
   WC2 . . . . 4D 15 (1A 76)
Goodwin St. N4 . . . . . . 4C 34
Goodwood Ct. W1 . . . . . 5E 5
   (off Devonshire St.)
Goodwood Ho. SE14 . . . 4A 94
   (off Goodwood St.)
Goodwood Rd. SE14 . . . 3A 94
Goodyear Pl. SE5 . . . . . 2E 91
Goodyer Ho. SW1 . . . . . 1F 89
   (off Tachbrook St.)
Goodyers Gdns. NW4 . . 1F 29

Goose Grn. Trad. Est.
   SE22 . . . . 2B 106
Gophir La.
   EC4 . . . . 4B 18 (1F 77)
Gopsall St. N1 . . . . 5F 49
Gordon Av. SW14 . . . . . 2A 98
Gordonbrock Rd.
   SE4 . . . . 3C 108
Gordon Cl. E17 . . . . 1C 38
   N19 . . . . 3E 33
Gordon Ct. W12 . . . . . . 5E 57
Gordondale Rd.
   SW19 . . . . 2C 114
Gordon Gro. SE5 . . . . . 5D 91
Gordon Ho. E1 . . . . 1E 79
   (off Glamis Rd.)
   SE10 . . . . 3D 95
   (off Tarves Way)
   SW1 . . . . 4E 75
   (off Greencoat Pl.)
Gordon Ho. Rd. NW5 . . . 1C 46
Gordon Mans. W14 . . . . 4F 71
   (off Addison Gdns.)
   WC1 . . . . 4B 6
   (off Torrington Pl.)
Gordon Pl. W8 . . . . 3C 72
Gordon Rd. E11 . . . . . . 1C 40
   E15 . . . . 1E 53
   SE15 . . . . 5D 93
Gordon Sq.
   WC1 . . . . 3B 6 (3F 61)
Gordon St. E13 . . . . 2C 68
   WC1 . . . . 3B 6 (3F 61)
Gorefield Ho. NW6 . . . . 1C 58
   (off Gorefield Pl.)
Gorefield Pl. NW6 . . . . . 1C 58
Gore Rd. E9 . . . . 5E 51
Gore St. SW7 . . . . 4E 73
Gorham Ho. SE16 . . . . . 3F 79
   (off Wolfe Cres.)
Gorham Pl. W11 . . . . . . 1A 72
Goring St. EC3 . . . . 2E 19
Gorleston St. W14 . . . . . 5A 72
   (not continuous)
Gorse Cl. E16 . . . . 5C 68
Gorsefield Ho. E14 . . . . 1C 80
   (off E. India Dock Rd.)
Gorse Ri. SW17 . . . . . . 5C 116
Gorst Rd. NW10 . . . . . . 3A 56
   SW11 . . . . 4B 102
Gorsuch Pl.
   E2 . . . . 1F 11 (2B 64)
Gorsuch St.
   E2 . . . . 1F 11 (1B 64)
Gosberton Rd.
   SW12 . . . . 1B 116
Gosfield St.
   W1 . . . . 1F 13 (4E 61)
Goslett Yd.
   WC2 . . . . 3C 14 (5F 61)
Gosling Ho. E1 . . . . 1E 79
   (off Sutton St.)
Gosling Way SW9 . . . . . 4C 90
GOSPEL OAK 1C 46
Gosport Rd. E17 . . . . . . 1B 38
Gosset St. E2 . . . . 2B 64
Gosterwood St. SE8 . . . 2A 94
Goswell Pl. EC1 . . . . . . 2E 9
Goswell Rd.
   EC1 . . . . 1D 9 (1D 63)

Gothic Ct. SE5 . . . . 3E 91
  (off Wyndham Rd.)
Gottfried M. NW5 . . . . . . 1E 47
Goudhurst Rd.
  BR1: Brom 5A 124
Gough Ho. N1. . . . . 5D 49
  (off Windsor St.)
Gough Rd. E15 . . . . 1B 54
Gough Sq.
  EC4 . . . . 2C 16 (5C 62)
Gough St.
  WC1 . . . . 3A 8 (3B 62)
Gough Wlk. E14 . . . . 5C 66
Goulden Ho. SW11 . . . . . 5A 88
Goulden Ho. App.
  SW11 . . . . 5A 88
Gouldman Ho. E1 . . . . . . 3E 65
  (off Wyllen Cl.)
Gould Ter. E8 . . . . 2D 51
Goulston St.
  E1. . . . . 2F 19 (5B 64)
Goulton Rd. E5 . . . . 1D 51
Gourley Pl. N15 . . . . 1A 36
Gourley St. N15 . . . . 1A 36
Govan St. E2. . . . . 5C 50
Gover Ct. SW4 . . . . 5A 90
Govier Cl. E15 . . . . 4A 54
Gowan Av. SW6 . . . . 4A 86
Gowan Ho. E2. . . . . 2F 11
  (off Chambord St.)
Gowan Rd. NW10 . . . . . . 3D 43
Gower Cl. SW4 . . . . 4E 103
Gower Ct.
  WC1 . . . . 3B 6 (3F 61)
Gower Ho. SE17 . . . . 1E 91
  (off Morecambe St.)
Gower M.
  WC1 . . . . 1C 14 (4F 61)
Gower M. Mans. WC1 . . . 5C 6
  (off Gower M.)
Gower Pl.
  WC1 . . . . 3A 6 (3F 61)
Gower Rd. E7 . . . . 3C 54
Gower St.
  WC1 . . . . 3A 6 (3E 61)
Gower's Wlk. E1 . . . . 5C 64
Gowlett Rd. SE15 . . . . . 1C 106
Gowrie Rd. SW11 . . . . . 1C 102
Gracechurch St.
  EC3. . . . . 4C 18 (1F 77)
Grace Cl. SE9 . . . . 3F 125
Gracedale Rd.
  SW16 . . . . 5D 117
Gracefield Gdns.
  SW16 . . . . 3A 118
Gracehill E1 . . . . 4E 65
  (off Hannibal Rd.)
Grace Ho. SE11 . . . . 2B 90
  (off Vauxhall St.)
Grace Jones Cl. E8 . . . . . 3C 50
Grace Path SE26. . . . . . 4E 121
Grace Pl. E3 . . . . 2D 67
Graces All. E1 . . . . 1C 78
Graces M. NW8 . . . . 1E 59
  SE5 . . . . 5F 91
Grace's Rd. SE5 . . . . 5A 92
Grace St. E3 . . . . 2D 67
Gradient, The SE26 . . . . 4E 121
Graduate Pl. SE1 . . . . . . 5D 27
Grafton Cres. NW1 . . . . . 3D 47

Grafton Gdns. N4 . . . . . . 1E 35
Grafton Ho. SE8 . . . . 1B 94
Grafton M. W1 . . . 4F 5 (3E 61)
Grafton Pl.
  NW1 . . . . 2C 6 (2F 61)
Grafton Rd. NW5 . . . . . . 2C 46
Graftons, The NW2 . . . . 5C 30
Grafton Sq. SW4 . . . . . . 1E 103
Grafton St.
  W1 . . . . 5E 13 (1D 75)
Grafton Ter. NW5 . . . . . . 2B 46
Grafton Way
  W1 . . . . 4F 5 (3E 61)
  WC1 . . . . 4A 6 (3E 61)
Grafton Yd. NW5 . . . . . . 3D 47
Graham Ct. SE14 . . . . . . 2F 93
  (off Myers La.)
Graham Lodge
  NW4 . . . . 1D 29
Graham Rd. E8. . . . . 3C 50
  E13 . . . . 3C 68
  NW4 . . . . 1D 29
Graham St.
  N1 . . . . 1F 9 (1D 63)
Graham Ter. SW1 . . . . . . 5C 74
Grainger Ct. SE5 . . . . . . 3E 91
Gramer Cl. E11 . . . . 4F 39
Grampian Gdns.
  NW2 . . . . 3A 30
Grampians, The W6 . . . . 3F 71
  (off Shepherd's Bush Rd.)
Gramsci Way SE6 . . . . . 3D 123
Granada St. SW17 . . . . . 5B 116
Granard Av. SW15 . . . . . 3D 99
Granard Ho. E9. . . . . 3F 51
Granard Rd. SW12. . . . . 5B 102
Granary Rd. E1 . . . . 3D 65
Granary Sq. N1 . . . . 3C 48
Granary St. NW1 . . . . . . 5F 47
Granby Pl. SE1. . . . . 4B 24
  (off Station App. Rd.)
Granby St. E2 . . . . 3C 64
  (not continuous)
Granby Ter.
  NW1 . . . . 1F 5 (1E 61)
Grand Av.
  EC1 . . . . 5E 9 (4D 63)
  (not continuous)
Grand Central Hgts.
  EC1 . . . . 1F 9
  (off Central St.)
Grandfield Ct. W4 . . . . . . 2A 84
Grandison Rd.
  SW11 . . . . 3B 102
Grand Junc. Wharf
  N1 . . . . 1E 63
Grand Pde. N4 . . . . 1D 35
Grand Pde. M.
  SW15 . . . . 3A 100
Grand Union W2 . . . . 4F 59
  (off Harbet Rd.)
Grand Union Cen.
  W10 . . . . 3F 57
  (off West Row)
Grand Union Cl. W9. . . . 4B 58
Grand Union Cres.
  E8 . . . . 5C 50
Grand Union Wlk.
  NW1 . . . . 4D 47
  (off Kentish Town Rd.)

Grand Vitesse Ind. Cen.
  SE1 . . . . 2E 25
  (off Dolben St.)
Grand Wlk. E1 . . . . 3A 66
Granfield St. SW11 . . . . . 4F 87
Grange, The E17 . . . . . . 1A 38
  (off Grange Rd.)
  SE1. . . . . 5F 27 (4B 78)
  SW19 . . . . 5F 113
  W14 . . . . 5B 72
Grange Ct. NW10 . . . . . . 5A 28
  (off Neasden La.)
  WC2. . . . . 3A 16 (5B 62)
Grangecourt Rd. N16. . . 3A 36
Grangefield NW1 . . . . . . 4F 47
  (off Marquis Rd.)
Grange Gdns. NW3 . . . . 5D 31
Grange Gro. N1 . . . . 3E 49
Grange Ho. NW10 . . . . . 4D 43
  SE1. . . . . 5F 27 (4B 78)
Grange La. SE21 . . . . . . 2B 120
Grange Lodge
  SW19 . . . . 5F 113
Grangemill Rd. SE6. . . . 3C 122
Grangemill Way
  SE6 . . . . 2C 122
Grange Pk. Rd. E10. . . . . 3D 39
Grange Pl. NW6 . . . . 4C 44
Grange Rd. E10 . . . . 3C 38
  E13 . . . . 2B 68
  E17 . . . . 1A 38
  (not continuous)
  N6. . . . . 1C 32
  NW10 . . . . 3D 43
  SE1. . . . . 5E 27 (4A 78)
  SW13 . . . . 4C 84
Grange St. N1. . . . . 5F 49
Grange Wlk.
  SE1. . . . . 5E 27 (4B 78)
Grange Wlk. M. SE1 . . . 5E 27
Grange Way NW6. . . . . . 4C 44
Grangewood St. E6. . . . . 5F 55
Grange Yd.
  SE1. . . . . 5F 27 (4B 78)
Granite Apartments
  E15 . . . . 3F 53
Granleigh Rd. E11 . . . . . 4A 40
Gransden Av. E8 . . . . . . 4D 51
Gransden Ho. SE8 . . . . . 1B 94
Gransden Rd. W12. . . . . 3B 70
Grantbridge St. N1. . . . . 1D 63
Grantham Ct. SE16. . . . . 3F 79
  (off Eleanor Cl.)
Grantham Ho. SE15. . . . 2C 92
  (off Friary Est.)
Grantham Pl.
  W1. . . . . 2D 21 (2D 75)
Grantham Rd. SW9 . . . . 5A 90
  W4 . . . . 3A 84
Grantley Ho. SE14 . . . . . 2F 93
  (off Myers La.)
Grantley St. E1 . . . . 2F 65
Grant Mus. of Zoology &
  Comparative Anatomy
  . . . . 4B 6
Grant Rd. SW11 . . . . . . 2F 101
Grants Quay Wharf
  EC3. . . . . 5C 18 (1F 77)

Grant St. E13 . . . . 2C 68
N1 . . . . 1C 62
Grant Ter. N16 . . . . 2C 36
(off Castlewood Rd.)
Grantully Rd. W9 . . . . . . 2D 59
Granville Arc. SW9 . . 2C 104
Granville Ct. N1 . . . . . 5A 50
N4 . . . . 1B 34
SE14 . . . . 3A 94
(off Nynehead St.)
Granville Gro. SE13 . . 1E 109
Granville Ho. E14 . . . . . 5C 66
(off E. India Dock Rd.)
Granville Mans. W12 . . 3E 71
(off Shepherd's Bush Grn.)
Granville Pk. SE13 . . 1E 109
Granville Pl. SW6 . . . . 3D 87
W1 . . . . 3B 12 (5C 60)
Granville Point NW2 . . 4B 30
Granville Rd. E17 . . . . 1D 39
N4 . . . . 1B 34
NW2 . . . . 4B 30
NW6 . . . . 1C 58
(not continuous)
SW18 . . . . 5B 100
Granville Sq. SE15 . . . 3A 92
WC1 . . . . 2A 8 (2B 62)
Granville St.
WC1 . . . . 2A 8 (2B 62)
Grape St.
WC2 . . . . . . 2D 15 (5A 62)
Graphite Sq. SE11 . . . 1B 90
Grasmere NW1 . . . . . . 2E 5
(off Osnaburgh St.)
Grasmere Av. SW15 . . 4A 112
Grasmere Ct. SE26 . . 5C 120
SW13 . . . . 2C 84
(off Verdun Rd.)
Grasmere Point SE15 . . 3E 93
(off Old Kent Rd.)
Grasmere Rd. E13 . . . . 1C 68
SW16 . . . . 5B 118
Grassmount SE23 . . . 2D 121
Gratton Rd. W14 . . . . 4A 72
Gratton Ter. NW2 . . . . 5F 29
Gravel La. E1 . . . 2F 19 (5B 64)
(off Chilton Gro.)
Gravely Ho. SE8 . . . . . 5A 80
Gravenel Gdns.
SW17 . . . . 5A 116
(off Nutwell St.)
Graveney Rd. SW17 . . 4A 116
Gravesend Rd. W12 . . 1C 70
Gray Ho. SE17 . . . . . . 1E 91
(off King & Queen St.)
Grayling Cl. E16 . . . . 3A 68
Grayling Rd. N16 . . . . 4F 35
Grayling Sq. E2 . . . . . 2C 64
(off Nelson Gdns.)
Grayshott Rd. SW11 . . 5C 88
Gray's Inn 5A 8 (4B 62)
Gray's Inn Bldgs. EC1 . . 4B 8
(off Rosebery Av.)
Gray's Inn Pl.
WC1 . . . . . . 1A 16 (4B 62)
Gray's Inn Rd.
WC1 . . . . . . 1E 7 (2A 62)
Gray's Inn Sq.
WC1 . . . . . . 5B 8 (4B 62)
Grayson Ho. EC1 . . . . 2A 10

Grays Ter. E7 . . . . . . 4C 55
Gray St. SE1 . . 4C 24 (3C 76)
Grayswood Point
SW15 . . . . 1C 112
Gray's Yd. W1 . . . . . . 3C 12
Grazebrook Rd. N16 . . 4F 35
Grazeley Ct. SE19 . . . 5A 120
Gt. Acre Ct. SW4 . . . 2F 103
Gt. Arthur Ho. EC1 . . . . 4F 9
(off Golden La. Est.)
Gt. Bell All.
EC2 . . . . . 2B 18 (5F 63)
Great Brownings
SE21 . . . . 4B 120
Gt. Castle St.
W1 . . . . . . 2E 13 (5D 61)
Gt. Central St. NW1 . . 4B 60
Gt. Central Way
NW10 . . . . 1A 42
Gt. Chapel St.
W1 . . . . . . 2B 14 (5F 61)
Gt. Chart St. SW11 . . 2F 101
Gt. Chertsey Rd. W4 . . 4A 84
Gt. Church La. W6 . . . 5F 71
Gt. College St.
SW1 . . . . . 5D 23 (4A 76)
Great Cft. WC1 . . . . . . 2E 7
(off Cromer St.)
Gt. Cross Av. SE10 . . . 3F 95
(not continuous)
Gt. Cumberland M.
W1 . . . . . . 3A 12 (5B 60)
Gt. Cumberland Pl.
W1 . . . . . . 3A 12 (5B 60)
Gt. Dover St.
SE1 . . . . . 4A 26 (3E 77)
Gt. Eastern Ent. Cen.
E14 . . . . 3D 81
Gt. Eastern Rd. E15 . . 4F 53
Gt. Eastern St.
EC2 . . . . . 2D 11 (2A 64)
Gt. Eastern Wlk. EC2 . . 1E 19
Gt. Eastern Wharf
SW11 . . . . 3A 88
Greatfield Cl. N19 . . . 1E 47
SE4 . . . . 2C 108
Gt. George St.
SW1 . . . . . 4C 22 (3F 75)
Gt. Guildford Bus. Sq.
SE1 . . . . . 2F 25 (2E 77)
Gt. Guildford St.
SE1 . . . . . 1F 25 (2E 77)
Greatham Wlk.
SW15 . . . . 1C 112
Gt. James St.
WC1 . . . . . . 5F 7 (4B 62)
Gt. Marlborough St.
W1 . . . . . . 3F 13 (5E 61)
Gt. Maze Pond
SE1 . . . . . 2C 26 (3F 77)
(not continuous)
Gt. Newport St.
WC2 . . . . . 4D 15 (1A 76)
Gt. New St.
EC4 . . . . . 2C 16 (5C 62)
Great Nth. Rd. N6 . . . 1B 32
Greatorex Ho. E1 . . . . 4C 64
(off Spelman St.)
Greatorex St. E1 . . . . 4C 64

Gt. Ormond St.
WC1 . . . . . . 5E 7 (4A 62)
Gt. Percy St.
WC1 . . . . . . 1A 8 (2B 62)
Gt. Peter St.
SW1 . . . . . 5B 22 (4F 75)
Gt. Portland St.
W1 . . . . . . 4E 5 (3D 61)
Gt. Pulteney St.
W1 . . . . . . 4A 14 (1E 75)
Gt. Queen St.
WC2 . . . . . 3E 15 (5A 62)
Gt. Russell St.
WC1 . . . . . 2C 14 (5F 61)
Gt. St Helen's
EC3 . . . . . 2D 19 (5A 64)
Gt. St Thomas Apostle
EC4 . . . . . 4A 18 (1E 77)
Gt. Scotland Yd.
SW1 . . . . . 2D 23 (2A 76)
Gt. Smith St.
SW1 . . . . . 5C 22 (4F 75)
Great Spilmans
SE22 . . . . 3A 106
Gt. Suffolk St.
SE1 . . . . . 2E 25 (2D 77)
Gt. Sutton St.
EC1 . . . . . . 4E 9 (3D 63)
Gt. Swan All.
EC2 . . . . . 2B 18 (5F 63)
(not continuous)
Gt. Titchfield St.
W1 . . . . . . 4E 5 (3D 61)
Gt. Tower St.
EC3 . . . . . 4D 19 (1A 78)
Gt. Trinity La.
EC4 . . . . . 4A 18 (1E 77)
Great Turnstile
WC1 . . . . . . 1A 16 (4B 62)
Gt. Western Rd. W9 . . 4B 58
W11 . . . . 4B 58
Gt. West Rd. W4 . . . . 1B 84
W6 . . . . 1B 84
Gt. Winchester St.
EC2 . . . . . 2C 18 (5F 63)
Gt. Windmill St.
W1 . . . . . . 4B 14 (1F 75)
Great Yd. SE1 . . . . . . 3E 27
Greaves Cotts. E14 . . 4A 66
Greaves Pl. SW17 . . 4A 116
Greaves Twr. SW10 . . 3E 87
(off Worlds End Est.)
Grebe Cl. E7 . . . . . . 2B 54
E17 . . . . 3E 81
(off River Barge Cl.)
SE8 . . . . 2B 94
(off Dorking Cl.)
Grecian Cres. SE19 . . 5D 119
Greek Ct. W1 . . 3C 14 (5F 61)
Greek St. W1 . . 3C 14 (5F 61)
Green, The
BR1: Brom 3C 124
(not continuous)
E11 . . . . 1D 41
E15 . . . . 3A 54
SW19 . . . . 5F 113
W3 . . . . 5A 56
Greenacre Sq. SE16 . . 3F 79
Grn. Arbour Ct. EC1 . . 2D 17
(off Old Bailey)

Greenaway Gdns.
NW3 . . . . 1D 45
Greenaway Ho. NW8 . . 5E 45
(off Boundary Rd.)
WC1 . . . . 2B 8
(off Fernsbury St.)
Green Bank E1 . . . . . . 2D 79
Greenbay Rd. SE7 . . . . 3F 97
Greenberry St. NW8 . . 1A 60
Green Cl. NW11 . . . . . . 2E 31
Greencoat Mans.
SW1 . . . . 4E 75
(off Greencoat Row)
Greencoat Pl.
SW1 . . . . 5A 22 (5E 75)
Greencoat Row SW1 . . 4E 75
Greencourt Ho. E1 . . . . 3F 65
(off Mile End Rd.)
Greencrest Pl. NW2 . . 5C 28
Greencroft Cl. E6 . . . . 4F 69
Greencroft Gdns.
NW6 . . . . 4D 45
Green Dale SE5 . . . . . 2F 105
SE22 . . . . 3A 106
Grn. Dale Cl. SE22 . . . 3A 106
Grn. Dragon Cl. SE1 . . 1B 26
Grn. Dragon Yd. E1 . . . 4C 64
Greene Ct. SE14 . . . . . 2F 93
(off Samuel Cl.)
Greene Ho. SE1 . . . . . 5B 26
(off Burbage Cl.)
Greenend Rd. W4 . . . . 3A 70
Greener Ho. SW4 . . . . 1F 103
Greenfell Mans. SE8 . . 2D 95
Greenfield Gdns.
NW2 . . . . 4A 30
Greenfield Ho.
SW19 . . . . 1F 113
Greenfield Rd. E1 . . . . 4C 64
N15 . . . . 1A 36
Greengate Lodge
E13 . . . . 1D 69
(off Hollybush St.)
Greengate St. E13 . . . 1D 69
Greenham Cl.
SE1 . . . . 4B 24 (3C 76)
Greenham Ho. E9 . . . . 5E 51
(off Templecombe Rd.)
Greenheath Bus. Cen.
E2 . . . . 3D 65
(off Three Colts La.)
Greenhill NW3 . . . . . . 1F 45
Greenhill Gro. E12 . . . 1F 55
Greenhill Pk. NW10 . . 5A 42
Greenhill Rd. NW10 . . 5A 42
Greenhill's Rents
EC1 . . . . 5D 9 (4D 63)
Greenhills Ter. N1 . . . 3F 49
Grn. Hundred Rd.
SE15 . . . . 2C 92
Greenhurst Rd.
SE27 . . . . 5C 118
Greenland Ho. E1 . . . . 3A 66
(off Ernest St.)
Greenland M. SE8 . . . . 1F 93
Greenland Pl. NW1 . . . 5D 47
Greenland Quay
SE16 . . . . 5F 79
Greenland Rd. NW1 . . 5E 47
Greenland St. NW1 . . . 5D 47

Green La. NW4 . . . . . . 1F 29
Green Lanes N4 . . . . . 3E 35
N16 . . . . 1D 35
Greenleaf Cl. SW2 . . . 5C 104
Greenleaf Rd. E6 . . . . 5E 55
GREEN MAN RDBT. . . . 2B 40
Greenman St. N1 . . . . 4E 49
Greenoak Way
SW19 . . . . 4F 113
Green Pk. 3E 21 (3D 75)
Green Point E15 . . . . . 3A 54
Greenroof Way
SE10 . . . . 4B 82
(off School Bank Rd.)
Greenscape SE10 . . . . 4B 82
(not continuous)
Green's Ct. W1 . . . . . . 4B 14
W11 . . . . 2B 72
(off Lansdowne M.)
Greenshields Ind. Est.
E16 . . . . 3C 82
Greenside Cl. SE6 . . . . 2F 123
Greenside Rd. W12 . . . 4C 70
Greenstead Gdns.
SW15 . . . . 3D 99
Greenstone M. E11 . . . 1C 40
Green St. E7 . . . . 3D 55
E13 . . . . 3D 55
W1 . . . . 4B 12 (1C 74)
Greenstreet Hill
SE14 . . . . 5F 93
Green Ter.
EC1 . . . . 2C 8 (2C 62)
Greenview Cl. W3 . . . . 2A 70
Green Wlk.
SE1 . . . . 5D 27 (4A 78)
Green Way SE9 . . . . . 3F 111
Greenway Cl. N4 . . . . 4E 35
Greenwell St.
W1 . . . . 4E 5 (3D 61)
GREENWICH 3E 95
Greenwich Bus. Pk.
SE10 . . . . 3D 95
Greenwich Chu. St.
SE10 . . . . 2E 95
Greenwich Cinema . . . 3E 95
Greenwich Commercial Cen.
SE10 . . . . 3D 95
Greenwich Ct. E1 . . . . 5D 65
(off Cavell St.)
Greenwich Cres. E6 . . 4F 69
Greenwich Gateway Vis. Cen.
. . . . 2E 95
Greenwich High Rd.
SE10 . . . . 4D 95
Greenwich Ind. Est.
SE7 . . . . 5D 83
SE10 . . . . 3D 95
Greenwich Mkt. SE10 . . 2E 95
GREENWICH MILLENNIUM
VILLAGE 4B 82
Greenwich Pk. 3F 95
Greenwich Pk. St.
SE10 . . . . 2F 95
Greenwich Quay SE8 . . 2D 95
Greenwich Shop. Pk.
SE7 . . . . 5D 83
Greenwich Sth. St.
SE10 . . . . 4D 95
Greenwich Theatre . . . 3E 95

Greenwich Vw. Pl.
E14 . . . . 4D 81
Greenwich Yacht Club
. . . . 4C 82
Greenwood Ho. SE4 . . 2F 107
Greenwood Pl. NW5 . . 2D 47
Greenwood Rd. E8 . . . 3C 50
E13 . . . . 1B 68
Greenwood Ter.
NW10 . . . . 5A 42
Green Yd.
WC1 . . . . 3A 8 (3B 62)
Green Yd., The EC3 . . . 3D 19
Greet Ho. SE1 . . . . . . 4C 24
Greet St. SE1 . . 2C 24 (2C 76)
Greg Cl. E10 . . . . 1E 39
Gregory Cres. SE9 . . . 5F 111
Gregory Pl. W8 . . . . . . 3D 73
Greig Ter. SE17 . . . . . 2D 91
Grenada Ho. E14 . . . . . 1B 80
(off Limehouse C'way.)
Grenada Rd. SE7 . . . . 3E 97
Grenade St. E14 . . . . . 1B 80
Grenard Cl. SE15 . . . . 3C 92
Grendon Ho. E9 . . . . . 4E 51
(off Shore Pl.)
N1 . . . . 1B 62
(off Calshot St.)
Grendon St. NW8 . . . . 3A 60
Grenfell Ho. SE5 . . . . . 3E 91
Grenfell Rd. W11 . . . . 1F 71
Grenfell Twr. W11 . . . . 1F 71
Grenfell Wlk. W11 . . . . 1F 71
Grenier Apartments
SE15 . . . . 3D 93
Grenville Ho. E3 . . . . . 1A 66
(off Arbery Rd.)
SE8 . . . . 2C 94
(off New King St.)
SW1 . . . . 2F 89
(off Dolphin Sq.)
Grenville M. N19 . . . . 3A 34
SW7 . . . . 5E 73
Grenville Pl. SW7 . . . . 4E 73
Grenville Rd. N19 . . . . 3A 34
Grenville St.
WC1 . . . . 4E 7 (3A 62)
Gresham Gdns.
NW11 . . . . 3A 30
Gresham Lodge E17 . . 1D 39
Gresham Pl. N19 . . . . 4F 33
Gresham Rd. E16 . . . . 5D 69
NW10 . . . . 2A 42
SW9 . . . . 1C 104
Gresham St.
EC2 . . . . 2F 17 (5E 63)
Gresham Way
SW19 . . . . 3D 115
Gresley Cl. E17 . . . . . 1A 38
Gresley Rd. N19 . . . . 3E 33
Gressenhall Rd.
SW18 . . . . 4B 100
Gresse St.
W1 . . . . 1B 14 (5F 61)
Greswell St. SW6 . . . . 4F 85
Gretton Ho. E2 . . . . . . 2E 65
(off Globe Rd.)
Greville Ct. E5 . . . . . . 1D 51
(off Napoleon Rd.)

Greville Hall NW6 . . . . . 1D 59
Greville Lodge E13 . . . . 5D 55
Greville M. *NW6* *5D 45*
   (off Greville Rd.)
Greville Pl. NW6 . . . . 1D 59
Greville Rd. NW6 . . . . . . 1D 59
Greville St.
  EC1 . . . . 1B 16 (4C 62)
   (not continuous)
Grey Cl. NW11 . . . . 1E 31
Greycoat Gdns. *SW1* . . . *4F 75*
   (off Greycoat St.)
Greycoat Pl.
  SW1 . . . . 5B 22 (4F 75)
Greycoat St. SW1 . . . . . . 4F 75
Greycot Rd.
  BR3: Beck. 5C 122
Grey Eagle St.
  E1. . . . . 4F 11 (3B 64)
Greyfriars SE26 . . . . . . *3C 120*
   (off Wells Pk. Rd.)
Greyfriars Pas.
  EC1 . . . . . . 2E 17 (5D 63)
Greyhound Ct.
  WC2 . . . . . . 4A 16 (1B 76)
Greyhound La.
  SW16 . . . . 5A 118
Greyhound Mans.
  W6 . . . . *2A 86*
   (off Greyhound Rd.)
Greyhound Rd.
  NW10 . . . . 2D 57
  W6. . . . . 2F 85
  W14. . . . . 2F 85
Grey Ho. *W12*. *1D 71*
   (off White City Est.)
Greyladies Gdns.
  SE10 . . . . 5E 95
Greystead Rd. SE23 . . . 5E 107
Greystoke Ho. *SE15*. . . . *2C 92*
   (off Peckham Pk. Rd.)
Greystoke Pl.
  EC4 . . . . . . 2B 16 (5C 62)
Greystone Path *E11* *2B 40*
   (off Mornington Rd.)
Greyswood St.
  SW16 . . . . 5D 117
Grey Turner Ho. W12. . . 5C 56
Grierson Ho. SW16 . . . . 4E 117
Grierson Rd. SE23 . . . . 5F 107
Griffin Cl. NW10. . . . . . . 2D 43
Griffin Ct. W4 . . . . 1B 84
Griffin Ct. *E14*. *5D 67*
   (off Ricardo St.)
  W6. . . . . *5F 71*
   (off Hammersmith Rd.)
Grigg's Pl. SE1 . . . . 5E 27
Griggs Rd. E10 . . . . 1E 39
Grimaldi Ho. *N1*. *1B 62*
   (off Calshot St.)
Grimsby St. E2 . . . . 3B 64
Grimsel Path SE5. . . . . . 3D 91
Grimshaw Cl. N6 . . . . . . 2C 32
Grimston Rd. SW6 . . . . . 5B 86
Grimthorpe Ho. EC1. . . . 3D 9
Grimwade Cl. SE15 . . . . 1E 107
Grindall Ho. *E1* *3D 65*
   (off Darling Row)
Grindal St.
  SE1 . . . . 4B 24 (3C 76)

Grindley Ho. *E3* *4B 66*
   (off Leopold St.)
Grinling Pl. SE8. . . . . . . 2C 94
Grinstead Rd. SE8 . . . . 1A 94
Grisedale *NW1* *1F 5*
   (off Cumberland Mkt.)
Grittleton Rd. W9. . . . . . 3C 58
Grizedale Ter. SE23 . . 2D 121
Grocer's Hall Ct.
  EC2. . . . . . . 3B 18 (5F 63)
Grocer's Hall Gdns.
  EC2. . . . . 3B 18
Groombridge Rd. E9. . . . 4F 51
Groom Cres. SW18. . . . 5F 101
Groome Ho. SE11 . . . . . 5B 76
Groomfield Cl.
  SW17 . . . . 4C 116
Groom Pl.
  SW1. . . . . . . 5C 20 (4C 74)
Grosse Way SW15. . . . . 4D 99
Grosvenor Av. N5 . . . . . 2E 49
  SW14 . . . . 1A 98
Grosvenor Cotts.
  SW1 . . . . 5C 74
Grosvenor Cres.
  SW1. . . . . . . 4C 20 (3C 74)
Grosvenor Cres. M.
  SW1. . . . . . . 4B 20 (3C 74)
Grosvenor Est. SW1 . . . 5F 75
Grosvenor Gdns. E6 . . . 2F 69
  NW2 . . . . 2E 43
  NW11 . . . . 1B 30
  SW1 . . . . 5D 21 (4D 75)
  SW14 . . . . 1A 98
Grosvenor Gdns. M. E.
  SW1 . . . . 5E 21
Grosvenor Gdns. M. Nth.
  SW1 . . . . 5D 21
Grosvenor Gdns. M. Sth.
  SW1 . . . . 5E 21
Grosvenor Ga.
  W1. . . . . . . 5B 12 (1C 74)
Grosvenor Hill
  SW19 . . . . 5A 114
  W1. . . . . . . 4D 13 (1D 75)
Grosvenor Hill Ct.
  W1 . . . . *4D 13*
   (off Bourdon St.)
Grosvenor Pk. SE5. . . . . 3E 91
Grosvenor Pk. Rd.
  E17. . . . . 1C 38
Grosvenor Pl.
  SW1. . . . . . . 4C 20 (3C 74)
Grosvenor Ri. E. E17. . . 1D 39
Grosvenor Rd. E6. . . . . 5F 55
  E7. . . . . 3D 55
  E10 . . . . 3E 39
  E11. . . . . 1D 41
  SW1 . . . . 2D 89
Grosvenor Sq.
  W1. . . . . . . 4C 12 (1C 74)
Grosvenor St.
  W1. . . . . . . 4D 13 (1D 75)
Grosvenor Ter. SE5. . . . 3E 91

Grosvenor Way E5 . . . . 4E 37
Grosvenor Wharf Rd.
  E14. . . . . 5F 81
Grotes Bldgs. SE3 . . . . 5A 96
Grote's Pl. SE3. . . . . . . 5A 96
Groton Rd. SW18. . . . . 2D 115
Grotto Cl.
  SE1 . . . . 3E 25 (3D 77)
Grotto Pas.
  W1 . . . . 5C 4 (4C 60)
Grove, THE 1C 120
Grove, The E15 . . . . . . 3A 54
  N4. . . . . 2B 34
  N6. . . . . 3C 32
  N8. . . . . 1F 33
  NW11 . . . . 2A 30
Grove Cl. SE23. . . . . . . 1A 122
Grove Cotts. *SW3*. *2A 88*
   (off Chelsea Mnr. St.)
  W4 . . . . 2A 84
Grove Ct. *NW8* *2F 59*
   (off Grove End Rd.)
  SW10 . . . . *1E 87*
   (off Drayton Gdns.)
Grove Cres. Rd. E15. . . 3F 53
Grovedale Rd. N19. . . . 4F 33
Grove Dwellings E1 . . . 4E 65
Grove End NW5 . . . . . . 1D 47
Grove End Gdns.
  NW8 . . . . 1F 59
Grove End Ho. *NW8* . . . *2F 59*
   (off Grove End Rd.)
Grove End Rd. NW8 . . . 1F 59
Grove Grn. Rd. E11 . . . 5E 39
Grove Hall Ct. NW8 . . . 2E 59
Grovehill Ct.
  BR1: Brom 5B 124
Grove Hill Rd. SE5. . . . 1A 106
Grove Ho. *SW3* *2A 88*
   (off Chelsea Mnr. St.)
Groveland Ct. EC4 . . . . 3A 18
Grovelands Cl. SE5 . . . 5A 92
Grovelands Rd. N15. . . . 1C 36
Grove La. SE5. . . . . 4F 91
Grove La. Ter SE5 . . . . 5F 91
Grove Mans. *W6* *3E 71*
   (off Hammersmith Gro.)
  W6 . . . . 4E 71
GROVE PARK 3D 125
Grove Pk. E11 . . . . 1D 41
  SE5. . . . . 5A 92
Grove Pk. Rd. SE9 . . . . 3E 125
Grove Pas. E2 . . . . 1D 65
Grove Pl. NW3 . . . . 5F 31
  SW12 . . . . 5D 103
Grover Ct. SE13. . . . . . . 5D 95
Grover Ho. SE11 . . . . . . 1B 90
Grove Rd. E3 . . . . 5F 51
  E11 . . . . 2B 40
  E17. . . . . 1D 39
  N15. . . . . 1A 36
  NW2 . . . . 3E 43
  SW13 . . . . 5B 84
Grove St. SE8. . . . . 5B 80
Grove Ter. NW5 . . . . . . 5D 33
Grove Ter. M. NW5 . . . . 5D 33
Grove Va. SE22 . . . . . . 2B 106
Grove Vs. E14 . . . . 1D 81
Groveway SW9. . . . . . . 4B 90

Grummant Rd. SE15 . . . . . 4B 92
Grundy St. E14 . . . . 5D 67
Guardian Ct. SE12 . . . 3A 110
Guards Memorial
. . . . 2C 22 (2F 75)
Guards' Mus.
. . . . 4A 22 (3E 75)
Gubyon Av. SE24 . . . . . 3D 105
Guerin Sq. E3 . . . . 2B 66
Guernsey Gro. SE24 . . 5E 105
Guernsey Ho. N1 . . . . 3E 49
(off Douglas Rd. Nth.)
Guernsey Rd. E11 . . . . . . 3F 39
N1 . . . . 3E 49
Guibal Rd. SE12 . . . . . 5D 111
Guildford Ct. SW8 . . . . . 3A 90
(off Guildford Rd.)
Guildford Gro. SE10 . . . 4D 95
Guildford Rd. SW8 . . . . 4A 90
Guildhall
City 2A 18 (5E 63)
Westminster 3A 76
Guildhall Art Gallery
. . . . 2B 18 (5F 63)
Guildhall Bldgs. EC2 . . 2B 18
Guildhall Library
. . . . 2A 18 (5E 63)
Guildhall Offices
EC2 . . . . 2A 18
Guildhall Yd.
EC2 . . . . 2A 18 (5E 63)
Guildhouse St. SW1 . . . 5E 75
Guild Rd. SE7 . . . . 2F 97
Guilford Pl.
WC1 . . . . 4F 7 (3B 62)
Guilford St.
WC1 . . . . 4D 7 (3A 62)
Guillemot St. SE8 . . . . . . 2B 94
(off Alexandra Cl.)
Guilsborough Cl.
NW10 . . . . 4A 42
Guinea Ct. E1 . . . . 1C 78
(off Royal Mint St.)
Guinness Cl. E9 . . . . 4A 52
Guinness Ct. E1 . . . . 3F 19
EC1 . . . . 2A 10
NW8 . . . . 5A 46
SE1 . . . . 3D 27
SW3 . . . . 5B 74
Guinness Sq. SE1 . . . . . 5A 78
Guinness Trust SW3 . . . 5B 74
Guinness Trust Bldgs.
SE11 . . . . 1D 91
W6 . . . . 1F 85
(off Fulham Pal. Rd.)
Guinness Trust Est.
E15 . . . . 5B 54
(off John St.)
N16 . . . . 3A 36
Guion Rd. SW6 . . . . 5B 86
Gulland Wlk. N1 . . . . 3E 49
(off Church Rd.)
Gulliver's Ho. EC1 . . . . . 4F 9
Gulliver St. SE16 . . . . . . 4A 80
Gulston Wlk. SW3 . . . . . 5B 74
(off Blackland Ter.)
Gun Ho. E1 . . . . 2D 79
(off Wapping High St.)
Gunmaker's La. E3 . . . . . 5A 52
E9 . . . . 5A 52

Gunnell Cl. SE26 . . . . . 4C 120
Gunners Rd. SW18 . . . 2F 115
Gunpowder Sq. EC4 . . . 2C 16
(off Gough Sq.,
not continuous)
Gunstor Rd. N16 . . . . . . 1A 50
Gun St. E1 . . . . . 1F 19 (4B 64)
Gunter Gro. SW10 . . . . . 2E 87
Gunterstone Rd.
W14 . . . . 5A 72
Gunthorpe St. E1 . . . . . . 4B 64
Gunton Rd. E5 . . . . 5D 37
Gunwhale Cl. SE16 . . . . 2F 79
Gun Wharf E1 . . . . 2E 79
(off Wapping High St.)
Gun Wharf Bus. Cen.
E3 . . . . 5A 52
(off Old Ford Rd.)
Gurdon Rd. E14 . . . . 5C 66
(off Dod St.)
Gurdon Rd. SE7 . . . . 1C 96
Gurney Cl. E15 . . . . 2A 54
Gurney Ho. E2 . . . . 1C 64
(off Goldsmiths Row)
Gurney Rd. E15 . . . . 2A 54
SW6 . . . . 1E 101
Guthrie Ct. SE1 . . . . 4C 24
Guthrie St. SW3 . . . . 1F 87
Gutter La.
EC2 . . . . 2F 17 (5E 63)
Guy Barnett Gro.
SE3 . . . . 1C 110
Guyscliff Rd. SE13 . . . . 3E 109
Guy St. SE1 . . . . 3C 26 (3F 77)
Gwalior Rd. SW15 . . . . . 2F 99
Gwendolen Av. SW15 . . 2F 99
Gwendolen Cl. SW15 . . 3F 99
Gwendoline Av. E13 . . . 5D 55
Gwendwr Rd. W14 . . . . . 1A 86
Gwent Cl. SE16 . . . . 2F 79
(off Rotherhithe St.)
Gwilym Maries Ho.
E2 . . . . 2D 65
(off Blythe St.)
Gwyn Cl. SW6 . . . . 3E 87
Gwynne Cl. W4 . . . . 2B 84
Gwynne Ho. E1 . . . . 4D 65
(off Turner St.)
WC1 . . . . 2B 8
(off Lloyd Baker St.)
Gwynne Pl.
WC1 . . . . 2A 8 (2B 62)
Gwynne Rd. SW11 . . . . 5F 87
Gylcote Cl. SE5 . . . . 2F 105

H

Haarlem Rd. W14 . . . . . . 4F 71
Haberdasher Est.
N1 . . . . 1C 10 (2F 63)
Haberdasher Pl.
N1 . . . . 1C 10 (2F 63)
Haberdashers Ct.
SE14 . . . . 1F 107
Haberdasher St.
N1 . . . . 1C 10 (2F 63)
Habington Ho. SE5 . . . . 3F 91
(off Notley St.)
Habitat Cl. SE15 . . . . . . 5D 93

Habitat Sq. SE10 . . . . . . 4B 82
(off Teal St.)
Hackford Rd. SW9 . . . . . 4B 90
Hackford Wlk. SW9 . . . . 4B 90
Hackington Cres.
BR3: Beck 5C 122
HACKNEY 3D 51
Hackney City Farm 1C 64
Hackney Empire Theatre
. . . . 3D 51
Hackney Gro. E8 . . . . . . 3D 51
Hackney Rd.
E2 . . . . 2F 11 (2B 64)
HACKNEY WICK 3B 52
HACKNEY WICK 3A 52
Haddington Ct. SE10 . . 3D 95
(off Tarves Way)
Haddington Rd.
BR1: Brom 3F 123
Haddo Ho. SE10 . . . . . . 2D 95
(off Haddo St.)
Haddon Ct. W3 . . . . 1B 70
Haddonfield SE8 . . . . . . 5B 79
Haddon Hall St. SE1 . . . 4F 77
(off Rephidim St.)
Haddo St. SE10 . . . . 2D 95
Haden Ct. N4 . . . . 4C 34
Hadfield Ho. E1 . . . . 5C 64
(off Ellen St.)
Hadleigh Cl. E1 . . . . 3E 65
Hadleigh Ho. E1 . . . . . . 3E 65
(off Hadleigh Cl.)
Hadleigh St. E2 . . . . 2E 65
Hadley Ct. N16 . . . . 3C 36
Hadley Gdns. W4 . . . . . 1A 84
Hadley St. NW1 . . . . 3D 47
(not continuous)
Hadlow Ho. SE17 . . . . . . 1A 92
(off Kinglake Est.)
Hadrian Est. E2 . . . . 1C 64
Hadrian St. SE10 . . . . . . 1A 96
Hadstock Ho. NW1 . . . . 1C 6
(off Ossulston St.)
Hadyn Pk. Ct. W12 . . . . 3C 70
(off Curwen Rd.)
Hadyn Pk. Rd. W12 . . . . 3C 70
Hafer Rd. SW11 . . . . . . 2B 102
Hafton Rd. SE6 . . . . 1A 124
HAGGERSTON 4B 50
Haggerston Rd. E8 . . . . 4B 50
Hague St. E2 . . . . 2C 64
Haig Ho. E2 . . . . 1C 64
(off Shipton St.)
Haig Rd. E. E13 . . . . 2E 69
Haig Rd. W. E13 . . . . 2E 69
Hailes Cl. SW19 . . . . . . 5E 115
Hailsham Av. SW2 . . . . 2B 118
Haimo Rd. SE9 . . . . 3F 111
Hainault Rd. E11 . . . . . . 3E 39
Haines St. SW8 . . . . 3E 89
Hainford Cl. SE4 . . . . . . 2F 107
Hainthorpe Rd.
SE27 . . . . 3D 119
Hainton Cl. E1 . . . . 5D 65
Halberd M. E5 . . . . 4D 37
Halcomb St. N1 . . . . 5A 50
Halcrow St. E1 . . . . 4D 65
Halcyon Wharf E1 . . . . . 2C 78
(off Hermitage Wall)
Haldane Pl. SW18 . . . . . 1D 115

Haldane Rd. E6. . . . . . . .2F **69**
  SW6 . . . . .3B **86**
Haldon Rd. SW18. . . . . .4B **100**
Hale Ho. *SW1* 1F **89**
  (off Lindsay Sq.)
Hale Path SE27 . . . . . .4D **119**
Hale Rd. E6. . . . . .3F **69**
  (not continuous)
Hales St. SE8 . . . . .3C **94**
Halesowen Cl. E5. . . . . .4E **37**
Halesworth Rd.
  SE13 . . . . .1D **109**
Haley Rd. NW4. . . . . . . .1E **29**
Half Moon Cl. E1 . . . . . .1F **17**
Half Moon Cres. N1 . . . .1B **62**
  (not continuous)
Half Moon La. SE24. . . .4E **105**
Half Moon Pas.
  E1. . . . . .3F **19** (5B **64**)
  (not continuous)
Half Moon St.
  W1. . . . . .1E **21** (2D **75**)
Halford Rd. E10 . . . . . . .1F **39**
  SW6 . . . . .2C **86**
Haliday Ho. *N1* *3F* **49**
  (off Mildmay St.)
Haliday Wlk. N1 . . . . . . .3F **49**
Halidon Cl. E9 . . . . .2E **51**
Halifax St. SE26 . . . . . .3D **121**
Haliwell Ho. *NW6* *5D* **45**
  (off Mortimer Cres.)
Halkett Ho. *E2* *5E* **51**
  (off Waterloo Gdns.)
Halkin Arc.
  SW1. . . . . . . .5A **20** (4B **74**)
Halkin M.
  SW1. . . . . . . .5B **20** (4C **74**)
Halkin Pl.
  SW1. . . . . . . .5B **20** (4C **74**)
Halkin St.
  SW1. . . . . . . .4C **20** (3C **74**)
Hall, The SE3 . . . . .1C **110**
Hallam Ct. *W1* *5E* **5**
  (off Hallam St.)
Hallam Ho. *SW1*. *1E* **89**
  (off Churchill Gdns.)
Hallam M. W1. . . .5E **5** (4D **61**)
Hallam Rd. SW13 . . . . .1D **99**
Hallam St.
  W1. . . . . .4E **5** (3D **61**)
Hallane Ho. SE27 . . . . .5E **119**
Hall Dr. SE26 . . . . .5E **121**
Halley Gdns. SE13 . . . .2F **109**
Halley Ho. *E2* *1C* **64**
  (off Pritchards Rd.)
  SE10 . . . .*1B* **96**
  (off Armitage Rd.)
Halley Rd. E7 . . . . .3E **55**
  E12 . . . . .3E **55**
Halley St. E14 . . . . .4A **66**
Hallfield Est. W2 . . . . . .5E **59**
  (not continuous)
Hall Ga. NW8 . . . . .2F **59**
Halliford St. N1 . . . . . . .4E **49**
Hallings Wharf Studios
  E15 . . . . .5F **53**
Halliwell Ct. SE22 . . . .3C **106**
Halliwell Rd. SW2 . . . .4B **104**

Hall Oak Wlk. NW6 . . . .3B **44**
Hall Pl. W2. . . . . .4F **59**
  (not continuous)
Hall Rd. E15. . . . . .1F **53**
  NW8 . . . . .2E **59**
Hall St. EC1. . . .1E **9** (2D **63**)
Hallsville Rd. E16 . . . . .5B **68**
Hallswelle Rd.
  NW11 . . . . .1B **30**
Hall Twr. *W2*. *4F* **59**
  (off Hall Pl.)
Hall Vw. SE9. . . . . .2F **125**
Halpin Pl. SE17 . . . . . . .5F **77**
Halsbrook Rd. SE3. . . .1E **111**
Halsbury Ho. *N7* *1B* **48**
  (off Biddestone Rd.)
Halsbury Rd. W12 . . . . .2D **71**
Halsey M. SW3 . . . . . . .5B **74**
Halsey St. SW3 . . . . . . .5B **74**
Halsmere Rd. SE5 . . . . .4D **91**
Halstead Ct. E17 . . . . . .2B **38**
  N1. . . . .*1C* **10**
  (off Fairbank Est.)
Halstead Rd. E11. . . . . .1C **40**
Halston Cl. SW11. . . . .4B **102**
Halstow Rd. NW10 . . . .2F **57**
  SE10. . . . . .1C **96**
Halton Cross St. N1 . . . .5D **49**
Halton Mans. N1 . . . . . .4D **49**
Halton Pl. N1 . . . . .5E **49**
Halton Rd. N1 . . . . .4D **49**
Halyard Ho. E14 . . . . . .4E **81**
Hamara Ghar E13. . . . . .5E **55**
Hambalt Rd. SW4 . . . . .3E **103**
Hambledon SE17 . . . . . .2F **91**
  (off Villa St.)
Hambledon Ct.
  SE22 . . . . .2A **106**
Hambledon Pl.
  SE21 . . . . .1A **120**
Hambledon Rd.
  SW18 . . . . .5B **100**
Hamble St. SW6 . . . . . .1D **101**
Hambley Ho. *SE16*. *5D* **79**
  (off Camilla Rd.)
Hambridge Way
  SW2 . . . . .5C **104**
Hamden Rd. SW16 . . . .5F **117**
Hamfrith Rd. E15. . . . . .3B **54**
Hamilton Bldgs. EC2 . . .4E **11**
Hamilton Cl. NW8 . . . . .2F **59**
  SE16 . . . . .3A **80**
Hamilton Ct. SE6 . . . . .1B **124**
  SW15 . . . . .1A **100**
  W9 . . . .*2E* **59**
  (off Maida Va.)
Hamilton Gdns. NW8 . . .2E **59**
Hamilton Ho. *E14* *1D* **95**
  (off St Davids Sq.)
  E14 . . . .*1B* **80**
  (off Victory Pl.)
  NW8 . . . .*2F* **59**
  (off Hall Rd.)
  W4 . . . . .2A **84**
Hamilton La. N5 . . . . . . .1D **49**
Hamilton Lodge *E1*. *3E* **65**
  (off Cleveland Gro.)
Hamilton M. SW18 . . . .1C **114**
  W1. . . . . .3D **21** (3D **75**)
Hamilton Pk. N5 . . . . . .1D **49**

Hamilton Pk. W. N5. . . .1D **49**
Hamilton Pl. N19 . . . . . .5F **33**
  W1. . . . . .2C **20** (2C **74**)
Hamilton Rd. E15. . . . . .2A **68**
  NW10 . . . . .2C **42**
  NW11 . . . . .2F **29**
  SE27 . . . . .4F **119**
  W4 . . . . .3A **70**
Hamilton Rd. Ind. Est.
  SE27 . . . .*4F* **119**
  (off Hamilton Rd.)
Hamilton Sq.
  SE1. . . . . .3C **26** (3F **77**)
Hamilton St. SE8 . . . . . .2C **94**
Hamilton Ter. NW8 . . . . .1D **59**
Hamlea Cl. SE12 . . . . . .3C **110**
Hamlet, The SE5 . . . . . .1F **105**
Hamlet Cl. SE13. . . . . . .2A **110**
Hamlet Ct. *SE11* *1D* **91**
  (off Opal St.)
  W6 . . . . .5C **70**
Hamlet Gdns. W6. . . . . .5C **70**
Hamlet Ind. Est. E9 . . . .4C **52**
Hamlet M. SE21 . . . . . .1F **119**
Hamlet Sq. NW2 . . . . . .5A **30**
Hamlets Way E3. . . . . . .3B **66**
Hamlet Way
  SE1. . . . . .3C **26** (3F **77**)
Hammelton Grn.
  SW9 . . . . .4D **91**
Hammerfield Ho.
  SW3 . . . .*1A* **88**
  (off Cale St.)
Hammersley Ho.
  SE14 . . . .*3E* **93**
  (off Pomeroy St.)
HAMMERSMITH 5E **71**
Hammersmith Bri.
  W6 . . . . .1D **85**
Hammersmith Bri. Rd.
  W6 . . . . .1E **85**
HAMMERSMITH BROADWAY
  . . . . .5E **71**
Hammersmith B'way.
  W6 . . . . .5E **71**
HAMMERSMITH FLYOVER
  . . . . .1E **85**
Hammersmith Flyover
  W6 . . . . .1E **85**
Hammersmith Gro.
  W6 . . . . .3E **71**
Hammersmith Ind. Est.
  W6 . . . . .2E **85**
Hammersmith Rd.
  W6. . . . . .5F **71**
  W14. . . . . .5F **71**
Hammersmith Ter.
  W6 . . . . .1C **84**
Hammett St.
  EC3. . . . . .4F **19** (1B **78**)
Hammond Ct. E10 . . . . .4D **39**
  (off Crescent Rd.)
Hammond Ho. *E14*. *4C* **80**
  (off Tiller Rd.)
  SE14 . . . .*3E* **93**
  (off Lubbock St.)
Hammond Lodge *W9*. . .*4C* **58**
  (off Admiral Wlk.)
Hammond St. NW5 . . . .3E **47**
Hamond Sq. N1 . . . . . . .1A **64**

Ham Pk. Rd. E7 . . . . 4B **54**
  E15 . . . . 4B **54**
Hampden Cl. NW1 . . . 1F **61**
Hampden Gurney St.
  W1 . . . . 3A **12** (5B **60**)
Hampden Ho. SW9 . . . . 5C **90**
Hampden Rd. N19 . . . . 4F **33**
Hampshire Hog La.
  W6 . . . . 1D **85**
Hampshire St. NW5 . . . 3F **47**
Hampson Way SW8 . . . 4B **90**
HAMPSTEAD 1F **45**
Hampstead Gdns.
  NW11 . . . . 1C **30**
HAMPSTEAD GARDEN
  SUBURB 1E **31**
Hampstead Grn.
  NW3 . . . . 2A **46**
Hampstead Gro.
  NW3 . . . . 5E **31**
Hampstead Heath 4F **31**
Hampstead Heath Info. Cen.
  . . . . 1C **46**
Hampstead High St.
  NW3 . . . . 1F **45**
Hampstead Hill Gdns.
  NW3 . . . . 1F **45**
Hampstead La. N6 . . . 3F **31**
  NW3 . . . . 3F **31**
Hampstead Mus. 1F **45**
  (in Burgh House)
Hampstead Rd.
  NW1 . . . . . . 1F **5** (1E **61**)
Hampstead Sq. NW3 . . 5E **31**
Hampstead Theatre. . . 4F **45**
Hampstead Wlk. E3 . . 5B **52**
Hampstead Way
  NW11 . . . . 1B **30**
Hampstead W. NW6 . . 3C **44**
Hampton Cl. NW6 . . . 2C **58**
Hampton Ct. N1 . . . . . 3D **49**
  SE16 . . . . 1F **79**
  (off King & Queen Wharf)
Hampton Rd. E7 . . . . . 2D **55**
  E11 . . . . 3F **39**
Hampton St. SE17 . . . 5D **77**
Ham Yd. W1 . . 4B **14** (1F **75**)
Hanameel St. E16 . . . 2C **82**
Hana M. E5 . . . . 1D **51**
Hanbury Dr. E11 . . . . 2B **40**
Hanbury Ho. E1 . . . . . 4C **64**
  (off Hanbury St.)
  SW8 . . . . 3A **90**
  (off Regent's Bri. Gdns.)
Hanbury M. N1 . . . . . 5E **49**
Hanbury St.
  E1 . . . . 5F **11** (4B **64**)
Hancock Nunn Ho.
  NW3 . . . . 3B **46**
  (off Fellows Rd.)
Hancock Rd. E3 . . . . . 2E **67**
Handa Wlk. N1 . . . . . 3F **49**
Hand Ct.
  WC1 . . . . . . 1A **16** (4B **62**)
Handel House Mus. . . 4D **13**
  (off Brook St.)
Handel Mans. SW13 . . 3E **85**
  WC1 . . . . 3E **7**
  (off Handel St.)
Handel Pl. NW10 . . . . 3A **42**

Handels Bus. Cen.
  SW8 . . . . 2A **90**
Handel St.
  WC1 . . . . 3D **7** (3A **62**)
Handen Rd. SE12 . . . . 3A **110**
Handforth Rd. SW9 . . . 3C **90**
Handley Gro. NW2 . . . 5F **29**
Handley Rd. E9 . . . . . 4E **51**
Hands Wlk. E16 . . . . . 5C **68**
Hanford Cl. SW18 . . . 1C **114**
Hanford Row SW19 . . 5E **113**
Hanging Sword All.
  EC4 . . . . 3C **16**
Hankey Pl.
  SE1 . . . . 4C **26** (3F **77**)
Hanley Gdns. N4 . . . . 3B **34**
Hanley Rd. N4 . . . . . . 3A **34**
Hanmer Wlk. N7 . . . . 4B **34**
Hannah Barlow Ho.
  SW8 . . . . 4B **90**
Hannah Mary Way
  SE1 . . . . 5C **78**
Hannay La. N8 . . . . . 2F **33**
Hannay Wlk. SW16 . . . 2F **117**
Hannell Rd. SW6 . . . . 3A **86**
Hannen Rd. SE27 . . . . 3D **119**
Hannibal Rd. E1 . . . . 4E **65**
Hannington Rd.
  SW4 . . . . 1D **103**
Hanover Av. E16 . . . . 2C **82**
Hanover Ct. SW15 . . . 2B **98**
  W12 . . . . 2C **70**
  (off Uxbridge Rd.)
Hanover Flats W1 . . . 4C **12**
  (off Binney St., not continuous)
Hanover Gdns. SE11 . . 2C **90**
Hanover Ga. NW1 . . . 2A **60**
Hanover Ga. Mans.
  NW1 . . . . 3A **60**
  (off Park Rd.)
Hanover Ho. E14 . . . . 2B **80**
  (off Westferry Cir.)
  NW8 . . . . 1A **60**
  (off St John's Wood High St.)
  SW9 . . . . 1C **104**
Hanover Mans.
  SW2 . . . . 3C **104**
  (off Barnwell Rd.)
Hanover Mead NW11 . . 1A **30**
Hanover Pk. SE15 . . . 4C **92**
Hanover Pl. E3 . . . . . 2B **66**
  WC2 . . . . 3E **15** (5A **62**)
Hanover Rd. NW10 . . . 4E **43**
Hanover Sq.
  W1 . . . . 3E **13** (5D **61**)
Hanover Steps W2 . . . 5A **60**
  (off St George's Flds.)
Hanover St.
  W1 . . . . 3E **13** (5D **61**)
Hanover Ter. NW1 . . . 2A **60**
Hanover Ter. M.
  NW1 . . . . 2A **60**
Hanover Trad. Est.
  N7 . . . . 2A **48**
Hanover Yd. N1 . . . . . 1E **63**
  (off Noel Rd.)
Hansard M. W14 . . . . 3F **71**
Hanscomb M. SW4 . . . 2E **103**
Hans Cres.
  SW1 . . . . 5A **20** (4B **74**)

Hansler Rd. SE22 . . . . 3B **106**
Hanson Cl. SW12 . . . . 5D **103**
Hanson Ct. E17 . . . . . 1D **39**
Hanson St. W1 . . . 5F **5** (4E **61**)
Hans Pl.
  SW1 . . . . 5A **20** (4B **74**)
Hans Rd.
  SW3 . . . . 5A **20** (4B **74**)
Hans St.
  SW1 . . . . 5A **20** (4B **74**)
Hanway Pl.
  W1 . . . . 2B **14** (5F **61**)
Hanway St.
  W1 . . . . 2B **14** (5F **61**)
Hanworth Ho. SE5 . . . 3D **91**
  (off Camberwell New Rd.,
  not continuous)
Harad's Pl. E1 . . . . . . 1C **78**
Harben Pde. NW3 . . . . 4E **45**
  (off Finchley Rd.)
Harben Rd. NW6 . . . . 4E **45**
Harberson Rd. E15 . . . 5B **54**
  SW12 . . . . 1D **117**
Harberton Rd. N19 . . . 3E **33**
Harbet Rd. W2 . . . . . . 4F **59**
Harbinger Rd. E14 . . . 5D **81**
Harbledown Ho. SE1 . . 4B **26**
  (off Manciple St.)
Harbledown Rd. SW6 . . 4C **86**
Harbord Cl. SE5 . . . . . 5F **91**
Harbord Ho. SE16 . . . . 5F **79**
  (off Cope St.)
Harbord St. SW6 . . . . 4F **85**
Harborough Rd.
  SW16 . . . . 4B **118**
Harbour Av. SW10 . . . 4E **87**
Harbour Club
  Leisure Cen.,The . . 5E **87**
Harbour Exchange Sq.
  E14 . . . . 3D **81**
Harbour Quay E14 . . . 2E **81**
Harbour Reach SW6 . . 4E **87**
Harbour Rd. SE5 . . . . 1E **105**
Harbour Yd. SW10 . . . 4E **87**
Harbridge Av. SW15 . . 5B **98**
Harbut Rd. SW11 . . . . 2F **101**
  (not continuous)
Harcombe Rd. N16 . . . 5A **36**
Harcourt Bldgs. EC4 . . 4B **16**
Harcourt Rd. E15 . . . . 1B **68**
  SE4 . . . . 1B **108**
Harcourt St. W1 . . . . 4A **60**
Harcourt Ter. SW10 . . 1D **87**
Hardcastle Ho. SE14 . . 4A **94**
  (off Loring Rd.)
Hardel Ri. SW2 . . . . . 1D **119**
Hardel Wlk. SW2 . . . . 5C **104**
Harden Ct. SE7 . . . . . 5F **83**
Harden Ho. SE5 . . . . . 5A **92**
Harden's Manorway
  SE7 . . . . 4F **83**
  (not continuous)
Harders Rd. SE15 . . . 5D **93**
Hardess St. SE24 . . . . 1E **105**
Harding Cl. SE17 . . . . 2E **91**
Harding La. E1 . . . . . 5E **65**
  (not continuous)
Hardinge Rd. NW10 . . 5D **43**
Hardinge St. E1 . . . . 1E **79**
  (not continuous)

Harding Ho. SW13 . . . . . 2D **85**
Hardington NW1 . . . . . . 4C **46**
   (off Belmont St.)
Hardman Rd. SE7 . . . . . 1D **97**
Hardwicke M. WC1 . . . . 2A **8**
Hardwick Ho. NW8 . . . . 3A **60**
   (off Lilestone St.)
Hardwick St.
  EC1 . . . . 2C **8** (2C **62**)
Hardwicks Way
  SW18 . . . . 3C **100**
Hardwidge St.
  SE1 . . . . . . 3D **27** (3A **78**)
Hardy Av. E16 . . . . 2C **82**
Hardy Cl. SE16 . . . . 3F **79**
Hardy Cotts. SE10 . . . . . 2F **95**
Hardy Ho. SW4 . . . . . . 5E **103**
Hardy Rd. SE3 . . . . 3B **96**
Hare & Billet Rd.
  SE3 . . . . 4F **95**
Hare Ct. EC4 . . 3B **16** (5C **62**)
Harecourt Rd. N1 . . . . . 3E **49**
Haredale Rd. SE24 . . . 2E **105**
Haredon Cl. SE23 . . . . 5F **107**
Harefield M. SE4 . . . . . 1B **108**
Harefield Rd. SE4 . . . . 1B **108**
Hare Marsh E2 . . . . 3C **64**
Hare Pl. EC4 . . . . 3C **16**
   (off Pleydell St.)
Hare Row E2 . . . . 1D **65**
Hare Wlk. N1 . . . . 1A **64**
   (not continuous)
Harewood Av. NW1 . . . . 3A **60**
Harewood Pl.
  W1 . . . . 3E **13** (5D **61**)
Harewood Row NW1 . . . 4A **60**
Harfield Gdns. SE5 . . . 1A **106**
Harfleur Ct. SE11 . . . . . . 5D **77**
   (off Opal St.)
Harford Ho. SE5 . . . . . . 2E **91**
   (off Bethwin Rd.)
  W11 . . . . 4B **58**
Harford M. N19 . . . . . . 5F **33**
Harford St. E1 . . . . 3A **66**
Hargood Rd. SE3 . . . . . 4E **97**
Hargrave Mans. N19 . . . 4F **33**
Hargrave Pk. N19 . . . . . 4E **33**
Hargrave Pl. NW5 . . . . . 2F **47**
Hargrave Rd. N19 . . . . . 4E **33**
Hargraves Ho. W12 . . . . 1D **71**
   (off White City Est.)
Hargwyne St. SW9 . . . . 1B **104**
Haringey Pk. N8 . . . . . . 1A **34**
Harkness Ho. E1 . . . . . . 5C **64**
   (off Christian St.)
Harland Rd. SE12 . . . . 1C **124**
Harlequin Ct. E1 . . . . . . 1C **78**
   (off Thomas More St.)
  NW10 . . . . 3A **42**
   (off Mitchellbrook Way)
Harlescott Rd. SE15 . . 2F **107**
HARLESDEN 1B **56**
Harlesden Gdns.
  NW10 . . . . 5B **42**
Harlesden La. NW10 . . 5C **42**
Harlesden Plaza
  NW10 . . . . 1B **56**
Harlesden Rd. NW10 . . 5C **42**
Harleston Cl. E5 . . . . . . 4E **37**

Harley Ct. E11 . . . . 2C **40**
Harleyford Ct. SE11 . . . 2B **90**
   (off Harleyford Rd.)
Harleyford Rd.
  SE11 . . . . 2B **90**
Harleyford St. SE11 . . . 2C **90**
Harley Gdns. SW10 . . . 1E **87**
Harley Gro. E3 . . . . 2B **66**
Harley Ho. E11 . . . . 2F **39**
  NW1 . . . . 4C **4**
Harley Pl.
  W1 . . . . . . 1D **13** (4D **61**)
Harley Rd. NW3 . . . . . . 4F **45**
  NW10 . . . . 1A **56**
Harley St. W1 . . 4D **5** (3D **61**)
Harley Vs. NW10 . . . . . 1A **56**
Harling Ct. SW11 . . . . . 5B **88**
Harlinger St. SE18 . . . . 4F **83**
Harlowe Cl. E8 . . . . 5C **50**
Harlowe Ho. E8 . . . . . . 5B **50**
   (off Clarissa St.)
Harlynwood SE5 . . . . . . 3E **91**
   (off Wyndham Rd.)
Harman Cl. NW2 . . . . . 5A **30**
  SE1 . . . . 1C **92**
Harman Dr. NW2 . . . . . 5A **30**
Harman Ho. SE8 . . . . . . 5B **80**
Harmont Ho. W1 . . . . . . 1D **13**
   (off Harley St.)
Harmony Cl. NW11 . . . . 1A **30**
Harmood Gro. NW1 . . . 4D **47**
Harmood Ho. NW1 . . . . 4D **47**
   (off Harmood St.)
Harmood Pl. NW1 . . . . 4D **47**
Harmood St. NW1 . . . . 3D **47**
Harmsworth M. SE11 . . 4D **77**
Harmsworth St.
  SE17 . . . . 1D **91**
Harold Ct. SE16 . . . . . . 3F **79**
   (off Christopher Cl.)
Harold Est. SE1 . . . . . . 4A **78**
Harold Gibbons Ct.
  SE7 . . . . 2E **97**
Harold Ho. E2 . . . . 1F **65**
   (off Mace St.)
Harold Laski Ho. EC1 . . . 2E **9**
   (off Percival St.)
Harold Maddison Ho.
  SE17 . . . . 1D **91**
   (off Penton Pl.)
Harold Pl. SE11 . . . . . . 1C **90**
Harold Rd. E11 . . . . 3A **40**
  E13 . . . . 5D **55**
  NW10 . . . . 2A **56**
Haroldstone Rd. E17 . . 1F **37**
Harold Wilson Ho.
  SW6 . . . . 2B **86**
   (off Clem Attlee Ct.)
Harp All.
  EC4 . . . . 2E **17**
Harp Bus. Cen. NW2 . . 3C **28**
   (off Apsley Way)
Harp Bus. Cen., The
  NW2 . . . . 4C **28**
Harpenden Rd. E12 . . . 4E **41**
  SE27 . . . . 3D **119**
Harpenmead Point
  NW2 . . . . 4B **30**
Harper Ho. SW9 . . . . . 1D **105**
Harper M. SW17 . . . . . 3E **115**

Harper Rd.
  SE1 . . . . . . 5A **26** (4E **77**)
Harp Island Cl.
  NW10 . . . . 4A **28**
Harp La. EC3 . . 5D **19** (1A **78**)
Harpley Sq. E1 . . . . . . 3E **65**
Harpsden St. SW11 . . . 4C **88**
Harpur M.
  WC1 . . . . 5F **7** (4B **62**)
Harpur St.
  WC1 . . . . 5F **7** (4B **62**)
Harraden Rd. SE3 . . . . 4E **97**
Harrier Av. E11 . . . . . . 1D **41**
Harriet Cl. E8 . . . . 5C **50**
Harriet Ho. SW6 . . . . . . 3D **87**
   (off Wandon Rd.)
Harriet St.
  SW1 . . . . . . 4A **20** (3B **74**)
Harriet Tubman Ho.
  SW2 . . . . 5B **104**
Harriet Wlk.
  SW1 . . . . . . 4A **20** (3B **74**)
HARRINGAY 1D **35**
Harrington Ct. W10 . . . 2B **58**
Harrington Gdns.
  SW7 . . . . 5D **73**
Harrington Hill E5 . . . . 3D **37**
Harrington Ho. NW1 . . . . 1F **5**
   (off Harrington St.)
Harrington Rd. E11 . . . 3A **40**
  SW7 . . . . 5F **73**
Harrington Sq.
  NW1 . . . . 1E **61**
Harrington St.
  NW1 . . . . . . 1F **5** (1E **61**)
   (not continuous)
Harrington Way SE18 . . 4F **83**
Harriott Cl. SE10 . . . . . 5B **82**
Harriott Ho. E1 . . . . 4E **65**
   (off Jamaica St.)
Harris Bldgs. E1 . . . . . . 5C **64**
   (off Burslem St.)
Harris Ho. SW9 . . . . . 1C **104**
   (off St James's Cres.)
Harris Lodge SE6 . . . . 1E **123**
Harrison Ho. SE17 . . . . . 1F **91**
   (off Brandon St.)
Harrisons Ct. SE14 . . . 2F **93**
   (off Myers La.)
Harrison St.
  WC1 . . . . 2E **7** (2A **62**)
Harris St. E17 . . . . 2B **38**
  SE5 . . . . 3F **91**
Harrods 5A **20** (4B **74**)
Harrogate Ct. SE12 . . 5C **110**
  SE26 . . . . 3C **120**
   (off Droitwich Cl.)
Harrold Ho. NW3 . . . . . 4F **45**
Harroway Rd. SW11 . . . 5F **87**
Harrowby St. W1 . . . . . 5A **60**
Harrow Club Sports Cen.
  . . . . 1F **71**
Harrowgate Ho. E9 . . . 3F **51**
Harrowgate Rd. E9 . . . 3A **52**
Harrow Grn. E11 . . . . . 5A **40**
Harrow La. E14 . . . . . . 1D **81**
Harrow Lodge NW8 . . . 3F **59**
   (off Northwick Ter.)
Harrow Pl.
  E1 . . . . 2E **19** (5A **64**)

Harrow Rd. E6 . . . . 5F 55
E11 . . . . 5A 40
NW10 . . . . 2D 57
W2 . . . . 4E 59
(not continuous)
W9 . . . . 3A 58
W10 . . . . 3A 58
Harrow Rd. Bri. W2 . . . 4E 59
Harrow St. NW1 . . . . 4A 60
(off Daventry St.)
Harry Hinkins Ho.
SE17 . . . . 1E 91
(off Bronti Cl.)
Harry Lambourn Ho.
SE15 . . . . 3D 93
(off Gervase St.)
Hartfield Ter. E3 . . . . 1C 66
Hartham Cl. N7 . . . . . . 2A 48
Hartham Rd. N7 . . . . . . 2A 48
Harting Rd. SE9 . . . . . 3F 125
Hartington Ct. SW8 . . . 4A 90
Hartington Ho.
SW1 . . . . 1F 89
(off Drummond Ga.)
Hartington Rd. E16 . . . 5D 69
E17 . . . . 1A 38
SW8 . . . . 4A 90
Hartismere Rd. SW6 . . . 3B 86
Hartlake Rd. E9 . . . . . . 3F 51
Hartland NW1 . . . . 5E 47
(off Royal College St.)
Hartland Rd. E15 . . . . 4B 54
NW1 . . . . 4D 47
NW6 . . . . 1B 58
Hartley Av. E6 . . . . . . 5F 55
Hartley Ho. SE1 . . . . . . 5B 78
(off Longfield Est.)
Hartley Rd. E11 . . . . . . 3B 40
Hartley St. E2 . . . . 2E 65
(not continuous)
Hartmann Rd. E16 . . . 2F 83
(not continuous)
Hartnoll St. N7 . . . . . . 2B 48
Harton St. SE8 . . . . . . 4C 94
Hartop Point SW6 . . . . . 3A 86
(off Pellant Rd.)
Hartshorn All. EC3 . . . 3E 19
Hart's La. SE14 . . . . . . 4A 94
Hart St. EC3 . . . 4E 19 (1A 78)
Hartswood Gdns.
W12 . . . . 4B 70
Hartswood Rd. W12 . . . 3B 70
Hartsworth Cl. E13 . . . 1B 68
Hartwell Ho. SE7 . . . . . 1D 97
(off Troughton Rd.)
Hartwell St. E8 . . . . . . 3B 50
Harvard Ct. NW6 . . . . . 2D 45
Harvard Ho. SE17 . . . . 2D 91
(off Doddington Gro.)
Harvard Rd. SE13 . . . 3E 109
SE7 . . . . 1E 97
Harvey Gdns. E11 . . . . 3B 40
Harvey Ho. E1 . . . . 3D 65
(off Brady St.)
N1 . . . . 5F 49
(off Colville Est.)
SW1 . . . . 1F 89
(off Aylesford St.)
Harvey Lodge W9 . . . . . 4C 58
(off Admiral Wlk.)

Harvey Point E16 . . . . . 4C 68
(off Fife Rd.)
Harvey Rd. E11 . . . . . . 3A 40
SE5 . . . . 4F 91
(not continuous)
Harvey's Bldgs.
WC2 . . . . 5E 15 (1A 76)
Harvey St. N1 . . . . . . 5F 49
Harvington Wlk. E8 . . . 4C 50
Harvist Est. N7 . . . . . . 1C 48
Harvist Rd. NW6 . . . . . 1F 57
Harwood Ct. N1 . . . . . . 5A 50
(off Colville Est.)
Harwood M. SW6 . . . . 3C 86
Harwood Point SE16 . . . 3B 80
Harwood Rd. SW6 . . . . 3C 86
Harwood Ter. SW6 . . . . 4D 87
Haseley End SE23 . . . 5E 107
Haselrigge Rd. SW4 . . 2F 103
Haseltine Rd. SE26 . . 4B 122
Hasker St. SW3 . . . . . 5A 74
Haslam Cl. N1 . . . . . . 4C 48
Haslam St. SE15 . . . . . 3B 92
Haslemere Av. NW4 . . . 1F 29
SW18 . . . . 2D 115
Haslemere Ind. Est.
SW18 . . . . 2D 115
Haslemere Rd. N8 . . . . 2F 33
Haslers Wharf E3 . . . . 5A 52
(off Old Ford Rd.)
Hassard St. E2 . . . . . . 1B 64
Hassendean Rd. SE3 . . 2D 97
Hassett Rd. E9 . . . . . . 3F 51
Hassocks Cl. SE26 . . . 3D 121
Hassop Rd. NW2 . . . . . 1F 43
Hassop Wlk. SE9 . . . . 4F 125
Hasted Rd. SE7 . . . . . . 1F 97
Hastings Cl. SE15 . . . 3C 92
Hastings Ho. W12 . . . 1D 71
(off White City Est.)
WC1 . . . . 2D 7
(off Hastings St.)
Hastings St.
WC1 . . . . . . 2D 7 (2A 62)
Hat & Mitre Ct. EC1 . . . 4E 9
Hatcham M. Bus. Cen.
SE14 . . . . 4F 93
(off Hatcham Pk. Rd.)
Hatcham Pk. M.
SE14 . . . . 4F 93
Hatcham Pk. Rd.
SE14 . . . . 4F 93
Hatcham Rd. SE15 . . . 2E 93
Hatchard Rd. N19 . . . . 4F 33
Hatchers M. SE1 . . . . . 4E 27
Hatchfield Ho. N15 . . . 1A 36
(off Albert Rd.)
Hatcliffe Almshouses
SE10 . . . . 1A 96
(off Tuskar St.)
Hatcliffe Cl. SE3 . . . . 1B 110
Hatcliffe St. SE10 . . . . 1B 96
Hatfield Cl. SE14 . . . . 3F 93
Hatfield Ct. SE3 . . . . . 3C 96
Hatfield Ho. EC1 . . . . . 4F 9
Hatfield Rd. E15 . . . . . 2A 54
W4 . . . . 3A 70
Hatfields
SE1 . . . . 1C 24 (2C 76)

Hathaway Ho.
N1 . . . . 1D 11 (1A 64)
Hatherley Ct. W2 . . . . . 5D 59
(off Hatherley Rd.)
Hatherley Gdns. E6 . . . 2F 69
N8 . . . . 1A 34
Hatherley Gro. W2 . . . 5D 59
Hatherley St. SW1 . . . . 5E 75
Hathersage Ct. N1 . . . . 2F 49
Hathorne Cl. SE15 . . . 5D 93
Hathway St. SE15 . . . . 5F 93
Hathway Ter. SE14 . . . 5F 93
(off Hathway St.)
Hatley Rd. N4 . . . . 4B 34
Hatteraick St. SE16 . . . 3E 79
Hatton Gdn.
EC1 . . . . 5C 8 (4C 62)
Hatton Pl. EC1 . . 5C 8 (4C 62)
Hatton Row NW8 . . . . . 3F 59
(off Hatton St.)
Hatton St. NW8 . . . . . . 3F 59
Hatton Wall
EC1 . . . . 5C 8 (4C 62)
Haunch of Venison Yd.
W1 . . . . 3D 13 (5D 61)
Hauteville Ct. Gdns.
W6 . . . . 4B 70
(off South Side)
Havana Rd. SW19 . . . 2C 114
Havannah St. E14 . . . . 3C 80
Havelock Cl. W12 . . . . 1D 71
Havelock Ho. SE23 . . . 1E 121
Havelock Rd.
SW19 . . . . 5E 115
Havelock St. N1 . . . . . 5A 48
Havelock Ter. SW8 . . . 4D 89
Havelock Ter. Arches
SW8 . . . . 4D 89
(off Havelock Ter.)
Havelock Wlk. SE23 . . 1E 121
Haven Cl. SW19 . . . . . 3F 113
Haven M. E3 . . . . 4B 66
N1 . . . . 4C 48
Havenpool NW8 . . . . . . 5D 45
(off Abbey Rd.)
Haven St. NW1 . . . . . . 4D 47
Haverfield Rd. E3 . . . . 2A 66
Haverhill Rd. SW12 . . 1E 117
Havering NW1 . . . . 4D 47
(off Castlehaven Rd.)
Havering St. E1 . . . . . 5F 65
Haversham Pl. N6 . . . . 4B 32
Haverstock Hill NW3 . . 2A 46
Haverstock Pl. N1 . . . . 1E 9
(off Haverstock St.)
Haverstock Rd. NW5 . . 2C 46
Haverstock St.
N1 . . . . 1E 9 (1D 63)
Havil St. SE5 . . . . 3A 92
Havisham Ho. SE16 . . . 3C 78
Hawarden Gro.
SE24 . . . . 5E 105
Hawarden Hill NW2 . . . 5C 28
Hawbridge Rd. E11 . . . 3F 39
Hawes St. N1 . . . . 4D 49
Hawgood St. E3 . . . . . 4C 66
Hawke Ho. E1 . . . . 3F 65
(off Ernest St.)
Hawke Pl. SE16 . . . . . 3F 79
Hawke Rd. SE19 . . . . 5F 119

Hawkesbury Rd.
SW15 . . . . 3D 99

Hawkesfield Rd.
SE23 . . . . 2A 122

Hawke Twr. SE14 . . . . 2A 94

Hawkins Ho. SE8 . . . 2C 94
(off New King St.)
SW1 . . . . 2E 89
(off Dolphin Sq.)

Hawkins Rd. NW10 . . . 4A 42

Hawkins Way SE6 . . . 5C 122

Hawkley Gdns.
SE27 . . . . 2D 119

Hawkshaw Cl. SW2 . . 5A 104

Hawkshead NW1 . . . . 1F 5

Hawkshead Rd.
NW10 . . . . 4B 42
W4 . . . . 3A 70

Hawkslade Rd.
SE15 . . . . 3F 107

Hawksley Rd. N16 . . . 5A 36

Hawks M. SE10 . . . . . 3E 95

Hawksmoor Cl. E6 . . . 5F 69

Hawksmoor Ho. E14 . . 4A 66
(off Aston St.)

Hawksmoor M. E1 . . . 1D 79

Hawksmoor Pl. E2 . . . 3C 64
(off Cheshire St.)

Hawksmoor St. W6 . . . 2F 85

Hawkstone Rd. SE16 . . 5E 79

Hawkwell Wlk. N1 . . . 5E 49
(off Maldon Cl.)

Hawkwood Mt. E5 . . . 3D 37

Hawley Cres. NW1 . . . 4D 47

Hawley M. NW1 . . . . . 4D 47

Hawley Rd. NW1 . . . . 4D 47
(not continuous)

Hawley St. NW1 . . . . . 4D 47

Hawstead Rd. SE6 . . . 4D 109

Hawthorn Av. E3 . . . . 5B 52

Hawthorn Cres.
SW17 . . . . 5C 116

Hawthorne Cl. N1 . . . . 3A 50

Hawthorne Ho. SW1 . . 1E 89
(off Churchill Gdns.)

Hawthorn Rd. NW10 . . 4C 42

Hawthorn Ter. N19 . . . 3F 33
(off Calverley Gro.)

Hawthorn Wlk. W10 . . 3A 58

Hawtrey Rd. NW3 . . . . 4A 46

Hay Cl. E15 . . . . 4A 54

Haycroft Gdns.
NW10 . . . . 5C 42

Haycroft Rd. SW2 . . . 3A 104

Hay Currie St. E14 . . . 5D 67

Hayday Rd. E16 . . . . . 4C 68
(not continuous)

Hayden's Pl. W11 . . . . 5B 58

Haydon Pk. Rd.
SW19 . . . . 5C 114

Haydons Rd. SW19 . . . 5D 115

Haydon St.
EC3 . . . . 4F 19 (1B 78)

Haydon Wlk.
E1 . . . . 3F 19 (5B 64)

Haydon Way SW11 . . 2F 101

Hayes Ct. SE5 . . . . . . 3E 91
(off Camberwell New Rd.)
SW2 . . . . 1A 118

Hayes Cres. NW11 . . . 1B 30

Hayesens Ho.
SW17 . . . . 4E 115

Hayes Gro. SE22 . . . . 1B 106

Hayes Pl. NW1 . . . . . . 3A 60

Hayfield Pas. E1 . . . . 3E 65

Hayfield Yd. E1 . . . . . 3E 65

Haygarth Pl. SW19 . . . 5F 113

Hay Hill W1 . . . 5E 13 (1D 75)

Hayles Bldgs. SE11 . . 5D 77
(off Elliotts Row)

Hayles St. SE11 . . . . . 5D 77

Hayling Cl. N16 . . . . . 2A 50

Haymans Point SE11 . . 5B 76

Hayman St. N1 . . . . . . 4D 49

Haymarket
SW1 . . . . 5B 14 (1F 75)

Haymarket Arc. SW1 . . 5B 14

Haymarket Ct. E8 . . . . 4B 50
(off Jacaranda Gro.)

Haymarket Theatre Royal
. . . . 5C 14
(off Haymarket)

Haymerle Ho. SE15 . . 2C 92
(off Haymerle Rd.)

Haymerle Rd. SE15 . . 2C 92

Haynes Cl. SE3 . . . . . 1A 110

Hayne St. EC1 . . . 5E 9 (4D 63)

Hay's Galleria
SE1 . . . . 1D 27 (2A 78)

Hays La.
SE1 . . . . 1D 27 (2A 78)

Hay's M. W1 . . 1D 21 (2D 75)

Hay St. E2 . . . . 5C 50

Hayter Ct. E11 . . . . . . 4D 41

Hayter Rd. SW2 . . . . . 3A 104

Hayton Cl. E8 . . . . . . 3B 50

Hayward Ct. SW4 . . . . 5A 90
(off Clapham Rd.)

Hayward Gallery 2A 24

Hayward Gdns.
SW15 . . . . 4E 99

Hayward's Pl.
EC1 . . . . 3D 9 (3D 63)

Haywards Yd. SE4 . . . 3B 108
(off Lindal Rd.)

Hazelbank Rd. SE6 . . . 2F 123

Hazelbourne Rd.
SW12 . . . . 4D 103

Hazeldean Rd. NW10 . . 4A 42

Hazeldon Rd. SE4 . . . 3A 108

Hazel Gro. SE26 . . . . 4F 121

Hazelhurst Ct. SE6 . . . 5E 123
(off Beckenham Hill Rd.)

Hazelhurst Rd.
SW17 . . . . 4E 115

Hazellville Rd. N19 . . . 2F 33

Hazelmere Ct. SW2 . . 1B 118

Hazelmere Rd. NW6 . . 5B 44

Hazel Rd. E15 . . . . . . 2A 54
NW10 . . . . 2D 57
(not continuous)

Hazel Way SE1 . . . . . . 5B 78

Hazelwood Ho. NW10 . . 5A 28

Hazelwood Ho. SE8 . . . 5A 80

Hazelwood Rd. E17 . . . 1A 38

Hazlebury Rd. SW6 . . 5D 87

Hazlewell Rd. SW15 . . 3E 99

Hazlewood Cl. E5 . . . . 5A 38

Hazlewood Cres.
W10 . . . . 3A 58

Hazlewood Twr. W10 . . 3A 58
(off Golborne Gdns.)

Hazlitt M. W14 . . . . . . 4A 72

Hazlitt Rd. W14 . . . . . 4A 72

Headbourne Ho.
SE1 . . . . 5C 26 (4F 77)

Headcorn Rd.
BR1: Brom 5B 124

Headfort Pl.
SW1 . . . . 4C 20 (3C 74)

Headington Rd.
SW18 . . . . 2E 115

Headlam Rd. SW4 . . . 4F 103
(not continuous)

Headlam St. E1 . . . . . 3D 65

Headley Ct. SE26 . . . . 5E 121

Head's M. W11 . . . . . . 5C 58

Head St. E1 . . . . 5F 65
(not continuous)

Heald St. SE14 . . . . . 4C 94

Healey Ho. SW9 . . . . . 3C 90

Healey St. NW1 . . . . . 3D 47

Hearn's Bldgs. SE17 . . 5F 77

Hearnshaw Ho. E14 . . 4A 66
(off Halley St.)

Hearnshaw St. E14 . . . 5A 66

Hearn St.
EC2 . . . . 4E 11 (3A 64)

Hearnville Rd.
SW12 . . . . 1C 116

Heath Brow NW3 . . . . 5E 31

Heath Cl. NW11 . . . . . 2D 31

Heathcock Ct. WC2 . . 5E 15
(off Exchange Ct.)

Heathcote St.
WC1 . . . . 3F 7 (3B 62)

Heath Cft. NW11 . . . . 3D 31

Heath Dr. NW3 . . . . . . 1D 45

Heathedge SE26 . . . . 2D 121

Heather Cl. N7 . . . . . . 5B 34
SE13 . . . . 5F 109
SW8 . . . . 1D 103

Heather Gdns. NW11 . . 1A 30

Heather Ho. E14 . . . . . 5E 67
(off Dee St.)

Heatherley Ct. E5 . . . . 5C 36

Heather Rd. NW2 . . . . 4B 28
SE12 . . . . 2C 124

Heather Wlk. W10 . . . 3A 58

Heatherwood Cl. E12 . . 4E 41

Heathfield Av. SW18 . . 5F 101

Heathfield Cl. E16 . . . . 4F 69

Heathfield Gdns.
NW11 . . . . 1F 29
SE3 . . . . 5A 96
(off Baizdon Rd.)
SW18 . . . . 4F 101

Heathfield Ho. SE3 . . . 5A 96

Heathfield Pk. NW2 . . . 3E 43

Heathfield Rd.
SW18 . . . . 4E 101

Heathfield Sq.
SW18 . . . . 5F 101

Heathfield St. W11 . . . 1A 72
(off Portland Rd.)

Heathgate NW11 . . . . 1D 31

Heathgate Pl. NW3 . . . 2B 46

Heath Hurst Rd. NW3 . . . 1A 46
Heathland Rd. N16 . . . . . . 3A 36
Heath La. SE3 . . . . 5F 95
    (not continuous)
Heathlee Rd. SE3 . . . . . . 2B 110
Heathmans Rd. SW6 . . . . 4B 86
Heathpool Ct. E1 . . . . 3D 65
Heath Ri. SW15 . . . . 4F 99
Heath Rd. SW8 . . . . 5D 89
Heath Royal SW15 . . . . . . 4F 99
Heath Side NW3 . . . . 1F 45
Heathside NW11 . . . . 3C 30
  SE13 . . . . 5E 95
Heathstan Rd. W12 . . . . . 5C 56
Heath St. NW3 . . . . 5E 31
Heathview NW5 . . . . 1C 46
Heathview Gdns.
  SW15 . . . . 5E 99
Heath Vs. NW3 . . . . 5F 31
Heathville Rd. N19 . . . . . . 2A 34
Heathwall St. SW11 . . . . 1B 102
Heathway SE3 . . . . 3C 96
Heathway Ct. NW3 . . . . . 4C 30
Heathwood Gdns.
  SE7 . . . . 5F 83
Heathwood Point
  SE23 . . . . 3F 121
Heaton Rd. SE15 . . . . 5D 93
Heaven Tree Cl. N1 . . . . . 3E 49
Heaver Rd. SW11 . . . . . . 1F 101
Hebden Ct. E2 . . . . 5B 50
Hebdon Rd. SW17 . . . . . 3A 116
Heber Mans. W14 . . . . . . 2A 86
    (off Queen's Club Gdns.)
Heber Rd. NW2 . . . . 2F 43
  SE22 . . . . 4B 106
Hebron Rd. W6 . . . . 4E 71
Heckfield Pl. SW6 . . . . . . 3C 86
Heckford Ho. E14 . . . . . . 5D 67
    (off Grundy St.)
Heckford St. E1 . . . . 1F 79
Hector Ct. SW9 . . . . 3C 90
    (off Caldwell St.)
Hector Ho. E2 . . . . 1D 65
    (off Old Bethnal Grn. Rd.)
Heddington Gro. N7 . . . . . 2B 48
Heddon St.
  W1 . . . . 4F 13 (1E 75)
    (not continuous)
Hedgegate Ct. W11 . . . . . 5B 58
    (off Powis Ter.)
Hedgers Gro. E9 . . . . 3A 52
Hedger St. SE11 . . . . 5D 77
Hedge Wlk. SE6 . . . . 5D 123
Hedgley M. SE12 . . . . . . 3B 110
Hedgley St. SE12 . . . . . . 3B 110
Hedingham Cl. N1 . . . . . . 4E 49
Hedley Ho. E14 . . . . 4E 81
    (off Stewart St.)
Hedley Row N5 . . . . 2F 49
Hedsor Ho. E2 . . . . 3F 11
    (off Ligonier St.)
Hega Ho. E14 . . . . 4E 67
    (off Ullin St.)
Heidegger Cres.
  SW13 . . . . 3D 85
Heigham Rd. E6 . . . . 4F 55
Heights, The SE7 . . . . . . 1E 97
Heiron St. SE17 . . . . 2D 91

Helby Rd. SW4 . . . . 4F 103
Heldar Ct.
  SE1 . . . . 4C 26 (3F 77)
Helder Gro. SE12 . . . . . . 5B 110
Helena Pl. E9 . . . . 5D 51
Helena Rd. E13 . . . . 1B 68
  E17 . . . . 1C 38
  NW10 . . . . 2D 43
Helena Sq. SE16 . . . . 1A 80
    (off Sovereign Cres.)
Helen Gladstone Ho.
  SE1 . . . . 3D 25
    (off Surrey Row)
Helen Ho. E2 . . . . 1D 65
    (off Old Bethnal Grn. Rd.)
Helen Mackay Ho.
  E14 . . . . 5F 67
    (off Blair St.)
Helen Peele Cotts.
  SE16 . . . . 4E 79
    (off Lower Rd.)
Helenslea Av. NW11 . . . . 3C 30
Helen's Pl. E2 . . . . 2E 65
Helen Taylor Ho.
  SE16 . . . . 4C 78
    (off Evelyn Lowe Est.)
Heliport Ind. Est.
  SW11 . . . . 5F 87
Helix Gdns. SW2 . . . . . . 4B 104
Helix Rd. SW2 . . . . 4B 104
Hellings St. E1 . . . . 2C 78
Helme Cl. SW19 . . . . 5B 114
Helmet Row
  EC1 . . . . 2A 10 (3E 63)
Helmsdale Ho. NW6 . . . . 1D 59
    (off Carlton Va.)
Helmsley Pl. E8 . . . . 4D 51
Helmsley St. E8 . . . . 4D 51
Helperby Rd. NW10 . . . . . 4A 42
Helsby St. NW8 . . . . 3F 59
    (off Pollitt Dr.)
Helsinki Sq. SE16 . . . . . . 4A 80
Helston NW1 . . . . 5E 47
    (off Camden St.)
Helston Ct. N15 . . . . 1A 36
    (off Culvert Rd.)
Helston Ho. SE11 . . . . . . 1C 90
    (off Kennings Way)
Helvetia St. SE6 . . . . 2B 122
Hemans St. SW8 . . . . 3F 89
Hemans St. Est.
  SW8 . . . . 3F 89
Hemberton Rd.
  SW9 . . . . 1A 104
Hemingford Rd. N1 . . . . . 5B 48
Hemingway Cl.
  NW5 . . . . 1C 46
Hemlington Ho. E14 . . . . 4A 66
    (off Aston St.)
Hemlock Rd. W12 . . . . . . 1B 70
    (not continuous)
Hemming St. E1 . . . . 3C 64
Hemp Wlk. SE17 . . . . 5F 77
Hemstal Rd. NW6 . . . . . . 4C 44
Hemsworth Ct. N1 . . . . . . 1A 64
Hemsworth St. N1 . . . . . . 1A 64
Hemus Pl. SW3 . . . . 1A 88
Hen & Chicken Ct.
  EC4 . . . . 3B 16
    (off Fleet St.)

Hen & Chickens Theatre
  . . . . 3D 49
    (off St Paul's Rd.)
Henchman St. W12 . . . . . 5B 56
Henderson Ct. NW3 . . . . . 2F 45
    (off Fitzjohn's Av.)
  SE14 . . . . 2F 93
    (off Myers La.)
Henderson Dr. NW8 . . . . . 3F 59
Henderson Rd. E7 . . . . . . 3E 55
  SW18 . . . . 5A 102
Hendham Rd.
  SW17 . . . . 2A 116
HENDON 1D 29
Hendon FC 3F 29
Hendon Ho. NW4 . . . . . . 1F 29
Hendon Pk. Mans.
  NW4 . . . . 1E 29
Hendon Pk. Row
  NW11 . . . . 1B 30
Hendon Way NW2 . . . . . . 2F 29
  NW4 . . . . 1D 29
Hendon Youth Sports Cen.
  . . . . 2F 29
Hendre Rd. SE1 . . . . 5A 78
Hendrick Av.
  SW12 . . . . 5B 102
Heneage La.
  EC3 . . . . 3E 19 (5A 64)
Heneage Pl.
  EC3 . . . . 3E 19 (5A 64)
Heneage St. E1 . . . . 4B 64
Henfield Cl. N19 . . . . 3E 33
Hengist Rd. SE12 . . . . . . 5D 111
Hengrave Rd. SE23 . . . . 4E 107
Henley Cl. SE16 . . . . 3E 79
    (off St Marychurch St.)
Henley Ct. NW2 . . . . 3F 43
Henley Dr. SE1 . . . . 5B 78
Henley Ho. E2 . . . . 3F 11
    (off Swanfield St.)
Henley Prior N1 . . . . 1F 7
    (off Affleck St.)
Henley Rd. NW10 . . . . . . 5E 43
Henley St. SW11 . . . . 5C 88
Hennel Cl. SE23 . . . . 3E 121
Henniker Gdns. E6 . . . . . 2F 69
Henniker M. SW3 . . . . 2F 87
Henniker Point E15 . . . . . 2A 54
    (off Leytonstone Rd.)
Henniker Rd. E15 . . . . . . 2F 53
Henning St. SW11 . . . . . . 4A 88
Henrietta Cl. SE8 . . . . 2C 94
Henrietta Ho. N15 . . . . . . 1A 36
    (off St Ann's Rd.)
  W6 . . . . 1E 85
    (off Queen Caroline St.)
Henrietta M.
  WC1 . . . . 3E 7 (3A 62)
Henrietta Pl.
  W1 . . . . 3D 13 (5D 61)
Henrietta St. E15 . . . . 2E 53
  WC2 . . . . 4E 15 (1A 76)
Henriques St. E1 . . . . 5C 64
Henry Cooper Way
  SE9 . . . . 3F 125
Henry Dickens Ct.
  W11 . . . . 1F 71
Henry Doulton Dr.
  SW17 . . . . 4C 116

Henry Ho.
SE1 . . . . 2B **24** (2C **76**)
SW8 . . . . 3A **90**
(off Wyvil Rd.)
Henry Jackson Rd.
SW15 . . . . 1F **99**
Henry Purcell Ho.
E16 . . . . 2D **83**
(off Evelyn Rd.)
Henry Rd. N4 . . . . 3E **35**
Henryson Rd. SE4 . . 3C **108**
Henry Tate M.
SW16 . . . . 5C **118**
Henry Wise Ho. SW1 . . 5E **75**
(off Vauxhall Bri. Rd.)
Hensford Gdns.
SE26 . . . . 4D **121**
Henshall St. N1 . . . . . 3F **49**
Henshaw St. SE17 . . . 5F **77**
Henslowe Rd. SE22 . . 3C **106**
Henslow Ho. SE15 . . . . 3C **92**
(off Peckham Pk. Rd.)
Henson Av. NW2 . . . . . 2E **43**
Henstridge Pl. NW8 . . 5A **46**
Henty Cl. SW11 . . . . . 3A **88**
Henty Wlk. SW15 . . . . 3D **99**
Henwick Rd. SE9 . . . . 1F **111**
Hepburn M. SW11 . . . 3B **102**
Hepplestone Cl.
SW15 . . . . 4D **99**
Hepscott Rd. E9 . . . . . 3C **52**
Hepworth Ct. N1 . . . . . 5D **49**
(off Gaskin St.)
NW3 . . . . 2A **46**
Hera Ct. E14 . . . . 5C **80**
(off Homer Dr.)
Herald's Pl. SE11 . . . . 5D **77**
(off Gilbert Rd.)
Herald St. E2 . . . . 3D **65**
Herbal Hill
EC1 . . . . 4C **8** (3C **62**)
Herbal Hill Gdns. EC1 . . 4C **8**
(off Herbal Hill)
Herbal Pl. EC1 . . . . 4C **8**
Herbert Cres.
SW1 . . . . 5A **20** (4B **74**)
Herbert Gdns. NW10 . . 1D **57**
Herbert Ho. E1 . . . . . . 2F **19**
(off Old Castle St.)
Herbert M. SW2 . . . . 4C **104**
Herbert Morrison Ho.
SW6 . . . . 2B **86**
(off Clem Attlee Ct.)
Herbert Rd. E12 . . . . . 1F **55**
E17 . . . . 2B **38**
NW9 . . . . 1C **28**
Herbert St. E13 . . . . . . 1C **68**
NW5 . . . . 3C **46**
Herbrand Est.
WC1 . . . . 3D **7** (3A **62**)
Herbrand St.
WC1 . . . . 3D **7** (3A **62**)
Hercules Ct. SE14 . . . . 2A **94**
Hercules Pl. N7 . . . . . 5A **34**
(not continuous)
Hercules Rd.
SE1 . . . . 5A **24** (4B **76**)
Hercules St. N7 . . . . . 5A **34**
Hercules Wharf E14 . . 1A **82**
(off Orchard Pl.)

Hercules Yd. N7 . . . . . 5A **34**
Hereford Bldgs.
SW3 . . . . 2F **87**
(off Old Chu. St.)
Hereford Gdns.
SE13 . . . . 3A **110**
Hereford Ho. NW6 . . . . 1C **58**
(off Carlton Va.)
SW3 . . . . 4A **74**
(off Ovington Gdns.)
SW10 . . . . 3D **87**
(off Fulham Rd.)
Hereford M. W2 . . . . . 5C **58**
Hereford Pl. SE14 . . . . 3B **94**
Hereford Retreat
SE15 . . . . 3C **92**
Hereford Rd. E11 . . . . 1D **41**
W2 . . . . 5C **58**
Hereford Sq. SW7 . . . . 5E **73**
Hereford St. E2 . . . . . 3C **64**
Hereward Rd.
SW17 . . . . 4B **116**
Heritage Cl. SW9 . . . . 1D **105**
Heritage Ct. SE8 . . . . . 1F **93**
(off Trundley's Rd.)
Heritage Pl. SW18 . . . 1E **115**
Herlwyn Gdns.
SW17 . . . . 4B **116**
Her Majesty's Theatre
. . . . 1B **22**
(off Haymarket)
Hermes Cl. W9 . . . . . . 3C **58**
Hermes St. SW2 . . . . . 4B **104**
SW9 . . . . 4C **90**
(off Southey Rd.)
Hermes St.
N1 . . . . 1B **8** (1C **62**)
Herm Ho. N1 . . . . 3E **49**
Hermiston Av. N8 . . . . 1A **34**
Hermitage, The
SE13 . . . . 5E **95**
SE23 . . . . 1E **121**
SW13 . . . . 4B **84**
Hermitage Ct. E1 . . . . 2C **78**
(off Knighten St.)
NW2 . . . . 5C **30**
Hermitage Gdns.
NW2 . . . . 5C **30**
Hermitage La. NW2 . . . 5C **30**
Hermitage Rd. N4 . . . . 2D **35**
SE19 . . . . 5F **119**
Hermitage Rooms 4A **16**
(off Embankment)
Hermitage Row E8 . . . 2C **50**
Hermitage St. W2 . . . . 4F **59**
Hermitage Vs. SW6 . . . 2C **86**
(off Lillie Rd.)
Hermitage Wall E1 . . . 2C **78**
Hermitage Waterside
E1 . . . . 2C **78**
(off Thomas More St.)
Hermit Pl. NW6 . . . . . 5D **45**
Hermit Rd. E16 . . . . . 4B **68**
Hermit St.
EC1 . . . . 1D **9** (2D **63**)
Hermon Hill E11 . . . . . 1C **40**
Herndon Rd. SW18 . . . 3E **101**
Herne Cl. NW10 . . . . . 2A **42**
HERNE HILL 3E **105**
Herne Hill SE24 . . . . . 4E **105**

Herne Hill Ho.
SE24 . . . . 4D **105**
(off Railton Rd.)
Herne Hill Rd. SE24 . . 1E **105**
Herne Hill Stadium . . . 4F **105**
Herne Pl. SE24 . . . . . 3D **105**
Heron Cl. NW10 . . . . . 3A **42**
Heron Ct. E14 . . . . 4E **81**
(off New Union Cl.)
Herondale Av.
SW18 . . . . 1F **115**
Heron Dr. N4 . . . . 4E **35**
Herongate Rd. E12 . . . 4E **41**
Heron Ho. E6 . . . . 4F **55**
NW8 . . . . 1A **60**
(off Newcourt St.)
SW11 . . . . 3A **88**
(off Searles Cl.)
Heron Ind. Est. E15 . . 1D **67**
Heron Pl. SE16 . . . . . . 2A **80**
W1 . . . . 2C **12**
(off Thayer St.)
Heron Quay E14 . . . . . 2C **80**
Heron Rd. SE24 . . . . . 2E **105**
Herons, The E11 . . . . . 1B **40**
Heron's Lea N6 . . . . . . 1B **32**
Herrick Ho. N16 . . . . . 1F **49**
(off Howard Rd.)
SE5 . . . . 3F **91**
(off Elmington Est.)
Herrick Rd. N5 . . . . . . 5E **35**
Herrick St. SW1 . . . . . 5F **75**
Herries St. W10 . . . . . 1A **58**
Herringham Rd. SE7 . . 4E **83**
Hersant Cl. NW10 . . . . 5C **42**
Herschell M. SE5 . . . . 1E **105**
Herschell Rd. SE23 . . 5A **108**
Hersham Cl. SW15 . . . 5C **98**
Hertford Av. SW14 . . . 3A **98**
Hertford Pl.
W1 . . . . 4A **6** (3E **61**)
Hertford Rd. N1 . . . . . 5A **50**
(not continuous)
Hertford St.
W1 . . . . 2D **21** (2D **75**)
Hertslet Rd. N7 . . . . . 5B **34**
Hertsmere Ho. E14 . . . 1C **80**
(off Hertsmere Rd.)
Hertsmere Rd. E14 . . . 2C **80**
Hervey Rd. SE3 . . . . . 4D **97**
Hesewall Cl. SW4 . . . . 5E **89**
Hesketh Pl. W11 . . . . . 1A **72**
Hesketh Rd. E7 . . . . . 5C **40**
Heslop Rd. SW12 . . . . 1B **116**
Hesper M. SW5 . . . . . 5D **73**
Hesperus Cl. E14 . . . . 5D **81**
Hesperus Cres. E14 . . 5D **81**
Hessel St. E1 . . . . 5D **65**
Hestercombe Av.
SW6 . . . . 5A **86**
Hester Rd. SW11 . . . . 3A **88**
Hestia Ho. SE1 . . . . . . 4D **27**
Heston Ho. SE8 . . . . . . 4C **94**
SE14 . . . . 4C **94**
Hetherington Rd.
SW4 . . . . 2A **104**
Hethpool Ho. W2 . . . . . 3F **59**
(off Hall Pl.)
Hetley Rd. W12 . . . . . 2D **71**
Hevelius Cl. SE10 . . . . 1B **96**

Hever Ho. *SE15* 2F **93**
   (off Lovelinch Cl.)
Heversham Ho. SE15 . . . 2E **93**
Hewer St. W10 . . . . 4F **57**
Hewett St.
  EC2 . . . . 4E **11** (3A **64**)
Hewison St. E3 . . . . 1B **66**
Hewitt Rd. N8 . . . . 1C **34**
Hewlett Ho. *SW8* 3D **89**
   (off Havelock Ter.)
Hewlett Rd. E3 . . . . 1A **66**
Hexagon, The N6 . . . . . . 3B **32**
Hexal Rd. SE6 . . . . 3A **124**
Hexham Rd. SE27 . . . . . 2E **119**
Heybridge *NW1* 3D **47**
   (off Lewis St.)
Heybridge Av.
  SW16 . . . . 5B **118**
Heybridge Way E10 . . . . 2A **38**
Heydon Ho. *SE14* 4E **93**
   (off Kender St.)
Heyford Av. SW8 . . . . . . 3A **90**
Heyford Ter. SW8 . . . . . . 3A **90**
Heygate St. SE17 . . . . . . 5E **77**
Heylyn Sq. E3 . . . . 2B **66**
Heysham La. NW3 . . . . . 5D **31**
Heysham Rd. N15 . . . . . . 1F **35**
Heythorp St. SW18 . . . . 1B **114**
Heywood Ho. *SE14* 2F **93**
   (off Myers La.)
Heyworth Rd. E5 . . . . . . 1D **51**
  E15 . . . . 2B **54**
Hibbert Ho. *E14* 4C **80**
   (off Tiller Rd.)
Hibbert Rd. E17 . . . . 2B **38**
Hibbert St. SW11 . . . . . . 1F **101**
Hichisson Rd. SE15 . . . . 3E **107**
Hickes Ho. NW6 . . . . . . 4F **45**
Hickin Cl. SE7 . . . . 5F **83**
Hickin St. E14 . . . . 4E **81**
Hickleton *NW1* 5E **47**
   (off Camden St.)
Hickling Ho. *SE16* 4D **79**
   (off Slippers Pl.)
Hickman Cl. E16 . . . . . . 4F **69**
Hickmore Wlk. SW4 . . . 1F **103**
Hicks Cl. SW11 . . . . 1A **102**
Hicks St. SE8 . . . . 1A **94**
Hide Pl. SW1 . . . . 5F **75**
Hider Cl. SE3 . . . . 3E **97**
Hides St. N7 . . . . 3B **48**
Hide Twr. *SW1* 5F **75**
   (off Regency St.)
Higgins Ho. *N1* 5A **50**
   (off Colville Est.)
Higginson Ho. *NW3* . . . 4B **46**
   (off Fellows Rd.)
Higgs Ind. Est.
  SE24 . . . . 1D **105**
Highbank Way N8 . . . . . 1C **34**
High Bri. SE10 . . . . 1F **95**
Highbridge Ct. *SE14* . . . 3E **93**
   (off Farrow La.)
High Bri. Wharf *SE10* . . 1F **95**
   (off High Bri.)
Highbrook Rd. SE3 . . . . 1F **111**
HIGHBURY 1D **49**
HIGHBURY CORNER . . . 3D **49**
Highbury Cres. N5 . . . . . 2D **49**
Highbury Est. N5 . . . . . . 2E **49**

Highbury Grange N5 . . . 1E **49**
Highbury Gro. N5 . . . . . 2D **49**
Highbury Gro. Ct. N5 . . . 3E **49**
Highbury Hill N5 . . . . . . 5C **34**
Highbury New Pk. N5 . . 2E **49**
Highbury Pk. N5 . . . . . . 5D **35**
Highbury Pk. M. N5 . . . . 1E **49**
Highbury Pl. N5 . . . . . . 3D **49**
Highbury Pool 3D **49**
Highbury Quad. N5 . . . . 5E **35**
Highbury Rd. SW19 . . . 5A **114**
Highbury Stadium 5D **35**
Highbury Sta. Rd. N1 . . 3C **48**
Highbury Ter. N5 . . . . . . 2D **49**
Highbury Ter. M. N5 . . . 2D **49**
Highclere St. SE26 . . . . 4A **122**
Highcliffe Dr. SW15 . . . . 4B **98**
   (not continuous)
Highcliffe Gdns.
  IG4: Ilf 1F **41**
Highcombe SE7 . . . . . . 2D **97**
Highcombe Cl. SE9 . . . 1F **125**
Highcroft Est. N19 . . . . . 2A **34**
Highcroft Gdns.
  NW11 . . . . 1B **30**
Highcroft Rd. N19 . . . . . 2A **34**
Highcross Way
  SW15 . . . . 1C **112**
Highdown Rd. SW15 . . . 4D **99**
Highfield Av. NW11 . . . . 2F **29**
Highfield Cl. SE13 . . . . . 4F **109**
Highfield Ct. NW11 . . . . 1A **30**
Highfield Gdns.
  NW11 . . . . 1A **30**
Highfield Rd. NW11 . . . . 1A **30**
Highfields Gro. N6 . . . . . 3B **32**
HIGHGATE 2C **32**
Highgate Av. N6 . . . . . . 2D **33**
Highgate Cemetery
  N6 . . . . 3C **32**
Highgate Cl. N6 . . . . . . 2C **32**
Highgate Edge N2 . . . . 1A **32**
Highgate Hgts. N6 . . . . . 1E **33**
Highgate High St. N6 . . 3C **32**
Highgate Hill N6 . . . . . . 3D **33**
  N19 . . . . 3D **33**
Highgate Ho. SE26 . . . . 3C **120**
Highgate Rd. NW5 . . . . 5C **32**
Highgate Spinney N8 . . 1F **33**
Highgate Wlk. SE23 . . . 2E **121**
Highgate W. Hill N6 . . . 3C **32**
Highgate West School
  Sports Cen. 1E **33**
High Hill Est. SE26 . . . . 3D **37**
High Hill Ferry E5 . . . . . 3D **37**
High Holborn
  WC1 . . . . 2D **15** (5A **62**)
Highland Cft.
  BR3: Beck. 5D **123**
Highland Rd. SE19 . . . . 5A **120**
Highlands Cl. N4 . . . . . . 2A **34**
Highlands Heath
  SW15 . . . . 5E **99**
Highland Ter. SE13 . . 1D **109**
   (off Algernon Rd.)
High Level Dr. SE26 . . . 4C **120**
Highlever Rd. W10 . . . . 4E **57**
High Meads Rd. E16 . . . 5F **69**
Highmore Rd. SE3 . . . . 3A **96**
High Mt. NW4 . . . . 1C **28**

High Pde., The
  SW16 . . . . 3A **118**
High Point N6 . . . . 2C **32**
High Rd. N15 . . . . 1B **36**
  NW10 . . . . 3A **42**
High Rd. Leyston
  E11 . . . . 5A **40**
High Rd. Leyton E10 . . . 1D **39**
  E15 . . . . 1E **53**
High Rd. Leytonstone
  E15 . . . . 1A **54**
High Sheldon N6 . . . . . 1B **32**
Highshore Rd. SE15 . . . 5B **92**
   (not continuous)
Highstone Av. E11 . . . . 1C **40**
Highstone Ct. *E11* 1B **40**
   (off New Wanstead)
Highstone Mans.
  NW1 . . . . 4E **47**
   (off Camden Rd.)
High St. E11 . . . . 1C **40**
  E13 . . . . 1C **68**
  E15 . . . . 1E **67**
  SW19 . . . . 5F **113**
High St. Colliers Wood
  SW19 . . . . 5A **116**
High St. Harlesden
  NW10 . . . . 1B **56**
High St. M. SW19 . . . . 5A **114**
High St. Nth. E12 . . . . . . 2F **55**
High Timber St.
  EC4 . . . . 4F **17** (1E **77**)
High Trees SW2 . . . . . . 1C **118**
Hightrees Ho.
  SW12 . . . . 4C **102**
Highview N6 . . . . 1E **33**
Highway, The E1 . . . . . . 1C **78**
Highway Bus. Pk., The
  E1 . . . . 1F **79**
   (off Heckford St.)
Highway Trad. Cen., The
  E1 . . . . 1F **79**
   (off Heckford St.)
Highwood Rd. N19 . . . . 5A **34**
Highworth St. *NW1* . . . 4A **60**
   (off Daventry St.)
Hi-Gloss Cen. SE8 . . . . 1A **94**
Hilary Cl. SW6 . . . . 3D **87**
Hilary Rd. W12 . . . . 5B **56**
   (not continuous)
Hilborough Ct. E8 . . . . . 4B **50**
Hilda Rd. E6 . . . . 4F **55**
  E16 . . . . 3A **68**
   (not continuous)
Hilda Ter. SW9 . . . . 5C **90**
Hildenborough Gdns.
  BR1: Brom 5A **124**
Hildreth St. SW12 . . . . 1D **117**
Hildreth St. M.
  SW12 . . . . 1D **117**
Hildyard Rd. SW6 . . . . . 2C **86**
Hiley Rd. NW10 . . . . 2E **57**
Hilgrove Rd. NW6 . . . . . 4E **45**
Hillary Ct. *W12* 3E **71**
   (off Titmuss St.)
Hillbeck Cl. SE15 . . . . . 3E **93**
Hillbeck Ho. *SE15* 2E **93**
   (off Hillbeck Cl.)
Hillboro Ct. E11 . . . . 2F **39**
Hillbrook Rd. SW17 . . . 3B **116**

Hillbury Rd. SW17 . . . . 3D **117**
Hill Cl. NW2 . . . . 5D **29**
   NW11 . . . . 1C **30**
Hillcourt Est. N16 . . . . . 3F **35**
Hillcourt Rd. SE22 . . . . 4D **107**
Hillcrest N6 . . . . 2C **32**
   SE24 . . . . 2F **105**
Hillcrest Cl. SE26 . . . . . 4C **120**
Hill Crest Gdns. NW2 . . 5C **28**
Hillcrest Rd.
   BR1: Brom 5C **124**
Hilldrop Cres. N7 . . . . . 2F **47**
Hilldrop Est. N7 . . . . . . 2F **47**
     (not continuous)
Hilldrop La. N7 . . . . 2F **47**
Hilldrop Rd.
   BR1: Brom 5D **125**
   N7 . . . . 2F **47**
Hillersden Ho. SW1 . . . . 1D **89**
     (off Ebury Bri. Rd.)
Hillersdon Av. SW13 . . . 5C **84**
Hillery Cl. SE17 . . . . 5F **77**
Hill Farm Rd. W10 . . . . 4E **57**
Hillfield Ct. NW3 . . . . . . 2A **46**
Hillfield Ho. N5 . . . . 2E **49**
Hillfield Rd. NW6 . . . . . 2B **44**
Hillgate Pl. SW12 . . . . . 5D **103**
   W8 . . . . 2C **72**
Hillgate St. W8 . . . . 2C **72**
Hillgate Wlk. N6 . . . . . . 1E **33**
Hill Ho. E5 . . . . 3D **37**
     (off Harrington Hill)
Hill Ho. Rd. SW16 . . . . 5B **118**
Hilliard Ho. E1 . . . . 2D **79**
     (off Prusom St.)
Hilliards Ct. E1 . . . . 2E **79**
Hillier Ho. NW1 . . . . 4F **47**
     (off Camden Sq.)
Hillier Rd. SW11 . . . . . . 4B **102**
Hillingdon St. SE17 . . . . 2D **91**
Hillman Dr. W10 . . . . . . 3E **57**
Hillman St. E8 . . . . 3D **51**
Hillmarton Rd. N7 . . . . . 2A **48**
Hillmead Dr. SW9 . . . . . 2D **105**
Hillmore Ct. SE13 . . . . . 1F **109**
     (off Belmont Hill)
Hillmore Gro. SE26 . . . . 5A **122**
Hill Path SW16 . . . . 5B **118**
Hill Ri. SE23 . . . . 1D **121**
Hillrise Mans. N19 . . . . . 2A **34**
     (off Warltersville Rd.)
Hillrise Rd. N19 . . . . 2A **34**
Hill Rd. NW8 . . . . 2E **59**
Hillsboro' Rd. SE22 . . . . 3A **106**
Hillsborough Ct.
   NW6 . . . . 5D **45**
     (off Mortimer Cres.)
Hillside N8 . . . . 1F **33**
   NW5 . . . . 5C **32**
   NW10 . . . . 5A **42**
   SE10 . . . . 3F **95**
     (off Crooms Hill)
Hillside Cl. NW8 . . . . . . 1D **59**
Hillside Est. N15 . . . . . . 1B **36**
Hillside Gdns. N6 . . . . . 1D **33**
   SW2 . . . . 2C **118**
Hillside Pas. SW16 . . . . 2B **118**
Hillside Rd. N15 . . . . . . 2A **36**
   SW2 . . . . 2B **118**
Hillsleigh Rd. W8 . . . . . 2B **72**

Hills Pl. W1 . . . . 3F **13** (5E **61**)
Hillstowe St. E5 . . . . . . 5E **37**
Hill St. W1 . . . . . . 1C **20** (2C **74**)
Hilltop Ct. NW8 . . . . 4E **45**
     (off Alexandra Rd.)
Hilltop Ho. N6 . . . . 2F **33**
Hilltop Rd. NW6 . . . . . . 4C **44**
Hill Vw. Gdns.
   NW9 . . . . 1A **28**
Hillway N6 . . . . 4C **32**
   NW9 . . . . 3A **28**
Hill-Wood Ho. NW1 . . . . 1A **6**
     (off Polygon Rd.)
Hillworth Rd. SW2 . . . . 5C **104**
Hillyard Rd. SW9 . . . . . 4C **90**
Hillyard St. SW9 . . . . . . 4C **90**
Hillyfield Cl. E9 . . . . 2A **52**
Hilly Flds. Cres.
   SE4 . . . . 1C **108**
   SE13 . . . . 1C **108**
Hilsea Point SW15 . . . . 1D **113**
Hilsea St. E5 . . . . 1E **51**
Hilton Ho. SE4 . . . . 2F **107**
Hilton's Wharf SE10 . . . 2D **95**
     (off Norman Rd.)
Hilversum Cres.
   SE22 . . . . 3A **106**
Himley Rd. SW17 . . . . . 5A **116**
Hinchinbrook Ho.
   NW6 . . . . 5D **45**
     (off Mortimer Cres.)
Hinckley Rd. SE15 . . . . 2C **106**
Hind Ct. EC4 . . . . . 3C **16** (5C **62**)
Hinde M. W1 . . . . 2C **12**
     (off Hinde St.)
Hinde M. W1 . . . . 2C **12**
Hinde St. W1 . . . . . 2C **12** (5C **60**)
Hind Gro. E14 . . . . 5C **66**
Hindhead Cl. N16 . . . . . 3A **36**
Hindhead Point
   SW15 . . . . 1D **113**
Hind Ho. N7 . . . . 1C **48**
   SE14 . . . . 2F **93**
     (off Myers La.)
Hindlip Ho. SW8 . . . . . . 4F **89**
Hindmans Rd. SE22 . . . 3C **106**
Hindmarsh Cl. E1 . . . . . 1C **78**
Hindon Ct. SW1 . . . . . . 5E **75**
     (off Guildhouse St.)
Hindrey Rd. E5 . . . . 2D **51**
Hindsley's Pl. SE23 . . . 2E **121**
Hinstock NW6 . . . . 5D **45**
     (off Belsize Rd.)
Hinton Ct. E10 . . . . 4D **39**
     (off Leyton Grange Est.)
Hinton Rd. SE24 . . . . . . 1D **105**
Hippodrome M. W11 . . . 1A **72**
Hippodrome Pl. W11 . . . 1A **72**
Hiroshima Prom.
   SE7 . . . . 4E **83**
Hitcham Rd. E17 . . . . . . 2B **38**
Hitchin Sq. E3 . . . . 1A **66**
Hithe Gro. SE16 . . . . . . 4E **79**
Hither Farm Rd.
   SE3 . . . . 1E **111**
Hitherfield Rd.
   SW16 . . . . 2B **118**
HITHER GREEN. 4A **110**
Hither Grn. La.
   SE13 . . . . 3E **109**

Hitherwood Dr.
   SE19 . . . . 4B **120**
HMP Brixton SW2 . . . . 4A **104**
HMP Pentonville N7 . . . 3B **48**
HMP Wormwood Scrubs
   W12 . . . . 5C **56**
Hoadly Rd. SW16 . . . . . 3F **117**
Hobart Pl.
   SW1 . . . . 5D **21** (4D **75**)
Hobbes Wlk. SW15 . . . . 3D **99**
Hobbs Ct. SE1 . . . . 3B **78**
     (off Mill St.)
Hobbs Pl. N1 . . . . 5A **50**
Hobbs Pl. Est. N1 . . . . . 1A **64**
     (off Hobbs Pl.)
Hobbs Rd. SE27 . . . . . . 4E **119**
Hobday St. E14 . . . . 5D **67**
Hobson's Pl. E1 . . . . 4C **64**
Hobury St. SW10 . . . . . 2E **87**
Hocker St. E2. . 2F **11** (2B **64**)
Hockett Cl. SE8 . . . . 5A **80**
Hockley Av. E6 . . . . 1F **69**
Hockliffe Ho. W10 . . . . . 4E **57**
     (off Sutton Way)
Hockney Ct. SE16 . . . . . 1D **93**
     (off Rossetti Rd.)
Hocroft Av. NW2 . . . . . . 5B **30**
Hocroft Ct. NW2 . . . . . . 5B **30**
Hocroft Rd. NW2 . . . . . . 5B **30**
Hocroft Wlk. NW2 . . . . . 5B **30**
Hodes Row NW3 . . . . . . 1C **46**
Hodford Rd. NW11 . . . . 3B **30**
Hodister Cl. SE5 . . . . . . 3E **91**
Hodnet Gro. SE16 . . . . . 5F **79**
Hoe St. E17 . . . . 1C **38**
Hoever Ho. SE6 . . . . 4E **123**
Hoffman Sq. N1 . . . . . . 1C **10**
Hofland Rd. W14 . . . . . . 4A **72**
Hogan M. W2 . . . . 4E **59**
Hogan Way E5 . . . . 4C **36**
Hogarth Bus. Pk. W4 . . 2A **84**
Hogarth Cl. E16 . . . . 4F **69**
Hogarth Ct. E1 . . . . 5C **64**
     (off Batty St.)
   EC3 . . . . 4E **19** (5A **64**)
   NW1 . . . . 4E **47**
     (off St Pancras Way)
   SE19 . . . . 4B **120**
Hogarth Ho. SW1 . . . . . 5F **75**
     (off Erasmus St.)
Hogarth Ind. Est.
   NW10 . . . . 3C **56**
Hogarth La. W4 . . . . 2A **84**
Hogarth Pl. SW5 . . . . . . 5D **73**
     (off Hogarth Rd.)
Hogarth Rd. SW5 . . . . . 5D **73**
HOGARTH RDBT. 2A **84**
Hogarth's House 2A **84**
     (off Hogarth La.)
Hogarth Ter. W4 . . . . . . 2A **84**
Hogshead Pas. E1 . . . . . 1D **79**
     (off Reunion Row)
Holbeach M. SW12 . . . . 1D **117**
Holbeach Rd. SE6 . . . . . 5C **108**
Holbeck Row SE15 . . . . 3C **92**
Holbein Ho. SW1 . . . . . . 1C **88**
     (off Holbein M.)
Holbein M. SW1 . . . . . . 1C **88**
Holbein Pl. SW1 . . . . . . 5C **74**

Holberton Gdns.
 NW10 . . . . 2D 57
HOLBORN . . 1F 15 (4C 62)
Holborn EC1 . . 1B 16 (4C 62)
Holborn Cir.
 EC1 . . . . 1C 16 (4C 62)
Holborn Pl. WC1 . . . . . 1F 15
Holborn Rd. E13. . . . . . 3D 69
Holborn Viaduct
 EC1 . . . . 1C 16 (4C 62)
Holbrook Cl. N19 . . . . . 3D 33
Holbrooke Ct. N7 . . . . . 5A 34
Holbrook Rd. E15. . . . . 1B 68
Holburne Cl. SE3 . . . . . 4E 97
Holburne Gdns. SE3 . . . 4F 97
Holburne Rd. SE3 . . . . 4E 97
Holcombe Ho.
 SW9 . . . . 1A 104
 (off Landor Rd.)
Holcombe Pl. SE4 . . . 1A 108
 (off St Asaph Rd.)
Holcombe St. W6 . . . . . 5D 71
Holcroft Ct. W1 . . . . 5F 5
Holcroft Rd. SW11 . . . 1F 101
Holcroft Rd. E9 . . . . . . 4E 51
Holdenby SE4 . . . . . 3A 108
Holden Ho. N1 . . . . . . 5E 49
 (off Prebend St.)
 SE8 . . . . 3C 94
Holden St. SW11 . . . . 5C 88
Holdernesse Rd.
 SW17 . . . . 3B 116
Holderness Ho. SE5 . . 1A 106
Holderness Way
 SE27 . . . . 5D 119
Holford Ho. SE16 . . . . 5D 79
 (off Camilla Rd.)
Holford M. WC1 . . . . . . 1B 8
Holford Pl.
 WC1 . . . . 1A 8 (2B 62)
Holford Rd. NW3 . . . . 5E 31
Holford St.
 WC1 . . . . 1B 8 (2B 62)
Holford Yd. WC1 . . . . . 1B 8
 (off Cruikshank St.)
Holgate Av. SW11 . . . 1F 101
Holgate St. SE7 . . . . . 4F 83
Holland Dr. SE23 . . . . 3A 122
Holland Gdns. W14 . . . 4A 72
Holland Gro. SW9 . . . . 3C 90
Holland Ho. NW10. . . . 1D 57
 (off Holland Rd.)
HOLLAND PARK 2B 72
Holland Pk. 3B 72
HOLLAND PARK 3F 71
Holland Pk. W11 . . . . . 2A 72
Holland Pk. Av. W11 . . . 3A 72
Holland Pk. Gdns.
 W14 . . . . 3A 72
Holland Pk. M. W11. . . . 2A 72
Holland Pk. Rd. W14 . . 4B 72
Holland Pk. Ter. W11. . . 2A 72
 (off Portland Rd.)
Holland Pk. Theatre
 (Open Air) 3B 72
 (in Holland Pk.)
Holland Pas. N1 . . . . . 5E 49
 (off Basire St.)
Holland Pl. W8. . . . . . . 3D 73
 (off Kensington Chu. St.)

Holland Pl. Chambers
 W8 . . . . 3D 73
 (off Holland Pl.)
Holland Ri. Ho. SW9 . . 3B 90
 (off Clapham Rd.)
Holland Rd. E15. . . . . . 2A 68
 NW10 . . . . 5C 42
 W14. . . . . 3F 71
Holland St.
 SE1 . . . . 1E 25 (2D 77)
 W8 . . . . 3C 72
Holland Vs. Rd.
 W14 . . . . 3A 72
Holland Wlk. N19 . . . . . 3F 33
 W8 . . . . 2B 72
Hollar Rd. N16. . . . . . . 5B 36
Hollen St.
 W1 . . . . 2B 14 (5F 61)
Holles Ho. SW9 . . . . . 5C 90
Holles St.
 W1 . . . . 2E 13 (5D 61)
Holley Rd. W3 . . . . 3A 70
Holliday Sq. SW11 . . . 1F 101
 (off Fowler Cl.)
Hollies, The E11 . . . . . 1C 40
 (off New Wanstead)
Hollies Way SW12 . . . 5C 102
Hollingbourne Rd.
 SE24 . . . . 3E 105
Hollins Ho. N7 . . . . . . 1A 48
Hollisfield WC1 . . . . . . 2E 7
 (off Cromer St.)
HOLLOWAY 5A 34
Holloway Ho. NW2. . . . 5E 29
 (off Stoll Cl.)
Holloway Rd. E11. . . . . 5F 39
 N7 . . . . 1B 48
 N19 . . . . 4F 33
Hollyberry La. NW3 . . . 1E 45
Hollybush Cl. E11 . . . . 1C 40
Hollybush Gdns. E2 . . . 2D 65
Hollybush Hill E11 . . . . 1B 40
 NW3 . . . . 1E 45
Hollybush Ho. E2 . . . . . 2D 65
Hollybush Pl. E2 . . . . . 2D 65
Hollybush Steps
 NW3 . . . . 1E 45
 (off Holly Mt.)
Hollybush St. E13 . . . . 2D 69
Holly Bush Va. NW3. . . 1E 45
Hollybush Wlk.
 SW9 . . . . 2D 105
Holly Cl. NW10 . . . . . . 4A 42
Hollycroft Av. NW3. . . . 5C 30
Hollydale Rd. SE15 . . . 4E 93
Holly Dene SE15 . . . . . 4D 93
Hollydown Way E11 . . . 5F 39
Holly Gro. SE15 . . . . . 5B 92
Holly Hedge Ter.
 SE13 . . . . 3F 109
Holly Hill NW3 . . . . . . 1E 45
Holly Ho. W10 . . . . . . 3A 58
 (off Hawthorn Wlk.)
Holly Lodge Gdns.
 N6. . . . . 4C 32
Holly Lodge Mans.
 N6. . . . . 4C 32
Holly Mt. NW3 . . . . . . 1E 45
Hollymount Cl. SE10 . . 4E 95

Holly Pk. N4 . . . . 2A 34
 (not continuation)
Holly Pk. Est. N4 . . . . . 2B 34
Holly Pl. NW3. . . . . 1E 45
 (off Holly Berry La.)
Holly Rd. E11. . . . . 2B 40
 W4 . . . . 5A 70
Holly St. E8 . . . . 4B 50
Holly Ter. N6 . . . . 3C 32
Holly Tree Cl. SW19. . . 1F 113
Holly Tree Ho. SE4. . . 1B 108
 (off Brockley Rd.)
Holly Vw. Cl. NW4 . . . . 1C 28
Holly Village N6. . . . . . 4D 33
Holly Vs. W6 . . . . 4D 71
 (off Wellesley Av.)
Holly Wlk. NW3 . . . . . . 1E 45
Hollywood Bowl
 Surrey Quays 4F 79
Hollywood M. SW10 . . . 2E 87
Hollywood Rd. SW10 . . 2E 87
Holman Ho. E2. . . . . . 2F 65
 (off Roman Rd.)
Holman Hunt Ho. W6. . . 1A 86
 (off Field Rd.)
Holman Rd. SW11 . . . . 5F 87
Holmbrook NW1. . . . . . 1E 61
 (off Eversholt St.)
Holmbury Ct. SW17 . . . 3B 116
Holmbury Ho. SE24. . . 3D 105
Holmbury Vw. E5. . . . . 3D 37
Holmbush Rd.
 SW15 . . . . 4A 100
Holmcote Gdns. N5 . . . 2E 49
Holm Ct. SE12 . . . . . . 3D 125
Holmdale Gdns. NW4. . 1F 29
Holmdale Rd. NW6 . . . 2C 44
Holmdale Ter. N15. . . . 2A 36
Holmdene Av. SE24 . . . 3E 105
Holmead Rd. SW6. . . . 3D 87
Holme Lacey Rd.
 SE12 . . . . 4B 110
Holmes Ho.
 NW6 . . . . 5C 44
 (off Kilburn Va.)
Holmesdale Ho. N6 . . . 2D 33
Holmesdale Rd. N6 . . . 2D 33
Holmes Pl. SW10 . . . . 2E 87
Holmes Place Health Club
 Barbican 5F 9
 (off Aldersgate St.)
 Hammersmith. 5F 71
 (off Hammersmith Rd.)
 Merton. 5E 115
 St Luke's 4B 10
Holmes Rd. NW5. . . . . 2D 47
Holmes Ter. SE1 . . . . . 3B 24
Holmewood Gdns.
 SW2 . . . . 5B 104
Holmewood Rd.
 SW2 . . . . 5A 104
Holmfield Ct. NW3. . . . 2A 46
Holmleigh Rd. N16 . . . 3A 36
Holmleigh Rd. Est.
 N16. . . . . 3A 36
Holmoak Cl. SW15. . . . 4B 100
Holm Oak M. SW4 . . . 3A 104
Holmsdale Ho. E14. . . . 1D 81
 (off Poplar High St.)

Holmshaw Cl. SE26 . . . 4A **122**
Holmside Rd.
  SW12 . . . . 4C **102**
Holmsley Ho. SW15. . . *5B* **98**
  (off Tangley Gro.)
Holm Wlk. SE3 . . . . 5C **96**
Holmwood Vs. SE7. . . . 1C **96**
Holne Chase N2 . . . . . . 1E **31**
Holness Rd. E15. . . . . . 3B **54**
Holocaust Memorial Garden
  . . . . 3A **20**
Holroyd Rd. SW15 . . . . 2E **99**
Holst Ct. SE1 . . . . *5B 24*
  (off Westminster Bri. Rd.)
Holst Mans. SW13. . . . 2E **85**
Holsworthy Sq. WC1 . . . 4A **8**
Holt Cl. E15 . . . . 2E **53**
Holt Ho. SW2 . . . . 4C **104**
Holton St. E1. . . . . 3F **65**
Holwood Pl. SW4 . . . . . 2F **103**
Holybourne Av.
  SW15 . . . . 5C **98**
Holyhead Cl. E3. . . . . . 2C **66**
Holyoake Ct. SE16 . . . . 3B **80**
Holyoak Rd. SE11 . . . . 5D **77**
Holyport Rd. SW6 . . . . 3F **85**
Holyrood M. E16 . . . . . . *2C 82*
  (off Badminton M.)
Holyrood St.
  SE1 . . . . 2D **27** (2A **78**)
Holywell Cen. *3D 11*
  (off Phipp St.)
Holywell Cl. SE3 . . . . . 2C **96**
  SE16 . . . . 1D **93**
Holywell La.
  EC2 . . . . 3E **11** (3A **64**)
Holywell Row
  EC2 . . . . 4D **11** (3A **64**)
Homecroft Rd. SE26. . . 5E **121**
Homefield Ho. SE23. . . 3F **121**
Homefield Rd.
  SW19 . . . . 5F **113**
  W4 . . . . 1B **84**
Homefield St.
  N1 . . . . 1D **11** (1A **64**)
Homeleigh Ct.
  SW16 . . . . 3A **118**
Homeleigh Rd.
  SE15 . . . . 3F **107**
Home Pk. Rd.
  SW19 . . . . 4B **114**
Homer Dr. E14 . . . . 5C **80**
Home Rd. SW11. . . . . . 5A **88**
Homer Rd. E9. . . . . 3A **52**
Homer Row W1 . . . . . . 4A **60**
Homer St. W1. . . . . 4A **60**
HOMERTON 2F **51**
Homerton Gro. E9. . . . . 2F **51**
Homerton High St.
  E9 . . . . 2F **51**
Homerton Rd. E9 . . . . . 2A **52**
Homerton Row E9. . . . . 2E **51**
Homerton Ter. E9 . . . . . 3E **51**
  (not continuous)
Homesdale Cl. E11 . . . . 1C **40**
Homestall Rd. SE22. . . 3E **107**
Homestead Pk. NW2 . . . 5B **28**
Homestead Rd. SW6 . . . 3B **86**
Homewoods SW12. . . . 5E **103**
Homildon Ho. SE26 . . . 3C **120**

Honduras St.
  EC1 . . . . 3F **9** (3E **63**)
Honeybourne Rd.
  NW6 . . . . 2D **45**
Honeybrook Rd.
  SW12 . . . . 5E **103**
Honey La. EC2 . . . . 3A **18**
Honeyman Cl. NW6 . . . 4F **43**
Honeywell Rd.
  SW11 . . . . 4B **102**
Honeywood Rd.
  NW10 . . . . 1B **56**
Honiton Gdns. SE15. . . *5E 93*
  (off Gibbon Rd.)
Honiton Rd. NW6. . . . . 1B **58**
Honley Rd. SE6 . . . . . . 5D **109**
HONOR OAK 4E **107**
Honor Oak Crematorium
  SE23 . . . . 5F **107**
HONOR OAK PARK . . . 5A **108**
Honor Oak Pk. SE23. . . 4E **107**
Honor Oak Ri. SE23 . . . 4E **107**
Honor Oak Rd.
  SE23 . . . . 1E **121**
Hood Ct. EC4 . . . . 3C **16**
Hood Ho. SE5. . . . . *3F 91*
  (off Elmington Est.)
  SW1 . . . . *1F 89*
  (off Dolphin Sq.)
Hooke Ho. E3. . . . . *1A 66*
  (off Gernon Rd.)
Hookham Ct. SW8 . . . . 4F **89**
Hooks Cl. SE15 . . . . . . 4D **93**
Hooper Ho. E16 . . . . . . 5C **68**
Hooper's Ct. SW3 . . . . 3B **74**
Hooper Sq. E1 . . . . *5C 64*
  (off Hooper St.)
Hooper St. E1. . . . . 5C **64**
Hoop La. NW11 . . . . . . 2B **30**
  (not continuous)
Hope Cl. N1 . . . . 3E **49**
  SE12. . . . . 3D **125**
Hope Ct. NW10. . . . . . . *2F 57*
  (off Chamberlayne Rd.)
Hopedale Rd. SE7 . . . . 2D **97**
Hopefield Av. NW6. . . . 1A **58**
Hope St. SW11 . . . . . . 1F **101**
Hopetown St. E1 . . . . . 4B **64**
Hopewell St. SE5. . . . . 3F **91**
Hopewell Yd. SE5. . . . . *3F 91*
  (off Hopewell St.)
Hope Wharf SE16. . . . . 3E **79**
Hop Gdns.
  WC2. . . . . 5D **15** (1A **76**)
Hopgood St. W12 . . . . . 2E **71**
Hopkins Ho. E14 . . . . . *5C 66*
  (off Canton St.)
Hopkins M. E15 . . . . . . 5B **54**
Hopkinsons Pl. NW1 . . . 5C **46**
Hopkins St.
  W1 . . . . 3A **14** (5E **61**)
Hopping La. N1 . . . . . . 3D **49**
Hop St. SE10 . . . . *5B 82*
  (off School Bank Rd.)
Hopton Rd. SW16 . . . . 5A **118**
Hopton's Gdns. SE1 . . . 1E **25**
Hopton St.
  SE1 . . . . 5D **17** (1D **77**)
Hopwood Cl. SW17 . . . 3E **115**
Hopwood Rd. SE17. . . . 2F **91**

Hopwood Wlk. E8. . . . . 4C **50**
Horace Rd. E7 . . . . 1D **55**
Horatio Ct. SE16. . . . . . *2E 79*
  (off Rotherhithe St.)
Horatio Ho. E2 . . . . *1B 64*
  (off Horatio St.)
  W6. . . . . *1F 85*
  (off Fulham Pal. Rd.)
Horatio Pl. E14 . . . . . . *2E 81*
  (off Preston's Rd.)
Horatio St. E2. . . . . 1B **64**
Horbury Cres. W11 . . . . 1C **72**
Horbury M. W11. . . . . . 1B **72**
Horder Rd. SW6 . . . . . . 4A **86**
Hordle Prom. E.
  SE15 . . . . 3B **92**
Hordle Prom. Sth.
  SE15. . . . . *3B 92*
  (off Quarley Way)
Horizon Bldg. E14 . . . . *1C 80*
  (off Hertsmere Rd.)
Horizon Way SE7 . . . . . 5D **83**
Horle Wlk. SE5 . . . . . . 5D **91**
Horley Rd. SE9 . . . . 4F **125**
Hormead Rd. W9 . . . . . 3B **58**
Hornbeam Cl. SE11. . . . 5C **76**
Hornbeam Sq. E3. . . . . 5B **52**
Hornblower Cl. SE16 . . 4A **80**
Hornby Cl. NW3 . . . . . . 4F **45**
Hornby Ho. SE11 . . . . . 2C **90**
  (off Clayton St.)
Horncastle Cl. SE12. . . 5C **110**
Horncastle Rd.
  SE12. . . . . 5C **110**
Horndean Cl. SW15 . . . 1C **112**
Horner Ho. N1 . . . . *5A 50*
  (off Whitmore Est.)
Horne Way SW15 . . . . . 5E **85**
Hornfair Rd. SE7 . . . . . 2E **97**
Horniman Dr. SE23 . . . 1D **121**
Horniman Mus. 1D **121**
Horn La. SE10 . . . . 1C **96**
  (not continuous)
Horn Link Way SE10 . . . 5C **82**
HORN PARK 3D **111**
Horn Pk. Cl. SE12 . . . . 3D **111**
Hornpark La. SE12. . . . 3D **111**
Hornsey Club, The 1F **33**
Hornsey La. N6 . . . . . . 3D **33**
Hornsey La. Est. N19. . . 2F **33**
Hornsey La. Gdns.
  N6 . . . . 2E **33**
Hornsey Ri. N19. . . . . . 2F **33**
Hornsey Ri. Gdns.
  N19 . . . . 2F **33**
Hornsey Rd. N7 . . . . . . 3A **34**
  N19 . . . . 3A **34**
Hornsey St. N7. . . . . . . 2B **48**
HORNSEY VALE 1B **34**
Hornshay St. SE15. . . . 2E **93**
Hornton Ct. W8 . . . . . . *3C 72*
  (off Kensington High St.)
Hornton Pl. W8 . . . . . . 3D **73**
Hornton St. W8 . . . . . . 3C **72**
Horsa Rd. SE12 . . . . . . 5E **111**
Horse & Dolphin Yd.
  W1 . . . . 4C **14**
Horseferry Pl. SE10 . . . 2E **95**
Horseferry Rd. E14 . . . . 1A **80**
  SW1 . . . . 4F **75**

Horseferry Rd. Est.
SW1 . . . . 5B **22**
Horseguards Av.
SW1 . . . . 2D **23** (2A **76**)
Horse Guards Parade
. . . . 2D **23** (2A **76**)
Horse Guards Rd.
SW1 . . . . 2C **22** (2E **75**)
Horsell Rd. N5 . . . . . 2C **48**
(not continuous)
Horselydown La.
SE1 . . . . 3F **27** (3B **78**)
Horselydown Mans.
SE1 . . . . 3F **27**
(off Lafone St.)
Horsemongers M.
SE1 . . . . 4A **26**
Horse Ride
SW1 . . . . 2B **22** (2E **75**)
Horseshoe Cl. E14 . . . . 1E **95**
NW2 . . . . 4D **29**
Horseshoe Ct. EC1 . . . . 3E **9**
(off Brewhouse Yd.)
Horseshoe Wharf
SE1 . . . . 1B **26**
(off Clink St.)
Horse Yd. N1 . . . . 5D **49**
(off Essex Rd.)
Horsfeld Gdns.
SE9 . . . . 3F **111**
Horsfeld Rd. SE9 . . . . 3F **111**
Horsfield Ho. N1 . . . . . 4E **49**
(off Northampton St.)
Horsford Rd. SW2 . . 3B **104**
Horsley St. SE17 . . . . . 2F **91**
Horsman Ho. SE5 . . . . . 2E **91**
(off Bethwin Rd.)
Horsman St. SE5 . . . . . 2E **91**
Horsmonden Rd.
SE4 . . . . 3B **108**
Hortensia Ho. SW10 . . . 3E **87**
(off Gunter Gro.)
Hortensia Rd. SW10 . . . 3E **87**
Horton Av. NW2 . . . . . 1A **44**
Horton Ho. SE15 . . . . . 2E **93**
SW8 . . . . 3B **90**
W6 . . . . 1A **86**
(off Field Rd.)
Horton Rd. E8 . . . . . . 3D **51**
Horton St. SE13 . . . . 1D **109**
Horwood Ho. E2 . . . . . 2D **65**
(off Pott St.)
NW8 . . . . 3A **60**
(off Paveley St.)
Hosack Rd. SW17 . . . 2C **116**
Hoser Av. SE12 . . . . . 2C **124**
Hosier La.
EC1 . . . . . 1D **17** (4D **63**)
Hoskins Cl. E16 . . . . . 5E **69**
Hoskins St. SE10 . . . . 1F **95**
Hospital Rd. E9 . . . . . 2F **51**
Hospital Way SE13 . . . 4F **109**
Hotham Rd. SW15 . . . . 1E **99**
Hotham St. E15 . . . . . 5A **54**
Hothfield Pl. SE16 . . . . 4E **79**
Hotspur St. SE11 . . . . 5C **76**
Houghton Cl. E8 . . . . . 3B **50**
Houghton St.
WC2 . . . . 3A **16** (5B **62**)
(not continuous)

Houndsditch
EC3 . . . . 2E **19** (5A **64**)
Houseman Way SE5 . . . 3F **91**
Houses of Parliament
. . . . 5E **23** (4A **76**)
Houston Rd. SE23 . . . 2A **122**
Hove Av. E17 . . . . 1B **38**
Hoveden Rd. NW2 . . . . 2A **44**
Hove St. SE15 . . . . 3E **93**
(off Culmore Rd.)
Howard Bldg. SW8 . . . . 2D **89**
Howard Cl. NW2 . . . . . 1A **44**
Howard Ho. E16 . . . . . 2D **83**
(off Wesley Av.)
SE8 . . . . 2B **94**
(off Evelyn St.)
SW1 . . . . 1E **89**
(off Dolphin Sq.)
SW9 . . . . 1D **105**
(off Barrington Rd.)
W1 . . . . 4E **5**
(off Cleveland St.)
Howard M. N5 . . . . . . 1D **49**
Howard Rd. E11 . . . . . 5A **40**
N15 . . . . 1A **36**
N16 . . . . 1F **49**
NW2 . . . . 1F **43**
Howard's La. SW15 . . . 2D **99**
Howards Rd. E13 . . . . 2C **68**
Howarth Ct. E15 . . . . . 2E **53**
(off Clays La.)
Howbury Rd. SE15 . . . 1E **107**
Howden St. SE15 . . . . 1C **106**
Howell Cl. E10 . . . . . . 2D **39**
Howell Wlk. SE1 . . . . . 5D **77**
Howick Pl.
SW1 . . . . 5A **22** (4E **75**)
Howie St. SW11 . . . . . 3A **88**
Howitt Cl. N16 . . . . . . 1A **50**
NW3 . . . . 3A **46**
Howitt Rd. NW3 . . . . . 3A **46**
Howland Est. SE16 . . . . 4E **79**
Howland Ho. SW16 . . . 3A **118**
Howland M. E.
W1 . . . . 5A **6** (4E **61**)
Howland St.
W1 . . . . 5F **5** (4E **61**)
Howland Way SE16 . . . 3A **80**
Howlett's Rd. SE24 . . . 4E **105**
Howley Pl. W2 . . . . . . 4E **59**
Howsman Rd. SW13 . . . 2C **84**
Howson Rd. SE4 . . . . 2A **108**
How's St. E2 . . . . 1B **64**
HOXTON 1A **64**
Hoxton Hall Theatre . . . 1A **64**
(off Hoxton Rd.)
Hoxton Mkt. N1 . . . . . 2D **11**
Hoxton Sq.
N1 . . . . 2D **11** (2A **64**)
Hoxton St.
N1 . . . . 2E **11** (5A **50**)
Hoylake Rd. W3 . . . . . 5A **56**
Hoyland Cl. SE15 . . . . 3D **93**
Hoyle Rd. SW17 . . . . . 5A **116**
Hoy St. E16 . . . . 5B **68**
HQS Wellington 5B **16**
Hubbard Rd. SE27 . . . 4E **119**
Hubbard St. E15 . . . . . 5A **54**
Huberd Ho. SE1 . . . . . 5C **26**
(off Manciple St.)

Hubert Gro. SW9 . . . . 1A **104**
Hubert Ho. NW8 . . . . . 3A **60**
(off Ashbridge St.)
Hubert Rd. E6 . . . . . . 2F **69**
Hucknall Ct. NW8 . . . . 3F **59**
(off Cunningham Pl.)
Huddart St. E3 . . . . . . 4B **66**
(Ackroyd Dr.)
E3 . . . . 4B **66**
(Weatherley Cl.)
Huddleston Cl. E2 . . . . 1E **65**
Huddlestone Rd. E7 . . . 1B **54**
NW2 . . . . 3D **43**
Huddleston Rd. N7 . . . 5E **33**
Hudson Cl. W12 . . . . . 1D **71**
Hudson Ct. E14 . . . . . 1C **94**
(off Maritime Quay)
Hudson's Pl. SW1 . . . . 5D **75**
Huggin Ct. EC4 . . . . . 4A **18**
Huggin Hill
EC4 . . . . 4A **18** (1E **77**)
Huggins Pl. SW2 . . . . 1B **118**
Hughan Rd. E15 . . . . . 2F **53**
Hugh Astor Ct. SE1 . . . 5E **25**
(off Keyworth St.)
Hugh Cubitt Ho. N1 . . . 1B **62**
(off Collier St.)
Hugh Dalton Av. SW6 . . 2B **86**
Hughenden Ho. NW8 . . 3A **60**
(off Jerome Cres.)
Hughenden Ter. E15 . . 1E **53**
Hughes Cl. N7 . . . . . . 2F **47**
Hughes Ho. E2 . . . . . . 2E **65**
(off Sceptre Ho.)
SE8 . . . . 2C **94**
(off Benbow St.)
SE17 . . . . 5D **77**
(off Peacock St.)
Hughes Mans. E1 . . . . 3C **64**
Hughes M. SW11 . . . . 3B **102**
Hughes Ter. E16 . . . . . 4B **68**
(off Clarkson Rd.)
SW9 . . . . 1D **105**
(off Styles Gdns.)
Hugh Gaitskell Cl.
SW6 . . . . 2B **86**
Hugh Gaitskell Ho.
N16 . . . . 4B **36**
SW6 . . . . 3C **86**
Hugh M. SW1 . . . . . . 5D **75**
Hugh Platt Ho. E2 . . . . 1D **65**
(off Patriot Sq.)
Hugh St. SW1 . . . . . . 5D **75**
Hugon Rd. SW6 . . . . . 1D **101**
Hugo Rd. N19 . . . . . . 1E **47**
Huguenot Pl. E1 . . . . . 4B **64**
SW18 . . . . 3E **101**
Huguenot Sq. SE15 . . . 1D **107**
Hullbridge M. N1 . . . . 5F **49**
Hull Cl. SE16 . . . . 3F **79**
Hull St. EC1 . . . . 2F **9** (2E **63**)
Hulme Pl.
SE1 . . . . 4A **26** (3E **77**)
Humber Dr. W10 . . . . . 3F **57**
Humber Rd. NW2 . . . . 4D **29**
SE3 . . . . 2B **96**
Humberstone Rd.
E13 . . . . 2E **69**
Humberton Cl. E9 . . . . 2A **52**
Humber Trad. Est.
NW2 . . . . 4D **29**

Humbolt Rd. W6 . . . . 2A **86**
Hume Ct. N1 . . . . 4D **49**
   (off Hawes St.)
Hume Ho. W11 . . . . 2F **71**
   (off Queensdale Cres.)
Hume Ter. E16 . . . . 4D **69**
Humphrey St. SE1 . . . . . 1B **92**
Hungerford Ho. SW1 . . . 2E **89**
   (off Churchill Gdns.)
Hungerford La. WC2. . . 1E **23**
   (not continuous)
Hungerford Rd. N7 . . . . 3F **47**
Hungerford St. E1 . . . . . 5D **65**
Hunsdon Rd. SE14 . . . . 3F **93**
Hunslett St. E2 . . . . 2E **65**
Hunstanton Ho. NW1 . . 4A **60**
   (off Cosway St.)
Hunt Cl. W11 . . . . 2F **71**
Hunter Cl.
  SE1 . . . . 5C **26** (4F **77**)
Hunter Ho. SE1 . . . . 4E **25**
   (off Lancaster St.)
  SW5 . . . . 1C **86**
   (off Old Brompton Rd.)
  SW8 . . . . 3F **89**
   (off Fount St.)
  WC1 . . . . 3E **7**
   (off Hunter St.)
Hunterian Mus., The . . 2A **16**
   (off Portugal St.)
Hunter Lodge W9 . . . . . 4C **58**
   (off Admiral Wlk.)
Hunters Cl. SW12 . . . . 1C **116**
Hunters Mdw. SE19 . . 4A **120**
Hunter St.
  WC1 . . . . 3E **7** (3A **62**)
Hunter Wlk. E13 . . . . . . 1C **68**
Huntingdon St. E16 . . . 5B **68**
  N1 . . . . 4B **48**
Huntingfield Rd.
  SW15 . . . . 2C **98**
Huntley St.
  WC1 . . . . 4A **6** (3E **61**)
Hunton St. E1 . . . . 4C **64**
Hunt's Cl. SE3 . . . . 5C **96**
Hunt's Ct.
  WC2 . . . . 5C **14** (1F **75**)
Hunts La. E15 . . . . 1E **67**
Huntsman St. SE17 . . . 5A **78**
Huntspill St. SW17 . . . 3E **115**
Hunts Slip Rd.
  SE21 . . . . 3A **120**
Huntsworth M.
  NW1 . . . . 3A **4** (3B **60**)
Hurdwick Pl. NW1 . . . . 1E **61**
   (off Hampstead Rd.)
Hurleston Ho. SE8 . . . . 1B **94**
Hurley Cres. SE16 . . . . 3F **79**
Hurley Ho. SE11. . . . . . 5D **77**
HURLINGHAM 1D **101**
Hurlingham Bus. Pk.
  SW6 . . . . 1C **100**
Hurlingham Club, The
  . . . . 1C **100**
Hurlingham Ct.
  SW6 . . . . 1B **100**
Hurlingham Gdns.
  SW6 . . . . 1B **100**
Hurlingham Retail Pk.
  SW6 . . . . 1D **101**

Hurlingham Rd.
  SW6 . . . . 5B **86**
Hurlingham Sq.
  SW6 . . . . 1C **100**
Hurlingham Stadium
  . . . . 1B **100**
Hurlock St. N5 . . . . 5D **35**
Huron Rd. SW17 . . . . . 2C **116**
Huron University 4F **73**
Hurren Cl. SE3 . . . . . . 1A **110**
Hurry Cl. E15 . . . . 4A **54**
Hurst Av. N6 . . . . 1E **33**
Hurstbourne Ho.
  SW15 . . . . 4B **98**
   (off Tangley Gro.)
Hurstbourne Rd.
  SE23 . . . . 1A **122**
Hurst Cl. NW11 . . . . . . 1D **31**
Hurst Cl. E6 . . . . 4F **69**
   (off Tollgate Rd.)
Hurstdene Gdns. N15. . 2A **36**
Hurst Ho. WC1 . . . . 1A **8**
   (off Penton Ri.)
Hurst St. SE24 . . . . . . 4D **105**
Hurstway Rd. W11 . . . . 1F **71**
Hurstway Wlk. W11 . . . 1F **71**
Husborne Ho. SE8 . . . . 5A **80**
   (off Chilton Gro.)
Huson Cl. NW3. . . . . . . 4A **46**
Hutchings St. E14 . . . . 3C **80**
Hutchings Wharf E14. . 3C **80**
   (off Hutchings St.)
Hutchins Cl. E15. . . . . . 4E **53**
Hutchinson Ho. NW3 . . 4B **46**
  SE14 . . . . 3E **93**
Hutton Cl. N4 . . . . 3B **34**
   (off Victoria Rd.)
Hutton St.
  EC4 . . . . 4C **16** (5D **63**)
Huxbear St. SE4. . . . . . 3B **108**
Huxley Ho. NW8 . . . . . . 3F **59**
   (off Fisherton St.)
Huxley Rd. E10. . . . . . . 4E **39**
Huxley St. W10 . . . . . . 2A **58**
Hyacinth Rd. SW15 . . . 1C **112**
HYDE, THE 1B **28**
Hyde, The NW9 . . . . 1B **28**
   (not continuous)
Hyde Cl. E13 . . . . 1C **68**
Hyde Cres. NW9. . . . . . 1A **28**
Hyde Est. Rd. NW9 . . . . 1B **28**
Hyde Farm M.
  SW12 . . . . 1F **117**
Hyde Ho. NW9 . . . . 1B **28**
Hyde Ind. Est., The
  NW9 . . . . 1B **28**
HYDE PARK CORNER
  . . . . 3D **75**
Hyde Pk. Cnr.
  W1 . . . . 3C **20** (3C **74**)
Hyde Pk. Cres. W2 . . . . 5A **60**
Hyde Pk. Gdns. W2 . . . 1F **73**
Hyde Pk. Gdns. M.
  W2 . . . . 1F **73**
   (not continuous)
Hyde Pk. Ga. SW7 . . . . 3E **73**
   (not continuous)
Hyde Pk. Ga. M.
  SW7 . . . . 3E **73**

Hyde Pk. Mans. NW1 . . 4A **60**
   (off Cabbell St.,
   not continuous)
Hyde Pk. Pl. W2 . . . . . . 1A **74**
Hyde Pk. Sq. W2 . . . . . 5A **60**
Hyde Pk. Sq. M. W2 . . 5A **60**
   (off Southwick Pl.)
Hyde Pk. St. W2 . . . . . . 5A **60**
Hyde Pk. Towers W2 . . 1E **73**
Hyderabad Way E15. . . 4A **54**
Hyde Rd. N1. . . . . 5A **50**
Hyde's Pl. N1 . . . . 4D **49**
Hyde St. SE8 . . . . 2C **94**
Hydethorpe Rd.
  SW12 . . . . 1E **117**
Hyde Va. SE10 . . . . 3E **95**
Hydra Bldg., The
  EC1 . . . . 2C **8**
Hyndewood SE23 . . . . 3F **121**
Hyndman St. SE15. . . . 2D **93**
Hyperion Ho. E3. . . . . . 1A **66**
   (off Arbery Rd.)
  SW2 . . . . 4B **104**
Hyson Rd. SE16. . . . . . 1D **93**
Hythe Ho. SE16 . . . . . . 3E **79**
   (off Swan Rd.)
  W6 . . . . 5E **71**
   (off Shepherd's Bush Rd.)
Hythe Rd. NW10 . . . . . 2B **56**
Hythe Rd. Ind. Est.
  NW10 . . . . 2C **56**

I

Ian Bowater Ct. N1. . . . 1C **10**
   (off East Rd.)
Ian Ct. SE23 . . . . 2E **121**
Ibberton Ho. SW8 . . . . 3B **90**
   (off Meadow Rd.)
  W14 . . . . 4A **72**
   (off Russell Rd.)
Ibbotson Av. E16 . . . . . 5B **68**
Ibbott St. E1 . . . . 3E **65**
Iberia Ho. N19 . . . . 2F **33**
Ibex Ho. E15. . . . . 2A **54**
   (off Forest La.)
Ibis Ct. SE8 . . . . 2B **94**
   (off Edward Pl.)
Ibsley Gdns. SW15 . . . 1C **112**
ICA Cinema 2C **22**
   (off Mall, The)
ICA Theatre 2C **22**
   (off Mall, The)
Iceland Rd. E3. . . . . 5C **52**
Ice Wharf Marina N1 . . 1A **62**
   (off New Wharf Rd.)
Ickburgh Est. E5. . . . . . 4D **37**
Ickburgh Rd. E5 . . . . . . 5D **37**
Icknield Ho. SW3. . . . . 1A **88**
   (off Cale St.)
Icon Apartments SE1 . . 5D **27**
   (off Cluny Pl.)
Ida St. E14 . . . . 5E **67**
   (not continuous)
Idlecombe Rd.
  SW17 . . . . 5C **116**
Idmiston Rd. E15. . . . . . 1B **54**
  SE27 . . . . 3E **119**
Idol La. EC3 . . . . 5D **19** (1A **78**)

Idonia St. SE8 . . . . 3C **94**
Iffley Rd. W6 . . . . 4D **71**
Ifield Rd. SW10 . . . . 2D **87**
Ifor Evans Pl. E1 . . . . . 3F **65**
Ightham Ho. SE17 . . . . 5A **78**
    (off Beckway St.)
Ilbert St. W10 . . . . 2F **57**
Ilchester Gdns. W2 . . . 1D **73**
Ilchester Pl. W14 . . . . . 4B **72**
Ildersly Gro. SE21 . . . 2F **119**
Ilderton Rd. SE16 . . . . 1E **93**
Ilderton Wharf SE15 . . . 2E **93**
    (off Rollins St.)
Ilex Rd. NW10 . . . . 3B **42**
Ilex Way SW16 . . . . . . 5C **118**
Ilford Ho. N1 . . . . 3F **49**
    (off Dove Rd.)
Ilfracombe Flats SE1 . . . 3A **26**
    (off Marshalsea Rd.)
Ilfracombe Rd.
  BR1: Brom 3B **124**
Iliffe St. SE17 . . . . 1D **91**
Iliffe Yd. SE17 . . . . 1D **91**
    (off Crampton St.)
Ilkeston Ct. E5 . . . . 1F **51**
    (off Overbury St.)
Ilkley Rd. E16 . . . . 4E **69**
Ilminster Gdns.
  SW11 . . . . 2A **102**
Ilsley Ct. SW8 . . . . 5E **89**
Imani Mans. SW11 . . . 5F **87**
IMAX Cinema
  . . . . 2B **8** (2C **76**)
Imber St. N1 . . . . 5F **49**
Imperial Av. N16 . . . . . . 1A **50**
Imperial College of Science,
  Technology & Medicine
  Imperial Coll. Rd. . . . 4F **73**
  Wilson House. 5A **60**
    (off Star La.)
Imperial Coll. Rd.
  SW7 . . . . 4F **73**
Imperial Ct. N6 . . . . 1E **33**
  NW8 . . . . 1A **60**
    (off Prince Albert Rd.)
  SE11 . . . . 1C **90**
Imperial Ho. E3 . . . . 2A **66**
    (off Grove Rd.)
  E14 . . . . 1B **80**
    (off Victory Pl.)
Imperial M. E6 . . . . 1F **69**
Imperial Pde. EC4 . . . . 3D **17**
    (off New Bri. St.)
Imperial Rd. SW6 . . . . 4D **87**
Imperial Sq. SW6 . . . . 4D **87**
Imperial War Mus.
  . . . . 5C **24** (4C **76**)
Imperial Wharf SW6. . . 5E **87**
Imre Cl. W12 . . . . 2D **71**
Inchmery Rd. SE6 . . . . 2D **123**
Independent Pl. E8. . . . 2B **50**
Independents Rd.
  SE3 . . . . 1B **110**
Inderwick Rd. N8 . . . . . 1B **34**
Indescon Ct. E14 . . . . . 3C **80**
India Pl. WC2 . . . . 4F **15**
India St. EC3 . . 3F **19** (5B **64**)
Indigo M. W12. . . . . . . 1D **71**
  N16 . . . . 5F **35**

Indus Rd. SE7 . . . . 3E **97**
Infirmary Ct. SW3 . . . . 2B **88**
    (off West Rd.)
Ingal Rd. E13 . . . . 3C **68**
Ingate Pl. SW8 . . . . . . 4D **89**
Ingatestone Rd.
  E12 . . . . 3E **41**
Ingelow Ho. W8 . . . . . . 3D **73**
    (off Holland St.)
Ingelow Rd. SW8 . . . . . 5D **89**
Ingersoll Rd. W12 . . . . 2D **71**
Ingestre Pl.
  W1 . . . . 3A **14** (5E **61**)
Ingestre Rd. E7 . . . . 1C **54**
  NW5 . . . . 1D **47**
Ingham Rd. NW6 . . . . . 1C **44**
Inglebert St.
  EC1 . . . . 1B **8** (2C **62**)
Ingleborough St.
  SW9 . . . . 5C **90**
Ingleby Rd. N7 . . . . 5A **34**
Inglefield Sq. E1 . . . . . 2D **79**
    (off Prusom St.)
Inglemere Rd. SE23 . . 3F **121**
Inglesham Wlk. E9. . . . 3B **52**
Ingleside Gro. SE3. . . . 2B **96**
Inglethorpe St. SW6 . . 4F **85**
Ingleton St. SW9 . . . . . 5C **90**
Inglewood Cl. E14 . . . . 5C **80**
Inglewood Rd. NW6. . . 2C **44**
Inglis St. SE5 . . . . 4D **91**
Ingoldisthorpe Gro.
  SE15 . . . . 2B **92**
Ingram Av. NW11 . . . . 2E **31**
Ingram Cl. SE11 . . . . . . 5B **76**
Ingram Ho. E3 . . . . 5A **52**
Ingrave St. SW11 . . . . 1F **101**
Ingrebourne Ho.
  BR1: Brom 5F **123**
    (off Brangbourne Rd.)
  NW8 . . . . 4F **59**
    (off Broadley St.)
Ingress St. W4 . . . . 1A **84**
Inigo Jones Rd. SE7 . . 3F **97**
Inigo Pl. WC2 . . . . 4D **15**
Inkerman Rd. NW5 . . . 3D **47**
Inkerman Ter. W8 . . . . . 4C **72**
    (off Allen St.)
Inman Rd. NW10 . . . . . 5A **42**
  SW18 . . . . 5E **101**
Inner Circ.
  NW1 . . . . 2B **4** (2C **60**)
Inner Pk. Rd. SW19 . . . 1F **113**
Inner Temple 4C **16**
Inner Temple Hall. 3B **16**
Inner Temple La.
  EC4 . . . . 3B **16** (5C **62**)
Innes Gdns. SW15 . . . 4D **99**
Innis Ho. SE17 . . . . . . 1A **92**
    (off East St.)
Inniskilling Rd. E13 . . . 1E **69**
Innis St. SE15 . . . . 3A **92**
Inn of Court &
  City Yeomanry Mus.
  . . . . 1A **16**
Innovation Cen., The
  E14 . . . . 3E **81**
    (off Marsh Wall)
Inskip Cl. E10. . . . . 4D **39**

Institute of Archaeology
  . . . . 3B **6**
    (off Gordon Sq.)
Institute of Classical Studies
  . . . . 3B **6**
    (off Gordon Sq.)
Institute of Contemporary Arts
  . . . . 2C **22**
Institute Pl. E8. . . . . . . 2D **51**
Integer Gdns. E11. . . . 2F **39**
International Bus. Pk.
  E15 . . . . 5F **53**
International Ho. E1. . . 5F **19**
    (off St Katharine's Way)
Inver Cl. E5. . . . . 4E **37**
Inver Ct. W2. . . . . 5D **59**
  W6 . . . . 4C **70**
Inverforth Cl. NW3 . . . 4E **31**
Invergarry Ho. NW6 . . . 1D **59**
    (off Carlton Va.)
Inverine Rd. SE7 . . . . . 1D **97**
Invermead Cl. W6 . . . . 4C **70**
Inverness Gdns. W8 . . 2C **72**
Inverness Gdns. W8 . . 2D **73**
Inverness M. W2 . . . . . 1D **73**
Inverness Pl. W2 . . . . . 1D **73**
Inverness St. NW1 . . . 5D **47**
Inverness Ter. W2 . . . . 5D **59**
Inverton Rd. SE15 . . . 2F **107**
Invicta Plaza
  SE1 . . . . 1D **25** (2D **77**)
Invicta Rd. SE3 . . . . . . 3C **96**
Invicta Sq. E3 . . . . 4C **66**
Inville Rd. SE17 . . . . . . 1F **91**
Inville Wlk. SE17 . . . . . 1F **91**
Inwen Ct. SE8. . . . . 1A **94**
Inwood Ct. NW1 . . . . . . 4E **47**
    (off Rochester Sq.)
Inworth St. SW11 . . . . 5A **88**
Inworth Wlk. N1 . . . . . . 5E **49**
    (off Popham St.)
Iona Cl. SE6 . . . . 5C **108**
Ion Ct. E2 . . . . 1C **64**
Ionian Bldg. E14 . . . . . 1A **80**
Ionian Ho. E1 . . . . 3F **65**
    (off Duckett St.)
Ion Sq. E2. . . . . 1C **64**
Ipsden Bldgs. SE1 . . . . 2C **24**
Ipswich Ho. SE4 . . . . . 3F **107**
Ireland Yd. EC4 . . . . . . 3E **17**
    (off St Andrew's Hill)
Irene Rd. SW6 . . . . 4C **86**
Ireton St. E3. . . . . 3C **66**
Iris Ct. SE14 . . . . 4E **93**
    (off Briant St.)
Iron Bri. Cl. NW10 . . . . 2A **42**
Iron Bri. Ho. NW1 . . . . 4B **46**
Iron Mill Pl. SW18. . . . 4D **101**
Iron Mill Rd. SW18 . . . 4D **101**
Ironmonger La.
  EC2 . . . . 3A **18** (5E **63**)
Ironmonger Pas. EC1. . 2A **10**
    (off Ironmonger Row)
Ironmonger Row
  EC1 . . . . 2A **10** (2E **63**)
Ironmonger Row Baths
  . . . . 2A **10**
    (off Ironmonger Row)
Ironmongers Pl. E14 . . 5C **80**
Ironside Cl. SE16 . . . . . 3F **79**

Ironside Ho. E9 . . . . 1A 52
Irvine Ho. N7 . . . . 3B 48
   (off Caledonian Rd.)
Irving Gro. SW9 . . . . 5B 90
Irving Ho. SE17 . . . . 1D 91
   (off Doddington Gro.)
Irving Mans. W14. . . . . . . 2A 86
   (off Queen's Club Gdns.)
Irving M. N1 . . . . 3E 49
Irving Rd. W14 . . . . 4F 71
Irving St.
  WC2 . . . . 5C 14 (1F 75)
Irving Way NW9 . . . . 1C 28
Irwell Est. SE16 . . . . 4E 79
Irwin Gdns. NW10 . . . . . . 5D 43
Isaac Way SE1 . . . . 3A 26
   (off Lant St.)
Isabella Ho. SE11 . . . . . . 1D 91
   (off Othello Cl.)
  W6 . . . . 1E 85
   (off Queen Caroline St.)
Isabella Rd. E9. . . . . 2E 51
Isabella St.
  SE1 . . . . 2D 25 (2D 77)
Isabel St. SW9 . . . . 4B 90
Isambard M. E14 . . . . 4E 81
Isambard Pl. SE16 . . . . . . 2E 79
Isel Way SE22 . . . . 3A 106
Isis Cl. SW15 . . . . 2E 99
Isis Ho. NW8 . . . . 3F 59
   (off Church St. Est.)
Isis St. SW18 . . . . 2E 115
Island Row E14 . . . . 5B 66
Islay Wlk. N1 . . . . 3E 49
   (off Douglas Rd. Sth.)
Isleden Ho. N1 . . . . 5E 49
   (off Prebend St.)
Isledon Rd. N7 . . . . 5C 34
ISLEDON VILLAGE 5C 34
Isley Ct. SW8 . . . . 5E 89
ISLINGTON 4D 49
Islington Grn. N1 . . . . . . 5D 49
Islington High St.
  N1 . . . . 1C 62
   (not continuous)
Islington Mus. 4D 49
Islington Pk. M. N1 . . . . . 4D 49
Islington Pk. St. N1 . . . . . 4C 48
Islington Tennis Cen.
  . . . . 3A 48
Islip St. NW5 . . . . 2E 47
Ismailia Rd. E7 . . . . 4D 55
Isom Cl. E13. . . . . 2D 69
Ivanhoe Ho. E3. . . . . 1A 66
   (off Grove Rd.)
Ivanhoe Rd. SE5. . . . . . . 1B 106
Ivatt Pl. W14 . . . . 1B 86
Iveagh Cl. E9 . . . . 5F 51
Iveagh Ct. E1 . . . . 3F 19
Iveagh Ho. SW9 . . . . 5D 91
  SW10 . . . . 3E 87
   (off King's Rd.)
Ive Farm Cl. E10 . . . . 4C 38
Ive Farm La. E10 . . . . 4C 38
Iveley Rd. SW4. . . . . 5E 89
Iverna Ct. W8 . . . . 4C 72
Iverna Gdns. W8 . . . . 4C 72
Iverson Rd. NW6 . . . . 3B 44
Ives Rd. E16. . . . . 4A 68
Ives St. SW3. . . . . 5A 74

Ivestor Ter. SE23 . . . . . . 5E 107
Ivimey St. E2 . . . . 2C 64
Ivinghoe Ho. N7 . . . . 2F 47
Ivor Ct. N8 . . . . 1A 34
  NW1 . . . . 3B 60
   (off Gloucester Pl.)
Ivories, The N1. . . . . 4E 49
   (off Northampton St.)
Ivor Pl. NW1 . . . . . . 4A 4 (3B 60)
Ivor St. NW1. . . . . 4E 47
Ivorydown
  BR1: Brom 4C 124
Ivory Ho. E1. . . . . 2B 78
Ivory Sq. SW11 . . . . 1E 101
Ivybridge Ct. NW1 . . . . . . 4D 47
   (off Lewis St.)
Ivybridge La.
  WC2 . . . . 5E 15 (1A 76)
Ivychurch La. SE17 . . . . . 1B 92
Ivy Cotts. E14 . . . . 1E 81
Ivy Ct. SE16 . . . . 1C 92
   (off Argyle Way)
Ivydale Rd. SE15 . . . . . . 1F 107
Ivyday Gro. SW16 . . . . . . 3B 118
Ivy Gdns. N8. . . . . 1A 34
Ivymount Rd.
  SE27 . . . . 3C 118
Ivy Rd. E16. . . . . 5C 68
  E17 . . . . 1C 38
  NW2 . . . . 1E 43
  SE4. . . . . 2B 108
  SW17 . . . . 5A 116
Ivy St. N1. . . . . 1A 64
Ixworth Pl. SW3 . . . . 1A 88

J

Jacana Ct. E1. . . . . 1B 78
   (off Star Pl.)
Jacaranda Gro. E8. . . . . . 4B 50
Jack Clow Rd. E15. . . . . . 1A 68
Jack Dash Ho. E14. . . . . . 3E 81
   (off Lawn Ho. Cl.)
Jack Dash Way E6 . . . . . . 3F 69
Jackman Ho. E1. . . . . 2D 79
   (off Watts St.)
Jackman M. NW10. . . . . . 5A 28
Jackman St. E8 . . . . 5D 51
Jackson Cl. E9 . . . . 4E 51
Jackson Ct. E7. . . . . 3D 55
Jackson Rd. N7 . . . . 1B 48
Jacksons La. N6. . . . . 2C 32
Jacksons Lane Theatre
  . . . . 1D 33
   (off Jacksons La.)
Jacks Pl. E1 . . . . 5F 11
   (off Corbet Pl.)
Jack Walker Ct. N5 . . . . . 1D 49
Jacobin Lodge N7 . . . . . . 2A 48
Jacobs Ho. E13 . . . . 2E 69
   (off New City Rd.)
Jacob St. SE1. . . . . 3C 78
Jacob's Well M.
  W1. . . . . 1C 12 (4C 60)
Jacotts Ho. W10. . . . . 3E 57
   (off Sutton Way)
Jacqueline Creft Ter.
  N6. . . . . 1C 32
   (off Grange Rd.)

Jade Cl. E16. . . . . 5F 69
  NW2 . . . . 2F 29
Jade Ter. NW6 . . . . 4E 45
Jaffray Pl. SE27 . . . . 4D 119
Jaggard Way SW12 . . . . . 5B 102
Jagger Ho. SW11. . . . . . . 4B 88
   (off Rosenau Rd.)
Jago Wlk. SE5 . . . . 3F 91
Jamaica Rd.
  SE1. . . . . 4F 27 (3B 78)
  SE16. . . . . 3B 78
Jamaica St. E1 . . . . 5E 65
James Allens School
  Swimming Pool 3A 106
James Anderson Ct.
  E2 . . . . 1A 64
   (off Kingsland Rd.)
James Av. NW2 . . . . 2E 43
James Boswell Cl.
  SW16 . . . . 4B 118
James Brine Ho.
  E2 . . . . 1F 11
   (off Ravenscroft St.)
James Campbell Ho.
  E2 . . . . 1E 65
   (off Old Ford Rd.)
James Cl. E13 . . . . 1C 68
  NW11 . . . . 1A 30
James Collins Cl.
  W9 . . . . 3B 58
James Ct. N1 . . . . 5E 49
   (off Raynor Pl.)
James Docherty Ho.
  E2 . . . . 1D 65
   (off Patriot Sq.)
James Hammett Ho.
  E2 . . . . 1F 11
   (off Ravenscroft St.)
James Ho. E1. . . . . 3A 66
   (off Solebay St.)
  SE16 . . . . 3F 79
   (off Wolfe Cres.)
James Joyce Wlk.
  SE24 . . . . 2D 105
James La. E10 . . . . 2E 39
  E11 . . . . 2F 39
James Lind Ho. SE8 . . . . . 5B 80
   (off Grove St.)
James Middleton Ho.
  E2 . . . . 2D 65
   (off Middleton St.)
Jameson Ct. E2 . . . . 1E 65
   (off Russia La.)
Jameson Ho. SE11. . . . . . 1B 90
   (off Glasshouse Wlk.)
Jameson Lodge N6 . . . . . 1E 33
Jameson St. W8. . . . . 2C 72
James Stewart Ho.
  NW6 . . . . 4B 44
James St.
  W1. . . . . 3C 12 (5C 60)
  WC2 . . . . 3E 15 (1A 76)
James Stroud Ho.
  SE11 . . . . 1E 91
   (off Bronti Cl.)
James Ter. SW14 . . . . . . 1A 98
   (off Church Path)
Jamestown Rd. NW1 . . . . 5D 47
Jamestown Way E14 . . . . 1F 81
Jamuna Cl. E14 . . . . 4A 66

Jane Austen Hall *E16*. . . **2D 83**
   (off Wesley Av.)
Jane Austen Ho.
  SW1. . . . . **1E 89**
   (off Churchill Gdns.)
Jane St. E1. . . . . **5D 65**
Janet Adegoke Leisure Cen.
  . . . . **1C 70**
Janet St. E14. . . . . **4C 80**
Janeway Pl. SE16. . . . . . . **3D 79**
Janeway St. SE16. . . . . . . **3C 78**
Jansen Wlk. SW11. . . . **1F 101**
Janson Cl. E15. . . . . **2A 54**
  NW10. . . . . **5A 28**
Janson Rd. E15. . . . . **2A 54**
Japan Cres. N4. . . . . **3B 34**
Jardine Rd. E1. . . . . **1F 79**
Jarman Ho. *E1*. **4E 65**
   (off Jubilee St.)
  SE16. . . . . **5F 79**
   (off Hawkstone Rd.)
Jarrett Cl. SW2. . . . . . . **1D 119**
Jarrow Rd. SE16. . . . . . . **5E 79**
Jarrow Way E9. . . . . **1B 52**
Jarvis Rd. SE22. . . . . . . **2A 106**
Jasmin Cl. SE12. . . . . . . **4B 110**
Jasmine Ct. SW19. . . . . **5C 114**
Jasmin Lodge *SW16*. . . **1D 93**
   (off Sherwood Gdns.)
Jason Ct. *SW9*. **4C 90**
   (off Southey Rd.)
  W1. . . . . **2C 12**
Jasper Pas. SE19. . . . . . **5B 120**
Jasper Rd. E16. . . . . **5F 69**
  SE19. . . . . **5B 120**
Jasper Wlk. N1. . . . . **1B 10**
Java Wharf *SE1*. **3B 78**
   (off Shad Thames)
Jay M. SW7. . . . . **3E 73**
Jean Darling Ho.
  SW10. . . . . **2F 87**
   (off Milman's St.)
Jean Ho. SW17. . . . . . . **5A 116**
Jean Pardies Ho. *E1*. . . **4E 65**
   (off Jubilee St.)
Jebb Av. SW2. . . . . **4A 104**
   (not continuous)
Jebb St. E3. . . . . **1C 66**
Jedburgh Rd. E13. . . . . . **2E 69**
Jedburgh St. SW11. . . . **2C 102**
Jeddo M. W12. . . . . **3B 70**
Jeddo Rd. W12. . . . . **3B 70**
Jefferson Bldg. E14. . . . . **3C 80**
Jeffrey Row SE12. . . . . **3D 111**
Jeffrey's Pl. NW1. . . . . . . **4E 47**
Jeffreys Rd. SW4. . . . . . . **5A 90**
Jeffrey's St. NW1. . . . . . . **4E 47**
Jeffreys Walk SW4. . . . . **5A 90**
Jeger Av. E2. . . . . **5B 50**
Jeken Rd. SE9. . . . . **2E 111**
Jelf Rd. SW2. . . . . **3C 104**
Jellicoe Ho. *E2*. **1C 64**
   (off Ropley St.)
  NW1. . . . . **3D 61**
Jellicoe Rd. E13. . . . . . . **3D 68**
Jemotts Ct. *SE14*. **2F 93**
   (off Myers La.)
Jenkinson Ho. *E2*. **2F 65**
   (off Usk St.)
Jenkins Rd. E13. . . . . . . **3D 69**

Jenner Av. W3. . . . . **4A 56**
Jenner Ho. SE3. . . . . **2A 96**
   (off Restell Cl.)
  WC1. . . . . **3E 7**
   (off Hunter St.)
Jenner Pl. SW13. . . . . . . **2D 85**
Jenner Rd. N16. . . . . **5B 36**
Jennifer Ho.
  SE11. . . . . **5C 76**
   (off Reedworth St.)
Jennifer Rd.
  BR1: Brom **3B 124**
Jenningsbury Ho.
  SW3. . . . . **1A 88**
   (off Cale St.)
Jennings Ho. *SE10*. . . . **1F 95**
   (off Old Woolwich Rd.)
Jennings Rd. SE22. . . . . **4B 106**
Jenny Hammond Cl.
  E11. . . . . **5B 40**
Jephson Ct. SW4. . . . . . . **5A 90**
Jephson Ho. *SE17*. . . . **2D 91**
   (off Doddington Gro.)
Jephson Rd. E7. . . . . **4E 55**
Jephson St. SE5. . . . . **4F 91**
Jephtha Rd.
  SW18. . . . . **4C 100**
Jepson Ho. *SW6*. **4D 87**
   (off Pearscroft Rd.)
Jerdan Pl. SW6. . . . . **3C 86**
Jeremiah St. E14. . . . . . . **5D 67**
Jeremy Bentham Ho.
  E2. . . . . **2C 64**
   (off Mansford St.)
Jermyn St.
  SW1. . . . . . . **1F 21** (2E 75)
Jermyn Street Theatre
  . . . . **5B 14**
   (off Jermyn St.)
Jerningham Ct. SE14. . . . **4A 94**
Jerningham Rd.
  SE14. . . . . **3A 94**
Jerome Cres. NW8. . . . . . **3A 60**
Jerome Ho. NW1. . . . . . . **4A 60**
   (off Lisson Gro.)
  SW7. . . . . **5F 73**
   (off Glendower Pl.)
Jerome St.
  E1. . . . . **5F 11** (3B 64)
Jerrard St. SE13. . . . . . **1D 109**
Jerrold St.
  N1. . . . . **1E 11** (1A 64)
Jersey Ho. N1. . . . . **3E 49**
Jersey Rd. E11. . . . . **3F 39**
  E16. . . . . **5E 69**
  N1. . . . . **3E 49**
Jersey St. E2. . . . . **2D 65**
Jerusalem Pas.
  EC1. . . . . . . **4D 9** (3D 63)
Jervis Bay Ho.
  E14. . . . . **5F 67**
   (off Blair St.)
Jervis Ct. *SE10*. **4E 95**
   (off Blissett St.)
  W1. . . . . **3E 13**
Jerviston Gdns.
  SW16. . . . . **5C 118**
Jerwood Space Art Gallery
  . . . . **3F 25**
Jessam Av. E5. . . . . **3D 37**

Jessel Ho. SW1. . . . . **5F 75**
   (off Page St.)
  WC1. . . . . **2D 7**
   (off Judd St.)
Jessel Mans. *W14*. **2A 86**
   (off Queen's Club Gdns.)
Jesse Rd. E10. . . . . **3E 39**
Jessica Rd. SW18. . . . . . **4E 101**
Jessie Blythe La.
  N19. . . . . **2A 34**
Jessie Duffett Ho.
  SE5. . . . . **3E 91**
   (off Pitman St.)
Jessie Wood Ct.
  SW9. . . . . **3C 90**
   (off Caldwell St.)
Jesson Ho. SE17. . . . . . . **5F 77**
   (off Orb St.)
Jessop Ct. N1. . . . . **1D 63**
Jessop Rd. SE24. . . . . . **2D 105**
Jessop Sq. *E14*. **2C 80**
   (off Heron Quay)
Jevington Way
  SE12. . . . . **1D 125**
Jewel House **5F 19**
   (in Tower of London)
Jewel Tower **5D 23**
   (off College M.)
Jewish Mus.
  Camden Town **5D 47**
Jewry St.
  EC3. . . . . . . **3F 19** (5B 64)
Jew's Row SW18. . . . . . **2D 101**
Jews' Wlk. SE26. . . . . . **4D 121**
Jeymer Av. NW2. . . . . . . **2D 43**
Jeypore Pas. SW18. . . . . **4E 101**
Jeypore Rd. SW18. . . . . **5E 101**
Jim Griffiths Ho.
  SW6. . . . . **2B 86**
   (off Clem Attlee Ct.)
  . . . . **2F 115**
Joan Bicknell Cen., The
  . . . . **2F 115**
Joan Cres. SE9. . . . . **5F 111**
Joanna Ho. *W6*. **1E 85**
   (off Queen Caroline St.)
Joan St. SE1. . . . **2D 25** (2D 77)
Jocelin Ho. *N1*. **5B 48**
   (off Barnsbury Est.)
Jocelyn St. SE15. . . . . . . **4C 92**
Jockey's Flds.
  WC1. . . . . . . **5A 8** (4B 62)
Jodane St. SE8. . . . . **5B 80**
Jodrell Rd. E3. . . . . **5B 52**
Joe Hunte Ct. SE27. . . . **5D 119**
Johanna St.
  SE1. . . . . . . **4B 24** (3C 76)
John Adam St.
  WC2. . . . . . . **5E 15** (1A 76)
John Aird Ct. *W2*. **4E 59**
   (off Howley Pl., not continuous)
John Archer Way
  SW18. . . . . **4F 101**
John Ashby Cl. SW2. . . . **4A 104**
John Baird Ct. SE26. . . . . **4E 121**
John Barker Ct. NW6. . . . **4A 44**
John Barnes Wlk.
  E15. . . . . **3B 54**
John Betts' Ho. W12. . . . **4B 70**
John Brent Ho. *SE8*. . . . **5F 79**
   (off Bush Rd.)

John Buck Ho.
NW10 . . . . 5B **42**
John Campbell Rd.
N16 . . . . 2A **50**
John Carpenter St.
EC4 . . . . . . 4D **17** (1D **77**)
John Cartwright Ho.
E2 . . . . *2D **65***
(off Old Bethnal Grn. Rd.)
John Drinkwater Cl.
E11 . . . . 2B **40**
John Fearon Wlk.
W10 . . . . *2A **58***
(off Dart St.)
John Felton Rd.
SE16 . . . . 3C **78**
John Fielden Ho. *E2* . . *2D **65***
(off Canrobert St.)
John Fisher St. E1 . . . . 1C **78**
John Harrison Way
SE10 . . . . 4B **82**
John Horner M. N1 . . . 1E **63**
John Islip St. SW1 . . . . 5F **75**
John Kennedy Ct. *N1* . . *3F **49***
(off Newington Grn. Rd.)
John Kennedy Ho.
SE16 . . . . *5F **79***
(off Rotherhithe Old Rd.)
John Knight Lodge
SW6 . . . . 3C **86**
John McDonald Ho.
E14 . . . . *4E **81***
(off Glengall Gro.)
John McKenna Wlk.
SE16 . . . . 4C **78**
John Masefield Ho.
N15 . . . . *1F **35***
(off Fladbury Rd.)
John Maurice Cl.
SE17 . . . . 5F **77**
John Orwell Sports Cen.
. . . . 2D **79**
John Parker Sq.
SW11 . . . . 1F **101**
John Parry Ct. *N1* *1A **64***
(off Hare Wlk.)
John Penn Ho. *SE14* . . . *3B **94***
(off Amersham Va.)
John Penn St. SE13 . . . 4D **95**
John Prince's St.
W1 . . . . 2E **13** (5D **61**)
John Pritchard Ho.
E1 . . . . *3C **64***
(off Buxton St.)
John Ratcliffe Ho.
NW6 . . . . *2C **58***
(off Chippenham Gdns.)
John Rennie Wlk. E1 . . 1D **79**
John Roll Way SE16. . . 4C **78**
John Ruskin St.
SE5. . . . . 3D **91**
John Scurr Ho. *E14* . . . *5A **66***
(off Ratcliffe La.)
John Silkin La. SE8 . . . 1F **93**
John's M.
WC1 . . . . 4A **8** (3B **62**)
John Smith Av.
SW6 . . . . 3B **86**
John Smith M. E14 . . . 1F **81**
Johnson Cl. E8 . . . . . . 5C **50**

Johnson Ho. *E2* *2C **64***
(off Roberta St.)
NW1 . . . . *1E **61***
(off Cranleigh St.)
NW3 . . . . *4B **46***
(off Adelaide Rd.)
SW1 . . . . 5C **74**
(off Cundy St.)
SW8 . . . . 3F **89**
(off Wandsworth Rd.)
Johnson Lodge *W9* . . . *4C **58***
(off Admiral Wlk.)
Johnson Mans. *W14* . . *2A **86***
(off Queen's Club Gdns.)
Johnson's Ct. EC4 . . . . 5C **62**
Johnson's Pl. SW1 . . . 1E **89**
Johnson St. E1 . . . . . . 1E **79**
John Spencer Sq. N1 . . 3D **49**
John's Pl. E1 . . . . 5D **65**
Johnston Cl. SW9 . . . . 4B **90**
Johnstone Ho. *SE13*. . . *1F **109***
(off Belmont Hill)
Johnston Ter. NW2 . . . 5F **29**
John Strachey Ho.
SW6 . . . . *2B **86***
(off Clem Attlee Ct.)
John St. E15. . . . . 5B **54**
WC1 . . . . 4A **8** (3B **62**)
John Strype St. E10. . . 3D **39**
John Trundle Ct. *EC2* . . 5F **9**
John Trundle Highwalk
EC2 . . . . *5F **9***
(off Beech St.)
John Tucker Ho. *E14* . . *4C **80***
(off Mellish St.)
John Wesley Highwalk
EC2 . . . . *1F **17***
(off Barbican)
John Wheatley Ho.
SW6 . . . . *2B **86***
(off Clem Attlee Ct.)
John Williams Cl.
SE14 . . . . 2F **93**
John Woolley Cl.
SE13 . . . . 2A **110**
Joiners Arms Yd.
SE5 . . . . 4F **91**
Joiners Pl. N5. . . . . . . 1F **49**
Joiner St.
SE1 . . . . 2C **26** (2F **77**)
Joiners Yd. *N1* *1E **7***
(off Caledonia St.)
Jonathan St. SE11 . . . 1B **90**
Jones Ho. E14 . . . . . . 5F **67**
(off Blair St.)
Jones M. SW15 . . . . . 2A **100**
Jones Rd. E13 . . . . . . 3D **69**
Jones St.
W1. . . . . 5D **13** (1D **75**)
Jonson Ho. *SE1* *5C **26***
(off Burbage Cl.)
Jordan Ct. SW15 . . . . 2F **99**
Jordan Ho. *N1* *5F **49***
(off Colville Est.)
SE4 . . . . *2F **107***
(off St Norbert Rd.)
Jordans Ho. *NW8* *3F **59***
(off Capland St.)
Joscoyne Ho. *E1* *5D **65***
(off Philpot St.)

Joseph Conrad Ho.
SW1 . . . . *5E **75***
(off Tachbrook St.)
Joseph Ct. N16. . . . . . *1A **36***
(off Amhurst Pk.)
Joseph Hardcastle Cl.
SE14 . . . . 3F **93**
Josephine Av. SW2 . . . 3B **104**
Joseph Irwin Ho. *E14*. . *1B **80***
(off Gill St.)
Joseph Lister Ct. E7. . . 4C **54**
Joseph Powell Cl.
SW12 . . . . 4E **103**
Joseph Priestley Ho.
E2. . . . . *2D **65***
(off Canrobert St.)
Joseph Ray Rd. E11. . . 4A **40**
Joseph St. E3. . . . . . . 3B **66**
Joseph Trotter Cl. EC1. . 2C **8**
Joshua St. E14 . . . . . . 5E **67**
Joslings Cl. W12 . . . . . 1C **70**
Josseline Ct. *E3* *1A **66***
(off Ford St.)
Joubert St. SW11. . . . . 5B **88**
Jowett St. SE15 . . . . . 3B **92**
Jowitt Ho. *E2* *2F **65***
(off Morpeth St.)
Joyce Page Cl. SE7 . . . 2F **97**
Joyce Wlk. SW2. . . . . . 4C **104**
Jubb Powell Ho. N15. . . 1A **36**
Jubilee, The SE10 . . . . 3D **95**
Jubilee Bldgs. NW8 . . . 5F **45**
Jubilee Cl. NW9. . . . . . 1A **28**
Jubilee Cres. E14. . . . . 4E **81**
Jubilee Hall Sports Cen.
. . . . 4E **15**
(off Tavistock St.)
Jubilee Ho. *SE11*. . . . *5C **76***
(off Reedworth St.)
WC1 . . . . 3F **7**
Jubilee Mans. *E1*. *5E **65***
(off Jubilee St.)
Jubilee Mkt. WC2. . . . . 4E **15**
Jubilee Pl. SW3 . . . . . 1A **88**
Jubilee Pl. Shop. Mall
E14. . . . . *2D **81***
(off Bank St.)
Jubilee Sports Cen. & Baths
. . . . 2B **58**
Jubilee St. E1. . . . . . . 5E **65**
Jubilee Walkway
SE1 . . . . 5E **17** (1D **77**)
Jubilee Yd. SE1 . . . . . . 3F **27**
Judd St. WC1 . . . 2D **7** (2A **62**)
Jude Ct. E16. . . . . 5B **68**
Judges Wlk. NW3. . . . . 5E **31**
Juer Ho. *SW11*. *3A **88***
(off Juer St.)
Juer St. SW11 . . . . . . 3A **88**
Julia Ct. E17 . . . . 1D **39**
Julia Garfield M. E16 . . 2D **83**
(not continuous)
Julian Ho. SE21 . . . . . 4A **120**
Julian Pl. E14 . . . . 1D **95**
Julian Tayler Path
SE23 . . . . 2D **121**
Julia St. NW5 . . . . 1C **46**
Juliet Ho. *N1* *1A **64***
(off Arden Est.)
Juliette Rd. E13 . . . . . 1C **68**

Julius Nyerere Cl.
  N1 . . . . 5B 48
    (off Copenhagen St.)
Junction App. SE13 . . . 1E 109
  SW11 . . . . 1A 102
Junction Av. NW10 . . . . 3E 57
Junction M. W2 . . . . . . 5A 60
Junction Pl. W2 . . . . . . 5F 59
    (off Praed St.)
Junction Rd. E13 . . . . . 1D 69
  N19 . . . . 1E 47
Juniper Cl. W8 . . . . . . 4D 73
    (off St Mary's Pl.)
Juniper Cres. NW1 . . . . 4C 46
Juniper Ho. SE14 . . . . . 3E 93
  W10 . . . . 3A 58
    (off Fourth Av.)
Juniper St. E1 . . . . 1E 79
Juno Ct. SW9 . . . . 3C 90
    (off Caldwell St.)
Juno Way SE14 . . . . . . 2F 93
Juno Way Ind. Est.
  SE14 . . . . 2F 93
Jupiter Cl. SW9 . . . . . . 3C 90
    (off Caldwell St.)
Jupiter Ho. E14 . . . . . . 1D 95
    (off St Davids Sq.)
Jupiter Way N7 . . . . . . 3B 48
Jupp Rd. E15 . . . . 4F 53
Jupp Rd. W. E15 . . . . . 5F 53
Jura Ho. SE16 . . . . 5F 79
    (off Plough Way)
Jurston Ct. SE1 . . . . . . 4C 24
Justice Wlk. SW3 . . . . . 2A 88
Justines Pl. E2 . . . . . . 2F 65
Jutland Cl. N19 . . . . . . 3A 34
Jutland Ho. SE5 . . . . . . 5E 91
Jutland Rd. E13 . . . . . . 3C 68
  SE6 . . . . 5E 109
Juxon Ho. EC4 . . . . . . 3E 17
    (off St Paul's Chyd.)
Juxon St. SE11 . . . . . . 5B 76
JVC Bus. Pk. NW2 . . . . 3C 28

K

Kambala Rd. SW11 . . . 1F 101
Kangley Bri. Rd.
  SE26 . . . . 5B 122
Kangley Bus. Cen.
  SE26 . . . . 5B 122
Karanjia Ct. NW2 . . . . . 3E 43
Kara Way NW2 . . . . . . 1F 43
Karen Ter. E11 . . . . . . 4B 40
Kashmir Rd. SE7 . . . . . 3F 97
Kassala Rd. SW11 . . . . 4B 88
Katherine Cl. SE16 . . . . 2F 79
Katherine Ct. SE23 . . . . 1D 121
Katherine Gdns.
  SE9 . . . . 2F 111
Katherine Rd. E6 . . . . . 2E 55
  E7 . . . . 2E 55
Katherine Sq. W11 . . . . 2A 72
Kathleen Godfree Ct.
  SW19 . . . . 5C 114
Kathleen Rd. SW11 . . . 1B 102
Kay Rd. SW9 . . . . 5A 90
Kay St. E2 . . . . 1C 64
  E15 . . . . 4F 53

Kean Ho. SE17 . . . . . . 2D 91
Kean St.
  WC2 . . . . 3F 15 (5B 62)
Keats Av. E16 . . . . 2D 83
Keats Cl. E11 . . . . 1D 41
  NW3 . . . . 1A 46
  SE1 . . . . 5B 78
  SW19 . . . . 5F 115
Keats Est. N16 . . . . . . 4B 36
    (off Kyverdale Rd.)
Keats Gro. NW3 . . . . . 1A 46
Keats House 1A 46
Keats Ho. E2 . . . . 2E 65
    (off Roman Rd.)
  SE5 . . . . 3E 91
    (off Elmington Est.)
  SW1 . . . . 2E 89
    (off Churchill Gdns.)
Keats Pl. EC2 . . . . 1B 18
    (off Moorfields)
Kebbell Ter. E7 . . . . . . 2D 55
    (off Claremont Rd.)
Keble Pl. SW13 . . . . . . 2D 85
Keble St. SW17 . . . . . . 4E 115
Kedge Ho. E14 . . . . . . 4C 80
    (off Tiller Rd.)
Kedleston Wlk. E2 . . . . 2D 65
Keedonwood Rd.
  BR1: Brom 5A 124
Keel Cl. SE16 . . . . 2F 79
Keel Ct. E14 . . . . 1F 81
    (off Newport Av.)
Keeley St.
  WC2 . . . . 3F 15 (5B 62)
Keeling Ho. E2 . . . . . . 1D 65
    (off Claredale St.)
Keeling Rd. SE9 . . . . . 3F 111
Keens Cl. SW16 . . . . . 5F 117
Keen's Yd. N1 . . . . 3D 49
Keep, The SE3 . . . . . . 5C 96
Keepier Wharf E14 . . . . 1F 79
    (off Narrow St.)
Keeton's Rd. SE16 . . . . 4D 79
    (not continuous)
Keevil Dr. SW19 . . . . . 5F 99
Keighley Cl. N7 . . . . . . 2A 48
Keildon Rd. SW11 . . . . 2B 102
Keir, The SW19 . . . . . . 5E 113
Keir Hardie Ct.
  NW10 . . . . 4B 42
Keir Hardie Est. E5 . . . 3D 37
Keir Hardie Ho. N19 . . . 2F 33
  W6 . . . . 2F 85
    (off Fulham Pal. Rd.)
Keith Connor Cl.
  SW8 . . . . 1D 103
Keith Gro. W12 . . . . . . 3C 70
Keith Ho. NW6 . . . . . . 1D 59
    (off Carlton Va.)
Kelbrook Rd. SE3 . . . . 5F 97
Kelby Ho. N7 . . . . 3B 48
    (off Sutterton St.)
Kelceda Cl. NW2 . . . . . 4C 28
Kelfield Ct. W10 . . . . . 5F 57
Kelfield Gdns. W10 . . . 5F 57
Kelfield M. W10 . . . . . . 5F 57
Kelland Rd. E13 . . . . . 3C 68
Kellaway Rd. SE3 . . . . 5F 97
Keller Cres. E12 . . . . . 1F 55
Kellerton Rd. SE13 . . . 3A 110

Kellet Ho's. WC1 . . . . . 2E 7
    (off Tankerton St.)
Kellett Ho. N1 . . . . 5A 50
    (off Colville Est.)
Kellett Rd. SW2 . . . . . . 2C 104
Kellino St. SW17 . . . . . 4B 116
Kellow Ho. SE1 . . . . . . 3B 26
    (off Tennis St.)
Kell St. SE1 . . . . . 5E 25 (4D 77)
Kelly Av. SE15 . . . . . . 3B 92
Kelly Cl. NW10 . . . . . . 5A 28
Kelly Ct. E14 . . . . 1C 80
    (off Garford St.)
Kelly M. W9 . . . . 3B 58
Kelly St. NW1 . . . . 3D 47
Kelman Cl. SW4 . . . . . 5F 89
Kelmore Gro. SE22 . . . 2C 106
Kelmscott Gdns.
  W12 . . . . 4C 70
Kelmscott Leisure Cen.
  . . . . 1B 38
Kelmscott Rd.
  SW11 . . . . 3A 102
Kelross Pas. N5 . . . . . 1E 49
Kelross Rd. N5 . . . . . . 1E 49
Kelsall Cl. SE3 . . . . . . 5D 97
Kelsey St. E2 . . . . 3C 64
Kelson Ho. E14 . . . . . . 4E 81
Kelvedon Ho. SW8 . . . . 4A 90
Kelvedon Rd. SW6 . . . . 3B 86
Kelvin Ct. W11 . . . . . . 1C 72
Kelvin Gro. SE26 . . . . . 3D 121
Kelvingrove Rd.
  SE15 . . . . 3F 107
Kelvin Rd. N5 . . . . 1E 49
Kember St. N1 . . . . . . 4B 48
Kemble Ho. SW9 . . . . . 1D 105
    (off Barrington Rd.)
Kemble Rd. SE23 . . . . 1F 121
Kemble St.
  WC2 . . . . 3F 15 (5B 62)
Kemerton Rd. SE5 . . . . 1E 105
Kemeys St. E9 . . . . . . 2A 52
Kemp Ct. SW8 . . . . . . 3A 90
    (off Hartington Rd.)
Kempe Ho. SE1 . . . . . . 4F 77
    (off Burge St.)
Kempe Rd. NW6 . . . . . 1F 57
Kemp Ho. E2 . . . . 1F 65
    (off Sewardstone Rd.)
  W1 . . . . 4B 14
    (off Berwick St.)
Kempis Way SE22 . . . . 3A 106
Kemplay Rd. NW3 . . . . 1F 45
Kemps Ct. W1 . . . . . . 3B 14
    (off Hopkins St.)
Kemps Dr. E14 . . . . . . 1C 80
Kempsford Gdns.
  SW5 . . . . 1C 86
Kempsford Rd. SE11 . . 5C 76
    (not continuous)
Kemps Gdns. SE13 . . . 3E 109
Kempson Rd. SW6 . . . . 4C 86
Kempthorne Rd. SE8 . . 5B 80
Kempton Ct. E1 . . . . . . 4D 65
Kemsing Ho. SE1 . . . . . 4C 26
    (off Long La.)
Kemsing Rd. SE10 . . . . 1C 96
Kemsley SE13 . . . . 3D 109

Kenbrook Ho. W14 . . . . . 4B 72
Kenbury Gdns. SE5. . . . . 5E 91
Kenbury Mans. SE5 . . . . 5E 91
(off Kenbury St.)
Kenbury St. SE5 . . . . . . 5E 91
Kenchester Cl. SW8. . . 3A 90
Kendal NW1 . . . . 1E 5
(off Augustus St.)
Kendal Cl. SW9. . . . . . . 3D 91
Kendale Rd.
BR1: Brom 5A 124
Kendal Ho. E9. . . . . 5E 51
N1. . . . . 1B 62
(off Priory Grn. Est.)
Kendall Pl.
W1 . . . . 1B 12 (4C 60)
Kendal M. SW15 . . . . . 3B 100
Kendal Rd. NW10 . . . . . 1C 42
Kendal Steps W2 . . . . . 5A 60
(off St George's Flds.)
Kendal St. W2 . . . . 5A 60
Kender Est. SE14 . . . . . 4E 93
(off Queen's Rd.)
Kender St. SE14 . . . . . . 3E 93
Kendoa Rd. SW4 . . . . . 2F 103
Kendon Cl. E11 . . . . 1D 41
Kendrick Ct. SE15 . . . . . 4D 93
(off Woods Rd.)
Kendrick M. SW7 . . . . . 5F 73
Kendrick Pl. SW7 . . . . . 5F 73
Kenilford Rd. SW12 . . . 5D 103
Kenilworth Av.
SW19 . . . . 5C 114
Kenilworth Rd. E3 . . . . . 1A 66
NW6 . . . . 5B 44
Kenley Wlk. W11 . . . . . 1A 72
Kenlor Rd. SW17 . . . . . 5F 115
Kenmont Gdns.
NW10 . . . . 2D 57
Kenmure Rd. E8 . . . . . . 2D 51
Kenmure Yd. E8 . . . . . . 2D 51
Kennacraig Cl. E16 . . . . 2C 82
Kennard Ho. SW11 . . . . 5C 88
Kennard Rd. E15 . . . . . . 4F 53
Kennard St. SW11 . . . . 4C 88
Kennedy Cl. E13 . . . . . . 1C 68
Kennedy Cox Ho.
E16 . . . . 4B 68
(off Burke St.)
Kennedy Ho. SE11 . . . . 1B 90
(off Vauxhall Wlk.)
Kennedy Wlk. SE17 . . . 5F 77
(off Elsted St.)
Kennet Cl. SW11 . . . . . 2F 101
Kennet Ct. W9 . . . . 4C 58
(off Elmfield Way)
Kenneth Campbell Ho.
NW8 . . . . 3F 59
(off Orchardson St.)
Kenneth Ct. SE11 . . . . . 5C 76
Kenneth Cres. NW2 . . . 2D 43
Kennet Ho. NW8 . . . . . 3F 59
(off Church St. Est.)
Kenneth Younger Ho.
SW6 . . . . 2B 86
(off Clem Attlee Ct.)
Kennet Rd. W9 . . . . 3B 58
Kennet St. E1 . . . . 2C 78
Kennett Wharf La.
EC4 . . . . 4A 18

Kenninghall Rd. E5 . . . . 5C 36
Kenning Ho. N1 . . . . . . 5A 50
(off Colville Est.)
Kenning St. SE16 . . . . . 3E 79
Kennings Way
SE11 . . . . 1C 90
KENNINGTON 2C 90
Kennington Grn.
SE11 . . . . 1C 90
Kennington Gro.
SE11 . . . . 2B 90
Kennington La. SE11 . . 1B 90
KENNINGTON OVAL . . 2C 90
Kennington Oval
SE11 . . . . 2B 90
Kennington Pal. Ct.
SE11 . . . . 1C 90
(off Sancroft St.)
Kennington Pk. Gdns.
SE11 . . . . 2D 91
Kennington Pk. Ho.
SE11 . . . . 1C 90
(off Kennington Pk. Pl.)
Kennington Pk. Pl.
SE11 . . . . 2C 90
Kennington Pk. Rd.
SE11 . . . . 2C 90
Kennington Rd.
SE11 . . . . . 5B 24 (4C 76)
SE1 . . . . . . 5B 24 (4C 76)
Kemistoun Ho.
NW5 . . . . 2E 47
Kennoldes SE21 . . . . . 2F 119
(off Croxted Rd.)
Kennyland Ct. NW4 . . . 1D 29
(off Hendon Way)
Kenrick Pl.
W1 . . . . 1B 12 (4C 60)
KENSAL GREEN 2E 57
Kensal Ho. W10 . . . . . . 3F 57
(off Ladbroke Gro.)
Kensal Rd. W10 . . . . . . 3A 58
KENSAL RISE 1F 57
Kensal Rd. W10 . . . . . . 3A 58
KENSAL TOWN 3A 58
Kensal Wharf W10 . . . . 3F 57
KENSINGTON 3D 73
Kensington Arc. W8 . . . 3D 73
(off Kensington High St.)
Kensington Cen.
W14 . . . . 5A 72
(not continuous)
Kensington Chu. Ct.
W8 . . . . 3D 73
Kensington Chu. St.
W8 . . . . 2C 72
Kensington Chu. Wlk.
W8 . . . . 3D 73
(not continuous)
Kensington Ct. SE16. . . 2F 79
(off King & Queen Wharf)
W8 . . . . 3D 73
Kensington Ct. Gdns.
W8 . . . . 4D 73
(off Kensington Ct. Pl.)
Kensington Ct. M.
W8 . . . . 4D 73
(off Kensington Ct. Pl.)
Kensington Ct. Pl.
W8 . . . . 4D 73
Kensington Gardens . . . 2E 73

Kensington Gdns. Sq.
W2 . . . . 5D 59
(not continuous)
Kensington Ga. W8 . . . . 4E 73
Kensington Gore
SW7 . . . . 3E 73
Kensington Hall Gdns.
W14 . . . . 1B 86
Kensington Hgts. W8 . . 2C 72
Kensington High St.
W8 . . . . 4B 72
W14 . . . . 4B 72
Kensington Ho. W14 . . . 3F 71
Kensington Mall W8 . . . 2C 72
Kensington Mans.
SW5 . . . . 1C 86
(off Trebovir Rd.,
not continuous)
Kensington Palace 3D 73
Kensington Pal. Gdns.
W8 . . . . 2D 73
Kensington Pk. Gdns.
W11 . . . . 1B 72
Kensington Pk. M.
W11 . . . . 5B 58
Kensington Pk. Rd.
W11 . . . . 5B 58
Kensington Pl. W8. . . . . 2C 72
Kensington Rd. SW7 . . . 3D 73
W8 . . . . 3D 73
Kensington Sports Cen. . 1A 72
Kensington Sq. W8 . . . . 4D 73
Kensington Village
W14 . . . . 5B 72
Kensington W. W14 . . . 5A 72
Kensworth Ho. EC1 . . . . 2C 10
(off Cranwood St.)
Kent Ct. E2 . . . . 1B 64
Kent Ho. SE1 . . . . 1B 92
SW1 . . . . 1F 89
(off Aylesford St.)
W4 . . . . 1A 84
(off Devonshire St.)
Kent Ho. La.
BR3: Beck. 5A 122
Kent Ho. Rd. SE26. . . . 5A 122
Kentish Bldgs.
SE1. . . . . 2B 26 (2F 77)
KENTISH TOWN 2D 47
Kentish Town Forum . . . 2D 47
Kentish Town Ind. Est.
NW5 . . . . 2D 47
Kentish Town Rd.
NW1 . . . . 4D 47
NW5 . . . . 4D 47
Kentish Town Sports Cen.
. . . . 3D 47
Kentmere Ho. SE15 . . . 2E 93
Kenton Cl. SE26. . . . . . 4A 122
(off Adamsrill Rd.)
W14 . . . . 4B 72
Kenton Ho. E1 . . . . 3E 65
(off Mantus Cl.)
Kenton Rd. E9. . . . . 3F 51
Kenton St.
WC1. . . . . . . 3D 7 (3A 62)
Kent Pk. Ind. Est.
SE15. . . . . 2D 93
Kent Pas. NW1. . . . . . . 3B 60

Kent St. E2 . . . . 1B 64
E13 . . . . 2E 69
Kent Ter. NW1 . . . . 2A 60
Kent Wlk. SW9 . . . . 2D 105
Kentwell Cl. SE4 . . . . . . 2A 108
Kent Wharf SE8 . . . . . . 3D 95
    (off Creekside)
Kentwode Grn. SW13 . . . 3C 84
Kent Yd. SW7 . . . . 3A 74
Kenward Rd. SE9 . . . . . . 3E 111
Kenward Way SW11 . . . . 5C 88
Kenway Rd. SW5 . . . . . . 5D 73
Ken Wilson Ho. E2 . . . . . 1C 64
    (off Pritchards Rd.)
Kenwood Cl. NW3 . . . . . 3F 31
Kenwood House 3A 32
Kenwood Ho. SW9 . . . . . 2D 105
Kenwood Ho. N6 . . . . . . 1B 32
Kenworthy Rd. E9 . . . . . 2A 52
Kenrick Ho. N1 . . . . 5B 48
    (off Barnsbury Est.)
Kenwyn Dr. NW2 . . . . . . 4A 28
Kenwyn Rd. SW4 . . . . . . 2F 103
Kenya Rd. SE7 . . . . 3F 97
Kenyon Mans. W14 . . . . 2A 86
    (off Queen's Club Gdns.)
Kenyon St. SW6 . . . . . . 4F 85
Keogh Rd. E15 . . . . 3A 54
Kepler Ho. SE10 . . . . . . 1B 96
    (off Armitage Rd.)
Kepler Rd. SW4 . . . . . . 2A 104
Keppel Ho. SE8 . . . . 1B 94
Keppel Row
  SE1 . . . . 2F 25 (2E 77)
Keppel St.
  WC1 . . . . 5C 6 (4F 61)
Kerbela St. E2 . . . . 3C 64
Kerbey St. E14 . . . . 5D 67
Kerfield Cres. SE5 . . . . . 4F 91
Kerfield Pl. SE5 . . . . 4F 91
Kerridge Ct. N1 . . . . 3A 50
    (off Balls Pond Rd.)
Kerrington Ct. W12 . . . . 3E 71
    (off Uxbridge Rd.)
Kerrison Rd. E15 . . . . . . 5F 53
  SW11 . . . . 1A 102
Kerry N7 . . . . 3A 48
Kerry Cl. E16 . . . . 5D 69
Kerry Ho. E1 . . . . 5E 65
    (off Sidney St.)
Kerry Path SE14 . . . . . . 2B 94
Kerry Rd. SE14 . . . . 2B 94
Kersey Gdns. SE9 . . . . . 4F 125
Kersfield Ho. SW15 . . . . 4F 99
Kersfield Rd. SW15 . . . . 4F 99
Kershaw Cl. SW18 . . . . . 4F 101
Kersley M. SW11 . . . . . . 4B 88
Kersley Rd. N16 . . . . . . 4A 36
Kersley St. SW11 . . . . . 5B 88
Kerswell Cl. N15 . . . . . . 1A 36
Kerwick Cl. N7 . . . . 4A 48
Keslake Mans. NW10 . . . 1F 57
    (off Station Rd.)
Keslake Rd. NW6 . . . . . . 1F 57
Keston Ho. SE17 . . . . . . 1A 92
    (off Kinglake St.)
Keston Rd. SE15 . . . . . . 1C 106
Kestrel Av. E6 . . . . 4F 69
  SE24 . . . . 3D 105
Kestrel Cl. NW10 . . . . . . 2A 42

Kestrel Ho. EC1 . . . . . . 1F 9
    (off Pickard St.)
Kestrel Pl. SE14 . . . . . . 2A 94
Keswick Av. SW15 . . . . . 5A 112
Keswick Ct. SE6 . . . . . . 1B 124
SE13 . . . . 3D 109
Keswick Ho. SE5 . . . . . . 5E 91
Keswick Rd. SW15 . . . . . 3A 100
Kett Gdns. SW2 . . . . . . 3B 104
Kettlebaston Rd. E10 . . . 3B 38
Kettleby Ho. SW9 . . . . . 1D 105
    (off Barrington Rd.)
Ketton Ho. W10 . . . . . . 3E 57
    (off Sutton Way)
Kevan Ho. SE5 . . . . 3E 91
Keybridge Ho. SW8 . . . . 2A 90
    (off Miles St.)
Key Cl. E1 . . . . 3E 65
Keyes Ho. SW1 . . . . 1F 89
    (off Dolphin Sq.)
Keyes Rd. NW2 . . . . 2F 43
Key Ho. SE11 . . . . 2C 90
Keymer Rd. SW2 . . . . . . 2B 118
Keynsham Gdns.
  SE9 . . . . 3F 111
Keynsham Rd. SE9 . . . . . 3F 111
Keyse Rd. SE1 . . . . 4B 78
Keystone Cres.
  N1 . . . . 1E 7 (1A 62)
Keyworth Cl. E5 . . . . . . 1A 52
Keyworth Pl. SE1 . . . . . 5E 25
Keyworth St.
  SE1 . . . . 5E 25 (4D 77)
Kezia St. SE8 . . . . 1A 94
Khama Rd. SW17 . . . . . . 4A 116
Khartoum Rd. E13 . . . . . 2D 69
  SW17 . . . . 4F 115
Khyber Rd. SW11 . . . . . 5A 88
Kibworth St. SW8 . . . . . 3B 90
KIDBROOKE 5D 97
Kidbrooke Est. SE3 . . . . 1E 111
Kidbrooke Gdns. SE3 . . . 5C 96
Kidbrooke Green
  Nature Reserve . . . 1E 111
Kidbrooke Gro. SE3 . . . . 4C 96
Kidbrooke La. SE9 . . . . . 2F 111
Kidbrooke Pk. Cl.
  SE3 . . . . 4D 97
Kidbrooke Pk. Rd.
  SE3 . . . . 4D 97
Kidbrooke Way SE3 . . . . 5D 97
Kidderpore Av. NW3 . . . 1C 44
Kidderpore Gdns.
  NW3 . . . . 1C 44
Kierbeck Bus. Complex
  E16 . . . . 3D 83
Kiffen St.
  EC2 . . . . 3C 10 (3F 63)
Kilbrennan Ho. E14 . . . . 5E 67
    (off Findhorn St.)
KILBURN 1B 58
Kilburn Bri. NW6 . . . . . . 5C 44
Kilburn Ga. NW6 . . . . . . 1D 59
Kilburn High Rd.
  NW6 . . . . 4B 44
Kilburn Ho. NW6 . . . . . . 1B 58
    (off Malvern Pl.)
Kilburn La. W10 . . . . . . 2F 57
Kilburn Pk. Rd. NW6 . . . 2C 58
Kilburn Pl. NW6 . . . . . . 5C 44

Kilburn Priory NW6 . . . . 5D 45
Kilburn Sq. NW6 . . . . . . 5C 44
Kilburn Va. NW6 . . . . . . 5D 45
Kilburn Va. Est. NW6 . . . 5D 45
    (off Kilburn Va.)
Kilby Ct. SE10 . . . . 4B 82
    (off School Bank Rd.)
Kildare Gdns. W2 . . . . . 5C 58
Kildare Rd. E16 . . . . 4C 68
Kildare Ter. W2 . . . . 5C 58
Kildare Wlk. E14 . . . . . . 5C 66
Kildoran Rd. SW2 . . . . . 3A 104
Kilgour Rd. SE23 . . . . . . 4A 108
Kilkie St. SW6 . . . . 5E 87
Killarney Rd.
  SW18 . . . . 4E 101
Killearn Rd. SE6 . . . . . . 1F 123
Killick St. N1 . . . . 1F 7 (1B 62)
Killieser Av. SW2 . . . . . 2A 118
Killip Cl. E16 . . . . 5B 68
Killoran Ho. E14 . . . . . . 4E 81
    (off Galbraith St.)
Killowen Rd. E9 . . . . 3F 51
Killyon Rd. SW8 . . . . . . 5E 89
Killyon Ter. SW8 . . . . . . 5E 89
Kilmaine Rd. SW6 . . . . . 3A 86
Kilmarsh Rd. W6 . . . . . . 5E 71
Kilmington Rd.
  SW13 . . . . 2C 84
Kilmore Ho. E14 . . . . . . 5D 67
    (off Vesey Path)
Kilmorie Rd. SE23 . . . . . 1A 122
Kilmuir Ho. SW1 . . . . . . 5C 74
    (off Bury St.)
Kiln Ct. E14 . . . . 1B 80
    (off Newell St.)
Kiln Ho. E16 . . . . 4D 69
    (off Freemasons Rd.)
SE11 . . . . 2C 90
    (off Clayton St.)
Kilner St. E14 . . . . 4C 66
Kiln M. SW17 . . . . 5F 115
Kiln Pl. NW5 . . . . 2C 46
Kilravock St. W10 . . . . . 2A 58
Kimbell Gdns. SW6 . . . . 4A 86
Kimbell Pl. SE3 . . . . 2E 111
Kimberley Av. E6 . . . . . . 1F 69
SE15 . . . . 5D 93
Kimberley Gdns. N4 . . . . 1D 35
Kimberley Ho. E14 . . . . . 4E 81
    (off Galbraith St.)
Kimberley Rd. E11 . . . . . 4F 39
E16 . . . . 3B 68
NW6 . . . . 5A 44
SW9 . . . . 5A 90
Kimber Rd. SW18 . . . . . 5C 100
Kimble Ho. NW8 . . . . . . 3A 60
    (off Lilestone St.)
Kimble Rd. SW19 . . . . . 5F 115
Kimbolton Cl. SE12 . . . . 4B 110
Kimbolton Row SW3 . . . 5A 74
    (off Fulham Rd.)
Kimmeridge Rd.
  SE9 . . . . 4F 125
Kimpton Ho. SW15 . . . . 5C 98
Kimpton Rd. SE5 . . . . . . 4F 91
Kinburn St. SE16 . . . . . . 3F 79
Kincaid Rd. SE15 . . . . . . 3D 93

Kincardine Gdns. *W9* . . . *3C 58*
   (off Harrow Rd.)
Kinder Ho. *N1* *1F 63*
   (off Cranston Est.)
Kindersley Ho. *E1* *5C 64*
   (off Pinchin St.)
Kinder St. E1 . . . . 5D 65
Kinefold Ho. N7 . . . . . . 3A 48
Kinfauns Rd. SW2 . . . . 2C 118
King Alfred Av. SE6 . . 4C 122
   (not continuous)
King & Queen St.
  SE17 . . . . 1E 91
King & Queen Wharf
  SE16 . . . . 1F 79
King Arthur Cl.
  SE15 . . . . 3E 93
King Charles I Island
  WC2 . . . . 1D 23
King Charles Ct.
  SE17 . . . . *2D 91*
   (off Royal Rd.)
King Charles Ho.
  SW6 . . . . *3D 87*
   (off Wandon Rd.)
King Charles's Ct.
  SE10 . . . . *2E 95*
   (off Park Row)
King Charles St.
  SW1 . . . . 3C 22 (3F 75)
King Charles Ter. *E1* . . *1D 79*
   (off Sovereign St.)
King Charles Wlk.
  SW19 . . . . 1A 114
King Ct. E10 . . . . 2D 39
King David La. E1. . . . . 1E 79
Kingdon Ho. *E14.* *4E 81*
   (off Galbraith St.)
Kingdon Rd. NW6. . . . . 3C 44
King Edward III M.
  SE16 . . . . 3D 79
King Edward Bldg.
  EC1 . . . . 5D 63
King Edward Mans.
  E8 . . . . *5D 51*
   (off Mare St.)
King Edward M.
  SW13 . . . . 4C 84
King Edward Rd. E10 . . 3E 39
King Edwards Mans.
  SW6 . . . . *3C 86*
   (off Fulham Rd.)
King Edward's Rd.
  E9. . . . . 5D 51
King Edward St.
  EC1. . . . . 2F 17 (5E 63)
King Edward Wlk.
  SE1 . . . . 5C 24 (4C 76)
Kingfield St. E14 . . . . . 5E 81
Kingfisher Av. E11 . . . . 1D 41
Kingfisher Ct. *E14* *3E 81*
   (off River Barge Cl.)
  SE1 . . . . *4A 26*
   (off Swan St.)
  SW19 . . . . 2F 113
Kingfisher Ho.
  SW18 . . . . 1E 101
Kingfisher M. SE13 . . 2C 108
Kingfisher Sq. *SE8*. . . . *2B 94*
   (off Clyde St.)

Kingfisher Way
  NW10 . . . . 3A 42
King Frederik IX Twr.
  SE16 . . . . 4B 80
King George IV Ct.
  SE17 . . . . *1F 91*
   (off Dawes St.)
King George VI Memorial
  . . . . 2B 22 (2F 75)
King George Av. E16 . . 5E 69
King George St.
  SE10 . . . . 3E 95
Kingham Cl. SW18. . . . 5E 101
  W11 . . . . 3A 72
King Henry's Reach
  W6 . . . . 2E 85
King Henry's Rd.
  NW3 . . . . 4A 46
King Henry's Stairs
  E1 . . . . 2D 79
King Henry St. N16 . . . 2A 50
King Henry's Wlk. N1. . 3A 50
King Henry Ter. *E1*. . . . *1D 79*
   (off Sovereign Cl.)
Kinghorn St.
  EC1. . . . . 1F 17 (4E 63)
King Ho. W12. . . . . 5D 57
King James Ct. SE1 . . . 4E 25
King James St.
  SE1 . . . . 4E 25 (3D 77)
King John Ct.
  EC2 . . . . 3E 11 (3A 64)
King John St. E1. . . . . . 4F 65
King John's Wlk.
  SE9 . . . . 5F 111
   (not continuous)
Kinglake Est. SE17. . . . 1A 92
Kinglake St. SE17. . . . . 1A 92
   (not continuous)
Kinglet Cl. E7 . . . . 3C 54
Kingly Ct. SW1. . . . . . . 4A 14
Kingly St. W1. . . 3F 13 (5E 61)
Kingsand Rd. SE12 . . . 2C 124
Kings Arms Ct. E1 . . . . 4C 64
Kings Arms Yd.
  EC2. . . . . 2B 18 (5F 63)
Kings Av.
  BR1: Brom 5B 124
  SW4 . . . . 1F 117
  SW12 . . . . 1F 117
King's Bench St.
  SE1 . . . . 3E 25 (3D 77)
King's Bench Wlk.
  EC4 . . . . 3C 16 (5C 62)
   (off Dockers Tanner Rd.)
Kingsbridge Ct. *E14*. . . *4C 80*
  NW1 . . . . *4D 47*
   (off Castlehaven Rd.)
Kingsbridge Rd. W10. . 5E 57
KINGSBURY GREEN . 1A 28
Kingsbury Rd. N1. . . . . 3A 50
  NW9 . . . . 1A 28
Kingsbury Ter. N1 . . . . 3A 50
Kingsbury Trad. Est.
  NW9 . . . . 1A 28
Kingsclere Cl.
  SW15 . . . . 5C 98
Kingscliffe Gdns.
  SW19 . . . . 1B 114
Kings Cl. E10 . . . . 2D 39

Kings Coll. Ct. NW3. . . 4A 46
Kings College London
  Dental Institute. 5F 91
  Hampstead Campus
  . . . . 1C 44
  Strand Campus
  . . . . 4A 16 (1B 76)
  Waterloo Campus . . 2B 24
King's Coll. Rd.
  NW3 . . . . 4A 46
King's College School of
  Medicine & Dentistry
  . . . . 5E 91
Kingscote St.
  EC4 . . . . 4D 17 (1D 77)
Kings Ct. E13 . . . . 5D 55
  N7. . . . . *4B 48*
   (off Caledonian Rd.)
  NW8 . . . . *5B 46*
   (off Prince Albert Rd.)
  SE1 . . . . 3E 25 (3D 77)
  W6 . . . . 5C 70
Kings Ct. Nth. SW3 . . . 1A 88
Kingscourt Rd.
  SW16 . . . . 3F 117
Kings Ct. Sth. *SW3* . . . *1A 88*
   (off Chelsea Mnr. Gdns.)
King's Cres. N4 . . . . . . 5E 35
Kings Cres. Est. N4 . . . 4E 35
Kingscroft SW4 . . . . . 4A 104
Kingscroft Rd. NW2 . . . 3B 44
KING'S CROSS 1A 62
King's Cross Bri. N1. . . 1E 7
King's Cross Rd.
  WC1 . . . . 1F 7 (2B 62)
Kingsdale Gdns. W11. . 2F 71
Kingsdown Av. W3 . . . 1A 70
Kingsdown Cl. *SE16* . . *1D 93*
   (off Masters Dr.)
  W10. . . . . 5F 57
Kingsdown Ho. E8 . . . . 2C 50
  N19. . . . . 4A 34
Kingsfield Ho. SE9 . . . 3F 125
Kingsford St. NW5 . . . 2B 46
King's Gdns. NW6 . . . . 4C 44
Kings Gth. M. SE23 . . . 2E 121
Kingsgate Est. N1 . . . . 3A 50
Kingsgate Ho. SW9 . . . 4C 90
Kingsgate Mans.
  WC1 . . . . *1F 15*
   (off Red Lion Sq.)
Kingsgate Pde. SW1 . . 5A 22
Kingsgate Pl. NW6. . . . 4C 44
Kingsgate Rd. NW6 . . . 4C 44
Kingsground SE9 . . . . 5F 111
King's Gro. SE15 . . . . . 3D 93
   (not continuous)
Kings Hall Leisure Cen.
  . . . . 2E 51
Kingshall M. SE13 . . . 1E 109
Kings Hall Rd.
  BR3: Beck. 5A 122
Kings Head Pas.
  SW4 . . . . *2F 103*
   (off Clapham Pk. Rd.)
Kings Head Theatre . . . *5D 49*
   (off Upper St.)
King's Head Yd.
  SE1. . . . . 2B 26 (2F 77)

Kingshill SE17 . . . . 5E 77
　　(off Brandon St.)
Kingshold Rd. E9 . . . . . . 4E 51
Kingsholm Gdns.
　SE9 . . . . 2F 111
Kings Ho. SW8 . . . . 3A 90
　　(off Sth. Lambeth Rd.)
Kingshurst Rd.
　SE12 . . . . 5C 110
Kings Keep SW15 . . . . . . 3F 99
KINGSLAND 3A 50
Kingsland NW8 . . . . 5A 46
Kingsland Grn. E8 . . . . . 3A 50
Kingsland High St.
　E8 . . . . 3B 50
Kingsland Pas. E8 . . . . . 3A 50
Kingsland Rd.
　E2 . . . . 2E 11 (2A 64)
　E8 . . . . 2A 64
　E13 . . . . 2E 69
Kingsland Shop. Cen.
　E8 . . . . 3B 50
Kingslawn Cl. SW15 . . . . 3D 99
Kingsley Ct. NW2 . . . . . . 3D 43
Kingsley Flats SE1 . . . . 5A 78
　　(off Old Kent Rd.)
Kingsley Ho. SW3 . . . . . 2F 87
　　(off Beaufort St.)
Kingsley Mans. W14 . . 2A 86
　　(off Greyhound Rd.)
Kingsley M. E1 . . . . 1D 79
　W8 . . . . 4D 73
Kingsley Pl. N6 . . . . 2C 32
Kingsley Rd. E7 . . . . 4C 54
　NW6 . . . . 5B 44
　SW19 . . . . 5D 115
Kingsley St. SW11 . . . . 1B 102
Kingsley Way N2 . . . . . . 1E 31
Kings Mall W6 . . . . 5E 71
Kingsmead Av. NW9 . . . 2A 28
Kingsmead Ct. N6 . . . . . 2F 33
Kingsmead Ho. E9 . . . . . 1A 52
Kingsmead Rd.
　SW2 . . . . 2C 118
King's Mead Way
　E9 . . . . 1A 52
Kingsmere Cl.
　SW15 . . . . 1F 99
Kingsmere Pl. N16 . . . . . 3F 35
Kingsmere Rd.
　SW19 . . . . 2F 113
King's M. SW4 . . . . 3A 104
　WC1 . . . . 4A 8 (3B 62)
Kingsmill NW8 . . . . 1F 59
　　(off Kingsmill Ter.)
Kingsmill Ho. SW3 . . . . 1A 88
　　(off Cale St.)
Kingsmill Ter. NW8 . . . . 1F 59
Kingsnorth Ho. W10 . . . 5F 57
Kings Pde. NW10 . . . . . 5E 43
　W12 . . . . 4C 70
Kings Pas. E11 . . . . 2A 40
King's Pl.
　SE1 . . . . 4F 25 (3E 77)
King Sq. EC1 . . . 2F 9 (2E 63)
King's Quay SW10 . . . . 4E 87
　　(off Chelsea Harbour Dr.)
Kings Reach Twr.
　SE1 . . . . 1C 24
Kingsridge SW19 . . . . . 2A 114

Kings Rd. E6 . . . . 5E 55
　E11 . . . . 2A 40
　NW10 . . . . 4D 43
　SW6 . . . . 3D 87
　SW10 . . . . 3D 87
　SW14 . . . . 1A 98
　SW19 . . . . 5C 114
King's Scholars' Pas.
　SW1 . . . . 4E 75
　　(off Carlisle Pl.)
King Stairs Cl. SE16 . . . 3D 79
King's Ter. NW1 . . . . 5E 47
Kingsthorpe Rd.
　SE26 . . . . 4F 121
Kingston By-Pass
　SW15 . . . . 5A 112
　SW20 . . . . 5A 112
Kingston Ho. NW6 . . . . 4A 44
Kingston Ho. E. SW7 . . 3A 74
　　(off Prince's Ga.)
Kingston Ho. Nth.
　SW7 . . . . 3A 74
　　(off Prince's Ga.)
Kingston Ho. Sth.
　SW7 . . . . 3A 74
　　(off Ennismore Gdns.)
Kingston Rd. SW15 . . . 2C 112
　SW19 . . . . 2C 112
Kingston Sq. SE19 . . . . 5F 119
Kingston University
　Kingston Hill 5A 112
　Roehampton Vale Cen.
　　. . . . . 3B 112
KINGSTON VALE 4A 112
Kingston Va. SW15 . . . 4A 112
Kingstown St. NW1 . . . 5C 46
　　(not continuous)
King St. E13 . . . . 3C 68
　EC2 . . . . 3A 18 (5E 63)
　SW1 . . . . 2A 22 (2E 75)
　W6 . . . . 5C 70
　WC2 . . . . 4D 15 (1A 76)
King St. Cloisters
　W6 . . . . 5D 71
　　(off Clifton Wlk.)
Kings Wlk. Shop. Cen.
　SW3 . . . . 1B 88
Kingswater Pl. SW11 . . 3A 88
Kingsway
　WC2 . . . . 2F 15 (5B 62)
Kingsway Mans. WC1 . . 5F 7
　　(off Red Lion Sq.)
Kingsway Pde. N16 . . . 5F 35
　　(off Albion Rd.)
Kingsway Pl. EC1 . . . . . 3C 8
　　(off Sans Wlk.)
Kingswear Rd. NW5 . . . 5D 33
Kings Wharf E8 . . . . 5A 50
　　(off Kingsland Rd.)
Kingswood E2 . . . . 1E 65
　　(off Cyprus St.)
Kingswood Av. NW6 . . . 5A 44
Kingswood Cl. SW8 . . . 3A 90
Kingswood Ct. NW6 . . . 4C 44
　　(off W. End La.)
Kingswood Dr.
　SE19 . . . . 4A 120
Kingswood Est.
　SE21 . . . . 4A 120
Kingswood Pl. SE13 . . 2A 110

Kingswood Rd.
　E11 . . . . 2A 40
　SW2 . . . . 4A 104
Kings Yd. E15 . . . . 3C 52
　SW15 . . . . 1E 99
　　(off Lwr. Richmond Rd.)
Kingthorpe Ter.
　NW10 . . . . 3A 42
Kington Ho. NW6 . . . . . 5D 45
　　(off Mortimer Cres.)
Kingward Ho. E1 . . . . . . 4C 64
　　(off Hanbury St.)
Kingweston Cl.
　NW2 . . . . 5A 30
King William La.
　SE10 . . . . 1A 96
King William's Ct.
　SE10 . . . . 2F 95
　　(off Park Row)
King William St.
　EC4 . . . . 3C 18 (5F 63)
King William Wlk.
　SE10 . . . . 2E 95
　　(not continuous)
Kingwood Rd. SW6 . . . 4A 86
Kinloch Dr. NW9 . . . . . . 2A 28
Kinloch St. N7 . . . . 5B 34
Kinnaird Av.
　BR1: Brom 5B 124
Kinnear Rd. W12 . . . . . 3B 70
Kinnerton Pl. Nth.
　SW1 . . . . 4A 20
Kinnerton Pl. Sth.
　SW1 . . . . 4A 20
Kinnerton St.
　SW1 . . . . 4B 20 (3C 74)
Kinnerton Yd. SW1 . . . 4B 20
Kinnoul Rd. W6 . . . . . . 2A 86
Kinross Ct. SE6 . . . . . . 1B 124
Kinsale Rd. SE15 . . . . . 1C 106
Kinsella Gdns.
　SW19 . . . . 5D 113
Kinsham Ho. E2 . . . . . . 3C 64
　　(off Ramsey St.)
Kintore Way SE1 . . . . . 5B 78
Kintyre Ct. SW2 . . . . . . 5A 104
Kintyre Ho. E14 . . . . . . 2E 81
　　(off Coldharbour)
Kinveachy Gdns.
　SE7 . . . . 1F 97
Kinver Rd. SE26 . . . . . . 4E 121
Kipling Dr. SW19 . . . . . 5F 115
Kipling Est.
　SE1 . . . . 4C 26 (3F 77)
Kipling Ho. SE15 . . . . . 2D 83
　　(off Southampton M.)
　SE5 . . . . 3F 91
　　(off Elmington Est.)
Kipling St.
　SE1 . . . . 4C 26 (3F 77)
Kippington Dr. SE9 . . . 1F 125
Kirby Est. SE16 . . . . . . 4D 79
Kirby Gro.
　SE1 . . . . 3D 27 (3A 78)
Kirby St. EC1 . . . 5C 8 (4C 62)
Kirkdale SE26 . . . . 2D 121
Kirkdale Cnr. SE26 . . . . 4E 121
Kirkdale Rd. E11 . . . . . 3A 40
Kirkeby Ho. EC1 . . . . . . 5B 8
　　(off Leather La.)

Kirkland Ho. *E14* *1D 95*
(off St Davids Sq.)
E14 . . . . *1D 95*
(off Westferry Rd.)
Kirkland Ter.
BR3: Beck 5C 122
Kirkland Wlk. E8 . . . . 3B 50
Kirkman Pl. W1 . . . . 1B 14
Kirkmichael Rd. E14 . . . . . 5E 67
Kirk Rd. E17 . . . . 1B 38
Kirkside Rd. SE3 . . . . 2C 96
Kirkstall Gdns.
SW2 . . . . 1A 118
Kirkstall Rd. SW2 . . . . . . 1F 117
Kirkstead Ct. E5 . . . . 1F 51
Kirkstone *NW1* *1F 5*
(off Harrington St.)
Kirk St. WC1 . . . . 4F 7
Kirkwall Pl. E2 . . . . 2E 65
Kirkwood Pl. NW1 . . . . . . 4C 46
Kirkwood Rd. SE15 . . . . . 5D 93
Kirtley Ho. SW8 . . . . 4E 89
Kirtley Rd. SE26 . . . . 4A 122
Kirtling St. SW8 . . . . 3E 89
Kirton Cl. W4 . . . . 5A 70
Kirton Gdns.
E2 . . . . 2F 11 (2B 64)
Kirton Lodge SW18 . . . . 4D 101
Kirton Rd. E13 . . . . 1E 69
Kirwyn Way SE5 . . . . 3D 91
Kitcat Ter. E3 . . . . 2C 66
Kitchener Rd. E7 . . . . 3D 55
Kite Pl. *E2* *2C 64*
(off Lampern Sq.)
Kite Yd. *SW11* *4B 88*
(off Cambridge Rd.)
Kitson Rd. SE5 . . . . 3F 91
SW13 . . . . 4C 84
Kittiwake Ct. *SE1* *4A 26*
(off Swan St.)
SE8 . . . . *2B 94*
(off Abinger Gro.)
Kitto Rd. SE14 . . . . 5F 93
Kiver Rd. N19 . . . . 4F 33
Klea Av. SW4 . . . . 4E 103
Klein's Wharf *E14*. *4C 80*
(off Westferry Rd.)
Knapdale Cl. SE23 . . . . . 2D 121
Knapmill Rd. SE6 . . . . . . 2C 122
Knapmill Way SE6 . . . . . 2D 123
Knapp Cl. NW10 . . . . 3A 42
Knapp Rd. E3 . . . . 3D 66
Knapton M. SW17 . . . . . 5C 116
Knaresborough Dr.
SW18 . . . . 1D 115
Knaresborough Pl.
SW5 . . . . 5D 73
Knatchbull Rd.
NW10 . . . . 5A 42
SE5 . . . . 5D 91
Knebworth Ho. SW8 . . . . . 5F 89
Knebworth Rd. N16 . . . . . 1A 50
Kneller Rd. SE4 . . . . 2A 108
Knighten St. E1 . . . . 2D 79
Knighthead Point
E14. . . . . 3C 80
Knight Ho. *SE17* *5A 78*
(off Tatum St.)
Knightland Rd. E5 . . . . . . 4D 37
Knightleas Ct. NW2 . . . . . 3E 43

Knightleys Ct. E10 . . . . . . *3A 38*
(off Wellington Rd.)
SE26 . . . . 5F 121
Knighton Pk. Rd.
SE26 . . . . 5F 121
Knighton Rd. E7 . . . . 5C 40
Knightrider Ct.
EC4 . . . . 4E 17
Knightrider St.
EC4 . . . . 4E 17 (5D 63)
Knights Arc. SW1 . . . . . . 4A 20
KNIGHTSBRIDGE 3A 74
Knightsbridge
SW1 . . . . 4A 20 (3B 74)
SW7 . . . . 3B 74
Knightsbridge Ct.
SW1 . . . . 4A 20
Knightsbridge Grn.
SW1 . . . . 3B 74
(not continuous)
Knights Cl. E9 . . . . 2E 51
Knights Ct.
BR1: Brom 3B 124
Knights Hill SE27 . . . . . . 5D 119
Knight's Hill Sq.
SE27 . . . . 4D 119
Knights Ho. *SW8* *3A 90*
(off Sth. Lambeth Rd.)
Knight's Rd. E16 . . . . 3C 82
Knight's Wlk. SE11 . . . . . 5D 77
(not continuous)
Knightswood Ct. N6 . . . . . 2F 33
Knivet Rd. SW6 . . . . 2C 86
Knobs Hill Rd. E15 . . . . . 5D 53
Knockholt Rd. SE9 . . . . . 3F 111
Knoll Ho. *NW8* *1E 59*
(off Carlton Hill)
Knoll Rd. SW18 . . . . 3E 101
Knollys Cl. SW16 . . . . . . 3C 118
Knolly's Ho. *WC1* *3D 7*
(off Tavistock Pl.)
Knollys Rd. SW16 . . . . . . 3B 118
Knottisford St. E2 . . . . . . 2E 65
Knotts Grn. M. E10 . . . . . 1D 39
Knotts Grn. Rd. E10 . . . . 1D 39
Knowlden Ho. *E1* *1E 79*
(off Cable St.)
Knowle Cl. SW9 . . . . 1C 104
Knowles Hill Cres.
SE13 . . . . 3F 109
Knowles Ho. *SW18* *4D 101*
(off Neville Gill Cl.)
Knowles Wlk. SW4 . . . . . 1E 103
Knowlton Ho. *SW9* *4C 90*
(off Cowley Rd.)
Knowsley Rd. SW11 . . . . . 5B 88
Knox Ct. SW4 . . . . 5A 90
Knox Rd. E7 . . . . 3B 54
Knox St. W1 . . . . 5A 4 (4B 60)
Knoyle St. SE14 . . . . 2A 94
Kohat Rd. SW19 . . . . . . 5D 115
Kossuth St. SE10 . . . . . . 1A 96
Kotree Way SE1 . . . . 5C 78
Kramer M. SW5 . . . . 1C 86
Kreedman Wlk. E8 . . . . . 2C 50
Krupnik Pl. EC2 . . . . 2E 11
Kubrick Bus. Est. *E7* . . . *1D 55*
(off Station App.)
Kuhn Way E7 . . . . 2C 54
Kylemore Cl. E6 . . . . 1F 69
Kylemore Rd. NW6 . . . . . 4C 44

Kylestrome Ho. *SW1* *5C 74*
(off Cundy St.)
Kynance M. SW7 . . . . . . 4D 73
Kynance Pl. SW7 . . . . . . 4E 73
Kynaston Av. N16 . . . . . . 5B 36
Kynaston Rd.
BR1: Brom 5C 124
N16 . . . . 5A 36
Kyrle Rd. SW11 . . . . 4C 102
Kyverdale Rd. N16 . . . . . 2B 36

L

Laburnum Cl. SE15 . . . . . 3E 93
Laburnum Ct. E2 . . . . . . 5B 50
SE16 . . . . *3E 79*
(off Albion St.)
Laburnum St. E2 . . . . . . 5B 50
La Caye Apartments
E14 . . . . *5F 81*
(off Glenaffric Av.)
Lacewing Cl. E13 . . . . . . 2C 68
Lacine Ct. *SE16* *3F 79*
(off Christopher Cl.)
Lackington St.
EC2 . . . . 5C 10 (4F 63)
Lackland Ho. *SE1* *1B 92*
(off Rowcross St.)
Lacland Ho. *SW10* *3F 87*
(off Worlds End Est.)
Lacon Ho. *WC1* *5F 7*
(off Theobalds Rd.)
Lacon Rd. SE22 . . . . . . 2C 106
Lacy Rd. SW15 . . . . 2F 99
(not continuous)
Ladas Rd. SE27 . . . . 4E 119
Ladbroke Cres. W11 . . . . 5A 58
Ladbroke Gdns. W11 . . . . 1B 72
Ladbroke Gro. W10 . . . . . 3F 57
Ladbroke Gro. Ho.
W11 . . . . *1B 72*
(off Ladbroke Gro.)
Ladbroke M. W11 . . . . . . 2A 72
Ladbroke Rd. W11 . . . . . 2B 72
Ladbroke Sq. W11 . . . . . 1B 72
Ladbroke Ter. W11 . . . . . 1B 72
Ladbroke Wlk. W11 . . . . . 2B 72
Ladlands SE22 . . . . 5C 106
Ladycroft Rd.
SE13 . . . . 1D 109
Lady Dock Path
SE16 . . . . 3A 80
Ladyfern Ho. *E3* *4A 66*
(off Gail St.)
Lady Margaret Rd.
N19 . . . . 2E 47
NW5 . . . . 2E 47
Lady Micos Almshouses
E1 . . . . *5E 65*
(off Aylward St.)
Ladyship Ter. SE22 . . . . 5C 106
Ladysmith Av. E6 . . . . . . 1F 69
Ladysmith Rd. E16 . . . . . 2B 68
Lady Somerset Rd.
NW5 . . . . 1D 47
LADYWELL 3D 109
Ladywell Arena 4D 109
Ladywell Cl. SE4 . . . . . . 3C 108
Ladywell Hgts. SE4 . . . . 4B 108

Ladywell Leisure Cen.
. . . . 3E 109
Ladywell Rd. SE13. . . 3C 108
Ladywell St. E15 . . . . 5B 54
LA Fitness
  Aldgate 4F 19
       (off Portsoken St.)
  Bayswater 1D 73
       (off Queen's M.)
  Bloomsbury 5F 7
       (off Conduit St.)
  Covent Garden 4F 15
  Golders Green 2B 30
  Gospel Oak 1D 47
  Leadenhall 3E 19
       (off Billiter St.)
  Marylebone
  . . . . 5A 4 (4B 60)
  Piccadilly 5B 14
       (off Regent St.)
  St Pauls. 1F 17
     (off King Edward St.)
  South Kensington . . 5A 74
  Sydenham 4E 121
  Victoria 5F 21
     (off Bressenden Pl.)
  West India Quay . . . 1C 80
Lafone St.
  SE1. . . . . . . 3F 27 (3B 78)
Lagado M. SE16 . . . . . 2F 79
Laing Ho. SE5. . . . . . . 3E 91
Lainson St. SW18 . . 5C 100
Lairdale Cl. SE21 . . . 1E 119
Laird Ho. SE5 . . . . 3E 91
      (off Redcar St.)
Lairs Cl. N7 . . . . 2A 48
Laitwood Rd. SW12 . . 1D 117
Lakanal SE5 . . . . 4A 92
     (off Dalwood St.)
Lake Av. BR1: Brom . . 5C 124
Lake Cl. SW19 . . . . . 5B 114
Lake Ho. SE1 . . . . 4F 25
    (off Southwark Bri. Rd.)
Lake Ho. Rd. E11. . . . 5C 40
Laker Ct. SW4 . . . . . . 4A 90
Laker Ind. Est.
  BR3. . . . . 5A 122
     (off Kent Ho. La.)
Lake Rd. SW19 . . . . . 5B 114
Laker Pl. SW15 . . . . . 4A 100
Lakeside Ct. N4 . . . . . 4E 35
Lakeside Rd. W14 . . . 4F 71
Lakeside Ter. EC2. . . . 5A 10
Lake Vw. Ct. SW1. . . . 5E 21
     (off Bressenden Pl.)
Lake Vw. Est. E3 . . . . 1A 66
Lakeview Rd. SE27 . . 5C 118
Lakis Cl. NW3. . . . . . . 1E 45
Laleham Ho. E2 . . . . . 3F 11
      (off Camlet St.)
Laleham Rd. SE6 . . . . 5E 109
Lalor St. SW6. . . . . . . 5A 86
Lambard Ho. SE10. . . . 3E 95
     (off Langdale Rd.)
Lamb Ct. E14 . . . . 1A 80
     (off Narrow St.)
Lamberhurst Ho.
  SE15. . . . . 2E 93
Lamberhurst Rd.
  SE27. . . . . 4C 118

Lambert Jones M. EC2. . . 5F 9
Lambert Rd. E16 . . . . 5D 69
  SW2. . . . . 3A 104
Lambert St. N1. . . . . . 4C 48
LAMBETH. 5F 23 (4B 76)
Lambeth Bri. SE1. . . . 5A 76
Lambeth Crematorium
  SW17 . . . . 4E 115
Lambeth High St.
  SE1. . . . . 5B 76
Lambeth Hill
  EC4. . . . . 4F 17 (1E 77)
Lambeth Palace
  . . . . 5F 23 (4B 76)
Lambeth Pal. Rd.
  SE1. . . . . 5F 23 (4B 76)
Lambeth Rd.
  SE1. . . . . . . 5B 24 (5B 76)
Lambeth Towers
  SE11 . . . . 5B 24
Lambeth Wlk. SE11 . . 5B 76
      (not continuous)
Lambfold Ho. N7 . . . . 3A 48
Lamb Ho. SE5 . . . . 3E 91
     (off Elmington Est.)
SE10 . . . . 2E 95
      (off Haddo St.)
Lamb La. E8. . . . . 4D 51
Lamble St. NW5. . . . . 2C 46
Lambolle Pl. NW3 . . . 3A 46
Lambolle Rd. NW3 . . . 3A 46
Lambourn Cl. NW5. . . 1E 47
Lambourne Av.
  SW19 . . . . 4B 114
Lambourne Gro.
  SE16 . . . . 1F 93
Lambourne Ho. NW8 . . . 4F 59
     (off Broadley St.)
  SE16 . . . . 5F 79
Lambourne Pl. SE3 . . 4D 97
Lambourne Rd. E11 . . 2E 39
Lambourn Rd. SW4 . . 1D 103
Lambrook Ho. SE15. . . 4C 92
Lambrook Ter. SW6 . . 4A 86
Lamb's Bldgs.
  EC1. . . . . . . 4B 10 (3F 63)
Lamb's Conduit Pas.
  WC1 . . . . 5F 7 (4B 62)
Lamb's Conduit St.
  WC1 . . . . 4F 7 (3B 62)
      (not continuous)
Lambscroft Av. SE9 . . 3E 125
Lambs Health & Fitness
  . . . . 4B 10
Lamb's M. N1 . . . . . . 5D 49
Lamb's Pas.
  EC1. . . . . . . 5B 10 (3F 63)
Lamb St. E1. . . . 5F 11 (4B 64)
Lambton M. N19 . . . . 3A 34
     (off Lambton Rd.)
Lambton Pl. W11. . . . 1B 72
Lambton Rd. N19. . . . 3A 34
Lamb Wlk.
  SE1 . . . . . . 4D 27 (3A 78)
LAMDA Theatre 5C 72
      (off Logan Pl.)
Lamerock Rd.
  BR1: Brom 4B 124
Lamerton St. SE8. . . . 2C 94
Lamington St. W6 . . . 5D 71

Lamlash St. SE11 . . . . 5D 77
Lamley Ho. SE10 . . . . 3D 95
     (off Ashburnham Pl.)
Lammas Grn. SE26 . . 3D 121
Lammas Rd. E9 . . . . . 4F 51
  E10. . . . . 4A 38
Lammermoor Rd.
  SW12 . . . . 5D 103
Lamont Rd. SW10 . . . 2F 87
Lamont Rd. Pas.
  SW10 . . . . 2F 87
     (off Lamont Rd.)
Lampard Gro. N16. . . . 3B 36
Lampern Sq. E2 . . . . . 2C 64
Lampeter Cl. NW9 . . . 1A 28
Lampeter Sq. W6. . . . 2A 86
Lamplighter Cl. E1. . . 3E 65
Lampmead Rd.
  SE12. . . . . 3B 110
Lamp Office Ct.
  WC1 . . . . 4F 7
Lamps Ct. SE5 . . . . . . 3E 91
    (off Thompson's Av.)
Lampton Ho. Cl.
  SW19 . . . . 4F 113
Lanain Ct. SE12 . . . . 5B 110
Lanark Ho. SE1 . . . . . 1C 92
     (off Old Kent Rd.)
Lanark Mans. W9. . . . . 3E 59
      (off Lanark Rd.)
  W12 . . . . 3E 71
     (off Pennard Rd.)
Lanark M. W9. . . . . . . 2E 59
Lanark Pl. W9 . . . . . . 3E 59
Lanark Rd. W9. . . . . . 1D 59
Lanark Sq. E14 . . . . . 4D 81
Lanbury Rd. SE15 . . . 2F 107
Lancashire Ct. W1 . . . 4E 13
Lancaster Av. SE27 . . 2D 119
  SW19 . . . . 5F 113
Lancaster Cl. N1 . . . . 4A 50
  W2 . . . . 1D 73
    (off St Petersburgh Pl.)
Lancaster Ct. SE27 . . 2D 119
  SW6 . . . . 3B 86
  W2 . . . . 1E 73
     (off Lancaster Ga.)
Lancaster Dr. E14. . . . 2E 81
  NW3. . . . . 3A 46
Lancaster Gdns.
  SW19 . . . . 5A 114
Lancaster Ga. W2 . . . 1E 73
Lancaster Gro. NW3. . 3F 45
Lancaster Hall E16. . . 2C 82
     (off Wesley Av.,
      not continuous)
Lancaster House 3A 22
Lancaster Lodge
  W11 . . . . 5A 58
     (off Lancaster Rd.)
Lancaster M. SW18. . 3D 101
  W2 . . . . 1E 73
Lancaster Pl. SW19 . . 5F 113
  WC2. . . . . . . 4F 15 (1B 76)
Lancaster Rd. E7 . . . . 4C 54
  E11. . . . . 4A 40
  N4. . . . . 2B 34
  NW10 . . . . 2C 42
  SW19 . . . . 5F 113
  W11 . . . . 5A 58

Lancaster Stables
NW3 . . . . 3A **46**
Lancaster Rd.
SE1 . . . . 4D **25** (3D **77**)
Lancaster Ter. W2. . . . . . . 1F **73**
Lancaster Wlk. W2. . . . . . 2E **73**
Lancefield Ct. W10 . . . 1A **58**
Lancefield Ho.
SE15 . . . . 2D **107**
Lancefield St. W10 . . . 2B **58**
Lancell St. N16 . . . . 4B **36**
Lancelot Pl. SW7 . . . . . 3B **74**
Lancer Sq. W8 . . . . 3D **73**
Lancey Cl. SE7 . . . . 5F **83**
Lanchester Ct. W2 . . . . . 5B **60**
(off Seymour St.)
Lanchester Rd. N6. . . . 1B **32**
Lancing St.
NW1 . . . . 2B **6** (2F **61**)
Lancresse Ct. N1 . . . . . 5A **50**
(off De Beauvoir Est.)
Landale Ho. SE16. . . . . 4E **79**
(off Lower Rd.)
Landcroft Rd. SE22 . . . 3B **106**
Landells Rd. SE22 . . . . 4B **106**
Landford Rd. SW15 . . . 1E **99**
Landgrove Rd.
SW19 . . . . 5C **114**
Landin Ho. E14. . . . . . . 5C **66**
(off Thomas Rd.)
Landleys Fld. NW5. . . . . 2F **47**
(off Long Mdw.)
Landmann Ho. SE16. . . 5D **79**
(off Rennie Est.)
Landmann Way SE14 . . 1F **93**
Landmark Hgts. E5. . . . 1A **52**
Landmark Ho. W6 . . . . . 1E **85**
(off Hammersmith Bri. Rd.)
Landon Pl.
SW1 . . . . 5A **20** (4B **74**)
Landon's Cl. E14 . . . . . . 2E **81**
Landon Wlk. E14 . . . . . . 1D **81**
Landor Ho. SE5. . . . . 3F **91**
(off Elmington Est.)
Landor Rd. SW9. . . . . . 1A **104**
Landor Theatre 1A **104**
Landor Wlk. W12 . . . . . . 3C **70**
Landrake NW1 . . . . 5E **47**
(off Plender St.)
Landridge Rd. SW6 . . . 5B **86**
Landrock Rd. N8 . . . . . . 1A **34**
Landseer Ho. NW8 . . . . 3F **59**
(off Frampton St.)
SW1 . . . . 5F **75**
(off Herrick St.)
SW11 . . . . 4C **88**
Landseer Rd. N19 . . . . 5A **34**
(not continuous)
Landulph Ho. SE11 . . . . 1C **90**
(off Kennings Way)
Landward Ct. W1 . . . . . 5A **60**
(off Harrowby St.)
Lane, The NW8. . . . . . . 1E **59**
SE3 . . . . 1C **110**
Lane Cl. NW2. . . . . 5D **29**
Lane End SW15 . . . . . . 4F **99**
Lanercost Cl. SW2 . . . . 2C **118**
Lanercost Rd. SW2 . . . 2C **118**
Lanesborough Ho. N1. . 1D **11**
(off Fanshaw St.)

Lanesborough Pl.
SW1 . . . . 3C **20**
Laneway SW15 . . . . . . 3D **99**
Laney Ho. EC1 . . . . 5B **8**
(off Leather La.)
Lanfranc Rd. E3 . . . . . . 1A **66**
Lanfrey Pl. W14. . . . . . . 1B **86**
Langbourne Av. N6 . . . . 4C **32**
Langbourne Ct. E17. . . 1A **38**
Langbourne Mans.
N6. . . . . 4C **32**
Langbourne Pl. E14. . . 1D **95**
Langbrook Rd. SE3. . . . 1F **111**
Langdale NW1 . . . . 1F **5**
(off Stanhope St.)
Langdale Cl. SE17 . . . . 2E **91**
Langdale Ho. SW1. . . . . 1E **89**
(off Churchill Gdns.)
Langdale Rd. SE10 . . . . 3E **95**
Langdale St. E1 . . . . 5D **65**
Langdon Ct. EC1. . . . . . . 1E **9**
(off City Rd.)
NW10 . . . . 5A **42**
Langdon Ho. E14 . . . . . . 5E **67**
Langdon Pk. Rd. N6. . . 2E **33**
Langdon Way SE1 . . . . 5C **78**
Langford Cl. E8 . . . . 2C **50**
NW8 . . . . 1E **59**
Langford Ct. NW8. . . . . . 1E **59**
(off Abbey Rd.)
Langford Grn. SE5 . . . . 1A **106**
Langford Ho. SE8. . . . . . 2C **94**
Langford Pl. NW8 . . . . . 1E **59**
Langford Rd. SW6 . . . . . 5D **87**
Langham Mans. SW5. . . 1D **87**
(off Earl's Ct. Sq.)
Langham Pl.
W1 . . . . 1E **13** (4D **61**)
W4 . . . . 2A **84**
Langham St.
W1 . . . . 1E **13** (4D **61**)
Langholm Cl. SW12 . . . 5F **103**
Langhorne Ct. NW8 . . . . 4F **45**
(off Dorman Way)
Lang Ho. SW8 . . . . 3A **90**
(off Hartington Rd.)
Langland Gdns. NW3. . . 2D **45**
Langland Ho. SE5. . . . . . 3F **91**
(off Edmund St.)
Langler Rd. NW10 . . . . . 1F **57**
Langley Ct.
WC2 . . . . 4D **15** (1A **76**)
Langley Cres. E11 . . . . . 2E **41**
Langley Dr. E11 . . . . 2D **41**
Langley Ho. W2 . . . . 4C **58**
(off Alfred Rd.)
Langley La. SW8 . . . . . . 2B **90**
Langley Mans. SW8. . . . 2B **90**
(off Langley La.)
Langley St.
WC2 . . . . 3D **15** (5A **62**)
Langmead St. SE27 . . . 4D **119**
Langmore Ho. E1. . . . . . 5C **64**
(off Stutfield St.)
Langport Ho. SW9 . . . . . 5D **91**
Langroyd Rd. SW17 . . . 2B **116**
Langside Av. SW15 . . . 2C **98**
Langston Hughes Cl.
SE24 . . . . 2D **105**
Lang St. E1. . . . . 3E **65**

Langthorn Ct.
EC2 . . . . 2B **18** (5F **63**)
Langthorne Ct.
BR1: Brom 4E **123**
Langthorne Rd. E11. . . . 5E **39**
Langthorne St. SW6 . . . 3F **85**
Langton Cl.
WC1 . . . . 3A **8** (3B **62**)
Langton Ho. SE11 . . . . . 5B **76**
(off Lambeth Wlk.)
Langton Pl. SW18 . . . . . 1C **114**
Langton Ri. SE23. . . . . . 5D **107**
Langton Rd. NW2 . . . . . . 5E **29**
SW9 . . . . 3D **91**
Langton St. SW10 . . . . . 2E **87**
Langton Way SE3 . . . . . 4B **96**
Langtry Pl. SW6. . . . . . . 2C **86**
Langtry Rd. NW8 . . . . . . 5D **45**
Langtry Wlk. NW8 . . . . . 5D **45**
Lanhill Rd. W9. . . . . 3C **58**
Lanier Rd. SE13 . . . . . . 4F **109**
Lannoy Point SW6 . . . . 3A **86**
(off Pellant Rd.)
Lanrick Ho. E14 . . . . 5F **67**
(off Lanrick Rd.)
Lanrick Rd. E14 . . . . 5F **67**
Lansbury Est. E14 . . . . . 5D **67**
Lansbury Gdns. E14 . . . 5F **67**
Lanscombe Wlk.
SW8 . . . . 4A **90**
Lansdell Ho. SW2 . . . . . 4C **104**
(off Tulse Hill)
Lansdowne Ct. W11. . . . 1A **72**
(off Lansdowne Ri.)
Lansdowne Cres.
W11 . . . . 1A **72**
Lansdowne Dr. E8 . . . . . 3C **50**
Lansdowne Gdns.
SW8 . . . . 4A **90**
Lansdowne Grn. Est.
SW8 . . . . 4A **90**
Lansdowne Gro.
NW10 . . . . 1A **42**
Lansdowne Hill
SE27 . . . . 3D **119**
Lansdowne La. SE7 . . . . 2F **97**
Lansdowne M. SE7. . . . . 1F **97**
W11 . . . . 2B **72**
Lansdowne Pl.
SE1. . . . . 5C **26** (4F **77**)
Lansdowne Ri. W11. . . . 1A **72**
Lansdowne Rd. E11 . . . . 4B **40**
E17. . . . . 1C **38**
W11 . . . . 1A **72**
Lansdowne Row
W1 . . . . 1E **21** (2D **75**)
Lansdowne Ter.
WC1 . . . . 4E **7** (3A **62**)
Lansdowne Wlk.
W11 . . . . 2B **72**
Lansdowne Way SW8. . . 4F **89**
Lansdowne Wood Cl.
SE27 . . . . 3D **119**
Lansdowne Workshops
SE7 . . . . 1E **97**
Lansdown Rd. E7 . . . . . . 4E **55**
Lantern Cl. SW15. . . . . . 2C **98**
Lanterns Ct. E14 . . . . . . 4C **80**
Lant Ho. SE1. . . . . 4F **25**
(off Toulmin St.)

Lant St. SE1 . . . . 3F **25** (3E **77**)
Lanvanor Rd.
SE15 . . . . 5E **93**
Lanyard Ho. SE8 . . . . 5B **80**
Lapford Cl. W9 . . . . . 3B **58**
Lapse Wood Wlk.
SE23 . . . . 1D **121**
Lapwing Ct. SE1 . . . . 4A **26**
(off Swan St.)
Lapwing Twr. SE8 . . . 2B **94**
(off Taylor Cl.)
Lapworth Ct. W2 . . . 4D **59**
(off Delamere Ter.)
Lara Cl. SE13 . . . . . . 4E **109**
Larch Av. W3 . . . . 2A **70**
Larch Cl. E13 . . . . . . 3D **69**
N19 . . . . 4E **33**
SE8 . . . . 2B **94**
SW12 . . . . 2D **117**
Larch Ct. SE1 . . . . . 4D **27**
(off Royal Oak Yd.)
W9 . . . . 4C **58**
(off Admiral Wlk.)
Larch Ho. SE16. . . . . 3E **79**
(off Ainsty Est.)
W10 . . . . 3A **58**
(off Rowan Wlk.)
Larch Rd. E10. . . . . . 4C **38**
NW2 . . . . 1E **43**
Larcom St. SE17. . . . 5E **77**
Larden Rd. W3. . . . . . 2A **70**
Larissa St. SE17. . . . 1F **91**
Larkbere Rd. SE26 . . 4A **122**
Larkhall La. SW4 . . . . 5F **89**
Larkhall Ri. SW4 . . . . 1E **103**
(not continuous)
Lark Row E2 . . . . 5E **51**
Larkspur Cl. E6 . . . . . 4F **69**
Larnach Rd. W6 . . . . . 2F **85**
Larpent Av. SW15. . . . 3E **99**
Lascelles Cl. E11 . . . . 4F **39**
Lascelles Ho. NW1 . . . 3A **60**
(off Harewood Av.)
Lassell St. SE10 . . . . 1F **95**
Lasseter Pl. SE3. . . . . 2A **96**
Latchmere Leisure Cen.
. . . . 5B **88**
Latchmere Pas.
SW11 . . . . 5A **88**
Latchmere Rd. SW11. . 5B **88**
Latchmere St. SW11 . . 5B **88**
Latham Cl. SW5 . . . . . 5C **72**
(off W. Cromwell Rd.)
Latham Ho. E1 . . . . . . 5F **65**
(off Chudleigh St.)
Latimer Ho. E9 . . . . . 3F **51**
W11 . . . . 1B **72**
(off Kensington Pk. Rd.)
Latimer Ind. Est.
W10 . . . . 5E **57**
Latimer Pl. W10. . . . . 5E **57**
Latimer Rd. E7. . . . . . 1D **55**
N15 . . . . 1A **36**
W10 . . . . 4E **57**
(not continuous)
Latona Ct. SW9 . . . . . 3C **90**
(off Caldwell St.)
Latona Rd. SE15 . . . . 2C **92**
Lattimer Pl. W4 . . . . . 3A **84**
Latymer Ct. W6. . . . . . 5F **71**

Latymer Upper School
Sports Cen. 1C **84**
Lauderdale House 3D **33**
Lauderdale Ho. SW9 . . 4C **90**
(off Gosling Way)
Lauderdale Mans.
W9 . . . . 2D **59**
(off Lauderdale Rd.,
not continuous)
Lauderdale Pde. W9 . . 3D **59**
Lauderdale Pl. EC2 . . . 5F **9**
(off Beech St.)
Lauderdale Rd. W9 . . . 2D **59**
Lauderdale Twr.
EC2 . . . . 5F **9**
Laud St. SE11 . . . . . . 1B **90**
Launcelot Rd.
BR1: Brom 4C **124**
Launcelot St.
SE1 . . . . . . 4B **24** (3C **76**)
Launceston Pl. W8. . . 4E **73**
Launch St. E14. . . . . . 4E **81**
Laundress La. N16. . . 5C **36**
Laundry La. N1. . . . . . 5E **49**
Laundry M. SE23 . . . 5A **108**
Laundry Rd. W6 . . . . . 2A **86**
Laura Pl. E5 . . . . 1E **51**
Laura Ter. N4 . . . . 4D **35**
Laurel Bank Gdns.
SW6 . . . . 5B **86**
Laurelbrook SE6. . . . 3A **124**
Laurel Cl. N19 . . . . . . 4E **33**
SW17 . . . . 5A **116**
Laurel Gro. SE26 . . . 4F **121**
Laurel Ho. SE8. . . . . . 2B **94**
Laurel Rd. SW13 . . . . 5C **84**
Laurels, The NW10 . . . 5D **43**
Laurel St. E8 . . . . 3B **50**
Laurence Ct. E10 . . . . 2D **39**
Laurence M. W12 . . . . 3C **70**
Laurence Pountney Hill
EC4 . . . . . . 4B **18** (1F **77**)
Laurence Pountney La.
EC4 . . . . . . 4B **18** (1F **77**)
Laurie Gro. SE14 . . . . 4A **94**
Laurie Ho. SE1 . . . . . 5E **25**
(off St George's Rd.)
Laurier Rd. NW5 . . . . 5D **33**
Lauriston Ho. E9 . . . . 4E **51**
(off Lauriston Rd.)
Lauriston Rd. E9 . . . . 4E **51**
SW19 . . . . 5F **113**
Lausanne Rd. SE15 . . 4E **93**
Lavell St. N16. . . . . . . 1F **49**
Lavender Cl. SW3 . . . 2F **87**
Lavender Gdns.
SW11 . . . . 2B **102**
Lavender Gro. E8 . . . . 4C **50**
Lavender Hill SW11. . 2A **102**
Lavender Ho. SE16. . . 2F **79**
(off Rotherhithe St.)
Lavender Pond Nature Pk.
. . . . 2A **80**
Lavender Rd. SE16 . . . 2A **80**
SW11 . . . . 1F **101**
Lavender Sq. E11 . . . . 5F **39**
Lavender St. E15 . . . . 3A **54**
Lavender Sweep
SW11 . . . . 2B **102**
Lavender Ter. SW11. . 1A **102**

Lavender Wlk.
SW11 . . . . 2B **102**
Lavendon Ho. NW8 . . 3A **60**
(off Paveley St.)
Lavengro Rd. SE27 . . 2E **119**
Lavenham Rd.
SW18 . . . . 2B **114**
Lavers Rd. N16 . . . . . 5A **36**
Laverstoke Gdns.
SW15 . . . . 5B **98**
Laverton M. SW5. . . . 5D **73**
Laverton Pl. SW5. . . . 5D **73**
Lavina Gro. N1. . . . . . 1B **62**
Lavington Cl. E9. . . . . 3B **52**
Lavington St.
SE1 . . . . . . 2E **25** (2D **77**)
Lavisham Ho.
BR1: Brom 5C **124**
Lawford Rd. N1 . . . . . 4A **50**
NW5 . . . . 3E **47**
Lawless Ho. E14 . . . . 1E **81**
(off Bazely St.)
Lawless St. E14. . . . . 1D **81**
Lawley St. E5 . . . . . . 1E **51**
Lawn Dr. E7 . . . . 1F **55**
Lawn Ho. Cl. E14 . . . . 3E **81**
Lawn La. SW8 . . . . . . 2A **90**
Lawn Rd. NW3 . . . . . . 2B **46**
Lawns, The SE3 . . . . . 1B **110**
SW19 . . . . 5B **114**
Lawnside SE3 . . . . . . 2B **110**
Lawn Ter. SE3 . . . . . . 1A **110**
Lawrence Av.
NW10 . . . . 5A **42**
Lawrence Bldgs.
N16 . . . . 5B **36**
Lawrence Cl. E3. . . . . 2C **66**
W12 . . . . 1D **71**
Lawrence Ct. N16 . . . 5B **36**
(off Smalley Rd. Est.)
Lawrence Ho. SW1. . . 5F **75**
(off Cureton St.)
Lawrence La.
EC2 . . . . . . 2A **18** (5E **63**)
Lawrence Pl. N1 . . . . 5A **48**
(off Brydon Wlk.)
Lawrence Rd. E6 . . . . 5F **55**
E13 . . . . 5D **55**
Lawrence St. E16. . . . 4B **68**
SW3 . . . . 2A **88**
Lawrence Trad. Est.
SE10 . . . . 5A **82**
Lawrie Pk. Av.
SE26 . . . . 5D **121**
Lawrie Pk. Cres.
SE26 . . . . 5D **121**
Lawrie Pk. Gdns.
SE26 . . . . 4D **121**
Lawrie Pk. Rd.
SE26 . . . . 5D **121**
Lawson Cl. E16 . . . . . 4E **69**
SW19 . . . . 3F **113**
Lawson Ct. N4 . . . . . . 3B **34**
(off Lorne Rd.)
Lawson Ho. W12. . . . . 1D **71**
(off White City Est.)
Law St. SE1. . . 5C **26** (4F **77**)
Lawton Rd. E3 . . . . . . 2A **66**
(not continuous)
E10 . . . . 3E **39**

Laxfield Ct. *E8* 5C **50**
   (off Pownall Rd.)
Laxford Ho. *SW1* 5C **74**
   (off Cundy St.)
Laxley Cl. *SE5* 3D **91**
Laxton Pl.
  NW1 . . . . 3E **5** (3D **61**)
Layard Rd. *SE16* 5D **79**
Layard Sq. *SE16* 5D **79**
Laybourne Ho. *E14* 3C **80**
   (off Admirals Way)
Laycock St. *N1* 3C **48**
Layfield Cl. *NW4* 2D **29**
Layfield Cres. *NW4* 2D **29**
Layfield Ho. *SE10* 1C **96**
   (off Kemsing Rd.)
Layfield Rd. *NW4* 2D **29**
Laystall Ct. *WC1* *4B* **8**
   (off Mount Pleasant)
Laystall St.
  EC1 . . . . . . 4B **8** (3C **62**)
Layton's Bldgs.
  SE1 . . . . . . 3B **26** (3F **77**)
Layzell Wlk. *SE9* 1F **125**
Lazar Wlk. *N7* 4B **34**
Lazenby Ct. *WC2* 4D **15**
Leabank Sq. *E9* 3D **52**
Leabank Vw. *N15* 1C **36**
Lea Bon Ct. *E15* 5B **54**
   (off Plaistow Gro.)
Leabourne Rd. *N16* 2F **37**
LEA BRIDGE 5F **37**
Lea Bri. Ind. Cen.
  E10 . . . . 3A **38**
Lea Bri. Rd. *E5* 5E **37**
  E10 . . . . 5E **37**
Lea Ct. *E13* 2C **68**
Leacroft Av. *SW12* 5B **102**
Leadale Rd. *N15* 1C **36**
  N16 . . . . 1C **36**
Leadenhall Mkt.
  EC3 . . . . 3D **19** (5A **64**)
Leadenhall Pl.
  EC3 . . . . 3D **19** (5A **64**)
Leadenhall St.
  EC3 . . . . 3D **19** (5A **64**)
Leadenham Ct. *E3* 3C **66**
Leaf Gro. *SE27* 5C **118**
Leafy Oak Rd. *SE12* . . 4E **125**
Leagrave St. *E5* 5E **37**
Lea Hall Gdns. *E10* 3C **38**
Lea Hall Rd. *E10* 3C **38**
Lea Ho. *NW8* 3A **60**
   (off Salisbury St.)
Leahurst Rd. *SE13* 3F **109**
   (not continuous)
LEA INTERCHANGE 2C **52**
Leake Ct.
  SE1 . . . . . . 4A **24** (3B **76**)
Leake St.
  SE1 . . . . . . 3A **24** (3B **76**)
   (not continuous)
Lealand Rd. *N15* 1B **36**
Leamington Av.
  BR1: Brom 5E **125**
  E17 . . . . 1C **38**
Leamington Cl.
  BR1: Brom 4E **125**
Leamington Rd. Vs.
  W11 . . . . 4B **58**

Leamore St. *W6* 5E **71**
LEAMOUTH 1A **82**
Leamouth Rd. *E6* 4F **69**
  E14 . . . . 5F **67**
Leander Ct. *SE8* 4C **94**
Leander Rd. *SW2* 4B **104**
Lea Pk. Trad. Est.
  E10 . . . . 2B **38**
Leary Ho. *SE11* 1B **90**
Leaside Rd. *E5* 3E **37**
Leasowes Rd. *E10* 3C **38**
Lea Sq. *E3* 5B **52**
Leatherdale St. *E1* 3E **65**
   (Harpley Sq.)
  E1 . . . . 2F **65**
   (Portelet Rd.)
Leather Gdns. *E15* 5A **54**
Leatherhead Cl.
  N16 . . . . 3B **36**
Leather La.
  EC1 . . . . . . 5B **8** (4C **62**)
   (not continuous)
Leathermarket, The
  SE1 . . . . 4D **27**
Leathermarket Ct.
  SE1 . . . . . . 4D **27** (3A **78**)
Leathermarket St.
  SE1 . . . . . . 4D **27** (3A **78**)
Leather St. *E1* 1F **79**
Leathwaite Rd.
  SW11 . . . . 2B **102**
Leathwell Rd. *SE8* 5D **95**
Lea Vw. Ho. *E5* 3D **37**
Leaway *E10* 3F **37**
Lebanon Gdns.
  SW18 . . . . 4C **100**
Lebanon Rd. *SW18* 3C **100**
Lebrun Sq. *SE3* 2D **111**
Lebus Ho. *NW8* 1A **60**
   (off Cochrane St.)
Lechmere Rd. *NW2* 3D **43**
Leckford Rd. *SW18* 2E **115**
Leckhampton Pl.
  SW2 . . . . 5C **104**
Lecky St. *SW7* 1F **87**
Leclair Ho. *SE3* 1D **111**
Leconfield Av. *SW13* . . 1B **98**
Leconfield Ho. *SE5* . . . 2A **106**
Leconfield Rd. *N5* 1F **49**
LEE 4C **110**
Lee Bri. *SE13* 1E **109**
Lee Chu. St. *SE13* 2A **110**
Lee Conservancy Rd.
  E9 . . . . 2B **52**

Lee Ct. *SE13* 2F **109**
   (off Lee High Rd.)
Leefern Rd. *W12* 3C **70**
Leegate *SE12* 3B **110**
LEE GREEN 3B **110**
Lee High Rd. *SE12* 1E **109**
  SE13 . . . . 1E **109**
Lee Ho. *EC2* 1A **18**
   (off Monkwell Sq.)
Leeke St. *WC1* 1F **7** (2B **62**)
Leeland Way *NW10* 1B **42**
Lee Pk. *SE3* 2B **110**
Leerdam Dr. *E14* 4E **81**
Lee Rd. *SE3* 1B **110**
Lees Ct. *W1* 4B **12**
   (off Lees Pl.)
Leeside Ct. *SE16* 2F **79**
   (off Rotherhithe St.)
Leeside Cres. *NW11* . . . 1A **30**
Leeson Rd. *SE24* 2C **104**
Lees Pl. *W1* 4B **12** (1C **74**)
Lee St. *E8* 5B **50**
Lee Ter. *SE3* 1A **110**
  SE13 . . . . 1A **110**
Lee Valley Cycle Circuit
   . . . . 2D **53**
Lee Valley Ice Cen. 4F **37**
Lee Valley Sports Cen.
   . . . . 1D **53**
Leeward Ct. *E1* 1C **78**
Leeward Gdns.
  SW19 . . . . 5A **114**
Leeway *SE8* 1B **94**
Leewood Cl. *SE12* 4B **110**
Lefevre Wlk. *E3* 1C **66**
Leff Ho. *NW6* 5A **44**
Lefroy Ho. *SE1* 4F **25**
   (off Southwark Bri. Rd.)
Lefroy Rd. *W12* 3B **70**
Legard Rd. *N5* 5D **35**
Legatt Rd. *SE9* 3F **111**
Leggatt Rd. *E15* 1E **67**
Legge St. *SE13* 3E **109**
Leghorn Rd. *NW10* 1B **56**
Legion Cl. *N1* 4C **48**
Legion Ter. *E3* 5B **52**
Leicester Ct. *W9* 4C **58**
   (off Elmfield Way)
  WC2 . . . . 4C **14**
Leicester Flds. *WC2* . . . 5C **14**
Leicester Ho. *SW9* 1D **105**
   (off Loughborough Rd.)
Leicester Pl.
  WC2 . . . . . . 4C **14** (1F **75**)
Leicester Rd. *E11* 1D **41**
  NW10 . . . . 4A **42**
Leicester Sq.
  WC2 . . . . 5C **14** (1F **75**)
Leicester St.
  WC2 . . . . . . 4C **14** (1F **75**)
Leigham Av. *SW16* 3A **118**
Leigham Cl. *SW16* 3B **118**
Leigham Ct. Rd.
  SW16 . . . . 2A **118**
Leigham Hall Pde.
  SW16 . . . . 3A **118**
   (off Streatham High Rd.)
Leigham Va. *SW2* 3B **118**
  SW16 . . . . 3B **118**
Leigh Gdns. *NW10* 1E **57**

Leigh Orchard Cl.
SW16 . . . . 3B **118**
Leigh Pl. EC1 . . . 5B **8** (4C **62**)
Leigh Rd. E10 . . . . . . 2E **39**
N5 . . . . 1D **49**
Leigh St. WC1 . . . 2D **7** (2A **62**)
Leighton Cres. NW5 . . . 2E **47**
Leighton Gdns.
NW10 . . . . 1D **57**
Leighton Gro. NW5 . . . . 2E **47**
Leighton Ho. SW1 . . . . 5F **75**
(off Herrick St.)
Leighton House Art Gallery &
Mus. 4B 72
Leighton Mans. W14 . . . 2A **86**
(off Greyhound Rd.)
Leighton Pl. NW5 . . . . 2E **47**
Leighton Rd. NW5 . . . . 2E **47**
Leila Parnell Pl. SE7 . . 3E **97**
Leinster Gdns. W2 . . . . 5E **59**
Leinster M. W2 . . . . . . 1E **73**
Leinster Pl. W2 . . . . . . 5E **59**
Leinster Sq. W2 . . . . . 5C **58**
(not continuous)
Leinster Ter. W2 . . . . . 1E **73**
Leithcote Gdns.
SW16 . . . . 4B **118**
Leithcote Path
SW16 . . . . 3B **118**
Leith Mans. W9 . . . . . . 2D **59**
(off Grantully Rd.)
Leith Yd. NW6 . . . . 5C **44**
(off Quex Rd.)
Lelitia Cl. E8 . . . . 5C **50**
Leman Pas. E1 . . . . . . 5C **64**
(off Leman St.)
Leman St. E1 . . . . 5B **64**
Le May Av. SE12 . . . . . 3D **125**
Lemmon Rd. SE10 . . . . 2A **96**
Lemna Rd. E11 . . . . . . 2B **40**
Le Moal Ho. E1 . . . . . . 4E **65**
(off Stepney Way)
Lemsford Cl. N15 . . . . 1C **36**
Lemsford Ct. N4 . . . . . 4E **35**
Lemuel St. SW18 . . . . 4E **101**
Lena Gdns. W6 . . . . . . 4E **71**
Lenanton Steps E14 . . 3C **80**
(off Manilla St.)
Lendal Ter. SW4 . . . . . 1F **103**
Len Freeman Pl.
SW6 . . . . 2B **86**
Lenham Ho. SE1 . . . . . 4C **26**
(off Long La.)
Lenham Rd. SE12 . . . . 2B **110**
Lennard Rd. SE20 . . . . 5F **121**
Lennon Rd. NW2 . . . . . 2E **43**
Lennox Gdns. NW10 . . 1B **42**
SW1 . . . . 4B **74**
Lennox Gdns. M.
SW1 . . . . 4B **74**
Lennox Lewis Cen.
E5 . . . . 4E **37**
(off Theydon Rd.)
Lennox Rd. E17 . . . . . 1B **38**
N4 . . . . 4B **34**
Lens Rd. E7 . . . . 4E **55**
Lenthall Ho. SW1 . . . . 1E **89**
(off Churchill Gdns.)
Lenthall Rd. E8 . . . . . . 4C **50**
Lenthorp Rd. SE10 . . . 5B **82**

Lentmead Rd.
BR1: Brom 3B **124**
Len Williams Ct.
NW6 . . . . 1C **58**
Leof Cres. SE6 . . . . . . 5D **123**
Leonard Ct.
WC1 . . . . 3C **6** (3F **61**)
Leonard Pl. N16 . . . . . 1A **50**
Leonard Rd. E7 . . . . . . 1C **54**
Leonard St.
EC2 . . . . 3C **10** (3F **63**)
Leonora Ho. W9 . . . . . 3E **59**
(off Lanark Rd.)
Leontine Cl. SE15 . . . . 3C **92**
Leopards Ct. EC1 . . . . 5B **8**
Leopold Av. SW19 . . . . 5B **114**
Leopold Bldgs. E2 . . . . 1F **11**
(off Columbia Rd.)
Leopold M. E9 . . . . . . 5E **51**
Leopold Rd. E17 . . . . . 1C **38**
NW10 . . . . 4A **42**
SW19 . . . . 4B **114**
Leopold St. E3 . . . . . . 4B **66**
Leopold Ter. SW19 . . . 5B **114**
Leo St. SE15 . . . . 3D **93**
Leo Yd. EC1 . . . . 4E **9**
Leppoc Rd. SW4 . . . . . 3F **103**
Leroy St. SE1 . . . . 5A **78**
Lerry Cl. W14 . . . . 2B **86**
Lescombe Cl. SE23 . . . 3A **122**
Lescombe Rd. SE23 . . 3A **122**
Leslie Prince Ct. SE5 . . 3F **91**
Leslie Rd. E11 . . . . . . 1E **53**
E16 . . . . 5D **69**
Lessar Av. SW4 . . . . . 4E **103**
Lessingham Av.
SW17 . . . . 4B **116**
Lessing St. SE23 . . . . 5A **108**
Lester Av. E15 . . . . . . 3A **68**
Leswin Pl. N16 . . . . . . 5B **36**
Leswin Rd. N16 . . . . . 5B **36**
Letchford Gdns.
NW10 . . . . 2C **56**
Letchford M. NW10 . . . 2C **56**
Letchmore Ho. W10 . . 3E **57**
(off Sutton Way)
Letchworth St.
SW17 . . . . 4B **116**
Lethbridge Cl. SE13 . . 4E **95**
Letterstone Rd. SW6 . . 3B **86**
Lettice St. SW6 . . . . . 4B **86**
Lett Rd. E15 . . . . 4F **53**
Lettsom St. SE5 . . . . . 5A **92**
Lettsom Wlk. E13 . . . . 1C **68**
Leucha Rd. E17 . . . . . 1A **38**
Levana Cl. SW19 . . . . 1A **114**
Levant Ho. E1 . . . . 3F **65**
(off Ernest St.)
Levehurst Ho. SE27 . . 5E **119**
Levendale Rd.
SE23 . . . . 2A **122**
Levenhurst Way SW4 . . 5A **90**
Leven Rd. E14 . . . . . . 4E **67**
Leverett St. SW3 . . . . 5A **74**
Leverington Pl.
N1 . . . . 2C **10** (2F **63**)
Leverson St. SW16 . . . 5B **117**
Leverstock Ho. SW3 . . 1A **88**
(off Cale St.)
Lever St. EC1 . . . 2E **9** (2D **63**)

Leverton Pl. NW5 . . . . 2E **47**
Leverton St. NW5 . . . . 2E **47**
Levison Way N19 . . . . 3F **33**
Levita Ho. NW1 . . . . . 1C **6**
(not continuous)
Lewesdon Cl. SW19 . . 1F **113**
Lewes Ho. SE1 . . . . . . 3E **27**
(off Druid St.)
SE15 . . . . 2C **92**
(off Friary Est.)
Leweston Pl. N16 . . . . 2B **36**
Lew Evans Ho.
SE22 . . . . 3C **106**
Lewey Ho. E3 . . . . 3B **66**
(off Joseph St.)
Lewin Rd. SW14 . . . . . 1A **98**
SW16 . . . . 5F **117**
Lewis Cl. SE16 . . . . . . 1D **93**
(off Stubbs Dr.)
Lewis Gro. SE13 . . . . . 2E **109**
LEWISHAM 1E **109**
Lewisham Bus. Cen.
SE14 . . . . 2F **93**
Lewisham Cen.
SE13 . . . . 2E **109**
Lewisham Crematorium
SE6 . . . . 2B **124**
Lewisham Hgts.
SE23 . . . . 1E **121**
Lewisham High St.
SE13 . . . . 4D **109**
Lewisham Hill SE13 . . . 5E **95**
Lewisham Lions Cen. . . 1E **93**
Lewisham Model Mkt.
SE13 . . . . 2E **109**
(off Lewisham High St.)
Lewisham Pk. SE13 . . . 3E **109**
Lewisham Rd. SE13 . . . 4D **95**
Lewisham St.
SW1 . . . . 4C **22** (3F **75**)
Lewisham Way SE4 . . . 4B **94**
SE14 . . . . 4B **94**
Lewis Ho. E14 . . . . . . 2E **81**
(off Coldharbour)
Lewis Pl. E8 . . . . 2C **50**
Lewis Silkin Ho.
SE15 . . . . 2E **93**
(off Lovelinch Cl.)
Lewis St. NW1 . . . . . . 3D **47**
(not continuous)
Lexham Gdns. W8 . . . . 5C **72**
Lexham Gdns. M.
W8 . . . . 4D **73**
Lexham M. W8 . . . . . . 5C **72**
Lexham Wlk. W8 . . . . . 4D **73**
Lexington Apartments
EC1 . . . . 3C **10** (3F **63**)
Lexington St.
W1 . . . . 4A **14** (1E **75**)
Lexton Gdns. SW12 . . . 1F **117**
Leybourne Ho. E14 . . . 5B **66**
(off Dod St.)
SE15 . . . . 2E **93**
Leybourne Rd. E11 . . . 3B **40**
NW1 . . . . 4D **47**
Leybourne St. NW1 . . . 4D **47**
Leybridge Ct. SE12 . . . 3C **110**
Leyden Mans. N19 . . . 2A **34**
Leyden St.
E1 . . . . 1F **19** (4B **64**)

Leydon Cl. SE16 . . . . . . 2F 79
Leyes Rd. E16 . . . . 1F 83
Leyland Ho. E14 . . . . . . 1D 81
　　　　　(off Hale St.)
Leyland Rd. SE12 . . . . . . 3C 110
Leylands SW18 . . . . . . 4B 100
Leylang Rd. SE14 . . . . . . 3F 93
Leys Cl. SW9 . . . . 5C 90
Leysdown Ho. SE17 . . . . 1A 92
　　　　　(off Madron St.)
Leysfield Rd. W12 . . . . . 4C 70
Leyspring Rd. E11 . . . . . 3B 40
LEYTON 4E 39
Leyton Bus. Cen. E10 . . . 4C 38
Leyton Ct. SE23 . . . . . . 1E 121
Leyton Grange Est.
　E10 . . . . 3C 38
Leyton Grn. Rd. E10 . . . . 1E 39
Leyton Grn. Twr. E10 . . . 1E 39
　　　　　(off Leyton Grn. Rd.)
Leyton Grn. Towers
　E10 . . . . 1E 39
　　　　　(off Leyton Grn. Rd.)
Leyton Ind. Village
　E10 . . . . 2F 37
Leyton Leisure Lagoon
　. . . . . 2D 39
Leyton Orient FC 5D 39
Leyton Pk. Rd. E10 . . . . 5E 39
Leyton Rd. E15 . . . . 2E 53
LEYTONSTONE 5A 40
Leytonstone Ho. E11 . . . 2B 40
　　　　　(off Hanbury Dr.)
Leytonstone Rd. E15 . . . 2A 54
Leyton Way E11 . . . . . . 2A 40
Leywick St. E15 . . . . . . 1A 68
Liardet St. SE14 . . . . . . 2A 94
Liberia Rd. N5 . . . . 3D 49
Liberty Ho. E1 . . . . 1C 78
　　　　　(off Ensign St.)
Liberty M. SW12 . . . . . . 4D 103
Liberty St. SW9 . . . . . . 4B 90
Libra Cl. E3 . . . . 1B 66
　E13 . . . . 1C 68
Library Mans. W12 . . . . . 3E 71
　　　　　(off Pennard Rd.)
Library Pde. NW10 . . . . . 5A 42
　　　　　(off Craven Pk. Rd.)
Library Pl. E1 . . . . 1D 79
Library St.
　SE1 . . . . 5D 25 (3D 77)
Lichfield Rd. E3 . . . . 2A 66
　E6 . . . . 2F 69
　NW2 . . . . 1A 44
Lickey Ho. W14 . . . . 2B 86
　　　　　(off Nth. End Rd.)
Lidcote Gdns. SW9 . . . . 5B 90
Liddell Gdns. NW10 . . . . 1E 57
Liddell Rd. NW6 . . . . . . 3C 44
Liddington Rd. E15 . . . . 5B 54
Liddon Rd. E13 . . . . 2D 69
Liden Cl. E17 . . . . 2B 38
Lidfield Rd. N16 . . . . . . 1F 49
Lidgate Rd. SE15 . . . . . 3B 92
Lidiard Rd. SW18 . . . . . 2E 115
Lidlington Pl. NW1 . . . . . 1E 61
Lidyard Rd. N19 . . . . . . 3E 33
Liffords Pl. SW13 . . . . . 5B 84
Lifford St. SW15 . . . . . . 2F 99
Lighter Cl. SE16 . . . . . . 5A 80

Lighterman Ho. E14 . . . . 1E 81
Lighterman M. E1 . . . . . 5F 65
Lightermans Rd. E14 . . . 3C 80
Lightermans Wlk.
　SW18 . . . . 2C 100
Light Horse Ct. SW3 . . . 1C 88
　　　　　(off Royal Hospital Rd.)
Ligonier St.
　E2 . . . . 3F 11 (3B 64)
Lilac Cl. E13 . . . . 5E 55
Lilac Ho. SE4 . . . . 1C 108
Lilac Pl. SE11 . . . . 5B 76
Lilac St. W12 . . . . 1C 70
Lilburne Rd. SE9 . . . . . . 3F 111
Lilestone Ho. NW8 . . . . . 3F 59
　　　　　(off Frampton St.)
Lilestone St. NW8 . . . . . 3A 60
Lilford Ho. SE5 . . . . 5E 91
Lilford Rd. SE5 . . . . 5D 91
Lilian Barker Cl.
　SE12 . . . . 3C 110
Lilian Cl. N16 . . . . 5A 36
Lilley Cl. E1 . . . . 2C 78
Lillian Rd. SW13 . . . . . . 2C 84
Lillie Mans. SW6 . . . . . . 2A 86
　　　　　(off Lillie Rd.)
Lillie Rd. SW6 . . . . 2A 86
Lillieshall Rd. SW4 . . . . 1D 103
Lillie Yd. SW6 . . . . 2C 86
Lillingston Ho. N7 . . . . . 1C 48
Lillington Gdns. Est.
　SW1 . . . . 5E 75
　　　　　(off Vauxhall Bri. Rd.)
Lilliput Ct. SE12 . . . . . . 3D 111
Lily Cl. W14 . . . . 5F 71
　　　　　(not continuous)
Lily Nichols Ho. E16 . . . 2F 83
　　　　　(off Connaught Rd.)
Lily Pl. EC1 . . . . 5C 8 (4C 62)
Lily Rd. E17 . . . . 1C 38
Lilyville Rd. SW6 . . . . . . 4B 86
Limborough Ho. E14 . . . 4C 66
　　　　　(off Thomas Rd.)
Limburg Rd. SW11 . . . . 2A 102
Lime Cl. E1 . . . . 2C 78
Lime Ct. E11 . . . . 4A 40
　　　　　(off Trinity Cl.)
　E17 . . . . 1E 39
Lime Gro. W12 . . . . 3E 71
Limeharbour E14 . . . . . . 4D 81
LIMEHOUSE 5B 66
Limehouse C'way.
　E14 . . . . 1B 80
Limehouse Ct. E14 . . . . 5C 66
Limehouse Cut E14 . . . . 4D 67
　　　　　(off Morris Rd.)
Limehouse Flds. Est.
　E14 . . . . 4A 66
Limehouse Link E14 . . . 5A 66
Lime Kiln Dr. SE7 . . . . . 2D 97
Limerick Cl. SW12 . . . . 5E 103
Limerston St. SW10 . . . 2E 87
Limes, The SW18 . . . . . 4C 100
　W2 . . . . 1C 72
Limes Av. NW11 . . . . . . 2A 30
　SW13 . . . . 5B 84

Limes Ct. NW6 . . . . 4A 44
　　　　　(off Brondesbury Pk.)
Limes Fld. Rd.
　SW14 . . . . 1A 98
Limesford Rd. SE15 . . . . 2F 107
Limes Gdns. SW18 . . . . 4C 100
Limes Gro. SE13 . . . . . . 2E 109
Limes Rd. SE3 . . . 4D 19 (1A 78)
Lime St. Pas.
　EC3 . . . . 3D 19 (5A 64)
Limes Wlk. SE15 . . . . . . 2E 107
Limetree Cl. SW2 . . . . . 1B 118
Limetree Ct. E3 . . . . 4C 66
Limetree Ter. SE6 . . . . . 1B 122
Limetree Wlk.
　SW17 . . . . 5C 116
Lime Wlk. E15 . . . . 5A 54
Limpsfield Av.
　SW19 . . . . 2F 113
Linacre Cl. SE15 . . . . . . 1D 107
Linacre Ct. W6 . . . . 1F 85
Linacre Rd. NW2 . . . . . . 3D 43
Linale Ho. N1 . . . . 1B 10
Linberry Wlk. SE8 . . . . . 5B 80
Linchmere Rd.
　SE12 . . . . 5B 110
Lincoln Av. SW19 . . . . . 3F 113
Lincoln Ct. N16 . . . . . . 2F 35
　SE12 . . . . 3E 125
Lincoln Ho. SE5 . . . . . . 3C 90
　SW3 . . . . 3B 74
Lincoln M. NW6 . . . . . . 5B 44
　SE21 . . . . 2F 119
Lincoln Rd. E7 . . . . 3F 55
　E13 . . . . 3D 69
Lincolns Inn Flds.
　WC2 . . . . 2F 15 (5B 62)
Lincoln's Inn Hall
　. . . . . 2A 16 (5B 62)
Lincoln St. E11 . . . . 4A 40
　SW3 . . . . 5B 74
Lincombe Rd.
　BR1: Brom 3B 124
Lindal Rd. SE4 . . . . 3B 108
Linden Av. NW10 . . . . . 1F 57
Linden Ct. W12 . . . . 2E 71
Linden Gdns. W2 . . . . . 1C 72
　W4 . . . . 1A 84
Linden Gro. SE15 . . . . . 1D 107
Linden Ho. SE8 . . . . 2B 94
　　　　　(off Abinger Gro.)
Linden Lea N2 . . . . 1E 31
Linden Mans. N6 . . . . . . 3D 33
　　　　　(off Hornsey La.)
Linden M. N1 . . . . 2F 49
　W2 . . . . 1C 72
Linden Wlk. N19 . . . . . . 4E 33
Lindfield Gdns. NW3 . . . 2D 45
Lindfield St. E14 . . . . . . 5C 66
Lindisfarne Way E19 . . . 1A 52
Lindley Est. SE15 . . . . . 3C 92
Lindley Ho. E1 . . . . 4E 65
　　　　　(off Lindley St.)
　SE15 . . . . 3C 92
　　　　　(off Peckham Pk. Rd.)
Lindley Rd. E10 . . . . 4E 39
Lindley St. E1 . . . . 4E 65
Lindop Ho. E1 . . . . 3A 66
　　　　　(off Mile End Rd.)
Lindore Rd. SW11 . . . . . 2B 102

Lindo St. SE15 . . . . 5E 93
Lindrop St. SW6 . . . . 5E 87
Lindsay Sq. SW1 . . . . . . 1F 89
Lindsell St. SE10 . . . . . . 4E 95
Lindsey M. N1 . . . . 4E 49
Lindsey St.
   EC1 . . . . 5E 9 (4D 63)
Lind St. SE8 . . . . 5C 94
Lindway SE27 . . . . 5D 119
Linfield WC1 . . . . .2F 7
      (off Sidmouth St.)
Linford Christie Stadium
   . . . . 4C 56
Linford St. SW8 . . . . . . 4E 89
Lingard Ho. E14 . . . . 4E 81
      (off Marshfield St.)
Lingards Rd. SE13 . . . 2E 109
Lingfield Ho. SE1 . . . . . 4E 25
Lingfield Rd.
   SW19 . . . . 5F 113
Lingham Ct. SW9 . . . . . . 5A 90
Lingham St. SW9 . . . . . . 5A 90
Ling Rd. E16 . . . . 4C 68
Lings Coppice SE21 . . 2F 119
Lingwell Rd. SW17 . . . 3A 116
Lingwood Rd. E5 . . . . . . 2C 36
Linhope St. NW1 . . . . . . 3B 60
Link, The NW2 . . . . 3C 28
Linkenholt Mans. W6 . . 5B 70
      (off Stamford Brook Av.)
Link Ho. E3 . . . . 1D 67
   W10 . . . . 5F 57
      (off Kingsdown Cl.)
Link Rd. E1 . . . . 1C 78
   E12 . . . . 4F 41
Links Rd. NW2 . . . . 4B 28
Link St. E9 . . . . 3E 51
Linksview N2 . . . . 1B 32
      (off Gt. North Rd.)
Links Yd. E1 . . . . 4B 64
      (off Spelman St.)
Linkway N4 . . . . 2E 35
Linkwood Wlk. NW1 . . . 4F 47
Linley Sambourne House
   . . . . 4C 72
      (off Stafford Ter.)
Linnell Cl. NW11 . . . . . 1D 31
Linnell Dr. NW11 . . . . . 1D 31
Linnell Ho. E1 . . . . 5F 11
      (off Folgate St.)
Linnell Rd. SE5 . . . . 5A 92
Linnet M. SW12 . . . . . 5C 102
Linom Rd. SW4 . . . . . . 2A 104
Linscott Rd. E5 . . . . 1E 51
Linsey Ct. E10 . . . . 3C 38
      (off Grange Rd.)
Linsey St. SE16 . . . . 5C 78
      (not continuous)
Linslade Ho. E2 . . . . . . 5C 50
   NW8 . . . . 3A 60
      (off Paveley St.)
Linstead Hall SW7 . . . . 4F 73
      (off Princes Gdns.)
Linstead St. NW6 . . . . . 4C 44
Linstead Way SW18 . . 5A 100
Lintaine Cl. W6 . . . . . . 2A 86
Linthorpe Rd. N16 . . . . 2A 36
Linton Cl. SE7 . . . . 1E 97
Linton Gdns. E6 . . . . . . 5F 69
Linton Gro. SE27 . . . . 5D 119

Linton Ho. E3 . . . . 4C 66
      (off St Paul's Way)
Linton St. N1 . . . . 5E 49
      (not continuous)
Linver Rd. SW6 . . . . 5C 86
Linwood Cl. SE5 . . . . . . 5B 92
Lion Cl. SE4 . . . . 4C 108
Lion Ct. E1 . . . . 1F 79
      (off Highway, The)
   N1 . . . . 5B 48
      (off Copenhagen St.)
   SE1 . . . . 2D 27
      (off Magdalen St.)
Lionel Gdns. SE9 . . . . . 3F 111
Lionel Mans. W14 . . . . 4F 71
      (off Haarlem Rd.)
Lionel M. W10 . . . . 4A 58
Lionel Rd. SE9 . . . . . . 3F 111
Lion Gate M.
   SW18 . . . . 5C 100
Lion Mills E2 . . . . 1C 64
Lions Cl. SE9 . . . . 3F 125
Lion Yd. SW4 . . . . 2F 103
Liphook Cres. SE23 . . 5E 107
Lipton Rd. E1 . . . . 5F 65
Lisburne Rd. NW3 . . . . 1B 46
Lisford St. SE15 . . . . . . 4B 92
Lisgar Ter. W14 . . . . . . 5B 72
Liskeard Gdns. SE3 . . . 4C 96
Liskeard Ho. SE11 . . . . 1C 90
      (off Kennings Way)
Lisle Cl. SW17 . . . . 4D 117
Lisle Ct. NW2 . . . . 5A 30
Lisle St.
   WC2 . . . . 4C 14 (1F 75)
Lismore SW19 . . . . 5B 114
      (off Woodside)
Lismore Cir. NW5 . . . . . 2C 46
Lismore Ho. SE15 . . . . 1D 107
Lismore Wlk. N1 . . . . . . 3E 49
      (off Clephane Rd. Nth.)
Lissenden Gdns.
   NW5 . . . . 1C 46
      (not continuous)
Lissenden Mans.
   NW5 . . . . 1C 46
Lisson Grn. Est.
   NW8 . . . . 3A 60
      (off Tresham Cres.)
LISSON GROVE 4A 60
Lisson Gro. NW1 . . . . . 3F 59
   NW8 . . . . 3F 59
Lisson Ho. NW1 . . . . . . 4A 60
      (off Lisson St.)
Lisson St. NW1 . . . . . . 4A 60
Lister Cl. W3 . . . . 4A 56
Listergate St. SW15 . . . 2E 99
Lister Ho. E1 . . . . 4C 64
   SE3 . . . . 2A 96
      (off Restell Cl.)
Lister Lodge W9 . . . . . . 4C 58
      (off Admiral Wlk.)
Lister Rd. E11 . . . . 3A 40
Liston Rd. SW4 . . . . . . 1E 103
Listowel Cl. SW9 . . . . . 3C 90
Listria Pk. N16 . . . . 4A 36
Litcham Ho. E1 . . . . . . 2F 65
      (off Longnor Rd.)
Litchfield Av. E15 . . . . 3A 54
Litchfield Ct. E17 . . . . . 1C 38

Litchfield Gdns.
   NW10 . . . . 3C 42
Litchfield St.
   WC2 . . . . 4C 14 (1F 75)
Lithos Rd. NW3 . . . . . . 3D 45
Lit. Albany St.
   NW1 . . . . 2E 5 (2D 61)
      (Albany St.)
   NW1 . . . . 1E 5
      (Longford St.)
Little Angel Theatre . . . 5D 49
      (off Cross St.)
Lit. Argyll St.
   W1 . . . . 3F 13 (5E 61)
Lit. Boltons, The
   SW5 . . . . 1D 87
   SW10 . . . . 1D 87
Little Bornes SE21 . . . 4A 120
Littlebourne SE13 . . . . 5A 110
Little Britain
   EC1 . . . . 1E 17 (4D 63)
Little Brownings
   SE23 . . . . 2D 121
Littlebury Rd.
   SW4 . . . . 1F 103
Lit. Chester St.
   SW1 . . . . 5D 21 (4D 75)
Little Cloisters
   SW1 . . . . 5D 23 (4A 76)
Lit. College La. EC4 . . . 4B 18
      (off College St.)
Lit. College St.
   SW1 . . . . 5D 23 (4A 76)
Littlecombe SE7 . . . . . 2D 97
Littlecombe Cl.
   SW15 . . . . 4F 99
Littlecote Cl. SW19 . . . 5A 100
Lit. Dean's Yd. SW1 . . . 5D 23
Little Dimocks
   SW12 . . . . 2D 117
Lit. Dorrit Ct.
   SE1 . . . . 3A 26 (3E 77)
Lit. Edward St.
   NW1 . . . . 1E 5 (2D 61)
Lit. Essex St. WC2 . . . . 4B 16
Littlefield Cl. N19. . . . . 1E 47
Lit. George St.
   SW1 . . . . 4D 23 (3A 76)
Little Grn. St. NW5 . . . . 1D 47
Little Heath SE7 . . . . . 2F 97
Little Holt E11 . . . . 1C 40
Lit. London Ct. SE1 . . . 3B 78
      (off Wolseley St.)
Lit. Marlborough St.
   W1 . . . . 3F 13
Lit. Newport St.
   WC2 . . . . 4C 14 (1F 75)
Lit. New St.
   EC4 . . . . 2C 16 (5C 62)
Lit. Portland St.
   W1 . . . . 2E 13 (5E 61)
Lit. Russell St.
   WC1 . . . . 1D 15 (4A 62)
Lit. St James's St.
   SW1 . . . . 2F 21 (2E 75)
Little Sanctuary
   SW1 . . . . 4C 22 (3F 75)
Lit. Smith St.
   SW1 . . . . 5C 22 (4F 75)

Lit. Somerset St.
E1 . . . . 3F **19** (5B **64**)
Lit. Titchfield St.
W1 . . . . 1F **13** (4E **61**)
Littleton Ho. *SW1* *1E 89*
(off Lupus St.)
Littleton St. SW18 . . . . . 2E **115**
Lit. Trinity La.
EC4 . . . . . . 4A **18** (1E **77**)
Little Turnstile
WC1 . . . . . . 1F **15** (4B **62**)
Littlewood SE13 . . . . . 4E **109**
Livermere Ct. *E8* *5B 50*
(off Queensbridge Rd.)
Livermere Rd. E8 . . . . . . 5B **50**
Liverpool Gro. SE17 . . . . . 1E **91**
Liverpool Rd. E10 . . . . . . 1E **39**
E16 . . . . 4A **68**
N1 . . . . 4C **48**
N7 . . . . 2C **48**
Liverpool St.
EC2 . . . . . . 1D **19** (4A **64**)
Livesey Mus. for Children
. . . . 2D **93**
Livesey Pl. SE15 . . . . . . 2C **92**
Livingstone Ct. E10 . . . . . 1E **39**
Livingstone Ho. *SE5* *3E 91*
(off Wyndham Rd.)
Livingstone Lodge
W9 . . . . *4C 58*
(off Admiral Wlk.)
Livingstone Mans.
W14 . . . . *2A 86*
(off Queen's Club Gdns.)
Livingstone Pl. E14 . . . . . 1E **95**
Livingstone Rd. E15 . . . . . 5E **53**
E17 . . . . 1D **39**
SW11 . . . . 1F **101**
LivingWell Health Club
. . . . 1D **59**
(within Regents Plaza)
Livonia St.
W1 . . . . 3A **14** (5E **61**)
Lizard St.
EC1 . . . . . . 2A **10** (2E **63**)
Lizban St. SE3 . . . . 3D **97**
Llandovery Ho. *E14* *3E 81*
(off Chipka St.)
Llanelly Rd. NW2 . . . . . . 4B **30**
Llanvanor Rd. NW2 . . . . . 4B **30**
Llewellyn St. SE16 . . . . . 3C **78**
Lloyd Baker St.
WC1 . . . . . . 2A **8** (2B **62**)
(not continuous)
Lloyd's Av.
EC3 . . . . . . 3E **19** (5A **64**)
Lloyds' Building
. . . . 3D **19** (5A **64**)
Lloyd's Pl. SE3 . . . . 5A **96**
Lloyd Sq.
WC1 . . . . 1B **8** (2C **62**)
Lloyd's Row
EC1 . . . . . . 2C **8** (2C **62**)
Lloyd St. WC1 . . . 1B **8** (2C **62**)
Lloyds Wharf *SE1* *3B 78*
(off Mill St.)
Lloyd Vs. SE4 . . . . 5C **94**
Loampit Hill SE13 . . . . . 5C **94**
LOAMPIT VALE 1E **109**
Loampit Va. SE13 . . . . 1D **109**

Loanda Cl. E8 . . . . 5B **50**
Loats Rd. SW2 . . . . . . 4A **104**
Lobelia Cl. E6 . . . . 4F **69**
Locarno Rd. SW16 . . . . . 5E **117**
Lochaber Rd. SE13 . . . . 2A **110**
Lochaline St. W6 . . . . . . 2E **85**
Lochinvar St.
SW12 . . . . 5D **103**
Lochmore Ho. *SW1* *5C 74*
(off Cundy St.)
Lochnagar St. E14 . . . . . 4E **67**
Lockbridge Ct. *W9* *4C 58*
(off Woodfield Rd.)
Lock Chase SE3 . . . . . 1A **110**
Locke Ho. *SW8* *4E 89*
(off Wadhurst Rd.)
Lockesfield Pl. E14 . . . . . 1D **95**
Lockgate Cl. E9 . . . . . . 2B **52**
Lockhart Cl. N7 . . . . . . 3B **48**
Lockhart Ho. *SE10* *3D 95*
(off Tarves Way)
Lockhart St. E3 . . . . . . 3B **66**
Lockhurst St. E5 . . . . . . 1F **51**
Lockington Rd. SW8 . . . . 4D **89**
Lock Keepers Quay
SE16 . . . . *4F 79*
(off Brunswick Quay)
Lockmead Rd. N15 . . . . 1C **36**
SE13 . . . . 1E **109**
Lock M. NW5 . . . . 3F **47**
(off Northpoint Sq.)
Locksfields *SE17* *5F 77*
(off Catesby St.)
Lockside *E14* *1A 80*
(off Narrow St.)
Locksley Est. E14 . . . . . 5B **66**
Locksley St. E14 . . . . . . 4B **66**
Lock Vw. Ct. *E14* *1A 80*
(off Narrow St.)
Lockwood Cl. SE26 . . . . 4F **121**
Lockwood Ho. SE11 . . . . 2C **90**
Lockwood Sq. SE16 . . . . 4D **79**
Lockyer Est. SE1 . . . . . . 4C **26**
(not continuous)
Lockyer Ho. *SE10* *1B 96*
(off Armitage Rd.)
SW8 . . . . *3F 89*
(off Wandsworth Rd.)
SW15 . . . . 1F **99**
Lockyer St.
SE1 . . . . . . 4C **26** (3F **77**)
Locton Grn. E3 . . . . . . 5B **52**
Loddiges Ho. E9 . . . . . . 4E **51**
Loddiges Rd. E9 . . . . . . 4E **51**
Loder St. SE15 . . . . . . 3E **93**
Lodge Av. SW14 . . . . . 1A **98**
Lodge Rd. NW8 . . . . . . 2F **59**
Lodore Gdns. NW9 . . . . 1A **28**
Lodore St. E14 . . . . . . 5E **67**
Loftie St. SE16 . . . . . . 3C **78**
Lofting Rd. N1 . . . . . . 4B **48**
Loftus Road 2D **71**
Loftus Rd. W12 . . . . . . 2D **71**
Loftus Vs. W12 . . . . . . 2D **71**
(off Loftus Rd.)
Logan M. W8 . . . . 5C **72**
Logan Pl. W8 . . . . 5C **72**
Loggetts SE21 . . . . . . 2A **120**
Lohmann Ho. *SE11* *2C 90*
(off Kennington Oval)

Lolesworth Cl.
E1 . . . . 1F **19** (4B **64**)
Lollard St. SE11 . . . . . . 5B **76**
(not continuous)
Loman St.
SE1 . . . . . . 3E **25** (3D **77**)
Lomas Dr. *E8* *4B 50*
(off Richmond Rd.)
Lomas St. E1 . . . . 4C **64**
Lombard Bus. Cen., The
. . . . 5F **87**
Lombard Ct.
EC3 . . . . . . 4C **18** (1F **77**)
Lombard La.
EC4 . . . . . . 3C **16** (5C **62**)
Lombard Rd. SW11 . . . . 5F **87**
Lombard St.
EC3 . . . . . . 3C **18** (5F **63**)
Lombard Trad. Est.
SE7 . . . . 5D **83**
Lombard Wall SE7 . . . . . 4D **83**
(not continuous)
Lombardy Pl. W2 . . . . . 1D **73**
Lomond Gro. SE5 . . . . . 3F **91**
Lomond Ho. SE5 . . . . . 3F **91**
Loncroft Rd. SE5 . . . . . 2A **92**
Londesborough Rd.
N16 . . . . 1A **50**
Londinium Twr. *E1* *4F 19*
(off W. Tenter St.)
London Academy of Music &
Dramatic Art *5C 72*
(off Cromwell Rd.)
London Apollo 1E **85**
London Aquarium
. . . . 3F **23** (3B **76**)
London Bri.
EC4 . . . . . . 5C **18** (2F **77**)
SE1 . . . . . . 1C **26** (2F **77**)
London Bri. St.
SE1 . . . . . . 2C **26** (2F **77**)
London Bri. Wlk.
SE1 . . . . *1C 26*
(off Duke St. Hill)
London Business School
. . . . 3A **4** (3B **60**)
London Canal Mus. 1A **62**
LONDON CITY AIRPORT
. . . . 1F **83**
London City College
. . . . 2B **24** (2C **76**)
(in Schiller University)
London Coliseum *5D 15*
(off St Martin's La.)
London College of
Fashion, The
Hackney *4E 51*
(off Mare St.)
St Luke's 4F **9** (3E **63**)
London Dungeon 2C **26**
London Eye 3F **23** (3B **76**)
London Flds. E. Side
E8 . . . . 4D **51**
London Flds. W. Side
E8 . . . . 4C **50**
London Fruit Exchange
E1 . . . . *1F 19*
(off Brushfield St.)
London Group Bus. Pk.
NW2 . . . . 3B **28**

London Guildhall University
Coke St. 5C 64
London Ho. NW8 . . . . 1A 60
(off Avenue Rd.)
WC1 . . . . 3F 7 (3B 62)
London La. E8 . . . . . . 4D 51
London Master Bakers
Almshouses E10 . . . 1D 39
London Metropolitan
University
Benwell Rd. 2C 48
City of London 3F 19
(off Jewry St.)
Hornsey St. 2B 48
Manningtree St.
. . . . 2F 19 (5C 64)
London M. W2 . . . . . . 5F 59
London Palladium . . . 3F 13
(off Argyll St.)
London Planetarium
. . . . 4B 4 (3C 60)
London Regatta Cen. . . 1F 83
London Rd. E13 . . . . . . 1C 68
SE1 . . . . 5D 25 (4D 77)
SE23 . . . . 1D 121
London School of Economics
& Politics, The
. . . . 3A 16 (5B 62)
London South Bank University
. . . . 5E 25 (4D 77)
London South Bank University
Sports Cen. 4D 77
(off Borough Rd.)
London Stock Exchange
. . . . 2E 17
(off Paternoster Sq.)
London St.
EC3 . . . . 4E 19 (1A 78)
W2 . . . . 5F 59
London Symphony Orchestra
. . . . 3A 10
(off St Lukes Cl.)
London Telecom Tower, The
. . . . 5F 5 (4E 61)
London Television Cen., The
. . . . 1B 24 (2C 76)
London Ter. E2 . . . . . . 1C 64
London Towers Basketball
Crystal Palace National
Sports Cen. 5C 120
London Transport Mus.
. . . . 4E 15 (1A 76)
London Wall
EC2 . . . . 1A 18 (4E 63)
London Wall Bldgs.
EC2 . . . . 1C 18
London Wetland Cen.
. . . . 4D 85
London Wharf E2 . . . . 5D 51
(off Wharf Pl.)
London Wildlife Trust
. . . . 5F 47
London Wildlife Trust Cen.
for Wildlife Gardening
. . . . 1B 106
London Zoo 1C 60
Long Acre
WC2 . . . . 4D 15 (1A 76)
Longbeach Rd.
SW11 . . . . 1B 102

Longberrys NW2 . . . . . 5B 30
Longbridge Way
SE13 . . . . 3E 109
Longdown Rd. SE6 . . . 4C 122
Long Dr. W3 . . . . 5A 56
Longfellow Rd. E17 . . . 1B 38
Longfellow Way SE1 . . 5B 78
Longfield Cres.
SE3 . . . . 3E 121
Longfield Est. SE1 . . . . 5B 78
Longfield Rd. SW18 . . 5C 100
Longford Ct. E5 . . . . . . 1F 51
(off Pedro St.)
Longford Ho.
BR1: Brom 5F 123
(off Brangbourne Rd.)
E1 . . . . 5E 65
(off Jubilee St.)
Longford St.
NW1 . . . . 3E 5 (3D 61)
Longford Wlk. SW2 . . . 5C 104
Longhedge Ho.
SE26 . . . . 4C 120
(off High Level Dr.)
Longhedge St. SW11 . . 5C 88
Longhill Rd. SE6 . . . . . 2F 123
Longhope Cl. SE15 . . . 2A 92
Longhurst Rd. SE13 . . . 3F 109
Longland Ct. SE1 . . . . . 1C 92
Longlands Ct. W11 . . . 1B 72
(off Westbourne Gro.)
Long La. EC1 . . . 1E 17 (4D 63)
SE1 . . . . 4B 26 (3F 77)
Longleat Ho. SW1 . . . . 1F 89
(off Rampayne St.)
Longleigh Ho. SE5 . . . . 4A 92
(off Peckham Rd.)
Long Lents Ho.
NW10 . . . . 5A 42
(off Fitzsimmons Ct.)
Longley Ct. SW8 . . . . . 4A 90
Longley Rd. SW17 . . . 5A 116
Longley St. SE1 . . . . . . 5C 78
Longley Way NW2 . . . . 5E 29
Longman Ho. E2 . . . . . 1F 65
(off Mace St.)
E8 . . . . 5B 50
(off Haggerston Rd.)
Long Mark Rd. E16 . . . 4F 69
Longmead Ho.
SE27 . . . . 5E 119
Long Mdw. NW5 . . . . . 2F 47
Longmead Rd.
SW17 . . . . 5B 116
Longmoore St. SW1 . . 5E 75
Longmoor Point
SW15 . . . . 1D 113
(off Norley Vale)
Longmore Gdns. Est.
SW1 . . . . 5E 75
(off Vauxhall Bri. Rd.)
Longnor Est. E1 . . . . . 2F 65
Longnor Rd. E1 . . . . . . 2F 65
Long Pond Rd. SE3 . . . 4A 96
Longridge Ho.
SE1 . . . . 5A 26 (4E 77)
Longridge Rd. SW5 . . . 5C 72
Long Rd. SW4 . . . . . . 2D 103
Long's Ct. WC2 . . . . . . 5C 14
Longshore SE8 . . . . . . 5B 80

Longshott Ct. SW5 . . . 5C 72
(off W. Cromwell Rd.)
Longstaff Cres.
SW18 . . . . 4C 100
Longstaff Rd. SW18 . . 4C 100
Longstone Av. NW10 . . 4B 42
Longstone Ct. SE1 . . . . 4B 26
(off Gt. Dover St.)
Longstone Rd.
SW17 . . . . 5D 117
Longthorpe Ct. W6 . . . 5C 70
(off Invermead Cl.)
Longton Av. SE26 . . . . 4C 120
Longton Gro. SE26 . . . 4D 121
Longville Rd. SE11 . . . 5D 77
Long Wlk. SE1 . . . . . . 5E 27
SW13 . . . . 5A 84
Long Wall E15 . . . . . . 2F 67
Longwood Dr. SW15 . . 4C 98
Long Yd. WC1 . . . 4F 7 (3B 62)
Lonsdale Av. E6 . . . . . 2F 69
Lonsdale Cl. E6 . . . . . . 3F 69
SE9 . . . . 3F 125
Lonsdale Ho. W11 . . . . 5B 58
(off Lonsdale Rd.)
Lonsdale M. W11 . . . . 5B 58
(off Lonsdale Rd.)
Lonsdale Pl. N1 . . . . . 4C 48
Lonsdale Rd. E11 . . . . 1B 40
NW6 . . . . 5B 44
SW13 . . . . 4B 84
W4 . . . . 5B 70
W11 . . . . 5B 58
Lonsdale Sq. N1 . . . . . 4C 48
Lonsdale Yd. W11 . . . . 1C 72
Lopez Ho. SW9 . . . . . 1A 104
Loraine Cotts. N7 . . . . 1B 48
Loraine Rd. N7 . . . . . . 1B 48
Lord Amory Way E14 . . 3E 81
Lordell Pl. SW19 . . . . 5E 113
Lorden Wlk. E2 . . . . . . 2C 64
Lord Hills Bri. W2 . . . . 4D 59
Lord Hills Rd. W2 . . . . 4D 59
Lord Holland La.
SW9 . . . . 5C 90
Lord Napier Pl. W6 . . . 1C 84
Lord North St.
SW1 . . . . . . 5D 23 (4A 76)
Lord Roberts M. SW6 . . 3D 87
Lords Cl. SE21 . . . . . . 2E 119
Lord's Cricket Ground
Marylebone & Middlesex
County Cricket Clubs
. . . . 2F 59
Lordship Gro. N16 . . . . 4F 35
Lordship La. SE22 . . . . 2B 106
Lordship La. Est.
SE21 . . . . 5C 106
Lordship Pk. N16 . . . . 4E 35
Lordship Pk. M. N16 . . 4E 35
Lordship Pl. SW3 . . . . 2A 88
Lordship Rd. N16 . . . . 3F 35
Lordship Ter. N16 . . . . 4F 35
Lords Vw. NW8 . . . . . . 2F 59
Loreburn Ho. N7 . . . . . 1B 48
Lorenzo St.
WC1 . . . . 1F 7 (2B 62)
Loring Rd. SE14 . . . . . 4A 94
Loris Rd. W6 . . . . 4E 71

Lorn Ct. SW9 . . . . 5C 90
Lorne Ho. NW8 . . . . 2A 60
Lorne Gdns. W11 . . . . 3F 71
Lorne Ho. E1 . . . . 4A 66
    (off Ben Jonson Rd.)
Lorne Rd. E7 . . . . 1D 55
E17 . . . . 1C 38
N4 . . . . 3B 34
Lorn Rd. SW9 . . . . 5B 90
Lorraine Ct. NW1 . . . . . . 4D 47
Lorrimore Rd. SE17 . . . . 2D 91
Lorrimore Sq. SE17 . . . . 2D 91
Lorton Ho. NW6 . . . . 5C 44
    (off Kilburn Va.)
Lothair Rd. Nth. N4 . . . . . 1D 35
Lothair Rd. Sth. N4 . . . . . 2C 34
Lothbury
    EC2 . . . . . . 2B 18 (5F 63)
Lothian Rd. SW9 . . . . . . 4D 91
Lothrop St. W10 . . . . . . 2A 58
Lots Rd. SW10 . . . . 3E 87
Lotus Cl. SE21 . . . . 3F 119
Loubet St. SW17 . . . . . . 5B 116
Loudoun Rd. NW8 . . . . . 5E 45
Loughborough Est.
    SW9 . . . . 1D 105
Loughborough Pk.
    SW9 . . . . 2D 105
Loughborough Rd.
    SW9 . . . . 5C 90
Loughborough St.
    SE11 . . . . 1B 90
Lough Rd. N7 . . . . 2B 48
Louisa Cl. E9 . . . . 5F 51
Louisa Gdns. E1 . . . . 3F 65
Louisa St. E1 . . . . 3F 65
Louise Aumonier Wlk.
    N19 . . . . 2A 34
    (off Jessie Blythe La.)
Louise Bennett Cl.
    SE24 . . . . 2D 105
Louise De Marillac Ho.
    E1 . . . . 4E 65
    (off Smithy St.)
Louise Rd. E15 . . . . 3A 54
Louise White Ho.
    N19 . . . . 3F 33
Louisville Rd.
    SW17 . . . . 3C 116
Louvaine Rd. SW11 . . . . 2F 101
Lovat Cl. NW2 . . . . 5B 28
Lovat La.
    EC3 . . . . . 4D 19 (1A 78)
    (not continuous)
Lovatt Ct. SW12 . . . . . . 1D 117
Lovegrove St. SE1 . . . . . 1C 92
Lovegrove Wlk. E14 . . . . 2E 81
Lovelace Ho. E8 . . . . 5B 50
    (off Haggerston Rd.)
Lovelace Rd. SE21 . . . . . 2E 119
Lovelinch Cl. SE15 . . . . . 2E 93
Lovell Ho. E8 . . . . 5C 50
    (off Shrubland Rd.)
Lovell Pl. SE16 . . . . 4A 80
Loveridge M. NW6 . . . . . 3B 44
Loveridge Rd. NW6 . . . . 3B 44
Lovers Wlk. SE10 . . . . . . 2F 95
    W1 . . . . 1B 20 (2C 74)
Love Wlk. SE5 . . . . 5F 91

Low Cross Wood La.
    SE21 . . . . 3B 120
Lowden Rd. SE24 . . . . . 2D 105
Lowder Ho. E1 . . . . 2D 79
    (off Wapping La.)
Lowe Av. E16 . . . . 4C 68
Lowell Ho. SE5 . . . . 3E 91
    (off Wyndham Est.)
Lowell St. E14 . . . . 5A 66
Lwr. Addison Gdns.
    W14 . . . . 3A 72
Lwr. Belgrave St.
    SW1 . . . . . . 5D 21 (4D 75)
LOWER CLAPTON 1D 51
Lwr. Clapton Rd. E5 . . . . 5D 37
Lwr. Clarendon Wlk.
    W11 . . . . 5A 58
    (off Clarendon Rd.)
Lwr. Common Sth.
    SW15 . . . . 1D 99
Lwr. Grosvenor Pl.
    SW1 . . . . . . 5E 21 (4D 75)
LOWER HOLLOWAY . . . 2B 48
Lwr. James St.
    W1 . . . . 4A 14 (1E 75)
Lwr. John St.
    W1 . . . . 4A 14 (1E 75)
Lwr. Lea Crossing
    E14 . . . . 1A 82
    E16 . . . . 1A 82
Lower Mall W6 . . . . 1D 85
Lower Marsh
    SE1 . . . . . . 4B 24 (3C 76)
Lwr. Merton Ri. NW3 . . . 4A 46
Lwr. Richmond Rd.
    SW15 . . . . 1D 99
Lower Rd.
    SE1 . . . . . . 3B 24 (3C 76)
    SE8 . . . . 5F 79
    SE16 . . . . 5F 79
    (not continuous)
Lwr. Robert St. WC2 . . . . 5E 15
    (in Robert St.)
Lwr. Sloane St. SW1 . . . . 5C 74
LOWER SYDENHAM
    . . . . 4F 121
Lwr. Sydenham Ind. Est.
    SE26 . . . . 5B 122
Lower Ter. NW3 . . . . . . 5E 31
    SE27 . . . . 5D 119
    (off Woodcote Pl.)
Lwr. Thames St.
    EC3 . . . . . 5C 18 (1F 77)
Lowerwood Ct. W11 . . . . 5A 58
    (off Westbourne Pk. Rd.)
Lowestoft Cl. E5 . . . . 4E 37
    (off Mundford Rd.)
Loweswater Ho. E3 . . . . . 3B 66
Lowfield Rd. NW6 . . . . . 4C 44
    W3 . . . . 5A 56
Low Hall La. E17 . . . . . . 1A 38
Low Hall Mnr. Bus. Cen.
    E17 . . . . 1A 38
Lowman Rd. N7 . . . . 1B 48
Lowndes Cl. SW1 . . . . . 4C 74
Lowndes Ct.
    SW1 . . . . . . 5A 20 (4B 74)
    W1 . . . . 3F 13
Lowndes Pl. SW1 . . . . . . 4C 74
Lowndes Sq.
    SW1 . . . . . . 4A 20 (3B 74)

Lowndes St.
    SW1 . . . . . . 5A 20 (4C 74)
Lowood Ho. E1 . . . . 1E 79
    (off Bewley St.)
Lowood St. E1 . . . . 1D 79
Lowry Ct. SE16 . . . . 1D 93
    (off Stubbs Dr.)
Lowther Gdns. SW7 . . . . 3F 73
Lowther Hill SE23 . . . . . 5A 108
Lowther Ho. E8 . . . . 5B 50
    (off Clarissa St.)
    SW1 . . . . 1E 89
    (off Churchill Gdns.)
Lowther Rd. N7 . . . . 2C 48
    SW13 . . . . 4B 84
Loxford Ho. SE5 . . . . 4E 91
Loxford Av. E6 . . . . 1F 69
Loxham St.
    WC1 . . . . . . 2E 7 (2A 62)
Loxley Cl. SE26 . . . . 5F 121
Loxley Rd. SW18 . . . . . . 1F 115
Loxton Rd. SE23 . . . . . . 1F 121
Lubbock Ho. E14 . . . . . . 1D 81
    (off Poplar High St.)
Lubbock St. SE14 . . . . . . 3E 93
Lucan Ho. N1 . . . . 5F 49
    (off Colville Est.)
Lucan Pl. SW3 . . . . 5A 74
Lucas Av. E13 . . . . 5D 55
Lucas Cl. NW10 . . . . 4C 42
Lucas Ct. SE26 . . . . 5A 122
    SW11 . . . . 4C 88
Lucas Ho. SW10 . . . . . . 3D 87
    (off Coleridge Gdns.)
Lucas Sq. NW11 . . . . . . 1C 30
Lucas St. SE8 . . . . 4C 94
Lucerne M. W8 . . . . 2C 72
Lucerne Rd. N5 . . . . 1D 49
Lucey Rd. SE16 . . . . 4C 78
Lucey Way SE16 . . . . . . 4C 78
Lucien Ho. SW17 . . . . . . 4C 116
    SW19 . . . . 2D 115
Lucorn Cl. SE12 . . . . 4B 110
Lucy Brown Ho. SE1 . . . . 2A 26
Ludgate B'way.
    EC4 . . . . . 3D 17 (5D 63)
Ludgate Cir.
    EC4 . . . . . 3D 17 (5D 63)
Ludgate Hill
    EC4 . . . . . 3D 17 (5D 63)
Ludgate Sq.
    EC4 . . . . . 3E 17 (5D 63)
Ludham NW5 . . . . 2B 46
Ludlow St.
    EC1 . . . . 3F 9 (3E 63)
Ludovick Wlk. SW15 . . . . 2A 98
Ludwick M. SE14 . . . . . . 3A 94
Luffman Rd. SE12 . . . . . 3D 125
Lugard Ho. W12 . . . . 2D 71
Lugard Rd. SE15 . . . . . . 5D 93
Luke Ho. E1 . . . . 5D 65
    (off Tillman St.)
Luke St. EC2 . . . 3D 11 (3A 64)
Lukin St. E1 . . . . 5E 65
Lullingstone Ho.
    SE15 . . . . 2E 93
    (off Lovelinch Cl.)
Lullingstone La.
    SE13 . . . . 4F 109
Lulot Gdns. N19 . . . . . . 4D 33

Lulworth NW1 . . . . 4F 47
(off Wrotham Rd.)
SE17 . . . . 1F 91
(off Portland St.)
Lulworth Ct. N1 . . . . 4A 50
(off St Peter's Way)
Lulworth Ho. SW8 . . . . 3B 90
Lulworth Rd. SE9 . . . . . 2F 125
SE15 . . . . 5D 93
Lumiere Bldg., The
E7 . . . . 2F 55
(off Romford Rd.)
Lumiere Ct. SW17 . . . . 2C 116
Lumina Bldgs. E14 . . . 2E 81
(off Prestons Rd.)
Lumley Ct.
WC2 . . . . 5E 15 (1A 76)
Lumley Flats SW1 . . . . . 1C 88
(off Holbein Pl.)
Lumley St.
W1 . . . . 3C 12 (5C 60)
Lumsdon Rd. 5D 45
(off Abbey Rd.)
Lund Point E15 . . . . . . 5E 53
Lundy Wlk. N1 . . . . . . 3E 49
Lunham Rd. SE19 . . . . 5A 120
Luntley Pl. E1 . . . . . . 4C 64
(off Chicksand St.)
Lupin Cl. SW2 . . . . . . 2D 119
Lupino Ct. SE11 . . . . . 5B 76
Lupin Point SE1 . . . . . 3B 78
(off Abbey St.)
Lupton Cl. SE12 . . . . . 3D 125
Lupton St. NW5 . . . . . 1E 47
(not continuous)
Lupus St. SW1 . . . . . . 1D 89
Luralda Wharf E14 . . . 1F 95
Lurgan Av. W6 . . . . . . 2F 85
Lurline Gdns. SW11 . . 4C 88
Luscombe Way SW8 . . 3A 90
Lushington Rd.
NW10 . . . . 1D 57
SE6 . . . . 4D 123
Lushington Ter. E8 . . . 2C 50
Luther King Cl. E17 . . . 1B 38
Luton Ho. E13 . . . . 3C 68
(off Luton Rd.)
Luton Pl. SE10 . . . . . . 3E 95
Luton Rd. E13 . . . . 3C 68
Luton St. NW8 . . . . . . 3F 59
Lutton Ter. NW3 . . . . . . 1E 45
(off Lakis Cl.)
Luttrell Av. SW15 . . . . 3D 99
Lutwyche Rd. SE6 . . . 2B 122
Lutyens Ho. SW1 . . . . . 1E 89
(off Churchill Gdns.)
Luxborough Ho. W1 . . . 5B 4
(off Luxborough St.)
Luxborough St.
W1 . . . . 5B 4 (4C 60)
Luxborough Twr. W1 . . 5B 4
Lux Cinema 2D 11
(off Hoxton Sq.)
Luxemburg M. E15 . . . 2A 54
Luxemburg Gdns. W6 . 5F 71
Luxfield Rd. SE9 . . . . 1F 125
Luxford St. SE16 . . . . 5F 79
Luxmore St. SE4 . . . . 4B 94
Luxor St. SE5 . . . . 1E 105
Lyall Av. SE21 . . . . . . 4A 120

Lyall M.
SW1 . . . . 5B 20 (4C 74)
Lyall M. W. SW1 . . . . . 4C 74
Lyall St.
SW1 . . . . 5B 20 (4C 74)
Lyal Rd. E3 . . . . 1A 66
Lycett Pl. W12 . . . . . . 3C 70
Lyceum Theatre 4F 15
Lydden Gro. SW18 . . . 5D 101
Lydden Rd. SW18 . . . 5D 101
Lyden Ho. E1 . . . . 2F 65
(off Westfield Way)
Lydford NW1 . . . . 5E 47
(off Royal College St.)
Lydford Cl. N16 . . . . . . 2A 50
(off Pellerin Rd.)
Lydford Rd. N15 . . . . . . 1F 35
NW2 . . . . 3E 43
W9 . . . . 3B 58
Lydhurst Av. SW2 . . . . 2B 118
Lydney Cl. SW19 . . . . 2A 114
Lydon Rd. SW4 . . . . . . 1E 103
Lyford Rd. SW18 . . . . 5F 101
Lygon Ho. E2 . . . . 2B 64
(off Gosset St.)
SW6 . . . . 4A 86
(off Fulham Pal. Rd.)
Lygon Pl.
SW1 . . . . 5D 21 (4D 75)
Lyham Cl. SW2 . . . . . 4A 104
Lyham Rd. SW2 . . . . . 3A 104
Lyly Ho. SE1 . . . . 5C 26
(off Burbage Cl.)
Lyme Farm Rd.
SE12 . . . . 2C 110
Lyme Gro. E9 . . . . 4E 51
Lyme Gro. Ho. E9 . . . . 4E 51
(off Lyme Gro.)
Lymer Av. SE19 . . . . . 5B 120
Lyme St. NW1 . . . . 4E 47
Lyme Ter. NW1 . . . . . . 4E 47
Lyminge Gdns.
SW18 . . . . 1A 116
Lymington Lodge E14 . . 4F 81
(off Schooner Cl.)
Lymington Rd. NW6 . . 3D 45
Lympstone Gdns.
SE15 . . . . 3C 92
Lynbrook Gro. SE15 . . 3A 92
Lynch Cl. SE3 . . . . . . 5B 96
Lynch Wlk. SE8 . . . . . 2B 94
(off Prince St.)
Lyncott Cres. SW4 . . . 2D 103
Lyncourt SE3 . . . . 5F 95
Lyncroft Gdns. NW6 . . 2C 44
Lyncroft Mans. NW6 . . 2C 44
Lyndale NW2 . . . . 1A 44
Lyndale Av. NW2 . . . . 5B 30
Lyndale Cl. SE3 . . . . . 2B 96
Lynde Ho. SW4 . . . . . . 1F 103
Lyndhurst Cl. NW10 . . 5A 28
Lyndhurst Ct. NW8 . . . . 5F 45
(off Finchley Rd.)
Lyndhurst Dr. E10 . . . 2E 39
Lyndhurst Gdns. NW3 . 2F 45
Lyndhurst Gro. SE15 . . 5A 92
Lyndhurst Lodge E14 . 5F 81
(off Millennium Dr.)
Lyndhurst Rd. NW3 . . 2F 45
Lyndhurst Sq. SE15 . . 4B 92

Lyndhurst Ter. NW3 . . . 2F 45
Lyndhurst Way SE15 . . 4B 92
Lyndon Yd. SW17 . . . . 4E 115
Lyneham Wlk. E5 . . . . 2A 52
Lynette Av. SW4 . . . . . 4D 103
Lyn M. E3 . . . . 2B 66
N16 . . . . 1A 50
Lynmouth Rd. E17 . . . . 1A 38
N16 . . . . 3B 36
Lynne Cl. SE23 . . . . . 5B 108
Lynn Ho. SE15 . . . . . . 2D 93
(off Friary Est.)
Lynn M. E11 . . . . 4A 40
Lynn Rd. E11 . . . . 4A 40
SW12 . . . . 5D 103
Lynsted Gdns. SE9 . . . 1F 111
Lynton Cl. NW10 . . . . . 2A 42
Lynton Est. SE1 . . . . . 5C 78
Lynton Ho. W2 . . . . 5E 59
(off Hallfield Est.)
Lynton Mans. SE1 . . . . 5B 24
(off Kennington Rd.)
Lynton Rd. N8 . . . . 1F 33
(not continuous)
NW6 . . . . 1B 58
SE1 . . . . 5B 78
Lynwood Rd. SW17 . . . 3B 116
Lynx Way E16 . . . . 1F 83
Lyon Ho. NW8 . . . . 3A 60
(off Broadley St.)
Lyon Ind. Est.
NW2 . . . . 4D 29
Lyons Pl. NW8 . . . . 3F 59
Lyon St. N1 . . . . 4B 48
Lyons Wlk. W14 . . . . . . 5A 72
Lyric Ct. E8 . . . . 4B 50
(off Holly St.)
Lyric M. SE26 . . . . 4E 121
Lyric Rd. SW13 . . . . . . 4B 84
Lyric Theatre
Hammersmith 5E 71
Westminster 4B 14
(off Shaftesbury Av.)
Lysander Gro. N19 . . . 3F 33
Lysander Ho. E2 . . . . . 1D 65
(off Temple St.)
Lysander M. N19 . . . . . 3E 33
Lysia Ct. SW6 . . . . 3F 85
(off Lysia St.)
Lysias Rd. SW12 . . . . 4D 103
Lysia St. SW6 . . . . 3F 85
Lysons Wlk. SW15 . . . 2C 98
Lytcott Gro. SE22 . . . . 3A 106
Lytham St. SE17 . . . . . 1F 91
Lyttelton Cl. NW3 . . . . 4A 46
Lyttelton Ho. E9 . . . . . . 4E 51
(off Well St.)
Lyttelton Rd. E10 . . . . 5D 39
Lyttelton Theatre 1B 24
(in Royal National Theatre)
Lytton Cl. N2 . . . . 1F 31
Lytton Gro. SW15 . . . . 3F 99
Lytton Rd. E11 . . . . . . 2A 40
Lyveden Rd. SE3 . . . . 3D 97

M

Mabledon Ct. WC1 . . . . . 2C 6
(off Mabledon Pl.)

Mabledon Pl.
  WC1 . . . . 2C 6 (2F 61)
Mablethorpe Rd.
  SW6 . . . . 3A 86
Mabley St. E9 . . . . 2A 52
Macarthur Cl. E7 . . . . 3C 54
Macarthur Ter. SE7 . . . . . . 2F 97
Macartney Ho. SE10 . . . . 3F 95
           (off Chesterfield Wlk.)
  SW9 . . . . 4C 90
           (off Gosling Way)
Macaulay Ct. SW4 . . . . . . 1D 103
Macaulay Rd. E6 . . . . 1F 69
  SW4 . . . . 1D 103
Macaulay Sq. SW4 . . . . . 2D 103
McAuley Cl. SE1 . . . . 5B 24
Macauley M. SE13 . . . . . . 4E 95
Macbeth Ho. N1 . . . . 1A 64
Macbeth St. W6 . . . . 1D 85
McCall Cl. SW4 . . . . 5A 90
McCall Cres. SE7 . . . . 1F 97
McCall Ho. N7 . . . . 1A 48
MCC Cricket Mus. and Tours
                  . . . . . 2F 59
Macclesfield Ho. EC1 . . . 2F 9
           (off Central St.)
Macclesfield Rd.
  EC1 . . . . 1F 9 (2E 63)
Macclesfield St.
  W1 . . . . 4C 14 (1F 75)
McCoid Way
  SE1 . . . . 4F 25 (3E 77)
McCrone M. NW3 . . . . . . 3F 45
McCullum Rd. E3 . . . . 5B 52
McDermott Cl.
  SW11 . . . . 1A 102
McDermott Rd.
  SE15 . . . . 1C 106
  N19 . . . . 4E 33
McDowall Cl. E16 . . . . 4B 68
McDowall Rd. SE5 . . . . . . 4E 91
Macduff Rd. SW11 . . . . . . 4C 88
Mace Cl. E1 . . . . 2D 79
Mace St. E2 . . . . 1F 65
McEwen Way E15 . . . . . . 5F 53
Macey St. SE10 . . . . 2E 95
          (off Thames St.)
Macfarlane Rd. W12 . . . . 2E 71
Macfarren Pl.
  NW1 . . . . 4C 4 (3C 60)
McGlashon Ho. E1 . . . . . 3C 64
          (off Hunton St.)
McGrath Rd. E15 . . . . 2B 54
McGregor Ct. N1 . . . . 1E 11
Macgregor Rd. E16 . . . . . 4E 69
McGregor Rd. W11 . . . . . . 5B 58
Machell Rd. SE15 . . . . 1E 107
McIndoe Ct. N1 . . . . 5F 49
        (off Sherborne St.)
Macintosh Ho. W1 . . . . . 5C 4
        (off Beaumont St.)
McIntosh Ho. SE16 . . . . 5E 79
        (off Millender Wlk.)
Mackay Ho. W12 . . . . . . 1D 71
        (off White City Est.)
Mackay Rd. SW4 . . . . . . 1D 103
McKay Trad. Est.
  W10 . . . . 3A 58
Mackennal St. NW8 . . . . . 1A 60

Mackenzie Cl. W12 . . . . . 1D 71
Mackenzie Ho. NW2 . . . . 5C 28
Mackenzie Rd. N7 . . . . . . 3B 48
Mackenzie Wlk. E14 . . . . 2C 80
McKerrell Rd. SE15 . . . . . 4C 92
Mackeson Rd. NW3 . . . . 1B 46
Mackie Rd. SW2 . . . . 5C 104
Mackintosh La. E9 . . . . . . 2F 51
Macklin St.
  WC2 . . . . 2E 15 (5A 62)
Mackonochie Ho. EC1 . . . 5B 8
       (off Baldwins Gdns.)
Mackrow Wlk. E14 . . . . . . 1E 81
Mack's Rd. SE16 . . . . 5C 78
Mackworth Ho. NW1 . . . 1F 5
       (off Augustus St.)
Mackworth St.
  NW1 . . . . 1F 5 (2E 61)
McLaren House SE1 . . . . 4D 25
       (off St Georges Cir.)
Maclaren M. SW15 . . . . . 2E 99
Maclean Rd. SE23 . . . . . . 4A 108
McLeod Ct. SE22 . . . . . . 1C 120
McLeod's M. SW7 . . . . . . 5D 73
Macleod St. SE17 . . . . . . 1E 91
Maclise Ho. SW1 . . . . . . 5A 76
       (off Marsham St.)
Maclise Rd. W14 . . . . 4A 72
McMillan Ho. SE4 . . . . . 1A 108
       (off Arica Rd.)
  SE14 . . . . 4A 94
McMillan St. SE8 . . . . . . 2C 94
Macmillan Way
  SW17 . . . . 4D 117
Macnamara Ho.
  SW10 . . . . 3F 87
       (off Worlds End Est.)
McNeil Rd. SE5 . . . . 5A 92
Maconochies Pl.
  E14 . . . . 1D 95
Macquarie Way E14 . . . . 5D 81
Macready Ho. W1 . . . . . 4A 60
       (off Crawford St.)
Macready Pl. N7 . . . . 1A 48
       (not continuous)
Macroom Rd. W9 . . . . . . 2B 58
Mac's Pl. EC4 . . . . 2B 16
Madame Tussaud's
          . . . . 4B 4 (3C 60)
Maddams St. E3 . . . . 3D 67
Maddocks Ho. E1 . . . . . . 1D 79
       (off Cornwall St.)
Maddock Way SE17 . . . . 2D 91
Maddox St.
  W1 . . . . 4E 13 (1D 75)
Madeira Rd. E11 . . . . 3F 39
  SW16 . . . . 5A 118
Madinah Rd. E8 . . . . 3C 50
Madison, The SE1 . . . . . 3B 26
       (off Long La.)
Madison Ho. E14 . . . . . . 1B 80
       (off Victory Pl.)
Madras Pl. N7 . . . . 3C 48
Madrid Rd. SW13 . . . . . . 4C 84
Madrigal La. SE5 . . . . 3D 91
Madron St. SE17 . . . . . . 1A 92
Mafeking Av. E6 . . . . 1F 69
Mafeking Rd. E16 . . . . . . 3B 68
Magazine Ga. W2 . . . . . . 2A 74
Magdala Av. N19 . . . . . . 4E 33

Magdalene Cl. SE15 . . . . 5D 93
Magdalen Ho. E16 . . . . 2D 83
       (off Keats Av.)
Magdalen Pas. E1 . . . . . . 1B 78
Magdalen Rd.
  SW18 . . . . 1E 115
Magdalen St.
  SE1 . . . . 2D 27 (2A 78)
Magee St. SE11 . . . . 2C 90
Magellan Cl. NW10 . . . . 4A 42
       (off Brentfield Rd.)
Magellan Ho. E1 . . . . . . 3F 65
       (off Ernest St.)
Magellan Pl. E14 . . . . 5C 80
Magnin Cl. E8 . . . . 5C 50
Magnolia Cl. E10 . . . . 4C 38
Magnolia Gdns. E10 . . . . 4C 38
Magnolia Ho. SE8 . . . . . 2B 94
       (off Evelyn St.)
Magnolia Lodge W8 . . . 4D 73
       (off St Mary's Ga.)
Magnolia Pl. SW4 . . . . . . 3A 104
Magpie All.
  EC4 . . . . 3C 16 (5C 62)
Magpie Cl. E7 . . . . 2B 54
Magpie Pl. SE14 . . . . 2A 94
Magri Wlk. E1 . . . . 4E 65
Maguire St. SE1 . . . . 3B 78
Mahatma Gandhi Ind. Est.
  SE24 . . . . 2D 105
Mahogany Cl. SE16 . . . . 2A 80
Maida Av. W2 . . . . 4E 59
MAIDA HILL 3B 58
MAIDA VALE 2D 59
Maida Va. W9 . . . . 1D 59
Maiden La. NW1 . . . . 4F 47
  SE1 . . . . 2A 26 (2E 77)
  WC2 . . . . 5E 15 (1A 76)
Maiden Pl. NW5 . . . . 5E 33
Maiden Rd. E15 . . . . 4A 54
Maidenstone Hill
  SE10 . . . . 4E 95
Maidstone Bldgs. M.
  SE1 . . . . 2A 26 (2E 77)
Maidstone Ho. E14 . . . . 5D 67
       (off Carmen St.)
Mail Coach Yd. E2 . . . . . 1E 11
Mais Ho. SE26 . . . . 2D 121
Maismore St. SE15 . . . . . 2C 92
Maitland Cl. SE10 . . . . . . 3D 95
Maitland Ct. W2 . . . . . . 1F 73
       (off Lancaster Ter.)
Maitland Ho. E2 . . . . . . 1E 65
       (off Waterloo Gdns.)
  SW1 . . . . 2E 89
       (off Churchill Gdns.)
Maitland Pk. Est.
  NW3 . . . . 3B 46
Maitland Pk. Rd.
  NW3 . . . . 3B 46
Maitland Pk. Vs.
  NW3 . . . . 3B 46
Maitland Pl. E5 . . . . 1D 51
Maitland Rd. E15 . . . . 3B 54
  SE26 . . . . 5F 121
Maize Row E14 . . . . 1B 80
Major Cl. SW9 . . . . 1D 105
Major Rd. E15 . . . . 2F 53
  SE16 . . . . 4C 78
Makepeace Av. N6 . . . . . 4C 32

Makepeace Mans.
N6 . . . . 4C 32
Makins St. SW3 . . . . 5A 74
Malabar Ct. W12 . . . . 1D 71
(off India Way)
Malabar St. E14 . . . . 3C 80
Malam Ct. SE11 . . . . 5C 76
Malam Gdns. E14 . . . 1D 81
Malbrook Rd. SW15 . . 2D 99
Malcolm Ct. E7 . . . . 3B 54
NW4 . . . . 1C 28
Malcolm Cres. NW4 . . 1C 28
Malcolm Ho. N1 . . . . 1A 64
(off Arden Est.)
Malcolm Pl. E2 . . . . . 3E 65
Malcolm Rd. E1 . . . . 3E 65
Malcolm Sargent Ho.
E16 . . . . 2D 83
(off Evelyn Rd.)
Malcolmson Ho. SW1 . . 1F 89
(off Aylesford St.)
Malden Ct. N4 . . . . . 1E 35
Malden Cres. NW1 . . . 3C 46
Malden Pl. NW5 . . . . 2C 46
Malden Rd. NW5 . . . . 2B 46
Maldon Cl. E15 . . . . . 2A 54
N1 . . . . 5E 49
SE5 . . . . 1A 106
Malet Pl. WC1 . . 4B 6 (3F 61)
Malet St. WC1 . . 4B 6 (3F 61)
Maley Av. SE27 . . . . 2D 119
Malfort Rd. SE5 . . . . 1A 106
Malham Rd. SE23 . . . . 1F 121
Malham Rd. Ind. Est.
SE23 . . . . 1F 121
Malibu Cl. SE26 . . . . 3D 121
Mall, The E15 . . . . . 4F 53
SW1 . . . . 2C 22 (3E 75)
Mallams M. SW9 . . . . 1D 105
Mallard Cl. E9 . . . . . 3B 52
NW6 . . . . 1C 58
Mallard Ho. NW8 . . . . 1A 60
(off Barrow Hill Est.)
Mallards E11 . . . . . . 2C 40
(off Blake Hall Rd.)
Mall Chambers W8 . . . 2C 72
(off Kensington Mall)
Mallet Rd. SE13 . . . . 4F 109
Mall Galleries 1C 22
Mall Gallery WC2 . . . . 3D 15
(in Thomas Neals Shop. Mall)
Malling SE13 . . . . . . 3D 109
Mallinson Rd.
SW11 . . . . 3A 102
Mallinson Sports Cen.
. . . . 2B 32
Mallon Gdns. E1 . . . . 2F 19
(off Commercial St.)
Mallord St. SW3 . . . . 2F 87
Mallory Cl. SE4 . . . . 2A 108
Mallory St. NW8 . . . . 3A 60
Mallow St.
EC1 . . . . . 3B 10 (3F 63)
Mall Rd. W6 . . . . . . 1D 85
Mall Vs. W6 . . . . . . 1D 85
(off Mall Rd.)
Malmesbury E2 . . . . . 1E 65
(off Cyprus St.)
Malmesbury Rd. E3 . . . 2B 66
E16 . . . . 4A 68

Malmesbury Ter.
E16 . . . . 4B 68
Malmsey Ho. SE11 . . . 1B 90
Malmsmead Ho. E9 . . . 2B 52
(off King's Mead Way)
Malpas Rd. E8 . . . . . 2D 51
SE4 . . . . 5B 94
Malta Rd. E10 . . . . . 3A 38
Malta St. EC1 . . 3D 9 (3D 63)
Maltby St.
SE1 . . . . . . 4F 27 (3B 78)
Malthouse Dr. W4 . . . 2B 84
Malthouse Pas.
SW13 . . . . 5B 84
(off Maltings Cl.)
Malting Ho. E14 . . . . 1B 80
(off Oak La.)
Maltings Cl. SW13 . . . 5B 84
SW6 . . . . 4D 87
Maltings Lodge W4 . . . 2A 84
(off Corney Reach Way)
Maltings Pl. SE1 . . . . 4E 27
SW6 . . . . 4D 87
Malton M. W10 . . . . . 5A 58
Malton Rd. W10 . . . . 5A 58
Maltravers St.
WC2 . . . . . 4A 16 (1B 76)
Malt St. SE1 . . . . . . 2C 92
Malva Cl. SW18 . . . . 3D 101
Malvern Cl. W10 . . . . 4B 58
Malvern Ct. SW7 . . . . 5F 73
(off Onslow Sq.)
W12 . . . . 1B 80
(off Hadyn Pk. Rd.)
Malvern Gdns. NW2 . . 4A 30
Malvern Ho. N16 . . . . 3B 36
Malvern M. NW6 . . . . 2C 58
Malvern Pl. NW6 . . . . 2B 58
Malvern Rd. E6 . . . . . 5F 55
E8 . . . . 4C 50
E11 . . . . 4A 40
NW6 . . . . 1B 58
(not continuous)
Malvern Ter. N1 . . . . 5C 48
Malwood Rd. SW12 . . . 4D 103
Malyons Rd. SE13 . . . 4D 109
Malyons Ter. SE13 . . . 3D 109
Managers St. E14 . . . . 2E 81
Manaton Cl. SE15 . . . 1D 107
Manbey Gro. E15 . . . . 3A 54
Manbey Pk. Rd. E15 . . 3A 54
Manbey Rd. E15 . . . . 3A 54
Manbey St. E15 . . . . . 3A 54
Manbre Rd. W6 . . . . . 2E 85
Manchester Ct. E16 . . . 5D 69
(off Garvary Rd.)
Manchester Dr. W10 . . 3A 58
Manchester Gro. E14 . . 1E 95
Manchester Ho. SE17 . . 1E 91
Manchester M. W1 . . . 1B 12
Manchester Rd. E14 . . 1E 95
N15 . . . . 1F 35
Manchester Sq.
W1 . . . . . . 2B 12 (5C 60)
Manchester St.
W1 . . . . . . 1B 12 (4C 60)
Manchuria Rd.
SW11 . . . . 4C 102
Manciple St.
SE1 . . . . . . 4B 26 (3F 77)
Mandalay Rd. SW4 . . . 3E 103

Mandarin Ct. NW10 . . . 3A 42
(off Mitchellbrook Way)
SE8 . . . . 2B 94
Mandarin St. E14 . . . . 1C 80
Mandela Cl. W12 . . . . 1D 71
Mandela Ho. E2 . . . . . 2F 11
(off Virginia Rd.)
SE5 . . . . 5D 91
Mandela Rd. E16 . . . . 5C 68
Mandela St. NW1 . . . . 5E 47
SW9 . . . . 3C 90
(not continuous)
Mandela Way SE1 . . . . 5A 78
Mandel Ho. SW18 . . . . 2C 100
Mandeville Cl. SE3 . . . 3B 96
Mandeville Ho. SE1 . . . 1B 92
(off Rolls Rd.)
SW4 . . . . 3E 103
Mandeville M. SW4 . . . 2F 103
Mandeville Pl.
W1 . . . . . . 2C 12 (5C 60)
Mandeville St. E5 . . . . 5A 38
Mandrake Rd.
SW17 . . . . 3B 116
Mandrake Way E15 . . . 4A 54
Mandrell Rd. SW2 . . . 3A 104
Manette St.
W1 . . . . . . 3C 14 (5F 61)
Manfred Rd.
SW15 . . . . 3B 100
Manger Rd. N7 . . . . . 3A 48
Manilla St. E14 . . . . . 3C 80
Manitoba Ct. SE16 . . . 3E 79
(off Canada Est.)
Manley Ct. N16 . . . . . 5B 36
Manley Ho. SE11 . . . . 5C 76
Manley St. NW1 . . . . 5C 46
Manneby Prior N1 . . . 1A 8
(off Cumming St.)
Manningford Cl.
EC1 . . . . . 1D 9 (2D 63)
Manningtree Cl.
SW19 . . . . 1A 114
Manningtree St. E1 . . . 5C 64
Manny Shinwell Ho.
SW6 . . . . 2B 86
(off Clem Attlee Ct.)
Manor, The SE23 . . . . 5E 107
SE4 . . . . 5B 94
Manor Av. E7 . . . . . . 1E 55
Manor Brook SE3 . . . . 2C 110
Manor Ct. E10 . . . . . 3D 39
N2 . . . . 1B 32
SW2 . . . . 3B 104
SW6 . . . . 4D 87
SW16 . . . . 3A 118
Manor Est. SE16 . . . . 5D 79
Manorfield Cl. N19 . . . 1E 47
(off Fulbrook M.)
Manor Flds. SW15 . . . 4F 99
Manor Gdns. N7 . . . . 5A 34
SW4 . . . . 5E 89
(off Larkhall Ri.)
W4 . . . . 1A 84
Manor Gro. SE15 . . . . 2E 93
Manorhall Gdns. E10 . . 3C 38
MANOR HOUSE 2F 35
MANOR HOUSE 2E 35
Manor Ho. NW1 . . . . . 4A 60
(off Marylebone Rd.)

Manor Ho. Ct. W9 . . . . . 3E **59**
(off Warrington Gdns.)
Manor Ho. Dr. NW6 . . . . 4F **43**
Manor Ho. Gdn.
E11 . . . . 1D **41**
Manor La. SE12 . . . . . 3A **110**
SE13 . . . . 3A **110**
Manor La. Ter.
SE13 . . . . 2A **110**
Manor M. NW6 . . . . 1C **58**
(off Cambridge Av.)
SE4 . . . . 5B **94**
Manor Mt. SE23 . . . . . 1E **121**
Manor Pde. N16 . . . . . 4B **36**
NW10 . . . . 1B **56**
(off High St. Harlesden)
MANOR PARK 1F **55**
Manor Pk. SE13 . . . . . 2F **109**
Manor Pk. Crematorium
E7 . . . . 1E **55**
Manor Pk. Pde.
SE13 . . . . 2F **109**
(off Lee High Rd.)
Manor Pk. Rd. E12 . . . . 1F **55**
(not continuous)
NW10 . . . . 5B **42**
Manor Pl. SE17 . . . . . . 1D **91**
Manor Rd. E10 . . . . 2C **38**
E15 . . . . 1A **68**
E16 . . . . 1A **68**
N16 . . . . 4F **35**
Manor Way SE3 . . . . . 2B **110**
Manorway SE7 . . . . 5F **83**
Manresa Rd. SW3 . . . . 1A **88**
Mansard Beeches
SW17 . . . . 5C **116**
Mansell St.
E1 . . . . 3F **19** (5B **64**)
Mansel Rd. SW19 . . . . 5A **114**
Manse Rd. N16 . . . . . . 5B **36**
Mansfield Ct. E2 . . . . . . 5B **50**
(off Whiston Rd.)
Mansfield Hgts. N2 . . . 1A **32**
Mansfield M.
W1 . . . . 1D **13** (4D **61**)
Mansfield Pl. NW3 . . . . 1E **45**
Mansfield Rd. E11 . . . . 1D **41**
NW3 . . . . 2B **46**
Mansfield St.
W1 . . . . 1D **13** (4D **61**)
Mansford St. E2 . . . . . . 1C **64**
Mansion Cl. SW9 . . . . . 4C **90**
(not continuous)
Mansion Cottage
Vis. Info. Cen. 3A **32**
Mansion Gdns. NW3 . . 5D **31**
Mansion House
. . . . 3B 18 (5F **63**)
Mansion Ho. Pl.
EC4 . . . . 3B **18** (5F **63**)
Mansion Ho. St. EC4 . . 3B **18**
Mansions, The SW5 . . . 1D **87**
Manson M. SW7 . . . . . . 5F **73**
Manson Pl. SW7 . . . . . 5F **73**
Manston NW1 . . . . 4E **47**
(off Agar Gro.)
Manstone Rd. NW2 . . . 2A **44**
Manston Ho. W14 . . . . . 4A **72**
(off Russell Rd.)
Mantilla Rd. SW17 . . . . 4C **116**

Mantle Ct. SW18 . . . . . 4D **101**
(off Mapleton Rd.)
Mantle Rd. SE4 . . . . . . 1A **108**
Mantle Way E15 . . . . . . 4A **54**
Mantua St. SW11 . . . . 1F **101**
Mantus Cl. E1 . . . . 3E **65**
Mantus Rd. E1 . . . . . . 3E **65**
Manville Gdns.
SW17 . . . . 3D **117**
Manville Rd. SW17 . . . 2C **116**
Manwood Rd. SE4 . . . . 3B **108**
Manygates SW12 . . . . 2D **117**
Mapesbury Ct. NW2 . . . 2A **44**
Mapesbury M. NW4 . . . 1C **28**
Mapesbury Rd. NW2 . . 4A **44**
Mapeshill Pl. NW2 . . . . 3E **43**
Mapes Ho. NW6 . . . . . . 4A **44**
Mape St. E2 . . . . 3D **65**
(not continuous)
Maple Av. W3 . . . . 2A **70**
Maple Cl. N16 . . . . 1C **36**
SW4 . . . . 4F **103**
Maple Ct. SE6 . . . . 1D **123**
Maplecroft Cl. E6 . . . . . 5F **69**
Mapledene Est. E8 . . . . 4C **50**
Mapledene Rd. E8 . . . . 4B **50**
Maple Ho. SE8 . . . . 3B **94**
(off Idonia St.)
Maple Leaf Sq. SE16 . . 3F **79**
Maple Lodge W8 . . . . . 4D **73**
(off Abbots Wlk.)
Maple M. NW6 . . . . 1D **59**
SW16 . . . . 5B **118**
Maple Pl. W1 . . . . 5A **6** (3E **61**)
Maple Rd. E11 . . . . 1A **40**
Maples Pl. E1 . . . . 4D **65**
Maplestead Rd.
SW2 . . . . 5B **104**
Maple St. W1 . . . . 5F **5** (4E **61**)
Mapleton Cres.
SW18 . . . . 4D **101**
Mapleton Rd. SW18 . . 4C **100**
(not continuous)
Maple Tree M. SE3 . . . . 4F **97**
Maple Wlk. W10 . . . . . . 2F **57**
Maplin Rd. E16 . . . . . . 5C **68**
Maplin St. E3 . . . . 2B **66**
Mapperley Cl. E11 . . . . 1B **40**
Marabou Cl. E12 . . . . . 2F **55**
Marathon Ho. NW1 . . . . 5A **4**
(off Marylebone Rd.)
Marban Rd. W9 . . . . . . 2B **58**
MARBLE ARCH 1B **74**
Marble Arch
W1 . . . . 4A **12** (1B **74**)
Marble Arch Apartments
W1 . . . . 5B **60**
(off Harrowby St.)
Marble Dr. NW2 . . . . . . 3F **29**
Marble Ho. W9 . . . . 3B **58**
Marble Quay E1 . . . . . . 2C **78**
Marbles Ho. SE5 . . . . . 2E **91**
(off Grosvenor Ter.)
Marbrook Ct. SE12 . . . 3E **125**
Marcella Rd. SW9 . . . . 5C **90**
Marchant Cl. SE1 . . . . . 1B **92**
Marchant Rd. E11 . . . . 4F **39**
Marchant St. SE14 . . . . 2A **94**
Marchbank Rd. W14 . . . 2B **86**

March Ct. SW15 . . . . . . 2D **99**
Marchmont St.
WC1 . . . . 3D **7** (3A **62**)
Marchwood Cl. SE5 . . . 3A **92**
Marcia Rd. SE1 . . . . . . 5A **78**
Marcilly Rd. SW18 . . . . 3F **101**
Marcon Ct. E8 . . . . 2D **51**
(off Amhurst Rd.)
Marconi Rd. E10 . . . . . 3C **38**
Marcon Pl. E8 . . . . 3D **51**
Marco Polo Ho.
SW8 . . . . 3D **89**
Marco Rd. W6 . . . . 4E **71**
Marcus Ct. E15 . . . . . . 5A **54**
Marcus Garvey M.
SE22 . . . . 4D **107**
Marcus Garvey Way
SE24 . . . . 2C **104**
Marcus St. E15 . . . . . . 5B **54**
SW18 . . . . 4D **101**
Marcus Ter. SW18 . . . . 4D **101**
Marden Ho. E8 . . . . 2D **51**
Marden Sq. SE16 . . . . 4D **79**
Mardyke Ho. SE17 . . . . 5F **77**
(off Mason St.)
Maresfield Gdns.
NW3 . . . . 2E **45**
Mare St. E2 . . . . 1D **65**
E8 . . . . 2D **51**
Margaret Bldgs. N16 . . 3B **36**
Margaret Ct. W1 . . . . . 2F **13**
Margaret Herbison Ho.
SW6 . . . . 2B **86**
(off Clem Attlee Ct.)
Margaret Ho. W6 . . . . . 1E **85**
(off Queen Caroline St.)
Margaret Ingram Cl.
SW6 . . . . 2B **86**
Margaret Rd. N16 . . . . 3B **36**
Margaret St.
W1 . . . . 2E **13** (5D **61**)
Margaretta Ter. SW3 . . 2A **88**
Margaretting Rd. E12 . . 3E **41**
Margaret Way IG4: Ilf . . 1F **41**
Margaret White Ho.
NW1 . . . . 1C **6**
(off Chalton St.)
Margate Rd. SW2 . . . . 3A **104**
Margery Fry Ct. N7 . . . . 5A **34**
Margery Pk. Rd. E7 . . . 3C **54**
Margery St.
WC1 . . . . 2B **8** (2C **62**)
Margery Ter. E7 . . . . . . 3C **54**
(off Margery Pk. Rd.)
Margin Dr. SW19 . . . . . 5F **113**
Margravine Gdns. W6 . . 1F **85**
Margravine Rd. W6 . . . 1F **85**
Marham Gdns.
SW18 . . . . 1A **116**
Maria Cl. SE1 . . . . 5D **79**
Marian Cl. E9 . . . . 2E **51**
Marian Pl. E2 . . . . 1D **65**
Marian St. E2 . . . . 1D **65**
Maria Ter. NW10 . . . . . 4B **42**
Maria Ter. E1 . . . . 4F **65**
Maribor SE10 . . . . 3E **95**
(off Burney St.)
Marie Curie SE5 . . . . . 4A **92**
Marie Lloyd Gdns.
N19 . . . . 2A **34**

Marie Lloyd Ho. *N1* *1B 10*
   (off Murray Gro.)
Marie Lloyd Wlk. E8 . . . 3B 50
Marigold All. SE1 . . . . . 5D 17
Marigold St. SE16 . . . . 3D 79
Marinefield Rd. SW6 . . 5D 87
Marinel Ho. SE5 . . . . . 3E 91
Mariners M. E14 . . . . . 5F 81
Marine St. SE16 . . . . . 4C 78
Marine Twr. *SE8* *2B 94*
   (off Abinger Gro.)
Marischal Rd. SE13 . . 1F 109
Maritime Ind. Est.
SE7 . . . . 5D 83
Maritime Quay E14 . . 1C 94
Maritime St. E3 . . . . . 3B 66
Marius Mans.
SW17 . . . . 2C 116
Marius Rd. SW17 . . . . 2C 116
Marjorie Gro. SW11 . . 2B 102
Marjorie M. E1 . . . . . . 5F 65
Market Ct. W1 . . . . . . 2F 13
Market Entrance SW8 . 3E 89
Market Est. N7 . . . . . . 3A 48
Market La. W12 . . . . . 3E 71
Market M.
W1 . . . . 2D 21 (2D 75)
Market Pde. *E10* *1E 39*
   (off High Rd.)
N16 . . . . *3C 36*
   (off Oldhill St.)
Market Pav. E10 . . . . . 5C 38
Market Pl. SE16 . . . . . 5C 78
   (not continuous)
W1 . . . . 2F 13 (5E 61)
Market Rd. N7 . . . . . . 3A 48
Market Row SW9 . . . . 2C 104
Market Sq. E14 . . . . . . 5D 67
Market Way E14 . . . . . 5D 67
Market Yd. M.
SE1 . . . . . . 5D 27 (3A 78)
Markham Pl. SW3 . . . . 1B 88
Markham Sq. SW3 . . . . 1B 88
Markham St. SW3 . . . . 1A 88
Mark Ho. *E2* *1F 65*
   (off Sewardstone Rd.)
Markhouse Av. E17 . . . 1A 38
Markhouse Pas. *E17* . . . *1B 38*
   (off Markhouse Rd.)
Markhouse Rd. E17 . . . 1B 38
Markland Ho. *W10* . . . *1F 71*
   (off Darfield Way)
Mark La. EC3 . . 4E 19 (1A 78)
Markmanor Av. E17 . . . 2A 38
Mark Sq.
EC2 . . . . 3D 11 (3A 64)
Markstone Ho. *SE1* . . . *4D 25*
   (off Lancaster St.)
Mark St. E15 . . . . 4A 54
EC2 . . . . 3D 11 (3A 64)
Mark Wade Cl. E12 . . . 3F 41
Markwell Cl. SE26 . . . 4D 121
Markyate Ho. *W10* . . . *3E 57*
   (off Sutton Way)
Marlborough *SW19* . . . *1F 113*
   (off Inner Pk. Rd.)
Marlborough Av. E8 . . 5C 50
   (not continuous)
Marlborough Cl.
SE17 . . . . 5E 77

Marlborough Ct. W1 . . . 4F 13
W8 . . . . 5C 72
   (off Pembroke Rd.)
Marlborough Cres.
W4 . . . . 4A 70
Marlborough Flats
SW3 . . . . 5A 74
   (off Walton St.)
Marlborough Gro.
SE1 . . . . 1C 92
Marlborough Hill
NW8 . . . . 1E 59
Marlborough House
. . . . 2A 22 (2E 75)
Marlborough Ho. *E16.* . . *2C 82*
   (off Hardy Av.)
NW1 . . . . *3E 5*
   (off Osnaburgh St.)
Marlborough La. SE7 . . 2E 97
Marlborough Mans.
NW6 . . . . *2D 45*
   (off Canon Hill)
Marlborough M.
SW2 . . . . 2B 104
Marlborough Pl.
NW8 . . . . 1E 59
Marlborough Rd.
E7 . . . . 4E 55
E15 . . . . 1A 54
N19 . . . . 4F 33
   (not continuous)
SW1 . . . . 2A 22 (2E 75)
Marlborough St.
SW3 . . . . 5A 74
Marlborough Yd. N19. . 4F 33
Marlbury *NW8* *5D 45*
   (off Abbey Rd.)
Marler Rd. SE23 . . . . 1A 122
Marley Ho. *W11* *1F 71*
   (off St Ann's Rd.)
Marley Wlk. NW2 . . . . 2E 43
Marloes Rd. W8. . . . . . 4D 73
Marlow Ct. NW6. . . . . . 4F 43
Marlowe Bus. Cen.
SE14 . . . . 3A 94
   (off Batavia Rd.)
Marlowe Ct. SW3. . . . . 5A 74
   (off Petyward)
Marlowe Ho. SE8 . . . . 1B 94
   (off Bowditch)
Marlowe Path SE8 . . . 2C 94
Marlowes, The NW8. . . 5F 45
Marlow Ho. *E2* *2F 11*
   (off Calvert Av.)
SE1 . . . . *5F 27*
   (off Maltby St.)
W2 . . . . *5D 59*
   (off Hallfield Est.)
Marlow Way SE16 . . . . 3F 79
Marlow Workshops
E2 . . . . *2F 11*
   (off Virginia Rd.)
Marl Rd. SW18. . . . . . 2E 101
Marlton St. SE10 . . . . 1B 96
Marmara Apartments
E16 . . . . *1C 82*
   (off Western Gateway)
Marmion M. SW11. . . . 1C 102
Marmion Rd. SW11 . . . 2C 102
Marmont Rd. SE15. . . . 4C 92

Marmora Ho. *E1.* *4A 66*
   (off Ben Jonson Rd.)
Marmora Rd. SE22. . . . 4E 107
Marne St. W10. . . . . . 2A 58
Marney Rd. SW11 . . . . 2C 102
Marnfield Cres.
SW2 . . . . 1C 118
Marnham Av. NW2 . . . 1A 44
Marnock Ho. *SE17* . . . *1F 91*
   (off Brandon St.)
Marnock Rd. SE4 . . . . 3B 108
Maroon Ho. E14 . . . . . 4A 66
Maroon St. E14 . . . . . 4A 66
Maroons Way
SE6 . . . . 5C 122
Marquess Rd. N1 . . . . 3F 49
Marquess Rd. Nth.
N1 . . . . 3F 49
Marquess Rd. Sth.
N1 . . . . 3E 49
Marquis Ct. *N4.* *3B 34*
   (off Marquis Rd.)
Marquis Rd. N4 . . . . . 3B 34
NW1 . . . . 3F 47
Marrick Cl. SW15. . . . . 2C 98
Marrick Ho. *NW6.* . . . *5D 45*
   (off Mortimer Cres.)
Marriett Ho. SE6 . . . . 4E 123
Marriott Rd. E15 . . . . 5A 54
N4. . . . . 3B 34
Marriotts Cl. NW9 . . . 1B 28
Marryat Ho. *SW1* *1E 89*
   (off Churchill Gdns.)
Marryat Pl. SW19 . . . . 4A 114
Marryat Rd. SW19 . . . 5F 113
Marryat Sq. SW6 . . . . 4A 86
Marsala Rd. SE13 . . . 2D 109
Marsden Rd. SE15. . . . 1B 106
Marsden St. NW5. . . . . 3C 46
   (not continuous)
Marshall Cl. SW18. . . . 4E 101
Marshall Ho. *N1.* *1F 63*
   (off Cranston St.)
NW6 . . . . *1B 58*
   (off Albert Rd.)
SE1 . . . . 5E 27
SE17 . . . . *1F 91*
   (off East St.)
Marshall Rd. E10. . . . . 5D 39
Marshall's Pl.
SE16. . . . . 5F 27 (4B 78)
Marshall St.
W1 . . . . 3A 14 (5E 61)
Marshall Street Leisure Cen.
. . . . 5E 61
Marshalsea Rd.
SE1 . . . . . . 3A 26 (3E 77)
Marsham Ct. SW1 . . . . 5F 75
Marsham St.
SW1 . . . . 5C 22 (4F 75)
Marshbrook Cl. SE3 . . 1F 111
Marsh Cen., The *E1.* . . *2F 19*
   (off Whitechapel St.)
Marsh Ct. SE8 . . . . . . 3C 50
Marsh Dr. NW9 . . . . . 1B 28
Marshfield St. E14 . . . 4E 81
Marsh Ga. Bus. Cen.
E15 . . . . 5E 53
Marshgate Cen., The
E15 . . . . 5D 53

Marshgate La. E15 . . . . . 4D **53**
   (not continuous)
Marshgate Sidings
  (Bow Depot)
  E15 . . . . 5D **53**
Marshgate Trad. Est.
  E15 . . . . 4D **53**
Marsh Hill E9 . . . . 2A **52**
Marsh Ho. SW1 . . . . . . 1F **89**
  (off Aylesford St.)
  SW8 . . . . 4E **89**
Marsh La. E10 . . . . 4B **38**
Marsh St. E14 . . . . 5D **81**
Marsh Wall E14 . . . . . . 2C **80**
Marshwood Ho. NW6 . . 5C **44**
  (off Kilburn Va.)
Marsland Cl. SE17 . . . . 1D **91**
Marsom Ho. N1 . . . . . . 1B **10**
  (off Fairbank Est.)
Marston Cl. NW6 . . . . . 4E **45**
Marston Ho. SW9 . . . . . 5C **90**
Marsworth Ho. E2 . . . . 2C **50**
  (off Whiston Rd.)
Martaban Rd. N16 . . . . 4B **36**
Martara M. SE17 . . . . . . 1E **91**
Martello St. E8 . . . . 4D **51**
Martello Ter. E8 . . . . . . 4D **51**
Martell Rd. SE21 . . . . 3F **119**
Martel Pl. E8 . . . . 3B **50**
Martha Ct. E2 . . . . 1D **65**
Martha Rd. E15 . . . . . . 3A **54**
Martha's Bldgs.
  EC1 . . . . 3B **10** (3F **63**)
Martha St. E1 . . . . 5E **65**
Martin Ct. E14 . . . . 3E **81**
  (off River Barge Cl.)
Martindale Av. E16 . . . . 1C **82**
Martindale Ho. E14 . . . 1D **81**
  (off Poplar High St.)
Martindale Rd.
  SW12 . . . . 5D **103**
Martineau Est. E1 . . . . 1E **79**
Martineau Ho. SW1 . . . 1E **89**
  (off Churchill Gdns.)
Martineau M. N5 . . . . . 1D **49**
Martineau Rd. N5 . . . . 1D **49**
Martin Ho.
  SE1 . . . . . . 5A **26** (4E **77**)
  SW8 . . . . 3A **90**
  (off Wyvil Rd.)
Martin La.
  EC4 . . . . 4C **18** (1F **77**)
  (not continuous)
Martlett Ct.
  WC2 . . . . 3E **15** (5A **62**)
Marton Cl. SE6 . . . . . . 3C **122**
Marton Rd. N16 . . . . . . 4A **36**
Martys Yd. NW3 . . . . . . 1F **45**
Marvell Ho. SE5 . . . . . . 3F **91**
  (off Camberwell Rd.)
Marvels Cl. SE12 . . . . 2D **125**
Marvels La. SE12 . . . . 2D **125**
  (not continuous)
Marville Rd. SW6 . . . . . 3B **86**
Marvin St. E8 . . . . 3D **51**
Mary Adelaide Cl.
  SW15 . . . . 4A **112**
Mary Ann Gdns. SE8 . . 2C **94**
Mary Datchelor Cl.
  SE5 . . . . 4F **91**

Mary Flux Ct. SW5 . . . . 1D **87**
  (off Bramham Gdns.)
Mary Grn. NW8 . . . . . . 5D **45**
Mary Holben Ho.
  SW16 . . . . 5E **117**
Mary Ho. W6 . . . . 1E **85**
  (off Queen Caroline St.)
Mary Jones Ho. E14 . . 1C **80**
  (off Garford St.)
Maryland Ind. Est.
  E15 . . . . 2A **54**
  (off Maryland Rd.)
Maryland Pk. E15 . . . . 2A **54**
  (not continuous)
Maryland Point E15 . . . 3A **54**
  (off Grove, The)
Maryland Rd. E15 . . . . 2F **53**
Maryland Sq. E15 . . . . 2A **54**
Marylands Rd. W9 . . . . 3C **58**
Maryland St. E15 . . . . . 2F **53**
Maryland Wlk. N1 . . . . 5E **49**
  (off Popham St.)
Mary Lawrenson Pl.
  SE3 . . . . 3C **96**
MARYLEBONE
  . . . . 5C **4** (4C **60**)
Marylebone Cricket Club
Lord's Cricket Ground
  . . . . 2F **59**
MARYLEBONE FLYOVER
  . . . . 4F **59**
Marylebone Fly-Over
  W2 . . . . 4F **59**
Marylebone High St.
  W1 . . . . 5C **4** (4C **60**)
Marylebone La.
  W1 . . . . 1C **12** (4C **60**)
Marylebone M.
  W1 . . . . 1D **13** (4D **61**)
Marylebone Pas.
  W1 . . . . 2A **14** (5E **61**)
Marylebone Rd.
  NW1 . . . . . . 5A **4** (4A **60**)
Marylebone St.
  W1 . . . . 1C **12** (4C **60**)
Marylee Way SE11 . . . 5B **76**
Mary MacArthur Ho.
  E2 . . . . 2F **65**
  (off Warley St.)
  W6 . . . . 2A **86**
Maryon M. NW3 . . . . . . 1A **46**
Maryon Rd. SE7 . . . . . . 5F **83**
  SE18 . . . . 5F **83**
Mary Pl. W11 . . . . 1A **72**
Mary Seacole Cl. E8 . . 5B **50**
Mary Smith Ct. SW5 . . 5C **72**
  (off Trebovir Rd.)
Marysmith Ho. SW1 . . 1F **89**
  (off Cureton St.)
Mary St. E16 . . . . 4B **68**
  N1 . . . . 5E **49**
Mary Ter. NW1 . . . . 5D **47**
Mary Wharrie Ho.
  NW3 . . . . 4B **46**
  (off Fellows Rd.)
Masbro' Rd. W14 . . . . . 4F **71**
Mascalls Ct. SE7 . . . . . 2E **97**
Mascalls Rd. SE7 . . . . . 2E **97**
Mascotte Rd. SW15 . . . 2F **99**
Mascotts Cl. NW2 . . . . 5D **29**

Masefield Ho. NW6 . . . 2C **58**
  (off Stafford Rd.)
Mashie Rd. W3 . . . . . . 5A **56**
Maskall Cl. SW2 . . . . . 1C **118**
Maskell Rd. SW17 . . . . 3E **115**
Maskelyne Cl. SW11 . . 4A **88**
Mason Cl. E16 . . . . 1C **82**
  SE16 . . . . 1C **92**
Mason Ho. E9 . . . . 4E **51**
  (off Frampton Pk. Rd.)
Mason's Arms M.
  W1 . . . . 3E **13** (5D **61**)
Mason's Av.
  EC2 . . . . 2B **18** (5F **63**)
Masons Pl.
  EC1 . . . . 1E **9** (2E **63**)
Mason St. SE17 . . . . . . 5F **77**
Masons Yd.
  EC1 . . . . 1E **9** (2D **63**)
  SW1 . . . . . . 1A **22** (2E **75**)
  SW19 . . . . 5F **113**
Massey Ct. E6 . . . . 5E **55**
  (off Florence Rd.)
Massie Rd. E8 . . . . 3C **50**
Massingberd Way
  SW17 . . . . 4D **117**
Massinger St. SE17 . . . 5A **78**
Massingham St. E1 . . . 3F **65**
Mast Cl. SE16 . . . . 5A **80**
  (off Boat Lifter Way)
Master Gunners Pl.
  SE18 . . . . 3F **97**
Masterman Ho. SE5 . . . 3F **91**
  (off Elmington Est.)
Masterman Rd. E6 . . . . 2F **69**
Masters Cl. SW16 . . . . 5E **117**
Masters Dr. SE16 . . . . . 1D **93**
Masters Lodge E1 . . . . 5E **65**
  (off Johnson St.)
Masters St. E1 . . . . 4F **65**
  (not continuous)
Mast Ho. Ter. E14 . . . . 5C **80**
Mastmaker Ct. E14 . . . 3C **80**
Mastmaker Rd. E14 . . . 3C **80**
Matcham Rd. E11 . . . . . 5A **40**
Matham Gro. SE22 . . . . 2B **106**
Matheson Lang Ho.
  SE1 . . . . 4B **24**
Matheson Rd. W14 . . . . 5B **72**
Mathews Pk. Av. E15 . . 3B **54**
Mathews Yd.
  WC2 . . . . . . 3D **15** (5A **62**)
Mathieson Ct. SE1 . . . . 4E **25**
  (off King James St.)
Mathison Ho. SW10 . . . 3E **87**
  (off Coleridge Gdns.)
Matilda Ho. E1 . . . . 2C **78**
  (off St Katherine's Way)
Matilda St. N1 . . . . 5B **48**
Matisse Ct.
  EC1 . . . . 3B **10** (3F **63**)
Matlock Cl. SE24 . . . . . 2E **105**
Matlock Ct. SE5 . . . . . . 2F **105**
Matlock Rd. E10 . . . . . . 1E **39**
Matlock St. E14 . . . . . . 5A **66**
Maton Ho. SW6 . . . . . . 3B **86**
  (off Estcourt Rd.)
Matrimony Pl. SW4 . . . 5E **89**
Matson Ho. SE16 . . . . . 4D **79**
Matthew Cl. W10 . . . . . 3F **57**

Matthew Parker St.
SW1 . . . . 4C **22** (3F **75**)
Matthews Ho. E14 . . . . . 4C **66**
(off Burgess St.)
Matthews St. SW11 . . . . . 5B **88**
Matthias Rd. N16 . . . . . . 2A **50**
Mattison Rd. N4 . . . . 1C **34**
Maude Ho. E2 . . . . 1C **64**
(off Ropley St.)
Maude Rd. SE5 . . . . 4A **92**
Maud Gdns. E13 . . . . . . 5B **54**
Maudlins Grn. E1 . . . . . . 2C **78**
Maud Rd. E10 . . . . 5E **39**
E13 . . . . 1B **68**
Maud St. E16 . . . . 4B **68**
Maud Wilkes Cl.
NW5 . . . . 2E **47**
Mauleverer Rd.
SW2 . . . . 3A **104**
Maundeby Wlk.
NW10 . . . . 3A **42**
Maunsel St. SW1 . . . . . . 5F **75**
Maurer Ct. SE10 . . . . . . 4B **82**
Mauretania Bldg. E1 . . . 1F **79**
(off Jardine Rd.)
Maurice Bishop Ter.
N6 . . . . 1C **32**
(off View Rd.)
Maurice Ct. E1 . . . . 2F **65**
Maurice Drummond Ho.
SE10 . . . . 4D **95**
(off Catherine Gro.)
Maurice St. W12 . . . . . . 5D **57**
Mauritius Rd. SE10 . . . . 5A **82**
Maury Rd. N16 . . . . 4C **36**
Maverton Rd. E3 . . . . . . 5C **52**
Mavis Wlk. E6 . . . . 4F **69**
(off Greenwich Cres.)
Mavor Ho. N1 . . . . 5B **48**
(off Barnsbury Est.)
Mawbey Ho. SE1 . . . . . . 1B **92**
Mawbey Pl. SE1 . . . . . . 1B **92**
Mawbey Rd. SE1 . . . . . . 1B **92**
Mawbey St. SW8 . . . . . . 3A **90**
Mawdley Ho. SE1 . . . . . 4D **25**
Mawson Ct. N1 . . . . 5F **49**
(off Gopsall St.)
Mawson Ho. EC1 . . . . . . 5B **8**
(off Baldwins Gdns.)
Mawson La. W4 . . . . . . 2B **84**
Maxden Ct. SE15 . . . . . 1B **106**
Maxilla Wlk. W10 . . . . . . 5F **57**
Maxted Rd. SE15 . . . . . 1B **106**
Maxwell Ct. SE22 . . . . . 1C **120**
SW4 . . . . 3F **103**
Maxwell Rd. SW6 . . . . . . 3D **87**
Maya Cl. SE15 . . . . 5D **93**
Mayall Rd. SE24 . . . . . . 3D **105**
Maybourne Cl.
SE26 . . . . 5D **121**
Maybury Ct. W1 . . . . . . 1C **12**
(off Marylebone St.)
Maybury Gdns.
NW10 . . . . 3D **43**
Maybury M. N6 . . . . 2E **33**
Maybury Rd. E13 . . . . . . 3E **69**
Maybury St. SW17 . . . . 5A **116**
Mayday Gdns. SE3 . . . . . 5F **97**
Maydew Ho. SE16 . . . . . 5E **79**
(off Abbeyfield Est.)

Maydwell Ho. E14 . . . . . 4C **66**
(off Thomas Rd.)
Mayerne Rd. SE9 . . . . . 3F **111**
Mayeswood Rd.
SE12 . . . . 4E **125**
MAYFAIR 5D **13** (1D **75**)
Mayfair M. NW1 . . . . 4B **46**
(off Regents Pk. Rd.)
Mayfair Pl.
W1 . . . . 1E **21** (2D **75**)
Mayfield Av. W4 . . . . . . 5A **70**
Mayfield Cl. E8 . . . . 3B **50**
SW4 . . . . 3F **103**
Mayfield Gdns.
NW4 . . . . 1F **29**
Mayfield Ho. E2 . . . . . . 1D **65**
(off Cambridge Heath Rd.)
Mayfield Mans.
SW15 . . . . 3B **100**
Mayfield Rd. E8 . . . . . . 4B **50**
E13 . . . . 3B **68**
N8 . . . . 1B **34**
W12 . . . . 3A **70**
Mayfield Rd. Flats
N8 . . . . 1B **34**
Mayflower Cl. SE16 . . . . 5F **79**
Mayflower Rd. SW9 . . . 1A **104**
Mayflower St. SE16 . . . . 3E **79**
Mayford NW1 . . . . 1E **61**
(not continuous)
Mayford Cl. SW12 . . . . . 5B **102**
Mayford Rd. SW12 . . . . . 5B **102**
Maygood St. N1 . . . . . . 1C **62**
Maygrove Rd. NW6 . . . . . 3B **44**
Mayhew Ct. SE5 . . . . . . 2F **105**
Mayhill Rd. SE7 . . . . . . 2D **97**
Maylands Ho. SW3 . . . . 5A **74**
(off Elystan St.)
Maynard Cl. SW6 . . . . . 3D **87**
Maynard Rd. E17 . . . . . . 1E **39**
Maynards Quay E1 . . . . . 1E **79**
Mayne Ct. SE26 . . . . . . 5D **121**
Mayo Ho. E1 . . . . 4E **65**
(off Lindley St.)
Mayola Rd. E5 . . . . 1E **51**
Mayo Rd. NW10 . . . . . . 3A **42**
Mayow Rd. SE23 . . . . . 3F **121**
SE26 . . . . 4F **121**
May Rd. E13 . . . . 1C **68**
May's Bldgs. M.
SE10 . . . . 3E **95**
Mays Ct. SE10 . . . . 3F **95**
WC2 . . . . 5D **15** (1A **76**)
Maysoule Rd. SW11 . . . 2F **101**
Mayston M. SE10 . . . . . . 1C **96**
(off Ormiston Rd.)
May St. W14 . . . . 1B **86**
Mayton St. N7 . . . . 5B **34**
May Tree Ho. SE4 . . . . . 1B **108**
(off Wickham Rd.)
Maytree Wlk. SW2 . . . . . 2C **118**
Mayville Est. N16 . . . . . . 2A **50**
Mayville Rd. E11 . . . . . . 4A **40**
May Wlk. E13 . . . . 1D **69**
Mayward Ho. SE5 . . . . . 4A **92**
(off Peckham Rd.)
May Wynne Ho. E16 . . . 1D **83**
(off Murray Sq.)
Maze Hill SE3 . . . . 3B **96**
SE10 . . . . 2A **96**

Maze Hill Lodge
SE10 . . . . 2F **95**
(off Park Vista)
Mazenod Av. NW6 . . . . . 4C **44**
Meadbank Studios
SW11 . . . . 3A **88**
(off Parkgate Rd.)
Mead Cl. NW1 . . . . 3C **46**
Meadcroft Rd. SE11 . . . . 2D **91**
(not continuous)
Meader Ct. SE14 . . . . . . 3F **93**
Mead Ho. W11 . . . . 2B **72**
(off Ladbroke Rd.)
Meadow Bank SE3 . . . . 1B **110**
Meadowbank NW3 . . . . . 4B **46**
Meadowbank Cl.
SW6 . . . . 3E **85**
Meadowbank Rd.
NW9 . . . . 2A **28**
Meadow Cl. SE6 . . . . . . 5C **122**
Meadow Ct. N1 . . . . 1A **64**
Meadowcourt Rd.
SE3 . . . . 2B **110**
Meadow La. SE12 . . . . . 3D **125**
Meadow Pl. SW8 . . . . . . 3A **90**
W4 . . . . 3A **84**
Meadow Rd. SW8 . . . . . . 3B **90**
Meadow Row SE1 . . . . . 4E **77**
Meadows Cl. E10 . . . . . . 4C **38**
Meadowside SE9 . . . . . 2E **111**
Meadowside Leisure Cen.
. . . . 2E **111**
Meadowsweet Cl.
E16 . . . . 4F **69**
Meadowview Rd.
SE6 . . . . 5B **122**
Mead Path SW17 . . . . . 4E **115**
Mead Pl. E9 . . . . 3E **51**
Mead Row
SE1 . . . . 5B **24** (4C **76**)
Meads Cl. E15 . . . . 3B **54**
Meadway NW11 . . . . 1C **30**
Meadway, The SE3 . . . . . 5F **95**
Meadway Cl. NW11 . . . . 1D **31**
Meadway Ga. NW11 . . . . 1C **30**
Meakin Est.
SE1 . . . . 5D **27** (4A **78**)
Meanley Rd. E12 . . . . . . 1F **55**
Meard St.
W1 . . . . 3B **14** (5F **61**)
(not continuous)
Meath Ho. SE24 . . . . . . 4D **105**
(off Dulwich Rd.)
Meath Rd. E15 . . . . 1B **68**
Meath St. SW11 . . . . . . 4D **89**
Mecca Bingo
Camden 5D **47**
(off Arlington Rd.)
Earlsfield 1D **115**
Fulham Broadway . . . 3C **86**
(off Vanston Pl.)
Haggerston 1B **64**
(off Hackney Rd.)
Islington 4E **49**
Kilburn 5C **44**
Mecklenburgh Pl.
WC1 . . . . 3F **7** (3B **62**)
Mecklenburgh Sq.
WC1 . . . . 3F **7** (3B **62**)

Mecklenburgh St.
WC1 . . . . 3F **7** (3B **62**)
Medburn St. NW1 . . . . . 1F **61**
Medebourne Cl.
SE3 . . . . 1C **110**
Mede Ho.
BR1: Brom 5D **125**
(off Pike Cl.)
Medfield St. SW15 . . . . 5C **98**
Medhurst Cl. E3 . . . . . 1A **66**
(not continuous)
Median Rd. E5 . . . . 2E **51**
Medina Gro. N7 . . . . . . 5C **34**
Medina Rd. N7 . . . . 5C **34**
Medland Ho. E14 . . . . . 1A **80**
Medlar St. SE5 . . . . 4E **91**
Medley Rd. NW6 . . . . . 3C **44**
Medora Rd. SW2 . . . . . 5B **104**
Medusa Rd. SE6 . . . . . 4D **109**
Medway Bldgs. E3 . . . . 1A **66**
(off Medway Rd.)
Medway Ct. NW11 . . . . 1D **31**
WC1 . . . . 2D **7**
(off Judd St.)
Medway Ho. NW8 . . . . . 3A **60**
(off Penfold St.)
SE1 . . . . 4C **26**
(off Hankey Pl.)
Medway M. E3 . . . . 1A **66**
Medway Rd. E3 . . . . . . 1A **66**
Medway St. SW1 . . . . . 4F **75**
Medwin St. SW4 . . . . . 2B **104**
Meerbrook Rd. SE3 . . . 1E **111**
Meeson Rd. E15 . . . . . 4B **54**
Meeson St. E5 . . . . 1A **52**
Meeson's Wharf E15 . . 1E **67**
Meeting Fld. Path E9 . . 3E **51**
Meeting Ho. All. E1 . . . 2D **79**
Meeting Ho. La.
SE15 . . . . 4D **93**
Megabowl 2A **118**
Mehetabel Rd. E9 . . . . 2E **51**
Melba Way SE13 . . . . . 4D **95**
Melbourne Ct. W9 . . . . 3E **59**
(off Randolph Av.)
Melbourne Gro.
SE22 . . . . 2A **106**
Melbourne Ho. W8 . . . . 2C **72**
(off Kensington Pl.)
Melbourne Mans.
W14 . . . . 2A **86**
(off Musard Rd.)
Melbourne Sq. SE6 . . . 5E **109**
SW9 . . . . 4C **90**
Melbourne Pl.
WC2 . . . . 3A **16** (5B **62**)
Melbourne Rd. E10 . . . 2D **39**
Melbourne Sq. SW9 . . . 4C **90**
Melbourne Ter. SW6 . . . 3D **87**
(off Moore Pk. Rd.)
Melbray M. SW6 . . . . . 5B **86**
Melbreak Ho. SE22 . . . 1A **106**
Melbury Ct. W8 . . . . . . 4B **72**
Melbury Dr. SE5 . . . . . 3A **92**
Melbury Ho. SW8 . . . . . 3B **90**
(off Richborne Ter.)
Melbury Rd. W14 . . . . . 4B **72**
Melbury Ter. NW1 . . . . 3A **60**
Melchester W11 . . . . . 5B **58**
(off Ledbury Rd.)

Melchester Ho. N19 . . . 5F **33**
(off Wedmore St.)
Melcombe Ct. NW1 . . . . 5A **4**
(off Melcombe Pl.)
Melcombe Ho. SW8 . . . 3B **90**
(off Dorset Rd.)
Melcombe Pl. NW1 . . . . 4B **60**
Melcombe Regis Ct.
W1 . . . . 1C **12**
(off Weymouth St.)
Melcombe St.
NW1 . . . . 4A **4** (3B **60**)
Meldon Cl. SW6 . . . . . . 4D **87**
Melfield Gdns. SE6 . . . 4E **123**
Melford Ct. SE1 . . . . . . 5E **27**
(off Fendall St.)
SE22 . . . . 1C **120**
(not continuous)
Melford Pas. SE22 . . . 5C **106**
Melford Rd. E11 . . . . . . 4A **40**
SE22 . . . . 5C **106**
Melgund Rd. N5 . . . . . . 2C **48**
Melina Ct. SW15 . . . . . 1C **98**
Melina Pl. NW8 . . . . . . 2F **59**
Melina Rd. W12 . . . . . . 3D **71**
Melior Ct. N6 . . . . 1E **33**
Melior Pl.
SE1 . . . . 3D **27** (3A **78**)
Melior St.
SE1 . . . . 3D **27** (3A **78**)
Meliot Rd. SE6 . . . . . . 2F **123**
Mellish Flats E10 . . . . . 2C **38**
Mellish Ho. E1 . . . . 5D **65**
(off Varden St.)
Mellish Ind. Est.
SE18 . . . . 4F **83**
Mellish St. E14 . . . . . . 4C **80**
Mellison Rd. SW17 . . . 5A **116**
Mellitus St. W12 . . . . . 4B **56**
Mell St. SE10 . . . . 1A **96**
Melody La. N5 . . . . 2E **49**
Melody Rd. SW18 . . . . 3E **101**
Melon Pl. W8 . . . . 3C **72**
Melon Rd. E11 . . . . 5A **40**
SE15 . . . . 4C **92**
Melrose Av. NW2 . . . . . 2D **43**
SW19 . . . . 2B **114**
Melrose Cl. SE12 . . . . . 1C **124**
Melrose Gdns. W6 . . . . 4E **71**
Melrose Ho. E14 . . . . . 4D **81**
(off Lanark Sq.)
NW6 . . . . 2C **58**
(off Carlton Va.)
Melrose Rd. SW13 . . . . 5B **84**
SW18 . . . . 4B **100**
Melrose Ter. W6 . . . . . . 4E **71**
Melthorpe Gdns. SE3 . . 4F **97**
Melton Ct. SW7 . . . . . . 5F **73**
(not continuous)
Melton St.
NW1 . . . . 2A **6** (2E **61**)
Melville Ct. SE8 . . . . . . 5A **80**
W12 . . . . 4D **71**
(off Goldhawk Rd.)
Melville Ho. SE10 . . . . . 4E **95**
Melville Pl. N1 . . . . 4E **49**
Melville Rd. SW13 . . . . 4C **84**
Melwood Ho. E1 . . . . . . 5D **65**
(off Watney Mkt.)
Melyn Cl. N7 . . . . 1E **47**

Memel Ct. EC1 . . . . 4F **9**
Memel St. EC1 . . 4F **9** (3E **63**)
Memorial Av. E12 . . . . . 4F **41**
E15 . . . . 2A **68**
Mendham Ho. SE1 . . . . 5D **27**
(off Cluny Pl.)
Mendip Cl. SE26 . . . . . 4E **121**
Mendip Ct. SE14 . . . . . 2E **93**
(off Avonley Rd.)
SW11 . . . . 1E **101**
Mendip Dr. NW2 . . . . . 4A **30**
Mendip Ho's. E2 . . . . . 2E **65**
(off Welwyn St.)
Mendip Rd. SW11 . . . . 1E **101**
Mendora Rd. SW6 . . . . 3A **86**
Menelik Rd. NW2 . . . . . 1A **44**
Menotti St. E2 . . . . 3C **64**
Menteath Ho. E14 . . . . 5C **66**
(off Dod St.)
Mentmore Ter. E8 . . . . 4D **51**
Mepham St.
SE1 . . . . 2B **24** (2C **76**)
Merbury Cl. SE13 . . . . . 3E **109**
Mercator Pl. E14 . . . . . 1C **94**
Mercator Rd. SE13 . . . . 2F **109**
Mercer Ho. SW1 . . . . . 1D **89**
(off Ebury Bri. Rd.)
Merceron Ho's. E2 . . . . 2E **65**
(off Globe Rd.)
Merceron St. E1 . . . . . . 3D **65**
Mercers Cl. SE10 . . . . . 5B **82**
Mercer's Cotts. E1 . . . . 5A **66**
(off White Horse Rd.)
Mercers M. N19 . . . . . . 5F **33**
Mercers Pl. W6 . . . . . . 5F **71**
Mercers Rd. N19 . . . . . 5F **33**
(not continuous)
Mercer St.
WC2 . . . . 3D **15** (5A **62**)
Merchant St. E3 . . . . . . 2B **66**
Merchants Ho. SE10 . . . 1F **95**
(off Collington St.)
Merchants Row SE10 . . 1F **95**
(off Hoskins St.)
Merchant St. E3 . . . . . . 2B **66**
Merchiston Rd. SE6 . . . 2F **123**
Mercia Gro. SE13 . . . . 2E **109**
Mercia Ho. SE5 . . . . . . 5E **91**
(off Denmark Rd.)
Mercier Rd. SW15 . . . . 3A **100**
Mercury Ct. E14 . . . . . . 5C **80**
(off Homer Dr.)
Mercury Way SE14 . . . 2F **93**
Mercy Ter. SE13 . . . . . . 3D **109**
Mere Cl. SW15 . . . . 5F **99**
Meredith Av. NW2 . . . . 2E **43**
Meredith Ho. N16 . . . . . 2A **50**
Meredith M. SE4 . . . . . 2B **108**
Meredith St. E13 . . . . . 2C **68**
EC1 . . . . 2D **9** (2D **63**)
Meredyth Rd. SW13 . . . 5C **84**
Meretone Cl. SE4 . . . . . 2A **108**
Mereton Mans. SE8 . . . 4C **94**
(off Brookmill Rd.)
Mereworth Ho. SE15 . . 2E **93**
Merganser Ct. SE8 . . . . 2B **94**
(off Edward St.)
Meriden Ct. SW3 . . . . . 1A **88**
(off Chelsea Mnr. St.)

Meridian Ga. E14 . . . . . . 3D 81
Meridian Ho. SE10 . . . . . 5A 82
(off Azof St.)
SE10 . . . . 3E 95
(off Royal Hill)
Meridian Pl. E14 . . . . . . 3D 81
Meridian Point SE8 . . . . 2D 95
Meridian Rd. SE7 . . . . . 3F 97
Meridian Sq. E15 . . . . . . 4F 53
Meridian Trad. Est.
SE7 . . . . 5D 83
Merifield Rd. SE9 . . . . . . 2E 111
Merivale Rd. SW15 . . . 2A 100
Merlin Gdns.
BR1: Brom 3C 124
Merlin Ho. SW18 . . . . . 2E 101
Merlin Rd. E12 . . . . 4F 41
Merlins Ct. WC1 . . . . . . 2B 8
(off Margery St.)
Merlin St.
WC1 . . . . 2B 8 (2C 62)
Mermaid Ct. E8 . . . . 4B 50
(off Celandine Dr.)
SE1 . . . . 3B 26 (3F 77)
SE16 . . . . 2B 80
Mermaid Ho. E14 . . . . . . 1E 81
(off Bazely St.)
Mermaid Twr. SE8 . . . . . 2B 94
(off Abinger Gro.)
Meroe Ct. N16 . . . . 4A 36
Merredene St. SW2 . . . 4B 104
Merriam Av. E9 . . . . 3B 52
Merrick Sq.
SE1 . . . . 5B 26 (4F 77)
Merriman Rd. SE3 . . . . . 4E 97
Merrington Rd. SW6 . . . 2C 86
Merritt Rd. SE4 . . . . 3B 108
Merritt's Bldgs. EC2 . . . 4D 11
Merrivale NW1 . . . . 5E 47
(off Camden St.)
Merrow St. SE17 . . . . . . 1F 91
Merrow Wlk. SE17 . . . . . 1F 91
Merryfield SE3 . . . . 5B 96
Merryfield Ho. SE9 . . . . 3E 125
(off Grove Pk. Rd.)
Merryfields Way
SE6 . . . . 5D 109
Merryweather Ct.
N19 . . . . 5E 33
Merthyr Ter. SW13 . . . . 2D 85
Merton Av. W4 . . . . 5B 70
Merton La. N6 . . . . 4B 32
Merton Ri. NW3 . . . . . . 4A 46
Merton Rd. E17 . . . . 1E 39
SW18 . . . . 4C 100
Mertoun Ter. W1 . . . . . . 4B 60
(off Seymour Pl.)
Merttins Rd. SE4 . . . . . . 3F 107
SE15 . . . . 3F 107
Meru Cl. NW5 . . . . 1C 46
Mervan Rd. SW2 . . . . . 2C 104
Messent Rd. SE9 . . . . . 3E 111
Messina Av. NW6 . . . . . 4C 44
Messiter Ho. N1 . . . . . . 5B 48
(off Barnsbury Est.)
Meteor St. SW11 . . . . . 2C 102
Methley St. SE11 . . . . . 1C 90
Methwold Rd. W10 . . . . 4F 57
Metro Bus. Cen., The
SE26 . . . . 5B 122

Metro Central Hgts.
SE1 . . . . 5F 25
Metropolis SE11 . . . . . . 4D 77
(off Oswin St.)
Metropolitan Bus. Cen.
N1 . . . . 4A 50
(off Enfield Rd.)
Metropolitan Cl. E14 . . . 4C 66
Metropolitan Sta. Bldgs.
W6 . . . . 5E 71
(off Beadon Rd.)
Metropolitan Wharf
E1 . . . . 2E 79
Mews, The IG4: Ilf 1F 41
N1 . . . . 5E 49
SE22 . . . . 3C 106
Mews St. E1 . . . . 2C 78
Mexborough NW1 . . . . . 5E 47
Mexfield Rd. SW15 . . . . 3B 100
Meymott St.
SE1 . . . . 2D 25 (2D 77)
Meynell Cres. E9 . . . . . . 4F 51
Meynell Gdns. E9 . . . . . 4F 51
Meynell Rd. E9 . . . . 4F 51
Meyrick Ho. E14 . . . . . . 4C 66
(off Burgess St.)
Meyrick Rd. NW10 . . . . 3C 42
SW11 . . . . 1F 101
Miah Ter. E1 . . . . 2C 78
Miall Wlk. SE26 . . . . . . 4A 122
Micawber Ct. N1 . . . . . . 1A 10
(off Windsor Ter.)
Micawber Ho. SE16 . . . . 3C 78
(off Llewellyn St.)
Micawber St.
N1 . . . . 1A 10 (2E 63)
Michael Cliffe Ho.
EC1 . . . . 2D 9
Michael Faraday Ho.
SE17 . . . . 1A 92
(off Beaconsfield Rd.)
Michael Manley Ind. Est.
SW8 . . . . 5E 89
(off Clyston St.)
Michael Rd. E11 . . . . . . 3B 40
SW6 . . . . 4D 87
Michaels Cl. SE13 . . . . 2A 110
Michael Sobell Leisure Cen.
. . . . 5B 34
Michael Stewart Ho.
SW6 . . . . 2B 86
(off Clem Attlee Ct.)
Michelangelo Ct.
SE16 . . . . 1D 93
(off Stubbs Dr.)
Micheldever Rd.
SE12 . . . . 4A 110
Michelle Ct. W3 . . . . . . 1A 70
Michelson Ho. SE11 . . . 5B 76
(off Black Prince Rd.)
Michigan Ho. E14 . . . . . 4C 80
Mickledore NW1 . . . . . . 1A 6
(off Ampthill Est.)
Micklethwaite Rd.
SW6 . . . . 2C 86
Middle Dartrey Wlk.
SW10 . . . . 3E 87
(off Dartrey Wlk.)
Middlefield NW8 . . . . . . 5F 45
Middle La. N8 . . . . 1A 34

Middle La. M. N8 . . . . . . 1A 34
Middle Pk. Av. SE9 . . . . 4F 111
Middle Rd. E13 . . . . 1C 68
Middle Row W10 . . . . . . 3A 58
Middlesex County Cricket Club
Lord's Cricket Ground
. . . . 2F 59
Middlesex Ct. W4 . . . . . 5B 70
Middlesex Filter Beds
Nature Reserve 5F 37
Middlesex Pas. EC1 . . . . 1E 17
Middlesex Pl. E9 . . . . . . 3E 51
(off Elsdale St.)
Middlesex St.
E1 . . . . 1E 19 (4A 64)
Middlesex University
Archway Campus, The
. . . . 3E 33
Middlesex Wharf E5 . . . . 4E 37
Middle St. EC1 . . . . 5F 9 (4E 63)
Middle Temple 4B 16
Middle Temple Hall 4B 16
(off Middle Temple La.)
Middle Temple La.
EC4 . . . . 3B 16 (5C 62)
Middleton Dr. SE16 . . . . 3F 79
Middleton Gro. N7 . . . . . 2A 48
Middleton Ho. E8 . . . . . 4C 50
SE1 . . . . 5B 26
(off Burbage Cl.)
SW1 . . . . 5F 75
(off Causton St.)
Middleton M. N7 . . . . . . 2A 48
Middleton Pl. W1 . . . . . 1F 13
Middleton Rd. E8 . . . . . 4B 50
NW11 . . . . 2C 30
Middleton St. E2 . . . . . . 2D 65
Middleton Way
SE13 . . . . 2F 109
Middleway NW11 . . . . . 1D 31
Middle Yd.
SE1 . . . . 1D 27 (2A 78)
Midford Pl.
W1 . . . . 4A 6 (3E 61)
Midhope Ho. WC1 . . . . . 2E 7
(off Midhope St.)
Midhope St.
WC1 . . . . 2E 7 (2A 62)
Midhurst SE26 . . . . 5E 121
Midhurst Ho. E14 . . . . . 5B 66
(off Salmon La.)
Midhurst Way E5 . . . . . 1C 50
Midland Pde. NW6 . . . . 3D 45
Midland Pl. E14 . . . . . . 1E 95
Midland Rd. E10 . . . . . . 2E 39
NW1 . . . . 1C 6 (1F 61)
Midland Ter. NW2 . . . . . 5F 29
NW10 . . . . 3A 56
Midmoor Rd. SW12 . . . 1E 117
Midship Cl. SE16 . . . . . 2F 79
Midship Point E14 . . . . . 3C 80
(off Quarterdeck, The)
Midstrath Rd. NW10 . . . 1A 42
Midway Ho. EC1 . . . . . . 1D 9
Midwood Cl. NW2 . . . . . 5D 29
Mighell Av. IG4: Ilf 1F 41
Milborne Gro. SW10 . . . 1E 87
Milborne St. E9 . . . . 3E 51
Milborough Cres.
SE12 . . . . 4A 110

Milcote St.
SE1 . . . . 4D **25** (3D **77**)
Mildenhall Rd. E5 . . . . 1E **51**
Mildmay Av. N1 . . . . . . 3F **49**
Mildmay Gro. Nth.
N1 . . . . 2F **49**
Mildmay Gro. Sth.
N1 . . . . 2F **49**
Mildmay Pk. N1 . . . . . . 2F **49**
Mildmay Pl. N16 . . . . . 2A **50**
Mildmay Rd. N1 . . . . . . 3F **49**
Mildmay St. N1 . . . . . . 3F **49**
MILE END 3B **66**
Mile End Pk. 3A **66**
Mile End Pl. E1 . . . . . . 3F **65**
Mile End Rd. E1 . . . . . 4E **65**
E3 . . . . 4E **65**
Mile End Stadium 4A **66**
Miles Bldgs. NW1 . . . . 4A **60**
(off Penfold Pl.)
Miles Ct. E1 . . . . 5D **65**
(off Tillman St.)
Miles Ho. SE10 . . . . . . 1A **96**
(off Tuskar St.)
Miles Pl. NW1 . . . . 4F **59**
(off Broadley St.)
Miles St. SW8 . . . . . . 2A **90**
(not continuous)
Miles St. Bus. Est.
SW8 . . . . 2A **90**
(off Miles St.)
Milfoil St. W12 . . . . . 1C **70**
Milford La.
WC2 . . . . . . 4A **16** (1C **76**)
Milford M. SW16 . . . . 3B **118**
Milford Towers SE6 . . 5D **109**
Milk St. BR1: Brom . . . 5D **125**
EC2 . . . . . . 3A **18** (5E **63**)
Milkwell Yd. SE5 . . . . . 4E **91**
Milkwood Rd. SE24 . . 3D **105**
Milk Yd. E1 . . . . 1E **79**
Millais Ho. SW1 . . . . . . 5A **76**
(off Marsham St.)
Millais Rd. E11 . . . . . 1E **53**
Millard Cl. N16 . . . . . . 2A **50**
Millard Rd. SE8 . . . . . . 1B **94**
(off Leeway)
Millbank
SW1 . . . . . . 5D **23** (4A **76**)
Millbank Ct. SW1 . . . . . 5A **76**
(off John Islip St.)
Millbank Twr. SW1 . . . 5A **76**
Millbank Way SE12 . . 3C **110**
Millbrook Ho. SE15 . . 2C **92**
(off Peckham Pk. Rd.)
Millbrook Pas. SW9 . . 1D **105**
Millbrook Pl. NW1 . . . . 1E **61**
(off Hampstead Rd.)
Millbrook Rd. SW9 . . . 1D **105**
Mill Ct. E10 . . . . 5E **39**
Millcroft Ho. SE6 . . . 4E **123**
(off Melfield Gdns.)
Millender Wlk. SE16 . . 5E **79**
(off New Rotherhithe Rd.)
Millennium Bridge
. . . . 5E **17** (1D **77**)
Millennium Bus. Cen.
NW2 . . . . 4D **29**
Millennium Cl. E16 . . . 5D **69**
Millennium Dome 2A **82**

Millennium Dr. E14 . . . 5F **81**
Millennium Pl. E2 . . . 1D **65**
Millennium Sq.
SE1 . . . . . . 3F **27** (3B **78**)
Millennium Way
SE10 . . . . 3A **82**
Miller Cl.
BR1: Brom 5D **125**
Miller Rd. SW19 . . . . 5F **115**
Miller's Av. E8 . . . . . . 2B **50**
Millers Mdw. Cl.
SE3 . . . . 2B **110**
Miller's Ter. E8 . . . . . . 2B **50**
Miller St. NW1 . . . . . . 1E **61**
(not continuous)
Millers Way W6 . . . . . 3E **71**
Millers Wharf Ho. E1 . . 2C **78**
(off St Katherine's Way)
Miller Wlk.
SE1 . . . . . . 2C **24** (2C **76**)
Millfield N4 . . . . 4C **34**
Millfield La. N6 . . . . . . 3A **32**
(not continuous)
Millfield Pl. N6 . . . . . . 4C **32**
Millfield Rd. E5 . . . . . 1E **51**
Mill Gdns. SE26 . . . . 3D **121**
Millgrove St. SW11 . . 4C **88**
Millharbour E14 . . . . 3D **81**
Mill Hill SW13 . . . . . . 5C **84**
Mill Hill Rd. SW13 . . . 5C **84**
Millhouse Pl. SE27 . . 4D **119**
Millicent Rd. E10 . . . . 3B **38**
Milligan St. E14 . . . . . 1B **80**
Milliners Ho. SW18 . . 2C **100**
Millington Ho. N16 . . . 5F **35**
Mill La. NW6 . . . . 2B **44**
Millman M.
WC1 . . . . . . 4F **7** (3B **62**)
Millman Pl. WC1 . . . . . 4A **8**
(off Millman St.)
Millman St.
WC1 . . . . . . 4F **7** (3B **62**)
Millmark Gro. SE14 . . . 5A **94**
MILL MEADS 1F **67**
Mill Pl. E14 . . . . 5A **66**
Mill Pond Cl. SW8 . . . . 3F **89**
Millpond Est. SE16 . . . 3D **79**
Mill Rd. E16 . . . . 2D **83**
Mill Row N1 . . . . 5A **50**
Mills Ct. EC2 . . . . 3D **11**
(off Curtain Rd.)
Mills Gro. E14 . . . . . . 4E **67**
Millshot Cl. SW6 . . . . . 4E **85**
Mills Ho. SW8 . . . . . . 4E **89**
(off Thessaly Rd.)
Millstream Ho. SE16 . . 3D **79**
(off Jamaica Rd.)
Millstream Rd.
SE1 . . . . . . 4F **27** (3B **78**)
Mill St. SE1 . . . . 3B **78**
W1 . . . . 4F **13** (1D **75**)
MILLWALL 5D **81**
Millwall Dock Rd.
E14 . . . . 4C **80**
Millwall FC 1E **93**
Millwood St. W10 . . . . 4A **58**
Mill Yd. E1 . . . . 1C **78**
Milman Rd. NW6 . . . . 1F **57**
Milman's St. SW10 . . . 2F **87**
Milne Gdns. SE9 . . . . 3F **111**

Milner Ct. SE15 . . . . . 3B **92**
(off Colegrove Rd.)
Milner Pl. N1 . . . . 5C **48**
Milner Rd. E15 . . . . . . 2A **68**
Milner Sq. N1 . . . . . . 4D **49**
Milner St. SW3 . . . . . . 5B **74**
Milo Gdns. SE22 . . . . 4B **106**
Milo Rd. SE22 . . . . . . 4B **106**
Milrood Ho. E1 . . . . . . 4F **65**
(off Stepney Grn.)
Milroy Wlk.
SE1 . . . . . . 1D **25** (2D **77**)
Milson Rd. W14 . . . . . 4F **71**
Milstead Ho. E5 . . . . . 2D **51**
Milton Av. E6 . . . . 4F **55**
N6 . . . . 2E **33**
Milton Cl. N2 . . . . 1E **31**
SE1 . . . . 5B **78**
Milton Ct.
EC2 . . . . . . 5B **10** (4F **63**)
SE14 . . . . 2B **94**
(not continuous)
SW18 . . . . 3C **100**
Milton Ct. Rd. SE14 . . . 2A **94**
Milton Ct. Wlk. EC2 . . . 5B **10**
(off Silk St.)
Milton Gdn. Est.
N16 . . . . 1F **49**
Milton Gro. N16 . . . . . 1F **49**
Milton Ho. E2 . . . . 2E **65**
(off Roman Rd.)
SE5 . . . . 3F **91**
(off Elmington Est.)
Milton Mans. W14 . . . . 2A **86**
(off Queen's Club Gdns.)
Milton Pk. N6 . . . . 2E **33**
Milton Rd. N7 . . . . 2C **48**
(off Eastwood Cl.)
N6 . . . . 2E **33**
NW9 . . . . 2C **28**
SE24 . . . . 3D **105**
SW19 . . . . 5E **115**
Milton St.
EC2 . . . . . . 5B **10** (4F **63**)
Milverton Ho. SE6 . . . 3A **122**
Milverton Rd. NW6 . . . 4E **43**
Milverton St. SE11 . . . 1C **90**
Milward St. E1 . . . . . . 4D **65**
Mimosa Lodge
NW10 . . . . 2B **42**
Mimosa St. SW6 . . . . . 4B **86**
Minard Rd. SE6 . . . . . 5A **110**
Mina Rd. SE17 . . . . . . 1A **92**
Minchin Ho. E14 . . . . . 5C **66**
(off Dod St.)
Mincing La.
EC3 . . . . . . 4D **19** (1A **78**)
Minehead Rd.
SW16 . . . . 5B **118**
Minera M. SW1 . . . . . 5C **74**
Minerva Cl. SW9 . . . . 3C **90**
(not continuous)
Minerva Rd. NW10 . . . 2A **56**
Minerva St. E2 . . . . . . 1D **65**
Minerva Wlk.
EC1 . . . . . . 2E **17** (5D **63**)
Minet Av. NW10 . . . . . 1A **56**
Minet Gdns. NW10 . . . 1A **56**
Minet Rd. SW9 . . . . . . 5D **91**
Minford Gdns. W14 . . . 3F **71**

Minford Ho. *W14* 3F **71**
(off Minford Gdns.)
Mingard Wlk. N7 . . . . . . 4B **34**
Ming St. E14. . . . . 1C **80**
Miniver Pl. EC4 . . . . . . 4A **18**
Minnow St. SE17 . . . . . 5A **78**
Minnow Wlk. SE17 . . . . 5A **78**
Minories EC3. . 3F **19** (5B **64**)
Minshull St. SW8 . . . . . 4F **89**
Minson Rd. E9 . . . . 5F **51**
Minstead Gdns.
SW15 . . . . 5B **98**
Minster Ct. EC3 . . . . . . 4E **19**
Minster Pavement
EC3 . . . . 4E **19**
(off Mincing La.)
Minster Rd. NW2 . . . . . 2A **44**
Mint Bus. Pk. E16 . . . . 4D **69**
Mintern St. N1 . . . . 1F **63**
Minton Ho. SE11 . . . . . 5C **76**
(off Walnut Tree Wlk.)
Mint Wlk. NW6 . . . . 3D **45**
Mint St. SE1. . . 3F **25** (3E **77**)
Mirabel Rd. SW6 . . . . . 3B **86**
Miranda Cl. E1 . . . . 4E **65**
Miranda Rd. N19 . . . . . 3E **33**
Mirfield St. SE7 . . . . . . 5F **83**
Mirror Path SE9 . . . . . . 3E **125**
Missenden SE17. . . . . . 1F **91**
(off Roland Way)
Missenden Ho. NW8 . . . 3A **60**
(off Jerome Cres.)
Mission, The *E14*. 5B **66**
(off Commercial Rd.)
Mission Pl. SE15 . . . . . 4C **92**
Mistral SE5. . . . . 4A **92**
Mitali Pas. E1. . . . . 5C **64**
(not continuous)
Mitcham Ho. SE5 . . . . . 4E **91**
Mitcham La. SW16. . . . . 5E **117**
Mitcham Rd. SW17 . . . . 5B **116**
Mitchellbrook Way
NW10 . . . . 3A **42**
Mitchell Ho. *W12*. 1D **71**
(off White City Est.)
Mitchell's Pl. *SE21*. . . 4A **106**
(off Aysgarth Rd.)
Mitchell St.
EC1. . . . . 3F **9** (3E **63**)
(not continuous)
Mitchell Wlk. *E6*. 4F **69**
(off Neats Ct. Rd.)
Mitchison Rd. N1 . . . . . 3F **49**
Mitford Rd. N19 . . . . . . 4A **34**
Mitre, The E14 . . . . 1B **80**
Mitre Bri. Ind. Pk.
NW10 . . . . 3D **57**
Mitre Ct. EC2 . . . . 2A **18**
Mitre Ct. E15 . . . . 1A **68**
SE1 . . . . 3C **24** (3C **76**)
Mitre Sq.
EC3 . . . . 3F **19** (5A **64**)
Mitre St. EC3. . 3F **19** (5A **64**)
Mitre Way NW10 . . . . . . 3D **57**
W10 . . . . 3D **57**
Mitre Yd. SW3 . . . . 5A **74**
Moat Dr. E13. . . . . 1E **69**
Moatfield NW6 . . . . 4A **44**
Moatlands Ho. *WC1*. . . . 2E **7**
(off Cromer St.)

Moat Pl. SW9. . . . . 1B **104**
Moberley Rd. SW4 . . . . 5F **103**
Mobil Ct. *WC2* 3A **16**
(off Clement's Inn)
Mocatta Ho. *E1* 3D **65**
(off Brady St.)
Modbury Gdns. NW5 . . . 3C **46**
Modder Pl. SW15 . . . . . 2F **99**
Model Bldgs. WC1 . . . . . 2A **8**
Model Farm Cl. SE9. . . . 3F **125**
Modern Ct. EC4 . . . . . . 2D **17**
Modling Ho. *E2*. 1F **65**
(off Mace St.)
Moelwyn N7 . . . . 2F **47**
Moffat Ct. SW19. . . . . . 5C **114**
Moffat Ho. SE5 . . . . 3E **91**
Moffat Rd. SW17 . . . . . 4B **116**
Mohawk Ho. *E3* 1A **66**
(off Gernon Rd.)
Mohmmad Khan Rd.
E11. . . . . 3B **40**
Moland Mead SE16 . . . . 1F **93**
(off Crane Mead)
Molasses Ho. SW11. . 1E **101**
(off Clove Hitch Quay)
Molasses Row
SW11 . . . . 1E **101**
Molesford Rd. SW6. . . . 4C **86**
Molesworth Ho.
SE17. . . . . 2D **91**
(off Brandon Est.)
Molesworth St.
SE13 . . . . 2E **109**
Mollis Ho. *E3*. 4C **66**
(off Gale St.)
Molly Huggins Cl.
SW12 . . . . 5E **103**
Molton Ho. *N1* 5B **48**
(off Barnsbury Est.)
Molyneux Dr. SW17. . . 4D **117**
Molyneux St. W1. . . . . . 4A **60**
Monarch Dr. E16. . . . . . 4F **69**
SW16 . . . . 5C **118**
Mona Rd. SE15 . . . . 5E **93**
Mona St. E16 . . . . 4B **68**
Moncks Row SW18 . . . . 4B **100**
Monck St.
SW1 . . . . 5C **22** (4F **75**)
Monclar Rd. SE5 . . . . . 2F **105**
Moncorvo Cl. SW7. . . . . 3A **74**
Moncrieff Cl. E6 . . . . . . 5F **69**
Moncrieff Pl. SE15. . . . . 5C **92**
Moncrieff St. SE15. . . . . 5C **92**
Monega Rd. E7. . . . . . . 3E **55**
E12. . . . . 3E **55**
Monet Ct. *SE16*. 1D **93**
(off Stubbs Dr.)
Moneyer Ho. *N1*. 1B **10**
(off Fairbank Est.)
Mongers Almshouses
E9 . . . . 4F **51**
(off Church Cres.)
Monica Shaw Ct.
NW1 . . . . 1F **61**
(off Purchese St.,
not continuous)
Monier Rd. E3 . . . . 4C **52**
Monk Ct. W12 . . . . 2C **70**
Monk Dr. E16 . . . . 1C **82**

Monk Pas. *E16*. 1C **82**
(off Monk Dr.)
Monkton Ho. E5 . . . . . . 2D **51**
SE16 . . . . 3F **79**
(off Wolfe Cres.)
Monkton St. SE11 . . . . . 5C **76**
Monkwell Sq.
EC2 . . . . 1A **18** (4E **63**)
Monmouth Pl. *W2* 5D **59**
(off Monmouth Rd.)
Monmouth Rd. W2. . . . . 5C **58**
Monmouth St.
WC2. . . . . 3D **15** (5A **62**)
Monnery Rd. N19. . . . . . 5E **33**
Monnow Rd. SE1. . . . . . 1C **92**
Monro Way E5 . . . . 1C **50**
Monsell Ct. N4. . . . . . . 5D **35**
Monsell Rd. N4 . . . . . . 5C **34**
Monson Rd. NW10. . . . . 1C **56**
SE14 . . . . 3F **93**
Montacute Rd.
SE6 . . . . 5B **108**
Montague Av. SE4 . . . . 2B **108**
Montague Cl.
SE1. . . . . 1B **26** (2F **77**)
Montague Ho. E16 . . . . 2D **83**
(off Wesley Av.)
Montague Pl.
WC1. . . . . 5C **6** (4F **61**)
Montague Rd. E8 . . . . . 2C **50**
E11. . . . . 4B **40**
N8. . . . . 1B **34**
Montague Sq. SE15 . . . 3E **93**
Montague St.
EC1. . . . . 1F **17** (4E **63**)
WC1. . . . . 5D **7** (4A **62**)
Montague Mans.
W1. . . . . 5A **4** (4B **60**)
Montagu M. Nth.
W1. . . . . 1A **12** (4B **60**)
Montagu M. Sth.
W1. . . . . 2A **12** (5B **60**)
Montagu M. W.
W1. . . . . 2A **12** (5B **60**)
Montagu Pl.
W1. . . . . 1A **12** (4B **60**)
Montagu Rd. NW4 . . . . . 1C **28**
Montagu Row
W1. . . . . 1A **12** (4B **60**)
Montagu Sq.
W1. . . . . 1A **12** (4B **60**)
Montagu St.
W1. . . . . 2A **12** (5B **60**)
Montaigne Cl. SW1 . . . . 5F **75**
Montana Gdns.
SE26 . . . . 5B **122**
Montana Rd. SW17 . . . . 3C **116**
Montcalm Ho. E14 . . . . 5B **80**
Montcalm Rd. SE7 . . . . 3F **97**
Montclare St.
E2. . . . . 3F **11** (3B **64**)
Monteagle Ct. N1. . . . . . 1A **64**
Monteagle Way E5. . . . . 5C **36**
SE15. . . . . 1D **107**
Montefiore Ct. N16 . . . . 3B **36**
Montefiore St. SW8 . . . . 5D **89**
Montego Cl. SE24 . . . . . 2C **104**
Montem Rd. SE23 . . . . . 5B **108**
Montem St. N4. . . . . . . 3B **34**
Montenotte Rd. N8. . . . . 1E **33**

Montesquieu Ter.
E16 . . . . 5B *68*
(off Clarkson Rd.)
Montevetro SW11 . . . . 4F *87*
Montford Pl. SE11 . . . . 1C *90*
Montfort Ho. E2 . . . . . . 2E *65*
(off Victoria Pk. Sq.)
E14 . . . . 4E *81*
(off Galbraith St.)
Montfort Pl. SW19 . . 1F *113*
Montgomery Lodge
E1 . . . . 3E *65*
(off Cleveland Gro.)
Montgomery St.
E14 . . . . 2D *81*
Montholme Rd.
SW11 . . . . 4B *102*
Monthope Rd. E1 . . . . 4C *64*
Montolieu Gdns.
SW15 . . . . 3D *99*
Montpelier Gdns. E6 . . 2F *69*
Montpelier Gro. NW5 . . 2E *47*
Montpelier M. SW7 . . . 4A *74*
Montpelier Pl. E1 . . . . 5E *65*
SW7 . . . . 4A *74*
Montpelier Ri. NW11 . . 2A *30*
Montpelier Rd.
SE15 . . . . 4D *93*
Montpelier Row
SE3 . . . . 5B *96*
Montpelier Sq. SW7 . . 3A *74*
Montpelier St. SW7 . . . 4A *74*
Montpelier Ter.
SW7 . . . . 3A *74*
Montpelier Va. SE3 . . . 5B *96*
Montpelier Wlk.
SW7 . . . . 4A *74*
Montpelier Way
NW11 . . . . 2A *30*
Montreal Pl.
WC2 . . . . 4F *15* (1B *76*)
Montrell Rd. SW2 . . . 1A *118*
Montrose Av. NW6 . . . 1A *58*
Montrose Ct. SE6 . . . . 2B *124*
SW7 . . . . 3F *73*
Montrose Ho. E14 . . . . 4C *80*
Montrose Pl.
SW1 . . . . 4C *20* (3C *74*)
Montrose Way SE23 . . 1F *121*
Montserrat Cl. SE19 . . 5F *119*
Montserrat Rd.
SW15 . . . . 2A *100*
Monument, The *4C 18*
(off Monument St.)
Monument Gdns.
SE13 . . . . 3E *109*
Monument St.
EC3 . . . . 4C *18* (1F *77*)
Monza St. E1 . . . . 1E *79*
Moodkee St. SE16 . . . . 4E *79*
Moody Rd. SE15 . . . . . 4B *92*
Moody St. E1 . . . . 2F *65*
Moon Ct. SE12 . . . . . . 2C *110*
Moon St. N1 . . . . 5D *49*
Moorcroft Rd.
SW16 . . . . 3A *118*
Moore Ct. N1 . . . . 5D *49*
(off Gaskin St.)
Moorehead Way
SE3 . . . . 1C *110*

Moore Ho. E1 . . . . 1E *79*
(off Cable St.)
E2 . . . . 2E *65*
(off Roman Rd.)
SE10 . . . . 1B *96*
(off Armitage St.)
Moore Pk. Ct. SW6 . . . 3D *87*
(off Fulham Rd.)
Moore Pk. Rd.
SW6 . . . . 3C *86*
Moore Rd. SE19 . . . . . 5E *119*
Moore St. SW3 . . . . . . 5B *74*
Moore Wlk. E7 . . . . . . 1C *54*
Moorey Cl. E15 . . . . . . 5B *54*
Moorfields
EC2 . . . . 1B *18* (4F *63*)
Moorfields Highwalk
EC2 . . . . *1B 18*
(off Moorfields,
not continuous)
Moorgate
EC2 . . . . 2B *18* (5F *63*)
Moorgate Pl. EC2 . . . . 2B *18*
Moorgreen Ho. EC1 . . . 1D *9*
Moorhouse Rd. W2 . . . 5C *58*
Moorings, The E16 . . . . 4E *69*
(off Prince Regent La.)
Moorland Rd. SW9 . . 2D *105*
Moor La. EC2 . . 1B *18* (4F *63*)
(not continuous)
Moor Pl. EC2 . . 1B *18* (4F *63*)
Moorside Rd.
BR1: Brom 3A *124*
Moor St. W1 . . . 3C *14* (5F *61*)
Moran Ho. E1 . . . . 2D *79*
(off Wapping La.)
Morant St. E14 . . . . . . 1C *80*
Mora Rd. NW2 . . . . . . 1E *43*
Mora St. EC1 . . 2A *10* (2E *63*)
Morat St. SW9 . . . . . . 4B *90*
Moravian Cl. SW10 . . . 2F *87*
Moravian Pl. SW10 . . . 2F *87*
Moravian St. E2 . . . . . 1E *65*
Moray Ho. E1 . . . . 3A *66*
(off Harford St.)
Moray M. N7 . . . . 4B *34*
Moray Rd. N4 . . . . 4B *34*
Mordaunt Ho. NW10 . . 5A *42*
Mordaunt Rd. NW10 . . 5A *42*
Mordaunt St. SW9 . . 1B *104*
Morden Hill SE13 . . . . 5E *95*
(not continuous)
Morden La. SE13 . . . . 4E *95*
Morden Rd. SE3 . . . . . 5C *96*
Morden Rd. M. SE3 . . . 5C *96*
Morden St. SE13 . . . . 4D *95*
Morden Wharf SE10 . . . *4A 82*
(off Morden Wharf Rd.)
Morden Wharf Rd.
SE10 . . . . 4A *82*
Mordern Ho. NW1 . . . . *3A 60*
(off Harewood Av.)
Mordred Rd. SE6 . . . . 2A *124*
Morecambe Cl. E1 . . . . 4F *65*
Morecambe St. SE17 . . 5E *77*
More Cl. E16 . . . . 5B *68*
W14 . . . . 5F *71*
Moreland Cotts. E3 . . . 1C *66*
(off Fairfield Rd.)
Moreland Ct. NW2 . . . . 5C *30*

Moreland St.
EC1 . . . . 1E *9* (2D *63*)
Morella Rd. SW12 . . . 5B *102*
More London Pl.
SE1 . . . . 2D *27* (2A *78*)
Moremead Rd. SE6 . . . 4B *122*
Morena St. SE6 . . . . . 5D *109*
Moresby Rd. E5 . . . . . 3D *37*
Moresby Wlk. SW8 . . . 5E *89*
More's Gdn. SW3 . . . . 2F *87*
(off Cheyne Wlk.)
Moreton Cl. E5 . . . . . . 4D *37*
N15 . . . . 1F *35*
SW1 . . . . 1E *89*
(off Moreton Ter.)
Moreton Ho. SE16 . . . . 4D *79*
Moreton Pl. SW1 . . . . . 1E *89*
Moreton Rd. N15 . . . . . 1F *35*
Moreton St. SW1 . . . . . 1E *89*
Moreton Ter. SW1 . . . . 1E *89*
Moreton Ter. M. Nth.
SW1 . . . . 1E *89*
Moreton Ter. M. Sth.
SW1 . . . . 1E *89*
Morgan Ho. SW1 . . . . . *5E 75*
(off Vauxhall Bri. Rd.)
SW8 . . . . *4E 89*
(off Wadhurst Rd.)
Morgan Mans. N7 . . . . *2C 48*
(off Morgan Rd.)
Morgan Rd. N7 . . . . . . 2C *48*
W10 . . . . 4B *58*
Morgan St. E3 . . . . . . 2A *66*
E16 . . . . 4B *68*
Moriatry Cl. N7 . . . . . . 1A *48*
Morie St. SW18 . . . . . 3D *101*
Morieux Rd. E10 . . . . . 3B *38*
Moring Rd. SW17 . . . 4C *116*
Morkyns Wlk. SE21 . . 3A *120*
Morland Cl. NW11 . . . 3D *31*
(off Coningham Rd.)
W12 . . . . *3D 71*
Morland Est. E8 . . . . . 4C *50*
Morland Gdns.
NW10 . . . . 4A *42*
Morland Ho. NW1 . . . . *1A 6*
(off Werrington St.)
NW6 . . . . 5C *44*
SW1 . . . . *5A 76*
(off Marsham St.)
W11 . . . . *5A 58*
(off Lancaster Rd.)
Morland M. N1 . . . . . . 4C *48*
Morland Rd. E17 . . . . . 1F *37*
Morley Ho. N16 . . . . . . 4C *36*
Morley Rd. E10 . . . . . . 3E *39*
E15 . . . . 1B *68*
SE13 . . . . 2E *109*
Morley St.
SE1 . . . . 5C *24* (4C *76*)
Morna Rd. SE5 . . . . . . 5E *91*
Morning La. E9 . . . . . . 3E *51*
Mornington Av.
W14 . . . . 5B *72*
Mornington Ct. NW1 . . . *1E 61*
(off Mornington Cres.)
Mornington Cres.
NW1 . . . . 1E *61*
Mornington Gro. E3 . . . 2C *66*
Mornington M. SE5 . . . 4E *91*

Mornington Pl. NW1 . . . . 1E **61**
SE8 . . . . 3B **94**
(off Mornington Rd.)
Mornington Rd.
E11 . . . . 2B **40**
(not continuous)
SE8 . . . . 3B **94**
Mornington Sports &
Leisure Cen. 5D **47**
(off Stanmore Pl.)
Mornington St. NW1 . . . . 1D **61**
Mornington Ter.
NW1 . . . . 5D **47**
Morocco St.
SE1 . . . . 4D **27** (3A **78**)
Morocco Wharf E1 . . . . 2D **79**
(off Wapping High St.)
Morpeth Gro. E9 . . . . . . 5F **51**
Morpeth Mans. SW1 . . . 5E **75**
(off Morpeth Ter.)
Morpeth Rd. E9 . . . . 5F **51**
Morpeth St. E2 . . . . 2E **65**
Morpeth Ter. SW1 . . . . . 4E **75**
Morrel Ct. E2 . . . . 1C **64**
(off Goldsmiths Row)
Morris Blitz Ct. N16 . . . 1B **50**
Morris Gdns. SW18 . . . 5C **100**
Morris Ho. E2 . . . . 2E **65**
(off Roman Rd.)
NW8 . . . . 3A **60**
(off Salisbury St.)
Morrish Rd. SW2 . . . . . 5A **104**
Morrison Bldgs. Nth.
E1 . . . . 5C **64**
(off Commercial Rd.)
Morrison Ho. SW2 . . . . 1C **118**
(off High Trees)
Morrison Rd. SW9 . . . . . 5C **90**
Morrison St. SW11 . . . . 1C **102**
Morris Pl. N4 . . . . 4C **34**
Morris Rd. E14 . . . . 4D **67**
E15 . . . . 1A **54**
Morriss Ho. SE16 . . . . . 3D **79**
(off Cherry Gdn. St.)
Morris St. E1 . . . . 5D **65**
Morse Cl. E13 . . . . 2C **68**
Morshead Mans. W9 . . . 2C **58**
(off Morshead Rd.)
Morshead Rd. W9 . . . . . 2C **58**
Mortain Ho. SE16 . . . . . 5D **79**
(off Roseberry St.)
Morten Cl. SW4 . . . . . . 4F **103**
Mortham St. E15 . . . . . . 5A **54**
Mortimer Cl. NW2 . . . . . 4B **30**
SW16 . . . . 2F **117**
Mortimer Ct. NW8 . . . . . 1E **59**
(off Abbey Rd.)
Mortimer Cres. NW6 . . . 5D **45**
Mortimer Est. NW6 . . . . 5D **45**
(off Mortimer Pl.)
Mortimer Ho. W11 . . . . . 2F **71**
W14 . . . . 5A **72**
(off Nth. End Rd.)
Mortimer Mkt.
WC1 . . . . 4A **6** (3E **61**)
Mortimer Pl. NW6 . . . . . 5D **45**
Mortimer Rd. N1 . . . . . . 4A **50**
(not continuous)
NW10 . . . . 2E **57**
Mortimer Sq. W11 . . . . . 1F **71**

Mortimer St.
W1 . . . . 2E **13** (5E **61**)
Mortimer Ter. NW5 . . . . 1D **47**
Mortlake High St.
SW14 . . . . 1A **98**
Mortlake Rd. E16 . . . . . 5D **69**
Mortlock Cl. SE15 . . . . . 4D **93**
Mortlock Ct. E7 . . . . 1F **55**
Morton M. SW5 . . . . 5D **73**
Morton Pl. SE1 . . . . 4C **76**
Morton Rd. E15 . . . . 4B **54**
N1 . . . . 4E **49**
Morval Rd. SW2 . . . . . 3C **104**
Morven Rd. SW17 . . . . 3B **116**
Morville Ho. SW18 . . . . 4F **101**
(off Fitzhugh Gro.)
Morville St. E3 . . . . 1C **66**
Morwell St.
WC1 . . . . 1B **14** (4F **61**)
Moscow Pl. W2 . . . . 1D **73**
Moscow Rd. W2 . . . . . . 1C **72**
Mosedale NW1 . . . . 2E **5**
(off Cumberland Mkt.)
Moseley Row SE10 . . . 5B **82**
(off School Bank Rd.)
Mosque Ter. E1 . . . . 4C **64**
(off Fieldgate St.)
Mosque Twr. E1 . . . . . . 4C **64**
(off Fieldgate St.)
E3 . . . . 1A **66**
(off Ford St.)
Mossbury Rd.
SW11 . . . . 1A **102**
Moss Cl. E1 . . . . 4C **64**
Mossford St. E3 . . . . . . 3B **66**
Mossington Gdns.
SE16 . . . . 5E **79**
Mossop St. SW3 . . . . . . 5A **74**
Mostyn Gdns. NW10 . . . 2F **57**
Mostyn Gro. E3 . . . . . . 1C **66**
Mostyn Rd. SW9 . . . . . . 4C **90**
Motcomb St.
SW1 . . . . 5B **20** (4C **74**)
Mothers Sq. E5 . . . . . . 1D **51**
(off Hana M.)
Motley Av. EC2 . . . . 4D **11**
Motley St. SW8 . . . . 5E **89**
MOTTINGHAM 2F **125**
Mottingham Gdns.
SE9 . . . . 1F **125**
Mottingham La.
SE9 . . . . 1E **125**
SE12 . . . . 1E **125**
Mottingham Rd.
SE9 . . . . 2F **125**
Moules Ct. SE5 . . . . . . 3E **91**
Moulins Rd. E9 . . . . 4E **51**
Moulsford Ho. N7 . . . . . 2F **47**
Moundfield Rd. N16 . . . 1C **36**
Mounsey Ho. W10 . . . . 2A **58**
(off Third Av.)
Mount, The E5 . . . . 4D **37**
(Alcester Cres.)
E5 . . . . 4D **37**
(Muston Rd.)
NW3 . . . . 1E **45**
Mountacre Cl. SE26 . . . 4B **120**
Mt. Adon Pk. SE22 . . . . 5C **106**
Mountain Ho. SE11 . . . . 5B **76**

Mt. Angelus Rd.
SW15 . . . . 5B **98**
Mt. Ash Rd. SE26 . . . . 3D **121**
Mountbatten Cl.
SE19 . . . . 5A **120**
Mountbatten Ct.
SE16 . . . . 2E **79**
(off Rotherhithe St.)
Mountbatten Ho. N6 . . . 2C **32**
(off Hillcrest)
Mountbatten M.
SW18 . . . . 5E **101**
Mt. Carmel Chambers
W8 . . . . 3C **72**
(off Dukes La.)
Mount Ct. SW15 . . . . . 1A **100**
Mountearl Gdns.
SW16 . . . . 3B **118**
Mt. Ephraim La.
SW16 . . . . 3F **117**
Mt. Ephraim Rd.
SW16 . . . . 3F **117**
Mountfield Cl. SE6 . . . . 5F **109**
Mountfield Ter.
SE13 . . . . 5F **109**
Mountford Rd. E8 . . . . . 2C **50**
Mountfort Cres. N1 . . . . 4C **48**
Mountfort Ter. N1 . . . . . 4C **48**
Mount Gdns. SE26 . . . . 3D **121**
Mountgrove Rd. N5 . . . . 5D **35**
Mountjoy Cl. EC2 . . . . . 1A **18**
(off Thomas More Highwalk)
Mountjoy Ho. EC2 . . . . . 1F **17**
Mount Lodge N6 . . . . . . 1E **33**
Mount Mills
EC1 . . . . 2E **9** (2D **63**)
Mt. Nod Rd. SW16 . . . . 3B **118**
Mount Pleasant
SE27 . . . . 4E **119**
WC1 . . . . 4B **8** (3C **62**)
Mt. Pleasant Cres.
N4 . . . . 3B **34**
Mt. Pleasant Hill E5 . . . 4D **37**
Mt. Pleasant La. E5 . . . 3D **37**
Mt. Pleasant Rd.
NW10 . . . . 4E **43**
SE13 . . . . 4D **109**
Mt. Pleasant Vs. N4 . . . 2B **34**
Mount Rd. NW2 . . . . . . 5D **29**
NW4 . . . . 1C **28**
SW19 . . . . 2C **114**
Mount Row
W1 . . . . 5D **13** (1D **75**)
Mountsfield Ct.
SE13 . . . . 4F **109**
Mounts Pond Rd.
SE3 . . . . 5F **95**
(not continuous)
Mount Sq., The NW3 . . . 5E **31**
Mount St.
W1 . . . . 5B **12** (1C **74**)
Mount St. M.
W1 . . . . 5D **13** (1D **75**)
Mount Ter. E1 . . . . 4D **65**
Mount Vernon NW3 . . . . 1E **45**
Mountview Cl. NW11 . . . 3D **31**
Mount Vw. Rd. N4 . . . . 2A **34**
Mount Vs. SE27 . . . . . 3D **119**
Mowatt Cl. N19 . . . . 3F **33**
Mowbray Rd. NW6 . . . . 4A **44**

Mowlem St. E2 . . . . 1D 65
Mowil St. SW9 . . . . 3C 90
Moxon Cl. E13 . . . . 1B 68
Moxon St.
  W1 . . . . 1B **12** (4C **60**)
Moye Cl. E2 . . . . 1C 64
Moyers Rd. E10 . . . . 2E 39
Moylan Rd. W6 . . . . 2A 86
Moyle Ho. SW1 . . . . 1E **89**
  (off Churchill Gdns.)
Moyne Ho. SW9 . . . . 3D **105**
Moyser Rd. SW16 . . . . . . 5D **117**
Mozart St. W10 . . . . 2B 58
Mozart Ter. SW1 . . . . 5C 74
Mudlarks Blvd. SE10 . . . . 4B **82**
Mudlarks Way SE10 . . . . 4B **82**
  (not continuous)
Muir Dr. SW18 . . . . 4A **102**
Muirfield W3 . . . . 5A 56
Muirfield Cl. SE16 . . . . . . 1D **93**
Muirfield Cres. E14 . . . . . 4D 81
Muirkirk Rd. SE6 . . . . 1E **123**
Muir Rd. E5 . . . . 1C 50
Mulberry Bus. Cen.
  SE16 . . . . 3F 79
Mulberry Cl. NW3 . . . . . . 1F 45
  SE7 . . . . 2F 97
  SE22 . . . . 3C **106**
  SW3 . . . . 2F 87
  SW16 . . . . 4E **117**
Mulberry Ct. E11 . . . . 1F **53**
  (off Langthorne Rd.)
  EC1 . . . . 2E **9**
  (off Tompion St.)
Mulberry Ho. E2 . . . . 2E **65**
  (off Victoria Pk. Sq.)
  SE8 . . . . 2B 94
Mulberry Housing Co-operative
  SE1 . . . . 1C 24
Mulberry Pl. SE14 . . . . . . 4B 94
Mulberry Pl. E14 . . . . 1E **81**
  (off Clove Cres.)
  SE9 . . . . 2F **111**
  W6 . . . . 1C 84
Mulberry Rd. E8 . . . . 4B 50
Mulberry St. E1 . . . . 5C 64
Mulberry Wlk. SW3 . . . . . 2F 87
Mulgrave Rd. NW10 . . . . 1B 42
  SW6 . . . . 2B 86
Mulkern Rd. N19 . . . . 3F 33
  (not continuous)
Mullen Twr. WC1 . . . . 4B **8**
  (off Mount Pleasant)
Muller Rd. SW4 . . . . 4F **103**
Mullet Gdns. E2 . . . . 2C 64
Mulletsfield WC1 . . . . 2E **7**
  (off Cromer St.)
Mull Wlk. N1 . . . . 3E **49**
  (off Clephane Rd.)
Mulready Ho. SW1 . . . . . 5A **76**
  (off Marsham St.)
Mulready St. NW8 . . . . . . 3A 60
Multi Way W3 . . . . 3A 70
Multon Ho. E9 . . . . 4E 51
Multon Rd. SW18 . . . . . . 5F **101**
Mulvaney Way
  SE1 . . . . 4C **26** (3F **77**)
  (not continuous)
Mumford Ct.
  EC2 . . . . 2A **18** (5E **63**)

Mumford Rd. SE24 . . . 3D **105**
Muncaster Rd.
  SW11 . . . . 3B **102**
Muncies M. SE6 . . . . 2E **123**
Mundania Ct. SE22 . . . . 4D **107**
Mundania Rd. SE22 . . . . 4D **107**
Munday Ho. SE1 . . . . 5B **26**
  (off Deverell St.)
Munday Rd. E16 . . . . 1C **82**
Munden St. W14 . . . . 5A **72**
Mundford Rd. E5 . . . . 4E **37**
Mund St. W14 . . . . 1B **86**
Mundy Ho. W10 . . . . 2A **58**
  (off Dart St.)
Mundy St.
  N1 . . . . 1D **11** (2A **64**)
Munnings Ho. E16 . . . . . . 2D **83**
  (off Portsmouth M.)
Munro Ho.
  SE1 . . . . 4B **24** (3C **76**)
Munro M. W10 . . . . 4A **58**
  (not continuous)
Munro Ter. SW10 . . . . . . 3F **87**
Munster Ct. SW6 . . . . . . 5B **86**
Munster M. SW6 . . . . . . 3A **86**
Munster Rd. SW6 . . . . . . 3A **86**
Munster Sq.
  NW1 . . . . 2E **5** (2D **61**)
Munton Rd. SE17 . . . . . . 5E **77**
Murchison Rd. E10 . . . . . 4E **39**
Murdoch Ho. SE16 . . . . . 4E **79**
  (off Moodkee St.)
Murdock Cl. E16 . . . . 5B **68**
Murdock St. SE15 . . . . . . 2D **93**
Murfett Cl. SW19 . . . . . . 2A **114**
Muriel Ct. E10 . . . . 2D **39**
Muriel St. N1 . . . . 1B **62**
  (not continuous)
Murillo Rd. SE13 . . . . . . 2F **109**
Murphy Ho. SE1 . . . . 5E **25**
  (off Borough Rd.)
Murphy St.
  SE1 . . . . 4B **24** (3C **76**)
Murray Gro.
  N1 . . . . 1A **10** (1E **63**)
Murray M. NW1 . . . . 4F **47**
Murray Rd. SW19 . . . . . . 5F **113**
Murray Sq. E16 . . . . 5C **68**
Murray St. NW1 . . . . 4E **47**
Murray Ter. NW3 . . . . . . 1E **45**
Mursell Est. SW8 . . . . . . 4B **90**
Musard Rd. W6 . . . . 2A **86**
  W14 . . . . 2A **86**
Musbury St. E1 . . . . 5E **65**
Muscal W6 . . . . 2A **86**
  (off Field Rd.)
Muscatel Pl. SE5 . . . . . . 4A **92**
Muschamp Rd.
  SE15 . . . . 1B **106**
Muscovy St.
  EC3 . . . . 4E **19** (1A **78**)
Museum Chambers
  WC1 . . . . 1D **15**
  (off Bury Pl.)
Mus. in Docklands, The
  . . . . 1C 80
Museum La. SW7 . . . . . . 4F **73**
Mus. of Classical Archaeology
  . . . . 3B **6**
  (off Gower Pl.)

Mus. of Garden History
  . . . . 4B **76**
Mus. of London
  . . . . 1F **17** (4E **63**)
Mus. of the Order of
  St John, The 4D **9**
  (off St John's La.)
Museum Pas. E2 . . . . . . 2E **65**
Museum St.
  WC1 . . . . 1D **15** (4A **62**)
Musgrave Ct. SW11 . . . . 4A **88**
Musgrave Cres.
  SW6 . . . . 3C **86**
Musgrove Rd. SE14 . . . . 4F **93**
Musjid Rd. SW11 . . . . . . 5F **87**
Muston Rd. E5 . . . . 4D **37**
Mustow Pl. SW6 . . . . 5B **86**
Muswell Hill Rd. N6 . . . . 1C **32**
  N10 . . . . 1D **33**
Mutrix Rd. NW6 . . . . 5C **44**
Mutton Pl. NW1 . . . . 3C **46**
Myatt Rd. SW9 . . . . 4D **91**
Myatts Flds. Sth.
  SW9 . . . . 5C **90**
  (off St Lawrence Way)
Mycenae Rd. SE3 . . . . . . 3C **96**
Myddelton Pas.
  EC1 . . . . 1C **8**
Myddelton Sq.
  EC1 . . . . 1C **8** (2C **62**)
Myddelton St.
  EC1 . . . . 2C **8** (2C **62**)
Myddleton Av. N4 . . . . . . 4E **35**
Myddleton Ho. N1 . . . . . . 1B **8**
Myers La. SE14 . . . . 2F **93**
Mylis Cl. SE26 . . . . 4D **121**
Mylius Cl. SE14 . . . . 3E **93**
Mylne Cl. W6 . . . . 1C **84**
Mylne St. EC1 . . . . 1B **8** (2C **62**)
Myrdle Ct. E1 . . . . 5C **64**
  (off Myrdle St.)
Myrdle St. E1 . . . . 4C **64**
Myron Pl. SE13 . . . . 1E **109**
Myrtleberry Cl. E8 . . . . . . 3B **50**
  (off Beechwood Rd.)
Myrtle Rd. E17 . . . . 1A **38**
Myrtle Wlk.
  N1 . . . . 1D **11** (1A **64**)
Mysore Rd. SW11 . . . . . . 1B **102**
Myton Rd. SE21 . . . . 3F **119**
Mytton Ho. SW8 . . . . 3B **90**
  (off St Stephens Ter.)

N

N1 Shop. Cen. N1 . . . . . . 1C **62**
N16 Fitness Cen. 1F **49**
Nadine St. SE7 . . . . 1E **97**
Nagasaki Wlk. SE7 . . . . . 4D **83**
NAG'S HEAD 5A **34**
Nags Head Ct. EC1 . . . . . 4A **10**
Nags Head Shop. Cen.
  N7 . . . . 1B **48**
Nainby Ho. SE11 . . . . . . 5C **76**
  (off Hotspur St.)
Nairne Gro. SE24 . . . . . . 3F **105**
Nairn St. E14 . . . . 4E **67**
Naish Ct. N1 . . . . 5A **48**
  (not continuous)

Naldera Gdns. SE3 . . . . . 2C 96
Namba Roy Cl.
SW16 . . . . 4B 118
Nankin St. E14 . . . . 5C 66
Nansen Rd.
SW11 . . . . 1C 102
Nant Ct. NW2 . . . . 4B 30
Nantes Cl. SW18 . . . . . 2E 101
Nantes Pas.
E1 . . . . 5F 11 (4B 64)
Nant Rd. NW2 . . . . 4B 30
Nant St. E2 . . . . 2D 65
Naoroji St.
WC1 . . . . 2B 8 (2C 62)
Napier Av. E14 . . . . 1C 94
SW6 . . . . 1B 100
Napier Cl. SE8 . . . . 3B 94
W14 . . . . 4A 72
Napier Ct. N1 . . . . 1F 63
(off Cropley St.)
SE12 . . . . 3D 125
SW6 . . . . 1B 100
(off Ranelagh Gdns.)
Napier Gro. N1 . . . . 1E 63
Napier Pl. W14 . . . . 4B 72
Napier Rd. E11 . . . . 1A 54
E15 . . . . 1A 68
(not continuous)
NW10 . . . . 2D 57
W14 . . . . 4B 72
Napier St. SE8 . . . . 3B 94
(off Napier Cl.)
Napier Ter. N1 . . . . 4D 49
Napoleon Rd. E5 . . . . . . 5D 37
Narbonne Av. SW4 . . . . . 3E 103
Narborough St. SW6 . . . . 5D 87
Narcissus Rd. NW6 . . . . . 2C 44
Narford Rd. E5 . . . . 5C 36
Narrow St. E14 . . . . 1A 80
Narvic Ho. SE5 . . . . 5E 91
Narwhal Inuit Art Gallery
. . . . 5A 70
Nascot St. W12 . . . . 5E 57
Naseby Cl. NW6 . . . . 4E 45
Naseby Rd. SE19 . . . . . . 5F 119
Nash Ct. E14 . . . . 2D 81
(off Nash Pl.)
Nashe Ho. SE1 . . . . 5B 26
(off Burbage Cl.)
Nash Ho. SW1 . . . . 1D 89
(off Lupus St.)
Nash Pl. E14 . . . . 2D 81
Nash Rd. SE4 . . . . 2A 108
Nash St. NW1 . . . 1E 5 (2D 61)
Nasmyth St. W6 . . . . 4D 71
Nassau Rd. SW13 . . . . . . 4B 84
Nassau St.
W1 . . . . 1F 13 (4E 61)
Nassington Rd. NW3 . . . . 1B 46
Natal Rd. SW16 . . . . 5F 117
Nathan Ho. SE11 . . . . . . 5C 76
(off Reedworth St.)
Nathaniel Cl.
E1 . . . . 1F 19 (4B 64)
Nathaniel Ct. E17 . . . . . . 2A 38
National Army Mus. . . . 2B 88
National Film Theatre, The
. . . . 1A 24
National Gallery
. . . . 5C 14 (1F 75)

National Gallery
(Sainsbury Wing) . . . 5C 14
(in National Gallery)
National Maritime Mus.
. . . . 2F 95
National Portrait Gallery
. . . . 5C 14
National Ter. SE16 . . . . . 3D 79
(off Bermondsey Wall E.)
Natural History Mus. . . . 4F 73
Nautilus Bldg., The
EC1 . . . . 1C 8
(off Myddelton Pas.)
Naval Ho. E14 . . . . 1F 81
(off Quixley St.)
Naval Row E14 . . . . 1E 81
Navarino Gro. E8 . . . . . . 3C 50
Navarino Mans.
E8 . . . . 3C 50
Navarino Rd. E8 . . . . . . 3C 50
Navarre St.
E2 . . . . 3F 11 (3B 64)
Navenby Wlk. E3 . . . . . . 3C 66
Navy St. SW4 . . . . 1F 103
Naxos Bldg. E14 . . . . . . 3B 80
Nayim Pl. E8 . . . . 2D 51
Nayland Ho. SE6 . . . . . . 4E 123
Naylor Ho. W10 . . . . 2A 58
(off Dart St.)
Naylor Rd. SE15 . . . . . . 3D 93
Nazareth Gdns. SE15 . . . 5D 93
Nazrul St. E2 . . . 1F 11 (2B 64)
Neagle Ho. NW2 . . . . . . 5E 29
(off Stoll Cl.)
Nealden St. SW9 . . . . . . 1B 104
Neal St.
WC2 . . . . 3D 15 (5A 62)
Neal's Yd.
WC2 . . . . 3D 15 (5A 62)
NEASDEN 5A 28
NEASDEN JUNC. 1A 42
Neasden Cl. NW10 . . . . . 2A 42
Neasden La. NW10 . . . . . 5A 28
(not continuous)
Neasden La. Nth.
NW10 . . . . 5A 28
Neate St. SE5 . . . . 2A 92
(not continuous)
Neathouse Pl. SW1 . . . . 5E 75
Neatscourt Rd. E6 . . . . . 4F 69
Nebraska St.
SE1 . . . . 4B 26 (3F 77)
Neckinger
SE16 . . . . 5F 27 (4B 78)
Neckinger Est.
SE16 . . . . 5F 27 (4B 78)
Neckinger St. SE1 . . . . . 3B 78
Nectarine Way SE13 . . . . 5D 95
Needham Ho. SE11 . . . . . 1C 90
(off Marylee Way)
Needham Rd. W11 . . . . . 5C 58
Needham Ter. NW2 . . . . . 5F 29
Needleman St. SE16 . . . . 3F 79
Needwood Ho. N4 . . . . . 3E 35
Neeld Cres. NW4 . . . . . . 1D 29
Neil Wates Cres.
SW2 . . . . 1C 118
Nelgarde Rd. SE6 . . . . . . 5C 108
Nella Rd. W6 . . . . 2F 85
Nelldale Rd. SE16 . . . . . 5E 79

Nello James Gdns.
SE27 . . . . 4F 119
Nelson Cl. NW6 . . . . 2C 58
Nelson Ct.
SE1 . . . . 3E 25 (3D 77)
SE16 . . . . 2E 79
(off Brunel Rd.)
Nelson Gdns. E2 . . . . . . 2C 64
Nelson Ho. SW1 . . . . 2E 89
(off Dolphin Sq.)
Nelson Mandela Rd.
SE3 . . . . 1E 111
Nelson Pas.
EC1 . . . . 1A 10 (2E 63)
Nelson Pl.
N1 . . . . 1E 9 (1D 63)
Nelson Rd. N8 . . . . 1B 34
SE10 . . . . 2E 95
Nelson's Column
. . . . 1D 23 (2A 76)
Nelson Sq.
SE1 . . . . 3D 25 (3D 77)
Nelson's Row SW4 . . . . . 2F 103
Nelson St. E1 . . . . 5D 65
E16 . . . . 1B 82
(not continuous)
Nelsons Yd. NW1 . . . . . . 1E 61
(off Mornington Cres.)
Nelson Ter.
N1 . . . . 1E 9 (1D 63)
Nelson Wlk. SE16 . . . . . . 2A 80
Nepaul Rd. SW11 . . . . . . 5A 88
Nepean St. SW15 . . . . . . 4C 98
Neptune Ct. E14 . . . . . . 5C 80
(off Homer Dr.)
Neptune Ho. SE16 . . . . . 4E 79
(off Moodkee St.)
Neptune St. SE16 . . . . . . 4E 79
Nesbit Rd. SE9 . . . . 2F 111
Nesbitt Cl. SE3 . . . . 1A 110
Nesham St. E1 . . . . 1C 78
Ness St. SE16 . . . . 4C 78
Nestor Ho. E2 . . . . 1D 65
(off Old Bethnal Grn. Rd.)
Netheravon Rd. W4 . . . . . 5B 70
Netheravon Rd. Sth.
W4 . . . . 1B 84
Netherby Rd. SE23 . . . . . 5E 107
Netherfield Rd.
SW17 . . . . 3C 116
Netherford Rd. SW4 . . . . 5E 89
Netherhall Gdns.
NW3 . . . . 3E 45
Netherhall Way NW3 . . . . 2E 45
Netherleigh Cl. N6 . . . . . 3D 33
Netherton Gro. SW10 . . . 2E 87
Netherton Rd. N15 . . . . . 1F 35
Netherwood Pl. W14 . . . . 4F 71
(off Netherwood Rd.)
Netherwood Rd. W14 . . . 4F 71
Netherwood St. NW6 . . . 4B 44
Netley SE5 . . . . 4A 92
(off Redbridge Gdns.)
Netley Rd. E17 . . . . 1B 38
Netley St. NW1 . . . 2F 5 (2E 61)
Nettlecombe NW1 . . . . . 4F 47
(off Agar Gro.)
Nettleden Ho. SW3 . . . . . 5A 74
(off Marlborough St.)
Nettlefold Pl. SE27 . . . . . 3D 119

Nettleton Ct. *EC2* 1F **17**
(off London Wall)
Nettleton Rd. SE14 . . . . . 4F **93**
Neuchatel Rd. SE6 . . . 2B **122**
Nevada St. SE10 . . . . 2E **95**
Nevern Pl. SW5 . . . . 5C **72**
Nevern Rd. SW5 . . . . 5C **72**
Nevern Sq. SW5 . . . . 5C **72**
Nevil Ho. *SW9* 5D **91**
(off Loughborough Est.)
Nevill Ct. EC4 . . . . 2C **16**
Neville Cl. E11 . . . . 5B **40**
NW1 . . . . 1F **61**
NW6 . . . . 1B **58**
SE15 . . . . 4C **92**
Neville Ct. *NW8* 1F **59**
(off Abbey Rd.)
Neville Dr. N2 . . . . 1E **31**
Neville Gill Cl.
SW18 . . . . 4C **100**
Neville Rd. E7 . . . . 4C **54**
NW6 . . . . 1B **58**
Nevilles Ct. NW2 . . . . . . 5C **28**
Neville St. SW7 . . . . 1F **87**
Neville Ter. SW7 . . . . . . 1F **87**
Nevill Rd. N16 . . . . 1A **50**
Nevinson Cl.
SW18 . . . . 4F **101**
Nevis Rd. SW17 . . . . . . 2C **116**
Nevitt Ho. *N1* 1F **63**
(off Cranston Est.)
Newall Ho. *SE1* 5A **26**
(off Bath Ter.)
Newarke Ho. SW9 . . . . . 5D **91**
Newark St. E1 . . . . 4D **65**
(not continuous)
New Atlas Wharf *E14* . . . 4C **80**
(off Arnhem Pl.)
New Baltic Wharf
SE8 . . . . 1A **94**
(off Evelyn St.)
New Barn St. E13 . . . . . . 3C **68**
NEW BECKENHAM 5B **122**
New Bentham Ct. *N1* . . . 4E **49**
(off Ecclesbourne Rd.)
Newbery Ho. *N1* 4E **49**
(off Northampton St.)
Newbold Cotts. E1 . . . . . 5E **65**
Newbolt Ho. *SE17* 1F **91**
(off Brandon St.)
New Bond St.
W1 . . . . 3D **13** (5D **61**)
Newbridge Point
SE23 . . . . 3F **121**
(off Windrush La.)
New Bri. St.
EC4 . . . . 3D **17** (5D **63**)
New Broad St.
EC2 . . . . 1D **19** (4A **64**)
Newburgh St.
W1 . . . . 3A **14** (5E **61**)
New Burlington M.
W1 . . . . 4F **13** (1E **75**)
New Burlington Pl.
W1 . . . . 4F **13** (1E **75**)
New Burlington St.
W1 . . . . 4F **13** (1E **75**)
Newburn Ho. *SE11* 1B **90**
(off Newburn St.)
Newburn St. SE11 . . . . . 1B **90**

Newbury Ho. SW9 . . . . . 5D **91**
W2 . . . . 5D **59**
(off Halfield Est.)
Newbury M. NW5 . . . . . . 3C **46**
Newbury St.
EC1 . . . . 1F **17** (4E **63**)
New Bus. Cen., The
NW10 . . . . 2B **56**
New Butt La. SE8 . . . . . . 3C **94**
New Butt La. Nth.
SE8 . . . . 3C **94**
(off Hales St.)
Newby *NW1* 2F **5**
(off Robert St.)
Newby Ho. *E14* 1E **81**
(off Newby Pl.)
Newby Pl. E14 . . . . 1E **81**
Newby St. SW8 . . . . . . 1D **103**
New Caledonian Mkt.
SE1 . . . . 5E **27**
New Caledonian Wharf
SE16 . . . . 4B **80**
Newcastle Cl.
EC4 . . . . 2D **17** (5D **63**)
Newcastle Ct. *EC4* 4A **18**
(off College Hill)
Newcastle Ho. *W1* 5B **4**
(off Luxborough St.)
Newcastle Pl. W2 . . . . . . 4F **59**
Newcastle Row
EC1 . . . . 4C **8** (3C **62**)
New Cavendish St.
W1 . . . . 1C **12** (4C **60**)
New Change
EC4 . . . . 3F **17** (5E **63**)
New Charles St.
EC1 . . . . 1E **9** (2D **63**)
NEW CHARLTON 5E **83**
New Chiswick Pool 3A **84**
New Church Rd.
SE5 . . . . 3E **91**
(not continuous)
New City Rd. E13 . . . . . . 2E **69**
New College Ct.
NW3 . . . . 3E **45**
(off Finchley Rd.)
New College M. N1 . . . . 4C **48**
New College Pde.
NW3 . . . . 3F **45**
(off Finchley Rd.)
Newcombe Gdns.
SW16 . . . . 4A **118**
Newcombe St. W8 . . . . . 2C **72**
Newcomen Rd. E11 . . . . . 5B **40**
SW11 . . . . 1F **101**
Newcomen St.
SE1 . . . . 3B **26** (3F **77**)
New Compton St.
WC2 . . . . 3C **14** (5F **61**)
New Concordia Wharf
SE1 . . . . 3C **78**
New Ct. EC4 . . . . 4B **16**
Newcourt Ho. *E2* 2D **65**
(off Pott St.)
Newcourt St. NW8 . . . . . 1A **60**
New Covent Garden Market
. . . . 3F **89**
New Coventry St.
W1 . . . . 5C **14** (1F **75**)
New Crane Pl. E1 . . . . . . 2E **79**

New Crane Wharf *E1* . . . 2E **79**
(off New Crane Pl.)
New Cres. Yd. NW10 . . . 1B **56**
NEW CROSS 3B **94**
NEW CROSS 4B **94**
NEW CROSS GATE 4F **93**
NEW CROSS GATE 4F **93**
New Cross Rd. SE15 . . . 3E **93**
Newdigate Ho. *E14* 5B **66**
(off Norbiton Rd.)
Newell St. E14 . . . . 5B **66**
New End NW3 . . . . 1E **45**
New End Sq. NW3 . . . . . 1F **45**
New End Theatre 5E **31**
Newent Cl. SE15 . . . . . . 3A **92**
New Era Est. *N1* 5A **50**
(off Phillipp St.)
New Fetter La.
EC4 . . . . 2C **16** (5C **62**)
Newfield Ri. NW2 . . . . . . 5C **28**
Newgate St.
EC1 . . . . 2E **17** (5D **63**)
New Globe Wlk.
SE1 . . . . 1F **25** (2E **77**)
New Goulston St.
E1 . . . . 2F **19** (5B **64**)
New Grn. Pl. SE19 . . . . . 5A **120**
Newham College of
Further Education
Stratford Campus 4A **54**
Newham Leisure Cen.
. . . . 4E **69**
Newham's Row
SE1 . . . . 4E **27** (4A **78**)
Newham Way E6 . . . . . . 4B **68**
E16 . . . . 4B **68**
Newhaven Gdns.
SE9 . . . . 2F **111**
Newhaven La. E16 . . . . . 3B **68**
Newick Rd. E5 . . . . 1D **51**
NEWINGTON 4E **77**
Newington Barrow Way
N7 . . . . 5B **34**
Newington Butts
SE1 . . . . 5D **77**
SE11 . . . . 5D **77**
Newington C'way.
SE1 . . . . 5E **25** (4D **77**)
Newington Ct. Bus. Cen.
SE1 . . . . 5F **25**
Newington Grn. N1 . . . . 2F **49**
N16 . . . . 2F **49**
Newington Grn. Mans.
N16 . . . . 2F **49**
Newington Grn. Rd.
N1 . . . . 3F **49**
Newington Ind. Est.
SE17 . . . . 5E **77**
New Inn B'way.
EC2 . . . . 3E **11** (3A **64**)
New Inn Pas. WC2 . . . . 3A **16**
New Inn Sq. EC2 . . . . . 3E **11**
New Inn St.
EC2 . . . . 3E **11** (3A **64**)
New Inn Yd.
EC2 . . . . 3E **11** (3A **64**)
New Jubilee Wharf
E1 . . . . 2E **79**
(off Wapping Wall)
New Kent Rd. SE1 . . . . . 4E **77**

New Kings Rd. SW6 . . . . . 5B 86
New King St. SE8 . . . . 2C 94
Newland Ct. EC1 . . . . 2B 10
Newland Ho. *SE14* *2F 93*
   (off John Williams Cl.)
NEWLANDS 3F 107
Newlands *NW1* *1F 5*
   (off Harrington St.)
Newlands Pk. SE26 . . . . . 5E 121
Newlands Quay E1 . . . . . 1E 79
New London St. EC3 . . . . . 4E 19
New London Theatre *2E 15*
   (off Drury La.)
New Lydenburg
  Commercial Est.
  SE7 . . . . 4E 83
New Lydenburg St.
  SE7 . . . . 4E 83
Newlyn *NW1* *5E 47*
   (off Plender St.)
Newman Pas.
  W1 . . . . 1A 14 (4E 61)
Newman Rd. E13 . . . . 2D 69
Newman's Ct. EC3 . . . . . . 3C 18
Newman's Row
  WC2 . . . . 1A 16 (4B 62)
Newman St.
  W1 . . . . 1A 14 (4E 61)
Newman Yd.
  W1 . . . . 2B 14 (5E 61)
Newmarket Grn.
  SE9 . . . . 5F 111
Newmill Ho. E3 . . . . 3E 67
New Mount St. E15 . . . . . 4F 53
Newnes Path SW15 . . . . . 2D 99
Newnham Ter.
  SE1 . . . . 5B 24 (4C 76)
New Nth. Pl.
  EC2 . . . . 3D 11 (3A 64)
New Nth. Rd.
  N1 . . . . 1C 10 (4E 49)
New Nth. St.
  WC1 . . . . 5F 7 (4B 62)
Newton Cl. N4 . . . . 2F 35
   (not continuous)
New Orleans Wlk.
  N19 . . . . 2F 33
New Oxford St.
  WC1 . . . . 2C 14 (5F 61)
New Pk. Pde. *SW2* . . . *5A 104*
   (off New Pk. Rd.)
New Pk. Rd. SW2 . . . . . 1F 117
New Pl. Sq. SE16 . . . . . . 4D 79
New Plaistow Rd.
  E15 . . . . 5A 54
Newport Av. E13 . . . . 3D 69
  E14 . . . . 1F 81
Newport Ct.
  WC2 . . . . 4C 14 (1F 75)
Newport Ho. *E3* *2A 66*
   (off Strahan Rd.)
Newport Pl.
  WC2 . . . . 4C 14 (1F 75)
Newport Rd. E10 . . . . . . 4E 39
  SW13 . . . . 4C 84
Newport St. SE11 . . . . . . 5B 76
New Priory Ct. *NW6* . . . *4C 44*
   (off Mazenod Av.)
New Providence Wharf
  E14 . . . . 2F 81

Newquay Ho. SE11 . . . . 1C 90
Newquay Rd.
  SE6 . . . . 2D 123
New Quebec St.
  W1 . . . . 3A 12 (5B 60)
New Ride
  SW7 . . . . 3A 20 (3A 74)
New River St. N5 . . . . . . 1E 49
New River Head
  EC1 . . . . 1C 8 (2C 62)
New River Wlk.
  N1 . . . . 3E 49
New River Way N4 . . . . . 2F 35
New Rd. E1 . . . . 4D 65
  E12 . . . . 4F 41
  N8 . . . . 1A 34
New Rochford St.
  NW5 . . . . 2B 46
New Row
  WC2 . . . . 4D 15 (1A 76)
New Spitalfields Mkt.
  E10 . . . . 5D 39
New Spring Gdns. Wlk.
  SE11 . . . . 1A 90
New Sq.
  WC2 . . . . 2B 16 (5C 62)
New Sq. Pas. WC2 . . . . . 2B 16
Newstead Rd. SE12 . . . 5B 110
Newstead Way
  SW19 . . . . 4F 113
New St. EC2 . . . . 1E 19 (4A 64)
New St. Hill
  BR1: Brom 5D 125
New St. Sq.
  EC4 . . . . 2C 16 (5C 62)
Newton Cl. E17 . . . . 1A 38
Newton Gro. W4 . . . . 5A 70
Newton Ho. *E1* *1D 79*
   (off Cornwall St.)
  NW8 . . . . *5D 45*
   (off Abbey Rd.)
Newton Mans. *W14* . . . *2A 86*
   (off Queen's Club Gdns.)
Newton Pl. E14 . . . . 5C 80
Newton Point *E16* *5B 68*
   (off Clarkson Rd.)
Newton Rd. E15 . . . . 2F 53
  NW2 . . . . 1E 43
  W2 . . . . 5D 59
Newton St.
  WC2 . . . . 2E 15 (5A 62)
Newton's Yd. SW18 . . . . 3C 100
New Twr. Bldgs. E1 . . . . 2D 79
Newtown St. SW11 . . . . . 4D 89
New Turnstile WC1 . . . . 1F 15
New Union Cl. E14 . . . . . 4E 81
New Union St.
  EC2 . . . . 1B 18 (4F 63)
New Wanstead E11 . . . . . 1B 40
New Wharf Rd. N1 . . . . . 1A 62
New Zealand Way
  W12 . . . . 1D 71
Next Generation Carlton Club
   . . . . 4C 58
Nexus Ct. E11 . . . . 3A 40
Niagra Cl. N1 . . . . 1E 63
Niagra Ct. *SE16* *4E 79*
   (off Canada Est.)
Nicholas Ct. *W4* *2A 84*
   (off Corney Reach Way)

Nicholas La.
  EC4 . . . . 4C 18 (1F 77)
   (not continuous)
Nicholas M. W4 . . . . 2A 84
Nicholas Pas. EC4 . . . . . 3C 18
Nicholas Rd. E1 . . . . 3E 65
Nicholas Stacey Ho.
  SE7 . . . . *1D 97*
   (off Frank Burton Cl.)
Nicholay Rd. N19 . . . . . . 3F 33
   (not continuous)
Nicholl Ho. N4 . . . . 3E 35
Nicholls Point *E15* *5C 54*
   (off Park Gro.)
Nicholl St. E2 . . . . 5C 50
Nichols Cl. *N4* *3C 34*
   (off Osborne Rd.)
Nichols Ct. E2 . . . . 1B 64
Nicholson Ho. SE17 . . . 1F 91
Nicholson St.
  SE1 . . . . 2D 25 (2D 77)
Nickleby Ho. *SE16* *3C 78*
   (off Parkers Row)
Nickols Wlk. SW18 . . . 2D 101
Nicolas Ct. E13 . . . . 2D 69
Nicoll Ct. NW10 . . . . 5A 42
Nicoll Pl. NW4 . . . . 1D 29
Nicoll Rd. NW10 . . . . . . 5A 42
Nicosia Rd. SW18 . . . . . 5A 102
Niederwald Rd.
  SE26 . . . . 4A 122
Nigel Ho. *EC1* *5B 8*
   (off Portpool La.)
Nigel Playfair Av.
  W6 . . . . 5D 71
Nigel Rd. E7 . . . . 2E 55
  SE15 . . . . 1C 106
Nigeria Rd. SE7 . . . . 3E 97
Nightingale Ct. *E14* *3E 81*
   (off Ovex Cl.)
  N4 . . . . *4B 34*
   (off Tollington Pk.)
  SW6 . . . . *4D 87*
   (off Maltings Pl.)
Nightingale Gro.
  SE13 . . . . 3F 109
Nightingale Ho. *E1* *2C 78*
   (off Thomas More St.)
  E2 . . . . *5A 50*
   (off Kingsland Rd.)
  W12 . . . . *5E 57*
   (off Du Cane Rd.)
Nightingale La.
  SW12 . . . . 5B 102
Nightingale Lodge
  W9 . . . . *4C 58*
   (off Admiral Wlk.)
Nightingale M. E3 . . . . . 1F 65
  E11 . . . . 1C 40
  SE11 . . . . 5D 77
Nightingale Pl.
  SW10 . . . . 2E 87
   (not continuous)
Nightingale Rd. E5 . . . . . 5D 37
  NW10 . . . . 1B 56
Nightingale Sq.
  SW12 . . . . 5C 102
Nightingale Wlk.
  SW4 . . . . 4D 103

Nile Cl. N16	5B 36
Nile Rd. E13	1E 69
Nile St. N1	1A 10 (2E 63)
Nile Ter. SE15	1B 92
Nimegen Way SE22	3A 106
Nimrod Ho. E16	4D 69
(off Vanguard Cl.)	
Nimrod Pas. N1	3A 50
Nimrod Rd. SW16	5D 117
Nina Mackay Cl. E15	5A 54
NINE ELMS	3E 89
Nine Elms La. SW8	3E 89
Nipponzan Myohoji Peace	
Pagoda	2B 88
Nirvana Apartments	
N1	5D 49
(off Islington Grn.)	
Nisbet Ho. E9	2F 51
Nita Ct. SE12	1C 124
Niton St. SW6	3F 85
Nobel Ho. SE5	5E 91
Noble Ct. E1	1D 79
Noblefield Hgts. N2	1A 32
Noble M. N16	5F 35
(off Albion Rd.)	
Noble St. EC2	2F 17 (5E 63)
Noel Coward Ho.	
SW1	5E 75
(off Vauxhall Bri. Rd.)	
Noel Ho. NW6	4F 45
(off Harben Rd.)	
Noel Rd. E6	3F 69
N1	1D 63
Noel St. W1	3A 14 (5E 61)
Noel Ter. SE23	2E 121
Nolan Way E5	1C 50
Norbiton Rd. E14	5B 66
Norbroke St. W12	1B 70
Norburn St. W10	4A 58
Norcombe Ho. N19	5F 33
(off Wedmore St.)	
Norcott Rd. N16	4C 36
Norcroft Gdns. SE22	5C 106
Norden Ho. E2	2D 65
(off Pott St.)	
Norfolk Av. N15	1B 36
Norfolk Cres. W2	5A 60
Norfolk Ho. SE3	2A 96
(off Restell Cl.)	
SE8	4C 94
SW1	5F 75
(off Page St.)	
Norfolk Ho. Rd.	
SW16	3F 117
Norfolk Mans. SW11	4B 88
(off Prince of Wales Dr.)	
Norfolk M. W10	4A 58
(off Blagrove Rd.)	
Norfolk Pl. W2	5F 59
(not continuous)	
Norfolk Rd. NW8	5F 45
NW10	4A 42
Norfolk Row SE1	5B 76
(not continuous)	
Norfolk Sq. W2	5F 59
Norfolk Sq. M. W2	5F 59
(off London Cl.)	
Norfolk St. E7	2C 54
Norfolk Ter. W6	1A 86
Norgrove St. SW12	5C 102

Norland Ho. W11	2F 71
(off Queensdale Cres.)	
Norland Pl. W11	2A 72
Norland Rd. W11	2F 71
Norland Sq. W11	2A 72
Norland Sq. Mans.	
W11	2A 72
(off Norland Sq.)	
Norley Va. SW15	1C 112
Norlington Rd. E10	3E 39
E11	3E 39
Normanby Cl. SW15	3B 100
Normanby Rd.	
NW10	1B 42
NW10	4C 42
Normand Gdns. W14	2A 86
(off Greyhound Rd.)	
Normand M. W14	2A 86
Normand Rd. W14	2B 86
Normandy Cl. SE26	3A 122
Normandy Ho. E14	3E 81
(off Plevna St.)	
Normandy Rd. SW9	4C 90
Normandy Ter. E16	5D 69
Norman Gro. E3	1A 66
Norman Ho. SW8	3A 90
(off Wyvil Rd.)	
Normanhurst Rd.	
SW2	2B 118
Norman Rd. E11	4F 39
SE10	3D 95
Norman St.	
EC1	2A 10 (2E 63)
Normanton Av.	
SW19	2C 114
Normanton St. SE23	2F 121
Normington Cl.	
SW16	5C 118
Norrice Lea N2	1F 31
Norris Ho. E9	5E 51
(off Handley Rd.)	
N1	5A 50
(off Colville Est.)	
SE8	1B 94
(off Grove St.)	
Norris St.	
SW1	5B 14 (1F 75)
Norroy Rd. SW15	2F 99
Norstead Pl. SW15	2C 112
NORTH ACTON	4A 56
Nth. Access Rd. E17	1F 37
Nth. Acton Rd. NW10	1A 56
Northampton Gro. N1	2F 49
Northampton Pk. N1	3E 49
Northampton Rd.	
EC1	3C 8 (3C 62)
Northampton Row EC1	3C 8
Northampton Sq.	
EC1	2D 9 (2D 63)
Northampton St. N1	4E 49
Nth. Audley St.	
W1	3B 12 (5C 60)
North Av. NW10	2E 57
North Bank NW8	2A 60
NORTH BECKTON	4F 69
Nth. Birkbeck Rd.	
E11	5F 39
North Block SE1	3A 24
(off York Rd.)	

Nth. Boundary Rd.	
E12	5F 41
Northbourne Rd.	
SW4	3F 103
Nth. Branch Av.	
NW10	2E 57
Northbrook Rd.	
SE13	3A 110
Northburgh St.	
EC1	4E 9 (3D 63)
Nth. Carriage Dr. W2	1A 74
(off Bayswater Rd.)	
Northchurch SE17	1F 91
(not continuous)	
Northchurch Rd. N1	4F 49
(not continuous)	
Northchurch Ter. N1	4A 50
Nth. Circular Rd.	
NW2	5A 28
NW4	2E 29
NW10	2A 42
NW11	1F 29
Nth. Colonnade, The	
E14	2C 80
Northcote M. SW11	2A 102
Northcote Rd. NW10	4A 42
SW11	3A 102
North Ct. SE24	1D 105
SW1	5D 23
(off St. Peter St.)	
W1	5A 6 (4E 61)
North Cres. E16	3F 67
WC1	5B 6 (4F 61)
Northcroft Ct. W12	3C 70
North Crofts SE23	1D 121
Nth. Cross Rd.	
SE22	3B 106
Northdene Gdns. N15	1B 36
Northdown St.	
N1	1F 7 (1A 62)
North Dr. SW16	4E 117
NORTH END	4E 31
North End NW3	4E 31
Nth. End Av. NW3	4E 31
(not continuous)	
Nth. End Cres. W14	5B 72
Nth. End Ho. W14	5A 72
Nth. End Pde. W14	5A 72
(off Nth. End Rd.)	
Nth. End Rd. NW11	3C 30
Nth. End Rd. W14	5A 72
Nth. End Way NW3	4E 31
Northern Hgts. N8	2F 33
(off Crescent Rd.)	
Northern Rd. E13	1D 69
Northesk Ho. E1	3D 65
(off Tent St.)	
Nth. Eyot Gdns. W6	1B 84
Northey St. E14	1A 80
Northfield Ho. SE15	2C 92
Northfield Rd. N16	2A 36
Northfields SW18	2C 100
Northfields Prospect Bus. Cen.	
SW18	2C 100
Northfleet Ho. SE1	3B 26
(off Tennis St.)	
Nth. Flock St. SE16	3C 78
Nth. Flower Wlk. W2	1E 73
(off Lancaster Wlk.)	
North Gdn. E14	2B 80

North Ga. NW8 . . . . 1A 60
(off Prince Albert Rd.)
Northgate Dr. NW9 . . . . . 1A 28
Northgate Ho. E14 . . . . 1C 80
(off E. India Dock Rd.)
Nth. Gower St.
NW1 . . . . 2A 6 (2E 61)
North Gro. N6 . . . . 2C 32
N15 . . . . 1F 35
North Hill N6 . . . . 1B 32
Nth. Hill Av. N6 . . . . . . 1C 32
North Ho. SE8 . . . . 1B 94
Northiam WC1 . . . . 2E 7
(off Cromer St.)
Northiam St. E9 . . . . . . 5D 51
Northington St.
WC1 . . . . 4A 8 (3B 62)
NORTH KENSINGTON
. . . . 4F 57
Northlands St. SE5 . . . . 5E 91
Northleach Ct. SE15 . . . 2A 92
(off Birdlip Cl.)
North Lodge E16 . . . . . 2D 83
(off Wesley Av.)
Nth. Lodge Cl. SW15 . . . 3F 99
North Mall SW18 . . . . 3D 101
(off Buckhold Rd.)
North M. WC1 . . 4A 8 (3B 62)
Northolme Rd. N5 . . . . . 1E 49
Northover
BR1: Brom 3B 124
North Pas. SE18 . . . . . 3C 100
Northpoint Sq. NW1 . . . 3F 47
Nth. Pole Rd. W10 . . . . 4E 57
Northport St. N1 . . . . . . 5F 49
North Ride W2 . . . . 1A 74
North Ri. W2 . . . . 5A 60
North Rd. N6 . . . . 2C 32
N7 . . . . 3A 48
SW19 . . . . 5E 115
North Row
W1 . . . . 4A 12 (1B 74)
Nth. Row Bldgs. W1 . . . 4B 12
(off North Row)
North Several SE3 . . . . 5F 95
Nth. Side Wandsworth Comn.
SW18 . . . . 3F 101
North Sq. NW11 . . . . . . 1C 30
Northstead Rd.
SW2 . . . . 2C 118
North St. E13 . . . . 1D 69
SW4 . . . . 1E 103
North St. Pas. E13 . . . . 1D 69
Nth. Tenter St. E1 . . . . . 5B 64
North Ter. SW3 . . . . . . 4A 74
Northumberland All.
EC3 . . . . 3E 19 (5A 64)
(not continuous)
Northumberland Av.
E12 . . . . 3E 41
WC2 . . . . . 1D 23 (2A 76)
Northumberland Ho.
SW1 . . . . 1D 23
(off Northumberland Av.)
Northumberland Pl.
W2 . . . . 5C 58
Northumberland Rd.
E17 . . . . 2C 38
Northumberland St.
WC2 . . . . . 1D 23 (2A 76)

Northumbria St. E14 . . . 5C 66
Nth. Verbena Gdns.
W6 . . . . 1C 84
North Vw. SW19 . . . . . 5E 113
Northview N7 . . . . 5A 34
Northview Cres.
NW10 . . . . 1B 42
North Vs. NW1 . . . . . . 3F 47
North Wlk. W8 . . . . . . 1D 73
(off Bayswater Rd.)
Northway NW11 . . . . . . 1D 31
Northway Rd. SE5 . . . . 1E 105
Northways Pde. NW3 . . 4F 45
(off College Cres.,
not continuous)
Nth. Western Commercial
Cen. NW1 . . . . 4A 48
NORTHWEST PL. N1 . . . 1C 62
North Wharf E14 . . . . . 2E 81
(off Coldharbour)
Nth. Wharf Rd. W2 . . . . 4F 59
Northwick Cl. NW8 . . . . 3F 59
Northwick Ho. NW8 . . . 3F 59
(off St John's Wood Rd.)
Northwick Ter. NW8 . . . 3F 59
Northwold Rd. E5 . . . . . 4B 36
N16 . . . . 4B 36
Northwood Est. E5 . . . . 4C 36
Northwood Hall N6 . . . . 2E 33
Northwood Ho.
SE27 . . . . 4F 119
Northwood Rd. N6 . . . . 2D 33
SE23 . . . . 1B 122
Northwood Way
SE19 . . . . 5F 119
Nth. Woolwich Rd.
E16 . . . . 2B 82
Nth. Worple Way
SW14 . . . . 1A 98
Norton Folgate
E1 . . . . 5E 11 (4A 64)
Norton Folgate Ho.
E1 . . . . 5F 11
(off Puma Ct.)
Norton Ho. E1 . . . . 5D 65
(off Bigland St.)
E2 . . . . 1F 65
(off Mace St.)
SW1 . . . . 4F 75
(off Arneway St.)
SW9 . . . . 5B 90
(off Aytoun Rd.)
Norton Rd. E10 . . . . . . 3B 38
Norway Ga. SE16 . . . . . 4A 80
Norway Pl. E14 . . . . . . 5B 66
Norway St. SE10 . . . . . 2D 95
Norway Wharf E14 . . . . 5B 66
(off Norway Pl.)
Norwich Ho. E14 . . . . . 5D 67
(off Cordelia St.)
Norwich Rd. E7 . . . . . . 2C 54
Norwich St.
EC4 . . . . . . 2B 16 (5C 62)
Norwood Cl. NW2 . . . . 5A 30
Norwood High St.
SE27 . . . . 3D 119
Norwood Ho. E14 . . . . . 1D 81
(off Poplar High St.)
NORWOOD NEW TOWN
. . . . 5E 119

Norwood Pk. Rd.
SE27 . . . . 5E 119
Norwood Rd. SE24 . . . 1D 119
SE27 . . . . 2D 119
Notley St. SE5 . . . . 3F 91
Notting Barn Rd.
W10 . . . . 3F 57
Nottingdale Sq. W11 . . 2A 72
Nottingham Av. E16 . . . 4E 69
Nottingham Ct.
WC2 . . . . . 3D 15 (5A 62)
Nottingham Ho.
WC2 . . . . 3D 15
(off Shorts Gdns.)
Nottingham Pl.
W1 . . . . 4B 4 (4C 60)
Nottingham Rd. E10 . . . 1E 39
SW17 . . . . 1B 116
Nottingham St.
W1 . . . . 5B 4 (4C 60)
Nottingham Ter. NW1 . . 4B 4
NOTTING HILL 1B 72
Notting Hill Ga. W11 . . 2C 72
Nottingwood Ho.
W11 . . . . 1A 72
(off Clarendon Rd.)
Nova Bldg. E14 . . . . . . 5C 80
Nova Ct. E. E14 . . . . . . 2E 81
(off Yabsley St.)
Nova Ct. W. E14 . . . . . 2E 81
(off Yabsley St.)
Novello St. SW6 . . . . . 4C 86
Novel Sq. SE10 . . . . . . 4B 82
(off School Bank Rd.)
Nowell Rd. SW13 . . . . . 2C 84
Noyna Rd. SW17 . . . . . 3B 116
Nubia Way
BR1: Brom 3A 124
Nuding Cl. SE13 . . . . . 1C 108
Nuffield Lodge N6 . . . . 1E 33
W9 . . . . 4C 58
(off Admiral Wlk.)
Nugent Rd. N19 . . . . . . 3A 34
Nugent Ter. NW8 . . . . . 1E 59
Nun Ct. EC2 . . . . 2B 18
NUNHEAD 1D 107
Nunhead Cres.
SE15 . . . . 1D 107
Nunhead Est. SE15 . . . 1D 107
Nunhead Grn. SE15 . . . 1D 107
Nunhead Gro. SE15 . . . 1D 107
Nunhead La. SE15 . . . . 1D 107
Nunhead Pas. SE15 . . . 1C 106
Nursery Cl. SE4 . . . . . . 5B 94
SW15 . . . . 2F 99
Nursery La. E2 . . . . 5B 50
E7 . . . . 3C 54
W10 . . . . 4E 57
Nursery Rd. E9 . . . . . . 3E 51
E12 . . . . 4F 41
SW9 . . . . 2B 104
Nutbourne St. W10 . . . 2A 58
Nutbrook St. SE15 . . . . 1C 106
Nutcroft Rd. SE15 . . . . 3D 93
Nutfield Rd. E15 . . . . . 1E 53
NW2 . . . . 5C 28
SE22 . . . . 2B 106
Nutford Pl. W1 . . . . . . 5B 60
Nuthurst Av. SW2 . . . . 2B 118
Nutley Ter. NW3 . . . . . 3E 45

Nutmeg Cl. E16 . . . . . . 3A 68
Nutmeg La. E14 . . . . . . 5F 67
Nuttall St. N1 . . . . 1A 64
Nutter La. E11 . . . . 1E 41
Nutt St. SE15 . . . . 3B 92
Nutwell St. SW17 . . . . 5A 116
Nye Bevan Est. E5 . . . . 5F 37
Nye Bevan Ho.
  SW6 . . . . 3B 86
    (off St Thomas's Way)
Nynehead St. SE14 . . . . 3A 94
Nyon Gro. SE6 . . . . . . 2B 122
Nyssa Ct. E15 . . . . 2A 68
    (off Teasel Way)
Nyton Cl. N19 . . . . 3A 34

O

Oak Apple Ct. SE12 . . . 1C 124
Oakbank Gro. SE24 . . . 2E 105
Oakbrook Cl.
  BR1: Brom 4D 125
Oakbury Rd. SW6 . . . . . 5D 87
Oak Cott. Cl. SE6 . . . . . 1B 124
Oak Ct. SE15 . . . . 3B 92
    (off Sumner Rd.)
Oak Cres. E16 . . . . 4A 68
Oakcroft Rd. SE13 . . . . . 5F 95
Oakdale Rd. E7 . . . . 4D 55
  E11 . . . . 4F 39
  N4 . . . . 1E 35
  SE4 . . . . 1E 107
  SE15 . . . . 1E 107
  SW16 . . . . 5A 118
Oakdene SE15 . . . . 4D 93
Oakden St. SE11 . . . . . . 5C 76
Oake Ct. SW15 . . . . 3A 100
Oakeford Ho. W14 . . . . . 4A 72
    (off Russell Rd.)
Oakend Ho. N4 . . . . 2F 35
Oakeshott Av. N6 . . . . . 4C 32
Oakey La.
  SE1 . . . . . . 5B 24 (4C 76)
Oakfield Cl. N8 . . . . 2A 34
  NW2 . . . . 2F 29
Oakfield Gdns.
  SE19 . . . . 5A 120
    (not continuous)
Oakfield Ho. E3 . . . . 4C 66
    (off Gale St.)
Oakfield Rd. E6 . . . . 5F 55
  N4 . . . . 1C 34
  SW19 . . . . 3F 113
Oakfields Rd. NW11 . . . 1A 30
Oakfield St. SW10 . . . . . 2E 87
Oakford Rd. NW5 . . . . . 1E 47
Oak Gro. NW2 . . . . 1A 44
Oakhall Ct. E11 . . . . 1D 41
Oak Hall Rd. E11 . . . . . . 1D 41
Oakham Cl. SE6 . . . . . . 2B 122
Oakham Ho. W10 . . . . . 3E 57
    (off Sutton Way)
Oakhill Av. NW3 . . . . . . 1D 45
Oakhill Ct. SE23 . . . . . . 4E 107
Oak Hill Pk. NW3 . . . . . 1D 45
Oak Hill Pk. M.
  NW3 . . . . 1E 45
Oakhill Pl. SW15 . . . . . . 3C 100
Oakhill Rd. SW15 . . . . . 3B 100

Oak Hill Way NW3 . . . . 1D 45
    (not continuous)
Oak Ho. W10 . . . . 3A 58
    (off Sycamore Wlk.)
Oakhurst Gro. SE22 . . . 2C 106
Oakington Rd. W9 . . . . . 3C 58
Oakington Way N8 . . . . 2A 34
Oakland Rd. E15 . . . . . . 1F 53
Oaklands Ct. NW10 . . . . 5A 42
    (off Nicoll Rd.)
Oaklands Est. SW4 . . . . 4E 103
Oaklands Gro. W12 . . . . 2C 70
Oaklands M. NW2 . . . . . 1F 43
    (off Oaklands Rd.)
Oaklands Pas. NW2 . . . 1F 43
    (off Oaklands Rd.)
Oaklands Pl. SW4 . . . . . 2E 103
Oaklands Rd.
  NW2 . . . . 1F 43
Oak La. E14 . . . . 1B 80
Oakley Cres. EC1 . . . . . 1D 63
Oakley Dr. SE13 . . . . . . 4F 109
Oakley Gdns. SW3 . . . . 2A 88
Oakley Ho. SW1 . . . . . . 5B 74
    (off Sloane St.)
Oakley Pl. SE1 . . . . 1B 92
Oakley Rd. N1 . . . . 4F 49
Oakley Sq. NW1 . . . . . . 1E 61
Oakley St. SW3 . . . . 2A 88
Oakley Wlk. W6 . . . . 2F 85
Oakley Yd. E2 . . . . 3B 64
Oak Lodge E11 . . . . 1C 40
    (off Chantry Sq.)
  W8 . . . . 4D 73
Oakman Ho. SW19 . . . . 1F 113
Oakmead Rd. SW12 . . . 1C 116
Oak Pk. Gdns.
  SW19 . . . . 1F 113
Oak Pk. M. N16 . . . . 5B 36
Oak Pl. SW18 . . . . 3D 101
Oakridge La.
  BR1: Brom 5F 123
Oakridge Rd.
  BR1: Brom 4F 123
Oaks, The NW6 . . . . 4F 43
    (off Brondesbury Pk.)
  NW10 . . . . 4D 43
Oaks Av. SE19 . . . . 5A 120
Oaksford Av. SE26 . . . . 3D 121
Oakshade Rd.
  BR1: Brom 4F 123
Oakshaw Rd. SW18 . . . 5D 101
Oakshott Ct.
  NW1 . . . . 1B 6 (1F 61)
    (not continuous)
Oak St. E14 . . . . 3E 81
    (off Stewart St.)
Oak Tree Gdns.
  BR1: Brom 5D 125
Oak Tree Ho. W9 . . . . . . 3C 58
    (off Shirland Rd.)
Oak Tree Rd. NW8 . . . . 2A 60
Oakview Lodge
  NW11 . . . . 2B 30
    (off Beechcroft Av.)
Oakview Rd. SE6 . . . . . . 5D 123
Oak Village NW5 . . . . . . 1C 46
Oak Vs. NW11 . . . . 1B 30
    (off Hendon Pk. Row)
Oak Way W3 . . . . 2A 70

Oakwood Bus. Pk.
  NW10 . . . . 3A 56
Oakwood Ct. E6 . . . . . . 5F 55
  W14 . . . . 4B 72
Oakwood Dr. SE19 . . . . 5F 119
Oakwood La. W14 . . . . . 4B 72
Oakworth Rd. W10 . . . . 4E 57
Oasis Sports Cen.
  . . . . 2D 15 (5A 62)
Oast Ct. E14 . . . . 1B 80
    (off Newell St.)
Oast Lodge W4 . . . . 3A 84
    (off Corney Reach Way)
Oatfield Ho. N15 . . . . . . 1A 36
    (off Perry Ct.)
Oat La. EC2 . . . . 2A 18 (5E 63)
Oatwell Ho. SW3 . . . . . . 1A 88
    (off Marlborough St.)
Oban Cl. E13 . . . . 3E 69
Oban Ho. E14 . . . . 5F 67
    (off Oban St.)
Oban Rd. E13 . . . . 2E 69
Oban St. E14 . . . . 5F 67
Oberon Ho. N1 . . . . 1A 64
    (off Arden Est.)
Oberstein Rd. SW11 . . . 2F 101
Oborne Cl. SE24 . . . . . . 3D 105
O'Brien Ho. E2 . . . . 2F 65
    (off Roman Rd.)
Observatory Gdns.
  W8 . . . . 3C 72
Observatory M. E14 . . . . 5F 81
Occupation Rd. SE17 . . 1E 91
Ocean Est. E1 . . . . 3F 65
    (Ernest St.)
  E1 . . . . 4A 66
    (Masters St.)
Ocean Music Venue . . . 3D 51
    (off Mare St.)
Ocean St. E1 . . . . 4F 65
Ocean Wharf E14 . . . . . 3B 80
Ockbrook E1 . . . . 4E 65
    (off Hannibal Rd.)
Ockendon M. N1 . . . . . . 3F 49
Ockendon Rd. N1 . . . . . 3F 49
Ockley Rd. SW16 . . . . . 4A 118
Octagon, The SW10 . . . 3D 87
    (off Coleridge Gdns.)
Octagon Arc.
  EC2 . . . . 1D 19 (4A 64)
Octagon Ct. SE16 . . . . . 2F 79
    (off Rotherhithe St.)
Octavia Ho. SW1 . . . . . . 4F 75
    (off Medway St.)
  W10 . . . . 3A 58
Octavia M. W10 . . . . 3B 58
Octavia St. SW11 . . . . . 4A 88
Octavius St. SE8 . . . . . . 3C 94
Odeon Cinema
  Camden Town 5D 47
    (off Parkway)
  Edgware Rd. 3A 12
    (off Edgware Rd.)
  Holloway 5A 34
  Kensington 4C 72
    (off Kensington High St.)
  Leicester Sq. 5C 14
    (off Leicester Sq.)
  Mezzanine 5C 14
    (off Leicester Sq.)

Odeon Cinema
Panton St. 5C 14
(off Panton St.)
Putney 1A 100
Shaftesbury Av. 3C 14
(off Shaftesbury Av.)
Streatham 3A 118
Streatham Hill 2A 118
Swiss Cen. 4B 14
(off Wardour St.)
Swiss Cottage 4F 45
Tottenham Ct. Rd. . . 1B 14
(off Tottenham Ct. Rd.)
West End 5C 14
(off Leicester Sq.)
Odeon Ct. E16 . . . . . . 4C 68
NW10 . . . . 5A 42
(off St Albans Rd.)
Odessa Rd. E7 . . . . . . 5B 40
NW10 . . . . 1C 56
Odessa St. SE16 . . . . . 3B 80
Odette Duval Ho. E1. . . 4E 65
(off Stepney Way)
Odger St. SW11 . . . . . 5B 88
Odhams Wlk.
WC2 . . . . 3E 15 (5A 62)
Odin Ho. SE5 . . . . . . 5E 91
O'Donnell Ct.
WC1 . . . . 3E 7 (3A 62)
Odontological Mus., The
. . . . 2A 16
(off Lincoln's Inn Flds.)
O'Driscoll Ho. W12 . . . 5D 57
Offa's Mead E9 . . . . . 1B 52
Offenbach Ho. E2 . . . . 1F 65
(off Mace St.)
Offerton Rd. SW4 . . . . 1E 103
Offham Ho. SE17 . . . . . 5A 78
(off Beckway St.)
Offley Rd. SW9. . . . . . 3C 90
Offord Rd. N1 . . . . . . 4B 48
Offord St. N1 . . . . 4B 48
Ogilvie Ho. E1. . . . . . . 5F 65
(off Stepney C'way.)
Oglander Rd. SE15. . . . 2B 106
Ogle St. W1 . . . 5F 5 (4E 61)
O'Gorman Ho. SW10 . . 3E 87
(off King's Rd.)
Ohio Rd. E13 . . . . 3B 68
Oil Mill La. W6. . . . . . 1C 84
Okeburn Rd. SW17. . . . 5C 116
Okehampton Rd.
NW10 . . . . 5E 43
Olaf St. W11 . . . . 1F 71
Oldacre M. SW12. . . . . 5C 102
Old Bailey
EC4 . . . . 3E 17 (5D 63)
Old Bailey
(Central Criminal Court)
. . . . 2E 17 (5D 63)
Old Barge Ho. All.
SE1 . . . . 5C 16
Old Barracks W8 . . . . . 3D 73
Old Barrack Yd.
SW1 . . . . 4B 20 (3C 74)
(not continuous)
Old Barrowfield E15 . . . 5A 54
Old Bellgate Pl. E14. . . . 4C 80
Old Bethnal Grn. Rd.
E2 . . . . 2C 64

Old Billingsgate Mkt.
EC3 . . . . 5C 18
(off Lwr. Thames St.)
Old Billingsgate Wlk.
EC3 . . . . . . 5D 19 (1A 78)
Old Bond St.
W1 . . . . . . 5F 13 (1E 75)
Old Brewer's Yd.
WC2 . . . . . . 3D 15 (5A 62)
Old Brewery M. NW3 . . 1F 45
Old Broad St.
EC2 . . . . . . 2C 18 (5F 63)
Old Bromley Rd.
BR1: Brom 5F 123
Old Brompton Rd.
SW5 . . . . 1C 86
SW7 . . . . 1C 86
Old Bldgs. WC2 . . . . . 2B 16
Old Burlington St.
W1 . . . . . . 4F 13 (1E 75)
Oldbury Pl.
W1 . . . . 5C 4 (4C 60)
Old Canal M. SE15. . . . 1B 92
(off Trafalgar Av.)
Old Castle St.
E1 . . . . 2F 19 (5B 64)
Old Cavendish St.
W1 . . . . . . 2D 13 (5D 61)
Old Change Ct. EC4 . . . 3F 17
Old Chapel Pl. SW9 . . . 5C 90
Old Chelsea M. SW3 . . 2A 88
Old Chiswick Yd.
W4 . . . . 2A 84
Old Church La. NW9 . . 4A 28
Old Church Rd. E1 . . . . 5F 65
Old Church St. SW3 . . . 1F 87
Old Compton St.
W1 . . . . 4B 14 (1F 75)
Old Ct. Ho. W8 . . . . . . 3D 73
(off Old Ct. Pl.)
Old Ct. Pl. W8 . . . . . . 3D 73
Old Curiosity Shop . . . 3A 16
(off Portsmouth St.)
Old Dairy M. NW5 . . . . 3D 47
SW12 . . . . 1C 116
Old Devonshire Rd.
SW12 . . . . 5D 103
Old Dover Rd. SE3 . . . 3C 96
Oldegate Ho. E6 . . . . . 4F 55
Old Farm Cl. SW17 . . . 2A 116
Oldfield Gro. SE16 . . . . 5F 79
Oldfield Ho. W4 . . . . . 1A 84
(off Devonshire Rd.)
Oldfield M. N6 . . . . . . 2E 33
Oldfield Rd. N16 . . . . . 5A 36
NW10 . . . . 4B 42
SW19 . . . . 5A 114
W3 . . . . 3B 70
Old Fish St. Hill EC4 . . 4F 17
(off Victoria St.)
Old Fleet La.
EC4 . . . . 2D 17 (5D 63)
OLD FORD 5C 52
Old Ford Rd. E2 . . . . . 2E 65
Old Forge M. W12 . . . . 3D 71
Old Forge Rd. N19 . . . . 4F 33
Old Gloucester St.
WC1 . . . . 5E 7 (4A 62)
Oldhill St. N16 . . . . . . 3C 36

Old Hospital Cl.
SW12 . . . . 1B 116
Old Ho. Cl. SW19. . . . . 5A 114
Old Jamaica Rd.
SE16 . . . . 4C 78
Old James St.
SE15 . . . . 1D 107
Old Jewry
EC2 . . . . . . 3B 18 (5F 63)
Old Kent Rd. SE1 . . . . 5A 78
SE15 . . . . 5A 78
Old Mnr. Ct. NW8. . . . . 1E 59
Old Mnr. Yd. SW5 . . . . 5D 73
Old Mkt. Sq.
E2 . . . . 1F 11 (2B 64)
Old Marylebone Rd.
NW1 . . . . 4A 60
Old Mitre Ct.
EC4 . . . . 3C 16 (5C 62)
Old Montague St. E1 . . 4C 64
Old Nichol St.
E2 . . . . 3F 11 (3B 64)
Old Nth. St. WC1 . . . . . 5F 7
OLD OAK COMMON . . 4A 56
Old Oak Comn. La.
NW10 . . . . 4A 56
W3 . . . . 4A 56
Old Oak La. NW10 . . . . 2A 56
Old Oak Rd. W3 . . . . . 1B 70
Old Orchard, The
NW3 . . . . 1B 46
Old Pal. Yd.
SW1 . . . . 5D 23 (4A 76)
Old Paradise St.
SE11 . . . . 5B 76
Old Pk. Av. SW12. . . . . 4C 102
Old Pk. La.
W1 . . . . 2D 21 (2D 75)
Old Post Office La.
SE3 . . . . 1D 111
Old Pye St.
SW1 . . . . . . 5B 22 (4F 75)
Old Pye St. Est. SW1 . . 5B 22
(off Old Pye St.)
Old Quebec St.
W1 . . . . 3A 12 (5B 60)
Old Queen St.
SW1 . . . . . . 4C 22 (3F 75)
Old Red Lion Theatre . . 1C 8
(off St John St.)
Oldridge Rd. SW12 . . . 5C 102
Old Rd. SE13 . . . . 2A 110
Old Royal Free Pl.
N1 . . . . 5C 48
Old Royal Free Sq.
N1 . . . . 5C 48
Old Royal Naval College
. . . . 1F 95
Old School Cl. SE10. . . 4A 82
Old School Cres. E7. . . 3C 54
Old School Sq. E14 . . . 5C 66
(off Pelling St.)
Old Seacoal La.
EC4 . . . . 3D 17 (5D 63)
Old Sth. Lambeth Rd.
SW8 . . . . 3A 90
Old Spitalfields Market
. . . . 5F 11 (4B 64)
Old Sq. WC2 . . . 2B 16 (5B 62)
Old Stable M. N5 . . . . . 5E 35

Oldstead Rd.
  BR1: Brom 4E **123**
OLD STREET 3F **63**
Old St. E13 . . . . 1D **69**
  EC1 . . . . 3F **9** (3E **63**)
Old Sun Wharf E14 . . . . 1A **80**
    (off Narrow St.)
Old Swan Wharf
  SW11 . . . . 4F **87**
Old Thackeray School
  SW8 . . . . 5D **89**
Old Theatre Ct. SE1 . . . 1A **26**
    (off Porter St.)
Old Town SW4 . . . . . . 1E **103**
Old Vic Theatre, The . . . 3C **24**
    (off Cut, The)
Old Woolwich Rd.
  SE10 . . . . 2F **95**
Old York Rd. SW18 . . . 3D **101**
O'Leary Sq. E1 . . . . . . 4E **65**
Olga St. E3 . . . . 1A **66**
Olinda Rd. N16 . . . . . . 1B **36**
Oliphant St. W10 . . . . . 2F **57**
Oliver Goldsmith Est.
  SE15 . . . . 4C **92**
Oliver Ho. SE16 . . . . . . 3C **78**
    (off George Row)
  SW8 . . . . 3F **89**
    (off Wyvil Rd.)
Oliver M. SE15 . . . . . . 5C **92**
Olive Rd. E13 . . . . 2E **69**
  NW2 . . . . 1E **43**
Oliver Rd. E10 . . . . 4D **39**
Olivers Wharf E1 . . . . . 2D **79**
    (off Wapping High St.)
Olivers Yd.
  EC1 . . . . 3C **10** (3F **63**)
Olive Tree Ho. SE15 . . . 2E **93**
    (off Sharratt St.)
Olivette St. SW15 . . . . . 1F **99**
Olive Waite Ho. NW6 . . 4C **44**
Olivier Theatre 1B **24**
Ollerton Grn. E3 . . . . . . 5B **52**
Ollgar Cl. W12 . . . . 2B **70**
Olliffe St. E14 . . . . 4E **81**
Olmar St. SE1 . . . . 2C **92**
Olney Ho. NW8 . . . . . . 3A **60**
    (off Tresham Cres.)
Olney Rd. SE17 . . . . . . 2D **91**
    (not continuous)
Olympia 4A **72**
Olympia M. W2 . . . . . . 1D **73**
Olympian Ct. E14 . . . . . 5C **80**
    (off Homer Dr.)
Olympia Way W14 . . . . 4A **72**
Olympus Sq. E5 . . . . . . 5C **36**
O'Mahoney Ct. SW17 . . 3E **115**
Oman Av. NW2 . . . . . . 1E **43**
O'Meara St.
  SE1 . . . . 2A **26** (2E **77**)
Omega Cl. E14 . . . . 4D **81**
Omega Pl. N1 . . . . 1E **7**
Omega St. SE14 . . . . . . 4C **94**
Ommaney Rd. SE14 . . . 4F **93**
Ondine Rd. SE15 . . . . . 2B **106**
Onega Ga. SE16 . . . . . . 4A **80**
O'Neill Ho. NW8 . . . . . 1A **60**
    (off Cochrane St.)
One Owen St. EC1 . . . . 1D **9**
    (off Goswell St.)

One Tree Cl. SE23 . . . . 4E **107**
Ongar Rd. SW6 . . . . . . 2C **86**
Onra Rd. E17 . . . . 2C **38**
Onslow Cl. W10 . . . . . . 2B **58**
Onslow Gdns.
  SW7 . . . . 5F **73**
Onslow M. E. SW7 . . . 5F **73**
Onslow M. W.
  SW7 . . . . 5F **73**
Onslow Sq. SW7 . . . . . 5F **73**
Ontario St.
  SE1 . . . . 4C **8** (3C **62**)
Ontario Way E14 . . . . . 1C **80**
    (not continuous)
Onyx M. E15 . . . . 3B **54**
Opal Cl. E16 . . . . 5F **69**
Opal M. NW6 . . . . 5B **44**
Opal St. SE11 . . . . 1D **91**
Open Air Stage 3A **32**
Open Air Theatre
  Roundwood Pk. 4C **42**
Open University, The
  (Parsifal College) . . . 1C **44**
Openview SW18 . . . . . . 1E **115**
Opera Ct. N19 . . . . 5F **33**
    (off Wedmore St.)
Operating Theatre Mus.
  . . . . 2C **26**
Ophelia Gdns. NW2 . . . 5A **30**
Ophelia Ho. W6 . . . . . . 1F **85**
    (off Fulham Pal. Rd.)
Ophir Ter. SE15 . . . . . . 4C **92**
Opie Ho. NW8 . . . . 1A **60**
    (off Townshend Est.)
Oppenheim Rd. SE13 . . 5E **95**
Oppidans Rd. NW3 . . . 4B **46**
Orange Gro. E11 . . . . . . 5A **40**
    (not continuous)
Orange Pl. SE16 . . . . . . 4E **79**
Orangery Gallery, The
  . . . . 3B **72**
Orange St.
  WC2 . . . . 5C **14** (1F **75**)
Orange Tree Ct. SE5 . . . 3A **92**
    (off Havil St.)
Orange Yd. W1 . . . . . . 3C **14**
Oransay Rd. N1 . . . . . . 3E **49**
Oratory La. SW3 . . . . . 1F **87**
Orbain Rd. SW6 . . . . . . 3A **86**
Orbel St. SW11 . . . . . . 4A **88**
Orb St. SE17 . . . . 5F **77**
Orchard, The NW11 . . . 1C **30**
  SE3 . . . . 5F **95**
  W4 . . . . 5A **70**
Orchard Bus. Cen.
  SE26 . . . . 5B **122**
Orchard Cl. N1 . . . . . . 4E **49**
  NW2 . . . . 5C **28**
  SE23 . . . . 4E **107**
  W10 . . . . 4B **58**
Orchard Ct. E10 . . . . . . 3D **39**
  SE3 . . . . 5F **95**
Orchard Hill SE13 . . . . 5D **95**
Orchard Ho. SE5 . . . . . 4E **91**
    (off County Gro.)
  SE16 . . . . 4E **79**
  SW6 . . . . 3B **86**
    (off Varna Rd.)

Orchard Ho. W1 . . . . . . 2B **12**
    (off Fitzhardinge St.)
  W12 . . . . 2C **70**
Orchard Mead Ho.
  NW2 . . . . 4C **30**
Orchard M. N1 . . . . . . 4F **49**
  N6 . . . . 2D **33**
Orchard Pl. E5 . . . . 2D **51**
  E14 . . . . 1A **82**
    (not continuous)
Orchard Rd. N6 . . . . . . 2D **33**
  SE3 . . . . 5A **96**
Orchardson Ho. NW8 . . 3F **59**
    (off Orchardson St.)
Orchardson St. NW8 . . 3F **59**
Orchard Sq. W14 . . . . . 1B **86**
Orchard St.
  W1 . . . . 3B **12** (5C **60**)
Orchard Studios W6 . . . 5F **71**
    (off Brook Grn.)
Orchard Ter. NW10 . . . 1B **42**
Orchard Wharf E14 . . . 1A **82**
    (off Orchard Pl.)
Orchid Cl. E6 . . . . 4F **69**
Orchid St. W12 . . . . . . 1C **70**
Orde Hall St.
  WC1 . . . . 4F **7** (3B **62**)
Ordell Rd. E3 . . . . 1B **66**
Ordnance Cres. SE10 . . 3F **81**
Ordnance Hill NW8 . . . 5F **45**
Ordnance M. NW8 . . . . 1F **59**
Ordnance Rd. E16 . . . . 4B **68**
Oregano Dr. E14 . . . . . 5F **67**
Orestes M. NW6 . . . . . 2C **44**
Orford Ct. SE27 . . . . . . 2D **119**
Orford Rd. E17 . . . . . . 1C **38**
  SE6 . . . . 3D **123**
Oriana Ho. E14 . . . . . . 1B **80**
    (off Victory Pl.)
Oriel Ct. NW3 . . . . 1E **45**
Oriel Dr. SW13 . . . . . . 2E **85**
Oriel M. NW3 . . . . 1E **45**
    (off Heath St.)
Oriel Rd. E9 . . . . 3F **51**
Oriental Rd. E16 . . . . . 2F **83**
Oriental St. E14 . . . . . . 1C **80**
    (off Pennyfields)
Orient Ind. Pk. E10 . . . 4C **38**
Orient St. SE11 . . . . . . 5D **77**
Orient Way E5 . . . . 5F **37**
  E10 . . . . 3A **38**
Orient Wharf E1 . . . . . 2E **79**
    (off Wapping High St.)
Orion E14 . . . . 5C **80**
    (off Crews St.)
Orion Bus. Cen. SE14. . 1F **93**
Orion Ho. E1 . . . . 3D **65**
    (off Coventry Rd.)
Orkney Ho. N1 . . . . 5B **48**
    (off Bemerton Est.)
Orkney St. SW11 . . . . . 5C **88**
Orlando Rd. SW4 . . . . . 1E **103**
Orleston M. N7 . . . . . . 3C **48**
Orleston Rd. N7 . . . . . . 3C **48**
Orlop St. SE10 . . . . 1A **96**
Ormanton Rd. SE26 . . . 4C **120**
Orme Ct. W2 . . . . 1D **73**
Orme Ct. M. W2. . . . . . 1D **73**
    (off Orme La.)
Orme Ho. E8 . . . . 5B **50**

Orme La. W2 . . . . 1D 73
Ormeley Rd. SW12 . . 1D 117
Orme Sq. W2 . . . . 1D 73
Ormiston Gro. W12 . . . 2D 71
Ormiston Rd. SE10. . 1C 96
Ormond Cl.
  WC1. . . . . 5E 7 (4A 62)
Ormonde Ct. NW8 . . . . 5B 46
  (off St Edmund's Cl.)
  SW15 . . . . 2E 99
Ormonde Ga. SW3 . . . . 1B 88
Ormonde Pl. SW1 . . . . 5C 74
Ormonde Ter. NW8. . . . 5B 46
Ormond Ho. N16. . . . . . 4F 35
Ormond M.
  WC1. . . . . 4E 7 (3A 62)
Ormond Rd. N19 . . . . . 3A 34
Ormond Yd.
  SW1. . . . . 1A 22 (2E 75)
Ormsby Lodge W4 . . . . 4A 70
Ormsby Pl. N16 . . . . . . 5B 36
Ormsby St. E2 . . . . 1B 64
Ormside St. SE15. . . . . 2E 93
Ornan Rd. NW3 . . . . . . 2A 46
Orpen Wlk. N16 . . . . . . 5A 36
Orpheus St. SE5 . . . . . 4F 91
Orsett M. W2 . . . . 5D 59
  (not continuous)
Orsett St. SE11. . . . . . . 1B 90
Orsett Ter. W2 . . . . 5D 59
Orsman Rd. N1. . . . . . . 5A 50
Orton St. E1 . . . . 2C 78
Orville Rd. SW11 . . . . . 5F 87
Orwell Ct. E8 . . . . 5C 50
  (off Pownall Rd.)
  N5. . . . . 1E 49
Orwell Rd. E13. . . . . . . 1E 69
Osbaldeston Rd. N16. . . 4C 36
Osberton Rd. SE12. . . . 3C 110
Osbert St. SW1. . . . . . . 5F 75
Osborn Cl. E8 . . . . 5C 50
Osborne Ct. E10 . . . . . 2D 39
Osborne Gro. N4 . . . . . 3C 34
Osborne Ho. E16 . . . . . 2C 82
  (off Wesley Av.)
Osborne Rd. E7 . . . . . . 2D 55
  E9. . . . . 3B 52
  E10. . . . . 4D 39
  N4. . . . . 3C 34
  NW2 . . . . 3D 43
Osborne Ter. SW17 . . . 5B 116
  (off Church La.)
Osborn La. SE23. . . . . . 5A 108
Osborn St. E1 . . . . 4B 64
Osborn Ter. SE3 . . . . . 2B 110
Oscar Faber Pl. N1. . . . 4A 50
Oscar St. SE8 . . . . 5C 94
  (Lewisham Way)
  SE8. . . . . 4C 94
  (Thornville St.)
Oseney Cres. NW5 . . . . 2E 47
O'Shea Gro. E3. . . . . . . 5B 52
Osier Ct. E1. . . . . 3F 65
  (off Osier St.)
Osier La. SE10. . . . . . . 4B 82
  (off School Bank Rd.)
Osier M. W4 . . . . 2A 84
Osiers Est., The
  SW18. . . . . 2C 100
Osiers Rd. SW18 . . . . . 2C 100

Osier St. E1 . . . . 3E 65
Osier Way E10. . . . . . . 5D 39
Oslac Rd. SE6 . . . . 5D 123
Oslo Ct. NW8 . . . . 1A 60
  (off Prince Albert Rd.)
Oslo Ho. SE5 . . . . 5E 91
  (off Carew St.)
Oslo Sq. SE16 . . . . 4A 80
Osman Cl. N15. . . . . . . 1F 35
Osmani School Sports Cen.
  . . . . 4C 64
Osman Rd. W6 . . . . 4E 71
Osmington Ho. SW8 . . . 3B 90
  (off Dorset Rd.)
Osmund St. W12 . . . . . 4B 56
Osnaburgh St.
  NW1. . . . . 4E 5 (3D 61)
  (Longford St.)
  NW1 . . . . 2E 5
  (Robert St.)
Osnaburgh Ter.
  NW1. . . . . 3E 5 (3D 61)
Osprey Cl. E6 . . . . 4F 69
Osprey Ct. E1. . . . . 1C 78
  (off Star Pl.)
Osprey Est. SE16 . . . . . 5A 80
Osprey Ho. E14 . . . . . . 1A 80
  (off Victory Pl.)
Ospringe Ho. SE1. . . . . 3C 24
  (off Wootton St.)
Ospringe Rd. NW5 . . . . 1E 47
Osram Ct. W6. . . . . 4E 71
Osric Path N1. . . . . 1A 64
Ossian M. N4 . . . . 2B 34
Ossian Rd. N4 . . . . 2B 34
Ossington Bldgs.
  W1. . . . . 5B 4 (4C 60)
Ossington Cl. W2. . . . . . 1C 72
Ossington St. W2. . . . . . 1C 72
Ossory Rd. SE1 . . . . . . 2C 92
Ossulston St.
  NW1. . . . . 1C 6 (1F 61)
Ostade Rd. SW2. . . . . . 5B 104
Ostend Pl. SE1 . . . . . . 5E 77
Osten M. SW7 . . . . 4D 73
Osterley Ho. E14 . . . . . 5D 67
  (off Giraud St.)
Osterley Rd. N16 . . . . . 1A 50
Oswald Bldg. SW8. . . . . 2D 89
Oswald's Mead E9 . . . . 1A 52
Oswald St. E5 . . . . 5F 37
Oswald Ter. NW2 . . . . . 5E 29
Osward SW17 . . . . 2B 116
Oswell Ho. E1 . . . . 2D 79
  (off Farthing Flds.)
Oswin St. SE11 . . . . . . 5D 77
Oswyth Rd. SE5 . . . . . . 5A 92
Otford Cres. SE4 . . . . . 4B 108
Otford Ho. SE1. . . . . . . 5C 26
  (off Staple St.)
  SE15. . . . . 2E 93
  (off Lovelinch Cl.)
Othello Cl. SE11 . . . . . 1D 91
Other Cinema, The . . . 4B 14
  (off Rupert St.)
Otis St. E3 . . . . 2E 67
Otley Ho. N5. . . . . 5C 34
Otley Rd. E16 . . . . 5E 69
Otley Ter. E5 . . . . 5F 37
Ottaway Ct. E5 . . . . . . 5C 36

Ottaway St. E5 . . . . . . 5C 36
Otterburn Ho. SE5 . . . . 3E 91
  (off Sultan St.)
Otterburn St. SW17 . . . 5B 116
Otter Cl. E15. . . . . 5E 53
Otterden St. SE6 . . . . . 4C 122
Otto Cl. SE26 . . . . 3D 121
Otto St. SE17 . . . . 2D 91
Oulton Cl. E5 . . . . 4E 37
Oulton Rd. N15. . . . . . . 1F 35
Ouseley Rd.
  SW12 . . . . 1B 116
Outer Circ.
  NW1 . . . . 1D 5 (1A 60)
Outgate Rd. NW10 . . . . 4B 42
Outram Pl. N1 . . . . 5A 48
Outram Rd. E6 . . . . 5F 55
Outwich St. EC3 . . . . . 2E 19
Outwood Ho. SW2 . . . . 5B 104
  (off Deepdene Gdns.)
Oval, The E2 . . . . 1D 65
Oval Cricket Ground, The
  . . . . 2B 90
Oval House Theatre . . . 2C 90
  (off Kennington Oval)
Oval Mans. SE11 . . . . . 2B 90
Oval Pl. SW8 . . . . 3B 90
Oval Rd. NW1 . . . . 5D 47
Oval Way SE11. . . . . . . 1B 90
Overbrae BR3: Beck. . 5C 122
Overbury Rd. N15. . . . . 1F 35
Overbury St. E5 . . . . . . 1F 51
Overcliff Rd. SE13 . . . . 1C 108
Overdown Rd. SE6. . . . 4C 122
Overhill Rd. SE22 . . . . 5C 106
Overlea Rd. E5. . . . . . . 2C 36
Oversley Ho. W2 . . . . . 4C 58
  (off Alfred Rd.)
Overstone Ho. E14. . . . 5C 66
  (off E. India Dock Rd.)
Overstone Rd. W6 . . . . 4E 71
Overstrand Mans.
  SW11 . . . . 4B 88
Overton Ct. E11 . . . . . . 2C 40
Overton Dr. E11 . . . . . . 2C 40
Overton Ho. SW15 . . . . 5B 98
  (off Tangley Gro.)
Overton Rd. E10. . . . . . 3A 38
  SW9 . . . . 5C 90
Overy Ho.
  SE1 . . . . 4D 25 (3D 77)
Ovex Cl. E14. . . . . 3E 81
Ovington Gdns. SW3 . . 4A 74
Ovington M. SW3. . . . . 4A 74
  (off Ovington Gdns.)
Ovington Sq. SW3. . . . . 4A 74
Ovington St. SW3. . . . . 5A 74
Owen Mans. W14. . . . . 2A 86
  (off Queen's Club Gdns.)
Owens M. E11 . . . . 4A 40
Owen's Row
  EC1 . . . . 1D 9 (2D 63)
Owen St. EC1 . . . 1D 9 (1D 63)
  (not continuous)
Owens Way SE23. . . . . 5A 108
Owgan Cl. SE5 . . . . 3F 91
Oxberry Av. SW6 . . . . . 5A 86
Oxendon St.
  SW1 . . . . 5B 14 (1F 75)
Oxenford St. SE15 . . . . 1B 106

Oxenham Ho. *SE8* 2C **94**
(off Benbow St.)
Oxenholme NW1 . . . . 1F **5**
(off Hampstead Rd.)
Oxestall's Rd. SE8 . . . . . . 1A **94**
Oxford & Cambridge Mans.
NW1 . . . . 4A **60**
(off Old Marylebone Rd.)
Oxford Av. NW10 . . . . . . 2D **57**
Oxford Cir. W1 . . . . 3F **13**
Oxford Cir. Av.
W1 . . . . 3F **13** (5E **61**)
Oxford Ct. EC4 . . . . 4B **18**
W9 . . . . 4C **58**
(off Elmfield Way)
Oxford Dr.
SE1 . . . . 2D **27** (2A **78**)
Oxford Gdns. W10 . . . . . 5E **57**
Oxford Ga. W6 . . . . 5F **71**
Oxford Pl. NW10 . . . . . . 5A **28**
(off Press Rd.)
Oxford Rd. E15 . . . . 3F **53**
(not continuous)
N4 . . . . 3C **34**
NW6 . . . . 1C **58**
SE19 . . . . 5F **119**
SW15 . . . . 2A **100**
Oxford Sq. W2 . . . . 5A **60**
Oxford St.
W1 . . . . 3B **12** (5C **60**)
Oxgate Cen. NW2 . . . . . 4D **29**
Oxgate Ct. NW2 . . . . 4C **28**
Oxgate Ct. Pde.
NW2 . . . . 4C **28**
Oxgate Gdns. NW2 . . . . . 5D **29**
Oxgate La. NW2 . . . . 4D **29**
Oxgate Pde. NW2 . . . . . . 4D **28**
Oxley Cl. SE1 . . . . 1B **92**
Oxleys Rd. NW2 . . . . 5D **29**
Oxonian St. SE22 . . . . . . 2B **106**
Oxo Tower Wharf
SE1 . . . . 5C **16** (1C **76**)
Oxygeem Sports Cen.
. . . . 4D **105**
Oystercatcher Cl.
E16 . . . . 5D **69**
Oystergate Wlk.
EC4 . . . . 5B **18**
Oyster Row E1 . . . . 5E **65**
Oyster Wharf SW11 . . . . 5F **87**
Ozolins Way E16 . . . . 5C **68**

P

Pablo Neruda Cl.
SE24 . . . . 2D **105**
Pace Pl. E1 . . . . 5D **65**
Pacific Ho. E1 . . . . 3F **65**
(off Ernest St.)
Pacific Rd. E16 . . . . 5C **68**
Pacific Wharf SE16 . . . . . 2F **79**
Packenham Ho. E2 . . . . . 2B **64**
(off Wellington Row)
Packington Sq. N1 . . . . . . 5E **49**
(not continuous)
Packington St. N1 . . . . . . 5D **49**
Padbury SE17 . . . . 1A **92**
(off Bagshot St.)
Padbury Ct. E2 . . . . 2B **64**

Padbury Ho. NW8 . . . . . . 3A **60**
(off Tresham Cres.)
Paddenswick Rd. W6 . . . 4C **70**
PADDINGTON 5F **59**
Paddington Bowling &
Sports Club 3D **59**
Paddington Grn.
W2 . . . . 4F **59**
Paddington St.
W1 . . . . 5B **4** (4C **60**)
Paddington Wlk. W2 . . . . 4F **59**
(off Hermitage St.)
Paddock Cl. SE3 . . . . 5C **96**
SE26 . . . . 4F **121**
Paddock Rd. NW2 . . . . . . 5C **28**
Paddock Way SW15 . . . . 5E **99**
Padfield Rd. SE5 . . . . . . 1E **105**
Padstow Ho. E14 . . . . 1B **80**
(off Three Colt St.)
Pagden St. SW8 . . . . 4D **89**
Pageant Cres. SE16 . . . . . 2A **80**
Pageantmaster Ct.
EC4 . . . . 3D **17**
Page Grn. Rd. N15 . . . . . . 1C **36**
Page Grn. Ter. N15 . . . . . 1B **36**
Page Ho. SE10 . . . . 2E **95**
(off Welland St.)
Page St. SW1 . . . . 5F **75**
Page's Wlk.
SE1 . . . . 5E **27** (5A **78**)
Pages Yd. W4 . . . . 2B **84**
Paget Ho. E2 . . . . 1E **65**
(off Bishop's Way)
Paget Rd. N16 . . . . 3F **35**
Paget St. EC1 . . . . 1D **9** (2D **63**)
Pagham Ho. W10 . . . . 3E **57**
(off Sutton Way)
Pagin Ho. N15 . . . . 1A **36**
(off Braemar Rd.)
Pagnell St. SE14 . . . . 3B **94**
Pagoda Gdns. SE3 . . . . . . 5F **95**
Paignton Rd. N15 . . . . . . 1A **36**
Painsthorpe Rd. N16 . . . . 5A **36**
Painswick Ct. SE15 . . . . . 3B **92**
(off Daniel Gdns.)
Painted Hall 2E **95**
Painters M. SE16 . . . . 5C **78**
Pakeman Ho. SE1 . . . . 3E **25**
(off Surrey Row)
Pakeman St. N7 . . . . 5B **34**
Pakenham Cl.
SW12 . . . . 1C **116**
Pakenham St.
WC1 . . . . 2A **8** (2B **62**)
Pakington Ho. SW9 . . . . . 5A **90**
(off Stockwell Gdns. Est.)
Palace Av. W8 . . . . 3D **73**
Palace Bingo 5E **77**
(off Walworth Rd.)
Palace Ct. NW3 . . . . 2D **45**
W2 . . . . 1D **73**
(off Moscow Rd.,
not continuous)
Palace Gdns. M. W8 . . . . 2D **73**
Palace Gdns. Ter.
W8 . . . . 2C **72**
Palace Ga. W8 . . . . 3E **73**
Palace Grn. W8 . . . . 2D **73**
Palace Mans. W14 . . . . . . 5A **72**
(off Hammersmith Rd.)

Palace M. SW1 . . . . 5C **74**
(off Eaton Ter.)
SW6 . . . . 3C **86**
Palace Pl.
SW1 . . . . 5F **21** (4E **75**)
Palace Pl. Mans. W8 . . . 3D **73**
(off Kensington Ct.)
Palace Rd. N8 . . . . 1F **33**
(not continuous)
SW2 . . . . 1B **118**
Palace St.
SW1 . . . . 5F **21** (4E **75**)
Palace Theatre
Soho 3C **14**
(off Shaftesbury Av.)
Palace Vw. SE12 . . . . . . 2C **124**
Palace Wharf W6 . . . . 3E **85**
(off Rainville Rd.)
Palamon Ct. SE1 . . . . 1B **92**
(off Cooper's Rd.)
Palamos Rd. E10 . . . . 3C **38**
Palatine Av. N16 . . . . 1A **50**
Palatine Rd. N16 . . . . 1A **50**
Palermo Rd.
NW10 . . . . 1C **56**
Palewell Comn. Dr.
SW14 . . . . 3A **98**
Palfrey Pl. SW8 . . . . 3B **90**
Palgrave Gdns. NW1 . . . . 3A **60**
Palgrave Ho. SE5 . . . . 3E **91**
(off Wyndham Est.)
Palgrave Rd. W12 . . . . . . 4B **70**
Palissy St.
E2 . . . . 2F **11** (2B **64**)
(not continuous)
Palladino Ho.
SW17 . . . . 5A **116**
(off Laurel Cl.)
Palladium Ct. E8 . . . . 4B **50**
(off Queensbridge Rd.)
Pallant Ho. SE1 . . . . 5C **26**
Pallet Way SE18 . . . . 4F **97**
Palliser Ct. W14 . . . . 1A **86**
(off Palliser Rd.)
Palliser Ho. E1 . . . . 3F **65**
(off Ernest St.)
SE10 . . . . 2F **95**
(off Trafalgar Rd.)
Palliser Rd. W14 . . . . 1A **86**
Pall Mall
SW1 . . . . 2A **22** (2E **75**)
Pall Mall E.
SW1 . . . . 1C **22** (2F **75**)
Pall Mall Pl. SW1 . . . . 2A **22**
Palm Cl. E10 . . . . 5D **39**
Palm Ct. SE15 . . . . 3B **92**
(off Garnies Cl.)
Palmer Pl. N7 . . . . 2C **48**
Palmer Rd. E13 . . . . 3D **69**
Palmer's Rd. E2 . . . . 1F **65**
Palmerston Ct. E3 . . . . . . 1F **65**
(off Old Ford Rd.)
Palmerston Ho. SE1 . . . . . 4B **24**
(off Westminster Bri. Rd.)
W8 . . . . 2C **72**
(off Kensington Pl.)
Palmerston Mans.
W14 . . . . 2A **86**
(off Queen's Club Gdns.)

Palmerston Rd. E7 . . . . . 3D **55**
    (not continuous)
NW6 . . . . 4B **44**
    (not continuous)
Palmerston Way
SW8 . . . . 3D **89**
Palmer St.
SW1 . . . . 5B **22** (4F **75**)
    (not continuous)
Palm Tree Ho. SE14 . . . . 3F **93**
    (off Barlborough St.)
Pamela Ho. E8 . . . . 5B **50**
    (off Haggerston Rd.)
Panama Ho. E1 . . . . 4F **65**
    (off Beaumont Sq.)
Pancras La.
EC4 . . . . 3B **18** (5E **63**)
Pancras Rd.
NW1 . . . . 1D **7** (1F **61**)
Pandian Way NW5 . . . . . 3F **47**
Pandora Rd. NW6 . . . . . 3C **44**
Pangbourne NW1 . . . . . . 2F **5**
    (off Stanhope St.)
Pangbourne Av.
W10 . . . . 4E **57**
Pankhurst Av. E16 . . . . . 2D **83**
Pankhurst Cl. SE14 . . . . 3F **93**
Panmure Cl. N5 . . . . 1D **49**
Panmure Rd. SE26 . . . . 3D **121**
Panorama Ct. N6 . . . . . . 1E **33**
Pansy Gdns. W12 . . . . . 1C **70**
Panton St.
SW1 . . . . 5B **14** (1F **75**)
Paper Bldgs. EC4 . . . . . 4C **16**
Papillons Wlk. SE3 . . . . 5C **96**
Papworth Gdns. N7 . . . . 2B **48**
Papworth Way SW2 . . . . 5C **104**
Parade, The N4 . . . . 3C **34**
SE4 . . . . 5B **94**
    (off Up. Brockley Rd.)
SE26 . . . . 3D **121**
    (off Wells Pk. Rd.)
SW11 . . . . 3B **88**
Parade Mans. NW4 . . . . 1D **29**
Parade M. SE27 . . . . . . 2D **119**
Paradise Pas. N7 . . . . . 2C **48**
Paradise Rd. SW4 . . . . . 5A **90**
Paradise Row E2 . . . . . . 2D **65**
Paradise St. SE16 . . . . . 3D **79**
Paradise Wlk. SW3 . . . . 2B **88**
Paragon, The SE3 . . . . . 5B **96**
Paragon Cl. E16 . . . . . . 5C **68**
Paragon M. SE1 . . . . . . 5F **77**
Paragon Pl. SE3 . . . . . . 5B **96**
Paragon Rd. E9 . . . . 3E **51**
Paramount Bldg. EC1 . . . 3D **9**
    (off St John St.)
Paramount St. WC1 . . . . 4A **6**
Parbury Rd. SE23 . . . . . 4A **108**
Pardoner Ho. SE1 . . . . . 5C **26**
    (off Pardoner St.)
Pardoner St.
SE1 . . . . 5C **26** (4F **77**)
    (not continuous)
Pardon St.
EC1 . . . . 3E **9** (3D **63**)
Parfett St. E1 . . . . 4C **64**
    (not continuous)
Parfitt Cl. NW3 . . . . 3E **31**
Parfrey St. W6 . . . . 2E **85**

Paris Gdn.
SE1 . . . . 1D **25** (2D **77**)
Paris Ho. E2 . . . . 1D **65**
    (off Old Bethnal Grn. Rd.)
Park, The N6 . . . . 1C **32**
NW11 . . . . 3D **31**
SE23 . . . . 1E **121**
Park App. SE16 . . . . . . 4D **79**
Park Av. E15 . . . . 3A **54**
NW2 . . . . 2D **43**
NW10 . . . . 2D **43**
NW11 . . . . 3D **31**
SW14 . . . . 2A **98**
Park Av. Nth. NW10 . . . . 2D **43**
Park Av. Sth. N8 . . . . . . 1F **33**
Park Bus. Cen. NW6 . . . 2C **58**
Park Cl. E9 . . . . 5E **51**
NW2 . . . . 5D **29**
SW1 . . . . 3B **74**
W4 . . . . 2A **84**
W14 . . . . 4B **72**
Park Club, The 2A **70**
Park Ct. E17 . . . . 1D **39**
SE26 . . . . 5D **121**
SW11 . . . . 4D **89**
W6 . . . . 5C **70**
Park Cres. W1 . . 4D **5** (3D **61**)
Park Cres. M. E.
W1 . . . . 4E **5** (3D **61**)
Park Cres. M. W.
W1 . . . . 4D **5** (3D **61**)
Parkcroft Rd. SE12 . . . . 5B **110**
Park Dr. NW11 . . . . 3D **31**
SE7 . . . . 2F **97**
SW14 . . . . 3A **98**
Park Dwellings NW3 . . . 2B **46**
Park End NW3 . . . . 1A **46**
Parker Cl. E16 . . . . 2F **83**
Parker Ho. E14 . . . . 3C **80**
    (off Admirals Way)
Parker M.
WC2 . . . . 2E **15** (5A **62**)
Parke Rd. SW13 . . . . . . 4C **84**
Parkers Row SE1 . . . . . 3C **78**
Parker St. E16 . . . . 2F **83**
WC2 . . . . 2E **15** (5A **62**)
Parkfield Av. SW14 . . . . 2A **98**
Parkfield Ct. SE14 . . . . . 4B **94**
    (off Parkfield Rd.)
Parkfield Ind. Est.
SW11 . . . . 5C **88**
Parkfield Rd. NW10 . . . . 4D **43**
SE14 . . . . 4B **94**
Parkfields SW15 . . . . . . 2E **99**
Parkfields Av. NW9 . . . . 3A **28**
Parkfield St. N1 . . . . . . 1C **62**
Park Gdns. E10 . . . . . . 2C **38**
Park Ga. SE3 . . . . 1B **110**
Parkgate M. N6 . . . . . . 2E **33**
Parkgate Rd. SW11 . . . . 3A **88**
Park Gro. E15 . . . . 5C **54**
Park Gro. Rd. E11 . . . . . 4A **40**
Park Hall SE10 . . . . 3F **95**
    (off Crooms Hill)
Pk. Hall Rd. SE21 . . . . . 3E **119**
Pk. Hall Trad. Est.
SE21 . . . . 3E **119**
Parkham St. SW11 . . . . 4A **88**
Park Hill SE23 . . . . 2D **121**
SW4 . . . . 3F **103**
Pk. Hill Ct. SW17 . . . . . 3B **116**

Parkhill Rd. NW3 . . . . . 2B **46**
Parkhill Wlk. NW3 . . . . . 2B **46**
Parkholme Rd. E8 . . . . . 3B **50**
Park Ho. E9 . . . . 4E **51**
    (off Shore Rd.)
Park Ho. Pas. N6 . . . . . 2C **32**
Parkhouse St. SE5 . . . . 3F **91**
Parkhurst Ct. N7 . . . . . . 1A **48**
Parkhurst Rd. N7 . . . . . 1A **48**
Parkinson Ho. E9 . . . . . 4E **51**
    (off Frampton Pk. Rd.)
SW1 . . . . 5E **75**
    (off Tachbrook St.)
Parkland Ct. E15 . . . . . . 2A **54**
    (off Maryland Pk.)
Parkland Gdns.
SW19 . . . . 1F **113**
Parklands N6 . . . . 2D **33**
Parklands Rd.
SW16 . . . . 5D **117**
Park La. E15 . . . . 5F **53**
W1 . . . . 4A **12** (1B **74**)
    (off Mandrell Rd.)
Park Lofts SW2 . . . . . . 3A **104**
    (off Mandrell Rd.)
Park Lorne NW8 . . . . . . 2A **60**
    (off Park Rd.)
Park Mans. NW4 . . . . . 1D **29**
NW8 . . . . 1A **60**
    (off Allitsen Rd.)
SW1 . . . . 4A **20**
    (off Knightsbridge)
SW8 . . . . 2A **90**
SW11 . . . . 4B **88**
    (off Prince of Wales Dr.)
Parkmead SW15 . . . . . . 4D **99**
Park M. SE24 . . . . 5E **105**
W10 . . . . 1A **58**
Park Pde. NW10 . . . . . . 1B **56**
Park Pl. E14 . . . . 2C **80**
N1 . . . . 4F **49**
    (off Downham Rd.)
SW1 . . . . 2F **21** (2E **75**)
Park Pl. Vs. W2 . . . . . . 4E **59**
Park Ri. SE23 . . . . 1A **122**
Park Ri. Rd. SE23 . . . . . 1A **122**
Park Rd. E6 . . . . 5E **55**
E10 . . . . 3C **38**
E12 . . . . 3D **41**
E15 . . . . 5C **54**
E17 . . . . 1B **38**
N8 . . . . 1F **33**
NW1 . . . . 3A **4** (2A **60**)
NW4 . . . . 2C **28**
NW8 . . . . 2A **60**
NW10 . . . . 5A **42**
SW19 . . . . 5A **116**
W4 . . . . 2A **84**
Park Rd. Nth. W4 . . . . . 1A **84**
Park Road Swimming Pool
    . . . . 1F **33**
Park Row SE10 . . . . 1F **95**
SW2 . . . . 4C **104**
Park Side NW2 . . . . 5C **28**
Parkside SE3 . . . . 3B **96**
SW1 . . . . 3A **20**
SW19 . . . . 3F **113**
W3 . . . . 2A **70**
Parkside Av. SW19 . . . . 5F **113**

Parkside Bus. Est.	**Parliament Sq.**	**Paternoster La.**
SE8 . . . . 2A **94**	SW1 . . . . . . 4D **23** (3A **76**)	EC4 . . . . 3E **17** (5D **63**)
(Blackhorse Rd.)	**Parliament St.**	**Paternoster Row**
SE8 . . . . 2A **94**	SW1 . . . . . . 3D **23** (3A **76**)	EC4 . . . . 3F **17** (5E **63**)
(Childers St.)	**Parliament Vw.** SE1 . . . . 5B **76**	**Paternoster Sq.**
Parkside Ct. E11 . . . . 1C **40**	**Parma Cres.** SW11 . . . 2B **102**	EC4 . . . . 3E **17** (5D **63**)
(off Wanstead Pl.)	**Parmiter Ind. Est.** E2 . . . 1D **65**	**Paterson Ct.** EC1 . . . . . . 2B **10**
Parkside Cres. N7 . . . . . 5C **34**	(off Parmiter St.)	**Pater St.** W8 . . . . 4C **72**
Parkside Est. E9 . . . . . . 5E **51**	**Parmiter St.** E2 . . . . 1D **65**	**Pathfield Rd.** SW16 . . . 5F **117**
Parkside Gdns.	**Parmoor Ct.** EC1 . . . . . . 3F **9**	**Patience Rd.** SW11 . . . . 5A **88**
SW19 . . . . 4F **113**	**Parnell Cl.** W12 . . . . 4D **71**	**Patio Cl.** SW4 . . . . 4F **103**
Parkside Rd. SW11 . . . . 4C **88**	**Parnell Ho.**	**Patmore Est.** SW8 . . . . . 4E **89**
Park Sq. E.	WC1 . . . . 1C **14** (4F **61**)	**Patmore Ho.** N16 . . . . . . 2A **50**
NW1 . . . . 3D **5** (3D **61**)	**Parnell Rd.** E3 . . . . 5B **52**	**Patmore St.** SW8 . . . . . . 4E **89**
Park Sq. M.	(not continuous)	**Patmos Lodge** SW9 . . . . 4D **91**
NW1 . . . . 4D **5** (3C **60**)	**Parnham St.** E14 . . . . . . 5A **66**	(off Elliott Rd.)
Park Sq. W.	(not continuous)	**Patmos Rd.** SW9 . . . . . . 3D **91**
NW1 . . . . 3D **5** (3D **61**)	**Parolles Rd.** N19 . . . . . . 3E **33**	**Paton Cl.** E3 . . . . 2C **66**
Parkstead Rd. SW15 . . . 3C **98**	**Parr Ct.** N1 . . . . 1F **63**	**Paton Ho.** SW9 . . . . 5B **90**
Park Steps W2 . . . . 1A **74**	(off New Nth. Rd.)	(off Stockwell Rd.)
(off St George's Flds.)	**Parr Ho.** E16 . . . . 2D **83**	**Paton St.** EC1 . . . . 2F **9** (2E **63**)
Parkstone Rd. SE15 . . . 5C **92**	(off Beaulieu Av.)	**Patrick Coman Ho.**
Park St. SE1 . . . . 1F **25** (2E **77**)	**Parr Rd.** E6 . . . . 5F **55**	EC1 . . . . 2D **9**
W1 . . . . 4B **12** (1C **74**)	**Parr St.** N1 . . . . 1F **63**	(off St John St.)
Parkthorne Rd.	**Parry Ho.** E1 . . . . 2D **79**	**Patrick Connolly Gdns.**
SW12 . . . . 5F **103**	(off Green Bank)	E3 . . . . 2D **67**
Park Towers W1 . . . . 2D **21**	**Parry Rd.** W10 . . . . 2A **58**	**Patrick Pas.** SW11 . . . . . 5A **88**
(off Brick St.)	(not continuous)	**Patrick Rd.** E13 . . . . 2E **69**
Park Vw. N5 . . . . 1E **49**	**Parry St.** SW8 . . . . 2A **90**	**Patriot Sq.** E2 . . . . 1D **65**
SE8 . . . . 1F **93**	**Parsifal Rd.** NW6 . . . . . . 2C **44**	**Patrol Pl.** SE6 . . . . 4D **109**
(off Trundleys Rd.)	**Parsonage St.** E14 . . . . . 5E **81**	**Pat Shaw Ho.** E1 . . . . . . 3F **65**
Park Vw. Apartments	**PARSONS GREEN** 5B **86**	(off Globe Rd.)
SE16 . . . . 4D **79**	**Parson's Grn.** SW6 . . . . 4C **86**	**Patshull Pl.** NW5 . . . . . . 3E **47**
(off Banyard Rd.)	**Parson's Grn. La.**	**Patshull Rd.** NW5 . . . . . 3E **47**
Parkview Ct. SW6 . . . . . 5A **86**	SW6 . . . . 4C **86**	**Pattenden Rd.** SE6 . . . . 1B **122**
SW18 . . . . 4C **100**	**Parsons Ho.** W2 . . . . 3F **59**	**Patten Ho.** N4 . . . . 3E **35**
Park Vw. Est. E2 . . . . . . 1F **65**	(off Hall Pl.)	**Patten Rd.** SW18 . . . . . . 5A **102**
Park Vw. Gdns. NW4 . . . 1E **29**	**Parsons Lodge** NW6 . . . 4D **45**	**Patterdale** NW1 . . . . 2E **5**
Park Vw. Ho. SE24 . . . . 4D **105**	(off Priory Rd.)	(off Osnaburgh St.)
(off Hurst St.)	**Parson's Rd.** E13 . . . . . . 1E **69**	**Patterdale Rd.** SE15 . . . 3E **93**
Pk. View Mans. N4 . . . . 1D **35**	**Parthenia Rd.** SW6 . . . . 4C **86**	**Pattern Ho.**
Park Vw. M. SW9 . . . . . . 5B **90**	**Partington Cl.** N19 . . . . . 3F **33**	EC1 . . . . 3D **9** (3D **63**)
Park Vw. Rd. NW10 . . . . 1B **42**	**Partridge Cl.** E16 . . . . . . 4F **69**	**Pattina Wlk.** SE16 . . . . . 2A **80**
Pk. Village E.	**Partridge Ct.** EC1 . . . . . . 3D **9**	(off Capstan Way)
NW1 . . . . 1E **5** (1D **61**)	**Pascall Ho.** SE17 . . . . . . 2E **91**	**Pattison Point** E16 . . . . . 4C **68**
Pk. Village W. NW1 . . . . 1D **61**	(off Draco St.)	(off Fife Rd.)
Parkville Rd. SW6 . . . . . 3B **86**	**Pascal St.** SW8 . . . . 3F **89**	**Pattison Ho.** E1 . . . . 5F **65**
Park Vista SE10 . . . . . . 2F **95**	**Pascoe Rd.** SE13 . . . . . 3F **109**	(off Wellesley St.)
SE10 . . . . 3F **95**	**Pasley Cl.** SE17 . . . . 1D **91**	SE1 . . . . 3A **26**
SW10 . . . . 2E **87**	**Passfield Dr.** E14 . . . . . . 4D **67**	(off Redcross Way)
Park Way NW11 . . . . 1A **30**	**Passfields** SE6 . . . . 3D **123**	**Pattison Rd.** NW2 . . . . . 5C **30**
Parkway NW1 . . . . 5D **47**	W14 . . . . 1B **86**	**Paul Cl.** E15 . . . . 4A **54**
Park W. W2 . . . . 5A **60**	(off Star St.)	**Paulet Rd.** SE5 . . . . 5D **91**
(off Edgware Rd.)	**Passing All.** EC1 . . . . 4E **9**	**Pauline Ho.** E1 . . . . 4C **64**
Park W. Pl. W2 . . . . 5A **60**	**Passmore House** E2 . . . 5B **50**	(off Old Montague St.)
Park Wharf SE8 . . . . 1A **94**	(off Kingsland Rd.)	**Paul Julius Cl.** E14 . . . . 1F **81**
(off Evelyn St.)	**Passmore St.** SW1 . . . . . 1C **88**	**Pauls Ho.** E3 . . . . 4B **66**
Parkwood NW8 . . . . 5B **46**	**Paston Cres.** SE12 . . . . 5D **111**	(off Timothy Rd.)
(off St Edmund's Ter.)	**Pastor Ct.** N6 . . . . 1E **33**	**Paul St.** E15 . . . . 5A **54**
Parkwood M. N6 . . . . 1D **33**	**Pastor St.** SE11 . . . . 5D **77**	EC2 . . . . 4C **10** (3F **63**)
Parkwood Rd.	(not continuous)	**Paul's Wlk.**
SW19 . . . . 5B **114**	**Pasture Rd.** SE6 . . . . . . 1B **124**	EC4 . . . . 4E **17** (1F **77**)
Parliament Ct. E1 . . . . . . 1E **19**	**Patcham Ter.** SW8 . . . . . 4D **89**	**Paultons Sq.** SW3 . . . . . 2F **87**
Parliament Fields 5C **32**	**Patent Ho.** E14 . . . . 4D **67**	**Paultons St.** SW3 . . . . . 2F **87**
Parliament Hill 5B **32**	(off Morris Rd.)	**Pauntley St.** N19 . . . . . . 3E **33**
Parliament Hill Lido . . . 1C **46**	**Patent Office, The**	**Pavan Ct.** E2 . . . . 2E **65**
Parliament Hill Mans.	EC4 . . . . 3C **16**	(off Sceptre Rd.)
NW5 . . . . 1C **46**	(off Bouverie St.)	**Paveley Dr.** SW11 . . . . . 3A **88**
		Paveley Ho. N1 . . . . 1B **62**
		(off Priory Grn. Est.)

Paveley St. NW8 . . . . 2A **60**
Pavement, The E11 . . . . 3E **39**
   (off Hainault Rd.)
SW4 . . . . 2E **103**
Pavilion NW8 . . . . 2F **59**
Pavilion, The SW8 . . . 3F **89**
Pavilion Ct. NW6 . . . . . 2C **58**
   (off Stafford Rd.)
Pavilion Pde. W12 . . . . 5E **57**
   (off Wood La.)
Pavilion Rd.
SW1 . . . . . . 4A **20** (4B **74**)
Pavilion Sq. SW17 . . . 3B **116**
Pavilion St.
SW1 . . . . . . 5A **20** (4B **74**)
Pavilion Ter. W12 . . . . . 5E **57**
   (off Wood La.)
Pawsey Cl. E13 . . . . . . 5D **55**
Paxton Ct. SE12 . . . . 3E **125**
SE26 . . . . 4A **122**
   (off Adamsrill Rd.)
Paxton Pl. SE27 . . . . 4A **120**
Paxton Rd. SE23 . . . . 3A **122**
W4 . . . . 2A **84**
Paxton Ter. SW1 . . . . 2D **89**
Paymal Ho. E1 . . . . 4E **65**
   (off Stepney Way)
Payne Ho. N1 . . . . 5B **48**
   (off Barnsbury Est.)
Paynell Ct. SE3 . . . . . 1A **110**
Payne Rd. E3 . . . . 1D **67**
Paynesfield Av.
SW14 . . . . 1A **98**
Payne St. SE8 . . . . 3B **94**
Paynes Wlk. W6 . . . . . . 2A **86**
Peabody Av. SW1 . . . . 1D **89**
Peabody Bldgs. E1 . . . 1C **78**
   (off John Fisher St.)
EC1 . . . . 4A **10**
   (off Roscoe St.)
SW3 . . . . 2A **88**
   (off Cheyne Row)
Peabody Cl. SE10 . . . . 4D **95**
SW1 . . . . 1D **89**
Peabody Ct. EC1 . . . . . 4A **10**
   (off Roscoe St.)
SE5 . . . . 4F **91**
   (off Kimpton Rd.)
Peabody Est. E1 . . . . . 1F **79**
   (off Glasmis Pl.)
E2 . . . . 1D **65**
   (off Minerva St.)
EC1 . . . . 4A **10**
   (off Dufferin St.,
   not continuous)
EC1 . . . . 4C **8**
   (off Farringdon La.)
N1 . . . . 5E **49**
SE1 . . . . . . 2C **24** (2C **76**)
   (Duchy St.)
SE1 . . . . . . 2F **25** (2E **77**)
   (Gt. Guildford St.)
SE1 . . . . 3A **26**
   (Mint St.)
SE24 . . . . 5D **105**
SW1 . . . . 5E **75**
   (off Vauxhall Bri. Rd.)
SW3 . . . . 2A **88**
Peabody Est. SW6 . . . 2C **86**
   (off Lillie Rd.)

Peabody Est. SW11 . . . 2A **102**
W6 . . . . 1E **85**
W10 . . . . 4E **57**
Peabody Hill SE21 . . . 1D **119**
Peabody Sq.
SE1 . . . . 4D **25** (3D **77**)
   (not continuous)
Peabody Ter. EC1 . . . . . 4C **8**
   (off Farringdon La.)
Peabody Twr. EC1 . . . . 4A **10**
   (off Golden La.)
Peabody Trust SE17 . . . 5F **77**
   (off Rodney Rd.)
Peabody Yd. N1 . . . . . . 5E **49**
Peachey Edwards Ho.
E2 . . . . 2D **65**
   (off Teesdale St.)
Peach Gro. E11 . . . . . . 5F **39**
Peach Rd. W10 . . . . 2F **57**
Peachum Rd. SE3 . . . . 2B **96**
Peachwalk M. E3 . . . . . 1F **65**
Peacock St. SE17 . . . . 5D **77**
   (off Portugal St.)
Peacock Wlk. E16 . . . . . 5D **69**
   (off Mortlake Rd.)
N6 . . . . 2D **33**
Peacock St SE17 . . . . 1D **91**
   (off Iliffe St.)
Peak, The SE26 . . . . . 3E **121**
Peak Fitness
Crossharbour 3D **81**
Peak Hill SE26 . . . . . . 4E **121**
Peak Hill Av.
SE26 . . . . 4E **121**
Peak Hill Gdns.
SE26 . . . . 4E **121**
Peak Ho. N4 . . . . 3E **35**
   (off Woodberry Down Est.)
Pearcefield Av.
SE23 . . . . 1E **121**
Pear Cl. SE14 . . . . 3A **94**
Pear Ct. SE15 . . . . 3B **92**
   (off Thruxton Way)
Pearcroft Rd. E11 . . . . 4F **39**
Peardon St. SW8 . . . . . 5D **89**
Pearfield Rd.
SE23 . . . . 3A **122**
Pearl Cl. NW2 . . . . 2F **29**
Pearl St. E1 . . . . 2D **79**
Pearman St.
SE1 . . . . . . 5C **24** (4C **76**)
Pear Pl. SE1 . . 3B **24** (3C **76**)
Pear Rd. E11 . . . . 5F **39**
Pearscroft Ct. SW6 . . . 4D **87**
Pearscroft Rd. SW6 . . . 4D **87**
Pearse St. SE15 . . . . . 2A **92**
Pearson Cl. SE5 . . . . . . 4C **91**
   (off Camberwell New Rd.)
Pearson M. SW4 . . . . . 1F **103**
   (off Slievemore Cl.)
Pearson's Av. SE14 . . . 4C **94**
Pearson St. E2 . . . . . . 1B **64**
Peartree SE26 . . . . . . 5A **122**
Peartree Av. SW17 . . . 3E **115**
Pear Tree Cl. E2 . . . . . 5B **50**
Pear Tree Ct.
EC1 . . . . . . 4C **8** (3C **62**)
Pear Tree Ho. SE4 . . . 1B **108**
Peartree La. E1 . . . . . . 1E **79**

Pear Tree St.
EC1 . . . . 3E **9** (3E **63**)
Peartree Way SE10 . . . 5C **82**
Peary Ho. NW10 . . . . . 4A **42**
Peary Pl. E2 . . . . 2E **65**
Peckarmans Wood
SE26 . . . . 3C **120**
Peckett St. N5 . . . . 1E **49**
Peckford Pl. SW9 . . . . 5C **90**
PECKHAM 3A **92**
Peckham Gro. SE15 . . . 3A **92**
Peckham High St.
SE15 . . . . 4C **92**
Peckham Hill St.
SE15 . . . . 3C **92**
Peckham Pk. Rd.
SE15 . . . . 3C **92**
Peckham Pulse Health &
Leisure Cen. 4C **92**
Peckham Rd. SE5 . . . . 4A **92**
SE15 . . . . 4A **92**
Peckham Rye SE15 . . . 1C **106**
SE22 . . . . 2C **106**
Peckham Sq. SE15 . . . 4C **92**
Peckwater St. NW5 . . . 2E **47**
Pedlar's Wlk. N7 . . . . . 2B **48**
Pedley St. E1 . . . . 3B **64**
Pedro St. E5 . . . . 5F **37**
Pedworth Gdns.
SE16 . . . . 5E **79**
Peek Cres. SW19 . . . . 5F **113**
Peel Gro. E2 . . . . 1E **65**
   (not continuous)
Peel Pas. W8 . . . . 2C **72**
Peel Pct. NW6 . . . . . . 1C **58**
Peel St. W8 . . . . 2C **72**
Peerless St.
EC1 . . . . . . 2B **10** (2F **63**)
Pegasus Cl. N16 . . . . . 1F **49**
Pegasus Cl. NW10 . . . 2D **57**
   (off Trenmar Gdns.)
Pegasus Ho. E1 . . . . . . 3F **65**
   (off Beaumont Sq.)
Pegasus Pl. SE11 . . . . 2C **90**
SW6 . . . . 4C **86**
Pegley Gdns. SE12 . . . 2C **124**
Pekin Cl. E14 . . . . 5C **66**
   (off Pekin St.)
Pekin St. E14 . . . . 5C **66**
Peldon Wlk. N1 . . . . . . 5D **49**
   (off Popham St.)
Pelham Cl. SE5 . . . . . 1A **106**
Pelham Ct. SW3 . . . . . . 5A **74**
   (off Fulham Rd.)
Pelham Cres. SW7 . . . . 5A **74**
Pelham Ho. W14 . . . . . 5B **72**
   (off Mornington Av.)
Pelham Pl. SW7 . . . . . . 5A **74**
Pelham St. SW7 . . . . . 5F **73**
Pelican Est. SE15 . . . . 4B **92**
Pelican Ho. SE8 . . . . . 5B **80**
Pelican Pas. E1 . . . . . . 3E **65**
Pelican Wlk. SW9 . . . . 2D **105**
Pelican Wharf E1 . . . . . 2E **79**
   (off Wapping Wall)
Pelier St. SE17 . . . . . . 2E **91**
Pelinore Rd. SE6 . . . . 2A **124**
Pella Ho. SE11 . . . . . . 1B **90**

Pellant Rd. SW6 . . . . 3A **86**
Pellatt Rd. SE22 . . . . 3B **106**
Pellerin Rd. N16 . . . . 2A **50**
Pellew Ho. E1 . . . . 3D **65**
   (off Somerford St.)
Pelling St. E14 . . . . 5C **66**
Pelly Rd. E13 . . . . 5C **54**
   (not continuous)
Pelter St. E2 . . . 1F **11** (2B **64**)
   (not continuous)
Pelton Rd. SE10 . . . . 1A **96**
Pember Rd. NW10 . . . . . . 2F **57**
Pemberton Ct. E1 . . . . . . 2F **65**
   (off Portelet Rd.)
Pemberton Gdns.
N19 . . . . 5E **33**
Pemberton Ho.
  SE26 . . . . 4C **120**
   (off High Level Dr.)
Pemberton Pl. E8 . . . . . . 4D **51**
Pemberton Rd. N4 . . . . . 1C **34**
Pemberton Row
  EC4 . . . . 2C **16** (5C **62**)
Pemberton Ter. N19 . . . . . 5E **33**
Pembridge Cres.
  W11 . . . . 1C **72**
Pembridge Gdns. W2 . . . 1C **72**
Pembridge M. W11 . . . . . 1C **72**
Pembridge Pl.
  SW15 . . . . 3C **100**
  W2 . . . . 1C **72**
Pembridge Rd. W11 . . . . . 1C **72**
Pembridge Sq. W2 . . . . . 1C **72**
Pembridge Vs. W2 . . . . . . 1C **72**
  W11 . . . . 1C **72**
Pembroke Av. N1 . . . . 5A **48**
Pembroke Bldgs.
  NW10 . . . . 2C **56**
Pembroke Cl.
  SW1 . . . . 4C **20** (3C **74**)
Pembroke Cotts. W8 . . . 4C **72**
   (off Pembroke Sq.)
Pembroke Gdns. W8 . . . . 5B **72**
Pembroke Gdns. Cl.
  W8 . . . . 4C **72**
Pembroke Ho. W2 . . . . . 5D **59**
   (off Hallfield Est.)
Pembroke M. E3. . . . . . . 2A **66**
  W8 . . . . 4C **72**
Pembroke Pl. W8 . . . . . . 4C **72**
Pembroke Rd. E17 . . . . . 1D **39**
  N15 . . . . 1B **36**
  W8 . . . . 5B **72**
Pembroke Sq. W8 . . . . . 4C **72**
Pembroke St. N1 . . . . . . 4A **48**
   (not continuous)
Pembroke Studios
  W8 . . . . 4B **72**
Pembroke Ter. NW8 . . . . 5F **45**
   (off Queen's Ter.)
Pembroke Vs. W8 . . . . . . 5C **72**
Pembroke Wlk. W8 . . . . . 5C **72**
Pembrook M. SW11 . . . . 2F **101**
Pembry Cl. SW9 . . . . 4C **90**
Pembury Cl. E5 . . . . 2D **51**
Pembury Pl. E5 . . . . 2D **51**
Pembury Rd. E5 . . . . 2D **51**
Pemell Cl. E1 . . . . 3E **65**
Pemell Ho. E1 . . . . 3E **65**
   (off Pemell Cl.)

Penally Pl. N1 . . . . 5F **49**
Penang Ho. E1 . . . . 2D **79**
   (off Prusom St.)
Penang St. E1 . . . . 2D **79**
Penarth Cen. SE15 . . . . . 2E **93**
Penarth St. SE15 . . . . . . 2E **93**
Penberth Rd. SE6 . . . . . 2E **123**
Pencombe M. W11 . . . . . 1B **72**
Pencraig Way SE15 . . . . . 2D **93**
Penda's Mead E9 . . . . . . 1A **52**
Pendennis Ho. SE8 . . . . . 5A **80**
Pendennis Rd.
  SW16 . . . . 4A **118**
Penderry Ri. SE6 . . . . . . 2F **123**
Penderyn Way N7 . . . . . . 1F **47**
Pendle Ho. SE26 . . . . . . 3C **120**
Pendle Rd. SW16 . . . . . 5D **117**
Pendlestone Rd. E17 . . . 1D **39**
Pendragon Rd.
  BR1: Brom 5B **124**
Pendragon Wlk. NW9 . . . 1A **28**
Pendrell Ho. WC2 . . . . . . 3C **14**
   (off New Compton St.)
Pendrell Rd. SE4 . . . . . . 5A **94**
Pendulum M. E8 . . . . 2B **50**
Penerley Rd. SE6 . . . . . 1D **123**
Penfield Lodge W9 . . . . . 4C **58**
   (off Admiral Wlk.)
Penfields Ho. N7 . . . . . . 3A **48**
Penfold Ho. N1 . . . . 4A **60**
Penfold St. NW1 . . . . 4A **60**
  NW8 . . . . 3F **59**
Penford Gdns. SE9 . . . . 1F **111**
Penford St. SE5 . . . . 5D **91**
Penge Ho. SW11 . . . . . . 1F **101**
Penge Rd. E13 . . . . 5E **55**
Penhall Rd. SE7 . . . . 5F **83**
Penhurst Pl. SE1 . . . . 5A **24**
Peninsula Apartments
  W2 . . . . 4A **60**
   (off Praed St.)
Peninsula Ct. E14 . . . . . . 4D **81**
   (off E. Ferry Rd.)
Peninsula Hgts. SE1 . . . 1A **90**
Peninsular Pk. SE7 . . . . . 5C **82**
Peninsular Pk. Rd.
  SE7 . . . . 5C **82**
Penley Ct.
  WC2 . . . . 4A **16** (1B **76**)
Penmayne Ho. SE11 . . . . 1C **90**
   (off Kennings Way)
Pennack Rd. SE15 . . . . . 2B **92**
Penn Almshouses
  SE10 . . . . 4E **95**
   (off Greenwich Sth. St.)
Pennant M. W8 . . . . 5D **73**
Pennard Mans. W12 . . . . 3E **71**
   (off Goldhawk Rd.)
Pennard Rd. W12 . . . . . . 3E **71**
Penner Cl. SW19 . . . . . . 2A **114**
Pennethorne Cl. E9 . . . . 5E **51**
Pennethorne Ho.
  SW11 . . . . 1F **101**
Pennethorne Rd.
  SE15 . . . . 3D **93**
Penn Ho. NW8 . . . . 3A **60**
   (off Mallory St.)
Pennine Dr. NW2 . . . . . . 4F **29**
Pennine La. NW2 . . . . . . 4A **30**
Pennine Pde. NW2 . . . . . 4A **30**

Pennington Cl.
  SE27 . . . . 4F **119**
Pennington Ct. SE16 . . . 2A **80**
Pennington St. E1 . . . . . 1D **79**
Pennington Way
  SE12 . . . . 2D **125**
Penn Rd. N7 . . . . 2A **48**
Penn St. N1 . . . . 5F **49**
Pennyfields E14 . . . . 1C **80**
   (not continuous)
Pennyford Ct. NW8 . . . . 3F **59**
   (off St John's Wood Rd.)
Penny M. SW12 . . . . . . 5D **103**
Pennymoor Wlk. W9 . . . . 3B **58**
   (off Ashmore Rd.)
Penpoll Rd. E8 . . . . 3D **51**
Penrith Cl. SW15 . . . . . 3A **100**
Penrith Pl. SE27 . . . . . . 2D **119**
Penrith Rd. N15 . . . . 1F **35**
Penrith St. SW16 . . . . . 5E **117**
Penrose Gro. SE17 . . . . . 1E **91**
Penrose Ho. SE17 . . . . . 1E **91**
   (not continuous)
Penrose St. SE17 . . . . . . 1E **91**
Penryn Ho. SE11 . . . . . . 1D **91**
   (off Seaton Cl.)
Penryn St. NW1 . . . . 1F **61**
Penry St. SE1 . . . . 5A **78**
Pensbury Pl. SW8 . . . . . 5E **89**
Pensbury St. SW8 . . . . . 5E **89**
Penshurst NW5 . . . . 3C **46**
Penshurst Ho. SE15 . . . . 2E **93**
   (off Lovelinch Cl.)
Penshurst Rd. E9 . . . . . 4F **51**
Pentland Cl. NW11 . . . . . 4A **30**
Pentland Gdns.
  SW18 . . . . 4E **101**
Pentland St. SW18 . . . . 4E **101**
Pentlow St. SW15 . . . . . 1E **99**
Pentney Rd. SW12 . . . . 1E **117**
Penton Gro. N1 . . . . 1C **62**
Penton Ho. N1 . . . . 1B **8**
   (off Pentonville Rd.)
Penton Pl. SE17 . . . . . . 1D **91**
Penton Ri.
  WC1 . . . . 1A **8** (2B **62**)
Penton St. N1 . . . . 1C **62**
PENTONVILLE 1B **62**
Pentonville Rd.
  N1 . . . . 1F **7** (1B **62**)
Pentridge St. SE15 . . . . . 3B **92**
Penwith Rd. SW18 . . . . 2C **114**
Penwood Ho. SW15 . . . . 4B **98**
Penwortham Rd.
  SW16 . . . . 5D **117**
Penywern Rd. SW5 . . . . . 1C **86**
Penzance Ho. SE11 . . . . 1C **90**
   (off Seaton Cl.)
Penzance Pl. W11 . . . . . 2A **72**
Penzance St. W11 . . . . . 2A **72**
Peony Gdns. W12 . . . . . 1C **70**
Peperfield WC1 . . . . 2F **7**
   (off Cromer St.)
Pepler Ho. W10 . . . . 3A **58**
   (off Wornington Rd.)
Pepler M. SE5 . . . . 1B **92**
Peploe Rd. NW6 . . . . . . 1F **57**
Peppermead Sq.
  SE13 . . . . 3C **108**
Peppermint Pl. E11 . . . . 5A **40**

Pepper St. E14 . . . . 4D **81**
   SE1 . . . . 3F **25** (3E **77**)
Peppie Cl. N16 . . . . 4A **36**
Pepys Cres. E16 . . . . 2C **82**
Pepys Ho. E2 . . . . 2E **65**
   (off Kirkwall Pl.)
Pepys Rd. SE14 . . . . 4F **93**
Pepys St.
   EC3 . . . . 4E **19** (1A **78**)
Perceval Av. NW3 . . . . 2A **46**
Perch St. E8 . . . . 1B **50**
Percival David Foundation of
   Chinese Art 3C **6**
Percival St.
   EC1 . . . . 3D **9** (3D **63**)
Percy Cir.
   WC1 . . . . 1A **8** (2B **62**)
Percy Laurie Ho.
   SW15 . . . . 2F **99**
   (off Nursery Cl.)
Percy M. W1 . . . . 1B **14**
Percy Pas. W1 . . . . 1B **14**
Percy Rd. E11 . . . . 2A **40**
   E16 . . . . 4A **68**
   W12 . . . . 3C **70**
Percy St. W1 . . . . 1B **14** (4F **61**)
Percy Yd.
   WC1 . . . . 1A **8** (2B **62**)
Peregrine Cl. NW10 . . . . 2A **42**
Peregrine Cl. SE8 . . . . 2C **94**
   (off Edward St.)
   SW16 . . . . 4B **118**
Peregrine Ho. EC1 . . . . 1E **9**
Perham Rd. W14 . . . . 1A **86**
Perifield SE21 . . . . 1E **119**
Periton Rd. SE9 . . . . 2F **111**
Perkins Ho. E14 . . . . 4B **66**
   (off Wallwood St.)
Perkin's Rents
   SW1 . . . . 5B **22** (4F **75**)
Perkins Sq.
   SE1 . . . . 1A **26** (2E **77**)
Perks Cl. SE3 . . . . 1A **110**
Perley Ho. E3 . . . . 4B **66**
   (off Weatherley Cl.)
Perran Rd. SW2 . . . . 1D **119**
Perren St. NW5 . . . . 3D **47**
Perrers Rd. W6 . . . . 5D **71**
Perring Est. E3 . . . . 4C **66**
   (off Gale St.)
Perrin Ho. NW6 . . . . 2C **58**
   (off Malvern Rd.)
Perrin's Ct. NW3 . . . . 1E **45**
Perrin's La. NW3 . . . . 1E **45**
Perrin's Wlk. NW3 . . . . 1E **45**
Perronet Ho. SE1 . . . . 5E **25**
Perry Av. W3 . . . . 5A **56**
Perry Ct. E14 . . . . 1C **94**
   (off Maritime Quay)
   N15 . . . . 1A **36**
Perryfield Way NW9 . . . . 1B **28**
Perry Hill SE6 . . . . 3B **122**
Perry Lodge E12 . . . . 3F **41**
Perrymead St. SW6 . . . . 4C **86**
Perryn Ho. W3 . . . . 1A **70**
Perryn Rd. SE16 . . . . 4D **79**
   W3 . . . . 2A **70**
Perry Ri. SE23 . . . . 3A **122**
Perry's Pl.
   W1 . . . . 2B **14** (5F **61**)

Perry Va. SE23 . . . . 2E **121**
Persant Rd. SE6 . . . . 2A **124**
Perseverance Pl.
   SW9 . . . . 3C **90**
Perseverance Works
   E2 . . . . 1E **11**
   (off Kingsland Rd.)
Perth Av. NW9 . . . . 2A **28**
Perth Cl. SE5 . . . . 2F **105**
Perth Ho. N1 . . . . 4B **48**
   (off Bemerton Est.)
Perth Rd. E10 . . . . 3A **38**
   E13 . . . . 1D **69**
   N4 . . . . 3C **34**
Perystreete SE23 . . . . 2E **121**
Peter Av. NW10 . . . . 4D **43**
Peter Best Ho. E1 . . . . 5D **65**
   (off Nelson St.)
Peterboat Cl. SE10 . . . . 5A **82**
Peterborough Ct.
   EC4 . . . . 3C **16** (5C **62**)
Peterborough M.
   SW6 . . . . 5C **86**
Peterborough Rd.
   E10 . . . . 1E **39**
   SW6 . . . . 5C **86**
Peterborough Vs.
   SW6 . . . . 4D **87**
Peter Butler Ho. SE1 . . . . 3C **78**
   (off Wolseley St.)
Peterchurch Ho.
   SE15 . . . . 2D **93**
   (off Commercial Way)
Petergate SW11 . . . . 2E **101**
Peter Heathfield Ho.
   E15 . . . . 5F **53**
   (off Wise Rd.)
Peter Ho. SW8 . . . . 3A **90**
   (off Luscombe Way)
Peterley Bus. Cen.
   E2 . . . . 1D **65**
Peter Pan Statue 2F **73**
Peter Scott Vis. Cen., The
   . . . . 4D **85**
Peters Ct. W2 . . . . 5D **59**
   (off Porchester Rd.)
Petersfield Ri.
   SW15 . . . . 1D **113**
Petersham Ho. SW7 . . . . 5F **73**
   (off Kendrick M.)
Petersham La. SW7 . . . . 4E **73**
Petersham M. SW7 . . . . 4E **73**
Petersham Pl. SW7 . . . . 4E **73**
Peter's Hill
   EC4 . . . . . . 4F **17** (1E **77**)
Peter Shore Ct. E1 . . . . 4F **65**
   (off Beaumont Sq.)
Peter's La.
   EC1 . . . . 5E **9** (4D **63**)
   (not continuous)
Peter's Path SE26 . . . . 4D **121**
Peterstow Cl. SW19 . . . . 2A **114**
Peter St. W1 . . . . 4B **14** (1F **75**)
Petherton Ct. NW10 . . . . 5F **43**
   (off Tiverton Rd.)
Petherton Ho. N4 . . . . 3E **35**
   (off Woodberry Down Est.)
Petherton Rd. N5 . . . . 2E **49**
Petiver Cl. E9 . . . . 4E **51**
Petley Rd. W6 . . . . 2F **85**

Peto Pl. NW1 . . . 3E **5** (3D **61**)
Peto St. Nth. E16 . . . . 5B **68**
Petrie Cl. NW2 . . . . 3A **44**
Petrie Mus. of
   Egyptian Archaeology
   . . . . 4B **6**
Petros Gdns. NW3 . . . . 3E **45**
Petticoat La.
   E1 . . . . 1F **19** (4A **64**)
Petticoat Lane Market
   . . . . 2F **19**
   (off Middlesex St.)
Petticoat Sq.
   E1 . . . . 2F **19** (5B **64**)
Petticoat Twr. E1 . . . . 2F **19**
Pettiward Cl. SW15 . . . . 2E **99**
Pett St. SE18 . . . . 5F **83**
Petty France
   SW1 . . . . 5A **22** (4E **75**)
Petworth St. SW11 . . . . 4A **88**
Petyt Pl. SW3 . . . . 2A **88**
Petyward SW3 . . . . 5A **74**
Pevensey Ho. E1 . . . . 4F **65**
   (off Ben Jonson Rd.)
Pevensey Rd. E7 . . . . 1B **54**
   SW17 . . . . 4F **115**
Peveril Ho. SE1 . . . . 5C **26**
Peyton Pl. SE10 . . . . 3E **95**
Pharamond NW2 . . . . 3F **43**
Pheasant Cl. E16 . . . . 5D **69**
Phelp St. SE17 . . . . 2F **91**
Phene St. SW3 . . . . 2A **88**
Philadelphia Ct.
   SW10 . . . . 3E **87**
   (off Uverdale Rd.)
Philbeach Gdns. SW5 . . . 1C **86**
Phil Brown Pl. SW8 . . . . 1D **103**
   (off Wandsworth Rd.)
Philchurch Pl. E1 . . . . 5C **64**
Philip Ct. W2 . . . . 4F **59**
   (off Hall Pl.)
Philip Ho. NW6 . . . . 5D **45**
   (off Mortimer Pl.)
Philip Jones Ct. N4 . . . . 3B **34**
Philip Mole Ho. W9 . . . . 3C **58**
   (off Chippenham Rd.)
Philippa Gdns. SE9 . . . . 3F **111**
Philip St. E13 . . . . 3C **68**
Philip Wlk. SE15 . . . . 1C **106**
   (not continuous)
Phillimore Gdns.
   NW10 . . . . 5E **43**
   W8 . . . . 3C **72**
Phillimore Gdns. Cl.
   W8 . . . . 4C **72**
Phillimore Pl. W8 . . . . 3C **72**
Phillimore Ter. W8 . . . . 4C **72**
   (off Allen St.)
Phillimore Wlk. W8 . . . . 4C **72**
Phillip St. N1 . . . . 5A **50**
Philpot La.
   EC3 . . . . . . 4D **19** (1A **78**)
Philpot Sq. SW6 . . . . 1D **101**
Philpot St. E1 . . . . 5D **65**
Phineas Pett Rd.
   SE9 . . . . 1F **111**
Phipps Ho. SE7 . . . . 1D **97**
   (off Woolwich Rd.)
   W12 . . . . 1D **71**
   (off White City Est.)

Phipp St.
EC2 . . . . 3D **11** (3A **64**)
Phoebeth Rd.
SE4 . . . . 3C **108**
Phoenix Bus. Cen.
E3 . . . . 4C **66**
(off Bow Comn. La.)
Phoenix Cl. E8 . . . . 5B **50**
Phoenix Ct. E1 . . . . 3D **65**
(off Buckhurst St.)
E14 . . . . 5C **80**
NW1 . . . . 1C **6**
(off Purchese St.)
SE14 . . . . 2A **94**
(off Chipley St.)
Phoenix Lodge Mans.
W6 . . . . 5F **71**
(off Brook Grn.)
Phoenix Pk. NW2 . . . . 4C **28**
Phoenix Pl.
WC1 . . . . 3A **8** (3B **62**)
Phoenix Rd.
NW1 . . . . 1B **6** (2F **61**)
Phoenix Sports &
Fitness Cen. 1C **70**
Phoenix St.
WC2 . . . . 3C **14** (5F **61**)
Phoenix Theatre 3C **14**
(off Charing Cross Rd.)
Phoenix Wharf E1 . . . 2D **79**
(off Wapping High St.)
Phoenix Wharf Rd.
SE1 . . . . 4F **27**
Phoenix Yd. WC1 . . . . 2A **8**
Photographers' Gallery
. . . . 4D **15**
(off Gt. Newport St.)
Physic Pl. SW3 . . . . . . 2B **88**
Piazza, The WC2 . . . . 4E **15**
(not continuous)
Piccadilly
W1 . . . . 2E **21** (3E **75**)
Piccadilly Arc. SW1 . . . 1F **21**
Piccadilly Circus
. . . . 5B **14** (1F **75**)
Piccadilly Cir.
W1 . . . . 5B **14** (1F **75**)
Piccadilly Pl. W1 . . . . . 5A **14**
Piccadilly Theatre 4A **14**
(off Denman St.)
Pickard St.
EC1 . . . . 1E **9** (2D **63**)
Pickering Cl. E9 . . . . . . 4F **51**
Pickering Ho. W2 . . . . . 5E **59**
(off Hallfield Est.)
Pickering M. W2 . . . . . 5D **59**
Pickering Pl. SW1 . . . . 2A **22**
Pickering St. N1 . . . . . 5D **49**
Pickets St. SW12 . . . . 5D **103**
Picketts Ter. SE22 . . . 3C **106**
Pickfords Wharf N1 . . . 1E **63**
SE1 . . . . 1B **26** (2F **77**)
Pickwick Ho. SE16 . . . 3C **78**
(off George Row)
W11 . . . . 2F **71**
(off St Ann's Rd.)
Pickwick Rd. SE21 . . . 5F **105**
Pickwick St.
SE1 . . . . 4F **25** (3E **77**)
Pickworth Cl. SW8 . . . 3A **90**

Picton Pl.
W1 . . . . 3C **12** (5C **60**)
Picton St. SE5 . . . . 3F **91**
Pied Bull Yard N1 . . . 5D **49**
(off Theberton St.)
Pier Head E1 . . . . 2D **79**
(not continuous)
Pierhead Wharf E1 . . . 2D **79**
(off Wapping High St.)
Pier Ho. SW3 . . . . 2A **88**
Piermont Grn. SE22 . . 3D **107**
Piermont Rd. SE22 . . . 3D **107**
Pierpoint Bldg. E14 . . . 3B **80**
Pierrepont Arc. N1 . . . . 1D **63**
(off Islington High St.)
Pierrepont Row N1 . . . 1D **63**
(off Camden Pas.)
Pier St. E14 . . . . 5E **81**
(not continuous)
Pier Ter. SW18 . . . . . . 2D **101**
Pietra Lara Bldg. EC1 . . . 3F **9**
(off Pear Tree St.)
Piggott Rd. E2 . . . . 1F **65**
(off Sewardstone Rd.)
Pigott St. E14 . . . . 5C **66**
Pike Cl. BR1: Brom . . . 5D **125**
Pikemans St. SW5 . . . 5C **72**
(off W. Cromwell Rd.)
Pikethorne SE23 . . . 2F **121**
Pilgrimage St.
SE1 . . . . 4B **26** (3F **77**)
Pilgrim Hill SE27 . . . . 4E **119**
Pilgrim Ho. SE1 . . . . . 5C **26**
(off Lansdowne Pl.)
Pilgrims Cloisters
SE5 . . . . 3A **92**
(off Sedgmoor Pl.)
Pilgrim's La. NW3 . . . . 1F **45**
Pilgrims M. E14 . . . . . . 1A **82**
Pilgrim's Pl. NW3 . . . . 1F **45**
Pilgrim St.
EC4 . . . . 3D **17** (5D **63**)
Pilgrims Way N19 . . . . 3F **33**
Pilkington Rd. SE15 . . . 5D **93**
Pilot Cl. SE8 . . . . 2B **94**
Pilot Ind. Cen. NW10 . . 3A **56**
Pilsden Cl. SW19 . . . . 1F **113**
Pilton Cl. SE17 . . . . 1E **91**
(off King & Queen St.)
Pilton Pl. Est. SE17 . . . 1E **91**
PIMLICO 1E **89**
Pimlico Ho. SW1 . . . . . 1D **89**
(off Ebury Bri. Rd.)
Pimlico Rd. SW1 . . . . . 1C **88**
Pimlico Wlk. N1 . . . . . . 1D **11**
Pinchin & Johnsons Yd.
E1 . . . . 1C **78**
(off Pinchin St.)
Pinchin St. E1 . . . . 1C **78**
Pincombe Ho. SE17 . . . 1F **91**
(off Orb St.)
Pincott Pl. SE4 . . . . . . 1F **107**
Pindar St.
EC2 . . . . 5D **11** (4A **64**)
Pindock M. W9 . . . . . . 3D **59**
Pineapple Ct. SW1 . . . 5A **22**
Pine Av. E15 . . . . 2F **53**
Pine Cl. E10 . . . . 4D **39**
N19 . . . . 4E **33**

Pinedene SE15 . . . . . . 4D **93**
Pinefield Cl. E14 . . . . . 1C **80**
Pine Gro. N4 . . . . 4A **34**
SW19 . . . . 5B **114**
Pine Ho. SE16 . . . . 3E **79**
(off Ainsty Est.)
W10 . . . . 3A **58**
(off Droop St.)
Pinehurst Ct. W11 . . . . 5B **58**
(off Colville Gdns.)
Pinemartin Cl. NW2 . . 5E **29**
Pine M. NW10 . . . . 1F **57**
Pine Rd. NW2 . . . . 1E **43**
Pine St. EC1 . . . 3C **8** (3C **62**)
Pine Tree Ho. SE14 . . . 3F **93**
(off Reaston St.)
Pinewood Cl. SW4 . . . 4F **103**
Pinfold Rd. SW16 . . . . 4A **118**
Pinkerton Pl. SW16 . . . 4F **117**
Pinnace Ho. E14 . . . . . 4E **81**
(off Manchester Rd.)
Pinnell Rd. SE9 . . . . . 2F **111**
Pinner Ct. NW8 . . . . . . 3F **59**
(off St John's Wood Rd.)
Pinners Pas. EC2 . . . . 2C **18**
(off Austin Friars)
Pintail Cl. E6 . . . . 4F **69**
Pintail Ct. SE8 . . . . . . 2B **94**
(off Pilot Cl.)
Pinter Ho. SW9 . . . . . . 5A **90**
(off Grantham Rd.)
Pinto Way SE3 . . . . . . 2D **111**
Pioneer St. SE15 . . . . 4C **92**
Pioneer Way W12 . . . . 5D **57**
Piper Cl. N7 . . . . 2B **48**
Pipers Ho. SE10 . . . . . . 1F **95**
(off Collington St.)
Pippin Cl. NW2 . . . . . . 5C **28**
Pirbright Rd. SW18 . . . 1B **114**
Pirie Cl. SE5 . . . . 1F **105**
Pirie St. E16 . . . . 2D **83**
Pitcairn Ho. E9 . . . . . . 4E **51**
Pitchford St. E15 . . . . 4F **53**
Pitfield Est.
N1 . . . . 1D **11** (2A **64**)
Pitfield St.
N1 . . . . 1D **11** (2A **64**)
Pitfold Cl. SE12 . . . . . 4C **110**
Pitfold Rd. SE12 . . . . . 4C **110**
Pitman Ho. SE8 . . . . . . 4C **94**
Pitman St. SE5 . . . . . . 3E **91**
(not continuous)
Pitmaston Ho. SE13 . . . 5E **95**
(off Lewisham Rd.)
Pitsea Pl. E1 . . . . 5F **65**
Pitsea St. E1 . . . . 5F **65**
Pitt Cres. SW19 . . . . . 4D **115**
Pitt's Head M.
W1 . . . . 2C **20** (2C **74**)
Pitt St. W8 . . . . 3C **72**
Pixley St. E14 . . . . 5B **66**
Place, The 2C **6**
(off Duke's Rd.)
Plaisterers Highwalk
EC2 . . . . 1F **17**
(off Noble St.)
PLAISTOW 1D **69**
Plaistow Gro. E15 . . . . 5B **54**
Plaistow Pk. Rd. E13 . . 1D **69**
Plaistow Rd. E15 . . . . . 5B **54**

Plaistow Wharf E16 . . . . 3C **82**
Plane St. SE26 . . . . 3D **121**
Planetree Cl. *W6* 5F **71**
(off Brook Grn.)
Plane Tree Ho. *SE8* 2A **94**
(off Etta St.)
Plane Tree Wlk.
SE19 . . . . .5A **120**
Plantain Gdns. *E11* 5F **39**
(off Hollydown Way,
not continuous)
Plantain Pl.
SE1 . . . . .3B **26** (3F **77**)
Plantation, The SE3 . . . .5C **96**
Plantation Pl. EC3 . . . .4D **19**
Plantation Wharf
SW11 . . . . .1E **101**
Plasel Ct. *E13* 5D **55**
(off Pawsey Cl.)
PLASHET 3F **55**
Plashet Gro. E6 . . . . . . .5E **55**
Plashet Rd. E13 . . . . . .5C **54**
Plassy Rd. SE6 . . . . . . .5D **109**
Plate Ho. *E14* 1D **95**
(off Burrells Wharf Sq.)
Platina St. EC2 . . . . . . .3C **10**
Plato Rd. SW2 . . . . . . .2A **104**
Platt, The SW15 . . . . . .1F **99**
Platt's La. NW3 . . . . . . .1C **44**
Platt St. NW1 . . . . .1F **61**
Plaxton Ct. E11 . . . . . . .5B **40**
Playfair Ho. *E14* 5C **66**
(off Saracen St.)
Playfair Mans. *W14* 2A **86**
(off Queen's Club Gdns.)
Playfair St. W6 . . . . . . .1E **85**
Playfield Cres. SE22 . . . .3B **106**
Playford Rd. N4 . . . . . . .4B **34**
(not continuous)
Playgreen Way SE6 . . . .3C **122**
Playhouse Ct. *SE1* 3F **25**
(off Southwark Bri. Rd.)
Playhouse Theatre 1E **23**
(off Northumberland Av.)
Playhouse Yd.
EC4 . . . . . . .3D **17** (5D **63**)
Playscape Pro Racing
Karting Track 5B **14**
Plaza Cinema 5B **14**
(off Regent St.)
Plaza Pde. NW6 . . . . . . .1D **59**
Plaza Shop. Cen., The
W1 . . . . .2A **14** (5E **61**)
Pleasance, The
SW15 . . . . .2D **99**
Pleasance Rd. SW15 . . . .3D **99**
Pleasance Theatre 3A **48**
(off Carpenters M.)
Pleasant Pl. N1 . . . . . . .4D **49**
Pleasant Row NW1 . . . . .5D **47**
Plender Pl. *NW1* 5E **47**
(off Plender St.)
Plender St. NW1 . . . . . . .5E **47**
Pleshey Rd. N7 . . . . . . .1F **47**
Plevna Cres. N15 . . . . . .1A **36**
Plevna St. E14 . . . . . . .4E **81**
Pleydell Av. W6 . . . . . . .5B **70**
Pleydell Ct. *EC4* 3C **16**
(off Lombard La.)
Pleydell Est. EC1 . . . . . .2A **10**

Pleydell St. EC4 . . . . . . .3C **16**
Plimsoll Cl. E14 . . . . . . .5D **67**
Plimsoll Rd. N4 . . . . . . .5C **34**
Plough Ct.
EC3 . . . . . . .4C **18** (1F **77**)
Plough La. SE22 . . . . . . .4B **106**
SW17 . . . . .5D **115**
SW19 . . . . .5D **115**
Ploughmans Cl.
NW1 . . . . .5F **47**
Plough M. SW11 . . . . . . .2F **101**
Plough Pl.
EC4 . . . . . . .2C **16** (5C **62**)
Plough Rd. SW11 . . . . . . .1F **101**
Plough St. E1 . . . . .5B **64**
Plough Ter. SW11 . . . . . .2F **101**
Plough Way SE16 . . . . . .5F **79**
Plough Yd.
EC2 . . . . . . .4E **11** (3A **64**)
Plover Ho. SW9 . . . . . . .3C **90**
(off Brixton Rd.)
Plover Way SE16 . . . . . .4A **80**
Plowden Bldgs. EC4 . . . .4B **16**
Plumber's Row E1 . . . . . .4C **64**
Plumbridge St. SE10 . . . .4E **95**
Plume Ho. *SE10* 2D **95**
(off Creek Rd.)
Plummer Rd. SW4 . . . . . .5F **103**
Plumtree Ct.
EC4 . . . . . . .2D **17** (5D **63**)
Plymouth Ho. *SE10* 4D **95**
(off Devonshire St.)
Plymouth Rd. E16 . . . . . .4C **68**
Plymouth Wharf E14 . . . .5F **81**
Plympton Av. NW6 . . . . . .4B **44**
Plympton Pl. NW8 . . . . . .3A **60**
Plympton Rd. NW6 . . . . . .4B **44**
Plympton St. NW8 . . . . . .3A **60**
Pocklington Cl. *W12* 4C **70**
(off Ashchurch Pk. Vs.)
Pocklington Ct.
SW15 . . . . .1C **112**
Pocklington Lodge
W12 . . . . .4C **70**
Pocock St.
SE1 . . . . . . .3D **25** (3D **77**)
Podmore Rd. SW18 . . . . .2E **101**
Poet's Rd. N5 . . . . .2F **49**
Point, The *W2* 5F **59**
(off Nth. Wharf Rd.)
Point Cl. SE10 . . . . .4E **95**
Pointers Cl. E14 . . . . . . .1D **95**
Point Hill SE10 . . . . . . .3E **95**
Point Pleasant
SW18 . . . . .2C **100**
Point Ter. *E7* 2D **55**
(off Claremont Rd.)
Point W. SW7 . . . . .5D **73**
Poland St.
W1 . . . . .3A **14** (5E **61**)
Polebrook Rd. SE3 . . . . .1E **111**
Polecroft La. SE6 . . . . . .2B **122**
Polesworth Ho. *W2* 4C **58**
(off Alfred Rd.)
Pollard Cl. E16 . . . . .1C **82**
N7 . . . . .1B **48**
Pollard Ho. *N1* 1F **7**
(off Northdown St.)
Pollard Row E2 . . . . .2C **64**
Pollard St. E2 . . . . .2C **64**

Pollen St.
W1 . . . . .3F **13** (5E **61**)
Pollitt Dr. NW8 . . . . .3F **59**
Pollock Ho. *W10* 3A **58**
(off Kensal Rd.)
Pollock's Toy Mus.
. . . . .5A **6** (4E **61**)
Polperro M. SE11 . . . . . .5D **77**
Polsted Rd. SE6 . . . . . . .5B **108**
Polworth Rd. SW16 . . . . .5A **118**
Polygon, The NW8 . . . . . .5F **45**
(off Avenue Rd.)
SW4 . . . . .2E **103**
Polygon Rd.
NW1 . . . . .1B **6** (1F **61**)
Pomell Way
E1 . . . . .2F **19** (5B **64**)
Pomeroy Ho. E2 . . . . . . .1F **65**
(off St James's Av.)
W11 . . . . .5A **58**
(off Lancaster Rd.)
Pomeroy St. SE14 . . . . . .3E **93**
Pomfret Rd. SE5 . . . . . . .1D **105**
Pomoja La. N19 . . . . . . .4A **34**
Pomona Ho. *SE8* 5A **80**
(off Evelyn St.)
Pond Cl. SE3 . . . . .5C **96**
Pond Cotts. SE21 . . . . . .1A **120**
Ponder St. N7 . . . . .4B **48**
(not continuous)
Pond Farm Est. E5 . . . . .5E **37**
Pondfield Ho. SE27 . . . . .5E **119**
Pond Ho. SW3 . . . . .5A **74**
Pond Mead SE21 . . . . . .4F **105**
Pond Pl. SW3 . . . . .5A **74**
Pond Rd. E15 . . . . .1A **68**
SE3 . . . . .5B **96**
Pond Sq. N6 . . . . .3C **32**
Pond St. NW3 . . . . .2A **46**
Ponler St. E1 . . . . .5D **65**
Ponsard Rd. NW10 . . . . .2D **57**
Ponsford St. E9 . . . . . . .3E **51**
Ponsonby Ho. E2 . . . . . .1E **65**
(off Bishop's Way)
Ponsonby Pl. SW1 . . . . . .1F **89**
Ponsonby Rd. SW15 . . . .5D **99**
Ponsonby Ter. SW1 . . . . .1F **89**
Pontefract Rd.
BR1: Brom 5B **124**
Ponton Rd. SW8 . . . . . . .2E **89**
Pont St. SW1 . . . .5A **20** (4B **74**)
Pont St. M.
SW1 . . . . . . .5A **20** (4B **74**)
Pontypool Pl.
SE1 . . . . . . .3D **25** (3D **77**)
Pool Cl. BR3: Beck 5C **122**
Pool Ct. SE6 . . . . .2C **122**
Poole Ct. *N1* 4A **50**
(off St Peter's Way)
Poole Ho. *SE11* 4C **76**
(off Lambeth Wlk.)
Poole Rd. E9 . . . . .3F **51**
Pooles Bldgs. WC1 . . . . .4B **8**
Pooles La. SW10 . . . . . . .3E **87**
Pooles Pk. N4 . . . . .4C **34**
Poole St. N1 . . . . .5F **49**
Pooley Ho. E1 . . . . .2F **65**
Pool Ho. NW8 . . . . .4F **59**
(off Penfold St.)
Poolmans St. SE16 . . . . .3F **79**

Poonah St. E1 . . . . 5E 65
Pope Ho. SE5 . . . . 3F 91
(off Elmington Est.)
SE16 . . . . 5D 79
(off Manor Est.)
Pope's Head All.
EC3 . . . . 3C 18 (5F 63)
Pope's Rd. SW9 . . . . . . 1C 104
Pope St. SE1 . . . 4E 27 (3A 78)
Popham Rd. N1 . . . . 5E 49
Popham St. N1 . . . . 5D 49
(not continuous)
POPLAR 1D 81
Poplar Bath St. E14 . . . 5D 67
Poplar Bus. Pk. E14 . . . 1E 81
Poplar Cl. E9 . . . . 2B 52
Poplar Ct. SW19 . . . . . . 5C 114
Poplar Gro. W6 . . . . 3E 71
Poplar High St. E14 . . . 1D 81
Poplar Ho. SE4 . . . . 2B 108
(off Wickham Rd.)
SE16 . . . . 3F 79
(off Woodland Cres.)
Poplar M. W12 . . . . 2E 71
Poplar Pl. W2 . . . . 1D 73
Poplar Rd. E12 . . . . 4F 41
SE24 . . . . 2E 105
Poplars Av. NW2 . . . . . . 3E 43
Poplars Rd. E17 . . . . . . 1D 39
Poplar Wlk. SE24 . . . . . 1E 105
(not continuous)
Poppins Ct.
EC4 . . . . 3D 17 (5D 63)
Poppleton Rd. E11 . . . . 1A 40
Porchester Cl. SE5 . . . 2E 105
Porchester Ct. W2 . . . 1D 73
(off Porchester Gdns.)
Porchester Gdns.
W2 . . . . 1D 73
Porchester Gdns. M.
W2 . . . . 5D 59
Porchester Ga. W2 . . . 1D 73
*(off Bayswater Rd.,
not continuous)*
Porchester Ho. E1 . . . 5D 65
(off Philpot St.)
Porchester Leisure Cen.
. . . . 5D 59
Porchester Mead
BR3: Beck. 5D 123
Porchester M. W2 . . . . 5D 59
Porchester Pl. W2 . . . . 5A 60
Porchester Rd. W2 . . . 5D 59
Porchester Sq. W2 . . . 5D 59
Porchester Ter. W2 . . . 1E 73
Porchester Ter. Nth.
W2 . . . . 5D 59
Porden Rd. SW2 . . . . . 2B 104
Porlock Ho. SE26 . . . 3C 120
Porlock St.
SE1 . . . . 3C 26 (3F 77)
Porson St. SE13 . . . . . 1D 109
Portal Cl. SE27 . . . . . . 3C 118
Portal Way W3 . . . . 4A 56
Portbury Cl. SE15 . . . . 4C 92
Port Cres. E13 . . . . 3D 69
Portcullis Ho. SW1 . . . 4D 23
Portelet Ho. N1 . . . . . . 5A 50
(off De Beauvoir Est.)
Portelet Rd. E1 . . . . . . 2F 65

Porten Ho's. W14 . . . . . 4A 72
(off Portland Rd.)
Porten Rd. W14 . . . . . . 4A 72
Porters Lodge, The
SW10 . . . . 3E 87
(off Coleridge Gdns.)
Porter Sq. N19 . . . . 3A 34
Porter St.
SE1 . . . . 1A 26 (2E 77)
W1 . . . . 5A 4 (4B 60)
Porters Wlk. E1 . . . . . . 1D 79
(off Balkan Wlk.)
Porteus Rd. W2 . . . . . . 4E 59
Portgate Cl. W9 . . . . . . 3B 58
Porthcawe Rd.
SE26 . . . . 4A 122
Port Ho. E14 . . . . 1D 95
(off Burrells Wharf Sq.)
Portia Ct. SE11 . . . . . . 1D 91
(off Opal St.)
Portia Way E3 . . . . 3B 66
Porticos, The
SW3 . . . . 2F 87
(off King's Rd.)
Portinscale Rd.
SW15 . . . . 3A 100
Portland Av. N16 . . . . . 2B 36
Portland Cl. N1 . . . . . . 4A 50
(off St Peter's Way)
SE1 . . . . 5B 26
(off Gt. Dover St.)
SE14 . . . . 2A 94
(off Whitcher Cl.)
Portland Cres. SE9 . . . 2F 125
Portland Gdns. N4 . . . 1D 35
Portland Gro. SW8 . . . 4B 90
Portland Ho. SW1 . . . . 5F 21
Portland M.
W1 . . . . 3A 14 (5E 61)
Portland Pl.
W1 . . . . 4D 5 (3D 61)
Portland Ri. N4 . . . . . . 3D 35
(not continuous)
Portland Rd.
BR1: Brom 4E 125
SE9 . . . . 2F 125
W11 . . . . 1A 72
Portland Sq. E1 . . . . . . 2D 79
Portland Wlk. SE17 . . . 2F 91
Portman Av. SW14 . . . 1A 98
Portman Cl.
W1 . . . . 2A 12 (5B 60)
Portman Ga. NW1 . . . . 3A 60
Portman Mans. W1 . . . 5A 4
(off Chiltern St.)
Portman M. Sth.
W1 . . . . 3B 12 (5C 60)
Portman Pl. E2 . . . . . . 2E 65
Portman Sq.
W1 . . . . 2B 12 (5C 60)
Portman St.
W1 . . . . 3B 12 (5C 60)
Portman Towers
W1 . . . . 2A 12 (5B 60)
Port Meers Cl. E17 . . . 1B 38
Portnall Rd. W9 . . . . . . 1B 58
Portobello Ct. Est.
W11 . . . . 5B 58
Portobello M. W11 . . . . 1C 72

Portobello Rd. W10 . . . 4A 58
W11 . . . . 5B 58
Portobello Road Market
. . . . 4A 58
Portpool La.
EC1 . . . . 5B 8 (4C 62)
Portree St. E14 . . . . . . 5F 67
Portsdown Av. NW11 . . 1B 30
Portsdown M. NW11 . . 1B 30
Portsea Hall W2 . . . . . 5B 60
(off Portsea Pl.)
Portsea M. W2 . . . . . . 5A 60
(off Portsea Pl.)
Portsea Pl. W2 . . . . . . 5A 60
Portslade Rd. SW8 . . . 5E 89
Portsmouth M. E16 . . . 2D 83
Portsmouth St. SW15 . . 5D 99
Portsmouth St.
WC2 . . . . 3F 15 (5B 62)
Portsoken St.
E1 . . . . 4F 19 (1B 78)
Portswood Pl. SW15 . . 4B 98
Portugal St.
WC2 . . . . 3F 15 (5B 62)
Portway E15 . . . . 5B 54
Portway Gdns. SE18 . . 3F 97
Pory Ho. SE11 . . . . . . 5B 76
(off Lambeth Wlk.)
Poseidon Ct. E14 . . . . 5C 80
(off Homer Dr.)
Postern, The EC2 . . . . 1A 18
Post Office App. E7 . . . 2D 55
Post Office Ct. EC3 . . . 3C 18
(off Barbican)
Post Office Way SW8 . . 3F 89
Potier St.
SE1 . . . . 5C 26 (4F 77)
Potterne Cl. SW19 . . . 5F 99
Potters Flds.
SE1 . . . . 2E 27 (2A 78)
Potter's La. SW16 . . . . 5F 117
Potters Lodge E14 . . . 1E 95
(off Manchester Rd.)
Potters Rd. SW6 . . . . . 5E 87
Pottery La. W11 . . . . . . 2A 72
Pottery St. SE16 . . . . . 3D 79
Pott St. E2 . . . . 2D 65
Poulton Cl. E8 . . . . 3D 51
Poultry EC2 . . . 3B 18 (5F 63)
Pound La. NW10 . . . . . 3C 42
Pound Pk. Rd. SE7 . . . 5F 83
Pountney Rd. SW11 . . 1C 102
Povey Ho. SE17 . . . . . 5A 78
(off Tatum St.)
Powell Ho. W2 . . . . . . 5D 59
(off Gloucester Ter.)
Powell Rd. E5 . . . . 5D 37
Powell's Wlk. W4 . . . . 2A 84
Powergate Bus. Pk.
NW10 . . . . 2A 56
Powerleague Soccer Cen.
. . . . 1C 122
Powerscroft Rd. E5 . . . 1E 51
Powis Ct. W11 . . . . . . 5B 58
(off Powis Gdns.)
Powis Gdns. NW11 . . . 2B 30
W11 . . . . 5B 58
Powis M. W11 . . . . 5B 58
Powis Pl. WC1 . . . 4E 7 (3A 62)
Powis Rd. E3 . . . . 2D 67

Powis Sq. W11 . . . . . . 5B 58
(not continuous)
Powis Ter. W11 . . . . . . 5B 58
Powlesland Ct. E1 . . . . . 5A 66
(off White Horse Rd.)
Powlett Ho. NW1 . . . . . 3D 47
(off Powlett Pl.)
Powlett Pl. NW1 . . . . . 4C 46
(not continuous)
Pownall Rd. E8 . . . . . . 5B 50
Powster Rd.
BR1: Brom 5C 124
Poynders Ct. SW4 . . . . 4E 103
Poynders Gdns.
SW4 . . . . 5E 103
Poynders Rd. SW4 . . . . 4E 103
Poynings Rd. N19 . . . . . 5E 33
Poynter Ho. NW8 . . . . . 3F 59
(off Fisherton St.)
W11 . . . . 2F 71
(off Queensdale Cres.)
Poyntz Rd. SW11 . . . . . 5B 88
Poyser St. E2 . . . . 1D 65
Praed M. W2 . . . . 5F 59
Praed St. W2 . . . . 5F 59
Pragel St. E13 . . . . . . 1E 69
Pragnell Rd. SE12 . . . . 2D 125
Prague Pl. SW2 . . . . . 3A 104
Prah Rd. N4 . . . . 4C 34
Prairie St. SW8 . . . . . . 5C 88
Pratt M. NW1 . . . . 5E 47
Pratt St. NW1 . . . . 5E 47
Pratt Wlk. SE11 . . . . . . 5B 76
Prayle Gro. NW2 . . . . . 3F 29
Preachers Ct. EC1 . . . . . 5E 9
(off Charterhouse Sq.)
Prebend Gdns. W4 . . . . 5B 70
W6 . . . . 5B 70
(not continuous)
Prebend Mans. W4 . . . 5B 70
(off Chiswick High Rd.)
Prebend St. N1 . . . . . . 5E 49
Precinct, The N1 . . . . . . 5E 49
Premier Cinema 5C 92
Premier Cnr. W9 . . . . . . 1B 58
Premiere Pl. E14 . . . . . 1C 80
Premier Ho. N1 . . . . . . 4D 49
(off Waterloo Ter.)
Premier Pl. SW15 . . . . 2A 100
Prendergast Rd.
SE3 . . . . 1A 110
Prentice Ct. SW19 . . . . 5B 114
Prentis Rd. SW16 . . . . . 4F 117
Prentiss Ct. SE7 . . . . . 5F 83
Presburg St. E5 . . . . . . 5F 37
Prescot St. E1 . . . . 1B 78
Prescott Ho. SE17 . . . . 2D 91
(off Hillingdon St.)
Prescott Pl. SW4 . . . . . 1F 103
Presentation M.
SW2 . . . . 2B 118
President Dr. E1 . . . . . 2D 79
President Ho.
EC1 . . . . . . 2E 9 (2D 63)
President Quay E1 . . . . 2B 78
(off St Katherine's Way)
President St. EC1 . . . . . 1F 9
Press Ho. NW10 . . . . . 5A 28
Press Rd. NW10 . . . . . 5A 28
Prestage Way E14 . . . . 1E 81

Prestbury Rd. E7 . . . . . 4E 55
Prested Rd. SW11 . . . . 2A 102
Preston Cl. SE1 . . . . . . 5A 78
Preston Dr. E11 . . . . . . 1E 41
Preston Gdns.
NW10 . . . . 3B 42
Preston Ho. SE1 . . . . . 5A 78
(off Preston Cl.)
SE1 . . . . 5F 27
(off Stanworth St.)
Preston Pl. NW2 . . . . . 3C 42
Preston Rd. E11 . . . . . 1A 40
SE19 . . . . 5D 119
Preston's Rd. E14 . . . . . 1E 81
Preston's Rd. E2 . . . . . 1F 65
Prestwich Ter. SW4 . . . 3E 103
Prestwood Ho. SE16 . . . 4D 79
(off Drummond Rd.)
Prestwood St.
N1 . . . . . . 1A 10 (1E 63)
Pretoria Rd. E11 . . . . . 3F 39
E16 . . . . 3B 68
SW16 . . . . 5D 117
Priam Ho. E2 . . . . 1D 65
(off Old Bethnal Grn. Rd.)
Price Cl. SW17 . . . . . . 3B 116
Price Ho. N1 . . . . 5E 49
(off Britannia Row)
Price's Ct. SW11 . . . . . 1F 101
Price's St.
SE1 . . . . . . 2E 25 (2D 77)
Price's Yd. N1 . . . . . . 5B 48
Prichard Ho. N7 . . . . . . 3B 48
Prideaux Pl. W3 . . . . . 1A 70
WC1 . . . . . . 1A 8 (2B 62)
Prideaux Rd. SW9 . . . . 1A 104
Priestfield Rd. SE23 . . . 3A 122
Priestley Cl. N16 . . . . . 2B 36
Priestley Ho. EC1 . . . . . 3A 10
(off Old St.)
Priestley Way NW2 . . . . 3C 28
Priest's Bri. SW14 . . . . 1A 98
Priest's Ct. EC2 . . . . . . 2F 17
(off Foster La.)
Prima Rd. SW9 . . . . . . 3C 90
Prime Meridian Line . . . 3F 95
Primrose Cl. E3 . . . . . . 1C 66
SE6 . . . . 5E 123
Primrose Ct. SW12 . . . 5F 103
Primrose Gdns. NW3 . . 3A 46
PRIMROSE HILL 5C 46
Primrose Hill
EC4 . . . . . . 3C 16 (5C 62)
Primrose Hill Ct.
NW3 . . . . 4B 46
Primrose Hill Rd.
NW3 . . . . 4B 46
Primrose Hill Studios
NW1 . . . . 5C 46
Primrose Mans.
SW11 . . . . 4C 88
Primrose M. NW1 . . . . 4B 46
(off Sharpleshall St.)
SE3 . . . . 3C 96
Primrose Rd. E10 . . . . . 3D 39
Primrose Sq. E9 . . . . . 4E 51
Primrose St.
EC2 . . . . . . 5D 11 (4A 64)
Primrose Wlk. SE14 . . . 3A 94
Primula St. W12 . . . . . 5C 56

Prince Albert Ct.
NW8 . . . . 5B 46
(off Prince Albert Rd.)
Prince Albert Rd.
NW1 . . . . 2A 60
NW8 . . . . 2A 60
Prince Arthur M.
NW3 . . . . 1E 45
Prince Arthur Rd.
NW3 . . . . 2E 45
Prince Charles Cinema . 4C 14
Prince Charles Dr.
NW4 . . . . 2E 29
Prince Charles Rd.
SE3 . . . . 5B 96
Prince Consort Rd.
SW7 . . . . 4E 73
Princedale Rd. W11 . . . 2A 72
Prince Edward Mans.
W2 . . . . 1C 72
(off Moscow Rd.)
Prince Edward Rd.
E9 . . . . 3B 52
Prince Edward Theatre
. . . . 3C 14
(off Old Compton St.)
Prince George Rd.
N16 . . . . 1A 50
Prince Henry Rd. SE7 . . 3F 97
Prince John Rd.
SE9 . . . . 3F 111
Princelet St.
E1 . . . . . . 5F 11 (4B 64)
Prince of Orange La.
SE10 . . . . 3E 95
Prince of Wales Dr.
SW8 . . . . 3D 89
SW11 . . . . 4A 88
Prince of Wales Mans.
SW11 . . . . 4C 88
Prince of Wales Pas.
NW1 . . . . 2F 5
Prince of Wales Rd.
E16 . . . . 5E 69
NW5 . . . . 3C 46
SE3 . . . . 5B 96
Prince of Wales Ter.
W4 . . . . 1A 84
W8 . . . . 3D 73
Prince of Wales Theatre
. . . . 5B 14
(off Coventry St.)
Prince Regent Ct.
NW8 . . . . 1A 60
(off Avenue Rd.)
SE16 . . . . 1A 80
(off Edward Sq.)
Prince Regent La.
E13 . . . . 2D 69
E16 . . . . 2D 69
Prince Regent M.
NW1 . . . . 2F 5
Prince Regents Ga.
NW8 . . . . 3A 60
Princes Arc. SW1 . . . . 1A 22
Princes Cir.
WC2 . . . . . . 2D 15 (5A 62)
Princes Cl. SW4 . . . . . 1E 103

Prince's Ct. SE16 . . . . . 4B 80
  SW3 . . . . 4B 74
  (off Brompton Rd.)
Princes Ct. Bus. Cen.
  E1 . . . . 1D 79
Prince's Gdns. SW7 . . . 4F 73
Prince's Ga. SW7 . . . . . 3F 73
  (not continuous)
Prince's Ga. Ct. SW7 . . 3F 73
Prince's Ga. M.
  SW7 . . . . 4F 73
Princes M. W2 . . . . . . 1D 73
  W6 . . . . 1D 85
  (off Down Pl.)
Princes Pde. NW11 . . . 1A 30
  (off Golders Grn. Rd.)
Princes Pk. Av.
  NW11 . . . . 1A 30
Princes Pl. SW1 . . . . . 1A 22
  W11 . . . . 2A 72
Prince's Ri. SE13 . . . . . 5E 95
Princes Riverside Rd.
  SE16 . . . . 2F 79
Princes Rd. SW14 . . . 1A 98
  SW19 . . . . 5C 114
Princess Alice Ho.
  W10 . . . . 3E 57
Princess Ct. N6 . . . . . . 2E 33
  W1 . . . . 4B 60
  (off Bryanston Pl.)
  W2 . . . . 1D 73
  (off Queensway)
Princess Cres. N4 . . . . 4D 35
Princess Louise Cl.
  W2 . . . . 4F 59
Princess Mary Ho.
  SW1 . . . . 5F 75
  (off Vincent St.)
Princess May Rd.
  N16 . . . . 1B 50
Princess M. NW3 . . . . 2F 45
Princes Sq. W2 . . . . . 1D 73
  (not continuous)
Princess Rd. NW1 . . . 5C 46
  NW6 . . . . 1C 58
Princess St.
  SE1 . . . . . . 5E 25 (4D 77)
Princes St.
  EC2 . . . . . . 3B 18 (5F 63)
  W1 . . . . . . 3E 13 (5D 61)
Princes Ter. E13 . . . . . 5D 55
Prince's Twr. SE16 . . . 3E 79
  (off Elephant La.)
Prince St. SE8 . . . . . . 2B 94
Princes Way SW19 . . . 5F 99
Prince's Yd. W11 . . . . 2A 72
Princethorpe Ho. W2 . . 4D 59
  (off Woodchester Sq.)
Princethorpe Rd.
  SE26 . . . . 4F 121
Princeton Ct. SW15 . . 1F 99
Princeton St.
  WC1 . . . . . . 1F 15 (4B 62)
Principal Sq. E9 . . . . . 2F 51
Pringle Gdns. SW16 . . 4E 117
  (not continuous)
Printers Inn Ct. EC4 . . 5C 62
Printers M. E3 . . . . . . 5A 52
Printer St.
  EC4 . . . . . . 2C 16 (5C 62)

Printing Ho. Yd.
  E2 . . . . 1E 11 (2A 64)
  (off Wallwood St.)
Printon Ho. E14 . . . . . 4B 66
  (off Wallwood St.)
Print Village SE15 . . . 5B 92
Printwork Apartments
  SE1 . . . . 5D 27
  (off Long La.)
Priolo Rd. SE7 . . . . . . 1E 97
Prior Bolton St.
  N1 . . . . 3D 49
Prioress Rd. SE27 . . . 3D 119
Prioress St.
  SE1 . . . . . . 5C 26 (4A 78)
Prior St. SE10 . . . . . . 3E 95
Priory, The SE3 . . . . . 2B 110
Priory Apartments, The
  SE6 . . . . 1D 123
Priory Av. W4 . . . . . . 5A 70
Priory Cl. E6 . . . . 5E 55
  E9 . . . . 2F 51
  EC4 . . . . 3E 17
  (off Pilgrim St.)
  SW8 . . . . 4F 89
Priory Gdns. N6 . . . . . 1D 33
  SW13 . . . . 1B 98
  W4 . . . . 5A 70
Priory Grn. Est. N1 . . . 1B 62
Priory Gro. SW8 . . . . 4A 90
Priory Ho. E1 . . . . 5F 11
  (off Folgate St.)
  EC1 . . . . 3D 9
  (off Sans Wlk.)
  SW1 . . . . 1F 89
  (off Rampayne St.)
Priory La. SW15 . . . . 4A 98
Priory M. SW8 . . . . . 4A 90
Priory Pk. SE3 . . . . . 1B 110
Priory Pk. Rd.
  NW6 . . . . 5B 44
  (not continuous)
Priory Rd. E6 . . . . . . 5F 55
  NW6 . . . . 5D 45
Priory St. E3 . . . . 2D 67
Priory Wlk. SW10 . . . 1E 87
Pritchard Ho. E2 . . . . 1D 65
  (off Ada Pl.)
Pritchard's Rd. E2 . . . 5C 50
Priter Rd. SE16 . . . . . 4C 78
Priter Way SE16 . . . . 4C 78
Probert Rd. SW2 . . . . 3C 104
Probyn Ho. SW1 . . . . 5F 75
  (off Page St.)
Probyn Rd. SW2 . . . . 2D 119
Procter Ho. SE1 . . . . 1C 92
  (off Avondale Sq.)
  SE5 . . . . 3F 91
  (off Picton St.)
Procter St.
  WC1 . . . . . . 1F 15 (4B 62)
Project Pk. E3 . . . . . . 3F 67
Prologis Pk. E16 . . . . 3F 67
Promenade, The
  W4 . . . . 5A 84
Promenade App. Rd.
  W4 . . . . 3A 84
Prospect Cl. SE26 . . . 4D 121
Prospect Cotts.
  SW18 . . . . 2C 100

Prospect Ho. N1 . . . . 1C 62
  (off Donegal St.)
  SE1 . . . . 5D 25
  W10 . . . . 5F 57
  (off Bridge Cl.)
Prospect Pl. E1 . . . . . 2E 79
  (not continuous)
  N7 . . . . 1A 48
  NW2 . . . . 5B 30
  NW3 . . . . 1E 45
  SE8 . . . . 2B 94
  (off Evelyn St.)
  W4 . . . . 1A 84
Prospect Quay
  SW18 . . . . 2C 100
  (off Lightermans Wlk.)
Prospect Rd. NW2 . . . 5B 30
Prospect St. SE16 . . . 4D 79
Prospect Va. SE18 . . . 5F 83
Prospect Wharf E1 . . . 1E 79
Prospero Rd. N19 . . . 3F 33
Protea Cl. E16 . . . . . . 3B 68
Prothero Rd. SW6 . . . 3A 86
Prout Gro. NW10 . . . 1A 42
Prout Rd. E5 . . . . 5D 37
Provence St. N1 . . . . 1E 63
Providence Cl. E9 . . . 5F 51
Providence Ct.
  W1 . . . . . . 4C 12 (1C 74)
Providence Pl. N1 . . . 5D 49
Providence Row N1 . . 1F 7
Providence Row Cl.
  E2 . . . . 2D 65
Providence Sq. SE1 . . 3C 78
Providence Twr.
  SE16 . . . . 3C 78
  (off Bermondsey Wall W.)
Providence Yd. E2 . . . 2C 64
  (off Ezra St.)
Provost Ct. NW3 . . . . 3B 46
  (off Eton Rd.)
Provost Est. N1 . . . . . 1B 10
Provost Rd. NW3 . . . . 4B 46
Provost St.
  N1 . . . . 1B 10 (1F 63)
Prowse Ho. NW1 . . . . 4E 47
Prudent Pas. EC2 . . . 2A 18
Prusom's Island E1 . . 2E 79
  (off Cinnamon St.)
Prusom St. E1 . . . . . . 2D 79
Pryors, The NW3 . . . . 5F 31
Pudding La.
  EC3 . . . . . . 5C 18 (1F 77)
Pudding Mill La. E15 . . 5D 53
Puddle Dock
  EC4 . . . . . . 4E 17 (1D 77)
  (not continuous)
Pugin Cl. N1 . . . . 4C 48
  (off Liverpool Rd.)
Pulborough Rd.
  SW18 . . . . 5B 100
Pulford St. N15 . . . . . 1F 35
Pulham Ho. SW8 . . . . 3B 90
  (off Dorset Rd.)
Pullen's Bldgs. SE17 . 1D 91
  (off Iliffe Cl.)
Pullman Ct. SW2 . . . . 1A 118
Pullman Gdns. SW15 . 4E 99
Pullman M. SE12 . . . 3D 125
Pulross Rd. SW9 . . . . 1B 104

Pulteney Cl. E3........5B **52**
Pulteney Ter. N1.......5B **48**
   (not continuous)
Pulton Ho. SE4........2A **108**
   (off Turnham Rd.)
Pulton Pl. SW6.......3C **86**
Puma Ct. E1....5F **11** (4B **64**)
Pump Ct.
EC4..........3B **16** (5C **62**)
Pump Ho. Cl. SE16......3E **79**
Pump House Gallery, The
.................3C **88**
Pump Ho. M. E1......1C **78**
   (off Hooper St.)
Pump House Steam &
Transport Mus......1A **38**
Pumping Ho. E14......1F **81**
   (off Naval Row)
Pumping Sta. Rd.
W4................3A **84**
Pump La. SE14........1E **93**
Punderson's Gdns.
E2................2D **65**
Purbeck Dr. NW2......4F **29**
Purbeck Ho. SW8......3B **90**
   (off Bolney St.)
Purbrook Est.
SE1........4E **27** (3A **78**)
Purbrook St.
SE1........5E **27** (4A **78**)
Purcell Cres. SW6.....3F **85**
   (not continuous)
Purcell Ho. SW10......2F **87**
   (off Milman's St.)
Purcell Mans. W14.....2A **86**
   (off Queen's Club Gdns.)
Purcell M. NW10......4A **42**
Purcell Room.......1A **24**
   (in South Bank)
Purcell St. N1........1A **64**
Purchese St.
NW1.......1C **6** (1F **61**)
Purdon Ho. SE15......4C **92**
   (off Peckham High St.)
Purdy St. E3.........3D **67**
Purelake M. SE13....1F **109**
   (off Marischal Rd.)
Purley Av. NW2.......4A **30**
Purley Pl. N1.........4D **49**
Purneys Rd. SE9......2F **111**
Purser Ho. SW2......4C **104**
   (off Tulse Hill)
Pursers Cross Rd.
SW6..............4B **86**
   (not continuous)
Purves Rd. NW10......2D **57**
Pusey Ho. E14.......5C **66**
   (off Saracen St.)
Puteaux Ho. E2......1F **65**
   (off Mace St.)
PUTNEY...........2F **99**
Putney Arts Theatre...2F **99**
Putney Bri. SW6......1A **100**
SW15............1A **100**
Putney Bri. App.
SW6............1A **100**
Putney Bri. Rd.
SW15............2A **100**
SW18............2A **100**
Putney Comn. SW15...1E **99**

Putney Exchange Shop. Cen.
SW15............2F **99**
PUTNEY HEATH......4E **99**
Putney Heath SW15...5D **99**
Putney Heath La.
SW15............4F **99**
Putney High St.
SW15............2F **99**
Putney Hill SW15......5F **99**
   (not continuous)
Putney Leisure Cen.....2E **99**
Putney Pk. Av. SW15...2C **98**
Putney Pk. La. SW15...2D **99**
   (not continuous)
PUTNEY VALE......3C **112**
Putney Vale Crematorium
SW15...........2C **112**
Putney Wharf
SW15...........1A **100**
Pylon Trad. Est. E16...3A **68**
Pymers Mead SE21...1E **119**
Pynfolds SE16........3D **79**
Pynnersmead SE24....1E **105**
Pyrford Ho. SW9......2D **105**
Pyrland Rd. N5.......2F **49**
Pyrmont Gro. SE27...3D **119**
Pytchley Rd. SE22....1A **106**

Q

Q Bldg., The E15.......3A **54**
   (off Grove, The)
Quadrangle, The
E15..............3A **54**
SE24............3E **105**
SW6.............3A **86**
SW10............4E **87**
W2..............5A **60**
W12.............5D **57**
   (off Du Cane Rd.)
Quadrangle Cl. SE1...5A **78**
Quadrant, The W10....2F **57**
Quadrant Arc. W1.....5A **14**
Quadrant Gro. NW5...2B **46**
Quadrant Ho. SE1.....1D **25**
Quaggy Wlk. SE3.....2C **110**
Quain Mans. W14.....2A **86**
   (off Queen's Club Gdns.)
Quainton St. NW10...5A **28**
Quaker Ct. E1........4F **11**
   (off Quaker St.)
EC1..............3B **10**
Quakers Pl. E7.......2F **55**
Quaker St. E1...4F **11** (3B **64**)
Quality Ct. WC2......2B **16**
Quantock Gdns. NW2...4F **29**
Quantock Ho. N16.....3B **36**
Quarley Way SE15....3B **92**
Quarrendon St. SW6...5C **86**
Quarry Rd. SW18.....4E **101**
Quarterdeck, The
E14..............3C **80**
Quarter Mile La. E10...1D **53**
Quastel Ho. SE1......4B **26**
   (off Long La.)
Quay Ho. E14........3C **80**
   (off Admirals Way)
Quayside Cotts. E1....2C **78**
   (off Mews St.)

Quayside Ct. SE16.....2F **79**
   (off Abbotshade Rd.)
Quayside Ho. E14......2B **80**
Quay Vw. Apartments
E14.............4C **80**
   (off Arden Cres.)
Quebec M.
W1..........3A **12** (5B **60**)
Quebec Way SE16.....3F **79**
Quebec Way Ind. Est.
SE16............3A **80**
Quebec Wharf E8.....5A **50**
   (off Kingsland Rd.)
E14.............5C **66**
Quedgeley Ct. SE15...2B **92**
   (off Ebley Cl.)
Queeens Ct. E11......2A **40**
Queen Alexandra Mans.
WC1............2D **7**
   (off Bidborough St.)
Queen Alexandra's Ct.
SW19...........5B **114**
Queen Anne Ho. E16...2C **82**
   (off Hardy Av.)
Queen Anne M.
W1........1E **13** (4D **61**)
Queen Anne Rd. E9....3F **51**
Queen Anne's Ct.
SE10............1F **95**
   (off Park Row)
Queen Anne's Gdns.
W4..............4A **70**
Queen Anne's Ga.
SW1........4B **22** (3F **75**)
Queen Anne's Gro.
W4..............4A **70**
Queen Anne St.
W1........2D **13** (5D **61**)
Queen Anne's Wlk.
WC1..............4E **7**
Queen Anne Ter. E1...1D **79**
   (off Sovereign Cl.)
Queenbridge Sports &
Community Cen....4B **50**
Queen Caroline St.
W6..............1E **85**
   (not continuous)
Queen Catherine Ho.
SW6............3D **87**
   (off Wandon Rd.)
Queen Elizabeth Bldgs.
EC4.............4B **16**
Queen Elizabeth Hall
.................1A **24**
Queen Elizabeth Ho.
SW12...........5C **102**
Queen Elizabeth II
Conference Cen.
.........4C **22** (3F **75**)
Queen Elizabeth's Cl.
N16.............4F **35**
Queen Elizabeth's Coll.
SE10............3E **95**
Queen Elizabeth St.
SE1........3E **27** (3A **78**)
Queen Elizabeth's Wlk.
N16.............3F **35**
Queen Elizabeth Wlk.
SW13...........4C **84**
   (not continuous)

Queenhithe
EC4 . . . . 4A **18** (1E **77**)
Queen Isabella Way
EC1 . . . . 2E **17**
(off King Edward St.)
Queen Margaret Flats
E2 . . . . 2D **65**
(off St Jude's Rd.)
Queen Margaret's Gro.
N1 . . . . 2A **50**
Queen Mary Ho. E16 . . . 2D **83**
(off Wesley Av.)
Queen Mary Rd.
SE19 . . . . 5D **119**
Queen Marys Bldgs.
SW1 . . . . 5E **75**
(off Stillington St.)
Queen Mary's Ct.
SE10 . . . . 2F **95**
(off Park Row)
Queen Mother Sports Cen., The
. . . . 5E **75**
(off Vauxhall Bri. Rd.)
Queen of Denmark Ct.
SE16 . . . . 4B **80**
Queensberry M. W.
SW7 . . . . 5F **73**
Queensberry Pl. E12. . . 2F **55**
SW7 . . . . 5F **73**
Queensberry Way
SW7 . . . . 5F **73**
Queensborough M.
W2 . . . . 1E **73**
Queensborough Pas.
W2 . . . . 1E **73**
(off Queensborough M.)
Queensborough Studios
W2 . . . . 1E **73**
(off Queensborough M.)
Queensborough Ter.
W2 . . . . 1D **73**
Queensbridge Ct. E2 . . 5B **50**
(off Queensbridge Rd.)
Queensbridge Rd. E2 . . 3B **50**
E8 . . . . 3B **50**
Queensbury St. N1 . . . . 4E **49**
Queen's Chapel of the Savoy
. . . . 5F **15**
(off Savoy St.)
Queen's Cir. SW8. . . . 3D **89**
Queen's Club Gdns.
W14 . . . . 2A **86**
Queen's Club, The (Tennis)
. . . . 1A **86**
Queens Ct. NW6. . . . . 2D **45**
NW8 . . . . 1F **59**
(off Queen's Ter.)
NW11 . . . . 1B **30**
SE23. . . . . 2D **121**
W2 . . . . 1D **73**
(off Queensway)
Queen's Cres. NW5 . . . 3C **46**
Queenscroft Rd.
SE9 . . . . 3F **111**
Queensdale Cres.
W11 . . . . 2F **71**
Queensdale Pl. W11 . . 2A **72**
Queensdale Rd. W11 . . 2F **71**
Queensdale Wlk.
W11 . . . . 2A **72**

Queensdown Rd. E5 . . 1D **51**
Queens Dr. E10 . . . . . 2C **38**
N4. . . . . 4D **35**
Queen's Elm Pde.
SW3 . . . . 1F **87**
(off Old Chu. St.)
Queen's Elm Sq. SW3. . 1F **87**
Queen's Gallery
. . . . 4F **21** (3D **75**)
Queen's Gdns. NW4 . . 1E **29**
W2 . . . . 1E **73**
Queens Ga. SW7 . . . . 3E **73**
Queens Ga. Gdns.
SW7 . . . . 4E **73**
SW15 . . . . 2D **99**
Queens Ga. M. SW7 . . 4E **73**
Queens Ga. Pl. SW7 . . 4E **73**
Queensgate Pl. NW6 . . 4C **44**
Queens Ga. Pl. M.
SW7 . . . . 4E **73**
Queens Ga. Ter.
SW7 . . . . 4E **73**
Queens Ga. Vs. E9. . . 4A **52**
Queens Gro. NW8 . . . 5F **45**
Queens Gro. Studios
NW8 . . . . 5F **45**
Queen's Head Pas.
EC4. . . . . . . 2F **17** (5E **63**)
Queen's Head St.
N1. . . . . 5D **49**
Queen's Head Yd.
SE1. . . . . 2B **26**
Queen's House, The . . 2F **95**
Queens Ho. SW8 . . . 3A **90**
(off Sth. Lambeth Rd.)
Queen's Ice Bowl 1D **73**
(off Queensway)
Queensland Pl. N7. . . 1C **48**
Queensland Rd. N7 . . 1C **48**
Queen's Mans. W6. . . 5F **71**
(off Brook Grn.)
Queensmead NW8 . . . 5F **45**
Queensmere Cl.
SW19 . . . . 2F **113**
Queensmere Ct.
SW13 . . . . 3B **84**
Queensmere Rd.
SW19 . . . . 2F **113**
Queen's M. W2 . . . . . 1D **73**
(not continuous)
Queensmill Rd.
SW6 . . . . 3F **85**
Queens Pde. NW2 . . . 3E **43**
(off Willesden La.)
NW4 . . . . 1E **29**
(off Queens Rd.)
Queens Pk. Ct. W10. . 2F **57**
Queen's Pk. Rangers FC
. . . . 2D **71**
Queens Pk. School
Sports Cen. 5F **43**
(within school)
Queen Sq.
WC1 . . . . 4E **7** (3A **62**)
Queen Sq. Pl. WC1 . . . 4E **7**
Queen's Quay EC4 . . . 4F **17**
(off Up. Thames St.)
Queens Ride SW13 . . . 1C **98**
SW15 . . . . 1C **98**

Queens Rd. E11 . . . . . 2F **39**
E13. . . . . 5D **55**
E17. . . . . 1B **38**
NW4 . . . . 1E **29**
SE14 . . . . 4E **93**
SE15. . . . . 4D **93**
SW14 . . . . 1A **98**
SW19 . . . . 5C **114**
Queens Rd. W. E13 . . 1C **68**
Queen's Row SE17 . . . 2F **91**
Queens Ter. E1 . . . . . 3E **65**
E13. . . . . 5D **55**
NW8 . . . . 5F **45**
Queen's Theatre
Westminster 4B **14**
(off Shaftesbury Av.)
Queensthorpe Rd.
SE26 . . . . 4F **121**
Queenstown M. SW8. . 5D **89**
Queen St.
EC4 . . . . 4A **18** (1E **77**)
(not continuous)
W1. . . . . 1D **21** (2D **75**)
Queen St. Pl.
EC4 . . . . 4A **18** (1E **77**)
Queensville Rd.
SW12 . . . . 5F **103**
Queen's Wlk. N5 . . . . 2D **49**
SW1 . . . . 2F **21** (2E **75**)
Queen's Wlk., The
SE1 . . . . 1C **26** (2A **78**)
(Morgan's La.)
SE1 . . . . 5C **16** (1C **76**)
(Oxo Tower Wharf)
SE1 . . . . 1A **24** (2B **76**)
(Waterloo Rd.)
Queen's Way NW4 . . . 1E **29**
Queensway W2 . . . . . 5D **59**
Queens Wharf W6 . . . 1E **85**
Queenswood Ct.
SE27 . . . . 4F **119**
SW4 . . . . 3A **104**
Queenswood Gdns.
E11. . . . . 3D **41**
Queens Wood Rd.
N10. . . . . 1D **33**
Queenswood Rd.
SE23 . . . . 3F **121**
Queen's Yd.
WC1 . . . . 4A **6** (4E **61**)
Queen Victoria Memorial
. . . . 4F **21** (3E **75**)
Queen Victoria Seaman's Rest
E14. . . . . 5D **67**
(off E. India Dock Rd.)
Queen Victoria St.
EC4 . . . . 4D **17** (1D **77**)
Queen Victoria Ter.
E1 . . . . 1D **79**
(off Sovereign Cl.)
Quemerford Rd. N7 . . 2B **48**
Quendon Ho. W10 . . . 3E **57**
(off Sutton Way)
Quenington Ct. SE15 . . 2B **92**
Quentin Ho. SE1. . . . . 4C **24**
(off Gray St., not continuous)
Quentin Pl. SE13 . . . . 1A **110**
Quentin Rd. SE13. . . . 1A **110**
Quernmore Cl.
BR1: Brom 5C **124**

Quernmore Rd.
BR1: Brom 5C 124
N4 . . . . 1C 34
Querrin St. SW6 . . . . 5E 87
Quested Ct. E8 . . . . 2D 51
(off Brett Rd.)
Quex M. NW6 . . . . 5C 44
Quex Rd. NW6 . . . . 5C 44
Quick Rd. W4 . . . . 1A 84
Quick St. N1 . . . . 1D 63
Quick St. M. N1 . . . . 1D 63
Quickswood NW3 . . . . . . 4A 46
Quill La. SW15 . . . . 2F 99
Quill St. N4 . . . . 5C 34
Quilp St.
SE1 . . . . 3F 25 (3E 77)
(not continuous)
Quilter Ho. W10 . . . . 2B 58
(off Dart St.)
Quilter St. E2 . . . . 2C 64
Quilting Ct. SE16 . . . . . . 3F 79
(off Garter Way)
Quince Ho. SE13 . . . . . . 5D 95
(off Quince Rd.)
Quinton Ho. SW8 . . . . . . 3A 90
(off Wyvil Rd.)
Quinton St. SW18 . . . . . . 2E 115
Quixley St. E14 . . . . 1F 81
Quorn Rd. SE22 . . . . 2A 106

R

Rabbit Row W8 . . . . 2C 72
Raby St. E14 . . . . 5A 66
Raceway, The (Go-Kart Track)
. . . . 5A 48
Racine SE5 . . . . 4A 92
(off Peckham Rd.)
Rackham M. SW16 . . . . . 5E 117
Rackstraw Ho. NW3 . . . . 4B 46
Racton Rd. SW6 . . . . 2C 86
RADA 5B 6
(off Chenies St.)
Radbourne Cl. E5 . . . . . . 1F 51
Radbourne Rd.
SW12 . . . . 5E 103
Radcliffe Av. NW10 . . . . 1C 56
Radcliffe Ho. SE16 . . . . . 5D 79
(off Anchor St.)
Radcliffe Path SW8 . . . . 5D 89
Radcliffe Rd.
SE1 . . . . 5E 27 (4A 78)
Radcliffe Sq. SW15 . . . . . 4F 99
Radcot Point SE23 . . . . . 3F 121
Radcot St. SE11 . . . . . . 1C 90
Raddington Rd. W10 . . . . 4A 58
Radford Est. NW10 . . . . . 2A 56
Radford Ho. E14 . . . . 4D 67
(off St Leonard's Rd.)
N7 . . . . 2B 48
Radford Rd. SE13 . . . . . 4E 109
Radipole Rd. SW6 . . . . . 4B 86
Radland Rd. E16 . . . . . . 5B 68
Radlet Av. SE26 . . . . 3D 121
Radlett Cl. E7 . . . . 3B 54
Radlett Pl. NW8 . . . . 5A 46
Radley Ct. SE16 . . . . 3F 79
Radley Ho. NW1 . . . . 3A 4
(off Gloucester Pl.)

Radley M. W8 . . . . 4C 72
Radley Sq. E5 . . . . 4E 37
Radley Ter. E16 . . . . 4B 68
(off Hermit Rd.)
Radlix Rd. E10 . . . . 3C 38
Radnor M. W2 . . . . 5F 59
Radnor Pl. W2 . . . . 5A 60
Radnor Rd. NW6 . . . . 5A 44
SE15 . . . . 3C 92
Radnor St.
EC1 . . . . 2A 10 (2E 63)
Radnor Ter. W14 . . . . 5B 72
Radnor Wlk. E14 . . . . 5C 80
(off Barnsdale Av.)
SW3 . . . . 1A 88
Radstock St. SW11 . . . . . 3A 88
(not continuous)
Raeburn Cl. NW11 . . . . . 1E 31
Raeburn St. SW2 . . . . . . 2A 104
Ragged School Mus.
. . . . 4A 66
Raglan Ct. SE12 . . . . . . 3C 110
Raglan Rd. E17 . . . . 1E 39
Raglan St. NW5 . . . . 3D 47
Railey M. NW5 . . . . 2E 47
Railton Rd. SE24 . . . . . . 2C 104
Railway App. N4 . . . . 1C 34
SE1 . . . . 2C 26 (2F 77)
Railway Arches E2 . . . . . 5B 50
(off Laburnum St.)
E2 . . . . 1F 11
(off Geffrye St.)
E7 . . . . 1C 54
(off Winchelsea Rd.)
E8 . . . . 4D 51
(off Mentmore Ter.)
E10 . . . . 2D 39
(off Capworth St.)
E11 . . . . 4A 40
(off Leytonstone High Rd.)
E11 . . . . 3F 39
(off Sidings, The)
E17 . . . . 1C 38
(off Yunus Khan Cl.)
W12 . . . . 3E 71
(off Shepherd's Bush Mkt.)
Railway Av. SE16 . . . . . . 3E 79
(not continuous)
Railway Children Wlk.
BR1: Brom 2C 124
SE12 . . . . 2C 124
Railway Cotts. E15 . . . . . 1A 68
(off Baker's Row)
SW19 . . . . 4D 115
W6 . . . . 3E 71
(off Sulgrave Rd.)
Railway Gro. SE14 . . . . . 3B 94
Railway M. E3 . . . . 2C 66
(off Wellington Way)
W11 . . . . 5A 58
Railway Ri. SE22 . . . . . . 2A 106
Railway Side SW13 . . . . 1A 98
(not continuous)
Railway St. N1 . . . . 1A 62
Railway Ter. SE13 . . . . . 3D 109
Rainbow Av. E14 . . . . . . 1D 95
Rainbow St. SE14 . . . . . 2A 94
(off Chipley St.)
Rainbow Quay SE16 . . . . 4A 80
(not continuous)

Rainbow St. SE5 . . . . . . 3A 92
Rainbow Theatre 4C 34
Raines Est. Ct. N16 . . . . 4B 36
Raine St. E1 . . . . 2D 79
Rainham Cl. SW11 . . . . . 4A 102
Rainham Ho. NW1 . . . . . 5E 47
(off Bayham Pl.)
Rainham Rd. NW10 . . . . . 2E 57
Rainhill Way E3 . . . . 2C 66
(not continuous)
Rainsborough Av.
SE8 . . . . 5A 80
Rainsford St. W2 . . . . . . 5A 60
Rainton Rd. SE7 . . . . . . 1C 96
Rainville Rd. W6 . . . . . . 2E 85
Raleana Rd. E14 . . . . . . 2E 81
Raleigh Ct. SE16 . . . . . . 2F 79
(off Clarence M.)
W12 . . . . 3E 71
(off Scott's Rd.)
Raleigh Gdns. SW2 . . . . 4B 104
Raleigh Ho. E14 . . . . 3D 81
(off Admirals Way)
SW1 . . . . 2F 89
(off Dolphin Sq.)
Raleigh M. N1 . . . . 5D 49
(off Packington St.)
Raleigh St. N1 . . . . 5D 49
Ralph Brook Ct. N1 . . . . 1C 10
(off Chart St.)
Ralph Ct. W2 . . . . 5D 59
(off Queensway)
Ralston St. SW3 . . . . 1B 88
Ramac Ind. Est. SE7 . . . . 5D 83
Ramac Way SE7 . . . . . . 5D 83
Ramar Ho. E1 . . . . 4C 64
(off Hanbury St.)
Rambler Cl. SW16 . . . . . 4E 117
Rame Cl. SW17 . . . . 5C 116
Ramilles Cl. SW2 . . . . . . 4A 104
Ramilles Pl.
W1 . . . . 3F 13 (5E 61)
Ramilles Rd. W4 . . . . . . 5A 70
Ramilles St.
W1 . . . . 3F 13 (5E 61)
Rampart St. E1 . . . . 5D 65
Rampayne St. SW1 . . . . . 1F 89
Ram Pl. E9 . . . . 3E 51
Ramsay M. NW8 . . . . 1A 60
(off Townshend Est.)
Ramsay M. SW3 . . . . 2A 88
Ramsay Rd. E7 . . . . 1A 54
Ramsdale Rd.
SW17 . . . . 5C 116
Ramsden Rd.
SW12 . . . . 4C 102
Ramsey Cl. NW9 . . . . . . 1B 28
Ramsey Ho. SW9 . . . . . . 3C 90
Ramsey St. E2 . . . . 3C 64
Ramsey Wlk. N1 . . . . 3F 49
(off Handa Wlk.)
Ramsfort Ho. SE16 . . . . . 5D 79
(off Camilla Rd.)
Ramsgate Cl. E16 . . . . . . 2D 83
Ramsgate St. E8 . . . . . . 3B 50
Ram St. SW18 . . . . 3D 101
Rancliffe Gdns.
SE9 . . . . 2F 111
Randall Av. NW2 . . . . . . 4A 28
Randall Cl. SW11 . . . . . . 4A 88

Randall Pl. SE10 . . . . . 3E **95**
Randall Rd. SE11 . . . . . 1B **90**
Randall Row SE11 . . . . . 5B **76**
Randalls Rents *SE16* . . . 4B **80**
(off Gulliver St.)
Randell's Rd. N1 . . . . . . 5A **48**
(not continuous)
Randisbourne Gdns.
SE6. . . . . 3D **123**
Randlesdown Rd.
SE6. . . . . 4C **122**
(not continuous)
Randolph App. E16. . . . . 5E **69**
Randolph Av. W9 . . . . . . 1D **59**
Randolph Cres. W9 . . . . 3E **59**
Randolph Gdns.
NW6 . . . . 1D **59**
Randolph M. W9 . . . . . . 3E **59**
Randolph Rd. E17 . . . . . 1D **39**
W9 . . . . 3E **59**
Randolph St. NW1 . . . . . 4E **47**
Ranelagh Av. SW6 . . . . . 1B **100**
SW13 . . . . 5C **84**
Ranelagh Bri. W2 . . . . . 4D **59**
Ranelagh Gdns.
SW6 . . . . 1A **100**
(not continuous)
W6 . . . . 5B **70**
Ranelagh Gdns. Mans.
SW6 . . . . 1A **100**
(off Ranelagh Gdns.)
Ranelagh Gro.
SW1 . . . . 1C **88**
Ranelagh Ho. *SW3* . . . 1B **88**
(off Elystan Pl.)
Ranelagh Rd. E11 . . . . . 1A **54**
E15 . . . . 1A **68**
NW10 . . . . 1B **56**
SW1 . . . . 1E **89**
Rangbourne Ho. N7 . . . . 2A **48**
Rangefield Rd.
BR1: Brom 5A **124**
Rangemoor Rd. N15 . . . . 1B **36**
Rangers House 4F **95**
Rangers Sq. SE10 . . . . . 4F **95**
Rangoon St. EC3 . . . . . . 3F **19**
Rankine Ho. *SE1* 5F **25**
(off Bath Ter.)
Ranmere St. SW12 . . . . 1D **117**
Rannoch Rd. W6 . . . . . . 2E **85**
Rannock Av. NW9 . . . . . 2A **28**
Ransome's Dock Bus. Cen.
SW11 . . . . 3A **88**
Ransom Rd. SE7 . . . . . . 5E **83**
Ranston St. NW1 . . . . . . 4A **60**
Ranulf Rd. NW2 . . . . . . 1B **44**
Ranwell Cl. E3 . . . . 5B **52**
Raphael Ct. *SE16* 1D **93**
(off Stubbs Dr.)
Raphael St. SW7 . . . . . . 3B **74**
Rapley Ho. *E2* 2C **64**
(off Turin St.)
Raquel Ct. *SE1* 3D **27**
(off Snowfields)
Rashleigh Ct. SW8. . . . . 5D **89**
Rashleigh Ho. *WC1* . . . 2D **7**
(off Thanet St.)
Rastell Av. SW2 . . . . . . 2F **117**
RATCLIFF 4A **66**
Ratcliffe Cl. SE12. . . . . . 5C **110**

Ratcliffe Ct. *SE1* 4A **26**
(off Gt. Dover St.)
Ratcliffe Cross St. E1. . . 5F **65**
Ratcliffe Ho. E14 . . . . . . 5A **66**
Ratcliffe La. E14 . . . . . . 5A **66**
Ratcliffe Orchard E1. . . . 1F **79**
Ratcliff Rd. E7 . . . . 2E **55**
Rathbone Ho. *E16* 5B **68**
(off Rathbone St.)
NW6 . . . . 5C **44**
Rathbone Mkt. E16 . . . . 4B **68**
Rathbone Pl.
W1 . . . . 1B **14** (4F **61**)
Rathbone St. E16. . . . . . 5B **68**
W1 . . . . 1A **14** (4E **61**)
Rathcoole Gdns. N8. . . . 1B **34**
Rathfern Rd. SE6. . . . . . 1B **122**
Rathgar Rd. SW9 . . . . . 1D **105**
Rathmell Dr. SW4 . . . . . 4F **103**
Rathmore Rd. SE7 . . . . . 1D **97**
Rattray Ct. SE6. . . . . . . 2B **124**
Rattray Rd. SW2 . . . . . . 2C **104**
Raul Rd. SE15 . . . . 5C **92**
Raveley St. NW5 . . . . . . 1E **47**
(not continuous)
Ravenet St. SW11 . . . . . 4D **89**
(not continuous)
Ravenfield Rd.
SW17 . . . . 3B **116**
Ravenhill Rd. E13 . . . . . 1E **69**
Raven Ho. *SE16* 5F **79**
(off Tawny Way)
Ravenna Rd. SW15 . . . . 3F **99**
Raven Row E1 . . . . 4D **65**
(not continuous)
Ravensbourne Ct.
SE6. . . . . 5C **108**
Ravensbourne Ho.
BR1: Brom 5F **123**
NW8 . . . . 4A **60**
(off Broadley St.)
Ravensbourne Mans.
SE8 . . . . 2C **94**
(off Berthon St.)
Ravensbourne Pk.
SE6. . . . . 5C **108**
Ravensbourne Pk. Cres.
SE6. . . . . 5B **108**
Ravensbourne Pl.
SE13 . . . . 5D **95**
Ravensbourne Rd.
SE6. . . . . 5B **108**
Ravensbury Rd.
SW18 . . . . 2C **114**
Ravensbury Ter.
SW18 . . . . 2D **115**
Ravenscar *NW1* 5E **47**
(off Bayham St.)
Ravenscar Rd.
BR1: Brom 4A **124**
Ravenscourt Av. W6. . . . 5C **70**
Ravenscourt Gdns.
W6 . . . . 5C **70**
Ravenscourt Pk. W6 . . . 4D **71**
Ravenscourt Pk. Mans.
W6 . . . . 4D **71**
(off Paddenswick Rd.)
Ravenscourt Pl. W6. . . . 5D **71**
Ravenscourt Rd. W6 . . . 5D **71**
(not continuous)

Ravenscourt Sq. W6 . . . 4C **70**
Ravenscroft Av.
NW11 . . . . 2B **30**
(not continuous)
Ravenscroft Cl. E16. . . . 4C **68**
Ravenscroft Rd. E16 . . . 4C **68**
Ravenscroft St. E2. . . . . 1B **64**
Ravensdale Mans.
N8. . . . . 1A **34**
(off Haringey Pk.)
Ravensdale Rd. N16 . . . 2B **36**
Ravensdon St. SE11 . . . 1C **90**
Ravenshaw St. NW6 . . . 2B **44**
Ravenslea Rd.
SW12 . . . . 5B **102**
Ravensleigh Gdns.
BR1: Brom 5D **125**
Ravensmede Way
W4 . . . . 5B **70**
Ravens M. SE12. . . . . . . 3C **110**
Ravenstone SE17 . . . . . 1A **92**
Ravenstone Rd. NW9. . . 1B **28**
Ravenstone St.
SW12 . . . . 1C **116**
Ravens Way SE12 . . . . . 3C **110**
Ravenswood Rd.
SW12 . . . . 5D **103**
Ravensworth Ct.
SW6 . . . . 3C **86**
(off Fulham Rd.)
Ravensworth Rd.
NW10 . . . . 2D **57**
Ravent Rd. SE11 . . . . . . 5B **76**
Raven Wharf *SE1* 3F **27**
(off Lafone St.)
Ravey St.
EC2 . . . . 3D **11** (3A **64**)
Rav Pinter Cl. N16. . . . . 2A **36**
Rawalpindi Ho. E16. . . . 3B **68**
Rawchester Cl.
SW18 . . . . 1B **114**
Rawlings St. SW3 . . . . . 5B **74**
Rawlinson Ct. NW2 . . . . 2E **29**
Rawlinson Ho. *SE13*. . . 2F **109**
(off Mercator Rd.)
Rawlinson Point *E16* . . 4B **68**
(off Fox Rd.)
Rawreth Wlk. N1 . . . . . . 5E **49**
(off Basire St.)
Rawson St. SW11 . . . . . 4C **88**
(not continuous)
Rawstone Wlk. E13 . . . . 1C **68**
Rawstorne Pl.
EC1 . . . . 1D **9** (2D **63**)
Rawstorne St.
EC1 . . . . 1D **9** (2D **63**)
Rayburne Ct. W14 . . . . . 4A **72**
Raydon St. N19 . . . . . . 4D **33**
Rayford Av. SE12 . . . . . 5B **110**
Ray Gunter Ho. *SE17*. . 1D **91**
(off Marsland Cl.)
Ray Ho. *N1*. 5A **50**
(off Colville Est.)
Rayleigh Rd. E16. . . . . . 2D **83**
Raymede Towers
W10. . . . . 4F **57**
(off Treverton St.)
Raymond Bldgs.
WC1. . . . . 5A **8** (4B **62**)

Raymond Cl. SE26 . . . . 5E **121**
Raymond Revuebar . . . 4B **14**
  (off Walkers Ct.)
Raymond Rd. E13. . . . . 5E **55**
SW19 . . . . 5A **114**
Raymouth Ho. SE16 . . . 5E **79**
  (off Raymouth Rd.)
Raymouth Rd. SE16. . . 5D **79**
Raynald Ho. SW16. . . . 3A **118**
Rayne Ho. *W9* 3D **59**
  (off Delaware Rd.)
Rayner Ct. *W12* 3E **71**
  (off Bamborough Gdns.)
Rayners Rd. SW15. . . . 3A **100**
Rayner Towers *E10*. . . 2C **38**
  (off Albany Rd.)
Raynes Av. E11. . . . . . . 2E **41**
Raynham *W2* 5A **60**
  (off Norfolk Cres.)
Raynham Ho. E1. . . . . . 3F **65**
  (off Harpley Sq.)
Raynham Rd. W6. . . . . 5D **71**
Raynor Pl. N1. . . . . 4E **49**
Ray St. EC1 . . . 4C **8** (3C **62**)
Ray St. Bri. EC1. . . . . . . 4C **8**
Ray Wlk. N7 . . . . 4B **34**
Reachview Cl. NW1. . . . 4E **47**
Read Ct. E17 . . . . 1C **38**
Reade Ho. *SE10*. 2F **95**
  (off Trafalgar Gro.)
Reade Wlk. NW10 . . . . 4A **42**
Read Ho. *SE11*. 2C **90**
  (off Clayton St.)
Reading Ho. *SE15* 2C **92**
  (off Friary Est.)
W2 . . . . 4F **59**
  (off Hallfield Est.)
Reading La. E8 . . . . 3D **51**
Reapers Cl. NW1 . . . . . 5F **47**
Reardon Ho. *E1* 2D **79**
  (off Reardon St.)
Reardon Path E1 . . . . . 2D **79**
  (not continuous)
Reardon St. E1. . . . . . . 2D **79**
Reaston St. SE14 . . . . . 3F **93**
Reckitt Rd. W4 . . . . 1A **84**
Record St. SE15. . . . . . 2E **93**
Recovery St. SW17 . . . 5A **116**
Recreation Rd.
  SE26 . . . . 4F **121**
Rector St. N1 . . . . 5E **49**
Rectory Cres. E11. . . . . 1E **41**
  (not continuous)
Rectory Fld. Cres.
  SE7 . . . . 3E **97**
Rectory Gdns. SW4 . . . 1E **103**
Rectory Gro. SW4. . . . . 1E **103**
Rectory La. SW17 . . . . 5C **116**
Rectory Orchard
  SW19 . . . . 4A **114**
Rectory Rd. N16. . . . . . 4B **36**
SW13 . . . . 5C **84**
Rectory Sq. E1 . . . . 4F **65**
Reculver Ho. *SE15*. . . . 2E **93**
  (off Lovelinch Cl.)
Reculver Rd. SE16 . . . . 1F **93**
Red Anchor Cl. SW3. . . 2F **87**
Redan Pl. W2. . . . . 5D **59**
Redan St. W14 . . . . 4F **71**
Redan Ter. SE5. . . . . . . 5D **91**

Redberry Gro. SE26 . . . 3E **121**
Redbourne Ho. E14 . . . 5B **66**
  (off Norbiton Rd.)
Redbourn Ho. *W10*. . . . 3E **57**
  (off Sutton Way)
REDBRIDGE 1F **41**
Redbridge Gdns. SE5. . 3A **92**
Redbridge La. E.
  IG4: Ilf. 1F **41**
Redbridge La. W.
  E11. . . . . 1D **41**
REDBRIDGE RDBT. . . . 1F **41**
Redburn St. SW3 . . . . . 2B **88**
Redcar St. SE5 . . . . 3E **91**
Redcastle Cl. E1. . . . . . 1E **79**
Redchurch St.
  E2. . . . . 3F **11** (3B **64**)
Redcliffe Cl. *SW5* 1D **87**
  (off Old Brompton Rd.)
Redcliffe Ct. E5 . . . . . . 5D **37**
  (off Napoleon Rd.)
Redcliffe Gdns. SW10 . . 1D **87**
Redcliffe M. SW10 . . . . 1D **87**
Redcliffe Pl. SW10 . . . . 2E **87**
Redcliffe Rd. SW10 . . . 1E **87**
Redcliffe Sq. SW10 . . . 1D **87**
Redcliffe St. SW10 . . . . 2D **87**
Redclyffe Rd. E6 . . . . . 5E **55**
Redclyf Ho. *E1* 3E **65**
  (off Cephas St.)
Red Cow La.
  EC1. . . . . 3F **9** (3E **63**)
Redcross Way
  SE1 . . . . 3A **26** (3E **77**)
Redding Ho. SE18 . . . . 4F **83**
Reddins Rd. SE15 . . . . 2C **92**
Redenham Ho. *SW15* . . 5C **98**
  (off Ellisfield Dr.)
Rede Pl. W2. . . . . 5C **58**
Redesdale St. SW3 . . . 2A **88**
Redfern Ho. *E13*. 5B **54**
  (off Redriffe Rd.)
Redfern Rd. NW10 . . . . 4A **42**
SE6 . . . . 5E **109**
Redfield La. SW5 . . . . . 5C **72**
Redfield M. SW5 . . . . . 5D **73**
Redford Ho. *W10*. 2B **58**
  (off Dowland St.)
Redford Wlk. N1 . . . . . . 5E **49**
  (off Popham St.)
Redgate Ter. SW15. . . . 4F **99**
Redgrave Rd. SW15. . . 1F **99**
Redgrave Ter. *E2* 2C **64**
  (off Derbyshire St.)
Redhill Ct. SW2 . . . . . . 2C **118**
Redhill St.
  NW1. . . . . 1E **5** (1D **61**)
Red Ho. Sq. N1 . . . . . . 3E **49**
Redington Gdns.
  NW3 . . . . 1D **45**
Redington Ho. *N1* 1B **62**
  (off Priory Grn. Est.)
Redington Rd. NW3 . . . 5D **31**
Redlands Way SW2 . . . 5B **104**
Red Lion Cl. *SE17* 2F **91**
  (off Red Lion Row)
Red Lion Ct.
  EC4 . . . . 3C **16** (5C **62**)
SE1 . . . . 1A **26** (2E **77**)
Red Lion Row SE17 . . . 2E **91**

Red Lion Sq. SW18 . . . 3C **100**
WC1 . . . . 1F **15** (4B **62**)
Red Lion St.
WC1 . . . . 5F **7** (4B **62**)
Redman Ho. *EC1* 5B **8**
  (off Bourne Est.)
SE1 . . . . 4A **26**
  (off Borough High St.)
Redman's Rd. E1 . . . . . 4E **65**
Redmead La. E1 . . . . . . 2C **78**
Redmill Ho. *E1* 3D **65**
  (off Headlam St.)
Redmond Ho. *N1*. 5B **48**
  (off Barnsbury Est.)
Redmore Rd. W6. . . . . 5D **71**
Red Path E9 . . . . 3A **52**
Red Pl. W1 . . . . 4B **12** (1C **74**)
Red Post Hill SE21. . . . 3F **105**
SE24 . . . . 2F **105**
Red Post Ho. E6. . . . . . 4F **55**
Redriffe Rd. E13 . . . . . . 5B **54**
Redriff Est. SE16. . . . . . 4B **80**
Redriff Rd. SE16. . . . . . 5F **79**
RED ROVER. 2C **98**
Redrup Ho. *SE14* 2F **93**
  (off John Williams Cl.)
Redruth Rd. E9. . . . . . . 5E **51**
Red Sq. N16. . . . . 5F **35**
Redstart Cl. E6 . . . . 4F **69**
SE14. . . . . 3A **94**
Redvers St. N1 . . . . 1E **11**
Redwald Rd. E5 . . . . . . 1F **51**
Redwing Ct. *SE1* 4A **26**
  (off Swan St.)
Redwood Cl. E3 . . . . . . 1C **66**
SE16. . . . . 2A **80**
Redwood Ct. N19 . . . . . 2F **33**
NW6. . . . . 4A **44**
Redwood Mans. *W8* . . 4D **73**
  (off Chantry Sq.)
Redwood M. SW4 . . . . 1D **103**
Redwoods SW15 . . . . . 1C **112**
Reece M. SW7 . . . . 5F **73**
Reed Cl. E16. . . . . 4C **68**
SE12. . . . . 3C **110**
Reedham St. SE15. . . . 5C **92**
Reedholm Vs. N16. . . . 1F **49**
Reed's Pl. NW1 . . . . . . 4E **47**
Reedworth St. SE11. . . 5C **76**
Reef Ho. *E14*. 4E **81**
  (off Manchester St.)
Rees St. N1 . . . . 5E **49**
Reets Farm Cl. NW9 . . 1A **28**
Reeves Av. NW9 . . . . . 2A **28**
Reeves Ho. *SE1* 4B **24**
  (off Baylis Rd.)
Reeves M.
  W1. . . . . 5B **12** (1C **74**)
Reeves Rd. E3 . . . . 3D **67**
Reflection Ho. *E2*. 3C **64**
  (off Cheshire St.)
Reform St. SW11. . . . . 5B **88**
Regal Cl. E1. . . . . 4C **64**
Regal Ho. *NW6* 1B **58**
  (off Malvern Rd.)
Regal La. NW1. . . . . . . 5C **46**
Regal Pl. E3. . . . . 2B **66**
SW6 . . . . 3D **87**
Regal Row SE15. . . . . . 4E **93**

Regan Way
  N1 . . . . 1D **11** (1A **64**)
Regatta Point *E14* *3C 80*
  (off Westferry Rd.)
Regency Ho. *E16* *2C 82*
  (off Pepys Cres.)
  NW1 . . . . *3E 5*
  (off Osnaburgh St.)
Regency Lawn NW5 . . . .5D **33**
Regency Lodge
  NW3 . . . . *4F 45*
  (off Adelaide Rd.)
Regency M. NW10 . . . . . . 3C **42**
  SW9 . . . . 3D **91**
Regency Pde. *NW3* *4F 45*
  (off Finchley Rd.)
Regency Pl. SW1 . . . . 5F **75**
Regency St. NW10 . . . . . 3A **56**
  SW1 . . . . 5F **75**
Regency Ter. *SW7* *1F 87*
  (off Fulham Rd.)
Regent Ct. *NW8* *2A 60*
  (off North Bank)
Regent Ho. *W14* *5A 72*
  (off Windsor Way)
Regent Pl. SW19 . . . . . . 5E **115**
  W1 . . . . . . 4A **14** (1E **75**)
Regent Rd. SE24 . . . . . 4D **105**
Regent's Bri. Gdns.
  SW8 . . . . 3A **90**
Regents Canal Ho.
  E14 . . . . *5A 66*
  (off Commercial Rd.)
Regents College 3A **4**
Regents Ct. *E8* *5B 50*
  (off Pownall Rd.)
Regents Ga. Ho. *E14* . . . 1A **80**
  (off Horseferry Rd.)
Regents M. NW8 . . . . 1E **59**
REGENT'S PARK
  . . . . 2E **5** (2D **61**)
Regent's Pk. . . . 1A **4** (1B **60**)
Regent's Pk. Barracks . . . 1E **5**
Regents Pk. Est. NW1 . . . 1F **5**
Regent's Pk. Gdns. M.
  NW1 . . . . 5B **46**
Regents Pk. Golf &
  Tennis School 1B **60**
Regent's Pk. Ho.
  NW8 . . . . *2A 60*
  (off Park Rd.)
Regent's Pk. Open Air Theatre
  . . . . 2B **4** (2C **60**)
Regent's Pk. Rd.
  NW1 . . . . 4B **46**
  (not continuous)
Regent's Pk. Ter.
  NW1 . . . . 5D **47**
Regent's Pl. SE3 . . . . 5C **96**
Regents Plaza *NW6* *1D 59*
  (off Kilburn High Rd.)
Regent Sq. E3 . . . . 2D **67**
  WC1 . . . . 2E **7** (2A **62**)
Regent's Row E8 . . . . 5C **50**
Regent St. NW10 . . . . 2F **57**
  SW1 . . . . . . 2E **13** (1F **75**)
  W1 . . . . 2E **13** (5D **61**)
Regents Wharf *E2* *5D 51*
  (off Wharf Pl.)
  N1 . . . . 1B **62**

Reginald Pl. *SE8* *3C 94*
  (off Deptford High St.)
Reginald Rd. E7 . . . . 4C **54**
  SE8 . . . . 3C **94**
Reginald Sorenson Ho.
  E11 . . . . 2F **39**
Reginald Sq. SE8 . . . . . . 3C **94**
Regina Point SE16 . . . . . . 4E **79**
Regina Rd. N4 . . . . 3B **34**
Regis Ct. *NW1* *4B 60*
  (off Melcombe Pl.)
Regis Ho. *W1* *5C 4*
  (off Beaumont St.)
Regis Pl. SW2 . . . . 2B **104**
Regis Rd. NW5 . . . . 2D **47**
Regnart Bldgs. NW1 . . . . 3A **6**
Reigate Rd.
  BR1: Brom 3B **124**
Reighton Rd. E5 . . . . 5C **36**
Reizel Cl. N16 . . . . 3B **36**
Relay Rd. W12 . . . . 2E **71**
Relf Rd. SE15 . . . . 1C **106**
Reliance Arc. SW9 . . . . 2C **104**
Reliance Sq.
  EC2 . . . . 3E **11** (3A **64**)
Relton M. SW7 . . . . 4A **74**
Rembold Ho. *SE10* *4E 95*
  (off Blissett St.)
Rembrandt Cl. E14 . . . . . . 4F **81**
  SW1 . . . . *1C 88*
  (off Graham Ter.)
Rembrandt Ct. *SE16* . . . *1D 93*
  (off Stubbs Dr.)
Rembrandt Rd.
  SE13 . . . . 2A **110**
Remembrance Rd.
  E7 . . . . 1F **55**
Remington Rd. E6 . . . . . . 5F **69**
  N15 . . . . 1F **35**
Remington St. N1 . . . . . . 1D **63**
Remnant St.
  WC2 . . . . 2F **15** (5B **62**)
Remsted Ho. *NW6* *5D 45*
  (off Mortimer Cres.)
Remus Bldg., The *EC1* . . *2C 8*
  (off Hardwick St.)
Remus Rd. E3 . . . . 4C **52**
Renaissance Wlk.
  SE10 . . . . *4B 82*
  (off Teal St.)
Rendlesham Rd. E5 . . . . 1C **50**
Renforth St. SE16 . . . . . . 4E **79**
Renfrew Rd. SE11 . . . . . 5D **77**
Renmuir St. SW17 . . . . 5B **116**
Rennell St. SE13 . . . . . . 1E **109**
Rennie Cotts. *E1* *3E 65*
  (off Pernell Cl.)
Rennie Ct. SE1 . . . . 1D **25**
Rennie Est. SE16 . . . . . . 5D **79**
Rennie Ho. *SE1* *5F 25*
  (off Bath Ter.)
Rennie St.
  SE1 . . . . 1D **25** (2D **77**)
  (not continuous)
Renoir Cinema
  . . . . 3E **7** (3A **62**)
Renoir Ct. *SE16* *1D 93*
  (off Stubbs Dr.)
Rensburg Rd. E17 . . . . . . 1F **37**
Renters Av. NW4 . . . . 1E **29**

Renton Cl. SW2 . . . . . . 4B **104**
Rephidim St.
  SE1 . . . . 5D **27** (4A **78**)
Replingham Rd.
  SW18 . . . . 1B **114**
Reporton Rd. SW6 . . . . . 3A **86**
Repton Ho. *E14* *5A 66*
  (off Repton St.)
  SW1 . . . . *5E 75*
  (off Charlwood St.)
Repton St. E14 . . . . 5A **66**
Reservoir Rd. SE4 . . . . . 5A **94**
Reservoir Studios
  E1 . . . . *5F 65*
  (off Cable St.)
Resolution Way *SE8* . . . *3C 94*
  (off Deptford High St.)
Restell Cl. SE3 . . . . 2A **96**
Reston Pl. SW7 . . . . 3E **73**
Restoration Sq.
  SW11 . . . . 4F **87**
Restormel Ho. *SE11* . . . *5C 76*
  (off Chester Way)
Retcar Cl. N19 . . . . 4D **33**
Retcar Pl. *N19* *4D 33*
  (off Retcar Cl.)
Retford St.
  N1 . . . . 1E **11** (1A **64**)
Retreat, The SW14 . . . . . 1A **98**
Retreat Ho. E9 . . . . 3E **51**
Retreat Pl. E9 . . . . 3E **51**
Reunion Row E1 . . . . 1D **79**
Reveley Sq. SE16 . . . . . . 3A **80**
Revelon Rd. SE4 . . . . . . 2A **108**
Revelstoke Rd.
  SW18 . . . . 2B **114**
Reverdy Rd. SE1 . . . . . . 5C **78**
Review Rd. NW2 . . . . 4B **28**
Rewell St. SW6 . . . . 3E **87**
Rex Pl. W1 . . . . 5C **12** (1C **74**)
Reydon Av. E11 . . . . 1E **41**
Reynard Cl. SE4 . . . . . . 1A **108**
Reynard Pl. SE14 . . . . . . 2A **94**
Reynolah Gdns. SE7 . . . 1D **97**
Reynolds Cl. NW11 . . . . 2D **31**
Reynolds Ho. *E2* *1E 65*
  (off Approach Rd.)
  NW8 . . . . *1F 59*
  (off Wellington Rd.)
  SW1 . . . . *5F 75*
  (off Erasmus St.)
Reynolds Pl. SE3 . . . . . . 3D **97**
Reynolds Rd. SE15 . . . . 2E **107**
Rheidol M. N1 . . . . 1E **63**
Rheidol Ter. N1 . . . . 5E **49**
Rhoda St. E2 . . . 3F **11** (3B **64**)
Rhodes Ho. *N1* *1B 10*
  (off Fairbank Est.)
Rhodesia Rd. E11 . . . . . . 4F **39**
  SW9 . . . . 5A **90**
Rhodes St. N7 . . . . 2B **48**
Rhodeswell Rd. E14 . . . . 4A **66**
  (Ben Jonson Rd.)
  E14 . . . . 5B **66**
  (Norbiton Rd., not continuous)
Rhondda Gro. E3 . . . . . . 2A **66**
Rhyl St. NW5 . . . . 3C **46**
Ribblesdale Ho.
  NW6 . . . . *5C 44*
  (off Kilburn Va.)

Ribblesdale Rd.
SW16 . . . . 5D **117**
Ribbon Dance M.
SE5 . . . . 4F **91**
Ricardo St. E14 . . . . . . 5D **67**
Ricards Rd. SW19 . . . 5B **114**
Riceyman Ho. WC1 . . . . . 2B **8**
(off Lloyd Baker St.)
Richard Anderson Ct.
SE14 . . . . 3F **93**
(off Monson Rd.)
Richard Burbidge Mans.
SW13 . . . . 2E **85**
(off Brasenose Dr.)
Richard Ho. SE16 . . . . . 5E **79**
(off Silwood St.)
Richard Ho. Dr. E16 . . . 5F **69**
Richard Neale Ho. E1 . . 1D **79**
(off Cornwall St.)
Richard Robert
Residence, The
E15 . . . . 3F **53**
(off Salway Rd.)
Richardson Cl. E8 . . . . . 5B **50**
Richardson Ct. SW4 . . . 5A **90**
(off Studley Rd.)
Richardson Rd. E15 . . . 1A **68**
Richardson's M. W1 . . . 4F **5**
Richard's Pl. SW3 . . . . 5A **74**
Richard St. E1 . . . . 5D **65**
Richbell Pl.
WC1 . . . . 5F **7** (4B **62**)
Richborne Ter. SW8 . . . 3B **90**
Richborough Ho.
SE15 . . . . 2E **93**
(off Sharratt St.)
Richborough Rd.
NW2 . . . . 1A **44**
Richbourne Ct. W1 . . . . 5A **60**
(off Harrowby St.)
Richford Ga. W6 . . . . . . 4E **71**
Richford Rd. E15 . . . . . 5B **54**
Richford St. W6 . . . . . . 3E **71**
Rich Ind. Est.
SE1 . . . . 5E **27** (4A **78**)
SE15 . . . . 1D **93**
Rich La. SW5 . . . . 1D **87**
Richman Ho. SE8 . . . . . 1B **94**
(off Grove St.)
Richmond American
International University
in London, The 4D **73**
(off Ansdell St.)
Richmond Av. N1 . . . . . 5B **48**
NW10 . . . . 3E **43**
Richmond Bldgs.
W1 . . . . 3B **14** (5F **61**)
Richmond Cl. E17 . . . . . 1B **38**
Richmond College
(American International
University in London, The)
. . . . 3D **73**
Richmond Cotts. W14 . . . 5A **72**
(off Hammersmith Rd.)
Richmond Ct. E8 . . . . . 4D **51**
(off Mare St.)
NW6 . . . . 4F **43**
(off Willesden La.)
SW1 . . . . 4A **20**
(off Sloane St.)

Richmond Cres. N1 . . . . 5B **48**
Richmond Gro. N1 . . . . 4D **49**
(not continuous)
Richmond Ho. NW1 . . . . 1E **5**
(off Pk. Village E.)
SE17 . . . . 1F **91**
(off Portland St.)
Richmond M.
W1 . . . . 3B **14** (5F **61**)
Richmond Rd. E7 . . . . . 2D **55**
(not continuous)
E8 . . . . 4B **50**
E11 . . . . 4F **39**
N15 . . . . 1A **36**
Richmond St. E13 . . . . . 1C **68**
Richmond Ter.
SW1 . . . . 3D **23** (3A **76**)
Richmond Way E11 . . . . 4C **40**
W12 . . . . 3F **71**
W14 . . . . 3F **71**
Richmount Gdns.
SE3 . . . . 1C **110**
Rich St. E14 . . . . 1B **80**
Rickard Cl. SW2 . . . . . 1C **118**
Rickett St. SW6 . . . . . . 2C **86**
Rickman Ho. E1 . . . . . . 2E **65**
(off Rickman St.)
Rickman St. E1 . . . . . . 3E **65**
Rick Roberts Way
E15 . . . . 5E **53**
Rickthorne Rd. N19 . . . . 4A **34**
Rickyard Path SE9 . . . . 2F **111**
Riddell Ct. SE5 . . . . . . 1B **92**
(off Albany Rd.)
Riddons Rd. SE12 . . . . 3E **125**
Ridgdale St. E3 . . . . . . 1D **67**
Ridgebrook Rd. SE3 . . . 1F **111**
Ridge Ct. SE22 . . . . . . 5C **106**
Ridge Hill NW11 . . . . . 3A **30**
Ridge Rd. N8 . . . . 1B **34**
NW2 . . . . 5B **30**
Ridge Way SE19 . . . . . 5A **120**
Ridgeway, The NW11 . . . 2A **30**
Ridgeway Dr.
BR1: Brom 4D **125**
Ridgeway Gdns. N6 . . . 2E **33**
Ridgewell Cl. N1 . . . . . 5E **49**
SE26 . . . . 4B **122**
Ridgmount Gdns.
WC1 . . . . 5B **6** (4F **61**)
Ridgmount Pl.
WC1 . . . . 5B **6** (4F **61**)
Ridgmount Rd.
SW18 . . . . 3D **101**
Ridgmount St.
WC1 . . . . 5B **6** (4F **61**)
Ridgway Pl. SW19 . . . . 5A **114**
Ridgway Rd. SW9 . . . . 1D **105**
Ridgwell Rd. E16 . . . . . 4E **69**
Riding, The NW11 . . . . 2B **30**
Riding Ho. St.
W1 . . . . 1E **13** (4D **61**)
Ridings Cl. N6 . . . . 2E **33**
Ridley Cl. SW16 . . . . . 5A **118**
Ridley Rd. E7 . . . . 1E **55**
E8 . . . . 2B **50**
NW10 . . . . 1C **56**
Riffel Rd. NW2 . . . . . . 2E **43**
Rifle Ct. SE11 . . . . 2C **90**
Rifle St. E14 . . . . 4D **67**

Riga Ho. E1 . . . . 4F **65**
(off Shandy St.)
Rigault Rd. SW6 . . . . . 5A **86**
Rigden St. E14 . . . . . . 5D **67**
Rigeley Rd. NW10 . . . . 2C **56**
Rigg App. E10 . . . . 3F **37**
Rigge Pl. SW4 . . . . . . 2F **103**
Riggindale Rd.
SW16 . . . . 5F **117**
Riley Ho. SW10 . . . . . . 3F **87**
Riley Rd.
SE1 . . . . 5E **27** (4B **78**)
Riley St. SW10 . . . . . . 2F **87**
Rill Ho. SE5 . . . . 3F **91**
(off Harris St.)
Rinaldo Rd. SW12 . . . . 5D **103**
Ring, The
W2 . . . . 4A **12** (1F **73**)
(not continuous)
Ringcroft St. N7 . . . . . 2C **48**
Ringford Rd. SW18 . . . . 3B **100**
Ring Ho. E1 . . . . 1E **79**
(off Sage St.)
Ringlet Cl. E16 . . . . . . 4D **69**
Ringmer Av. SW6 . . . . . 4A **86**
Ringmer Gdns. N19 . . . 4A **34**
Ringmore Ri. SE23 . . . 5D **107**
Ring Rd. W12 . . . . 2E **71**
Ringsfield Ho. SE17 . . . 1E **91**
(off Bronti Cl.)
Ringstead Rd. SE6 . . . . 5D **109**
Ringwood Gdns. E14 . . 5C **80**
SW15 . . . . 1C **112**
Ringwood Rd. E17 . . . . 1B **38**
Rio Cinema 2A **50**
(off Kingsland High St.)
Ripley Gdns. SW14 . . . 1A **98**
Ripley Ho. SW1 . . . . . . 2E **89**
(off Churchill Gdns.)
Ripley M. E11 . . . . 1A **40**
Ripley Rd. E16 . . . . . . 5E **69**
Ripon Gdns. IG1: Ilf . . . 1F **41**
Ripplevale Gro. N1 . . . 4B **48**
Risborough SE17 . . . . . 5E **77**
(off Deacon Way)
Risborough Ho. NW8 . . 3A **60**
(off Mallory St.)
Risborough St.
SE1 . . . . 3E **25** (3D **77**)
Risdon Ho. SE16 . . . . . 3E **79**
(off Risdon St.)
Risdon St. SE16 . . . . . 4E **79**
Rise, The E11 . . . . 1C **40**
NW10 . . . . 1A **42**
Riseholme Ct. E9 . . . . . 3B **52**
Riseldine Rd. SE23 . . . 4A **108**
Risinghill St. N1 . . . . . 1B **62**
Rising Sun Ct. EC1 . . . . 5E **9**
Rita Rd. SW8 . . . . 2A **90**
Ritches Rd. N15 . . . . . 1E **35**
Ritchie Ho. E14 . . . . . . 5F **67**
(off Blair St.)
N19 . . . . 3F **33**
SE16 . . . . 4E **79**
(off Howland St.)
Ritchie St. N1 . . . . 1C **62**
Ritherdon Rd.
SW17 . . . . 2C **116**
Ritson Ho. N1 . . . . 5B **48**
(off Barnsbury Est.)

Ritson Rd. E8 . . . . 3C 50
Riva Bingo 1A 118
Rivaz Pl. E9 . . . . 3E 51
Riven Ct. W2 . . . . 5D 59
    (off Inverness Ter.)
Riverbank Rd.
  BR1: Brom 3C 124
River Barge Cl. E14 . . . 3E 81
River Cl. E11 . . . . 1E 41
River Ct.
  SE1 . . . . 5D 17 (1D 77)
Rivercourt Rd. W6 . . . . 5D 71
Riverdale SE13 . . . . 2E 109
Riverdale Dr. SW18 . . . 1D 115
Riverdale Shop. Cen.
  SE13 . . . . 1E 109
    (off Birkenhead St.)
Riverfleet WC1 . . . . 1E 7
    (off Birkenhead St.)
River Ho. SE26 . . . . 3D 121
Rivermead Ct. SW6 . . . 1B 100
Rivermead Ho. E9 . . . . . 2A 52
River Pl. N1 . . . . 4E 49
Riversdale Rd. N5 . . . . . 5D 35
Riverside NW4 . . . . 2D 29
  SE7 . . . . 4D 83
  WC1 . . . . 1E 7
    (off Birkenhead St.)
Riverside Apartments
  SE1 . . . . . . 2F 27 (2B 78)
Riverside Bus. Cen.
  SW18 . . . . 1D 115
Riverside Cl. E5 . . . . . . 3E 37
Riverside Cl. SE3 . . . . . 2B 110
  SW8 . . . . 2F 89
Riverside Dr. NW11 . . . 1A 30
  W4 . . . . 3A 84
Riverside Gdns. W6 . . . 1D 85
Riverside Ho. N1 . . . . . . 4E 49
    (off Canonbury St.)
Riverside Mans. E1 . . . . 2E 79
    (off Milk Yd.)
Riverside Rd. E15 . . . . . 1E 67
  N15 . . . . 1C 36
  SW17 . . . . 4D 115
Riverside Studios 1E 85
    (off River Ter.)
Riverside Twr. SW6 . . . . 5E 87
    (off Boulevard, The)
Riverside Wlk. SE10 . . . 4A 82
    (off Morden Wharf Rd.)
  SE10 . . . . 3F 81
    (Tunnel Av.)
  SW6 . . . . 4A 100
  W4 . . . . 2B 84
    (off Chiswick Wharf)
Riverside Workshops
  SE1 . . . . 1A 26
    (off Park St.)
Riverside Yd. SW17 . . . 4E 115
River St. EC1 . . . 1B 8 (2C 62)
  WC2 . . . . 5F 15
River Ter. W6 . . . . 1E 85
Riverton Cl. W9 . . . . . . 2B 58
Riverview Ct. E14 . . . . . 4B 80
Riverview Gdns.
  SW13 . . . . 2D 85
River Vw. Hgts.
  SE16 . . . . 3C 78
    (off Bermondsey Wall W.)
Riverview Pk. SE6 . . . . 2C 122

River Wlk. W6 . . . . 3E 85
River Way SE10 . . . . . . 4B 82
Rivet Ho. SE1 . . . . 1B 92
    (off Coopers Rd.)
Rivington Ct.
  NW10 . . . . 5C 42
Rivington Pl.
  EC2 . . . . . . 2E 11 (2A 64)
Rivington St.
  EC2 . . . . . . 2D 11 (2A 64)
Rivington Wlk. E8 . . . . 5C 50
Rixon St. N7 . . . . 5C 34
Roach Rd. E3 . . . . 4C 52
Roads Pl. N19 . . . . 4A 34
Roan St. SE10 . . . . 2E 95
Robert Adam St.
  W1 . . . . 2B 12 (5C 60)
Roberta St. E2 . . . . 2C 64
Robert Bell Ho. SE16 . . 5C 78
    (off Rouel Rd.)
Robert Burns M.
  SE24 . . . . 3D 105
Robert Cl. W9 . . . . 3E 59
Robert Dashwood Way
  SE17 . . . . 5E 77
Robert Gentry Ho.
  W14 . . . . 1A 86
    (off Gledstanes Rd.)
Robert Jones Ho.
  SE16 . . . . 5C 78
    (off Rouel Rd.)
Robert Keen Cl.
  SE15 . . . . 4C 92
Robert Lowe Cl.
  SE14 . . . . 3F 93
Robert Owen Ho.
  SW6 . . . . 4F 85
Robert Runcie Ct.
  SW2 . . . . 2B 104
Roberts Cl. SE16 . . . . . 3F 79
Roberts Ct. N1 . . . . 5D 49
    (off Essex Rd.)
  NW10 . . . . 3A 42
Roberts M.
  SW1 . . . . . . 5B 20 (4C 74)
Robertson Gro.
  SW17 . . . . 5A 116
Robertson Rd. E15 . . . . 5E 53
Robertson St. SW8 . . . 1D 103
Roberts Pl.
  EC1 . . . . 3C 8 (3C 62)
Robert St.
  NW1 . . . . . . 2E 5 (2D 61)
  WC2 . . . . . . 5E 15 (1A 76)
Robert Sutton Ho. E1 . . 5E 65
    (off Tarling St.)
Robeson St. E3 . . . . . . 4B 66
Robin Cl. E14 . . . . 3E 81
  SE16 . . . . 5C 78
Robin Cres. E6 . . . . 4F 69
Robin Gro. N6 . . . . 4C 32
ROBIN HOOD 3A 112
Robin Hood Ct. EC4 . . . 2C 16
    (off Shoe La.)
Robin Hood Gdns.
  E14 . . . . 1E 81
    (off Woolmore St.,
    not continuous)
Robin Hood La. E14 . . . 1E 81
  SW15 . . . . 3A 112

Robin Hood Rd.
  SW19 . . . . 5C 112
Robin Hood Way
  SW15 . . . . 3A 112
  SW20 . . . . 3A 112
Robin Ho. NW8 . . . . 1A 60
    (off Barrow Hill Est.)
Robin Howard Dance Theatre
  . . . . 2C 6
    (in Place, The)
Robinia Cres. E10 . . . . 4D 39
Robins Ct. SE12 . . . . . 3E 125
Robinscroft M. SE10 . . 4E 95
Robinson Cl. E11 . . . . . 5A 40
Robinson Ct. N1 . . . . . . 5D 49
    (off St Mary's Path)
Robinson Ho. E14 . . . . 4C 66
    (off Selsey St.)
  W10 . . . . 5F 57
    (off Bramley Rd.)
Robinson Rd. E2 . . . . . . 1E 65
  SW17 . . . . 5A 116
Robinson St. SW3 . . . . 2B 88
Robinwood Pl.
  SW15 . . . . 4A 112
Robsart St. SW9 . . . . . 5B 90
Robson Av. NW10 . . . . 4C 42
Robson Cl. E6 . . . . 5F 69
Robson Rd. SE27 . . . . 3D 119
Roby Ho. EC1 . . . . 3F 9
    (off Mitchell St.)
Rocastle Rd. SE4 . . . . 3A 108
Rochdale Rd. E17 . . . . 2C 38
Rochdale Way SE8 . . . 3C 94
    (not continuous)
Roche Ho. E14 . . . . 1B 80
    (off Beccles St.)
Rochelle Cl. SW11 . . . 2F 101
Rochelle St.
  E2 . . . . 2F 11 (2B 64)
    (not continuous)
Rochemont Wlk. E8 . . . 5C 50
    (off Pownall Rd.)
Rochester Av. E13 . . . . 5E 55
Rochester Ct. E2 . . . . . 3D 65
    (off Wilmot St.)
  NW1 . . . . 4E 47
    (off Rochester Sq.)
Rochester Ho. SE1 . . . 4C 26
    (off Manciple St.)
  SE15 . . . . 2E 93
    (off Sharratt St.)
Rochester M. NW1 . . . 4E 47
Rochester Pl. NW1 . . . 3E 47
Rochester Rd. NW1 . . . 3E 47
Rochester Row SW1 . . 5E 75
Rochester Sq. NW1 . . . 4E 47
Rochester St. SW1 . . . 4F 75
Rochester Ter. NW1 . . . 3E 47
Rochester Wlk.
  SE1 . . . . 1B 26 (2F 77)
Rochester Way SE3 . . . 4D 97
  SE9 . . . . 5E 97
Rochester Way Relief Rd.
  SE3 . . . . 4D 97
  SE9 . . . . 2E 111
Rochford Cl. E6 . . . . . . 1F 69
Rochford Wlk. E8 . . . . . 4C 50
Rochfort Ho. SE8 . . . . . 1B 94
Rock Av. SW14 . . . . . . 1A 98

Rockbourne M.
SE23 . . . . 1F **121**
Rockbourne Rd.
SE23 . . . . 1F **121**
Rockell's Pl. SE22 . . . . 4D **107**
Rockfield Ho. SE10 . . . . 2E **95**
(off Welland St.)
Rock Gro. Way
SE16 . . . . 5C **78**
(not continuous)
Rockhall Rd. NW2 . . . . 1F **43**
Rockhall Way NW2 . . . . 5F **29**
Rockhampton Cl.
SE27 . . . . 4C **118**
Rockhampton Rd.
SE27 . . . . 4C **118**
Rock Hill SE26 . . . . . . 4B **120**
(not continuous)
Rockingham Cl.
SW15 . . . . 2B **98**
Rockingham St.
SE1 . . . . 5F **25** (4E **77**)
Rockland Rd.
SW15 . . . . 2A **100**
Rockley Ct. W14 . . . . . . 3F **71**
(off Rockley Rd.)
Rockley Rd. W14 . . . . . . 3F **71**
Rocks La. SW13 . . . . . . 4C **84**
Rock St. N4 . . . . 4C **34**
Rockwell Gdns.
SE19 . . . . 5A **120**
Rockwood Pl. W12 . . . . 3E **71**
Rocliffe St. N1 . . . . 1D **63**
Rocombe Cres.
SE23 . . . . 5E **107**
Rocque Ho. SW6 . . . . . . 3B **86**
(off Estcourt Rd.)
Rocque La. SE3 . . . . . 1B **110**
Rodale Mans.
SW18 . . . . 4D **101**
Rodborough Ct. W9 . . . . 3C **58**
(off Hermes Cl.)
Rodborough Rd.
NW11 . . . . 3C **30**
Roden Ct. N6 . . . . 2F **33**
Rodenhurst Rd.
SW4 . . . . 4E **103**
Roden St. N7 . . . . 5B **34**
Roderick Ho. SE16 . . . . 5E **79**
(off Raymouth Rd.)
Roderick Rd.
NW3 . . . . 1B **46**
Rodgers Ho. SW4 . . . . 5F **103**
(off Clapham Pk. Est.)
Rodin Ct. N1 . . . . 5D **49**
(off Essex Rd.)
Roding Ho. N1 . . . . 5C **48**
(off Barnsbury Est.)
Roding La. Sth.
IG4: Ilf, Wfd G 1F **41**
(not continuous)
Roding M. E1 . . . . 2C **78**
Roding Rd. E5 . . . . 1F **51**
Rodmarton St.
W1 . . . . 1A **12** (4B **60**)
Rodmell WC1 . . . . 2E **7**
(off Regent Sq.)
Rodmere St. SE10 . . . . 1A **96**
Rodmill La. SW2 . . . . . . 5A **104**
Rodney Ct. W9 . . . . 3E **59**

Rodney Ho. E14 . . . . . . 5D **81**
(off Cahir St.)
N1 . . . . 1B **62**
(off Donegal St.)
SW1 . . . . 1E **89**
(off Dolphin Sq.)
W11 . . . . 1C **72**
(off Pembridge Cres.)
Rodney Pl. SE17 . . . . . . 5E **77**
Rodney Rd. SE17 . . . . . 5E **77**
(not continuous)
Rodney St. N1 . . 1A **8** (1B **62**)
Rodway Rd. SW15 . . . . 5C **98**
Rodwell Rd. SE22 . . . . 4B **106**
Roebuck Ho. SW1 . . . . . 5F **21**
(off Palace St.)
Roedean Cres. SW15 . . 4A **98**
ROEHAMPTON 5C **98**
Roehampton Cl.
SW15 . . . . 2C **98**
Roehampton Ga.
SW15 . . . . 4A **98**
Roehampton High St.
SW15 . . . . 5C **98**
ROEHAMPTON LANE
. . . . 1D **113**
Roehampton La.
SW15 . . . . 2C **98**
Roehampton Recreation Cen.
. . . . 5C **98**
Roehampton Va.
SW15 . . . . 3B **112**
Roffey St. E14 . . . . 3E **81**
Rogate Ho. E5 . . . . 5C **36**
Roger Dowley Ct. E2 . . 1E **65**
Roger Harriss Almshouses
E15 . . . . 5B **54**
(off Gift La.)
Rogers Ct. E14 . . . . 1C **80**
(off Premiere Pl.)
Rogers Est. E2 . . . . 2E **65**
Rogers Ho. SW1 . . . . . . 5F **75**
(off Page St.)
Rogers Rd. E16 . . . . . . 5B **68**
SW17 . . . . 4F **115**
Roger St.
WC1 . . . . 4A **8** (3B **62**)
Rohere Ho.
EC1 . . . . 2F **9** (2E **63**)
Rojack Rd. SE23 . . . . . 1F **121**
Rokeby Ho. SW12 . . . . 5D **103**
(off Lochinvar St.)
Rokeby Rd. SE4 . . . . . . 5B **94**
Rokeby St. E15 . . . . . . 5F **53**
Rokell Ho.
BR3: Beck 5D **123**
(off Beckenham Hill Rd.)
Roland Gdns. SW7 . . . . 1E **87**
Roland Ho. SW7 . . . . . . 1E **87**
(off Old Brompton Rd.)
Roland M. E1 . . . . 4F **65**
Roland Way SE17 . . . . . 1F **91**
SW7 . . . . 1E **87**
Rollins St. SE15 . . . . . . 2E **93**
Rollit St. N7 . . . . 2C **48**
Rolls Bldgs.
EC4 . . . . 2B **16** (5C **62**)
Rollscourt Av. SE24 . . . 3E **105**
Rolls Pas. EC4 . . . . 2B **16**
Rolls Rd. SE1 . . . . 1B **92**

Rolt St. SE8 . . . . 2A **94**
(not continuous)
Roman Ct. N7 . . . . 3B **48**
Romanfield Rd.
SW2 . . . . 5B **104**
Roman Ho. EC2 . . . . . . 1A **18**
Roman Ri. SE19 . . . . . . 5F **119**
Roman Rd. E2 . . . . 2E **65**
E3 . . . . 5B **52**
E6 . . . . 3F **69**
NW2 . . . . 5E **29**
W4 . . . . 5A **70**
Roman Rd. Mkt. E3 . . . . 5B **52**
(off Roman Rd.)
Roman Way N7 . . . . 3B **48**
SE15 . . . . 3E **93**
Roman Way Ind. Est.
N7 . . . . 4B **48**
(off Roman Way)
Roma Read Cl.
SW15 . . . . 5D **99**
Romayne Ho. SW4 . . . . 1F **103**
Romberg Rd. SW17 . . . 3C **116**
Romborough Gdns.
SE13 . . . . 3E **109**
Romborough Way
SE13 . . . . 3E **109**
Romer Ho. W10 . . . . . . 2B **58**
(off Dowland St.)
Romero Cl. SW9 . . . . . . 1B **104**
Romero Sq. SE3 . . . . . . 2E **111**
Romeyn Rd. SW16 . . . . 3B **118**
Romford Rd. E7 . . . . . . 3A **54**
E12 . . . . 2E **55**
E15 . . . . 3A **54**
Romford St. E1 . . . . 4C **64**
Romilly Rd. N4 . . . . 4D **35**
Romilly St.
W1 . . . . 4C **14** (1F **75**)
Romily Ct. SW6 . . . . 5B **86**
Rommany Rd. SE27 . . . 4F **119**
(not continuous)
Romney Cl. NW11 . . . . . 3E **31**
SE14 . . . . 3E **93**
Romney Ct. NW3 . . . . . . 3A **46**
W12 . . . . 3F **71**
(off Shepherd's Bush Grn.)
Romney M.
W1 . . . . 5B **4** (4C **60**)
Romney Rd. SE10 . . . . . 2F **95**
Romney Row NW2 . . . . 4F **29**
(off Brent Ter.)
Romney St. SW1 . . . . . . 4A **76**
Romola Rd. SE24 . . . . . 1D **119**
Ronald Av. E15 . . . . 2A **68**
Ronald Buckingham Ct.
SE16 . . . . 3E **79**
(off Kenning St.)
Ronald Ho. SE3 . . . . . . 2E **111**
Ronaldshay N4 . . . . 2C **34**
Ronald St. E1 . . . . 5E **65**
Ronalds Rd. N5 . . . . 2C **48**
(not continuous)
Ronald St. E1 . . . . 5E **65**
Rona Rd. NW3 . . . . 1C **46**
Rona Wlk. N1 . . . . 3F **49**
(off Ramsey Wlk.)
Rondu Rd. NW2 . . . . . . 2A **44**
Ronver Rd. SE12 . . . . . 1B **124**
Rood La.
EC3 . . . . 4D **19** (1A **78**)

Roof Ter. Apartments, The
EC1 . . . . 4E *9*
(off Gt. Sutton St.)
Rookery Rd. SW4 . . . . . 2E **103**
Rookery Way NW9 . . . . . 1B **28**
Rooke Way SE10 . . . . . . 1B **96**
Rookstone Rd.
SW17 . . . . 5B **116**
Rook Wlk. E6 . . . . 5F **69**
Rookwood Rd. N16 . . . . 2B **36**
Roosevelt Memorial
. . . . 4C 12 (1C **74**)
Rootes Dr. W10 . . . . 4F **57**
Ropemaker Rd.
SE16 . . . . 3A **80**
Ropemaker's Flds.
E14 . . . . 1B **80**
Ropemaker St.
EC2 . . . . 5B **10** (4F **63**)
Roper La.
SE1 . . . . 4E **27** (3A **78**)
Ropers Orchard SW3 . . . 2A *88*
(off Danvers St.)
Ropers Wlk. SW2 . . . . . 5C **104**
Ropery Bus. Pk. SE7 . . . 5E **83**
Ropery St. E3 . . . . 3B **66**
Rope St. SE16 . . . . 5A **80**
Rope Wlk. Gdns. E1 . . . . 5C **64**
Ropewalk M. E8 . . . . 4C *50*
(off Middleton Rd.)
Ropley St. E2 . . . . 1C **64**
Rosa Alba M. N5 . . . . . . 1E **49**
Rosalind Ho. N1 . . . . 1A *64*
(off Arden Ho.)
Rosaline Rd. SW6 . . . . . 3A **86**
Rosaline Ter. SW6 . . . . . 3A *86*
(off Rosaline Rd.)
Rosamond St. SE26 . . . . 3D **121**
Rosary Gdns. SW7 . . . . . 5E **73**
Rosaville Rd. SW6 . . . . . 3B **86**
Roscoe St.
EC1 . . . . 4A **10** (3E **63**)
(not continuous)
Roscoe St. Est.
EC1 . . . . 4A **10** (3E **63**)
Rose All. EC2 . . . . 1E *19*
(off Bishopsgate)
SE1 . . . . 1A **26** (2E *77*)
Rose & Crown Ct.
EC2 . . . . 2A *18*
Rose & Crown Yd.
SW1 . . . . 1A **22** (2E *75*)
Rosebank SW6 . . . . 3E **85**
Rosebank Gdns. E3 . . . . 1B **66**
Rosebank Rd. E17 . . . . . 1D **39**
Rosebank Wlk. NW1 . . . . 4F **47**
Roseberry Gdns. N4 . . . . 1D **35**
Roseberry Pl. E8 . . . . . . 3B **50**
Roseberry St. SE16 . . . . 5D **79**
Rosebery Av. E12 . . . . . 3F **55**
EC1 . . . . 4B **8** (3C **62**)
Rosebery Ct. EC1 . . . . . . 4B *8*
(off Rosebery Av.)
Rosebery Gdns. N8 . . . . 1A **34**
Rosebery Ho. E2 . . . . . . 1E *65*
(off Sewardstone Rd.)
Rosebery Rd. SW2 . . . . . 4A **104**
Rosebery Sq. EC1 . . . . . 4B *8*
Rosebury Rd. SW6 . . . . . 5D **87**
Rose Bush Ct. NW3 . . . . 2B **46**

Rose Ct. E1 . . . . 1F **19**
E8 . . . . 4B *50*
(off Richmond Rd.)
N1 . . . . 5D *49*
(off Collin's Yd.)
SE8 . . . . 5F **79**
Rosecroft Av. NW3 . . . . 5C **30**
Rosecroft Gdns. NW2 . . . 5C **28**
Rosedale Ct. N5 . . . . . . 1D **49**
Rosedale Ho. N16 . . . . . 3F **35**
Rosedale Rd. E7 . . . . . . 2E **55**
Rosedale Ter. W6 . . . . . . 4D *71*
(off Dalling Rd.)
Rosedene NW6 . . . . 5F **43**
(not continuous)
Rosedene Av. SW16 . . . . 3B **118**
Rosedene Ter. E10 . . . . . 4D **39**
Rosedew Rd. W6 . . . . . . 2F **85**
Rosefield Gdns. E14 . . . . 1C **80**
Roseford Ct. W12 . . . . . . 3F *71*
(off Shepherd's Bush Grn.)
Rosehart M. W11 . . . . . . 5C **58**
Rosehill Rd. SW18 . . . . . 4E **101**
Roseleigh Av. N5 . . . . . . 1D **49**
Rosemary Branch Theatre
. . . . 5F *49*
(off Penally Pl.)
Rosemary Ct. SE8 . . . . . 2B *94*
(off Dorking Cl.)
Rosemary Dr. E14 . . . . . 5F **67**
IG4: Ilf 1F **41**
Rosemary Ho. N1 . . . . . . 5F *49*
(off Branch Pl.)
Rosemary Rd. SE15 . . . . 3B **92**
SW17 . . . . 3E **115**
Rosemary St. N1 . . . . . . 5F **49**
Rosemead NW9 . . . . 2B **28**
Rosemont Rd. NW3 . . . . 3E **45**
Rosemoor St. SW3 . . . . . 5B **74**
Rosemount Point
SE23 . . . . 3F **121**
Rosenau Cres. SW11 . . . 4B **88**
Rosenau Rd. SW11 . . . . 4A **88**
Rosendale Rd. SE21 . . . . 3F **119**
SE24 . . . . 5E **105**
Roseneath Rd.
SW11 . . . . 4C **102**
Rosenthal Rd. SE6 . . . . . 4D **109**
Rosenthorpe Rd.
SE15 . . . . 3F **107**
Rose Sq. SW7 . . . . 1F **87**
Rose St. EC4 . . . 2E **17** (5D **63**)
WC2 . . . . 4D **15** (1A *76*)
(not continuous)
Rosethorn Cl. SW12 . . . . 5F **103**
Rosetta Cl. SW8 . . . . . . 3A *90*
(off Kenchester Cl.)
Roseveare Rd.
SE12 . . . . 4E **125**
Rose Way SE12 . . . . 3C **110**
Roseway SE21 . . . . 4F **105**
Rosewood Ct. E11 . . . . . 1F **53**
Rosewood Gdns.
SE13 . . . . 5E **95**
Rosewood Ho. SW8 . . . . 2B *90*
(off Sth. Lambeth Rd.)
Rosewood Sq. W12 . . . . 5C **56**
Rosher Cl. E15 . . . . 4F **53**
Roshni Ho. SW17 . . . . . 5A **116**

Rosina St. E9 . . . . 3F **51**
Roskell Rd. SW15 . . . . . 1F **99**
Roslin Ho. E1 . . . . 1F *79*
(off Brodlove La.)
Roslin Way
BR1: Brom 5C **124**
Rosmead Rd. W11 . . . . . 1A **72**
Rosoman Pl.
EC1 . . . . 3C **8** (3C **62**)
Rosoman St.
EC1 . . . . 2C **8** (2C **62**)
Ross Ct. E5 . . . . 1D *51*
(off Napoleon St.)
SW15 . . . . 5F **99**
Rosscourt Mans.
SW1 . . . . 5F *21*
(off Buckingham Pal. Rd.)
Rossdale Rd. SW15 . . . . 2E **99**
Rosse M. SE3 . . . . 4D **97**
Rossendale St. E5 . . . . . 4D **37**
Rossendale Way
NW1 . . . . 5E *47*
Rossetti Ct. WC1 . . . . . . 5B *6*
(off Ridgmount Pl.)
Rossetti Ho. SW1 . . . . . 5F *75*
(off Erasmus St.)
Rossetti M. NW8 . . . . . . 5F **45**
Rossetti Rd. SE16 . . . . . 1D **93**
Ross Ho. E1 . . . . 2D *79*
(off Prusom St.)
Rossington St. E5 . . . . . 4C **36**
Rossiter Rd. SW12 . . . . . 1D **117**
Rosslyn Av. SW13 . . . . . 1A **98**
Rosslyn Hill NW3 . . . . . . 1F **45**
Rosslyn Mans. NW6 . . . . 4E *45*
(off Goldhurst Ter.)
Rosslyn M. NW3 . . . . . . 1F **45**
Rosslyn Pk. M. NW3 . . . . 2F **45**
Rosslyn Pk. RUFC 2B **98**
Rossmore Cl. NW1 . . . . . 3A *60*
(off Rossmore Rd.)
Rossmore Ct. NW1 . . . . . 3B **60**
Rossmore Rd. NW1 . . . . 3A **60**
Ross Way SE9 . . . . 1F **111**
Rostella Rd. SW17 . . . . . 4F **115**
Rostrevor Av. N15 . . . . . 1B **36**
Rostrevor M. SW6 . . . . . 4B **86**
Rostrevor Rd. SW6 . . . . . 4B **86**
SW19 . . . . 5C **114**
Rotary St.
SE1 . . . . 5D **25** (4D *77*)
Rothay NW1 . . . . 1E *5*
(off Albany St.)
Rothbury Hall SE10 . . . . 5A **82**
Rothbury Rd. E9 . . . . . . 4B **52**
Rotheley Ho. E9 . . . . 4E *51*
(off Balcorne St.)
Rotherfield Ct. N1 . . . . . 4F *49*
(off Rotherfield St.)
not continuous)
Rotherfield St. N1 . . . . . 4E **49**
Rotherham Wlk. SE1 . . . . 2D **25**
ROTHERHITHE 3E **79**
Rotherhithe New Rd.
SE16 . . . . 1D **93**
Rotherhithe Old Rd.
SE16 . . . . 5F **79**
Rotherhithe St. SE16 . . . 3E **79**
Rotherhithe Tunnel
SE16 . . . . 2F **79**

Rother Ho. SE15 . . . . 2D 107
Rotherwick Ho. E1 . . . . . . 1C 78
  (off Thomas More St.)
Rotherwick Rd.
NW11 . . . . 2C 30
Rotherwood Rd.
SW15 . . . . 1F 99
Rothery St. N1 . . . . 5D 49
  (off St Marys Path)
Rothesay Ct. SE6 . . . . . . 2B 124
SE11 . . . . 2C 90
  (off Harleyford St.)
SE12 . . . . 3D 125
Rothley Ct. NW8 . . . . 3F 59
  (off St John's Wood Rd.)
Rothsay Rd. E7 . . . . 4E 55
Rothsay St.
SE1 . . . . 5D 27 (4A 78)
Rothsay Wlk. E14 . . . . . . 5C 80
  (off Charnwood Gdns.)
Rothschild St. SE27 . . . . 4D 119
Roth Wlk. N7 . . . . 4B 34
Rothwell St. NW1 . . . . . . 5B 46
Rotten Row NW3 . . . . . . 3E 45
SW1 . . . . 3A 20 (3A 74)
SW7 . . . . 3A 74
Rotterdam Dr. E14 . . . . . 4E 81
Rouel Rd. SE16 . . . . 4C 78
  (Dockley Rd.)
SE16 . . . . 5C 78
  (Southwark Pk. Rd.)
Roundacre SW19 . . . . . . 2F 113
Roundel Cl. SE4 . . . . 2B 108
Roundhay Cl. SE23 . . . . . 2F 121
Round Hill SE26 . . . . 2E 121
  (not continuous)
Roundhouse, The 4C 46
  (off Chalk Farm Rd.)
Roundtable Rd.
BR1: Brom 3B 124
Roundwood Rd.
NW10 . . . . 3B 42
Rounton Rd. E3 . . . . 3C 66
Roupell Rd. SW2 . . . . . . 1B 118
Roupell St.
SE1 . . . . 2C 24 (2C 76)
Rousden St. NW1 . . . . . . 4E 47
Rouse Gdns. SE21 . . . . . 4A 120
Routemaster Cl.
E13 . . . . 2D 69
Routh Rd. SW18 . . . . 5A 102
Rover Ho. N1 . . . . 5A 50
  (off Mill Row)
Rowallan Rd. SW6 . . . . . 3A 86
Rowan Ct. E13 . . . . 1D 69
  (off High St.)
SE15 . . . . 3B 92
  (off Garnies Cl.)
SW11 . . . . 4B 102
Rowan Ho. SE16 . . . . 3F 79
  (off Woodland Cres.)
Rowan Lodge W8 . . . . . . 4D 73
  (off Chantry Sq.)
Rowan Rd. W6 . . . . 5F 71
Rowans Complex N4 . . . . 4C 34
Rowan Ter. W6 . . . . 5F 71
Rowan Wlk. N2 . . . . 1E 31
N19 . . . . 4E 33
W10 . . . . 3A 58
Rowberry Cl. SW6 . . . . . 3E 85

Rowcross St. SE1 . . . . . . 1B 92
Rowditch La. SW11 . . . . . 5C 88
Rowdon Av. NW10 . . . . . 4D 43
Rowe Ho. E9 . . . . 3E 51
Rowe La. E9 . . . . 2E 51
Rowena Cres. SW11 . . . . 5A 88
Rowfant Rd. SW17 . . . . . 1C 116
Rowhill Rd. E5 . . . . 1D 51
Rowington Cl. W2 . . . . . . 4D 59
Rowland Ct. E16 . . . . 3B 68
Rowland Gro. SE26 . . . . . 3D 121
Rowland Hill Ho.
SE1 . . . . 3D 25 (3D 77)
Rowland Hill St.
NW3 . . . . 2A 46
Rowlands Cl. N6 . . . . 1C 32
Rowley Gdns. N4 . . . . . . 2E 35
Rowley Ho. SE8 . . . . 1C 94
  (off Watergate St.)
Rowley Rd. N15 . . . . 1E 35
Rowley Way NW8 . . . . . . 5D 45
Rowntree Clifford Cl.
E13 . . . . 3C 68
Rowntree Cl. NW6 . . . . . 3C 44
Rowse Cl. E15 . . . . 5E 53
Rowstock Gdns. N7 . . . . . 2F 47
Roxburgh Rd. SE27 . . . . 5D 119
Roxby Pl. SW6 . . . . 2C 86
Roxley Rd. SE13 . . . . 4D 109
Roxwell NW1 . . . . 3D 47
  (off Hartland Rd.)
Roxwell Rd. W12 . . . . . . 3C 70
Roxwell Trad. Pk.
E10 . . . . 2A 38
Royal Academy of Arts
(Burlington House)
. . . . 5F 13 (1E 75)
Royal Academy of Music Mus.
. . . . 4C 4 (3C 60)
Royal Air Force Memorial
. . . . 2E 23 (2A 76)
Royal Albert Hall 3F 73
Royal Albert Rdbt.
E16 . . . . 1F 83
  (off Royal Albert Way)
Royal Albert Way E16 . . . 1F 83
Royal Arc. W1 . . . . 5F 13
Royal Av. SW3 . . . . 1B 88
Royal Av. Ho. SW3 . . . . . 1B 88
  (off Royal Av.)
Royal Belgrave Ho.
SW1 . . . . 5D 75
  (off Hugh St.)
Royal Ceremonial Dress
Collection, The 2D 73
  (in Kensington Palace)
Royal Cir. SE27 . . . . 3C 118
Royal Cl. N16 . . . . 3A 36
SE8 . . . . 2B 94
SW19 . . . . 3F 113
Royal College of Art 3F 73
Royal College of Music
. . . . 4F 73
Royal College of Obstetricians
  & Gynaecologists . . . 3B 60
Royal College of Physicians
. . . . 3D 5 (3D 61)
Royal College of Surgeons
. . . . 2A 16 (5B 62)
Royal Coll. St. NW1 . . . . 4E 47

Royal Connaught Apartments
E16 . . . . 2F 83
  (off Connaught Rd.)
Royal Ct. EC3 . . . . 3C 18
  (off Finch La.)
SE16 . . . . 4B 80
Royal Courts of Justice
. . . . 3A 16 (5C 62)
Royal Court Theatre
. . . . 5D 75
  (off Sloane Sq.)
Royal Cres. W11 . . . . 2F 71
Royal Cres. M. W11 . . . . 2F 71
Royal Duchess M.
SW12 . . . . 5D 103
Royal Exchange
. . . . 3C 18 (5F 63)
Royal Exchange Av.
EC3 . . . . 3C 18
Royal Exchange Bldgs.
EC3 . . . . 3C 18
Royal Festival Hall
. . . . 2A 24 (2B 76)
Royal Fusiliers Mus.
. . . . 5F 19
  (in Tower of London)
Royal Geographical Society
. . . . 3F 73
  (off Kensington Gore)
Royal Hill SE10 . . . . 3E 95
Royal Hill Ct. SE10 . . . . . 3E 95
  (off Greenwich High St.)
Royal Hospital Chelsea Mus.
. . . . 1C 88
Royal Hospital Rd.
SW3 . . . . 2B 88
Royal London Ind. Est.
NW10 . . . . 1A 56
Royal Mews, The
. . . . 5E 21 (4D 75)
Royal M.
SW1 . . . . 5E 21 (4D 75)
Royal Mint Ct.
EC3 . . . . 5F 19 (1B 78)
Royal Mint Pl. E1 . . . . . . 1C 78
Royal Mint St. E1 . . . . . . 1B 78
Royal National Theatre
. . . . 1A 24 (2B 76)
Royal Naval Pl. SE14 . . . . 3B 94
Royal Oak Ct. N1 . . . . . . 1D 11
  (off Pitfield St.)
Royal Oak Pl. SE22 . . . . . 4D 107
Royal Oak Rd. E8 . . . . . . 3D 51
Royal Oak Yd.
SE1 . . . . 4D 27 (3A 78)
Royal Observatory Greenwich
. . . . 3A 96
Royal Opera Arc.
SW1 . . . . 1B 22 (2F 75)
Royal Opera House
. . . . 3E 15 (5A 62)
Royal Orchard Cl.
SW18 . . . . 5A 100
Royal Pde. SE3 . . . . 5B 96
SW6 . . . . 3A 86
Royal Pde. M. SE3 . . . . . 5B 96
  (off Royal Pde.)
Royal Pl. SE10 . . . . 3E 95
Royal Rd. E16 . . . . 5F 69
SE17 . . . . 2D 91

Royal St.
SE1 . . . . 5A **24** (4B **76**)
Royal Twr. Lodge E1 . . 1C **78**
  (off Cartwright St.)
Royalty M.
W1 . . . . 3B **14** (5F **61**)
Royalty Studios W11 . . . 5A **58**
  (off Lancaster Rd.)
Royal Veterinary College
  Camden Town 5F **47**
Royal Victoria Docks
  Watersports Cen. . . 1C **82**
Royal Victoria Patriotic Bldg.
SW18 . . . . 4F **101**
Royal Victoria Pl.
E16 . . . . 2D **83**
Royal Victoria Sq.
E16 . . . . 1D **83**
Royal Victor Pl. E3 . . . 1F **65**
Royal Westminster Lodge
SW1 . . . . 5F **75**
  (off Elverton St.)
Roycroft Cl. SW2 . . . . . 1C **118**
Roydon Cl. SW11 . . . . . 5B **88**
  (off Battersea Pk. Rd.)
Royle Bldg. N1 . . . . 1E **63**
  (off Wenlock Rd.)
Roy Sq. E14 . . . . 1A **80**
Royston Ct. E13 . . . . . . 5C **54**
  (off Stopford Rd.)
SE24 . . . . 4E **105**
Royston Gdns.
IG1: Ilf. 1F **41**
Royston Ho. SE15 . . . . . 2D **93**
  (off Friary Est.)
Royston Pde. IG1: Ilf. . . 1F **41**
Royston St. E2 . . . . 1E **65**
Rozel Ct. N1 . . . . 5A **50**
Rozel Rd. SW4 . . . . 1E **103**
Rq33 SW18 . . . . 2C **100**
Rubens Gdns. SE22 . . . 5C **106**
  (off Lordship La.)
Rubens Pl. SW4 . . . . . . 2A **104**
Rubens St. SE6 . . . . 2B **122**
Ruby St. SE15 . . . . 2D **93**
Ruby Triangle SE15 . . . 2D **93**
Ruckholt Cl. E10 . . . . . . 5D **39**
Ruckholt Rd. E9 . . . . . . 1C **52**
E10 . . . . 1C **52**
Rucklidge Av. NW10. . . 1B **56**
Rucklidge Pas.
NW10 . . . . 1B **56**
  (off Rucklidge Av.)
Rudall Cres. NW3 . . . . . 1F **45**
Rudbeck Ho. SE15 . . . 3C **92**
  (off Peckham Pk. Rd.)
Ruddington Cl. E5 . . . . . 1A **52**
Rudge Ho. SE16 . . . . . 4C **78**
  (off Jamaica Rd.)
Rudgwick Ter. NW8 . . . 5A **46**
Rudloe Rd. SW12 . . . . . 5E **103**
Rudolf Pl. SW8 . . . . 2A **90**
Rudolph Rd. E13 . . . . . . 1B **68**
NW6 . . . . 1C **58**
Rufford St. N1 . . . . 5A **48**
Rufus Bus. Cen.
SW18 . . . . 2D **115**
Rufus Ho. SE1 . . . . 5F **27**
  (off Abbey St.)
Rufus St. N1 . . 2D **11** (2A **64**)

Rugby Mans. W14 . . . . . 5A **72**
  (off Bishop King's Rd.)
Rugby Rd. W4 . . . . 3A **70**
Rugby St.
WC1 . . . . 4F **7** (3B **62**)
Rugg St. E14 . . . . 1C **80**
Rugless Ho. E14 . . . . . . 3E **81**
  (off E. Ferry Rd.)
Rugmere NW1 . . . . 4C **46**
  (off Ferdinand St.)
Ruislip St. SW17 . . . . . 4B **116**
Rumball Ho. SE5 . . . . . 3A **92**
  (off Harris St.)
Rumbold Rd. SW6 . . . . 3D **87**
Rum Cl. E1 . . . . 1E **79**
Rumford Ho. SE1 . . . . . 5F **25**
  (off Tiverton St.)
Rumsey M. N4 . . . . 5D **35**
Rumsey Rd. SW9 . . . . . 1B **104**
Runacres Ct. SE17 . . . . 1E **91**
Runbury Circ. NW9 . . . . 4A **28**
Runcorn Pl. W11 . . . . . . 1A **72**
Rundell Cres.
NW4 . . . . 1D **29**
Rundell Twr. SW8 . . . . . 4B **90**
Runnymede Ct.
SW15 . . . . 1C **112**
Runnymede Ho. E9 . . . . 1A **52**
Rupack St. SE16 . . . . . . 3E **79**
Rupert Ct.
W1 . . . . 4B **14** (1F **75**)
Rupert Gdns. SW9 . . . . 5D **91**
Rupert Ho. SE11 . . . . . . 5C **76**
Rupert Ho. N19. . . . . . . 5F **33**
  (not continuous)
NW6 . . . . 1B **58**
W4 . . . . 4A **70**
Rupert St.
W1 . . . . 4B **14** (1F **75**)
Rusbridge Cl. E8 . . . . . . 2C **50**
Ruscoe Rd. E16 . . . . . . 5B **68**
Rusham Rd. SW12 . . . . 4B **102**
Rush Comn. M.
SW2 . . . . 5B **104**
  (Cotherstone Rd.)
SW2 . . . . 4B **104**
  (New Pk. Rd.)
Rushcroft Rd. SW2 . . . . 2C **104**
Rushcutters Ct. SE16 . . 5A **80**
  (off Boat Lifter Way)
Rushey Grn. SE6 . . . . . . 5D **109**
Rushey Mead SE4 . . . . . 3C **108**
Rushford Rd. SE4 . . . . . 4B **108**
Rushgrove Pde. NW9 . . 1A **28**
Rush Hill M. SW11 . . . 1C **102**
  (off Rush Hill Rd.)
Rush Hill Rd. SW11 . . . 1C **102**
Rushmead E2 . . . . 2D **65**
Rushmere Pl. SW19. . . . 5F **113**
Rushmore Cres. E5 . . . . 1F **51**
Rushmore Ho. SW15 . . . 5C **98**
W14 . . . . 4A **72**
  (off Russell Rd.)
Rushmore Rd. E5 . . . . . 1E **51**
  (not continuous)
Rusholme Gro.
SE19 . . . . 5A **120**
Rusholme Rd. SW15 . . . 4F **99**
Rushton Ho. SW8 . . . . . 5F **89**
Rushton St. N1 . . . . 1F **63**

Rushworth St.
SE1 . . . . 3E **25** (3D **77**)
Ruskin Av. E12 . . . . 3F **55**
Ruskin Cl. NW11 . . . . . . 1D **31**
Ruskin Ct. SE5 . . . . 1F **105**
  (off Champion Hill)
Ruskin Ho. SW1 . . . . . . 5F **75**
  (off Herrick St.)
Ruskin Mans. W14. . . . . 2A **86**
  (off Queen's Club Gdns.)
Ruskin Pk. Ho. SE5 . . . 1F **105**
Ruskin Wlk. SE24. . . . . . 3E **105**
Rusper Cl. NW2 . . . . 5E **29**
Rusper Ct. SW9 . . . . . . 5A **90**
  (off Clapham Rd.)
Russell Cl. SE7 . . . . 3E **97**
W4 . . . . 2B **84**
Russell Ct. E10 . . . . 2D **39**
SE15 . . . . 5D **93**
  (off Heaton Rd.)
SW1 . . . . 2A **22**
SW16 . . . . 5B **118**
WC1 . . . . 4D **7**
Russell Flint Ho. E16. . . 2D **83**
  (off Pankhurst Av.)
Russell Gdns. NW11 . . . 1A **30**
W14 . . . . 4A **72**
Russell Gdns. M.
W14 . . . . 3A **72**
Russell Gro. SW9 . . . . . 3C **90**
Russell Ho. E14. . . . . . . 5C **66**
  (off Saracen St.)
SW1 . . . . 1E **89**
  (off Cambridge St.)
Russell Lodge SE1. . . . . 5B **26**
  (off Spurgeon St.)
Russell Pde. NW11 . . . . 1A **30**
  (off Golders Grn. Rd.)
Russell Pl. NW3. . . . . . . 2A **46**
SE16 . . . . 4A **80**
Russell Rd. E10. . . . . . . 1D **39**
E16 . . . . 5C **68**
N8 . . . . 1F **33**
N15. . . . . 1A **36**
NW9 . . . . 1B **28**
W14 . . . . 4A **72**
Russell's Footpath
SW16 . . . . 5A **118**
Russell Sq.
WC1. . . . . 4D **7** (4A **62**)
Russell St.
WC2 . . . . 4E **15** (1A **76**)
Russet Yd. SW15 . . . . . 2A **100**
Russet Cres. N7 . . . . 2B **48**
Russet Way SE13 . . . . . 5D **95**
Russia Ct. EC2 . . . . 2A **18**
Russia Dock Rd.
SE16 . . . . 2A **80**
Russia La. E2 . . . . 1E **65**
Russia Row
EC2 . . . . 3A **18** (5E **63**)
Russia Wlk. SE16 . . . . . 3A **80**
Rusthall Av. W4 . . . . 5A **70**
Rustic Wlk. E16. . . . . . . 5D **69**
  (off Lambert Rd.)
Ruston M. W11 . . . . 5A **58**
Ruston Rd. SE18 . . . . . . 4F **83**
Ruston St. E3 . . . . 5B **52**
Rust Sq. SE5. . . . . 3F **91**
Rutford Rd. SW16 . . . . . 5A **118**

Ruth Ct. E3 . . . . 1A 66
Rutherford Ho. *E1* *3D 65*
  (off Brady St.)
Rutherford St. SW1 . . . . . 5F 75
Ruth Ho. *W10* *3A 58*
  (off Kensal Rd.)
Ruthin Cl. NW9 . . . . 1A 28
Ruthin Rd. SE3 . . . . 2C 96
Ruthven St. E9 . . . . 5F 51
Rutland Ct. SE5 . . . . . . 2F 105
  SW7 . . . . 3A 74
  (off Rutland Gdns.)
Rutland Gdns. N4 . . . . . . 1D 35
  SW7 . . . . 3A 74
Rutland Gdns. M.
  SW7 . . . . 3A 74
Rutland Ga. SW7 . . . . . . 3A 74
Rutland Ga. M. *SW7* 3A 74
  (off Rutland Ga.)
Rutland Gro. W6 . . . . 1D 85
Rutland Ho. *W8* *4D 73*
  (off Marloes Rd.)
Rutland M. NW8 . . . . 5D 45
Rutland M. E. *SW7* *4A 74*
  (off Ennismore Ga.)
Rutland M. Sth. *SW7* . . *4A 74*
  (off Ennismore Ga.)
Rutland M. W. *SW7* *4A 74*
  (off Rutland Ga.)
Rutland Pk. NW2 . . . . . . 3E 43
  SE6 . . . . 2B 122
Rutland Pk. Gdns.
  NW2 . . . . *3E 43*
  (off Rutland Pk.)
Rutland Pk. Mans.
  NW2 . . . . 3E 43
Rutland Pl.
  EC1 . . . . . . 5E **9** (3D **63**)
Rutland Rd. E7 . . . . 4F 55
  E9 . . . . 5F 51
  E17 . . . . 1C 38
Rutland St. SW7 . . . . 4A 74
Rutland Wlk. SE6 . . . . . 2B 122
Rutley Cl. SE17 . . . . 2D 91
Rutt's Ter. SE14 . . . . 4F 93
Ruvigny Gdns. SW15 . . . 1F 99
Ryan Cl. SE3 . . . . 2D 111
Rycott Path SE22 . . . . . 5C 106
Ryculff Sq. SE3 . . . . 5B 96
Rydal Gdns. NW9 . . . . . . 1A 28
  SW15 . . . . 3A 112
Rydal Rd. SW16 . . . . 4F 117
Rydal Water
  NW1 . . . . 2F **5** (2E **61**)
Rydens Ho. SE9 . . . . . . 3E 125
Ryder Ho.
  BR1: Brom 5D 125
Ryder Ct. E10 . . . . 4D 39
  SW1 . . . . 1A 22
Ryder Dr. SE16 . . . . 1D 93
Ryder Ho. *E1* *3E 65*
  (off Colebert Av.)
Ryder M. E9 . . . . 2E 51
Ryder's Ter. NW8 . . . . . . 1E 59
Ryder St.
  SW1 . . . . . . 1A **22** (2E **75**)
Ryder Yd.
  SW1 . . . . . . 1A **22** (2E **75**)
Ryde Va. Rd. SW12 . . . . 2E 117
Rydons Cl. SE9 . . . . 1F 111

Rydon St. N1 . . . . 5E 49
Rydston Cl. N7 . . . . 4A 48
Ryecotes Mead
  SE21 . . . . 1A 120
Ryecroft Rd. SE13 . . . . . 3E 109
  SW16 . . . . 5C 118
Ryecroft St. SW6 . . . . . . 4D 87
Ryedale SE22 . . . . 4D 107
Ryefield Path SW15 . . . 1C 112
Ryefield Rd. SE19 . . . . . 5E 119
Rye Ho. *SE16* *3E 79*
  (off Swan Rd.)
  SW1 . . . . *1D 89*
  (off Ebury Bri. Rd.)
Ryelands Cres.
  SE12 . . . . 4E 111
Rye La. SE15 . . . . 4C 92
Rye Pas. SE15 . . . . 1C 106
Rye Rd. SE15 . . . . 2F 107
Rye Wlk. SW15 . . . . 3F 99
Ryfold Rd. SW19 . . . . . 3C 114
Rylandes Rd. NW2 . . . . . 5C 28
Ryland Rd. NW5 . . . . 3D 47
Rylett Cres. W12 . . . . . . 3B 70
Rylett Rd. W12 . . . . 3B 70
Rylston Rd. SW6 . . . . . . 2B 86
Rymer St. SE24 . . . . . . 4D 105
Rysbrack St.
  SW3 . . . . . . 5A **20** (4B **74**)

S

Saatchi Collection 3F 23
Sabbarton St. E16 . . . . . 5B 68
Sabella Ct. E3 . . . . 1B 66
Sabine Rd. SW11 . . . . . 1B 102
Sable St. N1 . . . . 4D 49
Sach Rd. E5 . . . . 4D 37
Sackville Ho.
  SW16 . . . . 3A 118
Sackville St.
  W1 . . . . . . 5A **14** (1E **75**)
Saddlers M. SW8 . . . . . . 4A 90
Saddle Yd.
  W1 . . . . 1D **21** (2D **75**)
Sadler Ho. *EC1* *1C 8*
  (off Spa Grn. Est.)
Sadler's Wells Theatre
  . . . . 1C 8
Saffron Av. E14 . . . . 1F 81
Saffron Cl. NW11 . . . . . 1B 30
Saffron Ct. E15 . . . . 2A 54
  (off Maryland Pk.)
Saffron Hill
  EC1 . . . . . . 5C **8** (4C **62**)
Saffron St.
  EC1 . . . . . . 5C **8** (4C **62**)
Saffron Wharf *SE1* *3B 78*
  (off Shad Thames)
Sage M. SE22 . . . . 3B 106
Sage St. E1 . . . . 1E 79
Sage Way WC1 . . . . 2F 7
Saigasso Cl. E16 . . . . . . 5F 69
Sail Ct. *E14* *1F 81*
  (off Newport Av.)
Sailmakers Ct. SW6 . . . 5E 87
Sail St. SE11 . . . . 5B 76
Sainfoin Rd. SW17 . . . . 2C 116

Sainsbury Rd. SE19 . . . 5A 120
St Agnes Cl. E9 . . . . 5E 51
St Agnes Pl. SE11 . . . . . 2C 90
St Agnes Well EC1 . . . . . 3C 10
St Aidan's Rd. SE22 . . . 4D 107
St Alban's Av. W4 . . . . . 4A 70
St Albans Cl. NW11 . . . . 3C 30
St Albans Ct. EC2 . . . . . 1A 18
St Alban's Gro. W8 . . . . 4D 73
St Alban's La. NW11 . . . 3C 30
St Albans Mans. *W8* . . . *4D 73*
  (off Kensington Ct. Pl.)
St Alban's Pl. N1 . . . . . . 5D 49
St Albans Rd. NW5 . . . . 5C 32
  NW10 . . . . 5A 42
St Alban's St.
  SW1 . . . . . . 5B **14** (1F **75**)
  (not continuous)
St Albans Studios
  W8 . . . . *4D 73*
  (off St Albans Gro.)
St Albans Ter. W6 . . . . . 2A 86
St Albans Vs. NW5 . . . . 5C 32
St Alfege Pas. SE10 . . . 2E 95
St Alfege Rd. SE7 . . . . . 2F 97
St Alphage Gdn.
  EC2 . . . . 1A **18** (4E **63**)
St Alphage Highwalk
  EC2 . . . . 1A 18
St Alphage Ho. EC2 . . . 1B 18
St Alphonsus Rd.
  SW4 . . . . 2E 103
St Amunds Cl. SE6 . . . . 4C 122
St Andrews Chambers
  W1 . . . . *1A 14*
  (off Wells St.)
St Andrews Cl. NW2 . . . 5D 29
  SE16 . . . . 1D 93
St Andrew's Ct.
  SW18 . . . . 2E 115
St Andrew's Gro. N16 . . 3F 35
St Andrew's Hill
  EC4 . . . . . . 4E **17** (1D **77**)
  (not continuous)
St Andrews Mans.
  W1 . . . . *1B 12*
  (off Dorset St.)
  W14 . . . . *2A 86*
  (off St Andrews Rd.)
St Andrews M. N16 . . . . 3A 36
  SE3 . . . . 3C 96
  SW12 . . . . 1F 117
St Andrew's Pl.
  NW1 . . . . . . 3E **5** (3D **61**)
St Andrews Rd. E11 . . . 1A 40
  E12 . . . . 4F 41
  E13 . . . . 2D 69
  NW10 . . . . 3D 43
  NW11 . . . . 1B 30
  W3 . . . . 1A 70
  W14 . . . . 2A 86
St Andrews Sq. W11 . . . 5A 58
St Andrew St.
  EC1 . . . . . . 1C **16** (4C **62**)
St Andrews Way E3 . . . . 3D 67
St Andrew's Wharf
  SE1 . . . . 3B 78
St Anne's Cl. N6 . . . . . . 5C 32
St Anne's Ct. NW6 . . . . 5A 44
  W1 . . . . 3B **14** (5F **61**)

St Anne's Flats *NW1* *1B 6*
(off Doric Way)
St Anne's Pas. E14. . . . . 5B 66
St Anne's Rd. E11. . . . . 4F 39
St Anne's Row E14. . . . . 5B 66
St Anne's Trad. Est.
E14. . . . . *5B 66*
(off St Anne's Row)
St Anne St. E14 . . . . . . 5B 66
St Ann's Cres.
SW18. . . . . 4D 101
St Ann's Gdns.
NW5. . . . . 3C 46
St Ann's Hill SW18. . . 3D 101
St Ann's Ho. *WC1*. *2B 8*
(off Margery St.)
St Ann's La.
SW1. . . . . 5C 22 (4F 75)
St Ann's Pk. Rd.
SW18. . . . . 4E 101
St Ann's Pas. SW13 . . . 1A 98
St Ann's Rd. N15 . . . . . 1D 35
SW13. . . . . 5B 84
W11. . . . . 1F 71
St Ann's St.
SW1. . . . . 5C 22 (4F 75)
St Ann's Ter. NW8. . . . . 1F 59
St Ann's Vs. W11 . . . . . 2F 71
St Anselm's Pl.
W1. . . . . 4D 13 (1D 75)
St Anthony's Cl. E1. . . . 2C 78
SW17. . . . . 2A 116
St Anthony's Ct.
SW17. . . . . 2C 116
St Anthony's Flats
NW1. . . . . *1B 6*
(off Aldenham St.)
St Antony's Rd. E7 . . . . 4D 55
St Asaph Rd. SE4 . . . . . 1F 107
St Aubins Ct. N1 . . . . . 5F 49
St Aubyn's Av.
SW19. . . . . 5B 114
St Augustine's Ho.
NW1. . . . . *1B 6*
(off Werrington St.)
St Augustine's Mans.
SW1. . . . . *5E 75*
(off Bloomburg St.)
St Augustine's Path
N5. . . . . 1E 49
St Augustine's Rd.
NW1. . . . . 4F 47
St Austell Rd. SE13 . . . . 5E 95
St Barnabas Cl.
SE22. . . . . 3A 106
St Barnabas Rd. E17 . . . 1C 38
St Barnabas St. SW1. . . 1C 88
St Barnabas Ter. E9 . . . 2F 51
St Barnabas Vs. SW8. . . 4A 90
St Bartholomew's Cl.
SE26. . . . . 4D 121
St Bartholomew's
Hospital Mus. 1E 17
St Benedict's Cl.
SW17. . . . . 5C 116
St Benet's Cl. SW17. . . 2A 116
St Benet's Pl.
EC3. . . . . 4C 18 (1F 77)
St Bernard's Cl.
SE27. . . . . 4F 119

St Bernards Ho. E14. . . . *4E 81*
(off Galbraith St.)
St Bernard's Rd. E6 . . . 5F 55
St Botolph Row
EC3. . . . . 3F 19 (5B 64)
St Botolph St.
EC3. . . . . 2F 19 (5B 64)
St Brelades Ct. N1. . . 5A 50
St Bride's Av. EC4 . . . 3D 17
St Bride's Crypt Mus.
. . . . 3D 17
(in St Bride's)
St Bride's Pas. EC4 . . . 3D 17
St Bride St.
EC4. . . . . 2D 17 (5D 63)
St Catherine's Cl.
SW17. . . . . 2A 116
St Catherine's Ct. W4. . .4A 70
St Catherine's Dr.
SE14 . . . . 5F 93
St Catherines M.
SW3 . . . . 5B 74
St Catherines Twr.
E10. . . . . 2D 39
St Chad's Pl.
WC1. . . . . 1E 7 (2A 62)
St Chad's St.
WC1. . . . . 1E 7 (2A 62)
(not continuous)
St Charles Pl. W10 . . . 4A 58
St Charles Sq. W10 . . . 4F 57
St Christopher's Ho.
NW1. . . . . *1E 61*
(off Bridgeway St.)
St Christopher's Pl.
W1. . . . . 2C 12 (5C 60)
St Clair Rd. E13. . . . . 1D 69
St Clare St.
EC3. . . . . 3F 19 (5B 64)
St Clements Ct. EC4. . . 4C 18
N7. . . . . 3B 48
SE14. . . . . *2F 93*
(off Myers La.)
W11. . . . . *1F 71*
(off Stoneleigh St.)
St Clement's Hgts.
SE26. . . . . 3C 120
St Clements Ho. E1 . . . 1F 19
(off Leyden St.)
St Clement's La.
WC2. . . . . 3A 16 (5B 62)
St Clements Mans.
SW6. . . . . *2F 85*
(off Lillie Rd.)
St Clements St. N7 . . . 3C 48
St Clements Yd.
SE22. . . . . 2B 106
St Cloud Rd. SE27 . . . 4E 119
St Crispin's Cl. NW3 . . 1A 46
St Cross St.
EC1. . . . . 5C 8 (4C 62)
St Cuthbert's Rd.
NW2. . . . . 3B 44
St Cyprian's St.
SW17. . . . . 4B 116
St Davids Cl. SE16. . . . *1D 93*
(off Masters Dr.)
St Davids M. *E3*. *2A 66*
(off Morgan St.)
St David's Pl. NW4 . . . 2D 29

St Davids Sq. E14. . . . . 1D 95
St Denis Rd. SE27 . . . . 4F 119
St Dionis Rd. E12. . . . . 5F 41
SW6. . . . . 5B 86
St Donatt's Rd. SE14 . . 4B 94
St Dunstan's All.
EC3. . . . . 4D 19
St Dunstans Av. W3 . . . 1A 70
St Dunstan's Ct.
EC4. . . . . 3C 16 (5C 62)
St Dunstans Hill
EC3. . . . . 5D 19 (1A 78)
St Dunstan's La.
EC3. . . . . 5D 19 (1A 78)
St Dunstan's Rd. E7. . . 3D 55
W6. . . . . 1F 85
St Edmund's Cl. NW8. . 5B 46
SW17. . . . . 2A 116
St Edmund's Ct. NW8. . *5B 46*
(off St Edmund's Ter.)
St Edmunds Sq.
SW13 . . . . 2E 85
St Edmund's Ter.
NW8 . . . . 5A 46
St Edward's Cl.
NW11. . . . . 1C 30
St Edwards Ct. E10 . . . 2D 39
NW11. . . . . 1C 30
St Elizabeth Ct. E10. . . 2D 39
St Elmo Rd. W12 . . . . . 2B 70
(not continuous)
St Elmos Rd. SE16. . . . 3A 80
St Ermin's Hill SW1 . . . 5B 22
St Ervan's Rd. W10 . . . 4B 58
St Eugene Ct. NW6 . . . *5A 44*
(off Salusbury Rd.)
St Faith's Rd. SE21 . . . 1D 119
St Fillans Rd. SE6 . . . . 1E 123
St Francis' Ho. *NW1*. . . *1F 61*
(off Bridgeway St.)
St Francis Rd. SE22. . . 2A 106
St Frideswide's M.
E14 . . . . 5E 67
St Gabriel's Cl. E11. . . 4D 41
E14. . . . . 4D 67
St Gabriels Mnr. *SE5*. . *4D 91*
(off Cormont Rd.)
St Gabriels Rd. NW2 . . 2F 43
St George's Av. E7. . . . 4D 55
N7 . . . . 1F 47
St George's Bldgs.
SE1. . . . . *4D 77*
(off St George's Rd.)
St George's Cathedral
. . . . 1E 5 (2D 61)
St George's Cir.
SE1 . . . . 5D 25 (4D 77)
St George's Cl.
NW11. . . . . 1B 30
SW8 . . . . 4E 89
St Georges Ct.
EC4. . . . . 2D 17 (5D 63)
SW1. . . . . *1E 89*
(off St George's Dr.)
SW15 . . . . 2B 100
St George's Dr. SW1 . . 5D 75
ST GEORGE'S FIELD . . . 1A 74
St George's Flds. W2. . 5A 60
St George's Gro.
SW17. . . . . 3F 115

St George's Ho. NW1 . . . 1F **61**
  (off Bridgeway St.)
St George's La. EC3 . . . . 4C **18**
St George's Mans.
  SW1 . . . . 1F **89**
  (off Causton St.)
St George's M. NW1 . . . 4B **46**
  SE1 . . . . 5C **24**
  SE8 . . . . 5B **80**
St Georges Pde.
  SE6 . . . . 2B **122**
St George's Path
  SE4 . . . . 2C **108**
  (off Adelaide Av.)
St George's RC Cathedral
  . . . . 5C **24** (4C **76**)
St George's Rd. E7 . . . . 4D **55**
  E10 . . . . 5E **39**
  NW11 . . . . 1B **30**
  SE1 . . . . 5C **24** (4C **76**)
  W4 . . . . 3A **70**
St Georges Sq. E7 . . . . 4D **55**
  E14 . . . . 1A **80**
  SE8 . . . . 5B **80**
  (not continuous)
  SW1 . . . . 1F **89**
St George's Sq. M.
  SW1 . . . . 1F **89**
St George's Ter. E6 . . . . 2F **69**
  (off Masterman Rd.)
  NW1 . . . . 4B **46**
  SE15 . . . . 3C **92**
  (off Peckham Hill St.)
St George's Theatre . . 1F **47**
St George St.
  W1 . . . . 3E **13** (1D **75**)
St George's Way
  SE15 . . . . 2A **92**
St George's Wharf
  SE1 . . . . 3F **27**
  (off Shad Thames)
St George Wharf
  SW8 . . . . 2A **90**
St Gerards Cl. SW4 . . 3E **103**
St German's Pl. SE3 . . 4C **96**
St German's Rd.
  SE23 . . . . 1A **122**
St Giles Cir.
  W1 . . . . 2C **14** (5F **61**)
St Giles Ct. WC2 . . . . . 2D **15**
St Giles High St.
  WC2 . . . . 2C **14** (5F **61**)
St Giles Pas. WC2 . . . . 3C **14**
St Giles Rd. SE5 . . . . . 3A **92**
St Giles Ter. EC2 . . . . . 1A **18**
  (off Beech St.)
St Giles Twr. SE5 . . . . 4A **92**
  (off Gables Cl.)
St Gilles Ho. E2 . . . . . . 1F **65**
  (off Mace St.)
St Gothard Rd.
  SE27 . . . . 4F **119**
  (not continuous)
St Helena Ho. WC1 . . . . 2B **8**
  (off Margery St.)
St Helena Rd. SE16 . . . 5F **79**
St Helena St.
  WC1 . . . . 2B **8** (2C **62**)
St Helen's Gdns.
  W10 . . . . 4F **57**

St Helen's Pl.
  EC3 . . . . 2D **19** (5A **64**)
St Helier Ct. N1 . . . . . . 5A **50**
  (off De Beauvoir Est.)
  SE16 . . . . 3F **79**
  (off Poolmans St.)
St Helier's Rd. E10 . . . . 1E **39**
St Hilda's Cl. NW6 . . . . 4F **43**
  SW17 . . . . 2A **116**
St Hilda's Rd. SW13 . . 2D **85**
St Hilda's Wharf E1 . . . 2E **79**
  (off Wapping High St.)
St Hubert's Ho. E14 . . . 4C **80**
  (off Janet St.)
St Hughes Cl. SW17 . . 2A **116**
St James SE14 . . . . . . 4A **94**
St James App.
  EC2 . . . . 4D **11** (3A **64**)
St James Ct. E2 . . . . . . 2C **64**
  (off Bethnal Grn. Rd.)
  E12 . . . . 4E **41**
  SE3 . . . . 4D **97**
  SW1 . . . . 5A **22** (4E **75**)
St James Gro. SW11 . . 5B **88**
St James' Mans.
  NW6 . . . . 4C **44**
  (off W. End La.)
St James M. E14 . . . . . 4E **81**
  E17 . . . . 1A **38**
  (off St James's St.)
St James Residences
  W1 . . . . 4B **14**
  (off Brewer St.)
St James' Rd. E15 . . . . 2B **54**
ST JAMES'S . . 1B **22** (2F **75**)
St James's
  SW1 . . . . 1A **22** (2E **75**)
St James's Av. E2 . . . . 1E **65**
St James's Chambers
  SW1 . . . . 1A **22**
  (off Jermyn St.)
St James's Cl. NW8 . . 5B **46**
  (off St James's Ter. M.)
  SW17 . . . . 2B **116**
St James's Cres.
  SW9 . . . . 1C **104**
St James's Dr. SW17 . 1B **116**
St James's Gdns.
  W11 . . . . 2A **72**
  (not continuous)
St James's Mkt.
  SW1 . . . . 5B **14** (1F **75**)
St James's Palace
  . . . . 2A **22** (3E **75**)
St James's Pk.
  . . . . 3B **22** (3F **75**)
St James's Pas. EC3 . . 3E **19**
St James's Pl.
  SW1 . . . . 2F **21** (2E **75**)
St James's Rd. SE1 . . . 2C **92**
  SE16 . . . . 4C **78**
St James's Sq.
  SW1 . . . . 1A **22** (2E **75**)
St James's St. E17 . . . 1A **38**
  SW1 . . . . 1F **21** (2E **75**)
St James's Ter. NW8 . . 5B **46**
  (off Prince Albert Rd.)
St James's Ter. M.
  NW8 . . . . 5B **46**
St James St. W6 . . . . . 1E **85**

St James's Wlk.
  EC1 . . . . 3D **9** (3D **63**)
St James Ter. SW12 . . 1C **116**
ST JOHNS 5C **94**
St John's Av. NW10 . . . 5B **42**
  SW15 . . . . 3F **99**
St Johns Chu. Rd.
  E9 . . . . 2E **51**
St John's Cl. SW6 . . . . 3C **86**
St John's Ct. E1 . . . . . . 2D **79**
  (off Scandrett St.)
  N4 . . . . 4D **35**
  N5 . . . . 1D **49**
  SE13 . . . . 5E **95**
  W6 . . . . 5D **71**
  (off Glenthorne Rd.)
St John's Cres.
  SW9 . . . . 1C **104**
St Johns Dr. SW18 . . . 1D **115**
St John's Est. N1 . . . . . 1F **63**
  SE1 . . . . 3F **27**
St John's Gdns. W11 . . 1A **72**
St John's Gate 4D **9**
St John's Gro. N19 . . . 4E **33**
  SW13 . . . . 5B **84**
St John's Hill SW11 . . 3F **101**
St John's Hill Gro.
  SW11 . . . . 2F **101**
St Johns Ho. E14 . . . . 5E **81**
  (off Pier St.)
  SE17 . . . . 2F **91**
  (off Lytham St.)
St John's La.
  EC1 . . . . 4D **9** (3D **63**)
St John's M. W11 . . . . 5C **58**
St John's Pk. SE3 . . . . 3B **96**
St John's Pk. Mans.
  N19 . . . . 5E **33**
St John's Path EC1 . . . 4D **9**
St Johns Pathway
  SE23 . . . . 1E **121**
St John's Pl.
  EC1 . . . . 4D **9** (3D **63**)
St John's Rd. E16 . . . . 5C **68**
  N15 . . . . 1A **36**
  NW11 . . . . 1B **30**
  SW11 . . . . 2A **102**
St John's Sq.
  EC1 . . . . 4D **9** (3D **63**)
St John's Ter. E7 . . . . . 3D **55**
  SW15 . . . . 3A **112**
  (off Kingston Va.)
  W10 . . . . 3F **57**
St John St.
  EC1 . . . . 1C **8** (1C **62**)
St John's Va. SE8 . . . . 5C **94**
St John's Vs. N19 . . . . 4F **33**
  W8 . . . . 4D **73**
  (off St Mary's Pl.)
St John's Way N19 . . . 4E **33**
ST JOHN'S WOOD . . . 1F **59**
St John's Wood Ct.
  NW8 . . . . 2F **59**
  (off St John's Wood Rd.)
St John's Wood High St.
  NW8 . . . . 1F **59**
St John's Wood Pk.
  NW8 . . . . 5F **45**
St John's Wood Rd.
  NW8 . . . . 3F **59**

St John's Wood Ter.
NW8 . . . . 1F 59
St Josephs Almshouses
W6. . . . . .5F 71
(off Brook Grn.)
St Joseph's Cl. W10. . . . 4A 58
St Joseph's College
Sports Cen. 5D 119
St Joseph's Cotts.
SW3 . . . . .5B 74
(off Cadogan St.)
St Joseph's Cl. SE7. . . . 2D 97
St Joseph's Flats
NW1 . . . . .1B 6
(off Drummond Cres.)
St Joseph's Ho. W6 . . . .5F 71
(off Brook Grn.)
St Joseph's St. SW8 . . . 4D 89
St Joseph's Va. SE3 . . . 1F 109
St Jude's Rd. E2. . . . . . 1D 65
St Jude St. N16 . . . . 2A 50
St Julian's Cl.
SW16 . . . . 4C 118
St Julian's Farm Rd.
SE27 . . . . 4C 118
St Julian's Rd. NW6. . . . 5C 44
St Katharine Docks
. . . . 5F 19 (2C 78)
St Katharine's Pct.
NW1 . . . . 1D 61
St Katharine's Way
E1. . . . . 1F 27 (2B 78)
(not continuous)
St Katherine's Row
EC3 . . . . 4E 19
St Katherines Wlk.
W11. . . . . 2F 71
(off St Ann's Rd.)
St Kilda's Rd. N16 . . . . . 3F 35
St Kitts Ter. SE19 . . . . .5A 120
St Laurence Cl. NW6 . . 5F 43
St Laurence Cotts.
E14 . . . . .2E 81
(off St Lawrence St.)
St Lawrence Cl. N1. . . . 4F 49
St Lawrence Ho. SE1 . . .5E 27
(off Purbrook St.)
St Lawrence St. E14. . . 2E 81
St Lawrence Ter.
W10 . . . . 4A 58
St Lawrence Way
SW9 . . . . 4C 90
St Leonard M. N1. . . . . .1A 64
(off Hoxton St.)
St Leonard's Ct. N1 . . . 1C 10
St Leonard's Rd. E14. . . 4D 67
(not continuous)
NW10 . . . . 3A 56
St Leonards Sq.
NW5 . . . . 3C 46
St Leonard's St. E3 . . . 2D 67
St Leonard's Ter.
SW3 . . . . .1B 88
St Loo Av. SW3. . . . . . . 2A 88
St Louis Rd. SE27. . . . . 4F 119
St Lucia Dr. E15. . . . . . .5B 54
ST LUKE'S 3A 10 (3E 63)
St Luke's Av. SW4. . . . . 2F 103
St Luke's Cl.
EC1 . . . . 3A 10 (3E 63)

St Lukes Ct. E10 . . . . . 2D 39
(off Capworth St.)
St Luke's Est.
EC1. . . . . 2B 10 (2F 63)
St Luke's M. W11. . . . . .5B 58
St Luke's Rd. W11. . . . . 4B 58
St Luke's Sq. E16. . . . . 5B 68
St Luke's St. SW3 . . . . . 1A 88
St Luke's Yd. W9 . . . . . 1B 58
(not continuous)
St Margarets Cl.
EC2 . . . . 5F 63
St Margarets Ct.
SE1 . . . . . . 2A 26 (2E 77)
SW15 . . . . 2D 99
St Margaret's Cres.
SW15 . . . . 3D 99
St Margaret's Gro.
E11 . . . . 5B 40
St Margaret's La. W8 . . 4D 73
St Margaret's Pas.
SE13 . . . . 1A 110
(not continuous)
St Margarets Rd. E12. . . 4E 41
NW10 . . . . 2E 57
SE4 . . . . 2B 108
(not continuous)
St Margaret St.
SW1. . . . . 4D 23 (3A 76)
St Marks Cl. SE10 . . . . 3E 95
SW6 . . . . 4C 86
St Marks Cl. E10 . . . . . 2D 39
(off Capworth St.)
NW8 . . . . 1E 59
(off Abercorn Pl.)
St Mark's Cres. NW1 . . . 5C 46
W11 . . . . 5A 58
St Mark's Gro. SW10. . . 3D 87
St Marks Ho. SE17 . . . . 2F 91
(off Lytham St.)
St Marks Ind. Est.
E16 . . . . 2F 83
St Mark's Pl.
SW19 . . . . 5B 114
W11 . . . . 5A 58
St Mark's Ri. E8 . . . . . . 2B 50
St Mark's Rd. W10. . . . . 4F 57
St Mark's Sq. NW1. . . . . 5C 46
St Mark St. E1 . . . . 5B 64
St Mark's Vs. N4 . . . . . .4B 34
(off Moray Rd.)
St Martin-in-the-Fields Church
. . . . .5D 15
(off St Martin's Pl.)
St Martin's Almshouses
NW1 . . . . 5E 47
St Martin's Av. E6. . . . . 1F 69
St Martins Cl. NW1 . . . . 5E 47
St Martins Ct. EC4 . . . . 2F 17
(off Paternoster Row)
N1. . . . . .5A 50
(off De Beauvoir Est.)
WC2. . . . . 4D 15 (1A 76)
St Martins Est. SW2. . . 1C 118
St Martin's La.
WC2. . . . . 4D 15 (1A 76)
St Martin's le-Grand
EC1. . . . . 2F 17 (5E 63)
St Martin's Pl.
WC2. . . . . 5D 15 (1A 76)
St Martin's Rd. SW9 . . . 5B 90

St Martin's St.
WC2. . . . . 5C 14 (1F 75)
(not continuous)
St Martin's Theatre. 4D 15
(off West St.)
St Martins Way
SW17 . . . . 3E 115
St Mary Abbot's Ct.
W14 . . . . .4B 72
(off Warwick Gdns.)
St Mary Abbot's Pl.
W8 . . . . 4A 72
St Mary Abbot's Ter.
W14 . . . . .4B 72
St Mary at Hill
EC3 . . . . 5D 19 (1A 78)
St Mary Axe
EC3 . . . . 3D 19 (5A 64)
St Marychurch St.
SE16 . . . . 3E 79
St Mary Graces Ct.
E1 . . . . 1B 78
St Marylebone Cl.
NW10 . . . . 5A 42
St Mary le-Park Ct.
SW11 . . . . 3A 88
(off Parkgate Rd.)
St Mary Newington Cl.
SE17 . . . . 1A 92
(off Surrey Sq.)
St Mary's Av. E11. . . . . 2D 41
St Mary's Cl. SE7 . . . . . 3F 97
W6 . . . . 4B 70
St Mary's Est. SE16 . . . 3E 79
(off St Marychurch St.)
St Mary's Flats NW1 . . . 1B 6
(off Drummond Cres.)
St Mary's Gdns.
SE11 . . . . 5C 76
St Mary's Ga. W8. . . . . 4D 73
St Mary's Gro. N1 . . . . 3D 49
SW13 . . . . 1D 99
St Mary's Ho. N1 . . . . . 5D 49
(off St Mary's Path)
St Mary's Mans. W2. . . .4F 59
St Mary's M. NW6 . . . . 4D 45
St Mary's Path E1. . . . .5C 64
(off Adler St.)
N1. . . . . 5D 49
St Mary's Pl. W8 . . . . . 4D 73
St Mary's Rd. E10 . . . . . 5E 39
E13. . . . . 1D 69
NW10 . . . . 5A 42
NW11 . . . . 2A 30
SE15 . . . . 4E 93
SW19 . . . . 5A 114
St Mary's Sq. W2. . . . . 4F 59
St Mary's Ter. W2. . . . . 4F 59
St Mary's Twr. EC1. . . . 4A 10
(off Fortune St.)
St Mary's Wlk. SE11 . . . 5C 76
St Matthews Cl. E10 . . . 2D 39
SE1 . . . . 4E 77
(off Meadow Row)
St Matthews Ho.
SE17 . . . . 2F 91
(off Phelp St.)
St Matthew's Lodge
NW1 . . . . 1E 61
(off Oakley Sq.)

St Matthew's Rd.
SW2 . . . . .2B **104**
St Matthew's Row E2 . . .2C **64**
St Matthew St.
SW1 . . . . .5B **22** (4F **75**)
St Maur Rd. SW6 . . . . . .4B **86**
St Michael's All.
EC3. . . . . .3C **18** (5F **63**)
St Michaels Cl. E16 . . . .4F **69**
St Michaels Cl. E14 . . . .4E **67**
(off St Leonards Rd.)
SE1 . . . . .4A **26**
(off Trinity St.)
St Michael's Flats
NW1 . . . . .1B **6**
(off Aldenham St.)
St Michael's Gdns.
W10 . . . . .4A **58**
St Michaels M. SW1 . . .5C **74**
St Michael's Rd.
NW2 . . . . .1E **43**
SW9 . . . . .5B **90**
St Michael's St. W2 . . .5F **59**
St Michaels Ter. N6 . . .3C **32**
(off South Gro.)
St Mildred's Ct.
EC2. . . . . .3B **18** (5F **63**)
St Mildreds Rd.
SE6 . . . . .5A **110**
SE12 . . . . .5A **110**
St Nicholas' Flats
NW1 . . . . .1B **6**
(off Werrington St.)
St Nicholas Glebe
SW17 . . . . .5C **116**
St Nicholas Ho. SE8 . . .2C **94**
(off Deptford Grn.)
St Nicholas St. SE8 . . .4B **94**
St Norbert Grn. SE4 . . .2A **108**
St Norbert Rd. SE4 . . .3F **107**
St Olaf Ho. SE1 . . . . . .1C **26**
St Olaf's Rd. SW6 . . . .3A **86**
St Olaf Stairs SE1 . . . .1C **26**
St Olave's Ct.
EC2. . . . . .3B **18** (5F **63**)
St Olave's Est.
SE1 . . . . .3E **27** (3A **78**)
St Olave's Gdns.
SE11 . . . . .5C **76**
St Olave's Mans.
SE11 . . . . .5C **76**
(off Walnut Tree Wlk.)
St Olave's Ter. SE1 . . . .3E **27**
St Olav's Sq. SE16 . . . .3E **79**
St Oswald's Pl. SE11 . . .1B **90**
St Oswalds Studios
SW6 . . . . .2C **86**
(off Sedlescombe Rd.)
St Oswulf St. SW1 . . . .5F **75**
St Owen Ho. SE1 . . . . . .5F **27**
(off Fendall St.)
ST PANCRAS . . .2E **7** (3B **62**)
St Pancras Commercial Cen.
NW1 . . . . .5E **47**
(off Pratt St.)
St Pancras Way NW1 . . .4E **47**
St Paul's All. EC4 . . . . . .3E **17**
St Paul's Arts Cen. 5C **80**
(off Westferry Rd.)

St Paul's Av. NW2 . . . .3D **43**
SE16 . . . . .2F **79**
St Paul's Bldgs. EC1 . . .3E **9**
(off Dallington St.)
St Paul's Cathedral
. . . . .3F **17** (5E **63**)
St Paul's Chyd.
EC4 . . . . .3E **17** (5D **63**)
(not continuous)
St Pauls Cl. SE7 . . . . . .1F **97**
St Pauls Ct. SW4 . . . . . .3F **103**
St Pauls Courtyard
SE8 . . . . .3C **94**
(off Crossfield St.)
St Paul's Cres. NW1 . . .4F **47**
(not continuous)
St Paul's Dr. E15 . . . . . .2F **53**
St Paul's M. NW1 . . . . . .4F **47**
St Paul's Pl. N1 . . . . . . .3F **49**
St Paul's Rd. N1 . . . . . .3D **49**
St Paul's Shrubbery
N1 . . . . .3F **49**
St Paul's Studios
W14 . . . . .1A **86**
(off Talgarth Rd.)
St Pauls Ter. SE17 . . . .2D **91**
St Pauls Twr. E10 . . . . . .2D **39**
(off Beaumont Rd.)
St Paul St. N1 . . . . .5E **49**
(not continuous)
St Pauls Vw. Apartments
EC1 . . . . .2B **8**
(off Amwell St.)
St Pauls Way E3 . . . . . .4B **66**
St Peter's All. EC3 . . . . . .3C **18**
(off Cornhill)
St Peter's Av. E2 . . . . . .1C **64**
St Petersburgh M.
W2 . . . . .1D **73**
St Petersburgh Pl.
W2 . . . . .1D **73**
St Peter's Cen. E1 . . . . . .2D **79**
(off Reardon St.)
St Peter's Chu. Ct.
N1 . . . . .5D **49**
(off St Peter's St.)
St Peter's Cl. E2 . . . . . .1C **64**
SW17 . . . . .2A **116**
St Peters Ct. NW4 . . . . . .1E **29**
SE12 . . . . .3B **110**
St Peter's Gdns.
SE27 . . . . .3C **118**
St Peter's Gro. W6 . . . .5C **70**
St Peters Ho. SE17 . . . .2F **91**
WC1 . . . . .2E **7**
(off Regent Sq.)
St Peters M. N8 . . . . . . .1C **34**
St Peters Pl. W9 . . . . . . .3D **59**
St Peter's Rd. W6 . . . . . .1C **84**
St Peter's Sq. E2 . . . . . .1C **64**
W6 . . . . .5B **70**
St Peter's St. N1 . . . . . . .5D **49**
St Peter's St. M. N1 . . . . .1D **63**
(off St Peters St.)
St Peter's Ter. SW6 . . . .3B **86**
St Peter's Vs. W6 . . . . . .5C **70**
St Peter's Way N1 . . . . . .4A **50**
St Peter's Wharf W4 . . .1C **84**
St Philip Ho. WC1 . . . . . .2B **8**
(off Lloyd Baker St.)

St Philip Sq. SW8 . . . . .5D **89**
St Philip's Rd. E8 . . . . . .3C **50**
St Philip St. SW8. . . . . .5D **89**
St Philip's Way N1 . . . . .5E **49**
St Quentin Ho.
SW18 . . . . .4F **101**
St Quintin Av. W10 . . . . .4E **57**
St Quintin Gdns.
W10 . . . . .4E **57**
St Quintin Rd. E13 . . . . . .2D **69**
St Regis Hgts. NW3 . . . .5D **31**
St Richard's Ho.
NW1 . . . . .1B **6**
(off Eversholt St.)
St Rule St. SW8 . . . . . . .5E **89**
St Saviour's Coll.
SE27 . . . . .4F **119**
St Saviour's Est.
SE1 . . . . .5F **27** (3B **78**)
St Saviour's Rd.
SW2 . . . . .3B **104**
St Saviour's Wharf
SE1 . . . . .3F **27**
(off Mill St.)
SE1 . . . . .3F **27**
(off Shad Thames)
Saints Cl. SE27 . . . . . . .4D **119**
Saints Dr. E7 . . . . .2F **55**
St Silas Pl. NW5 . . . . . . .3C **46**
St Simon's Av. SW15 . . .3E **99**
St Stephen's Av. E17 . . .1E **39**
W12 . . . . .2D **71**
(not continuous)
St Stephen's Cl. E17 . . .1D **39**
NW8 . . . . .5A **46**
St Stephens Ct. N8 . . . . .1B **34**
St Stephen's Cres.
W2 . . . . .5C **58**
St Stephen's Gdns.
SW15 . . . . .3B **100**
W2 . . . . .5C **58**
(not continuous)
St Stephens Gro.
SE13 . . . . .1E **109**
St Stephens Ho.
SE17 . . . . .2F **91**
(off Lytham St.)
St Stephens M. W2 . . . .4C **58**
St Stephens Pde. E7 . . .4E **55**
St Stephen's Rd. E3. . . .5A **52**
E6 . . . . .4E **55**
E17 . . . . .1D **39**
St Stephen's Row
EC4 . . . . .3B **18**
St Stephen's Ter.
SW8 . . . . .3B **90**
St Stephen's Wlk.
SW7 . . . . .5E **73**
(off Southwell Gdns.)
St Swithins La.
EC4. . . . . .4B **18** (1F **77**)
St Swithun's Rd.
SE13 . . . . .4F **109**
St Thomas Ho. E10. . . . .2D **39**
(off Beaumont Rd.)
NW1 . . . . .4E **47**
(off Wrotham Rd.)
St Thomas Ho. E1 . . . . . .5F **65**
(off W. Arbour St.)
St Thomas Rd. E16 . . . .5C **68**

St Thomas's Gdns.
NW5 . . . . 3C 46
St Thomas's Pl. E9 . . . . . . 4E 51
St Thomas's Rd. N4 . . 4C 34
NW10 . . . . 5A 42
St Thomas's Sq. E9 . . . 4E 51
St Thomas St.
SE1 . . . . . . 2C 26 (2F 77)
St Thomas's Way
SW6 . . . . 3B 86
St Vincent Cl. SE27 . . 5D 119
St Vincent De Paul Ho.
E1 . . . . 4E 65
(off Jubilee Cl.)
St Vincent Ho. SE1 . . . 5F 27
(off Fendall St.)
St Vincent St.
W1 . . . . . . 1C 12 (4C 60)
Sala Ho. SE3 . . . . 2D 111
Salamanca Pl. SE1 . . 5B 76
Salamanca Sq. SE1 . . 5B 76
(off Salamanca Pl.)
Salamanca St. SE1 . . 5B 76
SE11 . . . . 5B 76
Salcombe Rd. E17 . . . . 2B 38
N16 . . . . 2A 50
Salcott Rd. SW11 . . . 3A 102
Salehurst Rd. SE4 . . 4B 108
Salem Rd. W2 . . . . . . 1D 73
Sale Pl. W2 . . . . 4A 60
Sale St. E2 . . . . 3C 64
Salford Rd. E14 . . . . . . 5E 81
(off Seyssel St.)
Salford Rd. SW2 . . . 1F 117
Salisbury Cl. SE17 . . 5F 77
Salisbury Ct.
EC4 . . . . . . 3D 17 (5D 63)
Salisbury Ho. E14 . . . 5D 67
(off Hobday St.)
EC2 . . . . 1C 18
(off London Wall)
N1 . . . . 5D 49
(off St Mary's Path)
SW1 . . . . 1F 89
(off Drummond Ga.)
SW9 . . . . 3C 90
(off Cranmer Rd.)
Salisbury Mans. N15 . . 1D 35
Salisbury M. SW6 . . . . 3B 86
Salisbury Pas. SW6 . . 3B 86
(off Dawes Rd.)
Salisbury Pavement
SW6 . . . . 3B 86
(off Dawes Rd.)
Salisbury Pl. SW9 . . . 3D 91
W1 . . . . . . 5A 4 (4B 60)
Salisbury Rd. E7 . . . . . 3C 54
E10 . . . . 4E 39
E12 . . . . 2F 55
E17 . . . . 1E 39
N4 . . . . 1D 35
Salisbury Sq.
EC4 . . . . . . 3C 16 (5C 62)
Salisbury St. NW8 . . . 3A 60
Salisbury Ter. SE15 . . 1E 107
Salisbury Wlk. N19 . . . 4E 33
Salmen Rd. E13 . . . . . 1B 68
Salmon La. E14 . . . . . 5A 66
Salmon M. NW6 . . . . . 2C 44
Salmon St. E14 . . . . . 5B 66

Salomons Rd. E13 . . . . 4E 69
Salop Rd. E17 . . . . 1F 37
Saltcoats Rd. W4 . . . . 3A 70
Saltdene N4 . . . . 3B 34
Salterford Rd.
SW17 . . . . 5C 116
Salter Rd. SE16 . . . . . 2F 79
Salters Ct. EC4 . . . . . 3A 18
Salter's Hall Ct. EC4 . . 4B 18
Salter's Hill SE19 . . . 5F 119
Salters Rd. W10 . . . . . 3F 57
Salter St. E14 . . . . 1B 80
NW10 . . . . 2C 56
Salterton Rd. N7 . . . . . 5B 34
Saltoun Rd. SW2 . . . . 2C 104
Saltram Cres. W9 . . . . 2B 58
Saltwell St. E14 . . . . . 1C 80
Saltwood Gro. SE17 . . 1F 91
Saltwood Ho. SE15 . . . 2E 93
(off Lovelinch Cl.)
Salusbury Rd. NW6 . . 5A 44
Salutation St. SE10 . . . 5A 82
Salvador SW17 . . . . . 5B 116
Salvin Rd. SW15 . . . . . 1F 99
Salway Pl. E15 . . . . . . 3F 53
Salway Rd. E15 . . . . . . 3F 53
Samantha Cl. E17 . . . . 2B 38
Sam Bartram Cl. SE7 . . 1E 97
Sambrook Ho. E1 . . . . 4E 65
(off Jubilee St.)
SE11 . . . . 5C 76
(off Hotspur St.)
Sambruck M. SE6 . . . 1D 123
Samels Ct. W6 . . . . . . 1C 84
Samford St. NW1 . . . . . 3F 59
Samira Cl. E17 . . . . . . 1C 38
Sam Manners Ho.
SE10 . . . . 1A 96
(off Tuskar St.)
Sam March Ho. E14 . . 5F 67
(off Blair St.)
Sampson Ho.
SE1 . . . . . . 1D 25 (2D 77)
Sampson St. E1 . . . . . 2C 78
Samson St. E13 . . . . . 1E 69
Samuda Est. E14 . . . . 4E 81
Samuel Cl. E8 . . . . 5B 50
SE14 . . . . 2F 93
Samuel Ho. E8 . . . . . . 5B 50
(off Clarissa St.)
Samuel Johnson Cl.
SW16 . . . . 4B 118
Samuel Jones Ind. Est.
SE15 . . . . 3B 92
Samuel Lewis Bldgs.
N1 . . . . 3C 48
Samuel Lewis Trust Dwellings
N16 . . . . 1A 36
SE5 . . . . 4E 91
(off Warner Rd.)
SW3 . . . . 5A 74
SW6 . . . . 3C 86
(off Vanston Pl.)
W14 . . . . 5B 72
(off Lisgar Ter.)
Samuel Richardson Ho.
W14 . . . . 5B 72
(off Nth. End Cres.)

Samuel's Cl. W6 . . . . . 5E 71
Samuel St. SE15 . . . . 3B 92
Sancroft Cl. NW2 . . . . 5D 29
Sancroft Ho. SE11 . . . 1B 90
(off Sancroft St.)
Sancroft St. SE11 . . . 1B 90
Sanctuary, The SW1 . . 5C 22
Sanctuary St.
SE1 . . . . . . 3A 26 (3E 77)
Sandale Cl. N16 . . . . . 5F 35
Sandall Ho. E3 . . . . . . 1A 66
Sandall Rd. NW5 . . . . 3E 47
Sandal St. E15 . . . . . . 5A 54
Sandalwood Cl. E1 . . . 3A 66
Sandalwood Mans.
W8 . . . . 4D 73
(off Stone Hall Gdns.)
Sandbourne NW8 . . . . 5D 45
(off Abbey Rd.)
W11 . . . . 5C 58
(off Dartmouth Cl.)
Sandbourne Rd. SE4 . . 5A 94
Sandbrook Rd. N16 . . . 5A 36
Sandby Ho. NW6 . . . . 5C 44
Sandell St.
SE1 . . . . . . 3B 24 (3C 76)
Sanderling Ct. SE8 . . . 2B 94
(off Abinger Gro.)
Sanderling Lodge E1 . . 1B 78
(off Star Pl.)
Sanders Ho. WC1 . . . . 1B 8
(off Gt. Percy St.)
Sanderson Cl. NW5 . . 1D 47
Sanderson Ho. SE8 . . 1B 94
(off Grove St.)
Sanderstead Av.
NW2 . . . . 4A 30
Sanderstead Cl.
SW12 . . . . 5E 103
Sanderstead Rd. E10 . . 3A 38
Sanders Way N19 . . . . 3F 33
Sandfield WC1 . . . . . . 2E 7
(off Cromer St.)
Sandford Cl. N16 . . . . 3A 36
Sandford Row SE17 . . 1F 91
Sandford St. SW6 . . . . 3D 87
Sandgate Ho. E5 . . . . 2D 51
Sandgate La. SW18 . . 1A 116
Sandgate St. SE15 . . . 2D 93
Sandgate Trad. Est.
SE15 . . . . 2D 93
(off Sandgate St.)
Sandham Ct. SW4 . . . 4A 90
Sandhills, The SW10 . . 2E 87
(off Limerston St.)
Sandhurst Ct. SW2 . . 2A 104
Sandhurst Ho. E1 . . . . 4E 65
(off Wolsy St.)
Sandhurst Mkt. SE6 . . 1E 123
(off Sandhurst Rd.)
Sandhurst Rd. SE6 . . 1F 123
Sandifer Dr. NW2 . . . . 5F 29
Sandilands Rd. SW6 . . 4D 87
Sandison St. SE15 . . . 1C 106
Sandland St.
WC1 . . . . . . 1A 16 (4B 62)
Sandlings Cl. SE15 . . . 5D 93
Sandmere Rd. SW4 . . 2A 104
Sandown Ct. SE26 . . . 3D 121
Sandpiper Cl. SE16 . . . 3B 80

Sandpiper Ct. E1 . . . . . . 1C 78
  (off Thomas More St.)
E14 . . . . 4E 81
  (off New Union Cl.)
SE8 . . . . 2C 94
  (off Edward Pl.)
Sandpiper Ho.
  SW18 . . . . 1E 101
Sandpit Rd.
  BR1: Brom 5A 124
Sandridge St. N19 . . . . . 4E 33
Sandringham Cl.
  SW19 . . . . 1F 113
Sandringham Ct.
  SE16 . . . . 2F 79
  (off King & Queen Wharf)
W1 . . . . 3A 14
  (off Dufour's Pl.)
W9 . . . . 2E 59
  (off Maida Va.)
Sandringham Flats
  WC2 . . . . 4C 14
  (off Charing Cross Rd.)
Sandringham Gdns.
  N8 . . . . 1A 34
Sandringham Ho.
  W14 . . . . 5A 72
  (off Windsor Way)
Sandringham Rd.
  BR1: Brom 5C 124
  E7 . . . . 2E 55
  E8 . . . . 2B 50
  E10 . . . . 1F 39
  NW2 . . . . 3D 43
  NW11 . . . . 2A 30
Sandrock Rd. SE13 . . 1C 108
SANDS END 4E 87
Sand's End La. SW6 . . 4D 87
Sandstone Pl. N19 . . . . 4D 33
Sandstone Rd.
  SE12 . . . . 2D 125
Sandtoft Rd. SE7 . . . . . 2D 97
Sandwell Cres. NW6 . . 3C 44
Sandwich Ho. SE16 . . . 3E 79
  (off Swan Rd.)
WC1 . . . . 2D 7
  (off Sandwich St.)
Sandwich St.
  WC1 . . . . 2D 7 (2A 62)
  (not continuous)
Sandy Rd. NW3 . . . . . . 4D 31
  (not continuous)
Sandys Row
  E1 . . . . 1E 19 (4A 64)
Sanford La. N16 . . . . . . 5B 36
Sanford St. SE14 . . . . . 2A 94
Sanford Ter. N16 . . . . . 5B 36
Sanford Wlk. N16 . . . . . 4B 36
  SE14 . . . . 2A 94
Sangley Rd. SE6 . . . . 5D 109
Sangora Rd. SW11 . . . 2F 101
Sankey Ho. E2 . . . . 1E 65
  (off St James's Av.)
Sansom Rd. E11 . . . . . . 4B 40
Sansom St. SE5 . . . . . . 4F 91
Sans Wlk.
  EC1 . . . . 3C 8 (3C 62)
Santley Ho.
  SE1 . . . . 4C 24 (3C 76)
Santley St. SW4 . . . . . 2B 104

Santos Rd. SW18 . . . . 3C 100
Sapcote Trad. Cen.
  NW10 . . . . 3B 42
Saperton Wlk. SE11 . . 5B 76
  (off Juxon St.)
Sapperton Ct. EC1 . . . . 3F 9
Sapphire Ct. E1 . . . . . . 1C 78
  (off Cable St.)
Sapphire Rd. SE8 . . . . . 5A 80
Saracens Head Yd.
  EC3 . . . . 3F 19
Saracen St. E14 . . . . . . 5C 66
Sarah Ho. E1 . . . . 5D 65
  (off Commercial Rd.)
Sarah St. N1 . . 1E 11 (2A 64)
Sarah Swift Ho. SE1 . . 3C 26
  (off Kipling St.)
Sara La. Ct. N1 . . . . . . 1A 64
  (off Stanway St.)
Saratoga Rd. E5 . . . . . . 1E 51
Sardinia St.
  WC2 . . . . 3F 15 (5B 62)
Sarjant Path SW19 . . . 2F 113
  (off Blincoe Cl.)
Sark Wlk. E16 . . . . 5D 69
Sarnesfield Ho. SE15 . 2D 93
  (off Pencraig Way)
Sarratt Ho. W10 . . . . . . 4E 57
  (off Sutton Way)
Sarre Rd. NW2 . . . . 2B 44
Sarsfeld Rd. SW12 . . . 1B 116
Sartor Rd. SE15 . . . . . 2F 107
Sarum Ter. E3. . . . . 3B 66
Satanita Cl. E16 . . . . . . 5F 69
Satchwell Rd. E2 . . . . . 2C 64
Satchwell St. E2. . . . . . 2C 64
Sattar M. N16 . . . . 5F 35
  (off Clissold Rd.)
Saul Ct. SE15 . . . . 2B 92
Sauls Grn. E11 . . . . 5A 40
Saunders Cl. E14 . . . . . 1B 80
  (off Limehouse C'way.)
Saunders Ho. SE16 . . . 3F 79
  (off Quebec Way)
Saunders Ness Rd.
  E14 . . . . 1E 95
Saunders St. SE11 . . . . 5C 76
Savage Gdns.
  EC3 . . . . 4E 19 (1A 78)
  (not continuous)
Savannah Cl. SE15 . . . . 3B 92
Savernake Ho. N4 . . . . 2E 35
Savernake Rd. NW3 . . . 1B 46
Savile Row
  W1 . . . . 4F 13 (1E 75)
Saville Rd. E16. . . . . . . 2F 83
Savill Ho. SW4 . . . . . . 4F 103
Savona Ho. SW8 . . . . . 3E 89
  (off Savona St.)
Savona St. SW8 . . . . . . 3E 89
Savoy Bldgs. WC2 . . . . 5F 15
SAVOY CIRCUS 1B 70
Savoy Ct. E15 . . . . 5A 54
Savoy Ct. NW3 . . . . 5E 31
  WC2 . . . . 5E 15 (1B 76)
Savoy Hill
  WC2 . . . . 5F 15 (1B 76)
Savoy Pl.
  WC2 . . . . 5E 15 (1A 76)
Savoy Row WC2 . . . . . 4F 15

Savoy Steps WC2 . . . . . 5F 15
Savoy St.
  WC2 . . . . 5F 15 (1B 76)
Savoy Theatre 5E 15
  (off Strand)
Savoy Way WC2 . . . . . . 5F 15
Sawkins Cl. SW19 . . . 2A 114
Sawley Rd. W12 . . . . . . 2C 70
Sawmill Yd. E3 . . . . 5A 52
Sawyer Ct. NW10 . . . . 4A 42
Sawyer St.
  SE1 . . . . 3F 25 (3E 77)
Saxby Rd. SW2 . . . . . 5A 104
Saxonbury Ct. N7 . . . . . 2A 48
Saxon Cl. E17. . . . . 2C 38
Saxonfield Cl.
  SW2 . . . . 1B 118
Saxon Ho. E1 . . . . 1F 19
  (off Thrawl St.)
Saxon Rd. E3 . . . . 1B 66
Saxon Ter. SE6 . . . . . . 2B 122
Saxton Cl. SE13 . . . . . 1F 109
Sayes Ct. SE8 . . . . 2B 94
Sayes Ct. St. SE8 . . . . . 2B 94
Scafell NW1 . . . . 1F 5
Scala St. W1 . . . 5A 6 (4E 61)
Scampston M. W10 . . . 5F 57
Scandrett St. E1 . . . . . . 2D 79
Scarba Wlk. N1 . . . . 3F 49
  (off Marquess Rd.)
Scarborough Rd. E11 . . 3F 39
  N4 . . . . 3C 34
Scarborough St. E1 . . . 5B 64
Scarlet Rd. SE6 . . . . . 3A 124
Scarlette Mnr. Way
  SW2 . . . . 5C 104
Scarsbrook Rd. SE3 . . 1F 111
Scarsdale Pl. W8 . . . . . 4D 73
Scarsdale Studios
  W8 . . . . 4C 72
  (off Stratford Rd.)
Scarsdale Vs. W8 . . . . . 4C 72
Scarth Rd. SW13 . . . . . 1B 98
Scawen Rd. SE8. . . . . . 1A 94
Scawfell St. E2. . . . . . . 1B 64
Sceaux Gdns. SE5 . . . . 4A 92
Sceptre Ct. EC3 . . . . . . 5F 19
  (off Tower Hill)
Sceptre Ho. E1 . . . . 3E 65
  (off Malcolm Rd.)
Sceptre Rd. E2 . . . . 2E 65
Schafer Ho.
  NW1 . . . . 2F 5 (2E 61)
Schiller International
  University 2B 24
  (off Stamford St.)
Schofield Wlk. SE3 . . . 3C 96
Scholars Pl. N16 . . . . . 5A 36
Scholars Rd. SW12 . . . 1E 117
Scholefield Rd. N19 . . . 4F 33
Scholey Ho. SW11 . . . 1A 102
Schomberg Ho. SW1 . . 5F 75
  (off Page St.)
Schonfeld Sq. N16 . . . . 4F 35
School App.
  E2. . . . . 1E 11 (2A 64)
Schoolbank Rd.
  SE10 . . . . 4B 82
Schoolbell M. E3 . . . . . 1A 66

School Ho. *SE1* *5A 78*
(off Page's Wlk.)
School Ho. La. E1. . . . . 1F 79
School of Hygiene &
Tropical Medicine. . . . 5C 6
School of Oriental &
African Studies. 4C 6
School Rd. NW10. . . . . . 3A 56
School Sq. SE10. . . . . . . 4B 82
Schooner Cl. E14. . . . . . 4F 81
SE16 . . . . 3F 79
Schubert Rd.
SW15. . . . . 3B 100
Science Mus. 4F 73
Sclater St.
E1. . . . . 3F 11 (3B 64)
Scoble Pl. N16. . . . . 1B 50
Scoles Cres. SW2 . . . . . 1C 118
Scoresby St.
SE1. . . . . 2D 25 (2D 77)
(off Whitmore Est.)
Scorton Ho. *N1*. 1A 64
(off Whitmore Est.)
SCOTCH HOUSE 3B 74
Scoter Ct. *SE8* 2B 94
(off Abinger Gro.)
Scotia Bldg. *E1*. 1F 79
(off Jardine Rd.)
Scotia Ct. *SE16*. 3E 79
(off Canada Est.)
Scotia Rd. SW2 . . . . . . 5C 104
Scotland Pl.
SW1. . . . . . . 2D 23 (2D 77)
Scotney Ho. E9 . . . . 3E 51
Scotsdale Rd. SE12 . . . 3D 111
Scotson Ho. *SE11*. 5C 76
(off Marylee Way)
Scotswood St.
EC1 . . . . 3C 8 (3C 62)
Scott Ellis Gdns.
NW8 . . . . 2F 59
Scott Ho. *E13*. 1C 68
(off Queens Rd. W.)
E14. . . . . 3C 80
(off Admirals Way)
N1. . . . . 5F 49
(off Sherborne St.)
N7. . . . . 3B 48
(off Caledonian Rd.)
NW8. . . . . 3A 60
(off Broadley St.)
NW10 . . . . 4A 42
(off Kingthorpe Rd.)
Scott Lidgett Cres.
SE16 . . . . 3C 78
Scott Russell Pl. E14. . . . 1D 95
Scotts Cl. *W12* 3E 71
(off Scott's Rd.)
Scott's Rd. E10. . . . . 3E 39
W12 . . . . 3D 71
Scott's Sufferance Wharf
SE1. . . . . 4F 27
Scotts Ter. SE9 . . . . . . 2F 125
Scott St. E1. . . . . 3D 65
Scott's Yd.
EC4. . . . . . . 4B 18 (1F 77)
Scoulding Ho.
E14. . . . . 4C 80
(off Mellish St.)
Scoulding Rd. E16. . . . . . 5C 68
Scouler St. E14. . . . . 1E 81

Scout App. NW10. . . . . . 1A 42
Scout La. SW4 . . . . 1E 103
Scovell Cres. SE1. . . . . . 4F 25
Scovell Rd.
SE1. . . . . 4F 25 (3E 77)
Screen on Baker Street
(Cinema) 5A 4
(off Baker St.)
Screen on the Green Cinema
. . . . 5D 49
(off Upper St.)
Screen on the Hill (Cinema)
Belsize Pk. 2A 46
Scriven Ct. E8 . . . . 5B 50
Scriven St. E8 . . . . 5B 50
Scrooby St. SE6. . . . . . 4D 109
Scrope Ho. *EC1* 5B 8
(off Bourne Est.)
Scrubs La. NW10. . . . . . 2C 56
W10. . . . . 2C 56
Scrutton Cl.
SW12 . . . . 5F 103
Scrutton St.
EC2. . . . . . . 4D 11 (3A 64)
Scutari Rd. SE22 . . . . . 3E 107
Scylla Rd. SE15. . . . . . 1C 106
(not continuous)
Seabright St. E2 . . . . . . 2D 65
Seacole Cl. W3 . . . . 5A 56
Seacon Twr. E14. . . . . . 3B 80
Seaford Ho. *SE16*. 3E 79
(off Swan Rd.)
Seaford St.
WC1. . . . . . . 2E 7 (2B 62)
Seaforth Cres. N5. . . . . . 2E 49
Seaforth Pl. SW1. . . . . . 5A 22
Seager Pl. E3. . . . . 4B 66
Seager Bldgs. SE8 . . . . . 4C 94
Seagrave Cl. E1 . . . . . . 4F 65
Seagrave Lodge *SW6* . . 2C 86
(off Seagrave Rd.)
Seagrave Rd. SW6. . . . . 2C 86
Seagry Rd. E11 . . . . 2C 40
Seagull La. E16 . . . . 1C 82
Seal Ho. *SE1* 5C 26
(off Pardoner St.)
Seal St. E8. . . . . 1B 50
Searles Cl. SW11. . . . . . 3A 88
Searles Rd. SE1. . . . . . . 5F 77
Searson Ho. *SE17* 5D 77
(off Canterbury Pl.)
Sears St. SE5 . . . . 3F 91
Seaton Cl. E13. . . . . 3C 68
SE11. . . . . 1C 90
SW15. . . . . 1D 113
Seaton Point *E5* 1C 50
(off Nolan Way)
Sebastian Ho. *N1*. 1D 11
(off Hoxton St.)
Sebastian St.
EC1. . . . . . . 2E 9 (2D 63)
Sebbon St. N1 . . . . 4D 49
Sebert Rd. E7. . . . . 2D 55
Sebright Ho. *E2* 1C 64
(off Coate St.)
Sebright Pas. E2 . . . . . . 1C 64
Secker Ho. SW9. . . . . . . 5D 91
(off Loughborough Est.)
Secker St.
SE1 . . . . 2B 24 (2C 76)

Second Av. E13 . . . . . . 2C 68
SW14 . . . . 1A 98
W3 . . . . 2B 70
W10 . . . . 3A 58
Sedan Way SE17 . . . . . . 1A 92
Sedding St. SW1 . . . . . . 5C 74
Sedding Studios
SW1 . . . . 5C 74
(off Sedding St.)
Seddon Highwalk *EC2* . . 5F 9
(off Seddon Ho.)
Seddon Ho. EC2. . . . . . . 5F 9
Seddon St.
WC1. . . . . . . 2A 8 (2B 62)
Sedgebrook Rd. SE3 . . . 5F 97
Sedgeford Rd. W12 . . . . 2B 70
Sedgehill Rd. SE6 . . . . 4C 122
Sedgeway SE6 . . . . 1B 124
Sedgmoor Pl. SE5 . . . . . 3A 92
Sedgwick Ho. *E3* 4C 66
(off Gale St.)
Sedgwick Rd. E10 . . . . . 4E 39
Sedgwick St. E9. . . . . . . 2F 51
Sedleigh Rd. SW18 . . . 4B 100
Sedlescombe Rd.
SW6 . . . . 2C 86
Sedley Ct. SE26. . . . . . 2D 121
Sedley Ho. *SE11* 1B 90
(off Newburn St.)
Sedley Pl.
W1. . . . . 3D 13 (5D 61)
Seeley Dr. SE21. . . . . . 4A 120
Seelig Av. NW9 . . . . 2C 28
Seely Rd. SW17. . . . . . 5C 116
Seething La.
EC3. . . . . . . 4E 19 (1A 78)
Sefton St. SW15. . . . . . . 1E 99
Segal Cl. SE23. . . . . . . 5A 108
Sekforde St.
EC1. . . . . . . 4D 9 (3D 63)
Selbie Av. NW10 . . . . . . 2B 42
Selborne Rd. SE5 . . . . . 5F 91
Selbourne Ho. SE1. . . . . 4B 26
Selby Cl. E6 . . . . 4F 69
Selby Ho. *W10*. 2A 58
(off Beethoven St.)
Selby Rd. E11 . . . . 5A 40
E13. . . . . 4D 69
Selby St. E1 . . . . 3C 64
Selcroft Ho. *SE10*. 1B 96
(off Glenister Rd.)
Selden Ho. SE15 . . . . . . 5E 93
(off Selden Rd.)
Selden Rd. SE15 . . . . . . 5E 93
Selden Wlk. N7 . . . . 4B 34
Seldon Ho. SW1. . . . . . . 1E 89
(off Churchill Gdns.)
SW8 . . . . 3B 89
(off Stewart's Rd.)
Selfridges 3B 12
(off Oxford St.)
Selhurst Cl. SW19 . . . . 1F 113
Selina Ho. *NW8* 3F 59
(off Frampton St.)
Selkirk Rd. SW17. . . . . 4A 116
Sellincourt Rd.
SW17 . . . . 5A 116
Sellons Av. NW10 . . . . . 5B 42
Selma Ho. *W12* 5D 57
(off Du Cane Rd.)

Selman Ho. E9 . . . . 3A 52
Selsdon Rd. E11. . . . . . 2C 40
E13 . . . . 5E 55
NW2 . . . . 4B 28
SE27 . . . . 3C 118
Selsdon Way E14. . . . . 4D 81
Selsea Pl. N16 . . . . 2A 50
Selsey St. E14 . . . . . . 4C 66
Selway Ho. SW8 . . . . . . 4A 90
(off Sth. Lambeth Rd.)
Selwood Pl. SW7 . . . . . 1F 87
Selwoods SW2 . . . . . . 5C 104
Selwood Ter. SW7 . . . . 1F 87
Selworthy Cl. E11. . . . . 1C 40
Selworthy Rd. SE6 . . . . 3B 122
Selwyn Ct. E17. . . . . . 1C 38
(off Yunus Khan Cl.)
SE3 . . . . 1B 110
Selwyn Rd. E3 . . . . 1B 66
E13 . . . . 5D 55
NW10 . . . . 4A 42
Semley Ga. E9 . . . . 3B 52
Semley Ho. SW1 . . . . . . 5D 75
(off Semley Pl.)
Semley Pl. SW1 . . . . . . 5C 74
Senate St. SE15 . . . . . . 5E 93
Senators Lodge E3 . . . . 1A 66
(off Roman Rd.)
Senior St. W2 . . . . 4D 59
Senlac Rd. SE12 . . . . . 1D 125
Senrab St. E1 . . . . 5F 65
Seraph Ct. EC1 . . . . 1F 9
(off Moreland St.)
Serbin Cl. E10 . . . . 2E 39
Serenaders Rd. SW9 . . . 5C 90
Sergeant Ind. Est.
SW18 . . . . 4D 101
Serica Ct. SE10 . . . . . . 3E 95
Serjeants Inn
EC4 . . . . 3C 16 (5C 62)
Serle St.
WC2 . . . . 2A 16 (5B 62)
Sermon La. EC4 . . . . . . 3F 17
Serpentine, The 2A 74
Serpentine Gallery 3F 73
Serpentine Rd.
W2 . . . . 2A 20 (2A 74)
Setchell Rd. SE1 . . . . . 5B 78
Setchell Way SE1. . . . . 5B 78
Seth St. SE16 . . . . 3E 79
Settle Point E13 . . . . . . 1C 68
(off London Rd.)
Settle Rd. E13 . . . . 1C 68
Settlers Ct. E14. . . . . . . 1F 81
Settles St. E1 . . . . 4C 64
Settrington Rd. SW6 . . . 5D 87
Seven Dials
WC2 . . . . 3D 15 (5A 62)
Seven Dials Ct. WC2 . . . 3D 15
(off Shorts Gdns.)
Seven Islands Leisure Cen.
. . . . 4E 79
Sevenoaks Rd. SE4 . . . . 4A 108
Seven Sisters Rd. N4. . . 5B 34
N7. . . . . 5B 34
N15 . . . . 4C 34
Seven Stars Cnr. W6 . . . 4C 70
Seven Stars Yd. E1. . . . . 5F 11
Severnake Cl. E14. . . . . 5C 80
Severn Way NW10 . . . . 2B 42

Severus Rd. SW11. . . . 2A 102
Seville Ho. E1 . . . . 2C 78
(off Hellings St.)
Seville M. N1. . . . . 4A 50
Seville St.
SW1 . . . . 4A 20 (3B 74)
Sevington Rd. NW4 . . . . 1D 29
Sevington St. W9. . . . . . 3D 59
Sewardstone Rd.
E2 . . . . 1E 65
Seward St.
EC1 . . . . 3E 9 (2D 63)
Sewdley St. E5 . . . . 5F 37
Sewell St. E13 . . . . 2C 68
Sextant Av. E14 . . . . . . 5F 81
Sexton Ct. E14 . . . . 1F 81
(off Newport Av.)
Sextons Ho. SE10 . . . . . 2E 95
(off Bardsley La.)
Seymour Ct. NW2 . . . . 4D 29
Seymour Gdns.
SE4 . . . . 1A 108
Seymour Ho. E16. . . . . 2C 82
(off De Quincey M.)
NW1 . . . . 1C 6
(off Churchway)
WC1 . . . . 3D 7
(off Tavistock Pl.)
Seymour M.
W1 . . . . 2B 12 (5C 60)
Seymour Pl.
W1 . . . . 2A 12 (4B 60)
Seymour Rd. E6 . . . . . . 1F 69
E10 . . . . 3B 38
N8. . . . . 1C 34
SW18 . . . . 5B 100
SW19 . . . . 3F 113
Seymour St.
W1 . . . . 3A 12 (5B 60)
W2 . . . . 5B 60
Seymour Wlk. SW10 . . . 2E 87
Seyssel St. E14 . . . . . . 5E 81
Shaa Rd. W3 . . . . 1A 70
Shabana Rd. W12 . . . . . 2D 71
Shackleton Cl.
SE23 . . . . 2D 121
Shackleton Ct. E14. . . . 1C 94
(off Maritime Quay)
W12 . . . . 3D 71
Shackleton Ho. E1 . . . . 2E 79
(off Prusom St.)
NW10 . . . . 4A 42
SHACKLEWELL 1B 50
Shacklewell Grn. E8 . . . 1B 50
Shacklewell Ho. E8 . . . . 1B 50
Shacklewell La. E8 . . . . 2B 50
Shacklewell Rd. N16. . . 1B 50
Shacklewell Row E8 . . . 1B 50
Shacklewell St. E2. . . . 2B 64
Shad Thames
SE1 . . . . 2F 27 (2B 78)
SHADWELL 1D 79
Shadwell Gdns. E1. . . . 1E 79
Shadwell Pierhead
E1 . . . . 1E 79
Shadwell Pl. E1 . . . . . . 1E 79
(off Shadwell Gdns.)
Shaftesbury Av.
W1 . . . . 5B 14 (1F 75)
WC2 . . . . 2D 15 (5A 62)

Shaftesbury Cen.
W10 . . . . 3F 57
(off Barlby Rd.)
Shaftesbury Ct. N1 . . . . 1F 63
(off Shaftesbury St.)
SW6 . . . . 4D 87
(off Maltings Pl.)
SW16 . . . . 3F 117
Shaftesbury Gdns.
NW10 . . . . 3A 56
Shaftesbury Lodge
E14 . . . . 5D 67
(off Up. North St.)
Shaftesbury M. SE1 . . . 5B 26
SW4 . . . . 3E 103
W8 . . . . 4C 72
(off Stratford Rd.)
Shaftesbury Pl. EC2 . . . 1F 17
(off London Wall)
W14 . . . . 5B 72
(off Warwick Rd.)
Shaftesbury Point
E13 . . . . 1C 68
(off High St.)
Shaftesbury Rd. E7 . . . . 4E 55
E10 . . . . 3C 38
E17 . . . . 1D 39
N19 . . . . 3A 34
Shaftesbury St. N1. . . . 1E 63
(not continuous)
Shaftesbury Theatre . . . 2D 15
(off Shaftesbury Av.)
Shafto M. SW1 . . . . . . 4B 74
Shafton M. E9. . . . . . . 5F 51
Shafton Rd. E9. . . . . . . 5F 51
Shaftsbury Ct. SE5 . . . 2F 105
Shafts Ct.
EC3 . . . . 3D 19 (5A 64)
Shahjalal Ho. E2 . . . . . 1C 64
(off Pritchards Rd.)
Shakespeare Ho. E9. . . 4E 51
(off Lyme Gro.)
Shakespeare Rd.
SE24 . . . . 3D 105
Shakespeare's Globe Theatre
& Exhibition
. . . . 5F 17 (2E 77)
Shakespeare Twr.
EC2 . . . . 5A 10
Shakspeare M. N16 . . . 1A 50
Shakspeare Wlk.
N16 . . . . 1A 50
Shalbourne Sq. E9. . . . 3B 52
Shalcomb St. SW10 . . . 2E 87
Shalden Ho. SW15. . . . 4B 98
Shalfleet Dr. W10. . . . . 1F 71
Shalford Ho.
SE1 . . . . 5C 26 (4F 77)
Shalford St. SW4 . . . . . 1F 103
Shandon Rd. SW4 . . . . 4E 103
Shand St.
SE1 . . . . 3E 27 (3A 78)
Shandy St. E1 . . . . 4F 65
Shanklin Rd. N8 . . . . . . 1F 33
Shannon Cl. NW2 . . . . 5F 29
Shannon Ct. N16 . . . . . 5A 36
Shannon Gro. SW9 . . . 2B 104
Shannon Pl. NW8 . . . . . 1A 60

Shanti Ct. SW18. . . . . . . 1C 114
Shap St. E2. . . . . 1B 64
Shardcroft Av. SE24. . . 3D 105
Shardeloes Rd. SE14. . . 5B 94
Shard's Sq. SE15. . . . . . . 2C 92
Sharnbrook Ho. W14. . . 2C 86
Sharon Gdns. E9. . . . . . . 5E 51
Sharp Ho. SW8. . . . . . . 1D 103
Sharpleshall St.
NW1. . . . . 4B 46
Sharpness Ct. SE15. . . . . 3B 92
(off Daniel Gdns.)
Sharratt St. SE15. . . . . . . 2E 93
Sharsted St. SE17. . . . . . 1D 91
Sharwood WC1. . . . . 1A 8
(off Penton Ri.)
Shaver's Pl. SW1. . . . . . . 5B 14
Shawbrooke Rd.
SE9. . . . . 3E 111
Shawbury Rd. SE22. . . 3B 106
Shaw Cres. E14. . . . . 5A 66
Shawfield St. SW3. . . . . . 1A 88
Shawford Ct. SW15. . . . . 5C 98
Shaw Path
BR1: Brom 3B 124
Shaw Rd.
BR1: Brom 3B 124
SE22. . . . . 2A 106
Shaws Cotts. SE23. . . . . 3A 122
Shaw Theatre . . . 2C 6 (2F 61)
Shearling Way N7. . . . . . 3A 48
Shearman Rd. SE3. . . . . 2B 110
Shearwater Ct. E1. . . . . . 1C 78
(off Star Pl.)
SE8. . . . . 2B 94
(off Abinger Gro.)
Sheba Pl. E1 . . . 4F 11 (3B 64)
Sheenewood SE26. . . . . 4D 121
Sheengate Mans.
SW14. . . . . 2A 98
Sheen Gro. N1. . . . . 5C 48
Sheen Sports & Fitness Cen.
. . . . 2A 98
Sheepcote La. SW11. . . . 5B 88
Sheep La. E8. . . . . 5D 51
Sheep Wlk. M.
SW19. . . . . 5F 113
Sheerwater Ho. E16. . . . 4F 69
Sheffield Sq. E3. . . . . . . 2B 66
Sheffield St.
WC2. . . . . 3F 15 (5B 62)
Sheffield Ter. W8. . . . . . . 2C 72
Shelburne Rd. N7. . . . . . 1B 48
Shelbury Rd. SE22. . . . . 3D 107
Sheldon Av. N6. . . . . 2A 32
Sheldon Cl. SE12. . . . . . 3D 111
Sheldon Ct. SW8 . . . . . . 3A 90
(off Lansdowne Grn.)
Sheldon Ho. N1. . . . . 5A 50
(off Kingsland Rd.)
Sheldon Pl. E2. . . . . 1C 64
(not continuous)
Sheldon Rd. NW2. . . . . . 1F 43
Sheldon Sq. W2. . . . . 4E 59
Sheldrake Ho. SE16. . . . 5F 79
(off Tawny Way)
Sheldrake Pl. W8. . . . . . . 3C 72
Shelduck Cl. E15. . . . . . . 2B 54
Shelduck Ct. SE8 . . . . . . 2B 94
(off Pilot Cl.)

Shelford Pl. N16. . . . . 5F 35
Shelgate Rd.
SW11. . . . . 3A 102
Shelley Av. E12. . . . . 3F 55
Shelley Cl. SE15. . . . . . . 5D 93
Shelley Ct. E10. . . . . 2D 39
(off Skelton's La.)
N19. . . . . 3B 34
SW3. . . . . 2B 88
(off Tite St.)
Shelley Ho. E2. . . . . 2E 65
(off Cornwall Av.)
N16. . . . . 1A 50
SE17. . . . . 1E 91
(off Browning St.)
SW1. . . . . 2E 89
(off Churchill Gdns.)
Shelley Rd. NW10. . . . . . 5A 42
Shelley Way SW19. . . . . 5F 115
Shellness Rd. E5. . . . . . . 2D 51
Shell Rd. SE13. . . . . 1D 109
Shellwood Rd.
SW11. . . . . 5B 88
Shelmerdine Cl. E3. . . . . 4C 66
Shelton St.
WC2. . . . . 3D 15 (5A 62)
(not continuous)
Shene Ho. EC1. . . . . 5B 8
(off Bourne Est.)
Shenfield Ho. SE18 . . . . 4F 97
(off Portway Gdns.)
Shenfield St.
N1. . . . . 1E 11 (1A 64)
(not continuous)
Shenley Rd. SE5. . . . . . . 4A 92
Shenstone Ho.
SW16. . . . . 5E 117
Shepherdess Pl.
N1. . . . . 1A 10 (2E 63)
Shepherdess Wlk.
N1. . . . . 1A 10 (1E 63)
Shepherd Ho. E14. . . . . . 5D 67
(off Annabel Cl.)
Shepherd Mkt.
W1. . . . . 1D 21 (2D 75)
SHEPHERD'S BUSH . . . 3E 71
Shepherds Bush
Empire Theatre 3E 71
W12. . . . . 3E 71
Shepherd's Bush Grn.
W12. . . . . 3E 71
Shepherd's Bush Mkt.
W12. . . . . 3E 71
(not continuous)
Shepherd's Bush Pl.
W12. . . . . 3F 71
Shepherd's Bush Rd.
W6. . . . . 5E 71
Shepherds Cl. N6. . . . . . 1D 33
W1. . . . . 4B 12
(off Lees Pl.)
Shepherds Ct. W12 . . . . 3F 71
(off Shepherd's Bush Grn.)
Shepherd's Hill N6. . . . . 1D 33
Shepherds La. E9. . . . . . 3F 51
Shepherd's Path W2. . . . 2F 45
(off Lyndhurst Rd.)
Shepherds Pl.
W1. . . . . 4B 12 (1C 74)
Shepherd St.
W1. . . . . 2D 21 (2D 75)

Shepherds Wlk.
NW2. . . . . 4C 28
NW3. . . . . 2F 45
(not continuous)
Sheppard Dr. SE16. . . . . 1D 93
Sheppard Ho. E2 . . . . . . 1C 64
(off Warner Pl.)
SW2. . . . . 1C 118
Sheppard St. E16. . . . . . 3B 68
Shepperton Rd. N1. . . . . 5E 49
Shepton Ho's. E2 . . . . . . 2E 65
(off Welwyn St.)
Sherard Ct. N7. . . . . 5A 34
Sherard Ho. E9. . . . . 4E 51
(off Frampton Pk. Rd.)
Sheraton Ho. SW1. . . . . 2D 89
(off Churchill Gdns.)
Sheraton St.
W1. . . . . 3B 14 (5F 61)
Sherborne Ho. SW1. . . . 1D 89
(off Winchester St.)
SW8 . . . . 3B 90
(off Bolney St.)
Sherborne La.
EC4. . . . . 4B 18 (1F 77)
Sherborne St. N1. . . . . . 5F 49
Sherboro Rd. N15. . . . . . 1B 36
Sherborne Ho. E2. . . . . . 1E 65
(off Bonner Rd.)
Sherbrooke Rd. SW6 . . . 3A 86
Sherbrooke Ter.
SW6 . . . . 3A 86
(off Sherbrook Rd.)
Shere Ho. SE1 . . . . 5B 26
Sherfield Gdns.
SW15. . . . . 4B 98
Sheridan Bldgs. WC2. . . 3E 15
(off Martlett Ct.)
Sheridan Ct. NW6 . . . . . 4E 45
(off Belsize Rd.)
Sheridan Ho. E1. . . . . . . 5E 65
(off Tarling St.)
SE11. . . . . 5C 76
(off Wincott St.)
Sheridan M. E11 . . . . . . 1D 41
Sheridan Pl. SW13 . . . . 1B 98
Sheridan Rd. E7. . . . . . . 5B 40
Sheridan St. E1. . . . . 5D 65
Sheridan Wlk.
NW11. . . . . 1C 30
Sheringham NW8. . . . . . 5F 45
Sheringham Ho.
NW1. . . . . 4A 60
(off Lisson St.)
Sheringham Rd. N7 . . . . 3B 48
Sherington Rd. SE7. . . . 2D 97
Sherlock Ct. NW8. . . . . . 5F 45
(off Dorman Way)
Sherlock Holmes Mus.
. . . . 4A 4
Sherlock M.
W1. . . . . 5B 4 (4C 60)
Shernhall St. E17 . . . . . . 1E 39
Sherrard Rd. E7. . . . . . . 3E 55
E12. . . . . 3E 55
Sherren Ho. E1. . . . . 3E 65
Sherrick Grn. Rd.
NW10. . . . . 2D 43
Sherriff Rd. NW6 . . . . . . 3C 44
Sherrin Rd. E10. . . . . . . 1D 53

Sherston Ct. *SE1* 5D **77**
  (off Newington Butts)
WC1 . . . . 2B **8**
Sherwin Ho. *SE11* 2C **90**
  (off Kennington Rd.)
Sherwin Rd. SE14. . . . . . 4F **93**
Sherwood NW6. . . . . 4A **44**
Sherwood Cl. SW13. . . 1D **99**
Sherwood Cl. SW11. . . 1E **101**
  W1 . . . . 4B **60**
  (off Bryanston Pl.)
Sherwood Gdns. E14 . . 5C **80**
  SE16. . . . . 1C **92**
Sherwood St.
  W1. . . . . 4A **14** (1E **75**)
Shetland St. E3 . . . . 1B **66**
Shifford Path SE23. . . . 3F **121**
Shillaker Ct. W3. . . . . . . 2B **70**
Shillibeer Pl. *W1* 4A **60**
  (off Harcourt St.)
Shillingford St. N1. . . . . 4D **49**
Shillingstone Ho.
  W14 . . . . 4A **72**
  (off Russell Rd.)
Shinfield St. W12. . . . . 5E **57**
Ship & Mermaid Row
  SE1. . . . . 3C **26** (3F **77**)
Shipka Rd. SW12. . . . . 1D **117**
Shiplake Ho. *E2* 2F **11**
  (off Arnold Cir.)
Shipman Rd. E16. . . . . 5D **69**
  SE23 . . . . 2F **121**
Ship St. SE8 . . . . 4C **94**
Ship Tavern Pas.
  EC3 . . . . 4D **19** (1A **78**)
Shipton Ho. *E2* 1B **64**
  (off Shipton St.)
Shipton St. E2 . . . . 1B **64**
Shipway Ter. N16. . . . . . 5B **36**
Shipwright Rd. SE16 . . . 3A **80**
Shipwright Yd.
  SE1 . . . . 2D **27** (2A **78**)
Ship Yd. E14 . . . . 1D **95**
Shirburn Cl. SE23. . . . . 5E **107**
Shirebrook Rd. SE3 . . . 1F **111**
Shirehall Cl. NW4 . . . . . 1F **29**
Shirehall Gdns. NW4 . . . 1F **29**
Shirehall La. NW4 . . . . . 1F **29**
Shirehall Pk. NW4 . . . . . 1F **29**
Shire Pl. SW18. . . . . . . 5E **101**
Shirland M. W9 . . . . 2B **58**
Shirland Rd. W9. . . . . . . 2B **58**
Shirlbutt St. E14. . . . . . . 1D **81**
Shirley Gro. SW11 . . . . 1C **102**
Shirley Ho. *SE5* 3F **91**
  (off Picton St.)
Shirley Ho. Dr. SE7 . . . . 3E **97**
Shirley Rd. E15 . . . . 4A **54**
  W4 . . . . 3A **70**
Shirley St. E16 . . . . 5B **68**
Shirlock Rd. NW3. . . . . 1B **46**
Shobroke Cl. NW2 . . . . 5E **29**
Shoe La.
  EC4 . . . . . . 2C **16** (5C **62**)
Shona Ho. E13 . . . . 4E **69**
Shooters Hill Rd.
  SE3 . . . . 4F **95**
  SE10. . . . . 4F **95**
  SE18. . . . . 3E **97**
Shoot Up Hill NW2. . . . 2A **44**

Shore Bus. Cen. E9 . . . . 4E **51**
SHOREDITCH
. . . . 1D **11** (2A **64**)
Shoreditch Ct. *E8*. 4B **50**
  (off Queensbridge Rd.)
Shoreditch High St.
  E1. . . . . 4E **11** (3A **64**)
Shoreham Cl.
  SW18. . . . . 3D **101**
Shore Ho. SW8 . . . . . . 1D **103**
Shore M. *E9* *4E **51***
  (off Shore Rd.)
Shore Pl. E9. . . . . 4E **51**
Shore Rd. E9 . . . . 4E **51**
Shorncliffe Rd. SE1. . . . 1B **92**
Shorndean St. SE6. . . . 1E **123**
Shorrold's Rd. SW6 . . . . 3B **86**
Shorter St. EC3 . . . . 1B **78**
Shortlands W6 . . . . 5F **71**
Shortlands Rd. E10 . . . . 2D **39**
Short Rd. E11. . . . . 4A **40**
  W4 . . . . 2A **84**
Shorts Gdns.
  WC2. . . . . . . 3D **15** (5A **62**)
Short St. SE1. . . 3C **24** (3C **76**)
Short Wall E15 . . . . 2E **67**
Short Way SE9 . . . . 1F **111**
Shottendane Rd.
  SW6 . . . . 4C **86**
Shottery Cl. SE9 . . . . . 3F **125**
Shottfield Av. SW14. . . 2A **98**
Shottsford *W2* 5C **58**
  (off Talbot Rd.)
Shoulder of Mutton All.
  E14. . . . . 1A **80**
Shouldham St. W1. . . . . 4A **60**
Shrewsbury Ct. EC1 . . . . 4A **10**
Shrewsbury Cres.
  NW10. . . . . 5A **42**
Shrewsbury Ho. *SW8*. . . 2B **90**
  (off Kennington Oval)
Shrewsbury M. *W2* 4C **58**
  (off Chepstow Rd.)
Shrewsbury Rd. E7. . . . 2F **55**
  W2 . . . . 5C **58**
Shrewsbury St. W10 . . 3E **57**
Shroffold Rd.
  BR1: Brom 4A **124**
Shropshire Pl.
  WC1. . . . . . . 4B **6** (3E **61**)
Shroton St. NW1 . . . . . . 4A **60**
Shrubbery, The E11 . . . 1D **41**
Shrubbery Cl. N1 . . . . . . 5E **49**
Shrubbery Rd.
  SW16 . . . . 4A **118**
Shrubland Rd. E8. . . . . . 5B **50**
  E10. . . . . 2C **38**
  E17. . . . . 1C **38**
Shrublands Cl.
  SE26 . . . . 3E **121**
Shuna Wlk. N1 . . . . 3F **49**
Shurland Gdns. SE15. . 3B **92**
Shuters Sq. SW14 . . . . 1B **86**
Shuttle St. E1. . . . . 3C **64**
Shuttleworth Rd.
  SW11 . . . . 5A **88**
Sibella Rd. SW4. . . . . . . 5F **89**
Sibthorpe Rd. SE12. . . 4D **111**
Sicilian Av. WC1 . . . . . . 1E **15**
Sidbury St. SW6. . . . . . . 4A **86**

Sidcup Rd. SE9 . . . . . . 4E **111**
  SE12. . . . . 4E **111**
Siddons La.
  NW1. . . . . 4A **4** (3B **60**)
Siddons Rd. SE23 . . . . 2A **122**
Side Rd. E17 . . . . 1B **38**
Sidford Ho. SE1 . . . . 5A **24**
Sidford Pl.
  SE1 . . . . 5A **24** (4C **76**)
Sidgwick Ho. *SW9* 5B **90**
  (off Lingham St.)
Sidings, The E11 . . . . . . 3E **39**
Sidings M. N7 . . . . 5C **34**
Sidlaw Ho. N16 . . . . 3B **36**
Sidmouth Ho. *SE15* 3C **92**
  (off Lympstone Gdns.)
  W1 . . . . *5A **60***
  (off Cato St.)
Sidmouth Pde. NW2. . . 4E **43**
Sidmouth Rd. E10 . . . . 5E **39**
  NW2 . . . . 4E **43**
Sidmouth St.
  WC1. . . . . . . 2E **7** (2B **62**)
Sidney Boyd Ct.
  NW6 . . . . 4C **44**
Sidney Est. E1 . . . . 5E **65**
  (Bromhead St.)
  E1 . . . . 5E **65**
  (Lindley St.)
Sidney Godley (VC) Ho.
  E2 . . . . *2E **65***
  (off Digby St.)
Sidney Gro.
  EC1 . . . . 1D **9** (1D **63**)
Sidney Ho. *E2*. *1F **65***
  (off Old Ford Rd.)
Sidney Rd. E7 . . . . 5C **40**
  SW9 . . . . 5B **90**
Sidney Sq. E1. . . . . 4E **65**
Sidney St. E1 . . . . 4D **65**
Sidworth St. E8 . . . . 4D **51**
Siebert Rd. SE3 . . . . . . 2C **96**
Siege Ho. *E1* 5D **65**
  (off Sidney St.)
Siemens Rd. SE18 . . . . 4F **83**
Sienna Ter. NW2 . . . . . 4C **28**
Sigdon Pas. E8. . . . . 2C **50**
Sigdon Rd. E8 . . . . 2C **50**
Sigmund Freud Statue
. . . . 3F **45**
Signal Ho. *E8*. *4D **51***
  (off Martello Ter.)
Signmakers Yd.
  NW1 . . . . 5D **47**
  (off Delancey St.)
Silbury Ho. SE26 . . . . 3C **120**
Silbury St.
  N1 . . . . 1B **10** (1F **63**)
Silchester Rd. W10 . . . 5F **57**
Silesia Bldgs. E8 . . . . . 4D **51**
Silex St. SE1. . . 4E **25** (3D **77**)
Silk Cl. SE12 . . . . 3C **110**
Silk Cl. *E2* 2C **64**
  (off Squirries St.)
Silk Mills Pas. SE13 . . . 5D **95**
Silk Mills Path SW11 . . 5D **95**
  (not continuous)
Silk Mills Sq. E9 . . . . . . 3B **52**
Silks Ct. E11. . . . . 3B **40**
Silk St. EC2. . . 5A **10** (4E **63**)

Sillitoe Ho. *N1* *5F 49*
   (off Colville Est.)
Silsoe Ho. NW1 . . . . 1D 61
Silver Birch Cl. SE6 . . 3B 122
Silverbirch Wlk.
  NW3 . . . . 3B 46
Silverburn Ho. *SW9* *4D 91*
   (off Lothian Rd.)
Silver Cl. SE14 . . . . 3A 94
Silverdale *NW1* *1F 5*
   (off Hampstead Rd.)
  SE26 . . . . 4E 121
Silverdale Ct. EC1 . . . . . . 3E 9
Silverdale Dr. SE9 . . . . . 2F 125
Silvermere Rd. SE6 . . . . 5D 109
Silver Pl. W1 . . . 4A 14 (5E 61)
Silver Rd. SE13 . . . . . . 1D 109
   (not continuous)
  W12 . . . . 1F 71
Silverthorn *NW8* *5D 45*
   (off Abbey Rd.)
Silverthorne Loft *SE5* . . *2F 91*
   (off Albany Rd.)
Silverthorne Rd. SW8 . . 5D 89
Silverton Rd. W6 . . . . . . 2F 85
SILVERTOWN 2E 83
Silvertown Viaduct
  E16 . . . . 5B 68
Silvertown Way E16 . . . 5A 68
   (not continuous)
Silver Wlk. SE16 . . . . . . 2A 80
Silvester Ho. *E1* *5D 65*
   (off Varden St.)
  E2 . . . . *2E 65*
   (off Sceptre Rd.)
  W11 . . . . *5B 58*
   (off Basing St.)
Silvester Rd. SE22 . . . 3B 106
Silvester St.
  SE1 . . . . 4B 26 (3F 77)
Silvocea Way E14 . . . . . 5F 67
Silwood Est. SE16 . . . . . 5E 79
Silwood St. *SE16* *5E 79*
   (off Rotherhithe New Rd.)
Simla Ho. *SE1* *4C 26*
   (off Kipling Est.)
Simms Rd. SE1 . . . . 5C 78
Simnel Rd. SE12 . . . . . . 5D 111
Simon Cl. W11 . . . . 1B 72
Simon Ct. *W9* *2C 58*
   (off Saltram Cres.)
Simonds Rd. E10 . . . . . . 4C 38
Simone Ct. SE26 . . . . . . 3E 121
Simons Cl. N16 . . . . 4B 36
Simons Wlk. E15 . . . . . . 2F 53
Simpson Dr. W3 . . . . 5A 56
Simpson Ho. NW8 . . . . . 3A 60
  SE11 . . . . 1B 90
Simpson's Rd. E14 . . . . . 1D 81
Simpson St. SW11 . . . . . 5A 88
Simrose Ct. SW18 . . . . . 3C 100
Sims Wlk. SE3 . . . . 2B 110
Sinclair Gdns. W14 . . . . 3F 71
Sinclair Gro. NW11 . . . . 1F 29
Sinclair Ho. *WC1* *2D 7*
   (off Sandwich St.)
Sinclair Mans. *W12* . . . *3F 71*
   (off Richmond Way)
Sinclair Pl. SE4 . . . . . . 4C 108
Sinclair Rd. W14 . . . . . . 3F 71

Singer St.
  EC2 . . . . . . 2C 10 (2F 63)
Sir Abraham Dawes Cotts.
  SW15 . . . . 2A 100
Sir Alexander Cl. W3 . . 2B 70
Sir Alexander Rd.
  W3 . . . . 2B 70
Sir Christopher France Ho.
  E1 . . . . 2A 66
Sirdar Rd. W11 . . . . 1F 71
Sirinham Point *SW8* . . *2B 90*
   (off Meadow Rd.)
Sirius Bldg. *E1* *1F 79*
   (off Jardine Rd.)
Sir John Cass Hall *E9* . *4E 51*
   (off Well St.)
Sir John Kirk Cl. SE5 . . 3E 91
Sir John Soane's Mus.
   . . . . 2F 15 (5B 62)
Sir Nicholas Garrow Ho.
  W10 . . . . *3A 58*
   (off Kensal Rd.)
Sir Oswald Stoll
  Foundation, The
  SW6 . . . . *3D 87*
   (off Fulham Rd.)
Sir Oswald Stoll Mans.
  SW6 . . . . *3D 87*
   (off Fulham Rd.)
Sir William Powell's
  Almshouses SW6 . . 5A 86
Sise La. EC4 . . . 3B 18 (5F 63)
Siskin Ho. *SE16* *5F 79*
   (off Tawny Way)
Sispara Gdns.
  SW18 . . . . 4B 100
Sissinghurst Cl.
  BR1: Brom 5A 124
Sissinghurst Ho.
  SE15 . . . . *2E 93*
   (off Sharratt St.)
Sissulu Ct. E6 . . . . 5F 55
Sister Mabel's Way
  SE15 . . . . 3C 92
Sisters Av. SW11 . . . . . . 1B 102
Sistova Rd. SW12 . . . . . 1D 117
Sisulu Pl. SW9 . . . . 1C 104
Sitarey Ct. W12 . . . . 2D 71
Sivill Ho. *E2* *1F 11*
   (off Columbia Rd.)
Siward Rd. SW17 . . . . . . 3E 115
Six Acres Est. N4 . . . . . 4B 34
Six Bridges Ind. Est.
  SE1 . . . . 1C 92
Sixth Av. W10 . . . . 2A 58
Skardu Rd. NW2 . . . . . . 2A 44
Skeena Hill SW18 . . . . . 5A 100
Skeggs Ho. *E14* *4E 81*
   (off Glengall St.)
Skegness Ho. *N7* *4B 48*
   (off Sutterton St.)
Skelbrook St. SW18 . . 2E 115
Skelgill Rd. SW15 . . . . 2B 100
Skelley Rd. E15 . . . . 4B 54
Skelton Cl. E8 . . . . 3B 50
Skelton Rd. E7 . . . . 3C 54
Skelton's La. E10 . . . . . . 2D 39
Skelwith Rd. W6 . . . . . . 2E 85
Skenfrith Ho. *SE15* . . . *2D 93*
   (off Commercial Way)

Sketchley Gdns.
  SE16 . . . . 1F 93
Skiers St. E15 . . . . 5A 54
Skiffington Cl. SW2 . . 1C 118
Skinner Pl. *SW1* *5C 74*
   (off Bourne St.)
Skinners La.
  EC4 . . . . . . 4A 18 (1E 77)
Skinner's Row SE10 . . . 4D 95
Skinner St.
  EC1 . . . . . . 2D 9 (2C 62)
Skipsea Ho.
  SW18 . . . . 4A 102
Skipton Ho. SE4 . . . . . . 2A 108
Skipwith Ho. *EC1* *5B 8*
   (off Bourne Est.)
Skipworth Rd. E9 . . . . . . 5E 51
Skua Cl. *SE8* *2B 94*
   (off Dorking Cl.)
Skylark Cl. *SE1* *4A 26*
   (off Swan St.)
Skyline Plaza Bldg.
  E1 . . . . *5C 64*
   (off Commercial Rd.)
Skylines E14 . . . . 3E 81
Skylines Village E14 . . 3E 81
Sladebrook Rd. SE3 . . 1F 111
Sladen Pl. E5 . . . . 1D 51
Slade Twr. E10 . . . . 4C 38
   (off Leyton Grange Est.)
Slade Wlk. SE17 . . . . . . 2D 91
Slagrove Pl. SE13 . . . . 3C 108
Slaidburn St. SW10 . . . 2E 87
Slaithwaite Rd.
  SE13 . . . . 2E 109
Slaney Cl. NW10 . . . . . . 4E 43
Slaney Pl. N7 . . . . 2C 48
Sleaford Ind. Est.
  SW8 . . . . 3E 89
Sleaford St. SW8 . . . . . 3E 89
Sleigh Ho. *E2* *2E 65*
   (off Bacton St.)
Slievemore Cl. SW4 . . 1F 103
Sligo Ho. *E1* *3F 65*
   (off Beaumont Gro.)
Slindon Ct. N16 . . . . 5B 36
Slingsby Pl.
  WC2 . . . . . . 4D 15 (1A 76)
Slippers Pl. SE16 . . . . . 4D 79
Slipway Ho. *E14* *1D 95*
   (off Burrells Wharf Sq.)
Sloane Av. SW3 . . . . . . 5A 74
Sloane Ct. E. SW3 . . . . 1C 88
Sloane Ct. W. SW3 . . . . 1C 88
Sloane Gdns.
  SW1 . . . . 5C 74
Sloane Ho. *E9* *4E 51*
   (off Loddiges Rd.)
Sloane Sq. SW1 . . . . 5C 74
Sloane St.
  SW1 . . . . . . 4A 20 (3B 74)
Sloane Ter. SW1 . . . . . . 5C 74
Sloane Ter. Mans.
  SW1 . . . . *5C 74*
   (off Sloane Ter.)
Sloman Ho. *W10* *2A 58*
   (off Beethoven St.)
Sly St. E1 . . . . 5D 65
Smallbrook M. W2 . . . . 5F 59
Smalley Cl. N16 . . . . . . 5B 36

Smalley Rd. Est.
N16. . . . . *5B 36*
(off Smalley Cl.)
Smallwood Rd.
SW17 . . . . 4F 115
Smart's Pl.
WC2. . . . . . . 2E 15 (5A 62)
Smart St. E2 . . . . 2F 65
Smeaton Ct.
SE1. . . . . 5F 25 (4E 77)
Smeaton Rd. SW18 . . . 5C 100
Smeaton St. E1 . . . . . . 2D 79
Smedley St. SW4 . . . . . 5F 89
Smeed Rd. E3 . . . . 4C 52
Smiles Pl. SE13 . . . . . . 5E 95
Smith Cl. SE16 . . . . 2F 79
Smithfield (Central Markets)
. . . . 1D 17
Smithfield St.
EC1 . . . . . 1D 17 (4D 63)
Smithies Ct. E15. . . . . . 2E 53
Smith's Ct. W1 . . . . 4A 14
Smiths Point *E13* *5C 54*
(off Brooks Rd.)
Smith Sq.
SW1 . . . . . 5D 23 (4A 76)
Smith St. SW3 . . . . 1B 88
Smith's Ter. SW18 . . . . 2E 115
Smith Ter. SW3 . . . . . . 1B 88
Smithwood Cl.
SW19 . . . . 1A 114
Smithy St. E1 . . . . 4E 65
Smokehouse Yd. *EC1*. . . *5E 9*
(off St John St.)
Smugglers Way
SW18 . . . . 2D 101
Smyrk's Rd. SE17. . . . . 1A 92
Smyrna Rd. NW6 . . . . . 4C 44
Smythe St. E14 . . . . . . 1D 81
SNARESBROOK 1C 40
Sneath Av. NW11 . . . . . 2B 30
Sneyd Rd. NW2 . . . . . . 2E 43
Snowberry Cl. E15 . . . . 1F 53
Snowbury Rd. SW6 . . . . 5D 87
Snowden St.
EC2 . . . . . 4D 11 (3A 64)
Snowdon Aviary *5B 46*
(in London Zoo)
Snowdon Dr. NW9 . . . . 1A 28
Snow Hill
EC1 . . . . . 1D 17 (5D 63)
Snow Hill Ct.
EC1 . . . . . 2E 17 (5D 63)
(not continuous)
Snowman Ho. NW6 . . . . 5D 45
Snowsfields
SE1 . . . . . . 3C 26 (3F 77)
Snowshill Rd. E12 . . . . 2F 55
Soames St. SE15 . . . . . 1B 106
Soane Ct. *NW1*. *4E 47*
(off St Pancras Way)
SOHO. 3B 14 (5E 61)
Soho Sq. W1 . . . 2B 14 (5F 61)
Soho St. W1 . . . 2B 14 (5F 61)
Soho Theatre & Writers Cen.
. . . . *3B 14*
(off Dean St.)
Sojourner Truth Cl.
E8 . . . . 3D 51

Solander Gdns. *E1*. . . *1D 79*
(off Cable St.)
E1 . . . . 1E 79
(Highway, The)
Solarium Ct. *SE1* *5B 78*
(off Alscot Rd.)
Soldene Ct. *N7*. *2B 48*
(off George's Rd.)
Solebay St. E1 . . . . 3A 66
Solent Ho. *E1*. *4A 66*
(off Ben Jonson Rd.)
Solent Ri. E13 . . . . 2C 68
Solent Rd. NW6 . . . . . . 2C 44
Soley M. WC1 . . . 1B 8 (2C 62)
Solna Av. SW15 . . . . . . 3E 99
Solomon's Pas.
SE15. . . . . 2D 107
Solon New Rd.
SW4 . . . . 2A 104
Solon New Rd. Est.
SW4 . . . . 2A 104
Solon Rd. SW2. . . . . . . 2A 104
Solway Cl. *E8*. *3B 50*
(off Queensbridge Rd.)
Solway Ho. *E1* *3F 65*
(off Ernest St.)
Solway Rd. SE22 . . . . . 2C 106
Somali Rd. NW2 . . . . . . 2B 44
Sombourne Ho.
SW15. . . . . *5C 98*
(off Fontley Way)
Somer Ct. *SW6* *2C 86*
(off Anselm Rd.)
Somerfield Ho. SE16 . . . 1F 93
Somerfield Rd. N4. . . . . 4D 35
(not continuous)
Somerfield St. SE16. . . . 1F 93
Somerford Gro. N16. . . . 1B 50
Somerford Gro. Est.
N16. . . . . 1B 50
Somerford St. E1. . . . . . 3D 65
Somerford Way SE16. . . 3A 80
Somerleyton Pas.
SW9 . . . . 2D 105
Somerleyton Rd.
SW9 . . . . 2C 104
Somers Cl. NW1 . . . . . . 1F 61
Somers Cres. W2. . . . . . 5A 60
Somerset Est. SW11 . . . 4F 87
Somerset Gdns. N6 . . . . 2C 32
SE13. . . . . 5D 95
Somerset House
. . . . 4F 15 (1B 76)
Somerset Ho. SW19. . . . 3F 113
Somerset Rd. E17 . . . . . 1C 38
SW19 . . . . 3F 113
Somerset Sq. W14. . . . . 3A 72
Somers Pl. SW2. . . . . . . 5B 104
Somers Rd. SW2 . . . . . . 4B 104
SOMERS TOWN
. . . . 1B 6 (2F 61)
Somers Town Community
Sports Cen. 1F 61
Somerton Rd. NW2 . . . . 5A 30
SE15. . . . . 2D 107
Somertrees Av.
SE12. . . . . 2D 125
Somerville Av. SW13. . . 2D 85
Somerville Point
SE16. . . . . 3B 80

Sonderburg Rd. N7 . . . . 4B 34
Sondes St. SE17. . . . . . 2F 91
Sonia Gdns. NW10. . . . . 1B 42
Sonning Ho. *E2*. *2F 11*
(off Swanfield St.)
Soper Cl. SE23 . . . . 1F 121
Sophia Cl. N7. . . . . 3B 48
Sophia Ho. *W6*. *1E 85*
(off Queen Caroline St.)
Sophia Rd. E10 . . . . 3D 39
E16. . . . . 5D 69
Sophia Sq. *SE16* *1A 80*
(off Sovereign Cres.)
Sopwith Way SW8 . . . . 3D 89
Sorensen Ct. *E10*. *4D 39*
(off Leyton Grange Est.)
Sorrel Gdns. E6 . . . . . . 4F 69
Sorrel La. E14 . . . . 5F 67
Sorrell Cl. SE14 . . . . . . 3A 94
SW9 . . . . 5C 90
Sotheby Rd. N5 . . . . 5D 35
Sotheran Cl. E8 . . . . 5C 50
Sotherby Lodge *E2*. . . . *1E 65*
(off Sewardstone Rd.)
Sotheron Rd. SW6. . . . . 3D 87
Soudan Rd. SW11 . . . . . 4B 88
Souldern Rd. W14 . . . . . 4F 71
Sth. Access Rd. E17 . . . 2A 38
Southacre *W2*. *5A 60*
(off Hyde Pk. Cres.)
Sth. Africa Rd. W12. . . . 2D 71
Southall Pl.
SE1. . . . . . . 4B 26 (3F 77)
Southampton Bldgs.
WC2. . . . . . . 1B 16 (4C 62)
Southampton M. E16. . . . 2D 83
Southampton Pl.
WC1 . . . . 1E 15 (4A 62)
Southampton Rd.
NW5 . . . . 2B 46
Southampton Row
WC1 . . . . 5E 7 (4A 62)
Southampton St.
WC2. . . . . . . 4E 15 (1A 76)
Southampton Way
SE5 . . . . 3F 91
Southam St. W10 . . . . . 3A 58
Sth. Audley St.
W1. . . . . 5C 12 (1C 74)
South Av. NW10 . . . . . . 3E 57
South Bank 1A 24 (2B 76)
Sth. Bank Bus. Cen.
SW8 . . . . 2F 89
Sth. Birkbeck Rd.
E11. . . . . 5F 39
Sth. Black Lion La.
W6 . . . . 1C 84
South Block *SE1* *4F 23*
(off Westminster Bri. Rd.)
Sth. Bolton Gdns.
SW5 . . . . 1E 87
Southborough Ho.
SE17. . . . . *1A 92*
(off Surrey Gro.)
Southborough Rd. E9. . . 5F 51
Southbourne Gdns.
SE12. . . . . 3D 111
Sth. Branch Av.
NW10 . . . . 3E 57
SOUTH BROMLEY. . . . 1E 81

Southbrook M.
SE12 . . . . 4B 110
Southbrook Rd.
SE12 . . . . 4B 110
Southbury NW8. . . . . . . 5E 45
(off Loudoun Rd.)
Sth. Carriage Dr.
SW1 . . . . 3A 20 (3B 74)
SW7 . . . . 3F 73
Sth. Circular Rd.
SW15 . . . . 2C 98
Sth. City Cl. SE15. . . . . 3A 92
South Cl. N6. . . . . 1D 33
Sth. Colonnade, The
E14 . . . . 2C 80
Southcombe St. W14 . . . 5A 72
Southcote Rd. N19 . . . . 1E 47
Southcott M. NW8 . . . . 1A 60
South Cres. E16 . . . . . . 3F 67
WC1 . . . . . . 1B 14 (4F 61)
Southcroft Rd.
SW16 . . . . 5D 117
SW17 . . . . 5C 116
Sth. Croxted Rd.
SE21 . . . . 3F 119
Southdean Gdns.
SW19 . . . . 2B 114
Southdown N7 . . . . 3A 48
South Eastern University
. . . . 5B 34
Sth. Eaton Pl. SW1 . . . . 5C 74
Sth. Edwardes Sq.
W8 . . . . 4B 72
SOUTHEND 4F 123
South End W8. . . . . . . 4D 73
Sth. End Cl. NW3 . . . . . 1A 46
Sth. End Grn. NW3 . . . . 1A 46
Southend La. SE6. . . . . 4B 122
SE26 . . . . 4B 122
Sth. End Rd. NW3 . . . . 1A 46
Southend Rd.
BR3: Beck. 5D 123
Sth. End Row W8 . . . . . 4D 73
Southerngate Way
SE14 . . . . 3A 94
Southern Gro. E3 . . . . . 2B 66
Southern Rd. E13 . . . . . 1D 69
Southern Oak W10 . . . . 3A 58
Southern St. N1 . . . . . . 1B 62
Southern Way SE10 . . . . 5B 82
(off School Bank Rd.)
Southernwood Retail Pk.
SE1 . . . . 1B 92
Southerton Rd. W6. . . . . 5E 71
Sth. Esk Rd. E7. . . . . . . 1E 55
Southey Ho. SE17. . . . . . 1E 91
(off Browning St.)
Southey M. E16 . . . . . . 2C 82
Southey Rd. N15 . . . . . . 1A 36
SW9 . . . . 4C 90
Southfield Cl. E11 . . . . . 5B 40
Southfield Rd. W4 . . . . . 3A 70
SOUTHFIELDS 1B 114
Southfields M.
SW18 . . . . 4C 100
Southfields Pas.
SW18 . . . . 4C 100
Southfields Rd.
SW18 . . . . 4C 100
Southfleet NW5 . . . . . . 3C 46

Southgate Ct. N1 . . . . . 4F 49
(off Downham Rd.)
Southgate Gro. N1 . . . . 4F 49
South Ga. Rd. E12 . . . . 5F 41
Southgate Rd. N1. . . . . 5F 49
South Gro. E17. . . . . . . 1B 38
N6. . . . . 3C 32
N15 . . . . 1F 35
South Gro. Ho. N6 . . . . 3C 32
SOUTH HACKNEY 4F 51
SOUTH HAMPSTEAD . . 4E 45
Sth. Hill Pk. NW3. . . . . 1A 46
Sth. Hill Pk. Gdns.
NW3 . . . . 5A 32
Sth. Island Pl. SW9 . . . . 3B 90
SOUTH KENSINGTON
. . . . 5F 73
Sth. Kensington Sta. Arc.
SW7 . . . . 5F 73
(off Pelham St.)
SOUTH LAMBETH 3A 90
Sth. Lambeth Pl.
SW8 . . . . 2A 90
Sth. Lambeth Rd.
SW8 . . . . 2A 90
Southlands Dr.
SW19 . . . . 2F 113
South Lodge E16 . . . . . 2D 83
(off Audley Dr.)
NW8 . . . . 1F 59
SW7 . . . . 3A 74
(off Knightsbridge)
South London Gallery
. . . . 4A 92
(off Peckham Rd.)
South London Theatre
. . . . 3D 119
(off Norwood High St.)
South Mall SW18. . . . . 4D 101
Southmead Rd.
SW19 . . . . 1A 114
Sth. Molton La.
W1. . . . . 3D 13 (5D 61)
Sth. Molton Rd. E16 . . . 5C 68
Sth. Molton St.
W1. . . . . 3D 13 (5D 61)
Southmoor Way E9 . . . . 3B 52
Sth. Oak Rd. SW16 . . . . 4E 117
Southolm St. SW11. . . . 4D 89
Southover
BR1: Brom 5C 124
South Pde. SW3 . . . . . . 1F 87
W4 . . . . 5A 70
South Pk. Cres. SE6. . . . 1A 124
South Pk. M. SW6. . . . . 1D 101
South Pk. Rd. SW19 . . . 5E 115
South Pl. EC2 . . . 5C 10 (4F 63)
South Pl. M.
EC2. . . . . 1C 18 (4F 63)
Sth. Quay Plaza E14 . . . 3D 81
South Ri. W2 . . . . 1A 74
(off St George's Flds.)
South Rd. SE23 . . . . . . 2F 121
South Row SE3. . . . . . . 5B 96
Sth. Sea St. SE16 . . . . . 4B 80
South Side W6 . . . . 4B 70
Southside N7 . . . . 1F 47
Southside Comn.
SW19 . . . . 5E 113

Southside Ind. Est.
SW8 . . . . 4E 89
(off Havelock Ter.)
Southside Shop. Cen.
SW18 . . . . 4D 101
South Sq. NW11 . . . . . . 1D 31
WC1 . . . . 1B 16 (4C 62)
Sth. Ter. SW1. . . 1C 20 (2C 74)
Sth. Tenter St. E1. . . . . 1B 78
South Ter. SW7 . . . . . . 5A 74
SOUTH TOTTENHAM . . 1B 36
Southvale Rd. SE3 . . . . 5A 96
Southview Av. NW10 . . . 2B 42
Southview Cl.
SW17 . . . . 5C 116
Southview Rd.
BR1: Brom 4F 123
South Vs. NW1 . . . . 3F 47
Southville SW8. . . . . . . 4F 89
SOUTHWARK
. . . . 3E 25 (2E 77)
Southwark Bri.
SE1 . . . . 5A 18 (1E 77)
Southwark Bri. Bus. Cen.
SE1 . . . . 2A 26
(off Southwark Bri. Rd.)
Southwark Bri. Office Village
SE1 . . . . 1A 26
Southwark Bri. Rd.
SE1 . . . . 5E 25 (4D 77)
Southwark Cathedral
. . . . 1B 26 (2F 77)
Southwark Pk. Est.
SE16. . . . . 4D 79
Southwark Pk. Rd.
SE16. . . . . 5B 78
Southwark Pk. Sports Cen.
Track 5E 79
Southwark Pk. Sports Complex
. . . . 5E 79
Southwark Playhouse
. . . . 2F 25
(off Gt. Guildford St.)
Southwark St.
SE1 . . . . 1D 25 (2D 77)
Southwater Cl. E14 . . . . 5B 66
Southway NW11 . . . . . . 1D 31
Southway Cl. W12. . . . . 3D 71
(off Scott's Rd.)
Southwell Gdns.
SW7 . . . . 5E 73
Southwell Gro. Rd.
E11 . . . . 4A 40
Southwell Ho. SE16. . . . 5D 79
(off Anchor St.)
Southwell Rd. SE5 . . . . 1E 105
South W. India Dock Entrance
E14 . . . . 3E 81
Southwest Rd. E11. . . . . 3F 39
Sth. Wharf Rd. W2. . . . . 5F 59
Southwick M. W2 . . . . . 5F 59
Southwick Pl. W2 . . . . . 5A 60
Southwick St. W2 . . . . . 5A 60
Southwick Yd. W2 . . . . . 5A 60
(off Titchborne Row)
SOUTH WIMBLEDON
. . . . 5D 115
Southwold Mans. W9. . . 2C 58
(off Widley Rd.)
Southwold Rd. E5 . . . . . 4D 37

Southwood Av. N6 . . . . . 2D 33
Southwood Ct. EC1 . . . . . 2D 9
   (off Wynyatt St.)
NW11 . . . . 1D 31
Sth. Woodford to
  Barking Relief Rd.
E11 . . . . 1F 41
IG4: Ilf 1F 41
Southwood Hall N6 . . . . 1D 33
Southwood Hgts. 2D 33
Southwood Ho. W11 . . . 1A 72
   (off Avondale Pk. Rd.)
Southwood La. N6 . . . . 3C 32
Southwood Lawn Rd.
N6 . . . . 2C 32
Southwood Mans. N6 . . 1C 32
   (off Southwood La.)
Southwood Pk. N6 . . . . 2C 32
Southwood Smith Ho.
E2 . . . . 2D 65
   (off Florida St.)
Southwood Smith St.
N1 . . . . 5D 49
Sth. Worple Av.
SW14 . . . . 1A 98
Sth. Worple Way
SW14 . . . . 1A 98
Southwyck Ho.
SW9 . . . . 2D 105
Sovereign Cl. E1 . . . . . 1D 79
Sovereign Cres.
SE16 . . . . 1A 80
Sovereign Ho. E1 . . . . 3D 65
   (off Cambridge Heath Rd.)
Sovereign M. E2 . . . . . . 1B 64
Spa Ct. SW16 . . . . 4B 118
Spafield St.
EC1 . . . . . 3B 8 (3C 62)
Spa Grn. Est.
EC1 . . . . . 1C 8 (2D 63)
Spalding Ho. SE4 . . . . . 2A 108
Spalding Rd. NW4 . . . . . 2E 29
SW17 . . . . 5D 117
Spanby Rd. E3 . . . . 3C 66
Spaniards Cl. NW11 . . . . 3F 31
Spaniards End NW3 . . . . 3E 31
Spaniards Rd. NW3 . . . . 4E 31
Spanish Pl.
W1 . . . . . . 2C 12 (5C 60)
Spanish Rd. SW18 . . . . . 3E 101
Sparkes Cotts. SW1 . . . . 5C 74
   (off Graham Ter.)
Sparke Ter. E16 . . . . . . 5B 68
   (off Clarkson Rd.)
Spa Rd. SE16 . . . 5F 27 (4B 78)
Sparrick's Row
SE1 . . . . 3C 26 (3F 77)
Sparrow Ho. E1 . . . . . . 3E 65
   (off Cephas Av.)
Sparsholt Rd. N19 . . . . 3B 34
Sparta St. SE10 . . . . . . 4E 95
Speakers' Corner
. . . . 4A 12 (1B 74)
Speakman Ho. SE4 . . . . 1A 108
   (off Arica Rd.)
Spearman Ho. E14 . . . . 5C 66
   (off Up. North St.)
Spear M. SW5 . . . . 5C 72
Spears Rd. N19 . . . . . . 3A 34
Spectacle Works E13 . . . 2E 69

Spectrum Pl. SE17 . . . . 2F 91
   (off Lytham St.)
Spedan Cl. NW3 . . . . . . 5E 31
Speechly M. E8 . . . . . . 2B 50
Speed Highwalk EC2 . . . 5A 10
   (off Silk St.)
Speed Ho. EC2 . . . . 5A 10
Speedwell St. SE8 . . . . 3C 94
Speedy Pl. WC1 . . . . . . 2D 7
Speke's Monument 2F 73
Speldhurst Rd. E9 . . . . . 4F 51
W4 . . . . 4A 70
Spellbrook Wlk. N1 . . . . 5E 49
Spelman Ho. E1 . . . . . . 4C 64
   (off Spelman St.)
Spelman St. E1 . . . . 4C 64
   (not continuous)
Spence Cl. SE16 . . . . . . 3B 80
Spencer Dr. N2 . . . . 1E 31
Spencer House 2F 21
Spencer Ho. NW4 . . . . . 1D 29
Spencer Mans. W14 . . . 2A 86
   (off Queen's Club Gdns.)
Spencer M. SW8 . . . . . . 4B 90
   (off Sth. Lambeth Rd.)
W6 . . . . 2A 86
SPENCER PARK 3F 101
Spencer Pk. SW18 . . . . 3F 101
Spencer Pl. N1 . . . . 4D 49
Spencer Ri. NW5 . . . . . . 1D 47
Spencer Rd. E6 . . . . 5F 55
N8 . . . . 1B 34
   (not continuous)
SW18 . . . . 2F 101
Spencer St.
EC1 . . . . . . 2D 9 (2D 63)
Spencer Wlk. NW3 . . . . 1E 45
   (off Perrin's Ct.)
NW3 . . . . 1F 45
   (Hampstead High St.)
SW15 . . . . 2F 99
Spenlow Ho. SE16 . . . . 4C 78
   (off Jamaica Rd.)
Spenser Gro. N16 . . . . . 2A 50
Spenser M. SE21 . . . . . 2F 119
Spenser Rd. SE24 . . . . . 3D 105
Spenser St.
SW1 . . . . . 5A 22 (4E 75)
Spensley Wlk. N16 . . . . 5F 35
Spert St. E14 . . . . 1A 80
Spey St. E14 . . . . 4E 67
Spezia Rd. NW10 . . . . . 1C 56
Spice Ct. E1 . . . . 1C 78
Spice Quay Hgts.
SE1 . . . . 2B 78
Spicer Cl. SW9 . . . . 5D 91
Spindrift Av. E14 . . . . . 5C 80
Spinnaker Ho. E14 . . . . 3C 80
   (off Byng St.)
Spinney, The SW13 . . . . 3D 85
SW16 . . . . 3E 117
Spinney Gdns. SE19 . . . 5B 120
Spire Ho. W2 . . . . 1E 73
   (off Lancaster Ga.)
Spirit Quay E1 . . . . 2C 78
SPITALFIELDS
. . . . 5F 11 (4B 64)
Spital Sq. E1 . . . 5E 11 (4A 64)
Spital St. E1 . . . . 4C 64
Spital Yd. E1 . . . 5E 11 (4A 64)

Splendour Wlk.
SE16 . . . . 1E 93
   (off Verney Rd.)
Spode Ho. SE11 . . . . . . 5B 24
Spode Wlk. NW6 . . . . . . 2D 45
Sportsbank St. SE6 . . . . 5E 109
Spratt Hall Rd. E11 . . . . 1C 40
Spriggs Ho. N1 . . . . 4D 49
   (off Canonbury Rd.)
Sprimont Pl. SW3 . . . . . 1B 88
Springall St. SE15 . . . . 3D 93
Springalls Wharf
SE16 . . . . 3C 78
   (off Bermondsey Wall W.)
Springbank Rd.
SE13 . . . . 4F 109
Springbank Wlk.
NW1 . . . . 4F 47
Spring Ct. NW6 . . . . . . 3B 44
Springdale M. N16 . . . . 1F 49
Springdale Rd. N16 . . . 1F 49
Springfield E5 . . . . 3D 37
Springfield Ct. NW3 . . . 4A 46
   (off Eton Av.)
Springfield Gdns. E5 . . . 3D 37
NW9 . . . . 1A 28
Springfield Gro. SE7 . . . 2E 97
Springfield La. NW6 . . . 5D 45
Springfield Ri.
SE26 . . . . 3D 121
   (not continuous)
Springfield Rd. E15 . . . . 2A 68
E17 . . . . 1B 38
NW8 . . . . 5E 45
SE26 . . . . 5D 121
SW19 . . . . 5B 114
Springfield Wlk.
NW6 . . . . 5D 45
Spring Gdns. N5 . . . . . . 2E 49
SW1 . . . . . 1C 22 (2F 75)
   (not continuous)
SE26 . . . . 2C 36
SE26 . . . . 4E 121
Springhill Cl. SE5 . . . . . 1F 105
Spring Ho. WC1 . . . . . . 2B 8
Spring La. E5 . . . . 2D 37
Spring M. W1 . . . 5A 4 (4B 60)
Spring Pk. Dr. N4 . . . . . 3E 35
Spring Pas. SW15 . . . . . 1F 99
Spring Path NW3 . . . . . 2F 45
Spring Pl. NW5 . . . . 2D 47
Springrice Rd. SE13 . . . 4F 109
Spring St. W2 . . . . 5F 59
Spring Tide Cl. SE15 . . . 4C 92
Spring Va. Ter. W14 . . . . 4F 71
Spring Wlk. E1 . . . . 4C 64
Springwater Av. NW10 . . 5B 42
Springwell Cl.
SW16 . . . . 4B 118
Springwell Rd.
SW16 . . . . 4C 118
Springwood Cl. E3 . . . . 1C 66
Sprowston M. E7 . . . . . 3C 54
Sprowston Rd. E7 . . . . . 2C 54
Spruce Ho. SE16 . . . . . 3F 79
   (off Woodland Cres.)
Sprules Rd. SE4 . . . . . . 5A 94
Spurgeon Rd. SE1 . . . . 5B 26
Spurling Rd. SE22 . . . . 2B 106

Spur Rd. SE1 . . . 3B **24** (3C **76**)
SW1 . . . . . . 4F **21** (3E **75**)
Spurstowe Rd. E8 . . . . . . 3D **51**
Spurstowe Ter. E8 . . . . . 2C **50**
Square, The E10 . . . . 5E **39**
W6 . . . . 1E **85**
Square Rigger Row
SW11 . . . . 1E **101**
Squarey St. SW17 . . . 3E **115**
Squire Gdns. NW8 . . . . 2F **59**
(off Grove End Rd.)
Squires Ct. SW4 . . . . . . 4A **90**
SW19 . . . . 4C **114**
Squires M. NW3 . . . . . . 5F **31**
Squirrels, The SE13 . . 1F **109**
Squirries St. E2 . . . . . . 2C **64**
Stable M. SE6 . . . . . . 1A **124**
Stables Gallery & Arts Cen.
. . . . 5C **28**
Stables Lodge E8. . . . . 4D **51**
(off Mare St.)
Stables Mkt., The
NW1 . . . . 4D **47**
Stables M. SE27 . . . . . 5E **119**
Stables Way SE11 . . . . 1C **90**
Stables Yd. SW18 . . . . 4C **100**
Stable Wlk. N1 . . . . 1A **62**
(off Wharfdale Rd.)
Stable Yd. SW1 . . . . . . 3F **21**
SW15 . . . . 1E **99**
Stableyard, The SW9 . . 5B **90**
Stable Yd. Rd.
SW1 . . . . . . 3A **22** (3E **75**)
(not continuous)
Stacey Cl. E10 . . . . 1F **39**
Stacey St. N7 . . . . 5C **34**
WC2 . . . . . 3C **14** (5F **61**)
Stack Ho. SW1 . . . . 5C **74**
(off Cundy St.)
Stackhouse St. SW3 . . 5A **20**
Stacy Path SE5 . . . . . . 3A **92**
Stadium Rd. E. NW4 . . . 2D **29**
Stadium St. SW10 . . . . . 3E **87**
Staffa Rd. E10 . . . . 3A **38**
Stafford Cl. E17 . . . . . . 1B **38**
(not continuous)
NW6 . . . . 2C **58**
Stafford Ct. SW8 . . . . . 3A **90**
Stafford Cripps Ho.
E2 . . . . 2E **65**
(off Globe Rd.)
SW6 . . . . 2B **86**
(off Clem Attlee Ct.)
Stafford Mans. SW1 . . 5F **21**
(off Stafford Pl.)
SW4 . . . . 2A **104**
SW11 . . . . 3B **88**
(off Albert Bri. Rd.)
W14 . . . . 4F **71**
(off Haarlem Rd.)
Stafford Pl.
SW1 . . . . . . 5F **21** (4E **75**)
Stafford Rd. E3 . . . . . . 1B **66**
E7 . . . . 4E **55**
NW6 . . . . 2C **58**
Staffordshire St.
SE15 . . . . 4C **92**
Stafford St.
W1 . . . . 1F **21** (2E **75**)

Stafford Ter. W8 . . . . . . 4C **72**
Staff St.
EC1 . . . . . . 2C **10** (2F **63**)
STAG LANE 2B **112**
Stag La. SW15 . . . . . . 3B **112**
Stag Pl. SW1 . . 5F **21** (4E **75**)
Stainer Ho. SE3 . . . . . 2E **111**
Stainer St.
SE1 . . . . . . 2C **26** (2F **77**)
Staining La.
EC2 . . . . . . 2A **18** (5E **63**)
Stainsbury St. E2 . . . . . 1E **65**
Stainsby Pl. E14 . . . . . . 5C **66**
Stainsby Rd. E14 . . . . . 5C **66**
Stainton Rd. SE6 . . . . . 4F **109**
Stalbridge Flats W1 . . . 3C **12**
(off Lumley St.)
Stalbridge St. NW1 . . 4A **60**
Stalham St. SE16 . . . . . 4D **79**
Stamford Bridge 3D **87**
Stamford Brook Arches
W6 . . . . 5C **70**
Stamford Brook Av.
W6 . . . . 4B **70**
Stamford Brook Gdns.
W6 . . . . 4B **70**
Stamford Brook Mans.
W6 . . . . 5B **70**
(off Goldhawk Rd.)
Stamford Brook Rd.
W6 . . . . 4B **70**
Stamford Cl. NW3 . . . . . 5E **31**
(off Heath St.)
Stamford Cotts.
SW10 . . . . 3D **87**
(off Billing St.)
Stamford Ct. W6 . . . . . 5C **70**
Stamford Ga. SW6 . . . . 3D **87**
Stamford Gro. E. N16 . . 3C **36**
Stamford Gro. W.
N16 . . . . 3C **36**
STAMFORD HILL 3B **36**
Stamford Hill N16 . . . . . 4B **36**
Stamford Lodge N16 . . 2B **36**
Stamford Rd. E6 . . . . . 5F **55**
N1 . . . . 4A **50**
Stamford St.
SE1 . . . . . . 2B **24** (2C **76**)
Stamp Pl. E2 . . 1F **11** (1B **64**)
Stanard Cl. N2 . . . . 2A **36**
Stanborough Pas. E8 . . 3B **50**
Stanbridge Rd. SW15 . . 1E **99**
Stanbury Ct. NW3 . . . . . 3B **46**
Stanbury Rd. SE15 . . . . 5D **93**
(not continuous)
Standard Cl. SE6 . . . . 1D **123**
Standard Pl. EC2 . . . . . 2E **11**
Standard Rd. NW10 . . 3A **56**
Standen Rd. SW18 . . . . 5B **100**
Standish Ho. SE3 . . . . 2D **111**
(off Elford Cl.)
W6 . . . . 5C **70**
(off St Peter's Gro.)
Standish Rd. W6 . . . . . . 5C **70**
Standlake Point
SE23 . . . . 3F **121**
Stane Pas. SW16 . . . . 5A **118**
Stanesgate Ho. SE15 . . 3C **92**
(off Friary Est.)
Stane Way SE18 . . . . . . 3F **97**

Stanfield Ho. NW8 . . . . . 3F **59**
(off Frampton St.)
Stanfield Rd. E3 . . . . . . 1A **66**
Stanford Ct. SW6 . . . . . 4D **87**
Stanford Pl. SE17 . . . . . 5A **78**
Stanford Rd. W8 . . . . . . 4D **73**
Stanford St. SW1 . . . . . 5F **75**
Stangate SE1 . . . . 5A **24**
Stanhope Cl. SE16 . . . . 3F **79**
Stanhope Gdns. N4 . . . 1D **35**
N6 . . . . 1D **33**
SW7 . . . . 5E **73**
Stanhope Ga.
W1 . . . . 2C **20** (2C **74**)
Stanhope Ho. SE8 . . . . . 3B **94**
(off Adolphus St.)
Stanhope M. E. SW7 . . . 5E **73**
Stanhope M. Sth.
SW7 . . . . 5E **73**
Stanhope M. W. SW7 . . 5E **73**
Stanhope Pde.
NW1 . . . . . . 1F **5** (2E **61**)
Stanhope Pl. W2 . . . . . . 1B **74**
Stanhope Rd. E17 . . . . . 1D **39**
N6 . . . . 1E **33**
Stanhope Row
W1 . . . . 2D **21** (2D **75**)
Stanhope St.
NW1 . . . . . . 1F **5** (1E **61**)
Stanhope Ter. W2 . . . . . 1F **73**
Stanier Cl. W14 . . . . . . 1B **86**
Stanlake M. W12 . . . . . 2E **71**
Stanlake Rd. W12 . . . . . 2E **71**
Stanlake Vs. W12 . . . . . 2E **71**
Stanley Cl. SW8 . . . . . . 2B **90**
Stanley Cohen Ho.
EC1 . . . . 4F **9**
(off Golden La. Est.)
Stanley Cres. W11 . . . . 1B **72**
Stanley Gdns. NW2 . . . 2E **43**
W3 . . . . 3A **70**
W11 . . . . 1B **72**
Stanley Gdns. M.
W11 . . . . 1B **72**
(off Kensington Pk. Rd.)
Stanley Gro. SW8 . . . . . 5C **88**
Stanley Holloway Ct.
E16 . . . . 5C **68**
(off Coolfin Rd.)
Stanley Ho. E14 . . . . . . 5C **66**
(off Saracen St.)
SW10 . . . . 3E **87**
(off Coleridge Gdns.)
Stanley M. SW10 . . . . . 3E **87**
(off Coleridge Gdns.)
Stanley Rd. E10 . . . . . . 1D **39**
E12 . . . . 2F **55**
E15 . . . . 5F **53**
NW9 . . . . 2C **28**
Stanley St. SE8 . . . . . . 3B **94**
Stanley Ter. N19 . . . . . . 4A **34**
Stanmer St. SW11 . . . . 4A **88**
Stanmore Pl. NW1 . . . . 5D **47**
Stanmore Rd. E11 . . . . 3B **40**
Stanmore St. N1 . . . . . 5B **48**
Stannard Cotts. E1 . . . . 3E **65**
(off Fox Cl.)
Stannard M. E8 . . . . . . 3C **50**
(off Stannard Rd.)
Stannard Rd. E8 . . . . . . 3C **50**

Stannary Pl. SE11 . . . . . 1C **90**
Stannary St. SE11 . . . . . 2C **90**
Stansbury Ho. W10 . . . . 2A **58**
  (off Beethoven St.)
Stansfield Rd. E6. . . . . . 4F **69**
  E16 . . . . 1F **83**
Stansfield Ho. SE1 . . . . . 5B **78**
  (off Balaclava Rd.)
Stansfield Rd. SW9 . . . 1B **104**
Stanstead Gro. SE6 . . . 1B **122**
Stanstead Rd. E11. . . . . 1D **41**
  SE6 . . . . 1A **122**
  SE23 . . . . 1F **121**
Stanswood Gdns.
  SE5 . . . . 3A **92**
Stanthorpe Cl.
  SW16 . . . . 5A **118**
Stanthorpe Rd.
  SW16 . . . . 5A **118**
Stanton Ho. SE10 . . . . . 2E **95**
  (off Thames St.)
  SE16 . . . . 3B **80**
  (off Rotherhithe St.)
Stanton Rd. SE26 . . . . . 4B **122**
  SW13 . . . . 5B **84**
Stanton Sq. SE26 . . . . . 4B **122**
Stanton Way SE26 . . . . 4B **122**
Stanway Ct. N1. . . . . . . 1A **64**
  (not continuous)
Stanway St. N1. . . . . . . 1A **64**
Stanwick Rd. W14 . . . . 5B **72**
Stanworth St.
  SE1 . . . . 4F **27** (4B **78**)
Stanyhurst SE23 . . . . . 1A **122**
Staplefield Cl. SW2 . . . 1A **118**
Stapleford Cl.
  SW19 . . . . 5A **100**
Staplehurst Rd.
  SE13 . . . . 3F **109**
Staple Inn WC1 . . . . . . 1B **16**
Staple Inn Bldgs.
  WC1 . . . . 1B **16** (4C **62**)
Staples Cl. SE16 . . . . . . 2A **80**
STAPLES CORNER 3D **29**
Staples Cnr. Bus. Pk.
  NW2 . . . . 3D **29**
Staple St.
  SE1 . . . . 4C **26** (3F **77**)
Stapleton Hall Rd.
  N4 . . . . 3B **34**
Stapleton Ho. E2 . . . . . 2D **65**
  (off Ellsworth St.)
Stapleton Rd.
  SW17 . . . . 3C **116**
Stapleton Vs. N16 . . . . 1A **50**
  (off Wordsworth Rd.)
Star All. EC3 . . . . 4E **19**
  (off Fenchurch St.)
Starboard Way E14 . . . 4C **80**
Starcross St.
  NW1 . . . . 2A **6** (2E **61**)
Starfield Rd. W12 . . . . . 3C **70**
Star La. E16 . . . . 3A **68**
Starling Ho. NW8 . . . . . 1A **60**
  (off Barrow Hill Est.)
Star Pl. E1 . . . . 1C **78**
Star Rd. W14 . . . . 2B **86**
Star St. W2 . . . . 5A **60**
Star Yd.
  WC2 . . . . 2B **16** (5C **62**)

Statham Gro. N16 . . . . . 1F **49**
Statham Ho.
  SW8 . . . . 4E **89**
  (off Wadhurst Rd.)
Station App. E7 . . . . . . 1D **55**
  NW1 . . . . 4A **4** (3B **60**)
  NW10 . . . . 2B **56**
  SE3 . . . . 1D **111**
  SE12 . . . . 4C **110**
  (off Burnt Ash Hill)
  SE26 . . . . 4E **121**
  SW6 . . . . 1A **100**
  SW16 . . . . 5F **117**
Station App. Rd.
  SE1 . . . . 4A **24** (3C **76**)
Station Arc. W1 . . . . 4E **5**
  (off Gt. Portland St.)
Station Av. SW9 . . . . . 1D **105**
Station Cres. SE3 . . . . . 1C **96**
Stationer's Hall Ct.
  EC4 . . . . 3E **17** (5D **63**)
Station Pde. E13 . . . . . . 5E **55**
  (off Green St.)
  NW2 . . . . 3E **43**
  SW12 . . . . 1C **116**
Station Pas. SE15 . . . . . 4E **93**
Station Path E8 . . . . 3D **51**
  (off Graham Rd.)
  SW6 . . . . 1B **100**
Station Pl. N4 . . . . 4C **34**
Station Ri. SE27 . . . . . . 2D **119**
Station Rd. E7 . . . . 1C **54**
  E12 . . . . 1F **55**
  E17 . . . . 1A **38**
  N19 . . . . 5E **33**
  NW4 . . . . 1C **28**
  NW10 . . . . 1B **56**
  SE13 . . . . 1E **109**
  SE20 . . . . 5E **121**
  SW13 . . . . 5B **84**
Station St. E15 . . . . 4F **53**
Station Ter. NW10 . . . . . 1F **57**
  SE5 . . . . 4E **91**
Station Ter. M. SE3 . . . 1C **96**
Station Way SE15 . . . . . 5C **92**
Staton Ct. E10 . . . . 2D **39**
  (off Kings Cl.)
Staunton Ho. SE17 . . . . 5A **78**
  (off Tatum St.)
Staunton St. SE8 . . . . . 2B **94**
Staveley NW1 . . . . 1F **5**
  (off Varndell St.)
Staveley Cl. E9 . . . . 2E **51**
  N7 . . . . 1A **48**
  SE15 . . . . 4D **93**
Staveley Gdns. W4 . . . . 4A **84**
Staveley Rd. W4 . . . . . . 3A **84**
Staverton Rd. NW2 . . . . 4E **43**
Stave Yd. Rd. SE16 . . . . 2A **80**
Stavordale Rd. N5 . . . . 1D **49**
Stayner's Rd. E1 . . . . . . 3F **65**
Steadman Ct. EC1 . . . . . 3A **10**
  (off Old St.)
Stead St. SE17 . . . . 5F **77**
Stean St. E8 . . . . 5B **50**
Stebbing Ho. W11 . . . . . 2F **71**
  (off Queensdale Cres.)
Stebondale St. E14 . . . . 5E **81**
Stedham Pl. WC1 . . . . . 2D **15**
Steedman St. SE17 . . . . 5E **77**

Steele Ho. E15 . . . . 1A **68**
  (off Eve Rd.)
Steele Rd. E11. . . . . 1A **54**
Steele's M. Nth.
  NW3 . . . . 3B **46**
Steele's M. Sth.
  NW3 . . . . 3B **46**
Steele's Rd. NW3. . . . . . 3B **46**
Steele's Studios
  NW3 . . . . 3B **46**
Steel's La. E1 . . . . 5E **65**
Steelyard Pas. EC4 . . . . 5B **18**
Steen Way SE22 . . . . . 3A **106**
Steep Hill SW16 . . . . . . 3F **117**
Steeple Cl. SW6 . . . . . . 5A **86**
  SW19 . . . . 5A **114**
Steeple Ct. E1 . . . . 3D **65**
Steeple Wlk. N1 . . . . 5E **49**
  (off New Nth. Rd.)
Steerforth St. SW18 . . . 2E **115**
Steers Way SE16 . . . . . 3A **80**
Stelfox Ho. WC1 . . . . . . 1A **8**
  (off Penton Ri.)
Stella Rd. SW17 . . . . . 5B **116**
Stellman Cl. E5 . . . . 5C **36**
Stephan Cl. E8 . . . . 5C **50**
Stephendale Rd.
  SW6 . . . . 1D **101**
Stephen Fox Ho. W4 . . . 1A **84**
  (off Chiswick La.)
Stephen M.
  W1 . . . . 1B **14** (4F **61**)
Stephen Pl. SW4 . . . . . 1E **103**
Stephens Ct. E16 . . . . . 3B **68**
  SE4 . . . . 1A **108**
Stephenson Ho.
  SE1 . . . . 5F **25** (4E **77**)
Stephenson Rd. E17 . . . 1A **38**
Stephenson St. E16 . . . 3A **68**
  NW10 . . . . 2A **56**
Stephenson Way
  NW1 . . . . 3A **6** (3E **61**)
Stephen's Rd. E15 . . . . 5A **54**
Stephen St.
  W1 . . . . 1B **14** (4F **61**)
STEPNEY 4F **65**
Stepney C'way. E1 . . . . 5F **65**
Stepney City Apartments
  E1 . . . . 4E **65**
Stepney Grn. E1 . . . . . . 4E **65**
Stepney Grn. Ct. E1 . . . 4E **65**
  (off Stepney Grn.)
Stepney High St. E1 . . . 4F **65**
Stepney Way E1 . . . . . . 4D **65**
Sterling Cl. NW10 . . . . . 4C **42**
Sterling Gdns. SE14 . . . 2A **94**
Sterling Ho. SE3 . . . . . 2D **111**
Sterling St. SW7 . . . . . . 4A **74**
Sterndale Rd. W14 . . . . 4F **71**
Sterne St. W12 . . . . 3F **71**
Sternhall La. SE15 . . . . 1C **106**
Sternhold Av. SW2 . . . 2F **117**
Sterry St.
  SE1 . . . . 4B **26** (3F **77**)
Steucers La. SE23 . . . . 1A **122**
Steve Biko La. SE6 . . . 4C **122**
Steve Biko Lodge
  E13 . . . . 1C **68**
  (off London Rd.)
Steve Biko Rd. N7 . . . . 5C **34**

Stevedore St. E1 . . . . 2D **79**
Stevenage Rd. SW6 . . . . . 3F **85**
Stevens Av. E9 . . . . 3E **51**
Stevens Cl.
  BR3: Beck. 5C **122**
Stevenson Cres.
  SE16 . . . . 1C **92**
Stevenson Ho. NW8 . . . *5E 45*
  (off Boundary Rd.)
Stevens Ho.
  SE1 . . . . 5E **27** (4A **78**)
Steventon Rd. W12 . . . . 1B **70**
Steward Ho.
  E1. . . . . 5E **11** (4A **64**)
    (not continuous)
Stewart Rd. E15 . . . . 1F **53**
Stewart's Gro. SW3 . . . . 1F **87**
Stewart's Rd. SW8 . . . . . 3E **89**
Stewart St. E14. . . . . 3E **81**
Stew La. EC4 . . 4F **17** (1E **77**)
Stifford Ho. E1 . . . . *4E 65*
  (off Stepney Way)
Stileman Ho. E3 . . . . *4B 66*
  (off Ackroyd Dr.)
Stillingfleet Rd.
  SW13 . . . . 2C **84**
Stillington St. SW1 . . . . . 5E **75**
Stillness Rd. SE23 . . . . 4A **108**
Stirling Rd. E13 . . . . 1D **69**
  SW9 . . . . 5A **90**
Stockbeck NW1 . . . . *1A 6*
  (off Ampthill Est.)
Stockfield Rd.
  SW16 . . . . 3B **118**
Stockholm Ho. E1. . . . . . 1C **78**
  (off Swedenborg Gdns.)
Stockholm Rd. SE16. . . . 1E **93**
Stockholm Way E1 . . . . . 2C **78**
Stockhurst Cl. SW15 . . . 5E **85**
Stockleigh Hall NW8 . . . *1A 60*
  (off Prince Albert Rd.)
Stock Orchard Cres.
  N7. . . . . 2B **48**
Stock Orchard St. N7 . . . 2B **48**
Stocks Pl. E14 . . . . 1B **80**
Stock St. E13 . . . . 1C **68**
Stockton Ho. E2 . . . . *2D 65*
  (off Ellsworth St.)
STOCKWELL 5B **90**
Stockwell Av. SW9 . . . . 1B **104**
Stockwell Gdns.
  SW9 . . . . 4B **90**
Stockwell Gdns. Est.
  SW9 . . . . 5A **90**
Stockwell Grn. SW9 . . . . 5B **90**
Stockwell Grn. Ct.
  SW9 . . . . 5B **90**
Stockwell La. SW9 . . . . . 5B **90**
Stockwell M. SW9 . . . . . 5B **90**
Stockwell Pk. Cres.
  SW9 . . . . 5B **90**
Stockwell Pk. Est.
  SW9 . . . . 5B **90**
Stockwell Pk. Rd.
  SW9 . . . . 4B **90**
Stockwell Pk. Wlk.
  SW9 . . . . 1C **104**
Stockwell Rd. SW9 . . . . 5B **90**
Stockwell St. SE10 . . . . . 2E **95**
Stockwell Ter. SW8 . . . . 4B **90**

Stoddart Ho. SW8 . . . . . 2B **90**
Stofield Gdns. SE9 . . . . 3F **125**
Stoford Cl. SW19 . . . . . 5A **100**
Stokenchurch St.
  SW6 . . . . 4D **87**
STOKE NEWINGTON . . . 5B **36**
Stoke Newington Chu. St.
  N16 . . . . 5F **35**
Stoke Newington Comn.
  N16 . . . . 4B **36**
Stoke Newington High St.
  N16 . . . . 5B **36**
Stoke Newington Rd.
  N16 . . . . 2B **50**
Stoke Pl. NW10 . . . . 2B **56**
Stokesley St. W12 . . . . . 5B **56**
Stokes Rd. E6 . . . . 3F **69**
Stoll Cl. NW2 . . . . 5E **29**
Stoms Path SE6 . . . . . . 5C **122**
  (off Maroons Way)
Stondon Ho. E15 . . . . . . 5B **54**
  (off John St.)
Stondon Pk. SE23 . . . . 4A **108**
Stondon Wlk. E6. . . . . . . 1F **69**
Stonebridge Cen.
  N15. . . . . 1B **36**
Stonebridge Rd. N15. . . 1B **36**
Stone Bldgs. WC2 . . . . 1A **16**
Stone Cl. SW4 . . . . 5E **89**
Stonecutter St.
  EC4 . . . . 2D **17** (5D **63**)
Stonefield N4 . . . . 4B **34**
Stonefield St. N1. . . . . . . 5C **48**
Stonefield Way SE7 . . . . 3F **97**
Stone Hall W8 . . . . *4D 73*
  (off Stone Hall Gdns.)
Stonehall Av. IG1: Ilf . . . 1F **41**
Stone Hall Gdns. W8. . . 4D **73**
Stone Hall Pl. W8 . . . . . . 4D **73**
Stonehills Ct. SE21 . . . 3A **120**
Stonehouse NW1 . . . . . *5E 47*
  (off Plender St.)
Stone Ho. Ct. EC3 . . . . . 2E **19**
Stone Lake Ind. Pk.
  SE7 . . . . 5E **83**
Stone Lake Retail Pk.
  SE7 . . . . 5E **83**
Stoneleigh M. E3 . . . . . . 1A **66**
Stoneleigh Pl. W11 . . . . 1F **71**
Stoneleigh St. W11 . . . . 1F **71**
Stoneleigh Ter. N19. . . . 4D **33**
Stonell's Rd. SW11 . . . 4B **102**
Stonenest St. N4 . . . . . . 3B **34**
Stones End St.
  SE1. . . . . 4F **25** (3E **77**)
Stoneyard La. E14 . . . . . 1D **81**
Stoneycroft Cl.
  SE12 . . . . 5B **110**
Stoney La.
  E1. . . . . 2E **19** (5B **64**)
Stoney St.
  SE1. . . . . 1B **26** (2F **77**)
Stonhouse St. SW4 . . . 2F **103**
Stonor Rd. W14 . . . . 5B **72**
Stopes St. SE15 . . . . . . 3B **92**
Stopford Rd. E13 . . . . . . 5C **54**
  SE17 . . . . 1E **91**
Stopher Ho. SE1. . . . . . . *4E 25*
  (off Webber St.)
Storers Quay E14 . . . . . 5F **81**

Store St. E15 . . . . 2F **53**
  WC1 . . . . 1B **14** (4F **61**)
Storey Ct. NW8 . . . . *2F 59*
  (off St John's Wood Rd.)
Storey Ho. E14 . . . . *1D 81*
  (off Cottage St.)
Storey Rd. N6. . . . . 1B **32**
Storey's Ga.
  SW1 . . . . 4C **22** (3F **75**)
Stories M. SE5 . . . . 5A **92**
Stories Rd. SE5 . . . . 1A **106**
Stork Rd. E7 . . . . 3B **54**
Stork's Rd. SE16 . . . . . . 4C **78**
Stormont Lawn Tennis &
  Squash Club. 1B **32**
Stormont Rd. N6 . . . . . . 2B **32**
  SW11 . . . . 1C **102**
Storrington WC1 . . . . . . *2E 7*
  (off Regent Sq.)
Story St. N1 . . . . 4B **48**
Stothard Ho. E1 . . . . *3E 65*
  (off Amiel St.)
Stothard St. E1 . . . . 3E **65**
Stott Cl. SW18 . . . . 4F **101**
Stoughton Cl. SE11 . . . . 5B **76**
  (off Gibson Rd.)
  SW15 . . . . 1C **112**
Stourcliffe Cl. W1 . . . . . 5B **60**
Stourcliffe St. W1 . . . . . 5B **60**
Stourhead Cl. SW19. . . 5F **99**
Stourhead Ho. SW1 . . . *1F 89*
  (off Tachbrook St.)
Stour Rd. E3. . . . . 4C **52**
Stowage SE8 . . . . 2C **94**
Stowe Ho. NW11 . . . . . . 1E **31**
Stowe Rd. W12 . . . . 3D **71**
Stracey Rd. E7. . . . . 1C **54**
  NW10 . . . . 5A **42**
Stradbroke Rd. N5 . . . . . 1E **49**
Stradella Rd. SE24. . . . 4E **105**
Strafford Ho. SE8. . . . . . *1B 94*
  (off Grove St.)
Strafford St. E14 . . . . . . 3C **80**
Strahan Rd. E3. . . . . 2A **66**
Straightsmouth
  SE10 . . . . 3E **95**
Strait Rd. E6. . . . . 1F **83**
Strakers Rd. SE15 . . . . 2D **107**
Strale Ho. N1 . . . . *5A 50*
  (off Whitmore Est.)
Strand WC2 . . . . 5E **15** (1A **76**)
Strand La.
  WC2 . . . . 4A **16** (1B **76**)
Strand Theatre *4F 15*
  (off Aldwych)
Strang Ho. N1. . . . . 5E **49**
Strang Print Room 3B **6**
Strangways Ter. W14 . . 4B **72**
Stranraer Way N1 . . . . . 4A **48**
Strasburg Rd. SW11 . . . 4C **88**
STRATFORD 4F **53**
Stratford Cen., The
  E15 . . . . 4F **53**
Stratford Circus
  (Performing Arts Cen.)
  . . . . 3F **53**
Stratford Gro. SW15. . . 2F **99**
STRATFORD MARSH. . . 4D **53**
STRATFORD NEW TOWN
  . . . . 2E **53**

Stratford Office Village, The
E15 . . . . 4A **54**
(off Romford Rd.)
Stratford Picture House
. . . . 3F **53**
Stratford Pl.
W1. . . . . 3D **13** (5D **61**)
Stratford Rd. E13 . . . . . 5B **54**
(not continuous)
W8 . . . . 4C **72**
Stratford Shop. Cen.
E15 . . . . *4F* **53**
(off Stratford Cen., The)
Stratford Studios W8 . . . 4C **72**
Stratford Vs. NW1 . . . . 4E **47**
Stratham Ct. *N19* *5A* **34**
(off Alexander Rd.)
Strathan Cl. SW18 . . . . 4A **100**
Strathaven Rd.
SE12. . . . . 4D **111**
Strathblaine Rd.
SW11 . . . . 3F **101**
Strathdale SW16 . . . . . 5B **118**
Strathdon Dr. SW17 . . . 3F **115**
Strathearn Pl. W2 . . . . 5A **60**
Strathearn Rd.
SW19 . . . . 5C **114**
Stratheden Pde. SE3 . . 3C **96**
Stratheden Rd. SE3 . . . 4C **96**
Strathleven Rd.
SW2 . . . . 3A **104**
Strathmore Ct. *NW8*. . . *2A* **60**
(off Park Rd.)
Strathmore Gdns.
W8 . . . . 2C **72**
Strathmore Rd.
SW19 . . . . 3C **114**
Strathnairn St. SE1 . . . 5C **78**
Strathray Gdns. NW3 . . 3A **46**
Strath Ter. SW11 . . . . 2A **102**
Strathville Rd.
SW18 . . . . 2C **114**
(not continuous)
Stratton Ct. *N1* *4A* **50**
(off Hertford Rd.)
Strattondale St. E14 . . . 4E **81**
Stratton St.
W1. . . . . . . 1E **21** (2D **75**)
Strauss Rd. W4 . . . . . . 3A **70**
Streakes Fld. Rd.
NW2 . . . . 4C **28**
Streamline Ct.
SE22 . . . . *1C* **120**
(off Streamline M.)
Streamline M. SE22. . . 1C **120**
STREATHAM 5A **118**
Streatham Cl.
SW16 . . . . 2A **118**
STREATHAM COMMON
. . . . 5A **118**
Streatham Comn. Nth.
SW16 . . . . 5A **118**
Streatham Comn. Sth.
SW16 . . . . 5A **118**
Streatham Ct.
SW16 . . . . 3A **118**
Streatham High Rd.
SW16 . . . . 4A **118**
STREATHAM HILL 2A **118**
Streatham Hill SW2 . . 2A **118**

Streatham Ice Arena
. . . . 5F **117**
Streatham Leisure Cen.
. . . . 5A **118**
STREATHAM PARK . . 5E **117**
Streatham Pl. SW2 . . 5A **104**
Streatham St.
WC1. . . . . 2D **15** (5A **62**)
Streathbourne Rd.
SW17 . . . . 2C **116**
Streatley Pl. NW3 . . . . 1E **45**
Streatley Rd. NW6 . . . 4B **44**
Streetfield M. SE3 . . . 1C **110**
Streimer Rd. E15 . . . . 1E **67**
Strelley Way W3 . . . . . 1A **70**
Stretton Mans. SE8 . . . 1C **94**
Strickland Ct. SE15 . . . 1C **106**
Strickland Ho. *E2* *2F* **11**
(off Chambord St.)
Strickland Row
SW18 . . . . 5F **101**
Strickland St. SE8 . . . . 5C **94**
Stride Rd. E13 . . . . 1B **68**
Stringer Ho. *N1* *5A* **50**
(off Whitmore Rd.)
Strode Rd. E7 . . . . 1C **54**
NW10 . . . . 3C **42**
SW6 . . . . 3A **86**
Strome Ho. *NW6* *1D* **59**
(off Carlton Va.)
Strone Rd. E7 . . . . 3E **55**
E12 . . . . 3E **55**
Stronsa Rd. W12 . . . . 3B **70**
Strood Ho. *SE1* *4C* **26**
(off Staple St.)
Stroud Cres. SW15 . . . 3C **112**
STROUD GREEN 2B **34**
Stroud Grn. Rd. N4 . . . 3B **34**
Stroudley Ho. SW8 . . . 4E **89**
Stroudley Wlk. E3 . . . . 2D **67**
Stroud Rd. SW19 . . . . 3C **114**
Strouts Pl. E2 . . 1E **11** (2B **64**)
Strudwick Ct. *SW4* *4A* **90**
(off Binfield Rd.)
Strutton Ground
SW1 . . . . 5B **22** (4F **75**)
Strype St. E1 . . 1F **19** (4B **64**)
Stuart Av. NW9 . . . . . . 2C **28**
Stuart Ho. *E16* *2D* **83**
(off Beaulieu Av.)
W14 . . . . *5A* **72**
(off Windsor Way)
Stuart Mill Ho. *N1* *1F* **7**
(off Killick St.)
Stuart Rd. NW6 . . . . . . 2C **58**
(not continuous)
SE15 . . . . 2E **107**
SW19 . . . . 3C **114**
Stuart Twr. *W9* *2E* **59**
(off Maida Va.)
Stubbs Dr. SE16. . . . . . 1D **93**
Stubbs Ho. *E2*. *2F* **65**
(off Bonner St.)
SW1 . . . . *5F* **75**
(off Erasmus St.)
Stubbs Point E13 . . . . 3C **68**
Stucley Pl. NW1. . . . . . 4D **47**
Studdridge St. SW6 . . . 5C **86**
(not continuous)
Studd St. N1. . . . . 5D **49**

Studholme Ct. NW3 . . . . 1C **44**
Studholme St. SE15. . . 3D **93**
Studio Pl. SW1 . . . . . . 4A **20**
Studland *SE17* *1F* **91**
(off Portland St.)
Studland Ho. *E14*. *5A* **66**
(off Aston St.)
Studland Rd. SE26 . . . 5F **121**
Studland W6. . . . . 5D **71**
Studley Cl. E5 . . . . 2A **52**
Studley Ct. *E14*. *1F* **81**
(off Jamestown Way)
Studley Dr. IG4: Ilf 1F **41**
Studley Est. SW4 . . . . . 4A **90**
Studley Rd. E7. . . . . 3D **55**
SW4 . . . . 4A **90**
Stukeley Rd. E7 . . . . . . 4D **55**
Stukeley St.
WC2. . . . . 2E **15** (5A **62**)
Stumps Hill La.
BR3: Beck. 5C **122**
Stunell Ho. *SE14* *2F* **93**
(off John Williams Cl.)
Sturdee Ho. *E2*. *1C* **64**
(off Horatio St.)
Sturdy Ho. *E3*. *1A* **66**
(off Gernon Rd.)
Sturdy Rd. SE15. . . . . . 5D **93**
Sturgeon Ho. SE17. . . . 1E **91**
Sturgess Av. NW4 . . . . 2D **29**
Sturge St.
SE1. . . . . 3F **25** (3E **77**)
Sturmer Way N7. . . . . . 2B **48**
Sturminster Ho. *SW8*. . *3B* **90**
(off Dorset Rd.)
Sturry St. E14 . . . . 5D **67**
Sturt St. N1. . . . 1A **10** (1E **63**)
Stutfield St. E1. . . . . . . 5C **64**
Styles Gdns. SW9 . . . . 1D **105**
Styles Ho. SE1 . . . . 3D **25**
Sudbourne Rd.
SW2 . . . . 3A **104**
Sudbrooke Rd.
SW12 . . . . 4B **102**
Sudbury Ct. *SW8* *4F* **89**
(off Allen Edwards Dr.)
Sudbury Cres.
BR1: Brom. 5C **124**
Sudbury Ho. SW18 . . . 3D **101**
Sudeley St. N1. . . . . . . 1D **63**
Sudlow Rd. SW18 . . . 3C **100**
Sudrey St.
SE1. . . . . 4F **25** (3E **77**)
Suffield Ho. *SE17* *1D* **91**
(off Berryfield Rd.)
Suffolk Ho. E10 . . . . . . 2C **38**
Suffolk La.
EC4. . . . . 4B **18** (1F **77**)
Suffolk Pl.
SW1 . . . . 1C **22** (2F **75**)
Suffolk Rd. E13 . . . . . . 2C **68**
N15. . . . . 1F **35**
NW10 . . . . 4A **42**
SW13 . . . . 3B **84**
Suffolk St. E7 . . . . 1C **54**
SW1. . . . . 5C **14** (1F **75**)
Sugar Bakers Ct. EC3. . 3E **19**
Sugar Ho. La. E15. . . . 1E **67**
Sugar Loaf Wlk. E2 . . . 2E **65**
Sugar Quay EC3. . . . . . 5E **19**

Sugar Quay Wlk.
  EC3 . . . . . . 5E **19** (1A **78**)
Sugden Rd. SW11 . . . . 1C **102**
Sugden St. SE5 . . . . . . 2F **91**
Sulby Ho. *SE4* 2A *108*
  (off Turnham Rd.)
Sulgrave Gdns. W6 . . . . 3E **71**
Sulgrave Rd. W6 . . . . . 4E **71**
Sulina Rd. SW2 . . . . . 5A **104**
Sulivan Ct. SW6 . . . . . 5C **86**
Sulivan Ent. Cen.
  SW6 . . . . 1D **101**
Sulivan Rd. SW6 . . . . . 1C **100**
Sulkin Ho. *E2* 2F *65*
  (off Knottisford St.)
Sullivan Av. E16 . . . . . 4F **69**
Sullivan Cl. SW11 . . . . 1A **102**
Sullivan Ct. N16 . . . . . 2B **36**
Sullivan Ho. *SE11* *5B 76*
  (off Vauxhall St.)
  SW1 . . . . *2D 89*
  (off Churchill Gdns.)
Sullivan Rd. SE11 . . . . 5C **76**
Sultan St. SE5 . . . . . . 3E **91**
Sumatra Rd. NW6 . . . . 2C **44**
Sumburgh Rd.
  SW12 . . . . 4C **102**
Summercourt Rd. E1 . . 5E **65**
Summerfield Av.
  NW6 . . . . 1A **58**
Summerfield St.
  SE12 . . . . 5B **110**
Summerhouse Rd.
  N16 . . . . 4A **36**
Summerley St.
  SW18 . . . . 2D **115**
Summersby Rd. N6 . . . 1D **33**
Summerskill Cl.
  SE15 . . . . 1D **107**
Summers St.
  EC1 . . . . . . 4B **8** (3C **62**)
SUMMERSTOWN 3E **115**
Summerstown
  SW17 . . . . 3E **115**
Summit Av. NW9 . . . . . 1A **28**
Summit Ct. NW2 . . . . . 2A **44**
Summit Est. N16 . . . . . 2C **36**
Sumner Av. SE15 . . . . . 4B **92**
Sumner Bldgs. SE1 . . . 1F **25**
Sumner Ct. SW8 . . . . . 3A **90**
Sumner Est. SE15 . . . . 3B **92**
Sumner Ho. *E3* *4D 67*
  (off Watts Gro.)
Sumner Pl. SW7 . . . . . 5F **73**
Sumner Pl. M. SW7 . . . 5F **73**
Sumner Rd. SE15 . . . . . 2B **92**
Sumner St.
  SE1 . . . . . . 1E **25** (2D **77**)
Sumpter Cl. NW3 . . . . . 3E **45**
Sunbeam Cres. W10 . . 3E **57**
Sunbeam Rd. NW10 . . 3A **56**
Sunbury Av. SW14 . . . . 2A **98**
Sunbury Av. Pas.
  SW14 . . . . 2A **98**
Sunbury Ho. *E2* *2F 11*
  (off Swanfield St.)
  SE14 . . . . *2F 93*
  (off Myers La.)
Sunbury La. SW11 . . . . 4B **87**
  (not continuous)

Sunbury Workshops
  E2 . . . . *2F 11*
  (off Swanfield St.)
Sun Ct. EC3 . . . . 3C **18**
Suncroft Pl. SE26 . . . . 3E **121**
Sunderland Ct.
  SE22 . . . . 5C **106**
Sunderland Mt.
  SE23 . . . . 2F **121**
Sunderland Rd.
  SE23 . . . . 1F **121**
Sunderland Ter. W2 . . . 5D **59**
Sunderland Way E12 . . 4F **41**
Sundew Av. W12 . . . . . 1C **70**
Sundew Cl. W12 . . . . . 1C **70**
Sundorne Rd. SE7 . . . . 1E **97**
Sundra Wlk. E1 . . . . . . 3F **65**
SUNDRIDGE 5D **125**
Sundridge Ho. *E9* *4F 51*
  (off Church Cres.)
Sunfields Pl. SE3 . . . . . 3D **97**
SUN-IN-THE-SANDS . . 3D **97**
Sun La. SE3 . . . . 3D **97**
Sunlight Cl. SW19 . . . . 5E **115**
Sunlight Sq. E2 . . . . . . 2D **65**
Sunningdale Av. W3 . . 1A **70**
Sunningdale Cl.
  SE16 . . . . 1D **93**
Sunningdale Gdns.
  W8 . . . . *4C 72*
  (off Stratford Rd.)
Sunninghill Rd. SE13 . . 5D **95**
Sunnydale Rd.
  SE12 . . . . 3D **111**
Sunnydene St. SE26 . . 4A **122**
Sunnyhill Cl. E5 . . . . . . 1A **52**
Sunnyhill Rd. SW16 . . . 4A **118**
Sunnymead Rd. NW9 . . 2A **28**
  SW15 . . . . 3D **99**
Sunnyside NW2 . . . . . . 5B **30**
  SW19 . . . . 5A **114**
Sunnyside Ho's.
  NW2 . . . . *5B 30*
  (off Sunnyside)
Sunnyside Pas.
  SW19 . . . . 5A **114**
Sunnyside Pl.
  SW19 . . . . 5A **114**
Sunnyside Rd. E10 . . . . 3C **38**
  N19 . . . . 2F **33**
Sun Pas. *SE16* *4C 78*
  (off Old Jamaica Rd.)
Sunray Av. SE24 . . . . . 2F **105**
Sun Rd. W14 . . . . 1B **86**
Sunset Rd. SE5 . . . . . . 2E **105**
  SW19 . . . . 5D **113**
Sun St. EC2 . . . . 5C **10** (4F **63**)
  (not continuous)
Sun St. Pas.
  EC2 . . . . . . 1D **19** (4A **64**)
Sun Wlk. E1 . . . . 1B **78**
Sunwell Cl. SE15 . . . . . 4D **93**
Sun Wharf *SE8* *3D 95*
  (off Creekside)
Surma Cl. E1 . . . . 3D **65**
Surrendale Pl. W9 . . . . 3C **58**
Surrey Canal Rd.
  SE15 . . . . 2E **93**
Surrey County Cricket Club
  . . . . 2B **90**

Surrey Docks Stadium
  . . . . 2F **79**
Surrey Docks Watersports Cen.
  . . . . 4A **80**
Surrey Gdns. N4 . . . . . 1E **35**
Surrey Gro. SE17 . . . . . 1A **92**
Surrey Ho. *SE16* *2F 79*
  (off Rotherhithe St.)
Surrey La. SW11 . . . . . 4A **88**
Surrey La. Est.
  SW11 . . . . 4A **88**
Surrey M. SE27 . . . . . . 4A **120**
Surrey Mt. SE23 . . . . . 1D **121**
Surrey Quays Rd.
  SE16 . . . . 4E **79**
Surrey Quays Shop. Cen.
  SE16 . . . . 5F **107**
Surrey Rd. SE15 . . . . . 3F **107**
Surrey Row
  SE1 . . . . 3D **25** (3D **77**)
Surrey Sq. SE17 . . . . . 1A **92**
Surrey Steps *WC2* *4A 16*
  (off Surrey St.)
Surrey St. E13 . . . . 2D **69**
  WC2 . . . . . . 4A **16** (1B **76**)
Surrey Ter. SE17 . . . . . 1A **92**
Surrey Water Rd.
  SE16 . . . . 2F **79**
Surridge Ct. *SW9* *5A 90*
  (off Clapham Rd.)
Surr St. N7 . . . . 2A **48**
Susan Constant Ct.
  E14 . . . . *1F 81*
  (off Newport Av.)
Susannah St. E14 . . . . 5D **67**
Susan Rd. SE3 . . . . . . 5D **97**
Sussex Cl. N19 . . . . . . 4A **34**
Sussex Ct. *SE10* *2E 95*
  (off Roan St.)
Sussex Gdns. N4 . . . . . 1E **35**
  N6 . . . . 1B **32**
  W2 . . . . 1F **73**
Sussex Ga. N6 . . . . 1B **32**
Sussex Lodge *W2*. . . . *5F 59*
  (off Sussex Pl.)
Sussex Mans. *SW7* . . . *5F 73*
  (off Old Brompton Rd.)
  WC2 . . . . *4E 15*
  (off Maiden La.)
Sussex M. SE6 . . . . . . 5C **108**
Sussex M. E. *W2* *5F 59*
  (off Clifton Pl.)
Sussex M. W. W2. . . . . 1F **73**
Sussex Pl.
  NW1 . . . . . . 3A **4** (3B **60**)
  W2 . . . . 5F **59**
  W6 . . . . 1E **85**
Sussex Sq. W2 . . . . 1F **73**
Sussex St. E13 . . . . 2D **69**
  SW1 . . . . 1D **89**
Sussex Way N7 . . . . . . 4A **34**
  N19 . . . . 3F **33**
  (not continuous)
Sutcliffe Cl. NW11 . . . . 1D **31**
Sutcliffe Pk. Athletics Track
  . . . . 3E **111**
Sutherland Av. W9 . . . . 3C **58**
Sutherland Ct. N16 . . . 5F **35**
  W9 . . . . *3C 58*
  (off Marylands Rd.)

Sutherland Gdns.
 SW14 . . . . 1A **98**
Sutherland Gro.
 SW18 . . . . 4A **100**
Sutherland Ho. W8 . . . . 4D **73**
Sutherland Pl. W2 . . . . 5C **58**
Sutherland Point E5 . . . 5D **37**
 (off Brackenfield Cl.)
Sutherland Rd. E3 . . . . 1B **66**
 W4 . . . . 2A **84**
Sutherland Row SW1 . . 1D **89**
Sutherland Sq. SE17 . . 1E **91**
Sutherland St. SW1 . . . 1D **89**
Sutherland Wlk.
 SE17 . . . . 1E **91**
Sutlej Rd. SE7 . . . . 3E **97**
Sutterton St. N7 . . . . . . 3B **48**
Sutton Ct. Rd. E13 . . . . 2E **69**
Sutton Est. EC1. . . . . . . 2C **10**
 W10 . . . . 4E **57**
Sutton La. EC1 . . . . 4E **9**
 (off Gt. Sutton St.)
Sutton Pl. E9 . . . . 2E **51**
Sutton Rd. E13 . . . . 3B **68**
Sutton Row
 W1 . . . . 2C **14** (5F **61**)
Sutton Sq. E9 . . . . 2E **51**
Sutton St. E1. . . . . 1E **79**
Sutton's Way
 EC1 . . . . 4A **10** (3E **63**)
Sutton Wlk.
 SE1 . . . . 2A **24** (2B **76**)
Sutton Way W10. . . . . . . 3E **57**
Swaby Rd. SW18 . . . . . 1E **115**
Swaffield Rd.
 SW18 . . . . 5D **101**
Swains La. N6 . . . . 3C **32**
Swainson Rd. W3 . . . . . 3B **70**
Swain St. NW8 . . . . 3A **60**
 (off Tresham Cres.)
Swallands Rd. SE6. . . . 3C **122**
 (not continuous)
Swallow Cl. SE14 . . . . 4F **93**
Swallow Ct. SE1 . . . . . . 4A **26**
 (off Swan St.)
 SE12 . . . . 5C **110**
 W9 . . . . 4C **58**
 (off Admiral Wlk.)
Swallow Dr. NW10 . . . . . 3A **42**
Swallowfield Rd.
 SE7 . . . . 1D **97**
Swallow Gdns.
 SW16 . . . . 5F **117**
Swallow Ho. NW8 . . . . . 1A **60**
 (off Barrow Hill Est.)
Swallow Pas. W1 . . . . . . 3E **13**
 (off Swallow Pl.)
Swallow Pl.
 W1 . . . . 3E **13** (5D **61**)
Swallow St.
 W1 . . . . 5A **14** (1E **75**)
Swanage Ct. N1 . . . . . . 4A **50**
 (off Hertford Rd.)
Swanage Ho. SW8 . . . . 3B **90**
 (off Dorset Rd.)
Swanage Rd. SW18 . . . 4E **101**
Swan App. E6 . . . . 4F **69**
Swanbourne SE17 . . . . 5E **77**
 (off Wansey St.)

Swanbourne Ho.
 NW8 . . . . 3A **60**
 (off Capland St.)
Swan Cen., The
 SW17 . . . . 3D **115**
Swan Ct. E1 . . . . 1C **78**
 (off Star Pl.)
 E14 . . . . 5B **66**
 (off Agnes St.)
 SW3 . . . . 1A **88**
 SW6 . . . . 3C **86**
 (off Fulham Rd.)
Swandon Way
 SW18 . . . . 3D **101**
Swanfield St.
 E2. . . . . 2F **11** (2B **64**)
Swan Ho. N1. . . . . 4F **49**
 (off Oakley Rd.)
Swan La.
 EC4. . . . . 5C **18** (1F **77**)
Swanley Ho.
 SE17 . . . . 1A **92**
 (off Kinglake Est.)
Swan Mead
 SE1 . . . . 5D **27** (4A **78**)
Swan M. SW6 . . . . 4B **86**
 SW9 . . . . 5B **90**
Swanne Ho. SE10. . . . . . 3E **95**
 (off Gloucester Cir.)
Swan Pas. E1 . . . . 1B **78**
 (off Royal Mint Pl.)
Swan Pl. SW13 . . . . 5B **84**
Swan Rd. SE16. . . . . 3E **79**
 SE18 . . . . 4F **83**
Swanscombe Ho.
 W11. . . . . 2F **71**
 (off St Ann's Rd.)
Swanscombe Point
 E16 . . . . 4B **68**
 (off Clarkson Rd.)
Swanscombe Rd. W4. . . 1A **84**
 W11. . . . . 2F **71**
Swan St. SE1 . . 5A **26** (4E **77**)
Swanton Gdns.
 SW19 . . . . 1F **113**
Swan Wlk. SW3 . . . . 2B **88**
Swanwick Cl. SW15. . . . 5B **98**
Swan Yd. N1 . . . . 3D **49**
Swathling Ho. SW15 . . . 4B **98**
 (off Tunworth Cres.)
Swaton Rd. E3 . . . . 3C **66**
Swedeland Ct. E1. . . . . . 1E **19**
Swedenborg Gdns.
 E1. . . . . 1D **79**
Swedenborg Pl. E1 . . . . 1D **79**
 (off Swedenborg Gdns.)
Sweden Ga. SE16 . . . . . 4A **80**
Swedish Quays SE16 . . 4A **80**
 (not continuous)
Sweeney Cres.
 SE1 . . . . 4F **27** (3B **78**)
Swell Ct. E17 . . . . 1C **38**
Swete St. E13. . . . . 1C **68**
Sweyn Pl. SE3 . . . . 5C **96**
Swift Lodge W9 . . . . . . 3C **58**
 (off Admiral Wlk.)
Swiftsden Way
 BR1: Brom 5A **124**
Swift St. SW6 . . . . 4B **86**
Swinbrook Rd. W10 . . . . 4A **58**

Swinburne Ct. SE5 . . . . 2F **105**
 (off Basingdon Way)
Swinburne Ho. E2 . . . . . 2E **65**
 (off Roman Rd.)
Swinburne Rd. SW15. . . 2C **98**
Swindon St. W12. . . . . . 2D **71**
Swinford Gdns.
 SW9 . . . . 1D **105**
Swingfield Ho. E9 . . . . . 5E **51**
 (off Templecombe Rd.)
Swinley Ho. NW1 . . . . . . 1E **5**
 (off Redhill St.)
Swinnerton St. E9 . . . . . 2A **52**
Swinton Pl.
 WC1 . . . . 1F **7** (2B **62**)
Swinton St.
 WC1 . . . . 1F **7** (2B **62**)
Swiss Cen. W1 . . . . 5B **14**
SWISS COTTAGE 4F **45**
Swiss Cottage Sports Cen.
 . . . . 4F **45**
Swiss Ct. WC2 . . . . 5C **14**
Swiss Re. 2E **19**
Swiss Ter. NW6 . . . . 4F **45**
Switch Ho. E14. . . . . . . 1F **81**
Sybil Ho. N4 . . . . 1D **35**
Sybil Phoenix Cl. SE8 . . 1F **93**
Sybil Thorndike Casson Ho.
 SW5 . . . . 1C **86**
 (off Kramer M.)
Sybourn St. E17 . . . . . . 2B **38**
Sycamore Av. E3 . . . . . . 5B **52**
Sycamore Cl. E16 . . . . . 3A **68**
 W3 . . . . 2A **70**
Sycamore Ct. E7 . . . . . . 3C **54**
 NW6 . . . . 5C **44**
 (off Bransdale Cl.)
Sycamore Gdns. W6 . . . 3D **71**
Sycamore Gro. SE6 . . . 4E **109**
Sycamore Ho. SE16 . . . 3F **79**
 (off Woodland Cres.)
 W6 . . . . 3D **71**
Sycamore Lodge W8. . . 4D **73**
 (off Stone Hall Pl.)
Sycamore M. SW4 . . . . 1E **103**
Sycamore Rd.
 SW19 . . . . 5E **113**
Sycamore St.
 EC1. . . . . 4F **9** (3E **63**)
Sycamore Wlk. W10 . . . 3A **58**
Sydcote SE21 . . . . 1E **119**
SYDENHAM 4E **121**
Sydenham Av. SE26. . . . 5D **121**
Sydenham Cotts.
 SE12 . . . . 2E **125**
Sydenham Hill
 SE23 . . . . 1D **121**
 SE26. . . . . 4B **120**
Sydenham Pk. SE26. . . . 3E **121**
Sydenham Pk. Mans.
 SE26 . . . . 3E **121**
 (off Sydenham Pk.)
Sydenham Pk. Rd.
 SE26 . . . . 3E **121**
Sydenham Pl. SE27. . . . 3D **119**
Sydenham Ri. SE23. . . . 2D **121**
Sydenham Rd.
 SE26 . . . . 4E **121**
Sydmons Ct. SE23 . . . . 5E **107**
Sydner M. N16. . . . . 1B **50**

Sydner Rd. N16 . . . . 1B **50**
Sydney Cl. SW3 . . . . 5F **73**
Sydney Gro. NW4 . . . . . . 1E **29**
Sydney M. SW3 . . . . 5F **73**
Sydney Pl. SW7 . . . . 5F **73**
Sydney Rd. E11 . . . . 1D **41**
Sydney St. SW3 . . . . 1A **88**
Sylvan Gro.
    NW2 . . . . 1F **43**
    SE15 . . . . 2D **93**
Sylvan Rd. E7 . . . . 3D **55**
    E17 . . . . 1C **38**
Sylvan Ter. SE15 . . . . . . 2D **93**
    (off Sylvan Gro.)
Sylvester Path E8 . . . . . . 3D **51**
Sylvester Rd. E8 . . . . . . 3D **51**
    E17 . . . . 2B **38**
Sylvia Ct. N1 . . . . 1F **63**
    (off Wenlock St.)
Symes M. NW1 . . . . 1E **61**
Symington Ho. SE1 . . . . 5B **26**
    (off Deverell St.)
Symington M.
    E9 . . . . 2F **51**
Symister M. N1 . . . . 2D **11**
Symons St. SW3 . . . . . . 5B **74**
Symphony M. W10 . . . . . 2A **58**
Syon Lodge SE12 . . . . . 5C **110**
Syringa Ho. SE4 . . . . . . 1B **108**

T

Tabard Ct. E14 . . . . 5E **67**
    (off Lodore St.)
Tabard Gdn. Est.
    SE1 . . . . 4B **26** (4F **77**)
Tabard Ho. SE1 . . . . 5C **26**
    (off Manciple St.)
Tabard St.
    SE1 . . . . 3A **26** (3E **77**)
Tabernacle Av. E13 . . . . 3C **68**
Tabernacle St.
    EC2 . . . . 4C **10** (3F **63**)
Tableer Av. SW4 . . . . . . 3E **103**
Tabley Rd. N7 . . . . 1A **48**
Tabor Rd. W6 . . . . 4D **71**
Tachbrook Est. SW1 . . . . 1F **89**
Tachbrook M. SW1 . . . . . 5E **75**
Tachbrook St. SW1 . . . . 5E **75**
    (not continuous)
Tack M. SE4 . . . . 1C **108**
Tadema Ho. NW8 . . . . . . 3F **59**
    (off Penfold St.)
Tadema Rd. SW10 . . . . . 3E **87**
Tadmor St. W12 . . . . 2F **71**
Tadworth Ho. SE1 . . . . . 4D **25**
Tadworth Rd. NW2 . . . . . 4C **28**
Taeping St. E14 . . . . 5D **81**
Taffrail Ho. E14 . . . . 1D **95**
    (off Burrells Wharf Sq.)
Taft Way E3 . . . . 2D **67**
Tailor Ho. WC1 . . . . 4E **7**
    (off Colonnade)
Tailworth St. E1 . . . . 4C **64**
    (off Chicksand St.)
Tait Ct. E3 . . . . 5B **52**
    (off St Stephen's Rd.)
    SW8 . . . . 4A **90**
    (off Lansdowne Grn.)

Tait Ho. SE1 . . . . 2C **24**
    (off Greet St.)
Takhar M. SW11 . . . . 5A **88**
Talacre Community
    Sports Cen.
    Kentish Town 3C **46**
Talacre Rd. NW5 . . . . . . 3C **46**
Talbot Ct. EC3 . . . . 4C **18**
Talbot Cres. NW4 . . . . . . 1C **28**
Talbot Gro. Ho.
    W11 . . . . 5A **58**
    (off Lancaster Rd.)
Talbot Ho. E14 . . . . 5D **67**
    (off Giraud St.)
    N7 . . . . 5C **34**
Talbot Pl. SE3 . . . . 5A **96**
Talbot Rd. E7 . . . . 1C **54**
    N6 . . . . 1C **32**
    SE22 . . . . 2A **106**
    W2 . . . . 5C **58**
    W11 . . . . 5B **58**
    (not continuous)
Talbot Sq. W2 . . . . 5F **59**
Talbot Wlk. NW10 . . . . . . 3A **42**
    W11 . . . . 5A **58**
Talbot Yd.
    SE1 . . . . 2B **26** (2F **77**)
Talcott Path SW2 . . . . . 1C **118**
Talfourd Pl. SE15 . . . . . . 4B **92**
Talfourd Rd. SE15 . . . . . 4B **92**
Talgarth Mans. W14 . . . . 1A **86**
    (off Talgarth Rd.)
Talgarth Rd. W6 . . . . . . 1F **85**
    W14 . . . . 1F **85**
Talia Ho. E14 . . . . 4E **81**
    (off Manchester Rd.)
Talina Cen. SW6 . . . . . . 4E **87**
Talisman Sq. SE26 . . . . 4C **120**
Tallack Rd. E10 . . . . 3B **38**
Talleyrand Ho. SE5 . . . . . 5E **91**
    (off Lilford Rd.)
Tallis Cl. E16 . . . . 5D **69**
Tallis Gro. SE7 . . . . 2D **97**
Tallis St. EC4 . . . 4C **16** (1C **76**)
Tallis Vw. NW10 . . . . . . 3A **42**
Talmage Cl. SE23 . . . . . 5E **107**
Talma Rd. SW2 . . . . . . 2C **104**
Talwin St. E3 . . . . 2D **67**
Tamar Cl. E3 . . . . 5B **52**
Tamar Ho. E14 . . . . 3E **81**
    (off Plevna St.)
    SE11 . . . . 1C **90**
    (off Kennington La.)
Tamarind Ho. W8 . . . . . . 4D **73**
    (off Stone Hall Gdns.)
Tamarind Yd. E1 . . . . 2C **78**
    (off Kennet St.)
Tamarisk Sq. W12 . . . . . 1B **70**
Tamar St. SE7 . . . . 4F **83**
Tamplin Ho. W10 . . . . . . 2B **58**
    (off Dowland St.)
Tamworth N7 . . . . 3A **48**
Tamworth St. SW6 . . . . . 2C **86**
Tancred Rd. N4 . . . . 1D **35**
Tanfield Av. NW2 . . . . . . 1B **42**
Tangley Gro. SW15 . . . . 4B **98**
Tangmere WC1 . . . . 2F **7**
    (off Sidmouth St.)
Tanhurst Ho. SW2 . . . . . 5B **104**
    (off Redlands Way)

Tankerton Ho's. WC1 . . . . 2E **7**
    (off Tankerton St.)
Tankerton St.
    WC1 . . . . 2E **7** (2A **62**)
Tankridge Rd. NW2 . . . . 4D **29**
Tanner Ho. SE1 . . . . 4E **27**
    (off Tanner St.)
Tanneries, The E1 . . . . . 3E **65**
    (off Cephas Av.)
Tanner Point E13 . . . . . . 5C **54**
    (off Pelly Rd.)
Tanner's Hill SE8 . . . . . . 4B **94**
Tanner St.
    SE1 . . . . 4E **27** (3A **78**)
    (not continuous)
Tannington Ter. N5 . . . . . 5D **35**
Tannsfeld Rd. SE26 . . . . 5F **121**
Tansley Cl. N7 . . . . 2F **47**
Tanswell St.
    SE1 . . . . 4B **24** (3C **76**)
Tantallon Rd. SW12 . . . . 1C **116**
Tant Av. E16 . . . . 5B **68**
Tanza Rd. NW3 . . . . 1B **46**
Tapley Ho. SE1 . . . . 3C **78**
    (off Wolseley St.)
Taplow SE17 . . . . 1F **91**
    (off Thurlow St.)
Taplow Ho. E2 . . . . 2F **11**
    (off Palissy St.)
Taplow St.
    N1 . . . . 1A **10** (1E **63**)
Tappesfield Rd.
    SE15 . . . . 1E **107**
Tapp St. E1 . . . . 3D **65**
Tara Arts Cen. 1D **115**
    (off Garratt La.)
Tara M. N8 . . . . 1A **34**
Taranto Ho. E1 . . . . 4F **65**
    (off Master's St.)
Tarbert Rd. SE22 . . . . . 3A **106**
Tarbert Wlk. E1 . . . . 1E **79**
Tariff Cres. SE8 . . . . 5B **80**
Tarleton Gdns.
    SE23 . . . . 2D **121**
Tarling Ho. E1 . . . . 5D **65**
    (off Tarling St.)
Tarling Rd. E16 . . . . 5B **68**
Tarling St. E1 . . . . 5D **65**
Tarling St. Est. E1 . . . . . 5E **65**
Tarns, The NW1 . . . . 1F **5**
    (off Varndell St.)
Tarn St. SE1 . . . . 4E **77**
Tarplett Ho. SE14 . . . . . . 2F **93**
    (off John Williams Cl.)
Tarquin Ho. SE26 . . . . . 4C **120**
    (off High Level Dr.)
Tarragon Cl. SE14 . . . . . 3A **94**
Tarragon Gro. SE26 . . . . 5F **121**
Tarranbrae NW6 . . . . . . 4A **44**
Tarrant Ho. E2 . . . . 2E **65**
    (off Roman Rd.)
Tarrant Pl. W1 . . . . 4B **60**
Tarrington Cl. SW16 . . . . 3F **117**
Tartan Ho. E14 . . . . 5E **67**
    (off Dee St.)
Tarver Rd. SE17 . . . . 1D **91**
Tarves Way SE10 . . . . . . 3D **95**
Tasker Ho. E14 . . . . 4B **66**
    (off Wallwood St.)
Tasker Rd. NW3 . . . . 2B **46**

Tasman Ct. *E14* 5D *81*
     (off Westferry Rd.)
Tasman Ho. *E1* 2D *79*
     (off College St.)
Tasman Rd. SW9 . . . . 1A *104*
Tasman Wlk. E16 . . . . 5F *69*
Tasso Rd. W6 . . . . 2A *86*
Tasso Yd. *W6* 2A *86*
     (off Tasso Rd.)
Tatchbury Ho. *SW6* 4B *98*
     (off Tunworth Cres.)
Tate Britain 5A *76*
Tate Ho. *E2* 1F *65*
     (off Mace St.)
Tate Modern 1E *25* (2D *77*)
Tatham Pl. NW8 . . . . 1F *59*
Tatnell Rd. SE23 . . . . 4A *108*
Tatsfield Ho. *SE1* 5C *26*
     (off Pardoner St.)
Tatton Cres. N16 . . . . 2B *36*
Tatum St. SE17 . . . . 5F *77*
Tauheed Cl. N4 . . . . 4E *35*
Taunton Ho. *W2* 5E *59*
     (off Hallfield Est.)
Taunton M. NW1 . . . . 3B *60*
Taunton Pl. NW1 . . . . 3B *60*
Taunton Rd. SE12 . . . . . 3A *110*
Tavern Ct. *SE1* 4E *77*
     (off Falmouth Rd.)
Taverners Cl. W11 . . . . . . 2A *72*
Taverners Ct. *E3* 2A *66*
     (off Grove Rd.)
Taverner Sq. N5 . . . . 1E *49*
Tavern La. SW9 . . . . 5C *90*
Tavern Quay SE16 . . . . . . 5A *80*
Tavistock Cl. N16 . . . . 2A *50*
Tavistock Ct. *WC1* 3C *6*
     (off Tavistock Sq.)
WC2 . . . . 4E *15*
     (off Tavistock St.)
Tavistock Cres. W11 . . . . 4B *58*
     (not continuous)
Tavistock Ho.
  WC1 . . . . 3C *6* (3F *61*)
Tavistock M. W11 . . . . . . 5B *58*
Tavistock Pl.
  WC1 . . . . 3D *7* (3A *62*)
Tavistock Rd. E7 . . . . 1B *54*
  E15 . . . . 3B *54*
  N4 . . . . 1F *35*
  NW10 . . . . 1B *56*
  W11 . . . . 5B *58*
     (not continuous)
Tavistock Sq.
  WC1 . . . . 3C *6* (3F *61*)
Tavistock St.
  WC2 . . . . 4E *15* (1A *76*)
     (not continuous)
Tavistock Ter. N19 . . . . . . 5F *33*
Tavistock Twr. SE16 . . . . 4A *80*
Taviton St.
  WC1 . . . . 3B *6* (3F *61*)
Tavy Cl. *SE11* 1C *90*
     (off White Hart St.,
     not continuous)
Tawny Way SE16 . . . . 5F *79*
Taybridge Rd.
  SW11 . . . . 1C *102*
Tay Burns SE 5D *27*
Tayburn Cl. E14 . . . . 5E *67*

Tayler Ct. NW8 . . . . 5F *45*
Taylor Cl. SE8 . . . . 2B *94*
Taylor Ct. E15 . . . . 2E *53*
Taylors Grn. W3 . . . . 5A *56*
Taylors La. NW10 . . . . . . 4A *42*
  SE26 . . . . 4D *121*
Taymount Grange
  SE23 . . . . 2E *121*
Taymount Ri. SE23 . . . . . 2E *121*
Tayport Cl. N1 . . . . 4A *48*
Tayside Ct. SE5 . . . . 2F *105*
Teak Cl. SE16 . . . . 2A *80*
Tealby Cl. *N7* 2B *48*
     (off George's St.)
Teal Cl. E16 . . . . 4F *69*
Teal Ct. *E1* 1C *78*
     (off Star Pl.)
  SE8 . . . . 2B *94*
     (off Abinger Gro.)
Teale St. E2 . . . . 1C *64*
Teal St. SE10 . . . . 4B *82*
Teasel Way E15 . . . . 2A *68*
Tea Trade Wharf *SE1* . . . 3B *78*
     (off Shad Thames)
Ted Roberts Ho. *E2* 1D *65*
     (off Parmiter St.)
Tedworth Gdns.
  SW3 . . . . 1B *88*
Tedworth Sq. SW3 . . . . . . 1B *88*
Tee, The W3 . . . . 5A *56*
Teesdale Cl. E2 . . . . 1C *64*
Teesdale Rd. E11 . . . . . . 1B *40*
Teesdale St. E2 . . . . 1C *64*
Teesdale Yd. *E2* 1D *65*
     (off Teesdale St.)
Teignmouth Cl.
  SW4 . . . . 2F *103*
Teignmouth Rd. NW2 . . . 2F *43*
Telegraph Hill NW3 . . . . . 5D *31*
Telegraph Pas. *SW2* . . . 5A *104*
     (off New Pk. Rd.)
Telegraph Pl. E14 . . . . . . 5D *81*
Telegraph Quarters
  SE10 . . . . 1F *95*
     (off Park Row)
Telegraph Rd. SW15 . . . 5B *98*
Telegraph St.
  EC2 . . . . 2B *18* (5F *63*)
Telemann Sq. SE3 . . . . 2D *111*
Telephone Pl. SW6 . . . . . 2B *86*
Telfer Ho. EC1 . . . . 2E *9*
Telferscot Rd. SW12 . . . 1F *117*
Telford Av. SW2 . . . . 1F *117*
Telford Ho. *SE1* 5F *25*
     (off Tiverton St.)
  W10 . . . . 4A *58*
Telfords St. E11 . . . . 1C *78*
Telford Ter. SW1 . . . . 2E *89*
Telford Way W3 . . . . 4A *56*
Tell Gro. SE22 . . . . 2B *106*
Tellson Av. SE18 . . . . 4F *97*
Temair Ho. *SE10* 3D *95*
     (off Tarves Way)
Temeraire St. SE16 . . . . . 3E *79*
Tempelhof Av. NW2 . . . . . 3E *29*
  NW4 . . . . 3E *29*
Temperley Rd.
  SW12 . . . . 5C *102*

Templar Ct. NW8 . . . . 2F *59*
     (off St John's Wood Rd.)
Templar Ho. NW2 . . . . 3B *44*
Templars Av. NW11 . . . . . 1B *30*
Templars Ho. E15 . . . . . . 2D *53*
Templar St. SE5 . . . . 5D *91*
Temple Av.
  EC4 . . . . 4C *16* (1C *76*)
Temple Bar 3B *16*
Temple Bar Gate 3E *17*
     (off Paternoster Sq.)
Temple Chambers
  EC4 . . . . 4C *16*
Temple Cl. E11 . . . . 2A *40*
Templecombe Rd. E9 . . . 5E *51*
Temple Cl. *E1* 4F *65*
     (off Rectory Sq.)
  SW8 . . . . 3A *90*
     (off Thorncroft St.)
Temple Dwellings *E2* . . 1D *65*
     (off Temple St.)
TEMPLE FORTUNE 1B *30*
Temple Fortune Hill
  NW11 . . . . 1C *30*
Temple Fortune La.
  NW11 . . . . 1B *30*
Temple Fortune Pde.
  NW11 . . . . 1B *30*
Temple Gdns. EC4 . . . . . . 4B *16*
     (off Middle Temple La.)
  NW11 . . . . 1B *30*
Temple Gro. NW11 . . . . . 1C *30*
Temple La.
  EC4 . . . . 3C *16* (5C *62*)
Templemead Cl. W3 . . . 5A *56*
Templemead Ho. E9 . . . . 1A *52*
Temple Mill La. E10 . . . . 1D *53*
     (not continuous)
  E15 . . . . 1E *53*
TEMPLE MILLS 1D *53*
Temple Mills E10 . . . . . . 5E *39*
Temple of Mithras (remains)
  . . . . 3B *18*
     (off Queen Victoria St.)
Temple Pl.
  WC2 . . . . 4A *16* (1B *76*)
Temple Rd. E6 . . . . 5F *55*
  NW2 . . . . 1E *43*
Temple St. E2 . . . . 1D *65*
Templeton Cl. N15 . . . . . 1F *35*
  N16 . . . . 2A *50*
Templeton Pl. SW5 . . . . . 5C *72*
Templeton Rd. N15 . . . . . 1F *35*
Temple W. M.
  SE11 . . . . 5D *25* (4D *77*)
Templewood Av.
  NW3 . . . . 5D *31*
Templewood Gdns.
  NW3 . . . . 5D *31*
Templewood Point
  NW2 . . . . 4B *30*
     (off Granville Rd.)
Temple Yd. *E2* 1D *65*
     (off Temple St.)
Tempus Wharf *SE16.* . . . 3C *78*
     (off Bermondsey Wall W.)
Tenbury Cl. E7 . . . . 2F *55*
Tenbury Ct. SW2 . . . . 1F *117*
Tenby Ho. *W2* 5E *59*
     (off Hallfield Est.)

Tenby Mans. *W1* *5C 4*
   (off Nottingham St.)
Tench St. E1 . . . . 2D 79
Tenda Rd. SE16 . . . . 5D 79
Tenham Av. SW2 . . . . . . 1F 117
Tenison Ct.
  W1 . . . . 4F 13 (1E 75)
Tenison Way
  SE1 . . . . 2A 24 (2B 76)
Tenniel Cl. W2 . . . . 1E 73
Tennis St.
  SE1 . . . . 3B 26 (3F 77)
Tennyson Av. E11 . . . . . . 2C 40
  E12 . . . . 4F 55
Tennyson Ct. SW6 . . . . . 4E 87
  (off Imperial Rd.)
Tennyson Ho. *SE17* *1E 91*
  (off Browning St.)
Tennyson Mans.
  W14 . . . . *2B 86*
  (off Queen's Club Gdns.)
Tennyson Rd. E10 . . . . . . 3D 39
  E15 . . . . 4A 54
  E17 . . . . 1B 38
  NW6 . . . . 5B 44
  (not continuous)
  SW19 . . . . 5E 115
Tennyson St. SW8 . . . . . 5D 89
Tenterden Ho. *SE17* *1A 92*
  (off Surrey Gro.)
Tenterden St.
  W1 . . . . 3E 13 (5D 61)
Tenter Ground
  E1 . . . . 1F 19 (4B 64)
Tenter Pas. *E1* *5B 64*
  (off Nth. Tenter St.)
Tent St. E1 . . . . 3D 65
Terborch Way SE22 . . . 3A 106
Teredo St. SE16 . . . . 4F 79
Terence McMillan Stadium
  . . . . 3E 69
Terence Messenger Twr.
  E10 . . . . 4D 39
  (off Alpine Rd.)
Terling Cl. E11 . . . . 5B 40
Terling Ho. *W10* *4E 57*
  (off Sutton Way)
Terling Wlk. *N1* *5E 49*
  (off Popham St.)
Terminus Pl. SW1 . . . . . 4D 75
Terrace, The *E2* *2E 65*
  (off Old Ford Rd.)
  EC4 . . . . 3C 16
  NW6 . . . . 5C 44
  SE8 . . . . *5B 80*
  (off Longshore)
  SE23 . . . . 5A 108
  SW13 . . . . 5A 84
Terrace Av. NW10 . . . . . 3E 57
Terrace Gdns. SW13 . . . 5B 84
Terrace Rd. E9 . . . . 4E 51
  E13 . . . . 1C 68
Terraces, The *NW8* *1F 59*
  (off Queen's Ter.)
Terrace Wlk. *SW11* *3B 88*
  (off Albert Bri. Rd.)
Terrapin Rd. SW17 . . . . 3D 117
Terretts Pl. *N1* *4D 49*
  (off Upper St.)
Terrick St. W12 . . . . 5D 57

Territorial Ho. *SE11* *5C 76*
  (off Reedworth St.)
Tessa Sanderson Pl.
  SW8 . . . . *1D 103*
  (off Daley Thompson Way)
Testerton Rd. *W11* *1F 71*
  (off Hurstway Wlk.)
Testerton Wlk. W11 . . . 1F 71
Tetbury Pl. N1 . . . . 5D 49
Tetcott Rd. SW10 . . . . . 3E 87
  (not continuous)
Teversham La. SW8 . . . 4A 90
Teviot Est. E14 . . . . 4D 67
Teviot St. E14 . . . . 3E 67
Tewkesbury Av.
  SE23 . . . . 1D 121
Tewkesbury Cl. N15 . . . 1F 35
Tewkesbury Rd. N15 . . . 1F 35
Thackeray Ct. SW3 . . . . 1B 88
  (off Elystan Pl.)
  W14 . . . . *4A 72*
  (off Blythe Rd.)
Thackeray Ho. WC1 . . . . 3D 7
Thackeray M. E8 . . . . . . 3C 50
Thackeray Rd. E6 . . . . . 1F 69
  SW8 . . . . 5D 89
Thackeray St. W8 . . . . . 4D 73
Thakeham Cl. SE26 . . . 4D 121
Thalia Cl. SE10 . . . . 2F 95
Thame Rd. SE16 . . . . . . 3F 79
Thames Av. SW10 . . . . . 4E 87
Thames Barrier Ind. Area
  SE18 . . . . *4F 83*
  (off Faraday Way)
Thames Barrier Vis. Cen.
  . . . . 4F 83
Thamesbrook *SW3* *1A 88*
  (off Dovehouse St.)
Thames Circ. E14 . . . . . 5C 80
Thames Ct. *SE15* *3B 92*
  (off Daniel Gdns.)
Thames Cres. W4 . . . . . 3A 84
Thames Exchange Bldg.
  EC4 . . . . 5A 18
Thames Ho. *EC4* *4A 18*
  (off Up. Thames St.)
  SW1 . . . . *5A 76*
  (off Millbank)
Thameside Ind. Est.
  E16 . . . . 3F 83
Thames Pl. SW15 . . . . . 1F 99
  (not continuous)
Thames Point SW6 . . . . 5E 87
Thames Quay E14 . . . . . 3D 81
  SW10 . . . . *4E 87*
  (off Chelsea Harbour)
Thames Reach *W6* *2E 85*
  (off Rainville Rd.)
Thames Rd. E16 . . . . . . 2F 83
Thames Rd. Ind. Est.
  E16 . . . . 3F 83
Thames St. SE10 . . . . . . 2D 95
Thames Wlk. SW11 . . . . 3A 88
Thames Wharf Studios
  W6 . . . . *2E 85*
  (off Rainville Rd.)
Thanet Ho. *WC1* *2D 7*
  (off Thanet St.)
Thanet Lodge *NW2* *3A 44*
  (off Mapesbury Rd.)

Thanet St.
  WC1 . . . . 2D 7 (2A 62)
Thanet Wharf *SE8* *2D 95*
  (off Copperas St.)
Thane Vs. N7 . . . . 5B 34
Thane Works N7 . . . . . . 5B 34
Thant Cl. E10 . . . . 5D 39
Thavie's Inn
  EC1 . . . . 2C 16 (5C 62)
Thaxted Ct. *N1* *1C 10*
  (off Fairbank Est.)
Thaxted Ho. *SE16* *5E 79*
  (off Abbeyfield Est.)
Thaxton Rd. W14 . . . . . . 2B 86
Thayer St.
  W1 . . . . 1C 12 (5C 60)
Theatre Mus. 4E 15
Theatrerites 2D 115
Theatre Royal
  Stratford 4F 53
Theatre Sq. E15 . . . . 3F 53
Theatre St. SW11 . . . . . 1B 102
Theatre Technis *5E 47*
  (off Crowndale Rd.)
Theberton St. N1 . . . . . . 5C 48
Theed St.
  SE1 . . . . 2C 24 (2C 76)
Thelma Gdns. SE3 . . . . . 4F 97
Theobald Rd. E17 . . . . . 2B 38
Theobalds Ct. N4 . . . . . . 5E 35
Theobald's Rd.
  WC1 . . . . 5F 7 (4B 62)
Theobald St. SE1 . . . . . . 4F 77
Theodore Ct. SE13 . . . . 4F 109
Theodore St. SE13 . . . . 4F 109
Therapia Rd. SE22 . . . . 4E 107
Theresa Rd. W6 . . . . 5C 70
Therfield Ct. N4 . . . . 4E 35
Thermopylae Ga.
  E14 . . . . 5D 81
Theseus Wlk. N1 . . . . . . 1E 9
Thessaly Ho. *SW8* *3E 89*
  (off Thessaly Rd.)
Thessaly Rd. SW8 . . . . . 3E 89
  (not continuous)
Thesus Ho. *E14* *5E 67*
  (off Blair St.)
Thetford Ho. *SE1* *5F 27*
  (off Maltby St.)
Theydon Rd. E5 . . . . 4E 37
Theydon St. E17 . . . . . . 2B 38
Third Av. E13 . . . . 2C 68
  E17 . . . . 1C 38
  W3 . . . . 2B 70
  W10 . . . . 2A 58
Thirleby Ho.
  SW1 . . . . 5A 22 (4E 75)
Thirlmere *NW1* *1E 5*
  (off Cumberland Mkt.)
Thirlmere Rd.
  SW16 . . . . 4F 119
Thirsk Rd. SW11 . . . . . . 1C 102
Thistle Gro. SW10 . . . . . 1E 87
Thistle Ho. *E14* *5E 67*
  (off Dee St.)
Thistlewaite Rd. E5 . . . . 5D 37
Thistlewood Cl. N7 . . . . 4B 34
Thistley Ct. SE8 . . . . 2D 95
Thomas Baines Rd.
  SW11 . . . . 1F 101

Thomas Burt Ho. *E2* **2D 65**
(off Canrobert St.)
Thomas Darby Ct.
W11 . . . . **5A 58**
(off Lancaster Rd.)
Thomas Dean Rd.
SE26 . . . . **4B 122**
Thomas Dinwiddy Rd.
SE12 . . . . **2D 125**
Thomas Doyle St.
SE1 . . . . **5D 25** (4D **77**)
Thomas Hollywood Ho.
E2 . . . . **1E 65**
(off Approach Rd.)
Thomas La. SE6 . . . . . . **5C 108**
Thomas More Highwalk
EC2 . . . . **1F 17**
(off Beech St.)
Thomas More Ho.
EC2 . . . . **1F 17**
Thomas More Sq. *E1* . . **1C 78**
(off Thomas More St.)
Thomas More St.
E1 . . . . **1C 78**
Thomas Neal's Shop. Mall
WC2 . . . . . . **3D 15** (5A **62**)
Thomas Nth. Ter.
E16 . . . . **4B 68**
(off Barking Rd.)
Thomas Pl. W8 . . . . **4D 73**
Thomas Rd. E14 . . . . . . **5B 66**
Thomas Rd. Ind. Est.
E14 . . . . **4C 66**
Thompson Ho. SE14 . . . . **2F 93**
(off John Williams Cl.)
Thompson Rd.
SE22 . . . . **4B 106**
Thompson's Av. SE5 . . . . **3E 91**
Thomson Ho. *E14* **5C 66**
(off Saracen St.)
SE17 . . . . **5A 78**
(off Tatum St.)
SW1 . . . . **1F 89**
(off Bessborough Pl.)
Thorburn Sq. SE1 . . . . . . **5C 78**
Thoresby St.
N1 . . . . **1A 10** (2E **63**)
Thornaby Ho. *E2* **2D 65**
(off Canrobert St.)
Thornbury Cl. N16 . . . . . **2A 50**
Thornbury Ct. *W11* **1C 72**
(off Chepstow Vs.)
Thornbury Rd.
SW2 . . . . **4A 104**
Thornbury Sq. N6 . . . . . . **3E 33**
Thornby Rd. E5 . . . . **5E 37**
Thorncliffe Rd.
SW2 . . . . **4A 104**
Thorncombe Rd.
SE22 . . . . **3A 106**
Thorncroft St. SW8 . . . . . **3A 90**
Thorndean St.
SW18 . . . . **2E 115**
Thorndike Cl. SW10 . . . . . **3E 87**
Thorndike Ho.
SW1 . . . . **1F 89**
(off Vauxhall Bri. Rd.)
Thorndike St. SW1 . . . . . **5F 75**
Thorne Cl. E11 . . . . **1F 53**
E16 . . . . **5C 68**

Thorne Ho. E2 . . . . **2E 65**
(off Roman Rd.)
E14 . . . . **4E 81**
(off Launch St.)
Thorne Pas. SW13 . . . . . **5A 84**
Thorne Rd. SW8 . . . . **3A 90**
Thorne St. SW13 . . . . . . **1A 98**
Thornewill Ho. *E1* **1E 79**
(off Cable St.)
Thorney Ct. W8 . . . . **3E 73**
(off Palace Ga.)
Thorney Cres. SW11 . . . . **3F 87**
Thorney St. SW1 . . . . . . **5A 76**
Thornfield Ho. E14 . . . . . **1C 80**
(off Rosefield Gdns.)
Thornfield Rd. W12 . . . . . **3D 71**
(not continuous)
Thornford Rd. SE13 . . . . **3E 109**
Thorngate Rd. W9 . . . . . . **3C 58**
Thorngrove Rd. E13 . . . . . **5D 55**
Thornham Gro. E15 . . . . . **2F 53**
Thornham Ind. Est.
E15 . . . . **3F 53**
Thornham St. SE10 . . . . . **2D 95**
Thornhaugh M.
WC1 . . . . **4C 6** (3F **61**)
Thornhaugh St.
WC1 . . . . **4C 6** (3F **61**)
Thornhill Bri. Wharf
N1 . . . . **5B 48**
Thornhill Cres. N1 . . . . . . **4B 48**
Thornhill Gdns. E10 . . . . . **4D 39**
Thornhill Gro. N1 . . . . **4B 48**
Thornhill Ho. W4 . . . . **1A 84**
(off Wood St.)
Thornhill Ho's. N1 . . . . . . **4C 48**
Thornhill Rd. E10 . . . . . . **4D 39**
N1 . . . . **4C 48**
Thornhill Sq. N1 . . . . **4B 48**
Thornicroft Ho. *SW9* **5B 90**
(off Stockwell Rd.)
Thornlaw Rd. SE27 . . . . **4C 118**
Thornley Pl. SE10 . . . . . . **1A 96**
Thornsbeach Rd.
SE6 . . . . **1E 123**
Thornsett Rd. SW18 . . . . **1D 115**
Thorn Ter. SE15 . . . . . . **1E 107**
Thornton Av. SW2 . . . . . **1F 117**
W4 . . . . **5A 70**
Thornton Gdns.
SW12 . . . . **1F 117**
Thornton Ho. *SE17* **5A 78**
(off Townsend St.)
Thornton Pl.
W1 . . . . **5A 4** (4B **60**)
Thornton Rd.
BR1: Brom **5C 124**
E11 . . . . **4F 39**
SW12 . . . . **5F 103**
Thornton Rd. SW9 . . . . . . **5C 90**
Thornton Way NW11 . . . . **1D 31**
Thorntree Rd. SE7 . . . . . . **1F 97**
Thornville St. SE8 . . . . . . **4C 94**
Thornwood Rd.
SE13 . . . . **3A 110**
Thornycroft Ho. W4 . . . . . **1A 84**
(off Fraser St.)
Thorogood Gdns. E15 . . . **2A 54**
Thorold Ho. *SE1* **3F 25**
(off Pepper St.)

Thorparch Rd. SW8 . . . . . **4F 89**
Thorpebank Rd. W12 . . . . **2C 70**
Thorpe Cl. SE26 . . . . **4F 121**
W10 . . . . **5A 58**
Thorpedale Rd. N4 . . . . . **4A 34**
Thorpe Ho. *N1* **5B 48**
(off Barnsbury Est.)
Thorpe Rd. E7 . . . . **1B 54**
N15 . . . . **1A 36**
Thorpewood Av.
SE26 . . . . **2D 121**
Thorsden Way SE19 . . . . **5A 120**
Thorverton Rd. NW2 . . . . . **5A 30**
Thoydon Rd. E3 . . . . **1A 66**
Thrale Rd. SW16 . . . . . . **4E 117**
Thrale St.
SE1 . . . . **2A 26** (2E **77**)
Thrasher Cl. E8 . . . . **5B 50**
Thrawl St. E1 . . . **1F 19** (4B **64**)
Thrayle Ho. *SW9* **1B 104**
(off Benedict Rd.)
Threadgold Ho. N1 . . . . . . **3F 49**
(off Dovercourt Est.)
Threadneedle St.
EC2 . . . . **3C 18** (5F **63**)
Three Barrels Wlk.
EC4 . . . . **5A 18**
(off Queen St. Pl.)
Three Colt Cnr. *E2* **3C 64**
(off Cheshire St.)
Three Colts La. E2 . . . . . . **3D 65**
Three Colt St. E14 . . . . . . **5B 66**
Three Cranes Wlk.
EC4 . . . . **5A 18**
Three Cups Yd. WC1 . . . . **1A 16**
Three Kings Yd.
W1 . . . . **4D 13** (1D **75**)
Three Mill La. E3 . . . . **2E 67**
(not continuous)
Three Mills **2E 67**
Three Oak La. SE1 . . . . . . **3F 27**
Three Quays EC3 . . . . . . **5E 19**
Three Quays Wlk.
EC3 . . . . **5E 19** (1A **78**)
Threshers Pl. W11 . . . . . . **1A 72**
Thriffwood SE26 . . . . **3E 121**
Thring Ho. *SW9* **5B 90**
(off Stockwell Rd.)
Throckmorten Rd.
E16 . . . . **5D 69**
Throgmorton Av.
EC2 . . . . **2C 18** (5F **63**)
(not continuous)
Throgmorton St.
EC2 . . . . **2C 18** (5F **63**)
Thrush St. SE17 . . . . **1E 91**
Thurbarn Rd. SE6 . . . . . **5D 123**
Thurland Ho. *SE16* **5D 79**
(off Camilla Rd.)
Thurland Rd. SE16 . . . . . . **4C 78**
Thurlby Rd. SE27 . . . . . . **4C 118**
Thurleigh Av. SW12 . . . . **4C 102**
Thurleigh Ct. SW12 . . . . **4C 102**
Thurleigh Rd.
SW12 . . . . **5B 102**
Thurlestone Rd.
SE27 . . . . **3C 118**
Thurloe Cl. SW7 . . . . **5A 74**
Thurloe Ct. SW3 . . . . **5A 74**
(off Fulham Ct.)

Thurloe Pl. SW7 . . . . 5F 73
Thurloe Pl. M. SW7 . . . . 5F 73
   (off Thurloe Pl.)
Thurloe Sq. SW7 . . . . . . 5A 74
Thurloe St. SW7 . . . . 5F 73
Thurlow Hill SE21 . . . . 1E 119
Thurlow Ho. SW16 . . . . 3A 118
Thurlow Pk. Rd.
  SE21 . . . . 2D 119
Thurlow Rd. NW3 . . . . . 2F 45
Thurlow St. SE17 . . . . . . 1F 91
   (not continuous)
Thurlow Ter. NW5 . . . . . 2C 46
Thurlow Wlk. SE17 . . . . 1A 92
   (not continuous)
Thurnscoe NW1 . . . . . . 5E 47
   (off Pratt St.)
Thursley Gdns.
  SW19 . . . . 2F 113
Thursley Ho. SW2 . . . . 5B 104
   (off Holmewood Gdns.)
Thurso Ho. NW6 . . . . . 1D 59
Thurso St. SW17 . . . . 4F 115
Thurstan Dwellings
  WC2 . . . . 2E 15
   (off Newton St.)
Thurston Ind. Est.
  SE13 . . . . 1D 109
Thurston Rd. SE13 . . . . 5D 95
Thurtle Rd. E2 . . . . 1B 64
Thyme Cl. SE3 . . . . 1E 111
Tibbatt's Rd. E3 . . . . . . 3D 67
Tibbenham Pl. SE6. . . . 2C 122
Tibbenham Wlk.
  E13 . . . . 1B 68
Tibberton Sq. N1 . . . . . 5E 49
Tibbet's Cl. SW19 . . . . 1F 113
TIBBET'S CORNER . . . 5F 99
Tibbet's Ride SW15 . . . 5F 99
Tiber Gdns. N1 . . . . 5A 48
Ticehurst Rd. SE23 . . . 2A 122
Tickford Ho. NW8 . . . . . 2A 60
Tidal Basin Rd. E16 . . . 1B 82
   (not continuous)
Tidbury Ct. SW8 . . . . . . 3E 89
   (off Stewart's Rd.)
Tideswell Rd. SW15. . . . 2E 99
Tideway Cl. SE16 . . . . . 2F 79
Tideway Ho. E14 . . . . . . 3C 80
   (off Strafford St.)
Tideway Ind. Est.
  SW8 . . . . 2E 89
Tideway Wlk. SW8 . . . . . 2E 89
Tidey St. E3 . . . . 4C 66
Tidworth Rd. E3 . . . . . . 3C 66
Tierney Rd. SW2 . . . . . 1A 118
Tiffany Hgts. SW18 . . . 5C 100
Tiger Way E5 . . . . 1D 51
Tilbrook Rd. SE3 . . . . . 1E 111
Tilbury Cl. SE15 . . . . . . 3B 92
Tilbury Ho. SE14 . . . . . . 2F 93
   (off Myers La.)
Tilbury Rd. E10 . . . . 2E 39
Tildesley Rd. SW15 . . . . 4E 99
Tilehurst Rd. SW18 . . . 1F 115
Tile Kiln La. N6 . . . . . . 3D 33
Tile Kiln Studios N6 . . . 2E 33
Tile Yd. E14 . . . . 5B 66
Tileyard Rd. N7 . . . . . . 4A 48
Tilford Gdns. SW19 . . . 1F 113

Tilford Ho. SW2 . . . . . . 5B 104
   (off Holmewood Gdns.)
Tilia Rd. E5 . . . . 1D 51
Tilia Wlk. SW9 . . . . 2D 105
Tilleard Ho. W10 . . . . . . 2A 58
   (off Herries St.)
Tiller Leisure Cen., The
  . . . . 4C 80
Tiller Rd. E14 . . . . 4C 80
Tillett Sq. SE16 . . . . . . 3A 80
Tilling Rd. NW2 . . . . . . 3E 29
Tillings Cl. SE5 . . . . 4E 91
Tillman St. E1 . . . . 5D 65
Tilloch St. N1 . . . . 4B 48
Tillotson Ct. SW8 . . . . . 3F 89
   (off Wandsworth Rd.)
Tilney Ct.
  EC1 . . . . 3A 10 (3E 63)
Tilney Gdns. N1 . . . . . . 3F 49
Tilney St.
  W1 . . . . 1C 20 (2C 74)
Tilson Cl. SE5 . . . . 3A 92
Tilson Gdns. SW2 . . . . 5A 104
Tilson Ho. SW2 . . . . . . 5A 104
Tilston Cl. E11 . . . . 5B 40
Tilton St. SW6 . . . . 2A 86
Timberland Cl. SE15 . . . 3C 92
Timberland Rd. E1 . . . . 5D 65
Timber Mill Way
  SW4 . . . . 1F 103
Timber Pond Rd.
  SE16 . . . . 2F 79
Timber St.
  EC1 . . . . 3F 9 (3E 63)
Timberwharf Rd.
  N16 . . . . 1C 36
Timber Wharves Est.
  E14 . . . . 5C 80
   (off Copeland Dr.)
Timbrell Pl. SE16 . . . . . 2B 80
Time Sq. E8 . . . . 2B 50
Timor Ho. E1 . . . . 3A 66
   (off Duckett St.)
Timothy Cl. SW4 . . . . . 3E 103
Timothy Rd. E3 . . . . . . 4B 66
Timsbury Wlk.
  SW15 . . . . 1C 112
Tindal St. SW9. . . . . . . 4D 91
Tinderbox All. SW14 . . . 1A 98
Tinniswood Cl. N5 . . . . 2C 48
Tinsley Rd. E1 . . . . 4E 65
Tintagel Cres. SE22 . . . 2B 106
Tintagel Gdns. SE22 . . . 2B 106
Tintern Cl. SW15 . . . . . 3A 100
Tintern Ho. NW1 . . . . . . 1E 5
   (off Augustus St.)
  SW1 . . . . 5D 75
   (off Abbots Mnr.)
Tintern Path NW9 . . . . . 1A 28
   (off Fryent Gro.)
Tintern St. SW4 . . . . . 2A 104
Tinto Rd. E16 . . . . 3C 68
Tinworth St. SE11 . . . . . 1A 90
Tipthorpe Rd. SW11 . . . 1C 102
Tiptree NW1 . . . . 4D 47
   (off Castlehaven Rd.)
Tisbury Ct. W1 . . . . 4B 14
Tisdall Pl. SE17 . . . . . . 5F 77
Tissington Ct. SE16 . . . 5E 79

Titan Bus. Est. SE8 . . . . 3C 94
   (off Ffinch St.)
Titchborne Row W2 . . . 5A 60
Titchfield Rd. NW8 . . . . 5A 46
Titchwell Rd. SW18 . . . 1F 115
Tite St. SW3 . . . . 1B 88
Titmuss St. W12 . . . . . . 3E 71
Tiverton Rd. N15 . . . . . . 1F 35
  NW10 . . . . 5F 43
Tiverton St.
  SE1 . . . . 5F 25 (4E 77)
Tivoli Ct. SE16 . . . . 2B 80
Tivoli Gdns. SE18 . . . . . 5F 83
   (not continuous)
Tivoli Rd. N8 . . . . 1F 33
  SE27 . . . . 5E 119
Tobacco Dock E1 . . . . . 1D 79
Tobacco Quay E1 . . . . . 1D 79
Tobago St. E14 . . . . 3C 80
Tobin Cl. NW3 . . . . 4A 46
Toby La. E1 . . . . 3A 66
Todds Wlk. N7 . . . . 4B 34
Tokenhouse Yd.
  EC2 . . . . 2B 18 (5F 63)
Token Yd. SW15 . . . . . 2A 100
Toland Sq. SW15 . . . . . 3C 98
Tolchurch W11 . . . . 5B 58
   (off Dartmouth Cl.)
Tollbridge Cl. W10 . . . . 3A 58
Tollet St. E1 . . . . 3F 65
Tollgate Dr. SE21 . . . . 2A 120
Tollgate Gdns. NW6 . . . 1D 59
Tollgate Ho. NW6 . . . . . 1D 59
   (off Tollgate Gdns.)
Tollgate Rd. E6. . . . . . . 4E 69
  E16 . . . . 4E 69
Tollhouse Way N19 . . . . 4E 33
Tollington Pk. N4 . . . . . 4B 34
Tollington Pl. N4 . . . . . . 4B 34
Tollington Rd. N7 . . . . . 1B 48
Tollington Way N7 . . . . 5A 34
Tolmers Sq.
  NW1 . . . . 3A 6 (3E 61)
   (not continuous)
Tolpaide Ho. SE11 . . . . 5C 76
   (off Marylee Way)
Tolpuddle Av. E13 . . . . . 5E 55
   (off Queens Rd.)
Tolpuddle St. N1 . . . . . . 1C 62
Tolsford Rd. E5 . . . . 2D 51
Tom Allen Arts Cen. . . . 3F 53
Tom Blau Gallery 3F 27
   (off Queen Elizabeth St.)
Tom Groves Cl. E15 . . . 2F 53
Tom Hood Cl. E15. . . . . 2F 53
Tom Jenkinson Rd.
  E16 . . . . 2C 82
Tomkyns Ho. SE11 . . . . 5C 76
   (off Distin St.)
Tomlin's Gro. E3 . . . . . . 2C 66
Tomlinson Cl. E2 . . . . . 2B 64
Tomlins Ter. E14 . . . . . . 5A 66
Tomlins Wlk. N7 . . . . . . 4B 34
Tom Nolan Cl. E15 . . . . 1A 68
Tompion Ho. EC1 . . . . . 3E 9
   (off Percival St.)
Tompion St.
  EC1 . . . . 2D 9 (2D 63)
   (not continuous)
Tom Smith Cl. SE10 . . . 2A 96

Tomson Ho. *SE1* 5F *27*
   (off Riley Rd.)
Tom Williams Ho.
  SW6 . . . . *2B 86*
   (off Clem Attlee Ct.)
Tonbridge Ho's. *WC1* 2D *7*
   (off Tonbridge St.)
Tonbridge St.
  WC1 . . . . 1D *7* (2A *62*)
Tonbridge Wlk. WC1 . . . 1D *7*
   (off Abbey Rd.)
Toneborough *NW8* *5D 45*
Tonsley Hill SW18 . . . 3D *101*
Tonsley Pl. SW18 . . . . . 3D *101*
Tonsley Rd. SW18 . . . . . 3D *101*
Tonsley St. SW18 . . . . . 3D *101*
Tony Cannell M. E3 . . . 2B *66*
Took's Ct.
  EC4 . . . . 2B *16* (5C *62*)
Tooley St.
  SE1 . . . . 1C *26* (2F *77*)
Toomy Cen. *E16* *2D 83*
   (off Evelyn Rd.)
TOOTING 5A *116*
TOOTING BEC 3B *116*
Tooting Bec Gdns.
  SW16 . . . . 4F *117*
   (not continuous)
Tooting Bec Lido 4E *117*
Tooting Bec Rd.
  SW16 . . . . 3C *116*
  SW17 . . . . 3C *116*
Tooting B'way.
  SW17 . . . . 5A *116*
TOOTING GRAVENEY
  . . . . 5B *116*
Tooting Gro. SW17 . . . . 5A *116*
Tooting High St.
  SW17 . . . . 5A *116*
Tooting Leisure Cen.
  . . . . 4F *115*
Tooting Mkt. SW17 . . . . 4B *116*
Topaz Wlk. NW2 . . . . 2F *29*
Topham Ho. *SE10* *3E 95*
   (off Prior St.)
Topham St.
  EC1 . . . . 3B *8* (3C *62*)
Topley St. SE9 . . . . 2E *111*
Topmast Point E14 . . . . 3C *80*
Topp Wlk. NW2 . . . . 4E *29*
Topsfield Cl. N8 . . . . 1F *33*
Topsfield Pde. *N8*. *1A 34*
   (off Tottenham La.)
Topsfield Rd. N8 . . . . . . 1A *34*
Topsham Rd. SW17 . . . 3B *116*
Torbay Ct. NW1 . . . . 4D *47*
Torbay Mans. *NW6*. *5B 44*
   (off Willesden La.)
Torbay Rd. NW6 . . . . 4B *44*
Torbay St. NW1 . . . . 4D *47*
Tor Ct. W8 . . . . 3C *72*
Torcross Dr. SE23 . . . . . 2E *121*
Tor Gdns. W8 . . . . 3C *72*
Tor Ho. N6 . . . . 1D *33*
Tornay Ho. E9 . . . . 4E *51*
  N1 . . . . *1B 62*
   (off Priory Grn. Est.)
Torquay St. W2. . . . . 4D *59*
Torrance Cl. SE7 . . . . . . 2F *97*
Torrens Ct. SE5 . . . . 1F *105*

Torrens Rd. E15 . . . . 3B *54*
  SW2 . . . . 3B *104*
Torrens Sq. E15 . . . . 3B *54*
Torrens St. EC1 . . . . 1C *62*
Torres Sq. E14 . . . . 1C *94*
Torrey Dr. SW9 . . . . 5C *90*
Torriano Av. NW5 . . . . . . 2F *47*
Torriano Cotts. NW5. . . . 2E *47*
Torriano M. NW5 . . . . 2E *47*
Torridge Gdns.
  SE15 . . . . 2E *107*
Torridon Ho. NW6 . . . . . *1D 59*
   (off Randolph Gdns.)
Torridon Rd. SE6 . . . . . 5F *109*
  SE13 . . . . 5A *110*
Torrington Ct. *SE26* . . . *5C 120*
   (off Crystal Pal. Pk. Rd.)
Torrington Pl. E1 . . . . . . 2C *78*
  WC1 . . . . 5B *6* (4F *61*)
Torrington Sq.
  WC1 . . . . 4C *6* (3F *61*)
Tortington Ho. *SE15* . . . *3C 92*
   (off Friary Est.)
Torwood Rd. SW15 . . . 3C *98*
Tothill Ho. *SW1* *5F 75*
   (off Page St.)
Tothill St.
  SW1 . . . . 4C *22* (3F *75*)
Tottan Ter. E1 . . . . 5F *65*
Tottenhall *NW1* *4C 46*
   (off Ferdinand St.)
Tottenham Ct. Rd.
  W1 . . . . 4A *6* (3E *61*)
Tottenham La. N8 . . . . . 1A *34*
Tottenham M.
  W1 . . . . 5A *6* (4E *61*)
Tottenham Rd. N1 . . . . 3A *50*
Tottenham St.
  W1 . . . . 1A *14* (4E *61*)
Totterdown St.
  SW17 . . . . 4B *116*
Totteridge Ho. *SW11* . . . *5F 87*
   (off Yelverton Rd.)
Toulmin St.
  SE1 . . . . 4F *25* (3E *77*)
Toulon St. SE5 . . . . 3E *91*
Toulouse Ct. *SE16* *1D 93*
   (off Rossetti Rd.)
Tourist Info. Cen.
  City of London
    . . . . 3F *17* (5E *63*)
  Greenwich 2E *95*
  Hackney 3D *51*
  King's Cross 1D *7*
  Leicester Sq.
    . . . . 5C *14* (1F *75*)
  Lewisham 2E *109*
  Southwark
    . . . . 1A *26* (2E *77*)
  Waterloo International
    Terminal 3A *24* (3C *76*)
Tournay Rd. SW6 . . . . . 3B *86*
Tours Pas. SW11 . . . . . 2E *101*
Toussaint Wlk. SE16 . . . 4C *78*
Tovy Ho. *SE1* *1C 92*
   (off Avondale Sq.)
Towcester Rd. E3 . . . . . 3D *67*
Tower 42 . . . . . 2D *19* (5A *64*)
Tower Bri. E1 . . . 1F *27* (2B *78*)
  SE1 . . . . 2F *27* (2B *78*)

Tower Bri. App.
  E1 . . . . 1F *27* (2B *78*)
Tower Bri. Bus. Complex
  SE16 . . . . 4C *78*
Tower Bri. Bus. Sq.
  SE16 . . . . 5D *79*
Tower Bridge Experience
  . . . . 1F *27*
Tower Bri. Plaza
  SE1 . . . . 2F *27* (2B *78*)
Tower Bri. Rd.
  SE1 . . . . 5D *27* (4A *78*)
Tower Bri. Sq. SE1. . . . . 3F *27*
Tower Bri. Wharf E1. . . . 2C *78*
Tower Bldgs. *E1*. *2D 79*
   (off Brewhouse La.)
Tower Cl. NW3 . . . . 2F *45*
Tower Cl. E5 . . . . 2B *36*
  N1 . . . . *4E 49*
   (off Canonbury St.)
  NW8 . . . . *1A 60*
   (off Mackennal St.)
  WC2 . . . . 3D *15*
Tower Hamlets Rd.
  E7 . . . . 1B *54*
TOWER HILL 1B *78*
Tower Hill
  EC3 . . . . 5E *19* (1A *78*)
Tower Hill Ter. EC3. . . . . 5E *19*
Tower Ho. *E1* *4C 64*
   (off Fieldgate St.)
Tower Mill Rd. SE15 . . . 2A *92*
   (not continuous)
Tower of London, The
  . . . . 5F *19* (1B *78*)
Tower of London Vis. Cen., The
  . . . . 5E *19* (1A *78*)
Tower Pl.
  EC3 . . . . 5E *19* (1A *78*)
Tower Pl. E. *EC3* *5E 19*
   (off Lwr. Thames St.)
Tower Pl. W. *EC3*. *5E 19*
   (off Lwr. Thames St.)
Tower Royal
  EC4 . . . . 4B *18* (1F *77*)
Tower St.
  WC2 . . . . 3D *15* (5A *62*)
Towncourt Path N4. . . . . 3E *35*
Town Hall Rd.
  SW11 . . . . 1B *102*
Town Hall Wlk. *N16* *1F 49*
   (off Albion Rd.)
Townley Ct. E15 . . . . . . 3B *54*
Townley Rd. SE22 . . . . 3A *106*
Townley St. SE17 . . . . . 1F *91*
   (not continuous)
Townmead Bus. Cen.
  SW6 . . . . 1E *101*
Townmead Rd.
  SW6 . . . . 1D *101*
Townsend Ho. *SE1* *5C 78*
   (off Strathnairn St.)
Townsend La. NW9 . . . . 2A *28*
Townsend Rd. N15. . . . . 1B *36*
Townsend St. SE17 . . . . 5A *78*
Townsend Yd. N6. . . . . . 3D *33*
Townshend Ct. *NW8* . . . *1A 60*
   (off Townshend Rd.)
Townshend Est. NW8 . . 1A *60*

Townshend Rd. NW8 . . . . . 5A **46**
   (not continuous)
Towns Ho. SW4. . . . . 1F **103**
Towpath, The SW10 . . . . . 4F **87**
Towpath Wlk. E9. . . . . 2B **52**
Towton Rd. SE27 . . . . . . 2E **119**
Toynbee St.
   E1. . . . . 1F **19** (4B **64**)
Toyne Way N6. . . . . 1B **32**
Tracey Av. NW2 . . . . 2E **43**
Tradescant Ho. E9 . . . . 4E **51**
   (off Frampton Pk. Rd.)
Tradescant Rd. SW8. . . . . 3A **90**
Tradewinds Ct. E1 . . . . . . 1C **78**
Trafalgar Av. SE15 . . . . . . 1B **92**
Trafalgar Chambers
   SW3 . . . . 1F **87**
   (off South Pde.)
Trafalgar Cl. SE16 . . . . . . 4A **80**
Trafalgar Ct. E1. . . . . 2E **79**
   (off Wapping Wall)
Trafalgar Gdns. E1 . . . . . . 4F **65**
   W8 . . . . 4D **73**
   (off Sth. End Row)
Trafalgar Gro. SE10 . . . . . 2F **95**
Trafalgar Ho. SE17. . . . . . 1E **91**
   (off Bronti Cl.)
Trafalgar M. E9. . . . . 3B **52**
Trafalgar Point N1. . . . . . . 4F **49**
   (off Downham Rd.)
Trafalgar Rd. SE10 . . . . . . 2F **95**
Trafalgar Square
   . . . . 1D **23** (2A **76**)
Trafalgar Sq.
   WC2 . . . . 1C **22** (2F **75**)
Trafalgar St. SE17. . . . . . . 1F **91**
Trafalgar Way E14 . . . . . . 2E **81**
Trafford Cl. E15 . . . . 2D **53**
Trafford Ho. N1. . . . . 1F **63**
   (off Cranston Est.)
Trahorn Cl. E1 . . . . 3D **65**
Traitors' Gate
   . . . . 1F **27** (2B **78**)
   (in Tower of London, The)
Tralee Ct. SE16 . . . . 1D **93**
   (off Masters Dr.)
Tramway Av. E15 . . . . 4A **54**
Tranley M. NW3 . . . . 1A **46**
   (off Fleet Rd.)
Tranmere Rd. SW18. . . . . 2E **115**
Tranquil Pas. SE3. . . . . . . 5B **96**
   (off Montpelier Va.)
Tranquil Va. SE3. . . . . 5A **96**
Transay Wlk. N1 . . . . 3F **49**
Transept St. NW1 . . . . 4A **60**
Transom Cl. SE16 . . . . . . 5A **80**
Transom Sq. E14 . . . . 1D **95**
Tranton Rd. SE16 . . . . . . 4C **78**
Trappes Ho. SE16 . . . . . . 5D **79**
   (off Camilla Rd.)
Travers Ho. SE10 . . . . 2F **95**
   (off Trafalgar Gro.)
Travers Rd. N7 . . . . 5C **34**
Travis Ho. SE10 . . . . 4E **95**
Treadgold Ho. W11. . . . . . 1F **71**
   (off Bomore Rd.)
Treadgold St. W11 . . . . . . 1F **71**
Treadway St. E2 . . . . 1D **65**
Treasury Pas. SW1 . . . . . . 3D **23**
Treaty St. N1. . . . . 5B **48**

Trebeck St.
   W1. . . . . 1D **21** (2D **75**)
Trebovir Rd. SW5. . . . . . . 1C **86**
Treby St. E3 . . . . 3B **66**
Trecastle Way N7 . . . . 1F **47**
Tredegar M. E3 . . . . 2B **66**
Tredegar Rd. E3 . . . . 1B **66**
Tredegar Sq. E3 . . . . 2B **66**
Tredegar Ter. E3 . . . . 2B **66**
Trederwen Rd. E8 . . . . 5C **50**
Tredown Rd. SE26 . . . . . . 5E **121**
Tredwell Cl. SW2. . . . . . . 2B **118**
Tredwell Rd. SE27 . . . . . . 4D **119**
Treen Av. SW13 . . . . 1B **98**
Treewall Gdns.
   BR1: Brom 4D **125**
Trefil Wlk. N7 . . . . 1A **48**
Trefoil Rd. SW18 . . . . 3E **101**
Tregaron Av. N8 . . . . 1A **34**
Tregarvon Rd.
   SW11 . . . . 2C **102**
Trego Rd. E9 . . . . 4C **52**
Tregothnan Rd.
   SW9 . . . . 1A **104**
Tregunter Rd.
   SW10 . . . . 2D **87**
Treherne Ct. SW9 . . . . 4D **91**
   SW17 . . . . 4C **116**
Trehern Rd. SW14 . . . . . . 1A **98**
Trehurst St. E5 . . . . 2A **52**
Trelawney Est. E9. . . . . . . 3E **51**
Trelawney Ho. SE1 . . . . . . 3F **25**
   (off Pepper St.)
Trelawn Rd. E10. . . . . 5E **39**
   SW2 . . . . 3C **104**
Trellick Twr. W10 . . . . 3B **58**
   (off Golborne Rd.)
Trellis Sq. E3 . . . . 2B **66**
Tremadoc Rd. SW4 . . . . . 2F **103**
Tremaine Cl. SE4. . . . . 5C **94**
Tremaine Ho. SE17 . . . . . . 1C **90**
   (off Kennings Way)
Tremlett Gro. N19 . . . . 5E **33**
Trenchard Ct. NW4. . . . . . 1C **28**
Trenchard St. SE10. . . . . . 1F **95**
Trenchold St. SW8. . . . . . 2A **90**
Trendell Ho. E14 . . . . 5C **66**
   (off Dod St.)
Trenmar Gdns. NW10 . . . 2D **57**
Trent Ho. SE15 . . . . 2E **107**
Trent Rd. SW2 . . . . 3B **104**
Treport St. SW18 . . . . 5D **101**
Tresco Ho. SE11 . . . . 1C **90**
   (off Sancroft St.)
Tresco Rd. SE15 . . . . 2D **107**
Tresham Cres.
   NW8 . . . . 3A **60**
Tresham Wlk. E9 . . . . 2E **51**
Tresidder Ho. SW4 . . . . . . 5F **103**
Tressell Cl. N1 . . . . 4D **49**
Tressillian Cres.
   SE4. . . . . 1C **108**
Tressillian Rd.
   SE4. . . . . 2B **108**
Tress Pl. SE1 . . . . 1D **25**
Trevanion Rd. W14 . . . . . 5A **72**
Trevelyan Gdns.
   NW10 . . . . 5E **43**

Trevelyan Ho. E2 . . . . 2F **65**
   (off Morpeth St.)
   SE17. . . . . 3D **91**
   (off John Ruskin St.)
Trevelyan Rd. E15 . . . . . . 1B **54**
   SW17 . . . . 5A **116**
Trevenna Ho. SE23. . . . . . 3F **121**
   (off Dacres Rd.)
Treveris St.
   SE1 . . . . 2E **25** (2D **77**)
Treverton St. W10 . . . . . . 3F **57**
Treverton Towers
   W10. . . . . 4F **57**
   (off Treverton St.)
Treves Ho. E1. . . . . 3C **64**
   (off Vallance Rd.)
Treville St. SW15. . . . . 5D **99**
Treviso Rd. SE23 . . . . 2F **121**
Trevithick Ho. SE16 . . . . . 5D **79**
   (off Rennie Est.)
Trevithick St. SE8. . . . . . . 2C **94**
Trevone Ct. SW2 . . . . 5A **104**
   (off Doverfield Rd.)
Trevor Pl. SW7. . . . . 3A **74**
Trevor Sq. SW7 . . . . 3B **74**
Trevor St. SW7 . . . . 3A **74**
Trevor Wlk. SW7 . . . . 3A **74**
   (off Trevor Pl., not continuous)
Trevose Ho. SE11. . . . . 1B **90**
   (off Orsett St.)
Trewint St. SW18. . . . . . . 2E **115**
Trewsbury Rd. SE26 . . . . 5F **121**
Triangle, The E8 . . . . 5D **51**
   EC1 . . . . 3E **9**
Triangle Bus. Cen., The
   NW10 . . . . 2B **56**
Triangle Ct. E16 . . . . 4F **69**
Triangle Pl. SW4 . . . . 2F **103**
Triangle Rd. E8 . . . . 5D **51**
Tricycle Cinema 4B **44**
   (in Tricycle Theatre)
Tricycle Theatre 4B **44**
   (off Kilburn High Rd.)
Trident Bus. Cen.
   SW17 . . . . 5B **116**
Trident Ho. E14 . . . . 5E **67**
   (off Blair St.)
Trident Pl. SW3 . . . . 2F **87**
   (off Old Chu. St.)
Trident St. SE16 . . . . 5F **79**
Trig La.
   EC4. . . . . 4F **17** (1E **77**)
Trigon Rd. SW8 . . . . 3B **90**
Trilby Rd. SE23. . . . . 2F **121**
Trimdon St. NW1 . . . . 5E **47**
Trim St. SE14 . . . . 2B **94**
Trinder Gdns. N19 . . . . . . 3A **34**
Trinder Rd. N19 . . . . 3A **34**
Trinidad Ho. E14 . . . . 1B **80**
   (off Gill St.)
Trinidad St. E14 . . . . 1B **80**
Trinity Buoy Wharf
   E14. . . . . 1A **82**
   (off Orchard Pl.)
Trinity Chu. Pas.
   SW13 . . . . 2D **85**
Trinity Chu. Rd.
   SW13 . . . . 2D **85**
Trinity Chu. Sq.
   SE1 . . . . 5A **26** (4E **77**)

Trinity Cl. E8 . . . . 3B 50
  E11 . . . . 4A 40
  NW3 . . . . 1F 45
  SE13 . . . . 2F 109
  SW4 . . . . 2E 103
Trinity College of Music
  . . . . 2E 95
Trinity Ct. N1 . . . . 5A 50
  (off Downham Rd.)
  NW2 . . . . 2E 43
  SE1 . . . . 5A 26
  (off Brockham St.)
  SE7 . . . . 5F 83
  SE26 . . . . 3E 121
  SW9 . . . . 1B 104
  W2 . . . . 5E 59
  (off Gloucester Ter.)
  WC1 . . . . 3F 7
Trinity Cres. SW17 . . . . 2B 116
Trinity Gdns. E16 . . . . . . 4B 68
  (not continuous)
  SW9 . . . . 2B 104
Trinity Grn. E1. . . . . 3E 65
Trinity Gro. SE10 . . . . . . 4E 95
Trinity Hospital (Almshouses)
  SE10 . . . . 1F 95
Trinity Ho. SE1 . . . . 5A 26
  (off Bath Ter.)
Trinity M. E1 . . . . 4E 65
  (off Redman's Rd.)
  W10. . . . . 5F 57
Trinity Path SE23 . . . . . 3E 121
Trinity Pl.
  EC3 . . . . 4F 19 (1B 78)
Trinity Ri. SW2 . . . . 1C 118
Trinity Rd. SW17 . . . . . 1A 116
  SW18 . . . . 2E 101
  SW19 . . . . 5C 114
Trinity Sq.
  EC3 . . . . 5E 19 (1A 78)
Trinity St. E16. . . . . 4B 68
  SE1 . . . . 4A 26 (3E 77)
  (not continuous)
Trinity Twr. E1 . . . . 1C 78
  (off Vaughan Way)
Trinity Wlk. NW3 . . . . . . 3E 45
Trinity Way W3 . . . . 1A 70
Trio Pl. SE1 . . . . 4A 26 (3E 77)
Tristan Ct. SE8 . . . . 2B 94
  (off Dorking Cl.)
Tristan Sq. SE3. . . . . . . 1A 110
Tristram Rd.
  BR1: Brom 4B 124
Triton Ho. E14 . . . . 5D 81
  (off Cahir St.)
Triton Sq.
  NW1. . . . . 3F 5 (3E 61)
Tritton Rd. SE21 . . . . . . 3F 119
Trocadero Cen.
  . . . . 5B 14 (1F 75)
Trocette Mans.
  SE1 . . . . 5D 27
  (off Bermondsey St.)
Trojan Ct. NW6 . . . . 4A 44
Trojan Ind. Est.
  NW10 . . . . 3B 42
Troon Cl. SE16 . . . . 1D 93
Troon Ho. E1 . . . . 5A 66
  (off White Horse Rd.)
Troon St. E1 . . . . 5A 66

Tropical Ct. W10 . . . . 2F 57
  (off Kilburn La.)
Trossachs Rd. SE22 . . . 3A 106
Trothy Rd. SE1 . . . . 5C 78
Trotman Ho. SE14 . . . . . 4E 93
  (off Pomeroy St.)
Trott St. SW11 . . . . 4A 88
Troughton Rd. SE7. . . . . 1D 97
Troutbeck NW1 . . . . 2E 5
Troutbeck Rd.
  SE14 . . . . 4A 94
Trouville Rd. SW4 . . . . . 4E 103
Trowbridge Rd. E9 . . . . . 3B 52
Troy Ct. W8 . . . . 4D 73
  (off Kensington High St.)
Troy Town SE15 . . . . . . 1C 106
Trumans Rd. N16 . . . . . . 2B 50
Trumpington Rd. E7 . . . . 1B 54
Trump St.
  EC2 . . . . . . 3A 18 (5E 63)
Trundle St.
  SE1 . . . . . . 3F 25 (3E 77)
Trundleys Rd. SE8 . . . . . 1F 93
Trundley's Ter. SE8. . . . . 5F 79
Truro Rd. NW5. . . . . 3C 46
Truslove Rd. SE27 . . . . 5C 118
Trussley Rd. W6. . . . . . . 4E 71
Trust Wlk. SE21 . . . . . . 1D 119
Tryfan Cl. IG4: Ilf 1F 41
Tryon Cres. E9 . . . . 5E 51
Tryon St. SW3 . . . . 1B 88
Tubbs Rd. NW10 . . . . . . 1B 56
Tucklow Wlk. SW15 . . . . 5B 98
Tudor Cl. N6 . . . . 2E 33
  NW3 . . . . 2A 46
  SW2 . . . . 4B 104
Tudor Ct. E17 . . . . 2B 38
  N1 . . . . 3A 50
  SE16 . . . . 2F 79
  (off Princes Riverside Rd.)
Tudor Gdns. SW13 . . . . 1A 98
Tudor Gro. E9 . . . . 4E 51
Tudor Ho. E9 . . . . 4E 51
  E16 . . . . 2D 83
  (off Wesley Av.)
  W14 . . . . 5F 71
  (off Windsor Way)
Tudor Rd. E6 . . . . 5B 68
  E9 . . . . 5D 51
Tudor Stacks SE24 . . . . 2E 105
Tudor St. EC4 . . 4C 16 (1C 76)
Tudway Rd. SE3 . . . . . . 1D 111
TUFNELL PARK 1E 47
Tufnell Pk. Rd. N7 . . . . . 1E 47
  N19 . . . . 1E 47
Tufton Ct. SW1. . . . . 5D 23
  (off Tufton St.)
Tufton St.
  SW1 . . . . . . 5D 23 (4A 76)
Tugela St. SE6 . . . . 2B 122
Tullis Ho. E9 . . . . 4E 51
  (off Frampton Pk. Rd.)
TULSE HILL 1D 119
Tulse Hill SW2 . . . . 4C 104
Tulse Hill Est. SW2 . . . . 4C 104
Tulsemere Rd. SE27 . . . 2E 119
Tunbridge Ho. EC1 . . . . 1C 8
Tunis Rd. W12 . . . . 2E 71
Tunley Grn. E14 . . . . 4B 66

Tunley Rd. NW10 . . . . . . 5A 42
  SW17 . . . . 1C 116
Tunmarsh La. E13 . . . . . 2D 69
Tunnel App. E14. . . . . . . 1A 80
  SE10 . . . . 3A 82
  SE16 . . . . 3E 79
Tunnel Av. SE10 . . . . . . 3F 81
  (not continuous)
Tunnel Av. Trad. Est.
  SE10 . . . . 3F 81
Tunnel Rd. SE16 . . . . . . 3E 79
Tunstall Rd. SW9 . . . . . 2B 104
Tunworth Cres. SW15 . . 4B 98
Tun Yd. SW8 . . . . 5D 89
  (off Silverthorne Rd.)
Tupelo Rd. E10 . . . . 4D 39
Tupman Ho. SE16 . . . . . 3C 78
  (off Scott Lidgett Cres.)
Turenne Cl. SW18 . . . . . 2E 101
Turin St. E2 . . . . 2C 64
Turk's Head Yd.
  EC1 . . . . 5D 9 (4D 63)
Turk's Row SW3 . . . . . . 1B 88
Turle Rd. N4 . . . . 4B 34
Turlewray Cl. N4 . . . . . . 3B 34
Turley Cl. E15 . . . . 5A 54
Turnagain La. EC4 . . . . . 2D 17
Turnberry Cl. SE16. . . . . 1D 93
Turnberry Quay E14 . . . . 4D 81
Turnbull Ho. N1 . . . . 5D 49
Turnchapel M. SW4. . . . 1D 103
Turner Cl. NW11 . . . . . . 1D 31
  SW9 . . . . 3D 91
Turner Ct. SE16 . . . . 3E 79
  (off Albion St.)
Turner Dr. NW11 . . . . . . 1D 31
Turner Ho. NW6 . . . . 2E 45
  (off Dresden Cl.)
  NW8 . . . . 1A 60
  (off Townshend Est.)
  SW1 . . . . 5F 75
  (off Herrick St.)
Turner Pl. SW11 . . . . . . 3A 102
Turner's All.
  EC3 . . . . 4D 19 (1A 78)
Turners Ct. N15 . . . . 1F 35
Turners Rd. E3 . . . . 4B 66
Turner St. E1 . . . . 4D 65
  E16 . . . . 5B 68
Turners Wood NW11 . . . 2E 31
Turneville Rd. W14 . . . . 2B 86
Turney Rd. SE21. . . . . . 5E 105
TURNHAM GREEN 5A 70
Turnham Grn. Ter.
  W4 . . . . 5A 70
Turnham Grn. Ter. M.
  W4 . . . . 5A 70
Turnham Rd. SE4 . . . . . 3A 108
Turnmill St.
  EC1 . . . . 4D 9 (3D 63)
Turnour Ho. E1 . . . . 5D 65
  (off Walburgh St.)
Turnpike Cl. SE8 . . . . . . 3B 94
Turnpike Ho.
  EC1 . . . . 2E 9 (2D 63)
Turnpin La. SE10 . . . . . . 2E 95
Turnstone Cl. E13. . . . . . 2C 68
Turnstone Ho. E1 . . . . . . 1C 78
  (off Star Pl.)
Turpentine La. SW1 . . . . 1D 89

Turpin Cl. E1 . . . . 1F 79
Turpin Ho. SW11 . . . . . . 4D 89
Turpin Way N19 . . . . 4F 33
   (not continuous)
Turquand St. SE17 . . . . . 5E 77
Turret Gro. SW4 . . . . . 1E 103
Turville Ho. NW8 . . . . . . 3A 60
   (off Grendon St.)
Turville St. E2 . . . . 3F 11
Tuscan Ho. E2 . . . . 2E 65
   (off Knottisford St.)
Tuskar St. SE10 . . . . 2A 96
Tustin Est. SE15 . . . . 2E 93
Tuttle Ho. SW1 . . . . 1F 89
   (off Aylesford St.)
Tweedale Ct. E15 . . . . . . 2E 53
Tweed Ho. E13 . . . . 1E 67
   (off Teviot St.)
Tweedmouth Rd. E13 . . . 1D 69
Tweezer's All. WC2 . . . . . 4B 16
Twelvetrees Cres. E3 . . . 3E 67
   (not continuous)
E16 . . . . 3F 67
Twickenham Rd. E11 . . . 4E 39
Twig Folly Cl. E2 . . . . 1F 65
Twilley St. SW18 . . . . . . 5D 101
Twine Ct. E1 . . . . 1E 79
Twine Ter. E3 . . . . 3B 66
   (off Ropery St.)
Twisden Rd. NW5 . . . . . . 1D 47
Twycross M. SE10 . . . . . . 1A 96
Twyford Ho. N5 . . . . 5D 35
N15 . . . . 1A 36
   (off Chisley Rd.)
Twyford Pl.
  WC2 . . . . . . 2F 15 (5B 62)
Twyford St. N1 . . . . 5B 48
Tyas Rd. E16 . . . . 3B 68
Tyburn Tree (site of) . . . 4A 12
Tyburn Way
  W1 . . . . . . 4A 12 (1B 74)
Tyers Est. SE1 . . . . 3D 27
Tyers Ga.
  SE1 . . . . . . 4D 27 (3A 78)
Tyers St. SE11 . . . . 1B 90
Tyers Ter. SE11 . . . . 1B 90
Tyler Cl. E2 . . . . 1B 64
Tyler's Ct. W1 . . . . 3B 14
Tyler St. SE10 . . . . 1A 96
   (not continuous)
Tylney Av. SE19 . . . . 5B 120
   (not continuous)
Tylney Ho. E1 . . . . 5D 65
   (off Nelson St.)
Tylney Rd. E7 . . . . 1E 55
Tyndale Ct. E14 . . . . 1D 95
   (off Transom Sq.)
Tyndale La. N1 . . . . 4D 49
Tyndale Mans. N1 . . . . . . 4D 49
   (off Upper St.)
Tyndale Ter. N1 . . . . 4D 49
Tyndall Gdns. E10 . . . . . 4E 39
Tyndall Rd. E10 . . . . 4E 39
Tyneham Cl. SW11 . . . . . 1C 102
Tyneham Rd. SW11 . . . . 5C 88
Tynemouth St. SW6 . . . . 5E 87
Tyne St. E1 . . . . 5B 64
Tynsdale Rd. NW10 . . . . 4A 42
Tynwald Ho. SE26 . . . . . 3C 120
Type St. E2 . . . . 1F 65

Tyrawley Rd. SW6 . . . . . 4D 87
Tyrell Ho.
  BR3: Beck 5D 123
   (off Beckenham Hill Rd.)
Tyrols Rd. SE23 . . . . 1F 121
Tyrrell Ho. SW1 . . . . 2E 89
   (off Churchill Gdns.)
Tyrrell Rd. SE22 . . . . 2C 106
Tyrrel Way NW9 . . . . 2B 28
Tyrwhitt Rd. SE4 . . . . . . 1C 108
Tysoe St. EC1 . . . 2C 8 (2C 62)
Tyson Gdns. SE23 . . . . . 5E 107
Tyson Rd. SE23 . . . . 5E 107
Tyssen Pas. E8 . . . . 3B 50
Tyssen Rd. N16 . . . . 5B 36
Tyssen St. E8 . . . . 3B 50
  N1 . . . . 1A 64
Tytherton E2 . . . . 1E 65
   (off Cyprus St.)
Tytherton Rd. N19 . . . . . 5F 33

U

Uamvar St. E14 . . . . 4D 67
UCI Cinema
  Rotherhithe 4F 79
  Whiteleys Cen. 5D 59
   (in Whiteleys Cen.)
UCI Filmworks 5B 82
Udall St. SW1 . . . . 5E 75
Udimore Ho. W10 . . . . . 4E 57
   (off Sutton Way)
Uffington Rd. NW10 . . . . 5C 42
  SE27 . . . . 4C 118
Ufford St.
  SE1 . . . . . . 3C 24 (3C 76)
Ufton Gro. N1 . . . . 4F 49
Ufton Rd. N1 . . . . 4F 49
   (not continuous)
UGC Cinema
  Fulham Rd. 1E 87
   (off Fulham Rd.)
  Hammersmith 5D 71
  Haymarket 5B 14
   (off Haymarket)
  King's Rd. 2F 87
   (off King's Rd.)
  Staples Corner 3D 29
  Trocadero 5B 14
   (off Coventry St.)
  West India Quay . . . 1C 80
Uhura Sq. N16 . . . . 5A 36
Ujima Ct. SW16 . . . . 4A 118
Ullathorne Rd. SW16 . . . 4E 117
Ullin St. E14 . . . . 4E 67
Ullswater Cl. SW15 . . . . 4A 112
Ullswater Cres.
  SW15 . . . . 4A 112
Ullswater Ho. SE15 . . . . 2E 93
   (off Hillbeck Cl.)
Ullswater Rd. SE27 . . . . 2D 119
  SW13 . . . . 3C 84
Ulster Pl. NW1 . . . 4D 5 (3D 61)
Ulster Ter.
  NW1 . . . . . . 3C 4 (3D 60)
Ulundi Rd. SE3 . . . . 2A 96
Ulva Rd. SW15 . . . . 3F 99
Ulverscroft Rd.
  SE22 . . . . 3B 106

Ulverstone Rd.
  SE27 . . . . 2D 119
Ulysses Rd. NW6 . . . . . . 2B 44
Umberston St. E1 . . . . . . 5C 64
Umbria St. SW15 . . . . . . 4C 98
Umfreville Rd. N4 . . . . . . 1D 35
Undercliff Rd. SE13 . . . . 1C 108
Underhill Ho. E14 . . . . . . 4C 66
   (off Burgess St.)
Underhill Pas. NW1 . . . . 5D 47
   (off Camden High St.)
Underhill Rd. SE22 . . . . . 3C 106
Underhill St. NW1 . . . . . . 5D 47
Undershaft
  EC3 . . . . . . 3D 19 (5A 64)
Undershaw Rd.
  BR1: Brom 3B 124
Underwood Ct. E10 . . . . 3D 39
   (off Leyton Grange Est.)
Underwood Ho. W6 . . . . 4D 71
   (off Sycamore Gdns.)
Underwood Rd. E1 . . . . . 3C 64
Underwood Row
  N1 . . . . 1A 10 (2E 63)
Underwood St.
  N1 . . . . 1A 10 (2E 63)
Undine Rd. E14 . . . . 5D 81
Undine St. SW17 . . . . . . 5B 116
Unicorn Bldg. E1 . . . . . . 1F 79
   (off Jardine Rd.)
Union Canal Wlk.
  W10 . . . . 3E 57
   (off Canal Way)
Union Cl. E11 . . . . 1F 53
Union Cotts. E15 . . . . . . 4A 54
Union Ct. EC2 . . . . 2D 19
  SW4 . . . . 5A 90
  W9 . . . . 4C 58
   (off Elmfield Way)
Union Dr. E1 . . . . 3A 66
Union Gro. SW8 . . . . 5F 89
Union M. SW4 . . . . 5A 90
Union Rd. SW4 . . . . 5F 89
  SW8 . . . . 5F 89
Union Sq. N1 . . . . 5E 49
Union St. E15 . . . . 5F 53
  SE1 . . . . . . 2D 25 (2D 77)
Union Theatre 2E 25
Union Wlk.
  E2 . . . . 1E 11 (2A 64)
Union Wharf N1 . . . . 1E 63
   (off Wenlock Rd.)
  N1 . . . . 5E 49
   (Arlington Av.)
Union Yd. W1 . . . 3E 13 (5D 61)
Unit Workshops E1 . . . . . 5C 64
   (off Adler St.)
Unity Cl. NW10 . . . . 3C 42
  SE19 . . . . 5E 119
Unity M. NW1 . . . . 1F 61
Unity Way SE18 . . . . 4F 83
Unity Wharf SE1 . . . . . . 3B 78
   (off Mill St.)
University College Department
  of Geological Sciences
  Collection 4B 6
University College London
  Gower St. 4B 6 (3F 61)
  Campbell House 3B 6
   (off Taviton St.)

University College London
  Chemistry Building . . . 3B 6
            (off Gordon St.)
University of East London
  Maryland Ho. 3A 54
  Stratford Campus . . . 3A 54
University of Greenwich
  Maritime Greenwich
  Campus 2E 95
University of London
  College Hall. 4B 6
            (off Malet St.)
  Institute of Education
      . . . . 3F 61
  Institute of Latin
  American Studies . . . 3F 61
  Senate Ho. . . . 5C 6 (4F 61)
University of London Union
      . . . . 4C 6
University of North London
  Highbury Cres. 3C 48
  Highbury Gro. 2E 49
  Hornsey Rd. 1C 48
University of Surrey
  Roehampton 4B 98
University of Westminster
  Cavendish Campus
      . . . . 5E 5 (4D 61)
  Hanson St. . . . 5F 5 (4E 61)
  Marylebone Campus
      . . . . 5B 4 (4C 60)
  Regent Campus . . . 1F 13
  Regent St. . . .
      . . . . 2E 13 (5D 61)
  Wells St. 1A 14
University St.
  WC1 . . . . 4A 6 (3E 61)
Unwin Cl. SE15 . . . . . 2C 92
Unwin Mans.
  W14 . . . . 2B 86
      (off Queen's Club Gdns.)
Unwin Rd. SW7 . . . . . 4F 73
Upbrook M. W2 . . . . . 5E 59
Upcerne Rd. SW10. . . 3E 87
Upcott Ho. E9 . . . . . . 4E 51
      (off Frampton Pk. Rd.)
Upgrove Mnr. Way
  SW2 . . . . 5C 104
Upham Pk. Rd.
  W4 . . . . 5A 70
Upland M. SE22 . . . . 3C 106
Upland Rd. E13 . . . . . 3C 68
  SE22. . . . . 3C 106
Uplands Rd. N8 . . . . . 1B 34
Upnall Ho. SE15 . . . . . 2E 93
Upnor Way SE17. . . . 1A 92
Up. Addison Gdns.
  W14 . . . . 3A 72
Upper Bank St.
  E14. . . . . 2D 81
Up. Bardsey Wlk.
  N1 . . . . 3E 49
      (off Douglas Rd. Nth.)
Up. Belgrave St.
  SW1 . . . . 5C 20 (4C 74)
Up. Berenger Wlk.
  SW10 . . . . 3F 87
      (off Berenger Wlk.)
Up. Berkeley St.
  W1 . . . . 3A 12 (5B 60)

Up. Blantyre Wlk.
  SW10 . . . . 3F 87
      (off Blantyre Wlk.)
Up. Brockley Rd.
  SE4 . . . . 1B 108
      (not continuous)
Up. Brook St.
  W1 . . . . 4B 12 (1C 74)
Up. Caldy Wlk.
  N1 . . . . 3E 49
      (off Arran Wlk.)
Up. Camelford Wlk.
  W11 . . . . 5A 58
      (off Cambourne M.)
  W11 . . . . 5A 58
      (off St Mark's Rd.)
Up. Cheyne Row
  SW3 . . . . 2A 88
      (off Old Chu. St.)
UPPER CLAPTON 4D 37
Up. Clapton Rd. E5 . . 3D 37
Up. Clarendon Wlk.
  W11 . . . . 5A 58
      (off Clarendon Rd.)
Up. Dartrey Wlk.
  SW10 . . . . 3F 87
      (off Whistler Wlk.)
Up. Dengie Wlk. N1 . . 5E 49
      (off Baddow Wlk.)
Upper Feilde W1 . . . . 4B 12
      (off Park St.)
Up. Grosvenor St.
  W1 . . . . 5B 12 (1C 74)
Upper Ground
  SE1 . . . . 1B 24 (2C 76)
Up. Gulland Wlk.
  N1 . . . . 4E 49
      (off Church Rd.)
Up. Hampstead Wlk.
  NW3 . . . . 1E 45
Up. Handa Wlk. N1 . . . 3F 49
      (off Handa Wlk.)
Up. Hawkwell Wlk.
  N1 . . . . 5E 49
      (off Maldon Cl.)
UPPER HOLLOWAY . . . 4E 33
Up. James St.
  W1 . . . . 4A 14 (1E 75)
Up. John St.
  W1 . . . . 4A 14 (1E 75)
Up. Lismore Wlk.
  N1 . . . . 3E 49
      (off Clephane Rd.)
Up. Lodge W8 . . . . . . 2D 73
      (off Palace Grn.)
Upper Mall W6. . . . . . 1C 84
      (not continuous)
Upper Marsh
  SE1 . . . . 5A 24 (4B 76)
Up. Montagu St.
  W1 . . . . 5A 4 (4B 60)
Up. North St. E14. . . . 4C 66
Up. Park Rd. NW3 . . . 2B 46
Up. Phillimore Gdns.
  W8 . . . . 3C 72
Up. Ramsey Wlk.
  N1 . . . . 3F 49
Up. Rawreth Wlk. N1. . 5E 49
      (off Basire St.)

Up. Richmond Rd.
  SW15 . . . . 2B 98
Up. Richmond Rd. W.
  SW14 . . . . 2A 98
Upper Rd. E13 . . . . . . 2C 68
Up. St Martin's La.
  WC2. . . . . . . 4D 15 (1A 76)
Upper St. N1 . . . . 1C 62
UPPER SYDENHAM . . . 3D 121
Up. Tachbrook St.
  SW1 . . . . 5E 75
Up. Talbot Wlk. W11 . . 5A 58
      (off Talbot Wlk.)
Upper Ter. NW3 . . . . . 5E 31
Up. Thames St.
  EC4 . . . . 4E 17 (1D 77)
Up. Tollington Pk.
  N4 . . . . 3C 34
      (not continuous)
Upperton Rd. E. E13 . . 2E 69
Upperton Rd. W. E13. . 2E 69
UPPER TOOTING . . . 4B 116
Up. Tooting Pk.
  SW17 . . . . 2B 116
Up. Tooting Rd.
  SW17 . . . . 4B 116
Up. Tulse Hill SW2 . . 5B 104
Up. Whistler Wlk.
  SW10 . . . . 3E 87
      (off Worlds End Est.)
Up. Wimpole St.
  W1 . . . . 5C 4 (4C 60)
Up. Woburn Pl.
  WC1 . . . . 2C 6 (2F 61)
Upstall St. SE5. . . . . . 4D 91
UPTON 4C 54
Upton Av. E7. . . . . . . 4C 54
Upton Cl. NW2 . . . . . 5A 30
Upton La. E7 . . . . 4C 54
Upton Lodge E7 . . . . 3C 54
UPTON PARK 5F 55
Upton Pk. Boleyn Cinema
      . . . . 1F 69
Upton Pk. Rd. E7 . . . . 4D 55
Upton Pk. Stadium . . . 1E 69
Upwey Ho. N1 . . . . . . 5A 50
Upwood Rd. SE12 . . . 4C 110
Urban M. N4 . . . . 1D 35
Urlwin St. SE5. . . . . . 2E 91
Urlwin Wlk. SW9 . . . . 4C 90
Urmston Dr. SW19 . . . 1A 114
Urmston Ho. E14 . . . . 5E 81
      (off Seyssel St.)
Ursula M. N4 . . . . 3E 35
Ursula St. SW11 . . . . 4A 88
Urswick Rd. E9. . . . . . 2E 51
Usborne M. SW8 . . . . 3B 90
Usher Rd. E3 . . . . 5B 52
Usk Rd. SW11 . . . . . . 2E 101
Usk St. E2. . . . . 2F 65
Utopia Village NW1. . . 4C 46
Uverdale Rd. SW10 . . 3E 87
Uxbridge Rd. W12 . . . 2C 70
Uxbridge St. W8. . . . . 2C 72

V

Vaine Ho. E9 . . . . 3A 52
Vaizeys Wharf SE7. . . 4D 83

Vale, The. NW11 . . . . 5F **29**
  SW3 . . . . 2F **87**
  W3 . . . . 2A **70**
Vale Cl. W9. . . . . 2E **59**
Vale Cotts. SW15 . . . . 3A **112**
Vale Ct. W3 . . . . 2B **70**
  W9 . . . . 2E **59**
Vale Cres. SW15 . . . . . 4A **112**
Vale End SE22 . . . . 2B **106**
Vale Est., The W3 . . . . . 2A **70**
Vale Gro. N4. . . . . 2E **35**
  W3 . . . . 3A **70**
Vale Lodge SE23 . . . . . 2E **121**
Valentia Pl. SW9 . . . . . 2C **104**
Valentine Ct.
  SE23 . . . . 2F **121**
    (not continuous)
Valentine Pl.
  SE1 . . . . 3D **25** (3D **77**)
Valentine Rd. E9. . . . . . . 3F **51**
Valentine Row
  SE1 . . . . 4D **25** (3D **77**)
VALE OF HEALTH 5E **31**
Vale of Health NW3 . . . . 5F **31**
Vale Pde. SW15 . . . . . . 3A **112**
Valerian Way E15 . . . . . . 2A **68**
Vale Ri. NW11 . . . . 3B **30**
Vale Rd. E7 . . . . 3D **55**
  N4 . . . . 2E **35**
Vale Row N5. . . . . 5D **35**
Vale Royal N7. . . . . 4A **48**
Vale Royal Ho. WC2. . . . 4C **14**
    (off Charing Cross Rd.)
Vale St. SE27 . . . . 3F **119**
Valeswood Rd.
  BR1: Brom 5B **124**
Vale Ter. N4 . . . . 1E **35**
Valetta Gro. E13 . . . . 1C **68**
Valetta Rd. W3. . . . . 3A **70**
Valette Ho. E9. . . . . 3E **51**
Valette St. E9 . . . . 3E **51**
Valiant Ho. E14. . . . . 3E **81**
    (off Plevna St.)
  SE7 . . . . 1E **97**
Vallance Rd. E1 . . . . 2C **64**
  E2 . . . . 2C **64**
Valley, The 1E **97**
Valleyfield Rd.
  SW16 . . . . 5B **118**
Valley Gro. SE7 . . . . 1E **97**
Valley Leisure Cen., The
  . . . . 1F **97**
    (off Valley, The)
Valley Rd. SW16 . . . . . 5B **118**
Valley Side SE7 . . . . 1F **97**
Valliere Rd. NW10 . . . . . 2C **56**
Valmar Rd. SE5 . . . . 4E **91**
Valmar Trad. Est.
  SE5 . . . . 4E **91**
Valnay St. SW17 . . . . . 5B **116**
Valois Ho. SE1 . . . . 5F **27**
    (off Grange, The)
Valonia Gdns.
  SW18 . . . . 4B **100**
Vanbrugh Castle SE3 . . 2A **96**
    (off Maze Hill)
Vanbrugh Cl. E16 . . . . . 4F **69**
Vanbrugh Ct. SE11 . . . . . 5C **76**
    (off Wincott St.)

Vanbrugh Flds. SE3 . . . 2B **96**
Vanbrugh Hill SE3 . . . . 2B **96**
  SE10 . . . . 1B **96**
Vanbrugh Ho. E9 . . . . . . 4E **51**
    (off Loddiges Rd.)
Vanbrugh Pk.
  SE3 . . . . 3B **96**
Vanbrugh Pk. Rd.
  SE3 . . . . 3B **96**
Vanbrugh Pk. Rd. W.
  SE3 . . . . 3B **96**
Vanbrugh Rd. W4. . . . . . 4A **70**
Vanbrugh Ter. SE3 . . . . 4B **96**
Vanburgh Ho. E1 . . . . . . 5F **11**
    (off Folgate St.)
Vancouver Ho. E1 . . . . . 2D **79**
    (off Reardon Path)
Vancouver Rd.
  SE23 . . . . 2A **122**
Vanderbilt Rd.
  SW18 . . . . 1D **115**
Vanderbilt Vs. W12 . . . . 3F **71**
    (off Sterne St.)
Vandome Cl. E16 . . . . . 5D **69**
Vandon Ct. SW1 . . . . . . 5A **22**
    (off Petty France)
Vandon Pas.
  SW1 . . . . . . 5A **22** (4E **75**)
Vandon St.
  SW1 . . . . . . 5A **22** (4E **75**)
Vandyke Cl. SW15 . . . . . 5F **99**
Vandyke Cross SE9. . . . 3F **111**
Vandy St.
  EC2 . . . . . . 4D **11** (3A **64**)
Vane Cl. NW3 . . . . 2F **45**
Vane St. SW1 . . . . 5E **75**
Vange Ho. W10 . . . . 4E **57**
    (off Sutton Way)
Van Gogh Ct. E14 . . . . . 4F **81**
Vanguard Bldg. E14 . . . 3B **80**
Vanguard Cl. E16 . . . . . 4C **68**
Vanguard Ct. SE5 . . . . . 4A **92**
Vanguard St. SE8 . . . . . 4C **94**
Vanguard Trad. Est.
  E15 . . . . 5E **53**
Vanneck Sq. SW15 . . . . 3C **98**
Vanoc Gdns.
  BR1: Brom 4C **124**
Vansittart Rd. E7 . . . . . . 1B **54**
Vansittart St. SE14 . . . . 3A **94**
Vanston Pl. SW6 . . . . . . 3C **86**
Vantage M. E14 . . . . 2E **81**
    (off Preston's Rd.)
Vantage Pl. W8 . . . . 4C **72**
Vantrey Ho. SE11 . . . . . 5C **76**
    (off Marylee Way)
Vant Rd. SW17. . . . . . . 5B **116**
Varcoe Rd. SE16 . . . . . 1D **93**
Vardens Rd. SW11 . . . . 2F **101**
Varden St. E1 . . . . 5D **65**
Vardon Cl. W3 . . . . 5A **56**
Vardon Ho. SE10 . . . . . 4E **95**
Varley Ho. NW6 . . . . . . 5C **44**
Varley Rd. E16. . . . . 5D **69**
Varna Rd. SW6 . . . . 3A **86**
Varndell St.
  NW1 . . . . 1F **5** (2E **61**)
Varnishers Yd. N1 . . . . . 1E **7**
    (off York Rd.)
Vartry Rd. N15 . . . . 1F **35**

Vassall Ho. E3 . . . . 2A **66**
    (off Antill Rd.)
Vassall Rd. SW9 . . . . . . 3C **90**
Vat Ho. SW8. . . . . 3A **90**
    (off Rita Rd.)
Vauban Est. SE16 . . . . . 4B **78**
Vauban St. SE16 . . . . . . 4B **78**
Vauban Ct. N4. . . . . 4C **34**
Vaudeville Theatre 5E **15**
    (off Strand)
Vaughan Av. NW4 . . . . . 1C **28**
  W6 . . . . 5B **70**
Vaughan Est. E2 . . . . . . 1F **11**
Vaughan Ho. SE1 . . . . . 3D **25**
    (off Blackfriars Rd.)
  SW4 . . . . 5E **103**
Vaughan Rd. E15 . . . . . 3B **54**
  SE5 . . . . 5E **91**
Vaughan St. SE16 . . . . 3B **80**
Vaughan Way E1 . . . . . 1C **78**
Vaughan Williams Cl.
  SE8 . . . . 3C **94**
VAUXHALL 2A **90**
Vauxhall Bri. SW1 . . . . . 1A **90**
Vauxhall Bri. Rd.
  SW1 . . . . 4E **75**
VAUXHALL CROSS 1A **90**
Vauxhall Distribution Pk.
  SW8 . . . . 2F **89**
    (off Post Office Way)
Vauxhall Gro. SW8 . . . . 2B **90**
Vauxhall St. SE11 . . . . . 1B **90**
Vauxhall Wlk. SE11 . . . . 1B **90**
Vawdrey Cl. E1. . . . . 3E **65**
Veda Rd. SE13 . . . . 2C **108**
Velde Way SE22. . . . . . 3A **106**
Velletri Ho. E2 . . . . 1F **65**
    (off Mace St.)
Venables St. NW8 . . . . . 3F **59**
Vencourt Pl. W6. . . . . . . 5C **70**
Venetian Rd. SE5 . . . . . 5E **91**
Venetia Rd. N4 . . . . 1D **35**
Venice Ct. NW8 . . . . 3F **59**
    (off Fisherton St.)
  SE5 . . . . 3E **91**
    (off Bowyer St.)
Venner Rd. SE26 . . . . . 5E **121**
    (not continuous)
Venn Ho. N1. . . . . 5B **48**
    (off Barnsbury Est.)
Venn St. SW4 . . . . 2E **103**
Ventnor Rd. SE14 . . . . . 3F **93**
Venture Ct. SE12 . . . . . 5C **110**
Venture Ho. W10 . . . . . 5F **57**
    (off Bridge Cl.)
Venue St. E14. . . . . 4E **67**
Venus Ho. E14. . . . . 5C **80**
    (off Westferry Rd.)
Vera Lynn Cl. E7 . . . . . . 1C **54**
Vera Rd. SW6 . . . . 4A **86**
Verbena Cl. E16. . . . . . . 3B **68**
Verbena Gdns. W6. . . . . 1C **84**
Verdant Ct. SE6 . . . . 5A **110**
    (off Verdant La.)
Verdant La. SE6 . . . . . . 5A **110**
Verdi Ho. W10 . . . . 1A **58**
    (off Herries St.)
Verdun Rd. SW13 . . . . . 2C **84**
Vereker Rd. W14 . . . . . 1A **86**
Vere St. W1 . . . 3D **13** (5D **61**)

Verity Cl. W11 . . . . 1A 72
Vermeer Ct. E14 . . . . . . 4F 81
Vermeer Gdns.
  SE15 . . . . 2E 107
Vermont Rd. SW18 . . . . 4D 101
Verney Ho. NW8 . . . . . . 3A 60
    (off Jerome Cres.)
Verney Rd. SE16 . . . . . . 2C 92
Verney St. NW10 . . . . . . 5A 28
Verney Way SE16 . . . . . 1D 93
Vernon Ho. SE11 . . . . . . 1B 90
    (off Vauxhall St.)
  WC1 . . . . 1E 15
    (off Vernon Pl.)
Vernon M. W14 . . . . 5A 72
Vernon Pl.
  WC1 . . . . . . 1E 15 (4A 62)
Vernon Ri.
  WC1 . . . . 1A 8 (2B 62)
Vernon Rd. E3 . . . . 1B 66
  E11 . . . . 3A 40
  E15 . . . . 4A 54
  SW14 . . . . 1A 98
Vernon Sq.
  WC1 . . . . 1A 8 (2B 62)
Vernon St. W14 . . . . 5A 72
Vernon Yd. W11 . . . . 1B 72
Verona Ct. SE14 . . . . 2F 93
    (off Myers La.)
  W4 . . . . 1A 84
Verona Rd. E7 . . . . 4C 54
Veronica Ho. SE4 . . . . . 1B 108
Veronica Rd. SW17 . . . . 2D 117
Verran Rd. SW12 . . . . . . 5D 103
Verulam Av. E17 . . . . . . 1B 38
Verulam Bldgs. WC1 . . . . . 5A 8
Verulam Ct. NW9 . . . . . . 2C 28
Verulam Ho. W6 . . . . 3E 71
    (off Hammersmith Gro.)
Verulam St.
  WC1 . . . . 5B 8 (4C 62)
Verwood Ho. SW8 . . . . . 3B 90
    (off Cobbett St.)
Verwood Lodge E14 . . . . 4F 81
    (off Manchester Rd.)
Veryan Ct. N8 . . . . 1F 33
Vesage Ct. EC1 . . . . 1C 16
    (off Leather La.)
Vesey Path E14 . . . . 5D 67
Vespan Rd. W12 . . . . . . 3C 70
Vesta Ct. SE1 . . . . 4D 27
Vesta Rd. SE4 . . . . 5A 94
Vestris Rd. SE23 . . . . . . 2F 121
Vestry Rd. SW1 . . . . 4F 75
    (off Monck St.)
Vestry M. SE5 . . . . 4A 92
Vestry Rd. SE5 . . . . 4A 92
Vestry St. N1 . . . . 1B 10 (2F 63)
Vevey St. SE6 . . . . 2B 122
Viaduct Bldgs.
  EC1 . . . . . . 1C 16 (4C 62)
Viaduct Pl. E2 . . . . 2D 65
Viaduct St. E2 . . . . 2D 65
Vian St. SE13 . . . . 1D 109
Vibart Gdns. SW2 . . . . . 5B 104
Vibart Wlk. N1 . . . . 5A 48
    (off Outram Pl.)
Vicarage Av. SE3 . . . . . . 3C 96
Vicarage Ct. W8 . . . . 3D 73

Vicarage Cres.
  SW11 . . . . 4F 87
Vicarage Gdns. W8 . . . . 2C 72
Vicarage Ga. W8 . . . . . . 2D 73
Vicarage Gro.
  SE5 . . . . 4F 91
Vicarage La. E15 . . . . . . 4A 54
Vicarage Path N8 . . . . . . 2A 34
Vicarage Rd. E10 . . . . . . 2C 38
  E15 . . . . 4B 54
  NW4 . . . . 1C 28
  SW14 . . . . 3A 98
Vicarage Wlk. SW11 . . . . 4F 87
Vicarage Way
  NW10 . . . . 5A 28
Vicars Cl. E9 . . . . 5C 51
  E15 . . . . 5C 54
Vicar's Hill SE13 . . . . . . 2D 109
Vicars Oak Rd.
  SE19 . . . . 5A 120
Vicar's Rd. NW5 . . . . . . 2C 46
Viceroy Ct. NW8 . . . . . . 1A 60
    (off Prince Albert Rd.)
Viceroy Rd. SW8 . . . . . . 4A 90
Vickery Ct. EC1 . . . . 3A 10
    (off Mitchell St.)
Victor Cazalet Ho.
  N1 . . . . 5D 49
    (off Gaskin St.)
Victoria & Albert Mus.
  . . . . 4F 73
Victoria Arc. SW1 . . . . . 5E 21
    (off Victoria St.)
Victoria Av. E6 . . . . 5F 55
  EC2 . . . . . . 1E 19 (4A 64)
Victoria Bldgs. E8 . . . . . 5D 51
    (off Mare St.)
Victoria Colonnade
  WC1 . . . . 1E 15
    (off Southampton Row)
Victoria Cotts. E1 . . . . . 4C 64
    (off Deal St.)
Victoria Ct. SE26 . . . . . 5E 121
Victoria Cres. N15 . . . . . 1A 36
  SE19 . . . . 5A 120
Victoria Dock Rd.
  E16 . . . . 5B 68
Victoria Dr. SW19 . . . . . 5F 99
Victoria Emb.
  EC4 . . . . . . 5A 16 (3A 76)
  SW1 . . . . . . 3E 23 (3A 76)
  WC2 . . . . . . 3E 23 (3A 76)
Victoria Gdns. W11 . . . . 2C 72
Victoria Gro. W8 . . . . . . 4E 73
Victoria Gro. M.
  W2 . . . . 1C 72
Victoria Hall E16 . . . . . . 2C 82
    (off Wesley Av.,
    not continuous)
Victoria Ho. SW1 . . . . . 5D 75
    (off Ebury Bri. Rd.)
  SW1 . . . . 3A 90
    (off Francis St.)
  SW8 . . . . 3A 90
    (off Sth. Lambeth Rd.)
Victoria Ind. Est.
  W3 . . . . 4A 56
Victoria Mans. NW10 . . . 4D 43
  SW8 . . . . 3A 90
    (off Sth. Lambeth Rd.)

Victoria M. E8 . . . . 3C 50
  NW6 . . . . 5C 44
  SW4 . . . . 2D 103
  SW18 . . . . 1E 115
Victoria Mills Studios
  E15 . . . . 5F 53
Victorian Gro.
  N16 . . . . 1A 50
Victorian Rd. N16 . . . . . 5A 36
Victoria Palace Theatre
  . . . . 5F 21
    (off Victoria St.)
Victoria Pk. Ct. E9 . . . . . 4E 51
    (off Well St.)
Victoria Pk. Ind. Cen.
  E9 . . . . 4C 52
    (off Rothbury Rd.)
Victoria Pk. Rd. E9 . . . . 5E 51
Victoria Pk. Sq. E2 . . . . 2E 65
Victoria Pas. NW8 . . . . . 3F 59
    (off Fisherton St.)
Victoria Pl. Shop. Cen.
  SW1 . . . . 5D 75
    (off Buckingham Pal. Rd.)
Victoria Point E13 . . . . . 1C 68
    (off Victoria Rd.)
Victoria Ri. NW6 . . . . . . 4E 45
    (off Hilgrove Rd.)
  SW4 . . . . 1D 103
Victoria Rd. E11 . . . . . . 1A 54
  E13 . . . . 1C 68
  N4 . . . . 2B 34
  NW6 . . . . 1B 58
  NW10 . . . . 4A 56
  W3 . . . . 4A 56
  W8 . . . . 4E 73
Victoria Sq. SW1 . . . . . 5E 21
Victoria St. E15 . . . . 4A 54
  SW1 . . . . . . 5E 21 (4E 75)
Victoria Ter. N4 . . . . 3C 34
  NW10 . . . . 3B 56
  SW8 . . . . 5D 89
Victoria Way SE7 . . . . . 1D 97
Victoria Wharf E2 . . . . . 1F 65
    (off Palmers Rd.)
  E14 . . . . 1A 80
  SE8 . . . . 1B 94
    (off Dragoon Rd.)
Victoria Works NW2 . . . . 4D 29
Victoria Yd. E1 . . . . 5C 64
Victor Rd. NW10 . . . . . . 2D 57
Victor Wharf SE1 . . . . . 1B 26
    (off Clink St.)
Victory Ct. W9 . . . . 3C 58
    (off Hermes Cl.)
Victory Pl. E14 . . . . 1A 80
  SE17 . . . . 5F 77
Victory Wlk. SE8 . . . . . . 4C 94
Victory Way SE16 . . . . . 3A 80
Video Ct. N4 . . . . 2B 34
View Cl. N6 . . . . 2B 32
View Ct. SE12 . . . . 3E 125
View Cres. N8 . . . . 1F 33
Viewfield Rd. SW18 . . . . 4B 100
View Rd. N6 . . . . 2B 32
Vigilant Cl. SE26 . . . . . 4C 120
Vigo St. W1 . . . . 5F 13 (1E 75)
Viking Cl. E3 . . . . 1A 66
Viking Ct. SW6 . . . . 2C 86
Viking Gdns. E6 . . . . . . 3F 69

Viking Ho. SE5 . . . . 5E **91**
(off Denmark Rd.)
Viking Pl. E10. . . . . 3B **38**
Village, The
  NW3 . . . . 4E **31**
  SE7 . . . . 2E **97**
Village Cl. NW3 . . . . 2F **45**
(off Belsize La.)
Village Ct. SE3 . . . . 1A **110**
(off Hurren Cl.)
Village Way NW10 . . . . . 1A **42**
  SE21 . . . . 4F **105**
Villa Rd. SW9. . . . . 1C **104**
Villas on the Heath
  NW3 . . . . 5E **31**
Villa St. SE17 . . . . 1F **91**
Villa Wlk. SE17. . . . . . . 1F **91**
(off Inville Rd.)
Villiers Cl. E10. . . . . 4C **38**
Villiers M. NW2 . . . . 3C **42**
Villiers Rd. NW2 . . . . . . 3C **42**
Villiers St.
  WC2. . . . . . . 5D **15** (2A **76**)
Vincennes Est.
  SE27 . . . . 4F **119**
Vincent Cl. SE16 . . . . . . 3A **80**
Vincent Ct. N4 . . . . 3A **34**
  SW9 . . . . 4B **90**
  W1 . . . . 2A **12**
(off Seymour Pl.)
Vincent Gdns. NW2 . . . . 5B **28**
Vincent Ho. SW1 . . . . . . 5F **75**
(off Vincent Sq.)
Vincent M. E3. . . . . 1C **66**
Vincent Sq. SW1. . . . . . 5F **75**
Vincent Sq. Mans.
  SW1 . . . . 5E **75**
(off Walcott St.)
Vincent St. E16. . . . . . . 4B **68**
  SW1 . . . . 5F **75**
Vincent Ter. N1. . . . . . . 1D **63**
Vince St. EC1. . . 2C **10** (2F **63**)
Vine Cotts. E1. . . . . 5E **65**
(off Sidney Sq.)
Vine Ct. E1. . . . . 4C **64**
Vinegar St. E1 . . . . 2D **79**
Vinegar Yd.
  SE1 . . . . 3D **27** (3A **78**)
Vine Hill EC1. . . 4B **8** (3C **62**)
Vine La. SE1 . . . 2E **27** (2A **78**)
Vineries, The SE6 . . . . . 1C **122**
Vine Rd. E15 . . . . 4B **54**
  SW13 . . . . 1B **98**
Vinery Row W6 . . . . 4D **71**
Vine Sq. W14 . . . . 1B **86**
(off Star Rd.)
Vine St. EC3. . . . 3F **19** (5B **64**)
  W1 . . . . 5A **14** (1E **75**)
Vine St. Bri.
  EC1 . . . . 4C **8** (3C **62**)
Vine Yd. SE1 . . . . 3A **26**
Vineyard Cl. SE6 . . . . . . 1C **122**
Vineyard Hill Rd.
  SW19 . . . . 4B **114**
Vineyard M. EC1 . . . . . . 3C **8**
Vineyard Wlk.
  EC1 . . . . 3B **8** (3C **62**)
Viney Rd. SE13 . . . . 1D **109**
Vining St. SW9 . . . . 2C **104**
Vinopolis 1A **26** (2E **77**)

Vinson Ho. N1 . . . . 1F **63**
(off Cranston Est.)
Vintners Ct.
  EC4 . . . . 5A **18** (1E **77**)
Vintner's Pl. EC4 . . . . . . 1E **77**
Viola Sq. W12 . . . . 1B **70**
Violet Cl. E16. . . . . 3A **68**
  SE8 . . . . 2B **94**
Violet Hill NW8 . . . . 1E **59**
Violet Hill Ho. NW8 . . . . 1E **59**
(off Violet Hill, not continuous)
Violet Rd. E3 . . . . 3D **67**
  E17 . . . . 1C **38**
Violet St. E2. . . . . 3D **65**
VIP Trading Est. SE7 . . . 5E **83**
Virgil Pl. W1 . . . . 4B **60**
Virgil St.
  SE1 . . . . 5A **24** (4B **76**)
Virginia Ct. SE16 . . . . . . 3F **79**
(off Eleanor Cl.)
  WC1 . . . . 3C **6**
(off Burton St.)
Virginia Ho. E14. . . . . . . 1E **81**
(off Newby Pl.)
Virginia Rd.
  E2. . . . . 2F **11** (2B **64**)
Virginia St. E1 . . . . 1C **78**
Virginia Wlk. SW2 . . . . . 4B **104**
Visage NW3 . . . . 4F **45**
(off Winchester Rd.)
Viscount Ct. W2 . . . . . . 5C **58**
(off Pembridge Vs.)
Viscount St.
  EC1. . . . . 4F **9** (3E **63**)
Vista, The SE9 . . . . 4F **111**
Vista Dr. IG4: Ilf 1F **41**
Vitae Apartments W6. . . 4C **70**
Vittoria Ho. N1. . . . . 5B **48**
(off High Rd.)
Vivian Av. NW4 . . . . 1D **29**
Vivian Comma Cl.
  N4. . . . . 5D **35**
Vivian Mans. NW4. . . . . 1D **29**
(off Vivian Av.)
Vivian Rd. E3 . . . . 1A **66**
Vivian Sq. SE15. . . . . . . 1D **107**
Vixen M. E8 . . . . 4B **50**
(off Haggerston Rd.)
Vogans Mill SE1. . . . . . . 3B **78**
Vogler Ho. E1. . . . . 1E **79**
(off Cable St.)
Vollasky Ho. E1 . . . . 4C **64**
(off Daplyn St.)
Voltaire Rd. SW4 . . . . . . 1F **103**
Volt Av. NW10 . . . . 2A **56**
Voluntary Pl. E11. . . . . . 1C **40**
Vorley Rd. N19. . . . . . . 4E **33**
Voss St. E2. . . . . 2C **64**
Voyager Bus. Est.
  SE16. . . . . 4C **78**
(off Spa Rd.)
Vue Cinema
  Finchley Rd. 3E **45**
    (in O2 Centre)
  Fulham Broadway. . . 3C **86**
  Islington 1C **62**
  Leicester Sq.. . . . . . 4C **14**
  Shepherds Bush . . . 3F **71**
Vulcan Rd. SE4 . . . . 5B **94**

Vulcan Sq. E14 . . . . 5D **81**
Vulcan Ter. SE4 . . . . . . 5B **94**
Vulcan Way N7. . . . . . . 3B **48**
Vyner Rd. W3. . . . . 1A **70**
Vyner St. E2. . . . . 5D **51**

W

W12 W12 . . . . 3F **71**
Wadding St. SE17 . . . . . 5F **77**
Waddington Rd. E15 . . . 2F **53**
Waddington St. E15. . . . 3F **53**
Wade Ho. SE1 . . . . 3C **78**
(off Parkers Row)
Wadeson St. E2 . . . . . . 1D **65**
Wade's Pl. E14. . . . . . . 1D **81**
Wadham Gdns. NW3 . . . 5A **46**
Wadham Rd.
  SW15 . . . . 2A **100**
Wadhurst Rd. SW8. . . . . 4E **89**
  W4 . . . . 4A **70**
Wadley Rd. E11. . . . . . . 2A **40**
Wager St. E3 . . . . 3B **66**
Waghorn Rd. E13. . . . . . 5E **55**
Waghorn St. SE15 . . . . . 1C **106**
Wagner St. SE15 . . . . . . 3E **93**
Wainford Cl. SW19. . . . . 1F **113**
Wainwright Ho. E1. . . . . 2E **79**
(off Garnet St.)
Waite Davies Rd.
  SE12. . . . . 5B **110**
Waite St. SE15. . . . . 2B **92**
Waithman St. EC4 . . . . . 3D **17**
(off Apothecary St.)
Wakefield Cl. SE26 . . . . 5E **121**
Wakefield Gdns.
  IG1: Ilf. 1F **41**
Wakefield Ho. SE15. . . . 4C **92**
Wakefield M.
  WC1 . . . . 2E **7** (2A **62**)
Wakefield Rd. N15. . . . . 1B **36**
Wakefield St. E6. . . . . . . 5F **55**
  WC1 . . . . 2E **7** (3A **62**)
Wakeford Cl. SW4 . . . . . 3E **103**
Wakeham St. N1 . . . . . . 3F **49**
Wakehurst Rd.
  SW11 . . . . 3A **102**
Wakeling St. E14. . . . . . 5A **66**
Wakelin Ho. N1. . . . . . . 4D **49**
(off Sebbon St.)
  SE23. . . . . 5A **108**
(off Brockley Pk.)
Wakelin Rd. E15 . . . . . . 1A **68**
Wakeman Ho. NW10 . . . 2F **57**
(off Wakeman Rd.)
Wakeman Rd. NW10 . . . 2E **57**
Wakley St.
  EC1 . . . . 1D **9** (2D **63**)
Walberswick St.
  SW8 . . . . 3A **90**
Walbrook
  EC4. . . . . 4B **18** (1F **77**)
(not continuous)
Walbrook Ct. N1. . . . . . . 1A **64**
(off Hemsworth St.)
Walbrook Wharf EC4 . . . 5A **18**
(off Bell Wharf La.)
Walburgh St. E1. . . . . . . 5D **65**
Walcorde Av. SE17. . . . . 5E **77**

Walcot Gdns. *SE11* 5C **76**
   (off Kennington Rd.)
Walcot Sq. SE11 . . . . . . 5C **76**
Walcott St. SW1 . . . . . . 5E **75**
Waldeck Gro. SE27 . . . 3D **119**
Waldemar Av. SW6 . . . . 4A **86**
Waldemar Rd.
   SW19 . . . . 5C **114**
Walden Ct. SW8 . . . . . . 4F **89**
Walden Ho. *SW1* 5C **74**
   (off Pimlico Rd.)
Waldenshaw Rd.
   SE23 . . . . 1E **121**
Walden St. E1 . . . . 5D **65**
   (not continuous)
Waldo Cl. SW4 . . . . . . 3E **103**
Waldo Ho. *NW10* 2D **57**
   (off Waldo Rd.)
Waldo Rd. NW10 . . . . . 2C **56**
   (not continuous)
Waldram Cres.
   SE23 . . . . 1E **121**
Waldram Pk. Rd.
   SE23 . . . . 1F **121**
Waldram Pl. SE23 . . . 1E **121**
Waldron M. SW3 . . . . . 2F **87**
Waldron Rd. SW18 . . . 3E **115**
Walerand Rd. SE13 . . . 5E **95**
Waleran Flats SE1 . . . 5A **78**
Wales Cl. SE15 . . . . . . 3D **93**
Wales Farm Rd. W3 . . . 4A **56**
Waley St. E1 . . . . 4A **66**
Walford Ho. E1 . . . . 5C **64**
Walford Rd. N16 . . . . . . 1A **50**
WALHAM GREEN 4C **86**
Walham Grn. Ct.
   SW6 . . . . 3D **87**
   (off Waterford Rd.)
Walham Gro. SW6 . . . 3C **86**
Walham Yd. SW6 . . . . 3C **86**
Walker Ho.
   NW1 . . . . 1B **6** (1F **61**)
Walker M. SW2 . . . . . 3C **104**
Walker's Ct. W1 . . . . . 4B **14**
Walkerscroft Mead
   SE21 . . . . 1E **119**
Walkers Lodge *E14* . . . 3E **81**
   (off Manchester Rd.)
Walkers Pl. SW15 . . . 2A **100**
Walkinshaw Ct. *N1* . . . 4E **49**
   (off Rotherfield St.)
Wallace Collection
   . . . . 2C **12** (5C **60**)
Wallace Ct. *NW1* 4A **60**
   (off Old Marylebone Rd.)
Wallace Ho. *N7* 3B **48**
   (off Caledonian Rd.)
Wallace Rd. N1 . . . . . . 3E **49**
Wallace Way *N19* 4F **33**
   (off St John's Way)
Wallbutton Rd. SE4 . . . 5A **94**
Wallcote Av. NW2 . . . . 3F **29**
Wall Ct. *N4* 3B **34**
   (off Stroud Grn. Rd.)
Waller Rd. SE14 . . . . . 4F **93**
Waller Way SE10 . . . . 3D **95**
Wallflower St. W12 . . . 1B **70**
Wallgrave Rd. SW5 . . . 5D **73**
Wallingford Av. W10 . . 4F **57**
Wallis All. SE1 . . . . . . 3A **26**

Wallis Cl. SW11 . . . . . 1F **101**
Wallis Ho. SE14 . . . . . 4A **94**
Wallis Rd. E9 . . . . 3B **52**
Wallis's Cotts. SW2 . . 5A **104**
Wallorton Gdns.
   SW14 . . . . 2A **98**
Wallside EC2 . . . . 1A **18**
Wall St. N1 . . . . 3F **49**
Wallwood Rd. E11 . . . . 2F **39**
Wallwood St. E14 . . . . 4B **66**
Walmer Ho. *W10* 5F **57**
   (off Bramley Rd.)
Walmer Pl. *W1* 4B **60**
   (off Walmer St.)
Walmer Rd. W10 . . . . . 5E **57**
   W11 . . . . 1A **72**
Walmer St. W1 . . . . . . 4B **60**
Walm La. NW2 . . . . . . 3E **43**
Walney Wlk. N1 . . . . . 3E **49**
Walnut Cl. SE8 . . . . . . 2B **94**
Walnut Ct. *W8* 4D **73**
   (off St Mary's Ga.)
Walnut Gdns. E15 . . . 2A **54**
Walnut Rd. E10 . . . . . 4C **38**
Walnut Tree Cl.
   SW13 . . . . 4B **84**
Walnut Tree Cotts.
   SW19 . . . . 5A **114**
Walnut Tree Ho.
   SW10 . . . . 2D **87**
   (off Tregunter Rd.)
Walnut Tree Rd.
   SE10 . . . . 1A **96**
   (not continuous)
Walnut Tree Wlk.
   SE11 . . . . 5C **76**
Walpole Ct. *W14* 4F **71**
   (off Blythe Rd.)
Walpole Ho. *SE1* 4B **24**
   (off Westminster Bri. Rd.)
Walpole M. NW8 . . . . . 5F **45**
Walpole Rd. E6 . . . . . . 4E **55**
   SW19 . . . . 5F **115**
Walpole St. SW3 . . . . . 1B **88**
Walsham Cl. N16 . . . . 3C **36**
Walsham Ho. SE14 . . . 5F **93**
   SE17 . . . . 1F **91**
   (off Blackwood St.)
Walsham Rd. SE14 . . . 5F **93**
Walsingham NW8 . . . . 5F **45**
Walsingham Lodge
   SW13 . . . . 4C **84**
Walsingham Mans.
   SW6 . . . . 3D **87**
   (off Fulham Rd.)
Walsingham Pl.
   SW4 . . . . 4C **102**
Walsingham Rd. E5 . . . 5C **36**
Walston Ho. *SW1* 1F **89**
   (off Aylesford St.)
Walter Besant Ho. *E1* . . 2F **65**
   (off Bancroft Rd.)
Walter Grn. Ho.
   SE15 . . . . 4E **93**
   (off Lausanne Rd.)
Walter Langley Ct.
   SE16 . . . . 3E **79**
   (off Brunel Rd.)
Walter Savil Twr. *E17* . 1C **38**
   (off Colchester Rd.)

Walters Cl. *SE17* 5F **77**
   (off Brandon St.)
Walters Ho. *SE17* 2D **91**
   (off Otto St.)
Walter St. E2 . . . . 2F **65**
Walters Way SE23 . . . 4F **107**
Walter Ter. E1 . . . . 5F **65**
Walterton Rd. W9 . . . . 3B **58**
Waltham Ho. NW8 . . . . 5E **45**
   NW2 . . . . 4D **29**
   SW8 . . . . 3A **90**
Walton Dr. NW10 . . . . 3A **42**
Walton Ho. *E2* 3F **11**
   (off Montclare St.)
Walton Pl.
   SW3 . . . . 5A **20** (4B **74**)
Walton Rd. E13 . . . . . . 1E **69**
Walton St. SW3 . . . . . 5A **74**
Walton Vs. *N1* 4A **50**
   (off Downham Rd.)
Walt Whitman Cl.
   SE24 . . . . 2D **105**
WALWORTH 1E **91**
Walworth Pl. SE17 . . . 1E **91**
Walworth Rd. SE1 . . . . 5E **77**
   SE17 . . . . 5E **77**
Wanborough Dr.
   SW15 . . . . 1D **113**
Wandle Ho.
   BR1: Brom 5F **123**
   NW8 . . . . 4A **60**
   (off Penfold St.)
Wandle Meadow Nature Pk.
   . . . . 5E **115**
Wandle Recreation Cen.
   . . . . 4D **101**
Wandle Rd. SW17 . . . 2A **116**
Wandle Way SW18 . . . 1D **115**
Wandon Rd. SW6 . . . . 3D **87**
   (not continuous)
Wandsdown Pl. SW6 . . 3D **87**
WANDSWORTH 3D **101**
Wandsworth Bri.
   SW6 . . . . 1D **101**
Wandsworth Bri. Rd.
   SW6 . . . . 4D **87**
WANDSWORTH COMMON
   . . . . 1B **116**
Wandsworth Comm. W. Side
   SW18 . . . . 3E **101**
WANDSWORTH GYRATORY
   . . . . 3D **101**
Wandsworth High St.
   SW18 . . . . 3C **100**
Wandsworth Mus. . . . 3D **101**
Wandsworth Plain
   SW18 . . . . 3D **101**
Wandsworth Rd.
   SW8 . . . . 1D **103**
Wangford Ho. *SW9* . . . 2D **105**
   (off Loughborough Pk.)
Wanless Rd. SE24 . . . 1E **105**
Wanley Rd. SE5 . . . . . 2F **105**
Wanlip Rd. E13 . . . . . . 3D **69**
Wansbeck Rd. E9 . . . . 4B **52**
Wansey St. SE17 . . . . 5E **77**
WANSTEAD 1D **41**
Wanstead Gdns.
   IG4: Ilf 1F **41**

Wanstead La. IG1: IIf . . . 1F **41**
Wanstead Leisure Cen.
. . . . 1E **41**
Wanstead Pk. Av.
E12 . . . . 3F **41**
Wanstead Pk. Rd.
IG1: IIf 1F **41**
Wanstead Pl. E11 . . . . . 1C **40**
Wantage Rd. SE12 . . . 3B **110**
WAPPING 2D **79**
Wapping Dock St.
E1 . . . . 2D **79**
Wapping High St. E1 . . 2C **78**
Wapping La. E1 . . . . . . 1D **79**
Wapping Wall E1 . . . . . 2E **79**
Warbeck Rd. W12 . . . . 3D **71**
Warburton Cl. N1 . . . . . 3A **50**
(off Culford St.)
Warburton Ho. E8 . . . . 5D **51**
(off Warburton St.)
Warburton Rd. E8 . . . . 5D **51**
Warburton St. E8 . . . . . 5D **51**
Wardalls Gro. SE14 . . . 3E **93**
Wardalls Ho. SE8 . . . . 2B **94**
(off Staunton St.)
Wardell Ho. SE10 . . . . . 2E **95**
(off Welland St.)
Warden Rd. NW5 . . . . . 3C **46**
Wardens Gro.
SE1 . . . . 2F **25** (2E **77**)
Wardle St. E9 . . . . 2F **51**
Wardley St. SW18 . . . 5D **101**
Wardo Av. SW6 . . . . . . 4A **86**
Wardour M. W1 . . . . . . 3A **14**
Wardour St.
W1 . . . . 2A **14** (5E **61**)
Ward Point SE11 . . . . . 5C **76**
Ward Rd. E15 . . . . 5F **53**
N19 . . . . 5E **33**
Wardrobe Pl. EC4 . . . . . 3E **17**
Wardrobe Ter. EC4 . . . . 4E **17**
Wards Wharf App.
E16 . . . . 2F **83**
Wareham Ct. N1 . . . . . . 4A **50**
(off Hertford Rd.)
Wareham Ho. SW8 . . . . 3B **90**
Warfield Rd. NW10 . . . 2F **57**
Warfield Yd. NW10 . . . . 2F **57**
(off Warfield Rd.)
Wargrave Av. N15 . . . . 1B **36**
Wargrave Ho. E2 . . . . . 2F **11**
(off Navarre St.)
Warham Rd. N4 . . . . . . 1C **34**
Warham St. SE5 . . . . . . 3D **91**
Waring St. SE27 . . . . . 4E **119**
Warley Ho. E10 . . . . . . 3B **38**
Warley Cl. E10 . . . . 3B **38**
Warley St. E2 . . . . 2F **65**
Warlock Rd. W9 . . . . . . 3B **58**
Warlters Cl. N7 . . . . 1A **48**
Warlters Rd. N7 . . . . . . 1A **48**
Warltersville Mans.
N19 . . . . 2A **34**
Warltersville Rd.
N19 . . . . 2A **34**
Warmington Cl. E5 . . . . 5F **37**
Warmington Rd.
SE24 . . . . 4E **105**
Warmington St. E13 . . . 3C **68**
Warmington Twr.
SE14 . . . . 4A **94**

Warmsworth NW1 . . . . . 5E **47**
(off Pratt St.)
Warndon St. SE16 . . . . 5F **79**
Warneford St. E9 . . . . . 5D **51**
Warner Cl. E15 . . . . . . 2A **54**
NW9 . . . . 2B **28**
Warner Ho.
BR3: Beck. 5D **123**
NW8 . . . . 2E **59**
SE13 . . . . 5D **95**
(off Russett Way)
Warner Pl. E2 . . . . 1C **64**
Warner Rd. SE5 . . . . . . 4E **91**
Warner St.
EC1 . . . . 4B **8** (3C **62**)
Warner Ter. E14 . . . . . . 4D **67**
(off Broomfield St.)
Warner Yd. EC1 . . . . . . 4B **8**
Warnford Ho. SW15 . . . 4A **98**
(off Tunworth Cres.)
Warnham WC1 . . . . 2F **7**
(off Sidmouth St.)
Warnham Ho.
SW2 . . . . 5B **104**
(off Up. Tulse Hill)
Warple M. W3 . . . . 3A **70**
Warple Way W3 . . . . . . 3A **70**
(not continuous)
Warren, The SE7 . . . . . 2E **97**
Warren Av. E10 . . . . . . 5E **39**
Warren Cl. SE21 . . . . . 5E **105**
Warren Ct. NW1 . . . . . . 3A **6**
(off Warren St.)
Warrender Rd. N19 . . . . 5E **33**
Warren Dr., The E11 . . . 2E **41**
Warren Gdns. E15 . . . . 2F **53**
Warren Ho. W14 . . . . . . 5B **72**
(off Beckford Cl.)
Warren M. W1 . . . 4F **5** (3E **61**)
Warren Pl. E1 . . . . 5F **65**
(off Caroline St.)
Warren Rd. E10 . . . . . . 5E **39**
E11 . . . . 1E **41**
(not continuous)
NW2 . . . . 4B **28**
Warren St. W1 . . . 4F **5** (3E **61**)
Warren Wlk. SE7 . . . . . 2E **97**
Warriner Gdns.
SW11 . . . . 4B **88**
Warrington Cres. W9 . . 3E **59**
Warrington Gdns.
W9 . . . . 3E **59**
Warspite Ho. E14 . . . . . 5D **81**
(off Cahir St.)
Warspite Rd. SE18 . . . . 4F **83**
Warton Rd. E15 . . . . . . 4E **53**
Warwick W14 . . . . 5B **72**
(off Kensington Village)
Warwick Av. W2 . . . . . . 3E **59**
W9 . . . . 3D **59**
Warwick Bldg. SW8 . . . 2D **89**
Warwick Chambers
W8 . . . . 4C **72**
(off Pater St.)
Warwick Ct. EC4 . . . . . 3E **17**
(off Warwick La.)
WC1 . . . . 1A **16** (4B **62**)
Warwick Cres. W2 . . . . 4E **59**
Warwick Dr. SW15 . . . . 1D **99**
Warwick Est. W2 . . . . . 4D **59**

Warwick Gdns. N4 . . . . 1E **35**
W14 . . . . 4B **72**
Warwick Gro. E5 . . . . . 3D **37**
Warwick Ho. E16 . . . . . 2C **82**
(off Wesley Av.)
SW9 . . . . 5C **90**
Warwick Ho. St.
SW1 . . . . 1C **22** (2F **75**)
Warwick La.
EC4 . . . . 2E **17** (5D **63**)
Warwick Pas. EC4 . . . . 2E **17**
(off Old Bailey)
Warwick Pl. W9 . . . . . . 4E **59**
Warwick Pl. Nth.
SW1 . . . . 5E **75**
Warwick Rd. E12 . . . . . 2F **55**
E15 . . . . 3B **54**
SW5 . . . . 5C **72**
W14 . . . . 5B **72**
Warwick Row
SW1 . . . . 5E **21** (4D **75**)
Warwickshire Path
SE8 . . . . 3B **94**
Warwickshire Rd.
N16 . . . . 1A **50**
Warwick Sq.
EC4 . . . . 2E **17** (5D **63**)
SW1 . . . . 1E **89**
(not continuous)
Warwick Sq. M. SW1 . . 5E **75**
Warwick St.
W1 . . . . 4A **14** (1E **75**)
Warwick Ter. E17 . . . . . 1F **39**
(off Lea Bri. Rd.)
Warwick Way SW1 . . . 1D **89**
Warwick Yd.
EC1 . . . . 4A **10** (3E **63**)
Washington Cl. E3 . . . . 2D **67**
Washington Rd. E6 . . . . 4E **55**
SW13 . . . . 3C **84**
Wastdale Rd. SE23 . . . 1F **121**
Waterbank Rd.
SE6 . . . . 3D **123**
Water Brook La.
NW4 . . . . 1E **29**
Watercress Pl. N1 . . . . 4A **50**
Waterden Cres. E15 . . . 2C **52**
Waterden Rd. E15 . . . . 2C **52**
Waterer Ho. SE6 . . . . . 4E **123**
Waterfall Cotts.
SW19 . . . . 5F **115**
Waterfall Rd. SW19 . . . 5F **115**
Waterfall Ter. SW17 . . . 5A **116**
Waterford Ho. W11 . . . . 1B **72**
(off Kensington Pk. Rd.)
Waterford Rd. SW6 . . . . 3D **87**
(not continuous)
Waterford Way
NW10 . . . . 2D **43**
Waterfront Studios Bus. Cen.
E16 . . . . 2C **82**
(off Dock Rd.)
Water Gdns., The W2 . . 5A **60**
Watergate
EC4 . . . . 4D **17** (1D **77**)
Watergate St. SE8 . . . . 2C **94**
Watergate Wlk.
WC2 . . . . 1E **23** (2A **76**)
Waterhead NW1 . . . . . . 1F **5**
(off Varndell St.)

Waterhouse Cl. E16 . . . . 4F 69
  NW3 . . . . 2F 45
  W6 . . . . 5F 71
Waterhouse Sq.
  EC1 . . . . 1B 16 (4C 62)
Wateridge Cl. E14 . . . . . 4C 80
Water La. E15 . . . . 3A 54
  EC3 . . . . . . 5E 19 (1A 78)
  NW1 . . . . 4D 47
  SE14 . . . . 3E 93
Waterloo Bri.
  SE1 . . . . . . 5A 16 (1B 76)
Waterloo Cl. E9 . . . . 2E 51
Waterloo Gdns. E2 . . . . . 1E 65
Waterloo Pas. NW6 . . . . 4B 44
Waterloo Pl.
  SW1 . . . . . . 1B 22 (2F 75)
Waterloo Rd. E6 . . . . 4E 55
  E7 . . . . 2B 54
  E10 . . . . 2C 38
  NW2 . . . . 3C 28
  SE1 . . . . . . 1A 24 (2B 76)
Waterloo Ter. N1 . . . . . . 4D 49
Waterlow Ct. NW11 . . . . 2D 31
Waterlow Rd. N19 . . . . . 3E 33
Waterman Bldg. E14 . . . 3B 80
Waterman St. SW15 . . . . 1F 99
Watermans Wlk. EC4 . . . 5B 18
  SE16 . . . . 3A 80
Waterman Way E1 . . . . . 2D 79
Watermead Ho. E9 . . . . . 2A 52
Watermeadow La.
  SW6 . . . . 5E 87
Watermead Rd. SE6 . . . 4E 123
Water M. SE15 . . . . 2E 107
Watermint Quay N16 . . . 2C 36
Water's Edge SW6 . . . . . 4E 85
  (off Palemead Cl.)
Waterside E17 . . . . 1E 37
  W2 . . . . 4F 59
  (off Nth. Wharf Rd.)
Waterside Cl. E3 . . . . . . 5B 52
  SE16 . . . . 3C 78
Waterside Ho. E14 . . . . . 3D 81
  (off Admirals Way)
Waterside Pl. NW1 . . . . . 5C 46
Waterside Point
  SW11 . . . . 3A 88
Waterside Twr. SW6 . . . . 5E 87
  (off Boulevard, The)
Waterside Way
  SW17 . . . . 4E 115
Waterson St.
  E2 . . . . 1E 11 (2A 64)
Waters Pl. SW15 . . . . . . 5E 85
Waters Rd. SE6 . . . . . . 3A 124
Water St. WC2 . . . . 4B 16
Water Twr. Pl. N1 . . . . . . 5C 48
Waterview Ho. E14 . . . . . 4A 66
  (off Carr St.)
Waterworks La. E5 . . . . . 4F 37
Waterworks Rd.
  SW2 . . . . 4B 104
Watford Cl. SW11 . . . . . 4A 88
Watford Rd. E16 . . . . . . 4C 68
Watford Way NW4 . . . . . 1D 29
Watkins Ho. E14 . . . . . . 3E 81
  (off Manchester Rd.)
Watkinson Rd. N7 . . . . . 3B 48
Watling Ct. EC4 . . . . 3A 18

Watling Gdns. NW2 . . . . 3A 44
Watling St.
  EC4 . . . . 3A 18 (5E 63)
  SE15 . . . . 2A 92
Watlington Gro.
  SE26 . . . . 5A 122
Watney Mkt. E1 . . . . 5D 65
Watney St. E1 . . . . 5D 65
Watson Cl. N16 . . . . 2F 49
Watson's M. W1 . . . . 4A 60
Watson St. E13 . . . . 1D 69
Watsons Sts. SE8 . . . . . 3C 94
Wattisfield Rd. E5 . . . . . 5E 37
Watts Gro. E3 . . . . 4C 66
Watts Point E13 . . . . 5C 54
  (off Brooks Rd.)
Watts St. E1 . . . . 2D 79
  SE15 . . . . 4B 92
Wat Tyler Rd. SE3 . . . . . 5E 95
  SE10 . . . . 5E 95
Wavel Ct. E1 . . . . 2E 79
  (off Garnet St.)
Wavelengths Leisure Pool
  . . . . 3C 94
Wavel M. NW6 . . . . 4D 45
Wavel Pl. SE26 . . . . 4B 120
Wavendon Av. W4 . . . . . 1A 84
Waveney Av. SE15 . . . . 2D 107
Waveney Cl. E1 . . . . 2C 78
Waverley Av. SE15 . . . . 2D 107
Waverley Ct. NW3 . . . . . 3B 46
  NW6 . . . . 4A 44
  SE26 . . . . 5E 121
Waverley Pl. N4 . . . . 4D 35
  NW8 . . . . 1F 59
Waverley Rd. N8 . . . . . . 1A 34
Waverton Rd. SW18 . . . . 5B 52
Waverton St. SE18 . . . . 5E 101
Waverton St.
  W1 . . . . 1D 21 (2C 74)
Wavertree Ct. SW2 . . . . 1A 118
Wavertree Rd. SW2 . . . 1B 118
Waxham NW3 . . . . 2B 46
Waxlow Rd. NW10 . . . . . 1A 56
Wayford St. SW11 . . . . . 5A 88
Wayland Av. E8 . . . . 2C 50
Wayland Ho. SW9 . . . . . 5C 90
  (off Robsart St.)
Waylett Ho. SE11 . . . . . . 1B 90
  (off Loughborough St.)
Waylett Pl. SE27 . . . . . . 3D 119
Wayman Ct. E8 . . . . 3D 51
Wayne Kirkum Way
  NW6 . . . . 2B 44
Waynflete Sq. W10 . . . . . 1F 71
Waynflete St. SW18 . . . 2E 115
Wayside NW11 . . . . 3A 30
Weald Cl. SE16 . . . . 1D 93
Weald Sq. E5 . . . . 4C 36
Weardale Rd. SE13 . . . . 2F 109
Wearmouth Ho. E3 . . . . . 4B 66
  (off Joseph St.)
Wear Pl. E2 . . . . 2D 65
  (not continuous)
Wearside Rd. SE13 . . . . 2D 109
Weatherbury W2 . . . . . . 5C 58
  (off Talbot Rd.)
Weatherbury Ho. N19 . . . 5F 33
  (off Wedmore St.)
Weatherley Cl. E3 . . . . . 4B 66

Weavers Almshouses
  E11 . . . . 1B 40
  (off Cambridge Rd.)
Weavers Ho. E11 . . . . . . 1C 40
  (off New Wanstead)
Weavers La.
  SE1 . . . . 2E 27 (2A 78)
Weavers Ter. SW6 . . . . . 2C 86
  (off Micklethwaite Rd.)
Weaver St. E1 . . . . 3C 64
Weavers Way NW1 . . . . 5F 47
Weaver Wlk.
  SE27 . . . . 4E 119
Webb Cl. W10 . . . . 3E 57
Webber Row SE1 . . . . . . 5C 24
Webber St.
  SE1 . . . . 3C 24 (3C 76)
Webb Est. E5 . . . . 2C 36
Webb Gdns. E13 . . . . . . 3C 68
Webb Ho. SW8 . . . . 3F 89
Webb Pl. NW10 . . . . 2B 56
Webb Rd. SE3 . . . . 2B 96
Webb's Rd. SW11 . . . . . 2B 102
Webb St.
  SE1 . . . . 5D 27 (4A 78)
Webheath NW6 . . . . 4B 44
  (not continuous)
Webster Rd. E11 . . . . . . 5E 39
  SE16 . . . . 4C 78
Weddell Ho. E1 . . . . 3F 65
  (off Duckett St.)
Wedderburn Rd. NW3 . . 2F 45
Wedgewood Ho.
  SW1 . . . . 1D 89
  (off Churchill Gdns.)
Wedgewood M.
  W1 . . . . 3C 14 (5F 61)
Wedgwood Ho. E2 . . . . . 2F 65
  (off Warley St.)
  SE11 . . . . 4C 76
  (off Lambeth Wlk.)
Wedgwood Wlk.
  NW6 . . . . 2D 45
  (off Dresden Cl.)
Wedlake St. W10 . . . . . . 3A 58
Wedmore Gdns. N19 . . . 4F 33
Wedmore M. N19 . . . . . . 5F 33
Wedmore St. N19 . . . . . 5F 33
Weech Rd. NW6 . . . . . . 1C 44
Weedington Rd. NW5 . . . 2C 46
Weedon Ho. W12 . . . . . . 5C 56
Weekley Sq. SW11 . . . . 1F 101
Weigall Rd. SE12 . . . . . 3C 110
Weighhouse St.
  W1 . . . . 3C 12 (5C 60)
Weimar St. SW15 . . . . . 1A 100
Weir Rd. SW12 . . . . 5E 103
  SW19 . . . . 3D 115
Weir's Pas.
  NW1 . . . . 1C 6 (2F 61)
Weiss Rd. SW15 . . . . . . 1F 99
Welbeck Av.
  BR1: Brom 4C 124
Welbeck Ct. W14 . . . . . . 5B 72
  (off Addison Bri. Pl.)
Welbeck Ho. W1 . . . . . . 2D 13
  (off Welbeck St.)
Welbeck Rd. E6 . . . . 2F 69
Welbeck St.
  W1 . . . . 1C 12 (4C 60)

Welbeck Way
  W1. . . . . . . 2D **13** (5D **61**)
Welby Ho. N19 . . . . . . 2F **33**
Welby St. SE5 . . . . . . 4D **91**
Welcome Ct. E17 . . . . . 2C **38**
  (off Boundary Rd.)
Welfare Rd. E15 . . . . . 4A **54**
Welford Cl. E5 . . . . 5F **37**
Welford Ct. NW1 . . . . . 4D **47**
  (off Castlehaven Rd.)
  SW8 . . . . 5E **89**
  W9 . . . . 4C **58**
  (off Elmfield Way)
Welford Pl. SW19 . . . 4A **114**
Welham Rd.
  SW16 . . . . 5D **117**
  SW17 . . . . 5C **116**
Welland Ct. SE6 . . . . . 2B **122**
  (off Oakham Cl.)
Welland Ho. SE15 . . . 2E **107**
Welland M. E1 . . . . . . 2C **78**
Welland St. SE10 . . . . 2E **95**
Wellby Ct. E13 . . . . . . 5E **55**
Well Cl. SW16 . . . . . 4B **118**
Wellclose Sq. E1 . . . . 1C **78**
Wellclose St. E1 . . . . . 1C **78**
  E3 . . . . 1A **66**
  (off Driffield Rd)
Wellcome Cen. for
  Medical Science . . . 3B **6**
Wellcome Mus. 2A **16**
  (off Portugal St.)
Well Cott. Cl. E11 . . . . 1E **41**
Well Ct. EC4 . . 3A **18** (5E **63**)
  (not continuous)
Weller Ho. SE16 . . . . . 3C **78**
  (off George Row)
Weller St.
  SE1 . . . . 3F **25** (3E **77**)
Welles Ct. E14 . . . . . . 1C **80**
  (off Premiere Pl.)
Wellesley Av. W6 . . . . 4D **71**
Wellesley Cl. SE7 . . . . 1E **97**
Wellesley Ct. NW2 . . . 4C **28**
  W9 . . . . 2E **59**
Wellesley Ho. NW1 . . . 2C **6**
  (off Wellesley Pl.)
  SW1 . . . . 1D **89**
  (off Ebury Bri. Rd.)
Wellesley Mans.
  W14 . . . . 1B **86**
  (off Edith Vs.)
Wellesley Pl.
  NW1 . . . . 2B **6** (2F **61**)
  NW5 . . . . 2C **46**
Wellesley Rd. E11 . . . . 1C **40**
  E17 . . . . 1C **38**
  NW5 . . . . 2C **46**
Wellesley St. E1 . . . . . 4F **65**
Wellesley Ter.
  N1 . . . . 1A **10** (2E **63**)
Wellfield Rd. SW16 . . 4A **118**
Wellfield Wlk.
  SW16 . . . . 5B **118**
  (not continuous)
Wellfit St. SE24 . . . . . 1D **105**
Wellgarth Rd. NW11 . . 3D **31**
Wellington Arch
  . . . . 3C **20** (3C **74**)
Wellington Av. N15 . . . . 1B **36**

Wellington Bldgs.
  SW1 . . . . 1C **88**
Wellington Cl. SE14 . . 4F **93**
  W11 . . . . 5C **58**
Wellington Ct. NW8 . . 1F **59**
  (off Wellington Rd.)
  SW1 . . . . 3B **74**
  (off Knightsbridge)
  SW6 . . . . 4D **87**
  (off Maltings Pl.)
Wellington Gdns.
  SE7 . . . . 2E **97**
Wellington Gro. SE10 . 3F **95**
Wellington Ho. E16 . . . 2C **82**
  (off Pepys Cres.)
  NW3 . . . . 3B **46**
  (off Eton Rd.)
Wellington Mans.
  E10 . . . . 3C **38**
Wellington M. N7 . . . . 3B **48**
  (off Roman Way)
  SE7 . . . . 2E **97**
  SE22 . . . . 2C **106**
  SW16 . . . . 3F **117**
Wellington Monument
  . . . . 3C **20**
Wellington Mus.
  . . . . 3C **20** (3C **74**)
Wellington Pk. Est.
  NW2 . . . . 4C **28**
Wellington Pas. E11 . . 1C **40**
  (off Wellington Rd.)
Wellington Pl. NW8 . . . 2F **59**
Wellington Rd. E7 . . . . 1B **54**
  E10 . . . . 3A **38**
  E11 . . . . 1C **40**
  NW8 . . . . 1F **59**
  NW10 . . . . 2F **57**
  SW19 . . . . 2C **114**
Wellington Row E2 . . . 2B **64**
Wellington Sq. SW3 . . 1B **88**
Wellington St.
  WC2 . . . . . . 4F **15** (1B **76**)
Wellington Ter. E1 . . . . 2D **79**
  W2 . . . . 1C **72**
Wellington Way E3 . . . 2C **66**
Wellmeadow Rd.
  SE13 . . . . 4A **110**
  (not continuous)
Well Pl. NW3 . . . . 5F **31**
Well Rd. NW3 . . . . 5F **31**
Wells Ct. NW6 . . . . . . 1C **58**
  (off Cambridge Av.)
Wells Gdns. IG1: Ilf . . 2F **41**
Wells Ho.
  BR1: Brom 5D **125**
  (off Pike Cl.)
  EC1 . . . . 1C **8**
  (off Spa Grn. Est.)
  SE16 . . . . 4E **79**
  (off Howland Est.)
Wells Ho. Rd. NW10 . . 4A **56**
Wells M. W1 . . . 1A **14** (4E **61**)
Wells Pk. Rd. SE26 . . 3C **120**
Wells Pl. SW18 . . . . . 5E **101**
Wells Ri. NW8 . . . . . . 5B **46**
Wells Rd. W12 . . . . . . 3E **71**
Wells Sq.
  WC1 . . . . 2F **7** (2B **62**)
Wells St. W1 . . 1F **13** (4E **61**)

Wells Ter. N4 . . . . 4C **34**
Well St. E9 . . . . 4E **51**
  E15 . . . . 3A **54**
Wells Way SE5 . . . . . . 2F **91**
  SW7 . . . . 4F **73**
Well Wlk. NW3 . . . . . . 1F **45**
Welmar M. SW4 . . . . . 3F **103**
  (off Northborne Rd.)
Welsford St. SE1 . . . . . 5C **78**
  (not continuous)
Welsh Cl. E13 . . . . 2C **68**
Welsh Harp Nature Reserve
Welsh Ho. E1 . . . . 2D **79**
  (off Wapping La.)
Welshpool Ho. E8 . . . . 5C **50**
  (off Welshpool St.)
Welshpool St. E8 . . . . 5C **50**
  (not continuous)
Welshside NW9 . . . . . . 1A **28**
  (off Ruthin Cl.)
Welshside Wlk. NW9 . . 1A **28**
Welstead Ho. E1 . . . . . 5D **65**
  (off Cannon St. Rd.)
Welstead Way
  W4 . . . . 5B **70**
Weltje Rd. W6 . . . . 5C **70**
Welton Ct. SE5 . . . . . . 4A **92**
Welton Ho. E1 . . . . 4F **65**
  (off Stepney Way)
Welwyn St. E2 . . . . 2E **65**
Wembury M. N6 . . . . . . 2E **33**
Wembury Rd. N6 . . . . . 2D **33**
Wemyss Rd. SE3 . . . . . 5B **96**
Wendell Rd. W12 . . . . 4B **70**
Wendle Ct. SW8 . . . . . 2A **90**
Wendling NW5 . . . . . . 2B **46**
Wendon St. E3 . . . . 5B **52**
Wendover SE17 . . . . . . 1A **92**
  (not continuous)
Wendover Ct. NW2 . . . 5C **30**
  W1 . . . . 1B **12**
  (off Chiltern St.)
Wendover Ho. W1 . . . . 1B **12**
  (off Chiltern St.)
Wendover Rd. NW10 . . 1B **56**
  SE9 . . . . 1F **111**
Wenham Ho. SW8 . . . . 3E **89**
Wenlake Ho. EC1 . . . . . 3F **9**
  (off Old St.)
Wenlock Barn Est. N1 . 1F **63**
  (off Wenlock St.)
Wenlock Ct.
  N1 . . . . 1C **10** (1F **63**)
Wenlock Rd.
  N1 . . . . 1A **10** (1E **63**)
Wenlock St.
  N1 . . . . 1A **10** (1E **63**)
Wennington Rd. E3 . . . 1F **65**
Wensdale Ho. E5 . . . . . 4C **36**
Wentland Cl. SE6 . . . . 2F **123**
Wentland Rd. SE6 . . . . 2F **123**
Wentworth Ct.
  SW18 . . . . 4D **101**
  (off Garratt La.)
  W6 . . . . 2A **86**
  (off Paynes Wlk.)
Wentworth Cres.
  SE15 . . . . 3C **92**

Wentworth Dwellings
  E1 . . . . 2F **19**
  (off Wentworth St.)
Wentworth M. E3 . . . . . . 3A **66**
Wentworth Rd. E12. . . . . 1F **55**
  NW11 . . . . 1B **30**
Wentworth St.
  E1. . . . . 2F **19** (5B **64**)
Werrington St.
  NW1 . . . . 1B **6** (1E **61**)
Werter Rd. SW15 . . . . . 2A **100**
Wesleyan Pl.
  NW5 . . . . 1D **47**
Wesley Av. E16. . . . . . . 2C **82**
  NW10 . . . . 2A **56**
Wesley Cl. N7. . . . . 4B **34**
  SE17 . . . . 5D **77**
Wesley Ct. SE16. . . . . . . 4D **79**
Wesley Rd. E10 . . . . 2E **39**
Wesley's House, Chapel &
  Mus. of Methodism
  . . . . 3C **10** (3F **63**)
Wesley Sq. W11. . . . . . . 5A **58**
Wesley St.
  W1. . . . . 1C **12** (4C **60**)
Wessex Gdns. NW11 . . . 3A **30**
Wessex Ho. SE1 . . . . . . 1B **92**
Wessex St. E2. . . . . 2E **65**
Wessex Way NW11 . . . . 3A **30**
Wesson Mead *SE5* 3E **91**
  (off Camberwell Rd.)
Westacott Cl. N19. . . . . . 3F **33**
W. Arbour St. E1. . . . . . . 5F **65**
West Av. NW4 . . . . 1F **29**
West Bank N16. . . . . 2A **36**
WEST BECKTON 5F **69**
Westbere Rd. NW2 . . . . . 1A **44**
West Block *SE1* 4A **24**
  (off Addington St.)
Westbourne Bri. W2. . . . 4E **59**
Westbourne Cres.
  W2. . . . . 1F **73**
Westbourne Cres. M.
  W2. . . . . 1F **73**
  (off Westbourne Cres.)
Westbourne Dr.
  SE23 . . . . 2F **121**
Westbourne Gdns.
  W2. . . . . 5D **59**
WESTBOURNE GREEN
  . . . . 5B **58**
Westbourne Green
  Sports Complex 4C **58**
Westbourne Gro. W2. . . 5C **58**
  W11 . . . . 1B **72**
Westbourne Gro. M.
  W11 . . . . 5C **58**
Westbourne Gro. Ter.
  W2. . . . . 5D **59**
Westbourne Ho.
  SW1 . . . . 1D **89**
  (off Ebury Bri. Rd.)
Westbourne Pk. Pas.
  W2 . . . . 4C **58**
  (not continuous)
Westbourne Pk. Rd.
  W2 . . . . 4C **58**
  W11 . . . . 5A **58**
Westbourne Pk. Vs.
  W2 . . . . 4C **58**

Westbourne Rd. N7 . . . 3B **48**
  SE26 . . . . 5F **121**
Westbourne St. W2 . . . 1F **73**
Westbourne Ter.
  SE23 . . . . 2F **121**
  (off Westbourne Dr.)
  W2 . . . . 5E **59**
Westbourne Ter. M.
  W2 . . . . 5E **59**
Westbourne Ter. Rd.
  W2 . . . . 4D **59**
Westbourne Ter. Rd. Bri.
  W2 . . . . 4E **59**
  (off Westbourne Ter. Rd.)
Westbridge Cl.
  W12 . . . . 3C **70**
Westbridge Rd.
  SW11 . . . . 4F **87**
WEST BROMPTON . . . 2E **87**
Westbrook Ho. *E2*. 2E **65**
  (off Victoria Pk. Sq.)
Westbrook Rd. SE3 . . . . 4D **97**
Westbury Rd. E7 . . . . . . 3D **55**
Westbury St. *SW8* 5E **89**
  (off Portslade Rd.)
Westbury Ter. E7 . . . . . . 3D **55**
W. Carriage Dr. W2 . . . 1A **74**
  (not continuous)
W. Central St.
  WC1 . . . . 2D **15** (5A **62**)
West Cen. Av. NW10 . . 3D **57**
Westcliffe Apartments
  W2. . . . . 4F **59**
Westcombe Ct. SE3 . . . 3B **96**
Westcombe Hill SE3 . . . 3C **96**
  SE10 . . . . 3C **96**
Westcombe Pk. Rd.
  SE3 . . . . 2A **96**
Westcote Rd. SW16 . . . 5E **117**
West Cotts. NW6 . . . . . . 2C **44**
Westcott Cl. N15 . . . . . . 1B **36**
Westcott Ho. E14 . . . . . . 1C **80**
Westcott Rd. SE17. . . . . 2D **91**
Westcroft NW2 . . . . 1A **44**
Westcroft Est. NW2 . . . . 1A **44**
Westcroft Sq. W6. . . . . . 5C **70**
Westcroft Way NW2 . . . 1A **44**
W. Cromwell Rd.
  SW5 . . . . 1B **86**
  W14 . . . . 1B **86**
W. Cross Route W10 . . 1F **71**
  W11. . . . . 1F **71**
  W12. . . . . 1F **71**
Westdean Av. SE12 . . . 1D **125**
Westdean Cl. SW18. . . . 4D **101**
Westdown Rd. E15. . . . . 1E **53**
  SE6 . . . . 5C **108**
West Dr. SW16. . . . . . . 4E **117**
WEST DULWICH 2F **119**
W. Eaton Pl. SW1. . . . . 5C **74**
W. Eaton Pl. M. *SW1* . . 5C **74**
  (off W. Eaton Pl.)
W. Ella Rd. NW10 . . . . . 4A **42**
W. End Av. E10 . . . . 1F **39**
W. End Ct. NW6 . . . . . . 4D **45**
W. End La. NW6 . . . . . . 2C **44**
  (not continuous)
W. End Quay W2 . . . . . 4F **59**
  (off Harbet Rd.)
Westerdale Rd. SE10. . . 1C **96**

Westerham *NW1* 5E **47**
  (off Bayham St.)
Westerham Rd. E10. . . . 2D **39**
Westerley Cres.
  SE26 . . . . 5B **122**
Western Av. NW11 . . . . 1F **29**
  W5 . . . . 5A **56**
Western Beach Apartments
  E16 . . . . 1C **82**
Western Ct. NW6 . . . . . 1B **58**
Western Gateway
  E16 . . . . 1C **82**
Western La. SW12 . . . . 5C **102**
Western M. W9 . . . . 3B **58**
Western Pl. SE16 . . . . . 3E **79**
Western Rd. E13 . . . . . 1E **69**
  E17 . . . . 1E **39**
  SW9 . . . . 1C **104**
Western Ter. *W6* 1C **84**
  (off Chiswick Mall)
Westferry Cir. E14. . . . . 2B **80**
Westferry Rd. E14 . . . . . 1B **80**
Westfield Cl. SW10 . . . . 3E **87**
Westfield Ct. *NW10* . . . 2F **57**
  (off Chamberlayne Rd.)
Westfield Ho. *SE16* . . . 5F **79**
  (off Rotherhithe New Rd.)
  SW18. . . . . 1D **115**
Westfields SW13 . . . . . 1B **98**
Westfields Av. SW13 . . . 1A **98**
Westfield St. SE18 . . . . 4F **83**
Westfield Way E1. . . . . . 2A **66**
West Gdn. Pl. W2 . . . . . 5A **60**
West Gdns. E1 . . . . 1D **79**
  SW17 . . . . 5A **116**
Westgate Cen., The
  E8 . . . . 5D **51**
  (off Bocking St.)
Westgate Ct. *SE12*. . . 1C **124**
  (off Burnt Ash Hill)
  SW9 . . . . 1C **104**
  (off Canterbury Cres.)
Westgate M. *W10* 3A **58**
  (off West Row)
Westgate St. E8. . . . . . . 5D **51**
Westgate Ter. SW10 . . . 2D **87**
Westgro. Ho. SE10 . . . . 4E **95**
Westgrove La. SE10. . . . 4E **95**
W. Halkin St.
  SW1. . . . . 5B **20** (4C **74**)
West Hallowes SE9 . . . 1F **125**
WEST HAM 5B **54**
W. Ham La. E15. . . . . . . 4F **53**
  (not continuous)
WEST HAMPSTEAD . . . 3D **45**
W. Hampstead M.
  NW6 . . . . 3D **45**
West Ham United FC. . . 1E **69**
W. Harding St.
  EC4 . . . . 2C **16** (5C **62**)
W. Heath Av. NW11 . . . 3C **30**
W. Heath Cl. NW3 . . . . . 5C **30**
W. Heath Ct. NW11 . . . . 3C **30**
W. Heath Dr. NW11 . . . . 3C **30**
W. Heath Gdns. NW3 . . 4C **30**
W. Heath Rd. NW3. . . . . 3C **30**
WEST HENDON 2C **28**
WEST HILL 4B **100**
West Hill SW15 . . . . . . 5F **99**

W. Hill Ct. N6. . . . . . . 5C **32**
W. Hill Pk. N6. . . . . . . 4B **32**
  (not continuous)
W. Hill Rd. SW18. . . . 4B **100**
Westhope Ho. E2 . . . . . 3C **64**
  (off Derbyshire St.)
Westhorne Av. SE9. . . . 4E **111**
SE12. . . . . 5C **110**
Westhorpe Rd. SW15. . 1E **90**
West Ho. Cl. SW19 . . . 1A **114**
W. India Av. E14. . . . . . 2C **80**
W. India Dock Rd.
E14 . . . . 1B **80**
  (not continuous)
W. India Ho. E14 . . . . . 1C **80**
  (off W. India Dock Rd.)
WEST KENSINGTON . . . 5B **72**
W. Kensington Ct.
W14 . . . . 1B **86**
  (off Edith Vs.)
W. Kensington Mans.
W14 . . . . 1B **86**
  (off Beaumont Cres.)
WEST KILBURN 2B **58**
Westlake SE16. . . . . . . 5E **79**
  (off Rotherhithe New Rd.)
Westland Pl.
N1 . . . . 1B **10** (2F **63**)
Westlands Ter.
SW12 . . . . 4E **103**
West La. SE16. . . . . . . 3D **79**
Westleigh Av. SW15 . . 3D **99**
Westleigh Ct. E11. . . . . 1C **40**
West Lodge E16. . . . . . 2C **82**
  (off Britannia Ga.)
West London Crematorium &
  Chapel NW10. . . . . . 3D **57**
Westmacott Ho. NW8 . . 3F **59**
  (off Hatton St.)
West Mall W8. . . . . 2C **72**
  (off Palace Gdns. Ter.)
Westmark Point
SW15 . . . . 1D **113**
  (off Norley Vale)
Westmead SW15. . . . . 4D **99**
W. Mersea Cl. E16. . . . 2D **83**
West M. SW1. . . . . 5D **75**
  (off W. Warwick Pl.)
Westmill Ct. N4 . . . . . . 4E **35**
WESTMINSTER
. . . . 4D **23** (3A **76**)
Westminster Abbey
. . . . 5D **23** (4F **75**)
Westminster Abbey
  Chapter House 5D **23**
  (in Westminster Abbey)
Westminster Abbey Mus.
. . . . 5D **23**
  (in Westminster Abbey)
Westminster Abbey Pyx
  Chamber 5D **23**
  (in Westminster Abbey)
Westminster Bri.
SW1. . . . . 4E **23** (3A **76**)
Westminster Bri. Rd.
SE1. . . . . 4F **23** (3B **76**)
Westminster Bus. Sq.
SE11 . . . . 1B **90**
Westminster Children's
  Sports Cen., The . . . 3F **59**

Westminster Ct.
E11 . . . . 1C **40**
  (off Cambridge Pk.)
SE16 . . . . 2F **79**
  (off King & Queen Wharf)
Westminster Gdns.
SW1 . . . . 5A **76**
  (off Marsham St.)
Westminster Hall 4D **23**
Westminster Ind. Est.
SE18 . . . . 4F **83**
Westminster Mans.
SW1 . . . . 5C **22**
  (off Gt. Smith St.)
Westminster Pal. Gdns.
SW1 . . . . 5B **22**
Westminster RC Cathedral
. . . . 4E **75**
Westminster Theatre. . 5F **21**
  (off Palace St.)
Westmoor St. SE7 . . . . 4E **83**
Westmore Ct.
SW15 . . . . 3A **100**
Westmoreland Ho.
E16 . . . . 2C **82**
  (off Gatcombe Rd.)
Westmoreland Pl.
SW1 . . . . 1D **89**
Westmoreland Rd.
SE17 . . . . 2F **91**
  (not continuous)
SW13 . . . . 4B **84**
Westmoreland St.
W1. . . . . 1C **12** (4C **60**)
Westmoreland Ter.
SW1 . . . . 1D **89**
Westmoreland Wlk.
SE17 . . . . 2F **91**
  (not continuous)
Westmorland Cl. E12. . 4F **41**
Westmorland Rd.
E17 . . . . 1C **38**
WEST NORWOOD 4E **119**
W. Norwood Crematorium
SE27 . . . . 3E **119**
Westonbirt St. SE15. . . 2B **92**
  (off Ebley Cl.)
Weston Ct. N4 . . . . 5E **35**
West One Ho. W1. . . . . 1F **13**
  (off Wells St.)
W. One Shop. Cen.
W1 . . . . 3C **12**
Weston Ho. E9 . . . . 5E **51**
  (off King Edward's Rd.)
NW6 . . . . 4A **44**
Weston London Heliport
. . . . 5F **87**
Weston Pk. N8 . . . . 1A **34**
Weston Ri.
WC1. . . . . . . 1A **8** (2B **62**)
Weston St.
SE1 . . . . 4C **26** (3A **78**)
  (not continuous)
Weston Wlk. E8. . . . . . 4D **51**
Westover Hill NW3 . . . 4C **30**
Westover Rd. SW18. . . 5E **101**
Westow Hill SE19 . . . . 5A **120**
West Pk. SE9 . . . . 2F **125**
West Parkside SE10. . . 3A **82**
West Pl. SW19. . . . . . . 5E **113**

West Point E14. . . . . . . 1B **80**
  (off Grenade St.)
SE1 . . . . 1C **92**
Westport Rd. E13. . . . . 3D **69**
Westport St. E1 . . . . . . 5F **65**
W. Poultry Av.
EC1 . . . . 1D **17** (4D **63**)
West Quarters W12 . . . 5C **56**
West Quay SW10 . . . . . 4E **87**
West Reservoir Cen. . . 3E **35**
West Ri. W2. . . . . 1A **74**
  (off St George's Flds.)
West Rd. E15. . . . . 5B **54**
SE1 . . . . 3A **24** (3B **76**)
SW3 . . . . 1B **88**
SW4 . . . . 3F **103**
West Row W10. . . . . . . 3A **58**
Westrow SW15. . . . . . . 4E **99**
W. Side Comn.
SW19 . . . . 5E **113**
Westside Ct. W9 . . . . . . 3C **58**
  (off Elgin Av.)
West Smithfield
EC1 . . . . 1D **17** (4D **63**)
West Sq.
SE11 . . . . 5D **25** (4D **77**)
West St. E2 . . . . 1D **65**
E11. . . . . 5A **40**
E17. . . . . 1D **39**
WC2 . . . . 3C **14** (5F **61**)
W. Tenter St.
E1. . . . . 3F **19** (5B **64**)
Westvale M. W3 . . . . . . 3A **70**
West Vw. Cl. NW10 . . . 2B **42**
Westview Cl. W10 . . . . 5E **57**
Westville Rd. W12 . . . . 3C **70**
W. Warwick Pl. SW1 . . 5E **75**
West Way NW10 . . . . . 5A **28**
Westway W2 . . . . 4B **58**
W10 . . . . 4B **58**
W11 . . . . 4B **58**
W12 . . . . 1B **70**
Westway Sports Cen.
. . . . 5F **57**
Westwell M. SW16 . . . 5A **118**
Westwell Rd. SW16. . . 5A **118**
Westwell Rd. App.
SW16 . . . . 5A **118**
Westwick Gdns. W14 . . 3F **71**
Westwood Bus. Cen.
NW10 . . . . 3A **56**
Westwood Gdns.
SW13 . . . . 1B **98**
Westwood Hill SE26 . . 5C **120**
Westwood Ho. W12 . . . 2E **71**
  (off Wood La.)
Westwood Pk.
SE23 . . . . 5D **107**
Westwood Pl. SE26 . . . 4C **120**
Westwood Rd. E16 . . . 2D **83**
SW13 . . . . 1B **98**
Wetherby Gdns. SW5. . 5E **73**
Wetherby Mans.
SW5 . . . . 1D **87**
  (off Earls Ct. Sq.)
Wetherby M. SW5 . . . . 1D **87**
Wetherby Pl. SW7 . . . . 5E **73**
Wetherden St. E17. . . . 2B **38**
Wetherell Rd. E9 . . . . . 5F **51**
Wevco Wharf SE15 . . . 2D **93**

Wevell Ho. *N6* *2C 32*
   (off Hillcrest)
Wexford Ho. *E1.* *4E 65*
   (off Sidney St.)
Wexford Rd. SW12 . . . . *5B 102*
Weybourne St.
  SW18 . . . . *2E 115*
Weybridge Ct. *SE16.* . . . *1D 93*
   (off Argyle Way)
Weybridge Point
  SW11 . . . . *5B 88*
Weydown Cl. SW19 . . . . *1A 104*
Weyhill Rd. E1. . . . . *5C 64*
Weyman Rd. SE3 . . . . . . *4E 97*
Weymouth Ct. *E2.* *1B 64*
   (off Weymouth Ter.)
Weymouth Ho. SW8. . . . . *3B 90*
   (off Bolney St.)
Weymouth M.
  W1 . . . . *5D 5 (4D 61)*
Weymouth St.
  W1 . . . . *1C 12 (4C 60)*
Weymouth Ter.
  E2 . . . . *1F 11 (1B 64)*
Weymouth Vs. *N4.* *4B 34*
   (off Moray Rd.)
Whadcoat St. N4 . . . . . . *4C 34*
Whalebone Ct. EC2 . . . . *2B 18*
Whalebone La. E15 . . . . . *4A 54*
Whales Yd. *E15* *4A 54*
   (off W. Ham La.)
Wharf, The
  EC3 . . . . *1E 27 (2B 78)*
Wharfdale Rd. N1 . . . . . . *1A 62*
Wharfedale Ct. E5 . . . . . *1F 51*
Wharfedale Ho. *NW6.* . . . *5D 45*
   (off Kilburn Va.)
Wharfedale St.
  SW10 . . . . *1D 87*
Wharfedale Yard *N1.* . . . *1A 62*
   (off Wharfedale Rd.)
Wharf Pl. E2. . . . . *5D 51*
Wharf Rd. N1 . . . *1F 9 (1E 63)*
   (Angel)
N1 . . . . *5F 47*
   (Camden Town)
Wharfside Rd. E16. . . . . . *4A 68*
Wharf St. E16. . . . . *4A 68*
Wharf Vw. Ct. *E14* *5E 67*
   (off Athol Sq.)
Wharton Cl. NW10 . . . . . *3A 42*
Wharton Cotts.
  WC1 . . . . *2B 8 (2C 62)*
Wharton Ho. *SE1* *5F 27*
   (off Maltby St.)
Wharton St.
  WC1 . . . . *2A 8 (2B 62)*
Whatcott's Yd. N16 . . . . *1A 50*
Whateley Rd. SE22 . . . . *3B 106*
Whatman Ho. *E14* *5B 66*
   (off Wallwood St.)
Whatman Rd. SE23 . . . *5F 107*
Wheatland Ho.
  SE22 . . . . *1A 106*
Wheatlands Rd.
  SW17 . . . . *3C 116*
Wheatley Ho. *SW15.* . . . *5C 98*
   (off Ellisfield Dr)
Wheatley St.
  W1 . . . . *1C 12 (4C 60)*

Wheat Sheaf Cl. E14 . . . *5D 81*
Wheatsheaf La.
  SW6 . . . . *3E 85*
  SW8 . . . . *3A 90*
   (not continuous)
Wheatsheaf Ter.
  SW6 . . . . *3B 86*
Wheatstone Rd.
  W10 . . . . *4A 58*
Wheeler Gdns. *N1* *5A 48*
   (off Outram Pl.)
Wheel Ho. *E14.* *1D 95*
   (off Burrells Wharf Sq.)
Wheelwright St. N7 . . . . *4B 48*
Wheler Ho. *E1* *4F 11*
   (off Quaker St.)
E1 . . . . *4F 11 (3B 64)*
Wheler St.
  E1 . . . . *4F 11 (3B 64)*
Whellock Rd. W4 . . . . . . *4A 70*
Whetstone Pk.
  WC2 . . . . *2F 15 (5B 62)*
Whetstone Rd. SE3 . . . . *5E 97*
Whewell Rd. N19 . . . . . . *4A 34*
Whidborne Bldgs.
  WC1 . . . . *2E 7*
   (off Whidborne St.)
Whidborne Cl. SE8. . . . . *5C 94*
Whidborne St.
  WC1 . . . . *2E 7 (2A 62)*
   (not continuous)
Whinfell Cl. SW16 . . . . . *5F 117*
Whinyates Rd. SE9. . . . . *1F 111*
Whipps Cross E17 . . . . . *1F 39*
Whipps Cross Rd.
  E11 . . . . *1F 39*
   (not continuous)
Whiskin St.
  EC1 . . . . *2D 9 (2D 63)*
Whistler M. SE15. . . . . . *3B 92*
Whistlers Av. SW11 . . . . *3F 87*
Whistler St. N5 . . . . *2D 49*
Whistler Twr. *SW10* *3E 87*
   (off Worlds End Est.)
Whistler Wlk. SW10. . . . . *3F 87*
Whiston Ho. *N1* *4D 49*
   (off Richmond Gro.)
Whiston Rd. E2 . . . . *1B 64*
Whitacre M. SE11 . . . . . *1C 90*
Whitbread Rd. SE4 . . . . *2A 108*
Whitburn Rd. SE13 . . . . *2D 109*
Whitby Ct. N7. . . . . *1A 48*
Whitby Ho. *NW8.* *5E 45*
   (off Boundary Rd.)
Whitby St. E1. . . *3F 11 (3B 64)*
   (not continuous)
Whitcher Cl. SE14 . . . . . *2A 94*
Whitcher Pl. NW1 . . . . . . *3E 47*
Whitchurch Ho. *W10* . . . *5F 57*
   (off Kingsdown Cl.)
Whitchurch Rd. W11 . . . *1F 71*
Whitcomb Ct. WC2. . . . . *5C 14*
Whitcomb St.
  WC2 . . . . *5C 14 (1F 75)*
Whiteadder Way E14 . . . *5D 81*
Whitear Wlk. E15 . . . . . . *3F 53*
Whitebeam Cl. SW9 . . . . *3B 90*
White Bear Pl. NW3 . . . . *1F 45*
White Bear Yd. EC1 . . . . *4B 8*
   (off Clerkenwell Rd.)
WHITECHAPEL *4C 64*

Whitechapel Art Gallery
  . . . . *5B 64*
   (off Whitechapel High St.)
Whitechapel High St.
  E1 . . . . *2F 19 (5B 64)*
Whitechapel Rd. E1. . . . . *4C 64*
Whitechapel Sports Cen.
  . . . . *4D 65*
White Chu. La. E1 . . . . . *5C 64*
White Chu. Pas.
  E1 . . . . *5C 64*
   (off White Chu. La.)
WHITE CITY *1D 71*
WHITE CITY *5E 57*
White City Cl. W12. . . . . . *1E 71*
White City Est. W12. . . . . *1D 71*
White City Rd. W12. . . . . *1E 71*
White Conduit St.
  N1 . . . . *1C 62*
Whitecross Pl.
  EC2 . . . . *5C 10 (4F 63)*
Whitecross St.
  EC1 . . . . *3A 10 (3E 63)*
Whitefield Av. NW2 . . . . . *3E 29*
Whitefield Cl.
  SW15 . . . . *4A 100*
Whitefoot La.
  BR1: Brom *4E 123*
Whitefoot Ter.
  BR1: Brom *3A 124*
Whitefriars Ct.
  EC4 . . . . *3C 16 (5C 62)*
Whitehall
  SW1 . . . . *2D 23 (2A 76)*
Whitehall Ct.
  SW1 . . . . *2D 23 (2A 76)*
   (not continuous)
Whitehall Gdns.
  SW1 . . . . *2D 23*
Whitehall Pk. N19 . . . . . . *3E 33*
Whitehall Pl. E7. . . . . *2C 54*
  SW1 . . . . *2D 23 (2A 76)*
Whitehall Theatre *1D 23*
   (off Whitehall)
White Hart Ct. EC2. . . . . *1D 19*
White Hart La. NW10. . . . *3B 42*
SW13 . . . . *1A 98*
White Hart St.
  EC4 . . . . *2E 17 (5D 63)*
SE11 . . . . *1C 90*
White Hart Yd.
  SE1 . . . . *2B 26 (2F 77)*
Whitehaven St. NW8 . . . . *3A 60*
Whitehead Cl.
  SW18 . . . . *5E 101*
Whiteheads Gro.
  SW3 . . . . *5A 74*
White Heather Ho.
  WC1 . . . . *2E 7*
   (off Cromer St.)
White Horse All. EC1. . . . *5D 9*
White Horse La. E1 . . . . . *3F 65*
Whitehorse M.
  SE1 . . . . *5C 24 (4C 76)*
White Horse Rd. E1. . . . . *4A 66*
   (not continuous)
White Horse St.
  W1 . . . . *2E 21 (2D 75)*
White Horse Yd.
  EC2. . . . . *2B 18 (5F 63)*

White Ho. SW4 . . . . . . 5F 103
  (off Clapham Pk. Est.)
  SW11 . . . . 4F 87
White Ho., The
  NW1 . . . . 3E 5
Whitehouse Est.
  E10 . . . . 1E 39
White Kennett St.
  E1 . . . . 2E 19 (5A 64)
Whitelands Ho. SW3 . . 1B 88
  (off Cheltenham Ter.)
Whitelegg Rd. E13 . . . . 1B 68
Whiteley Rd. SE19 . . . . 5F 119
Whiteleys Cen. W2 . . . . 5D 59
Whiteley's Cotts.
  W14 . . . . 5B 72
White Lion Ct. EC3 . . . . 3D 19
  SE15 . . . . 2E 93
White Lion Hill
  EC4 . . . . . . 4E 17 (1D 77)
White Lion St. N1 . . . . . 1C 62
White Lodge Cl. N2 . . . . 1F 31
White Lyon Ct. EC2 . . . . 5F 9
White Post La. E9 . . . . . 4B 52
White Post St. SE15 . . . 3E 93
White Rd. E15 . . . . 4A 54
White's Grounds
  SE1 . . . . . . 4E 27 (3A 78)
White's Grounds Est.
  SE1 . . . . 3E 27
White's Row
  E1 . . . . 1F 19 (4B 64)
Whites Sq. SW4 . . . . . . 2F 103
Whitestone La. NW3 . . . 5E 31
Whitestone Wlk.
  NW3 . . . . 5E 31
Whiteswan M. W4 . . . . 1A 84
Whitethorn Ho. E1 . . . . 2E 79
  (off Prusom St.)
Whitethorn Pas. E3 . . . 3C 66
  (off Whitethorn St.)
Whitethorn St. E3 . . . . 4C 66
White Tower. 5F 19
  (in Tower of London, The)
Whitfield Ho. NW8 . . . . 3A 60
  (off Salisbury St.)
Whitfield Pl. W1 . . . . . . 4F 5
Whitfield Rd. E6 . . . . . . 4E 55
  SE3 . . . . 4F 95
Whitfield St.
  W1 . . . . 4F 5 (3E 61)
Whitgift Ho. SE11 . . . . . 5B 76
Whitgift St. SE11 . . . . . 5B 76
Whitley Ho. SW1 . . . . . 2E 89
  (off Churchill Gdns.)
Whitlock Dr. SW19 . . . . 5A 100
Whitman Ho. E2 . . . . . . 2E 65
  (off Cornwall Av.)
Whitman Rd. E3 . . . . . . 3A 66
Whitmore Est. N1 . . . . . 5A 50
Whitmore Gdns.
  NW10 . . . . 1E 57
Whitmore Ho. N1 . . . . . 5A 50
  (off Whitmore Est.)
Whitmore Rd. N1 . . . . . 5A 50
Whitnell Way SW15 . . . 3E 99
Whitney Rd. E10 . . . . . . 2D 39
Whitstable Ho. W10 . . . 5F 57
  (off Silchester Rd.)
Whittaker Rd. E6 . . . . . 4E 55

Whittaker St. SW1 . . . . 5C 74
Whittaker Way SE1 . . . . 5C 78
Whitta Rd. E12 . . . . 1F 55
Whittell Gdns. SE26 . . . 3E 121
Whittingham Ct. W4 . . . 3A 84
Whittingstall Rd.
  SW6 . . . . 4B 86
Whittington Av.
  EC3 . . . . 3D 19 (5A 64)
Whittington Cl. N2 . . . . 1B 32
Whittle Cl. E17 . . . . 1A 38
Whittlesey St.
  SE1 . . . . 2B 24 (2C 76)
Whitton Wlk. E3 . . . . . . 2C 66
Whitwell Rd. E13 . . . . . 2C 68
Whitworth Ho.
  SE1 . . . . 5A 26 (4E 77)
Whitworth St. SE10 . . . 1A 96
Whorlton Rd. SE15 . . . . 1D 107
Whychcote Point
  NW2 . . . . 3E 29
Whyteville Rd. E7 . . . . . 3D 55
Whytlaw Ho. E3 . . . . . . 4B 66
  (off Baythorne St.)
Wickersley Rd.
  SW11 . . . . 5C 88
Wickers Oake SE19 . . . 4B 120
Wicker St. E1 . . . . 5D 65
Wickfield Ho. SE16 . . . . 3D 79
  (off Wilson Gro.)
Wickford Ho. E1 . . . . . . 3E 65
  (off Wickford St.)
Wickford St. E1 . . . . . . 3E 65
Wickham Cl. E1 . . . . . . 4E 65
Wickham Gdns.
  SE4 . . . . 1B 108
Wickham M. SE4 . . . . . 5B 94
Wickham Rd. SE4 . . . . . 2B 108
Wickham St. SE11 . . . . 1B 90
Wick La. E3 . . . . 5C 52
Wicklow Ho. N16 . . . . . 3B 36
Wicklow St.
  WC1 . . . . 1F 7 (2B 62)
Wick M. E9 . . . . 3A 52
Wick Rd. E9 . . . . 3F 51
Wicks Cl. SE9 . . . . 4F 125
Wick Sq. E9 . . . . 3B 52
Wicksteed Ho. SE1 . . . . 4E 77
Wickway Ct. SE15 . . . . 2B 92
  (off Cator St.)
Wickwood St. SE5 . . . . 5D 91
Widdenham Rd. N7 . . . . 1B 48
Widdin St. E15 . . . . 4A 54
Widegate St.
  E1 . . . . 1E 19 (4A 64)
Widford NW1 . . . . 3D 47
  (off Lewis St.)
Widford Ho. N1 . . . . . . 1D 63
  (off Colebrooke Rd.)
Widgeon Cl. E16 . . . . . 5D 69
Widley Rd. W9 . . . . 2C 58
Wigan Rd. E5 . . . . 3D 37
Wightman Rd. N4 . . . . . 1C 34
  N8 . . . . 1C 34
Wigmore Hall 2D 13
Wigmore Pl.
  W1 . . . . 2D 13 (5D 61)
Wigmore St.
  W1 . . . . 2C 12 (5C 60)

Wigram Ho. E14 . . . . . . 1D 81
  (off Wade's Pl.)
Wigram Rd. E11 . . . . . . 1E 41
Wigston Rd. E13 . . . . . . 3D 69
Wigton Pl. SE11 . . . . . . 1C 90
Wilberforce M. SW4 . . . 2F 103
Wilberforce Rd. N4 . . . . 4D 35
  (not continuous)
  NW9 . . . . 1C 28
Wilberforce Way
  SW19 . . . . 5F 113
Wilbraham Ho. SW8 . . . 3A 90
  (off Wandsworth Rd.)
Wilbraham Pl. SW1 . . . 5B 74
Wilby M. W11 . . . . 2B 72
Wilcox Cl. SW8 . . . . . . 3A 90
  (not continuous)
Wilcox Ho. E3 . . . . 4B 66
  (off Ackroyd Dr.)
Wilcox Pl.
  SW1 . . . . 5A 22 (4E 75)
Wilcox Rd. SW8 . . . . . . 3A 90
Wild Ct. WC2 . . . 3F 15 (5B 62)
  (not continuous)
Wildcroft Mnr. SW15 . . 5E 99
Wildcroft Rd. SW15 . . . 5E 99
Wilde Cl. E8 . . . . 5C 50
Wilde Ho. W2 . . . . 5D 59
  (off Gloucester Ter.)
Wilde Pl. SW18 . . . . . . 5F 101
Wilderness M. SW4 . . . 2D 103
Wilderton Rd. N16 . . . . 2A 36
Wildfell Rd. SE6 . . . . . . 5D 109
Wild Goose Dr. SE14 . . 4E 93
Wild Hatch NW11 . . . . 1C 30
Wild's Rents
  SE1 . . . . 5D 27 (4A 78)
Wild St. WC2 . . 3E 15 (5A 62)
Wildwood Cl. SE12 . . . 5B 110
Wildwood Gro. NW3 . . 3E 31
Wildwood Ri. NW11 . . . 3E 31
Wildwood Rd. NW11 . . 1D 31
Wilfred Ct. N15 . . . . . . 1F 35
  (off South Gro.)
Wilfred Owen Cl.
  SW19 . . . . 5E 115
Wilfred St.
  SW1 . . . . 5F 21 (4E 75)
Wilkes St. E1 . . . 5F 11 (4B 64)
Wilkie Ho. SW1 . . . . . . 1F 89
  (off Cureton St.)
Wilkins Ho. SW1 . . . . . 2D 89
  (off Churchill Gdns.)
Wilkinson Ct. SW17 . . . 4F 115
Wilkinson Ho. N1 . . . . . 1F 63
  (off Cranston Est.)
Wilkinson Rd. E16 . . . . 5E 69
Wilkinson St. SW8 . . . . 3B 90
Wilkin St. NW5 . . . . . . 3C 46
Wilkin St. M. NW5 . . . . 3D 47
Wilks Pl. N1 . . . . 1A 64
Willan Wall E16 . . . . . . 1B 82
Willard St. SW8 . . . . . . 1D 103
Will Crooks Gdns.
  SE9 . . . . 2E 111
WILLESDEN 3C 42
Willesden Belle Vue Cinema
  . . . . 3D 43
  (off Grange Rd.)
WILLESDEN GREEN . . . 3D 43

Willesden La. NW2 . . . . 3E 43
  NW6 . . . . 3F 43
Willesden Section Ho.
  NW2 . . . . 3F 43
      (off Willesden La.)
Willesden Sports Cen.
  . . . . 5D 43
Willesden Sports Stadium
  . . . . 5D 43
Willes Rd. NW5 . . . . 3D 47
Willett Ho. E13 . . . . 1D 69
    (off Queens Rd. W.)
William IV St.
  WC2 . . . . . . 5D 15 (1A 76)
William Banfield Ho.
  SW6 . . . . 5B 86
     (off Munster Rd.)
William Blake Ho.
  SW11 . . . . 4A 88
William Bonney Est.
  SW4 . . . . 2F 103
William Caslon Ho.
  E2 . . . . 1D 65
     (off Patriot Sq.)
William Channing Ho.
  E2 . . . . 2D 65
    (off Canrobert St.)
William Cl. SE13 . . . . . . 1E 109
William Cobbett Ho.
  W8 . . . . 4D 73
    (off Scarsdale Pl.)
William Dromey Ct.
  NW6 . . . . 4B 44
William Dunbar Ho.
  NW6 . . . . 1B 58
     (off Albert Rd.)
William Dyce M.
  SW16 . . . . 4F 117
William Ellis Way
  SE16 . . . . 4C 78
    (off St James's Rd.)
William Evans Ho.
  SE8 . . . . 5F 79
     (off Bush Rd.)
William Farm La.
  SW15 . . . . 1D 99
William Fenn Ho.
  E2 . . . . 2C 64
    (off Shipton Rd.)
William Gdns. SW15 . . 3D 99
William Gibbs Ct.
  SW1 . . . . 5B 22
    (off Old Pye St.)
William Gunn Ho.
  NW3 . . . . 2A 46
William Guy Gdns.
  E3 . . . . 2D 67
William Harvey Ho.
  SW19 . . . . 1A 114
    (off Whitlock Dr.)
William Henry Wlk.
  SW8 . . . . 2F 89
William Hunt Mans.
  SW13 . . . . 2E 85
William Margrie Cl.
  SE15 . . . . 5C 92
William M.
  SW1 . . . . . . 4A 20 (3B 74)
William Morley Cl.
  E6 . . . . 5F 55

William Morris Ho.
  W6 . . . . 2F 85
William Morris Way
  SW6 . . . . 1E 101
William Paton Ho.
  E16 . . . . 5D 69
William Pl. E3 . . . . 1B 66
William Rathbone Ho.
  E2 . . . . 2D 65
    (off Florida St.)
William Rd.
  NW1 . . . . . . 2F 5 (2E 61)
William Rushbrooke Ho.
  SE16 . . . . 5C 78
     (off Rouel Rd.)
William Saville Ho.
  NW6 . . . . 1B 58
    (off Denmark Rd.)
William's Bldgs. E2 . . 3E 65
Williams Cl. N8 . . . . . . 1F 33
  SW6 . . . . 3A 86
Williams Ho. E9 . . . . . . 5D 51
    (off King Edward's Rd.)
  NW2 . . . . 5E 29
     (off Stoll Cl.)
Williamson Cl. SE10 . . 1B 96
Williamson Ct.
  SE17 . . . . 1E 91
Williamson Rd. N4 . . . 1D 35
Williamson St. N7 . . . . 1A 48
William Sq. SE16 . . . . . 1A 80
    (off Sovereign Cres.)
William St. E10 . . . . . . 1D 39
  SW1 . . . . . . 4A 20 (3B 74)
William White Ct.
  E13 . . . . 5E 55
     (off Green St.)
William Wood Ho.
  SE26 . . . . 3E 121
    (off Shrublands Cl.)
Willifield Way NW11 . . 1C 30
Willingham Cl. NW5 . . 2E 47
Willingham Ter. NW5 . . 2E 47
Willington Ct. E5 . . . . . 5A 38
Willington Rd. SW9 . . 1A 104
Willis Ho. E14 . . . . 1D 81
     (off Hale St.)
Willis Rd. E15 . . . . 1B 68
Willis St. E14 . . . . 5D 67
Willoughby Highwalk
  EC2 . . . . 1B 18
     (off Moor La.)
Willoughby Ho. E1 . . . 2D 79
    (off Reardon Path)
  EC2 . . . . 5B 10
    (off W. India Av.)
Willoughby Rd. NW3 . . 1F 45
Willoughbys, The
  SW14 . . . . 1A 98
Willoughby St. WC1 . . 1D 15
Willoughby Way SE7 . . 5D 83
Willow Av. SW13 . . . . . 5B 84
Willow Bank SW6 . . . . 1A 98
Willow Bri. Rd. N1 . . . . 3E 49
    (not continuous)
Willowbrook Est.
  SE15 . . . . 3C 92
Willow Brook Rd.
  SE15 . . . . 3B 92

Willow Bus. Pk.
  SE26 . . . . 3E 121
Willow Cl. SE6 . . . . . . 1B 124
Willow Ct. E11 . . . . 4A 40
     (off Trinity Cl.)
  EC2 . . . . 3D 11
  NW6 . . . . 4A 44
  W4 . . . . 3A 84
   (off Corney Reach Way)
  W9 . . . . 4C 58
    (off Admiral Wlk.)
Willowdene N6 . . . . 2B 32
  SE15 . . . . 3D 93
Willow Gro. E13 . . . . . 1C 68
Willow Ho. W10 . . . . . . 3F 57
     (off Maple Wlk.)
Willow Lodge SW6 . . . 4F 85
Willow Pl. SW1 . . . . . . 5E 75
Willow Rd. NW3 . . . . . . 1F 45
Willows Ter. NW10 . . . 1B 56
    (off Rucklidge Av.)
Willow St.
  EC2 . . . . . . 3D 11 (3A 64)
Willow Tree Cl. E3 . . . 5A 52
  SW18 . . . . 1D 115
Willow Va. W12 . . . . . . 2C 70
Willow Wlk. SE1 . . . . . . 4A 78
Willow Way SE26 . . . . 3E 121
  W11 . . . . 1F 71
Willsbridge Ct.
  SE15 . . . . 2A 92
Wilman Gro. E8 . . . . . . 4C 50
Wilmcote Ho. W2 . . . . . 4D 59
   (off Woodchester Sq.)
Wilment Ct. NW2 . . . . . 5E 29
Wilmer Gdns. N1 . . . . 5A 50
    (not continuous)
Wilmer Lea Cl. E15 . . 4E 53
Wilmer Pl. N16 . . . . . . 4B 36
Wilmers Ct. NW10 . . . 5A 42
    (off Stracey Rd.)
Wilmington Sq.
  WC1 . . . . . . 2B 8 (2C 62)
     (not continuous)
Wilmington St.
  WC1 . . . . . . 2B 8 (2C 62)
Wilmot Cl. SE15 . . . . . 3C 92
Wilmot Pl. NW1 . . . . . . 4E 47
Wilmot Rd. E10 . . . . . . 4D 39
Wilmot St. E2 . . . . 3D 65
Wilna Rd. SW18 . . . . . . 5E 101
Wilsham St. W11 . . . . . 2F 71
Wilshaw Ho. SE8 . . . . . 3C 94
Wilshaw St. SE14 . . . . 4C 94
Wilson Gro. SE16 . . . . 3D 79
Wilson Rd. E6 . . . . 2F 69
  SE5 . . . . 4A 92
Wilson's Pl. E14 . . . . . 5B 66
Wilson's Rd. W6 . . . . . . 1F 85
Wilson St.
  EC2 . . . . . . 5C 10 (4F 63)
Wilson Wlk. W4 . . . . . . 5B 70
    (off Prebend Gdns.)
Wiltern Ct. NW2 . . . . . . 3A 44
Wilton Av. W4 . . . . 1A 84
Wilton Cl. E1 . . . . 5D 65
     (off Cavell St.)
Wilton Cres.
  SW1 . . . . . . 4B 20 (3C 74)
Wilton Est. E8 . . . . 3C 50

Wilton M. E8 . . . . 3D **51**
  SW1 . . . . 5C **20** (4C **74**)
Wilton Pl.
  SW1 . . . . 4B **20** (3C **74**)
Wilton Rd. SW1 . . . . . . 4D **75**
Wilton Row
  SW1 . . . . 4B **20** (3C **74**)
Wilton Sq. N1 . . . . 5F **49**
Wilton St.
  SW1 . . . . 5D **21** (4D **75**)
Wilton Ter.
  SW1 . . . . 5B **20** (4C **74**)
Wilton Vs. N1 . . . . .5F **49**
    (off Wilton Sq.)
Wilton Way E8 . . . . 3C **50**
Wiltshire Cl. SW3 . . . . 5B **74**
Wiltshire Ct. N4 . . . . . . 3B **34**
    (off Marquis Rd.)
Wiltshire Gdns. N4 . . . 1E **35**
Wiltshire Rd. SW9 . . . 1C **104**
Wiltshire Row N1 . . . . 5F **49**
Wimbart Rd. SW2 . . . 5B **104**
WIMBLEDON 5B **114**
Wimbledon (All England Lawn
  Tennis & Croquet Club)
  . . . . 4A **114**
Wimbledon Common
  . . . . 4C **112**
Wimbledon Greyhound &
  Speedway Stadium
  . . . . 4E **115**
Wimbledon Hill Rd.
  SW19 . . . . 5A **114**
Wimbledon Lawn Tennis Mus.
  . . . . 4A **114**
Wimbledon Mus. of
  Local History 5A **114**
WIMBLEDON PARK . 3C **114**
Wimbledon Pk. Ct.
  SW19 . . . . 1B **114**
Wimbledon Pk. Rd.
  SW18 . . . . 2A **114**
  SW19 . . . . 2A **114**
Wimbledon Pk. Side
  SW19 . . . . 3F **113**
Wimbledon Rd.
  SW17 . . . . 4E **115**
Wimbledon Stadium Bus. Cen.
  SW17 . . . . 3D **115**
Wimbledon Windmill Mus.
  . . . . 2D **113**
Wimbolt St. E2 . . . . 2C **64**
Wimborne Cl. SE12 . . 3B **110**
Wimborne Ct.
  SW12 . . . . 3E **117**
Wimborne Ho. E16 . . . 1B **82**
    (off Victoria Dock Rd.)
  NW1 . . . . 3A **60**
    (off Harewood Av.)
  SW8 . . . . 3B **90**
    (off Dorset Rd.)
  SW12 . . . . 3E **117**
Wimbourne Ct. N1 . . . 1F **63**
    (off Wimbourne St.)
Wimbourne St. N1 . . . 1F **63**
Wimpole M.
  W1 . . . . 5D **5** (4D **61**)
Wimpole St.
  W1 . . . . 1D **13** (4D **61**)
Winans Wlk. SW9 . . . . . 5C **90**

Winant Ho. E14 . . . . . . 1D **81**
    (off Simpson's Rd.)
Wincanton Rd.
  SW18 . . . . 5B **100**
Winchcomb Gdns.
  SE9 . . . . 1F **111**
Winchelsea Cl.
  SW15 . . . . 3F **99**
Winchelsea Ho.
  SE16 . . . . 3E **79**
    (off Swan Rd.)
Winchelsea Rd. E7 . . . 5C **40**
  NW10 . . . . 5A **42**
Winchendon Rd.
  SW6 . . . . 4B **86**
Winchester Av. NW6 . . 5A **44**
Winchester Cl.
  SE17 . . . . 5D **77**
Winchester Ct. W8 . . . 3C **72**
    (off Vicarage Ga.)
  SW3 . . . . 2F **87**
    (off Beaufort St.)
  SW9 . . . . 3C **90**
  W2 . . . . 5E **59**
    (off Hallfield Est.)
Winchester Pl. E8 . . . . 2B **50**
  N6 . . . . 3D **33**
Winchester Rd. N6 . . . 2D **33**
  NW3 . . . . 4F **45**
Winchester Sq. SE1 . . 1B **26**
Winchester St. SW1 . . 1D **89**
Winchester Wlk.
  SE1 . . . . 1B **26** (2F **77**)
Winchester Wharf
  SE1 . . . . 1B **26**
    (off Clink St.)
Winchfield Ho.
  SW15 . . . . 4B **98**
Winchfield Rd.
  SE26 . . . . 5A **122**
Winch Ho. E14 . . . . . . 4D **81**
    (off Tiller Rd.)
  SW10 . . . . 3E **87**
    (off King's Rd.)
Winchilsea Ho. NW8 . . 2F **59**
    (off St John's Wood Rd.)
Wincott St. SE11 . . . . . 5C **76**
Windermere NW1 . . . . . 2E **5**
    (off Albany St.)
Windermere Av.
  NW6 . . . . 5A **44**
Windermere Ct.
  SW13 . . . . 2B **84**
Windermere Ho. E3 . . . 3B **66**
Windermere Point
  SE15 . . . . 3E **93**
    (off Old Kent Rd.)
Windermere Rd. N19 . . 4E **33**
  SW15 . . . . 4A **112**
Winders Rd. SW11 . . . 5A **88**
    (not continuous)
Windfield Cl. SE26 . . . 4F **121**
Winding, The W2 . . . . . 4F **59**
    (off Nth. Wharf Rd.)
Windlass Pl. SE8 . . . . . 5A **80**
Windlesham Gro.
  SW19 . . . . 1F **113**
Windley Cl. SE23 . . . . 2E **121**

Windmill WC1 . . . . 5F **7**
    (off New Nth. St.)
Windmill Cl. SE1 . . . . . 5C **78**
    (off Beatrice Rd.)
  SE13 . . . . 5E **95**
Windmill Ct. NW2 . . . . 3A **44**
Windmill Dr. NW2 . . . . 5A **30**
  SW4 . . . . 3D **103**
Windmill Hill NW3 . . . . 5E **31**
Windmill Ho. E14 . . . . . 5C **80**
Windmill La. E15 . . . . . 3F **53**
Windmill M. W4 . . . . . . 5A **70**
Windmill Pas. W4 . . . . 5A **70**
Windmill Rd. SW18 . . . 4F **101**
  SW19 . . . . 2D **113**
  W4 . . . . 5A **70**
Windmill Row SE11 . . 1C **90**
Windmill St.
  W1 . . . . 1B **14** (4F **61**)
    (not continuous)
Windmill Wlk.
  SE1 . . . . . . 2C **24** (2C **76**)
Windrose Cl. SE16 . . . 3F **79**
Windrush Cl. SW11 . . . 2F **101**
Windrush La. SE23 . . . 3F **121**
Windsock Cl. SE16 . . . 5B **80**
Windsor Cen., The
  N1 . . . . 5D **49**
    (off Windsor St.)
Windsor Cl. SE27 . . . . 4E **119**
Windsor Cotts. SE14 . . 3B **94**
    (off Amersham Rd.)
Windsor Ct. NW2 . . . . . 3A **44**
    (off Chatsworth Rd.)
  NW3 . . . . 1C **44**
  NW11 . . . . 1A **30**
    (off Golders Grn. Rd.)
  SE16 . . . . 1F **79**
    (off King & Queen Wharf)
  SW3 . . . . 1A **88**
    (off Jubilee Pl.)
  SW11 . . . . 5F **87**
  W2 . . . . 1D **73**
    (off Moscow Rd.)
  W10 . . . . 5F **57**
    (off Bramley Rd.)
Windsor Gdns. W9 . . . 4C **58**
Windsor Gro. SE27 . . . 4E **119**
Windsor Hall E16 . . . . 2D **83**
    (off Wesley Av.)
Windsor Ho. E2 . . . . . . 2F **65**
    (off Knottisford St.)
  N1 . . . . 1E **63**
  NW1 . . . . 1E **5**
Windsor M. SE6 . . . . . 1E **123**
  SE23 . . . . 1A **122**
  SW18 . . . . 5E **101**
    (off Wilna Rd.)
Windsor Pl. SW1 . . . . . 4E **75**
Windsor Rd. E7 . . . . . . 2D **55**
  E10 . . . . 4D **39**
  E11 . . . . 3C **40**
  N7 . . . . 5A **34**
  NW2 . . . . 3D **43**
Windsor St. N1 . . . . . . 5D **49**
Windsor Ter.
  N1 . . . . 1A **10** (2E **63**)
Windsor Wlk. SE5 . . . . 5F **91**
Windsor Way W14 . . . . 5F **71**
Windsor Wharf E9 . . . . 3C **52**

Windspoint Dr. SE15 . . . 2D **93**
Windus Rd. N16 . . . . 3B **36**
Windus Wlk. N16 . . . . . 3B **36**
Windy Ridge Cl.
  SW19 . . . . 5F **113**
  (not continuous)
Wine Cl. E1 . . . . 1E **79**
Wine Office Ct. EC4 . . . . 5C **62**
Winford Ct. SE15 . . . . . 1D **93**
Winford Ho. E3 . . . . 4B **52**
Winforton St. SE10 . . . . 4E **95**
Winfrith Rd. SW18 . . . . 5E **101**
Wingate Rd. W6 . . . . 4D **71**
Wingfield Ct. E14 . . . . . . 1F **81**
  (off John Smith M.)
Wingfield Ho. E2 . . . . 2F **11**
  (off Virginia Rd.)
  NW6 . . . . 1D **59**
  (off Tollgate Gdns.)
Wingfield M. SE15 . . . . 1C **106**
Wingfield Rd. E15 . . . . . 1A **54**
  E17 . . . . 1D **39**
Wingfield St. SE15 . . . . 1C **106**
Wingford Rd. SW2 . . . . 4A **104**
Wingmore Rd. SE24 . . . 1E **105**
Wingrad Ho. E1 . . . . 4E **65**
  (off Jubilee St.)
Wingrave SE17 . . . . 5F **77**
  (not continuous)
Wingrave Rd. W6 . . . . . 2E **85**
Wingreen NW8 . . . . 5D **45**
  (off Abbey Rd.)
Wingrove Rd. SE6 . . . . 2A **124**
Winicotte Ho. W2 . . . . . 4F **59**
  (off Paddington Grn.)
Winifred Ter. E13 . . . . . 1C **68**
  (off Upper Rd.)
Winkfield Rd. E13 . . . . . 1D **69**
Winkley St. E2 . . . . 1D **65**
Winkworth Cotts. E1 . . . 3E **65**
  (off Cephas St.)
Winlaton Rd.
  BR1: Brom 4F **123**
Winnett St.
  W1 . . . . 4B **14** (1F **75**)
Winnington Cl. N2 . . . . . 1F **31**
Winnington Ho. SE5 . . . . 3E **91**
  (off Wyndham Est.)
Winnington Rd. N2 . . . . . 1F **31**
Winn Rd. SE12 . . . . 1C **124**
Winscombe St. N19 . . . . 4D **33**
Winsford Rd. SE6 . . . . . 3B **122**
Winsham Gro.
  SW11 . . . . 3C **102**
Winsham Ho. NW1 . . . . . 1C **6**
  (off Churchway)
Winslade Rd. SW2 . . . . 3A **104**
Winslade Way SE6 . . . . 5D **109**
Winsland M. W2 . . . . . . 5F **59**
Winsland St. W2 . . . . . . 5F **59**
Winsley St.
  W1 . . . . 2A **14** (5E **61**)
Winslow SE17 . . . . 1A **92**
Winslow Cl. NW10 . . . . 5A **28**
Winslow Rd. W6 . . . . . . 2E **85**
Winstanley Est.
  SW11 . . . . 1F **101**
Winstanley Rd.
  SW11 . . . . 1F **101**
  (not continuous)

Winston Av. NW9 . . . . . . 2A **28**
Winston Ho. WC1 . . . . 3C **6**
Winston Rd. N16 . . . . . . 1F **49**
Winterbourne Ho.
  W11 . . . . 1A **72**
  (off Portland Rd.)
Winterbourne Rd.
  SE6 . . . . 1B **122**
Winterbrook Rd.
  SE24 . . . . 4E **105**
Winterfold Cl.
  SW19 . . . . 2A **114**
Wintergreen Cl. E6 . . . . 4F **69**
Winterleys NW6 . . . . . . 1B **58**
  (off Denmark Rd.)
Winter Lodge SE16 . . . . 1C **92**
  (off Fern Wlk.)
Winterslow Ho. SE5 . . . . 5E **91**
  (off Flaxman Rd.)
Winterstoke Rd.
  SE6 . . . . 1B **122**
Winterton Ho. E1 . . . . . . 5E **65**
  (off Deancross St.)
Winterton Pl.
  SW10 . . . . 2E **87**
Winterwell Rd.
  SW2 . . . . 3A **104**
Winthorpe Rd.
  SW15 . . . . 2A **100**
Winthrop Ho. W12 . . . . . 1D **71**
  (off White City Est.)
Winthrop St. E1 . . . . . . 4D **65**
Winton Way SW16 . . . . 5C **118**
Wirrall Ho. SE26 . . . . . 3C **120**
Wisbech N4 . . . . 3B **34**
  (off Lorne Rd.)
Wisden Ho. SW8 . . . . . 2B **90**
Wiseman Rd. E10 . . . . . 4C **38**
Wise Rd. E15 . . . . 5F **53**
Wiseton Rd. SW17 . . . . 1A **116**
Wishart Rd. SE3 . . . . . . 5F **97**
Wisley Ho. SW1 . . . . . . 1F **89**
  (off Rampayne St.)
Wisley Rd. SW11 . . . . . 3C **102**
Wisteria Rd. SE13 . . . . 2F **109**
Witanhurst La. N6 . . . . . 3C **32**
Witan St. E2 . . . . 2D **65**
Witham Cl. E10 . . . . 5D **39**
  SW17 . . . . 3B **116**
Witherington Rd. N5 . . . 2C **48**
Withers Pl.
  EC1 . . . . 3A **10** (3E **63**)
Withycombe Rd.
  SW19 . . . . 5F **99**
Withy Ho. E1 . . . . 3F **65**
  (off Globe Rd.)
Witley Ct. WC1 . . . . 4D **7**
Witley Ho. SW2 . . . . . . 5A **104**
Witley Point SW15 . . . . 1D **113**
  (off Wanborough Dr.)
Witley Rd. N19 . . . . 4E **33**
Witney Path SE23 . . . . 3F **121**
Wittersham Rd.
  BR1: Brom 5B **124**
Wivenhoe Cl. SE15 . . . 1D **107**
Wiverton Rd. SE26 . . . . 5E **121**
Wixom Rd. SE3 . . . . . . 2E **111**
Wix's La. SW4 . . . . 1D **103**
Woburn Cl. SE16 . . . . . 1D **93**
  (off Masters Dr.)

Woburn M.
  WC1 . . . . 4C **6** (3F **61**)
Woburn Pl.
  WC1 . . . . 4D **7** (3A **62**)
Woburn Sq.
  WC1 . . . . 4C **6** (3F **61**)
Woburn Wlk.
  WC1 . . . . 2C **6** (2F **61**)
Wodeham Gdns. E1 . . . . 4C **64**
Wodehouse Av. SE5 . . . 4B **92**
Woking Cl. SW15 . . . . . 2B **98**
Wolcot Ho. NW1 . . . . 1A **6**
  (off Aldenham St.)
Wolfe Cres. SE7 . . . . . . 1F **97**
  SE16 . . . . 3F **79**
Wolfe Ho. W12 . . . . 1D **71**
  (off White City Est.)
Wolffe Gdns. E15 . . . . . 3B **54**
Wolfington Rd.
  SE27 . . . . 4D **119**
Wolfram Cl. SE13 . . . . 3A **110**
Wolftencroft Cl.
  SW11 . . . . 1A **102**
Wollaston Cl. SE1 . . . . . 5E **77**
Wollett Ct. NW1 . . . . . . 4E **47**
  (off St Pancras Way)
Wolseley Av. SW19 . . . 2C **114**
Wolseley Rd. E7 . . . . . . 4D **55**
  N8 . . . . 1F **33**
Wolseley St. SE1 . . . . . 3C **78**
Wolsey Cl. NW6 . . . . . . 4E **45**
  SW11 . . . . 4A **88**
  (off Westbridge Rd.)
Wolsey M. NW5 . . . . 3E **47**
Wolsey Rd. N1 . . . . 2F **49**
Wolsey St. E1 . . . . 4E **65**
Wolverley St. E2 . . . . . . 2D **65**
Wolverton SE17 . . . . . . 1A **92**
Wolverton Gdns. W6 . . . 5F **71**
Womersley Rd. N8 . . . . 1B **34**
Wontner Cl. N1 . . . . 4E **49**
Wontner Rd. SW17 . . . 2B **116**
Woodall Cl. E14 . . . . . . 1D **81**
Woodbank Rd.
  BR1: Brom 3B **124**
Woodbastwick Rd.
  SE26 . . . . 5F **121**
Woodberry Down N4 . . . 2E **35**
Woodberry Down Est.
  N4 . . . . 3E **35**
  (Woodberry Down)
  N4 . . . . 2E **35**
  (Woodberry Gro.)
Woodberry Gro. N4 . . . . 2E **35**
Woodbine Pl. E11 . . . . . 1C **40**
Woodbine Ter. E9 . . . . . 3E **51**
Woodborough Rd.
  SW15 . . . . 2D **99**
Woodbourne Av.
  SW16 . . . . 3F **117**
Woodbourne Cl.
  SW16 . . . . 3A **118**
Woodbridge Cl. N7 . . . . 4B **34**
  NW2 . . . . 5C **28**
Woodbridge Ho. E11 . . . 3B **40**
Woodbridge St.
  EC1 . . . . 3D **9** (3D **63**)
  (not continuous)
Woodburn Cl. NW4 . . . . 1F **29**
Woodbury Ho. SE26 . . . 3C **120**

Woodbury St. SW17 . . . 5A 116
Woodchester Sq. W2 . . 4D 59
Woodchurch Rd.
  NW6 . . . . 4C 44
Wood Cl. E2 . . . . 3C 64
  NW9 . . . . 2A 28
Woodcock Ho. E14 . . . . 4C 66
  (off Burgess St.)
Woodcocks E16 . . . . . . 4E 69
Woodcombe Cres.
  SE23 . . . . 1E 121
Woodcote Ho. SE8 . . . . 2B 94
  (off Prince St.)
Woodcote Pl. SE27 . . . 5D 119
Woodcote Rd. E11 . . . . 2C 40
Woodcote's. SE27 . . . 5E 119
  (off Woodcote Pl.)
Woodcroft. SE8 . . . . . . 5A 80
Wood Dene SE15 . . . . . 4D 93
  (off Queen's Rd.)
Wood Dr. BR7: Chst . . . 5F 125
Woodend SE19 . . . . . . 5E 119
Wooder Gdns. E7 . . . . . 1C 54
Woodfall Rd. N4 . . . . . . 4C 34
Woodfall St. SW3 . . . . . 1B 88
Woodfarrs SE5 . . . . . . 2F 105
Wood Fld. NW3 . . . . . . 2B 46
Woodfield Av. SW16 . . . 3F 117
Woodfield Gro.
  SW16 . . . . 3F 117
Woodfield Ho. SE23 . . . 3F 121
  (off Dacres Rd.)
Woodfield La.
  SW16 . . . . 3F 117
Woodfield Pl. W9 . . . . . 3B 58
Woodfield Rd. W9 . . . . . 4B 58
Woodford Ct. W12 . . . . 3F 71
  (off Shepherd's Bush Grn.)
Woodford Rd. E7 . . . . . 5D 41
Woodger Rd. W12 . . . . . 3E 71
Woodget Cl. E6 . . . . . . 5F 69
Woodgrange Rd. E7 . . . 2D 55
Woodhall NW1 . . . . . . 2F 5
  (off Robert St.)
Woodhall Av. SE21 . . . . 3B 120
Woodhall Dr. SE21 . . . . 3B 120
Woodhall Ho. SW18 . . . 4F 101
Woodham Rd. SE6 . . . . 3E 123
Woodhatch Cl. E6 . . . . 4F 69
Woodheyes Rd.
  NW10 . . . . 2A 42
Woodhouse Gro. E12 . . 3F 55
Woodhouse Rd. E11 . . . 5B 40
Woodland Cl. SE19 . . . . 5A 120
Woodland Ct. E11 . . . . 1C 40
  (off New Wanstead)
Woodland Cres.
  SE10 . . . . 2A 96
  SE16 . . . . 3F 79
Woodland Gro. SE10 . . 1A 96
Woodland Hill SE19 . . . 5A 120
Woodland M. SW16 . . . 3A 118
Woodland Rd. SE19 . . . 5A 120
Woodlands NW11 . . . . 1A 30
Woodlands, The N5 . . . 1E 49
  SE13 . . . . 5F 109
Woodlands Art Gallery
  . . . . 2C 96
Woodlands Av. E11 . . . . 3D 41
Woodlands Cl. NW11 . . 1A 30

Woodlands Ct. NW10 . . 5F 43
  (off Wrentham Av.)
  SE23 . . . . 5D 107
Woodlands Ga.
  SW15 . . . . 3B 100
  (off Woodlands Way)
Woodlands Hgts.
  SE3 . . . . 2B 96
  (off Vanburgh Hill)
Woodlands Pk. Rd.
  N15 . . . . 1D 35
  SE10 . . . . 2A 96
  (not continuous)
Woodlands Rd. E11 . . . 4A 40
  SW13 . . . . 1B 98
Woodlands St. SE13 . . . 5F 109
Woodland St. E8 . . . . . 3B 50
Woodlands Way
  SW15 . . . . 3B 100
Woodland Ter. SE7 . . . . 5F 83
Woodland Wlk.
  BR1: Brom 4F 123
  (not continuous)
  NW3 . . . . 2A 46
  SE10 . . . . 1A 96
Wood La. N6 . . . . 1D 33
  NW9 . . . . 2A 28
  W12 . . . . 5E 57
Woodlawn Cl.
  SW15 . . . . 3B 100
Woodlawn Rd. SW6 . . . 3F 85
Woodlea Rd. N16 . . . . . 5A 36
Woodleigh Gdns.
  SW16 . . . . 3A 118
Woodmans Gro.
  NW10 . . . . 2B 42
Woodman's M.
  W12 . . . . 4D 57
Woodmere Cl.
  SW11 . . . . 1C 102
Woodnook Rd.
  SW16 . . . . 5D 117
Woodpecker M.
  SE13 . . . . 2F 109
  (off Freshfield Cl.)
Woodpecker Rd.
  SE14 . . . . 2A 94
Wood Point E16 . . . . . . 4C 68
  (off Fife Rd.)
Woodquest Av.
  SE24 . . . . 3E 105
Woodriffe Rd. E11 . . . . 2F 39
Woodrush Cl. SE14 . . . 3A 94
Wood's Bldgs. E1 . . . . 4D 65
  (off Winthrop St.)
Woodseer St. E1 . . . . . 4B 64
Woodsford SE17 . . . . . 1F 91
  (off Portland St.)
Woodside Sq. W14 . . . 3A 72
Woodside SW19 . . . . . 5B 114
Woodside Av. N6 . . . . . 1B 32
Woodside Ct. E12 . . . . 3E 41
Woodside Ho.
  SW19 . . . . 5B 114
Woodside M. SE22 . . . 3B 106
Woodside Rd. E13 . . . . 3E 69
Woods M.
  W1 . . . . 4B 12 (1C 74)
Woodsome Rd. NW5 . . . 5C 32

Woods Pl.
  SE1 . . . . 5E 27 (4A 78)
Woodspring Rd.
  SW19 . . . . 2A 114
Woods Rd. SE15 . . . . . 4D 93
Woodstock Av. NW11 . . 2A 30
Woodstock Ct. SE11 . . . 1B 90
  SE12 . . . . 4C 110
Woodstock Gro. W12 . . 3F 71
Woodstock M. W1 . . . . 1C 12
Woodstock Rd. E7 . . . . 4E 55
  N4 . . . . 3C 34
  NW11 . . . . 2B 30
  W4 . . . . 5A 70
Woodstock St.
  W1 . . . . 3D 13 (5D 61)
Woodstock Ter. E14 . . . 1D 81
Wood St. E16 . . . . 1D 83
  EC2 . . . . 2A 18 (5E 63)
  W4 . . . . 1A 84
Woodsyre SE26 . . . . . . 4B 120
Wood Va. NW2 . . . . . . 5D 29
Woodthorpe Rd.
  SW15 . . . . 2D 99
Wood Va. N10 . . . . 1E 33
  SE23 . . . . 1D 121
Wood Va. Est. SE23 . . . 5E 107
Woodvale Wlk.
  SE27 . . . . 5E 119
Woodvale Way NW11 . . 5F 29
Woodview Cl. N4 . . . . . 2D 35
  SW15 . . . . 4A 112
Woodville SE3 . . . . 3D 97
Woodville Cl. SE12 . . . . 3C 110
Woodville Gdns.
  NW11 . . . . 2F 29
Woodville Ho. SE1 . . . . 5F 27
  (off Grange Wlk.)
Woodville Rd. E11 . . . . 3B 40
  N16 . . . . 2A 50
  NW6 . . . . 1B 58
  NW11 . . . . 2F 29
Woodward Av. NW4 . . . 1C 28
Woodwarde Rd.
  SE22 . . . . 4A 106
Woodwell St. SW18 . . . 3E 101
Wood Wharf SE10 . . . . 2E 95
Wood Wharf Bus. Pk.
  E14 . . . . 2D 81
  (not continuous)
Woodyard Cl. NW5 . . . 2C 46
Woodyard La. SE21 . . . 5A 106
Woodyates Rd.
  SE12 . . . . 4C 110
Woolacombe Rd. SE3 . . 4E 97
Woolcombes St.
  SE16 . . . . 2F 79
  (off Princes Riverside Rd.)
Wooler St. SE17 . . . . . 1F 91
Woolf M. WC1 . . . . 3C 6
  (off Burton Pl.)
Woolgar M. N16 . . . . . . 2A 50
  (off Gillett St.)
Woollaston Rd. N4 . . . . 1D 35
Woolley Ho. SW9 . . . . . 1D 105
  (off Loughborough Rd.)
Woollon Rd. E1 . . . . . . 5E 65
  (off Clark St.)
Woolmead Av. NW9 . . . 2C 28
Woolmore St. E14 . . . . 1E 81

Woolneigh St. SW6 . . . 1D **101**
Woolridge Way E9 . . . . 4E **51**
Woolstaplers Way
SE16. . . . . 4C **78**
Woolstone Rd.
SE23. . . . . 2A **122**
Woolwich Chu. St.
SE18 . . . . 4F **83**
Woolwich Dockyard Ind. Est.
SE18 . . . . 4F **83**
Woolwich Rd. SE7 . . . 1C **96**
SE10. . . . . 1B **96**
Wooster Gdns. E14. . . 5F **67**
Wooster Pl. SE1 . . . . . 5F **77**
(off Searles Rd.)
Wootton St.
SE1. . . . . 2C **24** (2C **76**)
Worcester Cl. NW2 . . . 5D **29**
Worcester Ct. W9. . . . 4C **58**
(off Elmfield Way)
Worcester Dr. W4. . . . 3A **70**
Worcester Gdns.
SW11 . . . . 3B **102**
(off Grandison Rd.)
Worcester Ho. SE11. . . . 5B **24**
(off Kennington Rd.)
SW9 . . . . 3C **90**
(off Cranmer Rd.)
W2 . . . . 5E **59**
(off Hallfield Est.)
Worcester M. NW6. . . 3D **45**
Worcester Rd.
SW19 . . . . 5B **114**
Wordsworth Av. E12 . . 4F **55**
Wordsworth Ho.
NW6 . . . . 2C **58**
(off Stafford Rd.)
Wordsworth Pl. NW3 . . 2B **46**
Wordsworth Rd. N16 . . 1A **50**
SE1. . . . . 5B **78**
Worfield St. SW11 . . . 3A **88**
Worgan St. SE11 . . . . 1B **90**
SE16. . . . . 5F **79**
Worland Rd. E15 . . . . 4A **54**
Worlds End Est.
SW10 . . . . 3F **87**
World's End Pas.
SW10 . . . . 3F **87**
(off Worlds End Est.)
World's End Pl.
SW10 . . . . 3F **87**
(off Worlds End Est.)
Worlidge St. W6. . . . . 1E **85**
Worlingham Rd.
SE22 . . . . 2B **106**
Wormholt Rd. W12. . . 1C **70**
Wormwood St.
EC2 . . . . 2D **19** (5A **64**)
Wornington Rd. W10 . . 3A **58**
(not continuous)
Wornum Ho. W10. . . . . 1A **58**
(off Kilburn La.)
Woronzow Rd. NW8 . . 5F **45**
Worple Rd. SW19. . . . 5B **114**
Worple Rd. M.
SW19 . . . . 5B **114**
Worple St. SW14 . . . . 1A **98**
Worship St.
EC2. . . . . 4C **10** (3F **63**)
Worslade Rd. SW17. . . 4F **115**

Worsley Bri. Rd.
BR3: Beck. 5C **122**
SE26. . . . . 4B **122**
Worsley Gro. EC1. . . . 1C **50**
Worsley Ho. SE23 . . . 2E **121**
Worsley Rd. E11. . . . . 1A **54**
Worsopp Dr. SW4. . . . 3E **103**
Worth Gro. SE17. . . . . 1F **91**
Worthing Cl. E15 . . . . 5A **54**
Worthington Ho. EC1. . . . 1C **8**
(off Myddelton Pas.)
Wortley Rd. E6 . . . . . 4F **55**
Wotton Ct. E14. . . . . . . 1F **81**
(off Jamestown Way)
Wotton Rd. NW2 . . . . 5E **29**
SE8. . . . . 2B **94**
Wouldham Rd. E16 . . . 5B **68**
Wragby Rd. E11. . . . . 5A **40**
Wrayburn Ho. SE16. . . . 3C **78**
(off Llewellyn St.)
Wray Cres. N4. . . . . . 4A **34**
Wren Av. NW2. . . . . . 2E **43**
Wren Cl. E16 . . . . 5B **68**
Wren Ho. E3. . . . . 1A **66**
(off Gernon Rd.)
SW1 . . . . 1F **89**
(off Aylesford St.)
Wren Landing E14 . . . 2C **80**
Wren Rd. SE5. . . . . . . 4F **91**
Wren's Pk. Ho. E5 . . . 4D **37**
Wren St. WC1 . . . 3A **8** (3B **62**)
Wrentham Av. NW10 . . 1F **57**
Wrenthorpe Rd.
BR1: Brom 4A **124**
Wren Vw. N6. . . . . . . 2E **33**
Wrestlers Ct. EC3. . . . 2D **19**
Wrexham Rd. E3 . . . . 1C **66**
Wricklemarsh Rd.
SE3. . . . . 5D **97**
(not continuous)
Wrigglesworth St.
SE14. . . . . 3F **93**
Wright Cl. SE13 . . . . . 2F **109**
Wright Rd. N1 . . . . . . 3A **50**
Wrights Grn. SW4 . . . 2F **103**
Wright's La. W8. . . . . 4D **73**
Wright's Rd. E3 . . . . . 1B **66**
(not continuous)
Wrotham Ho. SE1 . . . . 5C **26**
(off Law St.)
Wrotham Rd. NW1 . . . 4E **47**
Wrottesley Rd.
NW10 . . . . 1C **56**
Wroughton Rd.
SW11 . . . . 3B **102**
Wroxton Rd. SE15 . . . 5E **93**
Wulfstan St. W12. . . . 4B **56**
Wyatt Cl. SE16. . . . . . 3B **80**
Wyatt Dr. SW13 . . . . . 2D **85**
Wyatt Ho. NW8. . . . . . 3F **59**
(off Frampton St.)
SE3. . . . . 5B **96**
Wyatt Pk. Rd. SW2 . . 2A **118**
Wyatt Rd. E7 . . . . 3C **54**
N5. . . . . 1E **35**
Wybert St.
NW1 . . . . 3F **5** (3E **61**)
Wychcombe Studios
NW3 . . . . 3B **46**

Wycherley Cl. SE3. . . . 3B **96**
Wychwood End N6 . . . 2E **33**
Wychwood Way
SE19 . . . . 5F **119**
Wyclif Ct. EC1 . . . . 2D **9**
(off Wyclif St.)
Wycliffe Rd. SW11. . . 5C **88**
Wyclif St. EC1. . 2D **9** (2D **63**)
Wycombe Gdns.
NW11 . . . . 4C **30**
Wycombe Ho. NW8 . . . 3A **60**
(off Grendon St.)
Wycombe Pl. SW18. . . 4E **101**
Wycombe Sq. W8 . . . 2B **72**
Wydeville Mnr. Rd.
SE12. . . . . 4D **125**
Wye St. SW11 . . . . . . 5F **87**
Wyfold Rd. SW6. . . . . 3A **86**
Wykeham Ct. NW4 . . . . 1E **29**
(off Wykeham Rd.)
Wykeham Rd. NW4 . . . 1E **29**
Wyke Rd. E3. . . . . 4C **52**
Wyldes Cl. NW11 . . . . 3E **31**
Wyleu St. SE23 . . . . 5A **108**
Wyllen Cl. E1. . . . . . . 3E **65**
Wymans Way E7 . . . . 1E **55**
Wymering Mans. W9. . . 2C **58**
*(off Wymering Rd.,
not continuous)*
Wymering Rd. W9 . . . 2C **58**
Wymond St. SW15. . . 1E **99**
Wynan Rd. E14 . . . . . 1D **95**
Wyndcliff Rd. SE7 . . . 2D **97**
Wyndham Cres. N19 . . 5E **33**
Wyndham Deedes Ho.
E2. . . . . 1C **64**
(off Hackney Rd.)
Wyndham Est. SE5. . . 3E **91**
Wyndham Ho. E14. . . . 3D **81**
(off Marsh Wall)
Wyndham M. W1 . . . . 4B **60**
Wyndham Pl.
W1 . . . . 1A **12** (4B **60**)
Wyndham Rd. E6 . . . . 4F **55**
SE5. . . . . 3E **91**
Wyndhams Ct. E8. . . . . 4B **50**
(off Celandine Dr.)
Wyndham's Theatre 4D **15**
(off St Martin's La.)
Wyndham St. W1 . . . . 4B **60**
Wyndham Yd. W1 . . . 4B **60**
Wyneham Rd. SE24 . . 3F **105**
Wynell Rd. SE23 . . . . 3F **121**
Wynford Ho. N1 . . . . . 1B **62**
(off Wynford Rd.)
Wynford Rd. N1 . . . . . 1B **62**
Wynne Ho. SE14. . . . . 4F **93**
Wynne Rd. SW9. . . . . 5C **90**
Wynnstay Gdns. W8. . . 4C **72**
Wynter St. SW11 . . . . 2E **101**
Wynyard Ho. SE11. . . . 1B **90**
Wynyard Ter. SE11. . . 1B **90**
Wynyatt St.
EC1 . . . . 2D **9** (2D **63**)
Wythburn Ct. W1 . . . . . 2A **12**
(off Wythburn Pl.)
Wythburn Pl.
W1 . . . . 3A **12** (5B **60**)
Wythes Rd. E16 . . . . . 2F **83**

Wyvil Rd. SW8 . . . . 3A **90**
Wyvis St. E14 . . . . 4D **67**

Y

Yabsley St. E14 . . . . . 2E **81**
Yalding Rd. SE16 . . . . . 4C **78**
Yale Ct. NW6 . . . . 2D **45**
Yard, The N1 . . . . 1E **7**
(off Caledonian Rd.)
Yardley St.
WC1 . . . . 2B **8** (2C **62**)
(not continuous)
Yarmouth Pl.
W1 . . . . 2D **21** (2D **75**)
Yarnfield Sq. SE15 . . . . 4C **92**
Yarrow Cres. E6 . . . . . 4F **69**
Yarrow Ho. E14 . . . . 4E **81**
(off Stewart St.)
W10 . . . . 4E **57**
(off Sutton Way)
Yateley St. SE18 . . . . . . 4F **83**
Yates Ct. NW2 . . . . 3F **43**
(off Willesden La.)
Yates Ho. E2 . . . . 2C **64**
(off Roberta St.)
Yatton Ho. W10 . . . . . 4E **57**
(off Sutton Way)
Yeadon Ho. W10. . . . . . 4E **57**
(off Sutton Way)
Yearby Ho. W10 . . . . . 3E **57**
(off Sutton Way)
Yeate St. N1 . . . . 4F **49**
Yeatman Rd. N6 . . . . . 1B **32**
Yeats Cl. NW10 . . . . . . 2A **42**
SE13 . . . . 5F **95**
Yeldham Ho. W6 . . . . . 1F **85**
(off Yeldham Rd.)
Yeldham Rd. W6. . . . . . 1F **85**
Yeldham Vs. W6 . . . . . 1F **85**
(off Yeldham Rd.)
Yelverton Rd. SW11 . . . 5F **87**
Yeoman Cl. SE27 . . . . 3D **119**
Yeoman Ct. SE1 . . . . . . 1B **92**
(off Cooper's Rd.)
Yeoman's Row
SW3 . . . . 4A **74**
Yeoman St. SE8 . . . . . 5A **80**
Yeoman's Yd. E1 . . . . . 1B **78**
(off Chamber St.)
Yeo St. E3. . . . . 4D **67**
Yeovil Ho. W10. . . . . . 3E **57**
(off Sutton Way)

Yerbury Rd. N19 . . . . . . 5F **33**
(not continuous)
Yetev Lev Ct. E5. . . . . . 3C **36**
Yewfield Rd. NW10 . . . . 3B **42**
Yew Gro. NW2 . . . . 1F **43**
Yew Ho. SE16. . . . . 3F **79**
(off Woodland Cres.)
Yew Tree Ct. NW11 . . . . 1B **30**
(off Bridge La.)
Yew Tree Lodge
SW16 . . . . 4E **117**
Yew Tree Rd. W12 . . . . 1B **70**
Yoakley Rd. N16 . . . . . 4A **36**
Yoke Cl. N7 . . . . 3A **48**
Yolande Gdns. SE9. . . . 3F **111**
Yonge Pk. N4 . . . . 5C **34**
York Av. SE17 . . . . 1E **91**
York Bri. NW1 . . 3B **4** (3C **60**)
York Bldgs.
WC2 . . . . 5E **15** (1A **76**)
York Cl. SE5 . . . . 5E **91**
(off Lilford Rd.)
York Ga. NW1 . . 4B **4** (3C **60**)
York Gro. SE15. . . . . . 4E **93**
York Hill SE27 . . . . . . 3D **119**
York Ho. E16 . . . . 2C **82**
(off De Quincey M.)
SE1 . . . . 5A **24** (4B **76**)
W1 . . . . 5A **4**
(off York St.)
York Ho. Pl. W8. . . . . . 3D **73**
Yorkley Ho. W10 . . . . . 3E **57**
(off Sutton Way)
York Mans. SW5 . . . . . 1D **87**
(off Earls Ct. Rd.)
SW11 . . . . 4B **88**
(off Prince of Wales Dr.)
W1 . . . . 5B **4**
(off Chiltern St.)
York M. NW5 . . . . 2D **47**
York Pas. W8 . . . . 3D **73**
(off York Ho. Pl.)
York Pl. SW11 . . . . . . 1F **101**
WC2 . . . . 5E **15**
York Pl. Mans. W1. . . . . 5A **4**
(off Baker St.)
York Ri. NW5 . . . . 5D **33**
York Rd. E7 . . . . 3C **54**
E10 . . . . 5E **39**
E17 . . . . 1F **37**
SE1 . . . . . . 3A **24** (3B **76**)
SW11 . . . . 2E **101**
SW18 . . . . 2E **101**
SW19 . . . . 5E **115**

Yorkshire Cl. N16. . . . . . 5A **36**
YORKSHIRE GREY. 3F **111**
Yorkshire Grey Pl.
NW3 . . . . 1E **45**
Yorkshire Grey Yd.
WC1 . . . . 1F **15**
Yorkshire Rd. E14 . . . . . 5A **66**
York Sq. E14. . . . . 5A **66**
York St. W1 . . . . 1A **12** (4B **60**)
York St. Chambers
W1 . . . . 4B **60**
(off York St.)
York Ter. E.
NW1 . . . . 4C **4** (3C **60**)
York Ter. W.
NW1 . . . . 4B **4** (3C **60**)
Yorkton St. E2 . . . . 1C **64**
York Way N1 . . 1E **7** (3A **48**)
N7 . . . . 3F **47**
York Way Ct. N1. . . . . . 5A **48**
York Way Est. N7 . . . . . 3A **48**
Young Ct. NW6. . . . . . . 4A **44**
Young Rd. E16 . . . . 5E **69**
Youngs Bldgs. EC1. . . . 3A **10**
Youngs Ct. SW11 . . . . . 4C **88**
Youngs St. W8. . . . . . . 3D **73**
Young Vic Theatre, The
. . . . 3C **24**
Yoxall Ho. W10 . . . . . . 3E **57**
(off Sutton Way)
Yukon Rd. SW12 . . . . . 5D **103**
Yunus Khan Cl. E17 . . . 1C **38**

Z

Zampa Rd. SE16 . . . . . . 1E **93**
Zander Ct. E2 . . . . 2C **64**
Zangwill Rd. SE3 . . . . . 4F **97**
Zealand Ho. SE5 . . . . . 5E **91**
(off Denmark Rd.)
Zealand Rd. E3 . . . . . . 1A **66**
Zennor Rd. SW12. . . . . 1E **117**
Zennor Rd. Ind. Est.
SW12 . . . . 1E **117**
Zenoria St. SE22 . . . . . 2B **106**
Zetland Ho. W8 . . . . . . 4D **73**
(off Marloes Rd.)
Zetland St. E14 . . . . . . 4D **67**
Zion Ho. E1. . . . . 5E **65**
(off Jubilee St.)
Zoar St. SE1. . . . 1F **25** (2E **77**)
Zoffany St. N19. . . . . . . 4F **33**

HOSPITALS and HOSPICES
covered by this atlas.

N.B. Where Hospitals and Hospices are not named on the map,
the reference given is for the road in which they are situated.

ABBEY CHURCHILL LONDON, THE
.................................4C **76** (5C **24**)
22 Barkham Terrace
LONDON
SE1 7PW
Tel: 020 79285633

ATHLONE HOUSE 3B **32**
Hampstead Lane
LONDON
N6 4RX
Tel: 020 83485231

BARNES HOSPITAL 1A **98**
South Worple Way
LONDON
SW14 8SU
Tel: 020 88784981

BELVEDERE DAY HOSPITAL 5C **42**
341 Harlesden Road
LONDON
NW10 3RX
Tel: 020 84593562

BLACKHEATH BMI HOSPITAL, THE 1B **110**
40-42 Lee Terrace
LONDON
SE3 9UD
Tel: 020 83187722

BOLINGBROKE HOSPITAL. 3A **102**
Bolingbroke Grove
LONDON
SW11 6HN
Tel: 020 72237411

BRITISH HOME 5D **119**
Crown Lane
LONDON
SW16 3JB
Tel: 020 86708261

CAMDEN MEWS DAY HOSPITAL 4E **47**
1-5 Camden Mews
LONDON
NW1 9DB
Tel: 020 75304780

CHARING CROSS HOSPITAL 2F **85**
Fulham Palace Road
LONDON
W6 8RF
Tel: 020 88461234

CHELSEA & WESTMINSTER HOSPITAL
.................................2E **87**
369 Fulham Road
LONDON
SW10 9NH
Tel: 020 87468000

CHILDREN'S HOSPITAL, THE (LEWISHAM)
.................................3D **109**
Lewisham University Hospital
Lewisham High Street
LONDON
SE13 6LH
Tel: 020 83333000

CROMWELL HOSPITAL, THE 5D **73**
162-174 Cromwell Road
LONDON
SW5 0TU
Tel: 020 74602000

DULWICH COMMUNITY HOSPITAL 2A **106**
East Dulwich Grove
LONDON
SE22 8PT
Tel: AWAITING NEW T

EASTMAN DENTAL HOSPITAL &
   DENTAL INSTITUTE, THE 3B **62** (3F **7**)
256 Gray's Inn Road
LONDON
WC1X 8LD
Tel: 020 79151000

EDENHALL MARIE CURIE CENTRE 2F **45**
11 Lyndhurst Gardens
LONDON
NW3 5NS
Tel: 020 78533400

ELIZABETH GARRETT ANDERSON &
   OBSTETRIC HOSPITAL, THE 3E **61** (4A **6**)
Huntley Street
LONDON
WC1E 6DH
Tel: 020 73879300

EVELINA CHILDREN'S HOSPITAL
.................................4B **76** (5F **23**)
St Thomas' Hospital
Lambeth Palace Road
LONDON
SE1 7EH
Tel: 0207 1887188

FLORENCE NIGHTINGALE DAY HOSPITAL
.................................4A **60**
1B Harewood Row
LONDON
NW1 6SE
Tel: 020 77259940

FLORENCE NIGHTINGALE HOSPITAL ...4A **60**
11-19 Lisson Grove
LONDON
NW1 6SH
Tel: 020 75357700

FORDWYCH ROAD DAY HOSPITAL 2B **44**
85-87 Fordwych Road
LONDON
NW2 3TL
Tel: 020 82081612

GORDON HOSPITAL 5F **75**
Bloomburg Street
LONDON
SW1V 2RH
Tel: 020 87468733

GREAT ORMOND STREET HOSPITAL FOR
CHILDREN 3A **62** (4E **7**)
Great Ormond Street
LONDON
WC1N 3JH
Tel: 020 74059200

GUY'S HOSPITAL 2F **77** (2C **26**)
St Thomas Street
LONDON
SE1 9RT
Tel: 020 71887188

GUY'S NUFFIELD HOUSE 3F **77** (3B **26**)
Newcomen Street
LONDON
SE1 1YR
Tel: 020 79554257

HAMMERSMITH HOSPITAL 5C **56**
Du Cane Road
LONDON
W12 0HS
Tel: 020 83831000

HARLEY STREET CLINIC, THE 4D **61** (5D **5**)
35 Weymouth Street
LONDON
W1G 8BJ
Tel: 020 79357700

HEART HOSPITAL, THE 4C **60** (1C **12**)
16-18 Westmoreland Street
LONDON
W1G 8PH
Tel: 020 75738888

HIGHGATE HOSPITAL 1B **32**
17 View Road
LONDON
N6 4DJ
Tel: 020 83414182

HOMERTON UNIVERSITY HOSPITAL 2F **51**
Homerton Row
LONDON
E9 6SR
Tel: 020 85105555

HOSPITAL FOR TROPICAL DISEASES
. . . . 3E **61** (4A **6**)
Mortimer Market,
Capper Street
LONDON
WC1E 6AU
Tel: 020 7387 9300

HOSPITAL OF ST JOHN & ST ELIZABETH
. . . . 1F **59**
60 Grove End Road
LONDON
NW8 9NH
Tel: 020 78064000

KING EDWARD VII'S HOSPITAL SISTER AGNES
. . . . 4C **60** (5C **4**)
5-10 Beaumont Street
LONDON
W1G 6AA
Tel: 020 74864411

KING'S COLLEGE HOSPITAL 5F **91**
Denmark Hill
LONDON
SE5 9RS
Tel: 020 77374000

LAMBETH HOSPITAL 1B **104**
108 Landor Road
LONDON
SW9 9NT
Tel: 020 74116100

LATIMER DAY HOSPITAL 4E **61** (5F **5**)
40 Hanson Street
LONDON
W1W 6UL
Tel: 020 73809187

LEWISHAM UNIVERSITY HOSPITAL . . . 3D **109**
Lewisham High Street
LONDON
SE13 6LH
Tel: 020 83333000

LISTER HOSPITAL, THE 1D **89**
Chelsea Bridge Road
LONDON
SW1W 8RH
Tel: 020 77303417

LONDON BRIDGE HOSPITAL . . . 2F **77** (1C **26**)
27 Tooley Street
LONDON
SE1 2PR
Tel: 020 74073100

LONDON CHEST HOSPITAL 1E **65**
Bonner Road
LONDON
E2 9JX
Tel: 020 73777000

LONDON CLINIC, THE 3C **60** (4C **4**)
20 Devonshire Place
LONDON
W1G 6BW
Tel: 020 79354444

LONDON FOOT HOSPITAL 3E **61** (4F **5**)
33 & 40 Fitzroy Square
LONDON
W1T 6AY
Tel: 020 75304500

LONDON INDEPENDENT BMI HOSPITAL, THE
. . . . 4F **65**
1 Beaumont Square
LONDON
E1 4NL
Tel: 020 77802400

LONDON LIGHTHOUSE 5A **58**
111-117 Lancaster Road
LONDON
W11 1QT
Tel: 020 77921200

LONDON WELBECK HOSPITAL
. . . . 4D **61** (1D **13**)
27 Welbeck Street
LONDON
W1G 8EN
Tel: 020 72242242

MAUDSLEY HOSPITAL, THE 5F **91**
Denmark Hill
LONDON
SE5 8AZ
Tel: 0207 7036333

MIDDLESEX HOSPITAL, THE 4E **61** (1A **14**)
Mortimer Street
LONDON
W1T 3AA
Tel: 020 76368333

MILDMAY MISSION HOSPITAL. . . 2B **64** (2F **11**)
Hackney Road
LONDON
E2 7NA
Tel: 020 76136300

MILE END HOSPITAL 3F **65**
Bancroft Road
LONDON
E1 4DG
Tel: 020 73777000

MOORFIELDS EYE HOSPITAL 2F **63** (2B **10**)
162 City Road
LONDON
EC1V 2PD
Tel: 020 72533411

NATIONAL HOSPITAL FOR NEUROLOGY &
NEUROSURGERY, THE 3A **62** (4E **7**)
Queen Square
LONDON
WC1N 3BG
Tel: 020 78373611

NEWHAM GENERAL HOSPITAL 3E **69**
Glen Road
LONDON
E13 8SL
Tel: 020 74764000

NHS WALK-IN CENTRE (CHARING CROSS)
. . . . 1F **85**
Charing Cross Hospital
Fulham Palace Road
LONDON
W6 8RF
Tel: 020 8383 0904

NHS WALK-IN CENTRE (HACKNEY) 2F **51**
Homerton University Hospital
Homerton Row
LONDON
E9 6SR
Tel: 020 8510 5342 / 7121

NHS WALK-IN CENTRE
(LEYTONSTONE - WHIPPS CROSS) 1F **39**
Whipps Cross Hospital
Whipps Cross Road
LONDON
E11 1NR
Tel: 020 8558 8965 / 4229

NHS WALK-IN CENTRE (NEW CROSS). . . 3A **94**
Henderson House
40 Goodwood Road
LONDON
SE14 6BL
Tel: 020 7206 3100

NHS WALK-IN CENTRE (NEWHAM). 3E **69**
Glen Road
LONDON
E13 8SH
Tel: 020 7363 9200

NHS WALK-IN CENTRE (PARSONS GREEN)
. . . . 4C **86**
5-7 Parsons Green
LONDON
SW6 4UL
Tel: 020 8846 6758

NHS WALK-IN CENTRE (SOHO). . . 5F **61** (3B **14**)
1 Frith Street
LONDON
W1D 3HZ
Tel: 020 7534 6500

NHS WALK-IN CENTRE (TOOTING) 5A **116**
Clare House
St. Georges Hospital
Blackshaw Road
LONDON
SW17 0QT
Tel: 020 8700 0505

NHS WALK-IN CENTRE (WHITECHAPEL)
. . . . 4D **65**
Royal London Hospital
174 Whitechapel Road
LONDON
E1 1BZ
Tel: 020 7943 1333

NHS WALK-IN CENTRE (WHITTINGTON)
. . . . 4E **33**
Whittington Hospital, Sterling Way
LONDON
N18 1QX
Tel: 020 7288 5216

PARKSIDE HOSPITAL 3F **113**
53 Parkside
LONDON
SW19 5NX
Tel: 020 89718000

PLAISTOW HOSPITAL 1E **69**
Samson Street
LONDON
E13 9EH
Tel: 020 85866200

PORTLAND HOSPITAL FOR WOMEN &
CHILDREN, THE 3D **61** (4E **5**)
209 Great Portland Street
LONDON
W1W 5AH
Tel: 020 75804400

PRINCESS GRACE HOSPITAL 3C **60** (4B **4**)
42-52 Nottingham Place
LONDON
W1U 5NY
Tel: 020 74861234

PRINCESS GRACE HOSPITAL ANNEXE
. . . . .4C **60** (5C **4**)
29-31 Devonshire Street
LONDON
W1G 6PU
Tel: 020 74861234

PRINCESS LOUISE DAY HOSPITAL 4F **57**
St. Quintin Avenue
LONDON
W10 6DL
Tel: 020 89690133

QUEEN CHARLOTTE'S & CHELSEA HOSPITAL
. . . . .5C **56**
Du Cane Road
LONDON
W12 0HS
Tel: 020 83831111

QUEEN MARY'S HOUSE 5E **31**
23 East Heath Road
LONDON
NW3 1DU
Tel: 020 74314111

QUEEN MARY'S UNIVERSITY HOSPITAL
. . . . .4C **98**
Roehampton Lane
LONDON
SW15 5PN
Tel: 020 87896611

RAVENSCOURT PARK HOSPITAL 5C **70**
Ravenscourt Park
LONDON
W6 0NT
Tel: 020 88467777

RICHARD HOUSE CHILDREN'S HOSPICE
. . . . .1F **83**
Richard House Drive
LONDON
E16 3RG
Tel: 020 75110222

ROEHAMPTON HUNTERCOMBE HOSPITAL
. . . . .5C **98**
Holybourne Avenue
LONDON
SW15 4JL
Tel: 0208 7806155

ROEHAMPTON PRIORY HOSPITAL 2B **98**
Priory Lane
LONDON
SW15 5JJ
Tel: 020 88768261

ROYAL BROMPTON HOSPITAL 1A **88**
Sydney Street
LONDON
SW3 6NP
Tel: 020 73528121

ROYAL BROMPTON HOSPITAL (ANNEXE)
. . . . .1F **87**
Fulham Road
LONDON
SW3 6HP
Tel: 020 73528121

ROYAL FREE HOSPITAL, THE 2A **46**
Pond Street
LONDON
NW3 2QG
Tel: 020 77940500

ROYAL HOSPITAL FOR NEURO-DISABILITY
. . . . .4A **100**
West Hill
LONDON
SW15 3SW
Tel: 020 87804500

ROYAL LONDON HOMOEOPATHIC HOSPITAL,
THE 4A **62** (5E **7**)
Great Ormond Street
LONDON
WC1N 3HR
Tel: 020 73918864

ROYAL LONDON HOSPITAL 4D **65**
Whitechapel Road
LONDON
E1 1BB
Tel: 020 73777000

ROYAL MARSDEN HOSPITAL (FULHAM), THE
. . . . .1F **87**
Fulham Road
LONDON
SW3 6JJ
Tel: 020 73528171

ROYAL NATIONAL ORTHOPAEDIC HOSPITAL
(OUTPATIENTS) 3D **61** (4E **5**)
45-51 Bolsover Street
LONDON
W1W 5AQ
Tel: 020 73875070

ROYAL NATIONAL THROAT, NOSE &
EAR HOSPITAL 2B **62** (1F **7**)
330 Gray's Inn Road
LONDON
WC1X 8DA
Tel: 020 79151300

ST ANDREW'S HOSPITAL 3D **67**
Devas Street
LONDON
E3 3NT
Tel: 020 74764000

ST ANN'S HOSPITAL 1E **35**
St Ann's Road
LONDON
N15 3TH
Tel: 020 84426000

ST BARTHOLOMEW'S HOSPITAL
. . . . .4D **63** (1E **17**)
West Smithfield
LONDON
EC1A 7BE
Tel: 020 73777000

ST CHARLES HOSPITAL 4F **57**
Exmoor Street
LONDON
W10 6DZ
Tel: 020 89692488

ST CHRISTOPHER'S HOSPICE 5E **121**
51-59 Lawrie Park Road
LONDON
SE26 6DZ
Tel: 020 87789252

ST CLEMENT'S HOSPITAL 2B **66**
2A Bow Road
LONDON
E3 4LL
Tel: 020 73777000

ST GEORGE'S HOSPITAL (TOOTING) . . . 5A **116**
Blackshaw Road
LONDON
SW17 0QT
Tel: 020 86721255

ST JOHN'S HOSPICE 1F **59**
Hospital of St John & St Elizabeth,
60 Grove End Road
LONDON
NW8 9NH
Tel: 020 78064040

ST JOSEPH'S HOSPICE 5D **51**
Mare Street
LONDON
E8 4SA
Tel: 020 85256000

ST LUKE'S HOSPITAL FOR THE CLERGY
. . . . .3E **61** (4F **5**)
14 Fitzroy Square
LONDON
W1T 6AH
Tel: 020 73884954

ST MARY'S HOSPITAL 5F **59**
Praed Street
LONDON
W2 1NY
Tel: 020 77256666

ST PANCRAS HOSPITAL 5F **47**
4 St Pancras Way
LONDON
NW1 0PE
Tel: 020 75303500

ST THOMAS' HOSPITAL 4B **76** (5F **23**)
Lambeth Palace Road
LONDON
SE1 7EH
Tel: 0207 1887188

SPRINGFIELD UNIVERSITY HOSPITAL . .3A **116**
61 Glenburnie Road
LONDON
SW17 7DJ
Tel: 020 86826000

TRINITY HOSPICE 2D **103**
30 Clapham Common North Side
LONDON
SW4 0RN
Tel: 020 77871000

UNIVERSITY COLLEGE HOSPITAL
. . . . .3E **61** (3A **6**)
Gower Street
LONDON
WC1E 6AU
Tel: 020 73879300

WELLINGTON HOSPITAL, THE 2F **59**
8a Wellington Place
LONDON
NW8 9LE
Tel: 0207 5865959

WESTERN EYE HOSPITAL 4B **60**
171 Marylebone Road
LONDON
NW1 5QH
Tel: 020 78866666

WHIPPS CROSS UNIVERSITY HOSPITAL
. . . . .1F **39**
Whipps Cross Road
LONDON
E11 1NR
Tel: 020 85395522

WHITTINGTON HOSPITAL 4E **33**
Highgate Hill
LONDON
N19 5NF
Tel: 020 72723070

WILLESDEN COMMUNITY HOSPITAL 4C **42**
Harlesden Road
LONDON
NW10 3RY
Tel: 020 84518017

RAIL, CROYDON TRAMLINK, DOCKLANDS LIGHT RAILWAY, RIVERBUS AND LONDON UNDERGROUND STATIONS

with their map square reference

A

Acton Central (Rail) 2A 70
Aldgate East (Tube) 2F 19 (5B 64)
Aldgate (Tube) 3F 19 (5B 64)
All Saints (DLR) 1D 81
Angel (Tube) 1C 62
Archway (Tube) 4E 33
Arsenal (Tube) 5C 34

B

Baker Street (Tube) 4A 4 (3B 60)
Balham (Rail & Tube) 1D 117
Bankside Pier (Riverbus) 5F 17 (1E 77)
Bank (Tube & DLR) 3B 18 (5B 63)
Barbican (Rail & Tube) 5F 9 (4E 63)
Barnes (Rail) 1C 98
Barnes Bridge (Rail) 5B 84
Barons Court (Tube) 1A 86
Battersea Park (Rail) 3D 89
Bayswater (Tube) 1D 73
Beckenham Hill (Rail) 5E 123
Bellingham (Rail) 3D 123
Belsize Park (Tube) 2A 46
Bermondsey (Tube) 4C 78
Bethnal Green (Rail) 3D 65
Bethnal Green (Tube) 2E 65
Blackfriars Millennium Pier (Riverbus)
. . . . 4C 16 (1C 76)
Blackfriars (Rail & Tube) 4D 17 (1D 77)
Blackheath (Rail) 1B 110
Blackwall (DLR) 1E 81
Bond Street (Tube) 3D 13 (5D 61)
Borough (Tube) 4A 26 (3E 77)
Bow Church (DLR) 2C 66
Bow Road (Tube) 2C 66
Brent Cross (Tube) 2F 29
Brixton (Rail & Tube) 2C 104
Brockley (Rail) 1A 108
Bromley-by-Bow (Tube) 2D 67
Brondesbury Park (Rail) 5A 44
Brondesbury (Rail) 4B 44

C

Cadogan Pier (Riverbus) 2A 88
Caledonian Road & Barnsbury (Rail)
. . . . 4B 48
Caledonian Road (Tube) 3B 48
Cambridge Heath (Rail) 1D 65
Camden Road (Rail) 4E 47
Camden Town (Tube) 5D 47
Canada Water (Tube) 3E 79
Canary Wharf (Tube) 2D 81
Canary Wharf (DLR) 2C 80

Canary Wharf Pier (Riverbus) 2B 80
Canning Town (Rail, Tube & DLR)
. . . . 5A 68
Cannon Street (Rail & Tube)
. . . . 4B 18 (1F 77)
Canonbury (Rail) 2E 49
Catford (Rail) 5C 108
Catford Bridge (Rail) 5C 108
Chalk Farm (Tube) 4C 46
Chancery Lane (Tube) 1B 16 (4C 62)
Charing Cross (Rail & Tube) . . 1D 23 (2A 76)
Charlton (Rail) 1E 97
City Thameslink (Rail)
  Holborn Viaduct 2D 17 (5D 63)
Clapham Common (Tube) 2E 103
Clapham High Street (Rail) 1F 103
Clapham Junction (Rail) 1A 102
Clapham North (Tube) 1A 104
Clapham South (Tube) 4D 103
Clapton (Rail) 4D 37
Covent Garden (Tube) 4E 15 (1A 76)
Cricklewood (Rail) 1F 43
Crofton Park (Rail) 3B 108
Crossharbour & London Arena (DLR)
. . . . 4D 81
Crouch Hill (Rail) 2B 34
Custom House for ExCeL (Rail & DLR)
. . . . 1D 83
Cutty Sark for Maritime Greenwich (DLR)
. . . . 2E 95

D

Dalston Kingsland (Rail) 2A 50
Denmark Hill (Rail) 5F 91
Deptford (Rail) 3C 94
Deptford Bridge (DLR) 4C 94
Devons Road (DLR) 3D 67
Dollis Hill (Tube) 2C 42
Drayton Park (Rail) 1C 48

E

Earl's Court (Tube) 5D 73
Earlsfield (Rail) 1E 115
East Acton (Tube) 5B 56
East Dulwich (Rail) 2A 106
East India (DLR) 1F 81
East Putney (Tube) 3A 100
Edgware Road (Tube) 4A 60
Elephant & Castle (Rail & Tube) 5E 77
Elmstead Woods (Rail) 5F 125
Elverson Road (DLR) 5D 95
Embankment Pier (Riverbus)
. . . . 1E 23 (2A 76)
Embankment (Tube) 1E 23 (2A 76)
Essex Road (Rail) 4E 49

Euston Square (Tube) 3A 6 (3E 61)
Euston (Rail & Tube) 2B 6 (2F 61)

F

Farringdon (Rail & Tube) 5D 9 (4D 63)
Fenchurch Street (Rail)
. . . . 4F 19 (1B 78)
Festival Pier (Riverbus) 2B 76
Finchley Road (Tube) 3E 45
Finchley Road & Frognal (Rail) 2E 45
Finsbury Park (Rail & Tube) 4C 34
Forest Gate (Rail) 2C 54
Forest Hill (Rail) 2E 121
Fulham Broadway (Tube) 3C 86

G

Gipsy Hill (Rail) 5A 120
Gloucester Road (Tube) 5E 73
Golders Green (Tube) 3C 30
Goldhawk Road (Tube) 3E 71
Goodge Street (Tube) 5B 6 (4F 61)
Gospel Oak (Rail) 1C 46
Great Portland Street (Tube)
. . . . 4E 5 (3D 61)
Greenland Pier (Riverbus) 4B 80
Green Park (Tube) 1E 21 (2E 75)
Greenwich (Rail & DLR) 3D 95
Greenwich Pier (Riverbus) 1E 95
Grove Park (Rail) 3D 125

H

Hackney Central (Rail) 3D 51
Hackney Downs (Rail) 2D 51
Hackney Wick (Rail) 3C 52
Hammersmith (Tube) 5E 71
Hampstead (Tube) 1E 45
Hampstead Heath (Rail) 1A 46
Harlesden (Rail & Tube) 1A 56
Harringay Green Lanes (Rail) 1D 35
Harringay (Rail) 1C 34
Haydons Road (Rail) 5E 115
Hendon (Rail) 1C 28
Hendon Central (Tube) 1D 29
Herne Hill (Rail) 4D 105
Heron Quays (DLR) 2C 80
Highbury & Islington (Rail & Tube) . . . 3D 49
Highgate (Tube) 1D 33
High Street Kensington (Tube) 3D 73
Hilton Docklands Pier (Riverbus) 2B 80
Hither Green (Rail) 4A 110
Holborn (Tube) 1F 15 (5B 62)
Holland Park (Tube) 2B 72
Holloway Road (Tube) 2B 48
Homerton (Rail) 3F 51
Honor Oak Park (Rail) 4F 107
Hyde Park Corner (Tube) 3C 20 (3C 74)

I

Imperial Wharf (Rail) 4E 87
Island Gardens (DLR) 5E 81

K

Kennington (Tube) 1D 91
Kensal Green (Rail & Tube) 2E 57
Kensal Rise (Rail) 1F 57
Kensington Olympia (Rail & Tube) 4A 72
Kentish Town (Rail & Tube) 2E 47
Kentish Town West (Rail) 3D 47
Kidbrooke (Rail) 1D 111
Kilburn (Tube) 3B 44
Kilburn High Road (Rail) 5D 45
Kilburn Park (Tube) 1C 58
King's Cross (Rail) 1E 7 (1A 62)
King's Cross St Pancras (Tube)
. . . . 1D 7 (2A 62)
King's Cross Thameslink (Rail)
. . . . 1E 7 (2A 62)
Knightsbridge (Tube) 4A 20 (3B 74)

L

Ladbroke Grove (Tube) 5A 58
Ladywell (Rail) 3D 109
Lambeth North (Tube) 5B 24 (4C 76)
Lancaster Gate (Tube) 1F 73
Latimer Road (Tube) 1F 71
Lee (Rail) 4C 110
Leicester Square (Tube) 4C 14 (1A 76)
Lewisham (Rail & DLR) 1E 109
Leyton (Tube) 5E 39
Leyton Midland Road (Rail) 3E 39
Leytonstone High Road (Rail) 4A 40
Leytonstone (Tube) 3A 40
Limehouse (Rail & DLR) 5A 66
Liverpool Street (Rail & Tube)
. . . . 1D 19 (4A 64)
London Bridge (Rail & Tube) . . 2C 26 (2F 77)
London Bridge City Pier (Riverbus)
. . . . 1D 27 (2A 78)
London Fields (Rail) 4D 51
Loughborough Junction (Rail) 1D 105
Lower Sydenham (Rail) 5B 122

M

Maida Vale (Tube) 2D 59
Manor Park (Rail) 1F 55
Mansion House (Tube) 4A 18 (1E 77)
Marble Arch (Tube) 3A 12 (5B 60)
Maryland (Rail) 3A 54
Marylebone (Rail & Tube) 3B 60
Masthouse Terrace Pier (Riverbus) . . . 1C 94
Maze Hill (Rail) 2A 96
Mile End (Tube) 3B 66
Millbank Millennium Pier (Riverbus). . 5A 76
Monument (Tube) 4C 18 (1F 77)
Moorgate (Rail & Tube) 1B 18 (4F 63)
Mornington Crescent (Tube) 1E 61
Mudchute (DLR) 5D 81

N

Neasden (Tube) 2A 42
New Cross (Rail & Tube) 3B 94

New Cross Gate (Rail & Tube) 4A 94
North Acton (Tube) 4A 56
North Dulwich (Rail) 3F 105
North Greenwich (Rail) 3A 82
Notting Hill Gate (Tube) 2C 72
Nunhead (Rail) 5E 93

O

Old Street (Rail & Tube) 2C 10 (3F 63)
Oval (Tube) 2C 90
Oxford Circus (Tube) 3F 13 (5E 61)

P

Paddington (Rail & Tube) 5F 59
Parsons Green (Tube) 4C 86
Peckham Rye (Rail) 5C 92
Penge East (Rail) 5E 121
Piccadilly Circus (Tube) 5B 14 (1F 75)
Pimlico (Tube) 1F 89
Plaistow (Tube) 1B 68
Pontoon Dock (DLR) 2E 83
Poplar (DLR) 1D 81
Prince Regent (DLR) 1E 83
Pudding Mill Lane (DLR) 5D 53
Putney (Rail) 2A 100
Putney Bridge (Tube) 1B 100

Q

Queen's Park (Rail & Tube) 1B 58
Queens Road (Peckham) (Rail) 4E 93
Queenstown Road (Battersea) (Rail)
. . . . 4D 89
Queensway (Tube) 1D 73

R

Ravenscourt Park (Tube) 5D 71
Rectory Road (Rail) 5B 36
Redbridge (Tube) 1F 41
Regent's Park (Tube) 4D 5 (3D 61)
Rotherhithe (Tube) 3E 79
Royal Albert (DLR) 1F 83
Royal Oak (Tube) 4D 59
Royal Victoria (DLR) 1C 82
Russell Square (Tube) 4D 7 (3A 62)

S

St James's Park (Tube) 5B 22 (3F 75)
St James Street Walthamstow (Rail)
. . . . 1A 38
St Johns (Rail) 5C 94
St John's Wood (Tube) 1F 59
St Katharine's Pier (Riverbus)
. . . . 1D 7 (2A 62)
St Pancras (Rail) 1F 27 (2B 78)
St Paul's (Tube) 2F 17 (5E 63)
Savoy Pier (Riverbus) 5F 15 (1B 76)
Seven Sisters (Rail & Tube) 1B 36
Shadwell (Tube & DLR) 1D 79

Shepherd's Bush (Rail & Tube)
    Central Line 3F 71
Shepherd's Bush (Tube)
    Hammersmith & City Line 2E 71
Shoreditch (Tube) 3B 64
Silvertown (Rail) 2F 83
Sloane Square (Tube) 5C 74
Snaresbrook (Tube) 1C 40
South Bermondsey (Rail) 1E 93
Southfields (Tube) 1B 114
South Hampstead (Rail) 4E 45
South Kensington (Tube) 5F 73
South Quay (DLR) 3D 81
South Tottenham (Rail) 1B 36
Southwark (Tube) 2D 25 (2D 77)
Stamford Brook (Tube) 5B 70
Stamford Hill (Rail) 2A 36
Stepney Green (Tube) 3F 65
Stockwell (Tube) 4A 90
Stoke Newington (Rail) 4B 36
Stratford Low Level (Rail, Tube & DLR)
. . . . 4F 53
Stratford (Rail) 3F 53
Streatham Hill (Rail) 2A 118
Streatham (Rail) 5F 117
Surrey Quays (Tube) 5F 79
Swiss Cottage (Tube) 4E 45
Sydenham Hill (Rail) 3B 120
Sydenham (Rail) 4E 121

T

Temple (Tube) 4B 16 (1B 76)
Tooting Bec (Tube) 3C 116
Tooting Broadway (Tube) 5A 116
Tottenham Court Road (Tube)
. . . . 2C 14 (5F 61)
Tower Gateway (DLR) 4F 19 (1B 78)
Tower Hill (Tube) 4F 19 (1B 78)
Tower Millennium Pier (Riverbus)
. . . . 1E 27 (2A 78)
Tufnell Park (Tube) 1E 47
Tulse Hill (Rail) 2D 119
Turnham Green (Tube) 5A 70

U

Upper Holloway (Rail) 4F 33
Upton Park (Tube) 5E 55

V

Vauxhall (Rail & Tube) 1A 90
Victoria (Rail & Tube) 5D 75
Victoria Coach (Bus) 5D 75

W

Walthamstow Queens Road (Rail)
. . . . 1C 38
Wandsworth Common (Rail) 1B 116
Wandsworth Road (Rail) 5E 89
Wandsworth Town (Rail) 2D 101
Wanstead (Tube) 1D 41

Index to Stations

Wanstead Park (Rail) 1D 55
Wapping (Tube) 2E 79
Warren Street (Tube) 3F 5 (3E 61)
Warwick Avenue (Tube). 3E 59
Waterloo East (Rail) 2C 24 (2C 76)
Waterloo International (Rail)
. . . . 3B 24 (3C 76)
Waterloo Millennium Pier (Riverbus)
. . . . 3F 23 (3B 76)
Waterloo (Rail & Tube) 3B 24 (3C 76)
Westbourne Park (Tube) 4B 58
West Brompton (Rail & Tube) · 2C 86
Westcombe Park (Rail) 1C 96
West Dulwich (Rail) 2F 119
Westferry (DLR) 1C 80
West Hampstead (Rail) 3C 44
West Hampstead (Tube) 3D 45

West Hampstead Thameslink (Rail) . . . 3C 44
West Ham (Rail & Tube) 2A 68
West India Quay (DLR) 1C 80
West Kensington (Tube) 1B 86
Westminster (Tube). 4D 23 (3A 76)
Westminster Millennium Pier (Riverbus)
. . . . 3E 23 (3A 76)
West Norwood (Rail) 4D 119
West Silvertown (DLR) 2C 82
Whitechapel (Tube) 4D 65
White City (Tube) 1E 71
Willesden Green (Tube) 3E 43
Willesden Junction (Rail & Tube)
. . . . 2B 56
Wimbledon (Rail, Tube & CT) 5B 114
Wimbledon Park (Tube). 3C 114
Woodgrange Park (Rail) 2F 55